Annual Abstract of Statistics

2001 edition
United Kingdom
No 137

Editor: Keith Tyrrell

London: The Stationery Office

Contact points
For enquiries about this publication, contact
the Editor, Keith Tyrrell
Tel: 020 7533 5722
E-mail: annual.abstract@ons.gov.uk

To order this publication, call The Stationery Office
on **0870 600 5522.** See also back cover.

For general enquiries, contact the National Statistics
Public Enquiry Service on **0845 601 3034**
(minicom: 01633 812399)
E-mail: info@statistics.gov.uk
Fax: 01633 652747
Letters: Zone DG/18, 1 Drummond Gate,
London SW1V 2QQ

You can also find National Statistics on the internet -
go to **www.statistics.gov.uk**

A National Statistics publication
Official statistics bearing the National Statistics logo are produced to high professional standards set out in the National Statistics Code of Practice. They undergo regular quality assurance reviews to ensure that they meet customer needs. They are produced free from any political interference.

About the Office for National Statistics
The Office for National Statistics (ONS) is the government agency responsible for compiling, analysing and disseminating many of the United Kingdom's economic, social and demographic statistics, including the retail prices index, trade figures and labour market data, as well as the periodic census of the population and health statistics. The Director of ONS is also the National Statistician and the Registrar General for England and Wales, and the agency that administers the statutory registration of births, marriages and deaths there.

CONTENTS

CONTENTS

CONTENTS

CONTENTS

CONTENTS

CONTENTS

CONTENTS

CONTENTS

22 Banking, insurance etc

23 Service industry

UNITS OF MEASUREMENT

Length

1 millimetre (mm)		= 0.039 370 1 inch
1 centimetre (cm)	= 10 millimetres	= 0.393 701 inch
1 metre (m)	= 1 000 millimetres	= 1.093 61 yards
1 kilometre (km)	= 1 000 metres	= 0.621 371 mile
1 inch (in.)		= 25.4 millimetres or 2.54 centimetres
1 foot (ft.)	= 12 inches	= 0.304 8 metre
1 yard (yd.)	= 3 feet	= 0.914 4 metre
1 mile	= 1 760 yards	= 1.609 34 kilometres

Area

1 square millimetre (mm^2)		= 0.001 55 square inch
1 square metre (m^2)	= one million square millimetres	= 1.195 99 square yards
1 hectare (ha)	= 10 000 square metres	= 2.471 05 acres
1 square kilometre (km^2)	= one million square metres	= 247.105 acres
1 square inch (sq. in.)		= 645.16 square millimetres or 6.451 6 square centimetres
1 square foot (sq. ft.)	= 144 square inches	= 0.092 903 square metre or 929.03 square centimetres
1 square yard (sq. yd.)	= 9 square feet	= 0.836 127 square metres
1 acre	= 4 840 square yards	= 4 046.86 square metres or 0.404 686 hectare
1 square mile (sq. mile)	= 640 acres	= 2.589 99 square kilometres or 258.999 hectares

Volume

1 cubic centimetre (cm^3)		= 0.061 023 7 cubic inch
1 cubic decimetre (dm^3)	= 1 000 cubic centimetres	= 0.035 314 7 cubic foot
1 cubic metre (m^3)	= one million cubic centimetres	= 1.307 95 cubic yards
1 cubic foot (cu. ft.)		= 0.028 316 8 cubic metre or 28.316 8 cubic decimetres
1 cubic yard (cu. yd.)	= 27 cubic feet	= 0.764 555 cubic metre

Capacity

1 litre (l)	= 1 cubic decimetre	= 0.220 gallon
1 hectolitre (hl)	= 100 litres	= 22.0 gallons
1 pint		= 0.568 litre
2 pints	= 1 quart	= 1.137 litres
8 pints	= 1 gallon	= 4.546 09 cubic decimetres or 4.546 litres
36 gallons (gal.)	= 1 bulk barrel	= 1.636 56 hectolitres

Weight

1 gram (g)		= 0.035 274 0 ounce
1 hectogram (hg)	= 100 grams	= 3.527 4 ounces or 0.220 462 pound
1 kilogram (kg)	= 1 000 grams or 10 hectograms	= 2.204 62 pounds
1 tonne (t)	= 1 000 kilograms	= 1.102 31 short tons or 0.984 2 long ton
1 ounce avoirdupois (oz.)		= 28.349 5 grams
1 pound avoirdupois (lb.)	= 16 ounces	= 0.453 592 37 kilogram
1 hundredweight (cwt.)	= 112 pounds	= 50.802 3 kilograms
1 short ton	= 2 000 pounds	= 907.184 74 kilograms or 0.907 184 74 tonne
1 long ton (referred to as ton)	= 2 240 pounds	= 1 016.05 kilograms or 1.016 05 tonnes
1 ounce troy	= 480 grains	= 31.103 5 grams

Energy

Energy	British thermal unit (Btu)	= 0.252 kilocalorie (kcal) = 1.05 506 kilojoule (kj)
	Therm	= 100 000 British thermal units = 25 200 kcal = 105 506 kj
	Megawatt (Mw)	= 10^6 watts
	Gigawatt hour (GWh)	= 10^6 kilowatt hours = 34 121 therms

Food and drink

Food and drink	Butter	23 310 litres milk = 1 tonne butter (average)
	Cheese	10 070 litres milk = 1 tonne cheese
	Condensed milk	2 550 litres milk = 1 tonne full cream condensed milk
		2 953 litres skimmed milk = 1 tonne skimmed condensed milk
	Milk	1 million litres = 1 030 tonnes
	Milk powder	8 054 litres milk = 1 tonne full cream milk powder
		10 740 litres skimmed milk = 1 tonne skimmed milk powder
	Eggs	17 126 eggs = 1 tonne (approximate)
	Sugar	100 tonnes raw sugar = 95 tonnes refined sugar
	Beer	1 bulk barrel = 36 gallons irrespective of gravity

Shipping

Shipping	Gross tonnage	= The total volume of all the enclosed spaces of a vessel, the unit of measurement being a ton of 100 cubic feet.
	Deadweight tonnage	= Deadweight tonnage is the total weight in tons of 2 240 lb. that a ship can legally carry, that is the total weight of cargo, bunkers, stores and crew.

INTRODUCTION

Welcome to the 2001 edition of the *Annual Abstract of Statistics*. This compendium draws together statistics from a wide range of official and other authoritative sources. Their help is gratefully acknowledged.

Regional information, supplementary to the national figures in this *Annual Abstract*, is published in *Regional Trends*, published by The Stationery Office (TSO).

The five Parts of the *Annual Abstract*, illustrated in the contents, align with their equivalents in the *Britain 2001: The Official Yearbook of the United Kingdom*, so that the two books can be consulted as complementary volumes, painting a picture of the UK in words and figures.

Current data for many of the series appearing in this *Annual Abstract* are contained in other ONS publications, such as *Economic Trends, Monthly Digest of Statistics, Population Trends, Health Statistics Quarterly* and *Financial Statistics*. All are published by TSO.

The name and telephone number of the organisation providing the statistics are shown under each table. In addition, a list of Sources is given at the back of the book, which sets out the official publications or other sources to which further reference can be made.

All the data series published in the *Annual Abstract* are contained on a database, and almost all are stored with a four letter identification code (e.g. LUJS). These codes appear at the start of most columns or rows of data and can be quoted if you contact us requiring any further information about the data.

Definitions and Classification

Time Series. So far as possible annual totals are given throughout, but quarterly or monthly figures are given where these are more suitable to the type of series.

Explanatory notes. Most sections are preceded by explanatory notes which should be read in conjunction with the tables. Definitions and explanatory notes for many of the terms occurring in the *Annual Abstract* are also given in the *Annual Supplement* to the *Monthly Digest of Statistics*, published annually in the January editions. Detailed notes on items which appear in both the *Abstract* and *Financial Statistics* are given in an annual supplement to the latter entitled *Financial Statistics: Explanatory Handbook*. The original sources listed in the Sources may also be consulted.

Standard Industrial Classification. A Standard Industrial Classification (SIC) was first introduced into the United Kingdom in 1948 for use in classifying business establishments and other statistical units by the type of economic activity in which they are engaged. The classification provides a framework for the collection, tabulation, presentation and analysis of data about economic activities. Its use promotes uniformity of data collected by various government departments and agencies.

Since 1948 the classification has been revised in 1958, 1968, 1980 and 1992. One of the principal objectives of the 1980 revision was to eliminate differences from the activity classification issued by the Statistical Office of the European Communities (Eurostat) and entitled 'Nomenclature générale des activités économiques dans les Communautés Européennes', usually abbreviated to NACE. In 1990, the European Communities introduced a new statistical classification of economic activities (NACE Rev 1) by regulation. The regulation made it obligatory for the UK to introduce a new Standard Industrial Classification SIC(92), based on NACE Rev 1.

UK SIC(92) is based exactly on NACE Rev 1 but, where it is thought necessary or helpful, a fifth digit has been added to form subclasses of the NACE 1 four digit system. There are 17 sections, 16 subsections, 60 divisions, 222 groups, 503 classes and 253 subclasses. Full details are available from *UK Standard Industrial Classification of Economic Activities 1992* (TSO 1997, price £25.00) and *Indexes to the UK Standard Industrial Classification of Economic Activities 1992* (TSO 1997, price £22.50).

Regional classification. Some tables have been reclassified using the Government Office Regions. This has changed from the Standard Statistical Regions. For further advice please contact the Office for National Statistics Geographic Support Service (01329 813536).

Revisions to contents

Revisions. Some of the figures, particularly for the latest year, are provisional and may be revised in a subsequent issue of the *Annual Abstract*.

This edition of the *Abstract* has again seen a number of changes to the content. The changes are numerous, with most tables being amended at least slightly. The more significant changes are outlined below:

Chapter 6 - Education. On advice, tables showing students in further and higher education have been split up to reflect the differences in the way these data are collected.

Chapter 14 - Transport and communications. There have been a number of changes, with new tables

INTRODUCTION

including *Journeys per person per year by main mode and purpose*, and *Private motoring:households with regular use of cars.*

Symbols and conventions used

Change of basis. Where consecutive figures have been compiled on different bases and are not strictly comparable, a footnote is added indicating the nature of the difference.

Units of measurement. The various units of measurement used are listed opposite the inside back cover.

Rounding of figures. In tables where figures have been rounded to the nearest final digit, the constituent items may not add up exactly to the total.

Symbols. The following symbols have been used throughout:

    .. = not available (also information suppressed to avoid disclosure).

    - = nil or less than half the final digit shown.

Contact point

The Editor welcomes any feedback on the content of the *Annual Abstract*, including comments on the format of the data and the selection of topics. Comments and requests for general information should be addressed to:

    Keith Tyrrell
    Social and Regional Division
    Room B5/06
    Office for National Statistics
    1, Drummond Gate
    London SW1V 2QQ

or

    E-mail: annual.abstract@ons.gov.uk

January 2001

1 Area

Area

The United Kingdom comprises Great Britain and Northern Ireland. Great Britain comprises England, Wales and Scotland only.

Physical Features

The United Kingdom (UK) constitutes the greater part of the British Isles. The largest of the islands is Great Britain. The next largest comprises Northern Ireland and the Irish Republic. Western Scotland is fringed by the large island chain known as the Hebrides, and to the north east of the Scottish mainland are the Orkney and Shetland Islands. All these, along with the Isle of Wight, Anglesey and the Isles of Scilly, have administrative ties with the mainland, but the Isle of Man in the Irish Sea and the Channel Islands between Great Britain and France are largely self-governing, and are not part of the United Kingdom. The UK is one of the 15 member states of the European Union (EU).

With an area of about 243 000 sq km (94 000 sq miles), the United Kingdom is just under 1 000 km (about 600 miles) from the south coast to the extreme north of Scotland and just under 500 km (around 300 miles) across at the widest point.

- Highest mountain: Ben Nevis, in the highlands of Scotland, at 1 343 m (4 406 ft)

- Longest river: the Severn, 354 km (220 miles) long, which rises in central Wales and flows through Shrewsbury, Worcester and Gloucester in England to the Bristol Channel

- Largest lake: Lough Neagh, Northern Ireland, at 396 sq km (153 sq miles)

- Deepest lake: Loch Morar in the Highlands of Scotland, 310 m (1 017 ft) deep

- Highest waterfall: Eas a'Chual Aluinn, from Glas Bheinn, in the highlands of Scotland, with a drop of 200 m (660 ft)

- Deepest cave: Ogof Ffynnon Ddu, Wales, at 308 m (1 010 ft) deep

- Most northerly point on the British mainland: Dunnet Head, north-east Scotland

- Most southerly point on the British mainland: Lizard Point, Cornwall

- Closest point to mainland continental Europe: Dover, Kent. The Channel Tunnel, which links England and France, is a little over 50 km (31 miles) long, of which nearly 38 km (24 miles) are actually under the Channel.

1.1 Area of the United Kingdom, 1998

	sq km		sq km
		Worcestershire County	1 761
UNITED KINGDOM	242 910		
		Herefordshire and Worcestershire	*3 923*
GREAT BRITAIN	229 334	*Former county of Shropshire*	*3 488*
		Former county of Staffordshire	*2 715*
ENGLAND AND WALES	151 201		
		EAST	19 120
ENGLAND	130 422		
		Luton UA	43
NORTH EAST	8 592	Peterborough UA	344
		Southend-on-Sea UA	42
Darlington UA	197	Thurrock UA	164
Hartlepool UA	94		
Middlesbrough UA	54	Bedfordshire County	1 192
Redcar and Cleveland UA	245	Cambridgeshire County	3 056
Stockton-on-Tees UA	204	Essex County	3 469
		Hertfordshire	1 639
Durham County	2 232	Norfolk	5 372
Northumberland	5 026	Suffolk	3 798
Tyne and Wear (Met County)	540		
		Former county of Bedfordshire	*1 236*
Tees Valley	..	*Former county of Cambridgeshire*	*3 400*
Tees Valley less Darlington	*597*	*Former county of Essex*	*3 675*
Former county of Durham	*2 429*		
		LONDON	1 580
NORTH WEST	14 165		
		Inner London	322
Blackburn with Darwen UA	137	Outer London	1 258
Blackpool UA	35		
Halton UA	74	**SOUTH EAST**	19 096
Warrington UA	176		
		Bracknell Forest UA	109
Cheshire County	2 081	Brighton and Hove UA	82
Cumbria	6 824	Isle of Wight UA	380
Greater Manchester (Met County)	1 286	Medway UA	192
Lancashire County	2 897	Milton Keynes UA	309
Merseyside (Met County)	655	Portsmouth UA	40
		Reading UA	40
Former county of Cheshire	*2 331*	Slough UA	27
Former county of Lancashire	*3 070*	Southampton UA	50
		West Berkshire UA	704
YORKSHIRE AND THE HUMBER	15 411	Windsor and Maidenhead UA	198
		Wokingham UA	179
East Riding of Yorkshire UA	2 415		
Kingston upon Hull, City of UA	71	Buckinghamshire County	1 568
North East Lincolnshire UA	192	East Sussex County	1 713
North Lincolnshire UA	833	Hampshire County	3 689
York UA	271	Kent County	3 543
		Oxfordshire	2 606
North Yorkshire County	8 038	Surrey	1 677
South Yorkshire (Met County)	1 559	West Sussex	1 988
West Yorkshire (Met County)	2 034		
		Former county of Berkshire	*1 259*
The Humber	*3 511*	*Former county of Buckinghamshire*	*1 877*
Former county of North Yorkshire	*8 309*	*Former county of East Sussex*	*1 795*
		Former county of Hampshire	*3 779*
EAST MIDLANDS	15 627	*Former county of Kent*	*3 735*
Derby UA	78	**SOUTH WEST**	23 829
Leicester UA	73		
Nottingham UA	75	Bath and North East Somerset UA	351
Rutland UA	394	Bournemouth UA	46
		Bristol, City of UA	110
Derbyshire County	2 551	North Somerset UA	373
Leicestershire County	2 084	Plymouth UA	80
Lincolnshire	5 921	Poole UA	65
Northamptonshire	2 367	South Gloucestershire UA	497
Nottinghamshire County	2 085	Swindon UA	230
		Torbay UA	63
Former county of Derbyshire	*2 629*		
Former county of Leicestershire	*2 551*	Cornwall and the Isles of Scilly	3 559
Former county of Nottinghamshire	*2 160*	Devon County	6 562
		Dorset County	2 542
WEST MIDLANDS	13 004	Gloucestershire	2 653
		Somerset	3 452
Herefordshire, County of UA	2 162	Wiltshire County	3 246
Stoke-on-Trent UA	93		
Telford and Wrekin UA	290	*Bristol/Bath area*	*1 333*
		Former county of Devon	*6 703*
Shropshire County	3 197	*Former county of Dorset*	*2 653*
Staffordshire County	2 623	*Former county of Wiltshire*	*3 476*
Warwickshire	1 979		
West Midlands (Met County)	899		

Source: Office for National Statistics

1.1 Area of the United Kingdom, 1998

	sq km		sq km
WALES	20 779	Dumfries & Galloway	6 439
Blaenau Gwent	109	Dundee City	65
Bridgend	246	East Ayrshire	1 252
Caerphilly	278	East Dunbartonshire	172
Cardiff	140	East Lothian	678
Carmarthenshire	2 395		
		East Renfrewshire	173
Ceredigion	1 795	Edinburgh, City of	262
Conwy	1 130	Eilean Siar (Western Isles)	3 134
Denbighshire	844	Falkirk	299
Flintshire	438	Fife	1 323
Gwynedd	2 548		
		Glasgow City	175
Isle of Anglesey	714	Highland	25 784
Merthyr Tydfil	111	Inverclyde	162
Monmouthshire	850	Midlothian	356
Neath Port Talbot	442	Moray	2 238
Newport	190		
Pembrokeshire	1 590	North Ayrshire	884
		North Lanarkshire	474
Powys	5 196	Orkney Islands	992
Rhondda, Cynon, Taff	424	Perth & Kinross	5 311
Swansea	378	Renfrewshire	261
Torfaen	126	Scottish Borders	4 734
The Vale of Glamorgan	335		
Wrexham	498	Shetland Islands	1 438
		South Ayrshire	1 202
		South Lanarkshire	1 771
SCOTLAND	78 133	Stirling	2 196
		West Dunbartonshire	162
Aberdeen City	186	West Lothian	425
Aberdeenshire	6 318		
Angus	2 181		
Argyll & Bute	6 930	**NORTHERN IRELAND**	13 576
Clackmannanshire	157		

Source: Office for National Statistics

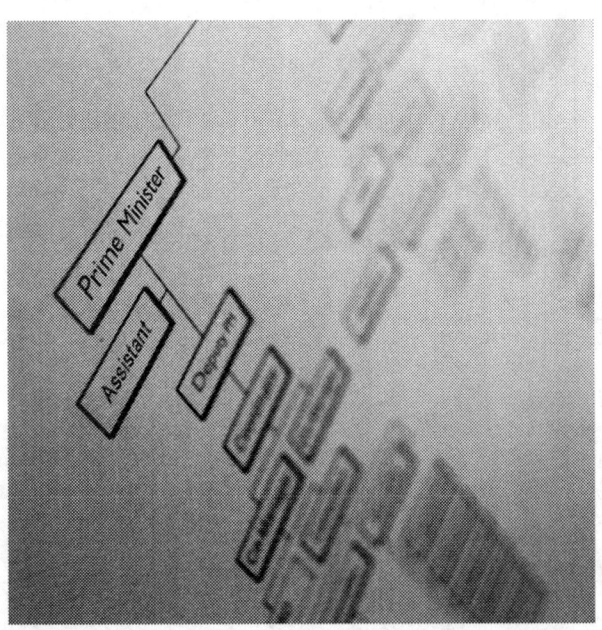

2 Parliamentary elections

Parliamentary elections

2.1 Parliamentary elections[1]

Thousands

	25 Oct 1951	26 May 1955	8 Oct 1959	15 Oct 1964	31 Mar 1966	18 June 1970[1]	28 Feb 1974	10 Oct 1974	3 May 1979	9 June 1983	11 June 1987	9 April 1992	1 May 1997[3]
United Kingdom													
Number of electors	34 919	34 852	35 397	35 894	35 957	39 615	40 256	40 256	41 573	42 704	43 666	43 719	43 830
Average-electors per seat	55.9	55.3	56.2	57.0	57.1	62.9	63.4	63.4	65.5	66.7	67.2	67.2	67.1
Number of valid votes counted	28 597	26 760	27 863	27 657	27 265	28 345	31 340	29 189	31 221	30 671	32 530	33 551	31 286
As percentage of electorate	81.9	76.8	78.7	77.1	75.8	71.5	77.9	72.5	75.1	71.8	74.5	76.7	71.4
England and Wales													
Number of electors	30 626	30 591	31 109	31 610	31 695	34 931	35 509	35 509	36 695	37 708	38 568	38 648	38 701
Average-electors per seat	56.5	55.9	56.9	57.8	57.9	63.9	64.3	64.3	66.5	67.2	68.8	68.8	68.6
Number of valid votes counted	25 356	23 570	24 619	24 384	24 116	24 877	27 735	25 729	27 609	27 082	28 832	29 813	27 679
As percentage of electorate	82.8	77.0	79.1	77.1	76.1	71.2	78.1	72.5	75.2	71.8	74.8	77.5	71.5
Scotland													
Number of electors	3 421	3 388	3 414	3 393	3 360	3 659	3 705	3 705	3 837	3 934	3 995	3 929	3 951
Average-electors per seat	48.2	47.7	48.1	47.8	47.3	51.5	52.2	52.2	54.0	54.6	55.5	54.6	54.9
Number of valid votes counted	2 778	2 543	2 668	2 635	2 553	2 688	2 887	2 758	2 917	2 825	2 968	2 913	2 817
As percentage of electorate	81.2	75.1	78.1	77.6	76.0	73.5	77.9	74.5	76.0	71.8	74.3	74.2	71.3
Northern Ireland													
Number of electors	872	873	875	891	902	1 025	1 027	1 037	1 028	1 050	1 090	1 141	1 178
Average-electors per seat	72.5	72.8	72.9	74.2	75.2	85.4	85.6	86.4	85.6	61.8	64.1	67.1	65.5
Number of valid votes counted	463	647	576	638	596	779	718	702	696	765	730	785	791
As percentage of electorate	53.1	74.1	65.8	71.7	66.1	76.0	69.9	67.7	67.7	72.9	67.0	68.8	67.1
Number of Members of Parliament elected:	625	630	630	630	630	630	635	635	635	650	650	651	659
Conservative	320	344	364	303	253	330	296	276	339	396	375	336	165
Labour	295	277	258	317	363	287	301	319	268	209	229	271	418
Liberal Democrat	6	6	6	9	12	6	14	13	11	17	17	20	46
Social Democratic Party	-	-	-	-	-	-	-	-	-	6	5	-	-
Scottish National Party	-	-	-	-	-	1	7	11	2	2	3	3	6
Plaid Cymru	-	-	-	-	-	-	2	3	2	2	3	4	4
Other[2]	4	3	2	1	2	6	15	13	13	18	18	17	20

1 The Representation of the People Act 1969 lowered the minimum voting age from 21 to 18 years with effect from 16 February 1970.
2 Including the Speaker.
3 Provisional.

Source: Home Office: 020 7273 3453

2.2 Parliamentary by-elections

	May 1979 - June 1983	Previous[1] General Election May 1979	June 1983 - June 1987	Previous[1] General Election June 1983	June 1987 - April 1992	Previous[1] General Election June 1987	April 1992 - August 1995	Previous[1] General Election April 1992	May 1997 - November 2000	Previous[1] General Election May 1997
Numbers of by-elections	20		31		24		16		16	
Votes recorded										
By party (percentages)										
Conservative	23.8	33.7	16.0	23.3	23.8	33.7	18.6	40.1	27.9	25.9
Labour	25.7	35.2	14.9	14.8	38.9	41.1	39.5	36.2	29.1	39.0
Liberal Democrat[2]	9.0	8.0	15.0	10.9	19.1	18.6	26.2	16.4	23.1	14.9
Social Democratic Party[2]	14.2	-	5.6	3.0	3.2	-	-	-	-	-
Scottish National Party	1.7	1.4	-	-	4.8	1.8	5.8	3.1	4.4	3.0
Plaid Cymru	0.5	0.4	0.3	0.3	2.3	0.6	0.5	0.2	2.6	2.4
Other	25.1[3]	21.2[3]	48.2[4]	47.6[4]	7.9	4.2	9.4	4.1	12.2[5]	14.0[6]
Total votes recorded										
(percentages)	100.0	100.0	100.0	100.0	100.0	100.0	100.0	100.0	100.0	100.0
(thousands)	715	852	1 235	1 410	878	1 130	560	808	416	684

1 Votes recorded in the same seats in the previous General Election. Does not apply to June 1983 in Northern Ireland.
2 The Social Democratic Party was launched on 26 March 1981. An SDP candidate contested a parliamentary seat for the first time at a by-election at Warrington on 16 July 1981. In the 1987 General Election the Liberals and the SDP contested the election jointly as the Liberal/SDP Alliance. Subsequently the Alliance split into its constituent parties and the Liberals are now known as the Liberal Democrats. The SDP effectively ceased to exist when its two remaining MPs lost their seats at the 1992 General Election.
3 The proportions of votes recorded for 'Other' is high because three of the 20 by-elections were in Northern Ireland (two were in the same constituency, Fermanagh and South Tyrone), and as votes recorded for the 1979 General Election have been included twice in the previous General Election Column.
4 The proportion of votes recorded for 'Other' is high because 15 of the 31 by-elections were in Northern Ireland.
5 Proportion of 'other' votes inflated by one by-election in Northern Ireland.
6 Proportion of 'other' votes inflated by a by-election in Northern Ireland, and the fact that at the general election, votes were cast for the retiring Speaker as 'The Speaker seeking re-election' and not as a party candidate.

Source: Home Office: 020 7273 3453

3 International development

International development

Overseas development assistance
(Tables 3.1 and 3.2)

The UK development assistance programme is administered by the Department for International Development (DFID) to promote the economic development of recipient countries. It is managed within financial years, the money being voted annually by Parliament. Since 1992 the statistics relating to the programme are also published on a financial year basis and on a calendar year basis for both international aid comparisons and for national purposes such as the balance of payments.

Aid flows can be measured before (gross) or after (net) deduction of repayments of principal on past loans. These tables show only the gross figures.

Assistance is provided in two main ways: *bilateral*, that is directly to governments of recipient countries or to institutions in the United Kingdom for work on behalf of such countries, or *multilateral*, that is to international institutions for their economic development programmes. Table 3.1 shows the main groups of multilateral agencies, the International Development Association being the largest in the World Bank Group.

Bilateral assistance takes various forms:

Project aid is finance for investment schemes primarily designed to increase the physical capital of the recipient country, including contributions for local and recurrent costs.

Sector-wide programmes (typically in education, health or agriculture) comprise a combination of assistance including direct budgetary aid and technical co-operation.

Programme aid is financial assistance to fund imports, sector support programmes or budgetary expenditure, usually as part of a World Bank/IMF co-ordinated structural adjustment programme.

Technical co-operation is the provision of know-how in the form of personnel, training, research and associated costs.

Grants and other aid in kind are used to provide equipment and supplies, and support to the development work of UK and international voluntary organisations.

Humanitarian assistance comprises food aid and other disaster relief.

Aid and Trade Provision is a special allocation to soften the terms of credit to developing countries by mixing aid funds with private export credits.

The *Commonwealth Development Corporation* invests in productive public or private sector projects in developing countries.

Other Government Departments' expenditure covers debt relief, drug-related assistance and support to voluntary organisations.

Most of the expenditure not allocable by region in Table 3.2, is for assistance provided through organisations in the United Kingdom.

Fuller statistics of the UK's development assistance effort are published annually in *Statistics on International Development* (obtainable from the Library, DFID, Abercrombie House, East Kilbride, Glasgow G75 8EA). International comparisons are available in the OECD Development Assistance Committee's annual report. The latest is *2000 Report: Development Co-operation* (available from The Stationery Office).

3.1 UK Gross public expenditure on aid (GPEX)

£ Thousands

		1991/92	1992/93	1993/94	1994/95	1995/96	1996/97	1997/98	1998/99	1999/00
Bilateral Assistance										
DFID										
Project or Sector Aid	LUJS	140 925	122 834	119 832	121 812	121 456	106 354	96 551	118 870	176 215
Programme Aid	LUJW	118 126	136 771	121 027	113 510	83 494	96 306	84 784	133 574	140 374
Technical Co-operation Projects	LUOS	375 832	398 637	401 560	430 447	446 788	456 449	483 352	485 073	531 813
Grants & Other Aid in Kind	LUOT	139 006	155 889	171 688	149 556	184 315	194 905	179 843	184 998	159 384
Humanitarian Assistance	LUOU	138 433	142 813	179 601	205 368	141 410	12 125	93 680	126 087	221 851
Debt Relief	LUOV	489	20 099	23 698	28 144	27 337	23 529	23 161	25 695	23 140
Aid and Trade Provision	LUOW	101 157	93 071	84 700	59 987	71 988	61 254	60 532	53 410	34 757
CDC Investments	LUOX	124 210	223 301	183 354	215 295	279 986	189 082	249 062	166 716	268 486
Other Government Departments	LUOY	38 666	60 475	22 796	33 034	61 606	34 224	170 171	87 147	100 721
Total Bilateral Assistance	LUOZ	1 176 844	1 353 890	1 308 256	1 357 153	1 418 381	1 283 498	1 441 135	1 381 570	1 656 738
Multilateral Assistance										
European Community	LUPA	459 930	476 065	529 823	612 080	693 690	636 418	557 287	754 548	692 367
World Bank Group	LUPB	228 198	249 682	229 613	227 728	206 877	174 398	189 851	175 254	170 631
International Monetary Fund	LUPC	1 500	10 000	20 000	90 000	30 000	20 000	20 000	18 000	17 000
UN Agencies	LUPD	112 875	122 366	142 527	127 880	116 772	130 775	141 278	130 983	176 465
Regional Development Banks	LUPE	69 122	91 933	76 413	71 212	69 513	58 833	60 411	66 096	66 720
Other	LUPF	20 735	21 360	17 829	27 904	27 036	30 665	30 846	31 216	34 994
Total Multilateral Assistance	LUPG	892 360	971 406	1 016 205	1 156 804	1 143 887	1 051 088	999 672	1 176 098	1 158 178
Administrative Costs	LUPH	63 155	58 823	65 329	70 314	72 198	79 753	88 992	97 235	103 682
Total Gross Public Expenditure on Aid	LUPI	2 132 359	2 384 119	2 389 790	2 584 270	2 634 465	2 414 339	2 529 799	2 654 903	2 918 598

Source: Department for International Development: 01355 843612

3.2 Total bilateral gross public expenditure on aid (GPEX) by main recipient countries and regions

£ Thousands

		1991/92	1992/93	1993/94	1994/95	1995/96	1996/97	1997/98	1998/99	1999/00
Main recipients										
India	LUPJ	135 983	116 108	102 367	98 622	154 730	112 359	114 562	111 409	110 720
States of Former Yugoslavia[1]	ZBXN	569	37 003	51 803	43 511	38 905	42 642	20 672	4 184	65 834
Uganda	LUPN	27 836	34 707	40 551	46 615	40 590	49 245	59 354	64 294	90 410
Tanzania	LUPK	32 430	62 457	32 499	31 633	29 900	56 287	51 200	77 515	74 949
Bangladesh	LUPM	59 217	64 934	56 068	57 441	54 282	44 938	39 620	67 688	71 868
Mozambique	LUPV	18 001	34 177	34 744	25 068	22 026	26 610	48 311	28 902	70 356
Indonesia	LUPZ	34 422	32 679	34 885	51 404	57 265	38 477	48 667	21 751	55 702
Ghana	LUPL	44 659	41 736	26 190	23 530	26 305	28 451	30 418	62 897	52 035
Malawi	LUPP	26 093	27 378	27 015	41 174	35 720	44 876	30 651	52 628	49 337
South Africa	LUPT	9 325	11 558	14 504	15 706	17 666	23 451	28 646	35 383	47 883
Zambia	LUPO	34 444	47 978	47 752	56 629	58 915	41 003	46 978	33 748	46 798
Bolivia	ZBXO	3 942	9 262	6 514	5 820	32 747	4 965	27 515	11 365	39 601
Dominican Republic	ZBXP	25	55	4 545	4	20 303	2 852	2 204	253	35 192
Kenya	LUPR	38 351	37 514	31 503	30 691	29 378	26 438	30 025	42 151	33 061
Sierra Leone	ZBXQ	2 486	6 483	4 003	8 345	8 963	10 841	3 293	9 153	30 044
Russian Federation	LUPW	26 686	11 795	20 749	32 753	30 884	32 205	33 617	30 887	27 743
China	LUPS	21 243	34 914	33 630	28 344	32 803	30 956	38 616	39 529	26 260
Pakistan	LUPY	37 236	35 063	48 197	63 487	60 234	59 367	32 817	27 678	23 510
Montserrat	LUPU	2 996	3 271	5 689	5 815	6 568	14 452	38 317	31 291	22 813
Zimbabwe	LUPX	47 690	44 268	41 390	35 394	20 191	21 105	13 807	29 440	17 373
Total Main Recipients	LUQD	603 634	693 340	664 598	701 986	777 568	711 520	739 290	782 146	991 489
Total Other Countries	LUQE	573 211	660 549	643 659	655 167	640 813	571 978	701 845	598 524	665 249
Regional Totals										
Africa	LUQF	440 598	526 833	457 991	475 626	437 146	445 848	450 709	575 035	635 457
America	LUQG	92 905	118 685	114 208	132 407	192 769	107 302	271 766	170 239	241 713
Asia	LUQH	403 782	424 574	410 387	415 812	465 945	402 920	393 476	349 952	383 381
Europe	LUQI	71 340	99 362	134 713	137 995	129 941	138 281	115 164	84 627	190 195
Pacific	LUQJ	22 462	28 715	14 935	16 291	14 053	12 458	26 890	20 251	7 248
World Unallocated[2]	LUQK	146 197	155 720	176 022	179 023	178 527	176 689	183 129	181 466	198 744
Total Bilateral GPEX	LUQL	1 176 845	1 353 889	1 308 257	1 357 153	1 418 381	1 283 498	1 441 135	1 381 570	1 656 738

1 The totals for the period prior to 1998/99 include amounts for the successor states of the Former Yugoslavia. The figures for 1998/99 onwards include expenditure for the Kosovo crisis.

2 World Unallocated comprises block grants to the British Council, Natural Resources Institute, VSO, NGOs, Research Institutions and Commonwealth Organisations based in the UK, and some ATP Technical Co-operation.

Source: Department for International Development: 01355 843612

4 Defence

Defence

This section includes figures on Defence expenditure, on the size and role of the Armed Forces and on related support activities.

Much of the material in this section can be found in *UK Defence Statistics 2000 (TSO)*.

Formation of the armed forces *(Table 4.1)*
This table shows the number of units which comprise the "teeth" elements of the Armed Forces and excludes supporting units.

Service personnel *(Tables 4.3 to 4.6 and 4.10)*
The Regular Forces consist entirely of volunteer members serving on a whole-time basis.

Locally Entered Personnel are recruited outside the United Kingdom for whole-time service in special formations with special conditions of service and normally restricted locations. The Brigade of Gurkhas is an example.

The Regular Forces are supported by Reserves and Auxiliary Forces. There are both regular and volunteer Reserves. Regular Reserves consist of former Service personnel with a Reserve liability. Volunteer Reserves are open to both former Service personnel and civilians. The call out liabilities of the various reserve forces differ in accordance with their roles.

All three Services run cadet forces for young people and the Combined Cadet Force, which is found in certain schools where education is continued to the age of 17 or above, may operate sections for any or all of the Services.

Deployment of Service personnel *(Table 4.6)*
The source from which the individual national totals are compiled is different from that used to obtain the total UK strength, and consequently the figures for England, Wales, Scotland and Northern Ireland do not add up to the UK figure. Royal Navy and Royal Marines personnel on board ship are included in the UK figure if the ship was in home waters on the situation date or otherwise against the appropriate overseas area. The overseas figures include personnel who are on loan to countries in the areas shown.

Service married accommodation and Defence land holdings *(Table 4.7)*
Accommodation is provided for Service families in the United Kingdom and abroad, partly by building to approved standards and partly by renting accommodation. Permanent holdings in the United Kingdom include a small number of unfurnished hirings taken on from local authorities which are not recorded separately. Multiple hirings relate to accommodation built by private developers and leased by the Federal German Authorities and the Government of Gibraltar on behalf of British Forces.
The table also presents statistics of land and foreshore in the United Kingdom owned by the Ministry of Defence or over which it has limited rights under grants or licences. Land declared as surplus to Defence requirements is also included.

Civilian personnel *(Table 4.8)*
This table gives an analysis of the number of civilians employed in the various management areas. The attribution of civilian staff can change according to circumstances so that figures for successive years may not always be comparable.

Some civilians from the United Kingdom serve tours of duty overseas. There were 4 403 such civilians serving abroad on 1 April 2000. Other civilian staff are engaged overseas to work locally as circumstances demand.

Health *(Tables 4.9 - 4.11)*
The Services operate a number of hospitals in this country and in areas abroad where there is a significant British military presence. These hospitals take as patients, members of all three Services and their dependants; in addition, the hospitals in the United Kingdom take civilian patients under arrangements agreed with the National Health Service. Medical support is also supplied by Service medical staff at individual units, ships and stations.

Sickness, medical discharges and deaths of UK Service personnel *(Table 4.11)*
It should be noted that, whereas the Royal Air Force content is for all episodes of bedded sickness lasting two days or more terminating in the year, that for the Army covers only those cases admitted to medical units (including hospitals) for two days or more, and the Royal Navy episodes exclude less than seven days sickness on shore.

Search and rescue *(Table 4.12)*
This table covers incidents in which Rescue Coordinating Centres (RCCs) in the United Kingdom coordinated search and rescue (SAR) action in which elements of the Armed Forces were involved. The table also includes urgent medical incidents in which the Forces SAR facilities gave assistance (eg inter-hospital transfers).

Defence services and the civilian community *(Table 4.13)*
The Ministry of Defence helps the civil community in a variety of ways, for example by providing assistance in time of natural disasters or other emergencies and by undertaking community projects which are of training value to the Services. In some cases facilities established primarily for defence purposes also provide benefits to the general public. Overall figures are not available, but the table presents information on a number of these activities and facilities.
Service assistance may be provided during an industrial dispute at the request of the civil ministries in order to maintain services essential to the life of the community (eg maintenance of emergency fire services in 1977/78).

The Royal Navy Fishery Protection squadron operates within the UK fishery limits on behalf of Fishery departments, who pay some of the running costs of the squadron.

The Hydrographer Office is the national authority responsible for hydrographic and oceanographic surveys and nautical charting. Many of the maps and charts are now available electronically, as well as in traditional paper format.

4.1 Formation of the UK armed forces
As at 1 April

Number

		Front Line Units[1]	1990	1991	1992	1993	1994	1995	1996	1997	1998	1999	2000
Royal Navy[2]													
Submarines	KCGA	Vessels	24	24	20	18	18	16	15	15	15	15	16
Carriers and assault ships	KCGB	Vessels	4	3	3	3	4	3	5	5	5	6	6
Cruisers. Destroyers and Frigates	KCGC	Vessels	43	41	43	38	32	30	36	35	35	35	32
Mine counter-measure	KCGE	Vessels	37	35	31	30	18	18	18	18	19	20	21
Patrol ships and craft	KCGF	Vessels	32	31	26	24	30	33	32	34	28	24	23
Fixed wing aircraft	KCGG	Squadrons	3	3	3	3	3	3	3	3	3	3	2
Helicopters[3]	KCGH	Squadrons	13	13	13	13	11	11	15	15	12	12	10
Royal Marines	KCGI	Commandos	3	3	3	3	3	3	3	3	3	3	3
Army													
Royal Armoured Corps	KCGJ	Regiments	19	19	19	14	12[4]	11	11	11	11	11	11[5]
Royal Artillery	KCGK	Regiments	22	22	21	18	16[4]	16	16	16	15	15	15
Royal Engineers	KCGL	Regiments	13	13	13	13	12	10	10	10	10[6]	10	11[7]
Infantry	KCGM	Battalions	55	55	55	48	45	41	41	40	40	40	40
Special Air Service	KCGN	Regiments	1	1	1	1	1	1	1	1	1	1	1
Army Air Corps	KCGO	Regiments	4	4	5	6	6	5	5	5	5	5	5
Royal Air Force													
Strike/attack	KCGP	Squadrons	11	11	9	8	6	6	6	6	6	5	5
Offensive support	KCGQ	Squadrons	5	5	5	5	5	5	5	5	5	5	5
Air defence	KCGR	Squadrons	9	11	9	7	6	6	6	6	6	5	5
Maritime patrol	KCGS	Squadrons	4	4	4	3	3	3	3	3	3	3	3
Reconnaissance	KCGT	Squadrons	3	5	5	5	5	5	5	5	5	5	5
Airborne early warning	KCGU	Squadrons	1	1	1	1	1	1	2	2	2	2	2
Air transport and tankers and helicopters[8]	KCGV	Squadrons	15	15	16	16	15	14	14	13	14	14	14
Search and rescue	KCGX	Squadrons	2	2	2	2	2	2	2	2	2	2	2
Surface to air missiles	KCGY	Squadrons	7	7	6	5	5	5	6	6	6	4	4
Ground defence[9]	KCGZ	Squadrons	6	5	5	5	5	5	5	5	5	5	5

1 Units which comprise the 'teeth' elements of the Armed Forces.
2 Excludes vessels undergoing construction, major refit, conversion, or on stand-by, etc.
3 Excludes training, search and rescue, fleet training and support squadrons.
4 Includes one training regiment.
5 Includes one Armoured Regiment which is committed to the new Joint NBC Regiment.
6 Does not include the Military Works force.

7 Includes an additional Close Support Regiment formed as a result of SDR. Excludes two Training Regiments and the Military Works Force.
8 Includes six support helicopter squadrons now part of the Joint Helicopter Command.
9 Includes the Queen's Colour Squadron, which since 1994 has a war role.

Source: Ministry of Defence/DASA (Tri-Service): 020 7218 4535

4.2 UK Defence expenditure

£ millions

		1988 /89	1989 /90	1990 /91	1991 /92	1992 /93	1993 /94	1994 /95	1995 /96	1996 /97	1997 /98	1998 /99
Total expenditure at												
outturn prices	KDAA	19 072	20 755	22 298	24 562	23 762	23 424	22 519	21 517	22 041	20 910	22 475
of which:												
Expenditure on personnel	KDAB	7 572	8 099	8 811	9 934	10 504	9 835	9 313	8 524	8 633	8 259	8 553
of the Armed Forces	KDAC	4 300	4 539	4 811	5 499	5 634	6 907	6 490	6 150	6 223	5 938	6 286
of the retired Armed Forces[1]	KDAD	1 060	1 197	1 406	1 613	1 950	..	..	..	..	..	..
of civilian staff	KDAE	2 212	2 363	2 594	2 822	2 920	2 928	2 823	2 374	2 409	2 321	2 267
Expenditure on equipment	KDAF	8 038	8 536	8 838	9 758	8 711	9 207	8 819	8 537	9 100	9 003	9 889
Sea systems	KDAG	2 633	2 890	2 955	3 142	2 891	2 589	2 441	2 110	2 190	2 142	2 319
Land systems	KDAH	1 554	1 738	1 927	2 157	1 846	1 806	1 642	1 576	1 806	1 658	1 665
Air systems	KDAI	3 085	3 102	3 197	3 574	3 152	3 246	3 184	3 356	3 507	3 843	4 572
Other	KDAJ	766	806	759	885	822	1 566	1 552	1 495	1 597	1 360	1 333
Other expenditure	KDAK	3 462	4 120	4 649	4 870	4 547	4 382	4 387	4 456	4 308	3 648	4 033
Works, buildings and land	KDAL	1 411	1 900	2 067	2 090	1 780	2 073	2 402	2 065	1 904	1 253	1 759
Miscellaneous stores and services	KDAM	2 051	2 220	2 582	2 780	2 767	2 309	1 985	2 391	2 404	2 395	2 274
Adjusted defence budget at 1998/99 prices[2]	KZBG	28 267	28 694	28 471	29 523	26 802	25 935	25 356	23 506	23 650	22 241	22 475

1 From 1990/91 to 1994/95, includes financial assistance to pre-1973 war widows.
2 The 'Adjusted Defence Budget' takes account of major definitional changes in defence spending and of major transfers of responsibility to and from Governmental Departments. It therefore provides a more consistent and reliable guide to trends. This is the basis upon which defence spending figures are presented in the MoD Department Return, the Statement on the Defence Estimates and certain Treasury publications. It excludes the element of receipts from the sale of the Married Quarters Estate. 1998/99 prices have been calculated using the GDP deflator.

Source: Ministry of Defence/DASA (Procurement): 0117 913 2552

Defence

4.3 UK Defence: service manpower strengths
As at 1 April

Thousands

		1990	1991	1992	1993	1994	1995	1996	1997	1998	1999	2000
UK service personnel												
Full-time trained strength[1]	ZBTR	284.5	281.6	278.3	267.1	248.4	226.3	211.6	197.4	194.0	191.1	190.5
Trained Naval Service	ZBTS	56.7	55.2	55.8	55.3	52.4	48.2	45.6	41.7	40.5	39.3	38.9
UK regulars	ZBTT	56.7	55.2	55.8	55.3	52.4	48.2	45.6	41.7	40.4	39.1	38.5
Full-time reserve service[2]	ZBTU	..	..	..	..	..	..	..	..	0.1	0.3	0.3
Trained Army	ZBTV	144.4	143.7	140.5	132.9	121.8	108.7	103.6	101.5	100.9	99.9	100.4
UK regulars	ZBTW	137.2	136.5	133.4	126.5	116.1	104.5	99.5	97.8	97.5	96.3	96.5
Full-time reserve service[2]	ZBTX	..	..	..	..	..	..	..	..	..	0.2	0.5
Gurkhas[3]	ZBTY	7.1	7.2	7.2	6.5	5.6	4.2	4.0	3.8	3.4	3.4	3.4
Trained Royal Air Force	ZBTZ	83.5	82.7	82.0	78.9	74.2	69.4	62.5	54.2	52.7	51.9	51.2
UK regulars	ZBUA	83.5	82.7	82.0	78.9	74.2	69.4	62.5	54.2	52.7	51.8	51.0
Full-time reserve service[2,4]	ZBUB	..	..	..	..	..	..	..	..	..	0.1	0.2
Untrained UK regulars	ZBUC	28.3	23.7	22.3	14.2	11.8	11.2	14.3	17.2	19.7	21.5	21.6
Naval Service	ZBUD	6.5	6.9	6.4	4.1	3.4	2.7	2.8	3.5	4.1	4.6	4.3
Army	ZBUE	15.6	11.1	12.0	8.1	6.9	7.2	9.3	11.1	12.4	13.4	13.6
Royal Air Force	ZBUF	6.2	5.7	4.0	2.0	1.5	1.3	2.2	2.7	3.2	3.5	3.7
Locally Entered Personnel[3] (excluding Gurkhas)	ZBUG	1.3	1.4	1.3	1.3	1.2	0.6	0.6	0.4	0.4	0.4	0.4
RIR (HS)[5]	ZBUH	6.2	6.1	6.0	5.6	5.4	5.3	5.0	4.8	4.6	4.4	4.2
Reserve personnel	ZBUI	267.8	276.9	273.6	265.3	264.4	263.3	267.7	269.9	273.3	273.4	268.0
Regular Reserves	ZBUJ	186.6	194.8	193.4	189.3	192.5	197.8	205.0	205.8	209.3	214.5	215.6
Naval Services	ZBUK	30.7	28.9	28.5	24.8	25.0	24.9	24.9	24.7	25.6	25.6	23.9
Army	ZBUL	119.2	126.6	123.8	122.2	124.8	130.4	136.8	136.6	139.2	144.4	147.3
Royal Air Force	ZBUM	36.7	39.3	41.1	42.3	42.8	42.6	43.3	44.5	44.5	44.5	44.4
Volunteer Reserves	ZBUN	81.2	82.1	80.2	75.9	71.9	65.5	62.7	64.1	63.9	58.9	52.4
RNR and RMR[6]	ZBUO	7.0	7.0	7.0	5.6	4.6	3.7	3.5	4.3	4.4	4.5	4.8
Territorial Army[7]	ZBUP	72.5	73.3	71.3	68.5	65.0	59.7	57.3	57.6	57.0	51.8	44.8
Royal Auxilliary Air Force	ZBUQ	1.7	1.8	1.8	1.8	2.3	2.1	1.9	2.2	2.5	2.6	2.7
Cadet Forces[8]	ZBUR	135.9	134.7	137.2	135.9	135.7	133.9	134.7	133.1	132.0	132.9	136.4
Naval Service	ZBUS	26.2	27.0	28.8	27.1	26.7	26.5	26.9	26.3	25.9	24.5	24.1
Army	ZBUT	65.5	64.6	64.8	65.1	65.2	63.7	65.4	65.1	64.9	65.7	68.5
Royal Air Force[5]	ZBUU	44.2	43.1	43.6	43.7	43.8	43.7	42.4	41.8	41.2	42.7	43.7

1 This table excludes reserve personnel mobilised for service in the former Yugoslavia.
2 FTRS Full-Time Reserve Service personnel, i.e. reserves serving full-time in regular posts, made possible by the Reserve Forces Act 1996. None existed before 1998.
3 Locally Entered Personnel and Gurkha figures for 1990 are at 1 July, not 1 April.
4 RAF Full-Time Reserve Service figures comprise Full Commitment, Limited Commitment and Home Commitment.

5 RIR (HS): Home Service batallions of the Royal Irish Regiment. Up until 1 July 1992, this was the Ulster Defence Regiment.
6 RNR: Royal Naval Reserve. RMR: Royal Marine Reserve.
7 Territorial Army figure includes Officer Training Corps and Non-Regular Permanent Staff.
8 Figures for each Service include Combined Cadet Force. Naval Service figures include Officers and Civilian Instructors. Army and RAF figures exclude Officers and Civilian Instructors.

Source: Ministry of Defence/DASA (Tri-Service): 020 7218 4535

4.4 Intake of UK regular forces from civilian life: by service

Number

		1989 /90	1990 /91	1991 /92	1992 /93	1993 /94	1994 /95	1995 /96	1996 /97	1997 /98	1998 /99	1999 /00
All services:												
Male	KCJB	32 297	26 782	24 357	13 067	10 616	11 154	15 495	19 121	20 169	22 545	22 374
Female	KCJC	4 115	4 428	3 550	1 750	1 333	1 853	2 175	3 038	3 336	3 431	3 159
Total	KCJA	36 412	31 210	27 907	14 817	11 949	13 007	17 670	22 165	23 505	25 976	25 533
Naval service:												
Male	KCJE	5 759	5 712	5 570	1 888	1 272	961	2 007	3 397	3 966	4 106	4 250
Female	KCJF	860	1 199	1 013	384	250	340	353	562	634	661	703
Total	KCJD	6 619	6 911	6 583	2 272	1 532	1 301	2 360	3 959	4 600	4 767	4 953
Army:												
Male	KCJJ	20 378	15 955	15 544	10 289	8 764	9 491	11 510	13 480	13 374	14 988	14 740
Female	KCJK	1 706	1 547	1 594	1 098	812	1 193	1 376	2 042	2 005	1 975	1 743
Total	KCJI	22 084	17 502	17 138	11 387	9 576	10 684	12 886	15 522	15 379	16 963	16 483
Royal Air Force:												
Male	KCJM	6 166	5 122	3 243	890	580	702	1 978	2 250	2 829	3 451	3 384
Female	KCJN	1 543	1 675	943	268	261	320	446	434	697	795	713
Total	KCJL	7 709	6 797	4 186	1 158	841	1 022	2 424	2 684	3 526	4 246	4 097

Source: Ministry of Defence/DASA (Tri-Service): 020 7218 4535

4.5 Outflow of UK regular forces: by service[1]

Number

		1989/90	1990/91	1991/92	1992/93	1993/94	1994/95	1995/96	1996/97	1997/98	1998/99	1999/00
All Services:												
Male	KDNA	39 461	36 017	30 057	31 138	29 699	31 046	25 746	29 325	21 775	24 459	23 767
Female	KDNB	3 106	3 062	2 748	2 517	2 429	2 994	3 118	3 675	2 483	2 976	2 739
Total	KDNC	42 567	39 079	32 805	33 655	32 128	34 040	28 864	33 000	24 258	27 435	26 506
Naval Service:												
Male	KDND	7 377	7 428	6 105	4 655	4 613	5 504	4 314	6 191	4 650	4 925	5 164
Female	KDNE	657	680	662	455	493	681	631	940	621	606	632
Total	KDNF	8 034	8 108	6 767	5 110	5 106	6 185	4 945	7 131	5 271	5 531	5 796
Army:												
Male	KDNI	23 760	21 582	18 304	20 993	19 633	20 234	13 935	13 758	13 103	15 282	14 520
Female	KDNJ	1 301	1 242	1 147	1 336	1 288	1 651	1 508	1 596	1 275	1 733	1 570
Total	KDNK	25 061	22 824	19 451	22 329	20 921	21 885	15 443	15 354	14 378	17 015	16 090
Royal Air Force:												
Male	KDNL	8 324	7 007	5 648	5 490	5 453	5 308	7 497	9 376	4 022	4 252	4 083
Female	KDNM	1 148	1 140	939	726	648	662	979	1 139	587	637	537
Total	KDNN	9 472	8 147	6 587	6 216	6 101	5 970	8 476	10 515	4 609	4 889	4 620

1 Comprises all those who left the Regular Forces and includes deaths.

Source: Ministry of Defence/DASA (Tri-Service): 020 7218 4535

4.6 Deployment of UK service personnel
As at 1 July

Thousands

		1989	1990	1991	1992	1993	1994	1995	1996	1997	1998	1999
UK Service personnel, Regular Forces:												
In United Kingdom[8]	KDOB	220.2	215.9	207.9	210.7	204.3	192.1	182.2	177.4	171.6	173.4	171.7
England	KDOC	183.3	179.6	173.3	174.2	167.1	156.5	149.4	146.6	142.6	144.6	144.3
Wales	KDOD	5.4	5.3	5.2	5.2	5.1	4.8	5.2	4.3	3.3	3.2	3.3
Scotland	KDOE	20.0	19.3	18.2	18.8	19.4	18.4	16.9	15.5	13.9	14.2	14.9
Northern Ireland[2]	KDOF	11.2	11.5	11.2	12.6	12.5	12.3	9.9	10.5	11.5	11.0	9.0
Overseas	KDOG	88.4	88.9	89.3	78.9	65.5	56.2	50.0	48.5	42.6	43.1	47.1
Germany[3,4,6]	KDOH	63.9	63.2	69.7	60.0	45.6	37.2	33.4	20.8	21.2	20.3	18.0
Elsewhere in Continental Europe[4,6]	KDOI	7.0	6.8	–	–	–	–	–	11.7	6.2	6.9	15.2
Gibraltar	KDOJ	1.6	1.8	1.0	1.0	1.3	1.5	0.6	0.6	0.5	0.5	0.6
Cyprus	KDOL	4.8	4.8	5.2	4.8	4.7	4.1	4.4	4.0	3.9	3.6	3.6
Mediterranean, Near East and Gulf	KDOM	1.8	1.3	1.1	2.2	2.8	2.4	0.6	0.5	0.3	1.2	1.3
Hong Kong	KDON	2.1	2.1	2.3	2.1	1.9	1.7	0.9	0.9	–	–	–
Elsewhere in the Far East	KDOP	0.6	0.5	0.5	2.1	0.3	0.3	0.3	0.3	1.5	0.3	0.3
Other locations[1,5]	KDOQ	6.6	8.4	9.5	6.7	8.8	8.9	9.4	9.8	9.0	10.4	8.2
Total[9]	KDOA	307.8	303.1	297.2	289.6	270.9	248.3	232.2	225.9	214.2	216.5	218.8
Locally entered service personnel:												
United Kingdom	KDOS	1.2	1.4	1.4	1.3	1.4	1.5	1.8	1.7	2.1	2.1	2.0
Gibraltar	KDOT	0.1	0.1	0.1	0.2	0.2	0.2	0.2	0.2	0.2	0.4	0.4
Hong Kong	KDOV	5.5	5.5	5.5	5.2	4.4	3.7	1.8	1.6	0.7	–	–
Brunei	KDOW	0.9	0.9	0.8	0.8	0.8	0.7	0.9	0.7	1.0	0.9	0.8
India/Nepal	KDOX	1.4	1.1	1.3	1.3	1.2	0.2	0.5	0.7	0.9	0.5	0.5
Total	KDOK	9.0	8.9	9.1	8.8	7.9	7.1	5.1	4.9	4.7	4.0	3.7

1 From 1984 to 1992 the England, Wales and Scotland national figures include personnel who were UK based but temporarily deployed in the South Atlantic. These have been included also in the Overseas numbers against 'Other locations'.

2 The figures for Northern Ireland include all personnel who are serving on emergency tours of duty but exclude the former Ulster Defence Regiment, now the Home Services element of the Royal Irish Regiment.

3 Prior to 1994, personnel serving in Northern Ireland on emergency tours of duty but remaining under the command of the Commander-in-Chief, British Army of the Rhine, are included in these numbers. Personnel serving on emergency tours of duty in other overseas areas are included in the numbers for that area.

4 These figures include personnel stationed in Berlin and Sardinia.

5 These figures include Defence Attaches/Advisers and their staffs.

6 From 1991-1995, figures for the Federal Republic of Germany and elsewhere in Continental Europe were combined.

7 Figures may not equate to totals because of rounding.

8 The figures for Service personnel in each country are obtained from a different source from that used to obtain the United Kingdom total. Consequently, the sum of the national figures can differ from the United Kingdom total.

9 The figures include service personnel who are on loan to countries in the areas shown. The Royal Navy and Royal Marines figures include personnel who are at sea at the situation date. All Defence Attaches and Advisers and their staffs are included under "Other Locations" and not identified within specific areas.

Source: Ministry of Defence/DASA (Tri-Service): 020 7218 4535

4.7 Service married accommodation and Defence land holdings
As at 1 April

			1990	1991	1992	1993	1994	1995	1996	1997	1998	1999	2000
Married accommodation		Thousands											
United Kingdom: total	KDPA	"	75.0	73.6	72.3	71.8	71.1	69.7	72.1	68.6	67.3	65.5	61.6
Permanent holdings[1]	KDPB	"	75.0	73.6	72.3	71.8	71.1	69.7	72.1	68.6	67.3	65.5	61.6
Hirings	KDPC	"	–	–	–	–	–	–	–	–	–	–	–
Overseas: total[2]	KDPD	"	46.7	48.9	45.1	42.4	36.9	28.8	26.3	..	..	..	..
Permanent holdings	KDPE	"	21.3	24.2	22.1	21.7	21.2	16.8	15.5	..	..	..	..
Hirings	KDPK	"	25.4	24.7	23.0	20.7	15.7	12.0	10.8	..	..	..	..
Land holdings		Thousand											
United Kingdom		hectares											
Land[3]	KDPF	"	222.6	224.8	225.4	224.1	223.5	221.0	222.6	221.0	220.0	220.2	219.9
Foreshore[3]	KDPH	"	18.0	18.0	18.0	18.4	18.5	18.4	18.5	18.6	18.6	18.6	18.6
Rights held[4]	KDPJ	"	103.4	121.3	120.7	100.2	100.4	122.3	124.3	124.5	124.5	124.8	124.8
Defence land													
Used for agricultural purposes	KDPL	"	110.8	109.9	109.3	107.1	107.6	107.9	107.4	96.2	103.5	114.5	92.2
Used for grazing only	KDPM	"	61.2	63.9	62.6	62.4	61.3	61.8	60.7	51.9	59.6	65.5	50.3
Full agricultural use	KDPN	"	49.6	46.0	46.7	44.6	46.3	46.1	46.7	44.3	43.9	49.0	41.9

1 Including a few unfurnished hirings taken from local authorities and from the Scottish Special Housing Association.
2 This information is no longer available.
3 Freehold and leasehold.
4 Land and foreshore not owned by, or leased to MOD, over which the Department has limited rights under grants or licenses.

Source: Ministry of Defence/DASA (Tri-Service): 020 7218 4535

4.8 UK Defence civilian manpower strengths
As at 1 April

Thousands

		1990	1991	1992	1993	1994	1995	1996	1997	1998	1999	2000
Ministry of Defence civilians												
Centre[5,7]												
Non-industrial	KDQE	17.7	21.8	22.9	23.7	18.9	17.3	20.0	21.2	20.6	20.0	18.1
Industrial	KDQF	0.4	0.7	0.8	0.8	0.8	0.7	0.9	1.1	1.1	1.0	0.9
Trading funds[4]												
Non-industrial	KYCU	..	..	..	..	..	..	12.1	13.4	12.3	11.9	14.2
Industrial	KYCV	..	..	..	..	..	..	1.9	1.7	1.3	1.1	–
Defence Logistics Organisation[8]												
Non-industrial	ZBTJ	..	..	..	..	..	..	..	..	..	..	19.0
Industrial	ZBTK	..	..	..	..	..	..	..	..	..	..	11.3
Naval Service[3]												
Non-industrial	KYCW	15.1	14.9	14.9	15.5	15.8	15.2	13.7	12.6	12.2	11.6	3.6
Industrial	KYCX	16.4	15.8	15.2	14.1	13.0	12.0	9.7	9.0	8.0	6.8	2.7
Army												
Non-industrial	KDQK	22.1	21.4	21.2	22.0	22.5	22.1	21.4	20.7	20.5	20.3	15.4
Industrial	KDQL	17.7	17.0	17.0	15.1	14.9	14.5	13.7	13.2	11.8	10.3	5.7
Royal Air Force												
Non-industrial	KDQM	12.4	10.2	10.7	10.3	10.3	10.1	9.9	10.0	10.1	10.6	5.6
Industrial	KDQN	8.0	7.7	7.7	7.2	7.0	6.7	6.5	6.4	6.1	7.1	3.4
Procurement Executive[6,7]												
Non-industrial	KDQO	22.6	22.0	21.0	16.4	15.3	15.1	–	–	–	–	–
Industrial	KDQP	9.1	8.6	8.1	4.1	3.1	2.5	–	–	–	–	–
Total UK based[2]	KDQB	141.4	140.2	139.5	129.2	121.6	116.1	109.9	109.2	104.0	100.9	100.0
Non-industrial	KDQC	89.9	90.3	90.7	87.9	82.8	79.8	77.1	77.9	75.7	74.5	76.0
Industrial	KDQD	51.5	49.9	48.8	41.3	38.8	36.3	32.7	31.3	28.3	26.4	24.0
Locally engaged overseas	KDQA	30.9	28.9	27.0	26.6	20.7	16.9	16.9	15.7	15.0	14.8	14.7
Non-industrial	KDQT	10.1	9.9	9.7	9.6	7.3	6.4	7.1	7.0	6.7	6.7	6.7
Industrial	KDQU	20.8	19.1	17.3	17.0	13.4	10.5	9.8	8.7	8.2	8.0	8.0
Total[1]	KFHT	172.3	169.1	166.5	155.8	142.3	133.0	126.8	124.9	119.0	115.7	114.7

1 Prior to April 1995 all part-timers were counted as half of full time. From that date they are counted as the number of hours worked as a proportion of normal conditioned hours. The average part timer works about 60% of full time.
2 Including UK-based civilians serving overseas.
3 The Devonport and Rosyth Dockyards were contractorised with effect from 6 April 1987.
4 Prior to becoming Trading Funds the Defence Evaluation Agency and the Hydrographic Office were included in Procurement Executive. From 1991 to 1995 Metrological Office was included in Central.
5 From 1989 the 'Centre' figure includes all MOD Police. From 1991 the 'Centre' figure includes staff in the Meteorological Office (transferred from 'Air Force'), staff in the Chemical Defence Establishment (transferred from 'Procurement Executive'), and all personnel serving overseas in support of the services (other than in BAOR or RAF Germany). Communications staff are excluded after 1993.
6 Atomic Weapons Establishment was contractorised with effect from 1 April 1992.
7 From 1996, those staff in the procurement executive are included in "Centre" figures.
8 As from 1 April 2000 a new TLB was formed in Central called DLO, replacing the TLBs CFS, QMG and RAF Logs Cmd.

Source: Ministry of Defence/DASA (Civilian): 020 7218 4277

4.9 Service hospitals

		1985	1986	1987	1988[4]	1989	1990	1991	1992	1993[5]	1994	1995
Average number of beds[1]												
United Kingdom	KDLA	1 986	1 959	1 846	1 765	1 661	1 441	1 264	1 375	1 348	1 358	1 209
Overseas	KDLB	1 184	1 117	1 029	985	985	825	815	723	581	445	345
Average number of admission by percentage[2]												
United Kingdom:	KDLE	62.0	59.2	58.2	59.6	59.7	60.0	56.2	57.5	53.0	50.4	43.3
Service personnel	KDLF	26.5	25.1	24.2	23.3	22.5	24.1	26.5	23.3	21.3	21.5	18.8
Service dependants	KDLG	7.8	6.5	6.9	6.0	5.6	5.4	4.9	4.8	3.5	2.5	1.5
NHS/Other	KDLH	27.7	27.7	27.0	30.3	31.6	30.4	24.8	29.3	28.2	26.4	23.0
Overseas:	KDLI	50.6	48.5	47.9	47.0	43.5	41.9	40.1	45.7	39.9	46.1	44.1
UK Service personnel	KDLJ	17.7	16.6	16.3	15.1	14.2	15.1	14.2	17.1	16.2	21.8	22.0
Service dependants	KDLK	20.6	20.6	21.9	22.1	21.3	23.9	23.1	25.4	20.9	21.3	19.9
Others	KDLL	12.4	11.4	9.7	9.6	8.0	2.9	2.8	3.1	2.8	3.0	2.2
Average number of admissions per bed[2]												
United Kingdom	KDLM	37.8	36.8	38.3	41.3	42.8	43.7	40.9	39.9	37.3	38.4	29.2
Overseas	KDLN	35.3	36.4	38.1	39.1	36.0	38.4	33.6	37.8	36.0	35.6	35.9
Average days in hospital per patient												
United Kingdom	KDLO	6.0	5.9	5.6	5.4	5.1	5.0	5.0	5.2	5.1	4.8	4.9
Overseas	KDLP	5.2	4.9	4.6	4.5	4.4	4.0	4.1	4.2	4.1	4.3	4.5
Outpatient attendances (thousands)[3]												
United Kingdom:	KDLQ	373.7	373.8	359.6	374.7	371.5	362.1	281.3	306.7	291.1	239.8	199.9
Service personnel	KDLR	119.3	117.2	116.4	119.8	111.4	109.0	93.3	103.9	102.8	96.5	82.2
Service dependants	KDLS	48.7	46.2	41.1	39.4	38.4	37.1	30.7	31.4	27.0	20.0	13.0
NHS/Others	KDLT	205.7	210.3	202.1	215.5	221.7	216.1	157.4	171.5	161.3	123.3	104.7
Overseas:	KDLU	229.6	212.9	202.8	179.6	171.2	138.7	134.8	138.7	123.9	81.5	64.2
UK Service personnel	KDLV	64.4	59.6	56.5	50.2	50.8	51.4	49.8	49.4	46.1	31.6	25.9
Service dependants	KDLW	102.9	96.5	94.0	84.1	81.8	75.8	75.2	78.9	67.5	42.2	33.1
Others	KDLX	62.3	56.8	52.2	45.3	38.5	11.4	9.9	10.8	10.2	7.7	5.2

1 These relate to the numbers of available beds.
2 Based on the number of beds as defined above.
3 In addition 3 300 patients were seen at outlying clinics of the hospitals and some 19 000 day patients were treated in the UK and 3 000 overseas in 1992.
4 Changes to the Statistical package used in certain hospitals to produce figures from 1988 onwards, mean that these figures are not fully comparable with those for earlier years.
5 Provisional.

Source: Ministry of Defence/DASA (Information Services): 01225 472963

4.10 Strength of uniformed UK medical staff[1]
At 1 April

Number

		1990	1991	1992	1993	1994	1995	1996	1997	1998	1999	2000
Qualified doctors:												
Naval Service	KDMA	275	267	263	270	268	262	238	211	209	209	211
Army	KDMB	501	649	530	522	490	473	431	434	431	437	452
Royal Air Force	KDMC	374	371	375	368	359	334	273	223	207	197	185
All Services	KDMD	1 150	1 287	1 168	1 160	1 117	1 069	942	868	847	843	848
Qualified dentists:												
Naval Services	KDME	83	77	75	76	75	73	62	65	64	65	60
Army	KDMF	197	194	183	178	168	154	145	139	140	141	144
Royal Air Force	KDMG	120	120	121	119	115	110	104	87	80	85	78
All Services	KDMH	400	391	379	373	358	337	311	291	284	291	282
Support staff:[2,3]												
Naval Services	KDMI	1 249	1 254	1 308	1 361	1 401	1 352	1 294	1 025	946	935	963
Nursing services	ZBTL	..	..	..	..	..	..	..	..	..	299	282
Support	ZBTM	..	..	..	..	..	..	..	..	..	636	681
Army	KDMJ	4 706	4 941	4 297	4 288	3 761	3 381	3 284	3 017	3 094	3 002	2 991
Nursing services	ZBTN	..	..	..	..	..	..	..	..	..	667	658
Support	ZBTO	..	..	..	..	..	..	..	..	..	2 335	2 333
Royal Air Force	KDMK	1 964	1 974	1 948	2 038	1 837	1 795	1 404	1 213	1 194	1 225	1 286
Nursing services	ZBTP	..	..	..	..	..	..	..	..	..	296	334
Support	ZBTQ	..	..	..	..	..	..	..	..	..	929	952
All Services	KDML	7 919	8 169	7 553	7 687	6 999	6 245	5 982	5 255	5 234	5 162	5 240

1 Includes staff employed at units (including ships) and in hospitals.
2 Includes all members of the Nursing Services/Nursing Corps.
3 Support staff have now been split so that nurses are separate from other support staff.

Source: Ministry of Defence/DASA (Tri- Service): 020 7218 4535

4.11 Health indicators for UK regular forces[1]

		1975	1980	1985	1990	1993	1994	1995	1996	1997[3]	1998	1999
Deaths[2]												
Total Number	LUIC	422	370	319	320	241	219	207	146	165[13]	164[13]	144
Male	LUID	414	367	314	314	230	212	198	144	156[13]	156[13]	141
Female	LUIE	8	3	5	6	11	7	9	2	9	8	3
Rates per thousand[3]												
Tri-service	LUIF	1.24	1.11	0.96	1.03	0.87	0.86	0.88	0.65	0.77[13]	0.77	0.68
Navy	LUIG	0.81	1.07	0.81	0.80	0.75	0.68	0.62	0.57	0.87[13]	0.59	0.60
Army[4]	LUIH	1.45	1.16	0.90	1.10	0.96	1.03	0.99	0.75	0.82	0.85[13]	0.76
RAF	LUII	1.21	1.05	1.18	1.06	0.81	0.70	0.89	0.53	0.58	0.75	0.58
By Diagnosis												
Diseases	LUIJ	0.53	0.36	0.33	0.33	0.26	0.27	0.26	0.18	0.27	0.26	0.22
Injuries	LUIK	0.72	0.75	0.63	0.70	0.61	0.59	0.62	0.47	0.50[13]	0.51	0.46
Others[5]	LUIL	–	–	–	–	–	–	–	–	–	–	–
Medical Discharges[6,7]												
Total Number	LUIM	1 822	1 010	1 398	1 419	1 220	1 345	1 626	1 727	1 636	1 598	1 667
Male	LUIN	1 746	962	1 365	1 367	1 134	1 190	1 406	1 416	1 407	1 327	1 336
Female	LUIO	76	48	33	52	86	155	220	311	229	271	331
Rates per thousand[3]												
Tri-service	LUIP	5.38	3.03	4.19	4.56	4.41	5.29	6.92	7.70	7.61	7.50	7.88
Navy	LUIQ	4.90	2.16	3.54	4.26	4.05	4.89	6.29	7.18	7.89	9.58	10.50
Army[4]	LUIR	6.35	3.66	5.97	6.32	6.03	7.62	9.60	10.47	9.38	9.01	9.23
RAF	LUIS	3.99	2.56	1.41	1.63	1.85	1.63	2.96	3.14	3.88	2.77	2.96
By Diagnosis												
Diseases	LUIT	4.53	2.53	3.16	3.95	3.75	4.09	4.60	4.77	4.93	4.91	4.69
Injuries	LUIU	0.84	0.50	1.03	0.61	0.66	1.20	2.31	2.93	2.67	2.40	2.60
Others[5]	LUIV	–	–	–	–	–	–	–	–	–	0.19	0.60
Causes of medical discharge[8]												
Musclo-skeletal disease	LUIW	..	0.66	1.42	2.39	2.22	2.55[13]	2.67	3.04	2.71	2.90[13]	2.71
Training & exercise injuries	LUIX	..	0.05	0.20	0.11	0.23	0.40	0.80	1.19	1.03	0.92[13]	1.07
Nervous system and sense organs[12]	LUIY	..	0.59	0.52	0.38	0.37	0.36	0.48	0.38	0.58	0.45	0.49
Fall & jump injuries	LUIZ	..	0.07	0.17	0.09	0.05	0.11	0.38	0.51	0.51	0.51[13]	0.43
All other causes	LUJA	..	1.77	2.03	1.67	1.54[13]	1.87[13]	2.59[13]	2.58[13]	2.81[13]	3.02[13]	3.18
Reported sickness events (provisional)[9,10]												
Total Number	LUJB	61 900	54 727	49 412	46 504	42 789[13]	36 826[13]	36 558[13]	26 902[13]	25 410[13]	23 927[13]	19 569
Male	LUJC	56 800	49 753	45 227	42 312	37 921[13]	32 566[13]	32 160[13]	23 576[13]	22 068[13]	20 581[13]	16 769
Female	LUJD	5 100	4 974	4 185	4 192	4 868	4 260	4 398[13]	3 326[13]	3 342[13]	3 346[13]	2 800
Rates per thousand[3]												
Tri-Service	LUJE	182	164	148	149	155	145	156[13]	120[13]	118[13]	112[13]	93
Navy	LUJF	..	157	140	108	110	99	99	87[13]	91[13]	83[13]	70
Army[4]	LUJG	..	159	147	150	134	129	132	106[13]	93[13]	89[13]	62
RAF	LUJH	..	180	156	177	223	206	234	169	189[13]	183[13]	173
By Diagnosis												
Diseases	LUJI	141	127	116	115	126	115	124	90	91	87[13]	71
Injuries	LUJJ	34	31	26	27	21	23	23	23	20	18[13]	17
Others[5]	LUJK	8	7	6	7	8	7	9	7	7[13]	7[13]	5
Average Strength[11]												
Tri-Service (thousands)	LUJL	339.2	332.8	333.7	311.1	276.5	254.2	235.0	224.3	215.1	213.2	211.5
Navy	LUJM	76.1	72.1	69.5	62.7	58.4	54.4	50.2	47.2	44.9	44.2	43.4
Army	LUJN	169.2	170.1	170.9	159.1	138.6	125.7	114.8	113.5	113.1	113.3	113.0
RAF	LUJO	93.9	90.6	93.3	89.3	79.4	74.1	70.0	63.6	57.1	55.7	55.1

1 These data have been revised since the previous edition as a result of updated information.
2 Includes deaths occuring on or off duty.
3 Rates per thousand have been calculated by taking the number of episodes in each year and dividing by the average strength for the year.
4 Army figures include Gurkhas, except those shown for 1975.
5 Used where no classificatory diagnosis was reported or where the person was not sick, e.g. admissions for investigation, preventive measures or elective surgery.
6 Those medically discharged out of the Services before the completion of their engagement.
7 Medical discharges by service in 1975 are for males only.
8 Main cause of medical discharge based on common causes in 1999.
9 Reported sickness events are based on the following events reported to DASA; all hospital events; all medical centre events over 48 hours and all sick at home events lasting more than 6 days. Deaths are also included but out-patient treatments are not. Readers should be aware that these data should be regarded as indicators of health activity only, they do not cover all aspects of health care since primary care and outpatients activity are not included. In addition DASA (Medical Statistics) are aware that not all sickness events are reported. Efforts are being made to quantify and improve this under reporting of sickness events.

10 For 1975 reported sickness events have been based on two days or more, whether occuring on or off duty, and terminating during the year. Episodes of Army personnel sickness not requiring admission into medical units and of Navy personnel sick on shore for less than 7 days are excluded. The number of reported sickness events for 1975 is rounded to the nearest hundred.
11 Average strength is calculated by taking the average strength at 1 Jan, 1 Apr, 1 Jul, 1 Oct of the year in question and 1 Jan of the following year.
12 All figures have been revised.
13 Figure has been revised.

Source: Ministry of Defence/DASA (Medical Statistics): 01225 472963

4.12 Search and rescue operations at home

Number

		1989	1990	1991	1992	1993	1994	1995	1996	1997	1998	1999
Call outs[1]												
of helicopters[2]	KCME	1 736	1 851	1 779	1 997	1 858	1 766	2 059	1 904	1 753	1 720	1 737
of other aircraft[2]	KCMF	84	86	87	69	77	82	85	70	82	72	65
of HM ships and Auxilliary Vessels[2]	KCMG	7	1	5	5	8	6	8	1	3	2	1
of mountain rescue teams	KCMH	76	83	92	125	149	140	125	162	88	82	117
Persons rescued[3]**:total**	KCMI	1 275	1 866	1 458	1 379	1 568	1 336	1 532	1 489	1 145	1 164	1 190
by helicopters	KCMJ	1 241	1 418	1 423	1 358	1 475	1 294	1 488	1 391	1 132	1 153	1 167
by HM ships and Auxilliary Vessels	KCMK	–	–	–	–	–	–	–	–	–	–	1
by mountain rescue teams[4]	KCML	34	448	35	21	93	42	40	98	13	11	22
Incidents: total	KCMM	1 675	1 851	1 783	2 015	1 879	1 791	2 035	1 896	1 739	1 687	1 781

1 More than one element of the Search and Rescue (SAR) services called to the same incident. Consequently, the number of callouts is likely to be greater than the number of incidents.

2 Not permanently on stand-by.

3 Civilian or Military personnel who were removed from a hazardous environment or were transported from the scene by SAR Units in order to receive urgent medical attention.

4 People assisted by Mountain Rescue Teams, but subsequently transported from the scene by helicopter are credited as having been rescued by the helicopter unit concerned. The total incidents figure also includes any HMCG incidents under the control of ARCC Kinloss.

Source: Ministry of Defence/DASA (Logistics): 01225 472295

4.13 UK Defence services and the civilian community

		1989	1990	1991	1992	1993	1994	1995	1996	1997	1998	1999
Military aid to civil ministries during industrial disputes (Manweeks of Service personnel deployed)	KCMN	11 550	–	–	–	–	–	1 827	256	389	1 394	–
Fishery protection[1]												
Vessels boarded	KCMO	2 284	1 992	2 284	2 465	2 540	2 080	1 878	2 224	1 758	1 829	1 777
Hydrographic services												
New charts produced	KCMP	148	240	96	94	–	–	–	–	–	–	–
New editions of charts	KCMQ	231	190	276	258	–	–	–	–	–	–	–
Charts printed(millions)	KCMR	2.5	2.9	3.1	3.1	–	–	–	–	–	–	–

1 This item relates to activities of the RN Fishery Squadron operating within British fishing limits under contract to MAFF. Boardings carried out by vessels of the Scottish Office Agriculture and Fisheries Department and the Department of Agriculture for Northern Ireland are not included.

Source: Ministry of Defence/DASA (Tri-Service): 020 7218 4535

5 Population and vital statistics

Population and vital statistics

This section begins with a summary of population figures for the United Kingdom and constituent countries for 1851 to 2031 and for Great Britain from 1801 (Table 5.1). Table 5.2 analyses the elements of population change. Table 5.3 gives details of the national sex and age structures for years up to the present date, with projected figures up to the year 2021. Legal marital condition of the population is shown in Table 5.4. The distribution of population at regional and local levels is summarised in Table 5.5.

In the main, historical series relate to census information, while mid-year estimates, which make allowance for under-enumeration in the census, are given for the recent past and the present (from 1961 onwards).

Population *(Tables 5.1 - 5.3)*

Figures shown in these tables relate to the population enumerated at successive censuses, (up to 1951), mid-year estimates (from 1961 to 1999) and population projections (up to 2021).

Definition of resident population
The estimated population of an area includes all those usually resident in the area, whatever their nationality. HM Forces serving abroad are excluded from, but non-UK Armed Forces stationed here are included within the estimates of resident population. Students are taken to be resident at their term-time addresses.

The current series of estimates are updated annually. Starting with estimates derived from results of the 1991 Census of Population, allowance is made for subsequent births, deaths and migration and for estimated underenumeration in the 1991 Census.

Table 5.4 shows the population estimates by marital status. The 1991 figures for England and Wales have been rebased using 1991 Census results. Rebased population estimates by marital status for England and Wales for 1991-1995 were published in an ONS First Release in October 1997 and are available from the Population Estimates Unit.

Projected resident population of the United Kingdom and constituent countries
(Tables 5.1 - 5.3)
These projections are prepared by the Government Actuary, in consultation with the Registrars General, as a common framework for use in national planning in a number of different fields. New projections are made at least every second year on assumptions regarding future fertility, mortality and migration which seem most appropriate on the basis of the statistical evidence available at the time. The population projections in Tables 5.1 - 5.3 are based on the estimates of the population of the United Kingdom at mid-1998 made by the Registrars General.

Geographical distribution of the population *(Table 5.5)*
The population enumerated in the censuses for 1911-1951, the mid-year population estimates for later years, and areas (1991 in km²), are provided for standard regions of the United Kingdom, for metropolitan areas, for broad groupings of local authority districts by type within England and Wales, and for some of the larger cities. Projections of future sub-national population levels are prepared from time to time by the Registrar General, but are not shown in this publication.

Migration into and out of the United Kingdom
(Tables 5.7 and 5.8)
A migrant into the United Kingdom is defined as a person who has resided abroad for a year or more and on entering has declared the intention to reside here for a year or more; and vice versa for a migrant from the United Kingdom. The estimates shown are derived from the International Passenger Survey (IPS), a sample survey covering the principal air and sea routes between the United Kingdom and overseas but excluding routes to and from the Irish Republic. Migration between the Channel Islands and the Isle of Man and the rest of the world has been excluded from these tables with effect from 1988. It is also highly likely that the data exclude asylum seekers and persons admitted as short-term visitors who are subsequently granted an extension of stay for a year or more for other reasons, for example as students or on the basis of marriage. After taking account of persons leaving the United Kingdom for a short-term period who stay overseas for periods longer than originally intended, adjustment is needed to net migration ranges from about 10 thousand in 1981 to 44 thousand in 1998, an average of approximately 31 thousand. The overall net inflow for 1998, including migration with the Irish Republic, is about 178 thousand.

Acceptances for settlement in the United Kingdom
(Table 5.9)
This table presents in geographic regions, the statistics of individual nationalities, arranged alphabetically within each region. The figures are on a different basis from those derived from IPS (Tables 5.6 and 5.7) and relate only to people subject to immigration control. Persons accepted for settlement are allowed to stay indefinitely in the United Kingdom. They exclude temporary migrants such as students and generally relate only to non-EEA nationals. Settlement can occur several years after entry to the country.

Applications received for asylum in the United Kingdom excluding dependants *(Table 5.10)*
This table shows statistics of applications for asylum in the United Kingdom. Figures are shown of the main applicant nationalities by geographic region. The basis of assessing asylum applications, and hence of deciding whether to grant asylum in the United Kingdom, is the 1951 United Nations Convention on Refugees.

Divorces *(Tables 5.12 and 5.13)*
Table 5.12 gives figures for dissolutions and annulments by duration of marriage and age of wife. Data in Table 5.13 give petitions filed for divorce, divorces by fact proven and separations.

Births *(Tables 5.14 and 5.15)*
For Scotland and Northern Ireland the number of births relate to those registered during the year. For England and Wales the figures up to and including 1930-32 are for those registered while later figures relate to births occurring in each year.

Deaths *(Tables 5.18 and 5.19)*
The figures relate to the number of deaths registered during each calendar year. However, from 1993 onwards, the figures for England and Wales represent occurrences. This change has little effect on annual totals.

Changes in coding practices for England and Wales, particularly coding of underlying cause of death, from January 1993 have led to some differences in the pattern of cause of death (eg. pneumonia) as compared with previous years. These changes result in a return to the rules in place prior to 1984 and bring England and Wales back into line with Scotland, Northern Ireland, and other countries. For further details, see the Introduction to *Mortality Statistics:* cause 1993 (revised) and 1994, Series DH2, no. 21, HMSO (1996).

Life tables *(Table 5.22)*
The interim life tables are constructed from the estimated populations in 1997-99 and the deaths occurring in those years for England and Wales and registered in those years for Scotland and Northern Ireland.

Population and vital statistics

5.1 Population summary

	United Kingdom			England and Wales			Wales	Scotland			Northern Ireland		
	Persons	Males	Females	Persons	Males	Females	Persons	Persons	Males	Females	Persons	Males	Females
Enumerated population: census figures													
1801	..	..	..	8 893	4 255	4 638	587	1 608	739	869	..	..	..
1851	22 259	10 855	11 404	17 928	8 781	9 146	1 163	2 889	1 376	1 513	1 442	698	745
1901	38 237	18 492	19 745	32 528	15 729	16 799	2 013	4 472	2 174	2 298	1 237	590	647
1911	42 082	20 357	21 725	36 070	17 446	18 625	2 421	4 761	2 309	2 452	1 251	603	648
1921[1]	44 027	21 033	22 994	37 887	18 075	19 811	2 656	4 882	2 348	2 535	1 258	610	648
1931[1]	46 038	22 060	23 978	39 952	19 133	20 819	2 593	4 843	2 326	2 517	1 243	601	642
1951	50 225	24 118	26 107	43 758	21 016	22 742	2 599	5 096	2 434	2 662	1 371	668	703
1961	52 709	25 481	27 228	46 105	22 304	23 801	2 644	5 179	2 483	2 697	1 425	694	731
Resident population: mid-year estimates													
	DYAY	BBAB	BBAC	BBAD	BBAE	BBAF	KGJM	BBAG	BBAH	BBAI	BBAJ	BBAK	BBAL
1964	53 991	26 191	27 800	47 324	22 979	24 346	2 677	5 209	2 501	2 707	1 458	711	747
1965	54 350	26 368	27 982	47 671	23 151	24 521	2 693	5 210	2 501	2 709	1 468	716	752
1966	54 643	26 511	28 132	47 967	23 296	24 671	2 702	5 201	2 496	2 704	1 476	719	757
1967	54 959	26 673	28 286	48 272	23 451	24 821	2 710	5 198	2 496	2 702	1 489	726	763
1968	55 214	26 784	28 429	48 511	23 554	24 957	2 715	5 200	2 498	2 702	1 503	733	770
1969	55 461	26 908	28 553	48 738	23 666	25 072	2 722	5 209	2 503	2 706	1 514	739	776
1970	55 632	26 992	28 641	48 891	23 738	25 153	2 729	5 214	2 507	2 707	1 527	747	781
1971	55 928	27 167	28 761	49 152	23 897	25 255	2 740	5 236	2 516	2 720	1 540	755	786
1972	56 097	27 259	28 837	49 327	23 989	25 339	2 755	5 231	2 513	2 717	1 539	758	782
1973	56 223	27 332	28 891	49 459	24 061	25 399	2 773	5 234	2 515	2 719	1 530	756	774
1974	56 236	27 349	28 887	49 468	24 075	25 393	2 785	5 241	2 519	2 722	1 527	755	772
1975	56 226	27 361	28 865	49 470	24 091	25 378	2 795	5 232	2 516	2 716	1 524	753	770
1976	56 216	27 360	28 856	49 459	24 089	25 370	2 799	5 233	2 517	2 716	1 524	754	770
1977	56 190	27 345	28 845	49 440	24 076	25 364	2 801	5 226	2 515	2 711	1 523	754	769
1978	56 178	27 330	28 849	49 443	24 067	25 375	2 804	5 212	2 509	2 704	1 523	754	770
1979	56 240	27 373	28 867	49 508	24 113	25 395	2 810	5 204	2 505	2 699	1 528	755	773
1980	56 330	27 411	28 919	49 603	24 156	25 448	2 816	5 194	2 501	2 693	1 533	755	778
1981	56 357	27 412	28 946	49 634	24 160	25 474	2 813	5 180	2 495	2 685	1 543	757	786
1982	56 325	27 394	28 931	49 613	24 148	25 466	2 806	5 167	2 490	2 677	1 545	757	788
1983	56 384	27 433	28 952	49 681	24 190	25 491	2 807	5 153	2 484	2 669	1 551	759	792
1984	56 513	27 513	29 000	49 810	24 270	25 540	2 806	5 146	2 482	2 664	1 557	761	796
1985	56 693	27 613	29 080	49 990	24 369	25 621	2 810	5 137	2 479	2 658	1 565	765	800
1986	56 859	27 698	29 160	50 162	24 456	25 706	2 820	5 123	2 474	2 649	1 574	768	805
1987	57 015	27 789	29 227	50 321	24 546	25 775	2 833	5 113	2 470	2 643	1 582	773	809
1988	57 166	27 875	29 290	50 487	24 641	25 846	2 854	5 093	2 461	2 632	1 585	774	812
1989	57 365	27 988	29 377	50 678	24 750	25 928	2 869	5 097	2 463	2 634	1 590	776	814
1990	57 567	28 116	29 452	50 869	24 872	25 998	2 878	5 102	2 466	2 636	1 596	778	818
1991	57 814	28 248	29 566	51 100	24 995	26 104	2 891	5 107	2 470	2 637	1 607	783	824
1992	58 013	28 365	29 648	51 277	25 099	26 178	2 899	5 111	2 473	2 638	1 625	793	831
1993	58 198	28 477	29 720	51 439	25 198	26 241	2 906	5 120	2 479	2 642	1 638	801	838
1994	58 395	28 595	29 805	51 621	25 304	26 317	2 913	5 132	2 486	2 646	1 648	805	842
1995	58 612	28 731	29 881	51 820	25 433	26 387	2 917	5 137	2 489	2 647	1 655	809	846
1996	58 807	28 860	29 948	52 010	25 557	26 453	2 921	5 128	2 486	2 642	1 669	816	853
1997	59 014	28 992	30 022	52 211	25 684	26 527	2 927	5 123	2 484	2 638	1 680	823	857
1998	59 237	29 128	30 108	52 428	25 817	26 611	2 933	5 120	2 484	2 636	1 689	827	861
1999	59 501	29 299	30 202	52 690	25 985	26 705	2 937	5 119	2 486	2 634	1 692	829	863
Resident population: projections (mid-year)[2]													
2001	59 954	29 581	30 372	53 137	26 258	26 879	2 950	5 109	2 485	2 624	1 708	839	869
2006	60 860	30 147	30 714	54 021	26 799	27 222	2 969	5 098	2 489	2 609	1 742	858	883
2011	61 773	30 696	31 077	54 915	27 328	27 587	2 993	5 087	2 492	2 595	1 771	876	895
2021	63 642	31 717	31 925	56 763	28 325	28 437	3 047	5 058	2 487	2 570	1 821	904	917

1 Figures for Northern Ireland are estimated. The population at the Census of 1926 was 1 257 thousand (608 thousand males and 649 thousand females).
2 These projections are 1998-based. More detail given in Table 5.3.

Sources: Office for National Statistics: 01329 813233; General Register Office (Northern Ireland); General Register Office (Scotland); Government Actuary's Department: 020 7211 2622

5.2 Population changes

Thousands

	Population[1] at start of period	Average annual change				
		Overall annual change	Births	Deaths[2]	Excess of births over deaths	Net migration and other adjustments[3]
United Kingdom						
1901 - 1911	38 237	385	1 091	624	467	-82
1911 - 1921	42 082	195	975	689	286	-92
1921 - 1931	44 027	201	824	555	268	-67
1931 - 1951	46 038	213	793	603	190	22
1951 - 1961	50 225	258	839	593	246	12
1961 - 1971	52 807	310	962	638	324	-14
1971 - 1981	55 928	42	736	666	69	-27
1981 - 1991	56 357	146	757	655	103	43
1991 - 1999	57 814	211	744	637	107	104
1999 - 2001[4]	59 501	228	716	627	88	140
2001 - 2011	59 954	182	701	614	87	95
2011 - 2021	61 773	187	712	620	92	95
England and Wales						
1901 - 1911	32 528	354	929	525	404	-50
1911 - 1921	36 070	182	828	584	244	-62
1921 - 1931	37 887	207	693	469	224	-17
1931 - 1951	39 952	193	673	518	155	38
1951 - 1961	43 758	244	714	516	197	47
1961 - 1971	46 196	296	832	560	272	23
1971 - 1981	49 152	48	638	585	53	-5
1981 - 1991	49 634	147	664	576	89	58
1991 - 1999	51 100	199	658	561	97	101
1999 - 2001[4]	52 690	223	636	554	81	142
2001 - 2011	53 137	178	623	542	81	97
2011 - 2021	54 915	185	635	547	88	97
Scotland						
1901 - 1911	4 472	29	131	76	54	-25
1911 - 1921	4 761	12	118	82	36	-24
1921 - 1931	4 882	-4	100	65	35	-39
1931 - 1951	4 843	13	92	67	25	
1951 - 1961	5 096	9	95	62	34	-25
1961 - 1971	5 184	3	97	63	34	-30
1971 - 1981	5 236	-6	70	64	6	-11
1981 - 1991	5 180	-7	66	63	3	-10
1991 - 1999	5 107	2	62	61	1	1
1999 - 2001[4]	5 119	-2	57	58	-1	-1
2001 - 2011	5 109	-2	55	56	-1	-1
2011 - 2021	5 087	-3	55	57	-2	-1
Northern Ireland						
1901 - 1911	1 237	1	31	23	8	-6
1911 - 1921	1 251	1	29	22	7	-6
1921 - 1931	1 258	-2	30	21	9	-11
1931 - 1951	1 243	6	28	18	10	-4
1951 - 1961	1 371	6	30	15	15	-9
1961 - 1971	1 427	11	33	16	17	-6
1971 - 1981	1 540	0	28	17	11	-11
1981 - 1991	1 538	6	27	16	12	-5
1991 - 1999	1 601	12	25	15	10	3
1999 - 2001[4]	1 692	7	23	15	8	-1
2001 - 2011	1 708	6	22	15	7	-1
2011 - 2021	1 771	5	21	16	5	-1

1 Census enumerated population up to 1951; mid-year estimates of resident population from 1961 to 1999 and mid-1998-based projections of resident population thereafter.

2 Including deaths of non-civilians and merchant seamen who died outside the country. These numbered 577 000 in 1911-1921 and 240 000 in 1931-1951 for England and Wales; 74 000 in 1911-1921 and 34 000 in 1931-1951 for Scotland; and 10 000 in 1911-1926 for Northern Ireland.

3 Changes in census visitor balance, in Armed Forces, asylum seekers, etc.

4 The population at the beginning of the period is the mid-year estimate for 1999 and is not fully consistent with the total increase/decrease figures which are calculated from the 1998-based projections of the population at mid-1999.

Sources: Government Actuary's Department: 020 7211 2622;
Office for National Statistics: 01329 813233;
General Register Office (Northern Ireland);
General Register Office (Scotland)

Population and vital statistics

5.3 Age distribution of the resident population

Thousands

		Population enumerated in Census			Estimated mid-year resident population					Projected mid-year resident population[1]				
		1901	1931	1951	1961	1971	1981	1991	1999	2001	2006	2011	2016	2021
Persons: All ages	KGUA	38 237	46 038	50 225	52 807	55 928	56 357	57 814	59 501	59 954	60 860	61 773	62 729	63 642
Under 1	KGUK	938	712	773	4 274[3]	899	730	794	708	712	696	699	711	713
1 - 4	KABA	3 443	2 818	3 553	..	3 654	2 726	3 094	2 916	2 875	2 813	2 781	2 822	2 857
5 - 9	KGUN	4 106	3 897	3 689	3 819	4 684	3 677	3 674	3 907	3 781	3 591	3 513	3 485	3 538
10 - 14	KGUO	3 934	3 746	3 310	4 267	4 232	4 470	3 501	3 856	3 926	3 790	3 601	3 523	3 495
15 - 19	KGUP	3 826	3 989	3 175	3 748	3 862	4 735	3 739	3 683	3 752	3 977	3 842	3 653	3 576
20 - 29	KABB	6 982	7 865	7 154	6 570	7 968	8 113	9 298	7 778	7 606	7 651	8 094	8 184	7 862
30 - 44	KABC	7 493	9 717	11 125	10 529	9 797	10 956	12 221	13 549	13 854	13 538	12 477	11 845	12 118
45 - 59	KABD	4 639	7 979	9 558	10 605	10 202	9 540	9 500	10 951	11 247	11 993	12 734	13 579	13 273
60 - 64	KGUY	1 067	1 897	2 422	2 788	3 222	2 935	2 888	2 861	2 859	3 244	3 824	3 532	4 000
65 - 74	KBCP	1 278	2 461	3 689	3 977	4 764	5 195	5 067	4 929	4 908	4 988	5 476	6 388	6 642
75 - 84	KBCU	470	844	1 555	1 885	2 159	2 677	3 139	3 222	3 264	3 344	3 382	3 561	4 000
85 Plus	KGVD	61	113	224	346	485	603	898	1 142	1 170	1 235	1 349	1 446	1 569
School ages (5-15)	KBWU	..	..	7 649	..	9 704	9 086	7 855	8 489	8 470	8 186	7 842	7 726	7 735
Under 18	KGUD	..	..	13 248	..	15 798	14 472	13 185	13 577	13 555	13 275	12 843	12 702	12 726
Pensionable ages [2]	KFIA	2 387	4 421	6 828	7 747	9 123	10 035	10 602	10 753	10 800	11 219	11 915	12 040	12 210
Males: All ages	KGWA	18 492	22 060	24 118	25 528	27 167	27 412	28 248	29 299	29 581	30 147	30 696	31 234	13 717
Under 1	KGWK	471	361	397	2 194[3]	461	374	407	363	364	356	358	364	365
1 - 4	KBCV	1 719	1 423	1 818	..	1 874	1 400	1 588	1 495	1 473	1 440	1 424	1 445	1 463
5 - 9	KGWN	2 052	1 967	1 885	1 956	2 401	1 889	1 888	2 001	1 939	1 841	1 800	1 786	1 813
10 - 14	KGWO	1 972	1 892	1 681	2 185	2 175	2 295	1 800	1 978	2 013	1 945	1 847	1 807	1 792
15 - 19	KGWP	1 898	1 987	1 564	1 897	1 976	2 424	1 925	1 891	1 923	2 034	1 966	1 868	1 828
20 - 29	KBCW	3 293	3 818	3 509	3 288	4 024	4 103	4 738	3 992	3 901	3 904	4 115	4 158	3 994
30 - 44	KBCX	3 597	4 495	5 461	5 237	4 938	5 513	6 141	6 879	7 053	6 925	6 383	6 043	6 157
45 - 59	KBUU	2 215	3 753	4 493	5 137	4 970	4 711	4 732	5 454	5 602	5 989	6 407	6 875	6 753
60 - 64	KGWY	490	894	1 061	1 250	1 507	1 376	1 390	1 400	1 401	1 592	1 883	1 744	1 989
65 - 74	KBWL	565	1 099	1 560	1 605	1 999	2 264	2 272	2 284	2 295	2 373	2 622	3 074	3 206
75 - 84	KBWM	196	335	617	675	716	922	1 152	1 255	1 297	1 383	1 458	1 574	1 787
85 plus	KGXD	23	36	70	105	126	141	215	306	319	363	433	497	569
School ages (5-15)	KBWV	..	..	3 895	..	4 982	4 666	4 038	4 353	4 345	4 198	4 021	3 961	3 965
Under 18	KGWD	..	..	6 753	..	8 108	7 430	6 776	6 963	6 950	6 804	6 583	6 508	6 521
Pensionable ages[2]	KFIB	785	1 471	2 247	2 385	2 841	3 327	3 639	3 845	3 911	4 119	4 513	5 145	5 562
Females: All ages	KGYA	19 745	23 978	26 107	27 279	28 761	28 946	29 566	30 202	30 372	30 714	31 077	31 495	31 925
Under 1	KGYK	466	351	376	2 079[3]	437	356	387	345	347	340	341	347	348
1 - 4	KBWN	1 724	1 397	1 735	..	1 779	1 327	1 505	1 421	1 403	1 373	1 357	1 377	1 394
5 - 9	KGYN	2 054	1 930	1 804	1 863	2 283	1 788	1 786	1 905	1 841	1 750	1 713	1 699	1 725
10 - 14	KGYO	1 962	1 854	1 629	2 083	2 057	2 175	1 701	1 878	1 913	1 845	1 754	1 717	1 703
15 - 19	KGYP	1 928	2 002	1 611	1 851	1 887	2 311	1 815	1 792	1 828	1 943	1 876	1 785	1 747
20 - 29	KBWO	3 690	4 047	3 644	3 282	3 945	4 009	4 560	3 785	3 704	3 747	3 979	4 026	3 869
30 - 44	KBWP	3 895	5 222	5 663	5 292	4 859	5 442	6 080	6 670	6 801	6 613	6 094	5 802	5 961
45 - 59	KBWR	2 424	4 226	5 065	5 467	5 231	4 829	4 769	5 497	5 645	6 004	6 328	6 703	6 520
60 - 64	KGYY	577	1 003	1 361	1 539	1 715	1 559	1 498	1 460	1 458	1 652	1 941	1 788	2 011
65 - 74	KBWS	713	1 361	2 127	2 372	2 765	2 931	2 795	2 645	2 613	2 615	2 854	3 314	3 435
75 - 84	KBWT	274	509	937	1 210	1 443	1 756	1 987	1 967	1 968	1 961	1 924	1 987	2 213
85 Plus	KGZD	38	77	154	241	359	462	683	836	851	872	916	949	1 000
School ages (5-15)	KBWW	..	..	3 753	..	4 722	4 421	3 817	4 137	4 125	3 988	3 820	3 765	3 770
Under 18	KGYD	..	..	6 495	..	7 690	7 042	6 409	6 614	6 605	6 471	6 260	6 194	6 205
Pensionable ages[2]	KFIC	1 601	2 950	4 580	5 362	6 282	6 708	6 963	6 908	6 889	7 099	7 401	6 895	6 648

1 1998-based projections are made as described in the introductory note on page 24.

2 The pensionable age population is that over state retirement age. The 2011, 2016 and 2021 figures take account of planned changes in retirement age from 65 for men and 60 for women at present to 65 for both sexes. This change will be phased in between April 2010 and March 2020.

3 This is for ages 0 - 4.

Sources: Government Actuary's Department: 020 7211 2622;
Office for National Statistics: 01329 813233

5.3 Age distribution of the resident population

continued

Thousands

		England						Wales				
		Estimated mid-year resident population			Projected population[1]			Estimated mid-year resident population			Projected population[1]	
		1981	1991	1999	2001	2011		1981	1991	1999	2001	2011
Persons: All ages	KCCI	46 821	48 208	49 753	50 187	51 922	KERY	2 813	2 891	2 937	2 950	2 993
Under 1	KCCJ	598	663	595	600	589	KFAC	36	39	33	33	33
1 - 4	KCCK	2 235	2 574	2 443	2 414	2 345	KFBX	136	154	138	136	131
5 - 9	KCCL	3 011	3 035	3 261	3 161	2 960	KFCA	185	187	191	182	165
10 - 14	KCCM	3 666	2 880	3 197	3 268	3 024	KFCB	222	178	198	198	174
15 - 19	KCCN	3 897	3 083	3 043	3 104	3 215	KFCC	233	188	190	193	188
20 - 29	KCEG	6 734	7 790	6 508	6 370	6 792	KFCD	381	422	352	348	394
30 - 44	KCEH	9 175	10 231	11 377	11 654	10 548	KFCE	536	587	617	627	552
45 - 59	KCEQ	7 948	7 920	9 169	9 423	10 686	KFCF	485	486	561	571	607
60 - 64	KCEW	2 449	2 399	2 378	2 377	3 211	KFCG	158	154	151	152	201
65 - 74	KCGD	4 347	4 222	4 098	4 081	4 580	KFCH	272	284	269	266	293
75 - 84	KCJG	2 249	2 645	2 707	2 739	2 829	KFCI	139	165	178	182	182
85 Plus	KCKJ	511	763	976	997	1 142	KFCK	29	47	60	62	75
School ages (5-15)	KCWX	7 451	6 473	7 059	7 060	6 594	KFCL	453	399	426	420	374
Under 18	KCWY	11 871	10 899	11 307	11 314	10 804	KFCM	721	665	671	666	611
Pensionable ages [2]	KEAA	8 403	8 870	8 990	9 025	9 983	KFEB	525	576	584	587	638
Males: All ages	KEAB	22 795	23 588	24 543	24 807	25 845	KFEI	1 365	1 407	1 442	1 451	1 482
Under 1	KEAC	306	340	305	307	302	KFEJ	18	20	17	17	17
1 - 4	KEAD	1 147	1 322	1 252	1 236	1 201	KFEK	70	79	71	70	67
5 - 9	KEAE	1 547	1 561	1 671	1 622	1 517	KFEL	95	96	97	93	84
10 - 14	KEAF	1 883	1 482	1 641	1 676	1 551	KFFA	113	92	101	102	89
15 - 19	KECA	1 996	1 588	1 565	1 593	1 646	KFFN	119	97	97	99	96
20 - 29	KECB	3 404	3 974	3 340	3 265	3 449	KFHA	193	214	184	181	201
30 - 44	KECC	4 623	5 148	5 795	5 954	5 406	KFHB	270	294	311	317	283
45 - 59	KECD	3 938	3 957	4 575	4 701	5 394	KFHW	240	242	279	284	303
60 - 64	KECE	1 154	1 159	1 169	1 169	1 584	KFQO	73	74	74	75	99
65 - 74	KECF	1 902	1 900	1 908	1 918	2 201	KFQV	118	128	125	125	141
75 - 84	KECG	777	975	1 060	1 094	1 227	KFUK	48	60	69	72	78
85 plus	KECH	119	183	263	273	369	KFUL	7	11	16	17	24
School ages (5-15)	KECI	3 827	3 330	3 621	3 622	3 381	KFUV	232	206	218	215	192
Under 18	KECJ	6 096	5 604	5 801	5 802	5 537	KFVE	370	342	344	341	313
Pensionable ages[2]	KECK	2 798	3 058	3 231	3 285	3 797	KFVF	173	199	210	214	242
Females: All ages	KEJV	24 026	24 620	25 210	25 380	26 077	KFVL	1 448	1 484	1 495	1 499	1 510
Under 1	KEJW	292	324	290	293	288	KFYW	18	19	..	16	16
1 - 4	KEJX	1 088	1 253	1 191	1 178	1 145	KFZJ	66	75	..	66	64
5 - 9	KEKP	1 464	1 474	1 590	1 539	1 444	KGCK	90	91	..	89	80
10 - 14	KEKQ	1 783	1 399	1 556	1 593	1 473	KGCM	109	86	..	97	85
15 - 19	KEKR	1 901	1 495	1 478	1 511	1 569	KGCN	114	91	..	95	92
20 - 29	KEKS	3 330	3 816	3 168	3 105	3 344	KGCO	189	208	..	166	192
30 - 44	KENR	4 553	5 083	5 583	5 701	5 141	KGCP	265	294	..	310	269
45 - 59	KEOQ	4 009	3 964	4 594	4 721	5 291	KGGZ	246	244	..	287	304
60 - 64	KEOZ	1 295	1 239	1 209	1 208	1 627	KGIY	85	80	..	77	102
65 - 74	KEQJ	2 445	2 323	2 190	2 163	2 380	KGKR	154	156	..	141	152
75 - 84	KEQK	1 472	1 670	1 647	1 645	1 601	KGTQ	91	105	..	110	103
85 Plus	KEQL	392	580	713	724	773	KGTZ	22	36	..	45	51
School ages (5-15)	KEQM	3 625	3 143	3 439	3 438	3 214	KGVG	221	194	..	205	182
Under 18	KEQN	5 775	5 295	5 506	5 513	5 267	KGVH	351	323	..	324	298
Pensionable ages[2]	KEQO	5 605	5 812	5 760	5 740	6 186	KGVK	352	377	..	373	396

1 1998-based projections are made as described in the introductory note on page 24.
2 The pensionable age population is that over state retirement age. The 2011 figures take account of planned changes in retirement age from 65 for men and 60 for women at present to 65 for both sexes. This change will be phased in between April 2010 and March 2020.

Sources: Government Actuary's Department: 020 7211 2622;
Office for National Statistics: 01329 813233

5.3 Age distribution of the resident population

continued

Thousands

| | | Scotland | | | | | | Northern Ireland | | | | |
| | | Estimated mid-year resident population | | | Projected population[1] | | | Estimated mid-year resident population | | | Projected population[1] | |
		1981	1991	1999	2001	2011		1981	1991	1999	2001	2011
Persons: All ages	KGVP	5 180	5 107	5 119	5 109	5 087	KIOY	1 543	1 607	1 692	1 708	1 771
Under 1	KHAQ	69	66	57	56	55	KIOZ	27	26	23	23	22
1 - 4	KHCT	249	259	238	230	218	KIPA	106	106	97	95	87
5 - 9	KHDN	348	321	325	313	275	KIPN	133	131	130	125	113
10 - 14	KHDQ	433	313	326	325	284	KIPP	148	129	135	135	120
15 - 19	KHDT	459	340	323	325	315	KIPQ	146	128	127	130	124
20 - 29	KHDU	771	834	678	651	662	KIPR	227	253	241	237	245
30 - 44	KHDV	971	1 088	1 187	1 195	1 009	KIPS	273	315	368	378	368
45 - 59	KHFK	880	853	942	966	1 100	KIPT	227	241	279	288	341
60 - 64	KHOZ	260	265	259	256	320	KIPU	68	70	72	74	93
65 - 74	KHTU	460	441	440	439	460	KIPV	116	120	122	122	143
75 - 84	KHUO	232	259	262	267	288	KIPW	57	69	75	77	84
85 Plus	KHUQ	49	69	83	86	101	KIPX	14	19	24	25	32
School ages (5-15)	KHVV	871	698	713	703	616	KIPY	311	285	291	287	257
Under 18	KIMT	1 377	1 153	1 136	1 117	1 012	KIQL	504	467	463	458	416
Pensionable ages [2]	KIMU	882	910	921	926	993	KIQM	224	246	258	262	300
Males: All ages	KIMV	2 495	2 470	2 486	2 485	2 492	KIQN	757	783	829	839	876
Under 1	KIMW	35	34	29	29	28	KIQO	14	13	12	12	11
1 - 4	KIMX	128	133	122	118	112	KIQP	54	54	50	49	45
5 - 9	KIMY	178	164	166	160	141	KIQQ	69	67	66	64	58
10 - 14	KIMZ	222	161	167	167	146	KIQR	76	66	69	69	61
15 - 19	KINA	234	174	164	165	161	KIQS	75	66	65	67	64
20 - 29	KINB	390	423	345	332	337	KIQT	117	127	124	123	128
30 - 44	KINC	483	543	592	596	507	KIQU	137	156	181	186	186
45 - 59	KIND	424	415	462	475	542	KIQV	109	118	137	142	167
60 - 64	KINE	118	124	123	122	155	KIQW	32	32	35	35	45
65 - 74	KINR	194	192	196	197	213	KIRJ	50	53	54	55	68
75 - 84	KINS	77	91	98	101	118	KIRK	21	26	28	30	35
85 plus	KINT	11	16	22	22	31	KIRL	4	5	6	7	10
School ages (5-15)	KINU	446	358	365	360	317	KIRM	160	146	149	147	132
Under 18	KINV	706	591	581	572	520	KIRN	259	239	237	235	213
Pensionable ages[2]	KINW	282	299	315	321	362	KIRO	75	83	89	91	112
Females: All ages	KINX	2 685	2 637	2 634	2 624	2 595	KIRP	786	824	863	869	895
Under 1	KINY	33	32	28	28	27	KIRQ	13	13	11	11	11
1 - 4	KINZ	121	126	116	112	106	KIRR	52	52	47	47	43
5 - 9	KIOA	170	157	159	153	133	KIRS	65	64	63	61	55
10 - 14	KIOB	211	153	159	158	138	KIRT	72	63	66	65	59
15 - 19	KIOC	225	166	158	159	154	KIRU	70	62	62	63	60
20 - 29	KIOO	381	411	333	319	325	KISH	110	126	117	114	118
30 - 44	KIOP	488	545	596	599	502	KISI	137	159	187	191	182
45 - 59	KIOQ	456	437	480	491	558	KISJ	118	123	141	146	175
60 - 64	KIOR	142	141	136	135	165	KISK	37	38	38	38	48
65 - 74	KIOS	265	249	244	241	247	KISL	66	67	68	67	76
75 - 84	KIOT	155	168	165	166	170	KISM	37	44	46	47	49
85 Plus	KIOU	38	53	61	63	70	KISN	10	14	17	18	22
School ages (5-15)	KIOV	424	340	348	343	299	KISO	151	139	142	140	125
Under 18	KIOW	671	562	555	545	492	KISP	245	228	226	223	203
Pensionable ages[2]	KIOX	600	611	606	605	631	KISQ	150	163	169	171	188

1 1998-based projections are made as described in the introductory note on page 24.
2 The pensionable age population is that over state retirement age. The 2011 figures take account of planned changes in retirement age from 65 for men and 60 for women at present to 65 for both sexes. This change will be phased in between April 2010 and March 2020.

Sources: Office for National Statistics: 01329 813233;
General Register Office (Scotland);
General Register Office (Northern Ireland);
Government Actuary's Department: 020 7211 2622

5.4 Marital condition (de jure): estimated population

Thousands

		United Kingdom[2] Males				United Kingdom[2] Females				England and Wales Males				England and Wales Females		
		1971	1981	1991[1]		1971	1981	1991[1]		1971	1981	1991		1971	1981	1991
All ages:																
Single	KQCA	12 120	12 168	12 874	KQDP	11 131	10 860	11 231	KRPL	10 507	10 614	11 320	KUBS	9 584	9 424	9 829
Married	KQCB	14 067	13 791	13 237	KQDQ	14 130	13 856	13 364	KRPM	12 522	12 238	11 745	KVCC	12 566	12 284	11 838
Widowed	KQCC	779	793	828	KQDR	3 178	3 331	3 370	KRPN	682	698	731	KVCD	2 810	2 939	2 978
Divorced	KQCD	201	657	1 306	KQDS	321	897	1 598	KRPO	187	611	1 200	KVCE	296	828	1 459
Age groups:																
0 - 14: Single	KQCE	6 912	5 956	5 683	KQDT	6 557	5 646	5 378	KRPP	5 984	5 181	4 991	KVCF	5 672	4 910	4 720
15 - 19: Single	KQCF	1 936	2 400	1 916	KQDU	1 726	2 203	1 778	KRPQ	1 677	2 095	1 677	KVCG	1 491	1 923	1 554
Married	KQCG	39	24	9	KQDV	160	107	36	KRPR	34	20	8	KVCH	142	93	32
Widowed	KQCH	–	–	–	KQDW	–	–	–	KRPS	–	–	–	KVCI	–	–	–
Divorced	KQCI	–	–	–	KQDX	–	–	–	KRPT	–	–	–	KVCJ	–	–	–
20 - 24: Single	KQCJ	1 376	1 618	2 004	KQDY	857	1 150	1 616	KRPU	1 211	1 420	1 764	KVCK	745	1 007	1 421
Married	KQCK	781	542	285	KQDZ	1 251	930	558	KRPV	689	466	249	KVCL	1 113	811	490
Widowed	KQCL	–	1	–	KQYZ	2	2	1	KRPW	–	1	–	KVCM	2	2	1
Divorced	KQCM	3	11	13	KQZA	10	30	32	KRPX	3	10	12	KVCN	9	27	29
25 - 34: Single	KQCN	722	1 020	1 925	KQZB	379	563	1 280	KRPY	637	906	1 718	KVCO	326	496	1 135
Married	KQCO	2 762	2 847	2 393	KQZC	2 980	3 160	2 831	KRPZ	2 450	2 508	2 100	KVCP	2 635	2 791	2 488
Widowed	KQCP	4	5	3	KQZD	14	16	9	KRQA	4	4	2	KVCQ	12	13	8
Divorced	KQCQ	41	163	270	KQZE	68	236	345	KRQB	38	151	245	KVCR	63	218	312
35 - 44: Single	KQCR	366	359	548	KQZF	242	198	322	KRQC	317	316	482	KVEH	201	170	280
Married	KQCS	2 838	2 845	3 002	KQZG	2 871	2 878	3 118	KRQD	2 513	2 519	2 658	KVEI	2 529	2 540	2 760
Widowed	KQCT	15	14	14	KQZH	57	49	41	KRQE	13	12	12	KVEJ	48	41	34
Divorced	KQCU	52	191	423	KQZI	72	240	487	KRQF	48	178	388	KVEK	66	222	444
45 - 54: Single	KQCV	326	293	287	KQZJ	298	203	168	KRQG	279	254	251	KVEL	248	169	144
Married	KQCW	2 924	2 640	2 648	KQZK	2 891	2 598	2 629	KUAR	2 605	2 338	2 347	KVEM	2 570	2 292	2 322
Widowed	KQCX	55	44	37	KQZL	218	176	138	KUBA	47	38	31	KVEN	187	150	118
Divorced	KQCY	50	144	315	KQZM	75	171	361	KUBB	46	134	290	KVEO	69	158	332
55 - 59: Single	KQCZ	140	149	116	KQZN	177	131	82	KUBC	118	128	101	KVEP	148	108	69
Married	KQDA	1 399	1 336	1 186	KQZO	1 293	1 267	1 114	KUBD	1 250	1 192	1 050	KVEQ	1 154	1 130	982
Widowed	KQDB	57	53	40	KQZP	247	216	159	KUBE	49	46	34	KVER	213	186	136
Divorced	KQDC	21	53	103	KQZQ	33	68	117	KUBF	20	49	95	KVES	31	63	107
60 - 64: Single	KQDD	125	115	120	KQZR	208	131	97	KUBG	105	98	104	KVET	174	109	80
Married	KQDE	1 276	1 149	1 121	KQZS	1 098	1 046	1 023	KUBH	1 140	1 029	997	KVEU	985	936	908
Widowed	KQDF	89	74	73	KQZT	382	328	289	KUBI	77	64	63	KVEV	332	284	250
Divorced	KQDG	17	38	76	KQZU	27	55	89	KUBJ	16	35	70	KVEW	25	51	82
65 - 74: Single	KQDH	159	178	177	KQZV	396	315	214	KUBK	132	149	150	KMGN	332	263	176
Married	KQDI	1 567	1 773	1 754	KQZW	1 254	1 431	1 464	KUBL	1 407	1 594	1 574	KMGO	1 133	1 291	1 317
Widowed	KQDJ	258	267	261	KQZX	1 087	1 112	1 002	KUBM	226	234	229	KMGP	959	978	879
Divorced	KQDK	15	46	80	KQZY	28	72	116	KUBN	14	43	74	KMGQ	26	68	107
75 and over: Single	KQDL	58	81	99	KQZZ	291	320	295	KU3O	47	67	81	KMGR	249	270	250
Married	KQDM	480	633	840	KRPI	332	440	592	KUBP	434	573	763	KMGS	304	401	541
Widowed	KQDN	301	336	401	KRPJ	1 172	1 433	1 731	KUBQ	266	300	360	KMGT	1 056	1 285	1 554
Divorced	KQDO	3	11	26	KRPK	7	24	50	KUBR	3	11	25	KMGU	6	23	46

1 Mid-1991 population estimates by marital status are still provisional.

2 Figures for Northern Ireland are more approximate than those for other countries: at each age/sex the proportions enumerated in the census in the various marital status groups have been applied to the estimated total (all statuses) population.

Sources: Office for National Statistics: 01329 813233; General Register Office (Northern Ireland); General Register Office (Scotland)

5.4 Marital condition (de jure): estimated population

continued

Thousands

| | | Scotland | | | | | | | | Northern Ireland[2] | | | | | | |
| | | Males | | | | Females | | | | Males | | | | Females | | |
		1971	1981	1991		1971	1981	1991		1971	1981	1991[1]		1971	1981	1991[1]
All ages:																
Single	KJPS	1 197	1 149	1 135	KJVG	1 155	1 066	1 029	KJWV	417	406	411	KJYK	392	370	373
Married	KJPT	1 227	1 227	1 159	KJVH	1 243	1 240	1 181	KJWW	318	327	339	KJYL	321	332	350
Widowed	KJPU	79	77	78	KJVI	297	317	306	KJWX	19	18	19	KJYM	71	75	80
Divorced	KJPV	13	42	97	KJVJ	24	62	122	KJWY	1	4	11	KJYN	2	6	18
Age groups:																
0 - 14: Single	KJPW	695	563	492	KJRI	660	535	468	KJWZ	232	212	200	KJYO	224	201	191
15 - 19: Single	KJPX	195	230	173	KJVL	178	214	163	KJXA	64	75	66	KJYP	58	67	61
Married	KJPY	5	4	1	KJVM	15	11	2	KJXB	1	1	–	KJYQ	3	3	1
Widowed	KJPZ	–	–	–	KJVN	–	–	–	KJXC	–	–	–	KJYR	–	–	–
Divorced	KJQQ	–	–	–	KJVO	–	–	–	KJXD	–	–	–	KJYS	–	–	–
20 - 24: Single	KJQR	120	149	184	KJVP	81	109	151	KJXE	45	48	57	KJYT	31	34	46
Married	KJQS	75	60	26	KJVQ	111	93	49	KJXF	18	16	9	KJYU	27	26	16
Widowed	KJQT	–	–	–	KJVR	–	–	–	KJXG	–	–	–	KJYV	–	–	–
Divorced	KJQU	–	1	1	KJVS	1	3	2	KJXH	–	–	–	KJYW	–	–	–
25 - 34: Single	KJQV	61	87	160	KJVT	37	51	113	KJXI	25	27	43	KJYX	16	16	30
Married	KJQW	243	266	224	KJVU	267	290	259	KJXJ	70	73	73	KJYY	77	80	86
Widowed	KJQX	–	1	–	KJVV	2	2	1	KJXK	–	–	–	KJYZ	–	1	1
Divorced	KJQY	3	11	23	KJVW	5	17	29	KJXL	–	1	2	KJZA	–	2	5
35 - 44: Single	KJQZ	35	32	49	KJVX	30	21	32	KJXM	13	11	14	KJZB	11	8	9
Married	KJRW	259	252	265	KJVY	271	262	276	KJXN	67	74	81	KJZC	70	76	83
Widowed	KJRX	2	2	2	KJVZ	7	6	5	KJXO	–	–	–	KJZD	2	2	2
Divorced	KJRY	3	12	31	KJWA	6	17	38	KJXP	–	1	4	KJZE	–	2	6
45 - 54: Single	KJRZ	34	28	26	KJWB	37	25	18	KJXQ	13	10	10	KJZF	13	9	7
Married	KJTD	254	241	232	KJWC	255	244	237	KJXR	64	61	69	KJZG	65	63	70
Widowed	KJTE	6	5	4	KJWD	25	21	15	KJXS	1	1	1	KJZH	6	6	5
Divorced	KJTF	3	9	22	KJWE	6	12	26	KJXT	–	1	3	KJZI	1	1	4
55 - 59: Single	KJTG	16	15	11	KJWF	22	17	10	KJXU	6	5	4	KJZJ	7	6	4
Married	KJTH	120	116	107	KJWG	112	110	105	KJXV	29	28	28	KJZK	27	27	28
Widowed	KJTI	6	6	5	KJWH	27	23	18	KJXW	1	1	1	KJZL	6	6	5
Divorced	KJTJ	1	3	8	KJWI	2	5	9	KJXX	–	–	1	KJZM	–	–	1
60 - 64: Single	KJTK	15	12	11	KJWJ	26	16	12	KJXY	6	5	5	KJZN	8	6	5
Married	KJTL	109	96	99	KJWK	92	88	92	KJXZ	27	24	25	KJZO	21	22	24
Widowed	KJTM	10	8	8	KJWL	40	35	30	KJYA	2	2	2	KJZP	9	9	8
Divorced	KJTN	1	2	5	KJWM	2	4	7	KJYB	–	–	1	KJZQ	–	–	1
65 - 74: Single	KJUY	20	21	18	KJWN	50	39	27	KJYC	8	8	8	KJZR	14	13	10
Married	KJUZ	129	144	143	KJWO	98	113	119	KJYD	31	35	38	KJZS	23	27	31
Widowed	KJVA	27	27	26	KJWP	104	109	95	KJYE	6	6	6	KJZT	24	26	26
Divorced	KJVB	1	2	5	KJWQ	2	4	8	KJYF	–	–	1	KJZU	–	–	1
75 and over: Single	KJVC	7	10	11	KJWR	34	39	34	KJYG	4	4	4	KJZV	9	10	11
Married	KJVD	36	48	62	KJWS	22	31	43	KJYH	11	13	16	KJZW	6	8	10
Widowed	KJVE	28	29	33	KJWT	93	121	141	KJYI	7	7	8	KJZX	23	26	34
Divorced	KJVF	–	1	1	KJWU	–	1	3	KJYJ	–	–	–	KJZY	–	–	–

1 Mid-1991 population estimates by marital status are still provisional.
2 Figures for Northern Ireland are more approximate than those for other countries: at each age/sex the proportions enumerated in the census in the census in the various marital status groups have been applied to the estimated total (all statuses) population.

Sources: Office for National Statistics: 01329 813233;
General Register Office (Northern Ireland);
General Register Office (Scotland)

5.5 Geographical distribution of the population

Thousands

		Area[1] Square Km	Population enumerated in Census			Mid-year population estimates				
			1911	1931	1951	1961	1971	1981	1991	1999
United Kingdom	KIUR	241 752	42 190	46 074	50 287	52 807	55 928	56 357	57 814	59 501
Great Britain	KISR	228 269	40 831	44 795	48 854	51 380	54 388	54 815	56 207	57 809
England	KKOJ	130 423	33 650	37 359	41 159	43 561	46 412	46 821	48 208	49 753
Standard Regions										
North	KKNA	15 415	2 729	2 938	3 009	3 246	3 152	3 117	3 092	3 073
Yorkshire and Humberside	KKNB	15 411	3 896	4 319	4 567	4 630	4 902	4 918	4 983	5 047
East Midlands	KKNC	15 627	2 467	2 732	3 118	3 108	3 652	3 853	4 035	4 191
East Anglia	KKND	12 570	1 191	1 231	1 381	1 489	1 688	1 894	2 082	2 196
South East	KKNE	27 224	11 613	13 349	14 877	16 346	17 125	17 011	17 637	18 586
South West	KKNF	23 829	2 818	2 984	3 479	3 436	4 112	4 381	4 718	4 936
West Midlands	KKNG	13 004	3 277	3 743	4 423	4 762	5 146	5 187	5 265	5 336
North West	KKNH	7 342	5 659	6 062	6 305	6 545	6 634	6 459	6 396	6 389
Government Office Regions	JZBT	130 412	..	..	..	43 561	46 412	46 821	48 208	49 753
North East	JZBU	8 594	..	..	..	..	2 679	2 636	2 603	2 581
North West	JZBV	13 510	..	..	..	..	5 446	5 418	5 436	5 477
Merseyside	JZBW	655	..	..	..	..	1 662	1 522	1 450	1 404
Yorkshire and The Humber	JZBX	15 400	..	..	..	..	4 902	4 918	4 983	5 047
East Midlands	JZBY	15 627	..	..	..	..	3 652	3 853	4 035	4 191
West Midlands	JZBZ	13 004	..	..	..	..	5 146	5 187	5 265	5 336
South West	JZCA	23 825	..	..	..	..	4 112	4 381	4 718	4 936
Eastern	JZCB	19 120	..	..	..	..	4 454	4 854	5 150	5 419
Greater London	JZCC	1 578	..	..	..	..	7 529	6 806	6 890	7 285
South East	JZCD	19 098	..	..	..	..	6 830	7 245	7 679	8 078
Wales	KKNI	20 766	2 421	2 593	2 599	2 635	2 740	2 813	2 891	2 937
Scotland	KGJB	77 179	4 761	4 843	5 096	5 184	5 236	5 180	5 107	5 119
Northern Ireland	KGJC	13 570	1 251	1 280[3]	1 371	1 427	1 540	1 543	1 607	1 692
Greater London	KKNJ	1 578	7 161	8 110	8 197	7 977	7 529	6 806	6 890	7 285
Inner London[2]	KISS	321	4 998	4 893	3 679	3 481	3 060	2 550	2 627	2 817
Outer London[2]	KITF	1 258	2 162	3 217	4 518	4 496	4 470	4 255	4 263	4 468
Metropolitan areas of England & Wales	KITG	6 974	9 716	10 770	11 365	11 686	11 862	11 353	11 166	11 133
Tyne and Wear	KGJN	540	1 105	1 201	1 201	1 241	1 218	1 155	1 130	1 108
West Yorkshire	KGJP	2 034	1 852	1 939	1 985	2 002	2 090	2 067	2 085	2 115
South Yorkshire	KGJO	1 559	963	1 173	1 253	1 298	1 331	1 317	1 302	1 302
West Midlands	KGJQ	899	1 780	2 143	2 547	2 724	2 811	2 673	2 629	2 627
Greater Manchester	KGJR	1 286	2 638	2 727	2 716	2 710	2 750	2 619	2 570	2 577
Merseyside	KGJS	655	1 378	1 587	1 663	1 711	1 662	1 522	1 450	1 404
Principal Metropolitan Cities[2]	KITH	1 535	3 154	3 906	3 915	4 204	3 910	3 550	3 451	3 433
Newcastle	KGJT	112	267	286	292	336	312	284	278	273
Leeds	KGJX	562	446	483	505	710	749	718	717	727
Sheffield	KGJV	367	455	512	513	581	579	548	529	531
Birmingham	KGKF	265	526	1 003	1 113	1 179	1 107	1 021	1 007	1 013
Manchester	KGKJ	116	714	766	703	657	554	463	439	431
Liverpool	KGKM	113	746	856	789	741	610	517	481	458
Other metropolitan districts[2]	KITI	5 438	6 562	6 864	7 450	7 482	7 952	7 803	7 716	7 701
Non-metropolitan districts of England & Wales	KITJ	142 637	19 194	21 072	24 196	26 533	29 761	31 475	33 043	34 271
Non-metropolitan cities[2,4]	KITK	2 094	..	..	..	4 670	4 715	4 617	4 676	..
Incl. Kingston-upon-Hull	KKNZ	71	278	314	299	302	288	274	267	258
Leicester	KKOA	73	227	239	285	286	285	283	285	291
Nottingham	KKNX	75	260	269	308	311	302	278	281	284
Bristol	KKNV	110	357	397	443	436	433	401	397	405
Plymouth	KITL	80	207	215	225	240	249	253	254	253
Stoke-on-Trent	KKOD	93	235	277	275	276	265	252	253	251
Cardiff	KKOB	120	182	224	244	289	291	281	294	324
Industrial districts[2,4]	KITM	17 132	..	..	..	6 004	6 486	6 713	6 852	..
New Towns[2,4]	KITN	5 054	..	..	..	1 552	1 895	2 194	2 382	..
Resort, port and retirement districts[2,4]	KITO	10 512	..	..	..	2 828	3 184	3 368	3 626	..
Urban and mixed urban/rural districts[2,4]	KITP	38 683	..	..	..	7 240	8 821	9 446	9 964	..
Remoter, mainly rural districts[2,4]	KITQ	69 161	..	..	..	4 239	4 661	5 137	5 544	..
City of Edinburgh local government district	KGKU	135	320	439	467	..	478	446	440	..
City of Glasgow local government district	KGKT	157	784	1 088	1 090	..	983	774	689	..
Belfast	KGKV	73	387	438[3]	444	..	..	315	294	..

1 Areas as constituted in 1991. Population figures for earlier years may relate to different areas where boundaries have changed.

2 Details of the classification by broad area type are given in recent issues of the ONS annual reference volume "Key Population and Vital Statistics; local and health authority areas" (Series VS). The ten broad area types include all local authorities in England and Wales.

3 Figures for Northern Ireland and the City of Belfast relate to the 1937 Census.

4 The breakdown of non-metropolitan districts by area type has not been provided for the mid-1996 population. This is because the effect of boundary changes due to the major local government reorganisation on 1 April 1995 and 1 April 1996 (particularly in Wales) which make the comparison of 1991 and 1996 data with data for earlier years invalid.

Sources: Office for National Statistics: 01329 813233;
General Register Office (Northern Ireland);
General Register Office (Scotland)

5.6 Population by age and ethnic group, Great Britain[1]
Average over the period Summer 1999 to Spring 2000

Percentages and thousands

	Age-group											All ages	
	0 to 4	5 to 9	10 to 14	15 to 19	20 to 24	25 to 29	30 to 34	35 to 44	45 to 59	60 to 74	75 and over	%	000's
Ethnic group													
Black - Caribbean	7	7	7	6	6	6	10	21	14	13	2	100	504
Black - African	13	10	9	7	8	8	13	20	9	3	0.4	100	374
Black - Other (non-mixed)	15	16	13	9	8	7	14	15	1	1	0.1	100	124
Black - Mixed	22	22	16	9	8	6	6	7	3	1	0.2	100	184
Indian	6	8	8	8	8	8	9	17	17	10	2	100	942
Pakistani	12	11	11	10	10	8	9	13	9	6	1	100	671
Bangladeshi	12	13	12	12	10	7	7	11	8	7	0.6	100	257
Chinese	4	6	6	7	11	10	12	18	17	7	2	100	133
Other - Asian (non-mixed)	6	6	6	5	9	10	12	23	17	5	0.6	100	217
Other - Other (non-mixed)	8	10	6	9	8	8	10	22	15	2	0.6	100	184
Other - Mixed	23	18	14	7	7	6	6	9	6	2	1	100	243
All ethnic minority groups	11	10	9	8	8	8	10	16	12	7	1	100	3 832
White	6	6	6	6	6	7	8	15	19	14	7	100	53 082
All ethnic groups[2]	6	7	7	6	6	7	8	15	19	13	7	100	56 927

1 Estimates whose relative standard errors exceed 20% appear in italics and should not be used in any analysis - they are provided as an approximate indication only

2 Includes ethnic group not stated.

Source: Office for National Statistics, Labour Force Survey

5.7 Migration into and out of the United Kingdom, estimates from International Passenger Survey*

Analysis by usual occupation[1] and sex

Thousands

	Total			Professional and managerial			Manual and clerical			Not gainfully employed[2]		
	Persons	Males	Females	Persons	Males	Females	Persons	Males	Females	Persons	Males	Females
Inflow												
	KGOA	KGOB	KGOC	KGOD	KGOE	KGOF	KGOG	KGOH	KGOI	KGOJ	KGOK	KGOL
1988	216	109	107	67	44	23	44	26	18	105	40	66
1989	250	110	140	76	47	28	49	22	26	125	40	86
1990	267	135	132	93	61	32	53	26	27	121	48	72
1991	267	122	144	80	51	29	56	23	33	131	48	83
1992	216	99	117	62	39	23	44	17	27	111	43	68
1993	213	101	112	66	41	25	43	21	22	105	39	66
1994	253	126	127	82	49	34	56	31	25	115	46	68
1995	245	130	115	86	57	29	46	20	26	113	53	60
1996	272	130	143	89	53	36	57	25	33	125	52	74
1997	285	143	142	93	59	34	44	24	20	147	60	87
1998	332	167	165	117	68	49	74	37	37	142	63	79
Outflow												
	KGPA	KGPB	KGPC	KGPD	KGPE	KGPF	KGPG	KGPH	KGPI	KGPJ	KGPK	KGPL
1988	237	125	113	68	44	23	52	25	27	118	55	63
1989	205	108	97	71	44	27	49	24	26	85	41	44
1990	231	113	118	75	47	27	56	25	31	100	41	59
1991	239	120	119	82	48	34	50	28	21	108	44	63
1992	227	113	114	82	50	33	47	23	24	98	40	58
1993	216	113	103	70	38	32	45	24	20	101	51	50
1994	191	92	98	55	32	23	48	24	25	87	37	50
1995	192	102	90	62	42	20	42	23	19	88	38	50
1996	216	105	111	84	53	31	46	23	24	86	30	56
1997	225	121	103	86	57	29	48	23	25	91	42	50
1998	199	100	99	79	46	33	41	21	20	79	32	47
Balance												
	KGRA	KGRB	KGRC	KGRD	KGRE	KGRF	KGRG	KGRH	KGRI	KGRJ	KGRK	KGRL
1988	−21	−15	−6	−1	−1	–	−8	1	−9	−13	−16	3
1989	44	1	43	5	4	1	−1	−1	1	40	−1	41
1990	36	22	14	19	14	5	−3	1	−4	21	7	13
1991	28	2	26	−2	3	−5	6	−5	11	24	4	19
1992	−11	−14	3	−21	−11	−10	−4	−6	3	13	3	10
1993	−2	−12	10	−4	3	−8	−2	−4	2	3	−12	15
1994	62	34	28	27	17	11	8	8	–	27	9	18
1995	54	28	26	24	15	9	5	−3	7	25	16	9
1996	56	24	32	5	1	5	11	2	9	39	22	18
1997	60	22	38	8	2	5	−4	1	−5	56	18	38
1998	133	68	66	38	22	16	33	16	17	63	30	32

*Data are from the International Passenger Survey and exclude migration with the Irish Republic and other categories. See Explanatory notes, at the beginning of the Population and Vital Statistics chapter.

Data also excludes the Channel Islands and Isle of Man from 1988.

1 Refers to regular occupation before migration.
2 Includes housewives, students, children and retired persons.

Source: Office for National Statistics: 01329 813255

5.8 Migration into and out of the United Kingdom, estimates from International Passenger Survey*

Analysis by citizenship and country of last or next residence   Thousands

| | All migrants | British citizens | | | | | | European Union citizens[1] (excl British) | | | |
| | | | Country of last/next residence | | | | | | Country of last/next residence | | |
	Total	Total	European[1] Union	Old[2] Common-wealth	New[3] Common-wealth	United States of America	Other countries	Total	European[1] Union	Other Europe	Other countries
Inflow											
	KEZR	KGLA	KGLB	KGLC	KGLD	KGLE	KGLF	KGLG	KGLH	KGLI	KGLJ
1988	216	89	27	20	18	8	16	27	26	–	2
1989	250	104	24	31	18	12	19	31	29	–	2
1990	267	106	30	29	22	10	15	37	33	–	4
1991	267	117	39	30	23	10	15	32	29	–	3
1992	216	99	47	22	13	8	10	24	23	–	2
1993	213	92	31	24	19	10	9	25	23	–	2
1994	253	118	45	22	21	16	14	31	27	1	3
1995	245	91	32	16	18	13	13	41	36	–	5
1996	272	104	33	21	22	14	13	54	49	1	4
1997	285	97	36	23	12	8	19	61	56	–	5
1998	332	111	29	33	16	17	17	68	63	–	5
Outflow											
	KEZS	KGMA	KGMB	KGMC	KGMD	KGME	KGMF	KGMG	KGMH	KGMI	KGMJ
1988	237	143	41	52	17	15	19	24	17	3	4
1989	205	122	27	47	18	13	17	22	18	–	4
1990	231	135	34	49	15	22	15	30	25	2	3
1991	239	137	46	42	19	13	18	32	23	2	6
1992	227	133	45	34	15	16	23	17	14	–	3
1993	216	127	45	34	16	16	16	23	21	–	3
1994	191	108	34	28	13	15	18	23	19	–	4
1995	192	118	38	34	13	17	16	20	16	–	4
1996	216	139	52	37	18	16	17	24	18	–	5
1997	225	131	40	37	12	15	26	32	27	1	4
1998	199	111	37	34	7	15	18	26	21	1	4
Balance											
	KEZT	KGNA	KGNB	KGNC	KGND	KGNE	KGNF	KGNG	KGNH	KGNI	KGNJ
1988	–21	–54	–14	–32	1	–7	–2	4	8	–2	–2
1989	44	–18	–3	–16	–	–	2	9	11	–	–2
1990	36	–30	–4	–20	7	–12	–1	7	8	–1	1
1991	28	–20	–7	–12	4	–3	–2	–	5	–2	–3
1992	–11	–34	2	–12	–3	–8	–13	8	9	–	–1
1993	–2	–35	–13	–10	2	–7	–7	2	2	–	–
1994	62	10	11	–6	8	1	–4	8	9	1	–2
1995	54	–27	–6	–17	5	–5	–4	21	21	–	1
1996	56	–36	–19	–16	4	–1	–3	30	31	1	–1
1997	60	–34	–5	–14	–1	–8	–7	29	29	–1	1
1998	133	–	–8	–2	9	2	–1	42	42	–1	1

*Data are from the International Passenger Survey and exclude migration with the Irish Republic and other categories. See Explanatory notes, at the beginning of the Population and Vital Statistics chapter.

Data also excludes the Channel Islands and Isle of Man from 1988.

1 Figures for the European Union have been revised for all the years in this table to show the Union as it was constituted on 1 January 1995.
2 Figures for all years include South Africa in the Old Commonwealth.
3 Figures for all years include Pakistan in the New Commonwealth.

Source: Office for National Statistics: 01329 813255

5.8 Migration into and out of the United Kingdom, estimates from International Passenger Survey*

continued   *Analysis by citizenship and country of last or next residence*   Thousands

| | Commonwealth citizens | | | | | | | | | | Other foreign citizens | | | | |
| | Country of last/next residence | | | | | | | | | | Country of last/next residence | | | | |
	Total	Aust-ralia	Canada	New Zealand	South Africa	Bangl-adesh, India, Sri Lanka	Pakistan	Other African Common-wealth	Carib-bean Common-wealth	Other count-ries	Total	Euro-pean[1] Union	Other Europe	United States of America	Other coun-tries
Inflow															
	KGLK	KGLL	KGLM	KGLN	KTDK	KGLO	KGLP	KGLQ	KGLR	KGLT	KGLU	KGLV	KGLW	KGLX	KGLY
1988	54	11	2	7	2	9	5	5	1	10	45	1	6	14	24
1989	71	10	3	10	4	12	6	8	1	13	43	2	4	18	19
1990	71	17	3	10	1	11	4	9	2	10	53	6	7	17	22
1991	68	12	4	7	1	10	7	9	2	14	50	6	7	14	23
1992	52	9	2	6	–	7	5	6	2	14	40	2	7	9	21
1993	53	11	3	5	2	9	4	5	–	10	44	2	12	12	18
1994	52	9	2	6	1	7	4	8	–	12	53	6	14	11	22
1995	63	12	5	7	2	8	3	4	–	19	50	2	10	11	26
1996	64	15	3	7	4	8	7	6	1	10	50	–	7	16	27
1997	80	15	5	7	5	16	5	7	1	19	47	–	7	12	28
1998	94	25	5	14	12	10	4	11	2	12	59	4	8	19	28
Outflow															
	KGMK	KGML	KGMM	KGMN	KTDL	KGMO	KGMP	KGMQ	KGMR	KGMT	KGMU	KGMV	KGMW	KGMX	KGMY
1988	36	6	2	3	1	3	2	6	2	8	34	–	5	14	15
1989	27	7	2	2	1	3	2	3	1	5	34	2	3	16	12
1990	31	8	3	5	2	1	1	4	1	5	34	–	4	18	12
1991	34	7	4	5	–	2	2	3	–	10	36	1	3	16	16
1992	29	6	2	5	1	2	1	2	1	7	48	1	11	19	17
1993	32	8	2	4	1	3	1	3	1	7	34	2	3	16	14
1994	29	5	2	4	1	2	3	2	1	7	31	1	9	8	13
1995	27	6	1	4	1	1	1	2	1	6	27	–	5	8	14
1996	29	7	2	3	2	2	–	2	–	8	24	1	6	5	11
1997	34	6	1	5	4	2	2	2	1	12	28	2	5	8	12
1998	29	8	1	3	4	2	1	2	–	6	33	2	6	9	16
Balance															
	KGNK	KGNL	KGNM	KGNN	KTDM	KGNO	KGNP	KGNQ	KGNR	KGNT	KGNU	KGNV	KGNW	KGNX	KGNY
1988	18	5	–	4	–	6	3	–	–1	2	11	–	2	–1	9
1989	44	4	2	8	3	9	4	4	–	8	9	–1	1	2	7
1990	40	9	–	5	–1	10	3	4	2	5	19	6	4	–1	10
1991	34	6	–	2	1	7	5	6	2	4	14	4	4	–2	7
1992	23	4	–	1	–1	5	4	3	1	7	–8	1	–4	–10	4
1993	21	3	1	1	1	6	3	2	–	2	10	–	9	–4	4
1994	23	4	–	2	–	5	1	6	–1	5	22	4	5	4	9
1995	36	6	4	3	1	7	3	2	–1	13	23	2	6	3	12
1996	35	8	1	5	2	6	7	4	1	1	27	–1	1	11	16
1997	46	8	4	3	1	14	4	4	–	8	20	–2	2	4	16
1998	65	17	3	11	7	8	3	9	1	5	26	2	1	11	12

'Data are from the International Passenger Survey and exclude migration with the Irish Republic and other categories. See Explanatory notes, at beginning of Population and Vital Statistics chapter.

Data also excludes the Channel Islands and Isle of Man from 1988.

1 Figures for the European Union have been revised for all the years in this table to show the Union as it was constituted on 1 January 1995. This includes Austria, Finland and Sweden.

Source: Office for National Statistics: 01329 813255

Population and vital statistics

5.9 Acceptances for settlement by nationality
United Kingdom

Geographical region and nationality		All acceptances for settlement 1996	1997	1998	1999	Geographical region and nationality		All acceptances for settlement 1996	1997	1998	1999
All nationalities	KGFA	61 730	58 720	69 790	97 120	**Africa(continued)**					
						Egypt	KGGW	330	330	360	380
Europe						Ethiopia	KGGX	140	210	190	2 170
European Economic Area						Ghana	KGGY	1 970	1 290	1 550	3 480
Austria	KGFM	–	–	–	–	Kenya	KGHA	590	500	530	760
Belgium	KGFB	–	–	–	–	Libya	KGHB	110	120	160	160
Denmark	KGFC	10	–	10	–	Mauritius	KGHC	460	380	450	460
Finland	KGFO	–	–	–	–	Morocco	KGHD	460	410	430	430
France	KGFD	30	10	30	–	Nigeria	KGHE	3 220	2 540	2 950	3 180
Germany	KGFE	10	10	30	–	Sierra Leone	KGHF	570	470	540	1 060
Greece	KGFF	10	10	20	–	Somalia	KGHG	680	990	2 950	3 180
Iceland	KOSQ	–	–	–	–	South Africa	KGHH	1 040	1 290	2 260	2 950
Italy	KGFG	20	10	20	–	Sudan	KGHI	360	2 180	470	540
Luxembourg	KGFH	–	–	–	–	Tanzania	KGHJ	220	150	220	240
Netherlands	KGFI	10	20	30	–	Tunisia	KGHK	90	70	110	160
Norway	KGFQ	10	10	–	–	Uganda	KGHL	1 040	690	500	1 400
Portugal	KGFJ	20	20	110	–	Zambia	KGHM	220	180	210	240
Spain	KGFK	–	10	20	–	Zimbabwe	KGHN	360	340	410	430
Sweden	KGFR	10	10	–	–	Other Africa	KOSU	600	550	870	1 570
European Economic Area[1]	KGFL	120	110	270	10	Africa	KGHO	12 970	13 200	16 090	27 020
Remainder of Europe						**Asia**					
Bulgaria	KGFW	200	160	180	280						
Cyprus	KGFN	240	240	280	430	**Indian sub-continent**					
Former Czechoslovakia	KGFX	290	280	400	500	Bangladesh	KGHP	2 720	2 870	3 630	3 280
Of which,						India	KGHQ	4 620	4 650	5 430	6 290
Czech Republic[2]	LQLS	..	..	240	270	Pakistan	KGHR	6 250	5 560	7 350	11 860
Slovakia	LQLT	..	..	160	230						
Hungary	KGFZ	200	180	180	190	Indian sub-continent	KGHS	13 590	13 080	16 420	21 440
Malta	KGFP	80	60	70	60						
Poland	KGGA	640	570	580	620	**Middle East**					
Romania	KGGB	270	220	240	290	Iran	KGHT	1 720	1 060	930	1 560
Switzerland	KGFS	210	200	250	220	Iraq	KGHU	1 580	1 610	1 650	2 210
Turkey	KGFT	3 720	4 230	2 360	5 220	Israel	KGHV	290	280	300	260
Former USSR	KGGC	820	870	1 180	1 390	Jordan	KGHW	120	150	130	140
Of which,						Kuwait	KGHX	20	40	60	60
Estonia	LQLU	..	..	20	20	Lebanon	KGHY	660	640	590	760
Latvia	LQLV	..	..	40	30	Saudi Arabia	KGHZ	40	30	50	60
Lithuania	LQLW	..	..	50	110	Syria	KGIA	110	120	110	140
Russia[3]	LQLX	..	..	860	870	Yemen	KOSV	180	150	230	260
Ukraine	LQLY	..	..	140	200	Other Middle East	KOSW	70	90	120	140
Other former USSR	LQLZ	..	..	80	160						
Former Yugoslavia	KGFU	680	590	1 500	6 650	Middle East	KGIB	4 790	4 160	4 180	5 590
Of which,											
Croatia	LQMA	..	..	180	320	**Remainder of Asia**					
Slovenia	LQMB	..	..	10	20	China	KGIC	1 180	1 230	1 550	1 520
Yugoslavia[4]	LQMC	..	..	870	5 760	Hong Kong[6]	KOSX	1 240	900	810	490
Other former Yugoslavia	LQMD	..	..	440	550	Indonesia	KGID	90	90	120	200
Other Europe	KOSO	20	30	60	130	Japan	KGIE	1 780	1 760	1 880	1 590
						Malaysia	KGIF	610	500	550	510
Remainder of Europe	KOSP	7 370	7 640	7 300	15 980	Philippines	KGIG	1 030	890	950	1 190
						Singapore	KGIH	150	160	120	170
Europe	KGGE	7 500	7 740	7 570	15 990	South Korea	KOTE	270	220	270	300
						Sri Lanka	KGII	2 180	1 620	2 100	5 370
Americas						Taiwan	KOSY	60	80	100	120
Argentina	KGGF	50	50	60	60	Thailand	KGIJ	550	500	540	830
Barbados	KGGG	80	60	100	70	Other Asia	KOSZ	350	420	530	770
Brazil	KGGH	390	330	350	410						
Canada	KGGI	970	980	1 050	1 010	Remainder of Asia	KGIL	9 500	8 370	9 520	13 060
Chile	KGGJ	60	70	50	50						
Colombia	KGGK	270	240	370	650	Asia	KGIM	27 880	25 610	30 120	40 090
Guyana	KGGM	200	170	180	130						
Jamaica	KGGN	1 420	1 030	1 120	1 060	**Oceania**					
Mexico	KGGO	110	130	120	90	Australia	KGIN	2 120	1 920	2 200	2 410
Peru	KGGP	80	110	100	140	New Zealand	KGIO	1 360	1 150	1 440	1 670
Trinidad and Tobago	KGGQ	340	280	320	280	Other Oceania	KOTA	40	30	50	40
USA	KGGR	4 030	3 900	3 940	3 760						
Venezuela	KGGT	50	50	60	60	Oceania	KGIP	3 520	3 100	3 690	4 120
Other Americas	KOSR	430	390	2 950	750						
						British Overseas citizens	KGIQ	620	540	960	560
Americas	KGGU	8 470	7 790	10 780	8 520	Stateless	KGIS	780	740	580	820
Africa						**All nationalities**	KGFA	61 730	58 720	69 790	97 120
Algeria	KGGV	400	370	710	1 130						
Angola	KOSS	30	60	90	520						
Congo (Dem. Rep.)[5]	KOST	90	90	120	2 580						

1 Includes Liechtenstein.
2 Includes Czechoslovakian passport holders.
3 Includes Soviet Union passport holders.

4 Includes holders of passports of the former Yugoslavia.
5 Democratic Republic of the Congo, formerly known as Zaire.
6 Includes Hong Kong stateless persons.

Source: Home Office: 020 8760 8289

5.10 Applications[1,2] received for asylum, excluding dependants, by nationality
United Kingdom

Number of principal applicants

Nationality		1991	1992	1993	1994	1995	1996[3]	1997	1998	1999[5]
Europe										
Albania	LQME	15	100	70	75	110	105	445	560	1 310
Czech Republic	LQMF	–	–	5	5	15	55	240	515	1 790
FYR	ZAFA	..	..	..	..	..	400	1 865	7 395	11 465
Poland	DMLX	20	90	155	360	1 210	900	565	1 585	1 860
Romania	KEAV	555	305	370	355	770	455	605	1 015	1 985
Russia	ZAEQ	..	..	..	..	..	205	180	185	685
Turkey	KEAW	2 110	1 865	1 480	2 045	1 820	1 495	1 445	2 015	2 850
Ukraine	ZAER	..	..	..	..	..	235	490	370	775
Other Former USSR	ZAES	245	270	385	595	795	960	1 345	2 260	2 640
Other Former Yugoslavia	ZAET	320	5 635	1 830	1 385	1 565	630	395	585	2 715
Other	ZAEU	425	170	245	535	770	1 035	1 575	1 260	200
Total	KEAZ	3 685	8 435	4 535	5 360	7 050	6 475	9 145	17 745	28 280
Americas										
Colombia	KEBZ	140	280	380	405	525	1 005	1 330	425	1 000
Ecuador	KYDB	5	15	60	105	250	435	1 205	280	610
Other	KECS	65	170	305	380	565	330	295	270	420
Total	KECT	210	465	745	890	1 340	1 765	2 825	975	2 025
Africa										
Algeria	KOTB	45	150	275	995	1 865	715	715	1 260	1 385
Angola	KECU	5 780	245	320	605	555	385	195	150	545
Congo (Dem. Rep.)	KEEH	7 010	880	635	775	935	680	690	660	1 240
Ethiopia	KECW	1 685	680	615	730	585	205	145	345	455
Gambia	DMMA	20	10	25	140	1 170	245	125	45	30
Ghana	KECX	2 405	1 600	1 785	2 035	1 915	780	350	225	195
Ivory Coast	DMLZ	1 415	310	330	705	245	125	70	95	190
Kenya	KOTC	70	110	630	1 130	1 395	1 170	605	885	485
Nigeria	KECY	335	615	1 665	4 340	5 825	2 900	1 480	1 380	945
Rwanda	ZAEV	25	10	10	100	135	80	90	280	820
Sierra Leone	KOTD	75	325	1 050	1 810	855	395	815	565	1 125
Somalia	KECZ	1 995	1 575	1 465	1 840	3 465	1 780	2 730	4 685	7 495
Sudan	KEEE	1 150	560	300	330	345	280	230	250	280
Tanzania	DMMC	25	30	110	205	1 535	225	90	80	80
Uganda	KEEG	1 450	295	595	360	365	215	220	210	420
Other	ZAEW	4 015	245	480	860	1 360	1 105	965	1 265	2 740
Total	KEEJ	27 500	7 630	10 295	16 960	22 545	11 290	9 515	12 380	18 435
Middle East										
Iran	KEEK	530	405	365	520	615	585	585	745	1 320
Iraq	KEEL	915	700	495	550	930	965	1 075	1 295	1 800
Other	ZAEX	1 095	875	655	910	755	600	675	745	1 045
Total	KEGY	2 540	1 980	1 520	1 985	2 295	2 150	2 335	2 785	4 165
Asia										
Afghanistan	DMLY	210	270	315	325	580	675	1 085	2 395	3 975
Bangladesh	ZAEY	460	150	155	310	685	645	545	460	530
China	KEGZ	525	330	215	425	790	820	1 945	1 925	2 625
India	KEIL	2 075	1 450	1 275	2 030	3 255	2 220	1 285	1 030	1 365
Pakistan	KEIM	3 245	1 700	1 125	1 810	2 915	1 915	1 615	1 975	2 615
Sri Lanka	KEIN	3 765	2 085	1 965	2 350	2 070	1 340	1 830	3 505	5 130
Other	ZAEZ	215	125	130	265	390	275	265	650	1 225
Total	KEJO	10 495	6 100	5 175	7 515	10 685	7 885	8 570	11 940	17 465
Other, and nationality not known[4]	KEJP	410	–	100	125	50	80	105	190	785
Grand Total	KEJQ	44 840	24 605	22 370	32 830	43 965	29 640	32 500	46 015	71 160

1 Figures do not include overseas applications.
2 Figures rounded to the nearest 5.
3 Includes revisions to the number of in-country applications lodged between September and December 1996.

4 Where the nationality was not known between 1991 and 1994 the most likely nationality was recorded.
5 Provisional figures.

Source: Home Office: 020 8760 8297

5.11 Marriages

Numbers

		1989	1990	1991	1992	1993	1994	1995	1996	1997[2]	1998[3]	1999
United Kingdom												
Marriages	KKAA	392 042	375 410	349 739	356 013	341 608	331 232	322 251	317 514	310 218	304 797	301 083
Persons marrying per 1 000 resident population	KKAB	13.7	13.1	12.1	12.3	11.7	11.3	11.0	10.8	10.5	10.3	10.1
Previous marital status												
Bachelors	KKAC	288 478	276 512	256 538	258 567	245 996	236 619	227 717	221 826	216 237	214 005	211 820
Divorced men	KKAD	92 033	88 199	83 069	87 419	85 824	85 261	85 743	87 113	85 625	82 977	81 750
Widowers	KKAE	11 531	10 699	10 132	10 027	9 788	9 352	8 791	8 575	8 356	7 815	7 513
Spinsters	KKAF	291 516	279 442	259 084	260 252	248 063	237 241	228 462	221 697	216 776	215 399	213 246
Divorced women	KKAG	89 234	85 608	81 224	86 361	84 268	85 220	85 396	87 618	85 648	82 016	80 816
Widows	KKAH	11 294	10 360	9 431	9 400	9 277	8 771	8 393	8 199	7 794	7 382	7 021
First marriage for both partners	KMGH	251 572	240 729	222 369	222 142	210 567	200 910	192 078	185 293	181 135	180 404	178 759
First marriage for one partner	KMGI	76 850	74 496	70 884	74 535	72 925	72 040	72 023	72 937	70 743	68 596	67 548
Remarriage for both partners	KMGJ	63 620	60 185	56 486	59 336	58 116	58 282	58 150	59 284	58 340	55 797	54 776
Males												
Under 21 years	KKAI	19 070	15 930	13 271	11 031	8 767	7 091	6 302	5 497	5 126	5 173	5 234
21-24	KKAJ	102 977	92 270	79 877	74 458	65 129	56 877	48 432	42 488	36 875	32 723	29 390
25-29	KKAK	123 491	122 800	115 637	118 255	114 101	111 108	105 218	101 647	97 345	94 696	90 412
30-34	KKAL	56 442	56 966	56 970	62 470	63 848	65 490	68 245	69 867	70 904	71 096	72 129
35-44	KKAM	51 411	49 984	48 147	51 125	50 553	51 310	53 350	56 513	58 292	59 838	62 114
45-54	KKAN	22 329	21 996	20 915	23 290	23 841	24 136	24 786	26 252	26 472	26 118	26 581
55 and over	KKAO	16 322	15 464	14 922	15 384	15 369	15 220	14 918	15 250	15 204	15 153	15 223
Females												
Under 21 years	KKAP	54 256	45 626	38 305	32 618	26 839	22 903	20 643	18 485	17 254	16 793	16 082
21-24	KKAQ	128 411	119 037	105 505	102 494	93 125	84 171	75 071	66 191	59 549	54 645	50 350
25-29	KKAR	100 531	103 209	99 851	105 223	104 517	102 803	100 644	99 651	97 932	97 181	94 703
30-34	KKAS	41 989	42 794	43 617	48 514	49 546	52 359	54 819	57 752	58 589	59 349	60 446
35-44	KKAT	40 290	38 983	37 582	40 075	40 090	41 213	43 115	45 969	47 267	47 721	50 136
45-54	KKAU	17 172	16 825	16 473	18 504	18 800	19 280	19 720	21 025	21 038	20 708	20 822
55 and over	KKAV	9 393	8 936	8 406	8 585	8 691	8 503	8 239	8 441	8 589	8 400	8 544
England and Wales												
Marriages	KKBA	346 697	331 150	306 756	311 564	299 197	291 069	283 012	278 975	272 536	267 303	263 515
Persons marrying per 1 000 resident population	KKBB	13.7	13.1	12.0	12.2	11.6	11.3	10.9	10.7	10.4	10.2	10.0
Previous marital status												
Bachelors	KKBC	252 230	241 274	222 823	224 152	213 476	206 077	198 208	193 306	188 268	186 329	184 266
Divorced men	KKBD	84 035	80 282	74 860	78 473	76 986	76 633	76 967	78 003	76 839	74 029	72 617
Widowers	KKBE	10 432	9 594	9 073	8 939	8 735	8 359	7 837	7 666	7 429	6 945	6 632
Spinsters	KKBF	254 763	243 825	224 812	225 608	214 987	206 332	198 603	192 707	188 457	187 391	185 328
Divorced women	KKBG	81 702	77 994	73 408	77 542	75 904	76 857	76 869	78 939	77 098	73 330	71 971
Widows	KKBH	10 232	9 331	8 536	8 414	8 306	7 880	7 540	7 329	6 981	6 582	6 216
First marriage for both partners	KMGK	218 904	209 043	192 238	191 732	181 956	174 200	166 418	160 680	156 907	156 539	155 027
First marriage for one partner	KMGL	69 185	67 013	63 159	66 296	64 551	64 009	63 975	64 653	62 911	60 642	59 540
Remarriage for both partners	KMGM	58 608	55 094	51 359	53 536	52 690	52 860	52 619	53 642	52 718	50 122	48 948
Males[1]												
Under 21 years	KKBI	16 312	13 772	11 416	9 471	7 540	6 173	5 520	4 877	4 574	4 608	4 629
21-24	KKBJ	89 263	79 818	68 547	63 932	55 963	49 072	42 711	36 713	31 907	28 389	25 424
25-29	KKBK	108 834	107 784	100 891	102 942	99 314	96 848	91 607	88 338	84 644	82 135	78 364
30-34	KKBL	50 409	50 600	50 403	55 012	56 129	57 854	60 014	61 582	62 265	62 323	63 212
35-44	KKBM	46 549	45 038	43 013	45 364	44 863	45 518	47 330	50 038	51 654	52 812	54 528
45-54	KKBN	20 365	19 991	18 929	20 925	21 440	21 794	22 349	23 661	23 688	23 385	23 676
55 and over	KKBO	14 965	14 147	13 557	13 918	13 948	13 803	13 481	13 766	13 804	13 651	13 682
Females[1]												
Under 21 years	KKBP	47 529	40 022	33 428	28 541	23 469	20 250	18 343	16 510	15 439	15 065	14 379
21-24	KKBQ	112 048	103 653	91 338	88 553	80 470	72 937	65 126	57 296	51 766	47 446	43 691
25-29	KKBR	88 662	90 629	87 244	91 735	91 134	89 941	87 680	86 838	85 352	84 399	82 250
30-34	KKBS	37 452	38 032	38 425	42 675	43 559	46 119	48 216	50 799	51 405	51 982	52 721
35-44	KKBT	36 678	35 315	33 755	35 660	35 662	36 651	38 367	40 889	41 838	42 245	44 199
45-54	KKBU	15 661	15 290	14 891	16 619	16 969	17 409	17 791	18 992	18 938	18 575	18 572
55 and over	KKBV	8 667	8 209	7 675	7 781	7 934	7 762	7 489	7 651	7 798	7 591	7 703

1 The figures for England and Wales include an assumed distribution of 'Age not stated'.
2 Provisional.
3 Later figures not available.

Source: Office for National Statistics: 01329 813772

5.11 Marriages

continued

Numbers

		1989	1990	1991	1992	1993	1994	1995	1996	1997	1998	1999
Scotland												
Marriages	KKCA	35 326	34 672	33 762	35 057	33 366	31 480	30 663	30 242	29 611	29 668	29 940
Persons marrying per 1 000 population	KKCB	13.9	13.6	13.2	13.7	13.0	12.3	11.9	11.8	11.6	11.6	11.7
Previous marital status												
Bachelors	KKCC	27 186	26 636	25 549	26 106	24 609	23 004	22 126	21 454	20 994	20 987	21 052
Divorced men	KKCD	7 224	7 108	7 344	8 027	7 879	7 654	7 741	8 048	7 845	7 934	8 142
Widowers	KKCE	916	928	869	924	878	822	796	740	772	747	746
Spinsters	KKCF	27 606	26 940	25 979	26 274	25 103	23 248	22 410	21 799	21 303	21 241	21 308
Divorced women	KKCG	6 832	6 869	7 048	7 935	7 469	7 487	7 542	7 718	7 621	7 754	7 949
Widows	KKCH	888	863	735	848	794	745	711	725	687	673	683
First marriage for both partners	KEZV	24 032	23 529	22 401	22 588	21 214	19 644	18 822	18 071	17 751	17 677	17 680
First marriage for one partner	KEZW	6 728	6 518	6 726	7 204	7 284	6 964	6 892	7 111	6 795	6 874	7 000
Remarriage for both partners	KEZX	4 566	4 625	4 635	5 265	4 868	4 872	4 949	5 060	5 065	5 117	5 260
Males												
Under 21 years	KKCI	2 042	1 626	1 378	1 172	902	680	577	452	406	421	490
21-24	KKCJ	10 295	9 454	8 572	7 958	6 870	5 693	4 915	4 191	3 494	3 147	2 853
25-29	KKCK	11 122	11 430	11 244	11 587	11 266	10 812	10 209	10 056	9 495	9 439	9 031
30-34	KKCL	4 831	5 061	5 290	6 022	6 214	6 176	6 574	6 574	6 911	6 988	7 179
35-44	KKCM	4 135	4 210	4 383	4 950	4 803	4 864	5 021	5 412	5 649	5 945	6 470
45-54	KKCN	1 721	1 760	1 733	2 083	2 093	2 050	2 124	2 288	2 459	2 412	2 575
55 and over	KKCO	1 180	1 131	1 162	1 285	1 218	1 205	1 243	1 269	1 197	1 316	1 342
Females												
Under 21 years	KKCP	4 951	4 161	3 589	3 060	2 461	1 959	1 728	1 423	1 302	1 289	1 322
21-24	KKCQ	12 386	11 666	10 735	10 503	9 506	8 291	7 264	6 474	5 568	5 248	4 778
25-29	KKCR	9 163	9 755	9 771	10 457	10 368	9 895	9 904	9 818	9 574	9 764	9 539
30-34	KKCS	3 728	3 925	4 331	4 822	5 002	5 145	5 401	5 675	5 927	6 036	6 433
35-44	KKCT	3 120	3 194	3 333	3 847	3 774	3 917	4 025	4 378	4 722	4 726	5 150
45-54	KKCU	1 345	1 351	1 386	1 673	1 606	1 648	1 689	1 794	1 844	1 900	1 994
55 and over	KKCV	633	620	617	695	649	625	652	680	674	705	724
Northern Ireland												
Marriages	KKDA	10 019	9 588	9 221	9 392	9 045	8 683	8 576	8 297	8 071	7 826	7 628
Persons marrying per 1 000 population	KKDB	12.7	12.1	11.7	11.5	11.0	10.6	10.4	10.0	9.6	9.3	9.0
Previous marital status												
Bachelors	KKDC	9 062	8 602	8 166	8 309	7 911	7 538	7 383	7 066	6 975	6 689	6 502
Divorced men	KKDD	774	809	865	919	959	974	1 035	1 062	941	1 014	991
Widowers	KKDE	183	177	190	164	175	171	158	169	155	123	135
Spinsters	KKDF	9 147	8 677	8 293	8 370	7 973	7 661	7 449	7 191	7 016	6 767	6 610
Divorced women	KKDG	700	745	768	884	895	876	985	961	929	932	896
Widows	KKDH	172	166	160	138	177	146	142	145	126	127	122
First marriage for both partners	KEZY	8 636	8 157	7 730	7 822	7 397	7 066	6 838	6 542	6 477	6 188	6 052
First marriage for one partner	KEZZ	937	965	999	1 035	1 090	1 067	1 156	1 173	1 037	1 080	1 008
Remarriage for both partners	KFBI	446	466	492	535	558	550	582	582	557	558	568
Males												
Under 21 years	KKDI	716	532	477	388	325	236	205	168	146	144	115
21-24	KKDJ	3 419	2 998	2 758	2 568	2 296	2 111	806	1 584	1 474	1 187	1 113
25-29	KKDK	3 535	3 586	3 502	3 726	3 521	3 434	3 402	3 253	3 206	3 122	3 017
30-34	KKDL	1 202	1 305	1 277	1 436	1 505	1 466	1 657	1 711	1 728	1 785	1 738
35-44	KKDM	727	736	751	811	887	932	999	1 063	989	1 081	1 116
45-54	KKDN	243	245	253	282	308	292	313	303	325	321	330
55 and over	KKDO	177	186	203	181	203	212	194	215	203	186	199
Females												
Under 21 years	KKDP	1 776	1 443	1 288	1 017	909	694	572	552	513	439	381
21-24	KKDQ	3 977	3 718	3 432	3 438	3 149	2 943	2 681	2 421	2 215	1 951	1 881
25-29	KKDR	2 706	2 825	2 836	3 031	3 015	2 967	3 060	2 995	3 006	3 018	2 914
30-34	KKDS	809	837	861	1 017	985	1 095	1 202	1 278	1 257	1 331	1 292
35-44	KKDT	492	474	494	568	654	645	723	702	707	750	787
45-54	KKDU	166	184	196	212	225	223	240	239	256	233	256
55 and over	KKDV	93	107	114	109	108	116	98	110	117	104	117

Sources: Office for National Statistics: 01329 813772;
General Register Office (Scotland);
General Register Office (Northern Ireland)

Population and vital statistics

5.12 Divorce

		1989	1990	1991	1992	1993	1994	1995	1996	1997	1998	1999
United Kingdom												
Decrees[1] absolute, granted:												
Number	ZBRL	164 349	167 555	173 454	175 144	180 018	173 611	170 050	171 729	161 087	160 057	158 746
Duration of marriage:												
0-4 years	ZBRM	37 844	38 624	40 123	39 191	39 530	37 978	36 594	37 016	33 719	33 087	31 047
5-9 years	ZBRN	46 067	46 169	46 884	47 990	50 883	49 215	48 309	48 670	45 040	44 243	43 357
10-14 years	ZBRO	28 933	30 053	31 773	32 261	33 221	31 177	30 257	30 159	29 085	29 706	30 270
15-19 years	ZBRP	21 347	21 761	22 233	22 179	22 324	21 336	21 040	21 379	20 211	20 078	20 147
20 years and over	ZBRQ	30 139	30 932	32 422	33 516	34 055	33 898	33 840	34 487	33 020	32 935	33 916
Not stated	ZBRR	19	16	19	7	5	7	10	18	12	8	9
Age of wife at marriage:												
16-19 years	ZBRS	47 359	45 905	45 356	44 347	43 368	38 464	35 145	33 590	28 987	27 627	25 440
20-24 years	ZBRT	75 525	78 110	80 969	81 574	83 806	80 594	78 341	78 075	72 971	71 416	69 509
25-29 years	ZBRU	21 876	23 260	25 813	27 109	29 213	30 576	31 611	33 634	33 452	34 195	35 585
30-34 years	ZBRV	9 113	9 457	10 180	10 582	11 272	11 716	12 322	13 122	12 968	13 719	14 420
35-39 years	ZBRW	4 907	5 171	5 300	5 531	6 018	5 979	6 172	6 470	6 155	6 571	6 848
40-44 years	ZBRX	2 684	2 749	2 897	3 017	3 260	3 247	3 335	3 507	3 375	3 360	3 357
45 years and over	ZBRY	2 850	2 863	2 877	2 933	3 004	2 952	3 052	3 239	3 094	3 086	3 291
Not stated	ZBRZ	35	40	62	51	77	83	72	92	85	83	96
Age of wife at divorce:												
16-24 years	ZBSA	17 893	16 778	16 150	14 604	13 895	11 845	10 517	9 298	7 371	6 758	5 671
25-29 years	ZBSB	37 731	38 504	39 059	38 186	38 632	35 824	33 354	32 808	28 814	26 968	24 120
30-34 years	ZBSC	32 611	34 326	36 434	38 220	39 879	39 456	38 839	39 497	37 257	36 795	36 052
35-39 years	ZBSD	26 402	26 596	28 097	29 044	30 746	30 000	30 280	31 497	30 641	31 688	32 605
40-44 years	ZBSE	22 308	23 156	23 928	23 756	23 943	22 847	22 791	22 843	22 246	22 810	23 614
45 years and over	ZBSF	27 350	28 139	29 705	31 276	32 841	33 549	34 187	35 684	34 662	34 947	36 578
Not stated	ZBSG	54	56	81	58	82	90	82	102	96	91	106
Divorces in which there were:												
No children[2] aged under 16	ZBSH	75 568	76 614	78 694	77 709	78 803	78 913	78 844	80 017	77 353	75 776	77 790
One or more children[2] aged under 16	ZBSI	88 781	90 941	94 760	97 435	101 215	94 698	91 206	91 712	83 734	84 281	80 956
England and Wales												
Decrees[1] absolute granted:												
Number	KKEA	150 872	153 386	158 745	160 385	165 018	158 175	155 499	157 107	146 689	145 214	144 556
Rate per 1,000 married couples	KKEB	*12.7*	*13.0*	*13.5*	*13.7*	*13.9*	*13.4*	*13.1*	*13.8*	*13.0*	*12.9*	*12.9*
Duration of marriage:												
0-4 years	KKEC	35 719	36 299	37 779	36 898	37 252	35 695	34 507	34 924	31 767	31 136	29 307
5-9 years	KKED	42 108	42 061	42 735	43 745	46 536	44 769	44 304	44 609	41 260	40 239	39 676
10-14 years	KKEE	26 281	27 310	28 791	29 285	30 156	28 073	27 365	27 332	26 215	26 698	27 384
15-19 years	KKEF	19 418	19 819	20 127	20 160	20 233	19 200	18 943	19 321	18 027	17 934	18 072
20 years and over	KKEG	27 327	27 881	29 294	30 290	30 836	30 431	30 370	30 912	29 408	29 199	30 108
Not stated	KKEH	19	16	19	7	5	7	10	9	12	8	9
Age of wife at marriage:												
16-19 years	KKEI	42 612	41 116	40 594	39 734	38 801	34 069	31 322	29 927	25 579	24 276	22 486
20-24 years	KKEJ	69 424	71 489	74 050	74 701	76 853	73 291	71 360	71 123	66 167	64 453	62 853
25-29 years	KKEK	20 369	21 701	24 025	25 173	27 178	28 360	29 441	31 396	31 022	31 533	32 867
30-34 years	KKEL	8 590	8 909	9 608	9 939	10 593	11 007	11 585	12 335	12 094	12 788	13 507
35-39 years	KKEM	4 643	4 880	5 024	5 200	5 673	5 615	5 800	6 051	5 767	6 153	6 432
40-44 years	KKEN	2 541	2 598	2 727	2 872	3 091	3 064	3 121	3 254	3 156	3 135	3 331
45 years and over	KKEO	2 693	2 693	2 717	2 766	2 819	2 769	2 870	3 021	2 904	2 876	3 080
Age of wife at divorce:												
16-24 years	KKEP	16 628	15 454	14 960	13 482	12 924	10 956	9 783	8 615	6 871	6 298	5 318
25-29 years	KKEQ	34 483	35 121	35 582	34 853	35 362	32 608	30 563	30 075	26 435	24 586	22 173
30-34 years	KKER	29 757	31 295	33 195	34 901	36 300	35 848	35 538	36 274	33 967	33 446	32 837
35-39 years	KKES	24 170	24 421	25 661	26 577	28 162	27 195	27 550	28 727	27 715	28 605	29 663
40-44 years	KKET	20 647	21 263	21 979	21 783	21 891	20 765	20 739	20 774	20 125	20 521	21 325
45 years and over	KKEU	25 168	25 816	27 349	28 782	30 374	30 796	31 316	32 633	31 564	31 750	33 231
Not stated	KKEV	19	16	19	7	5	7	10	9	12	8	9
Divorces in which there were:												
No children[2] aged under 16	ZBSJ	68 077	68 635	70 399	68 960	70 103	69 684	69 632	70 174	66 019	64 738	65 258
One or more children[2] aged under 16	ZBSK	82 795	84 751	88 346	91 425	94 915	88 491	85 867	86 933	80 670	80 476	79 298

Sources: Office for National Statistics: 01329 813772;
General Register Office (Scotland);
Scottish Courts Administration

5.12 Divorce
continued

		1989	1990	1991	1992	1993	1994	1995	1996	1997	1998	1999
Scotland												
Decrees[1] absolute granted												
Number	KKFA	11 659	12 272	12 399	12 479	12 787	13 133	12 249	12 308[4]	12 222	12 384	11 864
Rate per 1,000 married couples	KKFB	_10.0_	_10.5_	_10.6_	_10.8_	_11.1_	_11.5_	_10.8_	_10.9_	_11.0_	_11.2_	_10.8_
Duration of marriage:												
0-4 years	KKFC	2 013	2 208	2 142	2 085	2 092	2 095	1 908	1 914	1 793	1 766	1 588
5-9 years	KKFD	3 420	3 546	3 508	3 610	3 722	3 790	3 399	3 432	3 224	3 360	3 095
10-14 years	KKFE	2 245	2 361	2 484	2 454	2 539	2 592	2 407	2 310	2 385	2 456	2 368
15-19 years	KKFF	1 633	1 617	1 718	1 675	1 745	1 786	1 698	1 709	1 804	1 729	1 686
20 years and over	KKFG	2 348	2 540	2 547	2 655	2 689	2 870	2 837	2 934	3 016	3 073	3 127
Not stated	ZBSL	..	..	..	..	..	..	..	9	..	..	..
Age of wife at marriage:												
16-19 years	ZBSM	3 998	4 040	3 894	3 755	3 768	3 641	3 091	2 939	2 749	2 654	2 374
20-24 years	ZBSN	5 275	5 745	5 845	5 821	5 890	6 197	5 845	5 822	5 714	5 744	5 453
25-29 years	KKFJ	1 363	1 377	1 545	1 685	1 812	1 926	1 887	1 933	2 151	2 314	2 333
30-34 years	KKFK	479	497	514	575	612	628	654	697	791	824	829
35-39 years	KKFL	235	275	249	301	312	329	338	393	360	382	379
40-44 years	KKFM	131	139	148	138	152	163	196	234	199	198	208
45 years and over	KKFN	143	159	142	153	164	166	166	198	173	185	192
Not stated	KKFO	35	40	62	51	77	83	72	92	85	83	96
Age of wife at divorce:												
16-24 years	KKFP	1 139	1 199	1 038	963	843	767	622	583	426	377	301
25-29 years	KKFQ	2 818	2 938	2 932	2 807	2 775	2 750	2 353	2 269	2 021	1 957	1 597
30-34 years	KKFR	2 442	2 611	2 741	2 785	3 037	3 045	2 747	2 708	2 736	2 767	2 642
35-39 years	KKFS	1 927	1 891	2 037	2 092	2 212	2 390	2 290	2 307	2 469	2 562	2 450
40-44 years	KKFT	1 436	1 614	1 665	1 685	1 771	1 788	1 734	1 761	1 819	1 951	1 929
45 years and over	KKFU	1 862	1 979	1 924	2 096	2 071	2 310	2 431	2 587	2 667	2 687	2 848
Not stated	KKFV	35	40	62	51	77	83	72	93	84	83	97
Divorces in which there were:												
No children[2] aged under 16	KKFW	6 091	6 555	6 521	6 927	6 951	7 390	7 515	8 167	9 761	9 231	10 883
One or more children[2] under 16	KKFX	5 568	5 717	5 878	5 552	5 836	5 743	4 734	4 141	2 461	3 153	981
Northern Ireland												
Decrees[1] absolute granted:												
Number	ZBSO	1 818	1 897	2 310	2 280	2 213	2 303	2 302	2 314	2 176	2 459	2 326
Duration of marriage:												
0-4 years	ZBSP	112	117	202	208	186	188	179	178	159	185	152
5-9 years	ZBSQ	539	562	641	635	625	656	606	629	556	644	586
10-14 years	ZBSR	407	382	498	522	526	512	485	517	485	552	518
15-19 years	ZBSS	296	325	388	344	346	350	399	349	380	415	389
20 years and over	ZBST	464	511	581	571	530	597	633	641	596	663	681
Age of wife at marriage:												
16-19 years	ZBSU	749	749	868	858	789	754	732	724	659	697	580
20-24 years	ZBSV	826	876	1 074	1 052	1 063	1 106	1 136	1 130	1 090	1 219	1 203
25-29 years	ZBSW	144	182	243	251	223	290	283	305	279	348	385
30-34 years	ZBSX	44	51	58	68	67	81	83	90	83	107	84
35-39 years	ZBSY	29	16	27	30	33	35	34	26	28	36	37
40-44 years	ZBSZ	12	12	22	7	17	20	18	19	20	27	18
45 years and over	ZBTA	14	11	18	14	21	17	16	20	17	25	19
Age of wife at divorce:												
16-24 years	ZBTB	126	125	152	159	127	122	112	100	74	83	52
25-29 years	ZBTC	430	445	545	526	495	466	438	464	358	425	350
30-34 years	ZBTD	412	420	498	534	542	563	554	515	554	582	573
35-39 years	ZBTE	305	284	399	375	372	415	440	463	457	521	492
40-44 years	ZBTF	225	279	284	288	281	294	318	308	302	338	360
45 years and over	ZBTG	320	344	432	398	396	443	440	464	431	510	499
Divorces in which there were:												
No children[2] aged under 16	ZBTH	1 400	1 424	1 774	1 822	1 749	1 839	1 697	1 676	1 573	1 807	1 649
One or more children[2] aged under 16	ZBTI	418	473	536	458	464	464	605	638	603	652	677

1 Includes nullities.
2 Children of the family as defined by the Matrimonial Causes Act 1973.

Sources: Office for National Statistics: 01329 813772;
General Register Office (Scotland);
Northern Ireland Statistics and Research Agency

5.13 Divorce proceedings

Number

					United Kingdom							
		1989	1990	1991	1992	1993	1994	1995	1996	1997	1998	1999
Dissolution of marriage[1,3]												
Decree absolute/decree granted	ZBXR	163 943	167 086	172 997	174 718	179 539	173 178	169 621	171 309	160 733	159 788	158 418
On grounds of:												
Adultery	ZBXS	45 496	45 457	46 161	45 458	45 759	42 743	41 313	41 127	38 652	37 302	35 545
Behaviour	ZBXT	70 465	73 481	77 294	77 648	78 686	75 029	71 733	72 581	68 546	68 685	67 851
Desertion	ZBXU	1 224	1 112	1 185	1 096	1 193	1 185	1 196	1 101	956	828	748
Separation (2 years and consent)	ZBXV	34 810	35 015	36 041	37 955	41 002	41 144	41 969	42 265	39 398	39 727	40 368
Separation(5 years)	ZBXW	11 131	11 195	11 528	11 806	12 183	12 317	12 699	13 547	12 552	12 697	13 389
Combination of more than one ground and other	ZBXX	817	826	788	755	716	760	711	688	629	549	517
Decree absolute[1,3]/decree granted to:												
the wife	ZBXY	117 447	119 715	124 472	125 833	128 797	123 256	118 869	119 570	111 912	111 556	109 828
the husband	ZBXZ	46 145	46 981	48 136	48 509	50 407	49 507	50 268	51 247	48 393	47 764	48 236
both	ZBYA	357	396	393	379	345	423	490	493	430	369	358
Nullity of marriage[1]												
Decrees absolute/decree granted	ZBYB	406	469	457	426	479	433	429	420	354	369	328

					England and Wales							
		1989	1990	1991	1992	1993	1994	1995	1996	1997	1998	1999
Dissolution of marriage												
Petitions filed	KKGA	184 610	191 615	179 103	189 329	184 471	175 510	173 966	177 970	163 769	165 870	162 775
Decree nisi granted	KKGM	151 309	157 344	153 258	149 126	160 625	154 241	155 739	157 588	148 310	144 231	143 106
Decree absolute granted	KKGN	150 477	152 927	158 301	159 967	164 556	157 756	155 076	156 692	146 339	144 851	144 233
On grounds of:												
Adultery	KKGB	44 031	44 038	44 737	44 128	44 466	41 449	40 178	40 012	37 592	36 319	34 584
Behaviour	KKGC	66 716	69 381	73 266	73 906	74 583	70 932	68 168	68 986	65 047	65 257	64 816
Desertion	KKGD	1 113	1 027	1 082	1 021	1 118	1 062	1 108	1 030	912	790	713
Separation (2 years and consent)	KKGE	28 806	28 710	29 414	30 995	34 144	33 996	35 030	35 422	32 638	32 394	33 482
Separation(5 years)	KKGF	9 033	8 964	9 031	9 181	9 556	9 589	9 930	10 626	9 592	9 616	10 193
Combination of more than one ground and other	ZBYC	778	807	771	736	689	728	662	616	558	475	445
Decree absolute granted to:												
the wife	ZBYD	107 769	109 571	113 947	115 393	118 127	112 415	108 764	109 489	102 173	101 583	100 469
the husband	ZBYE	42 351	42 960	43 961	44 195	46 084	44 918	45 823	46 712	43 739	42 902	43 413
both	ZBYF	357	396	393	379	345	423	489	491	427	366	351
Nullity of marriage												
Petitions filed	KKGO	478	665	619	535	634	822	881	702	485	505	549
Decrees nisi granted	KKGR	365	430	508	369	365	705	425	332	248	281	495
Decrees absolute granted	KKGS	395	459	444	418	462	419	423	415	350	363	323
Judicial separation												
Petitions filed	KKGT	2 741	2 900	2 588	2 434	2 251	4 358	3 349	2 795	1 078	916	2 446
Decrees granted	KKGW	1 678	1 794	1 747	1 452	1 413	1 350	1 543	1 199	589	519	2 282

5.13 Divorce proceedings
continued

Number

		Scotland										
		1989	1990	1991	1992	1993	1994	1995	1996	1997	1998	1999
Dissolution of marriage[1,3]												
Decree granted	ZBYG	11 653	12 266	12 395	12 476	12 777	13 125	12 243	12 307	12 220	12 483	11 860
On grounds of:												
Adultery	ZBYH	1 291	1 232	1 198	1 136	1 092	1 099	956	943	909	832	770
Behaviour	ZBYI	3 532	3 847	3 688	3 407	3 757	3 711	3 203	3 184	3 081	3 005	2 611
Desertion	ZBYJ	100	68	82	58	56	103	72	61	33	28	18
Separation (2 years and consent)	ZBYK	5 098	5 362	5 508	5 823	5 800	6 078	5 846	5 835	5 773	6 221	5 908
Separation(5 years)	ZBYL	1 632	1 757	1 919	2 052	2 072	2 134	2 166	2 284	2 424	2 397	2 553
Decree granted to[2,3]:												
the wife	ZBYM	8 439	8 862	8 930	8 865	9 190	9 278	8 545	8 559	8 266	8 329	7 774
the husband	ZBYN	3 220	3 410	3 469	3 614	3 597	3 855	3 704	3 749	3 956	4 055	4 090
Nullity of marriage												
Decree granted	ZBYO	6	6	4	3	10	8	6	1	2	1	4

		Northern Ireland										
		1989	1990	1991	1992	1993	1994	1995	1996	1997	1998	1999
Dissolution of marriage												
Petitions filed	ZBYP	2 385	2 258	2 591	2 597	2 610	2 875	2 875	2 695	2 808	2 760	2 414
Decree nisi granted	ZBYQ	2 029	2 190	2 344	2 386	2 384	2 535	2 535	2 419	2 532	2 904	2 393
Decree absolute granted	ZBYR	1 813	1 893	2 301	2 275	2 206	2 297	2 302	2 310	2 174	2 454	2 325
On grounds of:												
Adultery	ZBYS	174	187	226	194	201	195	179	172	151	151	191
Behaviour	ZBYT	217	253	340	335	346	386	362	411	418	423	424
Desertion	ZBYU	11	17	21	17	19	20	16	10	11	10	17
Separation (2 years and consent)	ZBYV	928	945	1 119	1 137	1 059	1 072	1 093	1 010	991	1 112	978
Separation(5 years)	ZBYW	466	474	578	573	555	594	603	637	536	684	643
Combination of more than one ground and other	ZBYX	17	17	17	19	26	30	49	70	67	74	72
Decree absolute granted to:												
the wife	ZBYY	1 239	1 282	1 595	1 575	1 480	1 563	1 560	1 522	1 473	1 644	1 585
the husband	ZBYZ	574	611	706	700	726	734	741	786	698	807	733
both	ZBZA	–	–	–	–	–	–	1	2	3	3	7
Nullity of marriage												
Petitions filed	ZBZB	6	7	5	1	2	5	5	5	7	2	4
Decrees nisi granted	ZBZC	6	9	10	3	2	3	5	5	2	6	2
Decrees absolute granted	ZBZD	5	4	9	5	7	6	–	4	2	5	1
Judicial separation												
Petitions filed	ZBZE	16	16	23	17	44	57	84	63	70	64	50
Decrees granted	ZBZF	16	16	13	22	6	15	30	22	34	40	31

1 The terms Petition Filed, Decree Nisi Granted, Decree Absolute and Judicial Separation are not used in Scotland.
2 Information on Decree granted for the wife or husband for Scotland includes nullities (these are identified separately under Nullity of Marriage); figures excluding nullities are not available.
3 Decree Granted for Both, and Combinations of More than One Ground are not procedures used in Scotland.

Sources: National Statistics: 01329 813772;
General Register Office Scotland (GRO(S));
Northern Ireland Statistics and Research Agency (NISRA)

Population and vital statistics

5.14 Births
Annual averages or calendar years

Thousands

	Live births				Rates				
	Total	Male	Female	Sex ratio[5]	Crude birth rate[1]	General fertility rate[2]	TFR[3]	Still-births[4]	Still-birth rate[4]
United Kingdom									
1900 - 02	1 095	558	537	1 037	28.6	115.1	..	..	..
1910 - 12	1 037	528	508	1 039	24.6	99.4	..	..	..
1920 - 22	1 018	522	496	1 052	23.1	93.0	..	..	..
1930 - 32	750	383	367	1 046	16.3	66.5	..	..	..
1940 - 42	723	372	351	1 062	15.0	..	1.89	26	..
1950 - 52	803	413	390	1 061	16.0	73.7	2.21	18	..
1960 - 62	946	487	459	1 063	17.9	90.3	2.80	18	..
1970 - 72	880	453	427	1 064	15.8	82.5	2.36	12	13
1980 - 82	735	377	358	1 053	13.0	62.5	1.83	5	7
	BBCA	**KBCZ**	**KBCY**	**KMFW**	**KBCT**	**KBCS**	**KBCR**	**KBCQ**	**KMFX**
1984	730	373	356	1 049	12.9	60.3	1.77	4	6
1985	751	385	366	1 053	13.3	61.4	1.80	4	6
1986	755	387	368	1 053	13.3	61.1	1.78	4	5
1987	776	398	378	1 053	13.6	62.3	1.82	4	5
1988	788	403	384	1 049	13.8	63.2	1.84	4	5
1989	777	398	379	1 051	13.6	62.4	1.81	4	5
1990	799	409	390	1 049	13.9	64.2	1.84	4	5
1991	793	406	386	1 052	13.7	63.6	1.82	4	5
1992	781	400	380	1 052	13.5	63.4	1.80	3	4
1993	762	391	371	1 054	13.1	62.4	1.76	4	6
1994	751	385	365	1 054	12.9	61.6	1.74	4	6
1995	732	375	357	1 052	12.5	60.1	1.71	4	6
1996	733	376	357	1 055	12.5	60.1	1.72	4	6
1997	727	373	354	1 051	12.3	59.5	1.72	4	5
1998	717	368	350	1 052	12.1	58.7	1.71	4	5
1999	700	360	341	1 056	11.8	57.2	1.69	4	5
England and Wales									
1900 - 02	932	475	458	1 037	28.6	114.7	..	..	..
1910 - 12	884	450	433	1 040	24.5	98.6	..	..	..
1920 - 22	862	442	420	1 051	22.8	91.1	..	..	..
1930 - 32	632	323	309	1 047	15.8	64.4	..	27	..
1940 - 42	607	312	295	1 057	15.6	61.3	1.81	22	..
1950 - 52	683	351	332	1 058	15.6	72.1	2.16	16	..
1960 - 62	812	418	394	1 061	17.6	88.9	2.77	16	..
1970 - 72	764	394	371	1 061	15.6	81.4	2.31	10	13
1980 - 82	639	328	311	1 053	12.9	61.8	1.81	4	7
	BBCB	**KMFY**	**KMFZ**	**KMGA**	**KMGB**	**KMGC**	**KMGD**	**KMGE**	**KMGF**
1984	637	326	311	1 049	12.8	59.8	1.75	4	6
1985	656	337	320	1 054	13.1	61.0	1.78	4	6
1986	661	339	322	1 052	13.2	60.6	1.77	4	5
1987	682	350	332	1 053	13.6	62.0	1.81	3	5
1988	694	355	339	1 048	13.8	63.0	1.82	3	5
1989	688	352	335	1 051	13.6	62.5	1.80	3	5
1990	706	361	345	1 048	13.9	64.3	1.84	3	5
1991	699	358	341	1 052	13.7	63.6	1.82	3	5
1992	690	354	336	1 053	13.4	63.5	1.80	3	4
1993	674	346	328	1 056	13.1	62.6	1.76	4	6
1994	665	341	323	1 055	12.9	61.9	1.75	4	6
1995	648	332	316	1 051	12.5	60.4	1.72	4	6
1996	650	333	316	1 055	12.5	60.5	1.73	4	5
1997	643	330	314	1 051	12.3	59.8	1.73	3	5
1998	636	326	310	1 051	12.1	59.0	1.72	3	5
1999	622	319	303	1 055	11.8	57.6	1.70	3	5

See footnotes on the second part of this table.

Source: Office for National Statistics: 020 7533 5113

5.14
Births
Annual averages or calendar years
continued

Thousands

	Live births				Rates				
	Total	Male	Female	Sex ratio[5]	Crude birth rate[1]	General fertility rate[2]	TFR[3]	Still-births[4]	Still-birth rate4
Scotland									
1900 - 02	132	67	65	1 046	29.5	120.6	..	..	..
1910 - 12	123	63	60	1 044	25.9	107.4	..	..	..
1920 - 22	125	64	61	1 046	25.6	105.9	..	..	..
1930 - 32	93	47	45	1 040	19.1	78.8	..	..	..
1940 - 42	89	46	43	1 051	18.5	73.7	..	4	..
1950 - 52	91	47	44	1 060	17.9	81.4	2.41	2	..
1960 - 62	102	53	50	1 060	19.7	97.8	2.98	2	..
1970 - 72	84	43	41	1 057	16.1	83.3	2.46	1	13
1980 - 82	68	35	33	1 051	13.1	62.2	1.80	-	6
	BBCD	KMEU	KMEV	KMEW	KMEX	KMEY	KMEZ	KMFM	KMFN
1984	65	33	32	1 037	12.7	58.4	1.68	–	6
1985	67	34	33	1 048	13.0	59.5	1.70	–	5
1986	66	34	32	1 061	12.8	58.5	1.67	–	6
1987	66	34	32	1 053	13.0	58.8	1.67	–	5
1988	66	34	32	1 059	13.0	59.1	1.68	–	5
1989	63	33	31	1 049	12.5	56.8	1.61	–	5
1990	66	34	32	1 057	12.9	58.8	1.66	–	5
1991	67	34	33	1 056	13.1	59.8	1.69	–	6
1992	66	34	32	1 044	12.9	59.3	1.68	–	5
1993	63	32	31	1 046	12.4	57.4	1.61	–	6
1994	62	31	30	1 038	12.0	56.0	1.58	–	6
1995	60	31	29	1 043	11.7	54.5	1.55	–	7
1996	59	31	29	1 061	11.6	54.0	1.55	–	6
1997	59	31	29	1 055	11.6	54.3	1.58	–	5
1998	57	29	28	1 060	11.2	52.6	1.55	–	6
1999	55	28	27	1 050	10.8	50.8	1.51	–	5
Northern Ireland									
1900 - 02	..	..	..	..	..	..	..	..	..
1910 - 12	..	..	..	..	..	..	..	..	..
1920 - 22	31	16	15	1 048	24.2	105.9	..	..	..
1930 - 32	26	13	12	1 047	20.5	78.8	..	..	..
1940 - 42	27	14	13	1 078	20.8	73.7	..	..	..
1950 - 52	29	15	14	1 066	20.9	81.4	..	..	..
1960 - 62	31	16	15	1 068	22.5	111.5	3.47	7	23
1970 - 72	31	16	15	1 074	20.4	105.7	3.13	3	14
1980 - 82	28	14	13	1 048	18.0	87.5	2.59	-	8
	BBCE	KMFO	KMFP	KMFQ	KMFR	KMFS	KMFT	KMFU	KMFV
1984	27	14	13	1 069	17.6	84.2	2.50	0.2	6
1985	27	14	13	1 054	17.5	83.1	2.45	0.2	6
1986	28	15	13	1 076	17.8	82.7	2.44	0.1	4
1987	28	14	13	1 055	17.5	82.2	2.39	0.2	6
1988	28	14	13	1 056	17.4	82.0	2.35	0.1	5
1989	26	13	13	1 063	16.2	76.9	2.19	0.1	5
1990	26	14	13	1 049	16.5	78.0	2.21	0.1	4
1991	26	13	13	1 066	16.2	75.1	2.16	0.1	5
1992	25	13	12	1 040	15.6	72.7	2.08	0.1	5
1993	25	13	12	1 025	15.1	70.3	2.01	0.1	4
1994	24	12	12	1 053	14.6	68.0	1.94	0.1	5
1995	24	12	11	1 078	14.3	66.4	1.91	0.1	5
1996	25	12	12	1 032	14.6	67.6	1.95	0.1	5
1997	24	12	12	1 048	14.3	66.3	1.92	0.1	4
1998	24	12	12	1 039	14.0	64.9	1.89	0.1	4
1999	23	12	11	1 084	13.6	62.9	1.85	0.1	5

1 Rate per 1 000 population.
2 Rate per 1 000 women aged 15 - 44.
3 Total period fertility rate is the average number of children which would be born per woman if women experienced the age-specific fertility rates of the period in question throughout their child-bearing life span. UK figures for the years 1970-72 and earlier are estimates.

4 Figures given are based on stillbirths of 28 completed weeks gestation or more. On 1 October 1992 the legal definition of a stillbirth was altered to include babies born dead between 24 and 27 completed weeks gestation. Between 1 October and 31 December 1992 in the UK there were 258 babies born dead between 24 and 27 completed weeks gestation (216 in England and Wales, 35 in Scotland and 7 in Northern Ireland). If these babies were included in the stillbirth figures given, the stillbirth rates would be 5 for the UK and England and Wales while the Scotland and Northern Ireland stillbirth rate would remain as stated.
5 Males per 1,000 females.

Sources: Office for National Statistics: 020 7533 5113;
General Register Office (Scotland);
General register Office (Northern Ireland)

5.15 Birth occurrence inside and outside marriage by age of mother

Thousands

	Inside marriage						Outside marriage					
	All ages	Under 20	20 - 24	25 - 29	Over 30	Mean age (Years)	All ages	Under 20	20 - 24	25 - 29	Over 30	Mean age (Years)
United Kingdom												
	KKEY	KKEZ	KKFY	KKFZ	KKGX	KKGY	KKGZ	KKIC	KKID	KKIE	KKIF	KKIG
1961	890	55	273	280	282	27.7	54	13	17	10	13	25.5
1971	828	70	301	271	185	26.4	74	24	25	13	12	23.8
1981	640	36	193	231	180	27.3	91	30	33	16	13	23.4
1986	597	21	159	231	185	27.9	158	45	60	31	22	23.7
1987	598	18	153	235	192	28.1	178	48	68	37	26	23.9
1988	590	16	144	235	195	28.2	198	51	76	42	29	24.1
1989	571	14	130	229	198	28.4	207	49	79	46	32	24.3
1990	576	13	121	233	209	28.6	223	51	83	53	37	24.5
1991	556	10	109	224	213	28.9	236	50	87	58	41	24.8
1992	540	9	98	216	218	29.1	241	46	86	62	46	25.1
1993	520	8	87	204	221	29.3	242	44	84	64	50	25.4
1994	511	7	78	195	231	29.6	240	41	80	65	55	25.7
1995	486	6	69	180	232	29.8	246	42	79	66	60	25.9
1996	473	6	61	170	237	30.1	260	45	80	69	66	26.0
1997	460	6	55	159	240	30.3	267	47	79	71	71	26.1
1998	447	6	51	149	243	30.5	270	49	77	70	74	26.2
1999	429	6	47	137	239	30.7	272	49	77	68	77	26.3
Great Britain												
	KKIH	KKII	KKIJ	KKIK	KKIL	KKIM	KKIN	KKIO	KKIP	KKIQ	KKIR	KKIS
1961	859	53	264	270	272	27.7	53	13	17	10	13	25.5
1971	797	68	293	261	176	26.4	73	24	25	13	12	23.8
1981	614	34	186	223	171	27.2	89	29	32	16	13	23.3
1986	572	20	153	222	177	27.9	155	44	59	30	22	22.9
1987	574	17	147	227	184	28.0	174	46	66	36	25	23.4
1988	566	16	138	226	186	28.2	194	49	74	42	29	23.6
1989	549	13	125	220	190	28.4	202	48	77	45	32	24.2
1990	554	12	116	225	201	28.6	218	49	81	52	36	24.6
1991	535	10	105	216	205	28.9	231	48	85	57	41	24.8
1992	520	9	94	208	210	29.1	235	45	84	61	46	25.1
1993	500	7	84	196	213	29.3	236	42	82	62	49	25.4
1994	492	7	75	188	222	29.6	235	41	78	63	53	25.7
1995	468	6	66	173	223	29.8	240	40	77	65	59	25.9
1996	455	6	59	163	227	30.1	254	44	78	68	65	26.0
1997	442	6	53	152	231	30.3	261	46	76	69	69	26.2
1998	430	6	49	143	233	30.5	263	48	74	68	73	26.3
1999	412	6	46	131	230	30.7	265	48	74	67	76	26.4

Source: Office for National Statistics: 020 7533 5113

5.16 Live births by age of mother

Number

All live births - United Kingdom[1,2]

Age-group:	Under 20	20 - 24	25 - 29	30 - 34	35 - 39	40 - 44	45 and over	All ages
	KMDV	KMDW	KMDX	KMDY	KMDZ	KMES	KMET	KMBZ
1989	63 163	208 945	274 845	164 215	55 531	9 965	540	777 285
1990	63 002	203 473	285 990	176 826	58 421	10 300	540	798 612
1991	59 708	196 213	282 153	182 739	60 577	10 453	549	792 506
1992	54 927	184 380	277 377	189 118	63 805	10 809	553	781 017
1993	51 467	171 109	267 462	193 643	66 273	11 128	582	761 713
1994	47 878	157 483	259 422	202 954	70 905	11 441	536	750 671
1995	47 652	147 067	246 062	204 664	73 981	12 014	585	732 049
1996	50 793	141 090	238 857	210 490	78 335	12 832	638	733 163
1997	52 853	133 274	229 468	212 235	84 557	13 741	618	726 812
1998	54 823	127 245	218 112	212 953	88 776	14 465	640	717 080
1999	54 925	124 053	204 872	209 062	91 319	15 218	695	700 192

Age-specific fertility rates - United Kingdom[1,2]

Age-group:	Under 20	20 - 24	25 - 29	30 - 34	35 - 39	40 - 44	45 and over	All ages
	KMBR	KMBS	KMBT	KMBU	KMBV	KMBW	KMBX	KMBY
1989	31.9	91.2	120.6	82.8	29.3	4.9	0.3	62.3
1990	33.1	90.8	122.9	86.5	31.0	5.0	0.3	64.1
1991	32.9	88.9	119.9	86.5	32.0	5.0	0.3	63.6
1992	31.8	85.5	117.6	87.1	33.2	5.5	0.3	63.4
1993	30.9	81.8	114.2	86.8	33.8	5.8	0.3	62.4
1994	28.8	78.2	112.1	88.5	35.4	6.0	0.3	61.6
1995	28.3	75.7	108.5	87.2	35.9	6.4	0.3	60.1
1996[1]	29.7	76.2	106.7	88.6	36.9	6.8	0.3	60.1
1997	30.3	75.4	104.6	88.9	38.7	7.1	0.3	59.5
1998	30.7	74.1	102.0	89.8	39.5	7.4	0.3	58.7
1999	30.7	72.4	98.9	89.0	39.5	7.6	0.4	57.2

All live births - England and Wales

Age-group:	Under 20	20 - 24	25 - 29	30 - 34	35 - 39	40 - 44	45 and over	All ages
	KGSA	KGSB	KGSC	KGSD	KGSE	KGSF	KGSG	KGSH
1989	55 543	185 239	242 822	145 320	49 465	8 845	491	687 725
1990	55 541	180 136	252 577	156 264	51 905	9 220	497	706 140
1991	52 396	173 356	248 727	161 259	53 644	9 316	519	699 217
1992	47 861	163 311	244 798	166 839	56 650	9 696	501	689 656
1993	45 121	151 975	235 961	171 061	58 824	9 986	539	673 467
1994	42 026	140 240	229 102	179 568	63 061	10 241	488	664 726
1995	41 938	130 744	217 418	181 202	65 517	10 779	540	648 138
1996	44 667	125 732	211 103	186 377	69 503	11 516	587	649 485
1997	46 372	118 589	202 792	187 528	74 900	12 332	582	643 095
1998	48 285	113 537	193 144	188 499	78 881	12 980	575	635 901
1999	48 375	110 722	181 931	185 311	81 281	13 617	635	621 872

Age-specific fertility rates - England and Wales

Age-group:	Under 20	20 - 24	25 - 29	30 - 34	35 - 39	40 - 44	45 and over	All ages
	KGSI	KGSJ	KGSK	KGSL	KGSM	KGSN	KGSO	KGSP
1989	32.0	91.7	120.4	83.2	29.4	4.9	0.3	62.5
1990	33.3	91.4	122.6	86.9	31.1	5.0	0.3	64.2
1991	33.0	89.3	119.4	86.7	32.1	5.1	0.3	63.6
1992	31.7	86.2	117.3	87.2	33.4	5.5	0.3	63.5
1993	31.0	82.7	114.1	87.0	34.1	5.9	0.3	62.6
1994	29.0	79.4	112.1	88.7	35.8	6.1	0.3	61.9
1995	28.5	76.8	108.6	87.3	36.2	6.5	0.3	60.4
1996	29.8	77.5	106.9	88.6	37.2	6.9	0.3	60.5
1997	30.2	76.6	104.8	88.8	38.9	7.3	0.3	59.8
1998	30.7	75.4	102.6	89.9	39.9	7.8	0.3	59.0
1999	30.8	73.7	99.2	89.2	39.8	7.7	0.4	57.6

Sources: Office for National Statistics: 020 7533 5113;
General Register Office (Northern Ireland);
General Register Office (Scotland)

Population and vital statistics

5.16 Live births by age of mother

Number

All live births - Scotland[1]

Age-group:	Under 20	20 - 24	25 - 29	30 - 34	35 - 39	40 - 44	45 and over	All ages
	KGTA	KGTB	KGTC	KGTD	KGTE	KGTF	KGTG	KGTH
1989	5 720	17 164	22 899	13 110	3 846	618	22	63 480
1990	5 603	16 953	24 203	14 379	4 143	603	24	65 973
1991	5 523	16 723	24 163	15 206	4 589	686	31	67 024
1992	5 206	15 405	23 571	15 973	4 877	674	23	65 789
1993[1]	4 750	13 923	22 758	16 088	5 049	697	23	63 337
1994	4 303	12 637	21 851	16 705	5 346	736	26	61 656
1995	4 280	11 913	20 395	16 803	5 799	811	26	60 051
1996	4 544	11 026	19 511	17 038	6 126	891	32	59 296
1997	4 835	10 607	18 782	17 455	6 740	936	19	59 440
1998	4 802	9 804	17 477	17 207	6 893	1 027	43	57 319
1999	4 755	9 440	16 011	16 722	7 034	1 096	41	55 147

Age-specific fertility rates - Scotland[1]

Age-group:	Under 20	20 - 24	25 - 29	30 - 34	35 - 39	40 - 44	45 and over	All ages
	KGTI	KGTJ	KGTK	KGTL	KGTM	KGTN	KGTO	KGTP
1989	31.2	82.3	113.5	72.0	22.9	3.7	0.1	56.8
1990	31.9	82.4	117.2	76.7	24.5	3.5	0.2	58.8
1991	33.3	82.3	116.5	78.3	26.8	4.0	0.2	59.8
1992	33.1	77.6	113.6	80.7	27.8	4.1	0.1	59.3
1993	31.2	72.4	109.7	79.7	28.0	4.3	0.1	57.4
1994	28.4	68.2	106.1	81.2	28.9	4.5	0.2	56.0
1995	28.1	66.7	100.8	80.5	30.5	5.0	0.2	54.5
1996	29.6	64.6	97.9	81.6	31.4	5.4	0.2	54.0
1997	30.9	65.5	97.0	83.5	33.9	5.5	0.1	54.3
1998	30.4	62.7	94.2	82.6	34.1	6.0	0.3	52.6
1999	30.0	60.7	90.4	81.3	34.2	6.2	0.2	50.8

All live births - Northern Ireland[2]

Age-group:	Under 20	20 - 24	25 - 29	30 - 34	35 - 39	40 - 44	45 and over	All ages
	KMDF	KMDG	KMDH	KMDI	KMDJ	KMDK	KMDL	KMDM
1989	1 888	6 517	9 033	5 676	2 192	498	27	25 831
1990	1 853	6 355	9 129	6 089	2 327	471	27	26 251
1991	1 783	6 114	9 179	6 172	2 306	447	27	26 028
1992	1 855	5 643	8 946	6 208	2 241	432	29	25 354
1993	1 592	5 198	8 694	6 416	2 362	440	20	24 722
1994	1 545	4 591	8 414	6 607	2 464	455	22	24 098
1995	1 428	4 399	8 204	6 596	2 629	418	19	23 693
1996	1 582	4 332	8 243	7 075	2 706	425	19	24 382
1997	1 644	4 061	7 855	7 179	2 868	463	17	24 087
1998	1 735	3 889	7 451	7 170	2 955	446	22	23 668
1999	1 791	3 874	6 866	6 953	2 957	498	19	22 957

Age-specific fertility rates - Northern Ireland[2]

Age - group:	Under 20	20 - 24	25 - 29	30 - 34	35 - 39	40 - 44	45 and over	All ages
	KMDN	KMDO	KMDP	KMDQ	KMDR	KMDS	KMDT	KMDU
1989	29.0	101.4	148.5	104.3	45.0	10.2	0.6	75.5
1990	29.2	100.4	148.0	107.6	47.4	9.6	0.6	76.5
1991	28.7	97.2	146.4	105.3	45.8	9.0	0.6	75.1
1992	30.2	90.1	141.3	103.1	43.0	8.8	0.6	72.7
1993	26.1	83.1	136.0	104.2	44.0	8.9	0.4	70.3
1994	25.4	74.8	130.8	104.9	44.4	9.2	0.4	68.0
1995	23.4	73.3	128.2	102.8	45.6	8.4	0.4	66.4
1996	25.6	73.5	128.3	108.2	45.4	8.4	0.4	67.6
1997	26.5	70.8	123.3	109.2	46.5	8.8	0.3	66.3
1998	27.9	69.5	117.9	108.2	47.1	8.2	0.4	64.9
1999	28.9	70.5	111.6	104.7	46.0	8.9	0.4	62.9

1 The 'All ages' figure for Scotland includes births to mothers whose age was not known. There were 101 such births in 1989, 65 in 1990, 103 in 1991, 60 in 1992, 49 in 1993, 52 in 1994, 24 in 1995, 128 in 1996, 66 in 1997, 66 in 1998 and 48 in 1999.

2 Births to non-resident mothers in Northern Ireland are excluded from the figures for Northern Ireland, but included in the figures for the United Kingdom.

Sources: Office for National Statistics: 01329 813772;
General Register Office (Northern Ireland);
General Register Office (Scotland)

5.17 Legal abortions
Total by age for residents

Numbers

England and Wales

	All ages	Under 15	15	16 - 19	20 - 24	25 - 29	30 - 34	35 - 39	40 - 44	45 and over	Not stated
1986	147 619	924	2 970	33 819	45 316	28 656	18 005	12 977	4 521	409	22
1987	156 191	907	2 858	35 167	49 256	31 243	18 960	12 639	4 757	390	14
1988	168 298	859	2 709	37 928	54 067	34 584	20 000	12 681	5 047	412	11
1989	170 463	803	2 580	36 182	54 880	36 604	21 284	12 713	5 020	388	9
1990	173 900	873	2 549	35 520	55 281	38 770	22 431	12 956	5 104	404	12
1991	167 376	886	2 272	31 130	52 678	38 611	23 445	13 035	4 901	408	10
1992	160 501	905	2 095	27 589	49 052	38 430	23 870	13 252	4 844	452	12
1993	157 846	964	2 119	25 806	46 846	38 139	24 690	13 885	4 889	494	14
1994	156 539	1 080	2 166	25 223	44 871	38 081	25 507	14 156	5 008	440	7
1995	154 315	946	2 324	24 945	43 394	37 254	25 759	14 352	4 868	457	16
1996	167 916	1 098	2 547	28 790	46 356	39 311	28 228	16 118	5 027	428	13
1997	170 145	1 020	2 414	29 947	44 960	40 159	28 892	16 858	5 413	482	-
1998	177 871	1 103	2 656	33 236	45 766	40 366	30 449	18 174	5 576	511	34
1999	173 701	1 066	2 537	32 807	45 004	38 492	29 139	18 341	5 755	502	58

Scotland

	All ages	Under 15	15	16 - 19	20 - 24	25 - 29	30 - 34	35 - 39	40 - 44	45 and over
1986	9 628	74	236	2 529	2 985	1 744	1 081	708	249	22
1987	9 460	70	210	2 417	2 996	1 729	1 082	697	242	17
1988	10 128	65	218	2 529	3 304	1 970	1 107	663	257	15
1989	10 209	53	209	2 561	3 202	1 968	1 229	706	266	15
1990	10 219	54	186	2 539	3 242	2 063	1 161	700	253	21
1991	11 068	77	203	2 571	3 486	2 253	1 445	743	262	28
1992	10 818	73	174	2 377	3 389	2 291	1 444	799	254	17
1993	11 076	92	193	2 300	3 368	2 447	1 492	891	264	29
1994	11 392	78	215	2 312	3 486	2 431	1 648	877	315	30
1995	11 143	79	233	2 169	3 399	2 438	1 609	887	296	33
1996	11 978	87	236	2 362	3 571	2 603	1 801	960	331	27
1997	12 109	85	204	2 431	3 444	2 651	1 854	1 093	322	25
1998	12 485	73	213	2 707	3 426	2 749	1 807	1 149	339	22
1999[1]	12 144	69	182	2 630	3 346	2 551	1 807	1 175	361	23

1 Provisional.

Sources: Office for National Statistics;
Scottish Executive

Population and vital statistics

5.18 Deaths: analysis by age and sex
Annual averages or calendar years

Number

		United Kingdom												
	All ages[1]	Under 1 year	1-4	5-9	10-14	15-19	20-24	25-34	35-44	45-54	55-64	65-74	75-84	85 and over
Males														
1900 - 02	340 664	87 242	37 834	8 429	4 696	7 047	8 766	19 154	24 739	30 488	37 610	39 765	28 320	6 563
1910 - 12	303 703	63 885	29 452	7 091	4 095	5 873	6 817	16 141	21 813	28 981	37 721	45 140	29 397	7 283
1920 - 22	284 876	48 044	19 008	6 052	3 953	5 906	6 572	13 663	19 702	29 256	40 583	49 398	34 937	7 801
1930 - 32	284 249	28 840	11 276	4 580	2 890	5 076	6 495	12 327	16 326	29 376	47 989	63 804	45 247	10 022
1940 - 42	314 643	24 624	6 949	3 400	2 474	4 653	4 246	11 506	17 296	30 082	57 076	79 652	59 733	12 900
1950 - 52	307 312	14 105	2 585	1 317	919	1 498	2 289	5 862	11 074	27 637	53 691	86 435	79 768	20 131
1960 - 62	318 850	12 234	1 733	971	871	1 718	1 857	3 842	8 753	26 422	63 009	87 542	83 291	26 605
1970 - 72	335 166	9 158	1 485	1 019	802	1 778	2 104	3 590	7 733	24 608	64 898	105 058	82 905	30 027
1980 - 82	330 495	4 829	774	527	652	1 999	1 943	3 736	6 568	19 728	54 159	105 155	98 488	31 936
1990 - 92	312 521	3 315	623	372	396	1 349	2 059	4 334	6 979	15 412	40 424	87 849	106 376	43 032
	KHUA	KHUB	KHUC	KHUD	KHUE	KHUF	KHUG	KHUH	KHUI	KHUJ	KHUK	KHUL	KHUM	KHUN
1979	339 568	5 447	748	708	707	2 042	1 969	4 012	6 868	21 828	56 944	110 172	96 026	32 097
1980	332 370	5 174	792	609	659	2 022	1 940	3 786	6 698	20 577	55 176	107 089	96 301	31 547
1981	329 145	4 759	771	517	666	2 008	1 919	3 761	6 544	19 740	53 770	104 950	97 881	31 859
1982	329 971	4 555	760	456	632	1 966	1 971	3 661	6 462	18 867	53 531	103 426	101 281	32 403
1983	328 824	4 230	695	469	609	1 834	1 899	3 601	6 537	18 238	54 493	100 469	103 038	32 712
1984	321 095	3 995	725	423	580	1 708	1 999	3 595	6 425	17 647	53 715	95 420	102 513	32 350
1985	331 562	4 003	728	393	583	1 612	2 031	3 452	6 728	17 316	52 502	97 458	109 241	35 515
1986	327 160	4 219	653	384	444	1 676	2 067	3 668	6 712	16 814	50 352	95 987	108 123	36 061
1987	318 282	4 105	657	377	470	1 612	2 125	3 776	6 793	15 950	47 675	93 348	105 773	35 621
1988	319 119	4 110	680	433	460	1 525	2 160	3 983	6 860	16 016	46 001	91 893	107 082	37 916
1989	320 193	3 799	699	414	398	1 537	2 118	3 968	6 832	15 560	43 693	90 304	109 450	41 421
1990	314 601	3 614	674	376	406	1 487	2 197	4 354	6 991	15 507	41 983	88 458	107 451	41 103
1991	314 427	3 377	636	395	404	1 417	2 049	4 270	7 102	15 493	40 256	88 014	107 416	43 598
1992	308 535	2 954	559	346	377	1 144	1 932	4 379	6 845	15 236	39 033	87 075	104 261	44 394
1993[2]	317 796	2 746	582	325	401	1 072	1 907	4 442	6 672	15 631	38 734	90 160	105 693	49 431
1994	303 333	2 660	497	319	400	1 041	1 829	4 741	6 661	14 983	36 469	86 896	98 982	47 855
1995	310 722	2 595	447	314	388	1 115	1 810	4 748	6 754	15 644	36 068	85 459	103 324	52 056
1996	305 323	2 562	489	267	352	1 104	1 693	4 746	6 789	15 796	35 033	81 333	102 090	53 069
1997	300 414	2 391	456	300	364	1 111	1 712	4 583	6 667	15 689	33 707	77 870	101 365	54 199
1998	300 160	2 327	463	283	343	1 058	1 539	4 684	6 902	15 825	33 778	75 718	101 468	55 772
1999	300 368	2 318	456	257	319	1 085	1 553	4 516	6 946	15 849	33 338	73 736	101 795	58 200
Females														
1900 - 02	322 058	68 770	36 164	8 757	5 034	6 818	8 264	18 702	21 887	25 679	34 521	42 456	34 907	10 099
1910 - 12	289 608	49 865	27 817	7 113	4 355	5 683	6 531	15 676	19 647	24 481	32 813	46 453	37 353	11 828
1920 - 22	274 772	35 356	17 323	5 808	4 133	5 729	6 753	14 878	18 121	24 347	34 026	48 573	45 521	14 203
1930 - 32	275 336	21 072	9 995	3 990	2 734	4 721	5 931	12 699	15 373	24 695	39 471	59 520	56 250	18 886
1940 - 42	296 646	17 936	5 952	2 743	2 068	4 180	5 028	11 261	14 255	23 629	42 651	70 907	71 377	24 658
1950 - 52	291 597	10 293	2 098	880	625	1 115	1 717	5 018	8 989	18 875	37 075	75 220	92 848	36 844
1960 - 62	304 871	8 887	1 334	627	522	684	811	2 504	6 513	16 720	36 078	73 118	105 956	51 117
1970 - 72	322 968	6 666	1 183	654	459	718	900	2 110	5 345	15 594	36 177	75 599	109 539	68 024
1980 - 82	330 269	3 561	585	355	425	733	772	2 099	4 360	12 206	32 052	72 618	117 760	82 743
1990 - 92	328 218	2 431	485	259	255	520	714	1 989	4 340	9 707	25 105	61 951	115 467	104 994
	KIUA	KIUB	KIUC	KIUD	KIUE	KIUF	KIUG	KIUH	KIUI	KIUJ	KIUK	KIUL	KIUM	KIUN
1979	336 009	4 026	617	428	462	701	738	2 244	4 544	13 667	33 274	75 610	118 859	80 839
1980	329 149	3 938	596	409	442	771	811	2 157	4 460	12 583	32 349	73 672	116 461	80 500
1981	328 829	3 402	599	352	424	738	737	2 083	4 309	12 275	31 625	72 476	117 458	82 351
1982	332 830	3 342	561	304	410	689	767	2 057	4 312	11 759	32 183	71 705	119 362	85 379
1983	330 277	3 126	568	318	374	719	698	1 914	4 318	11 384	32 197	69 266	118 940	86 455
1984	323 823	3 005	537	304	344	665	722	1 932	4 269	10 947	32 262	66 432	116 649	85 756
1985	339 094	3 027	574	314	355	626	729	1 852	4 397	10 581	32 010	68 505	122 445	93 679
1986	333 575	2 961	561	275	307	635	769	1 882	4 387	10 211	29 954	67 313	120 663	93 657
1987	326 060	2 972	550	265	288	614	733	1 974	4 454	10 177	29 037	65 570	117 266	92 160
1988	330 059	2 951	552	264 ·	251	612	745	1 915	4 615	9 887	28 154	65 020	117 731	97 362
1989	337 540	2 743	551	271	268	598	773	1 955	4 506	9 834	27 324	64 575	120 975	103 167
1990	327 198	2 658	489	249	273	534	700	1 967	4 463	9 718	26 350	62 019	116 357	101 421
1991	331 754	2 448	512	280	264	538	738	2 005	4 295	9 699	24 952	62 200	116 924	106 899
1992	325 703	2 187	455	249	228	489	704	1 994	4 262	9 705	24 013	61 635	113 119	106 663
1993[2]	340 685	2 084	436	239	283	465	659	2 121	4 204	9 973	23 900	63 767	114 905	117 649
1994	324 303	1 989	410	205	232	406	626	2 053	4 285	10 081	22 401	62 069	106 816	112 730
1995	334 771	1 931	370	224	250	449	592	2 140	4 203	10 389	22 093	60 988	110 247	120 895
1996	330 701	1 904	355	214	224	493	589	2 140	4 215	10 301	21 406	57 889	109 578	121 393
1997	329 332	1 862	333	215	239	487	574	1 960	4 323	10 412	20 999	55 687	108 276	123 965
1998	329 012	1 752	347	213	215	486	568	1 971	4 289	10 430	20 874	54 200	107 135	126 532
1999	331 694	1 727	338	195	240	473	553	1 924	4 372	10 430	21 045	52 240	106 841	131 316

1 In some years the totals include a small number of persons whose age was not stated.
2 See chapter text.

Source: Office for National Statistics: 020 7533 5249

5.18 Deaths: analysis by age and sex
Annual averages or calendar years

continued

Number

	All ages[1]	Under 1 year	1-4	5-9	10-14	15-19	20-24	25-34	35-44	45-54	55-64	65-74	75-84	85 and over
						England and Wales								
Males														
1900 - 02	288 886	76 095	32 051	7 066	3 818	5 611	7 028	15 869	21 135	26 065	31 600	33 568	23 835	5 144
1910 - 12	257 253	54 678	24 676	5 907	3 348	4 765	5 596	13 603	18 665	24 820	32 217	38 016	24 928	6 036
1920 - 22	240 605	39 796	15 565	5 151	3 314	4 901	5 447	11 551	17 004	25 073	34 639	42 025	29 685	6 455
1930 - 32	243 147	23 331	9 099	3 844	2 435	4 354	5 580	10 600	14 041	25 657	41 581	54 910	39 091	8 624
1940 - 42	268 876	19 393	5 616	2 834	2 051	3 832	3 156	9 484	14 744	25 983	50 058	68 791	51 779	11 158
1950 - 52	266 879	11 498	2 131	1 087	778	1 248	1 947	4 990	9 489	23 815	46 948	75 774	69 496	17 677
1960 - 62	278 369	10 157	1 444	812	742	1 523	1 624	3 278	7 524	22 813	54 908	77 000	73 180	23 364
1970 - 72	293 934	7 818	1 259	860	677	1 524	1 788	3 079	6 637	21 348	56 667	92 389	73 365	26 522
1980 - 82	290 352	4 168	657	452	555	1 716	1 619	3 169	5 590	16 909	47 144	92 485	87 338	28 551
1990 - 92	275 550	2 926	545	325	338	1 157	1 757	3 717	6 057	13 258	34 977	77 063	94 672	38 757
	KHVA	KHVB	KHVC	KHVD	KHVE	KHVF	KHVG	KHVH	KHVI	KHVJ	KHVK	KHVL	KHVM	KHVN
1979	297 862	4 731	641	602	605	1 727	1 649	3 426	5 822	18 607	49 586	96 764	85 091	28 611
1980	291 869	4 471	668	517	546	1 745	1 613	3 203	5 710	17 693	48 053	94 188	85 300	28 162
1981	289 022	4 119	651	447	573	1 734	1 576	3 181	5 535	16 889	46 858	92 189	86 774	28 496
1982	290 166	3 914	652	391	546	1 669	1 668	3 122	5 526	16 144	46 521	91 079	89 940	28 994
1983	289 419	3 654	604	391	514	1 580	1 635	3 071	5 581	15 632	47 315	88 622	91 531	29 289
1984	282 357	3 443	610	348	501	1 484	1 728	3 033	5 512	15 113	46 904	83 728	90 983	28 970
1985	292 327	3 510	638	328	503	1 374	1 738	2 953	5 776	14 838	45 704	85 695	97 362	31 908
1986	287 894	3 724	573	325	380	1 429	1 746	3 104	5 767	14 370	43 637	84 437	96 201	32 201
1987	280 177	3 637	578	309	404	1 389	1 811	3 218	5 823	13 678	41 367	82 021	94 060	31 882
1988	280 931	3 649	587	374	402	1 279	1 802	3 367	5 855	13 701	39 791	80 870	95 306	33 948
1989	281 290	3 368	606	371	337	1 325	1 782	3 380	5 947	13 407	37 680	79 012	97 027	37 048
1990	277 336	3 207	593	333	338	1 295	1 889	3 714	6 060	13 342	36 405	77 604	95 539	37 017
1991	277 582	2 966	554	341	354	1 208	1 760	3 687	6 160	13 316	34 853	77 227	95 815	39 341
1992	271 732	2 606	487	302	322	969	1 621	3 751	5 952	13 117	33 674	76 357	92 662	39 912
1993[2]	279 561	2 407	510	276	340	912	1 596	3 813	5 784	13 416	33 347	78 881	93 754	44 525
1994	267 555	2 367	432	278	331	843	1 550	4 065	5 769	12 923	31 320	76 270	88 230	43 177
1995	274 449	2 305	391	269	340	910	1 533	4 043	5 880	13 487	30 973	74 970	92 291	47 057
1996	268 682	2 272	441	236	291	925	1 409	4 064	5 843	13 565	30 066	71 046	90 708	47 816
1997	264 865	2 137	412	267	325	947	1 442	3 940	5 707	13 484	28 907	68 024	90 207	49 066
1998	264 707	2 070	413	240	291	875	1 292	4 013	5 895	13 595	29 052	66 099	90 450	50 422
1999	264 299	2 075	405	218	275	902	1 270	3 847	5 934	13 620	28 689	64 296	90 431	52 337
Females														
1900 - 02	269 432	60 090	30 674	7 278	4 010	5 265	6 497	15 065	18 253	21 474	28 424	35 307	29 118	7 977
1910 - 12	242 079	42 642	23 335	5 883	3 519	4 522	5 256	12 742	16 363	20 611	27 571	38 489	31 363	9 782
1920 - 22	229 908	29 178	14 174	4 928	3 456	4 719	5 533	12 244	15 142	20 580	28 633	41 010	38 439	11 871
1930 - 32	233 915	16 929	8 013	3 338	2 293	3 969	5 039	10 716	13 022	21 190	33 798	50 844	48 531	16 234
1940 - 42	253 702	14 174	4 726	2 265	1 695	3 426	4 198	9 470	12 093	20 413	36 814	60 987	61 891	21 550
1950 - 52	252 176	8 367	1 727	732	520	893	1 365	4 131	7 586	16 161	31 875	65 087	81 154	32 579
1960 - 62	266 849	7 409	1 103	527	444	591	700	2 147	5 576	14 389	31 083	63 543	93 548	45 789
1970 - 72	284 181	5 677	1 020	562	396	620	806	1 814	4 585	13 417	31 222	65 817	96 952	61 293
1980 - 82	290 026	3 064	511	301	365	635	670	1 821	3 740	10 420	27 606	63 023	103 676	74 194
1990 - 92	288 851	2 161	420	227	217	455	625	1 718	3 765	8 347	21 466	53 783	101 752	93 914
	KIVA	KIVB	KIVC	KIVD	KIVE	KIVF	KIVG	KIVH	KIVI	KIVJ	KIVK	KIVL	KIVM	KIVN
1979	295 157	3 447	527	368	386	622	635	1 938	3 868	11 671	28 624	65 646	104 807	72 618
1980	289 516	3 428	518	349	373	667	696	1 861	3 771	10 757	27 857	64 087	102 728	72 424
1981	288 868	2 902	529	302	368	650	642	1 821	3 742	10 513	27 211	62 762	103 554	73 872
1982	291 695	2 861	485	253	353	588	672	1 781	3 708	9 990	27 751	62 221	104 745	76 287
1983	290 189	2 727	489	269	332	629	597	1 655	3 708	9 786	27 792	59 913	104 844	77 448
1984	284 524	2 594	454	260	302	575	621	1 676	3 658	9 343	27 764	57 813	102 744	76 720
1985	298 407	2 631	497	260	308	544	630	1 583	3 803	9 111	27 664	59 285	108 099	83 992
1986	293 309	2 589	491	248	272	562	674	1 646	3 834	8 761	25 785	58 360	106 463	83 624
1987	286 817	2 635	489	237	246	525	639	1 708	3 897	8 774	25 000	56 858	103 354	82 455
1988	290 477	2 621	498	232	218	542	650	1 670	4 025	8 448	24 104	56 567	103 666	87 236
1989	295 582	2 440	472	241	226	531	650	1 678	3 925	8 406	23 336	55 932	106 000	91 745
1990	287 510	2 357	434	220	230	472	616	1 702	3 875	8 337	22 511	53 770	102 440	90 546
1991	292 462	2 192	439	248	222	462	644	1 729	3 703	8 369	21 303	54 156	103 268	95 727
1992	286 581	1 933	387	214	199	432	615	1 722	3 717	8 336	20 585	53 423	99 548	95 470
1993[2]	299 238	1 835	374	194	246	394	575	1 802	3 625	8 914	20 423	55 245	100 947	104 964
1994	285 639	1 753	364	187	204	357	535	1 771	3 669	8 688	19 039	53 921	94 197	100 954
1995	295 234	1 677	333	196	210	382	502	1 859	3 644	9 001	18 891	52 987	97 162	108 390
1996	291 453	1 687	320	175	196	430	507	1 852	3 658	8 852	18 244	50 195	96 679	108 658
1997	290 416	1 663	297	177	209	426	490	1 718	3 737	9 016	17 949	48 293	95 508	110 933
1998	290 308	1 555	309	177	189	407	480	1 724	3 678	9 066	17 927	46 894	94 713	113 189
1999	291 819	1 546	300	168	215	385	470	1 668	3 786	9 029	18 031	45 100	93 878	117 243

1 In some years the totals include a small number of persons whose age was not stated.

2 See chapter text.

Source: Office for National Statistics: 020 7533 5249

5.18 Deaths: analysis by age and sex
Annual averages or calendar years
continued

Number

	All ages[1]	Under 1 year	1-4	5-9	10-14	15-19	20-24	25-34	35-44	45-54	55-64	65-74	75-84	85 and over
Scotland														
Males														
1900 - 02	40 224	9 189	4 798	1 083	672	1 069	1 292	2 506	2 935	3 591	4 597	4 531	3 117	834
1910 - 12	35 981	7 510	3 935	962	595	826	910	1 969	2 469	3 325	4 356	5 113	3 182	813
1920 - 22	34 649	6 757	2 847	710	489	747	791	1 616	2 128	3 314	4 785	5 624	3 928	911
1930 - 32	32 476	4 426	1 771	610	365	568	706	1 352	1 848	2 979	5 095	6 906	4 839	1 010
1940 - 42	36 384	3 973	1 011	449	321	668	888	1 643	2 090	3 348	5 728	8 556	6 317	1 337
1950 - 52	32 236	1 949	349	175	105	200	265	693	1 267	3 151	5 574	8 544	8 094	1 871
1960 - 62	32 401	1 578	222	121	102	146	185	456	1 013	2 986	6 682	8 505	7 980	2 425
1970 - 72	32 446	944	168	119	93	178	233	396	875	2 617	6 641	10 176	7 383	2 624
1980 - 82	31 723	451	80	56	71	206	233	423	776	2 280	5 601	10 152	8 804	2 591
	KHWA	KHWB	KHWC	KHWD	KHWE	KHWF	KHWG	KHWH	KHWI	KHWJ	KHWK	KHWL	KHWM	KHWN
1979	32 884	490	79	79	71	219	215	442	805	2 599	5 851	10 804	8 543	2 687
1980	31 669	481	93	65	78	190	223	421	778	2 316	5 628	10 248	8 571	2 577
1981	31 700	435	71	50	66	208	250	439	816	2 330	5 506	10 193	8 788	2 548
1982	31 801	436	77	53	69	220	225	410	733	2 195	5 669	10 015	9 052	2 647
1983	31 196	380	67	53	65	185	178	406	764	2 131	5 769	9 414	9 204	2 580
1984	30 731	389	87	53	65	172	202	429	696	2 017	5 493	9 337	9 222	2 569
1985	31 147	342	57	49	58	174	208	390	759	1 959	5 486	9 339	9 569	2 757
1986	31 111	334	66	44	49	177	238	436	757	1 967	5 354	9 169	9 574	2 946
1987	30 384	331	54	46	47	163	212	415	779	1 870	5 131	9 058	9 383	2 895
1988	30 195	324	64	39	42	181	246	475	808	1 915	4 997	8 763	9 314	3 027
1989	31 025	331	62	24	45	150	246	445	719	1 721	4 889	9 028	9 922	3 443
1990	29 617	297	62	31	50	138	240	502	745	1 734	4 512	8 635	9 499	3 172
1991	29 312	299	59	42	34	150	211	441	757	1 741	4 382	8 657	9 209	3 330
1992	29 334	265	51	28	36	123	238	511	731	1 716	4 313	8 541	9 225	3 556
1993[2]	30 504	240	50	39	37	107	225	490	725	1 817	4 375	9 031	9 470	3 898
1994	28 416	212	42	27	48	133	212	538	715	1 684	4 114	8 575	8 446	3 670
1995	28 791	197	37	30	30	152	195	563	698	1 746	4 144	8 449	8 604	3 946
1996	29 223	206	41	23	46	139	212	556	755	1 845	4 087	8 259	8 926	4 128
1997	28 305	186	32	22	27	114	208	521	788	1 794	3 876	7 909	8 791	4 037
1998	28 132	183	37	34	39	134	200	524	843	1 796	3 828	7 746	8 585	4 183
1999	28 605	161	31	23	33	138	215	545	818	1 820	3 773	7 569	8 908	4 571
Females														
1900 - 02	39 891	7 143	4 477	1 162	747	1 058	1 246	2 625	2 732	3 130	4 485	5 273	4 305	1 508
1910 - 12	36 132	5 854	3 674	981	618	836	910	2 149	2 473	2 909	3 960	5 636	4 588	1 552
1920 - 22	34 449	5 029	2 602	687	489	711	889	1 947	2 266	2 828	4 157	5 587	5 443	1 814
1930 - 32	32 377	3 319	1 602	527	339	568	666	1 508	1 812	2 731	4 380	6 630	6 178	2 117
1940 - 42	33 715	2 852	921	373	283	595	656	1 382	1 672	2 528	4 630	7 674	7 613	2 536
1950 - 52	31 525	1 432	284	115	84	185	293	714	1 127	2 188	4 204	8 157	9 310	3 431
1960 - 62	30 559	1 107	170	80	63	72	87	287	762	1 897	4 115	7 752	9 991	4 177
1970 - 72	30 978	694	118	69	46	73	74	231	608	1 769	4 036	7 823	10 112	5 324
1980 - 82	32 326	337	49	37	44	74	73	213	493	1 456	3 565	7 781	11 333	6 871
	KIWA	KIWB	KIWC	KIWD	KIWE	KIWF	KIWG	KIWH	KIWI	KIWJ	KIWK	KIWL	KIWM	KIWN
1979	32 863	388	69	37	58	59	81	247	551	1 635	3 776	8 045	11 309	6 608
1980	31 630	350	51	41	44	77	90	222	547	1 511	3 587	7 673	10 988	6 449
1981	32 128	345	46	35	43	68	69	213	453	1 414	3 556	7 935	11 144	6 807
1982	33 221	317	50	35	45	78	60	203	479	1 444	3 552	7 735	11 867	7 356
1983	32 258	266	51	33	33	67	76	201	504	1 317	3 568	7 558	11 340	7 244
1984	31 614	283	62	32	37	72	78	205	475	1 320	3 703	6 979	11 134	7 234
1985	32 820	282	55	37	34	63	76	207	481	1 179	3 563	7 449	11 604	7 790
1986	32 356	247	50	16	24	50	77	188	441	1 181	3 372	7 251	11 476	7 983
1987	31 630	232	44	21	34	60	70	195	429	1 160	3 301	7 032	11 262	7 790
1988	31 762	219	33	22	21	54	63	197	470	1 115	3 250	6 879	11 361	8 078
1989	33 992	223	56	23	27	54	104	224	470	1 156	3 279	7 052	12 100	9 224
1990	31 910	213	32	16	34	46	68	204	468	1 099	3 109	6 685	11 233	8 703
1991	31 729	174	54	22	31	57	74	225	463	1 070	2 974	6 542	11 059	8 984
1992	31 603	184	50	23	21	45	73	225	442	1 109	2 816	6 663	10 944	9 008
1993[2]	33 545	172	45	34	27	55	60	258	460	1 089	2 793	6 918	11 330	10 304
1994	30 912	170	29	11	19	33	74	229	495	1 102	2 723	6 617	10 008	9 402
1995	31 709	178	26	16	26	50	70	231	435	1 100	2 601	6 449	10 452	10 075
1996	31 448	159	24	31	21	49	67	218	453	1 172	2 573	6 206	10 256	10 219
1997	31 189	130	23	28	21	43	71	199	496	1 128	2 480	5 985	10 164	10 421
1998	31 032	137	26	28	19	55	68	198	485	1 106	2 416	5 955	9 913	10 626
1999	31 676	115	26	20	17	65	58	201	467	1 128	2 431	5 837	10 198	11 113

1 In some years the totals include a small number of persons whose age was not stated.
2 See chapter text.

Sources: Office for National Statistics: 020 7533 5249;
General Register Office (Scotland)

5.18 Deaths: analysis by age and sex
Annual averages or calendar years

continued

Number

	All ages[1]	Under 1 year	1-4	5-9	10-14	15-19	20-24	25-34	35-44	45-54	55-64	65-74	75-84	85 and over
						Northern Ireland								
Males														
1900 - 02	11 554	1 958	985	280	206	367	446	779	669	832	1 413	1 666	1 368	585
1910 - 12	10 469	1 697	841	222	152	282	311	569	679	836	1 148	2 011	1 287	434
1920 - 22	9 622	1 491	596	191	150	258	334	496	570	869	1 159	1 749	1 324	435
1930 - 32	8 626	1 083	406	126	90	154	209	375	437	740	1 313	1 988	1 317	388
1940 - 42	9 383	1 258	322	117	102	153	202	379	462	751	1 290	2 305	1 637	405
1950 - 52	8 197	658	105	55	36	50	77	179	318	671	1 169	2 117	2 178	583
1960 - 62	8 080	499	67	38	27	49	48	108	216	623	1 419	2 037	2 131	816
1970 - 72	8 786	396	58	40	32	76	83	115	221	643	1 590	2 493	2 157	881
1980 - 82	8 420	211	37	20	26	77	92	144	202	539	1 414	2 518	2 346	795
	KHXA	KHXB	KHXC	KHXD	KHXE	KHXF	KHXG	KHXH	KHXI	KHXJ	KHXK	KHXL	KHXM	KHXN
1979	8 822	226	28	27	31	96	105	144	241	622	1 507	2 604	2 392	799
1980	8 832	222	31	27	35	87	104	162	210	568	1 495	2 653	2 430	808
1981	8 423	205	49	20	27	66	93	141	193	521	1 406	2 568	2 319	815
1982	8 004	205	31	12	17	77	78	129	203	528	1 341	2 332	2 289	762
1983	8 209	196	24	25	30	69	86	124	192	475	1 409	2 433	2 303	843
1984	8 007	163	28	22	14	52	69	133	217	517	1 318	2 355	2 308	811
1985	8 088	151	33	16	22	64	85	109	193	519	1 312	2 424	2 310	850
1986	8 155	161	14	15	15	70	83	128	188	477	1 361	2 381	2 348	914
1987	7 721	137	25	22	19	60	102	143	191	402	1 177	2 269	2 330	844
1988	7 993	137	29	20	16	65	112	141	197	400	1 213	2 260	2 462	941
1989	7 878	100	31	19	16	62	90	143	166	432	1 124	2 264	2 501	930
1990	7 648	110	19	12	18	54	68	138	186	431	1 066	2 219	2 413	914
1991	7 533	112	23	12	16	59	78	142	185	436	1 021	2 130	2 392	927
1992	7 469	83	21	16	19	52	73	117	162	403	1 046	2 177	2 374	926
1993[2]	7 731	99	22	10	24	53	86	139	163	398	1 012	2 248	2 469	1 008
1994	7 362	81	23	14	21	65	67	138	177	376	1 035	2 051	2 306	1 008
1995	7 482	93	19	15	18	53	82	142	176	411	951	2 040	2 429	1 053
1996	7 418	84	7	8	15	40	72	126	191	386	880	2 028	2 456	1 125
1997	7 244	68	12	11	12	50	62	122	172	411	924	1 937	2 367	1 096
1998	7 321	74	13	9	13	49	47	147	164	434	898	1 873	2 433	1 167
1999	7 464	82	20	16	11	45	68	124	194	409	876	1 871	2 456	1 292
Females														
1900 - 02	12 735	1 537	1 013	317	277	495	521	1 012	902	1 075	1 612	1 876	1 484	614
1910 - 12	11 397	1 369	808	249	218	325	365	785	811	961	1 282	2 328	1 402	494
1920 - 22	10 415	1 149	547	193	188	299	331	687	713	939	1 236	1 976	1 639	518
1930 - 32	9 044	824	380	125	102	184	226	475	539	774	1 293	2 046	1 541	535
1940 - 42	9 229	910	305	105	90	159	174	409	490	688	1 207	2 246	1 873	572
1950 - 52	7 896	494	87	33	21	37	59	173	276	526	996	1 976	2 384	834
1960 - 62	7 463	371	61	20	15	21	24	70	175	434	880	1 823	2 417	1 151
1970 - 72	7 809	295	45	23	17	25	20	65	152	408	919	1 959	2 475	1 407
1980 - 82	7 917	160	26	17	17	23	29	65	127	329	881	1 813	2 752	1 678
	KIXA	KIXB	KIXC	KIXD	KIXE	KIXF	KIXG	KIXH	KIXI	KIXJ	KIXK	KIXL	KIXM	KIXN
1979	7 989	191	21	23	18	20	22	59	125	361	874	1 919	2 743	1 613
1980	8 003	160	27	19	25	27	25	74	142	315	905	1 912	2 745	1 627
1981	7 833	155	24	15	13	20	26	49	114	348	858	1 779	2 760	1 672
1982	7 914	164	26	16	12	23	35	73	125	325	880	1 749	2 750	1 736
1983	7 830	133	28	16	9	23	25	58	106	281	837	1 795	2 756	1 763
1984	7 685	128	21	12	5	18	23	51	136	284	795	1 640	2 770	1 802
1985	7 867	114	22	17	13	19	23	62	113	291	783	1 771	2 742	1 897
1986	7 910	125	20	11	11	23	18	48	112	269	797	1 702	2 724	2 050
1987	7 613	105	17	7	8	29	24	71	128	243	736	1 680	2 650	1 915
1988	7 820	111	21	10	12	16	32	48	120	324	800	1 574	2 704	2 048
1989	7 966	80	23	7	15	13	19	53	111	272	709	1 591	2 875	2 198
1990	7 778	88	23	13	9	16	16	61	120	282	730	1 564	2 684	2 172
1991	7 563	82	19	10	11	19	20	51	129	260	675	1 502	2 597	2 188
1992	7 519	70	18	12	8	12	16	47	103	260	612	1 549	2 627	2 185
1993[2]	7 902	77	17	11	10	16	24	61	119	270	684	1 604	2 628	2 381
1994	7 752	66	17	7	9	16	17	53	121	291	639	1 531	2 611	2 374
1995	7 828	76	11	12	14	17	20	50	124	288	601	1 552	2 633	2 430
1996	7 800	58	11	8	7	14	15	70	104	277	589	1 488	2 643	2 516
1997	7 727	69	13	10	9	18	13	43	90	268	570	1 409	2 604	2 611
1998	7 672	60	12	8	7	24	20	49	126	258	531	1 351	2 509	2 717
1999	8 199	66	12	7	8	23	25	55	119	273	583	1 303	2 765	2 960

1 In some years the totals include a small number of persons whose age was not stated.

2 See chapter text.

Sources: Office for National Statistics: 020 7533 5249; General Register Office (Northern Ireland)

5.19 Deaths: analysed by cause
International Statistical Classification of Diseases, Injuries and Causes of Death
Ninth Revision, 1979

Number

		ICD 9 code	England and Wales							
			1992[1]	1993[1,5]	1994	1995[4]	1996[4]	1997	1998	1999
Total deaths	KHEA		558 313	578 799	553 194	569 683	560 135	555 281	555 015	556 118
Deaths from natural causes [2]	KHEB		538 677	559 649	534 354	550 936	541 429	536 422	536 396	537 166
Infectious and parasitic diseases[3]	KHEC	001-139	2 633	3 257	3 318	3 682	3 636	3 496	3 410	3 613
Intestinal infectious diseases	KJZZ	001-009	240	194	222	277	339	384	418	476
Tuberculosis of the respiratory system	KHEH	010-012	309	423	418	353	310	289	283	299
Other tuberculosis, including late effects	KHEI	013-018,137	263	193	180	161	166	148	170	138
Whooping cough	KHEK	033	1	–	3	2	2	1	4	2
Meningococcal infection	KHEM	036	162	173	149	196	235	242	210	217
Measles	KHEP	055	2	4	1	1	–	3	3	3
Malaria	KHER	084	9	4	11	4	11	12	8	13
Syphilis	KHES	090-097	22	6	11	9	6	9	3	9
Neoplasms	KHET	140-239	145 963	142 535	141 747	141 297	139 459	137 618	138 306	136 181
Malignant neoplasm of stomach	KHEU	151	8 285	7 548	7 590	7 077	6 756	6 613	6 442	6 139
Malignant neoplasm of trachea, bronchus and lung	KHEV	162	33 662	32 614	32 143	31 627	30 810	29 976	30 199	29 493
Malignant neoplasm of breast	KHEW	174-175	13 755	13 115	12 918	12 623	12 246	12 047	11 835	11 670
Malignant neoplasm of uterus	KWUP	179+182	1 389	1 308	1 241	1 329	1 303	1 291	1 296	1 231
Malignant neoplasm of cervix	KWUQ	180	1 647	1 483	1 370	1 339	1 315	1 225	1 158	1 107
Leukaemia	KHEY	204-208	3 616	3 559	3 507	3 540	3 464	3 587	3 551	3 680
Benign and unspecified neoplasms	KHEZ	210-229,239	1 368	1 544	1 580	1 784	1 647	1 624	1 605	1 656
Endocrine, nutritional and metabolic diseases and immunity disorders	KHFA	240-279	10 605	7 924	7 430	7 883	7 502	7 383	7 542	7 560
Diabetes mellitus	KHFB	250	8 067	6 266	5 938	6 240	5 994	5 890	5 938	5 963
Nutritional deficiencies	KHFC	260-269	104	85	66	80	70	65	72	59
Other metabolic and immunity disorders[3]	KMBO	270-279	1 747	1 119	1 052	1 138	1 048	1 038	1 169	1 150
Diseases of blood and blood-forming organs	KHFD	280-289	2 417	1 974	1 898	1 929	1 986	2 008	1 937	1 855
Anaemias	KHFE	280-285	1 056	786	660	711	724	681	641	584
Mental disorders	KHFF	290-319	12 950	7 780	8 042	9 149	9 296	9 725	10 430	11 173
Diseases of nervous system and sense organs	KHFG	320-389	11 577	9 143	9 010	9 724	9 772	9 772	10 035	10 192
Meningitis	KHFH	320-322	208	218	170	209	245	224	216	182
Diseases of the circulatory system	KHFI	390-459	254 683	257 989	242 213	243 390	237 669	228 446	226 677	219 087
Rheumatic heart disease	KHFJ	393-398	2 136	1 834	1 719	1 714	1 682	1 481	1 629	1 638
Hypertensive disease	KHFL	401-405	3 144	3 052	2 800	2 882	3 026	3 084	3 122	3 324
Ischaemic heart disease	KHFM	410-414	145 904	146 302	135 440	133 861	129 047	122 432	121 037	115 119
Diseases of pulmonary circulation and other forms of heart disease	KHFN	415-429	18 352	21 341	25 795	26 891	26 170	26 609	26 377	26 462
Cerebrovascular disease	KHFO	430-438	66 291	61 172	58 768	59 957	59 723	57 747	57 516	56 051
Diseases of the respiratory system	KHFP	460-519	60 388	90 981	81 485	91 298	88 630	92 517	90 192	97 755
Influenza	KHFQ	487	262	439	62	251	179	347	129	585
Pneumonia	KHFR	480-486	26 257	54 624	48 917	55 318	54 137	56 719	54 631	59 273
Bronchitis, emphysema	KHFS	490-492	6 070	5 715	4 969	4 907	4 249	4 116	3 523	3 452
Asthma	KHFT	493	1 791	1 701	1 516	1 459	1 349	1 439	1 366	1 364
Diseases of the digestive system	KHFU	520-579	18 742	18 399	18 635	19 466	19 946	20 406	21 025	21 698
Ulcer of stomach and duodenum	KHFV	531-533	4 296	4 222	4 111	3 999	4 111	3 959	3 935	4 011
Appendicitis	KHFW	540-543	130	124	113	101	102	125	144	133
Hernia of the abdominal cavity and other intestinal obstruction	KHFX	550-553,560	2 025	1 855	1 814	1 975	1 967	2 106	2 042	2 126
Chronic liver disease and cirrhosis	KHFY	571	3 056	2 979	3 244	3 612	3 789	4 107	4 494	4 718
Diseases of the genito-urinary system	KHFZ	580-629	5 306	6 727	6 812	7 118	6 752	6 757	6 946	7 299
Nephritis, nephrotic syndrome and nephrosis	KHGA	580-589	2 072	3 401	3 246	3 283	3 057	2 930	2 946	2 952
Hyperplasia of prostate	KHGB	600	343	275	283	273	235	247	207	200
Complications of pregnancy, childbirth, etc	KHGC	630-676	45	36	50	45	41	35	43	30
Abortion	KHGD	630-639	6	3	6	8	4	2	7	5
Diseases of the skin and subcutaneous tissue	KHGE	680-709	907	1 019	1 107	1 088	1 075	1 025	1 070	1 152
Diseases of the musculo-skeletal system	KHGF	710-739	5 376	3 559	3 406	3 646	3 517	3 559	3 566	3 554
Congenital anomalies	KHGG	740-759	1 565	1 338	1 301	1 290	1 227	1 283	1 247	1 194
Certain conditions originating in the perinatal period	KHGH	760-779	242	259	147	148	149	131	124	116
Birth trauma, hypoxia, birth asphyxia and other respiratory conditions	KHGI	767-770	67	169	133	116	114	99	94	72
Signs, symptoms and ill-defined conditions	KHGJ	780-799	5 278	6 729	7 754	9 783	10 772	12 292	13 846	14 707
Sudden infant death syndrome	KMBP	798-0	456	391	371	315	345	327	236	222
Deaths from injury and poisoning[2]	KHGK	E800-E999	16 681	16 354	16 091	16 049	16 061	16 311	16 201	16 517
All accidents	KHGL	E800-E929	10 435	10 396	10 219	10 156	10 479	10 661	10 351	10 625
Motor vehicle accidents	KHGM	E810-E825	4 114	3 437	3 279	3 123	3 184	3 184	2 946	3 003
Suicide and self-inflicted injury	KHGN	E950-E959	3 952	3 719	3 619	3 570	3 445	3 424	3 614	3 690
All other external causes	KHGO	(E930-E949)+ (E960-E999)	2 294	2 239	2 253	2 323	2 137	2 226	2 236	2 202

1 On 1 January 1986, a new certificate for deaths within the first 28 days of life was introduced. It is not possible to assign one underlying cause of death from this certificate. The 'cause' figures in this table for 1986 onwards exclude all deaths at ages under 28 days.

2 Within certain main categories only selected causes of death are shown.

3 Deaths assigned to AIDS & AIDS - related diseases are included in ICD 270 279 for England and Wales up to 1992 and Scotland up until 1995. Northern Ireland has always assigned such deaths to the Chapter on Infectious Diseases (001 - 139). England and Wales adopted this practice from 1993 and Scotland from 1996 onwards.

4 Data for 1995 and 1996 has been amended to show the number of deaths that occurred during the calendar year. Data up to 1992 gives the number of deaths that were registered in the calendar year and subsequent years give the number that occurred during the calendar year.

5 See chapter text.

Source: Office for National Statistics: 020 7533 5249

5.19
continued

Deaths: analysed by cause
International Statistical Classification of Diseases, Injuries and Causes of Death
Ninth Revision, 1979

Number

			Scotland							
			1992	1993	1994	1995	1996	1997	1998	1999
		ICD 9 code								
Total deaths	KHHA		60 937	64 049	59 328	60 500	60 671	59 494	59 164	60 281
Deaths from natural causes[1]	KHHB		58 098	61 306	56 710	57 864	57 941	56 932	56 579	57 649
Infectious and parasitic diseases	KHHC	001-139	270	340	306	326	493	431	486	498
Intestinal infectious diseases	KFBP	001-009	18	19	19	17	22	19	34	31
Tuberculosis of respiratory system	KHHH	010-012	40	45	41	31	38	48	36	42
Other tuberculosis, including late effects	KHHI	013-018,137	23	42	24	–	15	23	22	23
Whooping cough	KHHL	033	–	–	1	–	–	1	–	–
Meningococcal infection	KHHN	036	9	13	8	15	12	12	20	14
Measles	KHHQ	055	–	–	2	1	–	–	–	–
Malaria	KHHS	084	–	1	2	–	1	–	1	–
Syphilis	KHHT	090-097	4	1	3	1	2	1	–	–
Neoplasms	KHHU	140-239	15 312	15 619	15 394	15 462	15 419	15 054	14 907	14 966
Malignant neoplasm of stomach	KHHV	151	828	766	754	758	699	710	680	650
Malignant neoplasm of the trachea, bronchus and lung	KHHW	162	4 308	4 299	4 237	4 221	4 126	4 106	3 984	3 961
Malignant neoplasm of breast	KHHX	174-175	1 256	1 285	1 278	1 249	1 200	1 161	1 147	1 136
Malignant neoplasm of uterus	KWUR	179+182	131	115	133	98	105	106	110	138
Malignant neoplasm of cervix	KWUS	180	183	170	154	147	138	144	145	122
Leukaemia	KHHZ	204-208	284	288	290	283	319	291	329	313
Benign neoplasms	KHIA	210-229,239	138	121	122	118	194	126	110	124
Endocrine, nutritional and metabolic diseases and immunity disorders	KHIB	240-279	742	775	768	738	722	727	797	870
Diabetes mellitus	KHIC	250	504	513	503	461	526	510	574	670
Nutritional deficiencies	KHID	260-269	17	16	14	6	16	7	12	17
Other metabolic and immunity disorders[2]	KMBN	270-279	193	215	217	235	140	167	175	147
Diseases of blood and blood-forming organs	KHIE	280-289	183	173	121	129	180	200	222	204
Anaemias	KHIF	280-285	75	71	60	67	76	71	81	80
Mental disorders	KHIG	290-319	1 133	1 322	1 306	1 583	1 595	1 611	1 725	1 901
Diseases of nervous system and sense organs	KHIH	320-389	877	879	853	832	852	900	894	971
Meningitis	KHII	320-322	27	17	24	18	14	17	6	19
Diseases of the circulatory system	KHIJ	390-459	28 776	29 909	27 138	27 079	26 728	25 911	25 253	24 787
Rheumatic heart disease	KHIL	393-398	186	201	175	178	154	183	151	173
Hypertensive disease	KHIM	401-405	323	325	312	324	281	294	277	353
Ischaemic heart disease	KHIN	410-414	16 536	16 925	15 234	14 977	14 650	14 013	13 419	13 337
Diseases of pulmonary circulation and other forms of heart disease	KHIO	415-429	2 291	2 470	2 200	2 351	3 063	2 900	2 784	2 638
Cerebrovascular disease	KHIP	430-438	7 861	8 392	7 684	7 748	7 130	6 959	6 900	6 785
Diseases of the respiratory system	KHIQ	460-519	6 999	8 409	6 981	7 668	7 863	7 891	8 011	8 870
Influenza	KHIR	487	29	127	11	33	45	83	12	62
Pneumonia	KHIS	480-486	3 729	4 495	3 757	4 021	4 158	4 028	4 064	4 526
Bronchitis, emphysema	KHIT	490-492	388	424	357	372	348	320	288	322
Asthma	KHIU	493	115	129	119	120	122	113	120	119
Diseases of the digestive system	KHIV	520-579	2 122	2 162	2 192	2 252	2 440	2 428	2 578	2 787
Ulcer of stomach and duodenum	KHIW	531-533	387	372	380	359	344	306	314	337
Appendicitis	KHIX	540-543	10	8	11	7	9	14	11	9
Hernia of abdominal cavity	KHIY	550-553, 560	197	200	183	173	196	168	211	213
Chronic liver disease and cirrhosis	KHIZ	571	446	494	555	607	723	767	806	896
Diseases of the genito-urinary system	KHJA	580-629	888	857	816	928	839	904	890	936
Nephritis, nephrotic syndrome and nephrosis	KHJB	580-589	574	581	562	606	549	576	570	540
Hyperplasia of prostate	KHJC	600	20	16	11	15	11	9	7	16
Complications of pregnancy, childbirth, etc	KHJD	630-676	7	7	9	6	6	4	5	7
Abortion	KHJE	630-639	–	1	–	–	–	–	–	–
Diseases of the skin and subcutaneous tissue	KHJF	680-709	82	100	101	80	75	87	94	90
Diseases of the musculo-skeletal system	KHJG	710-739	306	269	279	303	252	268	284	295
Congenital anomalies	KHJH	740-759	209	216	170	176	192	182	176	157
Certain conditions originating in the perinatal period	KHJI	760-779	216	174	191	178	181	140	165	137
Birth trauma, hypoxia, birth asphyxia and other respiratory conditions	KHJJ	767-770	107	101	104	90	94	71	82	54
Signs, symptoms and ill-defined conditions	KHJK	780-779	280	344	331	365	337	383	398	355
Sudden infant death syndrome	KMBM	7980	64	58	48	48	43	52	79	41
Deaths from injury and poisoning[1]	KHJL	E800-E999	2 535	2 489	2 372	2 395	2 497	2 373	2 379	2 450
All accidents	KHJM	E800-E929	1 580	1 469	1 413	1 439	1 497	1 398	1 388	1 428
Motor vehicle accidents	KHJN	E810-E825	468	402	354	422	363	384	387	320
Suicide and self-inflicted injuries	KHJO	E950-E959	569	615	624	623	596	599	649	637
All other external causes	KMBQ	(E930-E949) (E960-E999)	386	405	335	333	404	376	342	385

1 Within certain main categories only selected causes of death are shown.
2 See chapter text.

Sources: Office for National Statistics: 020 7533 5249;
General Register Office (Scotland)

5.19
continued

Deaths: analysed by cause
International Statistical Classification of Diseases, Injuries and Causes of Death
Ninth Revision, 1979

Number

			Northern Ireland							
		ICD 9 code	1992	1993	1994	1995	1996	1997	1998	1999
Total deaths	KHKA		14 988	15 633	15 114	15 310	15 218	14 971	14 993	15 663
Deaths from natural causes[1]	KHKB		14 303	14 871	14 325	14 516	14 528	14 276	14 331	14 942
Infectious and parasitic diseases	KHKC	001-139	41	55	39	44	54	61	53	47
Intestinal and infectious diseases	KHKD	001-009	–	–	2	1	1	–	–	1
Tuberculosis of the respiratory system	KHKE	010-012	8	9	6	13	–	8	4	7
Other tuberculosis, including late effects	KHKF	013-018,137	5	6	3	1	3	3	2	–
Whooping cough	KHKG	033	–	–	–	–	–	–	–	–
Meningococcal infection	KHKH	036	7	4	4	4	5	4	6	4
Measles	KHKI	055	–	–	1	–	–	–	–	–
Malaria	KHKJ	084	–	1	–	–	–	–	–	1
Syphilis	KHKK	090-097	–	1	–	–	–	–	–	–
Neoplasms	KHKL	140-239	3 621	3 705	3 665	3 585	3 715	3 669	3 769	3 654
Malignant neoplasm of stomach	KHKM	151	213	194	201	170	200	171	215	187
Malignant neoplasm of the trachea, bronchus and lung	KHKN	162	771	812	768	752	816	773	775	781
Malignant neoplasm of breast	KHKO	174-175	308	339	338	329	309	267	299	286
Malignant neoplasm of uterus	KWUT	179+182	31	32	37	28	28	35	34	26
Malignant neoplasm of cervix	KWUU	180	33	33	38	19	45	26	33	36
Leukaemia	KHKQ	204-208	66	84	94	83	92	107	93	104
Benign neoplasms and neoplasms of unspecified nature	KHKR	210-229,239	38	55	47	51	60	53	121	67
Endocrine, nutritional and metabolic diseases	KHKS	240-279	60	75	74	86	81	106	85	118
Diabetes mellitus	KHKT	250	23	44	45	43	49	77	55	93
Nutritional deficiencies	KHKU	260-269	–	–	1	2	–	1	1	3
Other metabolic and immunity disorders[2]	KHKV	270-279	26	25	20	38	28	17	26	20
Diseases of blood and blood-forming organs	KHKW	280-289	18	29	29	29	22	20	24	24
Anaemias	KHKX	280-285	11	8	15	10	11	9	14	9
Mental disorders	KHKY	290-319	52	56	91	78	100	138	145	190
Diseases of nervous system and sense organs	KHKZ	320-389	181	189	187	224	236	235	240	284
Meningitis	KHLA	320-322	7	15	4	1	7	8	4	3
Diseases of the circulatory system	KHLB	390-459	7 112	7 137	7 011	6 929	6 633	6 505	6 367	6 423
Rheumatic heart disease	KHLC	393-398	58	47	30	47	29	38	29	35
Hypertensive disease	KHLD	401-405	69	67	79	94	75	73	72	68
Ischaemic heart disease	KHLE	410-414	4 313	4 245	4 168	4 086	3 856	3 764	3 654	3 568
Diseases of pulmonary circulation and other forms of heart disease	KHLF	415-429	633	678	633	641	655	635	680	768
Cerebrovascular disease	KHLG	430-438	1 691	1 722	1 738	1 690	1 653	1 646	1 602	1 680
Diseases of the respiratory system	KHLH	460-519	2 423	2 756	2 398	2 656	2 749	2 664	2 627	3 161
Influenza	KHLI	487	6	17	3	9	6	8	2	5
Pneumonia	KHLJ	480-486	1 547	1 814	1 595	1 781	1 817	1 775	1 727	2 130
Bronchitis, emphysema	KHLK	490-492	143	151	116	104	137	99	108	93
Asthma	KHLL	493	53	58	30	42	31	32	44	38
Diseases of the digestive system	KHLM	520-579	405	445	424	449	483	450	499	507
Ulcer of stomach and duodenum	KHLN	531-533	97	97	100	87	102	95	80	80
Appendicitis	KHLO	540-543	–	1	3	6	–	4	2	3
Hernia of the abdominal cavity and other intestinal obstruction	KHLP	550-553,560	51	43	50	39	52	42	47	49
Chronic liver disease and cirrhosis	KHLQ	571	69	66	66	71	88	68	104	92
Diseases of the genito-urinary system	KHLR	580-629	238	261	250	251	254	243	265	242
Nephritis, nephrotic syndrome and nephrosis	KHLS	580-589	168	171	165	162	168	175	164	155
Hyperplasia of prostate	KHLT	600	6	5	3	7	3	4	5	4
Complications of pregnancy, childbirth, etc	KHLU	630-676	–	–	–	–	1	–	1	–
Abortion	KHLV	630-639	–	–	–	–	–	–	–	–
Diseases of the skin and subcutaneous tissue	KHLW	680-709	27	33	27	37	29	25	36	27
Diseases of the musculo-skeletal system	KHLX	710-739	43	35	31	40	35	44	30	54
Congenital anomalies	KHLY	740-759	77	116	87	91	72	59	70	93
Certain conditions originating in the perinatal period	KHLZ	760-779	63	62	69	93	68	67	64	69
Birth trauma, hypoxia, birth asphyxia and other respiratory conditions	KHMA	767-770	26	22	29	27	28	24	21	21
Signs, symptoms and ill-defined conditions	KHMB	780-799	46	40	44	55	88	92	149	161
Sudden infant death syndrome	KHMC	7980	11	6	7	9	15	8	4	3
Deaths from injury and poisoning[1]	KHMD	E800-E999	581	639	688	663	598	593	569	609
All accidents	KHME	E800-E929	376	391	430	391	402	427	381	430
Motor vehicle accidents	KHMF	E810-E825	165	152	172	140	121	153	129	134
Suicide and self-inflicted injuries	KHMG	E950-E959	107	129	138	122	124	120	126	121
All other external causes	KHMH	(E930-E949) (E960-E999)	98	119	120	150	72	45	62	58

1 Within certain main categories only selected causes of death are shown.
2 See chapter text.

Sources: Office for National Statistics: 020 7533 5249;
General Register Office (Northern Ireland)

5.20 Infant and maternal mortality

| | Deaths of Infants under 1 year of age per thousand live births | | | | | | | | | | | | Maternal deaths per thousand live births[2] | | | |
| | United Kingdom | | | England and Wales[1] | | | Scotland | | | Northern Ireland[3] | | | United Kingdom | England and Wales | Scotland | Northern Ireland |
	Total	Males	Females	Total	Males	Females	Total	Males	Females	Total	Males	Females				
1900 - 02	142	156	128	146	160	131	124	136	111	113	123	103	4.71	4.67	4.74	6.03
1910 - 12	110	121	98	110	121	98	109	120	97	101	110	92	3.95	3.67	5.65	5.28
1920 - 22	82	92	71	80	90	69	94	106	82	86	95	77	4.37	4.03	6.36	5.62
1930 - 32	67	75	58	64	72	55	84	94	73	75	83	66	4.54	4.24	6.40	5.24
1940 - 42	59	66	51	55	62	48	77	87	66	80	89	70	3.29	2.74	4.50	3.79
1950 - 52	30	34	26	29	33	25	37	42	32	40	45	36	0.88	0.79	1.09	1.09
1960 - 62	22	25	19	22	24	19	26	30	22	27	30	24	0.36	0.36	0.37	0.43
1970 - 72	18	20	16	18	20	15	19	22	17	22	24	20	0.17	0.17	0.17	0.12
1980 - 82	12	13	10	11	13	10	12	13	10	13	15	12	0.09	0.09	0.14	0.06
1990 - 92	7	8	6	7	8	6	7	8	6	7	8	6	0.07	0.07	0.10	-
	KKAW	KKAX	KKAY	KKAZ	KKBW	KKBX	KKBY	KKBZ	KKCW	KKCX	KKCY	KKCZ	KKDW	KKDX	KKDY	KKDZ
1978	13.3	14.8	11.7	13.2	14.7	11.6	12.9	14.5	11.2	15.9	17.3	14.5	0.10	0.11	0.06	–
1979	12.9	14.4	11.3	12.8	14.4	11.1	12.8	13.9	11.8	14.8	15.6	13.9	0.11	0.12	0.10	0.04
1980	12.2	13.4	10.6	12.0	13.3	10.7	12.1	13.6	10.4	13.4	15.1	11.5	0.11	0.11	0.15	0.07
1981	11.2	12.7	9.5	11.1	12.6	9.4	11.3	12.3	10.2	13.2	14.7	11.6	0.09	0.09	0.19	0.04
1982	11.0	12.3	9.5	10.8	12.2	9.4	11.4	12.9	9.8	13.6	14.8	12.4	0.07	0.07	0.09	0.07
1983	10.1	11.3	8.9	10.1	11.3	8.9	9.9	11.3	8.5	12.1	13.9	10.1	0.09	0.09	0.12	0.15
1984	9.6	10.7	8.4	9.5	10.6	8.3	10.3	11.7	8.9	10.5	11.4	9.6	0.09	0.08	0.12	0.11
1985	9.4	10.4	8.3	9.4	10.4	8.2	9.4	10.0	8.7	9.6	10.6	8.5	0.07	0.07	0.13	0.07
1986	9.5	10.9	8.1	9.6	11.0	8.0	8.8	9.9	7.7	10.2	11.0	9.2	0.07	0.07	0.11	–
1987	9.1	10.3	7.9	9.2	10.4	7.9	8.5	9.7	7.2	8.7	9.6	7.7	0.06	0.07	0.03	0.04
1988	9.0	10.2	7.7	9.0	10.3	7.7	8.2	9.5	6.8	8.9	9.6	8.2	0.06	0.06	0.12	0.07
1989	8.4	9.5	7.2	8.4	9.6	7.3	8.7	10.2	7.2	6.9	7.4	6.3	0.08	0.08	0.06	–
1990	7.9	8.8	6.8	7.9	8.9	6.8	7.7	8.8	6.6	7.5	8.1	6.8	0.08	0.08	0.06	–
1991	7.4	8.3	6.3	7.4	8.3	6.4	7.1	8.7	5.3	7.4	8.3	6.4	0.07	0.06	0.13	0.04
1992	6.6	7.4	5.7	6.6	7.4	5.8	6.8	7.9	5.7	6.0	6.4	5.6	0.07	0.07	0.11	–
1993	6.3	7.0	5.6	6.3	7.0	5.6	6.5	7.4	5.6	7.1	7.8	6.3	0.06	0.05	0.11	–
1994	6.2	6.9	5.4	6.2	6.9	5.4	6.2	6.8	5.6	6.1	6.5	5.6	0.08	0.08	0.15	–
1995	6.2	6.9	5.4	6.1	6.9	5.3	6.2	6.4	6.1	7.1	7.5	6.6	0.07	0.07	0.10	–
1996	6.1	6.8	5.4	6.1	6.9	5.4	6.2	6.7	5.5	5.8	6.7	4.8	0.07	0.07	0.10	0.04
1997	5.8	6.4	5.3	5.9	6.5	5.3	5.3	6.1	4.5	5.6	5.5	5.8	0.06	0.06	0.07	–
1998	5.7	6.3	5.0	5.7	6.4	5.0	5.6	6.2	4.9	5.6	6.1	5.1	0.07	0.07	0.09	0.04
1999	5.8	6.4	5.1	5.8	6.5	5.1	5.0	5.7	4.3	6.4	6.8	5.9	0.05	0.05	0.13	–

1 From 1937 to 1956 death rates are based on the births to which they relate in the current and preceding years.
2 Deaths in pregnancy and childbirth.

Sources: Office for National Statistics: 020 7533 5641;
General Register Office (Northern Ireland);
General Register Office (Scotland)

5.20 Infant and maternal mortality
continued

Deaths per thousand live births

		Analysis by sex of infant												
		1986	1987	1988	1989	1990	1991	1992	1993	1994	1995	1996	1997	1998	1999

Total

United Kingdom:
Stillbirths[1]	KHNQ	5.3	5.0	4.9	4.7	4.6	4.7	4.3	5.7	5.8	5.6	5.5	5.3	5.4	5.3
Perinatal[1]	KHNR	9.6	9.0	8.8	8.3	8.1	8.1	7.7	9.0	8.9	8.9	8.7	8.3	8.3	8.2
Neonatal	KHNS	5.3	5.0	4.9	4.7	4.5	4.4	4.3	4.2	4.1	4.2	4.1	3.9	3.8	3.9
Post neonatal	KHNT	4.2	4.1	4.1	3.7	3.3	3.0	2.3	2.2	2.1	2.0	2.0	2.0	1.9	1.9

England and Wales:
Stillbirths[1]	KHNU	5.3	5.0	4.9	4.7	4.6	4.6	4.3	5.7	5.7	5.5	5.4	5.3	5.3	5.3
Perinatal[1]	KHNV	9.6	8.9	8.7	8.3	8.1	8.0	7.6	8.9	8.9	8.7	8.6	8.3	8.2	8.2
Neonatal	KHNW	5.3	5.1	4.9	4.8	4.6	4.4	4.3	4.2	4.1	4.1	4.1	3.9	3.8	3.9
Post neonatal	KHNX	4.3	4.1	4.1	3.7	3.3	3.0	2.3	2.1	2.1	2.0	2.0	2.0	1.9	1.9

Scotland:
Stillbirths[1]	KHNY	5.8	5.1	5.4	5.0	5.3	5.5	4.9	6.4	6.1	6.6	6.4	5.3	6.1	5.2
Perinatal[1]	KHNZ	10.2	8.9	8.9	8.7	8.7	8.6	8.5	9.6	9.0	9.6	9.2	7.8	8.7	7.6
Neonatal	KHOA	5.2	4.7	4.5	4.7	4.4	4.4	4.6	4.0	4.0	4.0	3.9	3.2	3.6	3.3
Post neonatal	KHOB	3.6	3.8	3.7	4.0	3.3	2.7	2.2	2.5	2.2	2.2	2.2	2.1	2.0	1.7

Northern Ireland:
Stillbirths[1]	KHOC	4.4	6.1	5.0	5.1	4.4	4.7	4.9	5.2	6.3	6.1	6.3	5.4	5.1	5.7
Perinatal[1]	KHOD	9.5	9.8	9.3	8.2	7.6	8.4	8.2	8.8	9.7	10.4	9.4	8.2	8.1	10.0
Neonatal	KHOE	6.0	4.8	5.4	4.0	4.0	4.6	4.1	4.9	4.2	5.5	3.7	4.2	3.9	4.8
Post neonatal	KHOF	4.2	3.8	3.6	2.9	3.5	2.8	1.9	2.1	1.9	1.6	2.0	1.4	1.7	1.6

Males

United Kingdom:
Perinatal[1]	KHOG	10.4	9.7	9.5	9.3	8.8	8.7	8.3	9.7	9.6	9.4	9.1	8.7	8.8	8.7
Neonatal	KHOH	6.0	5.7	5.5	5.4	5.0	4.9	4.8	4.7	4.6	4.6	4.6	4.2	4.2	4.3
Infant mortality	KHOI	10.9	10.3	10.2	9.5	8.8	8.3	7.4	7.0	6.9	6.9	6.8	6.4	6.3	6.4

England and Wales:
Perinatal[1]	KHOK	10.4	9.8	9.4	9.2	8.8	8.6	8.1	9.5	9.6	9.3	9.0	8.7	8.8	8.6
Neonatal	KHOL	6.0	5.7	5.5	5.4	5.1	4.8	4.7	4.6	4.6	4.6	4.6	4.2	4.3	4.3
Infant mortality	KHOM	11.0	10.4	10.3	9.6	8.9	8.3	7.4	7.0	6.9	6.9	6.9	6.5	6.4	6.5

Scotland:
Perinatal[1]	KHOO	10.9	8.9	9.7	10.0	9.1	9.8	9.8	10.8	9.6	10.1	10.0	8.1	9.6	8.4
Neonatal	KHOP	5.6	5.3	5.3	5.3	4.7	5.5	5.5	4.5	4.4	4.1	4.3	3.4	4.0	3.8
Infant mortality	KHOQ	9.9	9.7	9.5	10.2	8.8	8.7	7.9	7.4	6.8	6.4	6.7	6.1	6.2	5.7

Northern Ireland:
Perinatal[1]	KHOS	9.7	10.5	10.9	8.7	8.7	7.9	8.6	10.3	10.4	10.4	10.1	8.5	8.9	10.5
Neonatal	KHOT	6.2	5.3	6.0	4.5	4.8	5.5	4.5	5.9	4.3	5.7	4.3	4.3	4.4	5.5
Infant mortality	KHOU	11.0	9.6	9.6	7.4	8.1	8.3	6.4	7.8	6.5	7.5	6.7	5.5	6.1	6.8

Females

United Kingdom:
Perinatal[1]	KHOW	8.8	8.1	8.0	7.4	7.4	7.5	7.0	8.2	8.2	8.3	8.2	7.9	7.7	7.8
Neonatal	KHOX	4.6	4.3	4.3	4.0	4.0	3.8	3.8	3.6	3.6	3.7	3.6	3.5	3.3	3.4
Infant mortality	KHOY	8.1	7.9	7.7	7.2	6.8	6.3	5.7	5.6	5.4	5.4	5.4	5.3	5.0	5.1

England and Wales:
Perinatal[1]	KHPA	8.7	8.0	8.0	7.4	7.4	7.5	7.0	8.3	8.1	8.1	8.2	7.9	7.7	7.8
Neonatal	KHPB	4.5	4.3	4.3	4.0	4.0	3.9	3.9	3.6	3.6	3.6	3.6	3.6	3.3	3.5
Infant mortality	KHPC	8.0	7.9	7.7	7.3	6.8	6.4	5.8	5.6	5.4	5.3	5.4	5.3	5.0	5.1

Scotland:
Perinatal[1]	KHPE	9.4	9.0	8.1	7.3	8.2	7.4	7.1	8.3	8.4	9.2	8.4	7.5	7.9	6.7
Neonatal	KHPF	4.8	4.1	3.7	4.1	4.1	3.2	3.7	3.5	3.6	3.9	3.5	2.9	3.2	2.8
Infant mortality	KHPG	7.7	7.2	6.8	7.2	6.6	5.3	5.7	5.6	5.6	6.1	5.5	4.5	4.9	4.3

Northern Ireland:
Perinatal[1]	KHPI	9.2	9.2	7.6	7.6	6.4	9.0	7.9	7.2	8.9	10.5	8.6	8.0	7.3	9.5
Neonatal	KHPJ	5.8	4.4	4.7	3.5	3.2	3.7	3.6	3.9	4.1	5.2	3.1	4.0	3.4	4.1
Infant mortality	KHPK	9.2	7.7	8.2	6.3	6.8	6.4	5.6	6.3	5.6	6.6	4.8	5.8	5.1	5.9

1 Deaths per 1 000 live and stillbirths. On 1 October 1992 the legal definition of a stillbirth was altered from baby born dead after 28 completed weeks gestation or more, to one born dead after 24 completed weeks gestation or more. The 258 stillbirths of 24 to 27 weeks gestation which occurred between 1 October and 31 December 1992 are excluded from this table.

Sources: Office for National Statistics: 020 7533 5641;
General Register Office (Northern Ireland);
General Register Office (Scotland)

5.21 Death rates per 1 000 population[1]
United Kingdom
Analysis by age and sex

	All ages	0-4	5-9	10-14	15-19	20-24	25-34	35-44	45-54	55-64	65-74	75-84	85 and over
Males													
1900 - 02	18.4	57.0	4.1	2.4	3.7	5.0	6.6	11.0	18.6	35.0	69.9	143.6	289.6
1910 - 12	14.9	40.5	3.3	2.0	3.0	3.9	5.0	8.0	14.9	29.8	62.1	133.8	261.5
1920 - 22	13.5	33.4	2.9	1.8	2.9	3.9	4.5	6.9	11.9	25.3	57.8	131.8	259.1
1930 - 32	12.9	22.3	2.3	1.5	2.6	3.3	3.5	5.7	11.3	23.7	57.9	134.2	277.0
1940 - 42	..	..	..	..	..	..	..	..	..	..	..	..	..
1950 - 52	12.6	7.7	0.7	0.5	0.9	1.4	1.6	3.0	8.5	23.2	55.2	127.6	272.0
1960 - 62	12.5	6.4	0.5	0.4	0.9	1.1	1.1	2.5	7.4	22.2	54.4	123.4	251.0
1970 - 72	12.4	4.6	0.4	0.4	0.9	1.0	1.0	2.4	7.3	20.9	52.9	116.3	246.1
1980 - 82	12.1	3.2	0.3	0.3	0.8	0.9	0.9	1.9	6.3	18.2	46.7	107.1	224.9
1990 - 92	11.1	2.0	0.2	0.2	0.7	0.9	0.9	1.8	4.6	14.3	38.7	92.9	195.7
	KHZA	KHZB	KHZC	KHZD	KHZE	KHZF	KHZG	KHZH	KHZJ	KHZK	KHZL	KHZM	KHZN
1978	12.3	3.4	0.3	0.3	0.9	1.0	1.0	2.1	7.0	19.3	49.3	111.8	232.0
1979	12.4	3.8	0.3	0.3	0.9	1.0	1.0	2.1	6.9	19.2	48.8	112.0	236.0
1980	12.1	3.4	0.3	0.3	0.8	0.9	0.9	2.0	6.5	18.7	47.2	108.6	227.0
1981	12.3	3.2	0.3	0.3	0.9	0.9	1.0	2.0	6.4	18.4	47.5	110.6	239.5
1982	12.0	2.9	0.3	0.3	0.8	0.9	0.9	1.8	6.1	17.9	46.4	106.4	225.0
1983	12.0	2.7	0.3	0.3	0.8	0.8	0.9	1.8	5.9	18.0	46.3	104.6	221.0
1984	11.7	2.6	0.3	0.3	0.7	0.9	0.9	1.7	5.7	17.5	44.9	100.9	212.8
1985	12.0	2.6	0.2	0.3	0.7	0.8	0.9	1.8	5.6	17.5	45.0	104.8	223.4
1986	11.8	2.6	0.2	0.2	0.7	0.9	0.9	1.7	5.5	17.0	43.6	102.0	217.1
1987	11.5	2.5	0.2	0.3	0.7	0.9	0.9	1.7	5.2	16.4	42.0	97.3	194.3
1988	11.5	2.5	0.2	0.3	0.7	0.9	0.9	1.7	5.1	16.0	41.2	96.6	193.9
1989	11.5	2.3	0.2	0.2	0.7	0.9	0.9	1.7	4.9	15.3	40.4	97.0	199.0
1990	11.2	2.2	0.2	0.2	0.7	0.9	1.0	1.8	4.8	14.8	39.5	94.3	187.8
1991	11.1	2.0	0.2	0.2	0.7	0.9	0.9	1.8	4.7	14.2	38.7	93.3	203.5
1992	10.9	1.8	0.2	0.2	0.6	0.9	0.9	1.7	4.4	13.8	37.9	91.2	195.8
1993	11.2	1.7	0.2	0.2	0.6	0.9	1.0	1.7	4.4	12.8	36.8	92.7	213.3
1994	10.6	1.6	0.2	0.2	0.6	0.9	1.0	1.7	4.1	12.8	36.8	90.3	190.5
1995	10.8	1.5	0.2	0.2	0.6	0.9	0.9	1.7	4.2	13.5	38.4	91.3	188.0
1996	10.6	1.6	0.1	0.2	0.6	0.9	1.0	1.7	4.2	12.4	35.4	86.5	195.5
1997	10.4	1.5	0.1	0.2	0.6	0.9	1.0	1.6	4.1	11.8	33.9	83.4	191.9
1998	10.3	1.5	0.1	0.2	0.6	0.9	1.0	1.6	4.1	11.7	33.1	82.0	188.1
1999	10.3	1.5	0.1	0.2	0.6	0.9	1.0	1.6	4.1	11.2	32.3	81.1	190.0
Females													
1900 - 02	16.3	47.9	4.3	2.6	3.5	4.3	5.8	9.0	14.4	27.9	59.3	127.0	262.6
1910 - 12	13.3	34.0	3.3	2.1	2.9	3.4	4.4	6.7	11.5	23.1	50.7	113.7	234.0
1920 - 22	11.9	26.9	2.8	1.9	2.8	3.4	4.1	5.6	9.3	19.2	45.6	111.5	232.4
1930 - 32	11.5	17.7	2.1	1.5	2.4	2.9	3.3	4.6	8.3	17.6	43.7	110.1	246.3
1940 - 42	..	..	..	..	..	..	..	..	..	..	..	..	..
1950 - 52	11.2	6.0	0.5	0.4	0.7	1.0	1.4	2.3	5.3	12.9	35.5	98.4	228.8
1960 - 62	11.2	4.9	0.3	0.3	0.4	0.5	0.8	1.8	4.5	11.0	30.8	87.3	218.5
1970 - 72	11.3	3.6	0.3	0.2	0.4	0.4	0.6	1.6	4.5	10.5	27.5	76.7	196.1
1980 - 82	11.4	2.3	0.2	0.2	0.3	0.4	0.5	1.3	3.9	9.9	24.8	67.2	179.5
1990 - 92	11.1	1.6	0.1	0.2	0.3	0.3	0.4	1.1	2.9	8.4	22.2	58.5	154.6
	KHZO	KHZP	KHZQ	KHZR	KHZS	KHZT	KHZU	KHZV	KHZW	KHZX	KHZY	KHZZ	KHZI
1978	11.5	2.8	0.2	0.2	0.4	0.4	0.6	1.5	4.3	10.1	25.7	70.5	184.5
1979	11.6	2.8	0.2	0.2	0.3	0.4	0.6	1.4	4.3	10.2	25.6	70.8	187.1
1980	11.4	2.7	0.2	0.2	0.3	0.4	0.5	1.3	4.0	10.0	25.0	67.7	181.3
1981	11.6	2.5	0.2	0.2	0.3	0.4	0.5	1.3	3.9	10.0	25.5	70.4	190.6
1982	11.5	2.3	0.2	0.2	0.3	0.4	0.5	1.2	3.8	9.9	24.8	66.8	179.4
1983	11.4	2.1	0.2	0.2	0.3	0.3	0.5	1.2	3.6	9.8	24.7	65.1	177.2
1984	11.2	2.0	0.2	0.2	0.3	0.3	0.5	1.2	3.5	9.7	24.3	62.6	170.2
1985	11.7	2.0	0.2	0.2	0.3	0.3	0.5	1.2	3.4	9.9	24.7	64.8	178.4
1986	11.5	2.0	0.2	0.2	0.3	0.3	0.5	1.1	3.3	9.5	24.0	63.2	172.4
1987	11.2	2.0	0.2	0.2	0.3	0.3	0.5	1.1	3.3	9.4	23.3	60.8	159.9
1988	11.3	1.9	0.2	0.2	0.3	0.3	0.5	1.2	3.2	9.2	23.2	60.4	162.3
1989	11.5	1.8	0.2	0.2	0.3	0.3	0.5	1.1	3.1	9.1	23.2	61.4	164.7
1990	11.1	1.7	0.1	0.2	0.3	0.3	0.5	1.1	3.0	8.8	22.4	58.9	156.7
1991	11.2	1.6	0.2	0.2	0.3	0.3	0.4	1.1	2.9	8.4	22.3	58.9	156.9
1992	11.0	1.4	0.1	0.1	0.3	0.3	0.4	1.1	2.8	8.1	22.0	57.8	150.3
1993	11.5	1.3	0.1	0.2	0.3	0.3	0.5	1.1	2.9	7.5	21.6	58.0	162.3
1994	10.9	1.3	0.1	0.1	0.2	0.3	0.4	1.1	2.8	7.6	21.7	57.5	148.4
1995	11.1	1.2	0.1	0.1	0.3	0.3	0.4	1.1	2.7	8.0	22.6	59.8	150.4
1996	11.1	1.2	0.1	0.1	0.3	0.3	0.5	1.1	2.7	7.3	21.2	56.8	153.7
1997	11.0	1.2	0.1	0.1	0.3	0.3	0.4	1.1	2.7	7.1	20.6	55.2	153.9
1998	10.9	1.2	0.1	0.1	0.3	0.3	0.4	1.0	2.7	7.0	20.3	54.4	153.3
1999	11.0	1.2	0.1	0.1	0.3	0.3	0.4	1.0	2.7	6.9	19.7	54.3	157.1

1 The figures 1974 to 1980 incorporate the revised intercensal estimates for England and Wales and Northern Ireland, but the old series for Scotland.

Sources: Office for National Statistics: 020 7533 5249;
General Register Office (Northern Ireland);
General Register Office (Scotland)

Population and vital statistics

5.22 Life tables

Interim life tables, 1997-99

	United Kingdom				England and Wales			
	Males		Females		Males		Females	
Age(x)	l_x	e^0_x	l_x	e^0_x	l_x	e^0_x	l_x	e^0_x
0 years	100 000	74.9	100 000	79.8	100 000	75.1	100 000	80.0
5 years	99 241	70.4	99 395	75.3	99 236	70.7	99 392	75.5
10 years	99 172	65.5	99 341	70.3	99 168	65.7	99 340	70.5
15 years	99 083	60.5	99 278	65.3	99 080	60.8	99 277	65.5
20 years	98 796	55.7	99 143	60.4	98 806	55.9	99 146	60.6
25 years	98 364	50.9	98 980	55.5	98 395	51.2	98 988	55.7
30 years	97 907	46.2	98 800	50.6	97 954	46.4	98 810	50.8
35 years	97 404	41.4	98 553	45.7	97 468	41.6	98 567	45.9
40 years	96 788	36.6	98 165	40.9	96 871	36.8	98 184	41.1
45 years	95 835	32.0	97 525	36.2	95 952	32.2	97 561	36.3
50 years	94 358	27.4	96 522	31.5	94 521	27.6	96 584	31.7
55 years	91 974	23.1	94 935	27.0	92 222	23.2	95 034	27.2
60 years	87 996	19.0	92 418	22.7	88 367	19.1	92 585	22.8
65 years	81 753	15.2	88 431	18.6	82 279	15.3	88 696	18.7
70 years	72 075	11.9	82 089	14.8	72 763	12.0	82 490	14.9
75 years	58 208	9.1	72 121	11.5	58 993	9.2	72 647	11.5
80 years	41 263	6.8	58 263	8.6	42 014	6.9	58 884	8.6
85 years	23 689	5.1	40 346	6.2	24 235	5.1	40 951	6.3
90 years	9 916	3.8	21 435	4.5	10 221	3.9	21 899	4.6

Interim life tables, 1997-99

	Scotland				Northern Ireland			
	Males		Females		Males		Females	
Age(x)	l_x	e^0_x	l_x	e^0_x	l_x	e^0_x	l_x	e^0_x
0 years	10 000	72.6	10 000	78.1	10 000	74.3	10 000	79.5
5 years	9 929	68.1	9 946	73.5	9 927	69.8	9 934	75.0
10 years	9 921	63.2	9 938	68.5	9 918	64.9	9 927	70.1
15 years	9 912	58.3	9 932	63.6	9 909	59.9	9 921	65.1
20 years	9 873	53.5	9 915	58.7	9 873	55.1	9 904	60.2
25 years	9 811	48.8	9 894	53.8	9 824	50.4	9 887	55.3
30 years	9 748	44.1	9 873	48.9	9 779	45.6	9 871	50.4
35 years	9 681	39.4	9 845	44.0	9 727	40.9	9 849	45.5
40 years	9 599	34.7	9 799	39.2	9 669	36.1	9 817	40.6
45 years	9 471	30.1	9 718	34.5	9 573	31.4	9 753	35.9
50 years	9 281	25.7	9 593	29.9	9 409	26.9	9 649	31.3
55 years	8 954	21.5	9 395	25.5	9 162	22.6	9 490	26.7
60 years	8 442	17.7	9 083	21.3	8 745	18.5	9 225	22.4
65 years	7 684	14.2	8 596	17.4	8 077	14.8	8 825	18.3
70 years	6 579	11.1	7 838	13.8	7 062	11.6	8 196	14.5
75 years	5 115	8.5	6 724	10.6	5 633	8.9	7 208	11.1
80 years	3 455	6.4	5 260	7.9	3 922	6.6	5 758	8.3
85 years	1 890	4.7	3 495	5.6	2 190	4.9	3 916	6.0
90 years	739	3.5	1 736	3.8	833	4.1	2 022	4.3

Note Column l_x shows the number who would survive to exact **age(x)**, out of 100 000 or 10 000 born, who were subject throughout their lives to the death rates experienced in the three-year period indicated.

Column e^0_x is 'the expectation of life', that is, the average future lifetime which would be lived by a person aged exactly x if likewise subject to the death rates experienced in the three-year period indicated. See introductory notes.

Source: Government Actuary's Department: 020 7211 2622

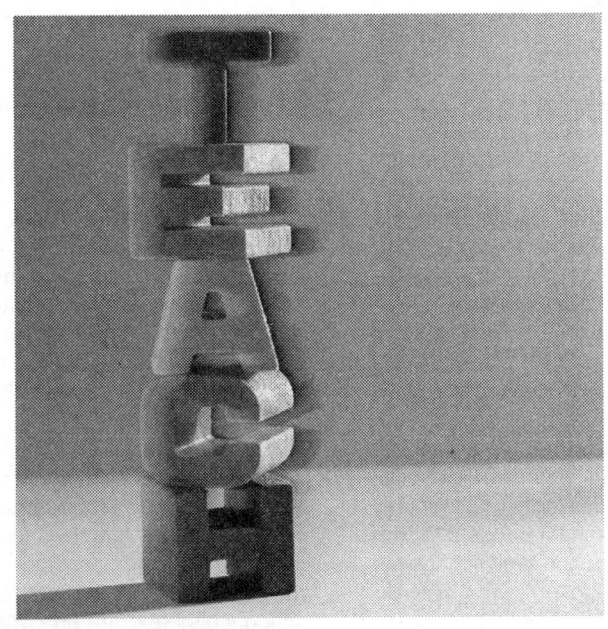

6 Education

Education

In general, the detailed provision and delivery of education in the United Kingdom is not subject to central administration. School quality assessment is undertaken in England by an inspectorate (OFSTED), in Wales by the Office of Her Majesty's Chief Inspector of Schools (OHMCI), in Scotland by Her Majesty's Inspectors of Schools (HMI) and in Northern Ireland by the Education and Training Inspectorate (ETI). Further education quality control is undertaken by the FEFC Inspectorate. In Wales external quality assurance is secured on behalf of the FEFCW through a contracted service provided by OHMCI. Higher Education Institutions (HEIs) are subject to quality assurance procedures of the HE Funding Councils and the Quality Assurance Agency (QAA). In practice, within the quanta of funds distributed by Funding Councils and Education Departments, Institutions are managed by their governing bodies which are able to select their own staff and decide how best to allocate funds to suit local needs. Some central control is however, exercised over the curriculum taught during compulsory schooling. In particular the Education Reform Act 1988 introduced the National Curriculum in England and Wales. However, unlike England Wales and Northern Ireland, the curriculum in Scotland is not statutorily prescribed, and pupils aged 5 - 14 study a broad curriculum based on national guidelines. The 1988 Act also provided for local authorities to delegate the management of school budgets to the schools themselves and for the schools to seek withdrawal from LEA control and become self-governing.

The four home Government Departments dealing with education statistics are:

Department for Education and Employment:
  which deals with all sectors of education in England.
National Assembly for Wales (NAFW):
  which deals with schools and higher and further education in Wales, excluding matters connected with the remuneration, superannuation and misconduct of teachers. From 1 April 1993, WOED has responsibility for the colleges of the University of Wales.
Scottish Executive (SE):
  all sectors of education in Scotland.
Department of Education, Northern Ireland:
  schools, institutes of further education, teacher training colleges and universities in Northern Ireland.

Each of the four home Education Departments have overall responsibility for funding the schools sectors in their own country. The FE and HE Funding Councils of England and of Wales and the Scottish HE Funding Council are responsible respectively for the distribution of funds made available by the Secretaries of State to FE colleges in England and Wales, and HEIs in England, Wales and Scotland. The SE is responsible for allocating funds to all but three of the FE colleges in Scotland. The remaining 3 are still funded by the relevant regional authorities. DENI allocates funds to further and higher education establishments in Northern Ireland.

Statistics for the separate systems obtained in England, Wales, Scotland and Northern Ireland are collected and processed separately in accordance with the particular needs of the responsible Departments. Since 1994/95 the data collection for all HEIs in the UK has been undertaken by the Higher Education Statistics Agency (HESA). This includes the former UFC funded UK universities previously collected by the Universities Statistical Record. There are some structural differences in the information collected for schools, further and higher education in each of the four home countries. In some tables the GB/UK data presented are an amalgamation from sources which are not entirely comparable.

Stages of education
There are five stages of education: nursery, primary, secondary, further and higher education. Primary and secondary education is compulsory for all children between the ages of five and sixteen years and the transition is normally at age eleven. The non compulsory fourth stage, further education, covers non-advanced education which can be taken at both further (including tertiary) education colleges, higher education institutions and increasingly in secondary schools. The fifth stage, higher education, is study beyond A levels and their equivalent which, for most full-time students, takes place in higher education institutions.

Nursery education
Many children under 5 attend state nursery schools or nursery classes attached to primary schools. Others may attend playgroups in the voluntary sector or in private run nurseries. In England and Wales many primary schools also operate an early admission policy where they admit children under 5 into what are called reception classes.

Primary education
Primary education normally provides for pupils aged five to eleven. In Northern Ireland children who attain the age of four on or before 1 July are required to commence primary school the following September. In Scotland children generally commence primary school when aged between 4.5 and 5.5 years, transferring to secondary school after seven years of primary schooling. The great majority of public sector primary schools take both boys and girls in mixed classes.

Middle schools
Some local education authorities in England operate a system of middle schools which cater for pupils on either side of the transition age, and these are deemed either primary or secondary according to the age range of the pupils.

Secondary education
Provision of secondary education in an area may include any combination of types of schools. The pattern is a reflection of historical circumstances and of the policy adopted by the local education authority. Comprehensive schools, on a variety of patterns as to forms of organisation and the age of the pupils attending, form the vast majority. In their 'pure' form, comprehensive schools admit pupils without reference to ability and aptitude, and cater for all the children in a neighbourhood. In 1997/98, over 86 percent of secondary school pupils in England attended comprehensive schools while all secondary schools in Wales are comprehensive schools. The majority of education authority secondary schools in Scotland are comprehensive in character and offer six years of secondary education; however in remote areas there are

several two-year and four-year secondary schools.

Specialist schools

City technology colleges, technology colleges and language colleges, sports colleges and arts colleges operate in England. The Specialist Schools Programme enables secondary schools to develop a strength in a particular subject area, often in partnership with an employer with an interest in some specialism, while still delivering a broad and balanced education through the National Curriculum. City technology colleges take the form of charitable companies limited by guarantee and are registered as independent schools.

Special schools

Special schools, both day and boarding, provide education for children with special educational needs, though the great majority are educated in ordinary schools. All children attending special schools are offered a curriculum designed to overcome their learning difficulties and to enable them to become self-reliant.

Further education

The term further education may be used in a general sense to cover all non-higher education, and embraces courses up to but not beyond, GCE A level or its equivalent. When undertaken immediately after compulsory schooling, it can be taken by continuing in school or transferring to further education colleges. Increasingly adults return to study at any stage of their lives, and are catered for full-time or part-time by FE colleges, or by adult education centres or by further education courses in some higher education institutions. From 1 April 1993 sixth form colleges are included in the further education sector.

Higher education

Higher education is defined as the academic standard beyond GNVQ/NVQ level 3, GCE A level or equivalent. This includes higher degrees and postgraduate diplomas and certificates, first degree and Edexcel (formerly BTEC) Higher National Certificate/Diploma as well as a wide range of professional qualifications at the higher education level. As a result of the 1992 Further and Higher Education Act former polytechnics and some other higher education institutions were designated as universities in 1992/93. Students normally attend HE courses at higher education institutions, but some attend at further education colleges. Some students also attend institutions which do not receive public grant (such as the University of Buckingham), and these numbers are excluded from the tables.

Education

6.1 Number of schools or departments[1] by type and establishments of further and higher education

Academic years

		1990 /91	1995 /96	1997 /98	1998[2] /99	1999[3] /00
United Kingdom:						
Public sector mainstream						
Nursery[4]	KBFK	1 364	1 486	1 681	2 329[5]	2 826[5]
Primary	KBFA	24 135	23 441[6]	23 230[6]	23 125[6]	23 052[6]
Secondary[7]	KBFF	4 790	4 463	4 434	4 418	4 406
of which 6th form colleges	KPGM	116	..	..	..	..
Non - maintained mainstream	KBFU	2 508	2 436	2 499[1]	2 482[1]	2 456[1]
Special - all	KBFP	1 830	1 565	1 517	1 522	1 523
maintained	KPVX	..	1 456	1 419	1 428	1 427
non maintained	KPGO	..	109	98	94	96
Pupil referral units	KXEP	..	315	332	325	322
Universities (including Open University)[8]	KAHG	48	89	88	88[9]	88
All other further and higher education institutions	KJPQ	588	609	596	581[9]	574
Higher education institutions	KPVY	..	66	63	58[9]	58
Further education institutions	KSNY	..	543	533	523	516
of which 6th form colleges	KPGP	..	110	108	107	105
England:						
Public sector mainstream						
Nursery	KBAK	566	547	533	520	514
Primary	KBAA	19 047	18 480	18 312	18 234	18 158
Secondary[7]	KBAF	3 897	3 594	3 567	3 560	3 550
of which 6th form colleges	KPGS	114	..	..	..	..
Non - maintained	KBAU	2 289	2 266	2 244	2 231	2 204
Special - all	KBAP	1 380	1 263	1 229	1 209	1 197
maintained	KPGT	..	1 191	1 164	1 148	1 134
non maintained	KPGU	..	72	65	61	63
Pupil referral units	KXEQ	..	291	309	298	295
Universities (including Open University)[8]	KAHM	37	72	71	70	70
All other further and higher education institutions	KJPR	460	503	491	482	475
Higher education institutions	KPXA	..	50	48	47	47
Further education institutions	KPWC	..	453	443	435	428
of which 6th form colleges	KPGV	..	110	108	107	105
Wales:						
Public sector mainstream						
Nursery	KBBK	54	52	47	46	46
Primary	KBBA	1 717	1 681	1 673	1 660	1 660
Secondary[7]	KBBF	230	228	228	229	229
of which 6th form colleges	KPGY	2	..	..	..	..
Non - maintained	KBBU	71	62	57	54	54
Special (Maintained)	KBBP	61	54	50	48	48
Pupil referral units	KZBF	..	24	23	27	27
Universities[8]	KAHS	1	2	2	2	2
All other further and higher education institutions	KJQP	38	31	30	28	28
Higher education institutions	KSNZ	..	5	4	4	4
Further education institutions	KPGZ	..	26	26	24	24
Scotland:						
Public sector mainstream						
Nursery	KBDK	659	796	1 010	1 672[5]	2 171[5]
Primary	KBDA	2 372	2 332	2 300	2 291	2 293
Secondary	KBDF	424	405	401	392	389
Non - maintained	KBDU	131	87	176[1]	175[1]	176[1]
Special - all	KBDP	343	201	191	218	228
maintained	KYCZ	343	164	158	185	195
non-maintained	KYDA	..	37	33	33	33
Universities[8]	KAHX	8	13	13	14[9]	14
All other further and higher education institutions	KJRA	64	56	56	52[9]	52
Higher education institutions	KPWE	..	9	9	5[9]	5
Further education institutions	KPHB	..	47	47	47	47
Northern Ireland:						
Grant aided mainstream						
Nursery[4]	KBEK	85	91	91	91	95
Primary	KBEA	999	948[6]	945[6]	940[6]	941[6]
Secondary	KBEF	239	236	238	237	238
Non - maintained	KBEU	17	21	22	22	22
Special (Maintained)	KBEP	46	47	47	47	50
Universities	KIAD	2	2	2	2	2
Colleges of education	KIAE	2	2	2	2	2
Further education colleges	KIAG	24	17	17	17	17

1 From 1997/98 non-maintained mainstream schools in Scotland with more than one department have been counted once for each department e.g. a school with nursery, primary and secondary departments has been counted 3 times.

2 Revised to include 1998/99 data for Wales and nursery schools data for Scotland.

3 Provisional. Data for Wales are for 1998/99.

4 Excludes voluntary and private pre-school education centres in Northern Ireland (268 in total in 1999/00).

5 Nursery schools figures for Scotland include pre-school education centres and are not therefore directlt comparable with previous years.

6 Includes Preparatory Departments in Northern Ireland Grammar Schools (24 in total in 1999/00). These figures were previously excluded from totals.

7 From 1993/94 excludes sixth form colleges in England and Wales which were reclassified as further education colleges on 1 April 1993.

8 From 1993/94 includes former polytechnics and colleges which became universities as a result of the Further and Higher Education Act 1992.

9 Figures for universities in Scotland have been revised to include one former college which became a university. Higher education figures now reflect a number of college mergers.

Source: Education Departments: 01325 392756

6.2 Full-time and part-time pupils in school[1] by age and gender
United Kingdom
All schools at January [2]

		1990	1991	1992	1993	1994	1995	1996	1997	1998	1999	2000[4]
Age at previous 31 August[3]												
Number (thousands)												
England[5]	KBIA	7 557	7 617	7 712	7 842	7 883	8 013	8 110	8 195	8 261	8 310	8 346
Wales	KBIB	480	482	487	493	498	504	..	..	501	513	513
Scotland	KBIC	821	821	826	832	841	845	846	848	850	844	874
Northern Ireland[6]	KBID	340	341	343	346	349	351	353	354	352	352	349
United Kingdom	KBIE	9 199	9 260	9 368	9 513	9 571	9 714	9 813	9 905	9 973	10 019	10 081
Boys and girls												
2 - 4[7]	KBIF	979	1 012	1 045	1 082	1 103	1 135	1 145	1 149	1 150	1 154	1 184
5 - 10	KBIG	4 312	4 346	4 356	4 392	4 462	4 517	4 581	4 627	4 666	4 663	4 633
11	KBIH	658	714	735	727	713	718	717	742	747	762	782
12 - 14	KBII	2 011	1 975	2 021	2 112	2 179	2 179	2 158	2 151	2 180	2 209	2 254
15	KBIK	726	691	664	638	651	700	721	717	701	706	705
16	KBIL	289	295	308	313	259	259	279	289	289	283	285
17	KBIM	194	197	206	215	180	181	191	206	216	218	213
18 and over	KBIN	29	32	34	35	23	24	22	22	24	25	27
Boys												
14	KBIO	358	344	332	338	367	376	371	365	368	367	380
15	KBIP	373	355	341	327	333	358	368	366	358	361	359
16	KBIQ	141	144	151	154	128	127	136	141	140	137	138
17	KBIR	96	96	100	104	88	88	92	100	104	104	101
18 and over	KBIS	16	17	18	18	12	13	12	12	13	12	14
Girls												
14	KBIT	339	326	314	322	347	358	355	349	350	352	363
15	KBIU	354	336	323	311	318	342	353	351	344	345	346
16	KBIV	147	151	156	159	131	132	142	148	149	146	147
17	KBIW	98	100	106	111	92	93	99	106	112	114	111
18 and over	KBIX	14	15	16	16	11	11	10	10	11	11	13

1 From 1 April 1993 excludes 6th form colleges in England and Wales which were reclassified as further education colleges.
2 In Wales and Scotland, as at the previous September.
3 1 July for Northern Ireland and 31 December for Scotland.
4 Provisional. Data for Wales are for 1998/99.
5 From 1992, figures for independent schools in England include pupils aged less than 2.

6 In Northern Ireland, a split is not collected by age but is available by year group and so this is used as a proxy.
7 Includes the so-called "rising 5s" (i.e. those pupils who become 5 during the autumn term.

Source: Education Departments: 01325 392756

6.3 Number of pupils and teachers: pupil/teacher ratios by school type
United Kingdom
At January[1]

		1996	1997	1998	1999[7]	2000[8]
All schools or departments						
Total						
Pupils (thousands)						
Full-time and full-time						
equivalent of part-time	KBCA	9 587.3	9 663.7	9 725.8	..	9 829.0
Teachers[2] (thousands)	KBCB	534.0	533.0	532.8	..	545.5
Pupils per teacher:						
United Kingdom[2]	KBCC	18.0	18.1	18.2	18.1	18.1
England	KBCD	18.2	18.3	18.5	18.4	18.3
Wales	KBCE	18.7	18.8	19.1	18.8	18.8
Scotland	KBCF	15.5	15.8	15.8	15.4	15.4
Northern Ireland	KBCG	17.1	16.7	16.7	16.7	16.8
Public sector mainstream[3] schools or departments						
Nursery						
Pupils (thousands)						
Full-time and full-time						
equivalent of part-time	KBFM	61.8	61.5	61.9	..	75.4
Teachers[2] (thousands)	KBFN	2.9	2.9	3.0	..	3.1
Pupils per teacher	KBFO	21.3	21.3	20.7	..	24.2
Primary[4]						
Pupils (thousands)						
Full-time and full-time						
equivalent of part-time	KBFB	5 144.9	5 184.9	5 213.3	..	5 171.4
Teachers[2] (thousands)	KBFD	227.0	227.0	225.6	..	228.0
Pupils per teacher	KBFE	22.7	22.8	23.1	..	22.7
Secondary[5]						
Pupils (thousands)						
Full-time and full-time						
equivalent of part-time	KBFG	3 677.4	3 714.1	3 741.1	..	3 855.2
Teachers[2] (thousands)	KBFH	228.2	228.9	228.7	..	232.8
Pupils per teacher	KBFI	16.1	16.2	16.4	..	16.6
Special schools						
Pupils (thousands)(ft and fte of pt)						
all	KBFQ	114.1	114.2	114.5	..	..
maintained	KPGE	107.7	107.8	108.4	..	107.4
non-maintained[6]	KPGF	6.4	6.4	6.0	..	..
Teachers (thousands)(ft and fte of pt)						
all	KBFS	18.6	18.3	18.1	..	..
maintained	KPGG	17.1	16.8	16.7	..	17.0
non-maintained[6]	KPGH	1.5	1.4	1.4	..	..
Pupils per teacher						
all	KBFT	6.2	6.2	6.3	..	..
maintained	KPGI	6.3	6.4	6.5	..	6.3
non-maintained[6]	KPGJ	4.4	4.4	4.4	..	..

1 In Scotland and Wales the school census date is September whereas that for the rest of the United Kingdom remains at January.
2 Figures of teachers and of pupil/teacher ratios take account of the full-time equivalent of part-time teachers.
3 Includes grant-maintained schools.
4 Includes preparatory departments attached to grammar schools in Northern Ireland.

5 Includes voluntary grammar schools in Northern Ireland.
6 England and Scotland only.
7 Revised to include 1998/99 data for Wales. Includes 1997/98 nursery data for Scotland.
8 Provisional. Includes 1998/99 data for Wales. Nursery schools for Scotland refer to pre-school education centres and are not therefore directly comparable with earlier years.

Source: Education Departments: 01325 392756

6.4 Full-time and part-time pupils with special educational needs (SEN)[1], 1999/00[2]
United Kingdom
By type of school

Thousands and percentages

	United Kingdom[2]	England	Wales[2]	Scotland	Northern Ireland
All schools					
Total pupils	10 085.2	8 345.8	512.8	874.4	352.2
SEN pupils with statements	294.5	252.9	17.1	16.1	8.5
Incidence (%)[3]	2.9	3.0	3.3	1.8	2.4
Maintained schools[4]					
Nursery[5,6]					
Total pupils	147.3	46.3	2.8	88.8	9.4
SEN pupils with statements	1.0	0.5	-	0.4	0.1
Incidence (%)[3]	0.7	1.0	1.2	0.5	0.7
Placement (%)[7]	0.3	0.2	0.2	2.7	0.8
Primary[8]					
Total pupils	5 340.5	4 435.3	291.7	431.4	182.0
SEN pupils without statements[9]	896.7	886.0	-	10.7	-
SEN pupils with statements	84.9	72.5	6.2	3.9	2.2
Pupils with statements - incidence (%)[3]	1.6	1.6	2.1	0.9	1.2
Pupils with statements - placement (%)[7]	28.8	28.7	36.3	24.5	26.3
Secondary					
Total pupils	3 855.2	3 181.8	204.2	314.3	155.0
SEN pupils without statements[9]	549.7	541.4	-	8.3	-
SEN pupils with statements	93.6	79.8	6.8	4.8	2.3
Pupils with statements - incidents (%)[3]	2.4	2.5	3.3	1.5	1.5
Pupils with statements - placement (%)[7]	31.8	31.6	39.6	29.8	26.9
Special[10,11]					
Total pupils	108.6	91.8	3.8	8.3	4.7
SEN pupils with statements	101.0	86.9	3.7	6.5	3.9
Incidence (%)[3]	93.0	94.6	96.1	78.7	83.3
Placement (%)[7]	34.3	34.4	21.4	40.7	46.0
Pupil referral units[10]					
Total pupils	9.1	8.5	0.7	..	..
SEN pupils with statements[9]	2.0	1.8	0.2	..	..
Incidence (%)[3]	21.4	20.8	28.3	..	..
Placement (%)[7]	0.7	0.7	1.1	..	..
Other schools					
Independent					
Total pupils	618.7	577.3	9.7	30.5	1.2
SEN pupils with statements[9]	7.1	6.8	0.2	-	..
Incidence (%)[3]	1.1	1.2	2.5	0.1	..
Placement (%)[7]	2.4	2.7	1.4	0.2	..
Non-maintained special[10]					
Total pupils	5.8	4.8	..	1.0	..
SEN pupils with statements	4.9	4.6	..	0.3	..
Incidents (%)[3]	84.7	96.6	..	30.7	..
Placement (%)[7]	1.7	1.8	..	2.0	..

1 For Scotland, pupils with a Record of Needs.
2 Provisional. Data for Wales are for 1998/99.
3 Incidence of pupils - the number of pupils with statements within each school type expressed as a proportion of the total number of pupils on roll in each school type.
4 Grant-Aided schools in Northern Ireland.
5 Includes pupils in Voluntary and Private Pre-School Centres in Northern Ireland funded under the Pre-School Expansion Programme which began in 1998/99.
6 Nursery school figures for Scotland include pre-school education centres and are not therefore directly comparable with earlier years.

7 Placement of pupils - the number of pupils with statements within each school type expressed as a proportion of the number of pupils with statements in all schools.
8 Includes nursery classes (except for Scotland, where they are included with Nursery schools) and reception classes in primary schools.
9 UK totals are slight undercounts as data are not available for Wales and not applicable for Northern Ireland.
10 England figures exclude dually registered pupils.
11 Including general and hospital special schools.

Source: Education Departments: 01325 392756

6.5 GCE, GCSE and SCE qualifications obtained at a typical age[1,2], and GCE, GCSE, SCE and GNVQ/GSVQ qualifications obtained by students of all ages

United Kingdom   Percentages and thousands

| | Pupils in their last year of compulsory education[1] | | | | | Pupils/students in education[2] | | | |
| | | | | | | % achieving GCE A Levels and equivalent | | | |
	5 or more grades A*-C[3]	1-4 grades A*-C[3]	Grades D-G[4] only	No graded results	Total (=100%) (Thousands)	2 or more passes[5,6]	1 pass[7]	1 or more passes	Population aged 17 (thousands)
Students at a typical age (percentages and thousands)									
1995/96[8]									
All	45.2	25.9	21.3	7.5	696.4	29.5	8.0	37.5	648.3
Males	40.4	25.4	25.4	8.7	355.7	26.7	7.3	34.0	333.6
Females	50.2	26.4	17.0	6.3	340.7	32.5	8.8	41.3	314.6
1996/97									
All	46.2	25.5	20.9	7.4	713.3	29.6	7.4	37.0	723.5
Males	41.4	25.3	24.9	8.5	363.5	26.5	6.7	33.2	372.4
Females	51.3	25.7	16.7	6.3	349.7	33.0	8.1	41.1	351.0
1997/98									
All	47.5	25.2[8]	21.1[8]	6.5	698.4	33.5	6.5	40.1	751.0
Males	42.3	25.4[8]	24.9[8]	7.5	356.1	29.9	6.0	35.9	384.9
Females	52.8	25.0[8]	17.1[8]	5.3	342.3	37.4	7.2	44.5	366.1
1998/99									
All	49.1	24.8	20.3	5.9	703.6	33.7	6.7	40.3	744.2
Males	43.8	25.2	24.1	6.9	359.6	30.1	6.1	36.2	381.4
Females	54.6	24.3	16.3	4.8	344.0	37.4	7.3	44.7	362.8

| | GCSE and SCE S Grade | | | | GCE A Level and SCE Higher Grade | | |
	5 or more grades A*-C[3,9]	1-4 grades A*-C[3,9]	Grades D-G[4,10] only	No graded results	2 or more passes[5,6]	1 pass[7]	Total 1 or more passes
Students of all ages (thousands)							
1995/96[11]							
All	331.4	371.7	236.5	51.3	204.5	78.2	282.6
Males	151.3	175.3	130.9	25.4	95.2	33.8	129.0
Females	180.1	196.4	105.6	25.9	109.3	44.3	153.6
1996/97[11]							
All	333.6	358.7	240.5	52.5	219.3	76.6	295.9
Males	152.3	169.6	133.5	26.1	101.2	33.2	134.3
Females	181.0	189.1	107.0	26.5	118.1	43.4	161.6
1997/98[11]							
All	335.3	336.4	233.9	47.4	260.4	70.3	330.6
Males	152.8	162.3	129.5	23.3	119.2	30.5	149.7
Females	182.5	174.1	104.5	24.1	141.2	39.8	181.0
1998/99							
All	341.0	323.7	229.8	40.8	257.9	69.9	327.8
Males	162.3	150.6	128.1	20.5	118.4	30.6	149.0
Females	178.7	173.2	101.7	20.3	139.5	39.3	178.8

1 Pupils aged 15 at the start of the academic year, pupils in year S4 in Scotland.

2 Pupils in schools and students in further education institutions aged 16-18 at the start of the academic year in England, Wales and Northern Ireland as a percentage of the 17 year old population. Pupils in Scotland generally sit Highers one year earlier and the figures tend to relate to the results of pupils in year S5/S6 as a percentage of the 16 year old population.

3 Standard Grades 1-3 in Scotland.

4 Grades D-G at GCSE and Scottish Standard Grades 4-7.

5 3 or more SCE Higher Grades in Scotland.

6 Includes Advanced level GNVQ/GSVQ which is equivalent to 2 GCE A Levels or AS equivalents/3 SCE Higher grades.

7 2 AS levels count as 1 A Level pass.

8 Great Britain only.

9 Includes GNVQ/GSVQ Intermediate Part 1, Full and Language unit which are equivalent to 2, 4 and 0.5 GCSE grades A*-C/SCE Standard grades 1-3 respectively. Figures include those with 4.5 GCSEs.

10 Includes GNVQ/GSVQ Foundation Part 1, Full and Language unit which are equivalent to 2, 4 and 0.5 GCSE grades D-G/SCE Standard grades 4-7 respectively.

11 Figures for Scotland have been revised to include students in year S7, which were not included in the 1999 Volume.

Source: Education Departments: 01325 392756

6.6 Students in further[1] education by country, mode of study[2], gender and age,[3] during 1998/99

United Kingdom (home and overseas students)

Thousands

	United Kingdom		England[4]		Wales		Scotland[5]		Northern Ireland	
	Full-time	Part-time	Full-time	Part-time	Full-time	Part-time	Full-time	Part-time	Full-time	Part-time
All										
Age under 16	9.1	56.3	7.2	29.0	0.6	3.2	1.2	21.4	0.1	2.5
16	246.5	83.7	218.7	58.8	13.1	3.9	7.6	15.3	7.2	5.6
17	214.9	94.1	189.8	70.3	10.9	4.6	7.4	14.6	6.9	4.6
18	112.3	100.9	97.1	80.3	5.7	5.0	5.3	12.4	4.2	3.2
19	47.8	84.6	42.2	68.8	2.3	4.4	2.3	9.0	1.1	2.4
20	28.5	68.2	25.6	57.1	1.1	3.4	1.4	6.1	0.4	1.7
21	22.1	64.9	20.2	55.0	0.8	3.2	1.0	5.1	0.2	1.5
22	20.2	67.2	18.6	57.2	0.6	3.4	0.8	5.2	0.1	1.4
23	18.9	68.6	17.6	58.8	0.5	3.3	0.8	5.1	0.1	1.3
24	17.8	70.1	16.6	60.3	0.5	3.4	0.7	5.1	0.1	1.4
25	16.8	72.4	15.8	62.5	0.4	3.5	0.6	5.1	-	1.3
26	16.2	75.2	15.2	65.2	0.4	3.6	0.5	5.2	-	1.3
27	16.0	77.7	15.0	67.3	0.5	3.9	0.5	5.3	-	1.2
28	15.4	76.4	14.5	65.9	0.4	3.9	0.5	5.5	-	1.2
29	14.8	76.4	13.9	65.6	0.4	4.0	0.4	5.5	-	1.3
30+	243.1	1 793.8	231.1	1 539.7	5.7	102.5	6.1	127.8	0.2	23.7
Unknown	4.6	47.6	4.5	44.1	0.1	3.1	-	-	-	0.4
All ages	1 065.0	2 977.9	963.5	2 506.1	43.9	162.4	37.0	253.6	20.6	55.8
Males										
Age under 16	5.3	28.9	4.2	15.7	0.4	1.7	0.8	9.9	0.1	1.6
16	122.3	43.2	107.5	31.7	6.6	2.1	4.5	7.2	3.7	2.3
17	104.7	51.5	92.0	39.2	5.2	2.7	4.0	7.7	3.5	1.9
18	58.5	54.1	50.8	42.6	2.8	2.9	2.7	7.1	2.3	1.4
19	26.4	42.0	23.3	33.5	1.2	2.5	1.3	4.9	0.6	1.1
20	15.5	31.6	13.9	26.3	0.6	1.7	0.8	3.0	0.2	0.6
21	11.6	28.0	10.6	23.8	0.4	1.4	0.5	2.3	0.1	0.5
22	10.3	27.9	9.5	23.9	0.3	1.4	0.5	2.2	0.1	0.4
23	9.8	28.5	9.2	24.5	0.2	1.3	0.4	2.2	-	0.4
24	9.1	29.2	8.5	25.4	0.2	1.4	0.3	2.0	-	0.4
25	8.2	30.0	7.7	26.3	0.2	1.3	0.3	2.0	-	0.4
26	8.0	31.4	7.6	27.6	0.2	1.4	0.2	2.0	-	0.4
27	7.8	32.5	7.4	28.5	0.2	1.4	0.2	2.1	-	0.4
28	7.4	32.0	7.1	28.1	0.1	1.5	0.2	2.1	-	0.4
29	7.1	32.1	6.8	28.0	0.1	1.5	0.2	2.2	-	0.4
30+	116.7	712.8	112.6	616.7	1.8	38.8	2.2	50.6	0.1	6.8
Unknown	2.7	21.4	2.7	19.7	-	1.6	-	-	-	0.1
All ages	531.6	1 257.0	481.3	1 061.5	20.6	66.6	19.0	109.5	10.7	19.4
Females										
Age under 16	3.8	27.4	3.0	13.3	0.3	1.5	0.4	11.5	-	1.0
16	124.2	40.4	111.2	27.2	6.5	1.8	3.0	8.1	3.5	3.3
17	110.2	42.6	97.7	31.2	5.7	1.9	3.4	6.9	3.4	2.6
18	53.7	46.8	46.4	37.7	2.8	2.1	2.6	5.3	2.0	1.8
19	21.4	42.6	18.8	35.3	1.1	1.9	1.0	4.1	0.5	1.3
20	13.0	36.7	11.7	30.8	0.5	1.8	0.6	3.1	0.2	1.1
21	10.5	36.9	9.6	31.2	0.4	1.8	0.5	2.9	0.1	1.0
22	9.8	39.3	9.0	33.4	0.3	2.0	0.4	2.9	0.1	1.0
23	9.1	40.1	8.4	34.3	0.3	2.0	0.4	2.9	-	0.9
24	8.7	40.9	8.1	34.9	0.3	2.1	0.4	3.0	-	1.0
25	8.6	42.3	8.1	36.2	0.2	2.2	0.3	3.1	-	0.9
26	8.2	43.8	7.7	37.6	0.3	2.2	0.3	3.2	-	0.9
27	8.1	45.2	7.6	38.7	0.3	2.4	0.3	3.2	-	0.8
28	8.0	44.4	7.4	37.8	0.3	2.4	0.3	3.4	-	0.9
29	7.7	44.3	7.1	37.6	0.3	2.5	0.3	3.3	-	0.9
30+	126.5	1 080.9	118.5	923.0	3.9	63.7	4.0	77.3	0.1	16.9
Unknown	1.9	26.2	1.9	24.4	-	1.6	-	-	-	0.3
All ages	533.4	1 720.9	482.3	1 444.6	23.3	95.8	18.0	144.1	9.9	36.4

1 Further education figures are whole year counts and differ from the higher education tables which use annual snapshots. Data for Northern Ireland however, are on a snapshot basis.

2 Full-time includes sandwich, and for Scotland, short full-time. Part-time comprises both day and evening, including block release (except Scotland) and open/distance learning.

3 Ages as at 31 August 1998 (1 July in Northern Ireland and 31 December in Scotland).

4 Excludes approximately 241,600 students in FE institutions in England since the information cannot be broken down in this way. External institutions and specialist designated colleges are also excluded.

5 Figures for Scotland further education institutions are enrolments rather than headcounts.

Source: Education Departments: 01325 392756

6.7 Students in further education[1] by country, mode of study[2], gender and subject group, during 1998/99

United Kingdom - Home and overseas students

Thousands

	United Kingdom		England[3]		Wales		Scotland[4]		Northern Ireland	
	Full-time	Part-time	Full-time	Part-time	Full-time	Part-time	Full-time	Part-time	Full-time	Part-time
All persons										
Subject group										
Medicine & Dentistry	-	-	-	-			-	-	-	-
Allied Medicine	105.9	161.3	101.2	145.7	-	-	3.3	13.9	1.5	1.7
Biological Sciences	1.0	1.4	0.9	0.5	-	-	0.1	0.9	-	-
Agriculture	36.1	150.6	35.0	144.7	-	-	1.0	5.3	0.1	0.6
Physical Sciences	14.7	10.5	14.0	5.4	-	-	0.7	5.0	-	0.1
Mathematical Science[5]	129.0	288.4	127.7	277.3	-	-	0.1	3.0	1.3	8.1
Engineering & Technology	50.3	113.0	43.6	91.4	-	-	4.8	17.9	2.0	3.6
Architecture	26.7	49.5	21.2	40.2	-	-	3.0	8.0	2.5	1.3
Social Sciences	15.7	62.0	11.2	46.8	-	-	3.8	12.3	0.7	2.9
Business & Financial	105.5	295.2	90.4	221.8	-	-	9.8	60.6	5.3	12.7
Documentation[5]	11.6	64.4	7.5	12.3	-	-	3.6	51.8	0.4	0.4
Languages	21.9	83.8	21.5	68.8	-	0.1	0.4	13.3	-	1.6
Humanities	6.8	9.4	6.4	7.2	-	-	0.4	2.2	-	-
Creative arts	67.9	65.9	63.3	54.8	0.1	-	2.4	7.8	2.2	3.3
Education[6]	17.1	48.2	15.5	26.8	-	0.4	1.0	18.4	0.6	2.4
Combined, gen	151.9	210.1	144.9	154.3	0.2	5.5	2.6	33.3	4.2	17.0
Unknown	302.8	1 364.3	259.3	1 208.0	43.5	156.3	-	-	-	-
All subjects	1 065.0	2 977.9	963.5	2 506.1	43.9	162.4	37.0	253.6	20.6	55.8
Males										
Subject group										
Medicine and Dentistry	-	-	-	-		-	-	-	-	-
Allied Medicine	33.8	61.4	33.6	57.2	-	-	0.2	4.0	0.1	0.2
Biological Sciences	0.3	0.4	0.3	0.2	-	-	-	0.2	-	-
Agriculture	16.1	55.6	15.4	51.9	-	-	0.7	3.4	-	0.3
Physical Sciences	10.2	6.0	9.9	3.4	-	-	0.3	2.5	-	0.1
Mathematical Science[5]	60.3	106.6	59.2	102.5	-	-	0.1	1.4	1.0	2.7
Engineering & Technology	47.0	103.4	40.5	85.1	-	-	4.6	14.9	1.9	3.4
Architecture	25.4	45.0	20.1	37.7	-	-	2.8	6.0	2.5	1.3
Social Sciences	1.9	9.0	1.4	6.2	-	-	0.5	2.5	-	0.3
Business & Financial	46.9	110.4	40.6	83.7	-	-	4.4	23.8	1.8	2.8
Documentation[5]	6.4	24.8	3.8	4.8	-	-	2.4	19.9	0.2	0.1
Languages	8.9	29.8	8.7	24.5	-	-	0.2	4.7	-	0.6
Humanities	3.2	3.9	3.0	3.2	-	-	0.1	0.7	-	-
Creative arts	25.3	12.5	23.4	9.9	-	-	1.1	2.1	0.8	0.5
Education[6]	10.0	18.0	9.4	9.8	-	0.1	0.3	7.3	0.4	0.8
Combined, gen	73.1	84.7	69.7	60.5	0.1	2.0	1.3	15.9	2.0	6.4
Unknown	162.8	585.3	142.3	520.9	20.4	64.4	-	-	-	-
All subjects	531.6	1 257.0	481.3	1 061.5	20.6	66.6	19.0	109.5	10.7	19.4
Females										
Subject group										
Medicine & Dentistry	-	-	-	-		-	-	-	-	-
Allied Medicine	72.1	99.9	67.6	88.5	-	-	3.1	9.9	1.4	1.5
Biological Sciences	0.6	0.9	0.6	0.3	-	-	0.1	0.6	-	-
Agriculture	20.1	95.0	19.6	92.8	-	-	0.4	1.9	0.1	0.3
Physical Sciences	4.5	4.5	4.2	2.0	-	-	0.3	2.5	-	-
Mathematical Science[5]	68.8	181.8	68.5	174.8	-	-	-	1.6	0.2	5.4
Engineering & Technology	3.3	9.5	3.1	6.3	-	-	0.2	3.0	-	0.3
Architecture	1.3	4.5	1.1	2.5	-	-	0.2	1.9	-	0.1
Social Sciences	13.8	53.0	9.8	40.6	-	-	3.3	9.8	0.7	2.6
Business & Financial	58.6	184.8	49.8	138.1	-	-	5.4	36.8	3.4	9.9
Documentation[5]	5.1	39.6	3.8	7.5	-	-	1.2	31.8	0.2	0.3
Languages	13.0	54.0	12.7	44.4	-	-	0.2	8.6	-	1.0
Humanities	3.6	5.5	3.4	4.0	-	-	0.2	1.5	-	-
Creative arts	42.6	53.4	39.8	44.9	-	-	1.3	5.7	1.4	2.8
Education[6]	7.1	30.1	6.2	17.1	-	0.3	0.7	11.1	0.2	1.6
Combined, gen	78.7	125.4	75.2	93.8	0.1	3.6	1.3	17.4	2.2	10.6
Unknown[6]	140.0	779.0	116.9	687.1	23.1	91.9	-	-	-	-
All subjects	533.4	1 720.9	482.3	1 444.6	23.3	95.8	18.0	144.1	9.9	36.4

1 Further education figures are whole year counts and differ from the higher education tables which use annual snapshots. Data for Northern Ireland however, are on a snapshot basis.

2 Full-time excludes sandwich, and for Scotland, short full-time. Part-time comprises both day and evening, including block release (except Scotland) and open/distance learning.

3 Excludes approximately 241,600 students in further education institutions in England since the information cannot be broken down in this way. External institutions and specialist designated colleges are also excluded.

4 Figures for Scotland further education institutions are enrolments rather than headcounts.

5 Computing Sciences figures for further education institutions in Scotland are included with Documention.

6 Includes ITT and INSET.

Source: Education Departments: 01325 392756

6.8 Students in higher[1] education by level, mode of study[2], gender and age[3], 1999/00[4,5]
United Kingdom (home and overseas students)

Thousands

	Postgraduate level						First degree		Other undergraduate		Total higher education	
	PHD's and equivalent		Masters and others		Total postgraduate							
	Full-time	Part-time	Full-time	Part-time	Full-time	Part-time	Full-time	Part-time	Full-time	Part-time	Full-time	Part-time
All												
Age under 16	-	-	-	-	-	-	-	-	-	0.2	0.1	0.2
16	-	-	-	-	-	-	0.4	-	0.7	0.5	1.1	0.6
17	-	-	-	-	-	-	10.2	-	4.2	1.1	14.4	1.1
18	-	-	-	-	-	-	145.9	0.7	22.6	6.4	168.6	7.1
19	-	-	0.1	0.1	0.1	0.1	202.7	2.2	30.5	10.1	233.3	12.4
20	-	-	1.0	0.2	1.1	0.2	205.9	3.7	25.3	10.5	232.3	14.5
21	0.8	-	12.5	1.1	13.3	1.1	130.7	4.3	17.0	9.8	161.0	15.2
22	2.7	0.1	16.5	3.4	19.2	3.5	60.6	4.3	12.3	10.0	92.0	17.8
23	4.0	0.3	14.8	5.2	18.8	5.4	31.4	3.9	9.1	10.8	59.4	20.2
24	4.5	1.3	11.4	6.4	15.9	7.7	19.0	3.6	6.9	11.6	41.7	22.9
25	3.6	2.2	8.9	7.0	12.4	9.2	13.6	3.6	5.4	12.1	31.4	24.9
26	3.1	2.4	7.1	7.7	10.2	10.1	10.9	3.5	4.6	12.6	25.6	26.2
27	2.6	2.2	5.9	8.3	8.5	10.5	9.3	3.4	4.1	13.4	21.9	27.3
28	2.1	2.0	5.0	8.5	7.1	10.5	8.2	3.6	3.6	13.4	18.9	27.4
29	1.7	1.9	4.0	8.4	5.8	10.3	6.9	3.3	3.3	13.2	16.0	26.7
30+	11.7	24.9	28.6	147.7	40.3	172.6	63.8	54.5	36.5	282.7	140.6	509.8
Unknown	-	0.1	0.3	2.2	0.3	2.3	0.7	0.4	0.4	7.5	1.4	10.2
All ages	36.9	37.4	116.3	206.3	153.1	243.6	920.1	95.1	186.4	425.7	1 259.7	764.4
Males												
Age under 16	-	-	-	-	-	-	-	-	-	0.1	-	0.1
16	-	-	-	-	-	-	0.2	-	0.3	0.3	0.5	0.3
17	-	-	-	-	-	-	4.5	-	1.8	0.6	6.3	0.6
18	-	-	-	-	-	-	66.6	0.4	10.6	3.9	77.2	4.3
19	-	-	-	-	-	-	94.4	1.3	14.2	6.3	108.7	7.7
20	-	-	0.4	0.1	0.5	0.1	96.6	2.2	11.4	6.1	108.5	8.4
21	0.4	-	5.1	0.4	5.6	0.4	64.3	2.4	7.2	5.1	77.1	7.9
22	1.6	-	7.4	1.4	9.0	1.4	32.1	2.4	5.2	4.7	46.3	8.6
23	2.4	0.1	6.9	2.1	9.3	2.2	17.1	2.0	3.9	4.7	30.2	8.9
24	2.6	0.8	5.4	2.7	8.0	3.4	10.2	1.7	2.9	4.8	21.1	9.9
25	2.1	1.3	4.3	2.9	6.3	4.2	7.1	1.6	2.3	5.1	15.7	11.0
26	1.7	1.4	3.6	3.4	5.3	4.8	5.6	1.5	1.9	5.3	12.8	11.6
27	1.5	1.3	3.1	3.6	4.5	4.9	4.7	1.5	1.7	5.7	10.9	12.1
28	1.3	1.2	2.7	4.0	3.9	5.1	4.0	1.5	1.4	5.8	9.3	12.4
29	1.0	1.1	2.2	4.0	3.2	5.1	3.3	1.4	1.3	5.9	7.8	12.4
30+	7.2	14.8	15.1	73.9	22.3	88.7	24.2	18.3	11.4	114.1	57.9	221.1
Unknown	-	-	0.2	0.8	0.2	0.8	0.4	0.2	0.2	2.8	0.7	3.7
All ages	21.8	22.1	56.5	99.3	78.3	121.4	435.1	38.6	77.7	181.2	591.1	341.2
Females												
Age under 16	-	-	-	-	-	-	-	-	-	0.1	-	0.1
16	-	-	-	-	-	-	0.2	-	0.4	0.3	0.6	0.3
17	-	-	-	-	-	-	5.7	-	2.4	0.5	8.1	0.5
18	-	-	-	-	-	-	79.4	0.3	12.0	2.5	91.4	2.7
19	-	-	-	-	-	-	108.3	0.9	16.3	3.7	124.6	4.7
20	-	-	0.6	0.1	0.6	0.1	109.3	1.5	13.8	4.4	123.7	6.0
21	0.4	-	7.4	0.7	7.7	0.7	66.4	1.8	9.7	4.7	83.9	7.3
22	1.1	-	9.1	2.0	10.2	2.1	28.4	1.9	7.0	5.3	45.7	9.3
23	1.7	0.1	7.8	3.1	9.5	3.2	14.4	1.9	5.3	6.1	29.1	11.2
24	1.9	0.5	6.0	3.8	7.9	4.3	8.8	1.9	3.9	6.8	20.6	13.0
25	1.5	0.9	4.6	4.1	6.1	4.9	6.5	2.0	3.2	7.0	15.8	13.9
26	1.3	1.0	3.5	4.3	4.9	5.3	5.3	2.0	2.7	7.3	12.9	14.6
27	1.1	0.9	2.9	4.7	4.0	5.6	4.6	2.0	2.4	7.7	11.0	15.2
28	0.9	0.9	2.3	4.5	3.2	5.3	4.2	2.1	2.2	7.6	9.6	15.0
29	0.7	0.8	1.8	4.4	2.6	5.1	3.6	1.9	2.1	7.3	8.2	14.3
30+	4.5	10.1	13.6	73.8	18.1	84.0	39.6	36.2	25.0	168.6	82.7	288.7
Unknown	-	-	0.1	1.5	0.1	1.5	0.3	0.3	0.3	4.7	0.7	6.5
All ages	15.0	15.3	59.8	106.9	74.9	122.2	485.0	56.5	108.7	244.5	668.6	423.2

1 Includes Open University students. Part-time figures include dormant modes, those writing up at home and on sabbaticals, which are not included in HESA SFR 38.

2 Full-time includes sandwich, and for Scotland, short full-time. Part-time comprises both day and evening, including block release (except Scotland) and open/distance learning.

3 Ages as at 31 August 1999 (1 July in Northern Ireland and 31 December in Scotland).

4 Figures are for students on courses at a particular point during the year. Therefore students starting courses after this date will not be counted.

5 Provisional. Figures for higher education students in further education institutions (except Northern Ireland) relate to 1998/99.

Source: Education Departments: 01325 392756

Education

6.9 Students in higher[1] education by type of course, mode of study[2], gender and subject group, 1999/00[3,4]

United Kingdom - Home and overseas students

Thousands

Subject group	Postgraduate level — PHD's & eqivalent Full-time	PHD's & eqivalent Part-time	Masters and others Full-time	Masters and others Part-time	Total postgraduate Full-time	Total postgraduate Part-time	First degree Full-time	First degree Part-time	Other undergraduate Full-time	Other undergraduate Part-time	Total higher education students Full-time	Total higher education students Part-time
All persons												
Subject group												
Medicine & Dentistry	2.3	3.3	2.9	5.2	5.2	8.4	29.5	0.1	0.1	-	34.8	8.6
Allied Medicine	1.6	1.7	2.8	14.5	4.4	16.2	50.2	22.5	53.3	43.0	108.0	81.7
Biological Sciences	5.8	4.0	4.0	4.9	9.8	8.9	64.2	3.0	2.5	1.7	76.5	13.6
Agriculture	0.9	0.6	1.2	0.9	2.2	1.5	10.4	0.3	4.7	2.1	17.3	3.9
Physical Sciences	6.0	3.4	4.5	3.0	10.5	6.4	47.5	2.1	1.8	2.8	59.8	11.3
Mathematical Science[5]	2.3	1.8	9.3	7.5	11.5	9.3	66.6	4.9	13.6	16.2	91.7	30.4
Engineering & Technology	5.5	4.4	9.0	8.5	14.5	12.9	74.4	7.1	12.6	26.9	101.5	46.8
Architecture	0.5	0.5	3.8	4.9	4.3	5.5	20.6	5.4	4.1	9.4	29.0	20.3
Social Sciences	3.9	4.6	20.3	21.7	24.2	26.3	109.6	11.3	11.2	22.4	145.0	60.0
Business & Financial	1.4	2.1	17.2	45.2	18.6	47.3	106.1	11.6	37.6	78.7	162.3	137.6
Documentation[5]	0.2	0.3	2.5	2.8	2.6	3.1	15.5	0.7	7.2	7.9	25.3	11.7
Languages	2.3	2.5	4.2	4.2	6.5	6.7	57.3	3.5	3.8	13.7	67.6	23.9
Humanities	2.3	2.9	3.6	5.5	5.9	8.4	31.6	2.4	0.7	8.4	38.2	19.3
Creative arts	0.5	0.9	5.3	3.6	5.8	4.5	76.4	3.1	12.4	5.8	94.6	13.4
Education[6]	0.8	3.6	23.5	42.7	24.3	46.2	48.2	4.2	3.9	15.6	76.4	66.1
Combined, gen	0.6	0.8	2.1	30.4	2.7	31.2	104.2	10.0	11.9	153.1	118.8	194.2
Unknown	-	-	0.1	0.8	0.1	0.8	7.8	2.9	5.1	18.0	13.0	21.7
All subjects	36.9	37.4	116.3	206.3	153.1	243.6	920.1	95.1	186.4	425.7	1 259.7	764.4
Males												
Subject group												
Medicine and Dentistry	1.0	1.8	1.3	2.6	2.3	4.4	13.6	0.1	-		16.0	4.5
Allied Medicine	0.7	0.7	0.9	4.0	1.6	4.7	12.1	2.5	7.9	4.1	21.6	11.3
Biological Sciences	2.5	1.9	1.6	1.7	4.1	3.5	24.4	1.2	1.3	0.6	29.7	5.3
Agriculture	0.5	0.4	0.6	0.4	1.1	0.8	4.1	0.1	2.4	1.2	7.7	2.1
Physical Sciences	4.1	2.4	2.7	1.8	6.8	4.2	29.5	1.2	1.0	1.6	37.3	7.1
Mathematical Science[5]	1.8	1.4	6.5	5.2	8.3	6.6	50.8	3.7	10.0	10.0	69.1	20.3
Engineering & Technology	4.5	3.7	7.2	7.4	11.7	11.1	62.9	6.6	11.1	24.9	85.7	42.6
Architecture	0.3	0.4	2.4	3.2	2.7	3.6	15.0	4.4	3.3	8.0	21.0	16.0
Social Sciences	2.1	2.6	9.0	9.5	11.1	12.0	43.9	4.7	2.7	5.1	57.7	21.9
Business & Financial	0.9	1.4	9.8	25.4	10.7	26.7	50.6	5.0	16.2	32.2	77.5	63.8
Documentation[5]	0.1	0.1	0.9	1.0	0.9	1.1	5.9	0.2	4.6	4.3	11.4	5.7
Languages	1.0	1.1	1.4	1.4	2.4	2.5	15.9	1.1	1.2	5.1	19.5	8.7
Humanities	1.4	1.7	1.7	2.7	3.1	4.4	14.6	1.0	0.3	2.9	18.0	8.3
Creative arts	0.3	0.5	2.2	1.6	2.5	2.0	31.1	1.0	6.3	2.1	39.9	5.2
Education[6]	0.3	1.7	7.2	12.7	7.5	14.4	12.7	1.0	2.0	4.5	22.2	19.8
Combined, gen	0.3	0.5	1.1	18.4	1.4	18.9	44.5	3.6	4.8	66.3	50.7	88.8
Unknown	-	-	-	0.3	-	0.3	3.5	1.2	2.5	8.2	6.1	9.8
All subjects	21.8	22.1	56.5	99.3	78.3	121.4	435.1	38.6	77.7	181.2	591.1	341.2
Females												
Subject group												
Medicine & Dentistry	1.3	1.5	1.6	2.6	2.9	4.0	15.8	-	0.1	-	18.8	4.1
Allied Medicine	0.9	1.0	1.9	10.5	2.8	11.5	38.2	19.9	45.4	38.9	86.4	70.4
Biological Sciences	3.3	2.1	2.4	3.2	5.7	5.3	39.8	1.9	1.2	1.0	46.7	8.2
Agriculture	0.4	0.2	0.6	0.5	1.0	0.7	6.3	0.2	2.3	0.9	9.6	1.7
Physical Sciences	1.9	1.0	1.8	1.2	3.7	2.2	18.1	0.9	0.7	1.2	22.5	4.3
Mathematical Science[5]	0.5	0.4	2.7	2.3	3.2	2.7	15.8	1.2	3.6	6.2	22.6	10.1
Engineering & Technology	1.1	0.7	1.8	1.1	2.8	1.8	11.5	0.5	1.5	2.0	15.8	4.2
Architecture	0.2	0.2	1.5	1.7	1.6	1.9	5.6	1.0	0.8	1.4	8.0	4.3
Social Sciences	1.8	2.0	11.3	12.2	13.1	14.3	65.7	6.6	8.5	17.2	87.3	38.1
Business & Financial	0.5	0.7	7.4	19.9	7.8	20.6	55.5	6.7	21.4	46.6	84.7	73.8
Documentation[5]	0.1	0.1	1.6	1.9	1.7	2.0	9.6	0.5	2.6	3.5	13.9	6.0
Languages	1.3	1.4	2.8	2.8	4.1	4.2	41.4	2.4	2.6	8.6	48.1	15.2
Humanities	0.9	1.2	1.9	2.8	2.8	4.0	17.0	1.5	0.4	5.5	20.2	11.0
Creative arts	0.3	0.4	3.1	2.1	3.4	2.5	45.3	2.1	6.1	3.7	54.7	8.3
Education[6]	0.5	1.9	16.3	29.9	16.8	31.9	35.5	3.2	1.9	11.2	54.2	46.2
Combined, gen	0.3	0.3	1.0	11.9	1.3	12.3	59.6	6.4	7.1	86.8	68.0	105.5
Unknown	-	-	0.1	0.5	0.1	0.5	4.3	1.7	2.6	9.8	6.9	11.9
All subjects	15.0	15.3	59.8	106.9	74.9	122.2	485.0	56.5	108.7	244.5	668.6	423.2

1 Higher education institutions include Open University students. Part-time figures include dormant modes, those writing up at home and on sabbaticals, which are not included in HESA SFR38.

2 Full-time includes sandwich, and for Scotland, short full-time. Part-time comprises both day and evening, including block release (except Scotland) and open/distance learning.

3 Provisional. Figures for higher education students in further education institutions (except for Northern Ireland) relate to 1998/99.

4 Figures for students (other than Scotland FE institutions) are snapshots counted at a particular point in the year (December for UK HE institutions and FE institutions in Wales, November for FE institutions in England and Northern Ireland). Students starting courses after these dates will not therefore be counted. Figures for Scotland are whole year enrolments (rather than headcounts) for 1998/99.

5 Computing Sciences figures for FE institutions in Scotland are included with Documentation.

6 Including ITT and INSET.

Source: Education Departments: 01325 392756

6.10 Students[1] obtaining higher education qualifications[2,3] by type of course, gender and subject group, 1998/99

United Kingdom

Thousands

| | Sub-degree[4] | First degree | Postgraduate | | | Total higher education |
			PHD's and equivalent	Other	Total	
All persons						
Subject group						
Medicine & Dentistry	-	5.8	0.9	1.9	2.8	8.7
Allied Medicine	19.3	17.6	0.5	4.5	5.1	41.9
Biological Sciences	1.3	17.4	1.7	2.5	4.2	22.8
Agriculture	1.3	2.9	0.3	0.8	1.1	5.3
Physical Sciences	1.0	13.1	1.9	2.4	4.3	18.4
Mathematical Science	4.9	14.6	0.7	4.5	5.2	24.7
Engineering & Technology	4.2	22.0	1.8	6.7	8.5	34.7
Architecture	1.6	7.2	0.1	3.4	3.5	12.4
Social Sciences	6.0	31.6	1.0	15.3	16.4	54.0
Business & Financial	11.0	30.9	0.4	20.0	20.4	62.4
Documentation	0.3	3.8	-	2.1	2.1	6.2
Languages	1.1	16.0	0.6	2.6	3.2	20.3
Humanities	0.8	10.4	0.6	2.5	3.1	14.3
Creative arts	2.9	20.3	0.1	3.3	3.4	26.6
Education[5]	3.9	13.5	0.4	26.3	26.7	44.1
Combined, gen	8.0	36.6	0.2	5.3	5.5	50.1
All subjects	67.7	263.7	11.3	104.3	115.6	446.9
Males						
Subject group						
Medicine and Dentistry	-	2.8	0.4	1.0	1.4	4.2
Allied Medicine	2.0	3.7	0.3	1.1	1.4	7.0
Biological Sciences	0.6	6.5	0.8	0.9	1.8	8.9
Agriculture	0.7	1.3	0.2	0.4	0.6	2.6
Physical Sciences	0.7	7.9	1.3	1.4	2.8	11.4
Mathematical Science	3.5	10.8	0.5	3.2	3.8	18.0
Engineering & Technology	3.8	18.8	1.5	5.5	7.0	29.5
Architecture	1.2	5.5	0.1	2.2	2.3	9.1
Social Sciences	1.9	12.9	0.6	6.8	7.5	22.2
Business & Financial	4.7	14.5	0.3	11.4	11.7	30.9
Documentation	0.1	1.4	-	0.7	0.8	2.3
Languages	0.4	4.4	0.3	0.9	1.2	5.9
Humanities	0.3	4.6	0.4	1.2	1.6	6.5
Creative arts	1.4	8.2	0.1	1.4	1.5	11.1
Education[5]	1.2	3.1	0.2	7.9	8.1	12.3
Combined, gen	3.2	15.3	0.1	3.3	3.4	21.9
All subjects	25.6	121.7	7.2	49.4	56.6	203.9
Females						
Subject group						
Medicine & Dentistry	-	3.0	0.5	1.0	1.4	4.4
Allied Medicine	17.3	13.9	0.3	3.4	3.7	34.9
Biological Sciences	0.6	10.8	0.9	1.6	2.4	13.9
Agriculture	0.6	1.6	0.1	0.4	0.5	2.6
Physical Sciences	0.4	5.1	0.6	1.0	1.6	7.0
Mathematical Science	1.4	3.9	0.1	1.3	1.4	6.7
Engineering & Technology	0.4	3.3	0.3	1.2	1.5	5.2
Architecture	0.4	1.7	-	1.2	1.2	3.3
Social Sciences	4.2	18.6	0.4	8.5	8.9	31.7
Business & Financial	6.4	16.4	0.1	8.6	8.7	31.5
Documentation	0.2	2.4	-	1.3	1.4	3.9
Languages	0.8	11.6	0.3	1.7	2.0	14.3
Humanities	0.5	5.8	0.2	1.3	1.5	7.8
Creative arts	1.5	12.1	-	1.9	1.9	15.5
Education[5]	2.7	10.5	0.2	18.4	18.6	31.8
Combined, gen	4.8	21.4	-	2.1	2.1	28.3
All subjects	42.0	142.0	4.2	54.8	59.0	243.0

1 Includes students on Open University courses.
2 Excludes qualifications from the private sector.
3 Includes higher education in higher education institutions in the UK only. Higher education qualifications in further education institutions (approximately 6% of the total number of students) are excluded.
4 Excludes students who successfully completed courses for which formal qualifications are not awarded.
5 Including ITT and INSET.

Source: Education Departments: 01325 392756

6.11 Qualified teachers: by type of school and gender

Thousands

	Public sector mainstream schools		Non-maintained mainstream schools	All special schools	Total
	Nursery and primary	Secondary[2]			
All full-time teachers					
Great Britain					
1990/91	200.3	223.2	44.9	18.2	486.6
1995/96	203.3	212.2	48.6	16.6	480.6
1996/97	202.7	211.3	48.2	16.4	478.6
1997/98[1]	201.1	209.6	49.1	16.0	476.0
United Kingdom					
1998/99	210.5	223.0	50.5	16.7	500.6
of which:					
England and Wales	181.1	190.6	47.9	14.0	433.4
Scotland	21.3	22.2	2.5	2.0	48.0
Northern Ireland	8.1	10.2	0.1	0.7	19.2
Full-time male teachers					
Great Britain					
1990/91	35.8	116.0	20.6	5.8	178.2
1995/96	33.8	103.4	21.1	5.3	163.5
1996/97	33.0	101.6	20.6	5.2	160.4
1997/98[1]	31.9	99.3	20.1	5.0	156.4
United Kingdom					
1998/99	32.9	103.9	20.8	5.1	162.8
of which:					
England and Wales	29.9	88.8	19.7	4.5	142.9
Scotland	1.5	10.9	1.1	0.4	13.9
Northern Ireland	1.5	4.3	-	0.1	5.9
Full-time female teachers					
Great Britain					
1990/91	164.5	107.1	24.3	12.4	308.4
1995/96	169.5	108.8	27.4	11.3	317.0
1996/97	169.7	109.7	27.6	11.2	318.2
1997/98[1]	169.2	110.3	28.5	11.0	319.0
United Kingdom					
1998/99	177.6	119.1	29.6	11.6	337.8
of which:					
England and Wales	151.2	101.8	28.1	9.4	290.6
Scotland	19.8	11.3	1.4	1.6	34.1
Northern Ireland	6.6	5.9	0.1	0.6	13.2
All part-time teachers[3]					
Great Britain					
1990/91	..	..	..	..	30.0
1995/96	18.7	17.6	8.9	1.5	46.7
1996/97	17.8	15.7	9.4	1.4	44.3
1997/98	18.0	16.2	10.7	1.4	46.4
United Kingdom					
1998/99	19.7	16.8	9.9	1.5	48.0

1 Includes revised data for England and Wales.
2 From 1993/94 excludes sixth form colleges in England and Wales which were reclassified as further education colleges on 1 April 1993.
3 Full-time equivalents of part-time teachers.

Source: Education Departments: 01325 392756

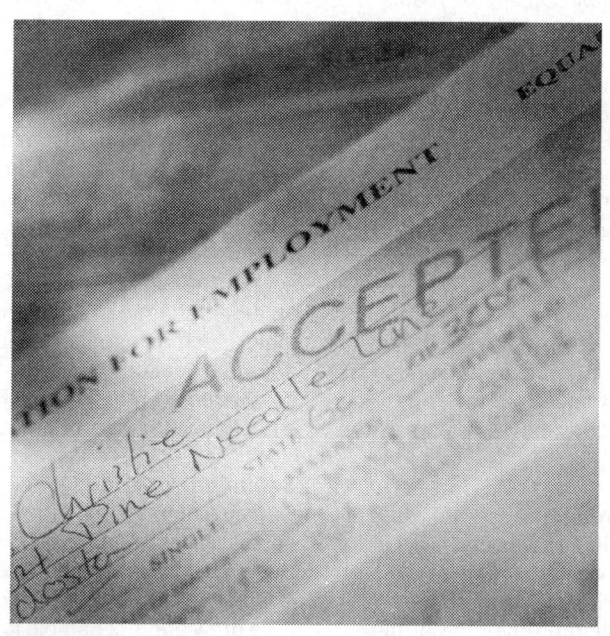

7 Labour market

Labour market

Labour Force Survey *(Tables 7.1 to 7.3, 7.6, 7.9, 7.10, 7.12 and 7.15 to 7.17)*

Background

The LFS is the largest regular household survey in the United Kingdom. LFS interviews are conducted continuously throughout the year. In any 3 month period, a nationally representative sample of approximately 120,000 people aged 16 or over in around 61,000 households are interviewed. Each household is interviewed five times, at 3 monthly intervals. The initial interview is done face-to-face by an interviewer visiting the address. The other interviews are done by telephone wherever possible. The survey asks a series of questions about respondents' personal circumstances and their labour market activity. Most questions refer to activity in the week before the interview.

The concepts and definitions used in the LFS are agreed by the International Labour Organisation (ILO) - an agency of the United Nations. The definitions are used by European Union member countries and members of the Organisation for Economic Co-operation and Development (OECD).

The Labour Force Survey was carried out every two years from 1973 to 1983. The ILO definition was first used in 1984. This was also the first year in which the survey was conducted on an annual basis with results available for every spring quarter (representing an average of the period from March to May). The survey moved to a continuous basis in spring 1992 in Great Britain and in winter 1994/5 in Northern Ireland, with average quarterly results published 4 times a year for seasonal quarters: spring (March to May), summer (June to August), autumn (September to November) and winter (December to February). From April 1998, results are published 12 times a year for the average of 3 consecutive months.

The LFS collects information on a sample of the population. To convert this information to give estimates for the population the data must be grossed. This is achieved by calculating weighting factors (often referred to simply as weights) which can be applied to each sampled individual in such a way that the weighted-up results match estimates or projections of the total population in terms of age distribution, sex, and region of residence. Estimates in the previous edition of this volume were derived using grossing control totals based on 1992-based population projections. These projections became progressively out of step with population estimates and have been superseded by figures which are more accurate and which relate to latest geographies. Therefore, all LFS data for autumn 1993 onwards have been regrossed using the best available population figures for any given period. See LFS User Guide volume 10 - Regrossing of LFS Data and 'LFS: regrossing and seasonal adjustment' in *Labour Market Trends*, May 2000. Whilst regrossing LFS data to the most up-to-date population estimates has resulted in an improvement in accuracy it has inevitably led to changes between the old and new series. These differences are in the absolute totals of the old and new series rather than in rates.

Strengths and limitations of the LFS

The LFS produces coherent labour market information on the basis of internationally standard concepts and definitions. It is a rich source of data on a wide variety of labour market and personal characteristics. It is the most suitable source for making comparisons between countries. The LFS is designed so that households interviewed in each three month period constitute a representative sample of UK households. The survey covers those living in private households and nurses in National Health Service accommodation. Students living in halls of residence have been included since 1992 as information about them is collected at their parents' address.

However the LFS has its limitations. It is a sample survey and is therefore subject to sampling variability. The survey does not include people living in institutions such as hostels or residential homes. 'Proxy' reporting (when members of the household are not present at the interview, another member of the household answers the questions on their behalf) can affect the quality of information on topics such as earnings, hours worked, benefit receipt and qualifications. Around one third of interviews are conducted 'by proxy', usually by a spouse or partner but sometimes by a parent or other near relation.

Sampling Variability

Survey estimates are prone to *sampling variability*. The easiest way to explain this concept is by example. In the September to November 1997 period, ILO unemployment in Great Britain (seasonally adjusted) stood at 1,847,000. If we drew another sample for the same period we could get a different result, perhaps 1,900,000 or 1,820,000.

In theory, we could draw many samples, and each would give a different result. This is because each sample would be made up of different people who would give different answers to the questions. The spread of these results is the sampling variability. Sampling variability is determined by a number of factors including the sample size, the variability of the population from which the sample is drawn and the sample design. Once we know the sampling variability we can calculate a range of values about the sample estimate that represents the expected variation with a given level of assurance. This is called a confidence interval. For a 95% confidence interval we expect that in 95% of the samples (19 times out of 20) the confidence interval will contain the true value that would be obtained by surveying the entire population. For the example given above, we can be 95% confident that the true value was in the range 1,791,000 to 1,903,000.

Unreliable estimates

Very small estimates have relatively wide confidence intervals making them unreliable. For this reason, the ONS does not publish LFS estimates below 10,000.

Non-Response

Non-response can introduce bias to a survey, particularly if the people not responding have characteristics that are different from those who do respond. The LFS has a response rate of around 80 per cent to the first interview, and over 90 per cent of those who are interviewed once go on to complete all five interviews. These are relatively high levels for a household survey. Any bias from non-response is minimised by *weighting* the results.

Weighting (or grossing) converts sample data to represent the full population. In the LFS, the data are weighted separately by age, sex and area of residence to population estimates based on the Census. Weighting also adjusts for people not in the survey and thus minimises non-response bias.

Labour Force Survey Concepts and Definitions

Discouraged workers - a sub-group of the economically inactive population, defined as those neither in employment nor unemployed (on the ILO measure) who said they would like a job and whose main reason for not seeking work was because they believed there were no jobs available.

Economically active - people aged 16 and over who are either in employment or ILO unemployed.

Economic activity rate - the percentage of people aged 16 and over who are economically active.

Economically inactive - people who are neither in employment nor unemployed. This group includes, for example, all those who were looking after a home or retired.

Employment - people aged 16 or over who did at least one hour of paid work in the reference week (whether as an employee or self-employed); those who had a job that they were temporarily away from (on holiday, for example); those on Government-supported training and employment programmes (from spring 1983); and those doing unpaid family work (from spring 1992).

Employees - the division between employees and self-employed is based on survey respondents' own assessment of their employment status.

Full Time - the classification of employees, self-employed and unpaid family workers in their main job as full-time or part-time is on the basis of self-assessment. Up until autumn 1995, people who were on government work-related training programmes are classified as full-time or part-time according to whether their usual hours of work per week were over 30 or 30 and under; from winter 1995/96 onwards, the full-time/part-time classification for this group has been changed to self-assessment, in line with the other groups outlined above. People on Government-supported training and employment programmes who are at college in the survey reference week are classified, by convention, as part-time.

Government-supported training and employment programmes - comprise all people aged 16 and over participating in one of the Government's employment and training programmes (Youth Training, Training for Work and Community Action), together with those on similar programmes administered by Training and Enterprise Councils in England and Wales, or Local Enterprise Companies in Scotland.

Hours worked - respondents to the LFS are asked a series of questions enabling the identification of both their usual hours and their actual hours. Total hours include overtime (paid and unpaid) and exclude lunchbreaks.

ILO unemployment - the International Labour Office (ILO) measure of unemployment used throughout this supplement refers to people without a job who were available to start work in the two weeks following their LFS interview and who had either looked for work in the four weeks prior to interview or were waiting to start a job they had already obtained. This definition of unemployment is in accordance with that adopted by the 13th International Conference of Labour Statisticians, further clarified at the 14th ICLS, and promulgated by the ILO in its publications.

ILO unemployment (rate) - the percentage of economically active people who are unemployed on the ILO measure.

ILO unemployment (duration) - defined as the shorter of the following two periods: (a) duration of active search for work; and (b) length of time since employment.

Part Time - see full-time

Second jobs - jobs which LFS respondents hold in addition to a main full-time or part-time job.

Self-employment - See Employees

Temporary employees - in the LFS these are defined as those employees who say that their main job is non permanent in one of the following ways: fixed period contract; agency temping; casual work; seasonal work; other temporary work.

Unpaid Family Workers - the separate identification from spring 1992 of this group in the LFS is in accordance with international recommendations. The group comprises persons doing unpaid work for a business they own or for a business that a relative owns.

Persons employed in local authorities
(Table 7.8)
The full-time equivalents for local authorities are derived by applying factors to the numbers of part-time workers in three groups based on average hours worked in each group nationally.

Jobseekers allowance claimant count
(Tables 7.13 and 7.14)
This is a count of all those people who are claiming unemployment-related benefits at Employment Service local offices and who have declared that they are unemployed, capable of, available for, and actively seeking work during the week in which their claim is made. All people claiming unemployment related benefits on the day of the monthly count are included in the claimant count, irrespective of whether they are actually receiving benefits.

Average earnings index
(Tables 7.21 and 7.22)
The Average Earnings Index (AEI) is designed to measure changes in the level of earnings i.e. wage inflation in Great Britain. Average earnings are calculated as the total wages and salaries paid by firms, divided by the number of employees paid. Like all indices, changes are measured against a base year, whose index value is set to 100. The current base

Labour market

year is 1995 for Table 7.21 and March 1996 for Table 7.22.

The Average Earnings Index was the subject of two reviews at the beginning of 1999. These were, *"Review of Methodology for the Average Earnings Index"* R Chambers and D Holmes, University of Southampton December 1998, and *"Review of the Revisions to the Average Earnings Index"* report submitted by Sir Andrew Turnbull and Mervyn King, The Stationery Office, March 1999. They made a number of recommendations for change in the methodology underpinning the index, and set out a long-term project for development. Work to implement the recommendations is underway and regular updates on progress will be published in the ONS' journal Labour Market Trends.

The AEI is published monthly in the Labour Market Statistics First Release. The main indicator of growth, the headline rate, is based on the annual change in the seasonally adjusted index values for the latest 3 months compared with the same period a year ago. The use of a 3-month average reduces the level of volatility seen in the data on a month-on-month basis.

Strengths of the AEI
The AEI, based on monthly survey data, is a timely indicator of changes in the level of earnings.

Limitations of the AEI
The index is not adjusted for any changes in the composition of the workforce such as changes in the share of full time and part time workers, or in the share of skilled and unskilled workers. Similarly, the index does not account for changes in the number of hours worked, or any temporary factors that affect earnings.

The sample of the Monthly Wages and Salaries Survey on which the AEI is based is not designed to provide information on the level of earnings. The sample is not completely representative of the economy as firms with fewer than 20 employees are excluded, as are the earnings of self employed persons.

The AEI only covers earnings in Great Britain as earnings information is not collected for Northern Ireland and regional data are not available.

Vacancies at jobcentres *(Table 7.27)*

Vacancy - This is a job opportunity notified by an employer to a Jobcentre.

Unfilled vacancy - (also known as "Stock of vacancies") This is the number of vacancies which have not been filled or cancelled on the count date.

Inflow of vacancy - (also known as "Notified vacancies") This is the number of job opportunities notified by employers to Jobcentres in the period between two successive count dates.

Outflow of vacancy - This is a derived statistic which represents the total of vacancies filled plus cancelled between count dates. This concept can also be expressed as "vacancy stock" at the beginning of the period plus notified vacancies (inflows) minus "vacancy stock" at the end of the period.

Placings - This is the number of Jobseekers placed into employment by individual Jobcentres.

Earnings *(Table 7.19 - 7.25)*
The total gross remuneration employees receive before any statutory deductions (tax, national insurance). Income in kind and pension funds are excluded.

7.1 Summary for United Kingdom labour force
Spring each year. Not seasonally adjusted.

Thousands

	All aged 16+[1]	All aged 16 & over				Economic activity rate 16-59/64 (%)[2]	Employment rate - all aged 16+ (%)[3]	Employment rate 16-59/64 (%)[4]	ILO unemployment rate (%)[5]
		Total economically active	Total in employment	ILO unemployed	Economically inactive				
All									
	BEAJ	BEAM	BEAP	BEAS	BEAV	BEAY	BEBK	BEBN	BEBQ
1990	45 107	28 909	26 935	1 974	16 198	80.2	59.7	74.7	6.8
1991	45 226	28 813	26 400	2 414	16 413	79.8	58.4	73.0	8.4
1992	45 310	28 581	25 812	2 769	16 728	78.8	57.0	71.1	9.7
1993	45 400	28 447	25 511	2 936	16 954	78.4	56.2	70.2	10.3
1994	45 488	28 455	25 717	2 738	17 032	78.2	56.5	70.6	9.6
1995	45 641	28 486	26 026	2 460	17 155	78.0	57.0	71.1	8.6
1996	45 835	28 663	26 323	2 340	17 172	78.2	57.4	71.6	8.2
1997	46 036	28 852	26 814	2 037	17 184	78.2	58.2	72.6	7.1
1998	46 253	28 892	27 116	1 776	17 361	78.0	58.6	73.1	6.1
1999	46 431	29 194	27 442	1 752	17 237	78.4	59.1	73.6	6.0
2000	46 581	29 412	27 793	1 619	17 169	78.7	59.7	74.3	5.5
Men									
	BEAK	BEAN	BEAQ	BEAT	BEAW	BEAZ	BEBL	BEBO	BEBR
1990	21 801	16 483	15 318	1 165	5 318	88.3	70.3	82.1	7.1
1991	21 871	16 401	14 887	1 514	5 470	87.7	68.1	79.6	9.2
1992	21 924	16 187	14 321	1 865	5 737	86.3	65.3	76.3	11.5
1993	21 985	16 021	14 035	1 986	5 964	85.6	63.8	74.8	12.4
1994	22 049	16 000	14 173	1 826	6 050	85.2	64.3	75.3	11.4
1995	22 156	16 009	14 397	1 612	6 146	84.7	65.0	76.1	10.1
1996	22 283	16 052	14 503	1 549	6 230	84.6	65.1	76.4	9.6
1997	22 412	16 098	14 792	1 306	6 314	84.4	66.0	77.5	8.1
1998	22 547	16 096	14 999	1 098	6 450	83.9	66.5	78.1	6.8
1999	22 657	16 234	15 138	1 095	6 423	84.1	66.8	78.4	6.7
2000	22 754	16 327	15 336	991	6 427	84.3	67.4	79.1	6.1
Women									
	BEAL	BEAO	BEAR	BEAU	BEAX	BEBJ	BEBM	BEBP	BEBS
1990	23 307	12 427	11 617	809	10 880	71.3	49.8	66.6	6.5
1991	23 354	12 412	11 512	900	10 942	71.0	49.3	65.8	7.2
1992	23 386	12 395	11 491	904	10 991	70.6	49.1	65.4	7.3
1993	23 415	12 426	11 476	949	10 989	70.6	49.0	65.1	7.6
1994	23 438	12 456	11 544	912	10 983	70.6	49.3	65.3	7.3
1995	23 486	12 477	11 629	849	11 009	70.6	49.5	65.6	6.8
1996	23 553	12 611	11 820	791	10 942	71.1	50.2	66.5	6.3
1997	23 624	12 754	12 022	732	10 871	71.4	50.9	67.2	5.7
1998	23 707	12 796	12 117	679	10 911	71.5	51.1	67.6	5.3
1999	23 774	12 960	12 304	657	10 813	72.1	51.8	68.3	5.1
2000	23 826	13 084	12 457	628	10 742	72.5	52.3	68.9	4.8

See chapter text for definitions.
1 Population in private households, and from 1992, student halls of residence.
2 Total economically active as a percentage of all persons of working age.
3 Total employed as a percentage of all persons 16 and over.

4 Total employed as a percentage of all persons of working age (men 16-64, women 16-59).
5 Total ILO unemployment as a percentage of all economically active.

Source: ONS, Labour Force Survey

7.2 Employment status, full-time/part-time, second jobs, temporary employees
United Kingdom
Spring each year. Not seasonally adjusted.

Thousands

	All in employment[1,2]					Total employment[2]		Employees[2]		Self-employed[2]			
	Total[3]	Employees	Self employed	Unpaid family workers[4]	Government[5] supported training & employment programmes	Full-time	Part-time	Full-time	Part-time	Full-time	Part-time	Workers with second jobs[6]	Temporary employees
All													
	BEAP	BEBT	BEBW	BEBZ	BECD	BECG	BECJ	BECM	BECP	BECS	BECV	BECY	BEDE
1990	26 935	22 887	3 572	–	471	21 030	5 889	17 773	5 112	3 008	563	1 101	1 195
1991	26 400	22 531	3 416	–	437	20 499	5 885	17 367	5 163	2 896	520	1 106	1 199
1992	25 812	22 018	3 227	181	386	19 753	6 052	16 835	5 180	2 683	544	988	1 220
1993	25 511	21 812	3 184	151	364	19 377	6 128	16 569	5 241	2 605	578	1 057	1 274
1994	25 717	21 929	3 301	146	342	19 423	6 286	16 543	5 379	2 692	607	1 164	1 410
1995	26 026	22 235	3 361	140	290	19 685	6 337	16 773	5 459	2 733	628	1 306	1 550
1996	26 323	22 643	3 300	127	254	19 748	6 574	16 927	5 715	2 652	648	1 311	1 591
1997	26 814	23 121	3 351	118	224	20 088	6 723	17 267	5 852	2 660	689	1 274	1 712
1998	27 116	23 554	3 280	102	179	20 335	6 776	17 645	5 906	2 560	718	1 207	1 668
1999	27 442	23 976	3 202	101	163	20 573	6 863	17 952	6 020	2 510	691	1 301	1 639
2000	27 793	24 396	3 139	109	149	20 820	6 967	18 269	6 123	2 443	694	1 209	1 653
Men													
	BEAQ	BEBU	BEBX	BECA	BECE	BECH	BECK	BECN	BECQ	BECT	BECW	BECZ	BEDF
1990	15 318	12 298	2 715	–	302	14 387	920	11 693	603	2 529	185	527	452
1991	14 887	12 016	2 599	–	264	13 958	919	11 374	640	2 437	161	519	466
1992	14 321	11 577	2 438	55	251	13 307	1 009	10 905	670	2 260	179	451	517
1993	14 035	11 370	2 384	43	237	12 993	1 039	10 680	690	2 184	200	477	563
1994	14 173	11 421	2 480	49	223	13 056	1 114	10 672	748	2 267	212	515	621
1995	14 397	11 620	2 549	42	187	13 226	1 169	10 804	815	2 316	232	550	719
1996	14 503	11 832	2 470	42	160	13 254	1 249	10 926	905	2 233	237	555	711
1997	14 792	12 130	2 486	37	139	13 460	1 330	11 128	1 001	2 233	253	561	788
1998	14 999	12 443	2 411	28	117	13 651	1 345	11 433	1 008	2 139	271	531	748
1999	15 138	12 617	2 378	35	109	13 746	1 389	11 556	1 058	2 118	258	552	783
2000	15 336	12 915	2 293	37	91	13 920	1 413	11 835	1 078	2 021	271	513	765
Women													
	BEAR	BEBV	BEBY	BECB	BECF	BECI	BECL	BECO	BECR	BECU	BECX	BEDD	BEDG
1990	11 617	10 589	857	–	169	6 643	4 968	6 079	4 509	479	379	574	742
1991	11 512	10 515	817	–	174	6 541	4 966	5 993	4 522	459	358	586	733
1992	11 491	10 441	789	126	135	6 445	5 042	5 930	4 510	423	365	537	702
1993	11 476	10 441	800	108	127	6 384	5 089	5 889	4 551	422	378	580	711
1994	11 544	10 508	820	97	119	6 366	5 172	5 871	4 632	425	395	649	788
1995	11 629	10 615	813	98	103	6 459	5 168	5 969	4 644	417	396	757	831
1996	11 820	10 810	830	85	94	6 494	5 326	6 000	4 810	419	411	757	880
1997	12 022	10 991	865	81	85	6 628	5 393	6 139	4 851	428	437	713	924
1998	12 117	11 112	869	73	62	6 683	5 431	6 212	4 897	421	448	676	921
1999	12 304	11 359	825	66	55	6 827	5 475	6 396	4 961	391	433	749	856
2000	12 457	11 481	845	72	58	6 900	5 554	6 434	5 045	422	423	696	888

1 See chapter text for definitions.
2 People whose main job is full or part-time.
3 Includes those who did not state whether they were employees or self employed in 1989-91.
4 Unpaid family workers have been classified as in employment since Spring 1992. Some may have reported themselves as employees or self employed in 1988-91.

5 Those on employment and training programmes are classified as in employment. Some of those on programmes may consider themselves to be employees or self employed so appear in other categories.
6 Second jobs reported in LFS in addition to person's main full or part-time job.

Source: ONS, Labour Force Survey

7.3 Employment
United Kingdom
By age group and gender. At Spring each year. Not seasonally adjusted.

Thousands and percentages.

	All aged 16 & over	16-59/64	16-17	18-24	16-24	25-34	35-49	50-64 (m) 50-59 (f)	65+ (m) 60+ (f)
All	**Numbers**								
	BEAP	BEDH	BEDK	BEDN	BEDQ	BEDT	BEDW	BEDZ	BEEC
1991	26 400	25 622	750	4 184	4 935	6 781	9 186	4 720	777
1992	25 812	24 996	648	3 814	4 462	6 720	9 176	4 638	816
1993	25 511	24 738	551	3 579	4 130	6 809	9 218	4 581	773
1994	25 717	24 936	558	3 432	3 990	6 930	9 327	4 688	782
1995	26 026	25 230	579	3 330	3 909	7 042	9 476	4 802	796
1996	26 323	25 552	631	3 283	3 914	7 081	9 653	4 906	771
1997	26 814	26 012	668	3 231	3 899	7 236	9 725	5 152	803
1998	27 116	26 341	665	3 199	3 864	7 212	9 870	5 395	775
1999	27 442	26 627	648	3 208	3 856	7 145	10 044	5 581	816
2000	27 793	26 966	645	3 275	3 919	7 026	10 286	5 734	827
Men									
	BEAQ	BEDI	BEDL	BEDO	BEDR	BEDU	BEDX	BEEA	BEED
1991	14 887	14 603	388	2 227	2 616	3 940	5 074	2 974	284
1992	14 321	14 021	332	1 998	2 329	3 846	4 980	2 866	300
1993	14 035	13 780	276	1 879	2 155	3 860	4 973	2 792	255
1994	14 173	13 909	284	1 819	2 103	3 931	5 041	2 835	264
1995	14 397	14 109	292	1 776	2 068	3 999	5 150	2 893	288
1996	14 503	14 238	321	1 736	2 057	4 008	5 207	2 965	266
1997	14 792	14 523	328	1 731	2 059	4 080	5 263	3 121	269
1998	14 999	14 725	332	1 714	2 045	4 086	5 355	3 238	274
1999	15 138	14 851	321	1 718	2 039	4 018	5 447	3 346	288
2000	15 336	15 049	322	1 757	2 079	3 956	5 603	3 412	287
Women									
	BEAR	BEDJ	BEDM	BEDP	BEDS	BEDV	BEDY	BEEB	BEEE
1991	11 512	11 020	362	1 957	2 319	2 842	4 112	1 747	493
1992	11 491	10 975	316	1 817	2 133	2 874	4 197	1 771	515
1993	11 476	10 958	275	1 701	1 976	2 949	4 244	1 790	518
1994	11 544	11 026	274	1 614	1 887	3 000	4 287	1 853	518
1995	11 629	11 121	287	1 554	1 841	3 044	4 326	1 910	508
1996	11 820	11 315	309	1 547	1 856	3 072	4 446	1 940	505
1997	12 022	11 488	340	1 500	1 840	3 155	4 461	2 031	534
1998	12 117	11 616	333	1 486	1 819	3 126	4 515	2 156	501
1999	12 304	11 776	327	1 490	1 817	3 127	4 597	2 235	528
2000	12 457	11 916	322	1 518	1 840	3 070	4 684	2 323	540
All	**Rates[1]**								
	BEBK	BEBN	BEEF	BEEI	BEEL	BEEO	BEER	BEEU	BEEX
1991	58.4	73.0	52.8	69.6	66.4	75.7	80.7	64.5	7.7
1992	57.0	71.1	46.9	64.9	61.5	74.0	79.7	63.3	8.0
1993	56.2	70.2	41.6	63.0	58.9	74.1	79.1	62.0	7.6
1994	56.5	70.6	43.0	62.7	58.9	74.7	79.2	62.5	7.7
1995	57.0	71.1	43.1	63.1	59.0	75.6	79.5	63.1	7.8
1996	57.4	71.6	44.3	64.6	60.2	75.8	79.8	63.5	7.6
1997	58.2	72.6	45.8	65.3	60.9	77.8	80.0	64.5	7.9
1998	58.6	73.1	45.7	65.2	60.8	78.5	80.7	65.4	7.6
1999	59.1	73.6	44.9	65.3	60.7	79.5	81.0	66.1	8.0
2000	59.7	74.3	44.8	66.4	61.5	80.4	81.7	66.6	8.1
Men									
	BEBL	BEBO	BEEG	BEEJ	BEEM	BEEP	BEES	BEEV	BEEY
1991	68.1	79.6	53.2	72.5	68.8	86.9	89.2	68.7	8.1
1992	65.3	76.3	46.9	66.6	62.8	83.6	86.6	66.2	8.5
1993	63.8	74.8	40.5	64.8	60.2	83.0	85.4	64.1	7.1
1994	64.3	75.3	42.7	65.0	60.7	83.6	85.6	64.3	7.4
1995	65.0	76.1	42.4	65.8	61.0	84.5	86.3	64.9	8.0
1996	65.1	76.4	44.0	66.9	61.9	84.5	85.9	65.8	7.3
1997	66.0	77.5	44.0	68.5	62.9	86.3	86.3	67.2	7.3
1998	66.5	78.1	44.6	68.4	63.0	87.3	87.1	67.8	7.4
1999	66.8	78.4	43.4	68.6	62.9	87.7	87.4	68.5	7.7
2000	67.4	79.1	43.7	69.9	63.9	88.8	88.4	68.6	7.7
Women									
	BEBM	BEBP	BEEH	BEEK	BEEN	BEEQ	BEET	BEEW	BEEZ
1991	49.3	65.8	52.4	66.5	63.8	64.2	72.2	58.3	7.5
1992	49.1	65.4	47.0	63.1	60.1	64.1	72.9	59.0	7.8
1993	49.0	65.1	42.6	61.1	57.6	65.0	72.8	58.9	7.9
1994	49.3	65.3	43.3	60.2	57.0	65.6	72.8	59.8	7.9
1995	49.5	65.6	43.8	60.2	56.9	66.3	72.6	60.5	7.8
1996	50.2	66.5	44.6	62.3	58.4	66.9	73.6	60.3	7.7
1997	50.9	67.2	47.8	62.0	58.8	69.1	73.7	60.7	8.2
1998	51.1	67.6	46.9	61.9	58.5	69.4	74.1	62.2	7.7
1999	51.8	68.3	46.4	61.9	58.4	71.0	74.6	62.8	8.1
2000	52.3	68.9	45.9	62.7	58.9	71.6	74.9	64.0	8.3

1 Total in employment as a percentage of all persons in the relevant group.

Source: ONS, Labour Force Survey

7.4 Distribution of the workforce
At mid-June each year

Thousands, seasonally adjusted

		1990	1991[7]	1992	1993	1994	1995	1996	1997	1998	1999	2000
United Kingdom												
Claimant unemployed[1]	KAMO	1 584	2 275	2 711	2 902	2 625	2 294	2 135	1 571	1 344	1 264	1 093
Males	KAMP	1 174	1 730	2 084	2 235	2 016	1 756	1 625	1 206	1 026	968	833
Females	KAMQ	410	545	627	667	609	538	509	364	318	297	260
Workforce jobs[2]	KAMR	28 013	27 103	26 406	26 050	26 198	26 492	26 768	27 305	27 628	27 917	28 075
Males	KAMS	15 772	15 077	14 486	14 141	14 201	14 366	14 402	14 798	14 933	15 096	15 120
Females	KAMT	12 241	12 026	11 920	11 909	11 998	12 126	12 366	12 507	12 695	12 821	12 955
HM Forces[3]	KAMU	303	297	290	271	250	230	222	210	210	209	207
Males	KAMV	286	278	270	252	232	214	206	195	194	192	190
Females	KAMW	18	19	20	19	18	16	16	15	16	16	17
Self-employment jobs[4]	KAMX	3 918	3 756	3 441	3 446	3 548	3 608	3 623	3 616	3 493	3 516	3 417
Males	KAMZ	2 949	2 828	2 573	2 537	2 630	2 680	2 680	2 629	2 530	2 556	2 470
Females	KANA	969	928	868	910	918	928	943	988	963	960	947
Employees jobs[5]	KANB	23 353	22 682	22 335	22 006	22 084	22 414	22 728	23 305	23 800	24 078	24 349
Males	KANC	12 270	11 747	11 430	11 150	11 139	11 316	11 396	11 867	12 132	12 278	12 398
Females	KAND	11 083	10 935	10 905	10 857	10 945	11 097	11 332	11 438	11 668	11 800	11 951
of whom												
Total, production and construction industries	KANF	6 435	5 895	5 524	5 200	5 180	5 228	5 251	5 373	5 503	5 373	5 370
Total, all manufacturing industries	KANG	4 780	4 362	4 137	3 951	3 967	4 069	4 110	4 173	4 194	4 049	3 967
Government-supported trainee[6]	KANH	438	369	340	326	317	240	195	173	125	114	102
Males	KANI	268	225	213	203	199	156	121	106	77	69	62
Females	KANJ	171	144	128	124	118	84	74	66	48	45	40
Great Britain												
Claimant unemployed[1]	KANN	1 490	2 176	2 607	2 798	2 527	2 207	2 048	1 509	1 287	1 213	1 051
Males	KANO	1 103	1 654	2 004	2 155	1 940	1 687	1 559	1 157	981	928	801
Females	KANP	387	522	603	643	587	519	489	352	305	285	250
Workforce jobs[2]	KANQ	27 369	26 446	25 758	25 403	25 539	25 809	26 087	26 603	26 914	27 200	27 351
Males	KANR	15 409	14 708	14 128	13 783	13 837	13 993	14 035	14 420	14 547	14 712	14 733
Females	KANS	11 960	11 738	11 630	11 620	11 701	11 816	12 052	12 183	12 367	12 488	12 617
HM Forces[3]	KANT	303	297	290	271	250	230	222	210	210	209	207
Males	KANU	286	278	270	252	232	214	206	195	194	192	190
Females	KANV	18	19	20	19	18	16	16	15	16	16	17
Self-employment jobs[4]	KANW	3 824	3 660	3 354	3 362	3 463	3 515	3 538	3 525	3 405	3 431	3 331
Males	KANX	2 871	2 748	2 501	2 464	2 556	2 603	2 608	2 555	2 457	2 487	2 401
Females	KANY	953	912	853	898	907	913	930	970	948	943	931
Employee jobs[5]	KANZ	22 816	22 140	21 792	21 460	21 525	21 839	22 149	22 709	23 189	23 458	23 721
Males	KAOA	11 994	11 471	11 156	10 875	10 860	11 031	11 110	11 572	11 829	11 971	12 088
Females	KAOB	10 822	10 669	10 636	10 585	10 665	10 808	11 039	11 137	11 360	11 487	11 634
of whom												
Total, production and construction industries	KAOC	6 292	5 755	5 389	5 068	5 048	5 094	5 118	5 233	5 362	5 232	5 229
Total, all manufacturing industries	KAOD	4 675	4 258	4 036	3 852	3 866	3 965	4 006	4 065	4 087	3 943	3 863
Government-supported trainees[6]	KAOE	426	348	322	310	301	224	179	159	110	102	91
Males	KAOF	259	211	201	192	189	145	111	97	67	61	55
Females	KAOG	166	137	121	118	112	79	68	61	43	41	37

Note: Because the figures have been rounded independently totals may differ from the sum of the components. Also the totals may include some employees whose industrial classification could not be ascertained.

1 Claimant unemployment: those people who were claiming unemployment-related benefits (Unemployment Benefit, Income Support or National Insurance credits) at Employment service local offices on the day of the monthly count. The seasonally adjusted claimant unemployment series allows for all relevant changes which, unless adjusted for, would distort comparisons over time.

2 The workforce jobs (formerly workforce in employment) comprises employee jobs, self-employment jobs (from the LFS), HM Forces and government supported trainees.

3 HM Forces figures, provided by the Ministry of Defence, represent the total number of UK service personnel, male and female, in HM Regular Forces, wherever serving and including those on release leave.

4 Estimates of self-employed jobs are based on the results of the Labour Force Survey. The Northern Ireland estimates are not seasonally adjusted.

5 Estimates of employee jobs from December 1987 to August 1989 include an allowance based on the Labour Force Survey to compensate for persistent undercounting in the regular sample enquiries (*Employment Gazette*, October 1989 p56). For all dates, individuals with two jobs as employees of different employers are counted twice.

6 Includes all participants on government training and employment programmes who are receiving some work experience on their placement but who do not have a contract of employment (those with a contract are included in the employee jobs series). The numbers are not subject to seasonal adjustment.

7 Estimates from September 1989 are based on data provided by the New Panel of employers (see article on p191 of the April 1992 edition of *Employment Gazette*).

Source: Earnings and Employment Division, ONS: 01633 812079

7.5 Employee jobs
Analysis by industry based on the Standard Industrial Classification 1992

At June in each year

Thousands, not seasonally adjusted

		SIC 1992	United Kingdom							Great Britain					
			1995	1996	1997	1998	1999	2000		1995	1996	1997	1998	1999	2000
All sections	KAOH	A - Q	22 454	22 732	23 268	23 764	24 043	24 314	KAPN	21 881	22 154	22 672	23 155	23 425	23 688
Index of production and construction industries	KAOI	C - F	5 218	5 240	5 350	5 481	5 350	5 350	KAPO	5 084	5 363	5 500	5 637	5 504	5 530
Index of production industries	KAOJ	C - E	4 301	4 334	4 390	4 401	4 256	4 162	KAPP	4 190	4 224	4 276	4 289	4 146	4 054
of which, manufacturing industries	KAOK	D	*4 064*	*4 106*	*4 162*	*4 185*	*4 041*	*3 958*	KAPQ	*3 960*	*4 002*	*4 055*	*4 078*	*3 936*	*3 855*
Service industries	KAOL	G - Q	16 964	17 213	17 604	17 963	18 377	18 621	KAPR	16 542	16 785	17 166	17 511	17 914	18 151
Agriculture, hunting and forestry and fishing	KAOM	A/B	272	279	314	321	317	342	KAPS	255	263	297	304	301	327
Agriculture hunting and forestry	KPHI	A	264	273	307	313	309	335	KOVW	247	257	291	297	294	320
Agriculture hunting & related activities	KPHJ	01	255	261	295	303	299	325	KOVX	238	245	279	287	284	310
Fishing	KPHK	B	6	6	7	7	8	8	KOVY	5	6	6	7	7	7
Mining and quarrying	KPHL	C	67	78	79	76	73	68	KOVZ	65	76	77	75	71	66
Mining and quarrying of energy producing materials	KPHM	CA	37	43	46	45	42	40	KOWA	37	43	46	45	42	40
Mining	KAPG	10/12	..	..	..	..	..	..	KOWB	11	15	16	15	15	13
Extraction of crude petroleum	KPHN	11	..	..	..	..	..	..	KOWC	26	28	30	30	27	27
Mining and quarrying except of energy producing materials	KPHO	CB(13/14)	30	34	33	31	30	29	KOWD	28	33	31	30	29	27
Energy and water supply industries	KAOO	C/E	237	228	227	216	215	204	KOWE	230	222	221	211	210	198
Manufacturing	KPHP	D	4 064	4 106	4 162	4 185	4 041	3 958	KOWF	3 960	4 002	4 055	4 078	3 936	3 855
Manufacture of food products Beverages and tobacco	KPHQ	DA	450	445	471	481	472	460	KOWG	430	426	451	462	453	441
Of food	KPHR	151 to 158	..	..	..	..	..	..	KOWH	368	372	395	403	395	385
Of beverages and tobacco	KPHS	159/16	..	..	..	..	..	..	KOWI	57	54	56	59	58	56
Manufacture of textiles and textile products	KPHT	DB	345	337	335	324	288	262	KOWJ	320	313	311	291	256	..
Of textiles	KPHU	17	187	184	184	177	163	155	KOWK	176	174	173	162	148	..
Of made-up textile articles except apparel	KPHV	174	..	..	..	..	..	..	KOWL	33	313	311	302	268	245
Of textiles excluding made-up textile	KPHW	Rest of 17	..	..	..	..	..	..	KOWM	142	174	173	167	154	146
Of wearing apparel,dressing and dyeing of fur	KPHX	18	158	153	151	147	125	107	KOWN	144	139	138	135	114	99
Manufacture of leather and leather products including footwear	KPHY	DC	39	39	34	31	28	26	KOWO	39	38	34	31	27	25
Of leather and leather goods	KPHZ	191/192	..	..	..	..	..	..	KOWP	13	14	12	12	11	12
Of footwear	KPIA	193	..	..	..	..	..	..	KOWQ	25	24	22	18	16	14
Manufacture of wood and wood products	KPIB	DD(20)	84	84	87	85	84	88	KOWR	81	81	83	82	81	85
Manufacture of pulp paper and paper products,publishing and printing	KPIC	DE	473	474	473	482	473	470	KOWS	467	467	467	475	466	463
Of pulp paper and paper products	KPID	21	124	123	117	116	109	103	KOWT	122	121	115	113	107	101
Publishing printing and reproduction of recorded media	KPIE	22	349	350	356	366	364	367	KOWU	345	347	352	362	360	362
Manufacture of coke refined petroleum products and nuclear fuel	KPIF	DF(23)	29	32	32	29	30	28	KOWV	28	32	32	29	30	28
Of refined petroleum products		232							KOWW	17	18	19	15	15	..
Manufacture of chemicals,chemical products and man-made fibres	KPIG	DG(24)	255	254	254	260	257	251	KOWX	251	250	250	256	254	248
Manufacture of rubber and plastics	KPIH	DH(25)	224	230	241	243	238	233	KOWY	218	224	235	236	231	226
Manufacture of other non-metallic mineral products	KPII	DI(26)	150	146	149	146	140	143	KOWZ	146	141	145	142	135	138
Manufacture of basic metals and fabricated metal products	KPIJ	DJ	555	569	566	549	527	521	KOXA	550	564	561	543	520	514
Of basic metals	KPIK	27	132	135	131	131	122	119	KOXB	132	134	131	130	122	118
except machinery	KPIL	28	423	435	435	419	404	402	KOXC	418	430	430	413	398	396

Sources: Department of Manpower Services (Northern Ireland);
Earnings and Employment Division, ONS: 01633 812079

7.5 Employee jobs
Analysis by industry based on the Standard Industrial Classification 1992

continued At June in each year

Thousands, not seasonally adjusted

			United Kingdom							Great Britain					
		SIC 1992	1995	1996	1997	1998	1999	2000		1995	1996	1997	1998	1999	2000
Manufacture of Machinery & Eqpt.Nec	KPIM	DK(29)	398	402	400	401	384	372	KOXD	391	395	394	394	377	366
Manufacture of electrical and optical equipment	KPIN	DL	488	510	520	531	507	501	KOXE	479	501	509	520	496	489
Of office machinery and computers	KPIO	30	52	49	47	56	56	54	KOXF	51	49	46	54	54	52
Of electrical machinery and apparatus	KPIP	31	167	178	181	187	176	174	KOXG	164	175	178	185	173	171
Of electric motors etc control apparatus and insulated cable	KPIQ	311 to 313	..	..	..	..	..	..	KOXH	97	99	101	107	102	100
Of accumulators, primary cells, batteries, lamps & electrical eqpt.	KPIR	314 to 316	..	..	..	..	..	..	KOXI	66	76	76	78	72	71
Radio television & communication eqpt	KPIS	32	123	130	132	131	124	129	KOXJ	118	126	126	125	119	124
Of electronic components	KPIT	321	..	..	..	..	..	..	KOXK	53	53	51	50	47	48
Of radio TV and telephone apparatus, sound and video recorders	KPIU	322/323	..	..	..	..	..	..	KOXL	66	73	75	75	72	75
Of medical precision & optical eqpt, watches	KPIV	33	147	153	160	157	151	144	KOXM	145	152	159	155	149	143
Manufacture of transport equipment	KPIW	DM	375	388	389	409	397	381	KOXN	364	377	378	396	384	368
Of motor vehicles and trailers	KPIX	34	218	227	228	234	222	212	KOXO	215	223	224	230	218	207
Of other transport equipment	KPIY	35	157	162	162	175	175	170	KOXP	149	154	154	166	166	161
Manufacturing NEC Of furniture	KPIZ	DN(36/37)	200	195	210	213	217	221	KOXQ	197	192	206	210	213	217
Electricity gas and water supply	KPJA	361	170	150	148	140	142	135	KOXR	111	110	121	126	127	129
Electricity gas steam and hot		E							KOXS	165	146	144	136	139	132
water supply	KPJB	40	..	..	..	..	..	..	KOXT	122	102	104	99	101	..
Collection purification and distribution of water	KPJC	41	..	..	..	..	..	..	KOXU	43	44	40	37	36	34
Construction	KPJD	F(45)	917	906	960	1 079	1 094	1 188	KOXW	893	883	933	1 051	1 064	1 156
Services	KPJE	G - Q	16 964	17 213	17 604	17 963	18 377	18 621	KOXX	16 542	16 785	17 166	17 511	17 914	18 151
Wholesale and retail trade; Repair of motor vehicles, motorcycles and personal household goods	KPJF	G (50 - 52)	3 770	3 816	3 933	3 989	4 042	4 095	KOXY	3 682	3 728	3 840	3 891	3 942	3 995
Sale maintenance and repair of motor vehicles,retail of automotive fuel	KPJG	50	556	563	557	551	552	552	KOXZ	544	551	545	537	539	538
Sale of motor vehicles, motorcycles and parts,motorcycle repair and sale of automotive fuel	KPJH	501/503 - 505	..	..	..	..	..	..	KOYA	327	376	381	387	387	380
Maintenance and repair of motor vehicles	KPJI	502	..	..	..	..	..	..	KOYB	171	175	164	150	152	158
Wholesale trade and commission trade except motor vehicles	KPJJ	51	998	1 009	1 080	1 075	1 098	1 114	KOYC	978	989	1 059	1 054	1 076	1 092
Wholesale on a fee of contract basis	KPJK	511	..	..	..	..	..	..	KOYD	38	43	43	47	56	59
Wholesale agricultural raw materials and live animals	KPJL	512	..	..	..	..	..	..	KPLD	22	21	22	25	24	22
Wholesale food beverages & tobacco	KPJM	513	..	..	..	..	..	..	KPLE	180	192	195	186	179	175
Wholesale household goods	KPJN	514	..	..	..	..	..	..	KPLF	200	226	245	245	251	255
Wholesale of non-agricultural intermediate products waste & scrap	KPJO	515	..	..	..	..	..	..	KPLG	234	232	231	230	239	249
Wholesale machinery eqpt. & supplies	KPJP	516	..	..	..	..	..	..	KPLH	189	201	230	240	240	237
Other wholesale	KPJQ	517	..	..	..	..	..	..	KPLI	73	74	91	81	87	94
Retail trade except of motor vehicles and motorcycles;repair of personal and household goods	KPJR	52	2 216	2 244	2 296	2 363	2 392	2 429	KPLJ	2 160	2 188	2 237	2 300	2 328	2 365
Non-specialised stores selling mainly food beverages & tobacco	KPJS	5211/5221-4,5227	..	..	..	..	..	..	KPLK	820	836	840	904	927	945
Other non-specialised stores second hand shops & sales not in stores	KPJT	5212/525-526	..	..	..	..	..	..	KPLL	316	255	294	313	328	329

Sources: Department of Manpower Services (Northern Ireland);
Earnings and Employment Division, ONS: 01633 812079

7.5 Employee jobs
continued
Analysis by industry based on the Standard Industrial Classification 1992
At June in each year

Thousands, not seasonally adjusted

		SIC 1992	United Kingdom							Great Britain					
			1995	1996	1997	1998	1999	2000		1995	1996	1997	1998	1999	2000
Alcoholic & other beverages, tobacco	KPJU	5225 to 5226	..	..	..	..	..	..	KPLM	25	43	56	57	49	52
Pharmaceutical & medical goods cosmetics & toilet articles	KPJV	523	..	..	..	..	..	..	KPLN	129	129	121	90	82	87
Clothing footwear & leather goods	KPJW	5242/5243	..	..	..	..	..	..	KPLO	235	225	249	272	275	286
Textile furniture lighting eqpt. electrical household appliances radio and TV paints glass hardware and household goods nec.	KPJX	5241/5244-46	..	..	..	..	..	..	KPLP	277	265	267	238	227	235
Books newspapers & stationary, other retail in specialised stores	KPJY	5247/5248	..	..	..	..	..	..	KPLQ	365	361	348	346	352	342
Repair of personal & household goods	KPJZ	527	..	..	..	..	..	..	KPLR	17	16	17	19	22	25
Hotels and restaurants	KPKA	H	1 231	1 274	1 299	1 357	1 391	1 413	KPLS	1 204	1 245	1 270	1 324	1 357	1 378
Hotels camp sites short-stay accom.	KPKB	551/552	..	..	..	..	..	..	KPLT	331	313	301	314	340	343
Restaurants	KPKC	553	..	..	..	..	..	..	KPLU	333	337	343	364	366	371
Bars	KPKD	554	..	..	..	..	..	..	KPLV	393	396	429	441	444	454
Canteens and catering	KPKE	555	..	..	..	..	..	..	KPLW	178	200	197	205	206	210
Transport storage & communication	KPKF	I	1 327	1 325	1 346	1 373	1 424	1 451	KPLX	1 305	1 302	1 322	1 349	1 399	1 425
Land transport,transport via pipelines	KPKG	60	487	470	466	484	500	517	KPLY	478	460	455	474	489	506
Transport via railways	KPKH	601	..	..	..	..	..	..	KPLZ	105	75	43	47	48	49
Other land transport & via pipelines	KPKI	602/603	..	..	..	..	..	..	KPMA	358	385	412	427	440	457
Water transport	KPKJ	61	28	25	22	19	20	20	KPMB	27	24	21	19	20	20
Air transport	KPKK	62	56	61	71	80	87	83	KPMC	56	60	71	80	86	82
Supporting and auxiliary transport activities,activities of travel agents	KPKL	63	325	324	340	336	345	356	KPMD	321	320	336	332	340	351
Travel agencies and tour operators	KPKM	633	..	..	..	..	..	..	KPME	82	88	97	98	106	110
Post and telecommunications	KPKN	64	431	445	447	453	472	474	KPMF	424	438	439	445	464	465
National post & courier activities	KPKO	641	..	..	..	..	..	..	KPMG	239	256	249	267	276	263
National post activities	KPKP	6411	..	..	..	..	..	..	KPMH	189	203	212	212	219	202
Courier activities	KPKQ	6412	..	..	..	..	..	..	KPMI	50	53	37	55	57	61
Telecommunications	KPKR	6420	..	..	..	..	..	..	KPMJ	185	182	190	178	188	202
Financial Intermediation	KPKS	J	993	972	996	1 009	1 011	988	KPMK	979	959	982	995	996	973
Financial intermediation except insurance and pension funding	KPKT	65	599	572	575	574	581	562	KPML	591	564	566	564	572	552
Insurance and pension funding except compulsory social security	KPKU	66	214	216	231	235	234	227	KPMM	211	214	229	233	231	224
Activities auxiliary to financial intermediation	KPKV	67	180	184	190	201	196	200	KPMN	178	181	187	198	194	197
Except insurance and pension funding	KPKW	671	..	..	..	..	..	..	KPMO	44	47	63	74	78	81
Auxiliary to insurance and pension funding	KPKX	672	..	..	..	..	..	..	KPMP	134	135	125	124	116	116
Real estate renting & business activities	KPKY	K	2 854	2 977	3 174	3 328	3 458	3 521	KPMQ	2 823	2 944	3 138	3 288	3 415	3 475
Real estate activities	KPKZ	70	277	271	288	288	302	321	KPMR	274	269	285	285	299	318
Activities with own property, letting of own property	KPLA	701/702	..	..	..	..	..	..	KPMS	156	152	154	162	170	187
Activities on a fee or contract basis	KPLB	703	..	..	..	..	..	..	KPMT	105	117	131	124	129	131

Sources: Department of Manpower Services (Northern Ireland);
Earnings and Employment Division, ONS: 01633 812079

7.5
Employee jobs
Analysis by industry based on the Standard Industrial Classification 1992

continued · At June in each year

Thousands, not seasonally adjusted

		SIC 1992	United Kingdom							Great Britain					
			1995	1996	1997	1998	1999	2000		1995	1996	1997	1998	1999	2000
Renting of machinery and eqpt. without operator & of personal & household goods	KPLC	71	119	124	139	141	156	158	KPMU	118	122	137	140	154	156
Construction and civil engineering machinery	KOUU	7132	..	..	..	..	..	..	KPMV	37	36	37	42	42	45
All other goods and equipment	KOUV	Rest of 71	..	..	..	..	..	..	KPMW	79	86	100	98	111	112
Computer and related equipment	KOUW	72	259	293	340	398	443	444	KPMX	257	291	338	395	440	440
Research and development	KOUX	73	88	94	93	96	97	101	KPMY	86	93	91	95	96	99
Other business activities	KOUY	74	2 112	2 195	2 314	2 404	2 460	2 497	KPMZ	2 087	2 170	2 286	2 373	2 426	2 461
Legal, accounting,book-keeping & auditing activities	KOUZ	741	..	..	..	..	..	..	KPNA	542	612	615	661	687	678
Legal activities	KOVA	7411	..	..	..	..	..	..	KPNB	191	196	204	210	212	216
Accounting, book-keeping auditing, tax consultancy	KOVB	7412	..	..	..	..	..	..	KPNC	138	160	138	161	175	184
Market research business and consultancy activities	KOVC	7413/7414	..	..	..	..	..	..	KPND	163	181	187	194	190	176
Management activities of holding co.	KOVD	7415	..	..	..	..	..	..	KPNE	50	75	86	96	110	102
Architectural engineering activities and related technical consultancy, technical testing	KOVE	742/743	..	..	..	..	..	..	KPNF	332	338	322	300	304	304
Advertising	KOVF	744	..	..	..	..	..	..	KPNG	63	81	83	84	93	93
Industrial cleaning	KOVG	747	..	..	..	..	..	..	KPNH	403	398	387	339	321	305
Public admin. & defence, compulsory social security	KOVH	L(75)	1 399	1 406	1 358	1 392	1 453	1 468	KPNI	1 339	1 346	1 299	1 333	1 394	1 409
Education	KOVI	M(80)	1 858	1 883	1 888	1 868	1 907	1 947	KPNJ	1 796	1 818	1 824	1 803	1 842	1 881
Health and social work	KOVJ	N	2 502	2 510	2 537	2 539	2 530	2 564	KPNK	2 410	2 419	2 444	2 446	2 436	2 469
Human health, vetinary activities	KOVK	851/852	..	..	..	..	..	..	KPNL	1 517	1 465	1 536	1 535	1 540	1 573
Social work activities	KOVL	853	..	..	..	..	..	..	KPNM	902	954	908	911	896	896
Other community social and personal service activities,private households with employed persons, extra-territorial organisations and bodies	KOVM	O - Q	1 029	1 050	1 074	1 110	1 161	1 175	KPNN	1 003	1 024	1 047	1 082	1 133	1 146
Sewage & refuse disposal; sanitation	KOVN	90	75	71	78	112	124	117	KPNO	72	69	76	110	122	115
Activities of membership organisations	KOVO	91	188	202	201	204	200	202	KPNP	179	194	193	196	191	193
Recreational cultural and sporting activities	KOVP	92	564	559	573	562	590	606	KPNQ	553	547	560	549	577	592
Motion picture video radio TV news agencies & entertainment activities	KOVQ	921 to 924	..	..	..	..	..	..	KPNR	133	162	162	161	173	175
Library archives museums and other cultural activities	KOVR	925	..	..	..	..	..	..	KPNS	78	78	79	78	75	88
Sporting activities and other recreational activities	KOVS	926/927	..	..	..	..	..	..	KPNT	320	307	319	311	329	330
Other service activities,private households with employed persons, extra territorial organisations	KOVT	93/95/99	202	217	222	231	247	250	KPNU	198	214	218	227	243	246
Washing dry cleaning of textile and fur products	KOVU	9301	..	..	..	..	..	..	KPNV	41	42	41	46	50	48
Hairdressing, other beauty treatment physical and well-being activities	KOVV	9302/9304	..	..	..	..	..	..	KPNW	74	78	74	81	81	79

Sources: Department of Manpower Services (Northern Ireland);
Earnings and Employment Division, ONS: 01633 812079

7.6 Weekly hours worked[1]
United Kingdom

At Spring each year. Not seasonally adjusted.

Hours

	All workers weekly hours[2]		Average actual weekly hours of work		
	Total (millions)	Average	Full-time workers[2]	Part-time workers[3]	Second jobs[4]
All					
	BEFA	BEFD	BEFG	BEFJ	BEFM
1990	926	34.4	39.1	15.4	9.2
1991	908	34.4	39.3	15.2	9.6
1992	856	33.3	38.4	14.8	9.3
1993	852	33.5	38.8	14.9	9.2
1994	866	33.8	39.2	15.2	9.1
1995	884	34.1	39.5	15.3	9.1
1996	890	33.9	39.5	15.3	8.8
1997	897	33.5	39.0	15.2	9.3
1998	905	33.4	39.0	15.2	9.0
1999	918	33.5	39.0	15.5	8.9
2000	923	33.3	38.7	15.6	8.8
Men					
	BEFB	BEFE	BEFH	BEFK	BEFN
1990	614	40.1	41.2	15.0	10.0
1991	596	40.1	41.2	14.8	10.6
1992	554	38.9	40.3	14.3	10.3
1993	548	39.3	40.8	14.4	10.2
1994	558	39.6	41.2	14.9	9.8
1995	571	39.9	41.6	14.7	10.0
1996	573	39.7	41.5	14.7	9.7
1997	577	39.1	41.1	14.8	10.6
1998	584	39.0	41.0	14.9	9.6
1999	587	38.9	40.9	14.9	9.5
2000	590	38.5	40.6	15.0	9.1
Women					
	BEFC	BEFF	BEFI	BEFL	BEFO
1990	312	26.9	34.6	15.4	8.5
1991	312	27.1	35.3	15.2	8.6
1992	302	26.4	34.6	14.9	8.5
1993	304	26.5	34.9	15.0	8.5
1994	308	26.8	35.2	15.3	8.5
1995	312	26.9	35.1	15.4	8.5
1996	317	26.8	35.3	15.4	8.2
1997	319	26.6	34.9	15.3	8.3
1998	321	26.5	34.8	15.3	8.5
1999	332	27.0	35.2	15.6	8.5
2000	333	26.8	34.9	15.7	8.7

1 Average hours actually worked in the reference week which includes hours worked in second jobs (see chapter text for definitions).
2 Main and second job.
3 Main job only.
4 Second jobs reported in the LFS in addition to persons main full time job.

Source: ONS, Labour Force Survey

7.7 Civil Service staff
Analysis by ministerial responsibility[1,2]

At 1 April each year

Full-time equivalents[2] (thousands)

		1989	1990	1991	1992	1993	1994	1995	1996	1997	1998	1999
Agriculture, Fisheries and Food[4]	BCDA	11.0	11.0	11.0	11.0	11.0	11.0	10.6	10.8	10.1	10.8	11.7
Cabinet Office[5,15]	KPQI	2.0	2.0	2.0	2.0	6.0	12.0	11.7	12.3	7.8	6.2	7.6
Chancellor of the Exchequer's Departments:												
Customs and Excise	BCDC	27.0	27.0	27.0	27.0	25.0	25.0	24.1	23.2	23.1	23.4	22.5
Inland Revenue[6,19]	BCDD	67.0	67.0	67.0	70.0	68.0	64.0	59.1	56.5	54.0	53.4	61.3
Department for National Savings[12]	BCDE	7.0	7.0	7.0	6.0	6.0	6.0	5.4	4.7	4.3	4.1	0.1
Treasury and others[5,18]	BCDF	8.0	10.0	10.0	10.0	5.0	5.0	4.3	6.0	5.1	5.1	5.0
Total	BCDB	110.0	111.0	111.0	113.0	105.0	99.0	92.9	90.3	86.4	86.0	89.0
Education	BCDG	3.0	3.0	3.0	3.0	3.0	2.0	2.5	–	–	–	–
Employment	BCDH	55.0	53.0	50.0	58.0	58.0	55.0	49.6	–	–	–	–
Education and Employment[4]	KTDI	..	..	..	..	..	..	..	40.8	34.1	33.6	34.6
Energy	BCDI	1.0	1.0	1.0	1.0	–	..	..	–	–	–	–
Environment[4]	BCDJ	31.0	29.0	26.0	23.0	18.0	10.0	9.4	10.9	9.6	–	–
Environment, Transport & Regions[4,20]	JYXS	..	..	..	..	..	..	..	..	..	21.2	21.3
Foreign and Commonwealth[4]	BCDK	10.0	10.0	10.0	10.0	10.0	8.0	7.5	7.1	6.6	5.4	5.5
International Development	JYXU	..	..	..	..	..	..	..	..	..	1.1	1.2
Health	BAKR	11.0	8.0	7.0	7.0	7.0	7.0	6.2	4.8	4.7	4.6	4.8
Home[4,5]	BCDL	41.0	43.0	45.0	50.0	52.0	51.0	51.4	50.8	50.4	50.7	50.0
Legal Departments	KPQJ	28.0	28.0	29.0	29.0	30.0	29.0	28.7	27.8	26.3	25.4	24.4
National Heritage	KPQK	–	–	–	1.0	1.0	1.0	1.0	1.0	1.0	–	–
Culture, Media & Sport	JYXT	..	..	..	..	..	..	..	..	..	0.6	0.6
Northern Ireland	KPQD	–	–	–	–	–	–	0.2	0.2	0.2	0.2	0.2
Scotland[4,13,14]	BCDN	12.0	13.0	13.0	13.0	14.0	13.0	12.1	11.7	11.8	12.0	13.6
Social Security[5,6]	BAKS	84.0	82.0	80.0	81.0	86.0	90.0	89.2	91.5	93.1	87.2	81.6
Health and Social Security	KAZL	–	–	–	–	–	–	–	–	–	–	–
Trade and Industry[4]	KAZM	15.0	14.0	13.0	13.0	13.0	12.0	11.1	11.2	10.3	10.4	10.5
Transport[4]	BCDR	14.0	16.0	15.0	15.0	15.0	14.0	12.9	11.3	11.4	–	–
Wales	BCDS	2.0	2.0	2.0	2.0	3.0	2.0	2.2	2.1	2.2	2.1	2.3
Total civil departments	BCDU	431.0	425.0	418.0	431.0	431.0	418.0	400.8	384.6	366.0	357.6	358.8
Defence[4,5,7,8,9,10]	BCDW	142.0	142.0	141.0	140.0	130.0	122.0	116.1	109.9	109.2	104.2	100.8
Total all departments	BCDX	573.0	567.0	559.0	571.0	560.0	540.0	516.9	494.5	475.2	461.7	459.6
of whom												
Non-industrial staff	BCDY	*503.0*	*499.0*	*495.0*	*509.0*	*509.0*	*494.0*	*474.1*	*458.7*	*439.3*	*430.5*	*428.9*
Industrial staff	BCDZ	*70.0*	*68.0*	*64.0*	*61.0*	*52.0*	*46.0*	*42.0*	*35.9*	*36.0*	*32.8*	*30.7*

1 The figures include non-industrial and industrial staff but exclude casual or seasonal staff and employees of the Northern Ireland Civil Service.

2 A comprehensive list of Machinery of Government changes is listed on the Cabinet Office's web site at www.cabinet-office.gov.uk/civilservice/index/statistics.htm Footnotes indicate the departments affected.

3 Figures included are measured as 'full-time equivalent' staff. Part-time staff are recorded as a proportion of full-time employees according to the proportion of a full week that they work.

4 1997

5 1998

6 Contributions Agency transferred from DSS to Inland Revenue (7580)

7 Ministry of Defence further privatisation and reorganisation (loss of 1200)

8 Defence Animal Centre merged with Army Training and Recruitment Agency.

9 Defence Codification Agency subsumed by MoD RAF.

10 Maintenance Group Defence Agency subsumed with Defence Aviation Repair Agency.

11 Office of the National Lottery became an NDPB and renamed the National Lottery Commission (loss of 33)

12 Much of National Savings privatised (loss of 4000)

13 Lord Advocate's Department subsumed in Scottish Office (19)

14 Scottish Records Office became The National Archives of Scotland.

15 UK Anti-Drugs Co-ordination Unit was transferred from Privy Council Office to the Cabinet Office.

16 UK Passport Agency recorded outsourced functions to Siemens Business Services (66)

17 Friendly Societies moved to the Financial Services Authority (FSA)(73)

18 Government Property Lawyers ceased to exist, remaining staff absorbed into Treasury Solicitors.

19 Family Credit Unit in the Benefits Agency transferred to the Tax Credit Office within the Inland Revenue.

20 The Rent Service, an Executive Agency of DETR was formed (80)

Source: Cabinet Office (OPS): 020 7270 5744

7.8 Persons employed in local authorities[1]

Thousands (Full-time equivalents)[2]

		1990	1991	1992	1993	1994	1995	1996	1997	1998	1999	2000
Service: England												
Education	ATAM	857.0	849.4	835.8	712.1	692.8	698.4	691.8	691.8	693.9	707.3	730.9
Construction	BCHC	93.7	85.7	77.1	70.9	67.4	63.5	58.8	55.0	51.9	52.3	51.2
Transport	BCHD	2.4	1.9	1.5	1.4	1.4	1.4	1.4	1.4	1.4	..	..
Social services	BCHE	236.0	235.6	232.3	225.8	233.3	234.3	230.6	227.3	221.3	215.9	213.5
Public libraries and museums	BCHF	33.6	33.3	32.4	31.9	31.8	32.7	31.5	31.4	31.1	31.5	31.1
Recreation, parks and baths	BCHG	77.2	75.7	72.7	68.6	67.2	65.2	63.6	60.7	59.8	58.1	57.2
Environmental health	BCHH	19.1	18.8	19.6	19.0	18.5	17.4	17.2	17.4	16.9	17.2	17.7
Refuse collection and disposal	BCHS	29.9	27.1	23.6	21.8	20.5	25.1	24.5	24.6	24.0	23.7	21.9
Housing	BCHT	64.5	65.5	65.4	65.5	65.7	68.0	66.8	65.5	64.7	65.4	65.1
Town and country planning	BCHU	22.9	23.1	23.1	22.5	22.2	25.9	27.1	27.3	26.8	27.7	27.7
Fire service												
regulars	BAIV	34.5	34.5	34.3	34.2	33.9	33.8	33.6	33.3	33.1	34.0	33.9
others	BAIW	6.0	5.7	5.8	5.7	5.7	5.8	5.7	5.6	5.6	6.3	6.2
Other services[3]	BCHM	243.7	244.7	238.0	226.7	217.0	191.3	183.8	177.9	173.1	178.1	177.8
Total of above	BCHN	1 720.5	1 701.0	1 661.6	1 506.1	1 477.4	1 462.8	1 436.4	1 419.2	1 403.6	1 417.5	1 434.2
Police Service												
police: all ranks	BCHO	120.2	120.9	120.8	121.4	121.0	118.8	118.4	118.5	119.2	119.2	117.0
cadets	BAIX	0.3	0.3	0.3	0.2	0.1	0.1	0.3	0.3	0.1	–	..
traffic wardens	BAIY	4.5	4.7	4.9	4.9	4.7	4.5	4.3	4.1	3.5	3.3	2.8
civilians	BAIZ	42.2	44.0	44.9	46.7	46.9	48.1	49.8	50.0	50.3	50.5	50.8
Magistrates courts	BAJA	9.4	10.0	10.0	10.0	9.9	10.0	9.9	9.2	8.9	9.0	8.9
Probation staff												
officers	BAJB	6.5	6.5	6.9	7.1	7.2	7.2	6.9	6.9	6.2	6.8	7.1
others	BAJC	7.0	7.3	7.5	7.9	8.0	8.5	7.2	7.1	5.4	7.1	7.5
Total law and order	BAJD	190.1	193.7	195.3	198.2	197.8	197.2	196.8	196.1	193.6	195.9	194.1
Agency staff	BAJE	1.3	1.5	1.1	1.4	1.6	0.9	0.8	0.8	0.8	–	..
Total(excluding special employment and training measures)	BCHR	1 911.9	1 896.2	1 858.0	1 705.7	1 676.8	1 660.9	1 634.0	1 616.1	1 598.0	1 613.4	1 628.3

		1990	1991	1992	1993	1994	1995	1996	1997	1998	1999	2000
Wales												
Education	ATAN	54.3	55.6	53.8	48.2	47.9	48.7	50.6	49.5	49.9	51.6	50.7
Construction	BCGC	7.4	7.0	6.5	5.9	5.8	5.9	6.0	5.5	5.5	5.7	5.6
Transport	BCGD	–	–	–	–	–	–	–	–	..	..	..
Social services	BCGE	15.0	15.0	16.0	16.0	17.0	18.3	18.5	19.0	18.8	19.2	19.2
Public libraries and museums	BCGF	1.6	1.7	1.7	1.7	1.7	1.7	1.5	1.6	1.5	1.6	1.6
Recreation, parks and baths	BCGG	5.8	5.9	5.8	6.0	6.0	6.3	5.8	6.4	6.1	6.1	6.0
Environmental health	BCGH	1.4	1.4	1.5	1.5	1.5	1.5	1.6	1.5	1.3	1.4	1.5
Refuse collection and disposal	BCGI	1.6	1.7	1.6	1.6	1.5	2.2	2.9	2.9	2.9	2.8	2.6
Housing	BCGJ	2.8	2.9	3.0	3.1	3.1	3.4	3.3	3.6	3.6	3.8	3.6
Town and country planning	BCGK	1.5	1.6	1.7	1.8	1.8	2.2	1.9	2.0	2.0	2.1	2.0
Fire service												
regulars	BAKT	1.8	1.8	1.8	1.8	1.8	1.8	1.9	1.9	1.9	1.9	1.9
others	BAKU	0.3	0.4	0.4	0.4	0.4	0.3	0.3	0.3	0.3	0.4	0.4
Other services	BCGM	19.0	18.8	18.7	23.5	19.8	15.6	14.2	14.6	14.0	15.1	15.1
Total of above	BCGN	112.9	114.3	112.5	111.5	108.1	107.9	108.5	108.8	107.8	111.7	109.9
Police Service												
police: all ranks	BCGO	6.5	6.6	6.6	6.6	6.5	6.4	6.4	6.6	6.6	6.6	6.6
cadets	BAKV	–	–	–	–	–	–	–	–	..	..	..
traffic wardens	BAKW	0.2	0.2	0.2	0.2	0.2	0.2	0.2	0.2	0.2	0.2	0.2
civilians	BAKX	2.0	2.1	2.1	2.1	2.2	2.2	2.5	2.4	2.4	2.8	2.7
Magistrates courts	BAKY	0.6	0.6	0.6	0.7	0.7	0.7	0.6	0.6	0.6	0.7	0.6
Probation staff												
officers	BAKZ	0.4	0.4	0.4	0.4	0.4	0.4	0.4	0.4	0.3	0.4	0.4
others	BALA	0.3	0.3	0.4	0.4	0.4	0.4	0.4	0.4	0.3	0.4	0.4
Total law and order	BALB	10.1	10.2	10.3	10.4	10.4	10.3	10.5	10.6	10.4	10.3	10.1
Agency staff	BALC	–	–	–	–	–	–	–	–	..	..	..
Total(excluding special employment and training measures)	BCGR	122.9	124.4	122.8	121.9	118.5	118.2	119.0	119.4	118.2	122.0	120.0

1 Figures are based on surveys undertaken on behalf of central and local government by the ONS and the Scottish Executive and the Convention of Scottish Local Authorities (COSLA).

2 Based on the following factors to convert part-time employees to approximate full-time equivalents: for teachers and lecturers in further education, 0.11; teachers in primary and secondary education and all other non-manual employees, 0.53; manual employees, 0.41.

3 Including civil service departments (eg engineers and treasurers) and all services not shown separately.

Sources: Department of the Environment, Transport and the Regions; Joint Staffing Watch; National Assembly for Wales

Labour market

7.8 Persons employed in local authorities[1]

continued

Thousands (Full-time equivalents)[2]

Service		1990	1991	1992	1993	1994	1995	1996	1997	1998	1999	2000
Scotland												
Education	ATAO	89.2	87.1	87.5	80.0	77.1	77.6	74.7	73.6	75.5	76.7	78.7
Construction	BCMC	23.4	23.5	23.1	22.9	22.0	21.7	20.7	20.6	20.5	20.4	20.5
Transport	BCMD	0.7	0.8	0.8	0.8	0.9	0.9	0.9	0.9	0.9	0.9	0.9
Social Services	BCME	36.2	36.2	36.8	37.3	38.3	39.1	38.4	37.9	37.0	34.6	34.6
Public libraries and museums	BCMF	4.4	4.4	4.5	4.6	4.7	4.7	4.2	4.2	4.2	4.1	4.0
Recreation, leisure and tourism	BCMG	13.8	13.6	13.3	13.7	13.9	13.9	11.4	11.4	11.3	11.3	11.3
Environmental health	BCMH	2.3	2.5	2.5	2.7	2.7	2.6	3.4	3.4	3.3	3.1	3.0
Cleansing	BCMI	8.4	8.2	8.1	8.2	8.1	8.0	7.3	7.2	7.2	7.2	7.2
Housing	BCMJ	7.3	7.3	7.2	7.4	7.8	7.9	7.9	8.4	8.5	8.5	8.5
Physical planning	BCMK	2.0	2.0	2.1	2.2	2.2	2.2	3.7	3.4	3.3	3.3	3.3
Fire service	BCML	5.1	5.2	5.2	5.3	5.3	5.2	5.8	5.6	5.7	5.7	5.7
Other services[3]	BCMM	44.3	46.8	48.1	48.0	52.1	51.5	40.7	40.7	38.5	39.0	38.1
Total of above	BCMN	237.1	237.6	239.2	233.1	235.1	235.3	219.1	217.3	215.9	214.8	215.8
Police service												
police (all ranks)	BCMO	13.7	13.9	13.9	14.2	14.2	14.4	13.7	14.2	14.3	14.4	14.4
others[4]	BCMP	4.7	4.6	4.8	5.1	5.2	5.2	5.2	5.3	5.4	5.4	5.4
Administration of district courts	BCMQ	0.2	0.2	0.1	0.2	0.2	0.2	0.2	0.2	0.2	0.2	0.2
Total (excluding special employment measures) and training	BCMR	255.7	256.3	258.0	252.6	254.7	255.1	238.2	237.0	235.8	234.8	235.8

1 See previous page.
2 Based on the following factors to convert part-time employees to approximate full-time equivalents: for lecturers and teachers, 0.40: non-manual staff (excluding teachers), 0.58; manual employees, 0.46.
3 Including central services departments (eg engineers and finance) and all services not shown separately.
4 Includes civilian employees of police forces and traffic wardens.

Sources: Department of the Environment, Transport and the Regions: 0117 987 8675;
Joint Staffing Watch;
National Assembly for Wales;
Scottish Executive;
Scottish Joint Staffing Watch.

7.9 Duration of ILO unemployment
United Kingdom

At Spring each year. Not seasonally adjusted.

Thousands

	All ILO unemployed	Less than 3 months	3 months & less than 6 months	6 months & less than 1 year	1 year & less than 2 years	2 years & less than 3 years	3 years & less than 4 years	4 years & less than 5 years	5 years or more	All 1 year or more	
										Number	As % of total
All											
	BEAS	BEFP	BEFS	BEFV	BEFY	BEGB	BEGE	BEGH	BEGK	BEGN	BEGQ
1990	1 974	686	324	310	211	107	73	51	210	653	33.1
1991	2 414	834	466	434	276	113	67	41	179	676	28.0
1992	2 769	668	500	607	529	174	75	37	179	993	35.9
1993	2 936	600	474	599	612	287	109	57	196	1 262	43.0
1994	2 738	610	389	488	514	310	166	81	178	1 248	45.6
1995	2 460	570	388	423	405	243	144	102	183	1 076	43.8
1996	2 340	602	381	421	344	190	130	85	185	933	39.9
1997	2 037	600	319	325	289	149	84	72	198	791	38.8
1998	1 776	595	327	265	218	109	68	42	149	587	33.1
1999	1 752	623	328	277	211	88	44	39	139	522	29.8
2000	1 619	605	308	249	198	79	36	32	111	456	28.2
Men											
	BEAT	BEFQ	BEFT	BEFW	BEFZ	BEGC	BEGF	BEGI	BEGL	BEGO	BEGR
1990	1 165	346	170	172	137	72	55	41	171	476	40.9
1991	1 514	455	288	281	189	76	50	31	142	488	32.3
1992	1 865	396	320	409	380	125	55	28	152	740	39.6
1993	1 986	348	313	385	439	212	84	43	160	938	47.2
1994	1 826	346	230	313	361	236	124	63	152	936	51.2
1995	1 612	301	240	268	280	182	115	79	144	801	49.7
1996	1 549	332	236	268	234	144	105	68	159	711	45.9
1997	1 306	323	195	198	195	104	63	58	167	588	45.0
1998	1 098	313	190	172	139	77	48	35	124	421	38.4
1999	1 095	341	203	171	143	61	31	31	113	379	34.6
2000	991	325	184	144	137	52	27	25	94	335	33.8
Women											
	BEAU	BEFR	BEFU	BEFX	BEGA	BEGD	BEGG	BEGJ	BEGM	BEGP	BEGS
1990	809	340	154	138	74	35	18	10	40	177	21.9
1991	900	378	178	153	87	36	17	10	37	188	20.9
1992	904	272	180	198	149	49	20	..	28	254	28.1
1993	949	251	161	214	173	74	25	15	37	323	34.1
1994	912	264	159	176	152	74	42	18	26	313	34.3
1995	849	270	148	155	125	61	28	23	39	275	32.4
1996	791	271	144	152	109	46	24	17	26	222	28.1
1997	732	277	124	127	94	45	20	14	31	203	27.8
1998	679	282	137	93	80	32	21	..	25	166	24.5
1999	657	282	126	106	69	27	13	..	25	143	21.7
2000	628	279	124	104	61	27	..	..	17	121	19.3

1 See chapter text for definitions.

Source: ONS, Labour Force Survey

Labour market

7.10 ILO Unemployment
United Kingdom

By age group and gender. At Spring each year. Not seasonally adjusted. Thousands and percentages

	All aged 16 and over	16-59/64	16-17	18-24	16-24	25-34	35-49	50-64 (m) 50-59 (f)	65+ (m) 60+ (f)
Numbers									
All									
	BEAS	BEGT	BEGW	BEGZ	BEHC	BEHF	BEHI	BEHL	BEHO
1991	2 414	2 373	131	643	775	656	577	365	41
1992	2 769	2 738	123	694	817	781	714	426	32
1993	2 936	2 902	112	755	867	801	748	487	33
1994	2 738	2 712	122	650	771	766	712	464	25
1995	2 460	2 443	122	586	708	693	654	388	17
1996	2 340	2 321	143	536	679	661	619	361	19
1997	2 037	2 015	144	464	608	537	546	324	23
1998	1 776	1 757	133	413	546	485	449	276	20
1999	1 752	1 732	142	400	541	437	478	276	19
2000	1 619	1 602	147	377	524	378	433	268	17
Men									
	BEAT	BEGU	BEGX	BEHA	BEHD	BEHG	BEHJ	BEHM	BEHP
1991	1 514	1 496	71	414	485	401	338	272	18
1992	1 865	1 850	71	469	541	517	459	333	15
1993	1 986	1 974	62	504	566	530	500	378	12
1994	1 826	1 816	66	434	499	510	455	352	10
1995	1 612	1 604	69	383	452	450	408	294	..
1996	1 549	1 538	87	360	446	417	401	273	11
1997	1 306	1 294	79	302	381	340	342	232	11
1998	1 098	1 088	73	259	332	291	264	201	..
1999	1 095	1 086	88	247	336	256	293	201	..
2000	991	984	81	235	316	221	253	193	..
Women									
	BEAU	BEGV	BEGY	BEHB	BEHE	BEHH	BEHK	BEHN	BEHQ
1991	900	877	61	229	290	255	240	92	23
1992	904	888	52	224	276	264	255	93	16
1993	949	928	49	251	300	271	248	109	21
1994	912	896	56	216	272	256	257	112	15
1995	849	839	53	203	256	243	246	95	..
1996	791	783	56	177	233	244	218	88	..
1997	732	720	65	162	227	197	204	92	11
1998	679	668	60	154	214	193	185	76	10
1999	657	646	53	152	206	181	184	75	10
2000	628	618	66	142	207	156	180	74	10
Rates[1]									
All									
	BEBQ	BEHR	BEHU	BEHX	BEIA	BEID	BEIG	BEIJ	BEIM
1991	8.4	8.5	14.9	13.3	13.6	8.8	5.9	7.2	5.0
1992	9.7	9.9	16.0	15.4	15.5	10.4	7.2	8.4	3.7
1993	10.3	10.5	16.8	17.4	17.3	10.5	7.5	9.6	4.1
1994	9.6	9.8	17.9	15.9	16.2	9.9	7.1	9.0	3.1
1995	8.6	8.8	17.4	15.0	15.3	9.0	6.5	7.5	2.1
1996	8.2	8.3	18.5	14.0	14.8	8.5	6.0	6.9	2.4
1997	7.1	7.2	17.7	12.6	13.5	6.9	5.3	5.9	2.7
1998	6.1	6.3	16.7	11.4	12.4	6.3	4.4	4.9	2.5
1999	6.0	6.1	17.9	11.1	12.3	5.8	4.5	4.7	2.3
2000	5.5	5.6	18.6	10.3	11.8	5.1	4.0	4.5	2.0
Men									
	BEBR	BEHS	BEHV	BEHY	BEIB	BEIE	BEIH	BEIK	BEIN
1991	.9.2	9.3	15.4	15.7	15.6	9.2	6.2	8.4	5.9
1992	11.5	11.7	17.7	19.0	18.8	11.9	8.4	10.4	4.9
1993	12.4	12.5	18.5	21.1	20.8	12.1	9.1	11.9	4.6
1994	11.4	11.5	18.8	19.3	19.2	11.5	8.3	11.0	3.7
1995	10.1	10.2	19.2	17.7	17.9	10.1	7.3	9.2	..
1996	9.6	9.7	21.3	17.2	17.8	9.4	7.2	8.4	4.0
1997	8.1	8.2	19.4	14.8	15.6	7.7	6.1	6.9	4.1
1998	6.8	6.9	18.1	13.1	14.0	6.7	4.7	5.8	..
1999	6.7	6.8	21.5	12.6	14.1	6.0	5.1	5.7	..
2000	6.1	6.1	20.1	11.8	13.2	5.3	4.3	5.4	..
Women									
	BEBS	BEHT	BEHW	BEHZ	BEIC	BEIF	BEII	BEIL	BEIO
1991	7.2	7.4	14.3	10.5	11.1	8.2	5.5	5.0	4.4
1992	7.3	7.5	14.0	11.0	11.5	8.4.	5.7	5.0	3.1
1993	7.6	7.8	15.1	12.9	13.2	8.4	5.5	5.7	3.9
1994	7.3	7.5	16.9	11.8	12.6	7.9	5.6	5.7	2.9
1995	6.8	7.0	15.5	11.6	12.2	7.4	5.4	4.7	..
1996	6.3	6.5	15.3	10.2	11.1	7.4	4.7	4.3	..
1997	5.7	5.9	16.0	9.8	11.0	5.9	4.4	4.3	2.1
1998	5.3	5.4	15.3	9.4	10.5	5.8	3.9	3.4	2.0
1999	5.1	5.2	14.0	9.3	10.2	5.5	3.9	3.3	1.9
2000	4.8	4.9	16.9	8.5	10.1	4.8	3.7	3.1	1.7

1 Total ILO unemployment as a percentage of all economically active persons in the relevant age group.

Source: ONS, Labour Force Survey

7.11 Claimant count by age and duration[1]
United Kingdom

		1996	1997	1998	1999
Annual averages					
Males					
All ages					
All durations	GEZG	1 601.0	1 216.3	1 031.0	954.6
Up to 6 months	GEZH	667.1	569.4	541.1	530.6
Over 6 and up to 12 months	GEZI	300.6	200.6	188.5	166.8
All over 12 months	GEZJ	633.4	446.3	301.4	257.1
All over 24 months	GEZK	372.7	269.7	169.8	128.9
Aged 18 to 24					
All durations	GEZL	378.1	284.6	237.5	205.2
Up to 6 months	GEZM	203.8	172.5	159.8	160.9
Over 6 and up to 12 months	GEZN	81.0	53.2	44.2	34.3
All over 12 months	GEZO	93.5	58.9	33.5	10.0
All over 24 months	GEZP	35.3	22.1	10.7	2.3
Aged 25 to 49					
All durations	IACI	957.7	729.1	619.4	582.9
Up to 6 months	IACK	363.5	313.7	303.2	291.3
Over 6 and up to 12 months	IACN	173.7	118.2	117.3	107.4
All over 12 months	IACQ	420.6	297.2	198.9	184.3
All over 24 months	IACT	257.5	185.6	112.4	88.0
Aged 50 and over					
All durations	IACW	255.6	193.0	165.8	158.0
Up to 6 months	IACZ	91.2	74.3	70.3	70.6
Over 6 and up to 12 months	IADC	45.1	28.6	26.6	24.6
All over 12 months	IADF	119.2	90.1	69.0	62.8
All over 24 months	IADI	80.0	62.0	46.7	38.6
Females					
All ages					
All durations	GEZR	506.9	373.5	321.8	296.3
Up to 6 months	GEZS	267.4	216.3	203.0	195.5
Over 6 and up to 12 months	GEZT	102.1	62.1	54.5	48.1
All over 12 months	GEZU	137.4	95.2	64.2	52.7
All over 24 months	GEZV	67.0	48.9	30.9	22.9
Aged 18 to 24					
All durations	GEZW	164.9	121.8	101.5	88.9
Up to 6 months	GEZX	100.1	80.1	72.4	71.1
Over 6 and up to 12 months	GEZY	33.6	21.6	17.3	14.0
All over 12 months	GEZZ	31.1	20.1	11.8	3.8
All over 24 months	GEYU	9.9	6.6	3.3	0.8
Aged 25 to 49					
All durations	IACJ	253.3	181.7	157.4	147.1
Up to 6 months	IACL	127.8	100.8	96.1	90.3
Over 6 and up to 12 months	IACO	52.3	29.9	27.0	24.7
All over 12 months	IACR	73.3	51.1	34.3	32.1
All over 24 months	IACU	37.2	27.5	16.9	13.4
Aged 50 and over					
All durations	IACX	81.5	62.8	56.7	54.0
Up to 6 months	IADA	33.0	28.6	28.6	28.2
Over 6 and up to 12 months	IADD	15.6	10.2	9.9	9.1
All over 12 months	IADG	32.9	23.9	18.1	16.7
All over 24 months	IADJ	20.0	14.9	10.7	8.7

Relationship between rows: 1=2+3+4; 6=7+8+9; 11=12+13+14; 16=17+18+19

1 Count of claimants of unemployment-related benefits.

Sources: Office for National Statistics: 020 7533 6094; Benefits Agency

Labour market

7.12 ILO unemployment rates[1]
At Spring each year. Not seasonally adjusted.

Percentages

		1993	1994	1995	1996	1997	1998	1999	2000
United Kingdom	BEBQ	10.3	9.6	8.6	8.2	7.1	6.1	6.0	5.5
North East	BENU	12.0	12.5	11.4	10.8	9.8	8.1	10.1	9.1
North West	BENV	10.8	10.3	9.0	8.4	6.8	6.6	6.2	5.3
Yorkshire and Humber	BENY	10.0	9.9	8.7	8.1	8.0	7.0	6.5	6.0
East Midlands	BENZ	9.1	8.3	7.4	7.4	6.3	4.9	5.2	5.1
West Midlands	BEOA	11.8	10.0	8.9	9.2	6.8	6.3	6.8	6.2
East	BEOB	9.2	8.2	7.5	6.1	5.8	5.0	4.1	3.6
London	BEOC	13.2	13.1	11.5	11.3	9.1	8.2	7.6	7.0
South East	BEOD	8.0	7.1	6.4	6.0	5.2	4.3	3.6	3.3
South West	BEOE	9.2	7.5	7.8	6.3	5.2	4.5	4.7	4.1
England	BEOF	10.3	9.5	8.6	8.1	6.8	6.0	5.8	5.2
Wales	BEOG	9.6	9.4	8.8	8.3	8.3	6.7	7.0	6.1
Scotland	BEOH	10.2	10.0	8.4	8.7	8.5	7.4	7.4	7.6
Northern Ireland	BEOI	12.5	11.6	11.0	9.5	7.5	7.2	7.2	7.0

1 See chapter text for definitions.

Source: ONS, Labour Force Survey

7.13 Claimant count rates[1,2]
Analysis by Government Office Regions[3]
Seasonally adjusted annual averages

Percentages

		1989	1990	1991	1992	1993	1994	1995	1996	1997	1998	1999
United Kingdom	BCJE	6.2	5.7	7.9	9.6	10.2	9.2	8.0	7.2	5.5	4.7	4.3
North East	DPDM	10.8	9.6	11.1	12.0	12.8	12.2	11.2	10.2	8.4	7.5	7.3
North West	IBWC	8.1	7.4	9.1	10.4	10.5	9.7	8.5	7.7	6.0	5.3	4.9
Yorkshire and the Humber	DPBI	7.3	6.6	8.6	9.8	10.1	9.5	8.5	7.8	6.3	5.6	5.2
East Midlands	DPBJ	5.3	5.1	7.2	8.9	9.4	8.6	7.4	6.7	4.8	4.1	3.8
West Midlands	DPBN	6.4	5.7	8.3	10.3	10.8	9.8	8.1	7.2	5.5	4.7	4.6
East	DPDP	3.4	3.5	6.3	8.6	9.3	8.0	6.5	5.9	4.1	3.3	3.0
London	DPDQ	5.0	5.0	8.0	10.4	11.5	10.6	9.4	8.5	6.4	5.2	4.7
South East	DPDR	2.8	3.0	5.7	7.9	8.6	7.2	5.9	5.0	3.4	2.7	2.4
South West	DPBM	4.3	4.2	6.8	9.1	9.4	8.0	6.8	6.1	4.3	3.5	3.1
Wales	DPBP	7.3	6.7	8.9	9.9	10.2	9.2	8.4	8.0	6.4	5.6	5.2
Scotland	DPBQ	9.3	8.1	8.7	9.3	9.6	9.2	7.9	7.6	6.4	5.7	5.4
Northern Ireland	DPBR	14.0	12.7	12.9	13.7	13.6	12.6	11.2	10.7	8.1	7.3	6.5
Great Britain	DPAJ	6.0	5.5	7.8	9.5	10.1	9.2	7.9	7.1	5.4	4.6	4.3

1 The number of unemployment-related benefit claimants as a percentage of the estimated total workforce (the sum of claimants, employee jobs self-employed, participants on work related government training programmes and HM Forces) at mid-year.
2 Seasonally adjusted and excluding claimants under 18, consistent with current coverage.

3 New geographical boundaries were introduced in May 1997 for UK regions and the data are only available from March 1986. Data for Standard Statistical Regions are available on request.

Source: ONS, Labour Market Statistics: 020 7533 6094

7.14 Claimant count[1,2]
Analysis by Government Office Regions[3]
Seasonally adjusted

Thousands

	North East	North West	Yorkshire and the Humber	East Midlands	West Midlands	East	London	South East	South West	England	Wales	Scotland	Great Britain	Northern Ireland	United Kingdom
	DPDG	IBWA	DPAX	DPAY	DPBC	DPDJ	DPDK	DPDL	DPBB	IBWK	DPBE	DPBF	DPAG	DPBG	BCJD
1986 Jan	..	..	286.4	186.3	324.3	..	382.3	..	192.2	2 439.9	169.2	319.5	2 928.6	115.9	3 044.5
Apr	197.1	442.4	289.2	186.8	326.1	191.3	390.9	246.6	194.4	2 464.3	169.0	322.5	2 956.3	120.0	3 076.3
Jul	196.2	443.4	291.3	188.1	326.8	190.5	393.5	245.6	195.8	2 474.4	167.8	329.0	2 968.0	122.0	3 090.0
Oct	192.5	437.3	287.5	186.2	322.6	186.8	388.1	241.2	192.6	2 432.8	162.9	331.5	2 929.2	123.5	3 052.7
1987 Jan	191.3	429.4	283.1	184.1	316.5	185.6	381.6	238.1	188.3	2 393.9	159.1	334.7	2 891.8	123.1	3 014.9
Apr	187.3	417.5	276.9	178.6	303.9	174.0	364.4	222.8	180.2	2 304.0	152.0	332.0	2 789.6	121.5	2 911.1
Jul	179.5	396.9	263.1	169.3	287.5	161.4	348.8	205.5	168.9	2 182.4	145.5	317.8	2 644.2	119.8	2 764.0
Oct	172.3	379.5	249.1	159.3	271.6	149.6	331.0	189.5	158.2	2 059.3	139.4	303.7	2 503.2	117.8	2 621.0
1988 Jan	164.7	363.6	237.6	150.7	256.1	138.3	313.7	171.7	150.4	1 943.7	132.9	294.6	2 374.3	114.3	2 488.6
Apr	158.8	347.1	229.2	143.1	241.4	124.0	299.8	154.6	140.1	1 835.6	128.7	283.5	2 250.3	112.1	2 362.4
Jul	151.7	328.4	216.1	134.1	224.4	110.8	277.6	140.1	129.6	1 713.8	120.9	270.4	2 104.1	110.3	2 214.4
Oct	146.2	319.0	207.0	127.2	210.0	101.4	265.4	130.8	122.3	1 629.0	117.1	265.0	2 011.4	108.6	2 120.0
1989 Jan	140.3	301.4	192.6	116.8	190.9	89.5	242.3	114.6	109.2	1 495.9	108.1	254.2	1 859.9	107.4	1 967.3
Apr	132.3	283.0	178.6	106.6	171.9	80.2	221.3	103.4	99.9	1 375.7	99.4	238.9	1 715.5	105.1	1 820.6
Jul	124.4	269.7	171.3	101.7	163.0	78.4	216.1	100.6	95.5	1 322.0	93.2	226.3	1 640.2	102.8	1 743.0
Oct	118.0	256.5	164.5	97.8	155.9	76.8	204.8	99.7	91.5	1 265.2	88.5	217.7	1 571.7	100.0	1 671.7
1990 Jan	112.5	243.7	159.5	93.8	151.1	74.3	199.4	95.5	86.5	1 215.7	84.4	207.9	1 508.6	97.3	1 605.9
Apr	109.3	238.0	154.0	92.7	145.0	75.3	194.7	95.1	86.5	1 189.9	82.8	200.8	1 474.2	96.0	1 570.2
Jul	109.1	237.7	156.1	96.1	147.1	83.8	203.9	107.2	94.1	1 234.7	83.2	194.3	1 512.6	94.4	1 607.0
Oct	112.3	248.0	165.0	104.8	157.3	98.2	226.6	127.5	106.4	1 345.5	88.7	197.3	1 632.1	93.8	1 725.9
1991 Jan	116.7	261.8	176.4	113.1	171.0	112.5	255.8	149.7	122.2	1 478.8	95.0	200.9	1 775.1	96.0	1 871.1
Apr	126.2	285.9	197.5	132.0	203.5	138.5	303.2	190.5	146.9	1 723.9	108.8	212.7	2 045.7	97.9	2 143.6
Jul	130.5	305.4	211.9	145.5	225.4	158.9	342.3	221.3	165.7	1 906.8	115.5	220.1	2 242.5	98.8	2 341.3
Oct	133.2	318.2	219.6	154.5	240.0	172.4	368.9	240.9	178.6	2 025.9	119.3	224.0	2 369.6	100.5	2 470.1
1992 Jan	133.9	325.4	222.7	160.4	250.6	183.3	389.8	258.4	188.4	2 112.6	121.3	228.0	2 462.2	102.2	2 564.4
Apr	135.7	332.8	227.6	168.0	260.0	196.0	409.6	277.7	199.0	2 205.5	123.4	231.8	2 561.6	103.4	2 665.0
Jul	136.7	335.2	232.4	172.1	266.1	205.1	426.2	288.9	206.6	2 268.9	124.1	235.2	2 628.6	104.6	2 733.2
Oct	141.4	343.6	240.2	178.8	277.4	218.6	448.0	308.4	215.3	2 371.1	129.2	242.4	2 743.3	105.1	2 848.4
1993 Jan	146.2	348.3	247.5	185.2	286.2	229.5	464.6	325.2	222.6	2 454.4	131.4	245.3	2 832.0	105.5	2 937.5
Apr	148.0	345.2	246.5	183.6	285.1	228.2	469.5	321.4	220.0	2 446.6	130.3	243.2	2 821.0	104.5	2 925.5
Jul	148.5	338.0	240.9	180.8	278.7	223.5	466.3	314.0	214.4	2 404.4	129.3	241.2	2 775.6	102.5	2 878.1
Oct	147.5	331.1	237.8	177.8	271.5	216.6	460.4	306.6	208.4	2 356.8	127.8	236.6	2 722.1	101.8	2 823.9
1994 Jan	145.6	325.1	233.7	174.7	262.3	210.0	451.4	296.7	203.6	2 302.3	126.7	236.0	2 665.8	100.2	2 766.0
Apr	141.6	314.5	227.4	170.7	252.0	200.4	440.4	280.9	194.5	2 221.7	123.3	231.7	2 577.4	98.9	2 676.3
Jul	139.1	304.2	222.7	166.3	242.3	191.0	428.1	268.1	188.1	2 148.8	119.0	227.4	2 496.3	97.2	2 593.5
Oct	136.0	291.7	215.9	160.1	230.5	180.5	415.4	251.1	178.9	2 059.0	112.9	218.1	2 391.1	93.8	2 484.9
1995 Jan	133.0	280.1	210.6	153.2	218.5	172.3	401.4	237.9	171.4	1 977.5	108.3	209.3	2 296.0	91.3	2 387.3
Apr	130.0	270.8	206.8	148.1	211.0	167.1	395.0	229.7	166.0	1 923.8	106.2	200.3	2 231.0	88.6	2 319.6
Jul	128.2	266.1	204.6	145.3	206.9	165.0	390.2	225.1	162.5	1 892.8	106.7	195.3	2 195.9	87.6	2 283.5
Oct	126.4	260.9	200.7	142.3	201.3	160.7	383.2	219.1	159.4	1 852.7	105.4	193.5	2 152.9	85.8	2 238.7
1996 Jan	123.1	255.8	197.0	140.0	196.5	157.2	376.8	213.3	155.6	1 814.6	104.0	193.2	2 112.5	85.9	2 198.4
Apr	121.7	254.9	195.7	137.7	194.2	153.5	367.9	207.6	152.3	1 785.1	104.6	194.9	2 085.0	86.1	2 171.1
Jul	116.9	248.2	188.8	131.8	187.6	146.8	357.5	198.9	146.8	1 722.5	101.8	191.9	2 017.0	86.4	2 103.4
Oct	110.5	238.4	181.1	124.9	177.8	138.5	341.6	185.5	137.9	1 635.0	98.2	186.3	1 920.7	81.7	2 002.4
1997 Jan	101.2	218.6	166.6	111.9	160.1	123.7	313.2	163.6	125.5	1 484.4	90.2	174.0	1 748.6	71.1	1 819.7
Apr	95.1	201.4	154.8	102.5	147.3	110.7	285.1	144.2	112.2	1 353.7	82.5	162.4	1 598.2	65.0	1 663.2
Jul	92.5	188.6	148.3	94.9	137.9	102.2	264.1	130.8	100.7	1 259.9	78.1	152.4	1 490.5	61.3	1 551.8
Oct	90.4	177.6	142.1	87.7	131.7	94.2	246.4	120.4	93.1	1 183.3	73.6	146.5	1 403.7	60.7	1 464.4
1998 Jan	87.9	170.8	137.4	82.7	126.2	88.7	234.9	112.6	87.7	1 129.0	70.9	142.0	1 341.8	60.0	1 401.8
Apr	84.1	165.6	134.2	80.0	122.4	85.3	229.7	107.9	85.0	1 094.2	69.3	138.7	1 302.2	57.7	1 359.9
Jul	81.7	163.3	133.0	79.8	121.0	83.4	224.6	105.3	84.1	1 075.9	68.5	137.5	1 282.2	57.1	1 339.3
Oct	82.0	160.8	130.9	80.0	121.4	82.0	219.1	102.5	82.0	1 060.3	68.1	136.7	1 265.5	56.2	1 321.7
1999 Jan	82.7	159.6	129.7	78.5	122.7	80.4	215.4	101.1	79.9	1 050.4	67.9	136.0	1 253.9	56.0	1 309.9
Apr	82.4	157.5	126.9	78.2	123.0	79.1	208.1	98.8	78.4	1 032.4	67.0	133.9	1 233.3	54.7	1 288.0
Jul	79.8	152.7	121.6	75.4	119.3	76.0	200.9	94.0	74.9	994.5	63.4	127.5	1 185.5	49.6	1 235.1
Oct	76.7	149.8	118.2	73.8	116.0	73.6	196.1	91.3	71.6	966.8	61.2	125.9	1 154.2	46.6	1 200.8
2000 Jan	75.8	145.7	114.4	72.5	112.4	70.0	190.1	86.7	66.5	934.5	59.3	123.8	1 117.2	44.2	1 161.4
Apr	73.6	140.6	109.6	70.6	108.7	66.9	181.4	82.0	64.2	897.6	57.6	119.7	1 075.1	42.5	1 117.6
Jul	71.5	134.6	104.8	68.4	106.4	62.6	171.1	77.7	61.1	858.1	56.8	113.6	1 028.5	40.8	1 069.3
Oct	70.1	131.2	103.0	68.1	106.6	60.8	164.8	74.4	58.4	837.3	56.7	111.9	1 006.0	41.3	1 047.3

1 The figures are based on the number of claimants receiving unemployment related benefits and are adjusted for seasonality and discontinuities to be consistent with current coverage.

2 The latest national and regional seasonally adjusted claimant count figures are provisional and subject to revision in the following month.

3 New geographical boundaries were introduced in May 1997 for UK regions and data for some regions are only available from March 1986.

Source: ONS, Labour Market Statistics: 020 7533 6094

7.15 Economic activity: by age and gender
United Kingdom
At Spring each year. Not seasonally adjusted.

Thousands and percentages

	All aged 16 and over	16-59/64	16-17	18-24	16-24	25-34	35-49	50-64 (m) 50-59 (f)	65+ (m) 60+ (f)
All	**Numbers**								
	BEAM	BEIP	BEIS	BEIV	BEIY	BEJB	BEJE	BEJH	BEJK
1991	28 813	27 995	882	4 828	5 709	7 438	9 763	5 085	818
1992	28 581	27 734	771	4 508	5 279	7 501	9 890	5 064	847
1993	28 447	27 640	663	4 334	4 997	7 610	9 966	5 068	806
1994	28 455	27 648	679	4 082	4 761	7 696	10 039	5 152	807
1995	28 486	27 673	701	3 916	4 617	7 735	10 130	5 191	813
1996	28 663	27 873	773	3 819	4 593	7 742	10 272	5 267	790
1997	28 852	28 026	812	3 695	4 507	7 773	10 271	5 476	825
1998	28 892	28 097	798	3 612	4 410	7 697	10 319	5 671	795
1999	29 194	28 359	790	3 608	4 398	7 582	10 522	5 858	835
2000	29 412	28 568	792	3 651	4 443	7 403	10 720	6 002	844
Men									
	BEAN	BEIQ	BEIT	BEIW	BEIZ	BEJC	BEJF	BEJI	BEJL
1991	16 401	16 099	459	2 641	3 100	4 341	5 412	3 246	302
1992	16 187	15 871	403	2 467	2 870	4 363	5 439	3 200	316
1993	16 021	15 754	338	2 382	2 721	4 390	5 473	3 170	267
1994	16 000	15 725	350	2 252	2 602	4 441	5 496	3 187	274
1995	16 009	15 713	362	2 158	2 520	4 449	5 558	3 186	296
1996	16 052	15 776	408	2 096	2 504	4 425	5 608	3 239	277
1997	16 098	15 818	407	2 032	2 440	4 421	5 605	3 353	280
1998	16 096	15 813	405	1 973	2 377	4 378	5 619	3 439	283
1999	16 234	15 937	409	1 966	2 375	4 274	5 741	3 548	297
2000	16 327	16 034	404	1 992	2 396	4 177	5 856	3 605	294
Women									
	BEAO	BEIR	BEIU	BEIX	BEJA	BEJD	BEJG	BEJJ	BEJM
1991	12 412	11 897	423	2 186	2 609	3 097	4 351	1 839	516
1992	12 395	11 863	368	2 041	2 409	3 138	4 452	1 864	532
1993	12 426	11 887	324	1 952	2 276	3 220	4 492	1 898	539
1994	12 456	11 923	329	1 830	2 159	3 255	4 543	1 965	533
1995	12 477	11 960	340	1 758	2 097	3 286	4 572	2 004	517
1996	12 611	12 098	365	1 723	2 089	3 316	4 664	2 028	513
1997	12 754	12 208	405	1 663	2 067	3 352	4 666	2 123	545
1998	12 796	12 284	393	1 640	2 033	3 320	4 700	2 232	511
1999	12 960	12 422	380	1 642	2 023	3 308	4 781	2 310	538
2000	13 084	12 534	388	1 660	2 047	3 227	4 863	2 397	550
All	**Rates[1]**								
	BEJN	BEAY	BEJQ	BEJT	BEJW	BEJZ	BEKC	BEKF	BEKI
1991	63.7	79.8	62.0	80.3	76.8	83.0	85.8	69.5	8.1
1992	63.1	78.8	55.9	76.7	72.7	82.6	86.0	69.1	8.4
1993	62.7	78.4	50.0	76.3	71.3	82.8	85.5	68.5	7.9
1994	62.6	78.2	52.3	74.5	70.3	83.0	85.2	68.6	8.0
1995	62.4	78.0	52.2	74.2	69.7	83.0	85.0	68.2	8.0
1996	62.5	78.2	54.4	75.2	70.6	82.9	84.9	68.2	7.8
1997	62.7	78.2	55.7	74.7	70.4	83.6	84.5	68.5	8.1
1998	62.5	78.0	54.8	73.7	69.4	83.8	84.3	68.8	7.8
1999	62.9	78.4	54.7	73.5	69.2	84.4	84.9	69.4	8.1
2000	63.1	78.7	55.0	74.0	69.7	84.7	85.1	69.8	8.2
Men									
	BEJO	BEAZ	BEJR	BEJU	BEJX	BEKA	BEKD	BEKG	BEKJ
1991	75.0	87.7	62.9	86.0	81.6	95.7	95.1	75.0	8.6
1992	73.8	86.3	56.9	82.3	77.4	94.9	94.6	73.9	8.9
1993	72.9	85.6	49.7	82.1	76.0	94.4	94.0	72.8	7.5
1994	72.6	85.2	52.5	80.5	75.1	94.5	93.3	72.3	7.6
1995	72.3	84.7	52.4	80.0	74.4	94.1	93.2	71.5	8.2
1996	72.0	84.6	56.0	80.7	75.3	93.3	92.5	71.8	7.6
1997	71.8	84.4	54.6	80.4	74.5	93.5	91.9	72.2	7.6
1998	71.4	83.9	54.4	78.8	73.2	93.5	91.4	72.0	7.7
1999	71.6	84.1	55.3	78.5	73.2	93.3	92.1	72.6	8.0
2000	71.8	84.3	54.8	79.2	73.7	93.8	92.4	72.5	7.9
Women									
	BEJP	BEBJ	BEJS	BEJV	BEJY	BEKB	BEKE	BEKH	BEKK
1991	53.1	71.0	61.1	74.3	71.8	69.9	76.4	61.4	7.8
1992	53.0	70.6	54.7	70.9	67.9	70.0	77.3	62.1	8.1
1993	53.1	70.6	50.2	70.2	66.4	71.0	77.1	62.5	8.2
1994	53.1	70.6	52.1	68.3	65.2	71.2	77.1	63.4	8.1
1995	53.1	70.6	51.9	68.1	64.8	71.6	76.7	63.5	7.9
1996	53.5	71.1	52.7	69.4	65.7	72.2	77.3	63.1	7.9
1997	54.0	71.4	56.9	68.7	66.0	73.4	77.0	63.4	8.4
1998	54.0	71.5	55.3	68.3	65.4	73.7	77.2	64.3	7.8
1999	54.5	72.1	54.0	68.3	65.0	75.1	77.6	64.9	8.2
2000	54.9	72.5	55.2	68.6	65.6	75.3	77.8	66.0	8.4

1 Total economically active (see chapter text for definitions) as a percentage
of all persons in the relevant age group.

Source: ONS, Labour Force Survey

7.16 Economically inactive: by age and gender
United Kingdom
At Spring each year. Not seasonally adjusted.

Thousands and percentages

	All aged 16 and over	16-59/64	16-17	18-24	16-24	25-34	35-49	50-64 (m) 50-59 (f)	65+ (m) 60+ (f)
Numbers									
All									
	BEAV	BEKL	BEKO	BEKR	BEKU	BEKX	BELA	BELD	BELG
1991	16 413	7 108	539	1 188	1 727	1 525	1 620	2 236	9 305
1992	16 728	7 439	609	1 368	1 978	1 581	1 616	2 264	9 289
1993	16 954	7 602	663	1 349	2 012	1 576	1 687	2 327	9 352
1994	17 032	7 690	619	1 396	2 015	1 578	1 742	2 355	9 343
1995	17 155	7 810	643	1 364	2 007	1 584	1 794	2 425	9 345
1996	17 172	7 790	649	1 261	1 911	1 594	1 828	2 457	9 382
1997	17 184	7 818	646	1 253	1 899	1 523	1 883	2 514	9 367
1998	17 361	7 929	657	1 292	1 949	1 487	1 916	2 576	9 433
1999	17 237	7 818	655	1 302	1 957	1 403	1 872	2 586	9 419
2000	17 169	7 744	649	1 284	1 932	1 338	1 872	2 602	9 425
Men									
	BEAW	BEKM	BEKP	BEKS	BEKV	BEKY	BELB	BELE	BELH
1991	5 470	2 251	271	430	700	193	277	1 080	3 219
1992	5 737	2 511	305	532	837	235	312	1 127	3 226
1993	5 964	2 661	342	518	860	262	352	1 187	3 304
1994	6 050	2 735	316	546	863	259	393	1 220	3 315
1995	6 146	2 828	328	540	868	281	409	1 270	3 318
1996	6 230	2 866	321	501	822	319	455	1 270	3 365
1997	6 314	2 926	339	496	835	309	491	1 290	3 388
1998	6 450	3 038	339	531	871	302	526	1 340	3 412
1999	6 423	3 006	330	539	869	306	492	1 339	3 418
2000	6 427	2 987	334	523	857	278	485	1 367	3 440
Women									
	BEAX	BEKN	BEKQ	BEKT	BEKW	BEKZ	BELC	BELF	BELI
1991	10 942	4 857	269	758	1 027	1 332	1 343	1 155	6 085
1992	10 991	4 928	305	837	1 141	1 347	1 304	1 136	6 063
1993	10 989	4 941	321	830	1 152	1 315	1 336	1 140	6 048
1994	10 983	4 955	302	850	1 152	1 320	1 349	1 135	6 028
1995	11 009	4 982	315	824	1 139	1 303	1 385	1 155	6 026
1996	10 942	4 924	328	761	1 089	1 275	1 373	1 188	6 017
1997	10 871	4 892	307	757	1 064	1 214	1 391	1 224	5 978
1998	10 911	4 890	318	760	1 078	1 185	1 390	1 237	6 021
1999	10 813	4 812	324	764	1 088	1 098	1 380	1 247	6 001
2000	10 742	4 758	315	761	1 076	1 060	1 387	1 235	5 985
Rates[1]									
All									
	BELJ	BELM	BELP	BELS	BELV	BELY	BEMB	BEME	BEMH
1991	36.3	20.2	38.0	19.7	23.2	17.0	14.2	30.5	91.9
1992	36.9	21.2	44.1	23.3	27.3	17.4	14.0	30.9	91.6
1993	37.3	21.6	50.0	23.7	28.7	17.2	14.5	31.5	92.1
1994	37.4	21.8	47.7	25.5	29.7	17.0	14.8	31.4	92.0
1995	37.6	22.0	47.8	25.8	30.3	17.0	15.0	31.8	92.0
1996	37.5	21.8	45.6	24.8	29.4	17.1	15.1	31.8	92.2
1997	37.3	21.8	44.3	25.3	29.6	16.4	15.5	31.5	91.9
1998	37.5	22.0	45.2	26.3	30.6	16.2	15.7	31.2	92.2
1999	37.1	21.6	45.3	26.5	30.8	15.6	15.1	30.6	91.9
2000	36.9	21.3	45.0	26.0	30.3	15.3	14.9	30.2	91.8
Men									
	BELK	BELN	BELQ	BELT	BELW	BELZ	BEMC	BEMF	BEMI
1991	25.0	12.3	37.1	14.0	18.4	4.3	4.9	25.0	91.4
1992	26.2	13.7	43.1	17.7	22.6	5.1	5.4	26.1	91.1
1993	27.1	14.4	50.3	17.9	24.0	5.6	6.0	27.2	92.5
1994	27.4	14.8	47.5	19.5	24.9	5.5	6.7	27.7	92.4
1995	27.7	15.3	47.6	20.0	25.6	5.9	6.8	28.5	91.8
1996	28.0	15.4	44.0	19.3	24.7	6.7	7.5	28.2	92.4
1997	28.2	15.6	45.4	19.6	25.5	6.5	8.1	27.8	92.4
1998	28.6	16.1	45.6	21.2	26.8	6.5	8.6	28.0	92.3
1999	28.4	15.9	44.7	21.5	26.8	6.7	7.9	27.4	92.0
2000	28.2	15.7	45.2	20.8	26.3	6.2	7.6	27.5	92.1
Women									
	BELL	BELO	BELR	BELU	BELX	BEMA	BEMD	BEMG	BEMJ
1991	46.9	29.0	38.9	25.7	28.2	30.1	23.6	38.6	92.2
1992	47.0	29.4	45.3	29.1	32.1	30.0	22.7	37.9	91.9
1993	46.9	29.4	49.8	29.8	33.6	29.0	22.9	37.5	91.8
1994	46.9	29.4	47.9	31.7	34.8	28.8	22.9	36.6	91.9
1995	46.9	29.4	48.1	31.9	35.2	28.4	23.3	36.5	92.1
1996	46.5	28.9	47.3	30.6	34.3	27.8	22.7	36.9	92.1
1997	46.0	28.6	43.1	31.3	34.0	26.6	23.0	36.6	91.6
1998	46.0	28.5	44.7	31.7	34.6	26.3	22.8	35.7	92.2
1999	45.5	27.9	46.0	31.7	35.0	24.9	22.4	35.1	91.8
2000	45.1	27.5	44.8	31.4	34.4	24.7	22.2	34.0	91.6

1 Total economically active (see chapter text for definitions) as a percentage of all persons in the relevant age group.

Source: ONS, Labour Force Survey

Labour market

7.17 Economically inactive: by reason
United Kingdom
At Spring each year. Not seasonally adjusted.

Thousands

| | Total economica-lly inactive | Does not want job | Wants job[1] but not seeking in last 4 weeks | | | | | | | | Wants job[1] and seeking work but not available to start[2] | | |
| | | | Total | Availability to start work in next 2 weeks | | Discourag-ed workers[3] | Long term sick/ disabled | Looking after family/ home | Students | Other | All | Students | Other |
				Available	Not available[2]								
All[4]													
	BEKL	BEMK	BEMN	BEMQ	BEMT	BEMW	BEMZ	BENC	BENF	BENI	BENL	BENO	BENR
1994	7 690	5 408	2 007	885	1 122	132	498	782	245	350	275	154	120
1995	7 810	5 510	2 017	889	1 128	105	518	763	256	374	283	173	109
1996	7 790	5 450	2 113	864	1 249	102	574	768	280	389	227	138	89
1997	7 818	5 394	2 174	753	1 421	89	686	738	288	373	249	145	104
1998	7 929	5 492	2 176	707	1 468	73	750	738	270	345	261	145	116
1999	7 818	5 456	2 108	663	1 446	70	751	674	264	349	253	140	113
2000	7 744	5 391	2 125	645	1 479	65	770	649	264	378	229	126	102
Men													
	BEKM	BEML	BEMO	BEMR	BEMU	BEMX	BENA	BEND	BENG	BENJ	BENM	BENP	BENS
1994	2 735	1 877	722	300	422	80	319	48	128	148	135	84	51
1995	2 828	1 969	726	298	428	62	321	49	137	157	133	85	48
1996	2 866	1 950	807	319	488	59	356	68	151	173	109	67	41
1997	2 926	1 965	842	254	587	52	414	69	149	159	119	79	40
1998	3 038	2 029	880	261	619	45	470	74	143	148	130	80	50
1999	3 006	2 037	856	258	598	42	461	71	136	146	113	68	45
2000	2 987	2 020	866	248	618	36	467	64	130	169	101	64	36
Women													
	BEKN	BEMM	BEMP	BEMS	BEMV	BEMY	BENB	BENE	BENH	BENK	BENN	BENQ	BENT
1994	4 955	3 531	1 285	584	701	53	179	734	117	202	139	70	69
1995	4 982	3 541	1 291	591	700	44	197	714	119	217	149	88	61
1996	4 924	3 500	1 306	545	761	42	218	700	129	216	119	71	48
1997	4 892	3 430	1 333	499	833	38	273	669	139	214	130	66	64
1998	4 890	3 463	1 296	446	850	28	280	664	127	197	131	65	66
1999	4 812	3 420	1 252	405	847	29	291	603	128	202	140	72	68
2000	4 758	3 371	1 259	397	862	29	302	584	134	209	128	62	66

1 According to responses to LFS question.
2 Not available to start work in next two weeks including a few people who could not state whether or not they were available.
3 People whose reason for not seeking work was that they believed no jobs were available.
4 All persons of working age (men 16-64, women 16-59).

Source: ONS, Labour Force Survey

7.18 Labour disputes
United Kingdom

Thousands

		1994	1995	1996	1997	1998	1999
SIC 1992							
Working days lost through all stoppages in progress: total	KBBZ	278	415	1 303	235	282	242
Analysis by industry							
Mining, quarrying, electricity, gas and water	DMME	1	1	2	2	–	–
Manufacturing	DMMF	58	65	97	86	34	57
Construction	DMMG	5	10	8	17	13	49
Transport, storage and communication	DMMH	110	120	884	36	139	50
Public administration and defence	DMMI	11	95	158	29	28	35
Education	DMMJ	70	67	128	28	6	25
Health and social work	DMMK	5	16	8	7	16	5
Other community, social and pesonal services	DMML	11	23	3	5	30	7
All other industries and services	DMMM	8	16	15	25	15	12
Analysis by number of working days lost in each stoppage							
Under 250 days	KBFC	11	11	14	12	8	11
250 and under 500 days	KBFJ	6	10	13	6	11	13
500 and under 1 000 days	KBFL	24	19	13	17	11	16
1 000 and under 5 000 days	KBFY	53	82	61	72	48	69
5 000 and under 25 000 days	KBFZ	68	195	123	101	118	133
25 000 and under 50 000 days	KBGS	–	29	54	26	–	–
50 000 days and over	KBGT	117	68	1 025	–	86	–
Working days lost per 1 000 employees all industries and services	KBHA	13	19	57	10	12	10
Workers directly and indirectly involved: total	KBHB	107	174	364	130	93	141
Analysis by industry							
Mining, quarrying, electricity, gas and water	DMMN	–	2	1	–	1	–
Manufacturing	DMMO	23	33	34	28	14	31
Construction	DMMP	1	2	3	13	2	18
Transport, storage and communications	DMMQ	37	54	146	24	39	42
Public administration and defence	DMMR	8	28	32	20	4	17
Education	DMMS	29	30	122	15	4	28
Health and social work	DMMT	2	4	5	5	2	–
Other community, social and personal services	DMMU	2	10	2	1	22	2
All other industries and services	DMMV	5	11	21	23	4	2
Analysis by duration of stoppage							
Not more than 5 days	KBHM	75	142	208	108	57	129
Over 5 but not more than 10 days	KBHN	5	11	133	7	32	8
Over 10 but not more than 20 days	KBJQ	1	2	4	14	1	3
Over 20 but not more than 30 days	KBJR	6	2	3	–	–	–
Over 30 but not more than 50 days	KBJS	–	10	16	1	1	–
Over 50 days	KBJT	20	7	1	–	1	–
Numbers of stoppages in progress: total	KBLG	205	235	244	216	166	205
Analysis by industry							
Mining, quarrying, electricity, gas and water	DMMW	1	5	6	1	1	–
Manufacturing	DMMX	71	68	67	53	36	37
Construction	DMMY	4	9	11	11	13	20
Transport, storage and communications	DMMZ	54	56	72	68	57	91
Public administration and defence	DMNA	27	26	22	23	10	17
Education	DMNB	13	27	35	35	19	21
Health and social work	DMNC	7	17	9	7	6	4
Other community, social and personal services	DMND	15	19	12	8	17	8
All other industries and services	DMNE	14	14	11	12	7	8
Analysis of number of stoppages by duration							
Not more than 5 days	KBNH	176	199	196	184	130	179
Over 5 but not more than 10 days	KBNI	14	12	20	15	21	8
Over 10 but not more than 20 days	KBNJ	6	9	7	8	3	9
Over 20 but not more than 30 days	KBNK	5	6	6	2	4	4
Over 30 but not more than 50 days	KBNL	1	2	10	6	3	3
Over 50 days	KBNM	3	7	5	1	5	2

NOTES These figures exclude details of stoppages involving fewer than ten workers or lasting less than one day except any in which the aggregate number of working days lost is 100 or more.

There may be some under-recording of small or short stoppages; this would have much more effect on the total of stoppages than of working days lost.

Some stoppages which affected more than one industry group have been counted under each of the industries but only once in the totals.

Stoppages have been classified using *Standard Industrial Classification (SIC) 1992.*

The figures for working days lost and workers involved have been rounded and consequently the sum of the constituent items may not agree with the totals.

Classifications by size are based on the full duration of stoppages where these continue into the following year.

Working days lost per thousand employees are based on the latest available mid-year (June) estimates of employee jobs.

Sources: Office for National Statistics,;
Labour Market Statistics: 01928 792825

7.18 Labour disputes
United Kingdom
continued

Thousands

SIC 1980		1986	1987	1988	1989	1990	1991	1992	1993	1994
Working days lost through all stoppages in progress: total	KBBZ	1 920	3 546	3 702	4 128	1 903	761	528	649	278
Analysis by industry										
Coal extraction	KBCH	143	217	222	50	59	29	8	27	–
Other energy and water	KBCI	6	9	16	20	39	4	26	–	–
Metals, minerals and chemicals	KBCJ	192	60	70	42	42	27	14	6	8
Engineering and vehicles	KBCK	744	422	1 409	617	922	160	63	91	36
Other manufacturing industries	KBCL	135	115	151	91	106	35	16	13	15
Construction	KBCM	33	22	17	128	14	14	10	1	5
Transport and communication	KBCN	190	1 705	1 491	624	177	60	13	160	87
Public admin., sanitary services and education	KBCO	449	939	254	2 237	175	362	328	339	92
Medical and health services	KBDZ	11	6	36	151	345	1	1	2	1
All other industries and services	KBEZ	20	53	30	167	20	69	50	9	35
Analysis by number of working days lost in each stoppage										
Under 250 days	KBFC	48	48	33	30	28	15	7	10	11
250 and under 500 days	KBFJ	50	54	34	28	24	16	15	9	6
500 and under 1 000 days	KBFL	89	88	78	51	45	34	22	15	24
1 000 and under 5 000 days	KBFY	369	360	310	221	216	123	114	74	53
5 000 and under 25 000 days	KBFZ	381	388	325	365	286	205	156	78	68
25 000 and under 50 000 days	KBGS	258	118	127	234	216	190	115	149	–
50 000 days and over	KBGT	726	2 490	2 795	3 198	1 087	178	98	314	117
Working days lost per 1 000 employees all industries and services	KBHA	90	164	166	182	83	34	24	30	13
Workers directly and indirectly involved: total	KBHB	720	887	790	727	298	176	148	385	107
Analysis by industry										
Coal extraction	KBHC	87	98	92	25	15	6	3	14	–
Other energy and water	KBHD	2	2	2	10	18	2	6	–	–
Metals, minerals and chemicals	KBHE	17	9	10	7	5	2	2	2	2
Engineering and vehicles	KBHF	147	174	137	99	92	34	21	25	17
Other manufacturing industries	KBHG	30	19	29	12	11	15	3	3	4
Construction	KBHH	8	4	4	20	5	6	4	1	1
Transport and communication	KBHI	72	207	321	112	68	12	7	71	25
Public admin., sanitary services and education	KBHJ	348	361	161	414	70	87	92	261	39
Medical and health services	KBHK	4	4	31	9	10	–	2	–	1
All other industries and services	KBHL	6	10	4	19	3	11	9	7	18
Analysis by duration of stoppage										
Not more than 5 days	KBHM	369	308	381	194	185	133	111	364	75
Over 5 but not more than 10 days	KBHN	47	66	280	97	24	2	8	5	5
Over 10 but not more than 20 days	KBJQ	24	153	19	388	27	11	4	13	1
Over 20 but not more than 30 days	KBJR	58	25	22	8	21	3	1	–	6
Over 30 but not more than 50 days	KBJS	17	23	57	12	22	1	12	–	–
Over 50 days	KBJT	206	313	32	29	19	26	11	3	20
Numbers of stoppages in progress: total	KBLG	1 074	1 016	781	701	630	369	253	211	205
Analysis by industry										
Coal extraction	KBLR	351	296	154	146	87	32	10	5	–
Other energy and water	KBLS	10	6	6	7	7	3	6	–	–
Metals, minerals and chemicals	KBLT	62	36	50	40	36	17	16	15	14
Engineering and vehicles	KBLU	202	209	162	126	132	67	44	34	42
Other manufacturing industries	KBLV	85	98	75	63	45	30	19	21	16
Construction	KBLW	26	24	16	40	12	18	12	4	4
Transport and communication	KBLX	145	191	176	79	124	37	20	34	52
Public admin., sanitary services and education	KBLY	132	99	104	154	164	124	105	89	55
Medical and health services	KBLZ	35	24	21	18	13	6	6	3	2
All other industries and services	KBNG	34	41	31	31	16	35	16	6	21
Analysis of number of stoppages by duration										
Not more than 5 days	KBNH	836	784	587	553	476	270	188	176	176
Over 5 but not more than 10 days	KBNI	108	103	89	52	44	20	13	9	14
Over 10 but not more than 20 days	KBNJ	65	78	60	45	45	24	17	11	6
Over 20 but not more than 30 days	KBNK	23	23	17	18	20	15	6	2	5
Over 30 but not more than 50 days	KBNL	18	12	12	18	22	10	9	2	1
Over 50 days	KBNM	24	16	16	15	23	30	20	11	3

NOTES These figures exclude details of stoppages involving fewer than ten workers or lasting less than one day except any in which the aggregate number of working days lost is 100 or more.

There may be some under-recording of small or short stoppages; this would have much more effect on the total of stoppages than of working days lost.

Some stoppages which affected more than one industry group have been counted under each of the industries but only once in the totals.

Stoppages have been classified using *Standard Industrial Classification (SIC) 1980*.

The figures for working days lost and workers involved have been rounded and consequently the sum of the constituent items may not agree with the totals.

Classifications by size are based on the full duration of stoppages where these continue into the following year.

Working days lost per thousand employees are based on the latest available mid-year (June) estimates of employee jobs.

Sources: *Office for National Statistics,;*
Labour Market Statistics: 01928 792825

7.19 Average earnings and hours of manual employees by industry division
Full time employees on adult rates: pay unaffected by absence: Great Britain
At April

	Agriculture Hunting and forestry	Fishing	Mining and Quarrying	Manufacturing	Electricity Gas and Water Supply	Construction	Wholesale and Retail Trade; repair of motor vehicles, cycles, personal and household goods
Standard Industrial Classification: Revised 1992							
Full-time manual men							
Weekly earnings							
	KOTK	KOTL	KOTM	KOTN	KOTO	KOTP	KOTQ
1995	237.3	..	340.3	313.4	367.8	294.7	257.8
1996	241.2	..	367.8	323.6	399.7	308.2	264.1
1997	252.1	..[1]	400.5	337.5	401.2	324.8	275.1
1998	260.3	..[1]	408.3	352.6	418.6	342.3	292.2
1999	272.4	..[1]	396.0	354.6	440.5	351.3	299.4
Hours worked							
	KOTZ	KPFV	KOUA	KOUB	KOUC	KOUD	KOUE
1995	48.2	..[1]	52.0	44.9	42.7	45.9	44.4
1996	47.5	46.5	50.8	44.2	42.6	45.8	44.4
1997	47.8	47.0	52.0	44.5	42.1	46.9	44.0
1998	47.0	..[1]	50.1	44.3	42.5	46.9	44.3
1999	47.5	..[1]	51.7	43.5	42.8	46.4	43.9
Hourly earnings							
	KOUN	KPFW	KOUO	KOUP	KOUQ	KOUR	KOUS
1995	4.93	..[1]	6.56	6.98	8.62	6.40	5.80
1996	5.06	..[1]	7.15	7.29	9.38	6.71	5.91
1997	5.27	..[1]	7.70	7.58	9.45	6.92	6.26
1998	5.54	..[1]	8.14	7.96	9.85	7.29	6.59
1999	5.75	..[1]	7.66	8.15	10.30	7.56	6.84
Full-time manual women							
Weekly earnings							
	KOYL	KPFX	KOYM	KOYN	KOYO	KOYP	KOYQ
1995	175.3	..[1]	..[1]	198.5	..[1]	..[1]	174.2
1996	177.9	..[1]	..[1]	205.0	..[1]	..[1]	185.4
1997	186.9	..[1]	..[1]	214.1	..[1]	..[1]	194.1
1998	185.7	..[1]	..[1]	224.2	..[1]	..[1]	203.6
1999	199.0	..[1]	..[1]	231.7	..[1]	..[1]	215.3
Hours worked							
	KOYZ	KPFY	KOZA	KOZB	KOZC	KOZD	KOZE
1995	41.6	..[1]	..[1]	40.9	..[1]	..[1]	39.6
1996	41.3	..[1]	..[1]	40.7	..[1]	..[1]	40.0
1997	40.9	..[1]	42.6	40.8	38.1	43.8	40.3
1998	42.0	..[1]	..[1]	40.7	..[1]	..[1]	40.3
1999	41.8	..[1]	..[1]	40.4	..[1]	..[1]	39.9
Hourly earnings							
	KOZN	KOZO	KOZP	KOZQ	KOZR	KOZS	KOZT
1995	4.21	..[1]	..[1]	4.86	..[1]	..[1]	4.39
1996	4.33	..[1]	..[1]	5.04	..[1]	..[1]	4.63
1997	4.50	..[1]	..[1]	5.26	..[1]	5.54	4.81
1998	4.43	..[1]	..[1]	5.52	..[1]	..[1]	5.06
1999	4.74	..[1]	..[1]	5.74	..[1]	..[1]	5.44
Full-time manual adults							
Weekly earnings							
	KPBO	KPFZ	KPBP	KPBQ	KPBR	KPBS	KPBT
1995	231.2	..[1]	338.9	290.7	366.6	293.4	246.0
1996	234.7	..[1]	366.5	300.8	398.5	307.0	253.5
1997	245.4	..[1]	398.9	314.6	399.6	323.4	264.3
1998	251.7	..[1]	403.8	329.9	416.2	340.9	280.3
1999	264.1	..[1]	392.5	333.7	439.5	350.9	287.7
Hours worked							
	KPCT	KPGA	KPCU	KPCV	KPCW	KPCX	KPCY
1995	47.6	45.6	50.8	44.1	..[1]	..[1]	43.7
1996	46.9	46.5	50.8	43.5	42.6	45.8	43.9
1997	47.1	47.0	51.9	43.8	42.0	46.8	43.5
1998	46.4	..[1]	49.9	43.7	42.4	46.9	43.8
1999	46.8	..[1]	51.6	43.0	42.7	46.4	43.4
Hourly earnings							
	KPDV	KPGB	KPDW	KPDX	KPDY	KPDZ	KPFA
1995	4.86	6.12	6.56	6.60	8.60	6.39	5.62
1996	5.00	..[1]	7.15	6.88	9.36	6.70	5.75
1997	5.20	5.42	7.69	7.18	9.42	6.90	6.08
1998	5.42	..[1]	8.07	7.56	9.81	7.27	6.40
1999	5.65	..[1]	7.61	7.77	10.29	7.56	6.66

1 Denotes sample number too low or standard error too high for reliable estimate.

Source: ONS, New Earnings Survey: 01928 792077

103

7.19
continued

Average earnings and hours of manual employees by industry division
Full time employees on adult rates: pay unaffected by absence: Great Britain
At April

	Hotels and restaur- ants	Transport, Storage and Communia- cation	Financ- ial- Inter- mediation	Real Estate, Renting and Business	Public Administration and Defence; compulsory social security	Educa- tion	Health and Social work	Other community, social and personal service activities

Standard Industrial Classification: Revised 1992

Full-time manual men

Weekly earnings

	KOTR	KOTS	KOTT	KOTU	KOTV	KOTW	KOTX	KOTY
1995	196.5	306.0	338.0	269.3	264.4	233.4	232.1	259.5
1996	203.3	314.9	373.8	275.6	275.4	243.5	241.3	264.4
1997	213.9	328.4	381.6	292.4	281.2	268.7	250.7	280.2
1998	227.0	344.0	394.8	302.7	289.0	277.9	264.4	289.0
1999	230.5	359.6	377.9	312.3	307.5	285.2	267.7	300.8

Hours worked

	KOUF	KOUG	KOUH	KOUI	KOUJ	KOUK	KOUL	KOUM
1995	42.3	47.8	41.9	47.0	42.0	..[1]	41.9	44.5
1996	42.1	47.6	42.5	46.4	42.4	41.7	41.8	44.0
1997	41.9	48.5	42.1	46.7	42.3	41.5	42.4	44.3
1998	42.5	48.0	42.5	46.4	41.9	41.7	42.1	44.8
1999	42.1	47.5	39.9	45.5	42.2	40.8	41.8	44.8

Hourly earnings

	KOUT	KOYE	KOYF	KOYG	KOYH	KOYI	KOYJ	KOYK
1995	4.65	6.38	8.07	5.74	6.31	5.55	5.55	5.86
1996	4.83	6.60	8.76	5.94	6.50	5.83	5.78	6.03
1997	5.10	6.77	9.07	6.27	6.66	6.48	5.92	6.33
1998	5.34	7.17	9.28	6.53	6.90	6.67	6.26	6.47
1999	5.48	7.56	9.46	6.86	7.30	7.00	6.41	6.72

Full-time manual women

Weekly earnings

	KOYR	KOYS	KOYT	KOYU	KOYV	KOYW	KOYX	KOYY
1995	147.2	279.9	..[1]	181.7	207.4	168.6	172.3	162.7
1996	156.7	286.7	..[1]	199.6	214.6	167.3	175.5	166.6
1997	160.5	278.3	..[1]	205.3	218.5	197.1	178.5	176.0
1998	170.8	292.7	..[1]	211.9	232.2	203.7	187.2	178.1
1999	180.5	311.5	..[1]	221.5	232.3	223.0	199.5	197.4

Hours worked

	KOZF	KOZG	KOZH	KOZI	KOZJ	KOZK	KOZL	KOZM
1995	39.0	42.4	..[1]	40.4	39.7	38.7	39.4	39.9
1996	39.4	42.4	37.9	41.6	39.6	38.6	39.1	40.0
1997	39.2	42.2	37.5	41.8	39.4	38.8	39.1	39.7
1998	39.4	42.0	..[1]	41.4	39.6	38.3	39.3	39.6
1999	39.3	41.5	..[1]	40.4	38.6	38.0	39.1	39.8

Hourly earnings

	KOZU	KOZV	KOZW	KOZX	KOZY	KOZZ	KPBN	KTDJ
1995	3.78	6.09	..[1]	4.54	5.23	4.34	4.38	4.07
1996	3.98	6.29	..[1]	4.81	5.43	4.35	4.49	4.17
1997	4.07	6.52	6.14	4.92	5.57	5.05	4.56	4.45
1998	4.30	6.98	..[1]	5.08	5.89	5.32	4.75	4.50
1999	4.55	7.52	..[1]	5.48	6.09	5.86	5.10	4.94

Full-time manual adults

Weekly earnings

	KPBU	KPBV	KPBW	KPBX	KPBY	KPBZ	KPCR	KPCS
1995	175.1	304.1	319.1	257.1	255.1	211.2	195.3	236.7
1996	182.4	312.5	349.7	264.6	264.7	220.0	199.7	241.8
1997	190.6	324.8	355.6	278.2	271.4	244.3	208.1	249.1
1998	203.6	340.0	367.3	289.1	280.7	254.8	218.9	258.3
1999	210.3	355.7	353.6	298.2	296.9	266.0	227.8	273.8

Hours worked

	KPCZ	KPDO	KPDP	KPDQ	KPDR	KPDS	KPDT	KPDU
1995	40.9	47.5	..[1]	46.1	41.6	40.9	40.4	43.4
1996	40.9	47.3	41.7	45.7	41.9	40.8	40.1	43.0
1997	40.7	48.1	41.3	45.9	41.8	40.6	40.5	42.9
1998	41.2	47.6	41.6	45.6	41.6	40.7	40.5	43.3
1999	41.0	47.0	39.7	44.7	41.7	40.0	40.2	43.5

Hourly earnings

	KPFB	KPFC	KPFD	KPFE	KPFF	KPFG	KPFT	KPFU
1995	4.29	6.37	7.76	5.60	6.14	5.16	4.85	5.47
1996	4.46	6.58	8.34	5.80	6.32	5.39	4.99	5.63
1997	4.67	6.76	8.61	6.07	6.50	6.02	5.14	5.82
1998	4.93	7.16	8.84	6.33	6.76	6.27	5.40	5.97
1999	5.12	7.56	8.92	6.67	7.15	6.66	5.66	6.29

1 Denotes sample number too low or standard error too high for reliable esti- mate.
2 It is now possible to recalculate data for previous years using SIC92. For further information contact the NES helpline on 01928 792077.

Source: ONS, New Earnings Survey: 01928 792077

7.20 Average weekly and hourly earnings and hours of full-time employees on adult rates: Great Britain

At April

	All Industries				Manufacturing industries			
	Average weekly earnings[1]	Average hours	Average hourly earnings		Average weekly earnings	Average hours	Average hourly earnings	
			including overtime	excluding overtime			including overtime	excluding overtime
	£		£	£	£		£	£
All adults								
	KBRZ	KBSA	KIUY	KIUZ	KBSD	KBSE	KIVO	KIVP
1994	325.7	40.1	8.03	8.03	321.6	41.7	7.62	7.58
1995	336.3	40.3	8.31	8.32	334.3	42.2	7.92	7.85
1996	351.7	40.2	8.71	8.72	349.2	41.9	8.29	8.22
1997	367.6	40.3	9.10	9.13	361.7	42.0	8.60	8.53
1998	384.5	40.2	9.53	9.54	384.5	41.8	9.17	9.10
1999	400.1	40.0	10.01	10.03	395.3	41.4	9.55	9.49
All men								
	KBSH	KBSI	KIVQ	KIWR	KBSL	KBSM	KIWS	KIWT
1994	362.1	41.6	8.61	8.65	350.9	42.5	8.16	8.12
1995	374.6	41.9	8.91	8.97	364.0	43.0	8.44	8.41
1996	391.6	41.7	9.34	9.39	380.0	42.7	8.86	8.81
1997	408.7	41.8	9.74	9.82	392.7	42.8	9.16	9.12
1998	427.1	41.7	10.20	10.26	416.8	42.6	9.75	9.72
1999	442.4	41.4	10.68	10.75	424.6	42.0	10.10	10.06
Manual men								
	KFHX	KFHY	KIWU	KIWV	KFJT	KFJU	KIWW	KIWX
1994	280.7	44.7	6.31	6.14	296.9	44.1	6.72	6.50
1995	291.3	45.2	6.44	6.25	313.4	44.9	6.98	6.74
1996	301.3	44.8	6.70	6.51	323.6	44.2	7.29	7.05
1997	314.3	45.1	6.97	6.79	337.5	44.5	7.58	7.34
1998	328.5	45.0	7.30	7.10	352.6	44.3	7.96	7.71
1999	335.0	44.4	7.54	7.36	354.6	43.5	8.15	7.92
Non-manual men								
	KFJX	KFJY	KIWY	KIWZ	KFMU	KFMV	KIXO	KIXP
1994	428.2	38.9	10.90	10.93	434.7	39.7	10.79	10.84
1995	443.3	39.0	11.33	11.36	449.2	39.9	11.24	11.29
1996	464.5	39.1	11.83	11.87	479.6	39.9	11.95	12.00
1997	483.5	39.1	12.33	12.39	489.2	39.8	12.28	12.32
1998	506.1	39.1	12.90	12.94	525.9	39.8	13.17	13.23
1999	525.5	39.0	13.49	13.52	541.6	39.6	13.68	13.73
All women								
	KBTF	KBTG	KIXQ	KIXR	KBTJ	KBTK	KIXS	KIXT
1994	261.5	37.6	6.89	6.88	226.8	39.1	5.76	5.72
1995	269.8	37.6	7.15	7.14	236.7	39.4	6.01	5.96
1996	283.0	37.6	7.51	7.50	246.7	39.3	6.27	6.23
1997	297.2	37.6	7.88	7.88	258.8	39.2	6.60	6.56
1998	309.6	37.6	8.23	8.22	274.5	39.2	7.01	6.97
1999	326.5	37.5	8.71	8.70	292.1	39.0	7.49	7.46
Manual women								
	KFMY	KFMZ	KIXU	KIXV	KFPS	KFPT	KIXW	KIXX
1994	181.9	40.1	4.53	4.45	186.4	40.6	4.59	4.49
1995	188.1	40.2	4.64	4.55	198.5	40.9	4.86	4.74
1996	195.2	40.2	4.81	4.72	205.0	40.7	5.04	4.92
1997	201.1	40.2	4.99	4.90	214.1	40.8	5.26	5.13
1998	210.8	40.2	5.23	5.14	224.2	40.7	5.52	5.39
1999	221.9	39.9	5.56	5.48	231.7	40.4	5.74	5.62
Non-manual women								
	KFRY	KFRZ	KIXY	KIYA	KFUY	KFUZ	KIYB	KIYC
1994	278.4	37.0	7.44	7.42	263.2	37.7	6.94	6.92
1995	288.1	37.0	7.76	7.75	275.0	37.8	7.26	7.23
1996	302.4	37.1	8.16	8.14	289.4	37.9	7.64	7.61
1997	317.8	37.1	8.56	8.55	300.0	37.8	7.94	7.92
1998	330.1	37.0	8.90	8.89	317.2	37.9	8.38	8.36
1999	346.9	37.0	9.37	9.36	341.5	37.9	9.02	9.01

1 Excluding those whose pay was affected by absence.

Source: ONS, New Earnings Survey: 01928 792077

7.21 Average earnings index: all employees: main industrial sectors
Great Britain
Analyses by industry based on Standard Industrial Classification 1992

1995 = 100

	Annual averages	January	February	March	April	May	June	July	August	September[1]	October	November	December
Unadjusted													
Whole economy (Divisions 01 - 93)													
	LNMM												
1998	113.5	110.7	112.9	116.6	113.1	113.2	112.9	114.4	112.1	112.6	112.4	113.5	117.5
1999	119.0	115.7	118.7	122.5	117.4	117.8	119.0	119.3	117.6	117.6	118.1	119.1	124.9
2000	..	123.2	125.3	129.3	122.5	122.4	123.3	123.6	122.5	122.3	..	..	..
Manufacturing industries (Divisions 15 - 37)													
	LNMN												
1998	113.7	110.5	112.8	116.7	113.5	112.8	113.2	114.6	112.5	112.5	113.7	114.8	116.7
1999	118.3	115.1	116.7	120.7	117.5	116.7	117.1	118.7	117.0	117.4	119.0	120.3	123.7
2000	..	121.8	122.1	126.1	122.8	122.7	122.4	124.0	121.8	122.6	..	..	..
Production industries (Divisions 10 - 41)													
	LNMO												
1998	113.4	110.3	112.5	116.5	113.4	112.5	112.9	114.3	112.2	112.1	113.4	114.4	116.4
1999	117.8	114.7	116.3	120.4	117.3	116.4	116.6	118.2	116.5	116.8	118.3	119.5	122.8
2000	..	121.2	121.6	125.4	122.0	121.9	121.8	123.0	120.9	121.6	..	..	..
Service industries (Divisions 50 - 93)													
	LNMP												
1998	113.4	110.9	113.3	117.0	113.2	113.4	112.8	114.2	111.9	112.3	111.8	112.8	117.7
1999	119.2	115.9	119.5	123.1	117.3	118.2	119.6	119.5	117.7	117.4	117.7	118.6	125.2
2000	..	123.7	126.5	130.2	122.4	122.3	123.5	123.5	122.8	121.9	..	..	..
Private sector services (unadjusted) (Divisions 50-99)													
	JJGF												
1998	115.2	110.9	113.3	117.0	113.2	113.4	112.8	114.2	111.9	112.3	111.8	112.8	117.7
1999	121.4	115.9	119.5	123.1	117.3	118.2	119.6	119.5	117.7	117.4	117.7	118.6	125.2
2000	..	123.7	126.5	130.2	122.4	122.3	123.5	123.5	122.8	121.9	..	..	..
Seasonally adjusted													
Whole economy (Divisions 01 - 93)													
	LNMQ												
1998	113.6	111.1	111.4	112.1	112.9	113.6	112.9	114.1	114.1	114.9	115.0	115.4	115.4
1999	119.0	116.0	116.7	117.2	117.6	118.3	118.9	119.3	119.8	120.2	120.9	121.1	122.4
2000	..	123.3	123.0	123.2	122.9	123.1	123.5	123.9	124.8	125.3	..	..	..
Manufacturing industries (Divisions 15 - 37)													
	LNMR												
1998	113.7	111.2	112.3	112.8	113.0	113.2	113.8	114.2	114.4	114.6	115.0	115.1	114.7
1999	118.3	115.7	116.1	116.7	117.1	117.2	117.8	118.4	119.1	119.4	120.1	120.5	121.3
2000	..	122.0	121.5	121.9	122.3	123.1	123.0	123.6	124.0	124.8	..	..	..
Production industries (Divisions 10 - 41)													
	LNMS												
1998	113.4	111.1	112.0	112.5	112.8	112.9	113.4	113.9	114.1	114.3	114.7	114.8	114.5
1999	117.8	115.3	115.8	116.3	116.8	116.7	117.3	117.9	118.5	118.8	119.5	119.8	120.5
2000	..	121.5	121.0	121.1	121.4	122.1	122.3	122.6	123.0	123.8	..	..	..
Service industries (Divisions 50 - 93)													
	LNMT												
1998	113.5	111.0	111.2	112.2	112.9	113.9	112.6	113.9	113.9	114.8	115.0	115.5	115.5
1999	119.3	115.8	117.0	117.4	117.4	118.8	119.4	119.6	120.0	120.5	121.1	121.5	122.6
2000	..	123.4	123.4	123.5	122.9	123.0	123.5	124.0	125.2	125.4	..	..	..
Private sector services (seasonally adjusted) (Divisions 50-93)													
	JJGH												
1998	115.3	111.0	111.2	112.2	112.9	113.9	112.6	113.9	113.9	114.8	115.0	115.5	
1999	121.5	115.8	117.0	117.4	117.4	118.8	119.4	119.6	120.0	120.5	121.1	121.5	
2000	..	123.4	123.4	123.5	122.9	123.0	123.5	124.0	125.2	125.4	..	..	..

The Average Earnings Index has been revised. More information available on website, WWW.Statistics.gov.uk, and helpline.
1 September 1999 data are provisional.

Source: Office for National Statistics: 01633 819002

7.22 Average earnings index[1] excluding bonus payments: all employee jobs: by industry (unadjusted)

Great Britain
March 1996 = 100

	Agriculture[2], forestry and fishing	Mining and quarrying	Food products, beverages and tobacco	Textiles	Clothing, leather and footwear	Wood, wood products and other manufacturing n.e.c.	Pulp, paper products, printing and publishing	Chemicals and chemical products	Rubber and plastic products	Other non-metallic mineral products	Basic metals	Fabricated metal products (excluding machinery)	Machinery and equipment n.e.c.
SIC 1992 Class	(01,02,05)	(10-14)	(15,16)	(17)	(18-19)	(20,23,36,37)	(21,22)	(24)	(25)	(26)	(27)	(28)	(29)
	LOTJ	LOTK	LOTL	LOTM	LOTN	LOTO	LOTP	LOTQ	LOTR	LOTS	LOTT	LOTU	LOTV
1997	–	104.8	103.6	105.1	105.0	107.0	104.4	105.2	105.4	105.1	107.7	104.8	105.1
1998	–	108.8	108.1	107.3	109.2	111.6	108.5	111.5	110.5	109.4	113.0	108.3	109.4
1996 May	–	100.5	100.6	100.4	100.6	100.9	100.2	101.1	101.1	101.0	103.3	100.2	100.7
Jun	–	100.5	101.1	102.2	100.9	101.2	100.6	101.6	101.8	101.3	103.8	100.5	101.2
Jul	–	100.6	101.6	103.2	101.2	101.5	101.1	101.6	102.3	101.5	105.5	100.7	101.5
Aug	–	100.2	101.3	103.4	101.0	101.1	101.5	101.3	102.1	101.3	106.1	100.9	101.2
Sep	–	100.4	100.9	102.6	101.3	101.9	101.7	101.5	102.1	101.3	106.8	101.2	101.2
Oct	–	100.6	100.2	102.9	101.5	102.0	102.0	101.4	102.0	101.1	104.7	101.6	101.0
Nov	–	101.7	100.8	103.7	102.3	103.1	102.3	101.9	102.5	101.7	105.1	102.4	101.9
Dec	–	102.6	101.2	104.1	102.4	103.4	102.7	102.3	102.9	101.9	106.2	102.5	102.1
1997 Jan	–	103.3	101.6	103.7	103.0	103.7	102.4	102.7	103.1	101.9	106.3	102.3	102.3
Feb	–	103.8	101.4	103.4	103.5	103.8	102.2	103.0	103.2	102.0	106.5	102.4	102.6
Mar	–	103.9	101.6	103.1	104.3	104.3	101.8	103.0	103.6	102.5	106.0	102.9	102.9
Apr	–	104.5	102.4	103.6	104.8	105.1	102.4	103.7	104.0	103.5	106.3	103.8	104.1
May	–	104.7	103.1	104.0	105.2	106.2	102.9	104.2	104.4	104.4	107.0	104.0	104.5
Jun	–	104.7	103.3	105.1	105.5	106.7	103.8	105.0	104.8	105.2	107.1	104.4	105.6
Jul	–	105.0	103.8	105.6	105.6	107.1	104.2	105.1	105.5	105.4	108.1	104.8	105.6
Aug	–	104.8	103.8	105.8	105.2	106.5	105.0	105.4	105.8	105.5	107.4	104.7	105.7
Sep	–	104.6	103.9	105.4	104.9	106.8	105.6	105.5	106.1	105.5	108.6	105.1	105.2
Oct	–	104.0	103.9	105.6	104.8	107.4	106.4	105.9	106.0	106.0	108.0	105.3	105.2
Nov	–	104.8	104.6	106.6	105.2	109.1	106.5	106.4	106.7	106.6	109.0	106.3	105.7
Dec	–	106.1	105.6	107.0	105.3	110.0	106.4	107.5	107.1	107.2	109.2	106.7	106.8
1998 Jan	–	106.4	105.9	106.4	105.8	110.7	105.8	108.2	107.7	107.7	109.5	106.9	107.0
Feb	–	106.8	105.9	105.3	106.5	110.6	105.5	109.0	108.0	108.0	110.0	107.0	107.4
Mar	–	106.8	105.9	105.0	107.7	111.2	105.6	109.1	108.6	108.0	110.3	107.1	107.6
Apr	–	108.0	106.6	105.8	108.6	111.8	106.4	109.6	109.6	108.2	112.0	108.0	108.5
May	–	108.7	107.7	106.3	109.1	112.6	107.4	110.0	110.4	108.6	113.1	108.6	109.0
Jun	–	108.9	108.4	107.5	109.4	112.1	108.0	110.9	110.5	109.1	113.5	108.8	109.5
Jul	–	108.7	108.8	107.7	109.8	112.2	108.3	111.3	110.4	109.8	114.4	108.9	110.1
Aug	–	108.4	108.2	108.2	109.7	111.4	108.7	111.8	110.5	110.1	114.6	108.7	110.5
Sep	–	108.7	108.2	107.8	109.8	111.3	109.3	111.7	111.2	110.2	114.8	108.8	110.4
Oct	–	109.3	108.0	107.9	109.4	110.9	110.1	112.1	111.5	110.0	114.1	108.2	110.1
Nov	–	110.0	109.0	108.7	109.8	111.8	110.7	112.9	111.7	110.3	113.7	108.4	110.0
Dec	–	110.6	109.9	108.7	109.8	111.9	111.1	114.5	111.7	110.5	113.4	108.5	110.0
1999 Jan[5]	–	110.7	110.1	108.6	110.2	111.6	111.4	115.3	111.7	110.4	111.7	108.6	109.9
1999 Feb[5]	–	109.8	109.6	107.5	110.0	111.1	111.1	115.6	111.6	110.1	110.9	108.0	109.7
Mar	–	109.1	109.1	107.4	110.5	111.3	110.7	115.5	111.4	110.5	111.4	107.7	109.6
Apr	–	108.8	108.9	107.9	110.4	111.8	110.7	116.6	111.4	111.4	112.0	108.1	110.1
May	–	109.1	109.3	109.2	110.9	112.6	111.2	117.4	111.8	112.2	114.0	108.7	110.7
Jun	–	109.4	109.5	110.6	111.0	113.4	111.8	118.5	112.2	112.6	115.2	109.5	111.3
Jul	–	109.4	109.8	111.6	111.4	114.3	112.1	118.7	112.5	113.0	117.0	110.0	111.7
Aug	–	109.7	110.0	112.3	111.1	115.0	112.7	119.1	113.3	113.6	117.2	109.8	112.0
Sep[3]	–	109.8	110.3	112.3	111.5	116.0	113.4	119.8	114.2	114.1	117.4	110.0	112.0
Oct	–	110.3	110.6	113.0	112.1	116.8	114.2	120.2	115.6	114.4	117.2	110.0	112.4
Nov	–	110.9	110.8	113.7	113.6	117.7	114.6	121.1	116.8	114.6	118.4	110.7	113.4
Dec	..	111.0	111.2	114.4	114.1	118.3	115.2	122.2	117.1	115.2	119.1	110.1	114.3
2000 Jan	..	111.3	111.8	113.4	112.0	118.1	114.8	122.9	116.9	116.3	120.5	110.0	114.4
Feb	..	111.4	112.4	112.4	110.9	118.3	114.5	123.0	115.5	117.8	120.5	110.0	114.6
Mar	..	112.1	113.1	111.8	108.6	118.6	114.1	122.9	115.0	118.5	120.6	110.6	115.1
Apr	..	112.1	114.6	112.0	108.7	119.3	114.4	123.3	114.7	119.3	120.6	110.4	116.0
May	..	112.0	115.8	112.6	107.2	119.2	115.0	123.6	115.7	120.2	121.4	110.8	116.3
Jun	..	111.9	116.1	113.5	107.6	119.6	115.2	123.7	117.0	120.6	122.8	111.0	117.1
Jul	..	112.3	114.8	114.7	108.0	120.3	115.6	123.8	118.3	120.1	125.8	111.9	117.8
Aug	..	112.5	113.9	115.2	108.2	121.4	115.7	124.0	118.6	119.0	126.7	111.4	118.0
Sep	..	112.7	113.7	115.5	109.4	122.2	116.9	124.2	118.8	118.5	127.1	111.3	117.5

The Average Earnings Index has been revised. More information available on website, WWW.Statistics.gov.uk, and helpline below.

1 Users should note that data contained in this table are not comparable with those previously published in Table 18.11 (prior to March 1999). Excluding bonuses and averaging the data over a three month period renders the data fundamentally different to the previous indices published for the same industries, but which included bonuses and related to single months only.

2 As a result of a discontinuity in the reporting of data for the agricultural sector, this series is not available.

3 Provisional.

4 The index for the sector Education, health and social work is based on a sample which excludes representatives of the private health and social work sector until June 1998. Monthly movements in the index for this sector therefore exclude health and social work up to May 1998.

5 As a result of a change in the survey questionnaire the series excluding bonuses are subject to a discontinuity between January and February 1999.

Source: Office for National Statistics: 01633 819002

7.22

Average earnings index[1] excluding bonus payments: all employee jobs: by industry (unadjusted)

continued

Great Britain

March 1996 = 100

	Electrical and optical equipment	Transport equipment	Electricity, gas and water supply	Constructi-on	Wholesale trade	Retail trade and repairs	Hotels and restauran-ts	Transport, storage and communica-tion	Financial intermedi-ation	Real estate, renting and business activities	Public administr-ation	Education, health and social work[4]	Other services
SIC 1992 Class	(30-33)	(34,35)	(40,41)	(45)	(51)	(50,52)	(55)	(60-64)	(65-67)	(70-74)	(75)	(80-85)	(90-93)
	LOTW	LOTX	LOTY	LOTZ	LOUA	LOUB	LOUC	LOUD	LOUE	LOUF	LOUG	LOUH	LOUI
1997	105.7	101.6	101.0	103.4	104.9	97.9	106.3	103.9	106.7	104.1	101.0	104.6	106.2
1998	110.1	106.3	103.9	110.4	110.8	101.8	110.8	107.9	113.3	110.3	103.5	107.6	114.8
1996 May	100.8	98.0	100.9	99.0	100.4	96.2	100.3	98.8	100.8	100.2	99.4	101.1	99.1
Jun	101.1	97.1	101.4	98.8	100.7	94.6	100.5	98.0	101.1	100.1	99.0	101.9	98.5
Jul	101.2	97.7	101.5	99.2	100.7	95.1	101.3	97.9	100.9	100.1	99.4	102.7	99.3
Aug	101.2	97.5	101.8	99.2	101.2	95.5	101.7	98.6	101.0	99.8	99.6	103.4	99.9
Sep	101.4	97.3	101.9	99.3	101.4	95.6	101.8	99.9	101.2	99.9	100.3	104.1	101.0
Oct	101.5	96.8	102.5	99.3	101.6	95.1	101.7	100.5	101.5	100.0	100.1	103.8	101.0
Nov	101.9	97.8	102.4	100.0	101.5	94.7	101.5	101.3	101.8	100.7	100.3	103.0	102.0
Dec	102.7	99.0	103.2	100.5	102.0	94.7	103.6	101.5	102.3	101.4	99.9	102.5	102.5
1997 Jan	102.9	99.5	101.8	100.9	102.1	95.1	104.5	102.1	102.9	102.0	100.1	102.6	103.3
Feb	103.4	99.8	100.9	101.2	102.5	95.5	105.2	102.0	103.4	102.5	100.2	102.9	102.9
Mar	103.6	99.9	99.2	101.5	102.6	96.9	104.3	101.8	103.7	102.5	100.3	103.0	104.0
Apr	104.5	100.5	99.4	101.7	103.4	97.3	103.9	102.3	104.5	102.7	100.2	103.5	104.2
May	105.0	100.9	100.4	102.1	104.1	98.1	104.5	102.4	105.5	103.1	100.0	103.8	104.6
Jun	105.6	100.9	101.2	102.4	104.5	97.6	104.9	102.5	106.5	103.5	99.8	104.1	103.4
Jul	106.4	101.4	101.6	103.1	104.9	98.2	106.2	102.9	107.2	104.2	99.9	104.6	103.8
Aug	106.6	101.2	101.0	103.1	105.2	98.6	106.9	103.7	107.7	104.3	100.5	105.6	105.2
Sep	106.5	101.5	101.0	103.7	105.5	99.0	107.1	105.1	107.9	104.5	101.1	106.5	107.1
Oct	106.2	101.7	101.1	104.2	105.7	98.8	107.2	105.2	108.1	104.6	101.9	106.3	108.5
Nov	106.6	103.0	102.1	105.3	105.9	98.4	107.1	105.8	108.2	105.0	102.5	105.4	109.3
Dec	107.1	104.0	102.5	106.0	106.9	98.2	108.8	106.3	108.7	105.8	102.9	104.8	110.2
1998 Jan	107.1	104.5	102.5	106.4	107.4	98.5	109.9	107.0	109.3	107.0	102.6	104.8	110.7
Feb	107.5	104.8	102.2	106.8	107.9	99.0	110.4	107.3	110.0	108.2	102.5	104.9	110.9
Mar	107.7	105.0	102.3	107.1	107.8	99.2	109.5	107.3	110.7	108.8	102.8	104.5	111.6
Apr	108.6	105.7	103.2	107.7	108.8	99.8	109.3	108.6	111.3	109.2	102.9	104.9	112.9
May	109.0	106.0	103.9	108.3	109.9	101.1	109.9	109.1	112.3	109.7	102.9	105.6	113.7
Jun	109.4	106.5	104.1	109.0	111.0	102.1	110.4	107.5	113.2	110.1	102.9	106.7	113.7
Jul	110.0	107.0	104.3	110.1	111.6	102.9	110.9	106.1	113.8	110.4	103.4	107.7	114.1
Aug	110.4	107.0	104.3	111.0	111.9	103.0	110.8	105.9	113.9	110.1	103.8	108.9	115.6
Sep	110.7	106.5	104.6	111.9	112.0	103.3	110.8	108.0	114.1	110.4	103.7	109.8	116.7
Oct	111.0	106.2	104.5	112.4	112.1	102.8	110.7	108.3	114.4	110.5	104.1	109.9	117.0
Nov	111.6	106.4	104.5	113.3	112.2	102.5	111.0	109.3	114.9	111.3	104.3	109.5	117.0
Dec	112.5	107.0	104.5	113.5	112.5	102.6	112.7	108.9	115.4	112.0	104.7	109.5	117.3
1999 Jan[5]	112.9	107.3	103.7	113.6	112.5	103.4	113.7	109.3	115.8	113.1	104.8	109.8	117.2
1999 Feb[5]	113.2	107.5	102.5	113.0	112.4	103.1	113.8	109.5	115.7	113.7	104.8	110.2	117.1
Mar	113.5	107.7	101.4	113.0	112.4	102.1	112.9	109.8	115.9	114.2	105.0	109.9	117.3
Apr	114.0	108.9	102.2	113.0	113.1	101.6	113.4	109.8	116.5	114.6	105.0	110.4	117.7
May	114.6	109.7	103.8	113.3	113.6	102.1	115.2	108.6	117.6	115.2	105.1	111.2	118.3
Jun	115.1	110.3	104.9	113.4	113.8	103.2	117.1	107.8	118.2	115.8	105.6	112.7	119.5
Jul	116.0	110.5	103.7	113.9	113.8	103.2	118.0	108.1	118.6	116.0	105.9	113.4	121.2
Aug	116.9	111.1	102.2	114.3	114.0	103.7	119.0	108.6	118.6	115.4	106.1	114.4	122.6
Sep[3]	118.0	111.5	101.0	115.5	114.3	104.0	118.7	109.9	118.6	115.0	105.9	114.7	123.8
Oct	118.7	112.1	100.8	116.5	114.4	103.9	118.7	109.8	118.2	114.6	106.4	114.8	124.5
Nov	119.3	112.8	100.9	117.8	114.3	103.3	118.2	110.0	118.5	115.1	107.2	114.5	125.8
Dec	119.4	113.3	101.2	118.0	114.6	102.8	120.8	110.5	119.3	115.6	107.6	114.3	126.9
2000 Jan	119.8	113.7	101.8	118.2	115.3	104.0	121.8	111.7	121.3	117.2	108.0	114.6	128.7
Feb	120.3	113.4	101.3	118.5	116.4	104.7	122.8	112.1	122.0	118.5	109.0	114.8	130.3
Mar	121.3	114.3	100.3	119.6	117.1	105.2	121.2	111.9	122.6	119.5	109.3	114.8	130.1
Apr	122.0	115.0	99.4	120.0	117.6	104.7	122.8	111.0	122.1	119.5	109.3	115.4	129.5
May	122.7	115.7	99.5	120.3	118.0	105.6	123.2	111.6	122.9	120.0	108.3	116.1	128.7
Jun	123.5	115.9	100.2	120.7	118.4	106.3	124.3	112.5	123.4	120.4	108.6	117.3	129.8
Jul	124.2	116.0	100.1	121.7	118.2	106.8	124.0	113.0	124.1	121.2	108.7	117.8	130.5
Aug	124.9	115.9	100.1	121.9	117.9	106.5	125.5	113.5	124.3	121.3	109.0	118.7	131.4
Sep	125.3	115.9	99.8	122.0	118.0	106.9	125.8	113.5	124.7	121.7	109.3	119.1	131.0

See footnotes on previous page.

Source: Office for National Statistics: 01928 792442

7.23 Gross weekly and hourly earnings of full-time adult employees
Great Britain
At April

	Gross weekly earnings					Gross hourly earnings				
	Lowest decile	Lower quartile	Median	Upper quartile	Highest decile	Lowest decile	Lower quartile	Median	Upper quartile	Highest decile
	£	£	£	£	£	£	£	£	£	£
All men										
	KBYD	KBYE	KBYF	KBYG	KBYH	KIYD	KIYE	KIYF	KIYG	KIYH
1991	160.7	206.9	277.5	376.5	507.8	3.87	4.88	6.53	9.12	12.99
1992	170.2	219.3	295.9	401.9	544.1	4.12	5.17	6.97	9.79	14.04
1993	174.7	226.0	304.6	417.3	567.2	4.22	5.35	7.25	10.28	14.55
1994	179.9	231.1	312.8	427.3	581.7	4.33	5.44	7.39	10.51	14.96
1995	182.0	237.1	323.2	442.7	600.8	4.33	5.55	7.60	10.90	15.60
1996	189.0	245.2	334.9	461.0	633.1	4.50	5.75	7.91	11.41	16.36
1997	198.6	256.4	349.7	480.0	656.9	4.71	6.00	8.24	11.89	17.01
1998	203.9	265.3	362.8	499.0	685.1	4.88	6.24	8.57	12.34	17.75
1999	211.1	274.5	374.3	517.3	711.6	5.09	6.50	8.92	12.96	18.63
Manual men										
	KFZY	KFZZ	KGAK	KGAL	KGAM	KIYN	KIYO	KIYP	KIYQ	KIYR
1991	149.3	186.0	235.4	298.2	375.5	3.60	4.36	5.40	6.70	8.10
1992	157.6	197.4	250.7	316.7	397.3	3.82	4.62	5.72	7.16	8.68
1993	160.9	201.2	256.4	324.0	407.1	3.87	4.72	5.89	7.35	8.98
1994	165.9	206.1	261.8	331.6	414.2	3.99	4.82	5.95	7.46	9.10
1995	166.9	211.1	271.8	347.1	437.5	3.97	4.86	6.09	7.66	9.43
1996	173.7	218.4	280.0	358.9	452.5	4.11	5.01	6.32	7.99	9.83
1997	182.4	228.8	292.5	373.9	472.8	4.32	5.25	6.60	8.28	10.17
1998	190.0	238.0	305.0	392.7	494.2	4.50	5.48	6.87	8.67	10.72
1999	194.9	244.8	312.8	399.0	500.6	4.68	5.69	7.11	8.95	11.04
Non-manual men										
	KGAS	KGAT	KGAU	KGAV	KGAW	KIYX	KIYY	KIYZ	KIZA	KIZB
1991	178.7	242.1	332.2	440.2	602.0	4.49	6.12	8.50	11.71	15.95
1992	188.0	257.6	353.4	473.3	641.2	4.77	6.51	9.05	12.57	17.11
1993	194.9	266.3	365.9	489.7	671.8	4.93	6.77	9.47	13.03	17.83
1994	200.4	274.4	376.0	503.9	688.5	5.03	6.90	9.67	13.30	18.20
1995	204.1	280.1	384.6	519.5	712.7	5.11	7.06	9.93	13.83	19.07
1996	211.1	287.9	399.5	545.9	755.1	5.28	7.28	10.29	14.42	19.90
1997	220.7	301.0	415.9	565.8	780.8	5.49	7.60	10.72	14.94	20.81
1998	225.5	309.1	430.7	586.1	823.4	5.62	7.79	11.09	15.54	21.74
1999	233.5	321.1	449.1	612.2	862.6	5.90	8.14	11.59	16.24	22.90

As percentages of the corresponding median

All men										
	KBZH	KBZI	KBZJ	KBZK	KBZL	KBZM	KBZN	KBZO	KBZP	KBZQ
1991	57.9	74.6	100.0	135.7	183.0	59.3	74.8	100.0	139.6	198.8
1992	57.5	74.1	100.0	135.8	183.9	59.0	74.2	100.0	140.3	201.3
1993	57.4	74.2	100.0	137.0	186.2	58.2	73.8	100.0	141.8	200.8
1994	57.5	73.9	100.0	136.6	186.0	58.5	73.6	100.0	142.3	202.5
1995	56.3	73.4	100.0	137.0	185.9	57.0	73.0	100.0	143.4	205.3
1996	56.4	73.2	100.0	137.6	189.0	56.9	72.7	100.0	144.3	206.9
1997	56.8	73.3	100.0	137.3	187.8	57.2	72.8	100.0	144.3	206.4
1998	56.2	73.1	100.0	137.6	188.8	56.9	72.7	100.0	143.9	207.1
1999	56.4	73.3	100.0	138.2	190.1	57.1	72.9	100.0	145.3	208.9
Manual men										
	KGBS	KGBT	KGBU	KGBV	KGBW	KGBX	KGBY	KGBZ	KGCH	KGCI
1991	83.4	79.0	100.0	126.7	159.5	66.7	80.7	100.0	124.0	149.9
1992	82.8	78.7	100.0	120.3	158.5	66.9	80.8	100.0	125.2	151.8
1993	62.7	78.5	100.0	126.4	158.7	65.8	80.2	100.0	124.9	152.6
1994	63.4	78.7	100.0	126.7	158.2	67.1	80.9	100.0	125.3	152.9
1995	61.4	77.7	100.0	127.7	161.0	65.2	79.8	100.0	125.8	154.8
1996	62.1	78.0	100.0	128.2	161.6	65.0	79.3	100.0	126.4	155.6
1997	62.4	78.2	100.0	127.8	161.6	65.4	79.5	100.0	125.3	154.0
1998	62.3	78.0	100.0	128.8	162.0	65.5	79.8	100.0	126.2	156.1
1999	62.3	78.3	100.0	127.6	160.0	65.8	80.0	100.0	125.9	155.3
Non-manual men										
	KGCJ	KGCQ	KGCR	KGCS	KGCT	KGCU	KGCV	KGCW	KGCX	KGCY
1991	53.8	72.9	100.0	132.5	181.2	52.8	71.9	100.0	137.7	187.5
1992	53.2	72.9	100.0	133.9	181.4	52.7	71.9	100.0	138.9	189.0
1993	53.3	72.8	100.0	133.6	183.6	52.1	71.5	100.0	137.6	188.3
1994	53.3	73.0	100.0	134.0	183.1	52.0	71.4	100.0	137.5	188.2
1995	53.1	72.8	100.0	135.1	185.3	51.5	71.1	100.0	139.3	192.0
1996	52.8	72.1	100.0	136.6	189.0	51.3	70.7	100.0	140.2	193.5
1997	53.1	72.4	100.0	136.1	187.7	51.2	70.9	100.0	139.3	194.1
1998	52.4	71.8	100.0	136.1	191.2	50.7	70.2	100.0	140.2	196.0
1999	52.0	71.5	100.0	136.3	192.1	50.9	70.2	100.0	140.1	197.6

Source: ONS, New Earnings Survey: 01928 792077

7.23

Gross weekly and hourly earnings of full-time adult employees
Great Britain
At April

	Gross weekly earnings					Gross hourly earnings				
	Lowest decile	Lower quartile	Median	Upper quartile	Highest decile	Lowest decile	Lower quartile	Median	Upper quartile	Highest decile
	£	£	£	£	£	£	£	£	£	£
All women										
	KCBK	KCBL	KCBM	KCBN	KCBO	KIZC	KIZD	KIZE	KIZF	KIZG
1991	120.8	150.6	195.7	271.6	353.3	3.20	3.96	5.16	7.20	9.97
1992	129.1	161.4	211.3	295.9	387.1	3.43	4.26	5.57	7.81	10.90
1993	134.0	168.2	221.6	309.1	402.3	3.55	4.44	5.86	8.19	11.30
1994	139.1	174.6	229.4	320.1	417.8	3.66	4.58	6.02	8.39	11.59
1995	141.1	179.5	237.2	332.5	430.7	3.70	4.69	6.24	8.87	12.30
1996	146.7	186.8	248.1	347.3	449.8	3.83	4.87	6.55	9.31	12.98
1997	154.5	196.1	260.5	364.7	472.1	4.03	5.11	6.84	9.79	13.54
1998	161.0	203.6	270.0	379.1	493.5	4.22	5.32	7.10	10.20	14.16
1999	169.5	213.3	284.0	398.2	521.1	4.47	5.59	7.47	10.75	14.98
Manual women										
	KGCZ	KGDA	KGDB	KGDC	KGDD	KIZM	KIZN	KIZO	KIZP	KIZQ
1991	100.5	119.9	147.4	185.5	233.8	2.68	3.12	3.76	4.59	5.67
1992	105.7	126.6	156.6	199.2	253.5	2.87	3.33	4.00	4.92	6.00
1993	109.6	130.5	162.2	205.8	263.7	2.95	3.41	4.12	5.12	6.25
1994	114.1	134.7	165.4	212.0	272.0	3.05	3.51	4.20	5.23	6.39
1995	114.8	137.4	171.0	222.1	282.6	3.02	3.56	4.32	5.37	6.61
1996	119.0	142.8	178.7	230.8	291.4	3.15	3.68	4.49	5.61	6.85
1997	122.4	148.7	185.4	237.3	300.0	3.25	3.83	4.66	5.81	7.16
1998	128.9	156.3	193.9	248.6	312.5	3.43	4.02	4.87	6.08	7.44
1999	140.4	164.7	201.4	260.9	327.8	3.73	4.27	5.08	6.37	7.93
Non-manual women										
	KGDJ	KGDK	KGDL	KGDM	KGDN	KIZW	KIZX	KIZY	KIZZ	KJAN
1991	131.0	162.8	211.1	289.8	365.4	3.52	4.37	5.62	7.82	10.55
1992	140.5	174.4	227.6	315.9	401.6	3.78	4.68	6.07	8.42	11.60
1993	146.4	182.5	238.4	329.6	414.1	3.93	4.90	6.35	8.83	11.98
1994	152.0	188.9	247.0	342.5	430.3	4.06	5.05	6.52	9.04	12.25
1995	155.6	194.7	256.2	355.5	445.3	4.13	5.22	6.83	9.61	13.09
1996	161.7	203.0	268.7	372.3	471.4	4.31	5.44	7.16	10.08	13.96
1997	171.4	212.8	283.3	390.7	495.1	4.53	5.68	7.53	10.61	14.38
1998	176.2	219.3	291.5	405.6	513.5	4.68	5.86	7.77	11.01	14.88
1999	184.0	230.3	305.0	422.3	540.9	4.92	6.14	8.16	11.52	15.78

As percentages of the corresponding median

All women										
	KGEO	KGEP	KGEQ	KGER	KGES	KGET	KGEU	KGEV	KGEW	KGEX
1991	61.7	76.9	100.0	138.8	180.6	62.0	76.7	100.0	139.4	193.2
1992	61.1	76.4	100.0	140.1	183.3	61.6	76.5	100.0	140.2	195.6
1993	60.5	75.9	100.0	139.5	181.5	60.6	75.8	100.0	139.8	192.9
1994	60.6	76.1	100.0	139.5	182.1	60.9	76.2	100.0	139.5	192.7
1995	59.5	75.6	100.0	140.2	181.5	59.3	75.2	100.0	142.1	197.1
1996	59.1	75.3	100.0	140.0	181.3	58.6	74.4	100.0	142.2	198.3
1997	59.3	75.3	100.0	140.0	181.2	58.8	74.7	100.0	143.0	197.8
1998	59.6	75.4	100.0	140.4	182.8	59.4	74.9	100.0	141.7	191.5
1999	59.7	75.1	100.0	140.2	183.5	59.8	74.8	100.0	143.9	200.5
Manual women										
	KGDT	KGDU	KGDV	KGDW	KGDX	KGDY	KGDZ	KGEA	KGEB	KGEC
1991	68.2	81.4	100.0	125.9	158.7	71.3	82.9	100.0	122.1	150.8
1992	67.5	80.8	100.0	127.2	161.8	71.7	83.1	100.0	123.0	149.8
1993	67.6	80.5	100.0	126.9	162.5	71.7	82.8	100.0	124.2	151.8
1994	69.0	81.4	100.0	128.2	164.4	72.6	83.5	100.0	124.4	151.9
1995	67.1	80.3	100.0	129.9	165.2	69.9	82.4	100.0	124.3	153.0
1996	66.5	79.9	100.0	129.1	163.0	70.1	82.0	100.0	125.0	152.6
1997	66.0	80.2	100.0	128.0	161.8	69.7	82.2	100.0	124.6	153.6
1998	66.5	80.6	100.0	128.2	161.2	70.4	82.6	100.0	124.9	152.7
1999	69.7	81.8	100.0	129.5	162.8	73.4	84.1	100.0	125.4	156.1
Non-manual women										
	KGED	KGEE	KGEF	KGEG	KGEH	KGEI	KGEJ	KGEK	KGEL	KGEM
1991	62.1	77.1	100.0	137.3	173.1	62.7	77.7	100.0	139.1	187.6
1992	61.7	76.6	100.0	138.8	176.5	62.3	77.1	100.0	138.9	191.3
1993	61.4	76.5	100.0	138.2	173.7	61.9	77.1	100.0	139.0	188.5
1994	61.5	76.5	100.0	138.6	174.2	62.3	77.5	100.0	138.7	188.0
1995	60.7	76.0	100.0	138.8	173.8	60.5	76.4	100.0	140.7	191.7
1996	60.2	75.6	100.0	138.6	175.4	60.2	76.0	100.0	140.7	192.1
1997	60.5	75.1	100.0	137.9	174.8	60.2	75.5	100.0	141.0	191.0
1998	60.4	75.2	100.0	139.1	176.2	60.2	75.5	100.0	141.7	191.5
1999	60.3	75.5	100.0	138.5	177.3	60.3	75.3	100.0	141.2	193.4

Source: ONS, New Earnings Survey: 01928 792077

7.24
Gross weekly and hourly earnings of full-time adults
Northern Ireland

April of each year

	Gross weekly earnings[1]					Gross hourly earnings[1]				
	Lowest decile	Lower quartile	Median	Upper quartile	Highest decile	Lowest decile	Lower quartile	Median	Upper quartile	Highest decile
	£	£	£	£	£	p	p	p	p	p
All men										
	KCIF	KCIG	KCIH	KCII	KCIJ	KCIK	KCIL	KCIM	KCIN	KCIO
1992	139.5	185.6	259.0	372.8	509.4	348.0	439.6	597.2	872.7	1 148.9
1993	147.1	195.0	274.3	393.6	534.2	368.3	465.6	636.0	964.2	1 256.6
1994	152.8	198.6	279.4	405.3	546.4	382.1	473.5	652.2	1 006.9	1 288.2
1995	161.0	205.3	285.6	419.4	548.5	394.6	491.2	674.6	1 043.5	1 371.6
1996	163.0	213.7	296.9	424.0	549.8	399.4	512.3	695.7	1 073.9	1 402.8
1997	171.1	222.2	307.1	449.6	575.8	414.8	522.1	724.4	1 106.2	1 452.0
1998	175.4	227.4	322.1	455.1	596.1	435.8	548.8	763.0	1 137.2	1 497.5
1999	183.9	237.0	328.9	467.7	607.6	457.0	572.3	778.4	1 167.1	1 545.9
Manual men										
	KCIP	KCIQ	KCIR	KCIS	KCIT	KCIU	KCIV	KCIW	KCIX	KCIY
1992	130.0	163.6	211.7	275.7	353.9	330.9	400.0	498.0	619.8	778.0
1993	135.9	172.2	218.2	281.9	356.9	339.8	412.2	513.3	627.0	761.8
1994	141.6	175.4	222.0	291.0	366.2	349.9	418.8	513.9	634.9	799.9
1995	149.7	181.5	230.9	299.4	383.3	359.7	435.5	527.0	664.6	826.5
1996	150.6	187.2	240.7	310.1	389.9	369.9	448.0	563.7	684.6	860.6
1997	158.4	192.9	249.4	321.4	402.7	385.0	460.0	570.5	709.5	882.0
1998	165.0	200.9	262.9	340.5	422.8	408.3	487.3	595.3	767.3	940.7
1999	175.6	216.4	270.4	355.0	454.6	435.5	515.0	624.5	786.0	994.7
Non-manual men										
	KCIZ	KCJO	KCJP	KCJQ	KCJR	KCJS	KCJT	KCJU	KCJV	KCJW
1992	161.2	237.2	337.6	467.4	573.4	404.0	577.0	851.7	1 078.3	1 356.5
1993	168.6	251.9	356.5	488.7	611.5	435.6	636.0	923.2	1 176.4	1 476.6
1994	174.8	253.8	366.4	501.5	615.2	445.9	641.7	956.2	1 222.5	1 461.7
1995	183.4	260.7	383.4	511.0	628.9	470.3	660.6	987.7	1 292.8	1 601.8
1996	192.5	268.4	387.1	506.4	617.2	482.4	682.5	1 013.0	1 322.7	1 612.2
1997	198.3	277.4	403.0	533.1	666.6	491.4	690.9	1 048.2	1 363.0	1 638.2
1998	200.5	284.2	418.4	543.8	685.9	500.0	715.7	1 074.7	1 404.5	1 739.5
1999	200.0	296.8	424.0	546.8	680.6	502.8	740.4	1 103.6	1 461.9	1 779.4

As percentages of the corresponding median

All men										
	KCJX	KCJY	KCJZ	KCKA	KCKB	KCKC	KCKD	KCKE	KCKF	KCKG
1992	53.9	71.7	100.0	143.9	196.7	58.3	73.6	100.0	146.1	192.4
1993	53.6	71.1	100.0	143.5	194.8	57.9	73.2	100.0	151.6	197.6
1994	54.7	71.1	100.0	145.1	195.6	58.6	72.6	100.0	154.4	197.5
1995	56.4	71.9	100.0	146.8	192.1	58.5	72.8	100.0	154.7	203.3
1996	54.9	72.0	100.0	142.8	185.2	57.4	73.6	100.0	154.4	201.6
1997	55.7	72.4	100.0	146.4	187.5	57.3	72.1	100.0	152.7	200.4
1998	54.5	70.6	100.0	141.3	185.1	57.1	71.9	100.0	149.0	196.3
1999	55.9	72.0	100.0	142.2	184.7	58.7	73.5	100.0	149.9	198.6
Manual men										
	KCKH	KCKI	KCKT	KCKK	KCKL	KCKM	KCKN	KCKO	KCKP	KCKR
1992	61.4	77.3	100.0	130.2	167.2	66.5	80.3	100.0	124.5	156.2
1993	62.3	78.9	100.0	129.2	163.6	66.2	80.3	100.0	122.2	148.4
1994	63.8	79.0	100.0	131.1	165.0	68.1	81.5	100.0	123.5	155.7
1995	64.8	78.6	100.0	129.7	166.0	68.3	82.6	100.0	126.1	156.8
1996	62.6	77.8	100.0	128.8	162.0	65.6	79.5	100.0	121.4	152.7
1997	63.5	77.3	100.0	128.9	161.5	67.5	80.6	100.0	124.4	154.6
1998	62.8	76.4	100.0	129.5	160.8	68.6	81.9	100.0	128.9	158.0
1999	64.9	80.0	100.0	131.3	168.1	69.7	82.5	100.0	125.9	159.3
Non-manual men										
	KCKQ	KCKS	KFZW	KCKU	KCKV	KCKW	KCKX	KCKY	KCKZ	KCLA
1992	47.8	70.3	100.0	138.5	169.9	47.4	67.8	100.0	126.6	159.3
1993	47.3	70.7	100.0	137.1	171.5	47.2	68.9	100.0	127.4	159.9
1994	47.7	69.3	100.0	136.9	167.9	46.6	67.1	100.0	127.8	152.9
1995	47.8	68.0	100.0	133.3	164.0	47.6	66.9	100.0	130.9	162.2
1996	49.7	69.3	100.0	130.8	159.4	47.6	67.4	100.0	130.6	159.2
1997	49.2	68.8	100.0	132.3	165.4	46.9	65.9	100.0	130.0	156.3
1998	47.9	67.9	100.0	130.0	163.9	46.5	66.6	100.0	130.7	161.9
1999	47.2	70.0	100.0	129.0	160.5	45.6	67.1	100.0	132.5	161.2

Sources: Department of Enterprise, Trade and Investment (Northern Ireland);
028 9052 9429

7.24
continued

Gross weekly and hourly earnings of full-time adults
Northern Ireland
April of each year

	Gross weekly earnings[1]					Gross hourly earnings[1]				
	Lowest decile	Lower quartile	Median	Upper quartile	Highest decile	Lowest decile	Lower quartile	Median	Upper quartile	Highest decile
	£	£	£	£	£	p	p	p	p	p
All women										
	KCDS	KCDT	KCDU	KCDV	KCDW	KCDX	KCDY	KCDZ	KCFF	KCFG
1992	113.3	141.2	193.1	291.2	385.7	293.4	350.0	482.0	670.2	937.4
1993	118.0	147.6	202.9	298.1	392.7	311.5	383.2	528.9	753.5	1 074.1
1994	120.4	149.0	201.5	303.7	399.0	321.3	398.0	545.5	809.4	1 138.4
1995	130.2	162.9	217.4	320.5	423.2	345.1	424.3	583.8	885.5	1 203.8
1996	133.3	165.5	226.2	331.9	434.8	354.5	431.0	595.8	893.6	1 256.9
1997	137.5	170.0	231.3	334.4	450.9	360.0	441.6	602.6	906.2	1 285.5
1998	148.1	181.4	243.9	348.0	465.2	390.2	471.5	652.5	950.9	1 304.5
1999	151.3	191.9	257.8	374.3	485.9	404.3	494.7	683.3	1 026.6	1 410.6
Manual women										
	KCFH	KCFI	KCFJ	KCFK	KCFL	KCFM	KCFN	KCFO	KCFP	KCFQ
1992	102.6	117.5	140.6	170.9	217.2	274.4	305.8	359.2	429.7	528.2
1993	103.9	121.6	142.9	173.7	218.7	276.2	314.6	371.0	431.0	533.1
1994	101.7	122.2	146.8	175.1	213.7	279.5	322.2	376.7	444.1	545.4
1995	109.1	131.5	161.0	193.7	247.7	287.6	343.0	401.7	483.0	616.2
1996	110.9	132.5	161.1	197.1	248.7	293.9	345.7	408.0	496.2	599.7
1997	113.4	138.3	160.0	201.8	250.8	308.3	354.4	413.7	500.0	593.0
1998	120.0	146.5	172.9	213.6	258.4	309.0	385.7	440.0	549.0	631.2
1999	136.1	151.3	175.1	219.0	275.8	360.0	397.2	451.3	546.8	633.8
Non-manual women										
	KCFR	KCFS	KCFT	KCFU	KCFV	KCFW	KCFX	KCFY	KCFZ	KCHA
1992	120.0	162.1	220.0	322.5	400.3	315.3	414.3	539.7	748.3	975.0
1993	129.6	169.2	229.4	332.3	402.2	334.8	442.0	595.3	837.0	1 127.7
1994	132.3	169.7	227.1	334.4	411.9	363.2	458.5	606.7	893.3	1 197.2
1995	139.1	176.9	241.4	346.3	435.8	375.2	473.9	650.1	943.0	1 269.6
1996	145.3	182.5	253.0	364.7	437.0	385.0	490.2	675.6	997.3	1 302.6
1997	149.7	188.6	254.0	364.3	451.3	389.0	501.6	679.4	996.7	1 342.9
1998	156.6	200.2	270.9	383.8	475.5	412.8	530.7	725.0	1 028.2	1 373.9
1999	167.4	211.5	289.3	409.2	500.9	442.1	569.7	773.3	1 137.8	1 459.0

As percentages of the corresponding median

All women										
	KCHB	KCHC	KCHD	KCHE	KCHF	KCHG	KCHH	KCHI	KCHJ	KCHK
1992	58.7	73.1	100.0	150.8	199.7	60.9	72.6	100.0	139.1	194.5
1993	58.2	72.8	100.0	146.9	193.5	58.9	72.5	100.0	142.5	203.1
1994	59.8	73.9	100.0	150.7	198.0	58.9	73.0	100.0	148.4	208.7
1995	59.9	74.9	100.0	147.4	194.7	59.1	72.7	100.0	151.7	206.2
1996	58.9	73.2	100.0	146.7	192.2	59.5	72.3	100.0	150.0	211.0
1997	59.4	73.5	100.0	144.6	194.9	59.7	73.3	100.0	150.4	213.3
1998	60.7	74.4	100.0	142.7	190.7	59.8	72.3	100.0	145.7	199.9
1999	58.7	74.5	100.0	145.2	188.5	59.2	72.4	100.0	150.2	206.5
Manual women										
	KCHL	KCHM	KCHN	KCHO	KCHP	KCHQ	KCHR	KCHS	KCHT	KCHU
1992	73.0	83.6	100.0	121.6	154.5	76.4	85.1	100.0	119.6	147.1
1993	72.7	85.1	100.0	121.6	153.0	74.4	84.8	100.0	116.2	143.7
1994	69.3	83.2	100.0	119.3	145.6	74.2	85.5	100.0	117.9	144.8
1995	67.8	81.7	100.0	120.3	153.9	71.6	85.4	100.0	120.2	153.4
1996	68.8	82.2	100.0	122.3	154.4	72.0	84.7	100.0	121.6	147.0
1997	70.9	86.4	100.0	126.1	156.8	74.5	85.7	100.0	120.9	143.3
1998	69.4	84.7	100.0	123.5	149.4	70.2	87.7	100.0	124.8	143.5
1999	77.7	86.4	100.0	125.1	157.5	79.8	88.0	100.0	121.2	140.4
Non-manual women										
	KCHV	KCHW	KCHX	KCHY	KCHZ	KCIA	KCIB	KCIC	KCID	KCIE
1992	54.6	73.7	100.0	146.6	182.0	58.4	76.8	100.0	138.7	180.7
1993	56.5	73.8	100.0	144.9	175.3	56.2	74.2	100.0	140.6	189.4
1994	58.3	74.7	100.0	147.2	181.4	59.9	75.6	100.0	147.2	197.3
1995	57.6	73.3	100.0	143.5	180.5	57.7	72.9	100.0	145.1	195.3
1996	57.4	72.1	100.0	144.2	172.7	57.0	72.6	100.0	147.6	192.8
1997	58.9	74.3	100.0	143.4	177.7	57.3	73.8	100.0	146.7	197.7
1998	57.8	73.9	100.0	141.7	175.5	56.9	73.2	100.0	141.8	189.5
1999	57.9	73.1	100.0	141.5	173.2	57.2	73.7	100.0	147.1	188.7

1 Those whose pay in the survey period was not affected by absence. Weekly earnings figures refer to April in each year and are gross before deductions, generally excluding the value of incomes in kind but including bonus, overtime and commission payments for the pay period.

Sources: Department of Enterprise, Trade and Investment (Northern Ireland);
028 9052 9429

7.25 Average earnings by age group of full-time employees whose pay for the survey pay period was not affected by absence: Great Britain

At April 1999

	Gross weekly earnings								Average weekly hours		Average hourly earnings excluding overtime pay
	Average		As a percentage of the median			As a percentage of the median		Percentage earning under £250			
	Total	Overtime pay	Lowest decile	Lower quartile	Median	Upper quartile	Highest decile		Total	Overtime	
	£	£	per cent	per cent	£	per cent	per cent				£
All males											
Under 18	142.8	8.8	58.1	77.2	136.7	125.2	149.6	95.4	40.9	1.8	3.43
18 to 20	209.9	15.5	70.0	82.3	191.9	126.2	159.7	78.1	41.3	2.3	5.00
21 to 24	307.3	20.6	63.7	78.4	267.9	128.6	166.3	42.5	41.1	2.4	7.41
25 to 29	368.8	25.3	60.6	77.4	332.8	129.6	170.0	22.9	41.4	2.7	8.89
30 to 39	458.6	28.7	57.8	74.4	394.9	135.1	184.7	14.5	41.5	2.8	11.12
40 to 49	495.9	27.7	55.8	73.0	427.8	134.9	185.8	12.2	41.1	2.7	12.17
50 to 59	473.3	26.1	57.0	73.7	388.5	140.1	197.6	16.1	41.5	2.8	11.50
60 to 64	385.7	25.2	60.9	75.9	318.8	135.4	189.2	27.3	42.0	2.9	9.21
All ages	438.3	26.4	55.5	73.0	370.6	138.7	191.3	19.8	41.4	2.7	10.64
Manual males											
Under 18	138.6	8.6	59.9	78.8	130.0	127.3	153.8	96.4	41.4	1.9	3.30
18 to 20	208.9	18.2	68.2	81.2	191.9	127.7	159.7	76.8	42.3	2.8	4.84
21 to 24	273.4	29.4	64.2	78.7	254.1	125.9	157.1	47.9	43.3	3.6	6.17
25 to 29	318.9	40.7	63.6	78.8	298.5	126.6	157.8	30.4	44.4	4.6	7.01
30 to 39	349.7	47.5	63.3	78.9	325.8	128.0	158.7	22.3	44.7	5.1	7.63
40 to 49	358.3	49.7	64.4	79.4	331.5	128.2	160.8	20.5	44.7	5.2	7.82
50 to 59	338.0	43.6	63.9	79.0	319.0	125.9	154.7	24.0	44.5	4.9	7.44
60 to 64	302.6	36.3	65.9	80.2	280.7	128.3	157.3	35.1	43.9	4.4	6.74
All ages	331.1	43.2	61.2	77.5	309.6	128.1	161.1	28.2	44.4	4.8	7.28
Non-manual males											
Under 18	155.0	9.5	54.7	71.9	153.3	118.9	153.3	92.4	39.4	1.5	3.86
18 to 20	211.2	11.7	71.7	83.1	191.9	124.4	159.5	79.8	39.9	1.6	5.23
21 to 24	334.6	13.6	63.9	78.9	278.5	129.9	175.6	38.2	39.4	1.5	8.46
25 to 29	404.9	14.1	59.9	76.5	364.4	131.0	170.5	17.5	39.2	1.3	10.33
30 to 39	539.5	14.8	55.7	74.0	467.0	133.7	186.1	8.7	39.0	1.2	13.85
40 to 49	588.9	12.8	56.1	75.9	510.6	132.5	184.8	6.6	38.6	1.0	15.30
50 to 59	590.5	11.1	52.0	71.3	492.4	136.4	194.9	9.2	38.8	0.9	15.23
60 to 64	498.9	10.0	52.7	72.7	400.3	142.9	201.4	16.5	39.5	0.9	12.75
All ages	522.2	13.2	51.7	71.1	445.6	136.7	192.9	13.2	39.0	1.1	13.44
All females											
Under 18	145.6	5.5	62.7	83.7	143.2	114.9	139.7	96.6	38.8	1.0	3.71
18 to 20	189.2	6.9	72.2	84.7	178.6	122.1	147.1	87.6	38.6	1.0	4.86
21 to 24	258.1	8.1	67.2	80.3	235.7	128.8	157.7	56.1	38.2	1.0	6.73
25 to 29	319.4	8.4	63.1	77.7	290.4	129.3	165.0	35.6	37.7	0.8	8.44
30 to 39	364.1	8.1	57.1	73.0	323.3	136.6	178.1	29.5	37.6	0.8	9.69
40 to 49	345.5	7.0	58.0	73.5	299.2	145.4	181.8	35.8	37.1	0.8	9.33
50 to 59	318.0	6.5	60.9	76.5	274.6	146.1	187.4	40.9	37.2	0.8	8.56
60 to 64	282.0	6.7	60.5	74.8	249.6	127.4	178.4	50.7	37.5	0.8	7.31
All ages	324.4	7.5	59.2	74.8	282.2	140.2	183.8	39.7	37.5	0.8	8.64
Manual females											
Under 18	144.9	6.5	67.2	83.7	143.3	110.6	139.4	96.9	40.0	1.5	3.59
18 to 20	175.9	7.4	68.7	81.9	169.7	120.6	144.9	90.6	39.5	1.2	4.40
21 to 24	207.6	11.8	70.3	82.3	192.1	126.1	154.9	77.6	40.3	1.8	5.10
25 to 29	236.9	13.2	66.7	79.5	217.6	129.1	158.6	65.2	40.0	1.7	5.83
30 to 39	235.8	15.5	67.1	80.7	214.5	131.1	166.9	65.5	40.1	2.1	5.80
40 to 49	222.8	14.7	70.3	82.2	203.7	127.7	160.5	70.8	39.8	2.0	5.51
50 to 59	217.5	13.7	71.2	82.5	197.9	129.9	160.0	72.8	39.7	1.9	5.39
60 to 64	206.6	11.0	73.5	82.9	184.9	124.0	167.4	79.3	39.2	1.7	5.07
All ages	220.5	13.5	69.4	81.6	200.2	129.8	163.3	71.8	39.9	1.9	5.45
Non-manual females											
Under 18	145.9	4.9	59.7	83.7	143.2	119.5	144.1	96.3	38.1	0.8	3.78
18 to 20	193.2	6.7	73.7	84.5	182.3	121.4	147.7	86.7	38.4	0.9	5.00
21 to 24	267.3	7.4	67.6	80.0	245.7	126.9	155.3	52.1	37.8	0.8	7.04
25 to 29	331.7	7.7	64.0	77.7	303.4	128.1	161.4	31.2	37.4	0.7	8.85
30 to 39	384.5	7.0	59.2	74.4	342.5	134.0	175.1	23.8	37.2	0.6	10.34
40 to 49	370.1	5.5	58.7	72.8	327.1	139.5	174.0	28.9	36.5	0.5	10.15
50 to 59	343.2	4.7	62.5	76.8	300.0	145.3	180.3	32.9	36.5	0.5	9.40
60 to 64	311.3	5.1	63.7	80.3	268.9	131.0	175.9	39.6	36.8	0.5	8.22
All ages	344.7	6.3	60.0	75.3	302.7	139.2	178.7	33.4	37.1	0.6	9.30

Source: ONS, New Earnings Survey: 01928 792077

7.26 Trade unions[1,2]
United Kingdom
At end of year

per cent

		1988	1989	1990	1991	1992	1993	1994	1995	1996	1997	1998
Number of trade unions	KCLB	315	309	287	275	268	254	243	238	226	221	206
Analysis by number of members:												
Under 100 members	KCLC	17.5	15.5	15.3	12.7	12.7	13.4	11.9	10.5	10.2	12.7	11.7
100 and under 500	KCLD	24.1	23.6	22.6	24.0	21.6	22.8	20.2	21.0	23.0	19.0	21.8
500 and under 1 000	KCLE	8.3	6.1	7.7	7.6	9.3	7.1	9.5	10.5	8.0	11.8	9.2
1 000 and under 2 500	KCLF	14.9	15.9	15.0	15.6	17.2	16.9	16.5	17.2	19.9	15.8	13.1
2 500 and under 5 000	KCLG	8.3	8.7	9.4	10.2	9.3	9.4	10.7	9.7	8.4	9.5	11.7
5 000 and under 10 000	KCLH	4.7	5.8	5.2	5.5	6.3	7.1	7.8	7.1	6.2	6.3	7.3
10 000 and under 15 000	KCLI	1.3	1.6	2.1	1.8	1.9	2.4	2.5	3.4	3.1	3.2	1.9
15 000 and under 25 000	KCLJ	3.5	3.9	3.1	3.3	3.7	3.1	2.9	2.5	2.2	2.3	2.9
25 000 and under 50 000	KCLK	7.6	7.8	8.7	7.6	7.1	7.9	8.2	8.4	9.3	9.0	9.7
50 000 and under 100 000	KCLL	2.5	2.3	2.4	3.3	3.4	3.1	2.9	2.9	2.2	2.7	2.9
100 000 and under 250 000	KCLM	4.1	4.2	4.9	4.4	4.1	3.5	4.1	3.4	3.5	3.6	2.9
250 000 and over	KCLN	3.2	3.2	3.1	3.6	3.4	3.1	2.9	3.4	4.0	4.1	4.9
Membership unknown	KCLO	–	1.3	0.3	–	–	–	–	–	–	–	–
All sizes	KCLP	100	100	100	100	100	100	100	100	100	100	100
Membership[3,4]												
Analysis by size of union:												
Under 100 members	KCLQ	–	–	–	0.02	0.02	0.02	–	–	–	–	–
100 and under 500	KCLR	0.2	0.2	0.2	0.2	0.2	0.2	0.2	0.2	0.2	0.1	0.1
500 and under 1 000	KCLS	0.2	0.1	0.2	0.2	0.2	0.2	0.2	0.2	0.1	0.2	0.2
1 000 and under 2 500	KCLT	0.8	0.8	0.7	0.8	0.9	0.9	0.8	0.8	0.9	0.8	0.6
2 500 and under 5 000	KCLU	0.9	0.9	1.0	1.1	1.0	1.0	1.1	1.0	0.9	1.0	1.1
5 000 and under 10 000	KCLV	1.0	1.2	1.0	1.2	1.3	1.5	1.6	1.5	1.2	1.2	1.4
10 000 and under 15 000	KCLW	0.5	0.6	0.7	0.6	0.6	0.9	0.9	1.3	1.2	1.1	0.7
15 000 and under 25 000	KCLX	2.0	2.3	1.7	1.7	2.0	1.6	1.5	1.3	1.1	1.1	1.4
25 000 and under 50 000	KCLY	8.5	8.6	9.0	7.8	7.7	8.4	8.9	9.2	9.2	8.5	8.4
50 000 and under 100 000	KCLZ	5.5	4.9	4.9	6.2	6.7	6.7	6.0	6.0	3.9	4.5	4.5
100 000 and under 250 000	KCMA	20.2	20.0	22.4	19.8	18.9	16.4	19.3	16.4	15.2	15.3	12.0
250 000 and over	KCMB	60.1	60.4	58.2	60.5	60.2	62.4	59.5	62.1	66.0	66.2	69.5
All sizes	KCMC	100	100	100	100	100	100	100	100	100	100	100
Total membership (Thousands)	KCMD	10 376	10 158	9 947	9 585	9 048	8 700	8 278	8 089	7 980	7 836	7 850

1 The statistics relate to all organisations of employees known to Certification Officer with head offices in the United Kingdom.

2 Figures are confined to organisations which appear to satisfy the statutory definition of a trade union in Section 28 of the Trade Union and Labour Relations Act 1974 and more recently section 1 of the Trade Union and Labour Relations (Consolidation) Act 1992.

3 Included in the data are home and overseas membership figures of contributory and non-contributory members. Employment status of members is not provided and the figures may therefore include some people who are self-employed, unemployed or retired.

4 The 1997 figures are provisional and subject to revision as later information becomes available. Figures published in earlier years have been revised in line with the latest information.

Source: Department of Trade and Industry: 020 7215 5780

7.27 Vacancies at jobcentres in the United Kingdom[1,2]
Seasonally adjusted

Thousands

	January	February	March	April	May	June	July	August	September	October	November	December
Numbers of vacancies remaining unfilled DPCB												
1990	198.3	194.1	191.0	195.9	194.4	186.6	173.5	168.3	163.2	149.9	139.9	128.6
1991	140.0	138.9	133.9	119.8	110.2	105.6	106.0	109.2	112.5	109.6	111.8	117.4
1992	117.0	118.2	118.2	117.1	118.8	119.8	120.2	118.6	113.1	112.9	114.4	117.0
1993	119.0	120.3	124.3	123.6	125.9	124.8	129.2	129.8	129.5	133.2	136.3	138.2
1994	140.4	142.7	143.4	146.2	149.1	154.9	158.8	165.0	165.4	175.3	176.9	177.6
1995	175.2	174.3	177.5	186.0	185.4	182.9	181.8	181.7	184.5	181.7	185.2	186.7
1996	190.4	189.3	196.9	201.2	209.2	220.7	233.0	238.8	247.4	248.7	257.5	265.5
1997	272.6	279.2	279.6	279.4	277.3	283.9	288.0	295.2	297.2	293.7	275.2	278.2
1998	275.4	285.2	286.1	289.8	298.0	300.1	303.5	302.7	301.5	301.3	303.2	302.8
1999	305.8	301.4	298.0	298.4	304.8	305.0	308.6	315.2	314.3	333.2	338.3	347.6
2000	343.1	343.4	346.9	355.9	354.0	357.4	362.1	362.2	365.5	363.5	..	..
Inflow of vacancies DRYW												
1990	201.4	224.5	217.1	215.1	214.2	200.9	197.6	198.3	196.7	186.9	185.2	176.4
1991	185.4	167.8	168.0	182.8	182.2	163.9	165.6	168.7	170.7	168.3	164.9	167.1
1992	166.4	166.9	171.7	166.0	166.2	176.4	173.3	164.0	167.1	171.3	164.7	173.8
1993	180.2	175.9	181.5	179.3	180.2	183.5	190.5	183.4	191.5	189.6	193.9	197.2
1994	199.2	199.5	199.1	203.7	205.2	212.2	208.3	223.6	216.6	219.1	223.1	226.8
1995	218.2	219.5	215.2	205.4	227.7	223.1	225.6	230.9	226.5	231.9	232.9	222.1
1996	228.9	222.2	219.8	231.7	221.4	219.5	224.4	223.1	221.7	203.4	230.2	232.8
1997	202.9	239.3	242.9	239.1	236.2	226.2	226.4	220.8	227.6	222.6	217.9	216.2
1998	181.6	222.3	222.6	223.3	210.4	225.2	219.7	219.2	222.8	231.1	222.6	218.2
1999	235.3	227.4	225.0	220.6	229.9	225.5	228.0	231.7	232.3	236.8	235.1	237.0
2000	225.9	231.2	233.5	235.3	198.9	222.2	218.9	218.3	227.2	222.7	..	..
Outflow of vacancies DRZL												
1990	204.7	228.7	219.4	216.9	216.3	208.1	211.6	203.4	202.1	200.4	197.0	180.4
1991	176.4	168.7	172.4	197.5	197.1	168.3	165.0	164.9	168.7	170.2	159.9	160.8
1992	169.7	165.6	170.5	168.4	168.6	174.1	172.5	164.1	170.5	169.8	160.8	170.6
1993	178.8	173.6	176.6	180.1	181.0	184.0	185.6	182.0	189.8	186.4	191.0	195.3
1994	196.8	196.7	198.3	202.3	203.4	205.8	202.8	217.1	214.8	210.8	221.6	227.0
1995	219.0	220.6	214.1	195.1	229.0	225.0	224.6	230.4	225.5	237.1	229.7	219.2
1996	225.6	222.1	213.8	222.7	212.9	211.1	214.3	218.4	213.9	200.9	220.9	229.8
1997	208.5	232.1	238.0	236.8	234.1	220.9	225.0	215.0	216.8	224.2	232.5	219.9
1998	204.9	212.9	217.6	215.9	201.8	221.1	218.2	219.8	218.3	228.8	220.3	226.5
1999	235.6	231.2	225.2	218.1	223.4	223.6	223.9	225.3	230.4	220.9	233.0	235.6
2000	240.1	232.7	229.9	224.0	205.5	217.4	212.5	219.0	222.8	217.4	..	..
Number of placings DTQR												
1990	144.9	159.9	153.7	151.4	151.1	144.7	148.5	145.9	144.9	144.7	142.6	131.4
1991	129.4	122.5	127.6	148.4	148.4	123.9	123.2	120.9	122.1	122.7	114.8	115.9
1992	124.6	119.7	123.6	122.6	123.0	126.5	126.5	119.6	125.9	127.6	120.6	130.2
1993	134.3	132.1	131.7	134.0	134.9	136.3	139.0	136.1	144.1	140.6	146.4	148.2
1994	149.5	150.6	151.5	156.6	157.7	161.9	157.7	169.6	166.4	162.3	170.3	173.2
1995	166.2	169.1	164.6	145.8	179.8	173.6	174.4	178.5	172.5	183.5	179.7	167.4
1996	176.1	164.6	151.5	152.8	151.6	148.2	149.7	153.6	148.9	135.4	150.4	159.3
1997	147.9	157.7	163.6	164.0	151.8	143.1	138.6	127.1	126.4	123.1	120.2	116.9
1998	108.6	115.2	118.3	116.1	107.4	114.7	114.4	115.6	118.0	122.1	118.0	118.0
1999	120.6	122.0	119.1	118.9	121.8	119.2	120.0	121.0	123.7	121.8	123.8	124.9
2000	123.1	117.9	118.3	116.1	102.0	108.3	105.5	109.4	111.8	110.1	..	..

Note: Vacancies notified to and placings made by jobcentres do not represent the total number of vacancies/engagements in the economy. Latest estimates suggest that about a third of all vacancies are notified to jobcentres: and about a quarter of all engagements are made through jobcentres. Inflow, outflow and placings figures are collected for four or five-week periods between count dates; the figures in this table are converted to a standard 4 $\frac{1}{3}$ week month.

1 Excluding vacancies on government programmes (except vacancies on Enterprise Ulster and Action for Community Employment (ACE) which are included in the seasonally adjusted figures for Northern Ireland). Note that Community Programme vacancies handled by jobcentres were excluded from the seasonally adjusted series when the coverage was revised in September 1985. The coverage of the seasonally adjusted series is therefore not affected by the cessation of C.P. vacancies with the introduction of Employment Training in September 1988. For further details, see the October 1985 *Employment Gazette* (now Labour Market Trends), 143.

2 The latest national seasonally adjusted vacancy figures are provisional and subject to revision in the following month.

Source: ONS, Labour Market Statistics: 020 7533 6094

8 Personal income, expenditure and wealth

Personal income, expenditure and wealth

Family Expenditure Survey
(Tables 8.3 - 8.5)

The Family Expenditure Survey, introduced in 1957, covers all types of private households in the United Kingdom. It is a continuous survey with fieldwork carried out in every month of the year. In 1999-2000 around 7,000 households in the UK provided information. The main purpose of the survey is to provide a source for the weighting pattern for the Index of Retail Prices, so it is primarily concerned with household expenditure on goods and services. However, it does have several other important uses.

Although the survey is primarily concerned with the expenditure of private households, much additional information is collected about income and the characteristics of co-operating households. Consequently, the survey provides a unique fund of important economic and social data.

Like all surveys based on a sample of the population, its results are subject to sampling error, and to some bias due to non-response.

The results of the survey are published in an annual report, the latest being *'Family Spending 1999-2000'*. The report includes a list of definitions used in the survey, items on which information is collected and a brief account of the fieldwork procedure.

Distribution of total incomes *(Table 8.2)*

The information shown in Table 8.2 comes from the Survey of Personal Incomes for the financial years 1995/96, 1996/97, 1997/98 and 1998/99. This is an annual survey that covers approximately 125 000 individuals across the whole of the UK. It is based on administrative data held by Inland Revenue offices on individuals who could be liable to tax.

8.1
Average incomes of households before and after taxes and benefits[1,2], 1998/99
United Kingdom

	Retired households[3]		Non-retired households								
	1 adult	2 or more adults	1 adult	2 adults	3 or more adults	1 adult with children[4]	2 adults with 1 child[4]	2 adults with 2 children[4]	2 adults with 3 or more children[4]	3 or more adults with children[4]	All house-holds
Number of households in the population (Thousands)	3 578	2 964	3 595	5 232	2 008	1 394	1 676	2 286	977	956	24 664
Average per household (£ per year)											
Original income	3 758	8 902	15 173	31 553	36 021	5 829	28 517	31 022	25 674	34 198	20 936
Disposable income	7 731	13 813	12 847	25 376	30 847	10 645	23 682	25 502	23 561	30 322	19 230
Post-tax income	6 379	10 866	10 138	20 444	23 897	8 261	18 787	20 368	18 534	23 362	15 261

1 Original income is the total income in cash and kind of the household before the deduction of taxes or the addition of state benefits. The addition of cash benefits (retirement pensions, child benefit, etc) and the deduction of income tax, council tax, water charges, domestic rates and employees' national insurance contributions give disposable income. By further allowing for taxes paid on goods and services purchased, such as VAT, an estimate of 'post-tax' income is derived. These income figures are derived from estimates made by the Office for National Statistics, based largely on information from the Family Expenditure Survey (FES), and published each year in *Economic Trends*.

2 Redistribution of Income, included in the Effects of taxes and benefits upon household income, 1998/99, article published in the April 2000 edition of *Economic Trends*.

3 A retired household is defined as one where the combined income of retired members amounts to at least half the total gross income of the household, where a retired person is defined as anyone who describes themselves as 'retired' or anyone over the minimum NI pension age describing themselves as 'unoccupied' or 'sick or injured but not intending to seek work'.

4 Children are defined as persons aged under 16 or aged between 16 and 18, unmarried and receiving non-advanced further education.

Source: Office for National Statistics: 020 7533 5772

Personal income, expenditure and wealth

8.2 Distribution of total incomes before and after tax
United Kingdom

Years ended 5 April

| | 1995/96 Annual Survey | | | | | 1996/97 Annual Survey | | | |
| | | £ million | | | | | £ million | | |
Lower limit of range of income	Number of individuals (000s)	Total income before tax	Total tax	Total income after tax	Lower limit of range of income	Number of individuals (000s)	Total income before tax	Total tax	Total income after tax
All incomes[1,2,3,4]	25 800	407 900	74 400	333 500	All incomes[1,2,3,4]	25 700	427 000	75 800	351 000
Income before tax £					**Income before tax £**				
3 525	547	2 070	24	2 040	3 765	259	1 010	6	1 000
4 000	582	2 460	76	2 390	4 000	567	2 400	49	2 360
4 500	714	3 410	120	3 290	4 500	589	2 800	100	2 700
5 000	885	4 640	200	4 440	5 000	896	4 710	180	4 530
5 500	861	4 950	280	4 670	5 500	810	4 660	220	4 430
6 000	1 610	10 400	760	9 680	6 000	1 640	10 700	680	9 990
7 000	1 730	12 900	1 090	11 900	7 000	1 570	11 800	910	10 900
8 000	3 040	27 300	2 990	24 300	8 000	3 080	27 800	2 690	25 100
10 000	2 720	29 800	3 970	25 900	10 000	2 830	31 100	3 770	27 300
12 000	3 470	46 500	7 070	39 500	12 000	3 470	46 700	6 630	40 100
15 000	3 930	67 800	11 600	56 200	15 000	3 980	69 000	10 900	58 000
20 000	3 790	90 700	17 000	73 700	20 000	3 770	90 800	16 000	74 800
30 000	1 360	50 300	11 700	38 600	30 000	1 550	57 500	12 600	44 800
50 000	455	29 700	8 770	21 000	50 000	491	32 400	9 270	23 100
100 000 and over	126	24 700	8 720	15 950	100 000 and over	154	33 800	11 840	22 000
Income after tax £					**Income after tax £**				
3 525	689	2 640	39	2 600	3 765	326	1 280	99	1 270
4 000	676	2 980	110	2 870	4 000	705	3 070	77	2 990
4 500	861	4 300	190	4 110	4 500	707	3 520	150	3 370
5 000	1 110	6 130	320	5 810	5 000	1 040	5 720	240	5 470
5 500	1 090	6 700	450	6 250	5 500	1 020	6 200	350	5 850
6 000	1 920	13 700	1 170	12 500	6 000	1 920	13 500	1 000	12 500
7 000	2 140	17 700	1 750	16 000	7 000	1 920	15 800	1 390	14 400
8 000	3 740	38 400	4 800	33 600	8 000	3 820	38 700	4 310	34 400
10 000	3 130	40 300	5 980	34 300	10 000	3 180	40 300	5 400	34 900
12 000	3 550	56 900	9 410	47 500	12 000	3 560	56 300	8 550	47 800
15 000	3 580	75 500	13 700	61 800	15 000	3 660	75 700	12 800	62 900
20 000	2 360	70 500	14 500	56 000	20 000	2 640	77 800	14 900	62 900
30 000	730	36 800	9 980	26 900	30 000	861	42 500	10 900	31 600
50 000	200	19 300	6 180	13 100	50 000	237	22 700	7 100	15 600
100 000 and over	55	16 030	5 800	10 230	100 000 and over	72	23 900	8 570	15 300

See footnotes on the second part of this table.

Source: Board of Inland Revenue: 020 7438 4335

8.2 Distribution of total incomes before and after tax
United Kingdom
continued · Years ended 5 April

	1997/98 Annual Survey					1998/99 Annual Survey			
		£ million					£ million		
	Number of individuals (000s)	Total income before tax	Total tax	Total income after tax		Number of individuals (000s)	Total income before tax	Total tax	Total income after tax
Lower limit of range of income					**Lower limit of range of income**				
All incomes[1,2,3,4]	26 200	461 000	79 500	381 100	All incomes[1,2,3,4]	26 900	498 000	88 000	409 000
Income before tax £					Income before tax £				
4 045	509	2 170	21	2 150	4 195	322	1 400	9	1 390
4 500	560	2 660	74	2 580	4 500	552	2 620	57	2 560
5 000	678	3 580	127	3 450	5 000	580	3 050	112	2 930
5 500	841	4 840	190	4 650	5 500	873	5 030	183	4 850
6 000	1 640	10 700	600	10 100	6 000	1 640	10 600	561	10 100
7 000	1 540	11 600	820	10 800	7 000	1 560	11 700	821	10 900
8 000	3 050	27 400	2 440	25 000	8 000	3 120	28 000	2 400	25 600
10 000	2 850	31 200	3 520	27 700	10 000	2 730	30 000	3 290	26 700
12 000	3 530	47 500	6 270	41 200	12 000	3 650	49 100	6 290	42 800
15 000	4 260	73 800	11 100	62 700	15 000	4 460	77 200	11 400	65 800
20 000	3 260	102 700	17 200	85 500	20 000	4 460	107 600	17 900	89 700
30 000	1 730	63 7000	13 100	50 600	30 000	2 060	75 900	15 300	60 600
50 000	582	38 400	10 600	27 700	50 000	702	46 400	12 800	33 600
100 000	135	18 000	5 850	12 100	100 000	160	21 300	6 940	14 300
200 000 and over	51	22 400	7 560	14 900	200 000 and over	62	27 600	9 980	17 700
Income after tax £					Income after tax £				
4 045	629	2 710	33	2 680	4 195	394	1 730	14	1 710
4 500	683	3 350	112	3 240	4 500	701	3 420	91	3 330
5 000	812	4 470	186	4 280	5 000	725	3 990	175	3 810
5 500	1 000	6 050	281	5 770	5 500	1 010	6 060	260	5 800
6 000	1 960	13 600	885	12 700	6 000	1 990	13 700	839	12 900
7 000	1 900	15 600	1 270	14 300	7 000	1 840	15 000	1 210	13 800
8 000	3 750	37 600	3 840	33 800	8 000	3 740	37 100	3 630	33 500
10 000	3 230	40 500	5 100	35 400	10 000	3 280	41 000	5 010	36 000
12 000	3 760	58 800	8 390	50 400	12 000	3 940	61 600	8 610	53 000
15 000	4 030	82 800	13 300	69 500	15 000	4 220	86 400	13 600	72 800
20 000	3 070	89 100	15 900	73 200	20 000	3 390	98 800	17 500	81 300
30 000	1 030	50 100	12 300	37 900	30 000	1 250	60 400	14 500	45 900
50 000	291	27 700	8 460	19 200	50 000	352	33 400	10 200	23 200
100 000	63	12 800	4 350	8 420	100 000	76	15 400	5 290	10 100
200 000 and over	23	15 500	5 150	10 400	200 000 and over	28	19 300	7 060	12 300

1 These tables relate only to those individuals who have some tax liability. The distributions cover only incomes as computed for tax purposes and above a level which for each year corresponds approximately to the single person's allowance. Incomes below these levels are not shown because the information about them is incomplete.

2 All figures have been independently rounded.

3 Investment income from which tax has been deducted at source is not always known to local tax offices. Estimates of missing bank and building society interest and dividends from United Kingdom companies are included in these tables. The missing investment income is distributed in a manner consistent with information from the Family Expenditure Survey and the National Accounts, to individuals where there is no investment income already reported by the tax office.

4 Superannuation contributions are estimated and included in total income. They have been distributed among earners in the Survey of Personal Incomes sample by a method consistent with information about the number of employees who are contracted in or out of the State Earnings Related Pension Scheme and the proportion of their earnings contributed.

Source: Board of Inland Revenue: 020 7438 4335

Personal income, expenditure and wealth

8.3 Sources of gross household income[1]
United Kingdom

		1989	1990	1991	1992	1993	1994 /95	1995 /96	1996 /97	1997 /98	1998[2] /99	1999[2] /00
Number of households supplying data	KPDA	7 410	7 046	7 056	7 418	6 979	6 853	6 797	6 415	6 409	6 630	7 097
Average weekly household income by source (£)												
Wages and salaries	KPCB	189.40	212.50	222.00	222.70	228.30	237.90	245.00	256.30	280.20	309.20	315.40
Self-employment	KPCC	28.50	32.10	29.70	29.60	29.20	35.30	32.90	37.50	32.90	37.20	46.00
Investments	KPCD	14.00	19.00	23.70	20.80	18.00	16.20	18.10	17.80	18.70	18.80	21.80
Annuities and pensions (other than social security benefits)	KPCE	14.40	15.50	17.30	19.60	21.90	23.50	26.00	26.00	28.90	30.30	32.80
Social security benefits	KPCF	32.70	35.30	40.10	45.00	48.90	49.90	52.40	54.10	55.00	55.80	58.00
Imputed income from owner/rent-free occupancy[2]	KPCG	16.60	18.60	24.50	..	..	..	..	..	..	..	..
Other sources	KPCH	4.50	4.50	5.30	5.20	6.70	6.50	6.60	5.30	5.20	5.70	5.90
Total	KPCI	300.00	337.60	362.70	342.90	353.00	359.30	380.90	396.90	420.80	457.00	479.90
Sources of household income as a percentage of total household income												
Wages and salaries	KPCJ	62	63	61	65	65	64	64	65	67	68	66
Self-employment	KPCK	9	10	8	9	8	10	9	9	8	8	10
Investments	KPCL	5	6	7	6	5	4	5	5	4	4	5
Annuities and pensions (other than social security benefits)	KPCM	5	5	5	6	6	6	7	7	7	7	7
Social security benefits	KPCN	11	11	11	13	14	14	14	14	13	12	12
Imputed income from owner/rent-free occupancy[2]	KPCO	6	6	7	..	..	..	..	..	..	..	..
Other sources	KPCP	2	1	2	2	2	2	2	1	1	1	1
Total	KPCQ	100	100	100	100	100	100	100	100	100	100	100

1 Information derived from the Family Expenditure Survey (FES).
2 Income based on weighted data.

Source: Office for National Statistics: 020 7533 5756

8.4 Availability in households of certain durable goods[1]
United Kingdom

Percentage

		1989	1990	1991	1992	1993	1994 /95	1995 /96	1996 /97	1997 /98	1998[2] /99	1999[2] /00
Number of households supplying data	KPDA	7 410	7 046	7 056	7 418	6 979	6 853	6 797	6 415	6 409	6 630	7 097
Car	KPDB	66	67	68	68	69	69	70	69	70	72	71
One	KPDC	45	44	45	45	46	45	47	43	44	44	43
Two	KPDD	18	19	19	19	19	20	19	22	21	23	21
Three or more	KPDE	4	4	4	4	4	4	4	5	5	5	6
Central heating, full or partial	KPDF	78	79	81	82	83	84	85	87	89	89	90
Washing machine	KPDG	86	86	87	88	89	89	91	91	91	92	91
Refrigerator or fridge/freezer	KPDH	98	98	98	99	99	99	99	..	..	..	..
Fridge/freezer or deep freezer	KPDI	79	80	82	84	87	86	87	91	90	92	91
Refrigerator	KPDJ	..	..	..	..	..	..	..	49	51	52	53
Television	KPDK	98	98	98	98	..	..	..	..	..	..	..
Telephone	KPDL	86	87	88	88	90	91	92	93	94	95	95
Home computer	KPDM	17	17	18	19	..	..	..	27	29	33	38
Video recorder	KPDN	57	61	65	69	73	76	79	82	84	85	86
Internet access	ZBUZ	..	..	..	..	..	..	..	..	..	10	19

1 Information derived from the Family Expenditure Survey (FES).
2 Percentages based on grossed number of households.

Source: Office for National Statistics: 020 7533 5756

8.5 Households and their expenditure[1]
United Kingdom

		1989	1990	1991	1992	1993	1994/95	1995/96	1996/97	1997[3]/98	1998[3,4,5]/99	1999[3,4,5]/00
Number of households supplying data	KPDA	7 410	7 046	7 056	7 418	6 979	6 853	6 797	6 415	6 409	6 630	7 097
Total number of persons	KPEA	18 590	17 437	17 089	18 174	17 291	16 617	16 586	15 732	15 430	16 218	16 786
Total number of adults[2]	KPEB	13 850	12 939	12 934	13 563	12 792	12 365	12 219	11 495	11 429	11 886	12 432
Household percentage distribution by tenure												
Rented unfurnished	KPED	30	29	28	28	28	28	29	28	29	28	28
Rented furnished	KPEE	3	3	3	4	4	4	4	5	3	3	3
Rent-free	KPEF	1	1	2	2	2	1	1	2	2	2	1
Owner-occupied	KPEG	65	66	67	66	67	67	66	66	67	67	67
Average number of persons per household												
All persons	KPEH	2.5	2.5	2.4	2.5	2.5	2.4	2.4	2.5	2.4	2.4	2.3
Males	KPEI	1.2	1.2	1.2	1.2	1.2	1.2	1.2	1.2	1.2	1.2	1.1
Females	KPEJ	1.3	1.3	1.3	1.3	1.3	1.3	1.3	1.3	1.3	1.2	1.2
Adults[2]	KPEK	1.9	1.8	1.8	1.8	1.8	1.8	1.8	1.8	1.8	1.8	1.8
Persons under 65	KPEL	1.5	1.5	1.5	1.5	1.5	1.4	1.4	1.4	1.4	1.5	1.4
Persons 65 and over	KPEM	0.4	0.4	0.4	0.4	0.4	0.4	0.4	0.4	0.3	0.4	0.3
Children[2]	KPEN	0.6	0.6	0.6	0.6	0.6	0.6	0.6	0.7	0.6	0.5	0.5
Children under 2	KPEO	0.1	0.1	0.1	0.1	0.1	0.1	0.1	0.1	0.1	0.1	0.1
Children 2 and under 5	KPEP	0.1	0.1	0.1	0.1	0.1	0.1	0.1	0.1	0.1	0.1	0.1
Children 5 and under 18	KPEQ	0.4	0.4	0.4	0.4	0.4	0.4	0.5	0.5	0.4	0.4	0.4
Persons economically active	KPER	1.2	1.2	1.2	1.2	1.2	1.2	1.1	1.2	1.1	1.2	1.1
Persons not economically active	KPES	1.3	1.3	1.3	1.3	1.3	1.3	1.3	1.3	1.3	1.2	1.2
Men 65 and over, women 60 and over	KPET	0.4	0.4	0.4	0.4	0.4	0.4	0.4	0.4	0.4	0.4	0.4
Others	KPEU	0.9	0.9	0.8	0.9	0.9	0.9	0.9	0.9	0.9	0.8	0.8
Average weekly household expenditure on commodities and services (£)												
Housing	KPEV	38.40	44.40	50.20	47.40	44.90	46.40	48.30	49.10	51.50	57.20	57.00
Fuel and power	KPEW	10.60	11.10	12.30	13.00	13.20	13.00	12.90	13.40	12.70	11.70	11.30
Food	KPEX	41.70	44.80	46.10	47.70	50.00	50.40	52.90	55.20	55.90	58.90	59.60
Alcoholic drink	KPEY	9.50	10.00	10.80	11.10	12.00	12.30	11.40	12.40	13.30	14.00	15.30
Tobacco	KPEZ	4.80	4.80	5.20	5.40	5.60	5.60	5.80	6.10	6.10	5.80	6.00
Clothing and footwear	KCWC	15.30	16.00	15.80	16.40	17.40	17.10	17.20	18.30	20.00	21.70	21.00
Household goods	KCWH	19.20	20.00	20.10	21.90	23.10	22.70	23.50	26.70	26.90	29.60	30.70
Household services	KCWI	9.70	12.30	13.00	13.40	15.40	15.10	15.10	16.40	17.90	18.90	18.90
Personal goods and services	KCWJ	8.50	9.50	10.00	10.20	11.00	10.80	11.60	11.60	12.50	13.30	13.90
Motoring expenditure	KCWK	30.40	33.80	34.10	35.70	36.30	36.20	37.00	41.20	46.60	51.70	52.60
Fares and other travel costs	KCWL	5.40	6.20	5.60	7.20	7.00	6.60	6.20	7.50	8.10	8.30	9.20
Leisure goods	KCWM	11.00	11.30	12.10	13.30	13.30	13.90	13.20	15.20	16.40	17.80	18.50
Leisure services	KCWN	19.00	21.50	22.20	27.60	25.60	31.20	32.10	34.00	38.80	41.90	43.90
Miscellaneous	KCWO	0.90	1.40	1.60	1.80	2.10	2.30	2.40	2.20	2.00	1.20	1.40
Total	KCWP	224.30	247.20	259.00	271.80	276.70	289.90	289.90	309.10	328.80	352.20	359.40

		1989	1990	1991	1992	1993	1994/95	1995/96	1996/97	1997[3]/98	1998[3,4,5]/99	1999[3,4,5]/00
Expenditure on commodity or service as a percentage of total expenditure												
Housing	KPFH	17	18	19	17	16	16	17	16	16	16	16
Fuel and power	KPFI	5	5	5	5	5	5	5	4	4	3	3
Food	KPFJ	19	18	18	18	18	18	18	18	17	17	17
Alcoholic drink	KPFK	4	4	4	4	4	4	4	4	4	4	4
Tobacco	KPFL	2	2	2	2	2	2	2	2	2	2	2
Clothing and footwear	KPFM	7	7	6	6	6	6	6	6	6	6	6
Household goods	KCWQ	9	8	8	8	8	8	8	9	8	8	9
Household services	KCWR	4	5	5	5	6	5	5	5	5	5	5
Personal goods and services	KCWS	4	4	4	4	4	4	4	4	4	4	4
Motoring expenditure	KCWT	14	14	13	13	13	13	13	13	14	15	15
Fares and other travel costs	KCWU	2	3	2	3	3	2	2	2	3	2	3
Leisure goods	KCWV	5	5	5	5	5	5	5	5	5	5	5
Leisure services	KCWW	9	9	9	10	9	11	11	11	12	12	12
Miscellaneous	KPFR	–	1	1	1	1	1	1	1	1	1	–	–
Total	KPFS	100	100	100	100	100	100	100	100	100	100	100

1 Information derived from the Family Expenditure Survey (FES).
2 Adults and children are: Adults = all persons 18 and over and married persons under 18. Children = all unmarried persons under 18.
3 Rented unfurnished includes Local Authority and Housing Association (furnished and unfurnished) and privately rented (unfurnished). Rented furnished only includes privately rented (furnished) Owner-occupied includes shared owners (who part own and part rent).

4 Averages based on grossed number of households
5 Expenditure based on weighted data and including children's expenditure

Source: Office for National Statistics: 020 7533 5756

9 Health

Health

Injuries at work *(Table 9.8)*

The appropriate 'responsible person' is required to report injuries arising from workplace activities to HSC or the local authority under the Reporting of Injuries, Diseases and Dangerous Occurrences Regulations 1995 (RIDDOR 95). This includes fatal injuries, non-fatal major injuries, as defined by the Regulations, and other injuries causing incapacity for work for more than 3 days. Statistics from 1996/97 onwards have been compiled from reports made under RIDDOR 95 which updated previous legislation (RIDDOR 85) on 1 April 1996. The main differences in the updated Regulations are that the definition of a major injury to a worker is now wider and injuries caused by acts of physical violence at work are reportable. Therefore, statistics from 1996/97 cannot be compared with those for previous years.

Details of fatal, non-fatal major and over-3-day injuries involving employees and self-employed people are shown in the table. The introduction of RIDDOR 95 has had no substantial effect on the number of recorded workplace fatalities. However, it is estimated that approximately 70 per cent of the increase in the total number of non-fatal major injuries between 1995/96 and 1996/97 was a result of expanded definitions under RIDDOR 95. The expansion also resulted in a decrease in the total number of over-3-day injuries, since some of the non-fatal major injuries in 1996/97 would have been previously reportable as over-3-day injuries. However, since injuries caused by violence at work also became reportable, the decrease in the number of over-3-day injuries appears to be relatively small.

Not all employers make reports of non-fatal injuries as they should. In 1990 the HSC commissioned a health and safety supplement to the Labour Force Survey (LFS) in order to establish the true levels of workplace injury. This has been continued annually since 1993/94. The results of the LFS suggest levels of non-fatal injury reporting for employees to be about 46 per cent in 1998/99 compared with 34 per cent in 1989/90. For the self-employed, reporting levels are less than 5 per cent in 1998/99.

9.1 Hospital and family health services
England and Wales

			England						Wales				
			1995	1996	1997	1998	1999		1995	1996	1997	1998	1999
Hospital services[3]													
Average daily number of available beds	KNMY	Thousands	206	199	194	190	..	KNHY	16.0	15.6	15.2	14.9	14.7
Average daily occupation of beds:													
All departments	KNMX	"	..	162	157	157	..	KNHX	12.4	12.2	12.0	11.8	11.8
Psychiatric departments	KNMW	"	..	41	39	37	..	KNGZ	3.1	3.0	2.9	2.7	2.6
Persons waiting for admission at 31 March[2]	KNMV	"	1 044	1 048	1 158	1 298	..	KNGY	60.3	65.0	69.9	61.8	75.4
Finished consultant episodes	KNLZ		..	..	..	..	..						
Day case admissions	KNLY	"	2 774	2 907	3 071	3 421	..	KNBZ	261.6	286.4	309.7	328.0	342.2
Ordinary admissions	KIBS	"	8 264	8 369	8 459	8 563	..	KNEO	516.0	516.4	521.1	522.7	516.3
Out-patients													
New cases	KNLX	"	10 988	11 293	11 529	11 778	..	KNBY	658.7	667.1	693.3	691.3	694.1
Total attendances	KNLW	"	40 116	40 872	41 635	42 154	..	KNBX	2 570.0	2 569.5	2 643.3	2 667.4	2 706.2
Accident and Emergency:													
New cases	KOTH	"	12 462	12 484	12 794	12 811	..	KTCO	804.1	798.4	826.6	831.0	868.0
Total attendances	KOTI	"	14 234	14 126	14 364	14 280	..	KTCP	995.8	975.3	997.9	982.0	1 026.4
Ward attendances	KOTJ	"	1 013	1 027	1 034	1 068	..	KTCQ	..	..	..	..	..
Family health services[14]													
Medical services:													
Doctors on the list[4]	KNKX	Number	26 702	26 855	27 099	..	..	KNBR	1 719	1 736	1 753	1 749	1 761
Number of UPEs[12]	LQZZ		..	..	..	27 392	27 591	ZCMA	1 721	1 739	1 756	1 755	1 770
Number of patients per doctor	KNKW	"	1 887	1 885	1 878	1 866	1 845	KNBQ	1 730	1 724	1 706	1 713	1 694
Paid to doctors[5,6]	KNKV	£ million	2 851.0	2 857.0	3 131.0	3 242.0	..	KNBP	166.0	170.5	179.4	186.0	201.3
Pharmaceutical services:[1,7]													
Number of prescription forms	KWUK	Million	284.4	282.9	287.4	291.1	293.6						
Number of prescription items	KWUL	"	473.3	484.9	500.2	513.2	529.8	KNBO	37.1	38.0	39.6	40.7	42.1
Total cost	KWUM	£ million	4 193.4	4 534.2	4 919.8	5 231.4	5 619.9	KNBN	303.8	325.6	351.9	372.7	403.9
Average total cost per prescription	KWUN	£	8.90	9.40	9.80	10.20	10.60	KNBK	8.18	8.56	8.89	9.17	9.60
Income from patients	KWUO	£ million	298.7	295.7	320.9	341.3	366.7	KNBM	17.9	16.9	18.8	19.6	21.6
Dental services:													
Principals on an FHSA/HA list at 30 September[8]	KIAZ	Number	15 064	15 280	15 509	15 820	16 089	KIBG	817	834	863	879	913
Number of adult courses of treatments	KIBA	Thousands	24 752	24 580	25 268	26 171	25 915	KIBH	1 350	1 357	1 446	1 514	1 525
Number of adult patients accepted into continuing care provision at 30 September[13]	KIBB	"	19 994	19 524	19 383	16 721	16 649	KIBI	1 197	1 177	1 184	1 043	1 055
Number of children accepted into capitation at 30 September[13]	KIBC	"	7 292	7 270	7 367	6 775	6 821	KIBJ	426	426	434	405	408
Gross expenditure[9]	KIBD	£ thousands	1 289 547	1 323 074	1 347 577	1 437 727	1 477 423	KIBK	70 424	72 248	76 816	82 262	86 093
Paid by patients[9]	KIBE	"	381 186	382 995	388 436	419 621	431 189	KIBL	19 185	19 483	20 665	22 293	23 456
Paid out of public funds[9]	KIBF	"	908 361	940 078	959 141	1 018 106	1 046 234	KIBM	51 239	52 765	56 151	59 969	62 637
General ophthalmic services:													
Sight tests[10,11]	KNJL	Thousands	6 512	6 808	6 991	6 992	9 399	KNBD	439	464	477	477	631
Pairs of spectacles for which NHS vouchers redeemed[11]	KNJK	"	3 815	3 967	3 935	3 777	3 662	KNBC	275	287	300	288	275
Cost of services (gross)[9]	KNJJ	£ million	223.5	237.2	241.4	239.6	281.0	KNBA	15.9	17.2	17.8	17.7	20.1
Paid out of public funds:[9]													
For sight testing	KNJH	"	90.9	97.5	102.8	103.5	146.1	KMZZ	6.2	6.7	7.1	7.2	9.8
For cost of vouchers[13]	KNHZ		132.6	139.8	138.6	136.0	134.4	KMZX	8.9	9.5	9.8	9.6	9.4

1 Data given are for calendar year for England. Welsh data is based on pricing bureau totals of prescriptions dispensed in a calendar year and paid during the financial year. Data shown reflect data for the year commencing the year in the heading (for example the figure under 1994 reflects 1994 - 95 data). Financial year is from 1 April to 31 March.

2 People awaiting elective admission at NHS Trusts in England and Wales, as an inpatient or a day case.

3 Data collection changed in 1987 from calendar year to a financial year basis. Data shown reflect data for the year commencing the year in the heading (for example the figure under 1994 reflects 1994 - 95 data). Out-patient figures do not include accident and emergency figures or ward attenders which are given separately as follows: Information on general practitioner maternity clinics was not collected separately from 1992-93 in England but included for Wales.

4 Principals providing unrestricted services as at 1 October.

5 Provisional data subject to change (England only).

6 Includes PFMA but excludes GPFH drugs and payments to providers.

7 The data cover all prescription items dispensed by community pharmacists and appliance contractors, dispensing doctors and prescriptions submitted by prescribing doctors for items personally administered. Total cost refers to the cost of the drug less discounts and includes on cost

allowance, dispensing fees, container allowance, oxygen payments and VAT. The figures for income from patients are for financial years. Figures for England include charges retained by pharmacists, received by dispensing doctors, income from pre-payment certificates, and recoveries from patients.

8 Principals only. Assistants and vocational trainees are not included. Some dentists may have a contract with more than one Family Health Service Authority/Health Authority. These dentists have been counted once only.

9 Figures are for financial year and are based on the Appropriation account.

10 Number of NHS sight tests paid for by FHSAs/HAs in the period.

11 Data given are for financial year and reflect the year commencing the year in the table heading (e.g. the figures for 1999 represents 1999/2000 data).

12 UPE's include Unrestricted Principals, PMS Contracted GP's and PMS salaried GP's. UPE data are as at 1 October.

13 Figures for 1998 onwards are affected by the shortening of the registration period to 15 months.

14 Welsh FHS expenditure and income is based upon cash payments and receipts in each financial year, as accrued data is not available in a common format for all years shown in this series. Welsh Dental Services data excludes refunds of dental charges. Welsh General Opthalmic Services data excludes the cost of replacement and repair of spectacles for children and handicapped adults.

Sources: Department of Health: 020 7972 2231;
National Assembly for Wales: 029 2082 5080

9.2 Hospital and primary care services
Scotland

		Unit	1989	1990	1991	1992	1993	1994	1995	1996	1997	1998	1999
Hospital and community services													
In-patients[1,2]:													
Average available staffed beds	KDEA	Thousands	53.4	52.1	50.6	48.7	46.7	44.2	42.4	40.6	38.4	36.8	35.2
Average occupied beds:													
All departments	KDEB	"	43.5	42.5	41.2	39.5	38.1	35.9	34.3	32.8	30.9	29.5	28.2
Psychiatric and learning disability	KDEC	"	17.6	17.0	16.3	15.5	14.6	13.2	12.6	11.7	10.8	10.0	9.1
Discharges or deaths[3]	KDED	"	882	896	912	920	942	952	960	973	965	977	975
Outpatients[2,4]:													
New cases	KDEE	"	2 325	2 381	2 403	2 426	2 457	2 503	2 577	2 666	2 675	2 715	2 734
Total attendances	KDEF	"	5 815	5 925	5 971	6 005	6 086	6 145	6 241	6 338	6 272	6 331	6 424
Medical and dental staff[5,6,7]:	JYXO	Number	7 777	7 936	7 890	8 069	8 078	8 317	8 524	8 774	9 098	9 157	9 367
Whole-time	KDEG	"	5 368	5 475	5 481	5 625	5 767	5 937	6 102	6 433	6 707	7 052	7 202
Part-time	KDEH	"	1 835	1 881	1 862	1 883	1 730	1 827	1 854	1 819	1 886	1 613	1 685
Honorary	JYXN	"	574	580	547	561	582	563	579	534	522	506	495
Professional and technical staff[8]:													
Whole-time	KDEI	"	9 320	9 291	9 387	9 759	9 953	10 062	10 452	10 584	10 740	10 884	11 261
Part-time	KDEJ	"	2 601	2 727	2 782	3 127	3 434	3 753	4 075	4 370	4 738	4 928	5 218
Nursing and midwifery staff[9,10,11]:													
Whole-time	KDEK	"	34 959	34 364	34 302	34 053	33 284	32 956	32 693	32 560	32 218	32 156	32 356
Part-time	KDEL	"	28 164	28 781	29 887	30 709	30 459	30 532	30 580	29 917	29 736	29 178	29 242
Administrative and clerical staff[12]:													
Whole-time	KDEM	"	12 648	13 223	13 718	14 447	15 125	15 723	15 815	15 155	14 707	14 564	14 541
Part-time	KDEN	"	4 769	4 985	5 276	5 815	6 113	6 624	7 005	6 986	7 174	7 265	7 465
Domestic, transport, etc. staff[13]:													
Whole-time	KDEO	"	15 214	12 468	11 622	10 805	10 205	9 574	9 037	8 596	8 187	8 090	7 972
Part-time	KDEP	"	16 059	16 685	16 167	15 753	15 403	14 464	14 105	13 554	13 082	12 716	12 424
Cost of services (gross)[14]	KDEQ	£ million	2 004.5	2 195.6	2 503.6	2 768.0	2 940.5	3 050.5	3 269.5	3 430.6	3 610.3	3 856.0	4 309.7
Payments by patients[14,26]	KDER	"	1.40	1.30	1.50	2.00	2.30	0.40	0.02	0.01	0.01	0.01	0.01
Payments out of public funds[14,26]	KDES	"	2 003.10	2 194.30	2 502.10	2 766.00	2 938.20	3 050.10	3 269.52	3 430.59	3 610.29	3 855.86	4 309.69
Primary care services													
Medical services													
Doctors on the list[15]:													
Principals[16]	KDET	Number	3 390	3 359	3 379	3 421	3 456	3 490	3 524	3 573	3 625	3 660	3 697
Assistants	KDEU	"	10	16	24	31	22	25	28	22	22	27	20
Average number of patients per principal doctor[17]	KDEV	"	1 590	1 593	1 580	1 556	1 542	1 524	1 506	1 488	1 468	1 450	1 441
Payments to doctor[18]	KDEW	£ million	183.3	222.2	247.2	263.8	275.3	291.7	311.9	333.2	356.4	365.9	..
Pharmaceutical services[19]													
Prescriptions dispensed	KDEX	Million	41.02	42.42	44.31	46.10	48.18	49.27	51.08	54.62	56.64	58.52	60.36
Payments to pharmacists (gross)	KDEY	£ million	269.99	298.16	329.82	370.20	406.07	434.85	474.22	543.40	588.38	627.18	693.65
Average gross cost per prescription	KDEZ	£	6.580	7.030	7.440	8.030	8.430	8.825	9.283	9.950	10.390	10.717	11.492
Dental services[20]													
Dentists on list[21]	KDFA	Number	1 585	1 645	1 676	1 702	1 772	1 763	1 764	1 772	1 798	1 854	1 833
Number of courses of treatment completed	KDFB	Thousands	3 143	3 057	2 485	2 569	2 647	2 723	2 711	2 825	3 406	3 349	3 406
Payments to dentists (gross)[22]	KDFC	£ million	97.7	99.9	132.8	133.6	128.4	136.1	137.3	139.2	154.9	157.5	160.6
Payments by patients	KDFD	"	46.4	48.0	41.6	40.5	40.0	42.2	41.7	41.4	45.9	47.4	48.8
Payments out of public funds[22]	KDFE	"	51.2	51.8	91.3	93.2	88.4	93.9	95.6	97.8	109.0	110.1	111.8
Average gross cost per course	KDFF	£	30.8	33.1	40.0	39.0	37.0	38.0	38.0	40.1	36.5	38.0	38.0
General ophthalmic services													
Number of sight tests given[23]	KDFG	Thousands	716	417	477	537	568	614	618	635	656	657	850
Number of pairs of glasses supplied[24]	KDFH	"	313	320	374	404	463	473	461	474	488	485	494
Cost of services (gross)[25]	KDFI	£ million	14.5	13.7	16.4	19.7	22.2	24.4	25.8	27.7	29.1	29.8	32.0
Payments by patients	KDFJ	"	–	–	..	..	..	..	..	..	..	..	..
Payments out of public funds:													
For sight testing and dispensing	KDFK	"	14.5	13.7	16.4	19.7	22.2	24.4	25.8	27.7	29.1	29.8	32.0

1 Excludes joint user and contractual hospitals.
2 In year to 31 March.
3 Includes transfers out.
4 Including attendances at accident and emergency consultant clinics.
5 At 30 September.
6 Figures exclude officers holding honorary locum appointments. Part-time includes maximum part-time appointments.
7 There is an element of double counting of "heads" in this table as doctors can hold more than one contract. For example, they may hold contracts of different type, e.g. part time and honorary. Doctors holding two or more contracts of the same type, e.g. part time, are not double counted. Doctors, whose sum of contracts amounts to whole time, are classed as such.
8 Comprises Scientific and Professional, Professions Allied to Medicine and Technical staff
9 Excludes nurse teachers, nurses in training and students on '1992' courses.
10 The apparent drop in whole time nurses numbers between 1989 and 1990 is due largely to reclassification.
11 Between 1992 and 1993 the criterion for excluding nursing staff on low hours was changed from 0.25 hours to 2 hours. This partially accounts for any decrease in staff numbers between these two years.
12 Comprises Senior Management and Administrative and Clerical staff. Assistant staff.
13 Comprises Ambulance, Works, Ancillary, Trades and Health Care Assistant staff.

14 Estimated from financial years.
15 At 1 October.
16 Unrestricted principals in post.
17 Unrestricted principals: establishment.
18 Provisional for 1997/98. Data relates to financial year, eg 1997 data are for year ending 31 March 1998. As 1994/95 data are unavailable for Dumfries and Galloway Health Board, 1993/94 data have been substituted for that board only.
19 For prescriptions dispensed in calendar year by all community pharmacists (including stock orders), dispensing doctors and appliance suppliers.
20 From 1990, when the new dental contract came into effect, the statistics available centrally changed significantly. From 1991, data refers to financial year (eg 1991 data is for year ending 31 March 1992).
21 Comprises principals only.
22 Before 1991 excludes capitation payments; from 1991 includes capitation, continuing care, weighted entry and item of service fees.
23 This figure represents sight tests paid for by health boards, hospital eye service referrals and GOS(s) ST (v) claimants.
24 Supply of spectacles restricted from 1 April 1985, includes hospital eye service.
25 Universal free eyesight testing ended in March 1989.
26 These figures are for Health Boards only and do not include the 2 NHS Trusts in 1992/93, 17 in 1993/94, 39 in 1994/95 and 47 in 1995/96.

Source: Scottish Health Service Common Services Agency: 0131 551 8899

9.3 Hospital and general health services
Northern Ireland

		Unit	1989	1990	1991	1992	1993	1994	1995	1996	1997	1998	1999
Hospital services[1]													
In-patients:													
Beds available[2]	KDGA	Number	14 154	13 487	12 600	11 712	10 878	10 356	10 054	9 475	9 007	8 819	8 639
Average daily occupation of beds	KDGB	Per cent	79.2	77.6	77.1	77.8	77.9	78.1	77.7	78.9	80.8	81.9	81.5
Discharges or deaths[3]	KDGC	Thousands	264	265	269	275	290	298	304	300	306	338	332
Out-patients[4]:													
New cases	KDGD	"	781	782	799	819	836	873	937	933	952	962	980
Total attendances	KDGE	"	1 989	1 954	1 963	1 969	1 967	2 051	2 087	2 072	2 083	2 091	2 106
General health services													
Medical services													
Doctors (principals) on the list[5]	KDGF	Number	933	928	928	942	953	991	1 005	1 028	1 039	1 042	1 054
Number of patients per doctor	KDGG	"	1 794	1 811	1 922	1 808	1 779	1 743	1 731	1 698	1 690	1 693	1 679
Payments to doctors	KDGH	£ thousand	48 651	47 850	53 675	55 715	59 253	61 742	64 027	66 733	69 889	71 340	76 829
Pharmaceutical services[6]													
Prescription forms dispensed	KDGI	Thousands	9 175	9 285	10 144	10 597	10 899	11 439	12 018	12 402	12 855	13 116	13 453
Number of prescriptions	KDGJ	"	15 726	15 404	16 754	17 496	18 043	18 561	19 894	20 581	21 430	22 171	23 249
Gross cost[7]	KDGK	£ thousand	97 721	108 144	133 134	146 925	160 420	173 064	197 580	213 258	229 852	241 973	266 535
Charges[7]	KDGL	"	4 185	4 893	4 745	5 582	6 017	6 529	6 255	6 028	6 607	6 853	8 183
Net Cost[7]	KDGM	"	93 536	103 751	119 694	141 343	154 403	172 412	191 325	207 230	223 245	235 120	258 353
Average gross cost per prescription	KDGN	£	6.50	7.00	7.70	8.40	8.90	9.44	9.93	10.36	10.73	10.91	11.46
Dental services													
Dentists on the list[5]	KDGO	Number	467	519	513	523	541	569	581	596	610	633[8]	660[8]
Number of courses of paid treatments	KDGP	Thousands	972	986	..	..	..	..	..	..	..	1 088[8]	1 097[8]
Gross cost[9]	KDGQ	£ thousand	31 697	35 026	47 210	47 637	43 904	47 076	48 781	51 512	53 735	56 835[8]	58 712[8]
Patients[9]	KDGR	"	8 009	8 732	9 922	11 036	10 378	11 417	11 530	11 870	12 433	13 686[8]	14 358[8]
Contributions (Net cost)[9]	KDGS	"	23 688	26 295	37 258	36 601	33 526	33 659	37 250	39 642	41 302	43 149[8]	44 353[8]
Average gross cost per paid treatment	KDGT	£	32.60	35.50	..	..	..	..	..	..	..	52.20[8]	53.50[8]
Ophthalmic services													
Number of sight tests given[10]	KDGU	Thousands	192	115	135	142	169	182	197	212	221	238	298
Number of optical appliances supplied[11,12]	KDGV	"	–	96	110	114	133	139	146	153	156	161	156
Cost of service (gross)[13]	KDGW	£ thousand	4 583	4 158	5 607	5 555	7 363	7 127	8 568	9 555	10 114	10 469	11 365
Payments by patients	KDGX	"	–	–	–	..	..	..	..	..	..	..	..
Payments out of public funds	KDGY	"	4 583	4 158	5 607	5 555	..	..	..	9 555	10 114	10 469	11 365
Health and social services[14]													
Medical and dental staff:													
Whole-time	KDGZ	Number	2 218	2 238	2 262	2 226	2 209	2 358	2 053	2 107	2 156	2 196	2 231
Part-time	KDHA	"	674	564	560	511	554	694	1 154	1 094	1 041	1 009	1 014
Nursing and midwifery staff:													
Whole-time	KDHB	"	14 425	14 071	13 451	12 381	11 445	11 047	10 896	10 578	10 114	10 117	10 135
Part-time	KDHC	"	6 477	6 841	7 144	7 417	7 952	8 662	9 169	8 943	9 015	8 287	8 813
Administrative and clerical staff:													
Whole-time	KDHD	"	5 409	5 843	6 398	6 573	6 696	7 006	7 078	7 055	6 915	7 019	7 230
Part-time	KDHE	"	1 583	1 680	1 831	1 924	2 050	2 186	2 306	2 518	2 708	2 776	2 910
Professional and technical staff:													
Whole-time	KDHF	"	2 522	2 563	2 673	2 695	2 695	2 786	2 862	2 939	2 933	3 014	3 177
Part-time	KDHG	"	475	513	559	636	710	804	921	985	1 060	1 146	1 226
Social services staff(excluding casual home helps):													
Whole-time	KDHH	"	3 646	3 649	3 641	3 607	3 550	3 480	3 470	3 441	3 349	3 262	3 319
Part-time	KDHI	"	1 546	1 687	1 695	1 707	1 766	1 933	2 110	2 250	2 394	2 241	2 358
Ancillary and other staff:													
Whole-time	KDHJ	"	6 960	6 433	5 551	4 954	4 679	4 364	3 982	3 812	3 569	3 423	3 426
Part-time	KDHK	"	5 480	4 989	4 728	4 862	4 767	4 609	3 685	3 558	3 482	3 558	3 913
Cost of services (gross)[15]	KDHL	£ thousand	750 918	822 795	889 422	947 354	1 002 326	1 043 745	1 111 507	1 120 563	1 153 741	1 292 348	1 422 920
Payments by recipients	KDHM	"	11 125	11 414	12 322	12 569	13 189	20 629	32 685	40 725	49 498	59 484	65 533
Payments out of public funds	KDHN	"	739 793	811 381	877 100	934 785	989 137	1 023 116	1 078 822	1 079 838	1 104 243	1 232 864	1 357 387

1 Financial Year.
2 Average available beds in wards open overnight during the year.
3 Includes transfers to other hospitals.
4 Includes consultant outpatient clinics and Accident and Emergency depart-
5 At 1st October. tments
6 Pharmaceutical services figures are at April 1999 - March 2000.
7 Prior to 1992, headings read, 'Payments to Pharmacists (Gross)', 'Payments by Patients', 'Payments out of Public funds'.
8 Dental services figures are at April 1999 - March 2000.
9 Prior to 1992, headings read, 'Payments to Dentists (Gross)', 'Payments by
Patients', 'Payments out of Public Funds'.
10 Excluding sight tests given in hospitals and under the school health service.

11 Due to the change in the Dental Contract which came into force in October
1990, dentists are now paid under a combination of headings relating to Capitation and Continuing care patients. Prior to this, payment was simply on an item
of service basis, which made statistics such as 'Number of courses of treatment completed' and Average gross cost per course' relevant and meaningful.
This is no longer the case.
12 Relates to the number of vouchers supplied.
13 Figures from 1977 include payments of superannuation.
14 Manpower figures refer to 31 December. From 1981, figures for medical and
dental staff exclude some joint appointees, information for whom is not held on
the computer payroll.
15 Figures relate to the cost of the hospital, community health, and personal social
services, and have been estimated from financial year data.

Sources: Central Service Agency Northern Ireland: 028 9032 4431;
Dept of Health & Social Services Northern Ireland: 028 9052 2509;
(For figures on Hospital Services: 028 9052 2800)

9.4 Health and personal social services: workforce summary
Great Britain

Number or whole-time equivalent

		1989	1990	1991	1992	1993	1994	1995	1996	1997	1998	1999
Health service staff and practitioners at 30 Sep:												
Medical staff: total[1]	KDBC	50 290	51 792	53 019	53 987	55 632	56 736	60 172	62 176	64 316	67 408	69 089
Hospital medical staff: total	KDBD	46 906	48 435	49 620	50 793	52 476	53 787	57 299	59 592	61 937	65 088	66 812
Consultant	KDBE	16 517	17 101	17 435	17 846	18 251	18 808	20 246	21 066	21 699	23 139	24 250
Staff grade[2]	KADJ	33	262	516	819	1 230	1 536	2 037	2 440	2 785	3 458	3 868
Associate specialist	KDBF	877	944	949	960	1 032	1 013	1 128	1 223	1 340	1 439	1 527
Registrar group[10]	KWUG	..	..	..	..	..	..	..	11 898	12 435	12 863	13 299
Senior registrar	KDBG	3 488	3 778	3 912	3 994	4 130	4 281	4 540	..	..	..	..
Registrar	KDBH	7 297	7 345	7 237	7 132	7 103	7 273	7 294	..	..	..	..
Senior house officer	KDBI	12 407	12 737	13 311	13 863	14 586	14 942	15 661	16 616	17 353	17 760	17 518
House officer	KADK	3 637	3 748	3 781	3 798	3 792	3 781	4 003	4 025	4 163	4 287	4 364
Hospital practitioner	KDBL	233	219	208	183	183	178	197	212	198	220	230
Part-time medical officer Clinical assistant	KDBM	2 402	2 285	2 255	2 189	2 162	1 964	2 182	2 094	1 924	1 907	1 744
Other staff[3]	KDBK	17	15	17	10	8	11	11	18	38	16	11
Community health medical staff[4]	KDBN	3 384	3 357	3 399	3 194	3 156	2 948	2 873	2 584	2 379	2 320	2 278
Dental staff: total[1]	KDBO	3 092	3 072	2 954	2 971	2 973	2 947	3 070	3 127	3 078	3 193	3 147
Hospital dental staff: total	KDBP	1 475	1 496	1 478	1 546	1 573	1 597	1 687	1 737	1 696	1 807	1 816
Consultant	KDBQ	512	497	498	541	521	537	549	556	524	570	581
Staff grade[2]	KADL	–	2	5	13	24	39	54	67	86	99	113
Associate specialist	KDBR	81	82	71	70	69	62	69	65	62	68	70
Registrar Group[10]	LQMZ	..	..	..	..	..	..	..	..	..	309	314
Senior registrar	KDBS	129	135	123	122	135	124	123	138	169	..	..
Registrar	KDBT	204	197	189	188	184	178	186	183	125	..	..
Senior house officer	KDBU	246	260	266	300	353	394	446	490	491	531	496
Dental house officer	KDBV	129	145	145	143	126	101	86	68	58	59	68
Hospital practitioner	KDBX	14	17	15	15	17	20	17	23	22	21	23
Clinical assistant	KDBY	158	160	165	154	142	141	158	145	152	144	146
Other staff[3]	KDBW	3	1	1	2	2	2	–	3	6	5	6
Community health dental staff[4]	KDBZ	1 617	1 576	1 476	1 425	1 400	1 350	1 383	1 390	1 382	1 386	1 331
Total non-medical staff	KWUH	912 481	910 455	912 028	906 236	899 234	876 630	859 213	851 185	894 309	757 143	772 059
Nursing and midwifery staff:[8,9] (excluding agency): total	KDCA	490 545	487 012	483 507	467 723	446 056	429 214	353 842	356 109	353 933	355 887	362 554
qualified	KSBR	299 527	297 320	298 299	300 698	295 245	291 070	292 248	264 744	262 732	299 010	267 575
unqualified	KSBS	116 088	114 273	114 474	115 431	116 360	116 138	116 053	89 998	90 595	91 447	94 408
learners	KSBT	74 929	71 645	59 615	44 879	27 560	13 945	7 580	..	..	2 177	1 962
unknown	KSBV	..	3 774	11 115	6 714	6 891	8 061	5 768	937	606	435	491
All Professional & Technical staff[8] (excluding works)	KSBM	97 149	100 226	103 572	107 367	109 463	111 597	100 350	105 496	107 158	110 350	114 011
Health care assistants	KWUI	..	..	..	..	..	..	..	18 025	19 260	21 992	22 708
Support staff	KWUJ	..	..	..	..	..	..	..	75 876	72 514	71 004	69 826
Ancillary, Works & Maintenance[8]	KSBN	156 277	145 573	132 321	123 100	118 867	110 577	102 669	..	..	13 916	13 579
Administrative & Clerical staff[5,6,8]	KSBO	144 041	157 519	165 467	179 300	180 820	186 446	180 132	178 461	177 957	164 931	170 306
Ambulance staff[8]	KSBP	22 443	21 698	21 369	21 744	21 424	21 379	15 681	16 330	16 424	16 041	16 195
Others[7,8]	KSBQ	..	..	5 696	7 165	639	1 250	8 759	6 834	3 337	832	938

1 Whole-time equivalent. Figures exclude locums and general medical practitioners participating in Hospital Staff Fund.
2 New grade introduced in 1989.
3 Figures include Senior Hospital Medical/Dental Officers (SHMO) without an allowance and other ungraded staff.
4 Whole-time equivalent. Figures exclude locums and occasional seasonal staff.
5 Figures exclude ambulance officers.
6 Includes Family Practitioner Service administrative and clerical staff and General Managers.
7 Due to changes in the collection procedure in 1991 a category of 'other staff' was introduced for these locally determined payscales. In previous years these staff were included in their respective main staff groups. Includes learners from 1996.

8 A new system for classifying NHS non-medical staff was used for the first time in September 1995 non-medical workforce census classifying staff according to what they do (known as new occupation codes). However in order to provide comparative information with earlier years, payscale based estimates were produced using data from organisations providing both payscale and occupation code information for at least 95 per cent of their non-medical staff. These estimates only provide a broad indication of 1995 levels of staff and therefore should be used with caution. For further information on the 1995 non-medical workforce see the Department of Health's statistical bulletin on non-medical staff in England (1985 - 95). These are England and Wales figures only from 1995.
9 Data for Scotland excludes bank nurses.
10 Includes Specialist Registrar (SpR), Senior Registrar and Registrar. The SpR grade was introduced formally on 1 April 1996.

Sources: Scottish Health Service Common Services Agency;
Department of Health: 020 7972 2231;
National Assembly for Wales

9.4

Health and personal social services: workforce summary
Great Britain

continued

Number or whole-time equivalent

		1989	1990	1991[7]	1992	1993	1994	1995	1996	1997	1998	1999
Family Health services:[3]												
General medical practitioners:												
Analysis by type of practitioners at 1 October												
Total												
All Practitioners	LQZN	33 308	33 056	33 462	33 834	34 134	34 421	34 594	34 825	35 205	35 611	35 954
Unrestricted Principals & equivalents (UPE's)[1]	LQZO	30 629	30 616	30 712	31 065	31 447	31 767	31 945	32 164	32 477	32 801	33 048
of which GMS UP's	LQZP	30 629	30 616	30 712	31 065	31 447	31 767	31 945	32 164	32 477	32 414	32 140
PMS contracted	LQZQ	..	..	..	..	..	..	..	..	..	324	837
PMS salaried	LQZP	30 629	30 616	30 712	31 065	31 447	31 767	31 945	32 164	32 477	32 414	32 140
Restricted principals	LQZS	179	163	151	152	161	156	137	126	111	106	98
Assistants	LQZT	261	221	471	521	539	626	684	890	891	750	691
GP Registrars[2]	LQZU	2 239	2 040	2 102	2 067	1 956	1 841	1 790	1 605	1 678	1 830	1 903
of which GMS[3]	LQZV	2 239	2 040	2 102	2 067	1 956	1 841	1 790	1 605	1 678	1 796	1 825
Salaried Doctors (Para 52 SFA)	LQZW	..	..	..	..	..	..	..	..	..	60	118
PMS Other[4]	LQZX	..	..	..	..	..	..	..	..	..	12	46
Associates[5]	LQZY	..	16	26	29	31	31	38	40	48	52	50
General dental practitioners: total[15]	KDCQ	17 830	18 011	18 037	18 019	18 467	18 600	18 736	19 147	19 598	20 216	20 750
Principals	KDCR	17 436	17 539	17 440	17 384	17 699	17 642	17 670	17 897	18 174	18 557	18 895
Assistants and Vocational trainees	KDCS	394	472	597	635	768	958	1 066	1 250	1 424	1 659	1 855
Ophthalmic medical practitioners [7,13]	KDCT	882	882	862	837	789	735	752	766	830	855	706
Ophthalmic opticians [7,13]	KDCU	6 557	6 685	6 841	6 997	7 124	7 179	7 445	7 652	7 847	8 160	6 811
Personal Social Services staff [10]:												
Total	KDDE	238 754	240 342	237 280	235 240	232 911	237 752	233 861	233 655	229 439	223 500	221 700
Management, administration and ancillary staff[14]	KADS	25 801	27 006	28 049	29 433	..	..	..	..	..	..	..
Home help service	KSBU	60 411	59 772	58 591	58 004	57 593	59 391	56 961	55 430	53 573	50 417	47 227
Field Social Workers[16]	KSBX	23 702	24 457	25 537	26 509	28 850	29 820	31 926	32 140	32 990	33 400	33 900
Day care establishments staff	KADV	28 857.0	28 612.0	28 442.0	28 596.0	30 221.3	31 270.1	31 109.2	31 605.0	30 839.0	30 300.0	30 800.0
Residential care staff	KADW	88 285.0	87 858.0	83 001.0	78 918.0	74 038.3	72 155.3	68 650.5	67 975.0	65 422.0	62 100.0	59 200.0
All other staff[14]	KADX	3 932	4 284	5 355	5 049	..	..	..	..	..	..	..

1 UPE's includes Unrestricted Principals, PMS Contracted GP's and PMS salaried GP's.
2 GP Registrars were formerly referred to as Trainees.
3 GP Registrars in GMS Partnerships.
4 PMS other includes 2 Salaried Restricted Principals who are working in Scotland.
6 Figures relate to 1 October.
7 Figures for England and Wales relate to 31 December. Figures for Scotland relate to 31 March of the following year.
8 In Scotland this is the Dental Practice Division (DPD).
9 The Prescription Pricing Authority in England is synonymous with the Prescription Pricing Division in Scotland. Figures for the Prescription Pricing Division in Scotland relate to 30 November.
10 Figures are for England only.

11 Due to changes in the collection procedure in 1991 a category of 'other staff' was introduced for these locally determined payscales. In previous years these staff were included in their respective occupation groups.
12 1991 figure revised.
13 OMPs and OOs holding contracts with FHSAs/HAs and/or Scottish Health Boards to carry out NHS sight tests. OOs with contracts with more than one Health Board and/or a Health Board and a FHSA/HA will be counted more than once.
14 Breakdown for England not available in this form from 1993.
15 Some dentists may have a contract with more than one Family Health Service Authority/Health Authority. These dentists have been counted only once.
16 Includes care managers from 1993.

Sources: Scottish Health Service Common Services Agency;
Department of Health: 020 7972 2231;
National Assembly for Wales

9.5 Notifications of infectious diseases

Number

		1989	1990	1991	1992	1993	1994	1995	1996	1997	1998	1999
United Kingdom												
Measles	KHQD	31 045	15 642	11 723	12 318	12 018	23 517	9 017	6 866	4 844	4 540	2 953
Mumps	KWNN	24 504	5 297	3 836	3 169	2 726	3 143	2 400	2 182	2 264	1 917	2 005
Rubella	KWNO	31 849	15 736	9 702	9 150	12 300	9 650	7 674	11 720	4 205	4 064	2 581
Whooping cough	KHQE	13 550	16 862	6 279	2 750	4 718	4 837	2 399	2 721	3 669	1 902	1 461
Scarlet fever	KHQC	10 386	9 505	6 876	5 978	7 341	8 031	6 863	6 101	4 639	4 708	2 951
Dysentery	KHQG	3 807	3 042	11 527	20 620	7 577	7 539	5 498	2 643	2 427	1 934	1 627
Food poisoning	KHQH	59 214	59 721	59 497	72 139	76 711	91 129	92 604	94 923	105 579	105 060	96 944
Typhoid and Paratyphoid fevers	KHQB	273	294	288	298	277	390	386	291	249	252	278
Hepatitis	KWNP	8 304	9 864	9 856	9 616	6 142	4 284	3 823	2 876	3 601	3 781	4 346
Tuberculosis	KHQI	6 059	5 898	6 078	6 442	6 565	6 229	6 176	6 238	6 367	6 605	6 703
Malaria	KWNQ	..	1 565	1 652	1 253	1 281	1 219	1 363	1 743	1 549	1 163	1 039
England and Wales[1]												
Measles	KHRD	26 222	13 302	9 680	10 268	9 612	16 375	7 447	5 614	3 962	3 728	2 438
Mumps	KWNR	20 713	4 277	2 924	2 412	2 153	2 494	1 936	1 747	1 914	1 587	1 691
Rubella	KWNS	24 570	11 491	7 174	6 212	9 724	6 326	6 196	9 081	3 260	3 208	1 954
Whooping cough	KHRE	11 646	15 286	5 201	2 309	4 091	3 964	1 869	2 387	2 989	1 577	1 139
Scarlet fever	KHRC	8 295	7 187	5 217	4 645	5 855	6 193	5 293	4 873	3 569	3 339	2 086
Dysentery	KHRG	3 278	2 756	9 935	16 960	6 841	6 956	4 651	2 312	2 274	1 813	1 538
Food poisoning	KHRH	52 557	52 145	52 543	63 347	68 587	81 833	82 041	83 233	93 901	93 932	86 316
Typhoid and Paratyphoid fevers	KHRB	252	271	281	282	268	370	370	276	241	243	276
Viral hepatitis	KWNT	7 071	9 005	8 860	8 993	5 557	3 722	3 296	2 437	3 186	3 183	3 424
Tuberculosis[2]	KHRJ	5 432	5 204	5 436	5 799	5 921	5 591	5 608	5 654	5 859	6 087	6 144
Malaria	KWNU	1 478	1 493	1 553	1 189	1 198	1 139	1 300	1 659	1 476	1 110	1 005
Total meningitis	KHRO	2 722	2 572	2 760	2 571	2 082	1 800	2 285	2 686	2 345	2 072	2 094
Meningococcal meningitis	KHRP	1 133	1 138	1 117	1 067	1 053	938	1 146	1 164	1 220	1 152	1 145
Meningococcal septicaemia	KWNV	229	277	273	277	398	430	707	1 129	1 440	1 509	1 822
Ophthalmia neonatorum	KHRI	427	440	433	424	340	268	245	246	224	198	163
Scotland												
Measles	KHSE	3 359	2 006	1 701	1 747	1 911	6 192	1 307	1 055	762	700	436
Mumps	KWNW	3 095	833	723	601	458	546	371	368	282	251	221
Rubella	KWNX	6 628	3 702	2 171	2 645	2 048	2 916	1 258	2 449	818	745	554
Whooping cough	KHSF	659	1 291	838	236	493	639	399	186	545	225	214
Scarlet fever	KHSD	1 345	1 546	1 084	808	911	1 319	1 065	750	645	883	433
Dysentery	KHSH	154	235	1 526	3 486	607	446	575	176	124	103	79
Food poisoning[3]	KHSI	6 156	6 757	6 318	7 877	7 170	8 291	9 297	10 234	10 144	9 186	8 595
Typhoid and Paratyphoid fevers	KHSB	18	20	7	15	7	18	16	14	6	6	2
Viral hepatitis	KWNY	831	546	556	319	290	296	405	360	359	490	844
Tuberculosis[4]	KHSL	533	563	546	559	554	546	478	509	433	457	498
Malaria	KWUC	60	68	91	50	75	74	58	70	57	30	21
Meningococcal infection	KWUD	190	216	178	207	207	201	190	201	271	313	327
Erysipelas	KHSC	152	125	155	128	130	118	125	84	95	66	63
Northern Ireland												
Measles	KHTD	1 464	334	342	303	495	950	263	197	120	112	79
Mumps	KHTR	696	187	189	156	115	103	93	67	68	79	93
Rubella	KHTQ	651	543	357	293	528	408	220	190	127	111	73
Whooping cough	KHTE	1 245	285	240	205	134	234	131	148	135	100	108
Scarlet fever	KHTC	746	772	575	525	575	519	502	478	425	486	432
Dysentery	KHTG	375	51	66	174	129	137	272	155	29	18	10
Food poisoning	KHTH	501	819	636	915	954	1 005	1 266	1 456	1 534	1 942	2 033
Typhoid and Paratyphoid fevers	KHTB	3	3	–	1	2	2	..	1	2	3	–
Infective hepatitis	KHTO	402	313	440	304	295	266	122	79	56	108	78
Tuberculosis	KHTI	94	131	96	84	90	92	90	75	75	61	61
Malaria	KWUE	..	4	8	14	8	6	5	14	16	23	13
Acute encephalitis/meningitis	KHTM	131	158	172	118	122	144	116	105	91	64	99
Meningococcal septicaemia	KWUF	..	2	23	27	34	39	42	67	56	87	145
Gastro-enteritis (children under 2 years)	KHTP	1 243	1 157	1 091	1 070	1 379	887	1 072	745	896	1 371	1 121

1 The figures show the corrected number of notifications, incorporating revisions of diagnosis, either by the notifying medical practitioner or by the medical superintendent of the infectious diseases hospital. Cases notified in Port Health Authorities are included.

2 Formal notifications of new cases only. The figures exclude chemoprophylaxis.

3 Scotland's food poisoning includes 'otherwise ascertained' for the first time in 1995.

4 Figures include cases of tuberculosis not notified before death.

Sources: Scottish Health Service Common Services Agency;
Department of Health and Social Services (Northern Ireland);
Communicable Diseases Surveillance Centre: 020 8200 6868

9.6 Deaths due to occupationally related lung disease [1]
Great Britain

		1988	1989	1990	1991	1992	1993	1994	1995	1996	1997	1998
Asbestosis (without mesothelioma)[2]	KADY	151	155	164	163	150	173	174	166	196	190	165
Mesothelioma [2]	KADZ	872	909	895	1 022	1 098	1 153	1 242	1 317	1 304	1 341	1 527
Pneumoconiosis (other than asbestosis)	KAEA	281	318	328	287	274	281	276	287	223	230	268
Byssinosis	KAEB	22	25	19	16	21	11	7	6	3	5	5
Farmer's lung and other occupational allergic alveolitis	KAEC	9	8	6	8	4	12	10	10	1	5	8
Total	KAED	1 335	1 415	1 412	1 496	1 547	1 630	1 709	1 786	1 727	1 771	1 973

1 The data in this table are derived from death certificates. For asbestosis and mesothelioma, the figure shown is the number of certificates mentioning the disease, those mentioning both diseases being counted as mesothelioma only. For the other diseases the figure is the number of deaths coded to the disease as underlying the case.

2 By definition every case of asbestosis is due to asbestos; the association with mesothelioma is also very strong, though there is thought to be a low natural background incidence.

Sources: Office for National Statistics;
Health and Safety Executive: 0151 951 4540

9.7 New cases of occupational diseases diagnosed under the Industrial Injuries and Pneumoconiosis, Byssinosis and Miscellaneous Diseases benefit schemes

Great Britain

		Disablement Benefit[1]										
		1989	1990	1991	1992	1993	1994	1995	1996	1997	1998	1999
A. Occupational lung diseases and deafness												
Pneumoconiosis (except asbestosis)[9]	KAEE	412	437[6]	447	428	456	657	433	362	249	554	461
Asbestosis	KAEF	268	306[6]	330	354	418	376	427	479	344	316	407
Byssinosis	KAEG	15	18[6]	7	4	5	2	6	4	1	2	2
Farmer's lung	KAEH	13	7	5	5	3	9	6	6	4	4	13
Occupational asthma	KAEI	220	216	293[3]	553	510	506	514	410	298	222	196
Mesothelioma	KAEJ	441	462	519	551	608	583	685	642	553	590	620
Lung cancer (asbestos)	KAEK	54	58	55	54	72	77	55	51	26	42	38
Lung cancer (other prescribed agents)[4]	KAEL	4	6	6	6	3	–	4	2	1	3	7
Pleural thickening[12]	KAEM	125	146	149	160	172	196	188	168	156	227	242
Other occupational lung disease	KAEN	–	4	6	5	2	–	–	1	–	–	–
Chronic bronchitis and/or emphysema[4,7]	KIUS	..	..	..	..	1 560	2 594	268	269	3 030	3 423	1 451
Occupational deafness[1]	KAEO	1 170	1 128	1 041	972	901	882	763	531	413	258	316
Total: Occupational lung disease and deafness	KAEP	2 722	2 788[6]	2 858	3 092	4 710	5 882	3 349	2 925	5 075	5 641	3 753

		Disablement Benefit[2,5]								
		1990 /91	1991 /92	1992 /93	1993 /94	1994 /95	1995 /96	1996 /97	1997 /98	1998 /99
B. Other diseases										
Dermatitis	KEAI	434	411	419	392	368	328	336	271	220
Tenosynovitis	KEAJ	556	649	911	800	787	548	513	415	344
Vibration white finger	KEAK	5 403	2 369	1 447	1 425	1 747	3 016	3 288	3 033	3 155
Beat conditions	KEAL	187	317	256	257	205	199	153	104	62
Carpal Tunnel Syndrome[4]	KIUV	..	..	20	267	277	265	297	400	478
Viral hepatitis	KEAM	2	4	1	3	3	4	4	2	3
Tuberculosis	KEAN	3	3	6	10	9	10	6	11	4
Leptospirosis	KEAO	–	1	1	1	–	–	–	–	–
Other infections	KEAP	5	4	3	2	5	2	3	6	2
Poisonings[10]	KEAQ	4	8	9	15	9	10	7	10	9
Occupational cancers[11]	KEAR	17	23	30	43	26	30	44	37	43
Other conditions	KEAS	72	68	132	144	133	147	119	98	75
Allergic rhinitis[8]	KIUW	13	75	494	528	589	720	352	199	135
Total: Other diseases	KEAT	6 696	3 932	3 729	3 887	4 158	5 279	5 122	4 586	4 530

1 Awards for occupational deafness are made only for disablement at 20% or more and cases with lesser degrees of disabilities are excluded from the figures.

2 From October 1986 disablement benefit for most diseases was paid only for cases with disibility assessed at 14% or more; the figures for 1987/88 and subsequent years include cases not qualifying for benefit but assessed at 1-13%. Exceptions are claims made before October 1986, but assessed in subsequent years and all claims made for pneumoconiosis, asbestosis, mesothelioma and byssinosis, where the 1% threshold still applies, and deafness. (see note 1).

3 Series affected by changes in prescription benefit rules.

4 The following diseases were first prescribed during the period covered by the table (Year benefit first payable shown in brackets): Lung cancer (other prescribed agents except nickel)(1993) Chronic bronchitis and/or emphysema (1993) Carpal Tunnel Syndrone (1993)

5 Years ending in September.

6 Figures from 1990 do not include cases awarded by Medical Appeals Tribunals.

7 Prescribed from September 1993 for coal miners with a specified level of lung function impairment, and a minimum 20 years employment underground. The sharp fall in numbers in 1995 is typical of the pattern seen after a disease has been newly prescribed. The larger numbers in the two preceeding years probably represents the clearance of a backlog of pre-existing cases. The sharp rise in numbers in 1997 and 1998 results from relaxations in eligibility rules; future numbers are expected to fall.

8 Before March 1996 defined as inflammation or ulceration of upper respiratory tract or mouth. The recent increase in numbers for this disease represents increases in claims following a take-up campaign by trade unions rather than a true increase in incidence.

9 Figures exclude a small number of cases assessed under the Pneumoconiosis, Byssinosis and Miscellaneous Diseases Benefit Scheme, which have been subject to revisions and are published elsewhere.

10 Excluding poisonings by nitrous fumes, beryllium or cadmium, which are included under 'other occupational lung disease'.

11 Excluding mesothelioma and lung cancer, see section A of table.

12 From 9 April 1997, the definition of this disease was changed to admit unilateral diffuse pleural thickening. Previously this was required to be bilateral.

Sources: Health and Safety Executive: 0151 951 4540;
Department of Social Security

9.8 Injuries to workers by industry and severity of injury
Great Britain
As reported to all enforcing authorities

	Code	Section	SIC (92)	Fatal 1996[7]/97	Fatal 1997/98	Fatal 1998/99	Code	Major[1] 1996[7]/97	Major 1997/98	Major 1998/99	Code	Over 3 Day[2] 1996[7]/97	Over 3 Day 1997/98	Over 3 Day 1998/99
Agriculture, hunting, forestry and fishing[3]	KSYS	A,B	01,02,05	55	40	46	KSZN	778	745	679	KTAZ	1 514	1 382	1 298
Energy and water supply industries[4]	KSYT	C,E	10-14,40/41	9	18	11	KSZO	694	684	555	KTBH	3 039	3 339	2 974
Mining and quarrying[4]	KSYU	C	10-14	7	14	7	KSZP	417	440	346	KTBI	1 476	1 920	1 773
Mining and quarrying of energy producing materials[4]	KSON	CA	10-12	6	10	5	KSZQ	228	297	213	KTBJ	861	1 359	1 238
Mining and quarrying except energy producing materials	KSOO	CB	13/14	1	4	2	KSZR	189	143	133	KTBK	615	561	535
Electricity, gas and water supply	KSOP	E	40/41	2	4	4	KSZS	277	244	209	KTBL	1 563	1 419	1 201
Manufacturing	KSOQ	D	15-37	59	61	69	KSZT	8 346	8 864	8 233	KTBM	40 159	41 742	39 264
of food products; beverages and tobacco	KSOR	DA	15/16	4	6	7	KSZU	1 501	1 556	1 525	KTBN	9 433	9 918	9 589
of textile and textile products	KSOS	DB	17/18	1	4	–	KSZV	338	353	290	KTBO	1 644	1 606	1 524
of leather and leather products	KSOT	DC	19	–	1	–	KSZW	33	43	25	KTBP	196	156	140
of wood and wood products	KSOU	DD	20	5	7	4	KSZX	390	373	346	KTBQ	1 144	1 168	1 026
of pulp, paper and paper products; publishing and printing	KSOV	DE	21/22	2	3	2	KSZY	552	598	503	KTBR	2 664	2 695	2 496
of coke, refined petroleum products and nuclear fuel	KSOW	DF	23	–	1	–	KSZZ	44	39	38	KTBS	140	138	132
of chemicals, chemical products and man-made fibres	KSOX	DG	24	4	2	4	KTAE	562	518	424	KTBT	2 187	2 054	1 782
of rubber and plastic products	KSOY	DH	25	3	2	5	KTAF	612	677	651	KTBU	3 270	3 618	3 437
of other non-metallic mineral products	KSOZ	DI	26	3	6	6	KTAG	433	483	426	KTBV	2 193	2 287	2 076
of basic metals and fabricated metal products	KSYV	DJ	27/28	13	14	22	KTAH	1 585	1 833	1 656	KTBW	5 911	6 407	6 144
of machinery and equipment n.e.c.	KSYW	DK	29	9	5	5	KTAI	780	765	685	KTBX	3 456	3 441	2 913
of electrical and optical equipment	KSYX	DL	30-33	1	2	–	KTAJ	442	513	481	KTBY	2 273	2 467	2 198
of transport equipment	KSYY	DM	34/35	10	5	5	KTAK	729	742	770	KTBZ	4 258	4 297	4 342
Manufacturing n.e.c.	KSYZ	DN	36/37	4	3	9	KTAL	345	371	413	KTCA	1 390	1 490	1 465
Construction	KSZA	F	45	90	80	65	KTAM	4 054	4 326	4 656	KTCB	9 666	10 265	9 576
Total service industries	KSZB	G-Q	50-99	74	75	62	KTAN	15 448	15 383	14 930	KTCC	75 190	79 045	80 032
Wholesale and retail trade, and repairs	KSZC	G	50-52	17	17	15	KTAO	3 493	3 527	3 158	KTCD	13 846	16 353	15 695
Hotel and restaurants	KSZD	H	55	4	1	1	KTAP	947	942	924	KTCE	2 696	3 234	3 434
Transport, storage and communication[5]	KSZE	I	60-64	18	27	25	KTAQ	2 906	2 771	2 879	KTCF	16 792	17 351	18 626
Financial intermediation	KSZF	J	65-67	–	–	–	KTAR	169	131	153	KTCG	658	623	653
Real estate, renting and business activities	KSZG	K	70-74	10	13	13	KTAS	1 015	1 013	1 050	KTCH	3 214	3 791	3 981
Public administration and defence	KSZH	L	75	8	3	2	KTAT	2 182	2 153	2 001	KTCI	14 744	13 895	14 266
Education	KSZI	M	80	3	–	1	KTAU	1 564	1 589	1 548	KTCJ	4 705	4 850	4 680
Health and social work	KSZJ	N	85	4	2	–	KTAV	1 871	1 966	1 930	KTCK	13 925	14 209	14 148
Other community, social and personal services activities	KSZK	O-Q	90-99	10	12	5	KTAW	1 301	1 291	1 287	KTCL	4 610	4 739	4 549
Unclassified	KSZL			–	–	–	KTAX	–	–	–	KTCM	–	–	–
All industries	KSZM			287	274	253	KTAY	29 320	30 002	29 053	KTCN	129 568	135 773	133 144

1 As defined in RIDDOR 85 prior to 1996/97 and RIDDOR 95 from 1996/97.
2 Injuries causing incapacity for normal work for more than 3 days.
3 Excludes sea fishing.
4 Includes the number of injuries in the oil and gas industry collected under offshore installations safety legislation.
5 Injuries arising from shore based services only. Excludes incidents reported under merchant shipping legislation.
6 n.e.c. not elsewhere classified.
7 1996/97 injury figures cannot be compared to previous years figures as they were reported under different legislation (RIDDOR 85 and 95).

Source: Health and Safety Executive (HSE): 0151 951 4842

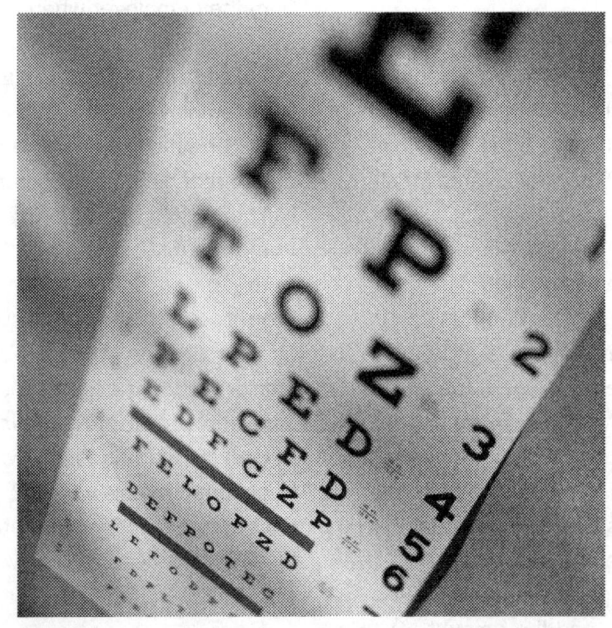

10 Social protection

Social protection

Social security
(Tables 10.2 - 10.8 and 10.10 to 10.16)

Tables 10.2 to 10.6 and 10.10 to 10.16 give details of contributors and beneficiaries under the National Insurance and Industrial Injury Acts, supplementary benefits and war pensions.

There are three types of contributor:

Class 1   Employed people, that is, people working for employers. Their contributions are paid partly by themselves and partly by their employers. They are covered for all benefits.

Class 2   Self-employed people, that is, people working on their own account. They are covered for all benefits other than unemployment and industrial injuries.

Class 3   Non-employed people, that is, people who do not work for gain. These people pay contributions on a voluntary basis. They are covered for benefits other than unemployment, sickness, industrial injuries and maternity allowances.

Class 4   Payable, in addition to Class 2 by self-employed people, and the amount payable is proportionate to profits or gains between a lower and upper limit in any one year.

An employer must pay a contribution for every employee whose earnings exceed a base level. Most employed people pay the full employee's contribution, but retirement pensioners working for an employer do not and some married women and some widows who are working need not, unless they so wish, contribute except for industrial injuries benefit. Thus the total numbers in the analysis by benefit for which the contributions were payable are less than the total numbers in the analysis by class of contributor.

Sickness benefit, Invalidity benefit and Incapacity benefit (Tables 10.7 and 10.8)

Incapacity Benefit replaced Sickness Benefit and Invalidity Benefit from 13 April 1995. The first condition for entitlement to these contributory benefits is that the claimants are incapable of work because of illness or disablement. Secondly, that they satisfy the contribution conditions which depend on contributions paid as an employed (Class 1) or self-employed person (Class 2). Under Sickness and Invalidity Benefits the contribution conditions were automatically treated as satisfied if a person was incapable of work because of an industrial accident or prescribed disease. Under Incapacity Benefit those who do not satisfy the contribution conditions in this case do not have them treated as satisfied. Class 1A contributions paid by employers are in respect of the benefit of cars provided for the private use of employees,

and the free fuel provided for private use. These contributions do not provide any type of benefit cover.

Since 6 April 1983, most people working for an employer and paying National Insurance contributions as employed persons, receive Statutory Sick Pay (SSP) from their employer when they are off work sick. SSP was payable for a maximum of 8 weeks until 5 April 1986, and 28 weeks thereafter. People who do not work for an employer, and employees who are excluded from the SSP scheme, or those who have run out of SSP before reaching the maximum of 28 weeks and are still sick can claim benefit. Any period of SSP is excluded from the tables.

From 14 September 1980, spells of incapacity of 3 days or less do not count as periods of interruption of employment, and are excluded from the tables. Exceptions are where people are receiving regular weekly treatment by dialysis, or treatment by radiotherapy, chemotherapy or plasmapheresis where 2 days in any 6 consecutive days make up a period of interruption of employment, and those whose incapacity for work ends within 3 days of the end of SSP entitlement.

At the beginning of a period of incapacity, benefit is subject to 3 waiting days, except where there was an earlier spell of incapacity of more than 3 days in the previous 8 weeks. Employees entitled to SSP for less than 28 weeks and who are still sick can get Sickness Benefit or Incapacity Benefit Short Term (Low) until they reach a total of 28 weeks provided they satisfy the conditions. After 28 weeks SSP and/or Sickness Benefit (SB), Invalidity Benefit (IVB) was payable up to pension age for as long as the incapacity lasts. From pension age Invalidity Benefit was paid at the person's Retirement Pension rate, until entitlement ceases when RP is paid or at deemed pension age (70 for a man, 65 for a woman). For people on Incapacity Benefit under State pension age there are two short-term rates: the lower rate is paid for the first 28 weeks of sickness and the higher rate for weeks 29 to 52. From week 53 the Long Term rate Incapacity Benefit is payable. The Short Term rate Incapacity Benefit is based on Retirement Pension entitlement for people over State pension age and is paid for up to a year if incapacity began before pension age.

The long-term rate of Incapacity Benefit applies to people under State pension age who have been sick for more than a year. People with a terminal illness or who are receiving the higher rate care component of Disability Living Allowance will get the Long Term rate. The Long Term rate is not paid for people over pension age.

Under Incapacity Benefit, for the first 28 weeks of incapacity, people previously in work will be assessed on the 'own occupation' test - the claimant's ability to do their own job. Otherwise, incapacity will be based on a new 'all work' test which will assess ability to carry out a range of work-related activities. The test will apply after 28 weeks of incapacity or from the start of the claim for people who did not previously have a job. Certain people will be exempted from this test.

The tables exclude all men aged over 65 and women aged over 60 who are in receipt of Retirement Pension, and all people over deemed pension age (70 for a man and 65 for a woman), members of the Armed Forces, mariners while at sea, and married women and certain widows who have chosen not to be insured for Sickness Benefit. In addition, employees of the Post Office are excluded prior to 29 March 1986, and the remainder of Civil Service Departments, British Telecom and fringe bodies prior to 25 August 1986. The tables include a number of individuals who were unemployed prior to incapacity.

The Short Term (Higher) and Long Term rates of incapacity Benefit are treated as taxable income.

There were transitional provisions for people who were on Sickness or Invalidity Benefit on 12 April 1995. They were automatically transferred to Incapacity Benefit, payable on the same basis as before. Former IVB recipients continue to get Additional Pension entitlement, but frozen at 1994 levels. Also their IVB is not subject to tax. If they were over State pension age on 12 April 1995 they may get Incapacity Benefit for up to 5 years beyond pension age.

Government expenditure on social services and housing *(Table 10.17 - 10.22)*

The tables of general government expenditure on the social services and housing in the United Kingdom comprise a summary table followed by separate tables for each of the social services and housing. The definition of government expenditure used in these tables follows that in Table 9.4 of *United Kingdom National Accounts 1994 Edition*, the CSO Blue Book, and covers both current and capital expenditure of the central government (including the National Insurance Fund) and local authorities. The housing table also includes the capital expenditure of public corporations concerned with housing. As in the Blue Book, government expenditure is measured after deducting fees and charges for services. Expenditure on administration includes the cost of common services (accommodation, stationery and printing, superannuation, etc) some of which is not directly borne by the departments administering each service. Transfers from one part of government to another have been eliminated to avoid double counting. The figures relate to years ended 31 March. Figures for the latest two years are the most

recent estimates available and are subject to revision.

It should be noted that the figures no longer include imputed rents for the use of fixed assets owned and used by general government. In the Blue Book, imputed rents have been replaced by capital consumption. Capital consumption, however, cannot be allocated to individual services and is therefore not included in these tables.

The following notes give brief descriptions of each of the main services shown in the tables.

Education (Table 10.18)

This covers expenditure by the Education Departments, local education authorities and the University Grants Committee on education in schools, training colleges, technical institutions and universities. It includes expenditure on school meals and milk.

The education statistics in Table 10.18 are provided by the Department for Education. They are not normally able to provide a full set of estimates, from their sources, for the latest financial year. The ONS has in the past made estimates from a variety of sources but, following a review of their accuracy, it has been decided that they do not give a reliable guide to the final outcome and have therefore been withdrawn.

National Health Service (Table 10.19)

This covers expenditure by central government on hospital and community health, family practitioner and other health services. The expenditure by local authorities on the provision of health centres, health visiting, home nursing, ambulance services, vaccination and immunisation, etc. was transferred to central government on 1 April 1974. Only the net costs of providing these services are included in total government expenditure, receipts from patients being shown separately.

Personal social services (Table 10.20)

This covers local authority expenditure on the aged, handicapped and homeless, child care, care of mothers and young children, mental health, domestic help, etc. Also included are central government grants to voluntary approved schools.

Welfare foods (Table 10.20)

This covers the cost of providing welfare foods at reduced prices to children and expectant mothers. Only the net costs of providing these services are included in the total government expenditure, payments by the recipients of the services being shown separately.

Social protection

Social security (Table 10.21)

This comprises both benefits under the Social Security schemes and non-contributory benefits and allowances, administered by the Department of Social Security. The analysis by type of Income Support is not exact; the estimates are derived from average numbers in receipt of benefit and average amounts paid. Unified housing benefit (rent rebates and allowances) is also included as social security expenditure and not as housing expenditure. This is now mainly administered by local authorities who receive grants from central government.

Housing (Table 10.22)

The table shows, in addition to government expenditure on housing, the capital expenditure of public corporations and the total expenditure of the public sector on housing. The government expenditure figures cover subsidies paid by the housing departments towards the provision of housing by local authorities, new town development corporations and housing associations; subsidies by local authorities to their housing revenue accounts; rent rebates for tenants of housing owned by local authorities and new towns; rent allowances for tenants of privately-owned housing; grants to persons for the reduction of mortgage interest payments; capital expenditure on the provision of houses for letting; capital grants to housing associations; grants by local authorities towards the cost of conversion and improvement of privately-owned houses; net lending by the central government and local authorities for private house purchase and improvement and loans for first time purchasers. The public corporations' figures cover capital expenditure on the provision of houses for letting and lending by the Housing Corporation to housing associations.

10.1 National Insurance Fund
United Kingdom
Years ended 31 March

£ thousands

		1990/91	1991/92	1992/93	1993/94	1994/95	1995/96	1996/97	1997/98	1998/99
Receipts										
Opening balance	KJFB	10 579 741	12 161 227	8 637 594	3 577 671	4 672 345	7 042 118	8 044 941	7 869 121	9 763 346
Contributions		31 480 868	33 156 696	34 331 672	35 090 000	38 712 218	40 874 579	42 806 429	46 754 687	50 023 377
Grant from Consolidated Fund	KOTF	..	..	..	..	7 785 000	6 445 000	3 680 000	1 951 500	966 200	3 430
Compensation for SSP/SMP	KJQM	..	1 089 811	1 124 500	1 158 289	563 400	474 700	541 800	600 500	576 400
Consolidated Fund Supplement	KJFD	..	..	..	..	..	..	..	..	..
Reimbursement for industrial Injury Benefit payments	KJQN	436 514		..	..	..	..	..	..	..
Transfers from GB	KOTG	225 000	125 000	40 000	40 000	145 000	125 000	75 000	150 000	315 000
Income from investments	KJFE	1 022 506	1 160 026	970 862	488 484	365 096	459 217	488 728	474 296	667 261
Other receipts	KJFF	944 680	19 359	24 813	- 41 989	60 625	76 487	85 126	97 206	92 292
Redundancy receipts[1]	KIBQ	2 024	19 091	26 942	25 688	25 288	23 899	26 193	24 720	21 210
Total		44 691 333	47 731 210	45 156 383	48 207 121	50 988 972	52 756 000	54 019 717	56 936 730	61 462 316
Expenditure										
Total benefits		30 590 421	37 430 154	39 823 984	42 366 510	42 270 821	43 198 045	44 517 872	45 321 420	46 822 291
Unemployment	KJFH	898 963	1 641 928	1 800 589	1 689 604	1 330 922	1 131 373	605 095	148	..
Sickness[2]	KJFI	226 968	286 455	378 136	378 407	350 700	14 711	..	..	..
Invalidity[2]	KJFJ	4 613 004	5 701 239	6 452 717	7 341 161	8 009 286	599 829	..	..	..
Incapacity[2]	JYXL	..	..	..	..	..	7 622 940	7 992 748	7 739 450	7 574 276
Maternity	KETY	34 590	32 071	32 660	34 230	28 230	29 897	34 283	36 715	39 329
Widows' pensions	KEWU	920 652	1 044 749	1 044 397	1 075 990	1 057 395	1 050 693	1 016 822	1 020 713	1 007 653
Guardians' allowances & Child's special allowance[3]	KJFK	1 643	1 562	2 091	1 111	1 111	1 842	1 569	1 637	1 834
Retirement pensions[4]		23 305 444	28 604 996	29 995 404	31 720 928	31 366 872	32 619 571	34 735 720	36 396 421	38 071 687
Disablement[5]	KAAU	419 756	..	..	..	..	..	..	..	..
Death	KAAV	47 920	..	..	..	..	..	..	..	..
Pensioners' lump sum payments	KAAW	118 259	117 154	117 990	125 079	126 305	127 189	131 635	126 336	127 512
Other benefits	KAAX	3 222	..	..	..	..	..	..	..	..
Other payments	KAAZ	9 623	9 682	10 523	35 045	8 879	14 174	17 392	19 037	18 305
Administration	KABE	1 056 787	1 243 488	1 379 212	1 604 510	1 323 631	1 218 772	1 065 338	1 073 350	1 052 820
Transfers to Northern Ireland	KABF	225 000	125 000	40 000	40 000	145 000	125 000	75 000	150 000	315 000
Redundancy payments	KIBR	..	285 291	324 994	271 636	198 523	155 068	133 621	119 961	140 075
Jobseeker's allowance (Contributory)[6]	LUQW	..	..	..	..	..	..	341 433	489 460	488 863
Total		31 881 831	39 093 615	41 578 713	44 317 701	43 946 854	44 711 059	46 150 656	47 173 228	48 837 354
Accumulated funds	KABH	12 161 227	8 637 594	3 577 671	4 672 345	7 042 118	8 044 941	7 869 121	9 763 346	12 624 962

1 The assets of the Redundancy Fund became those of the National Insurance Fund on 31 January 1991.
2 Incapacity Benefit replaced Sickness Benefit and Invalidity Benefit from April 1995.
3 Including figures of Child's special allowance for Northern Ireland.
4 Includes figures for Personal Pensions.

5 From 1/4/90, industrial injury benefits are no longer paid for out of of the National Insurance Fund; this amount is reimbursement for expenditure incurred by the fund for the period 1/4/90 to 31/12/90.
6 Jobseeker's Allowance (Contributory) was introduced in October 1996 and replaced Unemployment Benefit.

Sources: Department of Social Security: 01253 856123 Ext 62436;
Department of Health and Social Services (Northern Ireland): 028 9052 2062

10.2 Persons who paid National Insurance contributions in a tax year ending April[1]
Great Britain

Millions

		Total					Men					Women			
		1994	1995	1996	1997		1994	1995	1996	1997		1994	1995	1996	1997
Total[2]	KABI	23.99	24.27	24.57	24.77	KEYF	13.69	13.80	13.90	13.90	KEYP	10.29	10.50	10.71	10.80
Class 1 Standard rate	KABJ	21.38	21.66	21.99	22.28	KEYG	11.58	11.68	11.81	11.94	KEYQ	9.80	9.99	10.19	10.33
Not contracted out[3]	KABK	12.53	12.76	12.96	13.28	KEYH	6.37	6.62	6.82	7.04	KEYR	5.98	6.15	6.14	6.23
Contracted out	KABL	7.51	7.28	7.26	7.35	KEYI	4.68	4.44	4.32	4.23	KEYS	2.83	2.84	2.84	3.12
Mixed contracted in/out	KABM	1.04	1.21	1.43	1.36	KEYJ	0.53	0.62	0.67	0.67	KEYT	0.51	0.59	0.76	..
Class 1 Reduced rate (including standard rate)	KABO	0.48	0.41	0.34	0.29	KEYL	–	–	–	–	KEYV	0.48	0.41	0.35	0.29
Class 2	KABP	2.08	2.08	2.08	2.05	KEYM	1.73	1.72	1.71	1.67	KEYW	0.34	0.36	0.37	0.38
Mixed Class 1 and Class 2	KABQ	0.33	0.33	0.33	0.35	KEYN	0.25	0.25	0.24	0.26	KEYX	0.08	0.08	0.09	0.09
Class 3[4]	KABR	0.20	0.20	0.17	0.09	KEYO	0.13	0.13	0.11	0.06	KEYY	0.07	0.07	0.06	0.03

1 The tax year commences on 6 April and ends on 5 April of the following year. The years shown at the head of the column refer to the end of the tax year.
2 Not all figures agree because of rounding.

3 Includes those persons with an Appropriate Personal Pension (such persons pay contributions at the not contracted out rate but then receive a rebate).
4 Persons who paid a mixture of Class 3 contributions and others are not included in this category.

Source: Department of Social Security: 0191 225 7373

10.3 Weekly rates of principal social security benefits
Great Britain

£

		1989 Apr	1990 Apr	1991 Apr	1992 Apr	1993 Apr	1994 Apr	1995 Apr	1996 Apr	1997 Apr	1998 Apr	1999 Apr	2000 Apr
Unemployment benefit:[1,6]													
Men and women	KJNA	34.70	37.35	41.40	43.10	44.65	45.45	46.45	48.25	–	–	–	..
Jobseeker's allowance:[6]													
Personal allowances													
Single													
Aged under 18(Depending	KXDH	..	..	..	..	..	..	..	..	29.60	30.30	30.95	31.45
on their circumstances)	KXDI	..	..	..	..	..	..	..	..	38.90	39.85	40.70	41.35
Aged 18 - 24	KXDJ	..	..	..	..	..	..	..	..	38.90	39.85	40.70	41.35
Aged 25 or over	KXDK	..	..	..	..	..	..	..	..	49.15	50.35	51.40	52.20
Couple													
Both aged under 18[7]	KXDL	..	..	..	..	..	..	..	..	58.70	30.30[8]	30.95[8]	31.45
One or both aged													
18 or over	KXDM	..	..	..	..	..	..	..	..	77.15	79.00	80.65	81.95
Dependant children and													
young people													
Aged under 11	KXDN	..	..	..	..	..	..	..	..	16.90	17.30	20.20	26.60
Aged 11 - 16	KXDO	..	..	..	..	..	..	..	..	24.75	25.35	25.90	26.60
Aged 16 - 18	KXDP	..	..	..	..	..	..	..	..	29.60	30.30	30.95	31.75
Sickness benefit:[1,4]													
Men and women	KJNB	33.20	35.70	39.60	41.20	42.70	43.45	–	–	–	–	–	–
Invalidity benefit:[4]													
Invalidity pension	KJNC	43.60	46.90	52.00	54.15	56.10	57.60	–	–	–	–	–	–
Invalidity allowance:[4]													
High rate	KJND	9.20	10.00	11.10	11.55	11.95	12.15	12.40	12.90	13.15	13.60	14.05	14.20
Middle rate	KJNE	5.80	6.20	6.90	7.20	7.50	7.60	7.80	8.10	8.30	8.60	8.90	9.00
Low rate	KJNF	2.90	3.10	3.45	3.60	3.75	3.80	3.90	4.05	4.15	4.30	4.45	4.50
Increase for dependants:[4]													
Adult	KJNG	26.20	28.20	31.25	32.55	33.70	34.50	35.25	36.60	37.35	38.70	39.95	40.40
Each child	KJNH	8.95	9.65	10.70	10.85	10.95	11.00[3]	11.05[3]	11.15[3]	11.20[3]	11.30[3]	11.35[3]	11.35[3]
Incapacity benefit:													
Short term (Lower) Under pension age	KOSB	..	..	..	..	..	..	44.40	46.15	47.10	48.80	50.35	50.90
Increase for adult dependant	KOSC	..	..	..	..	..	..	27.50	28.55	29.15	30.20	31.15	31.50
Short term (Lower) Over pension age	KOSD	..	..	..	..	..	..	56.45	58.65	59.90	62.05	64.05[8]	64.75
Increase for adult dependant	KOSE	..	..	..	..	..	..	33.85	35.15	35.90	37.20	38.40[8]	38.80
Short term (Higher)	KOSF	..	..	..	..	..	..	52.50	54.55	55.70	57.70	59.55	60.20
Increase for dependants:													
Adult	KOSG	..	..	..	..	..	..	27.50	28.55	29.15	30.20	31.15	31.50
Child	KOSH	..	..	..	..	..	..	11.05[3]	11.15[3]	11.20[3]	11.30[3]	11.35[3]	11.35[3]
Long term	KOSI	..	..	..	..	..	..	58.85	61.15	62.45	64.70	66.75	67.50
Increase for dependants:													
Adult	KOSJ	..	..	..	..	..	..	35.25	36.60	37.35	38.70	39.95	40.40
Child	KOSK	..	..	..	..	..	..	11.05[3]	11.15[3]	11.20[3]	11.30[3]	11.35[3]	11.35[3]
Incapacity age addition:[5]													
Higher rate	KOSL	..	..	..	..	..	..	12.40	12.90	13.15	13.60	14.05	14.20
Lower rate	KOSM	..	..	..	..	..	..	6.20	6.45	6.60	6.80	7.05	7.10
Attendance allowance:													
Higher rate	KJNI	34.90	37.55	41.65	43.35	44.90	45.70	46.70	48.50	49.50	51.30	52.95	53.55
Lower rate	KJNJ	23.30	25.05	27.10	28.95	30.00	30.55	31.20	32.40	33.10	34.30	35.40	35.80
Mobility allowance[2]	KJNK	24.40	26.25	29.80	–	–	–	–	–	–	–	–	..
Disability living allowance:													
care component													
Higher rate	KXDC	..	..	..	43.35	44.90	45.70	46.70	48.50	49.50	51.30	52.95	53.55
Middle rate	KXDD	..	..	..	28.95	30.00	30.55	31.20	32.40	33.10	34.30	35.40	35.80
Lower rate	KXDE	..	..	..	11.55	11.95	12.15	12.40	12.90	13.15	13.60	14.05	14.20
mobility component													
Higher rate	KXDF	..	..	..	30.30	31.40	31.95	32.65	33.90	34.60	35.85	37.00	37.40
Lower rate	KXDG	..	..	..	11.55	11.95	12.15	12.40	12.90	13.15	13.60	14.05	14.20

1 Persons under the age of 18 are entitled to the appropriate adult rate.
2 Mobility allowance was introduced from 1 January 1976 at the £5.00 rate. Disability living allowance has replaced Mobility allowance from April 1992.
3 For the first child only, the Child Dependency increase is reduced by £1.30 to £9.90 because of child benefit.
4 Incapacity benefit introduced from 13 April 1995, has replaced sickness benefit and invalidity benefit.

5 The rate of age addition depends on age at date of onset of incapacity: Higher rate = under age 35 Lower rate = age 35-44.
6 Jobseeker's allowance introduced 7 October 1996 has replaced Unemployment benefit and is for the unemployed.
7 From 12 April 1999 the personal allowance for couples where both members not yet 18 or one of the couple is aged 18 or over depends on the couple's circumstances. They may be entitled to a couple allowance or a single persons allowance dependant on certain criteria.
8 Figure has been revised.

Source: Department of Social Security: 0191 225 7373

10.3 Weekly rates of principal social security benefits
Great Britain
continued

£

		1989 Apr	1990 Apr	1991 Apr	1992 Apr	1993 Apr	1994 Apr	1995 Apr	1996 Apr	1997 Apr	1998 Apr	1999 Apr	2000 Apr
Maternity benefit:													
Maternity allowances for insured women													
Higher rate[6]	KOSN	–	–	–	–	–	–	52.50	54.55	55.70	57.70	59.55	60.20
Lower rate[7]	KJNL	33.20	35.70	40.60	42.25	43.75	44.55	45.55	47.35	48.35	50.10	51.70	52.25
Death grant[2]	KJNM	–	–	–	–	–	–	–	–	–	–	–	–
Guardian's allowance	KJNN	8.95	9.65	10.70	10.85	10.95	11.00	11.05	11.15	11.20	11.30	11.35	11.35
Widow's benefit:													
Widow's pension	KJNO	43.60	46.90	52.00	54.15	56.10	57.60	58.85	61.15	62.45	64.70	66.75	67.50
Widowed mother's allowance	KJNP	43.60	46.90	52.00	54.15	56.10	57.60	58.85	61.15	62.45	64.70	66.75	67.50
Addition for each child	KJNQ	8.95	9.65	10.70	10.85	10.95	11.00	11.05	11.15	11.20	11.30	11.35	11.35
Retirement pension:[3]													
Single person	KJNR	43.60	46.90	52.00	54.15	56.10	57.60	58.85	61.15	62.45	64.70	66.75	67.50
Married couple	KJNS	69.80	75.10	83.25	86.70	89.80	92.10	94.10	97.75	99.80	103.40	106.70	107.90
Non-contributory retirement pension:													
Man or woman	KJNT	26.20	28.20	31.25	32.55	33.70	34.50	35.25	36.60	37.35	38.70	39.95	40.40
Married woman	KJNU	15.65	16.85	18.70	19.45	20.15	20.65	21.10	21.90	22.35	23.15	23.90	24.15
Industrial injuries benefit													
Injury benefit[5]	KJNV	–	–	–	–	–	–	–	–	–	–	–	–
Disablement pension at 100 per cent rate	KJNW	71.20	76.60	84.90	88.40	91.60	93.20	95.30	99.00	101.10	104.70	108.10[13]	109.30
Widow's or widower's pension	KJNX	43.60	46.90	52.00	54.15	56.10	57.60	58.85	61.15	62.45	..	..	..
Increase for dependants:[4]													
Adult	KJNY	21.40	23.05	25.55	26.60	27.55	28.05	28.65	29.75	–	–	..	..
Each child	KJNZ	–	–	–	–	–	–	–	–	–	–	..	..
Child benefit:[8]													
First child	KJOA	7.25	7.25	8.25	9.65	10.00	10.20	10.40	10.80	11.05	11.45	14.40	15.00
Subsequent children	KETZ	–	–	–	7.80	8.10	8.25	8.45	8.80	9.00	9.30	9.60	10.00
Family Credit[9,10,11] (maximum awards payable):[1]													
Families with 1 child													
Birth to September following 11th birthday	KJOB	40.90	44.60	48.00	51.40	53.25	55.15	56.50	58.20	59.70	61.15	64.95	..
From September following 11th birthday to September following 16th birthday	KJOC	46.50	50.50	54.40	58.25	60.35	62.45	64.00	65.90	67.60	69.25	70.70	..
From September following 16th birthday to day before 19th birthday	KJOD	49.95	54.15	58.35	62.45	64.70	67.00	68.55	70.60	72.45	74.20	75.95	..
Increase for each additional child													
Birth to September following 11th birthday	KJOF	7.30	8.25	9.70	10.40	10.75	11.15	11.40	11.75	12.05	12.35	15.15	..
From September following 11th birthday to September following 16th birthday	KJOG	12.90	14.15	16.10	17.25	17.85	18.45	18.90	19.45	19.95	20.45	20.90	..
From September following 16th birthday to day before 19th birthday	KJOH	16.35	17.80	20.05	21.45	22.20	23.00	23.45	24.15	24.80	25.40	25.95	..
War pension:													
Ex-private (100 per cent assessment)	KJOJ	71.20	76.60	84.90	89.00	97.20	98.90	101.10	105.00	107.20	111.10	114.70	116.00
War widow	KJOK	56.65	60.95	67.60	70.35	72.90	74.70	76.35	79.35	81.00	83.90	86.60	87.55
Single householder:[12]													
Ordinary rate	KJON	–	–	–	–	–	–	–	–	–	–	..	..
Long-term rate	KJOO	–	–	–	–	–	–	–	–	–	–	..	..

1 Maximum award does not include the 30 hour credit.
2 Death grant is not payable in respect of the death of a person who on 4 July 1948 was aged 65 or over (men) and 60 or over (women). This benefit was abolished from April 1987 and replaced by payments from Social Fund.
3 Retirement pensioners over 80 receive 25p addition.
4 An allowance for one adult dependent is payable, where appropriate, with unemployment benefit, sickness benefit, retirement pension, injury benefit and maternity allowance. Allowances for dependent children are payable with any of these benefits. Changes in these increases take effect from the same date as the main benefit.
5 Injury benefit ceased on 6 April 1983.
6 Following an EU Directive employees' maternity benefit is aligned with the state benefit they would receive if off work sick.

7 Women who are either not employed or self employed will receive the lower rate.
8 From October 1991 first child receives £9.25 and each subsequent child £7.50.
9 Family credit superseded Family Income Supplement from April 1988.
10 Age bandings for children's personal allowances have been revised from 7 April 1997. Some children have protected rights. Rates are as follows: Age 11 before 7 October 1997 £20.45, age 16 before 7 October 1997 £25.40 and age 18 before 7 October 1997 £35.55.
11 Family Credit was replaced by Working Families Tax Credit in October 1999.
12 Including any single person who is directly responsible for rent.
13 Figure has been revised.

Source: Department of Social Security: 0191 225 7373

10.3 Weekly rates of principal social security benefits
Great Britain

continued

£

		1989 Apr	1990 Apr	1991 Apr	1992 Apr	1993 Apr	1994 Apr	1995 Apr	1996 Apr	1997 Apr	1998 Apr	1999 Apr	2000 Apr
Non-householder aged:													
18 or over													
Ordinary rate	KJOP	–	–	–	–	–	–	–	–	–	–	–	–
Long-term rate	KJOQ	–	–	–	–	–	–	–	–	–	–	–	–
16-17													
Ordinary rate	KJOR	–	–	–	–	–	–	–	–	–	–	–	–
Long-term rate	KEUZ	–	–	–	–	–	–	–	–	–	–	–	–
Increase for children aged:													
11-15	KJOS	–	–	–	–	–	–	–	–	–	–	–	–
Under 10	KJOV	–	–	–	–	–	–	–	–	–	–	–	–
Income Support:													
Personal allowances[1]													
Single													
aged 16-17 either	KJOW	20.80	21.90	23.65[2]	25.55	26.45	27.50	28.00	28.85	29.60	30.30	30.95	31.45
or depending on their													
circumstances	KABS	–	28.80	31.15[3]	33.60	34.80	36.15	36.80	37.90	38.90	39.85	40.70	41.35
aged 18-24	KJOX	27.40	28.80	31.15	33.60	34.80	36.15	36.80	37.90	38.90	39.85	40.70	41.35
aged 25 or over	KJOY	34.90	36.70	39.65	42.45	44.00	45.70	46.50	47.90	49.15	50.35	51.40	52.20
Couple													
both aged under 18[6]	KJOZ	41.60	43.80	47.30	50.60	52.40	54.55	55.55	57.20	58.70	60.10	61.90	..
one or both 18 or over	KJPA	54.80	57.60	62.25	66.60	69.00	71.70	73.00	75.20	77.15	79.00	80.65	81.95
Lone parent													
aged 16-17 either	KJPB	20.80	21.90	23.65	25.55	26.45	27.50	28.00	28.85	29.60	30.30	30.95	31.45
or depending on their													
circumstances	KABT	..	28.80	31.15[3]	33.60	34.80	36.15	36.80	37.90	38.90	39.85	40.70	41.35
aged 18 or over	KJPC	34.90	36.70	39.65	42.45	44.00	45.70	46.50	47.90	49.15	50.35	51.40	52.20
Dependant children and young people[5]													
aged under 11	KJPD	11.75	12.35	13.35[4]	14.55	15.05	15.65	15.95	16.45	–	–	..	..
aged 11-15	KJPE	17.35	18.25	19.75	21.40	22.15	23.00	23.40	24.10	–	–	..	..
aged 16-17	KJPF	20.80	21.90	23.65	25.65	26.45	27.50	28.00	28.85	–	–	..	..
aged 18	KABU	27.40	28.80	31.15	33.60	34.80	36.15	36.80	37.90	–	–	..	..
Birth to September following 11th birthday	KXDQ	..	..	..	..	..	..	..	..	16.90	17.30	20.20	
From September following 11th birthday to September following 16th birthday	ZBXM KXDR	..	..	..	..	..	..	..	..	24.75	25.35	25.90	26.60
From September following 16th birthday to day before 19th birthday	KXDS	..	..	..	..	..	..	..	..	29.60	30.30	30.95	31.75

1 In addition to personal allowances a claimant may also be entitled to premium(s). The types of premium are family, lone parent, pensioner, higher pensioner, disability, severe disability and disabled child.
2 From October 1991 the rate is £23.90.
3 From October 1991 the rate is £31.40.
4 From October 1991 each rate increases by 25p.

5 Age bandings for childrens personal allowances have been revised from 7 April 1997. Some children have protected rights. 1997 rates are as follows: age 11 before 7 April 1997 £24.75, age 16 before 7 April 1997 £29.60 and age 18 before 7 April 1997 £38.90. Rates for 1998: age 11 before 7 April 1997 £25.35, age 16 before 7 April 1997 £30.30 and age 18 before 7 April 1997 £39.85.
6 From 12 April 1999 the personal allowance for couples where both members not yet 18 or one of the couple is aged 18 or over depends on the couple's circumstances. They may be entitled to a couple allowance or a single persons allowance dependant on certain criteria.

Source: Department of Social Security: 0191 225 7373

10.4 National Insurance contributions

	Employee's standard contributions (%)[1]		Employer's standard contributions (%)[1]	
	not contracted-out rate ·	contracted-out rate[2]	not contracted-out rate	contracted-out rate[3]
Class 1				
Weekly earnings				
1995/96				
Below 58.00 (LEL)	-	-	-	-
58.00-104.99	2% on first £58.00;	2% on first £58.00;	3.00	-
105.00-149.99	10% on balance	8.2% on balance	5.00	2.00
150.00-204.99			7.00	4.00
205.00-440.00			10.20	7.20
Above 440.00 (UEL)	£39.36	£32.48	10.20	10.20
1996/97				
Below 61.00 (LEL)	-	-	-	-
61.00-109.99	2% on first £61.00;	2% on first £61.00;	3.00	-
110.00-154.99	10% on balance	8.2% on balance	5.00	2.00
155.00-209.99			7.00	4.00
210.00-455.00			10.20	7.20
Above 440.00 (UEL)	£39.36	£32.48	10.20	10.20
1997/98				
Below 62.00 (LEL)	-	-	-	-
62.00-109.99	2% on first £62.00;	2% on first £62.00;	3.00	-
110.00-154.99	10% on balance	8.4% on balance	5.00	2.00
155.00-209.99			7.00	4.00
216.00-465.00			10.00	7.00
Above 455.00 (LEL)	£41.54	£35.09	10.00	10.00
1998/99				
Below 64.00 (LEL)	-	-	-	-
64.00-109.99	2% on first £64.00;	2% on first £64.00;	3.00	-
110.00-154.99	10% on balance	8.4% on balance	5.00	2.00
155.00-209.99			7.00	4.00
210.00-485.00			10.00	7.00
Above 485.00 (UEL)	£43.38	£36.64	10.00	10.00
1999/2000				
Below 66.00 (LEL)	-	-	-	-
66.00-83.00	10.0%	8.4%		
83.00-500.00	10.0%	8.4%	12.2	9.2
Above 500.00 (UEL)	£43.40	£36.46	12.2	12.2
2000/01				
Below 67.00 (LEL)	-	-	-	-
67.00-76.00 (PT)	-	See note 4	-	See note 5
76.00-84.00 (ST)	10.0%		-	
84.00-535.00 (UEL)	10.0%		12.2	
Above 535.00 (UEL)	£45.90	£38.41	12.2	12.2

	1995/96	1996/97	1997/98	1998/99	1999/00	2000/01
Class 2						
Flat rate weekly	£5.75	£6.05	£6.15	£6.35	£6.55	£2.00
Small earnings exception[6] (per annum)	£3,260	£3,430	£3,480	£3,590	£3,770	£3,825
Class 3						
Flat-rate voluntary weekly contributions	£5.65	£5.95	£6.05	£6.25	£6.45	£6.55
Class 4 (Self-employed; profit-related)						
Rate on profits between LPL and UPL	7.3%	6.0%	6.0%	6.0%	6.0%	7.0%
Lower profits limit (LPL)	£6,640	£6,860	£7,010	£7,310	£7,530	£4,385
Upper profits limit (UPL)	£22,880	£23,660	£24,180	£25,220	£26,000	£27,820

1 Married women opting to pay contributions at the reduced rate (3.85%) earn no entitlement to contributory National Insurance benefits as a result of these contributions. No women have been allowed to exercise this option since 1977, but around 200,000 women who have been continually married or widowed and in the labour market since that time have retained their right to pay the reduced rate.

2 The contracted-out rebate for employees' contributions is applied only between LEL and UEL. Earnings below LEL are charged at the appropriate not contracted-out rate (which depends on total earnings). Earnings above the UEL are not subject to employee NICs.

3 The rates shown only apply to Contracted-Out Salary Related schemes. (COSR). Earnings below the LEL and above the UEL are charged at the appropriate not-contracted out rate. The employers' contracted-out rate applies only between the LEL and the UEL.

4 The contracted-out rebate for primary contributions in 2000/01 is 1.6 per cent of earnings between the LEL and the UEL for all forms of contracting-out.

5 The contracted-out rebate for secondary contributions is 3 per cent of earnings between the LEL and the UEL.

6 If earnings from self-employment are below this annual limit and the contributor applies for and is granted a small earnings exception Class 2 contributions need not be paid. Class 2 or 3 contributions may be paid voluntarily.

Source: Board of Inland Revenue: 020 7438 4335

10.5 Social Security Acts: number of persons receiving benefit[1]
Great Britain
At any one time

Thousands

		1990	1991	1992	1993	1994	1995	1996	1997	1998	1999	2000
Persons receiving:												
Unemployment benefit[10]	KJHA	331.4	569.5	685.2	671.9	553.5	426.5	397.8	–	–	–	–
Jobseeker's allowance[23]	JYXM	..	..	..	..	..	..	..	1 406.3	1 181.2	1 105.8[26]	972.7[26]
Sickness and Invalidity benefit[2,3]	KJHB	1 312.3	1 415.6	1 577.3	1 727.0	1 808.6	1 894.1	–	–	–	_[27]	_[27]
Incapacity benefit[16,17]	KXDT	..	..	..	..	..	..	1 812.8	1 749.2	1 671.2	1 557.1[27]	1 504.3[27]
Attendance allowance[19,24]	KXDU	871.0	957.0	1 092.0	945.0	1 018.0	1 109.0	1 161.0	1 229.0	1 276.0	1 297.0	..
Mobility allowance[20]	KXDV	615	659	718	–	–	–	–	–	–	_[27]	_[27]
Disability living allowance[21,24]	KXDW	–	–	–	1 187.0	1 376.0	1 579.0	1 786.0	1 963.0	2 099.0	2 167.0[27]	..[27]
Guardians' allowances[25]	KJHE	1.8	1.9	1.9	2.0	2.1	2.1	2.2	2.3	2.3	2.3[27]	2.5[27]
Widows' benefits[4]	KJHF	365.2	362.3	351.0	345.3	335.0	323.1	311.6	284.6	277.6	263.7[27]	261.0[27]
National Insurance retirement pensions[3]:												
Males	KJHH	3 553.9	3 512.8	3 613.7	3 623.6	3 657.5	3 728.7	3 836.6	3 926.7	4 010.6	4 015.3[27]	4 039.4[27]
Females	KJHL	6 625.7	6 515.3	6 683.0	6 680.0	6 727.1	6 777.2	6 948.5	6 983.2	7 031.1	6 925.4[27]	6 928.0[27]
Total	KJHG	10 179.6	10 028.1	10 296.8	10 303.6	10 384.7	10 505.9	10 785.1	10 909.9	11 041.9	10 940.7[27]	10 967.4[27]
Non-contributory retirement pensions[3]:												
Males	KJHI	6.7	6.1	6.1	6.1	6.1	6.5	6.1	5.9	5.7	5.1[27]	5.2[27]
Females	KJHJ	29.4	25.3	25.7	24.9	24.1	24.5	23.5	22.5	21.3	18.7[27]	18.3[27]
Total	KJHK	36.0	31.4	31.8	31.0	30.2	31.0	29.6	28.3	27.0	23.8[27]	23.4[27]
Industrial Injuries disablement pensions assessments[5,24]	KJHN	196.3	200.3	204.3	212.4	225.6[15]	235.2	249.2	257.8[15]	269.1[15]	272.0[28]	..[28]
Reduced earnings allowance/ Retirement allowance assessments[5]	KEYC	160.0	163.7	159.7	156.0	154.3[15]	152.1	154.9	155.6[15]	152.8[15]	152.2[28]	..[28]
Child benefit[3]												
Families receiving benefit[26]	KJHO	6 732.0	6 805.0	7 078.3	6 913.0	6 954.7	6 996.0	7 024.1	6 956.1	6 976.1	6 989.4[28]	7 107.8[28]
Family income supplement	KJHP	–	–	–	–	–	–	–	–	–	–	..
Family Credit[6]	ZCGF	315	347	397	488	551	608	693	748	767	791	..
Supplementary benefits[7]	KJHQ	–	–	–	–	–	–	–	–	–	–	–
Income Support[7]	KABV	4 376.0	5 683.0	5 292.9	5 858.4	5 693.7	5 670.2	5 548.9	3 958.1	3 853.1	3 814.4	3 810.5
Housing Benefit and Council Tax Benefit[8]												
Rent rebate[11]	KABY	2 928.1	2 944.0	3 033.9	3 052.5	3 016.1	2 964.3	2 898.3	2 792.7	2 664.1	2 518.5	2 287.8
Rent allowance[11,18]	KABZ	1 067.2	1 082.4	1 291.6	1 480.6	1 633.9	1 770.1	1 877.6	1 847.5	1 810.6	1 794.6	1 745.7
Rate rebate[12]	KACA	..	..	..	..	..	..	..	..	..	..	..
Community charge benefit[9,12]	KACB	6 518.4	6 290.7	6 563.9	..	..	..	..	..	..	..	..
Community charge rebate[9,12]	KEZU	..	..	..	..	..	..	..	..	..	..	..
Council tax benefit[13,14]	KJPO	..	..	..	5 251.8	5 496.5	5 623.9	5 611.2	5 500.3	5 325.7	5 166.1	4 829.6
War pensions[3]	KJHR	248.0	249.6	260.1	292.9	309.2	315.4	327.5	320.7	302.0	306.0	295.7

1 Caseload counts at a specific date in the year which varies from benefit to benefit.

2 A relatively small number of claims do not result in the payment of benefit but are included here because they indicate notified incapacity for work.

3 Includes overseas cases.

4 Excluding widows' allowances paid during the first twenty-six weeks of widowhood. The number of such allowances does not exceed 35 000 in a six month period. Widows' allowance was replaced by widows' payment on 11 April 1988.

5 Industrial injuries disablement pension, reduced earnings allowance retirement allowance assessments starting 1 October up to 1986/87: first Monday in April thereafter.

6 Family Income Supplement was replaced by Family Credit from April 1988. Family Credit was replaced by Working Families' Tax Credit from October 1999.

7 From April 1988 Supplementary Benefit was replaced by Income Support. From 9 October 1996 Income Support for the unemployed was replaced by Income-based Jobseeker's Allowance. Figures in this table up to and including 1996 include unemployed Income Support claimants. Figures from 1997 exclude unemployed who will be counted in the Jobseeker's Allowance claims.

8 Data prior to 1988 is not available.

9 Claimants with partners are treated as one recipient.

10 Figures are given at May each year.

11 The housing benefit scheme was reformed in April 1988.

12 Rate rebate in Scotland was replaced by community charge rebate (CCR) in April 1989. In April 1990 rate rebate in England and Wales, and CCR in Scotland was replaced by Community Charge Benefit.

13 Community Charge Benefit was replaced by Council Tax Benefit in April 1993.

14 Excluding Second Adult Rebate Claims.

15 Includes an allowance for late returns.

16 Incapacity Benefit replaced Sickness Benefit and Invalidity Benefit from 13 April 1995.

17 Incapacity Benefit figures are taken at the last day in February.

18 Rent Allowance figures include housing association tenants.

19 Attendance Allowance figures are based at 31 March until 1995 then at the end of February.

20 Mobility Allowance figures are based at 31 December until 1991 and then 31 March 1992.

21 Disability Living Allowance figures are based at the end of February each year.

22 Figures provided by the Child Benefit Centre Management Information Statistics as a new scan is being developed.

23 Jobseeker's Allowance introduced 7 October 1996, replacing unemployment benefit.

24 Figure for 1998 has been revised.

25 Figure for 1999 as at May 2000.

26 Figure for 1999 as at November.

27 Figure for 1999 as at September. Figure for 2000 as at March.

28 Figure for 1999 as at November. Figure for 2000 as at August.

Source: Department of Social Security: 0191 225 7373

10.6 Unemployed benefit/jobseekers allowance claimants analysed by benefit entitlement

Great Britain at any one time

Thousands

		Jobseekers Allowance November[1] 1996	Jobseekers Allowance May 1997	Jobseekers Allowance May 1998	Jobseekers Allowance May 1999	Jobseekers Allowance May 2000
All Persons						
All with benefit - total	KXDX	1 643.2	1 406.3	1 181.2	1 105.2	972.7
Contribution-based JSA only	KXDY	293.5	181.1	154.2	158.2	148.2
Contribution based JSA & income-based JSA	KXDZ	41.5	28.3	23.5	27.1	19.0
Income-based JSA only payment	KXEA	1 308.2	1 196.8	1 003.6	920.4	805.5
No benefit in payment	KXEB	158.7	156.2	114.5	118.7	94.6
Total	KXEC	1 801.9	1 562.4	1 295.8	1 224.5	1 067.3
Males						
All with benefit - total	KXED	1 264.8	1 096.9	918.2	862.3	755.0
Contribution-based JSA only	KXEE	189.6	119.5	101.6	109.0	104.2
Contribution based JSA & income-based JSA	KXEF	37.1	25.4	20.7	24.4	17.2
Income-based JSA only payment	KXEG	1 038.1	952.0	795.9	728.9	633.6
No benefit in payment	KXEH	105.6	106.8	75.5	79.2	63.4
Total	KXEI	1 370.4	1 203.7	993.7	941.5	818.4
Females						
All with benefit - total	KXEJ	378.5	309.4	263.0	243.4	217.7
Contribution-based JSA only	KXEK	104.0	61.6	52.6	49.2	44.0
Contribution based JSA & income-based JSA	KXEL	4.5	3.0	2.8	2.7	1.8
Income-based JSA only payment	KXEM	270.0	244.8	207.7	191.5	171.9
No benefit in payment	KXEN	53.0	49.4	39.1	39.5	31.2
Total	KXEO	431.5	358.8	302.1	283.0	248.9

1 Jobseeker's Allowance replaced Unemployment Benefit and Income Support for unemployed claimants on 7 October 1996. It is a unified benefit with two routes of entry: contribution-based which depends mainly upon national insurance contributions and income-based which depends mainly upon a means test. Some claimants can qualify by either route. In practice they receive income-based JSA but have underlying entitlement to the contribution-based element.

2 Figures quoted as at May of each year apart from 1996 which is November.

Source: Department of Social Security: 0191 225 7373

10.6

Unemployed benefit/jobseekers allowance claimants analysed by benefit entitlement

continued

Great Britain at any one time

Thousands

		Unemployment Benefit[1,3]										
		1985	1986	1987	1988	1989	1990	1991	1992	1993	1994	1995
All Persons												
Unemployment benefit in payment - total	KJIB	872.0	955.0	676.0	521.6	304.4	356.1	641.7	671.1	598.3	471.6	386.5
Unemployment benefit only	KJIC	679.0	768.0	549.0	402.2	220.3	294.0	520.2	548.3	495.6	333.6	266.3
Unemployment benefit and Income Support[2]	KJIF	193.0	187.0	127.0	119.3	82.1	62.0	121.5	122.8	102.7	138.0	120.2
Income Support only in payment[2]	KJIG	1 690.0	1 715.0	1 407.0	1 143.0	995.5	1 044.4	1 464.0	1 746.8	1 823.1	1 714.2	1 515.0
Neither Unemployment benefit nor Income Support in payment[2]	KJIH	461.0	500.0	425.0	347.3	252.0	2 529.0	306.6	374.2	316.9	250.1	215.7
Total	KJIA	3 023.0	3 170.0	2 508.0	2 012.8	1 551.9	1 653.3	2 412.3	2 792.1	2 738.3	2 435.9	2 117.1
Males												
Unemployment benefit in payment - total	KJIJ	541.0	596.0	442.0	328.2	200.5	254.1	472.1	488.4	425.8	326.0	265.4
Unemployment benefit only	KJIK	375.0	435.0	331.0	227.5	128.9	197.3	362.0	378.6	335.3	212.8	168.2
Unemployment benefit and Income Support[2]	KJIN	166.0	161.0	111.0	100.7	71.6	56.9	110.1	109.8	90.5	113.1	97.3
Income Support only in payment[2]	KJIO	1 281.0	1 308.0	1 140.0	886.0	778.2	825.4	1 171.7	1 410.3	1 465.1	1 366.3	1 198.8
Neither Unemployment benefit nor Income Support in payment[2]	KJIP	252.0	275.0	279.0	209.9	157.6	166.8	205.3	255.3	215.2	167.0	144.5
Total	KJII	2 074.0	2 179.0	1 861.0	1 424.1	1 136.3	1 246.3	1 849.4	2 154.0	2 106.1	1 859.2	1 608.7
Females												
Unemployment benefit in payment - total	KJIR	331.0	359.0	250.0	278.0	1 039.0	101.9	169.7	182.7	172.6	145.8	121.1
Unemployment benefit only	KJIS	304.0	333.0	231.0	174.8	92.5	96.8	158.1	169.8	160.4	120.8	98.2
Unemployment benefit and Income Support[2]	KJIV	27.0	26.0	19.0	18.6	11.5	5.1	11.5	12.9	12.2	25.0	22.9
Income Support only in payment[2]	KJIW	409.0	407.0	354.0	258.0	217.3	219.0	291.9	336.5	358.0	347.9	316.2
Neither Unemployment benefit nor Income Support in payment[2]	KJIX	209.0	225.0	184.0	138.3	95.4	86.1	101.4	119.0	101.8	83.1	71.2
Total	KJIQ	949.0	991.0	788.0	588.7	416.7	407.0	562.9	638.1	632.4	576.7	508.4

1 Figures actually at November.
2 Income Support replaced Supplementary Benefit from April 1988.
3 Unemployment Benefit and Income Support for unemployed claimants were replaced by Jobseeker's Allowane on 7 October 1996.

Source: Department of Social Security: 0191 225 7373

10.7 Sickness benefit, invalidity benefit and incapacity benefit
Claimants analysed by age and duration of spell

Great Britain at end of statistical year[1]

Thousands

		1989	1990	1991	1992	1993	1994	1995[3]	1996	1997	1998	1999
Age at 31 March[2]												
Males												
All durations: All ages	KJJA	1 011.3	1 085.8	1 187.1	1 327.1	1 468.0	1 544.4	1 629.9	1 627.0	1 577.9	1 530.1	1 458.4
Under 20	KJJB	4.8	5.9	5.7	6.2	7.1	6.8	7.8	8.7	8.8	10.7	10.7
20-29	KJJC	46.4	49.0	61.3	75.7	86.2	97.2	106.0	119.3	118.8	119.1	115.0
30-39	KJJD	77.6	83.2	101.3	125.2	145.7	160.4	189.7	202.6	208.5	216.6	217.6
40-49	KJJE	142.5	154.6	169.5	194.5	228.1	245.2	260.4	274.3	272.4	271.4	271.0
50-59	KJJF	304.5	326.8	347.9	386.6	426.1	441.7	468.7	475.4	473.4	474.1	467.3
60-64	KJJG	283.5	289.3	299.8	319.7	344.7	356.6	362.5	352.1	349.7	344.2	336.0
65 and over	KJJH	152.0	177.0	201.6	219.2	230.1	236.5	234.8	194.6	146.2	94.0	40.7
Over six months: All ages	KJJI	865.6	940.7	1 024.0	1 148.5	1 273.8	1 361.5	1 442.1	1 440.9	1 385.7	1 349.2	1 287.0
Under 20	KJJJ	1.70	2.20	1.80	2.90	2.80	2.90	3.00	3.90	3.60	4.70	4.90
20-29	KJJK	26.5	29.6	37.7	50.2	59.6	65.7	74.3	86.4	83.1	84.5	81.4
30-39	KJJL	57.8	62.5	71.3	94.5	112.9	126.5	152.1	165.1	166.8	177.2	181.2
40-49	KJJM	114.0	122.0	138.1	159.6	184.8	208.6	219.7	235.9	232.3	234.0	237.6
50-59	KJJN	256.0	283.7	300.8	331.7	367.2	389.2	418.2	426.5	423.8	428.2	423.8
60-64	KJJO	258.3	264.4	273.2	291.1	317.1	332.6	340.2	329.7	330.4	326.8	317.6
65 and over	KJJP	151.3	176.3	201.1	218.5	229.4	236.0	234.6	193.3	145.6	93.7	40.6
Females												
All durations: All ages	KJJQ	381.2	432.3	491.2	570.2	646.1	704.7	776.5	779.1	795.1	810.8	815.5
Under 20	KJJR	8.0	8.0	9.1	9.3	9.5	11.0	12.0	12.5	12.3	13.0	14.1
20-29	KJJS	46.6	52.8	56.1	70.8	75.9	74.9	79.4	88.6	89.0	87.8	85.3
30-39	KJJT	61.6	66.8	73.0	86.7	95.5	108.5	122.4	134.6	137.6	144.7	149.4
40-49	KJJU	92.0	103.9	120.4	140.6	162.6	176.0	200.7	201.9	206.5	209.7	217.2
50-59	KJJV	148.0	168.8	192.7	213.1	244.6	266.6	290.7	285.1	303.3	323.1	333.2
60 and over	KJJW	25.0	32.0	39.9	49.7	58.0	67.7	71.3	56.3	46.4	32.5	16.3
Over six months: All ages	KJJX	307.3	353.6	415.4	483.1	552.9	611.4	673.1	672.9	686.6	701.7	707.9
Under 20	KJJY	2.3	3.0	3.9	3.4	3.6	4.7	4.2	6.2	4.8	5.7	6.1
20-29	KJJZ	29.0	33.1	38.9	47.3	54.0	55.9	60.3	66.3	66.1	65.8	64.2
30-39	KJKA	48.0	52.8	57.7	70.5	79.3	92.3	103.2	113.2	117.5	120.9	126.3
40-49	KJKB	75.3	85.5	102.6	120.0	138.4	151.8	170.8	176.4	179.6	183.3	190.1
50-59	KJKC	128.5	148.3	173.0	193.0	220.8	239.9	263.7	256.6	273.1	294.1	305.2
60 and over	KJKD	24.2	30.9	39.3	48.9	56.8	66.8	70.9	54.3	45.4	31.9	16.0

Note Figures are based on a 1 per cent sample up to 1995 and 5% sample thereafter.

1 The end of the statistical year up to 1993/94 was the Saturday before the first Monday in April.

2 Until 1995/96 then at 1 March. From 1995/96 the duration is taken on the last day of February.

3 The statistical year for 1994/95 was extended to 12/4/95, the day before the introduction of the new Incapacity Benefit which replaced Sickness and In-validity Benefit from 13/4/95.

Source: Department of Social Security: 0191 225 7373

10.8 Sickness, invalidity and incapacity benefit: days of certified incapacity
Great Britain analysis by age at end of period[1]

Years starting on first Monday in April[4]

Millions

		1988 /89	1989 /90	1990 /91	1991 /92	1992 /93	1993 /94	1994[3] /95	1995 /96	1996 /97	1997 /98	1998 /99
Age at 31 March[2]												
Males: All ages	KJKH	304.9	327.5	356.0	402.7	445.5	468.8	507.9	596.2	576.3	563.5	538.6
Under 20	KJKI	1.3	1.4	1.6	1.7	1.5	1.6	1.8	3.4	3.1	3.5	3.7
20 - 29	KJKJ	12.9	13.8	16.9	21.6	24.5	27.0	30.4	43.7	42.4	43.2	41.7
30 - 39	KJKK	22.6	24.4	28.1	36.1	41.4	46.6	56.0	72.3	73.9	77.7	78.2
40 - 49	KJKL	41.9	44.8	49.2	57.1	64.6	72.7	78.9	98.5	98.5	97.7	97.6
50 - 59	KJKM	87.5	96.2	100.8	112.8	121.7	129.8	141.4	172.0	170.7	172.2	170.0
60 - 64	KJKN	84.4	85.3	89.3	96.1	102.4	107.3	112.6	127.9	127.8	126.7	124.3
65 and over	KJKO	54.3	61.5	70.1	77.4	80.4	83.9	86.8	78.4	59.9	41.7	23.0
Females: All ages	KJKP	112.4	127.6	147.0	170.8	190.7	211.4	237.5	279.5	285.8	292.8	294.8
Under 20	KJKQ	1.8	2.2	2.3	2.2	2.1	2.4	2.6	4.8	4.1	4.4	4.5
20 - 29	KJKR	13.7	15.2	16.7	19.7	22.1	22.1	23.9	31.9	32.0	32.1	31.3
30 - 39	KJKS	18.8	20.1	21.7	25.6	28.5	32.7	37.6	48.0	49.8	51.4	53.4
40 - 49	KJKT	26.7	29.7	34.9	41.2	46.6	51.5	58.9	72.1	74.0	75.8	77.1
50 - 59	KJKU	42.5	49.0	56.7	63.8	71.3	79.1	88.4	101.0	107.5	115.3	120.0
60 and over	KJKV	9.0	11.5	14.6	18.2	20.1	23.6	26.1	21.7	18.4	13.8	8.4

1 The end of the statistical year up to 1993/94 was the Saturday before the first Monday in April.

2 Until 1995/96 then at 1 March.

3 The statistical year for 1994/95 was extended to 12/4/95, the day before the introduction of the new Incapacity Benefit which replaced Sickness and In-validity Benefit from 13/4/95.

4 Up to and including 1994/95 years start first Monday in April. The 1995/96 year started 13 April and ended 31 March. From 1996/97 years start 1 March.

Source: Department of Social Security: 0191 225 7373

10.9 Widows' benefit (excluding widows' allowance: widows' payment[1])
Great Britain
Number in payment analysed by type of benefit and age of widow

Thousands

		September										
		1990	1991	1992	1993	1994	1995	1996	1997	1998	1999	2000[3]
All widows' benefit (excluding widows' allowance)												
All ages	KJGA	365.2	357.2	351.0	345.3	335.0	323.1	311.6	293.2	277.6	263.7	261.0
Under 30	KJGB	2.4	2.1	2.1	2.0	1.9	1.6	1.4	1.2	1.1	1.6	1.5
30 - 39	KJGC	16.2	15.5	15.9	15.0	14.5	13.9	13.5	13.0	12.3	10.8	11.0
40 - 49	KJGD	63.7	61.0	57.8	56.0	53.0	52.8	50.1	44.9	41.3	38.5	38.1
50 - 59	KJGE	239.6	230.8	224.2	219.9	216.7	206.9	202.5	197.3	187.7	181.8	182.2
60 and over	KJGF	43.3	47.7	51.1	52.5	48.8	47.8	44.0	36.8	35.2	31.1	28.4
Widowed mothers' allowance - with dependant children												
All ages	KJGG	54.4	52.4	53.2	53.2	53.3	52.8	51.7	49.5	47.1	44.9	47.0
Under 30	KJGH	2.3	2.0	2.0	1.9	1.7	1.6	1.4	1.2	1.1	1.6	1.4
30 - 39	KJGI	14.5	14.1	14.5	13.8	13.9	13.3	12.9	12.4	11.8	10.4	10.6
40 - 49	KJGJ	25.7	25.3	25.8	27.1	26.9	27.5	26.7	24.6	33.3	22.5	23.3
50 - 59	KJGK	11.5	10.8	10.6	10.2	10.7	10.1	10.2	10.7	10.5	10.3	11.6
60 and over	KJGL	0.3	0.2	0.2	0.2	0.2	0.4	0.3	0.3	0.2	0.2	0.2
Widowed mothers' allowance - without dependant children												
All ages	KJGM	17.8	14.2	10.7	8.3	6.7	6.2	5.6	4.6	3.4	3.1	2.9
Under 30	KJGN	0.1	0.2	0.1	–	0.1	0.1	–	–	–	–	–
30 - 39	KJGO	1.8	1.6	1.3	1.1	0.8	0.6	0.6	0.5	0.5	0.4	0.4
40 - 49	KJGP	8.0	6.4	5.1	3.9	3.4	3.3	2.8	2.3	1.9	1.4	1.2
50 - 59	KJGQ	7.8	5.8	4.0	2.9	2.2	1.9	2.1	1.7	1.0	1.2	1.1
60 and over	KJGR	0.3	0.3	0.2	0.2	0.2	0.1	0.1	0.1	–	0.1	0.1
Widows' pension												
All ages	KJGS	157.9	145.9	134.4	122.8	108.1	95.1	84.3	71.9	63.4	57.1	54.5
40 - 49	KJGT	–	–	–	–	–	–	–	–	–	–	–
50 - 59	KJGU	119.2	103.5	89.1	76.5	65.8	54.6	48.4	43.0	37.1	35.7	35.6
60 and over	KJGV	38.6	42.6	45.3	46.3	42.1	40.5	36.0	28.9	26.3	21.4	18.9
Age-related widows' pension[2]												
All ages	KJGW	135.0	144.6	152.7	161.0	166.9	168.9	170.0	167.1	163.7	158.6	156.6
40 - 49	KJGX	30.0	29.2	27.0	25.0	22.7	21.9	20.4	17.8	16.0	14.6	13.5
50 - 59	KJGY	100.9	110.8	120.4	130.3	137.9	140.2	141.9	141.6	139.0	134.6	133.8
60 and over	KJGZ	4.0	4.6	5.2	5.7	6.3	6.8	7.6	7.6	8.7	9.4	9.3

1 This is an especially high rate of benefit which is payable for the first 26 weeks of widowhood, provided that the widow is under pensionable age (age 60) or, if she is over that age, provided that her husband was not entitled to retirement pension. Widows' allowance was replaced by widows' payment on 11.4.88.

2 Figures for widows' basic pension are included in age-related widows' pension.
3 Figures as at March.

Source: Department of Social Security: 0191 225 7874

10.10 Child benefits
Great Britain
At 31 December

Thousands

		1990	1991	1992	1993	1994	1995	1996	1997[1]	1998[1]	1999[2]	2000[3]
Families receiving allowances:												
Total	KJMU	6 732	6 805	7 079	6 913	6 955	6 996	7 024	6 956	6 976	6 989	7 108
With 1 child	KJMV	2 877	2 898	2 986	2 920	2 941	2 970	2 983	..	..	3 007	3 037
2 children	KJMW	2 713	2 733	2 829	2 773	2 781	2 784	2 794	..	..	2 759	2 815
3 children	KJMX	854	879	934	908	920	928	929	..	..	916	938
4 children	KJMY	215	221	–	231	228	231	236	..	..	231	238
5 or more children	KJMZ	73	75	–	81	84	84	82	..	..	76	80

1 Figures provided by Child Benefit Centre Management Information Statistics as a new scan is being developed.
2 Figures for 1999 are at November.
3 Figures for 2000 are at August.

Source: Department of Social Security: 0191 225 7373

10.11 Contributory and non-contributory retirement pensions
Great Britain
Numbers in payment analysed by age-group[1]

Thousands (percentages in italics)

		At 30 September										
		1990	1991	1992	1993	1994	1995	1996	1997	1998	1999	2000[2]
Men:												
Age-groups:												
65-69	KJSB	1 163.8	1 124.6	1 095.5	1 063.9	1 053.6	1 079.1	1 142.5	1 200.5	1 249.9	1 267.9	1 288.8
Percentage	KJSC	*32.7*	*31.3*	*30.3*	*29.3*	*28.8*	*28.9*	*29.8*	*30.5*	*31.1*	*31.5*	*31.9*
70-74	KJSD	999.2	1 046.0	1 104.0	1 155.3	1 196.2	1 155.0	1 146.6	1 138.2	1 131.1	1 115.4	1 117.5
Percentage	KJSE	*28.1*	*29.1*	*30.5*	*31.8*	*32.7*	*31.0*	*29.9*	*28.9*	*28.2*	*27.7*	*27.6*
75-79	KJSF	761.4	761.7	738.5	706.3	681.8	748.8	787.3	831.3	876.6	889.3	867.4
Percentage	KJSG	*21.4*	*21.2*	*20.4*	*19.5*	*18.6*	*20.1*	*20.5*	*21.1*	*21.8*	*22.1*	*21.5*
80-84	KJSH	427.1	437.3	448.9	458.2	468.0	477.4	481.8	471.2	454.5	433.6	457.7
Percentage	KJSI	*12.0*	*12.2*	*12.4*	*12.6*	*12.8*	*12.8*	*12.6*	*12.0*	*11.3*	*10.8*	*11.3*
85-89	KJSJ	164.0	172.9	180.5	189.6	197.4	204.4	209.4	217.2	225.0	231.6	231.1
Percentage	KJSK	*4.6*	*4.8*	*5.0*	*5.2*	*5.4*	*5.5*	*5.5*	*5.5*	*5.6*	*5.8*	*5.7*
90 and over	KJSL	46.0	49.1	53.8	57.2	60.6	64.5	69.4	75.3	79.3	82.6	82.1
Percentage	KJSM	*1.3*	*1.4*	*1.5*	*1.6*	*1.7*	*1.7*	*1.8*	*1.9*	*2.0*	*2.1*	*2.0*
Total all ages	KJSA	3 560.5	3 591.5	3 621.3	3 630.4	3 657.5	3 729.2	3 837.0	3 933.8	4 016.3	4 020.4	4 044.6
Women:												
Age-groups:												
60-64	KJSO	1 138.7	1 124.2	1 121.1	1 099.1	1 090.6	1 094.3	1 200.6	1 245.0	1 296.2	1 310.5	1 332.2
Percentage	KJSP	*17.1*	*16.9*	*16.7*	*16.4*	*16.2*	*16.1*	*17.3*	*17.8*	*18.4*	*18.9*	*19.2*
65-69	KJSQ	1 533.3	1 484.6	1 472.7	1 447.0	1 436.6	1 437.6	1 461.2	1 458.9	1 442.8	1 398.8	1 396.5
Percentage	KJSR	*23.0*	*22.3*	*21.9*	*21.5*	*21.4*	*21.2*	*21.0*	*20.8*	*20.5*	*20.1*	*20.2*
70-74	KJSS	1 285.8	1 336.9	1 403.8	1 469.3	1 515.9	1 447.3	1 423.7	1 398.6	1 379.6	1 341.5	1 339.8
Percentage	KJST	*19.3*	*20.1*	*20.9*	*21.9*	*22.5*	*21.3*	*20.5*	*20.0*	*19.6*	*19.3*	*19.3*
75-79	KJSU	1 170.3	1 161.5	1 126.0	1 068.0	1 023.0	1 100.6	1 148.7	1 197.2	1 255.7	1 267.3	1 227.9
Percentage	KJSV	*17.6*	*17.5*	*16.8*	*15.9*	*15.2*	*16.2*	*16.5*	*17.1*	*17.8*	*18.3*	*17.7*
80-84	KJSW	855.6	864.2	868.0	873.9	882.0	892.9	888.4	861.0	814.6	762.9	786.4
Percentage	KJSX	*12.9*	*13.0*	*12.9*	*13.0*	*13.1*	*13.2*	*12.8*	*12.3*	*11.6*	*11.0*	*11.4*
85-89	KJSY	465.7	438.8	499.2	514.1	521.9	534.3	542.2	545.9	552.3	548.9	539.7
Percentage	KJSZ	*7.0*	*6.6*	*7.4*	*7.7*	*7.8*	*7.9*	*7.8*	*7.8*	*7.8*	*7.9*	*7.8*
90 and over	KJTA	205.7	219.1	231.0	244.9	256.8	271.9	285.3	300.4	311.4	314.1	305.5
Percentage	KJTB	*3.1*	*3.3*	*3.4*	*3.6*	*3.8*	*4.0*	*4.1*	*4.3*	*4.4*	*4.5*	*4.4*
Total all ages	KJSN	6 655.1	6 648.2	6 721.7	6 716.3	6 727.1	6 779.0	6 950.2	7 006.8	7 052.5	6 944.1	6 928.0

1 Including pensions payable to persons residing overseas.
2 Figures are at 31 March.

Source: Department of Social Security: 0191 225 7874

10.12 Family credit[1]
Great Britain
At 31 December

Thousands

		1991	1992	1993	1994	1995	1996	1997	1998	1999[2]
Families receiving payments:										
Total	KJTO	344.3	459.3	518.3	578.0	646.5	716.7	751.4	779.7	784.6
Two-parent families: total	KJTP	210.1	266.5	291.0	324.6	356.9	390.2	388.0	383.4	379.0
With 1 child	KJTQ	50.6	66.9	73.3	80.1	89.7	98.6	96.6	95.4	94.1
2 children	KJTR	76.1	100.4	110.1	122.4	135.1	146.1	144.4	141.7	139.9
3 children	KJTS	49.1	61.4	66.9	76.4	83.4	91.1	91.4	89.1	88.5
4 children	KJTT	21.7	24.9	27.0	31.0	32.9	37.2	37.8	39.0	38.7
5 children	KJTU	8.3	8.5	8.9	9.5	10.2	11.7	11.9	12.5	12.4
6 or more children	KJTV	4.4	4.5	4.8	5.3	5.5	5.5	5.9	5.8	5.5
One-parent families: total	KJTW	134.2	192.7	227.3	253.4	289.6	326.5	363.4	396.3	405.6
With 1 child	KJTX	72.7	100.1	117.8	133.8	152.2	170.4	189.3	203.4	207.3
2 children	KJTY	44.8	66.7	79.2	86.0	99.1	111.2	121.8	136.1	139.0
3 or more children	KJTZ	17.1	25.8	30.4	33.5	38.3	45.0	52.3	56.9	59.2

1 Family Credit was replaced by Working Families Tax Credit in October 1999.
2 1999 figures are as at 31 August.

Source: Department of Social Security: 0191 225 7373

Social protection

10.13 Income support: number of beneficiaries receiving weekly payment[1]
Great Britain

On a day in May

Thousands

		1992	1993	1994	1995	1996	1997[4]	1998[4]	1999[4]	2000[4]
All income support	KACC	3 259	3 561	3 689	3 889	3 963	3 958	3 853	3 814	3 811
All aged 60 and over	KACD	1 626	1 760	1 749	1 770	1 753	1 720	1 659	1 624	1 615
Retirement pensioners	KACE	1 318	1 426	1 407	1 417	1 404	1 383	1 338	1 308	1 305
In receipt of other NI benefit[2]	KACF	59	72	81	92	89	81	74	67	64
Others[5]	KACG	249	262	261	261	260	256	248	249	246
All under 60	KACH	1 633	1 801	1 940	2 120	2 211	2 238	2 194	2 190	2 196
Disabled with contributory benefit[2,5]	KACK	82	94	113	146	161	180	195	196	207
Disabled without contributory benefit[2,5]	KFBJ	327	402	481	570	604	646	685	718	755
Lone parent premium not in other groups[3]	KACL	938	988	1 017	1 040	1 044	1 013	961	936	910
Others	KACM	287	317	328	363	402	398	353	341	324

1 Data are extracted from the Annual Statistical Enquiry undertaken in May 1988, 1989 , 1990, 1991, 1992 and 1993, and the Quarterly Statistical Enquiries May 1994 to May 2000.
2 Contributory/NI benefits other than Retirement pension are Incapacity Benefit (previously IVB & Sickness Benefit), Widows Pension and Widowed Mothers Allowance.

3 Figures relate to one-parent families headed by a man or a woman, where the claimant is not receiving a pensioner or disability premium.
4 Figures exclude unemployed claimants who transferred to Jobseeker's Allowance from 7 October 1996.

Source: Department of Social Security: 0191 225 7373

10.14 Income support
Great Britain[1,2]

On a day in May

Thousands

		1992	1993	1994	1995	1996	1997	1998	1999	2000
Number of regular weekly payments	KACN	3 259	3 561	3 689	3 889	3 963	3 958	3 853	3 814	3 811
Total number of persons provided for	KACO	5 618	6 146	6 465	6 858	7 004	6 973	6 769	6 689	6 666
Number of dependants	KACP	1 984	2 147	2 296	2 440	2 494	2 464	2 379	2 344	2 317
Partners	KACQ	374	438	480	528	546	551	537	531	539
Total children under 16 years	KACR	1 869	2 020	2 156	2 292	2 340	2 303	2 224	2 188	2 158
Under 11	KACS	1 444	1 543	1 623	1 708	1 728	1 685	1 605	1 557	1 524
11 - 15 years	KACT	425	477	533	584	612	618	618	631	634
16 - 17 years	KACU	97	104	112	119	129	134	129	128	131
Other dependants										
18 years and over	KACV	18	24	28	28	25	28	26	28	28

1 Data are extracted from the Annual Statistical Enquiry undertaken in May 1992-1993 and the Quarterly Statistical Enquiries undertaken in May 1994 to May 2000.
2 Figures exclude unemployed claimants in receipt of Income Support prior to the introduction of Jobseeker's Allowance in October 1996.

Source: Department of Social Security: 0191 225 7373

10.15 Income support: average weekly amounts of benefit
Great Britain[1]

May

Thousands

		1992	1993	1994	1995	1996	1997[4]	1998[4]	1999[4]	2000[4]
All income support	KACW	51.77	54.75	56.16	56.29	57.26	58.03	58.72	61.42	65.72
All aged 60 and over	KJUB	40.79	43.59	42.45	41.18	41.69	42.24	42.29	45.30	48.18
Retirement pensioners	KACX	35.42	38.28	36.14	34.61	34.66	34.90	34.50	36.99	39.50
In receipt of other NI benefit[2]	KJUD	27.44	27.17	27.83	27.28	29.17	30.73	32.42	35.58	40.76
Others	KACY	72.41	77.09	80.97	81.72	83.99	85.57	87.29	91.70	96.20
All under 60	KACZ	62.71	65.65	68.51	68.91	69.61	70.17	71.14	73.36	78.61
Disabled with contributory benefit[2]	KADC	27.91	27.22	29.54	31.96	33.05	33.87	33.56	34.40	36.85
Disabled without contributory benefit[2]	KADD	53.11	59.18	64.14	66.84	68.55	70.38	72.86	75.88	79.25
Lone parent premium not in other groups[3]	KADE	67.59	70.31	74.93	76.63	78.19	79.21	79.67	82.01	91.21
Others	KADF	67.60	70.73	68.44	64.92	63.59	63.24	65.38	66.71	68.37

1 Data are extracted from the Annual Statistical Enquiry undertaken in May 1988, 1989, 1990, 1991, 1992 and 1993, and from the Quarterly Statistical Enquiries May 1994 to May 2000.
2 Contributory/NI benefits other than Retirement pension are Incapacity Benefit (previously IVB & Sickness Benefit), Widows Pension and Widowed Mothers Allowance.

3 Figures relate to one-parent families headed by a man or a woman, where the claimant is not receiving a pensioner or disability premium.
4 Figures exclude unemployed claimants who transferred to Jobseeker's Allowance from 7 October 1996.

Source: Department of Social Security: 0191 225 7373

10.16 War pensions
Estimated number of pensioners

Great Britain at 31 March in each year

Thousands

		1990	1991	1992	1993	1994	1995	1996	1997	1998	1999	2000
Total	KADG	249.96	247.67	249.95	266.92	296.30	309.84	323.74	324.64	317.65	306.06	295.67
Disablement -												
1914 war; 1939 war and later service	KADH	192.47	192.04	196.19	214.53	245.44	260.30	265.37	264.59	259.16	248.93	240.76
Widows and dependants -												
1914 war; 1939 war and later service	KADI	57.48	55.83	53.76	52.39	50.86	49.54	58.37	60.05	58.49	55.85	54.92

Source: Department of Social Security: 0191 225 7373

Social protection

10.17 Summary of government expenditure on social services and housing
Years ended 31 March

£ millions

		1990/91	1991/92	1992/93	1993/94	1994/95	1995/96	1996/97	1997/98	1998/99	1999/00
Education[1]	KJAA	26 728	29 550	31 576	33 544	35 367	36 810	37 953	39 078	38 435	..
National health service	KJAB	27 911	31 842	35 413	37 259	39 879	40 691	42 383	43 878	48 096	49 148
Welfare services	CSWL	5 745	4 873	6 683	7 700	9 016	10 312	11 521	11 713	11 984	12 168
Social security benefits	KJAE	58 261	69 121	78 846	85 805	87 941	90 534	92 217	92 146	94 051	97 078
Housing	KJAF	6 065	5 547	6 984	5 919	5 634	5 445	4 593	3 415	3 605	2 825
Total government expenditure	KJAG	124 710	140 933	159 502	170 227	177 863	189 736	187 334	190 230	..	..
Current expenditure	KJAH	117 243	133 848	151 010	163 289	171 303	183 297	183 054	186 640	..	..
Capital expenditure	KJAI	7 467	7 085	8 492	6 938	6 560	6 439	4 280	3 590	..	..
Total government expenditure	KJAG	124 710	140 933	159 502	170 227	177 863	189 736	187 334	190 230	..	..
Central government	KJAK	90 224	103 304	116 357	126 407	130 828	136 993	136 766	139 269	..	..
Local authorities	KJAL	34 486	37 629	43 145	43 820	47 035	52 743	50 568	50 961	..	..
Total government expenditure	KJAG	124 710	140 933	159 502	170 227	177 863	189 736	187 334	190 230	..	..
Total government expenditure on social services and housing as a percentage of GDP[2]		22.10	23.83	25.97	26.24	25.88	26.21	24.40	23.28	..	..

1 Includes school meals and milk.
2 GDP adjusted to take account of change from rates to community charge.

Source: Office for National Statistics: 020 7533 5990

10.18 Government expenditure on education[1,3]
Years ended 31 march

£ millions

			1988 /89	1989 /90	1990 /91	1991 /92	1992 /93	1993 /94	1994 /95	1995 /96	1996 /97	1997 /98	1998[14] /99
Current expenditure													
Nursery schools	KEZN	KJBA	5 259	5 889	6 458	7 247	8 262	8 712	9 094	9 352	9 697	10 405	..
Primary schools		KJBB											
Secondary schools	KJBC		6 437	6 832	7 147	7 787	8 347	8 615	8 875	8 844	9 194	9 322	–
Special schools	KJBD		888	1 008	1 121	1 245	1 354	1 420	1 451	1 493	1 578	1 655	–
Universities[3]	KJBG		1 958	2 104	2 265	2 437	3 361	..	..	..	..	..	..
Other Higher, Further and adult education[4]	KJBE		3 277	3 729	4 128	4 454	4 136	..	..	..	..	..	..
Higher Education Funding Council[4,5]	CSWM		..	..	..	..	..	4 908	5 192	5 472	5 729	5 693	4 746
Further Education Funding Council[6]	CSWO		..	..	..	..	..	3 072	3 200	3 392	3 694	3 718	5 007
Continuing Education	CSWP		..	..	..	..	..	380	294	1 801	1 891	1 960	–
Other education expenditure	KJBH		1 009	1 191	1 325	1 361	1 009	905	963	948	1 277	1 355	5 067
Related current expenditure:													
Training of teachers: residence[7]	KJBI		..	..	..	..	..	..	..	..	..	..	..
School welfare[8]	KJBJ		70	91	155	214	270	346	359	328	336	372	–
Meals and milk[9]	KJBK		469	485	506	556	161	149	147	148	147	138	–
Youth service and physical training	KJBL		277	328	348	360	393	392	401	396	389	389	–
Maintenance grants and allowances to pupils and students[10,11]	KJBM		900	934	1 028	1 379	1 705	1 972	2 204	1 660	1 440	1 289	–
Transport of pupils	KJBN		311	335	393	442	417	444	486	507	526	584	–
Miscellaneous expenditure	KJBO		10	17	2	3	8	10	31	31	49	45	–
Total current expenditure[12]	KJBQ		20 865	22 943	24 876	27 485	29 424	31 325	32 697	34 372	35 947	36 925	36 946
Capital expenditure													
Nursery schools	KEZP	KJBR	246	314	353	376	384	414	517	497	482	546	..
Primary schools		KJBS											
Secondary schools	KJBT		195	397	465	493	518	485	565	482	515	601	–
Special schools	KJBU		33	38	36	35	32	31	37	51	52	44	–
Universities[3]	KJBX		172	196	211	231	236	..	..	..	..	..	..
Other Higher, Further and adult education[4]	KJBV		180	248	230	293	285	..	..	..	..	..	..
Higher Education Funding Council[2,4,5]	CSWQ		..	..	..	..	..	406	412	424	74	61	31
Further Education Funding Council[6]	CSWR		..	..	..	..	..	194	201	187	33	29	44
Continuing Education	CSWS		..	..	..	..	..	6	8	8	5	–	–
Other education expenditure	KJBY		22	41	39	33	25	12	45	25	24	30	57
Related capital expenditure	KJBZ		25	32	26	20	17	23	25	17	20	24	–
Total capital expenditure[12]	KJCA		873	1 266	1 359	1 481	1 496	1 571	1 810	1 691	1 205	1 335	1 489
VAT refunds to local authorities	KJBP		399	455	493	584	656	648	860	747	801	818	–
Total expenditure													
Central government	KJCB		3 025	4 337	4 582	4 288	4 722	8 186	9 490	10 853	11 388	12 167	11 207
Local authorities	KJCC		19 112	20 325	22 146	25 261	26 853	25 354	25 900	25 954	26 562	26 910	27 228
Total government expenditure on education[13]	KJAA		22 137	24 664	26 728	29 550	31 576	33 544	35 367	36 810	37 953	39 078	38 435
Total government education expenditure as a percentage of GDP[12]			4.61	4.71	4.74	5.00	5.14	5.17	5.15	5.09	4.94	4.78	4.47

1 Includes expenditure on University departments of Education for England and Wales.
2 Including tuition fees.
3 Includes expenditure on Higher Education Institutions in Northern Ireland.
4 Includes expenditure on Further Education Institutions in Northern Ireland.
5 With effect from 1987/8 included with maintenance grants and allowances.
6 Expenditure on the school health service is included in the National Health Service.
7 Expenditure on meals and milk in England has been recharged across other expenditure headings.

8 Excludes the secondment of teachers on further training.
9 Includes student loans expenditure.
10 Due to rounding constituent figures may not sum to totals.
11 Excludes additional adjustment to allow for Capital consumption made for National Accounts purposes amounting to £1109m in 1996/97.
12 GDP includes adjustments to remove the distortion caused by the abolition of domestic rates.
13 From 1995/96, figures include expenditure on training programmes in England (such as Work Based Training for Young People) reclassified as education. Therefore figures are not comparable with earlier years.
14 From 1998/99 figures have been taken from HM Treasury Public Expenditure Statistical Analyses. They are not comparable with earlier years which used different sources.

Sources: Department for Education and Employment;
Office for National Statistics: 020 7533 5990

10.19 Government expenditure on the National Health Service
Years ended 31 March

£ millions

		1989/90	1990/91	1991/92	1992/93	1993/94	1994/95	1995/96	1996/97	1997/98	1998/99	1999/00
Current expenditure												
Central government:												
Hospitals and Community Health Services[1] and Family Health Services[2]	KJQA	22 197	25 276	29 061	32 195	35 567	37 698	38 514	39 425	40 993	43 600	48 279
Administration[3]	KJQB	855	979	1 119	1 258	–	–	–	–	–	–	–
less Payments by patients:												
Hospital services	KJQC	–407	–510	–540	–505	–368	–111	–42	–42	–48	–84	–168
Pharmaceutical services	KJQD	–242	–247	–270	–297	–324	–342	–383	–376	–396	–390	–408
Dental services	KJQE	–340	–441	–477	–470	–440	–464	–494	–447	–475	–470	–513
Ophthalmic services	KJQF	–	–	–	–	–	–	–	–	–	–	–
Total	KJQG	–989	–1 198	–1 287	–1 272	–1 132	–917	–919	–865	–919	–944	–1 089
Departmental administration	KJQH	202	268	293	319	270	256	242	265	245	227	231
Other central services	KJQI	693	738	865	1 301	1 651	2 304	2 538	3 124	3 242	4 980	1 601
Total current expenditure	KJQJ	22 958	26 063	30 051	33 801	36 356	39 341	40 375	41 949	43 561	47 863	49 022
Capital expenditure												
Central government	KJQK	2 071	1 848	1 791	1 612	903	538	316	434	317	233	126
Total government NHS Expenditure												
Central government	KJAB	25 029	27 911	31 842	35 413	37 259	39 879	40 691	42 383	43 878	48 096	49 148
Total NHS expenditure as a percentage of GDP[4]		4.78	4.95	5.38	5.77	5.74	5.80	5.62	5.52	5.37	5.59	5.44

1 Including the school health service.
2 General Medical Services have been included in the expenditure of the Health Authorities. Therefore, Hospitals and Community Health Services and Family Practitioner Services (now Family Health Services) are not identifiable separately.
3 Administration costs are not separately identifiable from 1993/94.
4 GDP adjusted to take account of change from rates to community charge.

Source: Office for National Statistics: 020 7533 5990

10.20 Government expenditure on welfare services[1]
Years ended 31 March

£ millions

		1989/90	1990/91	1991/92	1992/93	1993/94	1994/95	1995/96	1996/97	1997/98	1998/99	1999/00
Personal social services												
Central government current expenditure	KJCG	143	163	190	202	216	197	140	101	73	53	50
Local authorities current expenditure:												
Running expenses	CTKQ	4 395	5 022	5 725	6 122	7 113	8 400	9 716	10 947	11 131	11 378	11 563
Capital expenditure	KJCI	213	227	200	189	190	235	229	210	204	199	145
Total	KJAC	4 877	5 626	4 732	6 513	7 519	8 832	10 085	11 258	11 408	11 630	11 758
Welfare foods service												
Central government current expenditure on welfare foods (including administration)	KJCK	108	120	142	171	182	185	228	264	306	355	411
less Receipts from the public	KJCL	–	–1	–1	–1	–1	–1	–1	–1	–1	–1	–1
Total	KJAD	108	119	141	170	181	184	227	263	305	354	410
Total government expenditure	CSWL	4 985	5 745	4 873	6 683	7 700	9 016	10 312	11 521	11 713	11 984	12 168
Total government expenditure as a percentage of GDP[2]		0.95	1.02	0.82	1.09	1.19	1.31	1.42	1.50	1.43	1.39	1.35

1 School meals and milk are included in Table 10.18.
2 GDP adjusted to take account of change from rates to community charge.

Source: Office for National Statistics: 020 7533 5990

10.21 Government expenditure on social security benefits
Years ended 31 March

£ millions

		1989 /90	1990 /91	1991 /92	1992 /93	1993 /94	1994 /95	1995 /96	1996 /97	1997 /98	1998 /99	1999 /00
Government current expenditure												
National insurance fund:												
Retirement pensions	EKXK	20 714	22 725	25 691	27 076	28 481	28 925	30 162	32 146	33 643	35 711	37 833
Lump sums to pensioners	KJDB	112	114	114	115	122	123	124	129	118	120	123
Widows and guardians allowances	CSDH	896	893	884	1 014	1 041	1 034	1 018	974	992	973	990
Unemployment benefit	CSDI	752	892	1 627	1 761	1 623	1 277	1 099	588	1	–	–1
Jobseeker's allowance[3]	CJTJ	–	–	–	–	–	–	–	379	590	474	462
Sickness benefit	CSDJ	209	222	278	365	294	426	12	–	–	–	–
Invalidity benefit	CSDK	3 935	4 544	5 461	6 198	7 146	8 042	271	–	–	–	–
Incapacity benefit[4]	CUNL	–	–	–	–	–	–	7 615	7 668	7 471	7 295	6 897
Maternity benefit	CSDL	32	35	40	42	32	17	28	32	36	39	40
Death grant	CSDM	–	–	–	–	–	–	–	–	–	–	–
Injury benefit	CSDN	–	–	–	–	–	–	–	–	–	–	–
Disablement benefit	CSDO	475	526	–	–	–	–	–	–	–	–	–
Industrial death benefit	CSDP	61	62	–	–	–	–	–	–	–	–	–
Statutory sick pay	CSDQ	996	966	725	688	688	24	24	24	28	28	28
Statutory maternity pay	GTKZ	292	344	396	416	440	498	476	500	516	552	585
Payments in lieu of benefits foregone	GTKV	–	–	–	–	–	–	–	–	–	–	–
Total	ACHH	28 474	31 323	35 216	37 675	39 867	40 366	40 829	42 440	43 395	45 192	46 957
Maternity Fund	GTKO	–	–	–	–	–	–	–	–	–	–	–
Redundancy Fund	GTKN	71	130	276	321	110	208	128	108	88	116	148
Social Fund	GTLQ	101	123	130	175	189	183	216	203	200	360	920
Non-contributory benefits:												
War pensions	KJDP	641	688	844	976	913	1 083	1 247	1 352	1 284	1 262	1 247
Family benefits:												
Child benefit	KJDQ	4 751	4 840	5 433	5 950	6 347	6 294	6 332	6 645	7 095	7 327	8 252
One parent benefit	KJDR	200	227	249	275	282	289	310	317	9	–	–
Family credit	KAAA	424	466	626	929	1 208	1 441	1 739	2 084	2 338	2 430	1 927
Family income supplement	KJDS	–	–	–	–	–	–	–	–	–	–	–
Maternity grants	KJDT	–	–					–	–	–	–	–
Income support/Supplementary benefits:												
Supplementary pensions	KJDU	–	–	–	–	–	–	–	–	–	–	–
Supplementary allowances	KJDV	–	–	–	–	–	–	–	–	–	–	–
Income support	KAAB	8 257	9 106	12 325	15 578	16 997	16 387	16 650	14 438	11 998	11 793	12 236
Other non-contributory benefits:												
Old persons' pensions	KJDX	35	38	36	36	36	35	36	30	29	29	28
Lump sums to pensioners	KJDY	9	8	11	13	14	13	15	15	17	17	17
Attendance allowance	KJDZ	1 262	1 698	1 706	1 553	1 795	1 963	2 194	2 393	2 640	2 682	2 834
Invalid care allowance	KJEA	184	229	285	345	442	526	617	736	745	783	821
Mobility allowance	KJEB	770	895	1 063	68	–	–	–	–	–	–	–
Disability living allowance	EKXL	–	–	–	1 973	2 772	3 125	3 802	4 498	5 018	5 367	5 651
Disability working allowance	EKYE	–	–	–	3	7	11	19	34	44	49	40
Severe disablement allowance	KJEC	347	407	596	640	703	776	820	906	1 007	984	1 016
Industrial injury benefits	EKXM	–	142	655	668	687	706	731	744	754	–	–
RPI Adjustment	KAAC	–	–									
Housing benefit[1]	KJED	4 095	4 735	6 053	7 670	9 163	10 345	10 773	11 276	11 315	11 311	11 247
Administration	KJEE	2 813	3 206	3 617	3 998	4 273	4 190	4 076	3 998	4 170	4 349	3 737
Total government benefit expenditure	KJAE	52 434	58 261	69 121	78 846	85 805	87 941	90 534	92 217	92 146	94 051	97 078
Total government benefit expenditure as a percentage of GDP[2]		10.01	10.32	11.69	12.84	13.23	12.79	12.51	12.01	11.27	10.93	10.74

1 From 1981-82 comprises expenditure by the Department of Health and Social Security under the unified housing benefit scheme.
2 GDP adjusted to take account of change from rates to community charge.
3 Jobseeker's allowance was introduced in October 1996 to replace Unemployment benefit and Income Support for the unemployed.
4 Sickness benefit and Invalidity benefit were replaced by a single incapacity benefit in 1995

Source: Office for National Statistics: 020 7533 5990

10.22 Government and other public sector expenditure on housing
Years ended 31 March

£ millions

		1989/90	1990/91	1991/92	1992/93	1993/94	1994/95	1995/96	1996/97	1997/98	1998/99	1999/00
Government expenditure												
Current expenditure												
Central government												
housing subsidies:												
to local authorities	**CTMN**	714	1 273	1 144	992	874	814	687	717	711	737	715
to public corporations	**ADVA**	285	284	260	208	214	228	228	236	244	218	230
to housing associations	**KJRC**	53	67	40	135	180	207	235	215	216	−22	−64
grants to housing associations	**KJRD**	7	85	117	59	13	3	1	1	–	–	–
Local authorities												
housing subsidies	**KJVK**	487	3	–	1	–	–	3	1	1	1	3
Grants under the option mortgage												
scheme	**KJRF**	–	–	–	–	–	–	–	–	–	–	–
Administration, etc	**KGVL**	249	320	373	394	364	405	402	447	509	575	590
Total current expenditure	**KJRH**	1 794	2 032	1 934	1 789	1 645	1 657	1 556	1 617	1 681	1 509	1 474
Capital expenditure												
Investment in housing by local												
authorities	**KGVM**	1 387	1 322	822	913	780	842	1 009	937	−52	59	−729
Capital grants to housing												
associations	**KJRJ**	552	1 495	2 045	2 583	2 136	1 774	1 329	1 393	1 102	1 021	975
Improvement grants	**ADCE**	885	863	1 152	1 240	1 287	1 105	846	980	1 157	779	766
Net lending for house purchase	**KJRL**	−259	−596	−782	−211	−402	−141	−136	−719	−816	−168	−82
Capital grants to public corporations	**KJRM**	241	774	482	631	439	387	837	386	400	415	431
Net lending to public corporations	**KJRN**	672	176	−104	39	34	10	7	−1	−57	−10	−10
Total capital expenditure	**KJRO**	3 479	4 033	3 613	5 195	4 274	3 977	3 889	2 976	1 734	2 096	1 351
Total expenditure												
Central government	**KJRP**	2 547	3 835	3 697	4 595	3 839	3 409	3 313	2 362	1 962	2 359	2 276
Local authorities	**KJRQ**	2 726	2 230	1 850	2 389	2 080	2 225	2 132	2 231	1 453	1 246	549
Total government expenditure	**KJAF**	5 273	6 065	5 547	6 984	5 919	5 634	5 445	4 593	3 415	3 605	2 825
Public corporations' capital												
expenditure												
Investment in housing	**KGVN**	451	519	673	549	568	560	580	574	452	424	420
Net lending to private sector	**AAFR**	−2	−3	−4	3	1	−1	−5	−1	−1	–	–
Total	**KJRU**	449	516	669	552	569	559	575	569	451	424	420
Total public sector housing expenditure[1]	**KJRV**	4 809	5 631	5 838	6 866	6 015	5 796	5 176	4 777	3 523	3 624	2 824
Total public sector housing expenditure as												
a percentage of GDP[2]		0.92	1.00	0.99	1.12	0.93	0.84	0.72	0.62	0.43	0.42	0.31

1 Total government expenditure *less* grants and loans to public corporations
 plus public corporations' capital expenditure.
2 GDP adjusted to take account of change from rates to community charge.

Source: Office for National Statistics: 020 7533 5990

11 Crime and justice

Crime and justice

There are differences in the legal and judicial systems of England and Wales, Scotland and Northern Ireland which make it impossible to provide tables covering the United Kingdom as a whole in this section. These differences concern the classification of offences, the meaning of certain terms used in the statistics, the effects of the several Criminal Justice Acts and recording practices.

Recorded crime statistics *(Table 11.1)*

Notifiable Offences recorded by the police provide a measure of the amount of crime committed. The statistics are based on counting rules, revised with effect from 1 April 1998, which are standard for all the police forces in England and Wales and now include all indictable and triable-either-way offences together with a few summary offences which are closely linked to these offences. The new rules have changed the emphasis of measurement more towards one crime per victim, and have also increased the coverage of offences. These changes have particularly impacted on the offence groups of violence against the person, fraud and forgery, drugs offences and other offences.

For a variety of reasons many offences are either not reported to the police or not recorded by them. The changes in the number of offences recorded do not necessarily provide an accurate reflection of changes in the amount of crime committed.

For further information please see the Home Office *Statistical Bulletin 12/00 on Recorded Crime Statistics.*

Court proceedings and police cautions
(Tables 11.3 - 11.8, 11.13 - 11.17, 11.20 - 11.22)

The statistical basis of the tables of court proceedings is broadly similar in England and Wales, Scotland and Northern Ireland; the tables show the number of persons found guilty, recording a person under the heading of the principal offence of which he is found guilty, excluding additional findings of guilt at the same proceedings. A person found guilty at a number of separate court proceedings is included more than once.

The statistics on offenders cautioned cover only those who, on admission of guilt, were given a formal caution by, or on the instructions of, a senior police officer as an alternative to prosecution (excluding Scotland). Written warnings by the police for motor offences and persons paying fixed penalties for certain motoring offences are excluded. There are no statistics on cautioning available for Northern Ireland.

In Scotland there are three criminal courts, the High

Court of Justiciary, the Sheriff Court and the District Court. The High Court deals with serious solemn (ie Jury) cases and has unlimited sentencing power. The Sheriff Court is limited to imprisonment of 3 years for solemn cases, or 3 months (6 months when specified in legislation for second or subsequent offences and 12 months for certain statutory offences) for summary cases. The District Court deals only with summary cases and is limited to 60 days imprisonment and level 4 fines. Stipendiary Magistrates sit in Glasgow District Court and have the summary sentencing powers of a Sheriff.

Indictable offences are offences which are (a) triable on indictment only (these are the most serious crimes such as murder and rape) and are tried at the Crown Court in England and Wales and the High Court in Scotland; (b) triable either way offences which may be tried at the Crown Court or Magistrates' Court in England and Wales or the High Court, Sheriff Court or District Court in Scotland; summary offences are those for which a defendant in England and Wales or accused in Scotland would normally be dealt with at the Magistrates' Courts and the Sheriff or District Court in Scotland.

The Criminal Justice Act 1991 led to the following main changes in the sentences available to the courts:
(a) introduction of combination orders, (b) introduction of the "unit fine scheme" at Magistrates' courts,
(c) abolishing the sentence of detention in a young offender institution for 14 year old boys and changing the minimum and maximum sentence lengths for 15 to 17 year olds to 10 and 12 months respectively, and
(d) abolishing partly suspended sentences of imprisonment and restricting the use of a fully suspended sentence.

The Criminal Justice Act 1993 abolished the "Unit Fine Scheme" in Magistrates' courts which had been introduced under the Criminal Justice Act 1991.

A *charging standard for assault* was introduced on 31 August 1994 with the aim to promote consistency between the police and prosecution on the appropriate level of charge to be brought.

The Criminal Justice and Public Order Act 1994 created several new offences, mainly in the area of Public Order, but also including male rape. The Act also (a) extended the provisions of section 53 of the Children and Young Persons Act 1993 for 10 to 13 year olds, (b) increased the maximum sentence length for 15 to 17 year olds to 2 years, (c) increased the upper limit from £2 000 to £5 000 for offences of criminal damage proceeded against as if triable only summarily, (d) introduced provisions for the reduction of sentences for early guilty pleas, and (e) increased the maximum sentence length for certain firearm offences.

Provisions within the Crime (Sentences) Act 1997 included: a) an automatic life sentence for a second serious violent or sexual offence unless there are exceptional circumstances; b) a minimum sentence of seven years for an offender convicted for a third time of a class A drug trafficking offence unless the court considers this to be unjust in all the circumstances, and c) the new section 38A of the Magistrates' Courts' Act 1980 extending the circumstances in which a magistrates' court may commit a person convicted of an offence triable either way to the Crown Court for sentence - it was implemented in conjunction with section 49 of the Criminal Procedure and Investigations Act 1996, which involves the magistrates' courts in asking defendants to indicate plea before the mode of trial decision is taken and compels the court to sentence or commit for sentence any defendant who indicates a guilty plea.

The Crime and Disorder Act 1998 created provisions in relation to reprimands and final warnings, new offences and orders which have been implemented nationally or piloted in certain areas. The Youth Justice and Criminal Evidence Act 1999 introduced a new sentence for young offenders of referral to a youth offender panel.

Section 45 of the Criminal Justice (Scotland) Act 1980 was implemented on 15 November 1983; this introduced unified custodial sentencing for under 21 offenders and abolished borstal training.

The system of Magistrates' courts and Crown Courts in Northern Ireland operates in a similar way to that in England and Wales. A particularly significant statutory development, however, has been the Criminal Justice (NI) Order 1996 which introduces a new sentencing regime into Northern Ireland, largely replicating that which was introduced into England and Wales by the Criminal Justice Acts of 1991 and 1993. The order makes many changes to both community and custodial sentences, while introducing new orders such as the combination order, the custody probation order and orders for release on licence of sexual offenders.

Previous convictions of prisoners *(Table 11.8)*
Information on previous convictions of prisoners published prior to 1995 was based upon Prison Service records. However, details of a prisoners previous conviction were often not recorded (eg this information was missing for 44 per cent of the 1990 male receptions under sentence). To overcome this problem the Home Office Offenders Index (a computerised database containing details of convictions for standard list offences) is now being used to provide information on prisoners previous convictions. Unfortunately, this means that the most up-to-date information on previous

convictions is not directly comparable with that previously published. Standard list offences include indictable offences and some of the more serious summary offences so the coverage is not as complete. The published information also does not relate to 'prison receptions' but to those sentenced to immediate custody for standard list offences (which accounted for 82 per cent of those sentenced to custody in 1993).

The problems with non-availability of previous history information are much less acute using the Offenders Index data source. Previous convictions were found for 95 per cent of the 1993 prison population sample. Some of the cases where information is missing, would be accounted for by prisoners who are not sentenced for a standard list offence and have no previous record for such offences.

11.1 Recorded crime statistics
England and Wales

Thousands

		Old counting rules											New counting rules	
		1989	1990	1991	1992	1993	1994	1995	1996	1997	1998[1] /99		1998 /99	1999 /00
Violence against the person	**BEAB**	177.0	184.7	190.3	201.8	205.1	218.4	212.6	239.3	250.8	230.8	**LQMP**	502.8	581.0
Sexual offences	**BEAC**	29.7	29.0	29.4	29.5	31.3	32.0	30.3	31.4	33.2	34.9	**LQMQ**	36.2	37.8
Burglary	**BEAD**	825.9	1 006.8	1 219.5	1 355.3	1 369.6	1 256.7	1 239.5	1 164.6	1 015.1	951.9	**LQMR**	953.2	906.5
Robbery	**BEAE**	33.2	36.2	45.3	52.9	57.8	60.0	68.1	74.0	63.1	66.2	**LQMS**	66.8	84.3
Theft and handling stolen goods	**BEAF**	2 012.8	2 374.4	2 761.1	2 851.6	2 751.9	2 564.6	2 452.1	2 383.9	2 165.0	2 126.7	**LQMT**	2 191.4	2 223.6
Fraud and forgery	**BEAG**	134.5	147.9	174.7	168.6	162.8	145.3	133.0	136.2	134.4	173.7	**LQMU**	279.5	334.8
Criminal damage	**BEAH**	630.1	733.4	821.1	892.6	906.7	928.3	914.0	951.3	877.0	834.4	**LQMV**	879.6	945.7
Drug offences[2]	**LQMO**	..	..	..	..	..	..	..	..	..	21.3	**LQYT**	135.9	121.9
Other offences[2]	**BEAI**	27.6	31.1	34.6	39.4	41.0	47.7	50.7	55.8	59.8	42.0	**LQYU**	63.6	65.7
Total	**BEAA**	3 870.7	4 543.6	5 276.2	5 591.7	5 526.3	5 253.0	5 100.2	5 036.6	4 598.3	4 481.8	**LQYV**	5 109.1	5 301.2

1 Estimates.
2 Prior to 1/4/98 th offence of drug trafficking was included in the "Other offences" group. From 1/4/99, under the new counting rules, drug trafficking became part of a new "Drug offences" group which, with the expanded coverage, now includes possession and other drug offences. For 1998/99, under the old counting rules, drug trafficking - the only drugs offence counted - has been listed under drugs offences.

Source: Home Office: 020 7273 2583

11.2 Police forces: strength
End of year

		1989	1990	1991	1992	1993	1994	1995[1]	1996[1]	1997[1]	1998[1]	1999[1]
England and Wales												
Regular police												
Strength:												
Men	KERB	110 466	110 790	110 396	111 027	108 967	108 030	107 022	106 549	105 691	104 606	103 083
Women	KERC	13 695	14 352	14 898	15 841	16 571	17 263	17 688	18 501	19 124	19 659	19 967
Seconded:[2]												
Men	KERD	1 815	1 787	1 670	1 766	1 938	1 881	1 896	1 864	1 814	2 007	2 158
Women	KERE	134	161	163	167	182	184	202	209	233	232	256
Additional officers:[3]												
Men	KERF	75	85	73	68	63	97	105	111	200	267	324
Women	KERG	1	5	3	3	12	17	22	57	158	514	582
Special constables												
Enrolled strength:												
Men	KERH	10 390	10 483	11 592	12 251	13 240	12 772	12 751	12 594	12 483	11 331	10 667
Women	KERI	5 199	5 419	6 480	6 992	7 326	7 060	6 904	6 857	6 680	5 965	5 060
Scotland												
Regular police												
Strength[4]:												
Men	KERK	12 656	12 583	12 566	12 629	12 580	12 634	12 341	12 347	12 495	12 479	12 258
Women	KERL	1 158	1 258	1 357	1 465	1 559	1 679	1 665	1 856	2 019	2 202	2 098
Central service:[4,5]												
Men	KERM	69	67	64	70	73	79	96	94	85	85	88
Women	KERN	4	6	6	5	5	4	7	8	4	6	9
Seconded:[4,6]												
Men	KERO	92	98	103	120	109	110	108	105	101	101	85
Women	KERP	8	8	6	10	16	16	16	16	13	10	12
Additional regular police:												
Strength	KERR	64	64	93	90	58	91	90	72	72	97	91
Special constables												
Strength:												
Men	KERS	1 521	1 475	1 436	1 454	1 466	1 518	1 411	1 336	1 286	1 289	1 229
Women	KERT	279	312	342	393	431	474	467	450	437	444	422
Northern Ireland												
Royal Ulster Constabulary [7]												
Strength:												
Men	KERU	7 571	7 535	7 510	7 687	7 646	7 640	7 528	7 531	7 562	7 527	7 406
Women	KERV	688	708	707	791	818	853	887	897	923	933	987
Royal Ulster Constabulary Reserve												
Strength:												
Men	KERW	4 200	4 097	4 069	4 060	4 027	4 052	3 976	3 727	3 587	3 469	3 199
Women	KERX	425	449	491	533	545	638	709	675	719	705	641

1 Figures for England and Wales are as at 30 September. Figures for Scotland are as at 31 March. From 1999 figures for Northern Ireland are as at 31 March. Prior to this, the figures were as at 31 December.
2 NCS, NCIS, other inter-force units and officers in central service.
3 Includes Police Officers on loan to organisations outside the British Police Service such as the Royal Hong Kong police, and those on career breaks.
4 'Strength' includes central service and seconded police.
5 Instructors at Training Establishments, etc formerly shown as secondments.
6 Scottish Crime Squad, officers on courses, etc.
7 Does not include officers on secondment.

Sources: Home Office: 020 7273 2583;
The Scottish Executive Justice Department: 0131 244 2225;
Royal Ulster Constabulary: 028 9065 0222 ext 24135

11.3 Offenders found guilty: by offence group Magistrates' courts and the Crown Court

England and Wales

Thousands

		1989	1990	1991	1992	1993	1994	1995	1996	1997	1998	1999
All ages[1]												
Indictable offences												
Violence against the person:	KJEJ	55.6	52.5	47.2	43.6	38.9	37.6	29.1	30.0	34.6	35.7	34.4
Murder	KESB	0.2	0.2	0.2	0.2	0.2	0.2	0.2	0.3	0.3	0.3	0.3
Manslaughter	KESC	0.3	0.2	0.2	0.3	0.2	0.2	0.2	0.3	0.3	0.3	0.3
Wounding	KESD	53.7	50.9	45.5	42.0	37.4	36.1	27.4	28.3	32.7	35.2	33.9
Other offences of violence against the person	KESE	1.4	1.2	1.2	1.1	1.0	1.0	1.2	1.2	1.3	1.3	1.3
Sexual offences	KESF	7.3	6.6	5.5	5.0	4.3	4.5	4.7	4.4	4.5	4.6	4.3
Burglary	KESG	43.4	43.6	46.1	44.3	40.3	38.0	35.3	32.2	31.7	30.8	29.3
Robbery	KESH	4.6	4.8	4.8	5.1	5.1	4.9	5.2	5.9	5.6	5.5	5.6
Theft and handling stolen goods	KESI	134.5	134.3	133.5	127.9	121.6	121.6	116.1	114.5	118.4	125.7	131.2
Fraud and forgery	KESJ	22.3	21.9	21.2	20.0	17.5	18.4	17.2	16.3	17.0	19.8	20.3
Criminal damage	KESK	9.4	11.2	10.2	9.8	9.4	10.0	9.6	9.8	10.5	10.9	10.9
Drugs	KBWX	22.6	24.6	23.5	22.7	21.9	27.8	31.6	34.1	40.7	48.8	48.7
Other offences (excluding motoring)	KESL	28.5	32.3	34.4	36.0	37.8	39.4	42.2	43.5	47.6	49.6	47.9
Motoring offences	KESM	11.3	11.1	11.3	10.7	10.8	12.0	11.2	9.9	9.5	9.0	8.1
Total	KESA	339.5	342.8	337.6	324.9	307.6	314.1	302.2	300.6	320.1	341.7	342.0
Summary offences[2]												
Assaults[3]	KESO	15.1	17.3	16.5	18.0	19.0	21.9	29.3	30.0	32.0	35.3	37.5
Betting and gaming	KESP	0.1	–	–	–	–	–	–	–	–	–	–
Offences with pedal cycles	KBWY	2.8	2.8	1.9	1.4	1.2	1.0	1.1	1.3	1.5	2.1	1.3
Other Highways Acts offences	KBWZ	8.6	7.9	5.9	4.5	3.6	3.4	2.6	2.8	3.2	3.1	2.9
Breach of local or other regulations	KESQ	10.1	12.6	8.5	8.2	10.5	9.4	6.7	5.9	6.4	5.8	6.5
Intoxicating Liquor Laws:												
Drunkenness	KESR	42.9	37.8	29.4	23.8	18.8	20.2	19.8	24.2	28.8	30.8	28.7
Other offences	KESS	2.7	2.2	1.5	1.2	0.8	0.7	0.7	0.5	0.6	0.6	0.5
Education Acts	KEST	2.8	3.0	2.8	2.0	2.3	2.8	3.1	3.5	3.7	5.0	5.1
Game Laws	KESU	0.1	0.1	1.0	0.8	0.6	0.6	0.4	0.4	0.3	0.4	0.3
Labour Laws	KESV	1.2	1.1	0.1	0.1	0.1	0.1	0.1	–	0.1	0.1	0.1
Summary offences of criminal damage and malicious damage	KESW	36.5	33.9	28.5	24.6	21.6	22.7	22.6	23.4	24.7	26.5	27.9
Offences by prostitutes	KESX	11.1	11.5	10.9	9.8	8.2	7.7	6.8	6.6	6.6	6.0	4.0
Railway offences	KESY	9.9	8.3	5.4	4.7	4.0	5.6	6.2	9.1	11.4	12.6	15.2
Revenue Laws[2]	KESZ	108.5	104.9	115.6	121.6	123.0	126.2	123.8	139.1	143.5	174.7	165.8
Vagrancy Acts	KETB	1.8	1.9	2.1	1.8	1.7	1.9	1.6	2.0	2.0	2.2	2.7
Wireless Telegraphy Acts[2]	KETC	123.7	126.4	138.7	170.3	168.7	162.9	113.8	164.9	77.0	76.6	55.8
Other summary offences	KETD	94.4	95.4	85.6	78.9	69.0	67.8	71.5	74.7	74.7	80.9	79.3
Motoring offences (summary)[2]	KETA	722.7	704.6	713.1	723.1	664.7	638.7	642.4	649.0	649.3	665.2	632.9
Total	KESN	1 195.0	1 171.8	1 167.5	1 194.8	1 117.7	1 093.5	1 052.4	1 137.4	1 065.8	1 128.0	1 066.5
Persons aged under 18[2,4]												
Indictable offences												
Violence against the person:	KETF	7.5	6.5	5.6	5.2	5.1	5.8	4.7	5.3	5.9	5.9	6.2
Murder	KBXA	–	–	–	–	–	–	–	–	–	–	–
Manslaughter	KBXB	–	–	–	–	–	–	–	–	–	–	0.2
Wounding	KBXC	7.4	6.4	5.5	5.2	5.1	5.7	4.7	5.3	5.8	5.9	5.9
Other offences of violence against the person	KCAA	0.1	0.1	0.1	–	–	–	–	–	0.1	0.1	–
Sexual offences	KETG	0.5	0.5	0.4	0.4	0.4	0.4	0.4	0.4	0.5	0.5	0.5
Burglary	KETH	12.0	11.2	10.4	9.5	8.7	8.9	9.1	8.6	8.6	8.5	7.8
Robbery	KETI	1.4	1.4	1.4	1.4	1.5	1.7	2.0	2.4	2.3	2.2	2.0
Theft and handling stolen goods	KETJ	20.0	19.1	17.0	15.2	14.1	14.4	18.2	19.0	19.6	21.9	22.7
Fraud and forgery	KETK	1.0	0.9	0.8	0.6	0.4	0.5	0.6	0.7	0.8	1.0	1.1
Criminal damage	KETL	2.0	2.1	1.8	1.6	1.7	2.0	2.1	2.2	2.3	2.3	2.7
Drugs	KCAB	1.0	1.2	1.2	1.0	0.8	1.1	1.3	1.6	1.8	2.7	3.1
Other offences (excluding motoring)	KETM	2.3	2.5	2.8	2.7	2.4	2.8	3.3	3.8	4.2	4.2	4.3
Motoring	KETN	0.6	0.6	0.7	0.5	0.3	0.3	0.4	0.4	0.4	0.4	0.4
Total	KETE	48.2	46.1	42.0	38.1	35.4	37.9	42.2	44.4	46.4	49.7	50.6
Summary offences[2]												
Offences with pedal cycles	KETP	0.5	0.5	0.3	0.2	0.1	0.1	0.2	0.2	0.2	0.3	0.3
Breach of local or other regulations	KETR	0.5	0.4	0.3	0.2	0.1	0.1	0.2	0.3	0.2	0.2	0.2
Summary offences of criminal damage and malicious damage	KETS	4.7	3.9	2.9	2.5	2.2	2.9	3.4	3.9	4.4	5.2	6.1
Railway offences	KETT	0.5	0.4	0.3	0.2	0.2	0.3	0.4	0.4	0.5	0.5	0.5
Other summary offences	KETU	18.3	16.4	14.1	11.3	8.3	9.7	7.2	8.8	10.1	12.1	11.7
Motoring offences (summary)[2]	KCAC	17.9	16.4	13.7	10.8	8.9	8.6	9.3	10.8	10.8	11.3	12.6
Total	KETO	42.4	38.1	31.6	25.2	19.9	21.7	25.6	30.3	22.0	36.8	39.6

1 Includes 'Companies', etc.
2 It is estimated that in 1995 there was a shortfall of 75 100 offenders found guilty for certain summary offences.
3 A new charging standard was introduced for assault in 1994 (see Introduction - Law enforcement).
4 Figures for persons aged under 18 are included in the totals above.

Source: Home Office: 020 8760 8270

11.4 Offenders cautioned: by offence group
England and Wales

Thousands

		1989	1990	1991	1992	1993	1994	1995	1996	1997	1998	1999
All ages[1]												
Indictable offences												
Violence against the person	KELB	14.7	16.8	19.4	23.5	24.1	23.6	20.4	21.8	23.6	23.5	21.2
Murder	KCAD	–	–	–	–	–	–	–	–	–	–	–
Manslaughter	KCAE	–	–	–	–	–	–	–	–	–	–	–
Wounding	KCAF	14.5	16.5	19.1	23.2	23.8	23.2	20.1	21.4	23.3	22.9	20.6
Other offences of violence against the person	KCAG	0.2	0.2	0.2	0.3	0.3	0.3	0.3	0.4	0.4	0.6	0.6
Sexual offences	KELC	3.5	3.4	3.3	3.4	3.3	3.0	2.3	2.0	1.9	1.7	1.5
Burglary	KELD	12.0	14.3	13.3	14.4	12.8	11.5	10.5	10.2	9.4	8.4	7.7
Robbery	KELE	0.4	0.6	0.6	0.6	0.7	0.6	0.6	0.6	0.7	0.6	0.6
Theft and handling stolen goods	KELF	81.9	99.8	108.5	130.3	117.2	104.8	104.9	93.6	82.8	83.6	75.4
Fraud and forgery	KELG	4.0	4.7	5.6	7.5	8.1	7.6	7.9	7.5	7.2	7.4	7.2
Criminal damage	KELH	3.7	4.2	3.8	4.0	4.1	4.3	3.8	3.1	2.8	2.7	3.0
Drugs	KCAI	13.1	18.7	21.2	27.6	35.1	44.4	48.2	47.5	56.0	58.7	49.4
Other offences (excluding motoring)	KELI	2.9	3.9	4.1	4.8	4.2	4.0	4.0	4.4	5.0	5.0	4.6
Motoring[2]	KCAJ	..	..	..	..	..	..	..	..	..	..	..
Total	KELA	136.0	166.3	179.9	216.2	209.6	209.8	202.6	190.8	189.4	191.7	170.6
Summary offences												
Assaults[3]	KELK	1.1	1.4	1.6	2.4	3.1	4.2	8.1	9.1	9.1	–	17.0
Betting and gaming	KELL	–	–	–	–	–	–	–	–	–	–	–
Offences with pedal cycles	KCAK	2.9	2.6	1.7	1.4	0.9	0.8	0.8	0.9	0.9	0.8	0.6
Other Highways Acts offences	KCAL	1.6	1.5	1.2	1.2	1.0	0.9	0.9	0.8	0.8	0.8	0.7
Breach of local or other regulations	KELM	1.2	1.2	1.3	1.5	1.1	1.1	0.9	0.8	0.9	0.9	0.7
Intoxicating Liquor Laws: Drunkenness	KELN	49.9	48.6	46.0	45.0	41.1	37.7	22.9	25.9	25.7	22.8	20.3
Other offences	KELO	3.6	2.8	1.7	1.7	1.2	1.0	1.0	0.9	0.9	0.7	0.4
Education Acts	KELP	–	–	–	–	–	–	–	–	–	–	–
Game Laws	KELQ	0.1	0.2	0.2	0.1	0.2	0.1	0.1	0.1	0.1	0.1	0.1
Labour Laws	KELR	–	–	–	–	–	–	–	–	–	–	–
Summary offences of criminal damage and malicious damage	KELS	14.3	16.2	17.3	20.5	22.1	23.1	25.1	27.7	27.6	28.3	28.7
Offences by prostitutes	KELT	5.3	4.5	4.1	4.2	4.0	3.6	3.3	3.5	3.5	3.5	2.1
Railway offences	KELU	0.6	0.4	0.3	0.3	0.2	0.2	0.3	0.2	0.1	–	–
Revenue Laws	KELV	0.6	0.5	0.7	0.8	0.5	0.2	0.2	0.1	0.1	0.1	0.1
Vagrancy Acts	KELX	0.4	0.5	0.7	1.3	1.5	1.0	1.0	0.6	0.6	1.2	0.8
Wireless Telegraphy Acts	KELY	–	–	–	–	–	–	–	–	–	–	–
Other summary offences	KELZ	20.3	22.5	22.1	25.0	24.9	24.6	24.2	24.7	22.3	37.0	24.1
Motoring offences[2]	KCAM	..	..	..	..	..	..	..	..	..	..	..
Total	KELJ	102.1	102.8	98.9	105.1	101.8	98.7	88.7	95.4	92.7	96.2	95.6
Persons aged 18 and under												
Indictable offences												
Violence against the person	KEMB	7.8	8.5	9.2	10.8	10.8	11.1	9.4	9.4	9.6	9.5	8.5
Murder	KCAN	–	–	–	–	–	–	–	–	–	–	–
Manslaughter	KCAO	–	–	–	–	–	–	–	–	–	–	–
Wounding	KCAP	7.8	8.5	9.2	10.7	10.8	11.1	9.4	9.4	9.6	9.4	8.4
Other offences of violence against the person	KCCE	–	–	–	–	–	–	–	–	–	–	–
Sexual offences	KEMC	1.8	1.6	1.4	1.3	1.1	1.1	0.8	0.7	0.7	0.6	0.6
Burglary	KEMD	11.1	13.1	11.7	12.0	10.3	9.6	8.5	8.2	7.5	6.7	6.1
Robbery	KEME	0.3	0.5	0.6	0.6	0.6	0.6	0.5	0.6	0.6	0.5	0.5
Theft and handling stolen goods	KEMF	51.6	63.1	62.3	69.8	58.9	58.6	57.4	48.2	40.9	44.0	39.6
Fraud and forgery	KEMG	1.4	1.5	1.5	1.7	1.5	1.4	1.6	1.5	1.4	1.6	1.7
Criminal damage	KEMH	3.1	3.2	2.6	2.6	2.6	2.8	2.4	2.0	1.8	1.7	1.9
Drugs	KCCF	2.3	4.0	5.0	5.4	6.7	8.5	8.7	7.9	9.7	11.0	9.6
Other offences (excluding motoring)	KEMI	0.9	1.0	1.2	1.4	1.4	1.4	1.3	1.3	1.5	1.5	1.4
Motoring[2]	KCCG	..	..	..	..	..	..	..	..	..	..	..
Total	KEMA	80.4	96.6	95.5	105.6	94.1	95.1	90.6	79.9	73.7	77.2	69.8
Summary offences												
Offences with pedal cycles	KEMK	1.6	1.5	0.9	0.7	0.4	0.5	0.4	0.5	0.5	0.4	0.3
Breach of local or other regulations	KEMM	0.5	0.5	0.5	0.6	0.3	0.4	0.3	0.3	0.3	0.3	0.2
Summary offences of criminal damage and malicious damage	KEMN	9.5	10.4	10.1	10.7	11.4	12.5	12.8	13.8	13.5	14.2	14.7
Railway offences	KEMO	0.2	0.2	0.1	0.1	0.1	0.1	0.1	0.1	0.1	–	–
Other summary offences	KEMP	16.6	18.0	15.5	16.0	15.3	15.6	10.3	10.8	9.1	13.8	9.9
Motoring offences[2]	KCCH	..	..	..	..	..	..	..	..	..	..	..
Total	KEMJ	28.4	30.5	27.1	28.1	27.5	29.2	30.0	33.2	30.8	32.5	34.2

1 Includes 'Companies', etc.
2 Not applicable as motoring offences may attract written warning.
3 A new charging standard was introduced for assault in 1994 (see Introduction - Law enforcement).

Source: Home Office: 020 8760 8270

11.5 Offenders found guilty of offences: by age and sex
England and Wales

Magistrates' courts and the Crown Court

Thousands

		1989	1990	1991	1992	1993	1994	1995	1996	1997	1998	1999
Males												
Indictable offences												
All ages	KEFA	293.7	295.7	293.5	282.8	268.2	273.2	263.2	261.1	276.5	292.9	291.7
10 and under 15 years	KEFB	6.5	6.0	5.1	4.9	5.5	6.9	7.1	6.6	7.1	8.1	8.9
15 and under 18 years	KEFC	36.8	35.0	32.3	28.9	26.2	28.7	30.2	32.5	33.6	35.2	35.1
18 and under 21 years	KEFD	63.7	65.8	65.3	58.9	53.0	50.3	47.4	46.3	48.4	51.8	52.6
21 years and over	KEFE	186.8	188.8	190.8	190.1	183.4	187.4	178.6	175.6	187.3	197.9	195.0
Summary offences[1]												
All ages	KEFF	996.2	968.9	956.3	959.6	892.0	871.0	862.0	903.6	880.9	929.0	886.6
10 and under 15 years	KEFG	2.3	2.0	1.8	1.8	1.8	2.3	2.9	2.8	3.0	3.9	5.1
15 and under 18 years	KEFH	37.7	27.6	21.7	21.7	16.8	17.7	20.5	24.6	25.9	28.5	30.3
18 and under 21 years	KEFI	128.9	125.1	109.8	97.6	85.7	82.9	84.0	88.4	91.0	96.3	94.8
21 years and over	KEFJ	827.3	808.0	816.9	838.5	787.7	768.2	754.6	787.9	761.0	800.3	756.5
Females												
Indictable offences												
All ages	KEFK	43.0	44.0	41.9	40.0	37.8	39.5	37.5	38.0	42.2	47.3	49.0
10 and under 15 years	KEFL	0.7	0.7	0.6	0.6	0.7	1.0	1.0	1.0	1.0	1.4	1.4
15 and under 18 years	KEFM	4.4	4.4	4.0	3.6	3.1	3.8	4.0	4.2	4.6	5.1	5.2
18 and under 21 years	KEFN	8.2	8.3	8.1	7.3	6.3	6.2	5.7	5.7	6.3	7.1	7.6
21 years and over	KEFO	29.8	30.6	29.2	28.5	27.7	28.6	26.8	27.2	30.4	33.7	34.7
Summary offences[1]												
All ages	KEFP	179.2	185.3	194.1	219.0	213.3	211.5	180.5	222.9	174.9	188.3	171.0
10 and under 15 years	KEFQ	0.1	0.1	0.1	0.1	0.2	0.2	0.4	0.4	0.5	0.6	0.8
15 and under 18 years	KEFR	2.4	2.3	2.0	1.7	1.2	1.5	1.8	2.6	3.4	3.8	3.4
18 and under 21 years	KEFS	12.4	12.6	12.1	11.2	10.0	9.6	10.4	12.1	11.1	12.1	10.8
21 years and over	KEFT	164.3	170.4	179.8	206.0	201.9	200.2	167.9	207.9	160.0	171.7	155.4
Companies, etc												
Indictable offences	KEFU	2.9	3.1	2.2	2.1	1.7	1.4	1.5	1.5	1.3	1.5	1.3
Summary offences[1]	KEFV	19.6	17.6	17.2	16.2	12.5	10.9	9.9	10.9	10.0	10.7	8.9

1 It is estimated that in 1995 there was a shortfall of 75 100 offenders found guilty for certain summary offences.

Source: Home Office: 020 8760 8270

11.6 Persons cautioned by the police: by age and sex
England and Wales

Thousands

		1989	1990	1991	1992	1993	1994	1995	1996	1997	1998	1999
Males												
Indictable offences												
All ages	KEGA	102.8	124.2	131.4	155.0	153.6	153.6	149.3	142.6	143.3	142.9	126.1
10 and under 15 years	KEGB	32.3	36.4	33.0	35.0	31.4	32.3	29.2	25.1	22.9	23.7	22.0
15 and under 18 years	KEGC	31.3	38.1	38.5	41.1	37.1	35.5	35.3	33.0	32.0	32.0	28.7
18 and under 21 years	KEGD	10.9	15.1	18.4	23.8	24.5	25.0	24.8	24.3	25.2	25.7	22.7
21 years and over	KEGE	28.3	34.6	41.4	55.1	60.6	60.7	60.0	60.2	63.2	61.5	52.7
Summary offences												
All ages	KEGF	86.9	88.2	85.3	90.0	86.3	83.6	73.8	79.2	75.7	76.9	76.1
10 and under 15 years	KEGG	9.2	9.8	8.9	9.3	9.4	10.5	10.1	10.3	9.9	10.6	11.7
15 and under 18 years	KEGH	15.9	16.9	14.8	15.1	14.4	14.7	15.4	18.0	16.1	16.1	16.1
18 and under 21 years	KEGI	9.1	9.4	9.7	11.3	11.4	11.3	11.1	13.0	12.9	13.2	13.0
21 years and over	KEGJ	52.7	52.1	51.9	54.3	51.0	47.0	37.1	37.9	36.9	37.0	35.3
Females												
Indictable offences												
All ages	KEGK	33.2	42.1	48.5	61.1	55.9	56.2	53.3	48.2	46.0	48.8	44.5
10 and under 15 years	KEGL	7.9	10.3	11.0	14.3	12.8	15.2	14.0	10.8	9.2	11.1	9.8
15 and under 18 years	KEGM	8.9	11.7	13.1	15.2	12.8	12.4	12.2	10.9	9.5	10.3	9.3
18 and under 21 years	KEGN	3.0	4.2	5.5	7.3	6.7	6.1	6.0	5.6	5.7	5.9	5.7
21 years and over	KEGO	13.5	15.8	19.0	24.4	23.6	22.4	21.1	20.9	21.5	21.4	19.6
Summary offences												
All ages	KEGP	15.2	14.6	13.6	15.1	18.5	15.1	14.8	16.2	17.0	19.2	9.4
10 and under 15 years	KEGQ	1.0	1.1	1.0	1.2	1.3	1.5	1.7	1.8	1.7	2.1	2.5
15 and under 18 years	KEGR	2.3	2.8	2.4	2.5	2.3	2.5	2.7	3.2	3.2	3.7	3.9
18 and under 21 years	KEGS	2.4	2.1	1.9	2.0	2.1	1.9	1.9	2.1	2.3	2.6	2.7
21 years and over	KEGT	9.5	8.7	8.3	9.5	9.8	9.2	8.6	9.1	9.9	10.8	10.3
Companies, etc												
Indictable offences	KEGU	–	–	–	–	–	–	–	–	–	–	–
Summary offences	KEGV	–	–	–	–	–	–	–	–	–	–	–

Source: Home Office: 020 8760 8270

11.7 Sentence or order passed on offenders sentenced for indictable offences: by sex
England and Wales

Magistrates' courts and the Crown Court

Percentages

		1989	1990	1991	1992	1993	1994	1995	1996	1997	1998	1999
Males												
Sentence or order												
Absolute discharge	KEJB	0.7	0.7	0.7	0.8	0.9	0.8	0.8	0.8	0.7	0.7	0.6
Conditional discharge	KEJC	12.4	14.2	16.1	18.0	18.6	17.4	16.2	15.6	15.5	15.3	15.0
Probation order	KEJD	8.5	9.1	9.3	9.1	9.3	10.2	10.0	9.9	10.0	10.0	10.1
Supervision order	KEJE	1.6	1.5	1.4	1.4	2.0	2.4	2.7	2.9	2.7	2.7	2.7
Fine	KEJF	40.4	40.1	36.0	34.2	33.8	31.8	30.0	28.6	28.2	28.4	27.7
Community service order	KEJG	7.6	8.5	9.5	10.3	11.4	11.1	10.6	9.9	9.5	9.3	9.3
Attendance centre order	KEJH	1.8	1.9	1.9	1.8	1.9	2.0	2.0	1.9	1.8	1.7	1.8
Combination orders	KIJW	..	..	..	0.3	2.1	2.7	3.0	3.5	3.7	3.8	3.7
Curfew order	LUJP	..	..	..	..	..	..	..	0.1	0.1	0.2	0.3
Care order	KEJJ	0.1	0.1	–	..	..	..	..	..	..	..	..
Sec 53	LUJQ	–	–	–	–	0.1	0.1	0.1	0.2	0.3	0.2	0.2
Young offender institution	KEJK	5.4	4.5	4.6	4.3	0.8	4.9	5.6	6.1	6.1	6.0	6.2
Secure training order	LUJR	..	..	..	..	..	..	..	..	..	–	0.1
Imprisonment												
Fully suspended	KEJL	6.4	6.3	6.4	5.4	0.9	0.7	0.7	0.8	0.8	0.7	0.6
Partly suspended[1]	KAFN	0.6	0.4	0.3	0.2	..	..	..	..	..	..	..
Unsuspended	KEJM	11.6	10.7	11.4	11.6	12.0	13.6	16.0	17.2	17.9	18.2	18.7
Other sentence or order	KEJN	2.0	2.1	2.2	2.5	2.5	2.3	2.2	2.4	3.0	2.6	3.1
Total number of offenders (thousands) = 100 per cent	KEJA	293.2	294.7	291.9	282.5	267.5	272.6	262.9	260.8	275.4	292.4	291.3
Females												
Sentence or order												
Absolute discharge	KEKB	0.9	1.0	0.9	1.0	0.9	0.9	0.8	0.9	0.8	0.7	0.7
Conditional discharge	KEKC	30.2	33.2	35.9	37.5	35.4	34.4	32.4	30.6	29.4	28.7	26.9
Probation order	KEKD	17.4	17.5	17.0	15.9	15.4	17.5	18.0	19.0	19.1	19.1	19.4
Supervision order	KEKE	1.1	1.1	1.1	1.3	1.8	2.4	2.7	2.9	2.9	3.1	2.9
Fine	KEKF	33.2	30.8	27.2	26.2	29.2	25.6	24.1	22.5	21.8	21.3	20.8
Community service order	KEKG	3.3	4.1	4.6	5.3	6.1	6.4	6.6	6.5	6.5	6.5	7.1
Attendance centre order	KEKH	0.3	0.3	0.4	0.4	0.5	0.8	1.0	1.0	1.0	0.9	0.9
Combination orders	KIJX	..	..	..	0.2	1.4	2.1	2.4	3.0	3.2	3.4	3.3
Curfew order	LUJT	..	..	..	..	..	..	..	–	0.1	0.1	0.3
Care order	KEKJ	0.1	0.1	–	..	..	..	..	..	..	..	..
Sec 53	LUJU	–	–	–	–	–	–	0.1	0.1	0.1	–	0.1
Young offender institution	KEKK	1.1	0.8	0.9	0.8	1.1	1.1	1.5	1.8	1.9	2.2	2.4
Secure training order	LUJV	..	..	..	..	..	..	..	..	..	–	–
Imprisonment												
Fully suspended	KEKL	6.0	5.3	5.9	4.8	1.2	1.1	1.4	1.5	1.6	1.5	1.3
Partly suspended[1]	KAFP	0.5	0.3	0.3	0.2	..	..	..	..	..	..	..
Unsuspended	KEKM	4.2	3.5	4.1	4.4	5.0	5.9	7.4	8.4	9.4	10.0	11.0
Other sentence or order	KEKN	1.8	1.9	1.8	2.2	1.9	1.7	1.8	2.0	2.2	2.5	3.0
Total number of offenders (thousands) = 100 per cent	KEKA	43.0	43.9	41.9	40.0	37.7	39.5	37.5	38.0	42.1	47.2	49.0

1 Abolished October 1992.

Source: Home Office: 020 8760 8270

11.8 Offenders sentenced to immediate custody for standard list offences[1]
England and Wales

Between 1993 and 1997: by gender and number of previous convictions   Percentage[2]

			Number of previous convictions[3]				
	Nil	1 - 2	3 - 6	7 - 10	11 and over	Total sentenced for standard list offences	Total sentenced to custody for all offences
Year and gender							
1994							
Males	19	14	24	18	25	51 874	66 036
Females	35	21	17	10	18	2 842	3 149
Total	20	14	23	18	25	54 716	69 185
1995							
Males	18	14	22	18	27	58 592	75 369
Females	41	20	14	9	15	3 429	3 768
Total	20	14	22	18	27	62 021	79 137
1996[4]							
Males	18	16	21	17	27	78 392 (65 656)	80 240
Females	36	18	18	11	17	4 273 (4 057)	4 374
Total	20	16	21	17	27	82 665 (69 713)	84 614
1997[4]							
Males	16	16	23	16	29	85 580	87 620
Females	31	18	22	12	17	5 345	5 473
Total	17	16	23	16	28	90 934	93 093
1998[4]							
Males	20	14	20	15	30	91 800	94 000
Females	37	16	18	10	18	6 400	6 600
Total	22	14	20	15	29	98 200	100 600

1 These consist of all the indictable offences plus some of the more serious summary offences.
2 The percentages are based on samples of 3 304, 2 975, 6 994, 7 562 and 6 096 males and 163, 160, 379, 459 and 426 females in the years 1994, 1995, 1996, 1997 and 1998 respectively. Percentages are rounded and therefore may not add to 100.
3 Counting one conviction per court appearance.

4 From 1 January 1996 a number of summary motoring offences became standard list offences. The sentencing figures shown in brackets for 1996 exclude those sentenced for these offences. Excluding the new standard list offences from the analysis would slightly alter the percentages with previous convictions.
Source: Home Office: 020 7273 3177

11.9 Population in Prison Service establishments under sentence[1]
England and Wales

On 30 June 1993, 1994, 1995, 1996 and 1997 : by gender and number of previous convictions   Percentage[2]

		Number of previous convictions[3]					
	Previous convictions not found[3]	Nil	1 - 2	3 - 6	7 - 10	11 and over	Number of prisoners
Year and gender							
1994							
Males	5	15	16	23	18	22	33 960
Females	10	36	18	18	8	9	1 266
Total	5	16	16	23	18	22	35 226
1995							
Males	5	16	16	21	16	25	37 479
Females	15	34	18	15	9	9	1 456
Total	6	17	16	21	16	25	38 935
1996[4]							
Males	9	22	16	19	14	20	41 187
Females	17	37	17	14	7	8	1 727
Total	9	22	16	19	14	19	42 914
1997[4]							
Males	9	15	16	20	15	24	46 611
Females	15	36	16	15	8	11	2 063
Total	9	16	16	20	15	24	48 674
1998[4]							
Males	5	16	14	19	15	31	49 793
Females	11	35	17	17	8	13	2 366
Total	5	17	14	19	14	30	52 159

1 Excludes fine defaulters.
2 The percentages are based on samples of 6 675, 9 105, 11 882, 11 800 and 12 303 males and 1 243, 1 414, 1 804, 2 032 and 2 291 females in the years 1993, 1994, 1995, 1996, 1997 and 1998. respectively. Percentages are rounded and therefore may not add to 100.

3 In some cases it was not possible to find details on previous convictions. This can happen when a prisoner is not sentenced for a standard list offence and has no previous record for such offences.
4 See footnote 1 of Table 11.8. Excluding the new standard list offences from the analysis would only alter the results very slightly.
Source: Home Office: 020 7273 3177

11.10 Receptions and average population in custody
England and Wales

Number

		1989	1990	1991	1992	1993	1994	1995	1996	1997	1998	1999
Receptions												
Type of inmate:												
Untried	KEDA	58 789	53 135	54 676	49 869	53 565	57 079	55 287	58 888	62 066	64 697	64 572
Convicted, unsentenced	KEDB	17 800	20 410	19 927	21 250	30 098	34 563	32 039	34 987	36 424	43 387	45 893
Sentenced	KEDE	76 430	67 510	72 313	69 832	72 966	83 657	89 173	82 861	87 168	91 282	93 965
Immediate custodial sentence	KEDF	59 445	50 851	53 340	50 006	50 563	61 188	69 016	74 306	80 832	85 908	90 238
Young offenders	KEDG	17 674	14 380	15 028	13 174	13 205	14 956	16 244	17 593	18 743	19 599	21 020
Up to 18 months	KEDH	14 764	11 758	12 447	10 862	11 114	12 739	13 783	14 156	14 893	15 965	17 338
Over 18 months up to 4 years	KEDJ	2 519	2 307	2 270	1 982	1 752	1 882	2 129	2 913	3 254	3 153	3 171
Over 4 years (including life)	KEDL	391	315	311	330	339	335	332	524	596	481	511
Adults	KFBO	41 771	36 471	38 312	36 832	37 358	46 232	52 772	56 713	62 089	66 309	69 218
Up to 18 months	KEDV	29 444	25 363	27 159	25 872	27 643	35 520	40 638	42 673	46 727	50 844	53 814
Over 18 months up to 4 years	KEDW	9 270	8 253	8 199	7 967	6 864	7 744	8 811	10 119	10 972	11 126	10 892
Over 4 years (including life)	KEDX	3 057	2 855	2 954	2 993	2 851	2 968	3 323	3 921	4 390	4 339	4 512
Committed in default of payment												
of a fine	KEDY	16 985	16 659	18 973	19 826	22 403	22 469	20 157	8 555	6 336	5 374	3 727
Young offenders	KEEA	3 671	3 522	4 209	4 282	3 353	3 268	2 846	885	555	568	366
Adults	KAFQ	13 314	13 137	14 764	15 544	19 050	19 201	17 311	7 670	5 781	4 806	3 361
Non-criminal prisoners	KEDM	3 021	2 314	2 791	3 109	5 073	4 507	3 789	3 128	3 204	3 290	3 271
Immigration Act 1971	KEDN	1 448	916	1 225	1 272	1 837	1 641	1 825	1 857	2 122	2 348	2 443
Others	KEDO	1 573	1 398	1 566	1 837	3 236	2 866	1 964	1 271	1 082	942	828
Average population[3]												
Total in custody	KEDP	48 610	45 636	45 897	45 817	44 565	48 794	51 047	55 281	61 114	65 298	64 771
Total in prison service establishments	KFBQ	48 500	44 975	44 809	44 718	44 551	48 621	50 962	55 281	61 114	65 298	64 771
Police cells[2]	KFBN	110	661	1 088	1 098	14	173	85	–	–	–	–
Untried	KEDQ	8 576	7 625	7 545	7 387	7 960	9 047	8 352	8 374	8 453	8 157	7 947
Convicted, unsentenced	KEDR	1 820	1 815	1 930	1 987	2 700	3 181	2 954	3 238	3 678	4 411	4 571
Remanded for medical examination[1]	KEDS	39	20	17	14	12	15	9	6	8	9	8
Others	KEDT	1 781	1 795	1 913	1 973	2 688	3 166	2 945	3 232	3 670	4 402	4 563
Sentenced	KEDU	37 885	35 336	35 034	35 037	33 317	35 753	39 040	43 043	48 413	52 176	51 691
Immediate custodial sentence	KFBR	37 427	34 972	34 665	34 707	32 825	35 308	38 636	42 863	48 272	52 045	51 596
Young offenders	KFBS	7 160	6 173	5 754	5 382	5 054	5 258	5 752	6 700	7 820	8 490	8 344
Up to 18 months	KFBU	3 638	3 143	3 095	2 808	2 671	2 736	2 911	2 930	3 267	3 507	3 394
Over 18 months up to 4 years	KFBV	2 749	2 328	2 033	1 999	1 800	1 902	2 159	2 606	3 019	3 155	3 158
Over 4 years (including life)	KFBW	773	699	623	575	583	620	682	1 164	1 534	1 828	1 792
Adults	KFCO	30 267	28 799	28 911	29 326	27 771	30 050	32 884	36 162	40 451	43 556	43 343
Up to 18 months	KFCP	7 646	7 001	7 194	7 170	7 054	8 051	8 845	8 199	9 724	10 308	9 441
Over 18 months up to 4 years	KFCQ	11 191	9 751	9 333	9 416	8 445	9 164	10 184	10 320	10 777	11 707	11 322
Over 4 years (including life)	KFCR	11 430	12 047	12 384	12 740	12 272	12 835	13 855	17 644	19 950	21 541	22 580
Committed in default of payment of a fine	KFCS	458	364	369	330	492	446	403	180	141	131	95
Young offenders	KFEW	71	80	85	65	77	62	54	22	13	15	9
Adults	KFEX	387	284	284	265	415	384	349	158	128	116	86
Non-criminal prisoners	KEEB	220	200	300	308	574	640	615	626	571	554	558
Immigration Act 1971	KEEC	157	144	222	227	431	487	483	516	485	476	485
Others	KEED	61	56	78	81	143	153	132	111	87	78	73

1 Under Section 30, Magistrates' Courts Act 1980.
2 Mostly untried prisoners.
3 Components may not add to totals because they have been rounded independently.

Source: Home Office: 020 7217 5567

11.11 Prison population serving sentences: analysis by age and offence[1]
England and Wales

Number

	Total	Age in years							
		14 - 16	17 - 20	21 - 24	25 - 29	30 - 39	40 - 49	50 - 59	60 and over
At 30 June 1994									
Offences									
Males									
Total	34 474	815	3 942	6 919	7 704	8 954	4 019	1 599	522
Violence against the person	7 744	99	669	1 376	1 738	2 270	1 055	397	140
Sexual offences	3 270	15	96	228	454	925	823	494	235
Burglary	5 136	257	1 037	1 524	1 178	887	180	64	9
Robbery	5 094	126	617	1 183	1 451	1 338	313	60	6
Theft, handling, fraud and forgery	4 005	167	479	784	795	965	573	195	47
Other offences	7 292	104	614	1 414	1 672	2 154	944	323	67
Offence not known	1 933	47	430	410	416	415	131	66	18
Females									
Total	1 289	27	105	238	295	382	175	53	14
Violence against the person	279	9	31	48	56	71	44	15	5
Sexual offences	12	-	-	1	2	4	4	1	-
Burglary	41	-	10	8	5	12	6	-	-
Robbery	96	5	13	30	21	23	4	-	-
Theft, handling, fraud and forgery	298	6	14	48	83	91	38	16	2
Other offences	466	5	28	78	108	157	65	18	7
Offence not known	97	2	9	25	20	24	14	3	-
At 30 June 1995									
Offences									
Males									
Total	37 897	957	4 702	7 202	8 261	10 021	4 386	1 792	576
Violence against the person	8 515	120	871	1 400	1 915	2 529	1 122	414	144
Sexual offences	3 658	19	121	231	456	1 029	936	575	291
Burglary	5 938	257	1 220	1 689	1 418	1 086	197	63	8
Robbery	5 267	184	795	1 132	1 314	1 448	332	52	10
Theft, handling, fraud and forgery	4 613	183	561	827	932	1 187	617	263	43
Drugs offences	3 863	11	188	511	874	1 316	677	241	45
Other offences	4 421	112	578	1 072	1 022	1 083	389	142	23
Offence not known	1 622	71	368	340	330	343	116	42	12
Females									
Total	1 482	31	152	233	324	443	224	59	16
Violence against the person	290	7	32	46	63	69	50	18	5
Sexual offences	12	1	2	1	2	3	2	1	-
Burglary	57	2	12	14	16	9	4	-	-
Robbery	108	9	27	27	19	22	4	-	-
Theft, handling, fraud and forgery	379	5	19	54	96	122	57	22	4
Drugs offences	398	-	36	51	79	143	74	12	3
Other offences	145	3	12	20	27	59	18	4	2
Offence not known	93	4	12	20	22	16	15	2	2

	Total	Age in years							
		15 - 17	18 - 20	21 - 24	25 - 29	30 - 39	40 - 49	50 - 59	60 and over
At 30 June 1996									
Offences									
Males									
Total	41 323	1 262	5 101	7 569	8 719	11 259	4 723	2 002	688
Violence against the person	9 236	177	937	1 547	1 986	2 747	1 174	501	167
Sexual offences	3 939	32	120	246	437	1 175	946	628	355
Burglary	6 351	373	1 287	1 753	1 484	1 199	202	49	4
Robbery	5 594	268	978	1 171	1 316	1 445	350	62	4
Theft, handling, fraud and forgery	4 709	180	540	798	893	1 311	678	266	43
Drugs offences	5 273	11	293	746	1 239	1 787	850	286	61
Other offences	4 729	119	600	1 050	1 102	1 248	419	160	31
Offence not known	1 492	102	346	258	262	347	104	50	23
Females									
Total	1 732	57	195	263	373	534	223	77	10
Violence against the person	355	16	51	55	60	89	57	22	5
Sexual offences	12	-	2	3	1	2	4	-	-
Burglary	80	5	23	25	12	11	4	-	-
Robbery	124	17	28	23	32	20	3	1	-
Theft, handling, fraud and forgery	433	7	29	48	115	141	62	27	4
Drugs offences	794	3	32	134	181	267	131	44	2
Other offences	166	5	23	31	32	52	16	7	-
Offence not known	76	7	4	13	15	27	9	1	-

1 Includes persons committed in default of payment of a fine.

Source: Home Office: 020 7217 5567

11.11
Prison population serving sentences: analysis by age and offence[1]
England and Wales

continued

Number

	Total	Age in years							
		15 - 17	18 - 20	21 - 24	25 - 29	30 - 39	40 - 49	50 - 59	60 and over
At 30 June 1997									
Offences									
Males									
Total	46 739	1 620	6 078	8 472	9 939	12 503	5 046	2 299	782
Violence against the person	10 045	216	1 039	1 631	2 181	3 014	1 234	549	181
Sexual offences	4 069	39	121	232	465	1 169	934	726	383
Burglary	7 983	448	1 574	2 184	1 938	1 515	245	71	8
Robbery	6 278	437	1 227	1 352	1 370	1 471	337	73	11
Theft, handling, fraud and forgery	5 052	167	605	865	1 020	1 417	638	272	68
Drugs offences	6 486	29	356	892	1 494	2 242	1 027	371	75
Other offences	1 746	142	437	296	324	321	141	64	21
Offence not known	5 080	142	719	1 020	1 147	1 354	490	173	35
Females									
Total	2 066	53	198	372	449	615	271	91	17
Violence against the person	391	18	43	72	61	105	62	22	8
Sexual offences	8	-	1	1	1	3	2	-	-
Burglary	101	4	13	29	31	17	6	1	-
Robbery	161	18	50	29	29	28	5	2	-
Theft, handling, fraud and forgery	455	3	25	78	100	148	71	25	5
Drugs offences	691	4	43	111	173	237	88	31	4
Other offences	68	-	8	12	15	25	4	4	-
Offence not known	191	6	15	40	39	52	33	6	-
At 30 June 1998									
Offences									
Males									
Total	49 902	1 627	5 807	8 780	10 590	14 109	5 485	2 608	896
Violence against the person	10 530	235	1 028	1 670	2 215	3 239	1 345	594	204
Sexual offences	4 781	51	140	224	560	1 366	1 113	872	455
Burglary	8 541	432	1 502	2 256	2 179	1 799	298	65	10
Robbery	6 452	449	1 244	1 319	1 427	1 587	350	61	15
Theft, handling, fraud & forgery	5 193	190	556	906	1 071	1 535	587	300	48
Drugs offences	7 103	38	308	944	1 616	2 569	1 092	441	95
Other offences	5 277	137	690	1 087	1 132	1 461	509	215	46
Offence not known	2 025	95	339	374	390	553	191	60	23
Females									
Total	2 367	62	210	425	501	709	332	116	12
Violence against the person	420	11	44	68	80	116	68	27	6
Sexual offences	16	1	1	1	2	5	5	1	-
Burglary	118	6	17	27	32	28	6	2	-
Robbery	177	24	45	33	36	28	8	3	-
Theft, handling, fraud & forgery	514	6	36	97	107	169	72	26	1
Drugs offences	794	3	32	134	181	267	131	44	2
Other offences	218	8	22	42	41	65	30	8	2
Offences not known	110	3	13	23	22	31	12	5	1
At 30 June 1999									
Offences									
Males									
Total	48 956	1 643	5 633	8 245	10 080	14 072	5 552	2 678	1 053
Violence against the person	10 435	250	1 070	1 548	2 033	3 260	1 428	608	238
Sexual offences	4 930	48	99	236	485	1 448	1 133	935	546
Burglary	8 626	447	1 441	2 207	2 230	1 899	322	73	7
Robbery	6 175	410	1 126	1 384	1 272	1 556	353	58	16
Theft, handling, fraud and forgery	5 027	208	585	886	1 065	1 418	529	279	57
Drugs offences	7 303	36	338	866	1 614	2 720	1 132	476	121
Other offences	5 224	185	742	968	1 120	1 422	541	197	49
Offence not known	1 236	59	232	150	261	349	114	52	19
Females									
Total	2 436	67	224	427	491	798	301	108	20
Violence against the person	429	17	65	50	77	125	63	25	7
Sexual offences	17	-	2	1	-	5	7	1	1
Burglary	158	7	27	37	38	41	6	2	-
Robbery	158	15	24	36	33	41	6	3	-
Theft, handling, fraud and forgery	502	11	33	113	99	159	58	24	5
Drugs offences	875	2	50	131	184	340	129	35	4
Other offences	220	13	9	45	43	68	26	16	-
Offence not known	77	2	14	14	17	19	6	2	3

1 Includes persons committed in default of payment of a fine.

Source: Home Office: 020 7217 5567

11.12 Expenditure on prisons
England and Wales

Operating cost and total capital employed, years ended 31 March

£ thousand

		1993 /94	1994 /95	1995 /96	1996 /97	1997 /98	1998 /99	1999 /00
Expenditure								
Staff costs	KWUV	833 900	866 600	895 700	948 700	939 700	995 200	1 044 700
Accommodation costs	KXCO	163 800	127 100	122 400	113 900	116 200	163 400	101 000
Other operating costs	KXCP	295 500	323 400	369 000	373 900	472 600	538 800	632 600
Depreciation	KXCQ	4 100	90 300	159 300	123 600	160 200	146 100	115 700
Cost of capital	KXCR	–	201 800	211 500	225 500	231 300	262 500	254 900
Total expenditure	KXCS	1 297 300	1 609 200	1 757 900	1 785 600	1 920 000	2 106 000	2 148 900
Income								
Contributions from industries	KXCT	−4 700	−4 600	−6 400	−6 600	−7 900	−8 300	−10 400
Other operating income	KXCU	−4 300	−3 300	−4 900	−5 300	−8 500	−8 500	−9 600
Total income	KXCV	−9 000	−7 900	−11 300	−11 900	−16 400	−16 800	−20 000
Net operating costs	KXCW	1 288 300	1 601 300	1 746 600	1 773 700	1 903 600	2 089 200	2 128 900
Total capital employed	KXCX	..	3 452 000	3 580 700	3 920 900	4 116 900	4 345 100	4 340 500

1 For 1993/94 figures are not directly comparable with subsequent years. No figure is available for cost of capital or capital employed as no balance sheet was produced.

Source: Home Office: 020 7217 5567

11.13 Crimes and offences recorded by the police
Scotland

Thousands

		1989	1990	1991	1992	1993	1994	1995	1996	1997	1998	1999
Non-sexual crimes of violence												
against the person	KAFR	18.4	18.2	21.7	23.3	19.4	19.8	21.1	21.5	19.2	21.1	23.4
Serious assault, etc[1]	KAFS	7.3	6.3	7.0	7.7	6.5	6.7	6.9	7.0	6.1	6.6	7.2
Handling offensive weapons	KAFT	4.8	5.1	6.2	6.5	5.2	5.3	6.5	6.8	6.0	6.7	7.9
Robbery	KAFU	4.4	4.7	6.2	6.8	5.6	5.3	5.3	5.3	4.5	5.0	5.1
Other	KAFV	1.9	2.2	2.4	2.2	2.1	2.5	2.4	2.5	2.6	2.8	3.3
Crimes involving indecency	KAFW	5.7	6.0	5.8	6.2	6.0	6.0	5.5	5.7	7.1	7.4	6.0
Sexual assault	KAFX	1.5	1.5	1.4	1.6	1.6	1.6	1.6	1.7	2.0	2.2	1.9
Lewd and indecent behaviour	KAFY	2.6	2.6	2.6	2.6	2.7	2.7	2.4	2.5	3.0	3.0	2.4
Other	KAFZ	1.7	2.0	1.8	2.0	1.7	1.7	1.5	1.5	2.2	2.3	1.7
Crimes involving dishonesty	KAGA	355.5	385.2	430.2	415.0	374.9	350.3	321.2	295.4	267.2	275.4	276.2
Housebreaking	KAGB	93.7	101.7	116.1	113.2	97.8	88.4	74.2	64.5	55.5	56.6	53.8
Theft by opening a lockfast places	KAGC	84.7	92.4	102.8	92.2	84.8	74.9	66.5	60.5	51.1	51.8	50.2
Theft of a motor vehicle	KAGD	29.1	36.1	44.3	47.4	42.8	42.0	37.5	34.2	28.6	28.4	29.8
Shoplifting	KAGE	26.3	26.8	30.1	29.7	26.7	26.6	28.0	26.9	26.3	29.6	32.0
Other theft	KAGF	92.7	97.8	104.6	98.8	93.3	88.9	87.7	82.6	79.6	80.1	81.1
Fraud	KAGG	19.3	19.6	22.0	22.6	19.1	17.7	17.1	16.1	15.7	18.6	18.6
Other	KAGH	9.7	10.8	10.3	11.1	10.3	12.0	10.2	10.8	10.3	10.2	10.6
Fire-raising, vandalism, etc	KAGI	79.1	86.5	89.7	92.2	84.2	88.5	86.5	89.0	81.0	79.2	79.6
Fire-raising	KAGJ	4.4	4.3	4.8	4.7	4.1	3.6	3.3	3.3	2.8	2.5	2.3
Vandalism, etc	KAGK	74.7	82.1	84.9	87.6	80.1	85.0	83.2	85.7	78.2	76.6	77.2
Other crimes[2]	KAGL	19.5	22.6	25.5	28.2	32.7	35.4	41.3	40.3	46.1	48.5	50.5
Crimes against public justice[2]	KAGM	12.3	12.9	13.3	14.4	14.5	16.0	16.4	16.1	16.6	16.9	18.5
Drugs	KAGN	7.0	9.6	12.0	13.6	18.0	19.3	24.8	24.0	29.4	31.5	31.9
Other	KAGO	0.2	0.2	0.2	0.2	0.2	0.2	0.2	0.1	0.1	0.1	0.1
Total crimes[2]	KAGQ	478.2	518.5	572.9	564.9	517.2	500.1	475.7	452.0	420.6	431.6	435.7
Miscellaneous offences	KAGR	124.9	127.0	122.3	127.5	126.6	133.2	134.4	146.1	155.9	153.7	151.0
Petty assault[1]	KAGS	37.7	39.6	41.0	42.5	41.3	45.1	46.6	47.6	50.1	51.0	54.0
Breach of the peace	KAGT	56.3	57.7	55.3	60.0	61.4	65.5	66.1	70.8	73.1	71.7	71.0
Drunkenness	KAGU	12.2	11.7	10.4	10.4	10.1	10.3	9.7	9.6	9.7	8.5	7.8
Other	KAGV	18.8	18.0	15.6	14.6	13.7	12.3	11.9	18.0	23.1	22.6	18.2
Motor vehicle offences	KAGW	283.8	296.2	305.6	306.4	315.1	330.7	317.5	305.9	331.0	362.1	353.4
Dangerous and careless driving	KAGX	25.8	25.3	23.1	22.5	20.0	21.1	18.7	17.3	16.3	15.8	14.0
Drunk driving	KAGY	10.9	11.4	11.0	11.3	10.9	10.8	10.7	11.8	11.2	10.6	10.8
Speeding	KAGZ	81.5	90.0	100.1	93.6	85.4	85.8	85.1	82.4	91.9	115.5	125.3
Unlawful use of a motor vehicle	KAHA	67.6	70.6	75.7	79.9	85.8	88.7	83.4	79.1	79.1	75.5	77.8
Vehicle defect offences	KAHB	48.2	47.5	46.8	47.8	51.4	56.9	56.3	53.5	60.1	63.6	52.9
Other	KAHC	49.8	51.5	48.9	51.5	61.7	67.4	63.2	61.8	72.3	81.2	72.5
Total offences	KAHD	408.6	423.2	427.9	433.9	441.7	463.9	451.9	452.0	486.9	515.8	504.5
Total crimes and offences[2]	KAHE	886.9	941.7	1 000.8	998.8	959.0	964.0	927.6	903.9	907.5	947.3	940.2

1 The definition of serious assault was changed in January 1990 to improve consistency between forces. It is estimated that the number of serious assaults that would have been recorded in 1989, using the revised definition, is some 1,150 fewer than actually recorded, with a corresponding rise in petty assaults.

2 Data from 1983 onwards has been revised as a result of a legislative change which came into force on 1 April 1996. From this date "offending while on bail" is no longer regarded as an offence in its own right.

Source: The Scottish Executive Justice Department: 0131 244 2225

173

Crime and justice

11.14 Persons proceeded against
Scotland

Number of persons

		1988	1989	1990	1991	1992	1993	1994	1995	1996	1997	1998
Non-sexual crimes of violence	KEHC	4 290	4 198	4 392	4 356	5 141	5 327	4 910	4 969	5 741	5 633	5 290
Homicide	KEHD	116	119	100	106	148	150	122	159	159	119	105
Serious assault, etc	KEHE	1 412	1 432	1 512	1 425	1 546	1 592	1 508	1 298	1 421	1 485	1 452
Handling offensive weapons	KEHF	1 444	1 430	1 427	1 504	2 028	2 028	2 001	2 357	2 946	2 882	2 664
Robbery	KEHG	906	786	846	885	949	1 006	990	855	929	848	758
Other violence	KEHH	412	431	507	436	470	371	289	302	286	299	311
Crimes of indecency	KEHI	1 366	1 371	1 825	1 660	1 563	1 683	1 587	1 452	1 154	1 379	1 496
Sexual assault	KEHJ	220	225	233	200	203	229	195	182	194	212	207
Lewd and libidinous practices	KEHK	451	438	440	429	363	370	399	350	376	399	400
Other indecency	KEHL	695	708	1 152	1 031	997	1 084	993	920	584	768	889
Crimes of dishonesty	KEHM	43 054	40 808	40 329	40 765	40 950	38 601	37 026	35 301	33 695	31 931	30 330
Housebreaking	KEHN	8 266	7 673	7 408	7 258	7 105	6 370	6 126	5 452	4 639	4 054	3 706
Theft by opening lockfast place	KEHO	3 832	3 847	3 586	3 906	3 698	3 640	3 565	3 111	2 906	2 665	2 302
Theft of motor vehicle	KEHP	3 363	3 082	3 226	3 476	3 688	3 480	3 494	3 449	3 497	3 259	2 849
Shoplifting	KEHQ	6 526	6 646	7 098	7 921	8 469	8 262	7 260	7 185	7 840	7 959	8 357
Other theft	KEHR	12 975	11 574	10 765	9 944	9 485	8 565	7 532	7 485	7 170	7 113	6 761
Fraud[1]	KEHS	3 514	3 531	3 753	3 438	3 326	3 519	4 191	4 073	3 566	3 202	2 915
Other dishonesty	KEHT	4 578	4 455	4 493	4 822	5 179	4 765	4 858	4 546	4 077	3 679	3 440
Fire-raising, vandalism, etc	KEHU	7 393	6 937	6 757	6 593	6 651	6 029	5 644	5 808	6 198	5 917	5 475
Fire-raising	KEHV	235	229	214	192	213	188	203	177	173	149	150
Vandalism, etc	KEHW	7 158	6 708	6 543	6 401	6 438	5 841	5 441	5 631	6 025	5 768	5 325
Other crime	KEHX	9 169	9 639	10 749	11 990	12 126	13 751	15 108	16 018	17 243	15 515	14 414
Crime against public justice	KFBK	6 485	6 854	7 272	7 537	7 377	8 407	8 892	9 424	9 748	7 248	6 224
Drugs offences	KFBL	2 638	2 756	3 436	4 413	4 713	5 313	6 185	6 556	7 454	8 219	8 153
Other	KFBM	46	29	41	40	36	31	31	38	41	48	37
Total crimes	KEHB	65 272	62 953	64 052	65 364	66 431	65 391	64 275	63 548	64 031	60 375	57 005
Miscellaneous offences	KEHZ	67 674	63 559	60 781	58 962	60 589	54 497	48 383	50 780	52 714	51 837	47 622
Petty assault	KEIA	16 146	16 858	15 990	15 116	14 715	14 452	13 962	14 809	15 577	15 875	15 165
Breach of the peace	KEIB	27 397	24 830	23 483	21 955	21 148	20 353	19 102	20 613	22 377	22 336	20 732
Drunkenness	KEIC	3 465	3 028	2 930	2 376	2 253	1 803	1 483	1 364	1 160	983	783
Other miscellaneous offences[1]	KEID	20 666	18 843	18 378	19 515	22 473	17 889	13 836	13 994	13 600	12 643	10 942
Motor vehicle offences	KEIE	65 627	67 392	73 784	76 566	72 055	64 580	66 009	62 840	58 712	60 344	54 605
Dangerous and careless driving	KEIF	7 363	8 603	8 862	7 840	7 177	5 883	5 162	5 273	5 193	5 150	4 199
Drunk driving	KEIG	10 680	8 875	8 997	8 679	8 314	7 812	7 601	7 798	8 313	8 900	7 527
Speeding	KEIH	11 216	13 959	18 202	21 807	19 519	15 405	16 787	15 159	12 645	11 805	12 059
Unlawful use of vehicle	KEII	22 820	20 002	20 881	21 742	22 033	21 951	22 947	21 528	21 124	22 213	20 062
Vehicle defect offences	KEIJ	5 197	5 071	5 035	4 489	4 111	3 308	3 560	3 683	3 548	3 775	2 960
Other motor vehicle offences	KEIK	8 351	10 882	11 807	12 009	10 901	10 221	9 952	9 399	7 889	8 501	7 798
Total offences	KEHY	133 301	130 951	134 565	135 528	132 644	119 077	114 392	113 620	111 426	112 181	102 227
Total crimes and offences	KEHA	198 573	193 904	198 617	200 892	199 075	184 468	178 667	177 168	175 457	172 556	159 232

1 For 1997 a net switch of around 850 persons proceeded against was made from the 'other miscellaneous offences' category to 'fraud'.

Source: Scottish Executive Justice Department: 0131 244 2229

11.15 Persons called to court
Scotland

Number of persons

		1988	1989	1990	1991	1992	1993	1994	1995	1996	1997	1998
Court procedure												
High Court[1]	KEIQ	1 062	1 056	1 099	1 227	1 419	1 601	1 228	1 390	1 420	1 356	1 225
Sheriff Court	KEIU	130 866	103 150	101 678	100 013	100 109	96 391	97 579	98 306	100 928	98 867	92 519
District Court	KEIV	81 063	80 153	83 591	87 186	84 704	74 920	68 183	66 037	62 485	61 648	57 182
Stipendiary Magistrate Court	KEIW	11 785	8 745	11 300	11 522	11 732	10 472	10 893	10 649	9 973	9 943	7 794
Total called to court[2]	KEIZ	197 805	193 162	197 722	200 002	198 038	183 674	178 067	176 423	174 844	171 932	158 815

1 Including cases remitted to the High Court from the Sheriff Court.
2 Includes court type not known.

Source: Scottish Executive Justice Department: 0131 244 2229

11.16 Persons with charge proved: by main penalty
Scotland

Number of persons

Main penalty		1988	1989	1990	1991	1992	1993	1994	1995	1996	1997	1998
Restriction of liberty order[1]	ZBRE	..	..	..	..	..	..	..	..	..	..	71
Supervised attendance order[2]	ZBRF	..	..	..	..	..	..	..	..	..	73	68
Absolute discharge	KEXA	669	699	869	887	967	989	839	939	1 008	1 064	964
Admonition or caution	KEXB	15 983	15 552	16 558	17 137	17 441	16 976	16 243	15 857	15 859	15 039	13 893
Probation	KEXC	3 343	3 840	4 268	4 877	5 385	5 722	6 145	6 145	6 435	6 814	7 144
Remit to children's hearing	KEXD	59	67	52	81	72	83	124	172	193	219	177
Community service order	KEXE	3 423	4 056	4 739	5 190	5 473	5 079	5 320	5 339	5 711	5 707	5 246
Fine	KEXF	139 283	133 817	135 273	135 479	131 842	116 918	112 748	110 337	105 384	103 861	94 910
Compensation order	KEXG	1 703	1 771	1 678	1 591	1 575	1 578	1 535	1 527	1 415	1 304	1 298
Insanity, hospital, guardianship order	KYAN	160	151	152	148	133	138	133	136	159	162	129
Prison	KEXI	9 669	9 091	8 796	9 222	10 085	10 832	11 583	11 561	12 134	11 621	11 447
Young offenders' institution[3]	KEXJ	4 799	4 531	4 150	4 318	4 488	4 461	4 472	4 646	4 744	4 557	4 459
Detention of child	KEXM	28	19	23	35	22	30	36	48	45	29	20
Total persons with charge proved	KEXO	179 119	173 594	176 558	178 965	177 483	162 806	159 178	156 707	153 087	150 450	139 826

1 A community sentence introduced by Section 5 of the Crime and Punishment (Scotland) Act 1995 and available on a pilot basis to 3 Scottish sheriff courts since August 1998.
2 A pilot scheme covering the provisions of the Criminal Procedure (Scotland) Act 1995 replacing fines for 16 & 17 year olds has been operating in a small number of Scottish courts.
3 Includes detention centres, which were only available to courts until 1988.

Source: Scottish Executive Justice Department: 0131 244 2229

11.17 Persons with charge proved: by age and sex
Scotland

Number of persons

		1988	1989	1990	1991	1992	1993	1994	1995	1996	1997	1998
Males	KEWA	154 360	148 157	150 105	150 482	147 692	136 127	136 533	133 330	130 961	129 461	120 482
Under 16	KEWB	276	215	173	189	138	138	171	180	149	137	135
16 to 20	KEWC	44 358	41 206	39 720	38 284	36 494	32 589	30 708	30 113	31 703	31 310	29 310
21 to 30	KEWD	58 375	56 509	59 114	59 532	59 561	56 052	56 517	54 184	52 217	50 684	46 121
Over 30	KEWE	48 317	46 602	48 390	49 802	49 093	45 701	47 788	47 648	45 799	46 281	44 047
Not known	KEWF	3 034	3 625	2 708	2 675	2 406	1 647	1 349	1 205	1 093	1 049	869
Females	KEWG	22 791	23 186	24 400	26 340	28 051	25 405	21 650	22 412	21 308	20 246	18 667
Under 16	KEWH	20	9	11	18	9	6	8	17	12	11	5
16 to 20	KEWI	3 982	3 700	3 903	3 927	3 885	3 589	2 939	3 098	3 302	3 424	3 361
21 to 30	KEWJ	9 184	9 110	10 077	10 958	11 998	10 557	9 190	9 284	8 461	8 095	7 456
Over 30	KEWK	8 760	9 261	9 507	10 519	11 409	10 611	9 002	9 439	8 894	8 266	7 531
Not known	KEWL	845	1 106	902	918	750	642	511	574	639	450	314
Males and Females	KEWM	177 151	171 343	174 505	176 822	175 743	161 532	158 183	155 742	152 269	149 707	139 149
Under 16	KEWN	296	224	184	207	147	144	179	197	161	148	140
16 to 20	KEWO	48 304	44 906	43 623	42 211	40 379	36 178	33 647	33 211	35 005	34 734	32 671
21 to 30	KEWP	67 559	65 619	69 194	70 490	71 559	66 609	65 707	63 468	60 678	58 779	53 577
Over 30	KEWQ	57 077	55 863	57 897	60 321	60 502	56 312	56 790	57 087	54 693	54 547	51 578
Not known	KEWR	3 879	4 731	3 610	3 593	3 156	2 289	1 860	1 779	1 732	1 499	1 183
Companies	KEWS	1 869	2 212	2 024	2 126	1 717	1 263	991	961	812	737	675
Total persons with charge proved[1]	KEWT	179 119	173 594	176 558	178 965	177 483	162 806	159 178	156 707	153 087	150 450	139 826

1 Includes sex not known.

Source: Scottish Executive Justice Department: 0131 244 2229

11.18 Penal establishments: average daily population and receptions
Scotland

Number

		1989	1990	1991	1992	1993	1994	1995	1996	1997	1998[1]	1999
Average daily population												
Male	KEPB	4 838	4 587	4 696	5 099	5 466	5 408	5 451	5 673	5 900	5 825	5 817
Female	KEPC	147	137	143	158	171	177	175	189	184	193	212
Total	KEPA	4 986	4 724	4 839	5 257	5 637	5 585	5 626	5 862	6 084	6 018	6 029
Analysis by type of custody												
Remand	KEPD	770	751	770	876	948	1 015	998	1 000	947	938	1 012
Persons under sentence: total	KEPE	4 209	3 961	4 056	4 375	4 686	4 569	4 624	4 861	5 134	5 077	5 016
Adult prisoners	KEPF	3 341	3 201	3 322	3 552	3 795	3 785	3 823	4 026	4 282	4 278	4 205
Young offenders	KEPI	813	708	684	769	819	720	719	770	787	712	692
Persons recalled from supervision/licence	KEPN	33	39	39	32	40	37	44	46	46	70	91
Others	KEPO	21	13	12	21	32	28	38	18	19	17	27
Persons sentenced by court martial	KEPP	6	11	12	6	2	1	3	–	1	2	1
Civil prisoners	KEPQ	1	1	1	1	1	1	–	1	1	1	1
Receptions to penal establishments												
Total[2]												
Remand	KEPR	14 276	15 168	13 127	13 546	13 412	14 922	14 253	14 977	14 826	15 098	15 291
Male	KEPS	13 486	14 323	12 360	12 722	12 478	13 985	13 377	13 976	13 850	13 979	14 090
Female	KEPT	790	845	767	824	934	937	876	1 001	976	1 119	1 201
Persons under sentence: total	KEPU	19 484	17 134	18 226	19 966	22 157	21 111	19 030	22 155	23 202	22 269	20 741
Male	KEPV	18 466	16 235	17 033	18 856	20 741	19 697	17 737	20 869	21 936	20 862	19 465
Female	KEPW	1 018	899	1 193	1 110	1 416	1 414	1 293	1 286	1 266	1 407	1 276
Imprisoned: Adults:												
directly	KEPX	7 619	7 551	7 951	8 543	9 444	9 349	8 730	10 040	9 698	9 959	9 484
in default of fine	KEPY	6 801	5 182	6 336	6 603	7 956	7 377	6 299	7 432	8 873	7 866	7 154
in default of compensation order	KEPZ	49	23	6	40	41	26	13	..[4]	..[4]	..[4]	..[4]
Sentenced to young offenders' institution:												
directly	KEQA	2 651	2 719	2 356	3 041	3 052	2 855	2 772	3 111	2 784	2 844	2 687
in default of fine	KEQB	2 353	1 653	1 573	1 736	1 660	1 498	1 210	1 567	1 847	1 593	1 411
in default of compensation order	KEQC	9	3	2	2	4	6	4	..[4]	..[4]	..[4]	..[4]
Persons recalled from supervised release orders	JYYD	2	3	2	1	–	–	2	5	11	7	5
Persons sentenced by court martial	KEQH	8	10	1	2	7	5	4	4	4	5	3
Civil prisoners[3]	KEQI	15	21	25	34	37	27	25	32	23	10	14

1 1998 figures have been revised to reflect improved treatment of missing data.
2 Total receptions cannot be calculated by adding together receptions in each category because there is double counting. This arises because a person received on remand and then under sentence in relation to the same set of charges is counted in both categories.
3 For 1995 and 1996 data is estimated.
4 From 1996 compensation orders are included in the figures for default of fine.

Source: The Scottish Executive Justice Department: 0131 244 2225

11.19 Expenditure on penal establishments
Scotland
Years ended 31 March

£ thousands

		1989 /90	1990 /91	1991 /92	1992 /93	1993 /94	1994 /95	1995 /96	1996 /97	1997 /98	1998 /99	1999 /00
Expenditure												
Manpower and Associated Services	**KPHC**	103 394	110 454	124 898	129 597	135 301	140 009	135 941	143 107	137 890	144 660	170 347
Prisoner and Associated Costs	**KPHD**	8 307	8 446	8 504	10 274	10 795	11 679	12 373	13 377	16 313	18 891	22 930
Capital Expenditure	**KPHE**	15 551	12 866	13 032	13 681	11 845	15 636	15 377	22 577	22 136	23 697	28 918
Gross Expenditure	**KPHF**	127 252	131 766	146 434	153 552	157 941	167 324	163 691	179 061	176 339	187 248	222 195
Less Receipts:-	**KPHG**	4 302	3 819	3 711	3 542	3 598	3 042	2 800	2 600	2 810	8 160	6 668
Net Operating Costs	**KPHH**	122 950	127 947	142 723	150 010	154 343	164 282	160 891	176 461	173 529	179 088	215 527

Source: The Scottish Executive Justice Department: 0131 244 2225

11.20 Disposals given to those convicted by court
Northern Ireland

Number

		1988	1989	1990	1991	1992	1993	1994	1995	1996	1997	1998
Magistrates court - all offences												
Prison	**KYAO**	1 222	1 006	1 009	960	830	1 027	945	1 046	1 003	989	..
Young offenders centre	**KYAP**	401	368	370	502	588	575	499	483	443	430	..
Training school	**KYAQ**	170	168	153	177	120	125	193	169	147	148	..
Total immediate custody	**KYAR**	1 793	1 542	1 532	1 639	1 538	1 727	1 637	1 698	1 593	1 567	..
Prison suspended	**KYAS**	1 647	1 544	1 513	1 379	1 420	1 529	1 558	1 674	1 722	1 506	..
YOC suspended	**KYAT**	310	319	310	432	507	447	447	385	444	461	..
Attendance centre	**KYAU**	139	108	118	90	66	94	89	101	91	66	..
Probations/supervision	**KYAV**	763	778	854	742	849	881	1 017	1 137	1 134	1 155	..
Community supervision order	**KYAW**	523	435	575	547	464	536	551	547	591	561	..
Fine	**KYAX**	28 019	26 306	26 644	19 569	23 418	25 166	24 390	22 726	20 612	21 313	..
Recognizance	**KYAY**	442	412	399	514	713	858	961	1 001	1 203	1 267	..
Conditional discharge	**KYAZ**	2 707	2 022	1 982	2 102	1 965	2 021	1 830	1 928	1 679	1 597	..
Absolute discharge	**KYBA**	1 656	1 305	1 274	845	732	690	661	608	509	424	..
Disqualification	**KYBB**	4 810	4 106	4 335	4 211	640	6	6	2	5	2	..
Other	**KYBC**	36	20	28	24	12	7	11	8	10	6	..
Total	**KYBD**	42 845	38 897	39 564	32 094	32 324	33 962	33 158	31 815	29 593	29 925	..
Crown court - all offences												
Prison	**KYBE**	536	472	493	493	447	555	471	533	469	475	345
Young offenders centre	**KYBF**	112	111	106	125	119	130	87	76	106	111	63
Training school	**KYBG**	5	10	4	13	5	2	5	6	–	4	2
Total immediate custody	**KYBH**	653	593	603	631	571	687	563	615	575	590	410
Prison suspended	**KYBI**	313	318	295	238	249	211	277	265	253	220	199
YOC suspended	**KYBJ**	93	73	78	46	63	37	43	63	71	60	49
Custody probation order	**ZAEO**	..	..	..	..	..	..	..	..	..	..	175
Combination order	**ZAEP**	..	..	..	..	..	..	..	..	..	..	13
Attendance centre	**KYBK**	1	2	–	–	–	–	1	–	–	–	–
Probation/supervision	**KYBL**	80	72	85	103	95	73	58	60	49	47	70
Community supervision order	**KYBM**	106	71	105	89	79	48	59	60	54	37	33
Fine	**KYBN**	35	39	33	23	17	33	23	27	39	40	25
Recognizance	**KYBO**	7	3	8	7	9	5	16	–	7	10	7
Conditional discharge	**KYBR**	65	51	37	53	36	19	15	64	30	31	23
Absolute discharge	**KYBS**	5	1	2	5	8	3	2	1	–	1	6
Disqualification	**KYBT**	4	8	10	6	2	–	–	–	–	–	1
Other	**KYBU**	5	3	–	8	6	6	1	2	3	3	6
Total	**KYBV**	1 367	1 234	1 256	1 209	1 135	1 122	1 058	1 157	1 081	1 039	1 017

Source: Northern Ireland Office: 028 9052 7534

11.21 Persons found guilty at all courts by offence group
Northern Ireland

Number

		1987	1988	1989	1990	1991	1992	1993	1994	1995	1996	1997
Violence against the person	KYCT	1 534	1 491	1 424	1 750	1 634	1 558	1 674	1 498	1 685	1 597	1 594
Sexual offences	KEVG	210	228	226	275	193	184	126	148	182	184	130
Burglary	KYBW	1 869	1 553	1 363	1 362	1 208	1 149	1 114	979	951	801	715
Robbery	KYBX	314	296	273	220	162	202	159	168	195	161	166
Theft	KYBY	4 108	3 614	3 298	3 399	3 429	3 158	3 254	3 044	3 128	2 765	2 596
Fraud and forgery	KYBZ	728	688	783	699	648	683	633	568	533	467	491
Criminal damage	KYCA	1 230	1 048	939	1 054	1 019	967	1 145	1 134	1 008	1 076	1 163
Offences against the state	KYCB	321	226	216	233	195	187	184	137	166	147	165
Other indictable	KYCC	319	429	380	287	368	448	606	669	863	899	739
Total indictable[1]	KYCD	10 633	9 573	8 902	9 279	8 856	8 536	8 895	8 345	8 711	8 097	7 759
Summary	KYCE	6 072	6 071	5 113	4 293	4 278	4 115	4 307	4 369	4 137	4 402	4 435
Motoring[2]	KYCF	28 218	28 568	26 116	27 248	20 169	20 808	21 882	21 502	20 124	18 177	18 770
All offences	KYCG	44 923	44 212	40 131	40 820	33 303	33 459	35 084	34 216	32 972	30 676	30 964

1 Excludes indictable motoring offences
2 Includes indictable motoring offences

Source: Northern Ireland Office: 028 9052 7534

11.22 Juveniles found guilty at all courts by offence group
Northern Ireland

Number

		1987	1988	1989	1990	1991	1992	1993	1994	1995	1996	1997
Violence against the person	KYCH	55	58	33	44	38	46	43	49	51	75	49
Sexual offences	KAHF	12	15	14	17	8	11	7	8	7	4	8
Burglary	KYCI	274	251	228	232	194	165	155	180	170	137	124
Robbery	KYCJ	11	19	11	10	7	8	4	9	22	13	18
Theft	KYCK	421	419	308	329	328	247	280	283	345	338	334
Fraud and forgery	KYCL	21	6	10	10	10	16	14	14	21	14	11
Criminal damage	KYCM	165	114	119	90	92	82	94	117	116	121	136
Offences against the state	KYCN	16	19	14	6	5	6	1	8	9	6	10
Other indictable	KYCO	8	11	15	10	11	8	2	6	14	24	10
Total indictable[1]	KYCP	983	912	752	748	693	589	600	674	755	732	700
Summary	KYCQ	262	190	186	138	111	113	125	131	180	182	198
Motoring[2]	KYCR	129	100	81	92	71	40	44	74	74	58	57
All offences[3]	KYCS	1 374	1 202	1 019	978	875	742	769	879	1 009	972	955

1 Excludes indictable motoring offences.
2 Includes indictable motoring offences.
3 Juveniles are aged 10 - 16 years inclusive.

Source: Northern Ireland Office: 028 9052 7534

11.23 Prisons and Young Offenders Centres
Northern Ireland
Receptions and average population

Number

		1988	1989	1990	1991	1992	1993	1994	1995	1996	1997	1998
Receptions:												
Reception of untried prisoners	KEOA	1 853	1 795	1 773	1 851	1 987	2 045	2 043	2 003	2 292	2 188	2 284
Reception of sentenced prisoners:												
Imprisonment under sentence of immediate custody[1]	KEOB	1 136	1 029	953	974	941	1 135	1 029	1 070	1 070	1 062	949
Imprisonment in default of payment of a fine	KEOC	1 493	1 291	1 264	1 282	1 352	1 221	1 190	1 248	1 374	1 513	1 530
Total	KEOD	2 629	2 320	2 217	2 256	2 293	2 356	2 219	2 318	2 444	2 575	2 479
Reception into Young Offender Centres:												
Detention under sentence of immediate custody	KEOE	437	422	371	348	371	416	346	371	362	331	347
Detention in default of payment of a fine	KEOF	457	378	309	356	364	353	276	351	373	366	385
Total	KEOG	894	800	680	704	735	769	622	722	735	697	732
Other receptions:												
Civil committals	KEOI	50	46	21	17	10	21	13	45	27	42	70
Total	KEOL	50	46	21	17	10	21	13	45	27	42	70
Daily average population:												
Total	KEOM	1 901	1 815	1 785	1 796	1 810	1 934	1 899	1 762	1 639	1 632	1 507
Unconvicted[2]	KEON	270	313	361	350	414	427	440	322	337	376	383
Convicted[3]	KEOP	1 631	1 502	1 424	1 446	1 396	1 507	1 459	1 440	1 302	1 256	1 124

1 Includes those detained under Section 73 of the Children and Young Persons (NI) Act 1968.
2 Prisoners on remand or awaiting trial and prisoners committed by civil process.
3 Includes those sentenced to immediate custody and fine defaulters.

Source: Northern Ireland Office: 028 9052 7534

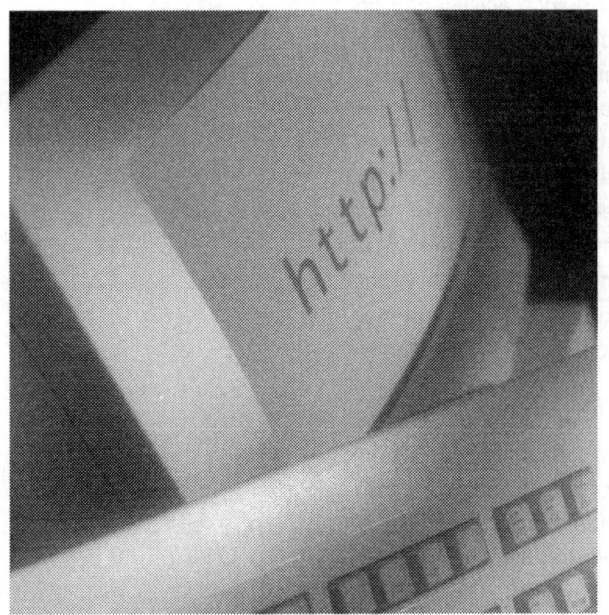

12 Lifestyles

Lifestyles

Cinema statistics *(Tables 12.3)*

These estimates represent the motion picture projection activity for all individual legal units (i.e. companies, sole proprietorships, partnerships etc.) whose main activity is motion picture projection (i.e. heading 92.13 of the UK Standard Industrial Classification 1992). However, where such activity can be identified, the estimates also include the film exhibition activity of a number of legal units where motion picture projection is not their main activity. The Office for National Statistics does not maintain registers of all sites where film exhibition takes place so that the estimates will not be completely comprehensive. It is believed, however, that the estimates cover the great majority of units engaged in cinema activity in Great Britain (i.e. England, Scotland and Wales but not Northern Ireland, the Isle of Man, the Channel Islands or the Republic of Ireland).

These figures are produced by combining information obtained by grossing data from a voluntary quarterly panel with estimates derived from the larger sample approached in the annual inquiry to the service trades.

All financial figures are exclusive of Value Added Tax.

12.1 Expenditure by the Department for Culture, Media and Sport

£ millions

	Museums and galleries (England)	Libraries (UK)	Museums library archives (UK)	The arts (England)	Sport (UK)	Historic buildings, monuments, and sites (England)	The Royal Parks (UK)	Tourism (UK)	Broadcast-ing and media (UK)	Central administr-ation (England)	National Lottery Commission	European regional developme-nt fund	Commemora-tive services and royal funerals
	KWFN	KWFO	LQYX	KWFP	KWFQ	KWFR	LQYY	KWFS	KWFT	KWFU	LQYZ	JYXQ	JYXP
1991/92	204	129	..	212	47	..	..	44	22	8	..	..	–
1992/93	217	133	..	235	50	..	..	46	79	17	..	..	–
1993/94	212	114	9	235	54	164	23	46	85	22	2	..	–
1994/95	217	146	9	195	53	164	24	44	93	21	–	..	3
1995/96	219	171	9	200	54	164	25	45	98	20	–	6	3
1996/97	212	114	10	195	52	162	23	46	97	21	–	16	–
1997/98	205	104	12	196	50	156	22	45	43	21	–	26	3
1998/99[1]	203	88	12	198	49	144	21	45	99	23	–	28	–
1999/00[2]	220	96	19	230	52	148	26	48	104	29	–	6	–
2000/01[2]	226	89	19	238	52	145	22	48	104	26	–	6	–
2001/02[2]	246	93	22	253	52	142	22	47	105	26	–	6	–

1 Data are Estimated Outturn.
2 Data are plans.

Source: Department for Culture, Media and Sport

12.2 Employment in tourism related industries
Great Britain
At June in each year

Thousands, not seasonally adjusted

	Hotels and other tourist accommodation	Restaurants, cafes etc.	Bars, pubs, clubs	Travel agents, tour operators	Libraries, museums, culture	Sport and other recreation	All	Total employees in tourist related industries	Estimated self employment
	KWFV	KWFW	KWFX	KWFY	KWFZ	KWGA	LQZA	KWGB	KWGC
1990	314.4	303.0	445.8	70.0	80.0	311.5	1 714.7	1 524.7	190.0
1991	307.9	297.7	435.0	69.7	75.6	316.5	1 685.4	1 502.4	183.0
1992	311.0	303.0	414.2	69.2	74.8	320.8	1 671.0	1 493.0	178.0
1993	317.6	298.0	370.6	69.3	75.6	316.5	1 643.6	1 447.6	196.0
1994	375.3	372.2	399.1	83.7	75.6	355.7	1 663.3	1 455.5	207.8
1995	385.8	386.2	445.1	90.7	77.3	363.5	1 751.6	1 536.6	215.0
1996	370.9	394.9	438.1	97.6	80.2	356.0	1 736.0	1 518.9	217.0
1997	344.0	410.3	479.9	108.8	78.4	363.3	1 786.4	1 568.2	218.2
1998	357.1	420.2	479.2	104.0	79.3	351.1	1 790.8	1 605.8	185.0
1999	378.1	423.2	465.8	113.7	77.8	361.4	1 819.9	1 659.9	160.0
2000	379.0	432.5	470.7	119.3	91.6	372.6	1 865.7	1 695.3	170.4

Source: Office for National Statistics, short term employment survey

Lifestyles

12.3 GB Cinema exhibitor statistics

	Sites	Screens	Total no. of admissions	Gross box office takings	Amount paid out for films	Revenue per admission	Revenue per screen
	number	number	millions	£ million	£ million	£	£ thousand
	CKNU	CKNV	CKQE	CKQF	CKQG	CKQH	CKQI
1989	481	1 177	82.9	169.5	65.4	2.04	143.7
1990	496	1 331	78.6	187.7	69.5	2.39	143.8
1991	537	1 544	88.9	229.7	78.5	2.58	152.4
1992	480	1 547	89.4	243.7	81.9	2.73	153.6
1993	495	1 591	99.3	271.3	95.9	2.73	171.0
1994	505	1 619	105.9	293.5	104.6	2.77	183.5
1995	475	1 620	96.9	286.5	96.3	2.96	176.7
1996	483	1 738	118.7	373.5	144.9	3.15	215.5
1997[1]	504	1 886	128.2	443.2	165.9	3.46	255.0
1998[1]	481	1 975	123.4	449.5	162.6	3.64	227.6
1999	507	2 276	127.9	501.1	181.9	3.92	220.2

1 Provisional.

Source: Office for National Statistics: 01633 812264

12.4 Films

	Production of UK films		Expenditure on feature films in UK				
	Films produced in the UK	Production costs	UK box office	Video rental	Video retail	Subscriptions to movie channels	Box office, video, subscription channels
	number	£ million 1998 prices	£ million current prices	£ million current prices	£ million current prices	£ million current prices	£ million current prices
	KWGD	KWGE	KWHU	KWHV	KWHW	KWHX	KWHY
1989	30	145.2	227	416	345	..	988
1990	60	271.8	273	418	374	47	1 112
1991	59	285.3	295	407	440	121	1 263
1992	47	208.6	291	389	506	283	1 469
1993	67	214.0	319	350	643	350	1 662
1994	78	436.0	364	339	698	540	1 941
1995	81	421.0	385	351	789	721	2 246
1996	127	726.0	426	382	803	1 319	2 930
1997	115	558.0	506	369	858	..	1 733
1998	91	487.0	515	437	940	..	1 892
1999	103	570.0	606	408	882	..	1 896

Sources: Department for Culture, Media and Sport;
(Screen Finance/ONS/BVA/EDI/BSKYB)

12.5 Tourism

International tourism

	Visits to the UK by overseas residents	Spending in the UK by overseas residents	Spending in the UK by overseas residents	Visits overseas by UK residents	Spending overseas by UK residents	Spending overseas by UK residents
	Thousands	£ million current prices	£ million constant 1995 prices	Thousand	£ million current prices	£ million constant 1995 prices
	KWGF	KWGG	KWGH	KWGI	KWGJ	KWGK
1989	17 338	6 945	9 567	31 030	9 357	12 861
1990	18 013	7 748	9 853	31 150	9 886	12 021
1991	17 125	7 386	8 627	30 808	9 951	11 775
1992	18 535	7 891	8 784	33 836	11 243	12 678
1993	19 863	9 487	10 188	36 720	12 972	13 184
1994	20 794	9 786	10 050	39 630	14 365	14 852
1995	23 537	11 763	11 763	41 345	15 386	15 386
1996	25 163	12 290	11 954	42 050	16 223	15 897
1997	25 515	12 244	11 542	45 957	16 931	18 652
1998	25 745	12 671	11 573	50 872	19 489	21 847
1999	25 394	12 498	11 227	53 881	22 020	24 676

UK Domestic tourism: one or more nights

	Number of trips	Number of nights spent	Expenditure at current prices	Average nights spent	Average expenditure per trip
	Millions	Millions	£ million	Numbers	£
	KWGL	KWGM	KWGN	KWGO	KWGP
1991	94.4	395.6	10 470	4.2	110.9
1992	95.6	399.7	10 665	4.2	111.6
1993	90.9	375.9	12 430	4.1	136.7
1994	109.8	416.5	13 215	3.8	120.4
1995	121.0	449.8	12 775	3.7	105.6
1996	127.0	454.6	13 895	3.6	109.4
1997	133.6	473.6	15 075	3.6	112.9
1998	122.3	437.6	14 030	3.6	114.7
1999	146.1	495.3	16 250	3.4	111.2

Holidays taken by GB residents

	Taking a holiday in GB	Taking a holiday abroad	Taking only one holiday (4+ nights)	Taking two holidays (4+ nights)	Taking 3 or more holidays (4+ nights)
	Percentage	Percentage	Percentage	Percentage	Percentage
	KWGQ	KWGR	KWGS	KWGT	KWGU
1988	39	30	37	16	8
1989	37	30	37	15	7
1990	38	30	36	15	8
1991	41	30	36	16	8
1992	36	32	35	15	9
1993	37	35	36	16	9
1994	35	36	34	16	10
1995	36	37	35	17	10
1996	35	34	35	15	9
1997	33	35	31	16	10
1998	31	38	34	16	9

UK Trends in number of visits to tourist attractions (index 1989 = 100)

	Historic properties	Gardens	Museums	Wildlife sites	Any types of attraction
	LQZB	LQZC	LQZD	LQZE	LQZG
1989	100	100	100	100	100
1990	102	102	106	101	103
1991	98	106	107	95	102
1992	98	105	110	87	102
1993	100	111	109	89	104
1994	99	116	110	87	105
1995	103	122	108	86	107
1996	106	125	111	90	110
1997	108	127	111	92	112
1998	107	118	112	92	110
1999	106	122	111	94	111

Sources: Department for Culture, Media and Sport;
Office for National Statistics;
British Tourist Authority

12.6 Participation in leisure activities[1]

Percentages

		1987	1990	1993	1996
Sports, games and physical activities					
Walking	KWHB	37.9	40.7	40.8	44.5
Swimming	KWHC	13.1	14.8	15.4	14.8
Cue sports	KWHD	15.1	13.6	12.2	11.3
Keep fit/yoga	KWHE	8.6	11.6	12.1	12.3
Cycling	KWHF	8.4	9.3	10.2	11.0
Darts	KWHG	8.8	7.1	5.6	..
Weight lifting)					1.3
Weight lifting/training)	KWHH	4.5	4.8	5.5	
Weight training)					..
					5.6
Golf	KWHI	3.9	5.0	5.3	4.7
Jogging	KWHJ	5.2	5.0	4.6	4.5
Football	KWHK	4.8	4.6	4.5	4.8
Any activity other than walking	KWHL	44.7	47.8	47.3	45.6
Selected leisure activities					
Watching TV	KWHM	99	99	99	99
Visiting/entertaining friends or relatives	KWHN	95	96	96	96
Listening to the radio	KWHO	88	89	89	88
Listening to tapes or records	KWHP	73	76	77	78
Reading books	KWHQ	60	62	65	65
Gardening	KWHR	46	48	48	48
DIY	KWHS	43	43	42	42
Dressmaking, needlework, knitting	KWHT	27	23	22	22

1 Percentage aged 16 and over participating in each activity in the four weeks before interview.

Source: Office for National Statistics

12.7 Gambling

		1986 /87	1987 /88	1988 /89	1989 /90	1990 /91	1991 /92	1992 /93	1993 /94	1994 /95
Money spent on gambling (£ million at 1994/95 prices)										
Lotteries (not including National Lottery)	KWHZ	32	31	28	29	31	60	49	44	39
Casinos	KWIA	2 382	2 437	2 296	2 329	2 178	2 063	2 154	2 291	2 461
Bingo clubs	KWIB	816	886	789	765	746	771	822	811	–

Source: Gaming Board for Great Britain

12.8 Private households with usual residents[1]: Census 1991[2]

Thousands

	All households	Owner occupied	Rented — From council or new town	Rented — Unfurnished	With no car
			Number of households — Selected tenures of households in permanent buildings		

Household and family type

Great Britain
All households

	All households	Owner occupied	From council or new town	Unfurnished	With no car
All households	21 441	14 288	4 589	765	7 095
Households with no family	6 344	3 297	1 778	363	3 936
One person	5 643	2 922	1 652	327	3 657
Two or more persons	701	375	126	36	280
Households with one family	14 898	10 856	2 760	398	3 113
Married couple family	11 847	9 279	1 719	273	1 889
With no children	5 208	3 994	796	156	1 145
With dependent child(ren)	4 802	3 813	651	85	526
With non-dependent child(ren) only	1 837	1 471	272	32	218
Cohabiting couple family	1 139	720	219	57	224
With no children	718	502	68	41	117
With dependent child(ren)	374	187	139	15	100
With non-dependent child(ren) only	47	31	12	1	7
Lone parent family	1 912	858	823	68	1 000
With dependent child(ren)	1 122	391	567	40	689
With non-dependent child(ren) only	790	467	256	28	311
Households with two or more families	199	134	50	4	46
England and Wales					
All households	19 458	13 252	3 838	717	6 253
Households with no family	5 725	3 053	1 498	341	3 500
One person	5 083	2 703	1 393	306	3 254
Two or more persons	642	351	105	34	247
Households with one family	13 551	10 071	2 298	373	2 713
Married couple family	10 779	8 589	1 411	254	1 645
With no children	4 762	3 714	661	146	1 015
With dependent child(ren)	4 358	3 517	534	78	448
With non-dependent child(ren) only	1 659	1 358	215	30	182
Cohabiting couple family	1 064	682	192	55	199
With no children	672	474	58	40	104
With dependent child(ren)	348	178	124	14	89
With non-dependent child(ren) only	43	29	10	1	6
Lone parent family	1 708	800	694	64	868
With dependent child(ren)	1 004	368	484	38	601
With non-dependent child(ren) only	703	432	210	26	267
Households with two or more families	183	127	42	3	40
Scotland					
All households	1 983	1 036	751	48	843
Households with no family	619	244	281	22	436
One person	560	219	260	20	403
Two or more persons	60	25	21	2	33
Households with one family	1 348	785	463	25	401
Married couple family	1 068	690	307	19	244
With no children	446	280	135	10	130
With dependent child(ren)	444	296	116	7	78
With non-dependent child(ren) only	178	113	56	2	36
Cohabiting couple family	75	38	27	2	25
With no children	45	28	10	1	13
With dependent child(ren)	26	9	15	1	11
With non-dependent child(ren) only	3	2	2	0	1
Lone parent family	204	58	129	4	132
With dependent child(ren)	118	23	83	2	88
With non-dependent child(ren) only	86	35	46	2	44
Households with two or more families	16	7	8	0	6

1 Number of households and family type by selected tenures of households in permanent buildings and with no car.
2 Later figures not available.

Sources: Office for National Statistics: 01329 813800; General Register Office (Scotland): 0131 314 4254

13 Environment, water and housing

Environment, water and housing

Environment *(Tables 13.1 to 13.17)*

Air Emissions *(Table 13.1 to 13.7)*

Emissions of air pollutants arise from a wide variety of sources. The National Atmospheric Emissions Inventory (NAEI) is prepared annually for the Government and the devolved administrations by the National Environmental Technology Centre (NETCEN), with the work being co-ordinated by DETR. Information is available for a range of point sources, including the most significant polluters. However, a different approach has to be taken for diffuse sources such as transport and domestic emissions where this type of information could not be available and estimates for these are derived from statistical information and from research on emission factors for stationary and mobile sources. Although for any given year considerable uncertainties surround the emission estimates for each pollutant, trends over time are likely to be more reliable.

UK national emission estimates are updated annually and any developments in methodology are applied retrospectively to earlier years. Adjustments in the methodology are made to accommodate new technical information and to improve international comparability.

Three different classification systems are used in the tables presented here: a National Accounts basis (Table 13.1); the format required by the Inter-governmental Panel on Climate Change (IPCC) (Table 13.2); and the CORINAIR format used by the United Nations Economic Commission for Europe (UNECE) (Tables 13.3-13.7).

The National Accounts figures in Table 13.1 differ from those on an IPCC basis in that they include estimated emissions from fuels purchased in the UK and used by international shipping and aircraft on international flights (marine and air bunkers). This is intended to bring them closer to the National Accounts treatment, which includes expenditures by residents abroad and excludes expenditures by non-residents.

The IPCC classification in Table 13.2 is used to report greenhouse gas emissions and includes land use change and all emissions from domestic aviation and shipping, but excludes international marine and aviation bunker fuels. Estimates of the relative contribution to global warming of the main greenhouse gases, or classes of gases, is presented weighted by their global warming potential.

The UNECE/CORINAIR classification used in Tables 13.3-13.7 excludes land use change and also international shipping, but includes aviation emissions below 1,000 metres to cover take-off and landing cycles.

Water quality *(Tables 13.8 and 13.9)*

The chemical quality of river and canal waters in the UK is monitored in a series of separate national surveys. The General Quality Assessment (GQA) Scheme used in the surveys provides a rigorous and objective method for assessing the basic chemical quality of rivers and canals based on three determinants – dissolved oxygen, biochemical oxygen demand (BOD), and ammoniacal nitrogen. The GQA grades river stretches into six categories (A-F) of chemical quality and these in turn have been grouped into four broader groups – good (classes A and B), fair (C and D), poor (E) and bad (F). In Scotland river and canal water quality is assessed using the following classes: unpolluted, fairly good, poor and grossly polluted. These classes are not directly comparable with those used in England and Wales and Northern Ireland.

To provide a more comprehensive picture of the health of rivers and canals, biological testing was carried out in parallel with chemical testing in the latest two quinquennial river quality surveys in England and Wales, Scotland and Northern Ireland. The biological grading is based on the monitoring of tiny animals (invertebrates) which live in or on the bed of the river. Research has shown that there is a relationship between species composition and water quality. Using a procedure known as the River Invertebrate Prediction and Classification System (RIVPACS), species groups recorded at a site were compared with those which would be expected to be present in the absence of pollution, allowing for the different environmental characteristics in different parts of the country. In England and Wales and in Northern Ireland two different summary statistics (known as ecological quality indices (EQI)) were calculated and then the biological quality was assigned to one of six bands based on a combination of these two statistics. In Scotland, a third EQI was also calculated by SEPA and the grading system based on a combination of all three statistics or EQIs. The results for Scotland are not directly comparable for this reason.

Bathing waters *(Table 13.12)*

Under the EC Bathing Water Directive, eleven physical, chemical and microbiological parameters are measured including total and faecal coliforms which are generally considered to be the most important indicators of the extent to which water is contaminated by sewage. The mandatory value for total coliforms is 10 000 per 100 ml, and for faecal coliforms 2 000 per 100 ml. For a bathing water to comply with the coliform standards, the Directive requires that at least 95 per cent of samples taken for each of these parameters over the bathing season are less than equal to the mandatory values. In the UK a minimum of 20 samples are normally taken at each site. In practice this means that where 20 samples are taken, a maximum of only one sample may exceed the mandatory value for the bathing water to comply, and where less than 20 samples are taken none may exceed the mandatory value for the bathing water to comply.

Radioactive wastes *(Table 13.13)*

Solid radioactive wastes are not discharged to the environment but stored and conditioned by processes such as supercompaction, cementation or turning into glass. Such wastes cover a wide range of materials and can be classified, according to the nature and quantity of radioactivity associated with them, as high level wastes (HLW), intermediate level wastes (ILW) or low level wastes (LLW). For explanation of what these three types of waste comprise see the footnotes to the table. HLW result from the reprocessing of nuclear fuel and are highly radioactive. Although small in volume, they contain over 95 per cent of all the radioactivity in wastes from nuclear establishments. Final disposal of HLW and ILW will be to deep underground repositories when these become available.

The table shows recent trends in the volume of radioactive waste stocks for particular groups of nuclear sites. Data for HLW and ILW are presented in two physical states – as-stored and conditioned – and conditioned for disposal for LLW (see footnotes to Table). There is also no simple relationship between as-stored and conditioned volumes of waste, since the effects of conditioning can vary with different wastes. Estimates of conditioned wastes are indicative only and should be interpreted with care.

Noise complaints *(Table 13.14)*

The table shows trends in the number of complaints received by local authority Environmental Health Officers. The figures are from those authorities making returns and are calculated per million people based on the population of the authorities making returns.

Recycling *(Table 13.16)*

The ratios shown reflect the amount of secondary material (scrap) used in the UK in a year as a proportion of consumption in that year. This gives some indication of the extent to which secondary material is displacing raw materials from the feedstock. This definition takes no account of the lifetime of the article being recovered ie that material which is being recycled now and related to current consumption might originally have been delivered to an end market some years ago.

Protected areas *(Table 13.17)*

National Parks, Areas of Outstanding Natural Beauty (AONBS) in England, Wales and Northern Ireland and National Scenic Areas in Scotland are the major areas which have been designated to protect their landscape importance.

Further details can be found in DETR's annual *Digest of Environmental Statistics*. If you would like to discuss the tables, Adrian Redfern can be contacted at the Department of the Environment, Transport and the Regions on 020 7890 6497.

Environment, water and housing

13.1 Estimated atmospheric emissions [1] 1998 on National Accounts basis
United Kingdom

Thousand tonnes

	Greenhouse gases	Acid rain precursors	Emissions affecting air quality								
	CO_2, CH_4 & N_2O, HFC PFC, SF_6 $KtCO_2$ equiv[2]	SO_2, NOx & NH_3 $KtSO_2$ equiv[3]	PM10[4]	CO[5]	NMVOC[6]	Benzene	Butadiene	Lead (tonnes)	Cadmium (tonnes)	Mercury (tonnes)
Agriculture	57 400	590	4.4	78.8	159.7	0.4	0.2	8.1	0.02	0.00
Mining and quarrying	34 600	90	31.4	143.0	195.3	0.5	0.1	4.4	0.04	0.02
Manufacturing	164 200	600	31.3	638.5	646.9	5.5	0.4	390.1	10.77	6.60
Electricity, gas and water supply	162 200	1 330	24.1	94.2	29.7	0.1	0.0	28.1	0.72	2.65
Construction	4 500	30	5.1	152.4	60.0	1.4	0.2	2.5	0.01	0.00
Wholesale and retail trade	14 900	50	6.0	200.8	156.8	1.7	0.4	28.2	0.05	0.00
Transport and communication	70 500	520	20.3	356.6	120.0	3.3	1.8	27.7	0.26	0.03
Financial intermediation	12 400	30	3.8	203.8	28.5	1.1	0.3	29.8	0.04	0.00
Public administration	9 500	40	1.3	13.5	2.5	0.1	0.0	2.1	0.02	0.03
Education, health and social work	11 900	30	2.3	39.3	7.4	0.2	0.1	7.3	0.04	0.05
Other services	20 600	60	1.5	25.5	18.6	0.2	0.1	7.0	0.49	2.17
Domestic	149 000	440	40.8	2 919.9	557.2	19.8	4.3	499.7	0.70	0.84
Totals	711 700	3 810	172.2	4 866.3	1 982.6	34.4	8.0	1 034.8	13.16	12.40
Of which, emissions from road transport	119 900	610	44.6	3 479.2	527.3	21.9	6.1	591.8	0.56	0.00

1 The National Accounts basis includes estimated emissions from fuels purchased in the UK and used by international shipping and aircraft on international flights
2 Carbon dioxide, methane, nitrous oxide, hydro-fluorocarbons, perfluorocarbons and sulphur hexafluoride expressed in thousand tonnes of carbon dioxide equivalent

3 Sulphur dioxide, nitrogen oxides and ammonia expressed as thousand tonnes of sulphur dioxide equivalent
4 PM_{10}s are carbon particles in air arising from incomplete combustion
5 Carbon monoxide
6 Non-methane Volatile Organic Compounds including benzene and 1,3-butadiene

Source: NETCEN, ONS

13.2 Estimated total emissions[1] of UK greenhouse gases on IPCC basis
United Kingdom

Million tonnes (CO_2 equivalent)

		1991	1992	1993	1994	1995	1996	1997	1998
Emissions weighted by global warming potential									
Carbon dioxide (CO_2(as CO_2))	JZCK	619.9	604.9	589.0	583.8	574.7	593.9	567.6	570.2
Methane (CH_4)	JZCL	76.17	74.20	66.75	61.81	61.26	59.93	58.02	55.35
Nitrous oxide (N_2O)	JZCM	63.73	56.74	53.04	57.67	55.06	57.04	58.71	55.98
Hydrofluorocarbons (HFC)	JZCN	11.86	12.35	12.90	13.81	15.21	16.29	18.45	20.18
Perfluorocarbons (PFC)	JZCO	1.79	0.96	0.81	0.98	1.09	0.91	0.66	0.65
Sulphur hexafluoride (SF_6)	JZCP	0.78	0.83	0.89	1.06	1.13	1.27	1.26	1.29
Total	JZCQ	774.2	750.0	723.4	719.2	708.4	729.4	704.7	703.7

1 Emissions inventories based on the methodology developed by the Intergovernmental Panel on Climate Change (IPCC) are used to report UK emissions to the Climate Change Convention.

Source: NETCEN

13.3 Estimated emissions of sulphur dioxide (SO_2) by source
United Kingdom

Thousand tonnes

		% of 1998 total	1970	1980	1985	1990	1991	1992	1993	1994	1995	1996	1997	1998
By source category (UNECE/CORINAIR94)														
Power stations	JZCR	66	2 913	3 007	2 627	2 723	2 535	2 434	2 084	1 762	1 591	1 320	1 025	1 072
Refineries	JZCS	11	254	270	139	155	164	182	208	184	178	180	175	172
Combustion in fuel extraction & transformation	JZCT	1	302	71	52	41	38	15	12	10	9	10	13	12
Domestic	JZCU	3	522	226	202	108	115	103	113	92	67	71	65	52
Commercial, public & agricultural combustion	JZCV	2	442	218	133	90	85	89	95	80	60	57	47	34
Iron and steel	JZCW	3	433	128	80	88	86	66	75	70	65	58	58	45
Other industrial combustion	JZCX	9	1 409	766	338	357	372	418	413	348	262	209	169	147
Production processes	JZCY	1	91	74	55	44	38	32	29	26	23	23	19	15
Road transport	JZCZ	1	44	42	45	63	58	62	59	63	51	37	28	23
Other transport	JZDA	25	92	61	49	47	50	49	48	46	44	44	42	38
Other sources	JZDB	-	9	10	14	21	10	12	9	10	8	8	7	7
Total	JZDC	100	6 511	4 871	3 734	3 736	3 552	3 462	3 144	2 689	2 356	2 017	1 647	1 615
Emissions from large combustion plants														
Large plants[1]	ZBZK			3 650	3 490	2 817	2 928	2 747	2 674	2 329	1 969	1 756	1 468	1 107	1 207
Index (1980=100)	ZBZL			105	100	81	84	79	77	67	56	50	42	32	35

1 Figures for 1991 onwards are totals of those reported by the Environment Agency to DETR on emissions from individual LCPs. For 1970-1990, estimates are made assuming all power station emissions from coal, fuel oil and orimulsion stations are included, plus 47 per cent of refineries' emissions, 12 per cent of iron and steel emissions and 39 per cent of other

industrial combustion in fuel extraction and transformation. It is not possible to calculate LCP figures using the categories presented in this table as refineries and other industrial combustion are both included in more than one category.

Source: NETCEN

13.4 Estimated emissions of PM_{10}[1] by source
United Kingdom

Thousand tonnes

By source category (UNECE/CORINAIR94)		Percentage of total in 1998	1970	1980	1985	1990	1991	1992	1993	1994	1995	1996	1997	1998
Power stations	JZDN	14	67	76	64	70	70	66	55	49	37	34	23	23
Domestic	JZDO	16	216	98	89	48	51	46	47	38	28	30	28	26
Commercial, public & agricultural combustion	JZDP	3	19	11	10	8	8	7	7	7	6	6	6	5
Industrial combustion[2]	JZDQ	10	74	31	25	25	27	28	27	25	23	21	18	17
Production processes[3]	JZDR	23	42	34	37	45	41	39	39	41	40	37	38	38
Road transport[4]	JZDS	24	46	55	58	67	66	63	60	59	54	51	45	40
Other transport	JZDT	3	6	5	5	5	5	5	5	4	4	5	4	4
Other sources	JZDV	6	22	12	10	9	9	9	9	10	9	9	9	9
Total	JZGA	100	495	322	296	276	276	262	249	233	201	194	171	163

1 Particles which pass through a size selective inlet with a 50 per cent efficiency cut-off at 10μm aerodynamics diameter.
2 Comprises emissions from Iron and Steel and Other Industrial Combustion.
3 Emissions from construction, mining, quarrying and industrial processes.
4 Includes emissions from tyre and brake wear.

Source: NETCEN

13.5 Estimated emissions[1] of nitrogen oxides (NOx)[2] by source
United Kingdom

Thousand tonnes

By source category (UNECE/CORINAIR94)		Percentage of total in 1998	1970	1980	1985	1990	1991	1992	1993	1994	1995	1996	1997	1998
Power stations	JZGB	21	812	861	753	781	683	671	568	526	493	448	371	364
Refineries	JZGC	3	43	44	39	42	44	44	47	47	48	48	48	52
Combustion in fuel extraction & transformation	JZGD	3	61	44	67	63	64	65	67	75	50	48	48	52
Domestic	JZGE	4	62	64	68	64	71	69	72	69	66	75	70	71
Commercial, public & agricultural combustion	JZGF	2	73	46	44	37	40	39	38	38	37	39	36	34
Iron and steel	JZGG	1	75	25	20	22	22	22	23	27	26	26	26	24
Other industrial combustion	JZGH	9	322	244	193	195	186	180	178	183	169	162	159	155
Production processes	JZGI	-	14	14	16	11	10	9	8	7	5	5	5	5
Road transport	JZGJ	46	769	989	1 096	1 328	1 313	1 251	1 181	1 115	1 028	984	899	799
Other transport	JZGK	11	250	229	225	226	225	222	217	207	202	212	203	195
Waste treatment and disposal	JZGL	-	5	11	9	8	8	8	7	7	7	6	4	3
Agriculture and managed forestry	JZGM	0	10	15	14	9	8	6	–	–	–	–	–	–
Other sources	JZGN	-	–	–	1	1	1	1	–	1	1	1	1	1
Total	JZGO	100	2 497	2 586	2 545	2 788	2 674	2 587	2 405	2 302	2 132	2 054	1 868	1 753

Emissions from large combustion plants

			1970	1980	1985	1990	1991	1992	1993	1994	1995	1996	1997	1998
Large plants[3]	ZBZM		931	956	822	846	749	742	636	572	524	471	371	369
Index (1980=100)	ZBZN		97	100	86	88	78	78	67	60	55	49	39	39

1 Most of the figures in this table are based on a single NOx emission factor for each fuel which are held constant over time.
2 Expressed as nitrogen dioxide equivalent.
3 Figures for 1991 onwards are totals of those reported by the Environment Agency to DETR on emissions from individual LCPs. For 1970-1990, estimates are made assuming all power station emissions from coal, fuel oil and orimulsion stations are included, plus 66 per cent of refineries' emissions, 11 per cent of iron and steel emissions and 38 per cent of other industrial combustion in fuel extraction and transformation. It is not possible to calculate LCP figures from the categories presented in this table as other industrial combustion is included under more than one category.

Source: NETCEN

Environment, water and housing

13.6 Estimated emissions[1] of carbon monoxide (CO) by source
United Kingdom

Thousand tonnes

By UNECE source category		Percentage of total in 1998	1970	1980	1985	1990	1991	1992	1993	1994	1995	1996	1997	1998
Power stations	JZGP	2	117	121	105	114	113	110	100	106	104	102	70	73
Combustion in fuel extraction & transformation	JZGQ	1	45	24	25	22	22	20	20	20	22	23	23	26
Domestic	JZGR	5	1 251	622	579	358	382	347	369	324	260	268	251	234
Commercial, public & agricultural combustion	JZGS	-	46	26	26	22	22	21	21	20	19	19	19	18
Industrial combustion[2]	JZGT	3	360	143	166	185	175	179	176	170	167	160	161	148
Production processes	JZGU	9	362	271	365	412	389	373	377	391	397	410	419	413
Road transport	JZGV	73	5 427	5 378	4 946	5 147	5 026	4 759	4 465	4 227	3 969	3 926	3 665	3 479
Other transport	JZGW	7	504	440	402	369	383	390	377	367	348	359	344	338
Waste treatment and disposal	JZGX	-	2	43	28	29	27	26	26	33	24	24	19	18
Agriculture and managed forestry	JZGY	0	288	449	416	266	228	165	4	–	–	–	–	–
Other sources	JZGZ	-	6	6	9	13	8	9	8	8	9	9	9	9
Total	JZHA	100	8 407	7 525	7 068	6 938	6 774	6 399	5 943	5 665	5 320	5 299	4 982	4 758

1 Most of the figures in this table are based on a single carbon monoxide emissions factor for each fuel which are held constant over time.
2 Comprises emissions from Iron and Steel and Other Industrial Combustion.

Source: NETCEN

13.7 Estimated emissions[1] of volatile organic compounds (VOCs)[2] by source
United Kingdom

Thousand tonnes

By source category (UNECE/CORINAIR94)		Percentage of total in 1998	1970	1980	1985	1990	1991	1992	1993	1994	1995	1996	1997	1998
Power stations	JZHB	-	7	8	7	7	7	7	7	8	8	9	8	6
Domestic	JZHC	2	293	129	117	64	67	61	61	48	37	40	37	37
Production processes	JZHD	15	372	363	349	361	352	353	344	328	324	307	295	289
Extraction and distribution of fossil fuels	JZHE	15	89	215	287	286	289	277	272	293	285	300	298	298
Solvent use	JZHF	27	576	569	581	660	628	594	585	593	579	562	541	532
Road transport[3]	JZHG	27	636	760	800	927	911	867	809	757	694	645	582	527
Other transport	JZHH	2	62	56	54	50	51	52	51	50	48	49	48	48
Waste treatment and disposal	JZHI	1	10	54	41	42	39	38	37	44	37	35	31	29
Agriculture and managed forestry	JZHJ	-	37	58	54	35	30	22	–	–	–	–	–	–
Forests[4]	JZHK	9	178	178	178	178	178	178	178	178	178	178	178	178
Other sources	JZHL	1	15	13	13	13	13	13	13	14	12	12	12	12
Total	JZHM	100	2 272	2 402	2 480	2 623	2 565	2 462	2 357	2 313	2 201	2 137	2 031	1 958

1 Most of the figures in this table are based on a single VOC emission factor for each source held constant over time.
2 Excluding methane.
3 Includes evaporative emissions from the petrol tank and carburettor of petrol-engined vehicles.
4 An order of magnitude estimate of natural emissions from managed and unmanaged forests.

Source: NETCEN

13.8 Chemical quality of rivers and canals[1]

	Years	Length[2] in km							Percentage of total	
		Good		Fair		Poor E	Bad F	Total	Good or fair	Poor or bad
		A	B	C	D					
England and Wales, Northern Ireland										
EA Region										
North West	1988-90	720	620	560	440	650	210	3 190	*73*	*27*
	1997-99	2 030	1 470	1 050	610	530	50	5 750	*90*	*10*
North East	1988-90	850	1 620	550	450	610	170	4 250	*82*	*18*
	1997-99	1 680	2 420	940	610	500	80	6 220	*91*	*9*
Midlands	1988-90	450	1 510	1 610	990	1000	130	5 700	*80*	*20*
	1997-99	930	2 700	1 840	590	570	40	6 670	*91*	*9*
Anglian	1988-90	40	760	1 690	1 190	790	100	4 560	*81*	*19*
	1997-99	320	1 290	1 630	870	660	30	4 810	*86*	*14*
Thames	1988-90	320	980	1 050	580	560	50	3 530	*83*	*17*
	1997-99	590	1 390	860	580	360	20	3 790	*90*	*10*
Southern	1988-90	240	710	670	290	240	30	2 180	*88*	*12*
	1997-99	370	890	530	210	190	-	2 200	*91*	*9*
South West	1988-90	1 640	2 670	1 240	740	360	70	6 720	*94*	*6*
	1997-99	2 400	2 480	850	130	190	-	6 040	*97*	*3*
Welsh	1988-90	1 780	1 410	430	230	130	40	4 020	*96*	*4*
	1997-99	3 440	1 200	240	100	60	10	5 040	*99*	*1*
England and Wales	1988-90	6 040	10 290	7 800	4 910	4 330	800	34 160	*85*	*15*
	1997-99	11 770	13 840	7 940	3 690	3 060	240	40 530	*92*	*8*
Northern Ireland[3]	1989-91	100	640	680	170	60	20	1 680	*95*	*5*
	1997-99	200	1 170	680	270	100	10	2 430	*96*	*4*

1 Based on the GQA chemical classification system.
2 Lengths are rounded to the nearest 10km and may not sum to totals.
3 No canals classified in Northern Ireland.

Sources: Environment Agency;
Environment and Heritage Service

	Year	Length[1] in km					Percentage of total	
		Unpolluted	Fairly good	Poor	Grossly polluted	Total	Unpolluted or fairly good	Poor or grossly polluted
Scotland								
Former River Purification Board								
Highland	1990	14 020	50	10	-	14 070	*100*	-
	1995	13 780	20	10	10	13 830	*100*	-
North East	1990	8 620	50	10	-	8 680	*100*	-
	1995	8 620	40	-	-	8 660	*100*	-
Tay	1990	6 230	60	-	-	6 290	*100*	-
	1995	6 110	30	-	-	6 150	*100*	-
Forth	1990	2 930	340	150	40	3 470	*94*	*6*
	1995	2 830	350	130	30	3 350	*95*	*5*
Tweed	1990	2 780	10	-	-	2 790	*100*	-
	1995	2 750	30	-	-	2 770	*100*	-
Solway	1990	4 890	70	10	10	4 980	*100*	-
	1995	4 940	20	-	-	4 960	*100*	-
Clyde	1990	9 990	630	60	20	10 690	*99*	*1*
	1995	9 860	590	70	10	10 530	*99*	*1*
Scotland	1990	49 450	1 200	240	70	50 960	*99*	*1*
	1995	48 890	1 090	220	60	50 260	*99*	*1*

1 Lengths are rounded to the nearest 10km and may not sum to totals. Figures for 1990 and 1995 include lengths of rivers on islands which were not included in previous surveys.

Source: Scottish Executive

13.9 Biological water quality of rivers and canals[1]

| | | Length[2] in km | | | | | | | Percentage of total | |
| | | Good | | Fair | | | | | | |
	Year	A	B	C	D	Poor E	Bad F	Total	Good or fair	Poor or bad
England and Wales, Northern Ireland										
EA Region										
North West	1990	430	1 070	690	330	620	880	4 020	63	37
	1995	960	1 530	900	500	810	260	4 970	78	22
North East	1990	1 340	1 170	520	410	380	310	4 130	83	17
	1995	2 260	1 200	730	520	480	270	5 460	86	14
Midlands	1990	330	810	1 210	770	470	220	3 810	82	18
	1995	970	1 680	1 790	920	360	120	5 840	92	8
Anglian	1990	470	1 420	1 520	480	210	70	4 170	93	7
	1995	1 050	2 020	1 170	350	120	20	4 730	97	3
Thames	1990	720	1 000	690	350	240	110	3 090	89	11
	1995	1 130	1 120	790	350	160	20	3 570	95	5
Southern	1990	400	450	400	130	30	10	1 420	97	3
	1995	980	720	300	160	30	-	2 190	98	2
South West	1990	2 140	2 110	830	220	150	90	5 550	96	4
	1995	3 330	1 900	530	100	50	20	5 940	99	1
Welsh	1990	1 400	1 440	610	240	100	20	3 810	97	3
	1995	2 320	1 680	680	150	30	-	4 860	99	1
England and Wales	1990	7 210	9 480	6 470	2 940	2 200	1 710	30 000	87	13
	1995	13 000	11 860	6 890	3 040	2 040	720	37 560	93	7
Northern Ireland	1991	710	950	410	100	10	-	2 190	100	-
	1995	850	910	440	120	10	-	2 330	100	-
	1996	670	1 010	500	160	-	-	2 340	100	-
	1997	700	1 020	490	150	-	-	2 350	100	-
	1998	680	1 040	480	150	-	-	2 350	100	-

1 Based on the new GQA biological classification system. Figures for 1990 and 1995 are not directly comparable.
2 Lengths are rounded to the nearest 10km and may not sum to totals.

Sources: Environment Agency; Environment and Heritage Service

| | | Length[1] in km of rivers and canals biologically classified | | | | | Percentage of total | |
	Year	Good A	Moderate B	Poor C	Very poor D	Total	Good or moderate	Poor or very poor
Scotland[2]								
Former River Purification Board								
Highland	1990	2 010	470	-	-	2 480	100	-
	1995	2 730	70	-	-	2 800	100	-
North East	1990	1 540	420	70	30	2 050	95	5
	1995	2 190	30	40	20	2 270	97	3
Tay	1990	1 240	160	20	-	1 420	98	2
	1995	2 870	130	40	10	3 060	98	2
Forth	1990	680	240	60	40	1 030	90	10
	1995	1 320	390	120	50	1 880	91	9
Tweed	1990	730	100	20	-	840	98	2
	1995	1 350	60	-	-	1 410	100	-
Solway	1990	1 070	130	10	-	1 210	99	1
	1995	1 540	40	10	-	1 590	99	1
Clyde	1990	1 260	460	60	70	1 850	93	7
	1995	2 970	640	60	30	3 700	97	3
Scotland	1990	8 530	1 960	230	140	10 870	97	3
	1995	14 960	1 360	280	110	16 710	98	2

1 Lengths are rounded to the nearest 10km and may not sum to totals.
2 The Scottish biological survey covered about 21 per cent of the freshwaters covered by the chemical classification system.

Source: Scottish Executive

13.10 Water pollution incidents and prosecutions
United Kingdom

		Incidents reported									Incidents substantiated					
		1992	1993	1994	1995	1996	1997	1998	1999		1994	1995	1996	1997	1998	1999
Water region																
North West	JZHN	4 206	4 842	4 776	5 014	4 000	3 433	3 839	6 274	JZIA	3 532	3 717	2 818	2 160	2 201	1 828
North East	JZHO	4 048	4 715	4 761	4 364	4 060	3 955	3 284	3 103	JZIB	3 243	2 576	2 143	2 404	1 993	1 668
Midlands	JZHP	6 301	6 689	6 633	6 310	5 953	5 848	5 376	6 567	JZKR	4 895	4 259	4 305	4 411	4 061	2 806
Anglian	JZHQ	3 369	3 504	3 693	3 416	3 318	3 246	2 945	3 838	JZKS	2 819	2 156	2 417	2 411	2 163	1 724
Thames	JZHR	3 595	3 538	3 763	3 977	3 782	3 525	3 257	3 539	JZKT	2 006	1 972	1 959	1 917	1 819	1 210
Southern	JZHS	1 578	1 853	1 719	2 389	2 507	2 357	2 594	3 303	JZKU	1 316	1 235	1 189	1 174	1 138	1 317
South West	JZHT	4 890	5 142	5 508	5 975	5 273	5 101	4 641	6 017	JZKV	4 340	4 558	3 042	2 847	2 603	2 461
Welsh	JZHU	3 686	4 013	4 438	4 445	3 516	3 234	2 734	4 025	JZKW	3 264	2 990	2 285	2 247	1 885	1 359
England and Wales	JZHV	31 673	34 296	35 291	35 890	32 409	30 699	28 670	36 666	JZKX	25 415	23 463	20 158	19 571	17 863	14 373
Scotland[1]	JZHW	..	..	..	..	..	..	..	..	JZKY	3 170	2 752	2 878	3 356	2 329	2 306
Northern Ireland	JZHX	1 845	1 877	2 216	2 380	2 880	2 681	2 508	2 415	JZKZ	..	..	2 063	1 824	1 644	1 510

1 Data for all years refer to financial years.

Sources: Environment Agency;
Scottish Environment Protection Agency;
Environment and Heritage Service

13.11 Estimated abstractions from all surface and groundwater sources by purpose[1]
England and Wales

Ml/day

		1988	1989	1990	1991	1992	1993	1994	1995	1996	1997	1998
Public water supply[2]	JZLA	17 597	18 205	18 337	17 562	17 953	16 651	16 735	17 346	17 453	16 820	16 765
Spray irrigation[3]	JZLB	133	298	377	366	269	164	283	352	369	292	282
Agriculture (excl spray irrigation)	JZLC	120	115	128	131	129	139	115	103	136	108	111
Electricity supply industry[4]	JZLD	28 868	33 302	30 768	30 359	37 693	26 581	27 732	25 805	31 294	33 307	34 587
Other industry	JZLE	7 875	8 854	9 275	5 469	5 326	6 017	4 292	7 513	4 960	4 352	4 964
Mineral washing[5]	JZLF	..	..	..	173	213	198	222	262	250	297	223
Fish farming, cress growing, amenity ponds[6]	JYXG	1 262	1 111	1 323	3 882	4 479	3 818	3 985	4 268	4 338	4 211	5 495
Private water supply[7]	JZLG	..	..	..	..	53	81	82	98	171	162	175
Other[2,8]	JZLH	..	..	..	1 254	1 794	93	194	223	531	408	289
Total	JZLI	55 855	61 885	60 208	59 196	67 909	53 742	53 640	55 970	59 503	59 957	62 891

1 From 1991 data were collected on a different basis. Figures are therefore not strictly comparable with those in previous years. Some regions report licensed and actual abstracts for financial rather than calendar years. As figures represent an average for the whole year expressed as daily amounts, differences between amounts reported for financial and calendar years are small.
2 The 1991 figures include some private water supply.
3 Includes small amounts of non-agricultural spray irrigation.
4 In South West region in 1991 and 1992, Hydroelectric licences were classified as "Other", in 1993 they were classified as "Other industry" and in 1994 and 1995 they were classified correctly as "Electricity supply".

5 "Mineral washing" included for the first time as a separate category in 1991 survey.
6 Category amended to include amenity ponds, but exclude miscellaneous in 1991.
7 Private abstractions for domestic use and individual households. New category in 1992. In the 1991 survey private water supply was included in either the "public supply" or "other" categories.
8 "Other" included for the first time as a separate category in 1991 survey. In 1991 "Other" included some private domestic water supply wells and boreholes, public water supply transfer licences and frost protection use. From 1992 "private water supply" shown as separate category.

Source: Environment Agency

13.12 Bathing water surveys
United Kingdom

Compliance with EC Bathing Water Directive[1] coliform standards[2] during the bathing season[3]

	Identified bathing waters					Numbers complying					Percentage complying				
	1995	1996	1997	1998	1999	1995	1996	1997	1998	1999	1995	1996	1997	1998	1999
Northumbrian[4,5]	34	34	34	34	33	33	29	32	26	32	97	85	94	76	97
Yorkshire[4]	22	22	22	22	22	20	20	19	21	20	91	91	86	95	91
Anglian	34	35	35	36	36	30	34	35	36	34	88	97	100	100	94
Thames	3	3	3	3	3	3	2	3	3	3	100	67	100	100	100
Southern	67	69	75	77	79	62	62	67	75	74	93	90	89	97	94
Wessex[4]	42	42	43	43	43	40	41	39	40	41	95	98	91	93	95
South West[4]	134	138	137	140	141	127	126	125	127	126	95	91	91	91	89
Wales[6]	55	56	64	68	70	49	52	60	64	69	89	93	94	94	99
North West[6]	34	34	34	34	34	15	20	17	21	23	44	59	50	62	68
England and Wales[5]	425	433	447	457	461	379	386	397	413	422	89	89	89	90	92
Scotland	23	23	23	23	58	19	21	18	12	51	83	91	78	52	88
Northern Ireland	16	16	16	16	16	15	16	14	15	16	94	100	88	94	100
United Kingdom[5]	464	472	486	496	535	413	423	429	440	489	89	90	88	89	91

1 76/160/EEC
2 At least 95 per cent of samples must have counts not exceeding the mandatory limit values for total and faecal coliforms.
3 Bathing waters which are closed for a season are excluded for that year.
4 In 1993, Northumbria and Yorkshire were amalgamated into one region, now called North East; and Wessex and South West were amalgamated into one region, now called South West. Results for the old regions are given for comparison with earlier years.

5 Figures for 1995-1998 include Alnmouth, which was dedesignated in 1999.
6 West Kirby is included in the figure for North West region for all years. In previous publications it was included in the Welsh region.

Sources: Environment Agency;
Scottish Environment Protection Agency;
Environment and Heritage Service

13.13 Radioactive waste stocks and arisings[1]
Great Britain

m³

	Stocks						
	1/1/86	1/1/87	1/1/88	1/1/89	1/1/91	1/4/94	1/4/98
High level waste[2]							
As stored[3]	1 351	1 430	1 463	1 575	1 686	1 639	1 804
Conditioned[4]	436	517	594	674	681	653	717
Intermediate level waste[5]							
As stored	41 887	43 602	47 783	45 313	51 558	61 494	70 948
Conditioned[6]	56 211	59 479	66 020	81 762	78 512	66 102	74 131
Low level waste[7,8]							
As stored	2 429	2 343	1 002	13 752	6 252	7 882	7 983

1 Excludes waste from defence establishments before 1991. Such intermediate and low level wastes will add no more than 20 per cent to the volumes of radioactive waste from civil sources before 1991.
2 "High level wastes" (HLW) come from the reprocessing of irradiated nuclear fuel and are intensely radioactive. They contain over 95 per cent of all the radioactivity in wastes from the nuclear cycle. HLWs are of relatively small volume, but have a high heat output as a result of the energy from radioactive decay.
3 "As stored" is the form in which the waste is currently stored. For the majority of low level waste, storage is short term prior to disposal.
4 Conditioned HLW is the form suitable for long-term storage (i.e. vitrified).

5 "Intermediate level waste" (ILW) have a lower radioactivity and heat output than HLW but radioactivity content that exceeds the upper limits for low level wastes. Examples of ILW include the irradiated metal cladding for nuclear reactor fuel, reactor components, and chemical process residues and filters.
6 "Conditioned" ILW is the form suitable for ultimate disposal to a deep repository.
7 "Low level wastes" (LLW) include concrete, rubble and soil from building demolition, discarded protective clothing and worn out or damaged plant and equipment. Unlike HLW and ILW, LLW does not normally require shielding against radiation emissions during handling and transport.
8 LLW volumes are reported in the form in which the waste will be disposed of in existing facilities or a future repository. For 1991 and 1994, the volumes are for the wastes after supercompaction.

Source: Electrowatt Engineering Services (UK) Ltd

13.14 Noise complaints received by Environmental Health Officers[1]

Number per million people

		1986/87	1987/88	1988/89	1989/90	1990/91	1991/92	1992/93	1993/94	1994/95	1995/96	1996/97	1997/98	1998/99	1999[12]/00
England and Wales															
Not controlled by the Act:[2]															
Road traffic[3]	JZLJ	41	41	42	47	46	65	59	59	60	66	62	52	39	39
Aircraft[4]	JZLK	19	20	47	48	34	72	73	64	111	48	58	92	109	135
Other	JZLL	54	48	35	59	60	99	105	84	91	90	74	229	..	..
Total	JZLM	114	109	124	154	140	236	237	207	262	204	194	373	..	..
Controlled by the Act:[2]															
Industrial/commercial premises	JZLN	654	670	713	811	913	1 037	1 108	1 120	1 320	1 466	1 455	1 647	1 280	1 323
Road works, construction and demolition[5]	JZLO	153	196	233	180	252	148	191	168	300	229	242	285	248	277
Domestic premises	JZLP	1 269	1 579	1 620	1 855	2 264	2 627	3 137	3 468	3 949	4 895	5 051	5 050	4 330	4 734
Vehicles, machinery & equipment in streets[5,6,11]	JZLQ	..	..	..	..	..	..	..	..	249	225	206	300	252	246
Total	JZLR	2 076	2 445	2 566	2 846	3 429	3 812	4 436	4 756	5 818	6 815	6 954	7 282	6 110	6 580
Controlled by Section 62 of the Act:[7]															
Noise in streets[5,8]	JZLS	55	52	69	60	75	100	76	92	89	109	111	..	..	..
Total complaints received	JZLT	2 245	2 606	2 759	3 060	3 644	4 148	4 749	5 055	6 169	7 128	7 259	..	..	..

		1986	1987	1988	1989	1990	1991	1992[10]/93	1993/94	1994/95	1995/96	1996/97	1997/98	1998/99	1999/00
Scotland															
Not controlled by the Act:[2]															
Road traffic[3]	JZLU	28	32	36	39	54	51	35	..	..	..	24	21	..	..
Aircraft[4]	JZLV	4	4	5	7	17	8	14	..	..	..	14	7	..	..
Other[9]	JZLW	6	4	6	7	87	128	172	..	..	..	304	229	..	..
Total	JZLX	38	40	47	53	158	187	221	..	..	..	342	257	..	..
Controlled by the Act:[2]															
Industrial/commercial premises	JZLY	437	411	436	501	537	519	560	..	..	..	845	504	..	..
Road works, construction and demolition	JZLZ	90	85	100	129	162	177	89	..	..	..	206	177	..	..
Domestic premises	JYWN	169	202	148	161	210	302	431	..	..	..	754	787	..	..
Vehicles, machinery & equipment in streets[6]	JYXH	..	..	..	..	..	..	..	..	..	..	12	41	..	..
Total	JYWO	696	698	684	791	909	998	1 080	..	..	..	1 817	1 509	..	..
Controlled by Section 62 of the Act:[7]															
Noise in streets[8]	JYXI	32	27	23	24	25	61	33	..	..	..	27	22	..	..
Total complaints received	JYWP	766	765	754	868	1 092	1 246	1 334	..	..	..	2 186	1 788	..	..

1 Figures relate to those authorities making returns.
2 Control of Pollution Act 1974 until 1990/91; Environmental Protection Act 1990 for 1991/92 onwards.
3 Most complaints about traffic noise are usually addressed to highways authorities or Department of Transport Regional Directors, and will not necessarily be included in these figures.
4 Complaints about noise from civil aircraft are generally received by aircraft operators, the airport companies, the Department of Transport or Civil Aviation Authority. Complaints about military flying are dealt with either by Station Commanding Officers or by Ministry of Defence headquarters. The figures in the table will not necessarily include these complaints.
5 From 1997/8 complaints about road works are included with 'vehicle machinery and equipment in streets'.

6 Noise & Statutory Nuisance Act 1993.
7 Control of Pollution Act 1974.
8 Primarily includes the chimes of ice-cream vendors and the use of loudspeakers other than for strictly defined purposes.
9 Complaints about barking dogs were included for the first time in 1990 figures for Scotland.
10 1992/93 figures cover a period of 15 months from January 1992 to March 1993 due to the change from calendar year to financial year in order to come into line with England and Wales.
11 From 1997/98 includes complaints about noise previously classified as
12 Figures are provisional.

Sources: The Chartered Institute of Environmental Health; Royal Environmental Health Institute of Scotland

13.15 Estimated total annual waste arisings by sector
United Kingdom

Sector	Annual arisings (million tonnes)	Date of estimate	Status[1]	Source	Percentage of total arisings
Agriculture[2]	87	1999	NC	DETR	20
Minerals (Mining & quarrying)[3]					
colliery[3]	15	1997	NC	DETR	4
coal[3]	9	1997	NC	DETR	2
china clay[3]	26	1997	NC	DETR	6
clay[3]	14	1997	NC	DETR	3
slate[3]	7	1997	NC	DETR	2
quarrying[3]	47	1997	NC	DETR	11
Sewage sludge[4,5]	1	1998/9	C	Water UK	0
Dredged material[6]	41	1997	C	MAFF	10
Municipal waste[7]	30	1998/99	C	DETR	7
of which household	27	1998/99	C	DETR	6
Commercial[8]	30	2000	C	EA	7
Industrial[8]	48	2000	C	EA	11
Demolition & construction[9]	72	2000	C	EA	17
Total	427				100

1 NC = Not classed as a controlled waste under the terms of the Environmental Protection Act (Controlled Waste Regulations) 1992; C = controlled wastes under the terms of the Environmental Protection Act (Controlled Waste Regulation) 1992.

2 Estimate is for Great Britain, derived from a survey of agricultural waste commissioned by DETR. It includes all waste streams, e.g. excreta from all livestock (both housed and grazing animals) and other wastes including straw, plastics and packaging, animal carcasses and slurries.

3 Minerals waste estimates based on ratios of waste to product. 1997 estimate used, as 1998 estimate is still provisional.

4 Dry weight arisings. Wet weight can be estimated on the basis of 4% solid content on averagegiving a total of 26,450,000 tonnes.

5 Water UK (formerly Water Services Association and Water Companies Association.)

6 The data are for all UK waters.

7 UK estimates based on returns made by Waste Disposal/Unitary Authorities in England and Wales to a DETR/National Assembly for Wales survey.

8 Estimated from Environment Agency survey. Figures only cover England and Wales and may change when detailed analysis is undertaken. Large waste streams, such as blast furnace and steel slag and power station ash were inadequately covered by the survey, and thus this is likely to be an underestimate of the total.

9 Estimated from Environment Agency survey. Figures only cover England and Wales.

Sources: Ministry of Agriculture, Fisheries and Food;
Department of the Environment, Transport and the Regions;
Environment Agency; Water UK

13.16 Recycling[1] of selected materials
United Kingdom

Scrap reused as a percentage of consumption

		1985	1986	1987	1988	1989	1990	1991	1992	1993	1994	1995	1996	1997	1998
Ferrous	JYWQ	39	36	38	34	36	38	36	45	42	42	40	44	45	35
Aluminium	JYWR	40	34	34	41	44	39	41	39	29	39	53	44	40	43
Copper	JYWS	43	44	47	49	49	50	49	35	35	32	34	36	37	38
Lead	JYWT	69	66	77	73	71	67	62	64	67	74	71	73	66	66
Zinc	JYWU	22	24	24	24	23	24	24	21	21	20	20	19	19	18
Paper & board	JYWV	28	27	27	27	28	32	34	34	32	34	37	38	38	38
Glass cullet	JYWW	12	..	10	11	12	15	17	20	22	22	22	22	21	22
Plastics	ZBZJ	..	..	..	..	..	..	2	2	2	2	3	3	3	3

1 The ratios shown reflect the amount of secondary material used (scrap collected less exported scrap plus imported scrap) in the UK in a year as a proportion of consumption in that year.

Sources: Iron and Steel Statistics Bureau;
Aluminium Federation;
Customs and Excise;
World Bureau of Metal Statistics;
British Paper & Board Industry Federation;
British Glass Manufacturers Confederation;
British Plastics Federation

13.17 Designated areas[1] by region at December 1997

	National Parks[3]		Areas of Outstanding Natural Beauty[3,4]		Defined Heritage Coasts Length (km)
	Area ('000 ha)	Percentage of total area in region	Area ('000 ha)	Percentage of total area in region	
Region					
Northern	362	23	226	15	128
Yorkshire and Humberside	315	20	92	6	82
East Midlands	92	6	52	3	-
East Anglia	-	-	91	7	121
South East	-	-	662	24	72
South West	165	7	712	30	638
West Midlands	20	2	127	10	-
North West	10	1	78	11	-
England	963	7	2 039	16	1 041
Wales	413	20	83	4	496
England and Wales	1 376	9	2 122	15	1 539
Scotland	-	-	1 002	13	-
Northern Ireland	-	-	285	20	-

1 Some areas may be in more than one category.
2 Estimated.
3 Figures may differ from those previously published due to redefinition or remeasurement of some National Parks and AONBs.
4 National Scenic Areas in Scotland.

Sources: Countryside Commission;
Environment & Heritage Service, Northern Ireland;
Countryside Council for Wales;
Scottish Natural Heritage

13.18 Stock of dwellings
Great Britain

		1988	1989	1990	1991	1992	1993	1994	1995	1996	1997	1998
Estimated annual gains and losses (Thousands)												
Gains: New construction[1]	KGAA	232.4	211.2	195.5	184.7	172.5	179.0	186.6	191.4	180.9	180.4	169.6
Other	KGAB	16.7	16.6	14.5	14.5	10.7	10.8	10.4	11.2	10.7	..	..
Losses: Slum clearance	KGAC	8.2	7.9	9.4	4.7	4.9	5.9	4.6	6.3	6.6	..	..
Other	KGAD	11.9	9.2	9.5	12.5	7.7	7.3	9.4	8.1	7.0	..	..
Net gain	KGAE	234.5	216.2	196.6	207.4	170.6	176.6	183.0	188.2	178.0	..	..
Stock at end of year[2]	KGAF	22 527	22 743	22 939	23 141	23 314	23 489	23 672	23 860	24 037	24 216	..
Estimated tenure distribution at end of year (percentage)												
Owner occupied	KGAG	64.0	65.2	65.8	66.3	66.3	66.6	66.8	66.8	67.0	67.2	..
Rented: From local authorities and new towns	KGAH	24.0	22.8	21.9	21.2	20.5	19.9	19.1	18.4	17.9	17.0	..
From housing associations	KGAI	2.7	2.9	3.1	3.1	3.3	3.6	4.0	4.3	4.6	4.9	..
From private owners including other tenants	KGAJ	9.2	9.1	9.2	9.6	9.8	9.9	10.1	10.4	10.6	10.6	..

Note: For statistical purposes the stock estimates are expressed to the nearest thousand, but should not be regarded as accurate to the last digit.

1 The figures for 1997 and 1998 have been revised.
2 Estimates are based on data from the 1981 and 1991 Censuses.

Sources: Department of the Environment, Transport and the Regions: 0117 987
8055;
Scottish Executive;
National Assembly for Wales

13.19 Renovations
Great Britain

Number of dwellings

		1989	1990	1991	1992	1993	1994	1995	1996	1997[5,9]	1998[6,9]	1999[7,8]
England												
Local authorities and new towns[1]	KGBA	238 957	231 558	179 584	171 202	244 582	297 613	311 640	321 802	..	..	..
Housing associations[2]	KGBB	13 024	10 657	6 425	7 532	6 012	6 881	..	..	..	..	..
Private owners: grants paid[3]	KGBC	89 686	90 864	84 696	82 866	80 734	91 233	93 090	95 230	83 045	94 148	108 575
Wales												
Local authorities[1]	KGBE	8 444	10 843	10 513	9 491	23 264	20 397	16 665	4 705	..	..	..
Housing associations[2]	KGBF	812	399	305	322	300	287	163	147	131	275	..
Private owners: grants paid[3]	KGBG	20 074	26 522	21 228	16 642	16 061	14 619	17 314	17 345	17 030	18 287	15 590
Scotland												
Local authorities and new towns[4]	KGBI	52 549	84 261	70 361	80 753	90 519	117 497	75 845	..	..	..	..
Housing associations[2]	KGBJ	1 122	816	1 680	1 785	1 524	1 229	1 328	767	337	..	..
Private owners: grants paid[3]	KGBK	26 915	23 586	23 478	37 934	21 194	19 697	19 027	15 800	13 585	12 711	12 048
Great Britain												
Local authorities and new towns[1,4]	KGBM	299 950	326 662	260 458	261 446	358 365	435 507	404 150	..	..	..	..
Housing associations[2]	KGBN	14 958	11 872	8 410	9 639	7 836	8 397	..	..	..	..	..
Private owners: grants paid[3]	KGBO	136 675	140 972	129 402	137 442	117 989	125 549	129 431	128 375	113 660	125 146	136 213

1 Work completed. Includes improvement for sale. Figures for Wales not available before 1984.

2 Figures for England are of work completed funded by the Housing Corporation and Local Authorities. Figures for Wales are for work completed by the Housing Corporation funded by housing associations only. Figures for Scotland are of work approved under specific housing association legislation. Figures from Scottish Homes not available for 1991.

3 Including grants paid to housing associations under private owner grant legislation. Figures include a small number of grants to tenants in both public and private sectors. Figures for 1997 and 1998 have been revised. Figures for 1999 are provisional.

4 Work approved in Scotland.

5 Of the 100 075 grants paid in 1997 to private owners and tenants in England and Wales, 41 605 were paid under the Housing Grants, Construction and Regeneration Act 1996 and 58 470 were paid under the Local Government and Housing Act 1989.

6 Of the 112 435 grants paid in 1998 to private owners and tenants in England and Wales, 102 615 were paid under the Housing Grants, Construction and Housing Act 1996 and 9 820 were paid under the Local Government and Housing Act 1989.

7 Of the 124 165 grants paid in 1999 to private owners and tenants in England and Wales, 121 512 were paid under the Housing Grants, Construction and Regeneration Act 1996 and 2 653 were paid under the Local Government and Housing Act 1989.

8 Provisional data.

9 Revised data.

Sources: Department of the Environment, Transport and the Regions: 0117 987 8055;
Scottish Executive;
National Assembly for Wales

13.20 Slum clearance: dwellings demolished or closed

Number

		1987 /88	1988 /89	1989 /90	1990 /91	1991 /92	1992 /93	1993 /94	1994 /95	1995 /96	1996 /97	1997 /98
England and Wales: total	KGCA	6 683	5 509	6 157	6 210	2 383	2 072	4 061	3 997	2 047	1 629	1 289
Demolished: In clearance areas	KGCB	3 617	2 290	3 433	4 421	1 221	1 221	1 461	2 044	1 180	861	847
Elsewhere	KGCC	1 605	1 456	2 031	1 465	459	347	261	1 953	493	391	332
Closed[1]	KGCD	1 461	1 763	713	324	703	504	2 339	−574	374	377	110
Scotland[2]: total	KGCE	1 801	1 175	1 007	2 224	1 816	3 685	4 311	4 371	5 542	3 437	5 014
Unfit[3]	KGCF	794	373	447	..	..	..	..	..	..	..	..
Other[1,3]	KGCG	1 007	802	560	..	..	..	..	..	..	..	..

1 Less dwellings included in numbers demolished which had previously been reported as closed.

2 Action under the Housing Acts, Town and Country Planning Acts and other specific statutory powers and other action. Unfit houses comprise houses failing to meet the tolerable standard introduced by the Housing (Scotland) Act 1969 and houses dealt with under earlier statutory provisions as being unfit for human habitation.

3 Figures after 31 March 1990 no longer include information about unfit or other dwellings demolished, as data collection on above and below tolerable standard demolitions ceased.

Sources: Department of the Environment, Transport and the Regions: 0117 987 8055;
Scottish Executive;
National Assembly for Wales

13.21 Permanent dwellings completed

Number

	United Kingdom				England and Wales			
	Total	For local housing authorities[1]	For private owners	Housing Associations and other[2]	Total	For local housing authorities[1]	For private owners	Housing Associations and other[2]
	KAAD	KAAE	KAAF	KAAG	KAAH	KAAI	KAAJ	KAAK
1976	324 769	151 824	155 229	17 716	278 660	124 152	128 477	16 031
1977	314 093	143 250	143 905	26 938	276 011	121 246	128 688	26 077
1978	288 603	112 340	152 166	24 097	254 001	96 752	134 578	22 671
1979	251 816	88 495	144 055	19 276	220 722	77 192	125 306	18 224
1980	242 001	87 974	131 989	22 038	214 934	78 012	116 179	20 743
1981	206 632	68 046	118 590	19 996	179 794	58 126	104 012	17 656
1982	182 863	39 960	129 022	13 881	159 407	33 430	113 893	12 084
1983	209 026	38 921	153 038	17 067	181 399	31 391	134 901	15 107
1984	220 492	37 408	165 574	17 510	191 190	31 187	145 282	14 721
1985	207 465	30 303	163 395	13 767	178 284	24 259	142 020	12 005
1986	216 592	25 070	178 017	13 505	187 758	20 303	156 065	11 390
1987	226 196	21 095	191 212	13 889	198 694	16 836	169 857	12 001
1988	242 359	21 129	207 423	13 807	214 156	16 687	185 733	11 736
1989	221 521	18 685	187 542	15 294	191 048	14 694	163 344	13 010
1990	203 380	17 651	167 473	18 256	175 099	14 483	144 849	15 767
1991	191 604	11 154	159 269	21 181	165 197	8 469	138 572	18 156
1992	180 246	5 473	147 322	27 451	154 088	3 414	127 020	23 654
1993	186 182	3 351	146 673	36 158	157 592	1 583	123 255	32 754
1994	193 591	2 882	153 341	37 368	165 210	1 321	130 066	33 823
1995	199 981	3 448	157 205	39 328	166 953	969	132 549	33 435
1996	189 016	1 744	154 202	33 070	159 436	576	129 278	29 582
1997	190 585	1 474	160 862	28 249	157 995	291	134 709	22 995
1998	179 768	1 058	154 516	24 194	149 266	289	127 563	21 414
1999	..	..	..	..	147 940	83	129 512	18 345

	Scotland				Northern Ireland			
	Total	For local housing authorities[1]	For private owners	Housing Associations and other[2]	Total	For local housing authorities[1]	For private owners	Housing Associations and other[2]
	KAAL	KAAM	KAAN	KAAO	KAAP	KAAQ	KAAR	KAAS
1976	36 527	21 154	13 704	1 669	9 582	6 518	3 048	16
1977	27 320	14 328	12 132	860	10 762	7 676	3 085	1
1978	25 759	9 907	14 443	1 409	8 843	5 681	3 145	17
1979	23 782	7 857	15 175	750	7 312	3 436	3 574	302
1980	20 611	7 455	12 242	914	6 456	2 507	3 568	381
1981	20 011	7 061	11 021	1 929	6 827	2 859	3 557	411
1982	16 423	3 716	11 523	1 184	7 033	2 814	3 606	613
1983	17 929	3 486	13 166	1 277	9 698	4 044	4 971	683
1984	18 838	2 633	14 115	2 090	10 464	3 588	6 177	699
1985	18 411	2 811	14 435	1 165	10 770	3 233	6 940	597
1986	18 637	2 187	14 870	1 580	10 197	2 580	7 082	535
1987	17 707	2 495	13 904	1 308	9 795	1 764	7 451	580
1988	18 272	2 730	14 179	1 363	9 931	1 712	7 511	708
1989	20 190	2 283	16 287	1 620	10 283	1 708	7 911	664
1990	20 362	1 869	16 461	2 032	7 919	1 299	6 163	457
1991	19 529	1 732	15 533	2 264	6 878	953	5 164	761
1992	18 443	1 010	14 389	3 044	7 715	1 049	5 913	753
1993	21 392	958	17 711	2 723	7 198	810	5 707	681
1994	21 404	661	17 753	2 990	6 977	900	5 522	555
1995	24 486	1 173	18 310	5 003	8 542	1 306	6 346	890
1996	21 306	278	18 345	.2 683	8 274	890	6 579	805
1997	22 422	108	17 807	4 507	10 168	1 075	8 346	747
1998	20 425	86	18 372	1 967	10 077	683	8 581	813
1999	..	..	..	..	9 225	196	7 911	1 118

1 Including the Commission for the New Towns and New Towns Development Corporations, the Scottish Special Housing Association, the Northern Ireland Housing Trust and the Northern Ireland Housing Executive.
2 Dwellings provided by housing associations other than the Scottish Special Housing Association and the Northern Ireland Housing Trust and provided or authorised by government departments for the families of police, prison staff, the Armed Forces and certain other services.

Sources: Department of the Environment, Transport and the Regions: 0117 987 8055;
Scottish Executive;
National Assembly for Wales;
Department for Social Development, Northern Ireland

13.22 Water industry expenditure[1,2,3,4]
England and Wales

£ millions

		1989 /90	1990 /91	1991 /92	1992 /93	1993 /94	1994 /95	1995 /96	1996 /97	1997 /98	1998 /99	1999 /00
Operating expenditure												
Water supply	KQQX	..	2 377.4	1 953.8	2 024.4	2 108.0	2 209.0	2 347.0	2 304.2	2 331.0	2 386.1	2 426.8
Sewerage services	KQQY	..	1 963.1	1 580.9	1 635.4	1 757.9	1 755.0	1 763.0	1 780.7	1 856.1	1 971.4	2 069.9
Capital expenditure												
Water supply	KQSX	632.9	986.4	1 307.0	1 358.2	1 386.7	1 081.0	1 074.5	1 314.3	1 467.2	1 294.1	1 290.0
Sewerage	KQSY	269.3	475.8	559.0	455.3	410.7	381.0	375.6	479.9	455.2	507.5	488.5
Sewage treatment and disposal	KQSZ	470.9	759.2	968.0	906.0	735.3	763.0	773.0	959.4	1 296.3	1 374.5	1 440.8

1 Data is taken from the annual and regulatory accounts of the water and sewerage companies and water companies of England and Wales.
2 Figures are given based on current cost rather than historical cost accounting principles.
3 The elements which make up operating expenditure are as follows:
Manpower costs
Other costs of employment
Power
Local Authority rates
Water charges

Local Authority sewerage agencies
Materials and consumables
Hired and contracted services
Charge for bad and doubtful debts
Depreciation
Infrastructure renewals expenditure
Infrastructure renewals accrual
Exceptional items
Other operating costs.
4 Capital expenditure figures are the addition to tangible fixed assets including management and general expenditure but excluding infrastructure renewals expenditure.

Source: Ofwat: 0121 625 1388

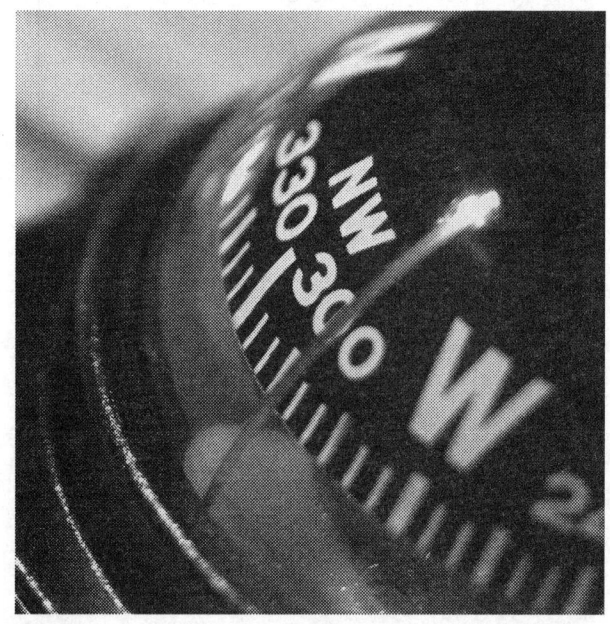

14 Transport and communications

Transport and communications

14.1 Passenger transport: by mode
Great Britain

	Road					Rail[1]	Air	All modes[2]
	Buses and coaches	Cars, vans and taxis	Motor cycles	Pedal cycles	All road			
Billion passenger kilometres								
	KCTP	KCTQ	KCTR	KCTS	ZCBD	KCTN	KCTM	KCTT
1989	47	581	6	5	639	39	4.9	683
1990	46	588	6	5	645	40	5.2	690
1991	44	582	6	5	637	39	4.8	681
1992	43	583	5	5	635	38	4.8	678
1993	44	584	4	4	636	37	5.1	678
1994	44	591	4	5	643	35	5.5	684
1995	44	596	4	4	648	37	5.9	691
1996	44	606	4	4	658	39	6.3	703
1997	44	614	4	4	666	42	6.8	715
1998	45	617[3]	4	4	671	44	7.0	722
1999	45	621[3]	5	4	675	46	7.3	728
Percentages								
	ZCBE	ZCBF	ZCBG	ZCBH	ZCBI	ZCBJ	ZCBK	ZCBL
1989	7	85	1	1	94	6	0.7	100
1990	7	85	1	1	93	6	0.8	100
1991	6	86	1	1	94	6	0.7	100
1992	6	86	1	1	94	6	0.7	100
1993	6	86	1	1	94	5	0.8	100
1994	6	86	1	1	94	5	0.8	100
1995	6	86	1	1	94	5	0.9	100
1996	6	86	1	1	94	6	0.9	100
1997	6	86	1	1	93	6	0.9	100
1998	6	86	1	1	93	6	1.0	100
1999	6	85	1	1	93	6	1.0	100

1 Financial years. Former British Rail companies and Urban Rail systems.
2 Excluding travel by water within the United Kingdom (including the Channel Islands), estimated at 0.6 billion passenger kilometres in 1999.
3 Provisional data.

Source: Department of the Environment, Transport and the Regions

14.2 Journeys per person per year by main mode[1] and purpose, 1997/99
Great Britain

Number

	Walk	Bicycle	Car/van driver	Car/van passenger	Motor-cycle	Other private	Buses in London
Commuting	19	6	95	19	2	1	3
Business	4	-	27	2	-	-	-
Education	30	1	3	18	-	3	2
Escort education	23	-	19	7	-	-	1
Shopping	67	2	80	49	-	1	4
Other escort	9	-	47	23	-	-	-
Other personal business	30	1	42	23	-	1	1
Visiting friends at home	30	2	53	44	-	-	1
Visiting friends elsewhere	13	-	12	14	-	-	-
Social/entertainment	10	1	23	21	-	1	1
Holidays/day trips	2	2	9	13	-	1	-
Other, including just walk	44	-	1	-	-	-	-
All purposes	**281**	**17**	**412**	**234**	**3**	**8**	**14**

	Other local bus	Non-local bus	LT Under-ground	Surface rail	Taxi/ minicab	Other public	All modes
Commuting	9	-	3	5	1	1	164
Business	-	-	-	1	-	-	37
Education	8	-	-	1	1	-	67
Escort education	1	-	-	-	-	-	50
Shopping	14	-	-	1	2	-	221
Other escort	1	-	-	-	-	-	81
Other personal business	4	-	1	-	1	-	105
Visiting friends at home	5	-	-	1	2	-	140
Visiting friends elsewhere	2	-	-	-	3	-	45
Social/entertainment	2	-	-	1	1	-	61
Holidays/day trips	1	1	-	1	-	-	30
Other, including just walk	-	-	-	-	-	-	45
All purposes	**46**	**2**	**6**	**11**	**12**	**2**	**1 046**

1 Main mode is that used for the longest part of the journey.

Source: Department of the Environment, Transport and the Regions (020) 7944 3097

14.3 Retail Prices Index: real changes in the cost of transport and disposable income
Great Britain

Constant prices

Index 1974=100

	Petrol/oil	All motoring	Rail	Bus and coach fares	Disposable income
	ZCFV	ZCFW	ZCFX	ZCFY	ZCFZ
1974	100.0	100.0	100.0	100.0	100.0
1975	109.5	104.4	91.1	108.9	100.7
1976	99.9	101.2	103.7	119.0	100.3
1977	92.0	99.9	104.3	115.0	98.3
1978	81.2	99.7	110.1	121.4	105.6
1979	94.1	104.0	107.4	119.8	111.5
1980	102.2	103.8	113.1	130.0	113.4
1981	108.5	103.9	115.6	130.8	112.8
1982	107.4	101.0	122.2	139.4	112.5
1983	109.8	103.2	123.9	140.8	115.3
1984	108.2	100.7	118.5	137.0	119.4
1985	108.5	99.4	118.8	134.9	123.5
1986	91.3	94.7	122.6	141.3	128.8
1987	88.4	96.3	123.8	144.5	133.3
1988	83.4	95.9	126.2	146.2	140.3
1989	82.9	93.9	127.8	145.9	146.4
1990	84.6	91.0	126.9	145.3	151.8
1991	85.9	92.3	132.4	151.2	154.1
1992	85.2	95.0	137.0	154.7	159.8
1993	90.5	97.6	144.3	159.5	164.6
1994	92.4	98.5	147.1	163.0	166.7
1995	93.9	97.0	148.5	164.8	171.1
1996	96.3	97.5	150.4	168.9	174.8
1997	102.7	99.6	149.3	172.3	181.4
1998	104.2	99.3	150.2	174.7	181.4
1999	111.3	100.2	153.4	179.7	187.1

Source: Office for National Statistics

14.4 Domestic freight transport: by mode
Great Britain

Goods moved

			1989	1990	1991[1]	1992	1993	1994	1995	1996	1997	1998	1999
Petroleum products		Billion tonnes kilometres/ percentage											
Road[2]	ZBZP		4.5	4.9	4.9	4.5	5.0	5.1	5.7	6.1	5.8	5.1	4.9
Rail	ZBZQ	"	2.2	2.1	2.0	2.0	1.9	1.8	1.8	..	..	..	..
Water[3]	ZBZR	"	47.9	45.4	46.0	42.7	41.7	43.0	42.5	45.9	38.3	45.2	42.5[7]
ow: coastwise	ZBZS	"	34.1	32.1	31.2	29.4	28.9	28.9	31.4	38.7	33.8	36.4	33.1[7]
Pipeline	ZBZT	"	9.8	11.1[4]	11.1	11.0	11.6	12.0	11.1	11.6	11.2	11.7	11.6
All modes	ZBZU	"	64.4	63.5	64.0	60.2	60.2	61.9	61.1	63.6	55.3[5]	62.0[5]	59.0[5,7]
Coal and coke													
Road[2]	ZBZV	"	4.0	4.2	3.7	3.5	3.1	2.9	2.7	2.5	2.7	2.0	2.2
Rail	ZBZW	"	4.8	5.0	5.0	5.4	3.9	3.3	3.6	3.8	4.4	4.5	4.9
Water[3]	ZBZX	"	2.6	1.4	1.8	1.8	1.5	1.4	2.3	0.6	0.6	0.5	0.5[7]
All modes	ZBZY	"	11.4	10.6	10.5	10.7	8.5	7.6	8.6	6.9	7.7	7.0	7.6[7]
Other traffic													
Road[2]	ZBZZ	"	129.3	127.2	121.4	118.5	126.4	135.7	141.2	145.3	148.6	153.0	149.6
Rail	ZCAA	"	10.3	8.7	8.3	8.1	7.9	7.9	7.9	11.3	12.5[6]	12.9[6]	13.5[6]
Water[3]	ZCAB	"	7.4	8.7	9.9	10.4	8.0	7.8	8.3	8.7	9.2	11.2	10.0[7]
All modes	ZCAC	"	147.0	144.6	139.6	137.0	142.3	151.4	157.4	165.3	170.3	177.1	173.1[7]
All traffic													
Road[2]	KCTA	"	137.8	136.3	130.0	126.5	134.5	143.7	149.6	153.9	157.1	159.5	156.7
Rail	KCTB	"	16.7	16.0	15.3	15.5	13.8	13.0	13.3	15.1	16.9	17.4	18.4
Water[3]	ZCAD	"	57.9	55.7	57.7	54.9	51.2	52.2	53.1	55.3	48.1	56.9	53.0[7]
Pipeline	KCTE	"	9.8	11.1[4]	11.1	11.0	11.6	12.0	11.1	11.6	11.2	11.7	11.6
All modes	KCTF	"	222.8	218.9	214.1	207.9	211.1	220.9	227.1	235.9	233.3	245.5	239.7[7]
Percentage of all traffic													
Road[2]	ZCAE	"	62	62	61	61	64	65	66	65	67	65	65
Rail	ZCAF	"	8	7	7	7	7	6	6	6	7	7	8
Water[3]	ZCAG	"	26	25	27	26	24	24	23	23	21	23	22
Pipeline	ZCAH	"	4	5	5	5	5	5	5	5	5	5	5
All modes	ZCAI	"	100	100	100	100	100	100	100	100	100	100	100

Goods lifted

			1989	1990	1991[1]	1992	1993	1994	1995	1996	1997	1998	1999
Petroleum products		Million tonnes/ percentage											
Road[2]	ZCAJ		65	74	73	63	67	68	71	75	73	61	61
Rail	ZCAK	"	10	10	10	10	9	8	6	..	..	..	..
Water[3]	ZCAL	"	70	68	67	66	64	70	72	71	69	76	71[7]
ow: coastwise	ZCAM	"	46	44	44	43	42	43	47	54	52	55	52[7]
Pipeline	ZCAN	"	93	121[4]	105	106	125	161	168	157	148	153	155
All modes	ZCAO	"	238	273	255	245	265	307	317	303	290[5]	290[5]	287[5,7]
Coal and coke													
Road[2]	ZCAP	"	73	62	57	55	48	42	34	32	37	22	28
Rail	ZCAQ	"	77	75	75	68	49	43	45	52	50	45	44
Water[3]	ZCAR	"	8	6	6	6	5	4	4	3	4	3	3[7]
All modes	ZCAS	"	158	143	138	129	102	89	83	87	91	70	75[7]
Other traffic													
Road[2]	ZCAT	"	1 674	1 613	1 470	1 437	1 500	1 579	1 596	1 623	1 630	1 646	1 572
Rail	ZCAU	"	59	56	51	45	45	47	50	50	55[6]	57[6]	58[6]
Water[3]	ZCAV	"	77	78	71	68	65	66	67	67	69	70	70[7]
All modes	ZCAW	"	1 810	1 747	1 592	1 550	1 610	1 692	1 713	1 740	1 754	1 773	1 700[7]
All traffic													
Road[2]	KCTG	"	1 812	1 749	1 600	1 555	1 615	1 689	1 701	1 730	1 740	1 727	1 661
Rail	KCTH	"	143.1	138.2	135.8	122.4	103.2	97.3	100.7	101.7	105.4	102.1	102.8
Water[3]	ZCAX	"	155	152	144	140	134	140	143	142	142	149	143[7]
Pipeline	KCTK	"	93	121[4]	105	106	125	161	168	157	148	153	155
All modes	KCTL	"	2 206	2 162	1 985	1 923	1 977	2 087	2 113	2 131	2 135	2 131	2 062[7]
Percentage of all traffic													
Road[2]	ZCAY	"	82	81	81	81	82	81	80	81	81	81	81
Rail	ZCAZ	"	7	6	7	6	5	5	5	5	5	5	5
Water[3]	ZCBA	"	7	7	7	7	7	7	7	7	7	7	7
Pipeline	ZCBB	"	4	6	5	6	6	8	8	7	7	7	8
All modes	ZCBC	"	100	100	100	100	100	100	100	100	100	100	100

1 Figures for rail from 1991 are for financial years.
2 All goods vehicles, including those under 3.5 tonnes gross vehicle weight. These estimates were revised following a survey in 1993.
3 Figures for water are for UK traffic.
4 The increase as compared to the corresponding figure for 1989 is believed to be largely due to changes in coverage.
5 Excludes rail.
6 Includes petroleum products.
7 Provisional data.

Source: Department of the Environment, Transport and the Regions

14.5 Public road length: by road type
Great Britain

Kilometres

		1989	1990	1991	1992	1993	1994	1995	1996	1997	1998	1999
Trunk motorway	ZCBM	2 903	2 993	3 033	3 063	3 061	3 092	3 118	3 181	3 250	3 295	3 316
Principal motorway	ZCBN	92	77	68	71	78	76	72	45	45	45	42
Non built-up major roads:												
Trunk	ZCBO	11 087	11 142	10 867	10 865	10 803	10 767	10 811	11 046	10 955	10 791	10 837
Principal	ZCBP	22 587	22 692	23 005	23 014	23 034	23 054	23 207	22 896	22 884	22 954	22 897
Total	ZCBQ	33 674	33 834	33 872	33 879	33 837	33 821	34 019	33 941	33 839	33 745	33 734
Built-up major roads												
Trunk	ZCBR	1 628	1 532	1 455	1 431	1 400	1 344	1 297	1 313	1 314	1 344	1 313
Principal	ZCBS	12 452	12 457	12 575	12 627	12 681	12 737	12 750	12 961	12 950	13 048	13 147
Total	ZCBT	14 080	13 989	14 030	14 058	14 081	14 081	14 047	14 274	14 264	14 392	14 460
Minor non built-up roads:												
B roads	ZCBU	21 990	22 048	22 290	22 161	22 093	21 872	21 686	21 293	21 169	21 149	20 952
C roads	ZCBV	67 015	67 096	67 360	67 350	67 448	66 980	67 509	66 903	66 472	66 571	65 811
Unclassified	ZCBW	81 375	81 584	81 773	81 108	80 973	79 450	78 944	78 390	77 318	77 083	76 572
All	ZCBX	170 380	170 727	171 424	170 618	170 514	168 302	168 139	166 585	164 958	164 804	163 335
Minor built-up roads:												
B roads	ZCBY	7 716	7 790	7 816	8 066	8 215	8 475	8 567	8 903	9 195	9 129	9 353
C roads	ZCBZ	13 526	13 621	13 713	13 984	14 376	15 125	15 065	15 626	16 435	16 582	16 989
Unclassified	ZCCA	114 231	115 004	116 010	118 572	120 050	121 995	123 974	126 267	127 881	129 553	130 684
All	ZCCB	135 473	136 415	137 538	140 622	142 641	145 594	147 606	150 795	153 511	155 264	157 026
All minor roads	ZCCC	305 854	307 142	308 962	311 241	313 155	313 897	315 744	317 380	318 470	320 068	320 361
All roads	KCTY	356 602	358 034	359 966	362 310	364 212	364 966	366 999	368 821	369 867	371 543	371 914

Source: Department of the Environment, Transport and the Regions (020) 7944 3095

14.6 Road traffic: by type of vehicle
Great Britain

Billion vehicle kilometres

		1989	1990	1991	1992	1993	1994	1995	1996	1997	1998	1999
Cars and taxis	KCWA	331.3	335.9	335.2	338.0	338.5	345.7	353.2	362.4	370.9	375.6	380.1
Motor cycles etc.	KCWB	5.9	5.6	5.4	4.5	4.1	4.2	4.1	4.2	4.1	3.9	4.6
Larger buses and coaches	KDZS	4.5	4.6	4.8	4.6	4.6	4.7	4.7	4.8	4.9	4.9	5.0
Light vans[1]	KDZT	39.7	39.9	41.7	41.2	41.1	42.5	43.8	45.1	45.6	48.1	49.2
Goods vehicles:												
2 axles rigid	ZCCD	11.7	11.6	11.5	11.4	11.3	12.1	11.4	11.4	11.7	10.9	11.7
3 axles rigid	ZCCE	1.8	1.6	1.5	1.4	1.3	1.4	1.5	1.5	1.8	1.9	1.7
4 or more axles rigid	ZCCF	1.8	1.7	1.5	1.4	1.5	1.5	1.5	1.4	1.4	1.4	1.5
3 and 4 axles artic.	ZCCG	5.0	4.6	4.3	3.9	3.4	3.4	3.3	3.5	3.4	3.1	3.0
5 axles artic.	ZCCH	3.9	4.1	4.3	4.3	4.8	5.3	5.6	6.1	6.5	6.7	6.9
6 or more axles artic.	ZCCI	1.2	1.3	1.4	1.4	1.5	1.7	1.8	2.1	2.4	2.6	3.2
All	KDZV	25.5	24.9	24.5	23.8	23.8	25.5	25.1	26.0	27.1	26.7	28.1
All motor vehicles	KCVZ	406.9	410.8	411.6	412.1	412.2	422.6	430.9	442.5	452.5	459.2	467.0
Pedal cycles	KDZW	5.2	5.3	5.2	4.7	4.5	4.5	4.5	4.3	4.1	3.9	4.2

1 Not exceeding 3,500 kgs gross vehicle weight.

Source: Department of the Environment, Transport and the Regions (020) 7944 3095

Transport and communications

14.7 Motor vehicle traffic: by road class
Great Britain

Billion vehicle kilometres

		1989	1990	1991	1992	1993	1994	1995	1996	1997	1998	1999
Motorways	ZCEF	59.0	61.6	61.0	61.5	63.9	66.7	70.9	73.7	77.9	81.3	83.6
Non built-up major roads												
Trunk	ZCEG	57.8	59.0	59.5	58.9	59.3	59.8	61.3	63.2	64.8	65.5	68.9
Principal	ZCEH	54.0	55.9	57.5	58.2	58.9	60.0	61.2	62.5	64.2	66.3	65.9
All	ZCEI	111.9	114.8	117.0	117.0	118.1	119.9	122.5	125.8	128.9	131.8	134.9
Built-up major roads[1]												
Trunk	ZCEJ	10.7	10.1	9.9	9.8	9.4	10.0	9.1	9.4	9.3	9.5	9.7
Principal	ZCEK	68.6	68.2	69.5	69.7	68.6	70.1	70.0	71.6	70.4	70.1	70.1
All	ZCEL	79.3	78.3	79.4	79.5	78.0	80.2	79.1	81.1	79.7	76.6	79.8
Minor roads												
Minor non built-up roads	ZCEM	51.5	51.6	50.7	49.7	45.5	44.9	44.8	46.3	48.3	48.5	48.4
Minor built-up roads	ZCEN	105.2	104.4	103.4	104.4	106.8	110.9	113.6	115.7	117.7	118.1	120.4
All	ZCEO	156.7	156.1	154.2	154.1	152.2	155.9	158.4	161.9	166.0	166.6	168.8
All roads	KCVZ	406.9	410.8	411.6	412.1	412.2	422.6	430.9	442.5	452.5	459.2	467.0

1 Built-up roads are those with a speed limit of 40 mph or less, irrespective of whether there are buildings or not.

Source: Department of the Environment, Transport and the Regions (020) 7944 3095

14.8 Motor vehicles currently licenced at end of year
Great Britain

Thousands

	Private and light goods		Motor cycles, scooters and mopeds	Public transport Hackney taxation class		Goods vehicles	Special machines/ special conces- sionary	Other vehicles	Crown & exempt vehicles	Special vehicles group	All vehicles	Body type cars	
	Body type cars	Other vehicles		Total	Buses							All	Company cars (%)
	BMBJ	BMBK	BMBB	ZCGQ	KCUD	BMBD	KSBY	BMBF	BMBL	KSBZ	BMBI	ZCGR	ZCGS
1989	19 248	2 199	875	122	73	505	384	77	785	..	24 196	19 720	13.0
1990	19 742	2 247	833	115	73	482	375	71	807	..	24 673	20 230	12.9
1991	19 737	2 215	750	109	72	449	346	65	840	..	24 511	20 253	12.0
1992[1]	19 870	2 198	684	107	72	432	324	59	903	..	24 577	20 444	11.1
1993	20 102	2 187	650	107	73	428	318	55	979	..	24 826	20 755	10.7
1994	20 479	2 192	630	107	75	434	309	50	1 030	..	25 231	21 199	10.4
1995[2]	20 505	2 217	594	..	74	421	274	44	1 169	28	25 369[3]	21 394	10.4
1996	21 172	2 267	609	..	77	413	254	40	1 424	48	26 302	22 238	10.3
1997	21 681	2 317	626	..	79	414	249	38	1 522	48	26 974	22 832	10.5
1998	22 115	2 362	684	..	80	412	243	37	1 558	47	27 538	23 293	10.4
1999	22 785	2 427	760	..	84	415	241	36	1 573	47	28 368	23 975	10.0

1 New methods of estimating vehicle stock were introduced in 1992.
2 The vehicle taxation system was subject to substantial revision from 1 July 1995.
3 Contains 44,000 vehicles still taxed in classes abolished from 1 July 1995.

Source: Department of the Environment, Transport and the Regions (020) 7944 6386

14.9 New vehicle registrations by taxation class
Great Britain

Thousands

		1988	1989	1990	1991	1992	1993	1994	1995[7]	1996	1997	1998
Total[1]	BMAX	2 723.5	2 828.9	2 438.7	1 921.5	1 901.8	2 074.0	2 249.0	2 306.5	2 410.1	2 597.2	2 740.3
Private and light goods[2]												
Private cars	BMAA	2 154.7	2 241.2	1 942.3	1 536.6	1 528.0	1 694.6	1 809.1	1 828.3	1 888.4	2 015.9	2 123.5
Other vehicles	BMAE	282.3	294.0	237.6	171.9	166.4	158.8	182.6	195.7	205.0	228.4	244.5
Total	KCUG	2 403.6	2 494.0	2 179.9	1 708.5	1 694.4	1 853.4	1 991.7	2 024.0	2 093.4	2 244.3	2 368.0
Motor cycles, etc:												
Up to 50c.c.	KCUH	24.7	22.9	18.8	13.1	9.1	6.5	6.9	6.3	8.9	14.2	22.6
Other	KCUI	65.4	74.4	75.9	63.6	56.5	51.9	57.7	62.6	80.7	107.1	120.7
Total	BMAD	90.1	97.3	94.4	76.5	65.6	58.4	64.6	68.9	89.6	121.3	143.3
Public road passenger vehicles												
Buses, coaches, taxis, etc												
Not over 8 seats	KCUJ	4.2	3.0	2.9	2.2	2.0	1.8	2.5	1.3[8]	..	..	..
Over 8 seats	KCUK	5.0	5.2	4.8	3.0	3.1	3.6	4.2	5.2	6.5	6.6	7.4
Total	BMAG	9.2	8.2	7.7	5.2	5.1	5.4	6.7	6.5	6.5	6.6	7.4
Heavy general goods[2] and farmers[3]												
Goods vehicles: by weight	KCUL	63.4	64.5	44.4	28.6	28.7	32.8	41.1	48.0	45.5	41.8	49.1
Privately owned agricultural tractors and engines[4]	BMAH	45.2	42.5	34.2	26.1	24.1	30.0	35.3	..	..	..	..
Special concession group	KSCB	..	..	..	..	..	..	..	33.0[9]	25.7	21.7	15.2
Other licensed vehicles[5]	KCUM	3.4	2.6	2.1	0.7	1.6	1.4	1.3	1.0	1.0	1.5	1.5
Special vehicles group	DMNR	..	..	..	..	..	..	..	3.3[10]	8.1	8.6	7.6
Exempt from license duty												
Crown vehicles	KCUN	4.1	4.4	4.0	3.2	3.7	3.1	4.1	3.3	1.2	0.7	1.1
All other exempt vehicles[1,6]	KCUO	66.0	74.2	72.2	72.6	78.7	89.4	104.3	118.1	139.1	150.7	146.6
Total	KCUP	70.1	78.6	76.2	75.8	82.3	92.4	108.4	121.4	140.3	151.4	147.7

1 Including personal and direct export vehicles.
2 For years up to 1990 retrospective counts within these new taxation classes have been estimated.
3 Owned by a farmer and available for hauling produce and requisites for his own farm.
4 Agricultural tractors are excluded unless driven on public roads.
5 Includes three wheelers, pedestrian controlled vehicles, general haulage and showmen's tractors and recovery vehicles. Recovery vehicle tax class introduced January 1988.
6 Between 1980 and 30 June 1995 electric vehicles were exempt from duty. From 1 July 1995 electric vehicles pay VED as part of the special conession group.
7 Various revisions to the vehicle taxation system were introduced on 1 July 1995 and on 29 November 1995. Separate taxation classes for farmers' goods vehicles were abolished on 1 July 1995; after this date new vehicles of this type were registered as general HGVs. The total includes 5 900 vehicles registered between 1 January and 30 June in the (now abolished)

agricultural and special machines group in classes which were not eligible to register in the special concession group.
8 From 1 July 1995 separate taxation of public transport vehicles with 8 or fewer seats was abolished. After this date new vehicles of this type were registered as PLG.
9 The old agricultural and special machines taxation group was abolished at end June 1995 and replaced by the special concession group from 1 July 1995. The group includes agricultural and mowing machines, snow ploughs and gritting vehicles. Electric vehicles are also included in this group and are no longer exempt from VED. Steam propelled vehicles were added to this group from November 1995.
10 The special vehicles group was created on 1 July 1995 and consists of various vehicle types over 3.5 tonnes gross weight but not required to pay VED as heavy goods vehicles. The group includes mobile cranes, works trucks, digging machines, road rollers and vehicles previously taxed as showman's goods and haulage. Figure shown for 1995 covers period from 1 July to 31 December only.

Source: Department of the Environment, Transport and the Regions: 020 7944 3077

14.10 Private motoring: full car driving licence holders by age and sex
Great Britain

Percentages

	Age							Estimated number of licence holders (millions)
	17-20	21-29	30-39	40-49	50-59	60-69	70 or over	
All adults								
1975/76	28	59	67	60	50	35	15	19.4
1985/86	33	63	74	71	60	47	27	24.4
1989/91	43	72	77	78	67	54	32	28.0
1992/94	48	75	82	79	72	57	33	29.0
1995/97	42	73	81	82	74	64	39	30.7
1997/99	42	74	83	83	78	67	39	31.6
Males								
1975/76	36	78	85	83	75	58	32	13.4
1985/86	37	73	86	87	81	72	51	15.3
1989/91	52	82	88	89	85	78	58	16.9
1992/94	54	83	91	88	88	81	59	17.1
1995/97	48	79	89	89	88	83	65	17.6
1997/99	46	80	90	91	89	84	64	18.0
Females								
1975/76	20	43	48	37	24	15	4	6.0
1985/86	29	54	62	56	41	24	11	9.2
1989/91	35	64	67	66	49	33	15	11.2
1992/94	42	68	73	70	57	37	16	12.1
1995/97	36	67	74	74	61	46	22	13.2
1997/99	39	69	76	75	67	51	22	13.7

Source: Department of the Environment, Transport and the Regions; (020) 7944 3097

14.11
Private motoring: households with regular use of cars
Great Britain

	No car	One car	Two cars	Three or more cars	Total (millions)
	ZCGA	ZCGB	ZCGC	ZCGD	ZCGE
1989	34	44	18	4	21.9
1990	33	44	19	4	22.1
1991	32	45	19	4	22.4
1992	32	45	20	4	22.6
1993	31	45	20	4	22.9
1994	32	45	20	4	23.1
1995	30	45	21	4	23.3
1996	30	45	21	4	23.5
1997	30	45	21	4	23.7
1998	28	44	23	5	23.9
1999	28	44	22	5	..

	No car	One car	Two cars	Three or more cars	Total
Government Office Regions, 1999					
Great Britain	28	44	22	5	100
North East	38	43	15	3	100
North West	30	44	22	4	100
Yorkshire and the Humber	31	43	21	5	100
East Midlands	26	45	24	5	100
West Midlands	28	43	24	5	100
East	21	47	26	6	100
London	36	45	16	3	100
South East	23	43	28	6	100
South West	23	46	24	7	100
England	28	44	23	5	100
Wales	27	46	23	4	100
Scotland	34	44	19	4	100

	No car	One car	Two cars	Three or more cars	Total
Area type, 1997/99					
London	38	45	15	2	100
Metropolitan areas	39	40	18	3	100
Other urban areas with population:					
Over 250,000	33	45	19	3	100
25,000 - 250,000	29	46	22	3	100
3,000 - 25,000	22	46	27	5	100
Rural areas	16	45	33	6	100
Great Britain	29	45	22	4	100

Source: ONS: Family Expenditure Survey, General Household Survey, National Travel Survey

Transport and communications

14.12 Vehicles with licences current[1]
Northern Ireland

Number

		1989	1990	1991	1992	1993	1994	1995	1996[2]	1997	1998	1999
Private cars, etc	KNKA	456 611	481 090	498 471	516 194	515 185	514 760	521 605	540 083	575 923	584 706	608 316
Cycles and tricycles	KNKB	9 460	10 167	9 684	9 023	8 634	8 775	9 142	10 026	10 932	11 663	13 088
Public road passenger vehicles:												
Taxis up to 4 seats	KNKD	741	603	656	494	462	623	739	..	..	..	..
Buses, coaches, over 4 seats	KNKE	2 221	2 183	2 231	2 280	2 217	2 455	1 353	2 090	2 144	2 175	2 204
Total	KNKC	2 962	2 786	2 887	2 744	2 679	3 078	2 092	2 090	2 144	2 175	2 204
General (HGV) goods vehicles:												
Unladen weight												
Not over 1 525kgs	KNKG	..	..	..	..	..	..	..	..	..	..	..
Over 1 525 and not over 12 000kgs	KNKH	18 424	..	..	..	..	..	..	..	..	..	..
Over 12 000kgs·	KNKI	..	..	..	..	..	..	..	..	..	..	..
Total	KNKF	23 514	16 191	13 907	14 286	14 576	14 810	15 844	17 401	18 172	18 312	17 075
Farmers' goods vehicles[3]	KNKJ	4 948	4 962	4 994	5 315	5 498	5 904	2 854	..	..	..	..
Tractors for general haulage	KNKK	120	..	..	..	..	..	..	..	..	..	..
Tower wagons	KNKL	22	..	..	..	..	..	..	..	..	..	..
Agricultural tractors and engines, etc[3]	KNKM	7 965	8 021	7 199	6 892	7 201	7 317	7 318	5 911	6 378	5 906	5 505
Other	KNKN	..	513	403	343	329	354	658	1 019	1 188	1 193	1 228
Vehicles exempt from duty:												
Government owned	KNKP	5 142	5 211	5 120	5 004	4 828	4 818	3 872	3 753	3 705	3 785	4 032
Other:												
Ambulances	KNKQ	56	74	98	97	101	104	250	371	389	425	417
Fire engines	KNKR	234	162	250	251	205	194	301	292	291	285	286
Other exempt[4]	KNKS	11 712	13 937	15 305	18 163	27 089	35 837	47 626	58 340	64 447	66 910	68 494
Total	KNKO	17 144	19 384	20 773	23 515	27 395	36 135	48 177	59 003	68 832	71 405	73 229
Total	KNKT	517 656	543 114	558 318	578 312	586 325	595 951	611 562	639 286	683 569	695 360	720 645

1 Licences current at any time during the quarter ended December.
2 Due to a revision of taxation classes, 1996 data are not directly comparable with previous years.
3 Owned by a farmer and available for hauling produce and requisites for his farm. From 1 July 1995 farmers goods taxation classes have been abolished
4 Changes in the Mobility Allowance (DSS) have contributed to the increase in Other exempt.

Source: Department of the Environment, Northern Ireland: 028 9054 0801

14.13 New vehicles registrations
Northern Ireland

Number

		1989	1990	1991	1992	1993	1994	1995	1996	1997	1998	1999
Private cars, etc	KNLA	67 112	68 918	63 739	62 777	65 360	70 765	73 718	77 817	83 968	91 141	89 078
Cycles and tricycles	KNLB	2 163	2 343	2 218	1 993	1 885	1 943	2 362	2 803	3 376	4 307	5 310
Public road passenger vehicles:												
Taxis[1]	KNLD	74	..	..	..	..	..	..	..	..	..	..
Buses, coaches etc	KNLE	528	..	..	..	..	..	..	..	..	..	..
Total	KNLC	602	606	620	551	466	1 143	622	724	714	486	568
Goods vehicles:												
General haulage vehicles:												
Unladen weight:												
Not over 1.5 tons	KNLH	3 813	4 301[5]	6 273	6 236	6 468	6 908	7 357	7 232	8 468	10 107	11 054
Over 1.5 tons and not over 3 tons[2]	KNLI	..	..	..	..	..	..	..	..	..	..	..
Over 3 tons	KNLJ	4 117	4 630[6]	2 619	2 471	2 593	2 668	2 935	3 492	3 521	3 572	3 697
Total	KNLG	7 930	..	..	..	..	..	..	..	..	..	..
Agricultural vans and lorries[3]	KNLK	466	..	..	..	..	..	..	..	..	..	..
Tractors for general haulage	KNLL	11	..	..	..	..	..	..	..	..	..	..
Goods vehicles: Total	KNLF	8 407	..	..	..	..	..	..	..	..	..	..
Agricultural tractors and engines, etc[4]	KNLM	1 805	1 610[7]	1 177	1 184	1 658	1 558	1 619	1 292	1 364	971	987
Vehicles exempt from duty:												
Ambulances	KNLO KGVE	9	332[8]	330	..	..	..	..	..	..	..	..
Fire engines	KNLP	–										
Road construction vehicles	KNLQ	2	..	..	..	..	..	..	..	..	..	..
Other exempt	KNLR	2 225	2 181	2 006	2 463	4 550	6 423	8 333	10 520	10 885	10 718	11 083
Total	KNLN	2 236	..	..	..	..	..	..	..	..	..	..
Total	KNLS	82 325	84 921	78 982	77 675	82 980	91 408	96 946	103 880	112 296	121 302	121 777

1 From 1990 figure is for Hackneys.
2 Goods vehicles 1.5 - 3 tons from 1988.
3 Owned by a farmer and available for hauling produce and requisites for his farm.
4 Agricultural tractors are excluded unless driven on public roads.
5 From 1990 figure is for light goods.
6 From 1990 figure is for heavy goods.
7 From 1990 figure is for tractors only.
8 From 1990 figure is for crown vehicles.

Source: Department of the Environment, Northern Ireland: 028 9054 0801

14.14 Local bus services: passenger journeys by area

Millions

		1989 /90	1990 /91	1991 /92	1992 /93	1993 /94	1994 /95	1995 /96	1996 /97	1997 /98	1998 /99	1999 /00
London	KILS	1 188	1 178	1 149	1 129	1 117	1 167	1 205	1 242	1 294	1 279	1 307
English metropolitan areas	KILT	1 648	1 547	1 478	1 383	1 337	1 331	1 292	1 246	1 233	1 195	1 160
English shire counties	KILU	1 474	1 396	1 333	1 307	1 274	1 277	1 265	1 265	1 247	1 246	1 269
England	ZCER	4 310	4 120	3 961	3 819	3 727	3 775	3 762	3 753	3 774	3 720	3 736
Scotland	KILV	613	585	571	532	525	513	494	467	438	413	431
Wales	KILW	151	145	133	129	133	132	127	130	120	116	111
All outside London	ZCES	3 886	3 672	3 516	3 351	3 268	3 253	3 178	3 108	3 036	2 969	2 972
Great Britain	ZCET	5 074	4 850	4 665	4 480	4 385	4 420	4 383	4 350	4 330	4 248	4 279

Source: Department of the Environment, Transport and the Regions (020) 7944 3076

14.15 Local bus services: fare indices by area
Current prices

Index 1995=100

		1989 /90	1990 /91	1991 /92	1992 /93	1993 /94	1994 /95	1995 /96	1996 /97	1997 /98	1998 /99	1999 /00
London	KNEP	64.7	71.4	78.2	84.2	90.9	96.2	101.1	105.4	109.3	113.7	117.2
English metropolitan areas	KILD	66.8	74.2	82.9	88.6	92.9	96.4	101.5	106.9	113.3	118.7	124.5
English shire counties	KILE	72.9	80.4	86.6	90.4	93.1	97.0	101.1	106.0	111.5	116.7	121.9
England	ZCEP	69.5	76.7	83.6	88.3	92.5	96.7	101.2	106.1	111.4	116.5	121.4
Scotland	KILF	71.2	76.6	82.5	88.2	91.3	96.9	100.8	108.0	116.5	121.8	125.3
Wales[1]	KILG	..	..	..	90.4	93.8	97.4	100.7	104.4	110.1	116.3	122.2
All outside London	ZCEQ	70.9	78.0	84.8	89.4	92.8	96.8	101.2	106.6	112.8	118.2	123.3
Great Britain	KNEU	69.8	76.8	83.6	88.4	92.4	96.7	101.2	106.3	112.0	117.1	121.9
Retail Prices Index	KNEV	78.7	86.4	90.5	93.3	94.9	97.5	100.7	103.1	106.5	109.9	111.6

1 Figures for Wales before 1992/93 are omitted as insufficient fares data were available.

Source: Department of the Environment, Transport and the Regions (020) 7944 3076

14.16 Road accident casualties : by road user type and severity
Great Britain

Number

		1989	1990	1991	1992	1993	1994	1995	1996	1997	1998	1999
Child pedestrians:												
Killed	ZCDH	254	242	225	180	165	160	132	131	138	103	107
KSI	KIJS	5 836	5 914	5 097	4 901	4 231	4 610	4 400	4 132	3 954	3 737	3 457
All severities	ZCDI	22 154	22 860	20 708	20 124	18 250	19 263	18 590	18 510	18 407	17 971	16 876
Adult pedestrians:												
Killed	ZCDJ	1 439	1 434	1 263	1 163	1 072	953	897	858	835	803	760
KSI	KIJT	11 460	11 228	9 733	9 125	8 260	8 114	7 716	7 300	6 925	6 592	6 221
All severities	ZCDK	36 820	36 318	32 229	30 354	28 750	28 129	27 178	26 827	26 223	25 827	24 806
Child pedal cyclists:												
Killed	ZCDL	73	59	50	48	37	42	48	54	33	32	36
KSI	KIJU	1 623	1 490	1 345	1 195	1 146	1 234	1 249	1 231	1 016	915	950
All severities	ZCDM	9 327	8 720	8 182	7 725	7 386	8 075	8 133	8 217	7 899	6 930	7 920
Adult pedal cyclists:												
Killed	ZCDN	220	197	192	156	148	129	164	148	150	126	135
KSI	KIJV	3 477	3 075	2 800	2 752	2 598	2 710	2 673	2 517	2 542	2 345	2 172
All severities	ZCDO	18 749	17 311	16 201	16 488	16 115	16 097	16 140	15 778	16 181	15 326	14 834
Motorcyclists[1] and passengers:												
Killed	ZCDP	683	659	548	469	427	444	445	440	509	498	547
KSI	ZCDQ	12 488	11 121	8 502	7 338	6 882	6 666	6 615	6 208	6 446	6 442	6 908
All severities	ZCDR	42 630	39 048	30 751	26 891	25 094	24 354	23 524	23 133	24 492	24 610	26 192
Car drivers and passengers:												
Killed	ZCDS	2 426	2 371	2 053	1 978	1 760	1 764	1 749	1 806	1 795	1 696	1 687
KSI	ZCDT	29 684	29 120	25 395	25 124	22 833	23 892	23 461	24 048	23 191	21 676	20 368
All severities	ZCDU	184 688	190 558	179 383	185 662	187 479	195 154	194 027	205 336	211 448	210 474	205 735
Bus/coach drivers and passengers:												
Killed	ZCDV	20	19	25	19	35	21	35	11	14	18	11
KSI	KCUZ	835	807	725	655	725	815	836	695	601	631	611
All severities	ZCDW	10 200	9 954	8 875	9 103	9 307	10 090	9 278	9 345	9 439	9 839	10 252
LGV drivers and passengers:												
Killed	ZCDX	144	129	119	117	91	64	69	61	64	67	65
KSI	ZCDY	1 827	1 627	1 427	1 308	1 082	1 101	1 106	989	928	949	867
All severities	ZCDZ	10 101	9 728	8 673	8 129	7 420	7 558	7 200	7 215	7 476	7 672	7 124
HGV drivers and passengers:												
Killed	ZCEA	82	67	65	70	59	41	57	63	45	60	52
KSI	ZCEB	846	772	695	659	635	571	635	555	573	560	540
All severities	ZCEC	4 063	3 844	3 603	3 326	3 333	3 370	3 331	3 245	3 302	3 444	3 484
All road users:[2]												
Killed	ZCED	5 373	5 217	4 568	4 229	3 814	3 650	3 621	3 598	3 599	3 421	3 423
KSI	ZCEE	68 531	65 658	56 186	53 485	48 834	50 190	49 154	48 097	46 583	44 255	42 545
All severities	KCVC	341 592	341 141	311 368	310 753	306 135	315 359	310 687	320 578	327 803	325 212	320 310

Note: KSI = Killed or seriously injured.
1 Includes mopeds and scooters.
2 Includes other motor or non-motor vehicle users, and unknown road user
type and casualty age.

Source: Department of the Environment, Transport and the Regions (020) 7944 3078

14.17

Freight transport by road: goods moved by goods vehicles over 3.5 tonnes[1]
Great Britain

Billion tonne-kilometres

		1989	1990	1991	1992	1993	1994	1995	1996	1997	1998	1999
By mode of working												
Mainly public haulage	KNND	95.3	94.7	85.8	86.4	93.2	100.8	106.5	109.1	112.2	114.3	110.9
Mainly own account	KNNC	36.8	36.0	38.8	34.9	35.4	37.0	37.2	37.7	37.4	37.6	38.3
All modes	KNNB	132.1	130.6	124.6	121.3	128.6	137.8	143.7	146.8	149.6	151.9	149.2
By gross weight of vehicle												
Rigid vehicles:												
3.5-17 tonnes	ZCIL	21.6	20.9	20.1	19.0	18.7	19.9	18.7	19.5	19.2	17.8	17.9
17-25 tonnes	ZCIM	8.0	7.4	7.1	6.5	6.6	6.1	5.6	5.3	4.7	4.2	4.3
25 tonnes and over	ZCIN	12.9	12.3	11.3	10.7	11.3	12.4	13.3	13.5	14.3	14.7	15.3
All rigids	ZCIO	42.4	40.6	38.5	36.2	36.5	38.4	37.5	38.3	38.1	36.6	37.5
Articulated vehicles[1]:												
3.5-33 tonnes	ZCIP	25.7	21.8	18.6	16.7	16.5	16.9	15.9	15.9	14.3	14.4	14.0
33 tonnes and over	ZCIQ	63.9	68.3	67.6	68.4	75.6	82.5	90.2	92.6	97.1	100.9	97.7
All articulated vehicles	ZCIR	89.7	90.1	86.1	85.0	92.1	99.4	106.1	108.5	111.4	115.3	111.7
All vehicles												
3.5-25 tonnes	ZCIS	30.6	29.2	28.0	26.3	25.9	26.6	24.7	25.3	24.3	22.5	22.7
25 tonnes and over	KNNG	101.5	101.4	96.6	95.0	102.7	111.2	119.0	121.5	125.2	129.4	126.5
All weights	ZCIT	132.1	130.6	124.6	121.3	128.6	137.8	143.7	146.8	149.6	151.9	149.2
By commodity												
Food, drink and tobacco	ZCIU	31.9	32.8	32.7	33.2	35.9	36.5	37.5	39.3	40.8	42.5	41.5
Wood, timber and cork	ZCIV	3.2	2.4	2.7	2.6	3.1	3.3	3.2	3.8	3.5	3.6	3.8
Fertiliser	ZCIW	1.5	1.6	1.5	1.4	1.5	1.3	1.4	1.5	1.3	1.2	1.4
Crude minerals	ZCIX	14.9	14.5	13.0	12.7	12.6	14.1	13.5	13.5	13.6	13.3	12.7
Ores	ZCIY	1.4	1.2	1.3	1.2	1.6	1.4	1.5	1.3	1.7	1.1	1.3
Crude materials	ZCIZ	1.9	1.7	1.7	2.0	1.7	2.0	1.9	2.1	2.1	2.6	2.6
Coal and coke	ZCJA	4.0	4.2	3.7	3.5	3.1	2.9	2.7	2.5	2.7	2.0	2.2
Petrol and petroleum products	ZCJB	4.5	4.9	4.9	4.5	5.0	5.1	5.7	6.1	5.8	5.2	5.0
Chemicals	ZCJC	8.3	8.0	7.3	6.8	7.2	8.1	7.4	7.7	8.2	7.9	7.4
Building materials	ZCJD	11.3	9.4	8.7	8.0	9.3	10.0	10.7	9.6	11.1	10.7	10.6
Iron and steel products	ZCJE	8.1	7.1	6.9	6.5	6.4	6.7	7.8	7.2	7.9	7.7	6.8
Other metal products	ZCJF	2.4	2.1	1.9	2.0	1.9	2.0	1.7	1.7	1.5	1.7	1.7
Machinery and transport equipment	ZCJG	7.5	6.7	5.9	6.0	5.7	6.8	7.4	7.7	8.4	9.1	8.7
Miscellaneous manufactures	ZCJH	12.7	13.3	12.4	12.0	12.4	13.4	13.3	14.2	14.2	15.9	15.7
Miscellaneous transactions	ZCJI	18.5	20.5	20.0	19.0	21.3	24.3	27.8	28.4	26.8	27.5	27.9
All commodities	ZCJJ	132.1	130.6	124.6	121.3	128.6	137.8	143.7	146.8	149.6	151.9	149.2

1 Rigid vehicles or articulated vehicles (tractive unit and trailer) with gross vehicle weight over 3.5 tonnes.

Source: Department of the Environment, Transport and the Regions; (020) 7944 3093

14.18 Freight transport by road: goods lifted by goods vehicles over 3.5 tonnes[1]
Great Britain

Million tonnes

		1989	1990	1991	1992	1993	1994	1995	1996	1997	1998	1999
By mode of working												
Mainly public haulage	ZCJK	1 020	978	862	843	911	980	987	1 011	1 044	1 041	991
Mainly own account	ZCJL	684	667	643	620	612	618	622	618	599	589	576
All modes	ZCJM	1 704	1 645	1 505	1 463	1 523	1 597	1 609	1 628	1 643	1 630	1 567
By gross weight of vehicle												
Rigid vehicles:												
3.5-17 tonnes	ZCJN	393	363	331	315	322	317	298	306	294	268	254
17-25 tonnes	ZCJO	264	258	236	219	211	202	162	133	120	106	86
25 tonnes and over	ZCJP	360	325	289	282	307	332	373	371	380	401	408
All rigids	ZCJQ	1 016	947	857	817	840	852	833	811	793	776	748
Articulated vehicles[1]:												
3.5-33 tonnes	ZCJR	231	192	165	142	144	142	139	138	124	125	113
33 tonnes and over	ZCJS	457	506	484	505	540	604	637	679	726	729	706
All articulated vehicles	ZCJT	688	698	648	646	683	746	776	817	850	854	819
All vehicles[1]												
3.5-25 tonnes	ZCJU	672	632	578	544	541	527	467	447	419	382	346
25 tonnes and over	ZCJV	1 033	1 013	927	919	982	1 070	1 142	1 181	1 224	1 248	1 221
All weights	ZCJW	1 704	1 645	1 505	1 463	1 523	1 597	1 609	1 628	1 643	1 630	1 567
By commodity												
Food, drink and tobacco	ZCJX	289	299	291	290	300	302	308	326	342	346	333
Wood, timber and cork	ZCJY	26	18	21	20	25	24	24	27	26	27	28
Fertiliser	ZCJZ	16	14	13	13	12	10	11	13	10	9	11
Crude minerals	ZCKA	399	354	298	327	310	355	319	320	329	327	297
Ores	ZCKB	21	17	14	15	21	18	18	18	25	18	20
Crude materials	ZCKC	18	13	15	17	14	16	16	18	17	20	20
Coal and coke	ZCKD	73	62	57	55	48	42	34	32	37	26	28
Petrol and petroleum products	ZCKE	65	74	73	63	67	68	71	75	73	61	61
Chemicals	ZCKF	55	53	45	42	47	51	50	51	53	53	47
Building materials	ZCKG	190	178	155	136	153	156	161	142	156	161	159
Iron and steel products	ZCKH	61	55	50	46	45	47	54	52	55	54	48
Other metal products	ZCKI	22	20	16	18	20	17	17	15	16	18	17
Machinery and transport equipment	ZCKJ	60	54	46	47	46	57	61	59	71	73	67
Miscellaneous manufactures	ZCKK	86	86	80	75	81	84	85	88	90	96	91
Miscellaneous transactions	ZCKL	323	348	331	300	332	351	379	393	343	342	340
All commodities	ZCKM	1 704	1 645	1 505	1 463	1 523	1 597	1 609	1 628	1 643	1 630	1 567

1 Rigid vehicles or articulated vehicles (tractive unit and trailer) with gross vehicle weight over 3.5 tonnes.

Source: Department of the Environment, Transport and the Regions; (020) 7944 3093

14.19 Rail systems summary

		1989/90	1990/91	1991/92	1992/93	1993/94	1994/95	1995/96	1996/97	1997/98	1998/99	1999/00
Passenger journeys (million)												
National Rail network[1]	ZCKN	812	809	792	770	740	735	761	801	846	892	947
London Underground	KNOE	765	775	751	728	735	764	784	772	832	866	927
Docklands Light Railway	ZCKO	9	8	8	7	8	12	14	17	21	28	31
Glasgow Underground	ZCKP	14	14	14	14	14	15	14	14	14	15	15
Nexus (Tyne & Wear Metro)	ZCKQ	46	44	41	39	39	37	36	35	35	34	33
Centro (W. Midlands Metro)[2]	ZCKR	..	..	..	..	..	..	..	..	..	..	5
Altram Manchester Metrolink[3]	ZCKS	..	..	..	8	11	12	13	13	14	13	14
Stagecoach Supertram (Sheffield)	ZCKT	..	..	..	..	..	2	5	8	9	10	11
All rail	ZCKU	1 646	1 649	1 605	1 565	1 547	1 577	1 627	1 660	1 771	1 858	1 983
Passenger receipts (£ million at current prices)												
National Rail network[1]	KNDL	1 907	2 057	2 117	2 154	2 193	2 171	2 379	2 573	2 821	3 089	3 368
London Underground	KNOA	462	531	559	589	637	718	765	797	899	977	1 060
Docklands Light Railway	ZCKV	3	3	3	3	5	6	9	12	14	20	22
Glasgow Underground	ZCKW	5	6	6	6	7	7	8	8	9	9	10
Nexus (Tyne & Wear Metro)	ZCKX	16	16	18	19	19	19	20	21	22	23	24
Centro (W. Midlands Metro)[2]	ZCKY	..	..	..	..	..	..	..	..	..	..	..
Altram Manchester Metrolink[3]	ZCKZ	..	..	..	7	10	10	11	13	14	..	..
Stagecoach Supertram (Sheffield)	ZCLA	..	..	..	..	..	2	4	5	6	6	7
All rail	ZCLB	2 394	2 613	2 703	2 778	2 870	2 933	3 196	3 429	3 785	..	..
Passenger kilometres (millions)												
National Rail network[1]	KNDZ	33 323	33 200	32 500	31 700	30 400	28 700	30 000	32 100	34 700	36 300	38 300
London Underground	KNOI	6 016	6 164	5 895	5 758	5 814	6 051	6 337	6 153	6 479	6 716	7 171
Docklands Light Railway	ZCLC	38	33	32	33	39	55	70	86	103	144	172
Glasgow Underground	ZCLD	39	40	39	39	41	43	41	40	45	47	49
Nexus (Tyne & Wear Metro)	ZCLE	319	290	277	271	273	271	261	254	249	238	230
Centro (W. Midlands Metro)[2]	ZCLF	..	..	..	..	..	..	..	..	..	..	12
Altram Manchester Metrolink[3]	ZCLG	..	..	..	53	73	79	81	86	88	117	153
Stagecoach Supertram (Sheffield)	ZCLH	..	..	..	..	..	8	20	29	34	35	37
All rail	ZCLI	39 735	39 727	38 744	37 854	36 640	35 206	36 810	38 748	41 698	43 597	46 125
Route kilometres open for passenger traffic (number)												
National Rail network[1]	ZCLJ	14 318	14 317	14 291	14 317	14 357	14 359	15 002	15 034	15 024	15 038	15 038
London Underground	ZCLK	394	394	394	394	394	392	392	392	392	392	408
Docklands Light Railway	ZCLM	12	12	14	14	14	22	22	22	22	22	27
Glasgow Underground	ZCLN	11	11	11	11	11	11	11	11	11	11	11
Nexus (Tyne & Wear Metro)	ZCLO	56	56	59	59	59	59	59	59	59	59	59
Centro (W. Midlands Metro)[2]	ZCLP	..	..	..	..	..	..	..	..	..	..	21
Altram Manchester Metrolink[3]	ZCLQ	..	..	..	31	31	31	31	31	31	31	39
Stagecoach Supertram (Sheffield)	ZCLR	..	..	..	..	7	22	29	29	29	29	29
All rail	ZCLS	14 791	14 790	14 769	14 826	14 873	14 896	15 546	15 578	15 568	15 582	15 632
Stations served (Number)												
National Rail network[1]	ZCLT	2 471	2 488	2 468	2 482	2 493	2 506	2 514	2 515	2 495	2 499	2 500
London Underground	KNOO	245	245	246	246	245	245	245	245	245	246	253
Docklands Light Railway	ZCLU	15	15	15	16	27	27	28	28	29	29	34
Glasgow Underground	ZCLV	15	15	15	15	15	15	15	15	15	15	15
Nexus (Tyne & Wear Metro)	ZCLW	44	44	46	46	46	46	46	46	46	46	46
Centro (W. Midlands Metro)[2]	ZCLX	..	..	..	..	..	..	..	..	..	..	23
Altram Manchester Metrolink[3]	ZCLY	..	..	..	26	26	26	26	26	26	26	36
Stagecoach Supertram (Sheffield)	ZCLZ	..	..	..	..	9	37	45	45	46	470	47
All rail	ZCLL	2 790	2 807	2 790	2 831	2 861	2 902	2 919	2 920	2 902	2 908	2 954

1 Franchised train operating companies from February 1996 following rail privatisation.
2 Centro Line 1 in the West Midlands opened in 1999.
3 Transfer of 20 stations from the national rail network to Manchester Metrolink.

Sources: Railtrack Group plc; Shadow Strategic Rail Authority; Transport for London, and various Passenger Transport Executives

14.20 National railways freight
Great Britain

Billion tonne-kilometres

		1989/90	1990/91	1991/92	1992/93	1993/94	1994/95	1995/96	1996[1]/97	1997[1]/98	1998[1]/99	1999[1]/00
Freight moved by commodity												
Coal	ZCGG	4.6	5.0	5.0	5.4	3.9	3.3	3.6	3.9	4.4	4.5	4.9
Metals	ZCGH	2.5	2.3	2.4	2.3	2.1	1.7	1.7	..	..	..	..
Construction	ZCGI	3.2	2.7	2.5	2.5	2.3	2.5	2.3	..	..	..	..
Oil and petroleum	ZCGJ	2.1	2.0	2.0	2.0	1.9	1.8	1.8	..	..	..	..
Other traffic	ZCGK	4.2	3.8	3.4	3.3	3.5	3.8	3.9	11.3	12.5	12.9	13.5
All traffic	KCTB	16.7	16.0	15.3	15.5	13.8	13.0	13.3	15.1	16.9	17.4	18.4

		1989/90	1990/91	1991/92	1992/93	1993/94	1994/95	1995/96	1996/97	1997/98	1998/99	1999/00
Freight lifted by commodity												
Coal	ZCGL	75.8	74.7	75.1	67.9	48.9	42.5	45.2	52.2	50.2	45.2	44.3
Metals	ZCGM	18.9	18.0	17.8	15.9	15.8	16.9	15.1	..	..	..	..
Construction	ZCGN	23.5	20.2	17.7	15.8	16.1	16.8	11.5	..	..	..	..
Oil and petroleum	ZCGO	10.2	10.0	10.0	9.5	9.0	8.1	6.3	..	..	..	..
Other traffic	ZCGP	14.7	15.1	15.3	13.2	13.4	13.0	22.6	49.5	55.2	56.9	58.5
All traffic	KCTH	143.1	138.2	135.8	122.4	103.2	97.3	100.7	101.7	105.4	102.1	102.8

1 Because of changes in the way freight traffic has been estimated following privatisation, figures since 1996/97 are not strictly comparable with those for previous years.

Source: Department of the Environment, Transport and the Regions (020) 7944 3089

14.21 Railways: permanent way and rolling stock
Northern Ireland

At end of year

Number

		1989	1990	1991	1992	1993	1994	1995	1996	1997	1998	1999
Length of road open for traffic[1] (km)	KNRA	332	332	332	332	330	331	333	335	335	335	335
Length of track open for traffic (km)												
Total	KNRB	553	553	553	553	504	503	506	506	505	526	526
Running lines	KNRC	500	500	500	500	463	462	464	464	464	484	484
Sidings (as single track)	KNRD	53	53	53	53	41	41	42	42	42	42	42
Locomotives												
Diesel-electrics	KNRE	12	9	9	9	9	11	11	8	6	5	6
Passenger carrying vehicles												
Total	KNRF	115	115	115	114	112	112	112	112	112	120	108
Rail motor vehicles:												
Diesel-electric, etc	KNRG	30	30	30	30	30	30	30	30	30	28	30
Trailer carriages:												
Total locomotive hauled	KNRH	28	28	28	28	28	28	28	28	28	38	21
Ordinary coaches	KNRI	26	26	26	26	26	26	26	26	26	36	19
Restaurant cars	KNRJ	2	2	2	2	2	2	2	2	2	2	2
Rail car trailers	KNRK	56	56	56	56	54	54	54	54	54	54	54
Non-passenger carrying vehicles												
Post Office and luggage vans, etc	KNRL	–	–	–	–	–	–	–	–	–	–	–
Trucks and wagons owned												
Total	KNRM	17	17	17	18	–	–	–	–	–	–	–
Merchandise wagons:												
Open	KNRN	–	–	–	–	–	–	–	–	–	–	–
Covered	KNRO	–	–	–	–	–	–	–	–	–	–	–
Rail and timber trucks	KNRP	–	–	–	–	–	–	–	–	–	–	–
Brake vans	KNRQ	–	–	–	–	–	–	–	–	–	–	–
Special wagons	KNRR	17	17	17	18	–	–	–	–	–	–	–
Containers	KNRS	–	–	–	–	–	–	–	–	–	–	–
Rolling stock for maintenance and repair	KNRT	55	55	55	36	42	41	41	41	41	26	18

1 The total length of railroad open for traffic irrespective of the number of tracks comprising the road.

Source: Department for Regional Development, Northern Ireland: 028 9054 0801

14.22 Operating statistics of railways
Northern Ireland

		Unit	1989	1990	1991	1992	1993	1994	1995	1996	1997	1998	1999
Maintenance of way and works														
Material used:														
Ballast	KNSA	Thousand m^2	33.0	25.0	22.5	30.2	16.0	33.2	22.5	27.0	51.3	38.5	40.0
Rails	KNSB	Thousand tonnes	1.60	0.91	1.68	2.26	2.00	1.80	1.76	2.12	0.37	2.50	3.00
Sleepers	KNSC	Thousands	18.00	19.00	23.20	31.23	14.60	22.40	22.90	27.50	5.10	32.00	30.00
Track renewed	KNSD	Km	9.70	8.80	10.40	14.00	16.00	12.00	16.00	20.00	2.40	22.50	7.00
New Track laid	KPGD	Km	..	..	..	..	..	3.2	2.5	–	–	–	–
Engine kilometres														
Total[1]	KNSE	Thousand Km	3 575	3 200	3 200	3 540	3 640	3 640	4 000	4 100	4 100	4 100	4 100
Train kilometres:														
Total	KNSF	"	3 391	3 844	3 410	3 210	3 210	3 210	3 570	3 670	3 670	3 670	3 670
Coaching	KNSG	"	3 393	3 840	3 406	3 206	3 206	3 206	3 566	3 666	3 666	3 666	3 666
Freight	KNSH	"	4	4	4	4	4	4	4	4	4	4	4

1 Including shunting, assisting, light, departmental, maintenance and repair.

Source: Department for Regional Development, Northern Ireland: 028 9054 0801

14.23 Main output[1] of United Kingdom airlines

		1989	1990	1991	1992	1993	1994	1995	1996	1997	1998	1999
All services: total	KNTA	18 920	20 375	20 166	23 145	25 144	27 714	29 904	32 210	35 538	40 021	42 002
Percentage growth on previous year	KNTB	*9.9*	*7.7*	*−1.0*	*14.8*	*8.5*	*10.2*	*7.4*	*7.7*	*10.3*	*12.5*	*5.0*
Scheduled services: total	KNTC	13 427	15 274	15 188	17 065	18 605	20 360	22 016	23 793	26 504	29 756	13 815
Percentage growth on previous year	KNTD	*8.2*	*13.8*	*−0.6*	*12.4*	*9.0*	*9.4*	*8.1*	*8.1*	*11.4*	*12.3*	*6.9*
Non-scheduled services: total	KNTE	5 496	5 103	4 978	6 079	6 510	7 265	7 695	8 044	9 034	10 265	10 186
Percentage growth on previous year	KNTF	*14.0*	*−7.2*	*−2.5*	*22.0*	*7.1*	*13.0*	*5.9*	*4.5*	*7.3*	*13.3*	*−0.7*

1 Available tonne kilometres (millions).

Source: Civil Aviation Authority: 020 7453 6246

Transport and communications

14.24 Air traffic between the United Kingdom and abroad[1]
Aircraft flights and passengers carried

Thousands

		1989	1990	1991	1992	1993	1994[3]	1995	1996	1997	1998	1999
Flights												
United Kingdom airlines												
Scheduled services	KNUA	245.0	271.0	250.5	283.0	290.8	325.8	342.1	373.0	410.3	443.7	480.9
Non-scheduled services	KNUB	221.3	207.9	202.6	236.2	215.2	195.0	204.8	198.0	208.2	218.7	212.6
Overseas airlines[2]												
Scheduled services	KNUC	269.9	294.8	300.4	328.0	336.2	351.3	363.3	390.0	399.6	426.4	467.6
Non-scheduled services	KNUD	46.1	45.5	34.6	33.9	38.0	35.1	31.5	31.3	32.5	34.8	31.7
Total	KNUE	782.3	819.2	788.1	881.1	880.2	907.2	941.7	992.3	1 050.6	1 223.6	1 192.8
Passengers carried												
United Kingdom airlines												
Scheduled services	KNUF	21 863.2	25 316.8	23 271.6	27 138.8	29 798.2	32 578.0	34 934.7	37 902.2	41 854.7	46 747.7	50 148.5
Non-scheduled services	KNUG	22 558.8	19 679.1	19 715.2	23 347.6	24 777.1	19 501.0	20 434.5	26 304.4	28 699.5	31 616.6	32 603.8
Overseas airlines[2]												
Scheduled services	KNUH	26 517.8	28 224.4	26 719.4	29 240.9	31 163.4	35 134.5	34 568.5	36 992.1	39 900.7	42 554.5	46 628.0
Non-scheduled services	KNUI	4 325.6	4 187.9	3 078.8	3 222.6	3 638.0	3 509.5	4 244.2	4 416.3	4 413.0	4 569.7	4 156.5
Total	KNUJ	75 265.3	77 408.2	72 785.0	82 949.9	89 376.7	90 723.0	94 231.9	105 615.0	114 867.9	125 488.5	133 536.8

1 Excludes travel to and from the Channel Islands.
2 Includes airlines of overseas UK Territories.

3 Due to the introduction of European licencing, off shore helicopter movements are no longer included in this figure.

Source: Civil Aviation Authority: 020 7453 6246

14.25 United Kingdom airlines[1]
Operations and traffic on scheduled services: revenue traffic

		Unit	1989	1990	1991	1992	1993	1994	1995	1996	1997	1998	1999
All services													
Aircraft stage flights:													
Number	KNFA	Number	606 505	617 477	568 122	601 500	601 620	621 272	658 958	702 492	749 806	797 682	835 031
Average length	KNFB	Kilometres	801	848	876	916	971	1 023	1 032	1 047	1 079	1 111	1 134
Aircraft-kilometres flown	KNFC	Millions	485.7	523.8	497.7	551.2	584.3	663.2	679.9	735.3	809.2	886.3	946.9
Passengers uplifted	KNFD	"	35.2	38.4	34.6	38.2	40.1	43.9	47.5	51.1	56.3	61.7	65.4
Seat-kilometres used	KNFE	"	70 196.0	79 579.6	74 615.4	86 731.4	94 670.1	104 294.5	115 347.1	124 846.5	136 388.2	151 969.1	160 336.4
Cargo uplifted:[2]													
Total	KNFF	Tonnes	453 430	485 535	466 622	507 356	541 986	618 067	643 181	690 806	782 855	831 436	860 291
Tonne-kilometres used:		Millions											
Passenger	KNFH	"	6 604.9	7 465.6	7 007.9	8 135.2	8 905.3	9 789.2	11 171.5	12 189.6	13 287.2	14 754.9	15 517.7
Freight	KNFI	"	2 206.4	2 388.7	2 379.9	2 644.1	2 919.6	3 378.1	3 567.3	3 831.9	4 454.0	4 663.3	4 924.9
Mail	KNFJ	"	162.3	168.6	182.6	161.1	141.5	147.3	151.1	176.0	172.2	177.7	153.0
Total	KNFG	"	8 973.5	10 023.0	9 570.5	10 940.5	11 966.4	13 314.6	14 889.9	16 197.5	17 913.4	19 595.9	20 595.6
Domestic services													
Aircraft stage flights:													
Number	KNFK	Number	303 147	300 683	285 346	299 893	300 416	301 652	318 884	331 109	336 218	352 936	354 864
Average length	KNFL	Kilometres	281.0	288.0	301.0	305.7	311.3	314.8	317.0	320.0	330.0	333.1	337.0
Aircraft-kilometres flown	KNFM	Millions	85.2	86.5	86.0	91.6	93.5	94.9	101.1	105.8	111.0	117.6	119.6
Passengers uplifted	KNFN	"	12.2	12.7	11.6	11.6	12.1	13.0	14.0	15.0	15.9	16.6	17.1
Seat-kilometres used	KNFO	"	4 767.6	5 020.8	4 663.7	4 728.2	4 933.8	5 334.0	5 753.6	6 204.3	6 645.7	6 947.5	7 183.9
Cargo uplifted:[2]													
Total	KNFP	Tonnes	46 660	45 818	37 739	35 420	30 660	32 670	33 659	35 432	30 679	31 879	25 964
Tonne-kilometres used:		Millions											
Passenger	KNFR	"	392.0	412.0	382.3	387.4	405.2	417.3	485.0	527.8	568.9	592.6	609.9
Freight	KNFS	"	8.9	8.7	6.7	6.6	5.6	6.3	6.9	7.4	6.1	6.0	6.0
Mail	KNFT	"	7.1	7.6	7.4	7.0	6.5	6.7	6.6	6.4	6.0	6.0	4.0
Total	KNFQ	"	408.0	428.3	396.5	401.1	417.3	430.3	498.5	541.6	581.0	604.7	619.9
International services													
Aircraft stage flights:													
Number	KNFU	Number	303 358	316 794	282 776	301 607	301 204	319 620	339 714	371 400	413 588	444 746	480 167
Average length	KNFV	Kilometres	1 320	1 381	1 456	1 523	1 629	1 693	1 703	1 695	1 688	1 729	1 723
Aircraft-kilometres flown	KNFW	Millions	400.5	437.4	411.7	459.5	490.8	541.4	578.8	629.5	698.2	768.8	827.3
Passengers uplifted	KNFX	"	22.9	25.7	22.9	26.5	28.0	30.9	33.5	36.1	40.4	45.1	48.2
Seat-kilometres used	KNFY	"	65 428.3	74 558.8	69 951.7	82 003.1	89 736.3	99.0	109.6	118.6	129.7	145.0	153.1
Cargo uplifted:[2]													
Total	KNFZ	Tonnes	406 770.0	439 717.0	428 883.0	471 936.0	511 326.0	585.4	609.5	655.4	752.2	799.6	834.3
Tonne-kilometres used:		Millions											
Passenger	KNJX	"	6 212.9	7 053.6	6 625.6	7 747.8	8 500.1	9 352.3	10 636.4	11 661.9	12 718.2	14 162.3	14 908.0
Freight	KNJY	"	2 197.4	2 380.1	2 373.2	2 637.4	2 914.0	3 371.8	3 560.4	3 824.5	4 448.0	4 657.2	4 919.0
Mail	KNJZ	"	155.2	161.1	175.2	154.0	135.0	140.5	144.4	169.5	166.3	171.7	149.0
Total	KNJW	"	8 565.6	9 594.7	9 174.0	10 539.3	11 549.1	12 864.6	14 391.2	15 655.9	17 332.5	18 991.2	19 976.0

1 Includes services of British Airways and other UK private companies (including operations performed by Cathay Pacific Airways on their scheduled service London - Hong Kong from May 1981 until December 1984).

2 Cargo has re-defined as freight and mail.

Source: Civil Aviation Authority: 020 7453 6246

Transport and communications

14.26 United Kingdom airlines
Accidents on scheduled fixed wing passenger-carrying services[1]

	Passenger casualties			Crew casualties		Thousand aircraft stage flights per fatal accident	Million aircraft-kms. flown per fatal accident	Thousand passengers carried per passenger killed	Million passenger kms. flown per passenger killed	Fatal accidents		Passengers killed per hundred million passenger-kms.
	Number of fatal accidents	Killed	Seriously injured	Killed	Seriously injured					per 100 000 aircraft stage flights	per hundred million aircraft-kms.	
1950-54	7	194	9	28	4	107.4	61.8	46.1	50.0	0.93	1.62	1.99
1955-59	7	123	28	29	8	158.3	92.1	155.2	158.5	0.63	1.09	0.63
1960-64	5	104	35	21	6	303.7	182.3	373.4	390.6	0.33	0.55	0.25
1965-69	6	273	2	32	2	282.7	194.9	222.2	255.2	0.35	0.52	0.39
1970-74	2	167	5	14	2	897.4	737.6	466.3	657.7	0.11	0.14	0.15
1975-79	1	54	6	9	-	1 797.2	1 481.6	1 697.0	3 240.0	0.06	0.07	0.03
1980-84	-	-	4	-	1	.	.	.	.	.	.	.
1985-89	2	47	79	1	8	1 220.0	1 014.5	3031.0	6 262.9	0.08	0.10	0.02
1990-94	-	-	1	-	9	.	.	.	.	.	.	.
	KCVN	KCVO	KCVP	KCVQ	KCVR							
1995	1	9	-	3	2	)						
1996	-	-	-	-	1	)						
1997	-	-	-	-	-	)	3700.0	4026.0	31265.6	76539.4	0.03	0.02	0.001
1998	-	-	1	-	-	)						
1999	-	-	-	-	-	)						

1 Excluding accidents involving the deaths of third parties only.

Source: Civil Aviation Authority: 01293 573346

14.27 Activity at civil aerodromes
United Kingdom

		1989	1990	1991	1992	1993	1994	1995	1996	1997	1998	1999
Movement of civil aircraft (Thousands)												
Commercial												
Transport	KNQC	1 359	1 420	1 365	1 448	1 487	1 552	1 615	1 686	1 764	1 871	1 959
Other[1]	KNQD	128	127	115	112	109	112	124	128	143	162	159
Total	KNQB	1 487	1 547	1 481	1 561	1 596	1 664	1 739	1 814	1 907	2 033	2 118
Non-commercial[2]	KNQE	1 650	1 708	1 466	1 321	1 523	1 684	1 809	1 281	1 330	1 343	1 263
Total	KNQA	3 137	3 255	2 947	2 881	3 119	3 348	3 548	3 095	3 237	3 376	3 381
Passengers handled												
Terminal	KNQG	98 898	102 417	95 768	106 123	112 278	122 364	129 586	135 998	146 823	158 997	168 478
Transit	KNQH	1 655	1 725	1 525	1 680	1 620	1 578	1 514	1 508	1 427	1 251	1 172
Total	KNQF	100 553	104 142	97 293	107 804	113 898	123 942	131 100	137 506	148 250	160 248	169 650
Commercial freight handled[3] (Tonnes)												
Set down	KNQJ	592 139	625 131	595 886	658 183	696 055	794 860	854 859	891 150	987 065	1 077 731	1 141 517
Picked up	KNQK	556 318	567 919	524 087	581 315	682 186	811 353	862 584	892 206	968 506	1 014 791	1 059 881
Total	KNQI	1 148 457	1 193 050	1 119 973	1 239 498	1 378 241	1 606 213	1 717 443	1 783 356	1 955 571	2 092 522	2 201 398
Mail handled												
Set down	KNQM	71 918	76 262	77 082	80 236	85 803	91 212	93 562	101 664	110 355	108 110	112 161
Picked up	KNQN	90 586	95 902	93 390	97 241	101 092	110 817	116 057	127 544	138 002	134 275	134 303
Total	KNQL	162 504	172 164	170 472	177 477	186 895	202 029	209 619	229 208	248 357	242 385	246 464

1 Local pleasure flights and non-transport charter flights for reward (for example: aerial survey work, crop dusting and delivery of empty aircraft).
2 Test and training flights, scheduled service positioning flights, private, aero-club and official flights, etc.
3 Figures include weight of vehicles carried on vehicle ferry services.

Source: Civil Aviation Authority: 020 7379 7311

14.28 Great Britain ports: foreign, coastwise and one-port traffic[1]

Million tonnes

		1989	1990	1991	1992	1993	1994	1995	1996	1997	1998	1999
Inwards:												
Foreign												
Bulk fuel	ZCHN	64.22	75.07	78.02	76.47	78.54	71.17	67.06	70.48	74.80	77.54	69.93
Other traffic	ZCHO	107.20	104.75	100.10	101.23	105.32	113.76	118.09	117.41	126.62	127.52	128.96
All traffic	ZCHP	171.42	179.82	178.12	177.70	183.86	184.93	185.15	187.88	201.42	205.06	198.88
Coastwise												
Bulk fuel	ZCHQ	44.71	41.26	41.73	38.52	40.21	42.80	47.29	49.10	46.51	48.07	44.65
Other traffic	ZCHR	10.99	10.78	11.50	11.63	10.96	10.81	10.81	10.72	11.09	12.39	11.59
All traffic	ZCHS	55.70	52.04	53.22	50.14	51.17	53.61	58.10	59.82	57.60	60.46	56.24
One-port												
Bulk fuel	ZCHT	13.33	13.86	13.45	14.11	10.06	13.73	10.85	10.86	6.87	10.59	20.22
Other traffic	ZCHU	21.70	20.24	16.40	14.86	13.65	14.85	15.88	14.24	14.97	15.50	16.20
All traffic	ZCHV	35.03	34.10	29.84	28.96	23.71	25.58	26.73	25.10	21.84	26.09	36.42
Total inwards												
Bulk fuel	ZCHW	122.26	130.19	133.19	129.10	128.81	127.70	125.20	130.44	128.19	136.20	134.80
Other traffic	ZCHX	139.89	135.77	128.00	127.71	129.93	139.42	144.78	142.37	152.68	155.41	156.74
All traffic	ZCHY	262.15	265.96	261.19	256.81	258.74	267.11	269.97	272.81	280.87	291.61	291.54
Outwards:												
Foreign												
Bulk fuel	ZCHZ	72.88	80.34	84.70	88.81	94.12	112.10	109.58	103.92	102.53	103.65	106.41
Other traffic	ZCIA	54.18	55.33	58.02	60.89	62.93	66.47	68.72	71.41	76.23	77.50	77.45
All traffic	ZCIB	127.06	135.67	142.71	149.70	157.05	178.57	178.30	175.32	178.76	181.16	183.86
Coastwise												
Bulk fuel	ZCIC	50.43	46.60	46.93	45.45	45.84	48.65	54.69	58.40	54.26	53.19	52.39
Other traffic	ZCID	11.12	11.42	12.21	11.45	11.94	11.60	12.86	12.40	13.14	13.95	13.33
All traffic	ZCIE	61.55	58.02	59.13	56.90	57.78	60.26	67.55	70.80	67.40	67.14	65.72
One-port												
Other traffic	ZCIF	14.62	15.64	14.77	14.66	13.78	12.11	12.06	12.04	11.91	8.52	3.21
All traffic	ZCIG	14.62	15.64	14.77	14.66	13.78	12.11	12.06	12.04	11.91	8.52	3.21
Total outwards												
Bulk fuel	ZCIH	123.32	126.94	131.62	134.26	139.96	160.76	164.27	162.32	156.79	156.84	158.80
Other traffic	ZCII	79.92	82.40	84.99	87.00	88.65	90.19	93.64	95.85	101.28	99.97	93.99
All traffic	ZCIJ	203.23	209.34	216.61	221.25	228.61	250.94	257.91	258.16	258.07	256.81	252.79
Total goods handled	ZCIK	465.39	475.30	477.80	478.06	487.35	518.06	527.89	530.97	538.94	548.42	544.33

1 Includes estimates of traffic at smaller ports from 1995 onwards.

Source: Department of the Environment, Transport and the Regions; (020) 7944 3087

14.29 Roll-on/roll-off ferry and Channel Tunnel traffic; road goods vehicles outward to mainland Europe: by country of registration

Thousands

		1989	1990	1991	1992	1993	1994	1995	1996	1997	1998	1999
Powered vehicles:												
United Kingdom	ZCGT	295.3	339.0	360.2	373.7	398.0	453.1	486.0	531.1	543.2	544.3	562.7
Austria	ZCGU	..	..	..	..	..	..	9.7	8.6	5.4	10.2	14.9
Belgium/Luxembourg	ZCGV	41.0	37.4	33.8	37.2	29.4	37.1	45.7	41.0	53.6	72.7	96.7
Denmark	ZCGW	7.3	8.4	6.5	6.9	4.9	5.0	4.5	4.6	5.5	7.3	8.7
Finland	ZCGX	..	..	..	..	..	..	0.3	0.2	0.8	0.6	0.7
Germany	ZCGY	36.4	33.8	29.8	30.8	27.7	28.1	28.0	30.4	39.3	52.4	73.1
France	ZCGZ	128.4	131.2	128.7	141.2	144.0	163.2	154.9	181.7	234.2	272.4	319.1
Greece	ZCHA	2.4	2.2	2.3	2.2	1.5	1.3	1.8	2.1	2.6	1.9	2.6
Irish Republic	ZCHB	19.2	21.0	24.3	24.7	35.6	32.4	31.0	30.1	32.3	38.8	44.7
Italy	ZCHC	18.4	15.2	13.7	13.5	13.0	22.7	29.3	28.8	30.4	35.3	45.8
Netherlands	ZCHD	76.1	71.0	69.0	71.9	73.3	76.3	84.6	87.2	107.0	125.4	153.3
Spain	ZCHE	27.5	27.2	25.3	32.4	29.5	35.2	38.4	39.4	45.1	56.3	67.7
Sweden	ZCHF	..	..	..	..	..	..	0.7	0.9	8.9	10.3	1.0
Portugal	ZCHG	1.8	2.8	2.5	3.4	3.3	3.7	3.4	3.1	5.1	6.7	9.2
European Union (excluding UK)	ZCHH	358.4	350.2	335.8	364.2	362.2	405.2	432.2	458.1	569.5	692.1	837.3
Non-European Union	ZCHI	34.2	34.5	29.5	31.9	36.0	38.2	32.0	28.5	26.6	38.1	53.7
Unknown	ZCHJ	1.9	1.7	2.4	2.1	5.8	4.0	4.0	2.2	5.7	4.5	6.3
All countries	ZCHK	690.1	723.7	725.5	769.8	796.2	896.5	950.2	1 017.7	1 146.4	1 274.5	1 453.7
Unaccompanied trailers	ZCHL	595.2	583.9	601.2	629.3	593.4	701.6	677.4	626.4	746.2	779.3	788.7
Powered vehicles and unaccompanied trailers	ZCHM	1 285.3	1 307.6	1 326.7	1 399.1	1 389.6	1 598.1	1 627.6	1 644.1	1 892.6	2 053.8	2 242.4

Source: Department of the Environment, Transport and the Regions; (0117)
987 8484

14.30 United Kingdom international passenger movements by air and sea
Arrivals plus departures

Thousands

		1989	1990	1991	1992	1993	1994	1995	1996	1997	1998	1999
By air												
EC Europe[1]	ZCDD	45 126	45 072	43 163	48 641	51 501	58 080	60 003	60 979	66 127	73 397	79 040
Other Western Europe[2]	ZCDE	7 957	8 040	6 735	8 102	8 507	8 812	9 372	9 481	10 397	11 099	11 252
Rest of the world	ZCDF	21 342	22 661	21 981	25 397	27 281	28 899	31 528	34 400	37 575	40 247	42 610
All air passenger movements	KMUP	74 424	75 772	71 879	82 141	87 289	95 790	100 902	104 861	114 099	124 744	132 903
By sea												
Republic of Ireland, European continent and Mediterranean Sea area[3]	ZCDG	28 807	30 088	31 419	32 912	34 713	36 767	34 355	34 571	36 258	33 306	31 381[6]
Rest of the world	BMMF	31.2	21.6	33.9	26.5	37.0	34.2	32.6	23.9	29.4	23.2	25.5[6]
Pleasure cruises[4]	KMRQ	129	153	172	138	193	236	207	233	..	..	450[6]
All sea passenger movements	KMUO	28 968	30 263	31 625	33 076	34 943	37 038	34 595	34 828	36 288[5]	33 330[5]	31 857[6]

1 Includes Azores, Madeira, Canary and Cape Verde Islands. Austria, Finland, and Sweden joined the EC in 1995, but are included in the EC section for all years to show a consistent time series.
2 Includes Iceland and the Faroe Islands.
3 Prior to 1997, includes passengers between the Isle of Man and the Irish Republic.
4 Cruise passengers, like other passengers are included at both departure and arrival if their journeys begin and end at United Kingdom seaports.
5 Excluding cruise passengers.
6 Provisional data.

Sources: Civil Aviation Authority;
Department of the Environment, Transport and the Regions

14.31 Postal services and television licences
United Kingdom
Years ended 31 March[1]

		1990	1991	1992	1993	1994	1995	1996	1997	1998	1999	2000
Letters, etc posted[2]	KMRA	15 293	15 902	16 038	16 364	16 651	17 468	18 322	18 101	18 389	18 942	19 787
of which:												
Registered and insured	KMRB	*22.2*	*21.3*	*20.7*	*21.5*	*21.8*	*21.5*	*23.5*	*25.6*	*28.7*	*31.6*	*30.2*
Airmail (Commonwealth and foreign)[3]	KMRC	444.0	467.7	544.5	534.4	545.0	567.1	655.1	684.5	658.4	693.2	672.3
Business reply and freepost items[4]	KMRD	438.7	416.7	428.9	481.3	482.9	477.6	493.1	505.8	524.7	503.6	475.3
Postal orders												
Total issued (thousands)[5]	KMRH	42 281	39 644	39 867	38 401	39 089	37 901	35 542	33 404	31 907	30 289	30 153
Television licences (thousands)												
in force on 31 March	KMQL	19 645	19 546	19 631	20 067	20 413	20 732	21 105	21 305	21 723	22 240	22 625
of which:												
Colour	KMQM	*17 964*	*18 111*	*18 426*	*19 031*	*19 524*	*19 957*	*20 505*	*20 849*	*21 344*	*21 944*	*22 413*

1 Years ended 31 March for letters, postal orders and telegrams sent. For all other items figures relate to 31 March in each year.
2 Including printed papers, newspapers, postcards and sample packets.
3 Including letters without special charge for air transport.
4 Business reply and Freepost is now known as Response Services.
5 Excluding those issued on HM ships, in many British possessions and in other places abroad. For 1990 to 1998 includes Postal Orders issued Overseas and by Ministry of Defence.

Sources: Royal Mail: 01246 547012;
Subscription Services Limited: 01179 219384;
Post Office Counters.Limited: 020 7921 9384

15 National accounts

National accounts

National accounts (Tables 15.1 to 15.22)

The tables which follow are based on those in the *Blue Book 2000 Edition*. Some of the figures are provisional and may have to be revised later; this applies particularly to the figures for 1998 and 1999.

The accounts are based on the European System of Accounts 1995 (ESA95). The *Blue Book* contains an introduction to the system of the UK accounts outlining some of the main concepts and principles of measurement used. It explains how key economic indicators are derived from the sequence of accounts and how the figures describing the whole economy are broken down by sector and by industry. A detailed description of the structure for the accounts is provided in a separate ONS publication *United Kingdom National Accounts*: *Concepts, Sources and Methods* (TSO 1998). Further information on the financial accounts is given in the *Financial Statistics Explanatory Handbook*.

In the tables in this chapter on national income, analyses by industry are based, as far as possible, on the Standard Industrial Classification Revised 1992. The first aggregate measured in these tables is the **Gross domestic product** (GDP). This is a concept of the value of the total economic activity taking place in UK territory. It can be viewed as incomes earned, as expenditures incurred, or as production. Adding all primary incomes received from the rest of the world and deducting all primary incomes payable to non-residents produces **Gross national income** (previously known as gross national product). This is a concept of the value of all incomes earned by UK residents.

ESA95, the new internationally compatible accounting framework, provides a systematic and detailed description of the UK economy. It includes the sector accounts which provide, by institutional sector, a description of the different stages of the economic process from production through income generation, distribution and use of income to capital accumulation and financing; and the input output framework, which describes the production process in more detail. It contains all the elements required to compile such aggregate measures as GDP, gross national income (GNI) and saving.

Gross domestic product and national income (Tables 15.1, 15.2, 15.3)

Table 15.1 shows the main national accounts aggregates, at current prices and at constant 1995 prices.

Table 15.2 shows the various money flows which generate the gross domestic product and gross national income. The output approach to GDP shows the total output of goods and services, the use of goods and services in the production process (intermediate consumption) and taxes and subsidies on products. The expenditure approach to GDP shows consumption expenditure by households and government, gross capital formation and expenditure on UK exports by overseas purchasers. The sum of these items overstates the amount of income generated in the United Kingdom by the value of imports of goods and services; this item is therefore subtracted to produce gross domestic product at market prices. The income approach to GDP shows gross operating surplus, mixed income and compensation of employees (previously known as income from employment). Taxes are added and subsidies are deducted to produce the total of the income-based components at market prices.

Table 15.2 also shows the primary incomes received from the rest of the world, which are added to GDP and primary incomes payable to non-residents, which are deducted from GDP, to arrive at **Gross national income.** Property income comprises compensation of employees, taxes *less* subsidies on production and property and entrepreneurial income.

Table 15.3 shows the expenditure approach to GDP at constant 1995 prices. When looking at the change in the economy over time the main concern is usually whether more goods and services are actually being produced now than at some time in the past. Over time changes in current price GDP show changes in the monetary value of the components of GDP and, as these changes in value can reflect changes in both price and volume, it is difficult to establish how much of an increase in the series is due either to increased activity in the economy or to an increase in the price level. As a result, when looking at the real growth in the economy over time it is useful to look at volume (or constant price) estimates of GDP. In constant price series, for all years the transactions are re-valued to a constant price level using the average prices of a selected year, known as the base year, presently 1995.

Industrial analysis (Tables 15.4, 15.5)
The analysis of gross value added by industry at current prices shown in Table 15.4 reflects the estimates based on the Standard Industrial Classification, Revised 1992 (SIC92). The table is based on current price data reconciled through the input-output process for 1992 to 1998. Figures for the latest year, 1999, are based on data reconciled through the national accounts balancing process. The estimates are valued at basic prices, that is, the only taxes included in the price will be taxes paid as part of the production process, such as business rates, and not any taxes specifically levied on the production of a unit of output, for example VAT.

Table 15.5 shows constant price estimates of gross value added at basic prices by industry. Constant price gross value added (output approach) provides the lead indicator of economic change in the short term.

Sector analysis - Distribution of income accounts and capital account (Tables 15.6-15.13)
The new national accounts accounting framework includes the sector accounts which provide, by institutional sector, a description of the different stages of the economic

process from production through income generation, distribution and use of income to capital accumulation and financing.

Tables 15.6-15.12 show the allocation of primary income account and the secondary distribution of income account for the non-financial corporations, financial corporations, government and households sectors. Additionally, Table 15.12 shows the use of income account for the households sector and Table 15.13 provides a summary of the capital account. The full sequence of accounts is shown in the *Blue Book*.

The allocation of primary income account shows the resident units and institutional sectors as recipients rather than as producers of primary income. It demonstrates the extent to which operating surpluses are distributed to the owners of the enterprises. The resources side of the allocation of primary income accounts includes the components of the income approach to measurement of GDP. The balance of this account is the gross balance of primary income (B.5g) for each sector, and if the gross balance is aggregated across all sectors of the economy the result is **gross national income.**

The secondary distribution of income account describes how the balance of income for each sector is allocated by redistribution; through transfers such as taxes on income, social contributions and benefits and other current transfers. The balancing item of this account is gross disposable income (B.6g). For the households sector, gross disposable income at constant prices is shown as real household disposable income.

Table 15.12 shows, for the households sector, the use of disposable income where the balancing item is saving (B.8g). For the non-financial corporations sector the balancing item of the secondary distribution of income account, gross disposable income (B.6g) is equal to saving (B.8g).

The summary capital account *(Table 15.13)* brings together the saving and investment of the several sectors of the economy. It shows saving, capital transfers, gross capital formation and net acquisition of non-financial assets for each of the four sectors.

Household and non-profit institutions serving households (NPISH) consumption expenditure at current and constant prices *(Tables 15.14-15.17)*
Household and NPISH consumption expenditure is a major component of the expenditure measure of gross domestic product at current prices *(Table 15.2)* and at constant prices *(Table 15.3)*.

Household final consumption expenditure includes the value of income-in-kind and imputed rent of owner-occupied dwellings but excludes business expenditure allowed as deductions in computing income for tax purposes. It includes expenditure on durable goods, for instance motor cars, which from the point of view of the individual

might more appropriately be treated as capital expenditure. The only exceptions are the purchase of land and dwellings and costs incurred in connection with the transfer of their ownership and expenditure on major improvements by occupiers, which are treated as personal capital expenditure.

The estimates of household consumption expenditure include purchases of second-hand as well as new goods, *less* the proceeds of sales of used goods.

The most detailed figures are published quarterly in *Consumer Trends*.

Change in inventories (previously known as value of physical increase in stocks and work in progress) *(Table 15.18)*
This table gives a broad analysis by industry, and, for manufacturing industry, by asset, of the value of entries *less* withdrawals and losses of inventories (stocks).

Gross fixed capital formation *(Tables 15.19-15.22)*
Gross fixed capital formation comprises expenditure on the replacement of, and additions to, fixed capital assets located in the United Kingdom, including all ships and aircraft of UK ownership.

15.1 UK national and domestic product
Main aggregates: index numbers and values
At current and constant 1995 prices

		1991	1992	1993	1994	1995	1996	1997	1998	1999
INDICES (1995=100)										
VALUES AT CURRENT PRICES										
Gross domestic product at current market prices										
("money GDP")	YBEU	81.9	85.2	89.5	94.9	100.0	105.9	112.8	119.3	124.9
Gross value added at current basic prices	YBEX	82.3	85.8	90.2	95.3	100.0	106.1	112.5	118.9	124.0
VALUES AT 1995 PRICES										
Gross domestic product at 1995 market prices	YBEZ	91.0	91.1	93.2	97.3	100.0	102.6	106.2	109.0	111.3
Gross national disposable income at 1995 market prices	YBFP	91.4	91.9	94.0	98.5	100.0	103.4	108.6	112.2	114.6
Gross value added at 1995 basic prices	CGCE	90.9	91.1	93.2	97.4	100.0	102.5	106.0	109.1	111.5
PRICES										
Implied deflator of GDP at market prices										
(expenditure based, "total home costs per unit of output")	YBGB	90.0	93.5	96.1	97.5	100.0	103.3	106.3	109.5	112.2
VALUES AT CURRENT PRICES (£ million)										
Gross measures, before deduction of										
fixed capital consumption										
at current market prices										
Gross domestic product at current market prices										
("money GDP")	YBHA	584 536	608 165	639 356	677 594	713 980	756 058	805 402	851 654	891 583
Employment, property and entrepreneurial income from										
the rest of the world (receipts *less* payments)	YBGG	−1 953	2 115	685	7 770	5 976	8 111	11 170	14 245	8 332
Subsidies (receipts) *less* taxes (payments) on										
production from/to the rest of the world	−QZOZ	−3 512	−4 253	−4 510	−3 063	−4 927	−3 888	−2 598	−3 437	−3 181
Gross national income at current market prices	ABMX	579 071	606 027	635 531	682 300	715 028	760 281	813 974	862 462	896 734
Current transfers from the rest of the world										
(receipts *less* payments)	−YBGF	2 849	−562	−98	−1 605	−1 987	−636	−2 455	−2 935	−905
Gross national disposable income at current market prices	NQCO	581 920	605 465	635 433	680 695	713 041	759 645	811 519	859 527	895 829
adjustment to current basic prices										
Gross domestic product at current market prices	YBHA	584 536	608 165	639 356	677 594	713 980	756 058	805 402	851 654	891 583
Adjustment to current basic prices										
(*less* taxes *plus* subsidies on products)	−NQBU	−61 399	−62 678	−65 979	−71 874	−78 482	−82 029	−90 275	−96 357	−103 720
Gross value added at current basic prices	ABML	523 137	545 487	573 377	605 720	635 498	674 029	715 127	755 297	787 863
Net measures, after deduction of										
fixed capital consumption	−NQAE	−74 623	−77 253	−83 595	−84 882	−86 720	−89 553	−94 524	−98 398	−103 313
Net domestic product at current market prices	NHRK	509 913	530 912	555 761	592 712	627 260	666 505	710 878	753 256	787 793
Net national income at current market prices	NSRX	504 448	528 774	551 936	597 418	628 308	670 728	719 450	764 064	792 944
Net national disposable income at current market prices	NQCP	507 297	528 212	551 838	595 813	626 321	670 092	716 995	761 129	792 039
VALUES AT 1995 PRICES (£ million)										
Gross measures, before deduction of										
fixed capital consumption										
at 1995 market prices										
Gross domestic product at 1995 market prices	ABMI	649 815	650 288	665 427	694 616	713 980	732 203	757 921	777 937	794 730
Terms of trade effect ("Trading gain or loss")	YBGJ	4 284	7 303	8 058	4 836	–	2 182	8 891	14 656	18 335
Real gross domestic income	YBGL	654 099	657 591	673 486	699 452	713 980	734 386	766 812	792 594	812 701
Real employment, property and entrepreneurial income										
from the rest of the world (receipts *less* payments)	YBGI	−2 187	2 289	722	8 019	5 976	7 882	10 638	13 288	7 637
Subsidies (receipts) *less* taxes (payments) on										
production from/to the rest of the world	−QZPB	−3 068	−3 801	−4 149	−3 205	−4 926	−4 649	−996	−2 830	−3 029
Gross national income at 1995 market prices	YBGM	648 844	656 079	670 059	704 266	715 030	737 619	776 454	803 052	817 309
Real current transfers from the rest of the world										
(receipts *less* payments)	−YBGP	3 184	−615	−102	−1 653	−1 985	−616	−2 336	−2 736	−795
Gross national disposable income at 1995 market prices	YBGO	652 045	655 467	669 962	702 613	713 045	737 003	774 118	800 316	816 514
adjustment to 1995 basic prices										
Gross domestic product at 1995 market prices	ABMI	649 815	650 288	665 427	694 616	713 980	732 203	757 921	777 937	794 730
Adjustment to 1995 basic prices										
(*less* taxes *plus* subsidies on products)	−NTAQ	−72 335	−71 524	−73 383	−75 775	−78 482	−80 538	−84 543	−84 379	−86 407
Gross value added at 1995 basic prices	ABMM	577 704	578 854	592 166	618 841	635 498	651 665	673 378	693 558	708 323
Net measures, after deduction of										
fixed capital consumption at 1995 prices	−YBFX	−79 605	−84 460	−89 138	−88 094	−86 720	−86 489	−88 433	−88 935	−88 920
Net national income at 1995 market prices	YBET	569 425	571 333	580 285	616 172	628 310	651 130	688 021	714 117	728 389
Net national disposable income at 1995 market prices	YBEY	572 706	570 726	580 189	614 519	626 325	650 514	685 685	711 381	727 594

Source: Office for National Statistics: 020 7533 6031

15.2 UK gross domestic product and national income
Current prices

£ millions

		1991	1992	1993	1994	1995	1996	1997	1998	1999
GROSS DOMESTIC PRODUCT										
Gross domestic product: output approach										
Gross value added, at basic prices										
Output of goods and services, at basic prices	NQAF	1 041 414	1 103 288	1 169 732	1 272 863	1 361 025	1 451 473	1 527 884	1 601 222	1 682 811
less intermediate consumption, at purchasers' prices	-NQAJ	-518 277	-557 801	-596 355	-667 143	-725 527	-777 444	-812 757	-845 925	-895 425
Total	ABML	523 137	545 487	573 377	605 720	635 498	674 029	715 127	755 297	787 863
Value added taxes (VAT) on products	QYRC	38 415	40 710	42 757	46 113	48 467	51 623	55 658	56 907	61 752
Other taxes on products	NSUI	29 206	28 888	30 651	33 311	37 724	39 457	42 661	46 849	50 426
less subsidies on products	-NZHC	-6 222	-6 920	-7 429	-7 550	-7 709	-9 051	-8 044	-7 399	-8 458
Gross domestic product at market prices	YBHA	584 536	608 165	639 356	677 594	713 980	756 058	805 402	851 654	891 583
Gross domestic product: expenditure approach										
Final consumption expenditure										
Actual individual consumption										
Household final consumption expenditure	ABPB	357 785	377 147	399 108	419 262	438 453	467 841	498 307	530 851	564 369
Final consumption expenditure of NPISH	ABNV	11 096	10 806	13 981	15 287	16 481	18 385	19 602	20 972	22 537
Individual government final consumption expenditure	NNAQ	66 524	73 205	75 000	77 512	82 311	85 638	88 451	92 079	96 663
Total actual individual consumption	ABRE	435 405	461 158	488 089	512 061	537 245	571 864	606 360	643 902	683 569
Collective government final consumption expenditure	NNAR	55 216	56 006	56 413	58 862	58 764	61 122	59 958	62 688	67 115
Total final consumption expenditure	ABKW	490 621	517 164	544 502	570 923	596 009	632 986	666 318	706 590	750 684
Households and NPISH	NSSG	368 881	387 953	413 089	434 549	454 934	486 226	517 909	551 823	586 906
Central government	NMBJ	73 171	78 245	81 425	84 523	86 861	90 388	91 481	95 798	99 464
Local government	NMMT	48 569	50 966	49 988	51 851	54 214	56 372	56 928	58 969	64 314
Gross capital formation										
Gross fixed capital formation	NPQX	104 680	100 278	101 230	107 390	116 360	125 675	134 153	148 071	158 372
Changes in inventories	ABMP	-4 927	-1 937	329	3 708	4 512	1 771	4 388	4 461	-1 946
Acquisitions less disposals of valuables	NPJO	-86	36	-9	136	-92	-185	39	487	346
Total gross capital formation	NPDN	99 667	98 377	101 550	111 234	120 780	127 261	138 580	153 019	156 772
Exports of goods and services	KTMW	135 365	143 291	162 078	178 767	202 412	220 303	229 326	225 474	229 649
less imports of goods and services	-KTMX	-141 117	-150 667	-168 774	-183 330	-205 221	-224 492	-228 822	-233 429	-244 878
External balance of goods and services	KTMY	-5 752	-7 376	-6 696	-4 563	-2 809	-4 189	504	-7 955	-15 229
Statistical discrepancy between expenditure components and GDP	GIXM	–	–	–	–	–	–	–	–	-644
Gross domestic product at market prices	YBHA	584 536	608 165	639 356	677 594	713 980	756 058	805 402	851 654	891 583
Gross domestic product: income approach										
Operating surplus, gross										
Non-financial corporations										
Public non-financial corporations	NRJT	2 207	2 237	3 206	3 627	5 367	5 114	4 205	4 054	3 738
Private non-financial corporations	NRJK	108 502	108 460	118 453	133 237	143 086	158 805	169 778	174 421	174 400
Financial corporations	NQNV	7 836	15 657	18 393	23 616	20 077	18 970	18 151	19 126	18 171
Adjustment for financial services	-NSRV	-15 828	-20 997	-20 025	-26 410	-25 499	-25 557	-25 678	-27 732	-30 411
General government	NMXV	10 662	10 619	10 720	11 167	11 570	12 305	12 476	13 140	13 101
Households and non-profit institutions serving households	QWLS	29 162	33 390	35 153	37 510	40 084	41 913	45 094	48 905	54 058
Total operating surplus, gross	ABNF	142 541	149 366	165 900	182 747	194 685	211 550	224 026	231 914	233 057
Mixed income	HAXH	31 635	33 872	36 096	38 336	40 239	41 570	41 665	42 811	43 856
Compensation of employees	HAEA	333 850	347 036	356 323	369 960	385 397	404 521	432 388	463 044	491 873
Taxes on production and imports	NZGX	82 732	84 811	88 466	94 101	101 368	107 468	115 367	121 284	130 290
less subsidies	-AAXJ	-6 222	-6 920	-7 429	-7 550	-7 709	-9 051	-8 044	-7 399	-8 458
Statistical discrepancy between income components and GDP	GIXQ	–	–	–	–	–	–	–	–	965
Gross domestic product at market prices	YBHA	584 536	608 165	639 356	677 594	713 980	756 058	805 402	851 654	891 583
GROSS NATIONAL INCOME at market prices										
Gross domestic product at market prices	YBHA	584 536	608 165	639 356	677 594	713 980	756 058	805 402	851 654	891 583
Compensation of employees										
receipts from the rest of the world	KTMN	551	551	595	681	887	911	1 007	840	960
less payments to the rest of the world	-KTMO	-614	-600	-560	-851	-1 183	-818	-924	-850	-759
Total	KTMP	-63	-49	35	-170	-296	93	83	-10	201
less Taxes on production paid to the rest of the world *plus* Subsidies received from the rest of the world	-QZOZ	-3 512	-4 253	-4 510	-3 063	-4 927	-3 888	-2 598	-3 437	-3 181
Property and entrepreneurial income										
receipts from the rest of the world	HMBN	84 419	74 549	78 825	82 639	97 086	101 669	106 898	108 392	108 139
less payments to the rest of the world	-HMBO	-86 309	-72 385	-78 175	-74 699	-90 814	-93 651	-95 811	-94 137	-100 008
Total	HMBM	-1 890	2 164	650	7 940	6 272	8 018	11 087	14 255	8 131
Gross national income at market prices	ABMX	579 071	606 027	635 531	682 300	715 028	760 281	813 974	862 462	896 734

Source: Office for National Statistics: 020 7533 6031

15.3 UK gross domestic product
Constant (1995) prices

£ millions

		1991	1992	1993	1994	1995	1996	1997	1998	1999
GROSS DOMESTIC PRODUCT										
Gross domestic product: expenditure approach										
Final consumption expenditure										
Actual individual consumption										
Household final consumption expenditure	ABPF	408 309	410 026	420 081	431 462	438 453	454 686	472 701	491 378	512 864
Final consumption expenditure of non-profit institutions serving households	ABNU	12 217	12 445	14 723	15 900	16 481	16 691	17 055	18 112	18 552
Individual government final consumption expenditure	NSZK	75 142	77 437	78 999	79 363	82 311	84 361	85 818	87 032	87 681
Total actual individual consumption	YBIO	495 220	499 495	513 691	526 725	537 245	555 738	575 574	596 522	619 097
Collective government final consumption expenditure	NSZL	62 399	60 772	58 038	59 551	58 764	59 140	55 677	56 021	59 632
Total final consumption expenditure	ABKX	557 707	560 347	571 743	586 276	596 009	614 878	631 251	652 543	678 729
Gross capital formation										
Gross fixed capital formation	NPQR	109 000	108 246	109 127	113 042	116 360	122 042	131 246	144 437	153 272
Changes in inventories	ABMQ	−5 349	−1 962	360	4 836	4 512	1 830	3 762	4 229	−1 386
Acquisitions less disposals of valuables	NPJP	−90	39	−9	140	−92	−186	14	457	323
Total gross capital formation	NPQU	104 505	106 940	109 888	118 018	120 780	123 686	135 022	149 123	152 209
Gross domestic final expenditure	YBIK	661 163	666 495	680 925	704 294	716 789	738 564	766 273	801 666	831 462
Exports of goods and services	KTMZ	156 362	162 819	169 225	184 873	202 412	217 600	236 283	242 498	250 429
Gross final expenditure	ABME	817 330	829 176	850 039	889 167	919 201	956 164	1 002 556	1 044 164	1 081 891
less imports of goods and services	-KTNB	−167 472	−178 879	−184 607	−194 551	−205 221	−223 961	−244 635	−266 227	−286 587
Statistical discrepancy between expenditure components and GDP	GIXS	–	–	–	–	–	–	–	–	−574
Gross domestic product at 1995 market prices	ABMI	649 815	650 288	665 427	694 616	713 980	732 203	757 921	777 937	794 730
of which External balance of goods and services	KTNC	−11 110	−16 060	−15 382	−9 678	−2 809	−6 361	−8 352	−23 729	−36 158

Source: Office for National Statistics: 020 7533 6031

15.4 Gross value added at current basic prices: by industry[1,2]

£ millions

		1991	1992	1993	1994	1995	1996	1997	1998	1999
Agriculture, hunting, forestry and fishing	EWSH	9 376	10 349	10 765	10 776	11 713	11 963	10 594	9 731	9 332
Mining & quarrying	EWSL	13 410	13 167	13 305	14 550	16 116	19 447	17 643	15 034	17 976
Manufacturing	EWSP	111 337	113 704	118 718	128 202	136 747	143 485	148 619	151 197	147 699
Electricity, gas & water supply	EWST	14 553	14 721	16 049	15 932	15 562	16 120	16 230	15 851	17 944
Construction	EWSX	31 995	29 965	29 144	31 347	32 948	34 563	36 927	38 945	41 273
Wholesale and retail trade	EWTB	75 349	79 652	83 823	88 224	92 557	99 170	108 450	115 650	117 554
Transport & communication	EWTF	43 909	45 714	47 294	50 708	52 297	53 994	57 916	62 200	69 208
Financial intermediation	EWTJ	121 861	133 501	141 698	154 498	159 069	168 448	184 163	205 549	220 601
Adjustment for financial services	-NSRV	–15 828	–20 997	–20 025	–26 410	–25 499	–25 557	–25 678	–27 732	–30 411
Public administration and defence	EWTN	36 617	39 416	40 189	39 713	39 869	39 835	39 646	39 651	40 199
Education, health & social work	EWTR	60 740	65 087	69 132	72 734	76 693	81 886	85 825	91 105	93 241
Other services	EWTV	19 819	21 204	23 280	25 439	27 422	30 670	34 786	38 116	41 498
All industries including adjustment for financial services	ABML	523 137	545 487	573 377	605 720	635 498	674 029	715 127	755 297	787 863

1 The contribution of each industry to the gross domestic product before providing for consumption of fixed capital. The industrial composition in this table is consistent with the Input-Output analyses. Although the industrial composition for 1989-91 is based on Input-Output analyses also, there are improvements to the underlying data from 1992. Between 1989 and 1991, the data were compiled on a different basis, which lead to step changes in 1991 and 1992.
2 Components may not sum to totals due to rounding.

Source: Office for National Statistics: 020 7533 6031

15.5 Gross value added at 1995 basic prices: by industry
Index numbers

Indices 1995=100

	Weight per 1000[1]		1991	1992	1993	1994	1995	1996	1997	1998	1999
	1995										
Agriculture, hunting & forestry; fishing	18.5	GDQA	105.7	110.1	101.2	100.0	100.0	102.0	103.5	101.8	103.1
Production											
Mining and quarrying											
Mining and quarrying of energy producing materials											
Mining of coal	1.9	CKZP	202.0	181.8	142.3	94.6	100.0	95.5	90.3	76.5	69.2
Extraction of mineral oil and natural gas	21.3	CKZO	63.8	68.4	77.5	96.1	100.0	105.6	104.7	107.5	112.2
Other mining and quarrying	2.3	CKZQ	107.9	103.4	105.6	105.4	100.0	88.9	87.5	98.1	101.4
Total mining and quarrying	25.4	CKYX	76.7	78.9	84.2	96.8	100.0	103.3	102.1	104.4	108.0
Manufacturing											
Food; beverages & tobacco	28.7	CKZA	97.0	98.7	99.0	101.5	100.0	101.0	104.6	101.9	101.2
Textiles & textile products	10.1	CKZB	101.0	101.9	101.3	103.6	100.0	99.6	96.4	89.2	82.3
Leather & leather products	1.4	CKZC	97.1	94.5	97.8	97.3	100.0	99.9	103.8	89.5	86.7
Wood & wood products	2.9	CKZD	99.4	98.2	100.4	108.2	100.0	97.6	95.8	94.7	89.9
Pulp, paper & paper products; publishing & printing	26.3	CKZE	92.0	93.1	96.1	98.5	100.0	98.0	98.2	98.8	98.8
Coke, petroleum products & nuclear fuel	4.7	CKZF	83.5	88.5	88.9	89.7	100.0	91.8	93.5	88.3	79.4
Chemicals, chemical products & man-made fibres	24.1	CKZG	85.8	88.5	90.4	95.1	100.0	100.7	102.4	103.8	107.7
Rubber & plastic products	10.5	CKZH	83.1	85.1	88.9	98.0	100.0	98.8	98.6	101.6	101.1
Other non-metallic mineral products	7.9	CKZI	99.1	94.7	99.1	102.8	100.0	96.5	99.0	96.4	95.3
Basic metals & fabricated metal products	24.6	CKZJ	101.0	96.0	95.0	97.3	100.0	99.7	101.2	99.0	94.4
Machinery & equipment not elsewhere classified	19.2	CKZK	98.8	94.8	94.7	99.9	100.0	98.0	95.8	95.8	90.0
Electrical & optical equipment	26.9	CKZL	77.6	78.9	83.2	93.3	100.0	104.0	105.9	112.4	121.5
Transport equipment	20.5	CKZM	101.8	99.8	98.1	100.7	100.0	105.7	109.5	115.8	117.6
Manufacturing not elsewhere classified	7.6	CKZN	98.5	98.0	99.4	102.4	100.0	100.2	101.7	102.2	102.3
Total manufacturing	215.7	CKYY	92.8	92.8	94.1	98.5	100.0	100.4	101.7	102.2	102.2
Electricity, gas and water supply	24.5	CKYZ	91.4	92.9	96.8	97.8	100.0	105.3	105.7	107.6	109.3
Total production	265.6	CKYW	91.0	91.3	93.3	98.3	100.0	101.1	102.1	102.9	103.4
Construction	52.0	GDQB	102.3	98.3	97.1	100.8	100.0	101.5	104.7	106.1	106.4
Service industries											
Wholesale & retail trade (including motor trade); repair of motor vehicles, personal & household goods	116.9	GDQC	86.3	87.5	92.5	97.5	100.0	103.4	107.3	110.1	112.2
Hotels and restaurants	29.0	GDQD	100.4	96.4	98.5	101.2	100.0	102.4	103.6	105.7	107.5
Transport, storage & communication											
Transport and storage	53.6	GDQF	84.4	87.5	89.3	96.3	100.0	100.7	106.5	113.9	117.2
Communication	28.9	GDQG	79.6	79.5	83.6	90.7	100.0	110.8	126.2	135.5	156.1
Total	82.5	GDQH	82.7	84.6	87.3	94.3	100.0	104.2	113.4	121.5	130.8
Financial intermediation	67.4	GDQI	98.7	94.2	96.3	97.3	100.0	104.3	109.9	113.0	112.5
Adjustment for financial services	−40.2	GDQJ	94.0	90.9	91.6	95.8	100.0	105.5	112.8	119.5	121.3
Real estate, renting & business activities											
Letting of dwellings, including imputed rent of owner occupiers	72.2	GDQL	94.8	95.3	96.5	97.8	100.0	101.4	103.5	107.1	110.3
Other real estate, renting & business activities	111.3	GDQK	84.1	82.6	84.7	93.5	100.0	106.8	117.6	128.5	135.7
Total	183.5	GDQM	87.9	86.8	88.9	95.2	100.0	104.7	112.0	120.1	125.7
Public administration & defence	61.2	GDQO	105.6	105.0	102.9	101.3	100.0	98.5	96.7	96.4	96.2
Education	56.0	GDQP	92.2	95.0	95.0	98.7	100.0	101.6	103.0	103.3	103.8
Health and social work	64.6	GDQQ	86.1	88.6	92.6	95.0	100.0	104.4	108.3	111.8	114.5
Other social & personal services, private households with employees and extra-territorial organisations	42.9	GDQR	81.4	83.2	90.1	95.7	100.0	103.7	106.7	112.4	112.7
Total service industries	663.9	GDQS	89.3	89.7	92.5	96.8	100.0	103.3	107.8	112.3	115.6
All industries	1 000.0	YBFR	90.9	91.1	93.1	97.5	100.0	102.6	106.1	109.3	111.6

1 The weights are in proportion to total gross value added in 1995. The GVA for sections L, M, and N in this table follows the SIC(92) and differs from that shown in table 2.3, which is based on Input-Output groups. Central government expenditure on teachers' pay is included in Education in table 2.4 but in PAD in table 2.3. The administation costs of the NHS are included in PAD in table 2.4 but are included in Health and social work in table 2.3.

2 The output analysis of gross value added is estimated in terms of change and expressed in index number form. It is therefore inappropriate to show as a statistical adjustment any divergence of an output measure of GDP derived from it from other measures of GDP. Such an adjustment does, however, exist implicitly.

Source: Office for National Statistics: 020 7533 6031

15.6 Non-financial corporations
Allocation of primary income account

£ millions

		1991	1992	1993	1994	1995	1996	1997	1998	1999
Resources										
Operating surplus, gross	**NQBE**	110 709	110 697	121 659	136 864	148 453	163 919	173 983	178 475	178 138
of which UK continental shelf companies										
gross trading profits	**CAGD**	8 322	8 345	9 312	10 654	12 018	15 538	13 786	11 208	13 602
of which other private non-financial corporations'										
gross trading profits	**CAED**	94 969	93 641	102 082	117 351	126 313	134 776	146 576	151 584	150 837
Property income, received										
Interest	**EABC**	13 907	11 263	7 883	7 902	9 772	9 989	10 468	14 423	11 586
Distributed income of corporations	**EABD**	14 797	16 430	15 943	18 437	24 517	25 458	29 223	27 363	23 228
Reinvested earnings on direct foreign investment	**HDVR**	5 461	4 539	7 468	11 704	10 861	12 782	11 366	10 428	15 458
Attributed property income of insurance policy-holders	**FAOF**	730	786	765	780	862	779	878	978	674
Rent	**FAOG**	109	108	106	108	109	115	120	120	120
Total	**FAKY**	35 004	33 126	32 165	38 931	46 121	49 123	52 055	53 312	51 066
Total resources	**FBXJ**	145 713	143 823	153 824	175 795	194 574	213 042	226 038	231 787	229 204
Uses										
Property income, paid										
Interest	**EABG**	32 784	29 804	23 718	23 594	26 943	26 218	27 983	33 572	32 597
Distributed income of corporations	**NVCS**	49 380	53 038	52 843	58 717	72 090	77 403	82 215	79 349	88 974
of which private non-financial corporations' dividends	**RVFT**	30 171	33 403	33 727	38 549	48 671	54 793	59 253	55 173	64 107
Reinvested earnings on direct foreign investment	**HDVB**	238	109	1 672	3 533	3 845	5 177	4 369	2 617	4 906
Rent	**FBXO**	697	682	734	693	719	753	752	568	446
Total	**FBXK**	83 099	83 633	78 967	86 537	103 597	109 551	115 319	116 106	126 923
Balance of primary incomes, gross	**NQBG**	62 614	60 190	74 857	89 258	90 977	103 491	110 719	115 681	102 281
Total uses	**FBXJ**	145 713	143 823	153 824	175 795	194 574	213 042	226 038	231 787	229 204

Source: Office for National Statistics: 020 7533 6031

15.7 Non-financial corporations
Secondary distribution of income account

£ millions

		1991	1992	1993	1994	1995	1996	1997	1998	1999
Resources										
Balance of primary incomes, gross	**NQBG**	62 614	60 190	74 857	89 258	90 977	103 491	110 719	115 681	102 281
Social contributions										
Imputed social contributions	**NSTJ**	2 478	3 031	3 226	3 805	3 371	2 983	2 872	3 108	3 350
Current transfers other than taxes, social contributions and benefits										
Non-life insurance claims	**FCBP**	10 464	11 147	9 834	9 286	10 287	10 121	9 538	9 934	10 967
Miscellaneous transfers	**NRJY**	37	112	256	420	494	537	557	595	611
Total	**NRJB**	10 501	11 259	10 090	9 706	10 781	10 658	10 095	10 529	11 578
Total resources	**FCBR**	75 593	74 480	88 173	102 769	105 129	117 132	123 686	129 318	117 209
Uses										
Current taxes on income, wealth etc.										
Taxes on income	**FCBS**	16 563	12 951	12 827	14 497	19 318	21 219	28 031	25 185	21 480
Social benefits other than social transfers in kind	**NSTJ**	2 478	3 031	3 226	3 805	3 371	2 983	2 872	3 108	3 350
Current transfers other than taxes, social contributions and benefits										
Net non-life insurance premiums	**FCBY**	10 464	11 147	9 834	9 286	10 287	10 121	9 538	9 930	10 960
Miscellaneous current transfers	**FDBI**	238	240	272	311	343	1 455	402	363	375
Total, other current transfers	**FCBX**	10 702	11 387	10 106	9 597	10 630	11 576	9 940	10 293	11 335
Disposable income, gross[1]	**NRJD**	45 850	47 111	62 014	74 870	71 810	81 354	82 843	90 732	81 044
Total uses	**FCBR**	75 593	74 480	88 173	102 769	105 129	117 132	123 686	129 318	117 209

1 Gross disposable income equals gross saving.

Source: Office for National Statistics: 020 7533 6031

15.8 General government
Allocation of primary income account

£ millions

		1991	1992	1993	1994	1995	1996	1997	1998	1999
Resources										
Operating surplus, gross	NMXV	10 662	10 619	10 720	11 167	11 570	12 305	12 476	13 140	13 101
Taxes on production and imports, received										
Taxes on products										
Value added tax (VAT)	NZGF	35 157	36 651	38 286	42 992	43 622	47 152	52 261	52 679	57 941
Taxes and duties on imports excluding VAT										
Import duties	NMBS	–	–	–	–	–	–	–	–	–
Taxes on imports excluding VAT and import duties	NMBT	–	–	–	–	–	–	–	–	–
Taxes on products excluding VAT and import duties	NMBV	27 242	26 891	28 422	31 079	35 211	37 113	40 290	44 731	48 356
Total taxes on products	NVCC	62 399	63 542	66 708	74 071	78 833	84 265	92 551	97 410	106 297
Other taxes on production	NMYD	15 111	15 213	15 058	14 677	15 177	16 388	17 048	17 528	18 112
Total taxes on production and imports, received	NMYE	77 510	78 755	81 766	88 748	94 010	100 653	109 595	114 938	124 409
less Subsidies, paid										
Subsidies on products	-NMYF	–4 512	–5 117	–5 239	–5 260	–5 278	–6 124	–4 870	–4 490	–5 758
Other subsidies on production	-NMCC	–	–	–	–	–	–	–	–	–
Total	-NMRL	–4 512	–5 117	–5 239	–5 260	–5 278	–6 124	–4 870	–4 490	–5 758
Property income, received										
Interest										
from general government	NMYI	4 774	4 606	4 055	3 866	3 767	3 901	4 004	4 060	4 073
from other sectors	NMYJ	4 407	4 042	3 965	4 562	4 846	4 997	4 313	4 133	3 936
Total	NMYL	9 181	8 648	8 020	8 428	8 613	8 898	8 317	8 193	8 009
Distributed income of corporations	NMYM	2 609	2 184	1 518	1 313	1 642	1 565	1 620	2 050	1 594
Property income attributed to insurance policy holders	NMYO	28	29	28	28	32	28	33	36	24
Rent										
from sectors other than general government	NMYQ	662	647	699	658	684	718	717	533	..
Total property income, received										
from general government	NMYS	4 774	4 606	4 055	3 866	3 767	3 901	4 004	4 060	4 073
from other sectors	NMYT	7 706	6 902	6 210	6 561	7 204	7 308	6 683	6 752	5 964
Total	NMYU	12 480	11 508	10 265	10 427	10 971	11 209	10 687	10 812	10 037
Total resources	NMYV	96 140	95 765	97 512	105 082	111 273	118 043	127 888	134 400	141 789
Uses										
Property income, paid										
Interest										
to general government	NMYW	4 774	4 606	4 055	3 866	3 767	3 901	4 004	4 060	4 073
to other sectors	NMYX	18 659	18 737	19 981	22 963	26 305	27 975	29 935	30 547	26 495
Total	NMYY	23 433	23 343	24 036	26 829	30 072	31 876	33 939	34 607	30 568
Balance of primary incomes, gross	NMZH	72 707	72 422	73 476	78 253	81 201	86 167	93 949	99 793	111 221
Total uses	NMYV	96 140	95 765	97 512	105 082	111 273	118 043	127 888	134 400	141 789

Source: Office for National Statistics: 020 7533 6031

15.9 General government
Secondary distribution of income account

£ millions

		1991	1992	1993	1994	1995	1996	1997	1998	1999
Resources										
Balance of primary incomes, gross	NMZH	72 707	72 422	73 476	78 253	81 201	86 167	93 949	99 793	111 221
Current taxes on income, wealth etc.										
Taxes on income	NMZJ	81 428	80 222	78 275	85 344	95 045	99 292	107 389	125 348	129 048
Other current taxes	NVCM	10 496	10 299	10 551	11 140	11 937	12 795	13 820	14 910	16 365
Total	NMZL	91 924	90 521	88 826	96 484	106 982	112 087	121 209	140 258	145 413
Social contributions										
Actual social contributions										
Employers' actual social contributions	NMZM	22 573	23 185	24 615	25 000	26 141	27 580	29 327	31 625	33 213
Employees' social contributions	NMZN	16 029	16 525	17 235	19 649	21 091	21 700	24 121	25 728	26 339
Social contributions by self- and non-employed persons	NMZO	1 206	1 281	1 472	1 469	1 541	1 771	1 848	1 760	1 836
Total	NMZP	39 808	40 991	43 322	46 118	48 773	51 051	55 296	59 113	61 388
Imputed social contributions	NMZQ	4 943	5 426	5 397	5 419	5 279	5 300	5 356	5 728	5 652
Total	NMZR	44 751	46 417	48 719	51 537	54 052	56 351	60 652	64 841	67 040
Other current transfers										
Non-life insurance claims	NMZS	382	408	361	340	377	371	349	363	401
Current transfers within general government	NMZT	48 859	54 527	55 891	57 736	58 587	59 458	59 506	60 421	64 437
Current international cooperation	NMZU	4 616	1 907	2 558	1 752	1 233	2 424	1 739	1 384	3 176
from institutions of the EC	NMEX	2 506	1 898	2 558	1 752	1 233	2 424	1 739	1 384	3 176
Miscellaneous current transfers										
from sectors other than general government	NMZX	353	178	296	420	469	429	476	390	269
Total, other current transfers										
from general government	NMZY	48 859	54 527	55 891	57 736	58 587	59 458	59 506	60 421	64 437
from other sectors	NMZZ	5 351	2 493	3 215	2 512	2 079	3 224	2 564	2 137	3 846
Total	NNAA	54 210	57 020	59 106	60 248	60 666	62 682	62 070	62 558	68 283
Total resources	NNAB	263 592	266 380	270 127	286 522	302 901	317 287	337 880	367 450	391 957
Uses										
Social benefits other than social transfers in kind	NNAD	81 753	94 766	102 585	106 187	109 877	112 568	116 302	116 874	120 187
Other current transfers										
Net non-life insurance premiums	NNAE	382	408	361	340	377	371	349	363	401
Current transfers within general government	NNAF	48 859	54 527	55 891	57 736	58 587	59 458	59 506	60 421	64 437
Current international cooperation	NNAG	1 677	1 931	1 774	1 825	2 018	1 598	1 527	1 503	1 460
to institutions of the EC	NMFA	–	–	2	7	8	8	31	-1	11
Miscellaneous current transfers										
to sectors other than general government	NNAI	4 965	5 096	9 055	10 760	11 369	13 386	14 531	16 586	17 714
GNP based fourth own resource	NMFH	813	914	1 558	2 071	1 826	2 454	2 458	3 920	4 632
Total other current transfers										
to general government	NNAL	48 859	54 527	55 891	57 736	58 587	59 458	59 506	60 421	64 437
to other sectors	NNAM	7 024	7 435	11 190	12 925	13 764	15 355	16 407	18 452	19 575
Total	NNAN	55 883	61 962	67 081	70 661	72 351	74 813	75 913	78 873	84 012
Disposable income, gross	NNAO	125 956	109 652	100 461	109 674	120 673	129 906	145 665	171 703	187 758
Total uses	NNAB	263 592	266 380	270 127	286 522	302 901	317 287	337 880	367 450	391 957

Source: Office for National Statistics: 020 7533 6031

15.10 Households and non-profit institutions serving households
Allocation of primary income account

£ millions

		1991	1992	1993	1994	1995	1996	1997	1998	1999
Resources										
Operating surplus, gross	QWLS	29 162	33 390	35 153	37 510	40 084	41 913	45 094	48 905	54 058
Mixed income, gross	QWLT	31 635	33 872	36 096	38 336	40 239	41 570	41 665	42 811	43 856
Compensation of employees										
Wages and salaries	QWLW	291 905	303 018	310 252	321 545	335 589	351 547	375 643	401 413	426 347
Employers' social contributions	QWLX	41 882	43 969	46 106	48 245	49 512	53 067	56 828	61 621	65 727
Total	QWLY	333 787	346 987	356 358	369 790	385 101	404 614	432 471	463 034	492 074
Property income										
Interest	QWLZ	36 922	33 122	23 802	22 339	26 043	23 681	26 043	30 021	25 003
Distributed income of corporations	QWMA	26 705	27 641	27 572	29 222	34 607	35 882	38 467	39 172	41 515
Attributed property income of insurance policy holders	QWMC	33 782	34 765	35 267	37 001	42 078	47 564	51 800	55 414	56 667
Rent	QWMD	98	99	95	96	99	103	104	103	106
Total	QWME	97 507	95 627	86 736	88 658	102 827	107 230	116 414	124 710	123 291
Total resources	QWMF	492 091	509 876	514 343	534 294	568 251	595 327	635 644	679 460	713 279
Uses										
Property income										
Interest	QWMG	49 861	45 796	36 253	36 985	39 887	38 376	42 045	51 441	47 605
Rent	QWMH	200	200	194	197	201	211	217	216	219
Total	QWMI	50 061	45 996	36 447	37 182	40 088	38 587	42 262	51 657	47 824
Balance of primary incomes, gross	QWMJ	442 030	463 880	477 896	497 112	528 163	556 740	593 382	627 803	665 455
Total uses	QWMF	492 091	509 876	514 343	534 294	568 251	595 327	635 644	679 460	713 279

Source: Office for National Statistics: 020 7533 6031

15.11 Households and non-profit institutions serving households
Secondary distribution of income account

£ millions

		1991	1992	1993	1994	1995	1996	1997	1998	1999
Resources										
Balance of primary incomes, gross	QWMJ	442 030	463 880	477 896	497 112	528 163	556 740	593 382	627 803	665 455
Imputed social contributions	RVFH	288	360	412	491	448	383	427	394	402
Social benefits other than social transfers in kind	QWML	109 677	126 932	136 370	143 303	149 234	156 429	165 245	170 389	175 176
Other current transfers										
Non-life insurance claims	QWMM	10 976	11 690	10 313	9 739	10 785	16 203	10 259	10 461	11 491
Miscellaneous current transfers	QWMN	11 254	11 248	15 481	17 013	17 722	20 060	20 478	21 146	21 901
Total	QWMO	22 230	22 938	25 794	26 752	28 507	36 263	30 737	31 607	33 392
Total resources	QWMP	574 225	614 110	640 472	667 658	706 352	749 815	789 791	830 193	874 425
Uses										
Current taxes on income, wealth etc										
Taxes on income	QWMQ	66 109	68 063	65 316	69 507	74 288	74 938	74 958	90 556	95 069
Other current taxes	NVCO	10 496	10 299	10 551	11 140	11 937	12 795	13 820	14 910	16 365
Total	QWMS	76 605	78 362	75 867	80 647	86 225	87 733	88 778	105 466	111 434
Social contributions										
Actual social contributions										
Employers' actual social contributions	QWMT	33 909	34 867	36 795	38 233	40 158	44 161	47 711	52 172	55 601
Employees' social contributions	QWMU	45 005	46 477	45 415	49 615	53 747	59 900	66 802	71 222	73 110
Social contributions by self and non-employed	QWMV	1 206	1 281	1 472	1 469	1 541	1 771	1 848	1 760	1 836
Total	QWMW	80 120	82 625	83 682	89 317	95 446	105 832	116 361	125 154	130 547
Imputed social contributions	QWMX	7 973	9 102	9 311	10 012	9 354	8 906	8 911	9 449	9 626
Total	QWMY	88 093	91 727	92 993	99 329	104 800	114 738	125 272	134 603	140 173
Social benefits other than social transfers in kind	QWMZ	560	691	871	946	918	853	897	866	874
Other current transfers										
Net non-life insurance premiums	QWNA	10 976	11 690	10 313	9 739	10 785	16 203	10 259	10 461	11 491
Miscellaneous current transfers	QWNB	6 675	6 802	7 618	8 114	8 287	8 199	9 067	9 301	9 494
Total	QWNC	17 651	18 492	17 931	17 853	19 072	24 402	19 326	19 762	20 985
Disposable income, gross	QWND	391 316	424 838	452 810	468 883	495 337	522 089	555 518	569 496	600 959
Total uses	QWMP	574 225	614 110	640 472	667 658	706 352	749 815	789 791	830 193	874 425
Read households' disposable income, at 1995 prices	RVGK	446 102	462 638	476 613	482 708	495 337	506 145	525 321	525 807	544 140

Source: Office for National Statistics: 020 7533 6031

15.12 Households and non-profit institutions serving households
Use of disposable income account

£ millions

		1991	1992	1993	1994	1995	1996	1997	1998	1999
Resources										
Disposable income, gross	QWND	391 316	424 838	452 810	468 883	495 337	522 089	555 518	569 496	600 959
Adjustment for the change in net equity of households in pension funds	NSSE	15 596	13 265	10 742	10 577	11 690	14 824	15 692	16 369	17 721
Total resources	NSSF	406 912	438 103	463 552	479 460	507 027	536 913	571 210	585 865	618 680
Uses										
Final consumption expenditure										
Individual consumption expenditure	NSSG	368 881	387 953	413 089	434 549	454 934	486 226	517 909	551 823	586 906
Saving, gross	NSSH	38 031	50 150	50 463	44 911	52 093	50 687	53 301	34 042	31 774
Total uses	NSSF	406 912	438 103	463 552	479 460	507 027	536 913	571 210	585 865	618 680
Saving ratio (per cent)	RVGL	9.4	11.5	11.0	9.4	10.3	9.5	9.3	5.8	5.1

Source: Office for National Statistics: 020 7533 6031

15.13 Summary capital accounts and net lending/net borrowing

£ millions

		1991	1992	1993	1994	1995	1996	1997	1998	1999
Non-financial corporations										
Gross saving[1]	RPJV	45 850	47 111	62 014	74 870	71 810	81 354	82 843	90 732	81 044
Capital transfers (net receipts)	GZQW	3 519	3 317	3 187	3 275	4 882	3 599	2 459	1 505	1 660
Gross capital formation[2]	RQBZ	53 430	52 474	55 434	60 357	68 514	74 481	85 293	93 283	95 572
Net acquisition of non-financial assets	RQAX	−39	41	254	214	301	117	195	723	726
Financial corporations										
Gross saving[1]	RPPS	3 196	10 593	9 407	16 695	13 534	11 474	11 803	11 229	7 384
Capital transfers (net receipts)	GZQE	–	–	−88	−518	–	–	–	–	–
Gross capital formation[2]	RPYP	6 249	4 969	3 748	5 566	4 984	5 212	5 087	9 411	7 773
Net acquisition of non-financial assets	RPYO	−8	−49	−203	86	−77	−1	−39	−4	26
General Government										
Gross saving[1]	RPQC	4 216	−19 559	−30 952	−26 700	−20 402	−16 854	−2 744	16 936	23 980
Capital transfers (net receipts)	GZQU	−6 702	−6 170	−6 985	−5 929	−7 097	−5 040	−3 910	−3 229	−3 580
Gross capital formation[2]	RPZF	14 213	14 227	13 698	13 807	13 851	11 482	10 012	10 585	9 918
Net acquisition of non-financial assets	RPZE	−396	−312	−497	−485	−143	−467	−372	−688	−696
Households & NPISH										
Gross saving[1]	RPQL	38 031	50 150	50 463	44 911	52 093	50 687	53 301	34 042	31 774
Capital transfers (net receipts)	GZQI	3 473	3 274	4 195	3 205	2 749	2 163	2 289	2 245	2 716
Gross capital formation[2]	RPZV	21 304	21 024	23 377	26 190	27 813	31 029	33 536	35 225	39 284
Net acquisition of non-financial assets	RPZU	443	320	446	185	−81	337	250	17	−36
Net lending(+)/net borrowing(-)[3]										
Non-financial corporations	RQAW	−8 493	−7 770	4 220	12 260	2 259	5 298	−4 839	−6 284	−17 819
Financial corporations	RPYN	−3 045	5 673	5 774	10 525	8 627	6 263	6 755	1 822	−415
General government	RPZD	−16 303	−39 644	−51 138	−45 951	−41 207	−32 909	−16 294	3 810	11 178
Households sector	RPZT	19 757	32 080	30 835	21 741	27 110	21 484	21 804	1 045	−4 758
Rest of the world[4]	RQCH	8 084	9 661	10 309	1 425	3 211	−136	−7 427	−393	10 205
Statistical Discrepancy[5]	RVFE	–	–	–	–	–	–	–	–	1 652

1 Before providing for depreciation, inventory holding gains.
2 Comprises gross fixed capital formation and changes in inventories and acquisitions less disposals of valuables.
3 This balance is equal to gross saving *plus* capital transfers *less* gross fixed capital formation, *less* Net acquisition of non-financial assets, *less* changes in inventories.
4 Equals, the current balance of payments accounts, *plus* capital transfers.
5 Series is only available annually.

Source: Office for National Statistics: 020 7533 6031

15.14 Household final consumption expenditure: classified by commodity
At current market prices

£ millions

		1991	1992	1993	1994	1995	1996	1997	1998	1999
Durable goods:										
Cars, motorcycles and other vehicles	CCDT	16 977	16 470	18 063	19 778	20 749	23 467	26 731	27 956	27 649
Other durable goods	ABZB	15 890	17 044	17 311	18 102	18 747	20 212	23 194	25 283	27 218
Total durable goods	AEIT	32 867	33 514	35 374	37 880	39 496	43 679	49 925	53 239	54 867
Non-Durable Goods:										
Food (household expenditure)	CCDW	44 044	45 193	46 334	47 122	49 274	52 513	53 188	53 789	54 862
Alchohol and tobacco	CDFH	32 680	33 553	34 865	36 624	37 456	39 618	40 858	41 938	44 611
Clothing and footwear	CDDE	22 209	23 404	24 777	26 893	28 347	29 564	31 115	32 376	33 530
Energy products	CCEC	24 955	25 399	26 136	26 857	27 118	28 822	28 593	27 998	28 861
Other goods	ABZN	42 171	44 461	46 738	48 935	51 947	57 094	61 921	67 533	72 867
Total non-durable goods	ABZR	166 059	172 010	178 850	186 431	194 142	207 611	215 675	223 634	234 731
Services:										
Rental and water charges	ABRG	42 411	48 637	52 405	56 297	59 798	62 197	66 421	70 792	77 916
Catering	CDEY	30 671	32 287	35 154	36 459	37 727	40 786	42 652	46 277	48 708
Transport and communication	ABOZ	32 843	34 610	37 840	39 603	41 360	43 211	46 247	50 246	54 390
Financial services	CEGK	14 549	14 801	16 316	16 226	16 784	18 958	21 461	23 847	25 917
Other services	AEJC	37 571	39 759	42 026	44 391	48 602	50 958	54 981	60 676	63 739
Total services	AELL	158 045	170 094	183 741	192 976	204 271	216 110	231 762	251 838	270 670
Total household final expenditure in the UK by resident and non-resident households (domestic concept)	ABQI	356 971	375 618	397 965	417 287	437 909	467 400	497 362	528 711	560 268
Final consumption expenditure outside the UK by UK resident households	ABTA	9 385	10 605	11 890	13 096	13 768	14 433	14 945	16 669	18 648
Less Final consumption expenditure in the UK by households resident in the rest of the world	CDFD	−8 571	−9 076	−10 747	−11 121	−13 224	−13 992	−14 000	−14 529	−14 547
Final consumption expenditure by UK resident households in the UK and abroad (national concept)	ABPB	357 785	377 147	399 108	419 262	438 453	467 841	498 307	530 851	564 369

Data for all series in this table are available in *Consumer Trends* or on the ONS Databank. Some of these quarterly data are published regularly in *UK Economic Accounts* in table A7.

Source: Office for National Statistics: 020 7533 6031

15.15 Household final consumption expenditure: classified by commodity
At 1995 market prices

£ millions

		1991	1992	1993	1994	1995	1996	1997	1998	1999
Durable goods:										
Cars, motorcycles and other vehicles	CCBJ	18 598	17 397	19 016	20 334	20 749	22 673	24 680	25 595	25 541
Other durable goods	ABZD	15 894	16 980	17 196	18 249	18 747	20 028	23 273	26 202	29 775
Total durable goods	AEIV	34 436	34 474	36 221	38 583	39 496	42 701	47 953	51 797	55 316
Non-Durable Goods:										
Food (household expenditure)	CCBM	47 114	47 664	48 282	48 931	49 274	50 931	51 786	51 627	52 277
Alchohol and tobacco	FCCA	40 258	38 415	37 861	38 441	37 456	38 007	37 533	36 467	36 788
Clothing and footwear	FCCB	22 502	23 683	24 875	26 928	28 347	29 773	31 076	32 544	34 662
Energy products	CCBS	28 281	27 961	28 123	27 754	27 118	28 210	27 427	27 106	26 982
Other goods	ABZP	47 567	47 817	49 035	50 119	51 947	55 419	59 165	63 419	68 501
Total non-durable goods	ABZT	184 760	185 041	187 926	192 173	194 142	202 340	206 987	211 163	219 210
Services:										
Rental and water charges	ABRI	56 743	57 191	58 015	58 862	59 798	60 344	60 934	61 555	62 633
Catering	CCHS	36 806	36 279	37 539	37 319	37 727	39 704	40 399	42 609	43 466
Transport and communication	ABPD	35 121	35 704	38 473	40 011	41 360	42 188	43 387	45 865	49 803
Financial services	CEGM	16 477	16 202	17 168	16 397	16 784	18 034	19 516	20 191	21 362
Other services	AEJZ	44 808	44 736	45 183	46 008	48 602	48 863	50 371	52 725	52 499
Total services	AELN	189 592	189 729	196 363	198 597	204 271	209 133	214 607	222 945	229 763
Total household final expenditure in the UK by resident and non-resident households (domestic concept)	ABQJ	407 322	408 208	419 536	429 353	437 909	454 174	469 547	485 905	504 289
Final consumption expenditure outside the UK by UK resident households	ABTC	11 081	11 953	12 093	13 525	13 768	14 125	16 357	18 739	21 531
Less Final consumption expenditure in the UK by households resident in the rest of the world	CCHX	−10 031	−10 086	−11 524	−11 416	−13 224	−13 613	−13 203	−13 266	−12 956
Final consumption expenditure by UK resident households in the UK and abroad (national concept)	ABPF	408 309	410 026	420 081	431 462	438 453	454 686	472 701	491 378	512 864

Data for all series in this table are available in *Consumer Trends* or on the ONS Databank. Some of these quarterly data are published regularly in *UK Economic Accounts* in table A7.

Source: Office for National Statistics: 020 7533 6031

15.16 Individual consumption expenditure at current market prices by households, NPISHs[1] and general government

Classified by function (COICOP/COPNI/COFOG)[1]

£ millions

		1991	1992	1993	1994	1995	1996	1997	1998	1999
FINAL CONSUMPTION EXPENDITURE OF HOUSEHOLDS										
Food and non-alcoholic beverages	ABZV	44 044	45 193	46 334	47 122	49 274	52 513	53 188	53 789	54 862
Food	ABZW	39 363	40 465	41 630	42 392	44 049	47 034	47 631	47 942	48 506
Non-alcoholic beverages	ADFK	4 681	4 728	4 704	4 730	5 225	5 479	5 557	5 847	6 356
Alcoholic beverages and tobacco	ADFL	32 680	33 553	34 865	36 624	37 456	39 618	40 858	41 938	44 611
Alcoholic beverages	ADFM	23 032	23 481	24 399	25 616	26 039	27 774	29 109	30 145	32 567
Tobacco	ADFN	9 648	10 072	10 466	11 008	11 417	11 844	11 749	11 793	12 044
Clothing and footwear	ADFP	22 977	24 165	25 511	27 625	29 140	30 370	31 978	33 350	34 601
Clothing	ADFQ	19 199	20 137	21 379	23 228	24 687	25 895	27 286	28 711	29 962
Footwear	ADFR	3 778	4 028	4 132	4 397	4 453	4 475	4 692	4 639	4 639
Housing, water, electricity, gas and other fuels	ADFS	65 270	71 951	75 651	79 772	83 473	87 440	91 855	96 321	103 887
Actual rentals for housing	ADFT	12 829	15 155	17 122	18 238	18 925	19 703	20 706	21 677	23 822
Imputed rentals for housing	ADFU	26 608	30 182	31 646	34 045	36 629	37 969	40 994	44 206	48 972
Maintenance and repair of the dwelling	ADFV	8 114	8 329	7 939	7 834	7 744	8 297	9 628	10 736	11 355
Water supply and miscellaneous dwelling services	ADFW	3 522	3 905	4 326	4 770	5 058	5 397	5 648	5 904	6 111
Electricity, gas and other fuels	ADFX	14 197	14 380	14 618	14 885	15 117	16 074	14 879	13 798	13 627
Furnishings, household equipment and routine maintenance of the house	ADFY	20 945	22 338	23 393	24 758	25 767	28 032	30 881	32 953	34 781
Furniture, furnishings, carpets and other floor coverings	ADFZ	6 667	7 281	7 771	8 589	9 109	10 286	11 603	12 305	12 933
Household textiles	ADGG	2 306	2 321	2 629	2 656	2 825	3 239	3 419	3 745	3 913
Household appliances	ADGL	5 396	5 642	5 387	5 487	5 603	5 905	6 656	7 089	7 514
Glassware, tableware and household utensils	ADGM	511	540	598	643	644	673	731	786	838
Tools and equipment for house and garden	ADGN	1 154	1 213	1 247	1 302	1 317	1 380	1 525	1 637	1 741
Goods and services for routine household maintenance	ADGO	4 911	5 341	5 761	6 081	6 269	6 549	6 947	7 391	7 842
Health	ADGP	4 232	4 669	4 774	5 298	5 463	5 881	5 906	6 478	6 919
Medical products, appliances and equipment	ADGQ	2 560	3 035	3 213	3 651	3 698	4 070	4 190	4 471	4 879
Out-patient services	ADGR	1 436	1 398	1 336	1 411	1 514	1 556	1 466	1 723	1 750
Hospital services	ADGS	236	236	225	236	251	255	250	284	290
Transport	ADGT	52 083	53 148	56 811	59 788	62 224	66 851	74 047	78 195	80 884
Purchase of vehicles	ADGU	19 754	19 509	21 024	22 551	23 192	25 621	28 722	29 403	28 536
Operation of personal transport equipment	ADGV	20 560	21 109	22 325	23 270	23 972	25 085	27 639	29 344	31 245
Transport services	ADGW	11 769	12 530	13 462	13 967	15 060	16 145	17 686	19 448	21 103
Communications										
Communications	ADGX	7 041	7 332	7 831	8 594	9 092	9 432	9 918	10 859	12 297
Recreation and culture	ADGY	36 739	38 145	40 409	41 750	45 236	48 247	53 334	60 072	65 467
Audio-visual, photographic and information processing equipment	ADGZ	6 606	6 970	7 179	6 966	7 479	7 662	9 032	10 519	11 534
Other major durables for recreation and culture	ADHL	2 381	2 093	2 309	2 532	2 850	3 279	3 697	4 636	5 611
Other recreational items and equipment; flowers, garden and pets	ADHZ	7 195	7 839	8 164	8 705	9 232	10 094	11 582	13 114	14 860
Recreational and cultural services	ADIA	12 780	13 176	13 756	14 614	16 683	17 380	18 683	20 731	21 697
Newspapers, books and stationery	ADIC	7 178	7 435	8 313	8 220	8 250	9 028	9 499	10 159	10 804
Package holidays	ADID	599	632	688	713	742	804	841	913	961
Education										
Educational services	ADIE	4 028	4 788	5 186	5 677	6 392	6 984	7 734	8 205	8 723
Restaurants and hotels	ADIF	24 671	25 475	28 113	29 450	31 196	34 344	36 254	39 919	42 303
Catering services	ADIG	19 377	19 127	21 239	22 303	23 432	26 315	28 296	31 678	33 929
Accommodation services	ADIH	5 294	6 348	6 874	7 147	7 764	8 029	7 958	8 241	8 374
Miscellaneous goods and services	ADII	42 261	44 861	49 087	50 829	53 196	57 688	61 409	66 632	70 933
Personal care	ADIJ	7 497	7 798	8 258	8 970	9 812	11 269	11 707	12 547	13 067
Personal effects n.e.c.	ADIK	4 453	4 491	4 769	5 053	5 992	6 284	6 511	7 011	7 342
Social protection	ADIL	6 462	7 303	7 550	7 631	7 343	7 389	7 498	7 717	7 982
Insurance	ADIM	14 649	15 442	17 410	17 273	16 834	17 613	18 839	20 472	20 917
Financial services n.e.c.	ADIN	4 540	4 948	5 864	6 168	6 677	7 895	8 972	9 832	11 584
Other services n.e.c.	ADIO	4 660	4 879	5 236	5 734	6 538	7 238	7 882	9 053	10 041
Final consumption expenditure in the UK by resident and non-resident households (domestic concept)	ABQI	356 971	375 618	397 965	417 287	437 909	467 400	497 362	528 711	560 268
Final consumption expenditure outside the UK by UK resident households	ABTA	9 385	10 605	11 890	13 096	13 768	14 433	14 945	16 669	18 648
less Final consumption expenditure in the UK by households resident in the rest of the world	CDFD	−8 571	−9 076	−10 747	−11 121	−13 224	−13 992	−14 000	−14 529	−14 547
Final consumption expenditure by UK resident Households in the UK and abroad(national concept)	ABPB	357 785	377 147	399 108	419 262	438 453	467 841	498 307	530 851	564 369

1 Non-profit institutions serving households.

Source: Office for National Statistics: 020 7533 6031

15.16
Individual consumption expenditure at current market prices by households, NPISHs[1] and general government

continued

Classified by function (COICOP/COPNI/COFOG)[1]

£ millions

		1991	1992	1993	1994	1995	1996	1997	1998	1999
CONSUMPTION EXPENDITURE OF UK RESIDENT HOUSEHOLDS										
Final consumption expenditure of UK resident households in the UK and abroad	ABPB	357 785	377 147	399 108	419 262	438 453	467 841	498 307	530 851	564 369
FINAL INDIVIDUAL CONSUMPTION EXPENDITURE OF NPISH										
Final individual consumption expenditure of NPISH	ABNV	11 096	10 806	13 981	15 287	16 481	18 385	19 602	20 972	22 537
FINAL INDIVIDUAL CONSUMPTION EXPENDITURE OF OF GENERAL GOVERNMENT										
Health	QYOT	29 583	33 263	35 518	37 356	39 018	41 498	42 683	45 730	48 647
Recreation and culture	QYSU	3 200	3 411	3 590	3 304	3 229	3 227	3 273	3 508	2 585
Education	QYSE	23 926	25 710	23 659	24 185	25 406	25 474	26 532	26 991	29 198
Social protection	QYSP	9 707	10 710	12 162	12 632	14 644	15 428	15 915	15 850	16 233
Housing	QYXO	–	–	–	–	–	–	–	–	–
Final individual consumption expenditure of of general government	NNAQ	66 524	73 205	75 000	77 512	82 311	85 638	88 451	92 079	96 663
Total, individual consumption expenditure/	NQEO	435 405	461 158	488 089	512 061	537 245	571 864	606 360	643 902	683 569
actual individual consumption	ABRE	435 405	461 158	488 089	512 061	537 245	571 864	606 360	643 902	683 569

1 "Purpose" or "function" classifications are designed to indicate the "socio-economic objectives" that institutional units aim to achieve through various kinds of outlays. COICOP is the Classification of Industrial Consumption by Purpose and applies to households. COPNI is the Classification of the Purposes of Non-profit Institutions Serving Households and COFOG the Classification of the Functions of Government. The introduction of ESA95 coincides with the redefinition of these classifications and data will be available on a consistent basis for all European Union member states.

Source: Office for National Statistics: 020 7533 6031

15.17 Individual consumption expenditure at 1995 market prices by households, NPISHs[1] and general government

Classified by function (COICOP/COPNI/COFOG)[1]

£ millions at 1995 prices

		1991	1992	1993	1994	1995	1996	1997	1998	1999
FINAL CONSUMPTION EXPENDITURE OF HOUSEHOLDS										
Food and non-alcoholic beverages	ADIP	47 114	47 664	48 282	48 931	49 274	50 931	51 786	51 627	52 277
Food	ADIQ	42 401	43 024	43 542	44 010	44 049	45 687	46 565	46 305	46 705
Non-alcoholic beverages	ADIR	4 714	4 650	4 749	4 921	5 225	5 244	5 221	5 322	5 572
Alcoholic beverages and tobacco	ADIS	40 258	38 415	37 861	38 441	37 456	38 007	37 533	36 467	36 788
Alcoholic beverages	ADIT	27 088	25 956	25 967	26 689	26 039	26 906	27 278	26 994	28 107
Tobacco	ADIU	13 342	12 603	11 959	11 752	11 417	11 101	10 255	9 473	8 681
Clothing and footwear	ADIW	23 359	24 508	25 645	27 686	29 141	30 555	31 885	33 414	35 578
Clothing	ADIX	19 451	20 348	21 461	23 267	24 688	25 997	26 979	28 475	30 570
Footwear	ADIY	3 918	4 171	4 189	4 419	4 453	4 558	4 906	4 939	5 008
Housing, water, electricity, gas and other fuels	ADIZ	82 003	81 951	82 700	82 955	83 470	85 190	86 178	87 365	88 859
Actual rentals for housing	ADJA	17 366	17 987	18 672	18 876	18 925	19 069	18 871	18 986	19 280
Imputed rentals for housing	ADJB	35 234	35 093	35 211	35 724	36 629	37 027	37 772	38 342	39 138
Maintenance and repair of the dwelling	ADJC	8 936	8 767	8 203	8 006	7 743	8 038	9 065	9 861	10 380
Water supply and miscellaneous dwelling services	ADJD	4 707	4 735	4 856	5 038	5 056	5 090	5 155	5 106	5 052
Electricity, gas and other fuels	ADJE	15 381	15 129	15 598	15 311	15 117	15 966	15 315	15 070	15 009
Furnishings, household equipment and routine maintenance of the house	ADJF	22 430	23 246	24 049	25 374	25 766	27 298	29 808	31 428	33 075
Furniture, furnishings, carpets and other floor coverings	ADJG	7 331	7 759	8 203	9 005	9 109	9 797	10 794	11 250	11 726
Household textiles	ADJH	2 305	2 349	2 692	2 695	2 825	3 170	3 333	3 621	3 800
Household appliances	ADJI	5 440	5 599	5 306	5 494	5 603	5 929	6 791	7 290	7 873
Glassware, tableware and household utensils	ADJJ	548	564	617	656	645	660	708	755	807
Tools and equipment for house and garden	ADJK	1 209	1 240	1 260	1 318	1 316	1 367	1 514	1 622	1 743
Goods and services for routine household maintenance	ADJL	5 555	5 694	5 944	6 206	6 268	6 375	6 668	6 890	7 126
Health	ADJM	4 918	5 089	5 069	5 387	5 462	5 671	5 497	5 751	5 922
Medical products, appliances and equipment	ADJN	2 928	3 248	3 366	3 684	3 698	3 907	3 901	3 990	4 201
Out-patient services	ADJO	1 717	1 579	1 457	1 458	1 515	1 515	1 366	1 516	1 479
Hospital services	ADJP	293	271	250	245	249	249	230	245	242
Transport	ADJQ	58 411	57 501	60 050	61 626	62 211	64 480	67 295	69 128	70 655
Purchase of vehicles	ADJR	21 537	20 456	22 076	23 106	23 179	24 780	26 638	27 336	27 179
Operation of personal transport equipment	ADJS	24 519	23 968	23 896	24 066	23 972	24 025	24 760	25 275	25 513
Transport services	ADJT	12 534	13 241	14 128	14 454	15 060	15 675	15 897	16 517	17 963
Communications										
Communications	ADJU	6 663	6 757	7 141	8 155	9 092	9 599	10 369	11 639	13 553
Recreation and culture	ADJV	40 229	40 347	41 709	42 602	45 250	46 972	51 335	57 296	63 095
Audio-visual, photographic and information processing equipment	ADJW	6 208	6 622	6 825	6 803	7 480	7 769	9 454	11 655	14 139
Other major durables for recreation and culture	ADJX	2 557	2 210	2 380	2 595	2 863	3 202	3 532	4 249	5 119
Other recreational items and equipment; flowers, gardens and pets	ADJY	7 704	8 146	8 373	8 844	9 232	9 907	11 218	12 720	14 752
Recreational and cultural services	ADJZ	14 877	14 507	14 649	15 029	16 683	16 784	17 553	18 738	18 875
Newspapers, books and stationery	ADKM	8 297	8 152	8 743	8 601	8 250	8 529	8 783	9 093	9 352
Package holidays	ADMI	719	708	733	730	742	781	795	841	858
Education										
Educational services	ADMJ	5 309	5 731	5 855	6 205	6 392	6 398	6 490	6 480	6 517
Restaurants and Hotels	ADMK	29 521	28 697	30 043	30 013	31 196	33 356	34 119	36 415	37 338
Catering services	ADML	23 575	21 886	23 077	23 219	23 432	25 290	26 206	28 223	29 104
Accommodation services	ADMM	5 984	6 795	6 958	6 794	7 764	8 066	7 913	8 192	8 234
Miscellaneous goods and services	ADMN	48 761	49 389	51 818	51 978	53 199	55 717	57 252	58 895	60 632
Personal care	ADMO	8 843	8 718	8 912	9 453	9 811	10 781	10 744	10 881	11 014
Personal effects n.e.c.	ADMP	4 891	4 807	4 902	5 081	5 992	6 232	6 448	6 933	7 342
Social protection	ADMQ	7 858	8 193	8 059	7 956	7 342	7 245	7 318	7 357	7 337
Insurance	ADMR	15 901	16 053	17 754	17 259	16 835	17 298	17 272	17 778	17 302
Financial services n.e.c.	ADMS	5 650	5 945	6 483	6 297	6 677	7 201	8 002	7 892	9 319
Other services n.e.c.	ADMT	5 625	5 715	5 674	5 932	6 542	6 960	7 468	8 054	8 318
Final consumption expenditure in the UK by resident and non-resident households (domestic concept)	ABQJ	407 322	408 208	419 536	429 353	437 909	454 174	469 547	485 905	504 289
Final consumption expenditure outside the UK by UK resident households	ABTC	11 081	11 953	12 093	13 525	13 768	14 125	16 357	18 739	21 531
less Final consumption expenditure in the UK by households resident in the rest of the world	CCHX	−10 031	−10 086	−11 524	−11 416	−13 224	−13 613	−13 203	−13 266	−12 956
Final consumption expenditure by UK resident households in the UK and abroad (national concept)	ABPF	408 309	410 026	420 081	431 462	438 453	454 686	472 701	491 378	512 864

1 Non-profit institutions serving households.

Source: Office for National Statistics: 020 7533 6031

15.17

Individual consumption expenditure at 1995 market prices by households, NPISHs[1] and general government

continued

Classified by function (COICOP/COPNI/COFOG)[1]

£ millions at 1995 prices

		1991	1992	1993	1994	1995	1996	1997	1998	1999
CONSUMPTION EXPENDITURE OF UK RESIDENT HOUSEHOLDS										
Final consumption expenditure of UK resident households in the UK and abroad	ABPF	408 309	410 026	420 081	431 462	438 453	454 686	472 701	491 378	512 864
FINAL INDIVIDUAL CONSUMPTION EXPENDITURE OF NPISH										
Final individual consumption expenditure of NPISH	ABNU	12 217	12 445	14 723	15 900	16 481	16 691	17 055	18 112	18 552
FINAL INDIVIDUAL CONSUMPTION EXPENDITURE OF GENERAL GOVERNMENT										
Health	QYXJ	33 716	34 980	36 544	37 573	39 032	40 100	41 003	42 601	44 015
Recreation and culture	QYXK	3 614	3 732	4 404	3 353	3 229	3 147	3 157	3 242	2 337
Education	QYXL	26 246	26 751	25 316	25 099	25 406	25 682	25 928	26 046	26 274
Social protection	QYXM	11 566	11 974	12 735	13 338	14 644	15 432	15 730	15 143	15 055
Housing	QYXO	–	–	–	–	–	–	–	–	–
Final individual consumption expenditure of general government	NSZK	75 142	77 437	78 999	79 363	82 311	84 361	85 818	87 032	87 681
Total, individual consumption expenditure/ actual individual consumption	YBIO	495 220	499 495	513 691	526 725	537 245	555 738	575 574	596 522	619 097

Source: Office for National Statistics: 020 7533 6031

1 "Purpose" or "function" classifications are designed to indicate the "socio-economic objectives" that institutional units aim to achieve through various kinds of outlays. COICOP is the Classification of Industrial Consumption by Purpose and applies to households. COPNI is the Classification of the Purposes of Non-profit Institutions Serving Households and COFOG the Classification of the Functions of Government. The introduction of ESA95 coincides with the redefinition of these classifications and data will be available on a consistent basis for all European Union member states.

15.18

Change in inventories at constant 1995 prices[1,2]

£ millions

		1991	1992	1993	1994	1995	1996	1997	1998	1999
Mining and quarrying	FADO	170	66	−45	−267	−123	−47	55	257	−191
Manufacturing industries										
Materials and fuel	FBID	−861	−211	20	433	514	−105	403	721	170
Work in progress	FBIE	−1 358	−1 124	−981	639	1 144	−217	−1 332	−588	−236
Finished goods	FBIF	−1 346	−47	−320	548	998	6	340	367	−1 103
Total	DHBH	−3 565	−1 382	−1 281	1 102	2 656	−316	−589	500	−1 169
Electricity, gas and water supply	FADP	200	−100	−270	−661	−205	15	103	−154	−180
Distributive trades										
Wholesale[3]	FAJM	−612	117	802	1 332	597	681	1 499	−16	−686
Retail[3]	FBYH	−404	216	368	884	811	638	799	987	674
Other industries[4]	DLWV	−420	−616	738	2 451	776	859	1 895	2 655	166
Change in inventories	ABMQ	−5 349	−1 962	360	4 836	4 512	1 830	3 762	4 229	−1 386

Source: Office for National Statistics: 020 7533 6031

1 Estimates are given to the nearest £ million but cannot be regarded as accurate to this degree.
2 Components may not sum to totals due to rounding.
3 Wholesaling and retailing estimates exclude the motor trades.
4 Quarterly alignment adjustment included in this series. For description see notes.

15.19 Gross fixed capital formation at current purchasers' prices
Analysis by broad sector and type of asset
Total economy

£ millions

		1991	1992	1993	1994	1995	1996	1997	1998	1999
Private sector										
New dwellings, excluding land	EQBT	15 577	16 246	17 124	18 285	18 784	20 467	22 018	24 001	25 996
Other buildings and structures	EQBU	21 347	18 378	15 743	16 213	17 841	20 408	24 352	26 973	31 100
Transport equipment	EQBV	7 574	6 972	8 357	10 049	10 021	11 279	12 283	15 054	16 387
Other machinery and equipment and cultivated assets	EQBW	32 387	31 553	32 616	34 968	41 532	46 606	49 980	55 889	57 302
Intangible fixed assets	EQBX	3 591	3 290	3 122	2 982	3 179	3 278	3 395	3 555	3 431
Costs associated with the transfer of ownership of non-produced assets	EQBY	5 729	3 926	5 089	5 208	5 222	7 065	7 599	7 821	9 612
Total	EQBZ	86 205	80 365	82 051	87 705	96 579	109 103	119 627	133 293	143 828
Public non-financial corporations										
New dwellings, excluding land	DEER	153	172	150	139	162	151	123	114	114
Other buildings and structures	DEES	3 015	3 332	3 416	3 492	3 781	3 397	2 675	2 691	2 489
Transport equipment	DEEP	383	678	516	512	354	225	191	157	150
Other machinery and equipment and cultivated assets	DEEQ	442	873	720	761	857	765	756	718	826
Intangible fixed assets	DLXJ	252	256	279	374	496	585	595	605	615
Costs associated with the transfer of ownership of non-produced assets	DLXQ	168	358	376	349	126	133	314	15	164
Total	FCCJ	4 413	5 669	5 457	5 627	5 776	5 256	4 654	4 300	4 358
General government										
New dwellings, excluding land	DFHW	2 609	2 407	2 618	2 809	2 642	2 148	1 786	1 716	1 489
Other buildings and structures	EQCH	10 010	9 928	9 940	10 010	9 997	9 193	7 920	8 030	8 107
Transport equipment	EQCI	711	747	721	768	680	659	689	717	760
Other machinery and equipment and cultivated assets	EQCJ	2 246	2 264	2 230	1 964	2 075	1 845	1 493	1 380	1 436
Intangible fixed assets	EQCK	220	236	247	257	264	273	259	387	424
Costs associated with the transfer of ownership of non-produced assets	EQCL	−1 734	−1 338	−2 034	−1 750	−1 653	−2 802	−2 275	−1 752	−2 030
Total	NNBF	14 062	14 244	13 722	14 058	14 005	11 316	9 872	10 478	10 186
Total gross fixed capital formation	NPQX	104 680	100 278	101 230	107 390	116 360	125 675	134 153	148 071	158 372

Source: Office for National Statistics: 020 7533 6031

15.20 Gross fixed capital formation at current purchasers' prices
Analysis by type of asset
Total economy

£ millions

		1991	1992	1993	1994	1995	1996	1997	1998	1999
Tangible fixed assets										
New dwellings, excluding land	DFDK	18 339	18 825	19 892	21 233	21 588	22 766	23 927	25 831	27 599
Other buildings and structures	DLWS	34 372	31 638	29 099	29 715	31 619	32 998	34 947	37 694	41 696
Transport equipment	DLWZ	8 668	8 397	9 594	11 329	11 055	12 163	13 186	15 928	17 297
Other machinery and equipment and cultivated assets	DLXI	35 075	34 690	35 566	37 693	44 464	49 216	52 206	57 987	59 564
Total	EQCQ	96 454	93 550	94 151	99 970	108 726	117 143	124 266	137 440	146 156
Intangible fixed assets	DLXP	4 063	3 782	3 648	3 613	3 939	4 136	4 249	4 547	4 470
Costs associated with the transfer of ownership of non-produced assets	DFBH	4 163	2 946	3 431	3 807	3 695	4 396	5 638	6 084	7 746
Total gross fixed capital formation	NPQX	104 680	100 278	101 230	107 390	116 360	125 675	134 153	148 071	158 372

Source: Office for National Statistics: 020 7533 6031

15.21 Gross fixed capital formation at 1995 purchasers' prices[1]
Analysis by broad sector and type of asset

Total economy
£ millions at 1995 prices

		1991	1992	1993	1994	1995	1996	1997	1998	1999
Private sector										
New dwellings, excluding land	DFDP	16 603	17 311	18 353	19 076	18 784	19 903	20 824	21 521	22 109
Other buildings and structures	EQCU	20 273	19 280	17 449	17 914	17 841	19 099	22 860	24 315	26 777
Transport equipment	EQCV	8 460	7 678	9 242	10 597	10 021	10 916	12 148	14 102	15 379
Other machinery and equipment and cultivated assets	EQCW	36 209	34 662	33 926	35 464	41 532	46 486	51 914	61 577	66 163
Intangible fixed assets	EQCX	3 960	3 414	3 152	2 997	3 179	3 298	3 288	3 249	3 070
Costs associated with the transfer of ownership of non-produced assets	EQCY	5 716	5 045	5 821	5 705	5 222	6 435	6 160	5 378	5 528
Total	EQCZ	91 844	87 965	88 081	91 753	96 579	106 137	117 194	130 142	139 026
Public non-financial corporations										
New dwellings, excluding land [2]	DEEW	..	..	..	150	162	147	119	106	100
Other buildings and structures [2]	DEEX	..	..	..	3 847	3 781	3 154	2 417	2 424	2 168
Transport equipment [2]	DEEU	..	..	..	529	354	223	181	144	139
Other machinery and equipment and cultivated assets [2]	DEEV	..	..	..	766	857	768	764	760	880
Intangible fixed assets	EQDE	281	274	295	387	496	571	553	554	545
Costs associated with the transfer of ownership of non-produced assets	EQDF	182	351	368	355	126	151	327	314	376
Total	EQDG	4 282	5 863	5 930	6 034	5 776	5 014	4 361	4 302	4 208
General government										
New dwellings, excluding land	DFID	2 633	2 570	2 932	3 041	2 642	2 104	1 726	1 604	1 313
Other buildings and structures	EQDI	9 211	10 296	11 174	11 162	9 997	8 511	7 313	7 213	7 191
Transport equipment	EQDJ	742	804	785	801	680	638	653	667	738
Other machinery and equipment and cultivated assets	EQDK	2 381	2 380	2 259	1 941	2 075	1 870	1 563	1 496	1 658
Intangible fixed assets	EQDL	232	227	231	247	264	293	262	353	373
Costs associated with the transfer of ownership of non-produced assets	EQDM	−1 724	−1 755	−2 343	−1 937	−1 653	−2 525	−1 826	−1 340	−1 235
Total	EQDN	13 339	14 436	15 043	15 255	14 005	10 891	9 691	9 993	10 038
Total gross fixed capital formation	NPQR	109 000	108 246	109 127	113 042	116 360	122 042	131 246	144 437	153 272

1 For the years before 1994, totals differ from the sum of their components.
2 Data not available for years before 1994.

Source: Office for National Statistics: 020 7533 6031

15.22 Gross fixed capital formation at 1995 purchasers' prices[1]
Analysis by type of asset

Total economy
£ millions at 1995 prices

		1991	1992	1993	1994	1995	1996	1997	1998	1999
Tangible fixed assets										
New dwellings, excluding land	DFDV	19 587	20 041	21 491	22 267	21 588	22 154	22 669	23 231	23 522
Other buildings and structures	EQDP	32 143	32 974	32 414	32 923	31 619	30 764	32 590	33 952	36 136
Transport equipment	DLWJ	9 656	9 253	10 589	11 927	11 055	11 777	12 982	14 913	16 256
Other machinery and equipment and cultivated assets	DLWM	39 086	38 031	36 958	38 171	44 464	49 124	54 241	63 833	68 701
Total	EQDS	100 464	100 751	101 630	105 288	108 726	113 819	122 482	135 929	144 615
Intangible fixed assets	EQDT	4 474	3 914	3 677	3 631	3 939	4 162	4 103	4 156	3 988
Costs associated with the transfer of ownership of non-produced assets	DFDW	4 176	3 640	3 857	4 123	3 695	4 061	4 661	4 352	4 669
Total gross fixed capital formation	NPQR	109 000	108 246	109 127	113 042	116 360	122 042	131 246	144 437	153 272

1 For the years before 1994, totals differ from the sum of their components.

Source: Office for National Statistics: 020 7533 6031

16 Prices

Prices

Producer price index numbers *(Tables 16.1 and 16.2)*

The producer price indices were published for the first time in August 1983, replacing the former wholesale price indices. Full details of the differences between the two indices were given in an article published in *British Business*, 15 April 1983. The producer price indices are calculated using the same general methodology as that used by the wholesale price indices.

The high level index numbers in Tables 16.1 and 16.2 are constructed on a net sector basis. That is to say, they are intended to measure only transactions between the sector concerned and other sectors. Within sector transactions are excluded. Index numbers for the whole of manufacturing are thus not weighted averages of sector index numbers.

The index numbers for selected industries in Tables 16.1 and 16.2 are constructed on a gross sector basis i.e. all transactions are included in deriving the weighting patterns, including sales within the same industry.

All the index numbers are compiled exclusive of value-added tax. Excise duties on cigarettes, manufactured tobacco and alcoholic liquor are included as is the duty on hydrocarbon oils.

The indices relate to the average prices for a year. The movement in these prices are weighted to reflect the relative importance of the composite products in a chosen year (known as the base year) currently 1995.

Since July 1995, PPIs have been published fully reclassified to the 1992 version of the Standard Industrial Classification (SIC). From 1998, high level PPIs on the 1980 SIC will also be shown in Tables 16.1 and 16.2.

Purchasing power of the pound *(Table 16.3)*

Changes in the internal purchasing power of a currency may be defined as the 'inverse' of changes in the levels of prices; when prices go up, the amount which can be purchased with a given sum of money goes down. Movements in the internal purchasing power of the pound are based on the consumers' expenditure deflator (CED) prior to 1962 and on the General index of retail prices (RPI) from January 1962 onwards. The CED shows the movement in prices implied by the national accounts estimates of consumers' expenditure valued at current and at constant prices, whilst the RPI is constructed directly by weighting together monthly movements in prices according to a given pattern of household expenditure derived from the Family Expenditure Survey. If the purchasing power of the pound is taken to be 100p in a particular month (quarter, year), the comparable purchasing power in a subsequent month (quarter, year) is:

$$100 \times \frac{\text{earlier period price index}}{\text{later period price index}}$$

where the price index used is the CED for years 1946-1961 and the RPI for periods after 1961.

Index of retail prices *(Table 16.4)*

The retail prices index measures the change from month to month in the average level of prices of goods and services purchased by most households in the United Kingdom. The expenditure pattern on which the index is based is revised each year using information from the Family Expenditure Survey. The expenditure of certain higher income households and households of retired people dependent mainly on social security benefits is excluded.

The index covers a large and representative selection of more than 600 separate goods and services, for which price movements are regularly measured in 146 locations throughout the country. Around 120 000 separate price quotations are used in compiling the index.

The index of retail prices replaced the interim index from January 1956 (indices of the interim index of retail prices for the period 1952 to January 1956 were last published in *Annual Abstract of Statistics* No 103, 1965). A new set of weights was introduced, based on expenditure in 1953-54, valued at January 1956 prices. Between January 1962 and 1974 the weights have been revised each January on the basis of expenditure in the three years ended in the previous June, valued at prices obtained at the date of revision. From 1975 the weights have been revised on expenditure for the latest available year.

Following the recommendations of the Retail Prices Index Advisory Committee, the index has been re-referenced to make January 13, 1987 = 100. Calculations of price changes which involve periods spanning the new reference date are made as follows:

$$\% \text{ change} = \frac{\text{Index for later month} \times \text{Index for Jan 1987}}{\text{Index for earlier month (Jan 1974 = 100)}}$$

Tax and price index (TPI) *(Table 16.5)*

The purpose and methodology of the TPI were described in an article in the August 1979 issue (No 310) of *Economic Trends* (The Stationery Office). The TPI measures the change in *gross* taxable income needed for taxpayers to maintain their purchasing power, allowing for changes in retail prices. The TPI thus takes account of the changes to direct taxes (and employees' National Insurance contributions) facing a representative cross-section of taxpayers as well as changes in the retail prices index (RPI).

When direct taxation or employees' National Insurance contributions change, the TPI will rise by less than or more than the RPI according to the type of changes made. Between Budgets, the monthly increase in the TPI is normally slightly larger than that in the RPI, since all the extra income needed to offset any rise in retail prices is fully taxed.

Index numbers of agricultural prices
(Tables 16.6 and 16.7)
The indices of agricultural prices for the United Kingdom are based on the calendar year 1990 and designed to provide an indication of movements in the purchase prices of the means of agricultural production and of the prices received by producers for their agricultural products. The methodology is comparable with that used for the other member states of the European Community and enables the compilation of indices for the Fifteen, which appear in the Communities Eurostat series of publications.

16.1

Producer price index numbers of materials and fuels purchased
All manufacturing and selected industries SIC(92)
United Kingdom

1995 = 100

			Annual averages							
			1992	1993	1994	1995	1996	1997	1998	1999
Net sector										
Materials and fuel purchased by manufacturing industry	PLKW	6292000000	86.2	90.2	91.9	100.0	98.8	90.6	82.5	83.7
Materials	PLKX	6292000010	83.7	88.8	90.3	100.0	99.7	90.9	81.6	83.0
Fuels	PLKY	6292000020	104.6	106.1	104.6	100.0	91.7	88.3	89.2	89.1
Materials and fuels purchased by manufacturing industry-seasonally adjusted	PLKZ	6292008900	86.2	90.2	91.9	100.0	98.8	90.6	82.3	83.6r
Materials and fuels purchased by manufacturing industry other than food, beverages, petroleum and tobacco	PLLA	6292990000	85.9	89.0	91.3	100.0	95.8	89.7	85.9	83.1
Materials purchased by manufacturing industry other than food, drink and tobacco	RWCJ	6292990010	81.0	84.9	88.5	100.0	96.6	90.0	85.2	81.9
Materials purchased by manufacturing industry other than food and beverages	RWCK	6292990020	104.5	106.0	104.6	100.0	91.7	88.2	89.1	89.0
Materials and fuels purchased by manufacturing industries other than food, beverages, petroleum and tobacco-seasonally adjusted	PLLB	6292998900	85.9	89.0	91.3	100.0	95.7	89.7	85.8	83.1r
Gross sector										
All manufacturing	RBBO	6192000000	89.5	92.0	94.0	100.0	100.3	97.0	93.2	92.5
Other mining & quarrying products	RABE	6112140000	90.2	93.1	95.7	100.0	101.9	102.9	104.0	105.1
Manufacture of food products	RBBQ	6192151600	87.2	93.1	94.2	100.0	99.8	94.2	90.3	88.9
Food products and beverages	RABF	6112150000	87.3	92.9	94.2	100.0	100.9	96.6	93.3	91.6
Tobacco products	RABG	6112160000	84.1	87.8	90.7	100.0	100.9	95.8	91.0	88.7
Manufacture of textiles	RBBR	6192171800	87.6	88.9	92.1	100.0	99.2	96.3	93.2	89.1
Textiles	RABH	6112170000	87.2	88.6	91.6	100.0	99.1	95.8	92.4	88.4
Wearing apparel	RABI	6112180000	88.3	89.6	92.9	100.0	99.5	97.0	94.6	90.2
Manufacture of leather	RBBS	6192190000	89.2	91.9	94.0	100.0	101.0	98.3	94.9	93.2
Manufacture of wood and wood products	RBBT	6192200000	84.4	88.6	93.7	100.0	99.0	98.1	95.3	93.6
Manufacture of pulp, paper, publishing & printing	RBBU	6192212200	85.1	85.4	88.4	100.0	99.2	93.1	90.4	88.9
Pulp and paper products	RABL	6112210000	85.0	85.5	88.3	100.0	99.1	93.1	90.5	89.0
Printed matter and recording material	RABM	6112220000	85.3	85.3	88.4	100.0	99.3	93.1	90.3	88.9
Manufacture of coke	RBBV	6192230000	97.4	101.5	94.7	100.0	118.1	107.4	78.9	103.5
Manufacture of chemical products	RBBW	6192240000	88.0	91.3	93.5	100.0	98.7	95.9	94.2	93.3
Manufacture of rubber products	RBBX	6192250000	81.8	84.3	87.4	100.0	94.7	90.2	84.3	82.2
Manufacture of other non-metallic mineral products	RBBY	6192260000	92.5	95.4	97.0	100.0	100.6	100.4	100.7	101.2
Manufacture of basic metals	RBBZ	6192272800	86.3	89.0	92.8	100.0	99.3	97.3	94.9	90.9
Basic metals	RABV	6112270000	85.2	88.1	92.2	100.0	98.8	96.3	93.3	88.5
Fabricated metal products	RABW	6112280000	87.7	90.2	93.5	100.0	99.9	98.5	96.9	93.7
Manufacture of machinery and equipment n.e.c.	RBCA	6192290000	90.6	92.7	95.2	100.0	100.8	100.5	99.6	97.8
Manufacture of electrical and optical equipment	RBCB	6192303300	99.2	96.8	98.0	100.0	97.8	93.6	88.6	85.2
Office machinery and computers	RABY	6112300000	110.6	103.0	102.6	100.0	95.3	87.7	78.8	73.9
Electrical machinery and apparatus n.e.c.	RACB	6112310000	90.3	91.3	94.0	100.0	99.4	97.6	95.0	92.5
Radio, television and communication equipment	RACC	6112320000	96.7	95.9	97.3	100.0	98.4	95.1	91.2	88.3
Medical, precision, optical instruments and clocks	RACD	6112330000	95.7	95.2	96.7	100.0	98.9	96.0	92.6	90.1
Manufacture of transport equipment	RBCC	6192343500	90.5	93.5	95.7	100.0	101.9	102.0	102.3	102.0
Motor vehicles, trailers and semi-trailers	RACE	6112340000	90.2	93.1	95.4	100.0	101.9	101.9	101.8	100.5

Source: Office for National Statistics: 01633 812106

16.1
Producer price index numbers of materials and fuels purchased
All manufacturing and selected industries SIC(92)
United Kingdom

1995 = 100

			Annual averages							
			1992	1993	1994	1995	1996	1997	1998	1999
Other transport equipment	RACF	6112350000	91.3	94.6	96.5	100.0	101.9	102.4	103.8	106.2
Manufacturing n.e.c.	RBCD	6192363700	87.1	89.6 .	93.1	100.0	100.0	98.8	96.8	94.8
Electricity	PQMX	4010990000	99.9	103.8	103.8	100.0	96.6	90.7	90.6	90.5
Gas	PQMZ	4020990000	113.5	109.2	107.1	100.0	76.4	79.1	83.3	82.8
Collected and purified water	PQNB	4100000000	83.3	91.3	96.8	100.0	104.9	109.6	115.3	119.7
Construction materials	RWDZ	6101451000	87.7	90.1	94.4	100.0	100.5	102.1	102.9	101.6
House building materials	RWEA	6101452000	87.7	90.2	94.6	100.0	100.7	102.2	103.0	102.1

SIC (80) Net sector

Materials and fuels purchased by manufacturing industry	DZBR	6200000000	84.9	89.7	91.7	100.0	96.4	89.0	84.1	82.0

Source: Office for National Statistics: 01633 812106

16.2 Producer price index numbers of output
All manufacturing and selected industries SIC(92)
United Kingdom

1995 = 100

			Annual averages							
			1992	1993	1994	1995	1996	1997	1998	1999
Net sector										
Output of manufactured products	PLLU	7209200000	90.2	93.8	96.1	100.0	102.6	103.6	104.2	105.4
All manufacturing excl. duty	PVNP	7209200010	90.7	94.2	96.2	100.0	102.3	102.5	102.1	102.2
All manufacturing excl. duty - seasonally adjusted	PVNQ	7209200890	90.7	94.2	96.2	100.0	102.3	102.5	102.0	102.2
Products of manufacturing industries other than the food, beverages, petroleum and tobacco manufacturing industries -unadjusted	PLLV	7209299000	91.5	93.9	96.1	100.0	102.0	102.2	102.1	101.7
All manufacturing excl. food, beverages, tobacco & petroleum - seasonally adjusted	PLLW	7209299890	91.5	93.9	96.0	100.0	101.9	102.2	102.1	101.7
Gross sector										
Manufactured product	POKE	7109200000	93.2	95.6	96.6	100.0	102.1	101.5	99.2	99.8
Manufactured products excl. food, drink, tobacco & petroleum	POKF	7109299000	92.8	94.0	95.8	100.0	101.4	100.9	100.1	99.2
Other mining & quarrying products	POKW	7112140000	90.0	91.1	94.3	100.0	105.0	108.1	111.2	112.3
Food products, beverages & tobacco	POKH	7111151600	89.6	94.7	96.3	100.0	103.1	103.0	102.7	102.6
Food products, beverages & tobacco including duty	RBGA	7111151680	89.4	94.5	96.6	100.0	103.3	103.9	104.7	106.4
Food products & beverages	POKX	7112150000	90.0	95.2	96.8	100.0	103.1	102.9	102.3	102.0
Food products excluding beverages	RBGD	7112159900	90.8	95.9	97.3	100.0	103.1	102.1	101.0	100.8
Tobacco products	POKY	7112160000	74.0	79.4	83.5	100.0	101.2	105.6	114.5	121.6
Textiles & textile products	POKI	7111171800	93.5 B	94.6 B	95.9 B	100.0 B	102.6 B	104.7	105.7	104.9
Textiles	POKZ	7112170000	93.0 B	94.0 B	95.5 B	100.0 B	102.3	104.1	104.9	103.5
Wearing apparel: Furs	POLA	7112180000	94.5 B	96.0 B	97.0 B	100.0 B	103.3	106.2	107.7	108.5
Leather & leather products	POKJ	7111190000	91.0	93.8	97.4	100.0	102.7	103.3	102.8	101.6
Wood & wood products	POKK	7111200000	86.3 B	90.2 B	94.0 B	100.0 B	98.8 B	100.3	98.9	96.4
Pulp, paper & paper products, recorded media & printing services	POKL	7111212200	88.8	91.0	92.9	100.0	103.4	102.0	102.5	102.9
Pulp, paper & paper products	POLD	7112210000	81.3	82.8	85.6	100.0	101.7	97.0	95.8	95.1
Printed matter & recorded media	POLE	7112220000	92.6	95.2	96.6	100.0	104.3	104.6	106.0	106.9
Chemicals, chemical, products & manmade fibres	POKN	7111240000	88.8	91.1	93.4	100.0	98.9	97.3	94.0	92.8
Rubber & plastic products	POKO	7111250000	89.9	91.2	92.3	100.0	101.4	100.8	98.4	96.3
Other non metallic mineral products	POKP	7111260000	89.9	91.8	95.9	100.0	101.1	103.5	106.5	108.3
Base metals & fabricated metal products	POKQ	7111272800	89.2	90.4	93.6	100.0	101.4	100.7	100.1	96.8
Base metals	POLJ	7112270000	82.8	84.5	90.0	100.0	98.8	96.0	93.0	87.3
Fabricated metal products, except machinery and equipment	POLK	7112280000	93.6 B	94.5 B	96.0 B	100.0 B	103.1	104.0	105.0	103.4
Machinery and equipment n.e.c.	POKR	7111290000	93.0 B	95.5 B	97.5 B	100.0 B	102.9 B	105.7	106.7	107.8
Electrical and optical equipment	POKS	7111343500	110.3	104.6	103.8	100.0	98.1	93.3	87.1	83.1
Office machinery and computers	POLM	7112300000	138.8	120.8	115.5	100.0	93.7	81.7	67.6	59.5
Electrical machinery and apparatus n.e.c.	POLN	7112310000	92.6 B	94.0 B	96.1 B	100.0 B	101.6	102.2	101.4	99.1
Radio, television and communication equipment and apparatus	POLO	7112320000	103.6	99.6	100.2	100.0	95.8	90.1	83.2	79.2
Medical precision and optical instruments, watches and clocks	POLP	7112330000	93.6 B	97.7 B	99.2 B	100.0 B	104.1	104.9	106.1	107.1

B = These index values are considered less reliable due to lack of market coverage.

Source: Office for National Statistics: 01633 812106

16.2
continued

Producer price index numbers of output
All manufacturing and selected industries SIC(92)
United Kingdom

			Annual averages							
			1992	1993	1994	1995	1996	1997	1998	1999
Gross sector continued										
Transport equipment	**POKT**	7111343500	90.8	94.5	96.5	100.0	103.0	104.4	106.4	108.0
Motor vehicles, trailers and semi-trailers	**POLQ**	7112340000	90.6	93.9	96.2	100.0	103.0	104.3	105.9	106.2
Other transport	**POLR**	7112350000	91.7 B	96.3 B	97.4 B	100.0 B	102.9	104.9	108.2	114.7
Furniture: other manufactured goods n.e.c.	**POLS**	7112360000	93.2 B	95.5 B	96.9 B	100.0 B	103.7	105.1	107.3	108.0
SIC (80) Net sector										
Output of manufactured products	**DZCV**	7200000000	91.4	94.3	96.3	100.0	102.3	102.8	103.2	103.6

B = These index values are considered less reliable due to lack of market coverage.

Source: Office for National Statistics: 01633 812106

16.3

Internal purchasing power of the pound (based on RPI)[1,2]
United Kingdom

Pence

	Year in which purchasing power was 100p																			
	1980	1981	1982	1983	1984	1985	1986	1987	1988	1989	1990	1991	1992	1993	1994	1995	1996	1997	1998	1999
	BAMM	BAMN	BAMO	BAMP	BAMQ	BAMR	BAMS	BAMT	BAMU	BAMV	BAMW	BASX	CZVM	CBXX	DOFX	DOHR	DOLM	DTUL	CDQG	JKZZ
1981	89	100	109	114	119	127	131	136	143	154	169	179	185	188	193	199	204	211	218	221
1982	82	92	100	105	110	116	120	125	132	142	155	164	171	173	177	184	188	194	201	204
1983	79	88	96	100	105	111	115	120	126	136	148	157	163	166	170	176	180	185	192	195
1984	75	84	91	95	100	106	110	114	120	129	141	150	155	158	162	167	171	177	183	185
1985	71	79	86	90	94	100	103	108	113	122	133	141	146	149	152	158	161	166	172	175
1986	68	76	83	87	91	97	100	104	109	118	129	136	142	144	147	152	156	161	167	169
1987	66	73	80	83	88	93	96	100	105	113	124	131	136	138	141	146	150	155	160	162
1988	63	70	76	79	83	88	92	95	100	108	118	125	130	132	135	139	143	147	152	155
1989	58	65	70	74	77	82	85	88	93	100	109	116	120	122	125	129	133	137	141	144
1990	53	59	64	67	71	75	78	81	85	91	100	106	110	112	114	118	121	125	129	131
1991	50	56	61	64	67	71	73	76	80	86	94	100	104	105	108	112	114	118	122	124
1992	48	54	59	61	64	68	71	74	77	83	91	96	100	102	104	108	110	114	118	119
1993	48	53	58	60	63	67	70	72	76	82	90	95	98	100	102	106	109	112	116	118
1994	46	52	56	59	62	66	68	71	74	80	88	93	96	98	100	103	106	109	113	115
1995	45	50	54	57	60	63	66	68	72	77	85	90	93	94	97	100	102	106	109	111
1996	44	49	53	56	58	62	64	67	70	75	83	87	91	92	94	98	100	103	107	108
1997	42	47	52	54	57	60	62	65	68	73	80	85	88	89	92	95	97	100	103	105
1998	41	46	50	52	55	58	60	63	66	71	77	82	85	86	88	92	94	97	100	102
1999	40	45	49	51	54	57	59	62	65	70	76	81	84	85	87	90	92	95	98	100

1 To find the purchasing power of the pound in 1993, given that it was 100 pence in 1980, select the column headed 1980 and look at the 1993 row. The result is 48 pence.

2 These figures are calculated by taking the inverse ratio of the respective annual averages of the Retail Prices Index.

Source: Office for National Statistics: 020 7533 5874

Prices

16.4 Retail Prices Index
United Kingdom

13 January 1987=100

| | ALL ITEMS (RPI) | All items excluding | | | | | Food and catering | Alcohol and tobacco | Housing and household expenditure | Personal expenditure | Travel and leisure | Consumer durables | All items excluding mortgage interest payments & indirect taxes (RPIY)[3] |
		mortgage interest payments (RPIX)	mortgage interest payments and depreciation[1]	housing	food	seasonal food[2]							
Weights													
	CZGU	CZGY	DOGZ	CZGX	CZGV	CZGW	CBVV	CBVW	CBVX	CBVY	CBVZ	CBWA	
1992	1 000	936	936	828	848	978	199	116	344	99	242	127	
1993	1 000	952	952	836	856	979	189	113	336	97	265	127	
1994	1 000	956	956	842	858	980	187	111	326	95	281	127	
1995	1 000	958	928	813	861	978	184	111	356	93	256	123	
1996	1 000	958	929	810	857	978	191	113	353	92	251	116	
1997	1 000	961	932	814	864	981	185	114	351	96	254	122	
1998	1 000	955	923	803	870	982	178	105	359	95	263	121	
1999	1 000	958	928	807	872	980	179	100	358	95	268	127	
2000	1 000	960	924	805	882	982	170	95	355	101	279	126	
Annual averages													
	CHAW	CHMK	CHON	CHAZ	CHAY	CHAX	CHBS	CHBT	CHBU	CHBV	CHBW	CHBY	CBZW
1990	126.1	122.1	122.1	119.2	127.4	126.4	120.9	120.6	139.0	117.6	119.8	111.3	121.4
1991	133.5	130.3	130.3	128.3	135.1	133.8	128.6	136.2	142.2	123.6	128.9	114.8	129.5
1992	138.5	136.4	136.4	134.3	140.5	139.1	132.6	146.8	144.2	126.9	136.8	115.5	135.1
1993	140.7	140.5	140.5	138.4	142.6	141.4	136.1	155.1	141.2	129.5	141.8	115.9	139.0
1994	144.1	143.8	143.8	141.6	146.5	144.8	138.5	161.4	144.4	131.9	145.7	115.5	141.3
1995	149.1	147.9	148.0	145.4	151.4	149.6	143.9	169.0	150.8	133.6	148.4	116.2	144.5
1996	152.7	152.3	152.3	149.3	154.9	153.4	148.9	175.9	153.0	135.1	152.8	117.1	148.2
1997	157.5	156.5	156.4	152.9	160.5	158.5	150.4	183.2	158.4	137.7	159.0	117.3	151.5
1998	162.9	160.6	160.3	156.2	166.5	163.8	153.4	192.3	166.2	139.9	162.8	115.9	154.5
1999	165.4	164.3	163.6	158.9	169.4	166.5	155.4	202.6	167.7	139.6	165.6	112.3	157.1
Monthly figures													
1997 Sep	159.3	157.8	157.6	154.1	162.5	160.3	151.1	185.0	160.7	139.8	160.8	118.4	152.6
Oct	159.5	157.9	157.8	154.2	162.8	160.5	151.4	185.4	161.0	139.7	161.0	117.9	152.9
Nov	159.6	158.0	157.8	154.2	163.0	160.6	151.0	184.9	161.5	140.8	160.7	119.0	152.9
Dec	160.0	158.3	158.1	154.5	163.5	161.0	151.1	185.6	162.4	140.7	160.7	119.7	152.8
1998 Jan	159.5	157.7	157.4	153.7	162.8	160.4	151.4	188.6	161.2	134.9	161.4	113.2	152.1
Feb	160.3	158.5	158.3	154.6	163.8	161.4	151.6	189.8	162.1	137.8	161.8	115.2	153.0
Mar	160.8	158.9	158.7	155.2	164.4	161.8	151.4	190.3	162.9	139.6	161.6	117.3	153.4
Apr	162.6	160.4	160.2	155.9	166.4	163.7	151.9	191.4	165.9	140.2	163.5	116.5	154.1
May	163.5	161.3	161.0	156.8	167.2	164.4	153.7	192.5	166.6	141.4	163.8	117.7	155.1
Jun	163.4	161.1	160.8	156.6	167.1	164.3	153.4	192.5	166.5	141.4	163.6	117.0	154.9
Jul	163.0	160.5	160.1	155.8	166.7	164.1	153.2	193.1	167.0	136.6	163.5	113.1	154.2
Aug	163.7	161.1	160.7	156.4	167.3	164.6	154.6	193.4	167.5	138.5	163.5	114.2	155.0
Sep	164.4	161.8	161.4	157.1	168.2	165.4	154.3	193.6	168.4	142.3	163.6	116.8	155.7
Oct	164.5	161.9	161.3	157.1	168.3	165.5	154.7	193.9	168.8	141.7	163.2	115.6	155.7
Nov	164.4	162.0	161.4	157.1	168.2	165.4	154.6	193.5	168.9	142.4	162.7	116.7	155.6
Dec	164.4	162.4	161.9	157.6	168.0	165.2	155.5	195.4	168.6	142.0	162.0	118.0	155.8
1999 Jan	163.4	161.8	161.2	156.8	166.7	164.2	156.1	198.2	165.9	136.3	162.8	110.6	155.1
Feb	163.7	162.3	161.7	157.4	167.0	164.5	156.4	198.6	165.9	138.5	162.6	112.3	155.8
Mar	164.1	163.2	162.6	158.4	167.7	165.0	155.8	200.8	165.5	139.8	164.0	114.2	156.0
Apr	165.2	164.3	163.7	159.0	169.1	166.3	155.4	201.9	166.8	140.3	166.1	113.1	156.9
May	165.6	164.7	164.1	159.4	169.5	166.5	156.1	202.6	167.3	140.8	166.2	114.0	157.4
Jun	165.6	164.7	164.0	159.2	169.6	166.6	155.7	203.4	167.3	140.9	165.9	113.1	157.3
Jul	165.1	164.1	163.4	158.6	169.1	166.3	155.1	204.2	166.9	136.9	166.3	109.6	156.7
Aug	165.5	164.5	163.8	158.9	169.7	166.8	154.7	204.5	167.6	138.3	166.6	110.5	157.2
Sep	166.2	165.2	164.4	159.6	170.6	167.4	154.6	204.5	168.5	141.6	166.5	112.7	157.8
Oct	166.5	165.4	164.4	159.6	171.0	167.7	154.6	204.7	169.2	140.8	167.1	111.6	158.1
Nov	166.7	165.6	164.6	159.7	171.1	167.8	155.1	204.3	170.0	141.1	166.6	112.3	158.3
Dec	167.3	165.9	164.9	160.1	171.8	168.4	155.3	204.0	171.7	140.3	166.8	113.2	158.6
2000 Jan	166.6	165.2	164.1	159.1	171.0	167.8	155.5	205.0	170.8	134.4	167.7	106.3	157.9
Feb	167.5	165.8	164.7	159.7	172.0	168.7	155.6	205.7	171.9	137.1	167.8	108.4	158.6
Mar	168.4	166.4	165.3	160.5	173.2	169.7	155.0	206.0	173.2	138.5	169.2	109.6	159.2
Apr	170.1	167.5	166.4	161.3	175.3	171.5	155.1	210.4	175.9	139.2	170.4	110.0	159.4
May	170.7	168.0	166.8	161.7	175.7	171.9	156.3	211.1	176.3	139.4	170.7	110.1	160.0
Jun	171.1	168.4	167.1	162.0	176.1	172.3	156.6	211.5	176.7	138.7	171.7	109.3	160.4
Jul	170.5	167.7	166.4	161.2	175.2	171.5	157.7	211.4	176.7	133.1	171.5	104.5	159.7
Aug	170.5	167.6	166.2	160.9	175.4	171.7	156.9	212.0	177.1	134.6	170.5	105.6	159.6
Sep	171.7	168.9	167.4	162.2	176.8	172.9	157.2	212.7	178.5	137.5	171.3	108.0	160.9

1 This series has been constructed using the index for all items excluding mortgage interest payments prior to February 1995.
2 Seasonal food is defined as items of food the prices of which show significant seasonal variations. These are fresh fruit and vegetables, fresh fish, eggs and home-killed lamb.

3 There are no weights available for RPIY.

Source: Office for National Statistics: 020 7533 5874

16.5 Tax and Price Index
United Kingdom

| | Tax and Price Index: January 1978 = 100 | | | | | January 1987 = 100 | | | | | | | | | | | | |
| | BSAA | | | | | DQAB | | | | | | | | | | | | |
	1983	1984	1985	1986	1987	1987	1988	1989	1990	1991	1992	1993	1994	1995	1996	1997	1998	1999
January	170.7	177.9	184.7	192.9	198.0	100.0	101.4	107.1	113.9	123.6	128.1	128.7	132.1	137.2	141.6	143.6	147.1	150.5
February	171.6	178.8	186.4	193.7	..	100.5	101.8	108.0	114.7	124.3	128.8	129.6	132.9	138.2	142.3	144.2	147.9	150.8
March	171.9	179.4	188.4	194.0	..	100.7	102.3	108.5	115.9	124.9	129.3	130.2	133.4	138.8	143.0	144.6	148.4	151.2
April	171.8	178.8	190.2	192.5	..	99.7	101.4	109.8	118.2	125.4	129.6	131.3	135.3	140.3	141.7	143.8	149.7	151.2
May	172.6	179.6	191.2	192.9	..	99.8	101.9	110.5	119.4	125.8	130.2	131.8	135.8	141.0	142.0	144.4	150.6	151.7
June	173.1	180.1	191.7	192.8	..	99.8	102.3	110.9	119.9	126.5	130.2	131.7	135.8	141.2	142.1	145.0	150.5	151.7
July	174.2	179.9	191.3	192.1	..	99.7	102.4	111.1	120.0	126.2	129.6	131.4	135.1	140.4	141.5	145.0	150.1	151.1
August	175.1	181.8	191.8	192.9	..	100.0	103.7	111.4	121.4	126.5	129.7	132.1	135.8	141.3	142.2	146.0	150.8	151.5
September	176.0	182.2	191.7	194.0	..	100.4	104.3	112.2	122.7	127.0	130.3	132.7	136.1	142.0	143.0	146.9	151.5	152.3
October	176.7	183.5	191.4	194.3	..	100.9	105.4	111.7	123.8	127.5	130.8	132.6	136.4	141.2	143.0	147.1	151.6	152.6
November	177.5	184.1	192.1	196.3	..	101.5	106.0	112.8	123.4	128.1	130.6	132.4	136.5	141.2	143.1	147.2	151.5	152.8
December	178.0	183.9	192.4	197.1	..	101.4	106.3	113.1	123.3	128.2	130.1	132.7	137.2	142.1	143.6	147.6	151.5	153.4

| | Retail Prices Index: January 1974 = 100 | | | | | January 1987 = 100 | | | | | | | | | | | | |
| | CBAB | | | | | CHAW | | | | | | | | | | | | |
	1983	1984	1985	1986	1987	1987	1988	1989	1990	1991	1992	1993	1994	1995	1996	1997	1998	1999
January	325.9	342.6	359.8	379.7	394.5	100.0	103.3	111.0	119.5	130.2	135.6	137.9	141.3	146.0	150.2	154.4	159.5	163.4
February	327.3	344.0	362.7	381.1	..	100.4	103.7	111.8	120.2	130.9	136.3	138.8	142.1	146.9	150.9	155.0	160.3	163.7
March	327.9	345.1	366.1	381.6	..	100.6	104.1	112.3	121.4	131.4	136.7	139.3	142.5	147.5	151.5	155.4	160.8	164.1
April	332.5	349.7	373.9	385.3	..	101.8	105.8	114.3	125.1	133.1	138.8	140.6	144.2	149.0	152.6	156.3	162.6	165.2
May	333.9	351.0	375.6	386.0	..	101.9	106.2	115.0	126.2	133.5	139.3	141.1	144.7	149.6	152.9	156.9	163.5	165.6
June	334.7	351.9	376.4	385.8	..	101.9	106.6	115.4	126.7	134.1	139.3	141.0	144.7	149.8	153.0	157.5	163.4	165.6
July	336.5	351.5	375.7	384.7	..	101.8	106.7	115.5	126.8	133.8	138.8	140.7	144.0	149.1	152.4	157.5	163.0	165.1
August	338.0	354.8	376.7	385.9	..	102.1	107.9	115.8	128.1	134.1	138.9	141.3	144.7	149.9	153.1	158.5	163.7	165.5
September	339.5	355.5	376.5	387.8	..	102.4	108.4	116.6	129.3	134.6	139.4	141.9	145.0	150.6	153.8	159.3	164.4	166.2
October	340.7	357.7	377.1	388.4	..	102.9	109.5	117.5	130.3	135.1	139.9	141.8	145.2	149.8	153.8	159.5	164.5	166.5
November	341.9	358.8	378.4	391.7	..	103.4	110.0	118.5	130.0	135.6	139.7	141.6	145.3	149.8	153.9	159.6	164.4	166.7
December	342.8	358.5	378.9	393.0	..	103.3	110.3	118.8	129.9	135.7	139.2	141.9	146.0	150.7	154.4	160.0	164.4	167.3

| | Percentage changes on one year earlier | | | | | | | | | | | | | | | | |
	1983	1984	1985	1986	1987	1988	1989	1990	1991	1992	1993	1994	1995	1996	1997	1998	1999
Tax and Price Index																	
January	5.2	4.2	3.8	4.4	2.6	1.4	5.6	6.3	8.5	3.6	0.5	2.6	3.9	3.2	1.4	2.4	2.3
February	5.7	4.2	4.3	3.9	2.7	1.3	6.1	6.2	8.4	3.6	0.6	2.5	4.0	3.0	1.3	2.6	2.0
March	4.8	4.4	5.0	3.0	2.8	1.6	6.1	6.8	7.8	3.5	0.7	2.5	4.0	3.0	1.1	2.6	1.9
April	3.5	4.1	6.4	1.2	2.5	1.7	8.3	7.7	6.1	3.3	1.3	3.0	3.7	1.0	1.5	4.1	1.0
May	3.1	4.1	6.5	0.9	2.4	2.1	8.4	8.1	5.4	3.5	1.2	3.0	3.8	0.7	1.7	4.3	0.7
June	3.0	4.0	6.4	0.6	2.5	2.5	8.4	8.1	5.5	2.9	1.2	3.1	4.0	0.6	2.0	3.8	0.8
July	3.1	3.3	6.3	0.4	2.8	2.7	8.5	8.0	5.2	2.7	1.4	2.8	3.9	0.8	2.5	3.5	0.7
August	3.6	3.8	5.5	0.6	2.6	3.7	7.4	9.0	4.2	2.5	1.9	2.8	4.1	0.6	2.7	3.3	0.5
September	4.2	3.5	5.2	1.2	2.4	3.9	7.6	9.4	3.5	2.6	1.8	2.6	4.3	0.7	2.7	3.1	0.5
October	4.0	3.8	4.3	1.5	2.9	4.5	6.0	10.8	3.0	2.6	1.4	2.9	3.5	1.3	2.9	3.1	0.7
November	3.9	3.7	4.3	2.2	2.4	4.4	6.4	9.4	3.8	2.0	1.4	3.1	3.4	1.3	2.9	2.9	0.9
December	4.4	3.3	4.6	2.4	1.9	4.8	6.4	9.0	4.0	1.5	2.0	3.4	3.6	1.1	2.8	2.6	1.3
Retail Prices Index																	
January	4.9	5.1	5.0	5.5	3.9	3.3	7.5	7.7	9.0	4.1	1.7	2.5	3.3	2.9	2.8	3.3	2.4
February	5.3	5.1	5.4	5.1	3.9	3.3	7.8	7.5	8.9	4.1	1.8	2.4	3.4	2.7	2.7	3.4	2.1
March	4.6	5.2	6.1	4.2	4.0	3.5	7.9	8.1	8.2	4.0	1.9	2.3	3.5	2.7	2.6	3.5	2.1
April	4.0	5.2	6.9	3.0	4.2	3.9	8.0	9.4	6.4	4.3	1.3	2.6	3.3	2.4	2.4	4.0	1.6
May	3.7	5.1	7.0	2.8	4.1	4.2	8.3	9.7	5.8	4.3	1.3	2.6	3.4	2.2	2.6	4.2	1.3
June	3.7	5.1	7.0	2.5	4.2	4.6	8.3	9.8	5.8	3.9	1.2	2.6	3.5	2.1	2.9	3.7	1.3
July	4.2	4.5	6.9	2.4	4.4	4.8	8.2	9.8	5.5	3.7	1.4	2.3	3.5	2.2	3.3	3.5	1.3
August	4.6	5.0	6.2	2.4	4.4	5.7	7.3	10.6	4.7	3.6	1.7	2.4	3.6	2.1	3.5	3.3	1.1
September	5.1	4.7	5.9	3.0	4.2	5.9	7.6	10.9	4.1	3.6	1.8	2.2	3.9	2.1	3.6	3.2	1.1
October	5.0	5.0	5.4	3.0	4.5	6.4	7.3	10.9	3.7	3.6	1.4	2.4	3.2	2.7	3.7	3.1	1.2
November	4.8	4.9	5.5	3.5	4.1	6.4	7.7	9.7	4.3	3.0	1.4	2.6	3.1	2.7	3.7	3.0	1.4
December	5.3	4.6	5.7	3.7	3.7	6.8	7.7	9.3	4.5	2.6	1.9	2.9	3.2	2.5	3.6	2.8	1.8

Note: The purpose and methodology of the Tax and Price Index were described in an article in the August 1979 issue of *Economic Trends* . The purpose is to produce a single index which measures changes in both direct taxes (including national insurance contributions) and in retail prices for a representative cross-section of taxpayers. Thus, while the Retail Prices Index may be used to measure changes in the purchasing power of after-tax income (and of the income of non-taxpayers) the Tax and Price Index takes account of the fact that taxpayers will have more or less to spend according to changes in direct taxation. The index measures the change in gross taxable income which would maintain their after tax-income in real terms.

Source: Office for National Statistics: 020 7533 5874

16.6 Index of purchase prices of the means of agricultural production
United Kingdom
Annual averages

1990 = 100

		Weights	1989	1990	1991	1992	1993	1994	1995	1996	1997	1998	1999
Goods and services currently consumed	BYEA	100	97.2	100.0	103.4	106.9	111.5	111.0	114.9	122.4	116.8	108.4	106.2
Seeds	BYEB	4.3	93.0	100.0	102.5	111.4	119.0	114.1	133.5	141.6	124.5	..	119.7
Animals for rearing and production	BYEC	0.5	99.7	100.0	93.9	100.5	88.1	111.6	139.1	139.2	133.4	127.8	118.7
Energy, lubricants	BYED	6.8	91.4	100.0	103.1	105.8	106.6	104.8	108.0	116.4	115.4	110.5	117.6
Fuels for heating	KVBA	2.0	85.0	100.0	97.8	89.5	96.6	88.9	92.5	110.4	102.1	82.2	92.9
Motor fuel	KVBB	2.1	98.1	100.0	102.4	107.9	109.4	111.5	122.0	133.1	141.5	149.5	162.4
Electricity	KVBC	2.4	91.3	100.0	106.8	116.5	112.3	111.2	107.7	107.2	103.6	99.0	97.2
Lubricants	KVBD	0.4	88.3	100.0	112.6	109.6	110.2	112.4	113.1	112.3	114.4	116.9	128.4
Fertilisers and soil improvers	BYEE	10.9	98.7	100.0	96.6	91.1	85.6	91.0	102.0	112.8	97.9	83.0	79.5
Straight fertilisers	KVBE	4.4	99.0	100.0	94.1	87.6	80.1	87.4	98.4	108.8	93.8	78.9	75.5
Compound fertilisers	KVBF	6.0	99.2	100.0	98.1	92.6	87.9	92.0	103.7	115.0	98.6	78.3	78.3
Other fertiliser	KVBG	0.5	90.7	100.0	100.6	102.8	106.3	111.4	113.2	122.2	124.3	127.4	128.5
Plant protection products	BYEF	6.6	91.5	100.0	108.4	110.1	111.5	117.5	115.9	123.5	124.4	116.1	112.7
Animal feedingstuffs	BYEG	40.5	101.4	100.0	101.1	105.2	112.9	107.8	109.3	119.0	108.5	92.5	86.1
Feed wheat	KVBI	2.3	97.2	100.0	104.6	105.7	107.9	93.5	100.4	102.5	81.0	68.8	66.9
Wheat feed	ZBUV	0.5	97.2	100.0	104.6	105.7	107.9	93.5	100.4	102.5	81.0	68.8	66.9
Whole barley	KVBJ	1.2	98.0	100.0	103.8	105.4	109.7	98.1	101.9	101.3	79.2	68.5	70.5
Whole oats	KVBL	0.1	93.9	100.0	101.5	109.6	124.8	101.0	93.3	100.6	78.7	63.4	68.7
Maize glutten feed	ZBUW	0.6	120.4	100.0	108.3	106.9	109.5	107.7	110.6	126.1	93.2	74.7	77.8
Oilcake	KVBM	2.5	104.4	100.0	100.2	107.2	113.6	111.1	119.4	126.8	113.1	92.8	84.0
White fish meal	KVBN	0.2	110.0	100.0	109.3	112.3	105.2	103.0	118.5	145.5	142.9	156.4	106.8
Other straight feedstuffs	ZBUX	3.9	98.6	100.0	102.3	113.9	116.3	120.4	126.6	131.9	117.9	95.0	95.3
All straight feedstuffs	KVBH	11.3	107.2	100.0	101.6	105.9	113.2	104.8	109.3	121.6	106.3	84.9	78.9
Compound feedingstuffs for:	KVBP	29.2	99.2	100.0	100.8	104.9	112.8	108.9	109.3	118.0	109.3	95.5	88.9
Cattle and calves	ZBUY	12.3	98.3	100.0	98.7	103.9	113.8	108.6	107.6	116.5	108.4	93.6	89.0
Pigs	KVBS	7.2	98.8	100.0	103.4	107.7	115.8	110.7	112.7	120.1	110.7	96.7	87.2
Poultry	KVBT	8.3	100.8	100.0	102.2	104.4	109.0	106.5	107.4	116.2	107.2	95.5	88.7
Sheep	KVBU	1.4	98.2	100.0	98.7	102.9	112.1	116.0	118.4	130.1	122.6	106.1	97.3
Material and small tools	BYEH	4.4	93.2	100.0	111.2	116.0	119.0	121.8	122.3	122.7	122.3	119.7	119.8
Maintenance and repair of plant	BYEI	10.0	91.9	100.0	110.6	119.0	126.2	129.0	132.2	139.3	145.2	149.8	155.1
Maintenance and repair of buildings	BYEJ	4.9	95.2	100.0	102.1	102.1	104.9	109.9	116.4	117.0	118.8	119.8	118.3
Veterinary services	BYEK	2.4	95.3	100.0	105.0	108.3	110.4	111.5	113.4	116.2	119.4	122.9	125.8
General expenses	BYEL	8.7	96.2	100.0	107.2	114.6	122.2	124.0	127.0	129.3	132.0	132.3	136.1
Goods and services contributing to investment in agriculture	BYEM	100	94.5	100.0	105.9	109.8	113.2	115.8	118.8	121.8	125.2	128.0	129.2
Machinery and other equipment	BYEN	50.9	95.0	100.0	106.6	111.7	115.7	117.0	117.7	121.8	123.9	124.8	125.1
Machinery and plant for cultivation	KVBV	6.2	94.0	100.0	109.0	117.2	118.9	119.8	121.2	125.0	128.1	130.7	131.5
Machinery and plant for harvesting	KVBW	11.2	95.7	100.0	106.3	110.8	113.8	113.8	113.8	113.8	113.8	113.8	113.8
Farm machinery and installations	KVBX	4.7	93.5	100.0	105.9	109.8	111.3	112.3	113.9	115.3	116.9	118.6	119.8
Tractors	KVBY	22.3	95.4	100.0	106.4	111.5	117.7	119.0	118.8	125.5	128.7	129.5	130.3
Other vehicles	KVBZ	6.5	95.2	100.0	106.4	111.2	116.4	118.4	119.1	125.1	128.1	128.7	128.9
Buildings	BYEO	49.1	94.0	100.0	105.2	107.8	110.6	114.5	120.0	121.7	126.5	131.3	133.5
Farm buildings	KVCA	33.6	94.3	100.0	104.5	106.5	109.3	113.7	119.4	121.9	126.7	130.7	132.8
Engineering and soil improvement operations	KVCB	15.5	93.1	100.0	106.8	110.8	113.5	116.2	121.4	121.2	126.0	132.7	135.0

The price indices shown are all on the 1990 = 100 series.

Source: Stats (C & S) H, Ministry of Agriculture, Fisheries and Food: 01904 455253

16.7 Index of producer prices of agricultural products
United Kingdom
Annual averages

1990 = 100

		Weights	1989	1990	1991	1992	1993	1994	1995	1996	1997	1998	1999
All products	BYEP	100	98.9	100.0	99.2	100.8	106.0	106.4	116.0	114.3	98.9	90.0	86.4
All crop products	BYEQ	40.4	96.1	100.0	101.2	96.4	96.0	98.0	111.5	103.4	86.0	87.6	83.6
Cereals	BYER	15.9	98.3	100.0	105.8	108.1	111.5	97.2	103.1	104.7	83.9	72.7	70.1
Wheat for:													
breadmaking	KVDA	3.9	98.6	100.0	111.4	116.6	122.5	102.3	106.6	108.6	92.5	83.5	75.3
other milling	KVDB	0.5	98.0	100.0	109.2	110.6	111.4	96.4	101.9	103.6	83.7	72.7	69.6
feeding	KVDC	6.6	97.2	100.0	104.6	105.7	107.9	93.5	100.4	102.5	81.0	68.8	66.9
Barley for:													
feeding	KVDD	2.9	98.0	100.0	103.8	105.4	109.7	98.1	101.9	101.3	79.2	68.5	70.8
malting	KVDE	1.7	102.8	100.0	100.6	102.1	102.0	97.9	109.1	110.8	84.0	71.9	69.7
Oats for:													
milling	KVDF	0.2	94.3	100.0	102.2	108.2	120.6	100.6	92.8	100.3	78.5	63.4	66.3
feeding	KVDG	0.1	93.9	100.0	101.5	109.6	124.8	101.0	93.3	100.6	78.7	63.4	68.5
Root crops	BYES	5.6	93.2	100.0	99.5	86.0	80.6	121.7	177.3	105.2	70.4	106.8	107.3
Potatoes:													
early	KVDH	0.3	174.1	100.0	224.7	100.7	110.1	257.7	197.8	139.1	99.5	194.8	93.9
main crop	KVDI	3.3	84.5	100.0	87.7	72.4	58.3	119.2	214.4	94.4	51.4	112.7	121.2
Sugar beet	KVDJ	2.1	96.1	100.0	101.6	105.5	111.9	107.6	116.0	117.8	96.5	88.0	87.2
Fresh vegetables	BYET	7.8	91.8	100.0	99.6	89.0	96.3	99.7	108.4	109.3	97.3	105.6	99.2
Cauliflowers	KVDK	0.5	93.8	100.0	111.5	95.7	104.4	106.6	97.1	107.7	88.2	100.3	93.3
Lettuce	KVDL	1.0	106.0	100.0	101.8	108.9	105.0	106.2	115.4	112.9	122.2	115.3	106.9
Tomatoes	KVDM	0.7	99.9	100.0	88.8	80.4	75.8	84.8	78.5	98.5	69.2	77.9	72.4
Carrots	KVDN	0.8	73.1	100.0	104.0	67.1	86.0	100.1	122.8	121.0	73.3	108.9	104.7
Cabbage	KVDO	0.7	87.8	100.0	98.5	85.6	106.4	94.5	120.5	112.1	102.4	119.4	113.4
Beans	KVDP	0.2	63.2	100.0	68.0	57.2	82.8	93.1	90.8	87.6	92.9	69.8	81.0
Onions	KVDQ	0.5	75.8	100.0	89.9	78.2	88.1	108.6	122.4	75.5	84.2	108.5	70.3
Mushrooms	KVDR	1.6	95.3	100.0	104.2	96.4	106.0	104.3	107.9	111.6	98.2	100.1	98.9
Fresh fruit	BYEU	2.1	91.9	100.0	104.5	100.5	87.5	87.0	95.8	107.5	98.4	98.5	90.1
Dessert apples	KVDS	0.7	94.7	100.0	117.3	124.7	79.6	74.8	96.4	112.6	97.1	93.5	88.5
Dessert pears	KVDT	0.1	80.3	100.0	90.9	90.3	77.8	78.9	86.6	82.9	78.6	75.3	71.5
Cooking apples	KVDU	0.3	70.9	100.0	99.3	78.0	76.3	86.9	88.5	105.6	112.8	125.5	83.8
Strawberries	KVDV	0.5	102.0	100.0	109.9	105.3	101.2	103.0	91.3	94.1	91.0	85.3	90.3
Raspberries	KVDW	0.2	101.6	100.0	85.9	69.0	95.5	93.1	124.7	156.8	106.1	111.6	102.4
Seeds	BYEV	1.1	96.7	100.0	99.1	101.1	92.2	107.3	143.3	122.7	92.1	89.6	93.0
Flowers and plants	BYEW	3.8	102.3	100.0	97.1	99.3	97.9	104.4	107.2	114.6	114.8	109.0	107.8
Other crop products	BYEX	4.1	96.1	100.0	91.3	73.7	60.3	62.6	63.2	66.8	60.2	58.7	45.1
Animals and animal products	BYEY	59.6	100.8	100.0	97.9	103.8	112.8	112.1	119.0	121.8	107.5	91.6	88.4
Animals for slaughter	BYEZ	33.8	103.0	100.0	94.9	102.1	111.8	109.1	112.7	115.5	102.2	84.7	83.2
Calves	KVDX	0.3	141.1	100.0	92.5	114.8	150.7	145.4	130.9	93.6	96.2	82.0	63.3
Clean cattle	KVDY	11.7	107.2	100.0	100.5	102.7	120.2	114.6	115.1	98.2	89.7	79.6	85.2
Cows and bulls	KVDZ	2.1	114.7	100.0	97.4	131.8	110.0	118.1	117.0	106.6	87.7	81.0	68.5
Clean pigs	KVEA	7.7	100.3	100.0	91.4	102.3	92.2	88.6	105.9	122.1	98.4	71.9	70.0
Sows and boars	KVEB	0.3	112.0	100.0	103.2	121.4	92.0	95.4	121.3	131.0	102.5	53.4	53.5
Sheep	KVEC	4.3	105.4	100.0	84.0	105.1	126.7	135.4	136.6	163.2	148.5	111.4	103.9
Ewe and ram	KVED	0.3	119.6	100.0	87.5	109.9	133.8	125.9	123.5	172.0	178.0	105.0	74.0
Poultry	KVEE	7.0	90.8	100.0	95.3	95.0	101.9	101.5	98.4	108.4	100.0	92.3	88.8
Chickens	KVEF	5.0	94.6	100.0	92.9	94.0	101.5	99.3	94.2	104.8	97.3	85.5	81.5
Turkeys	KVEG	1.6	77.4	100.0	100.8	95.9	102.3	107.2	108.6	117.4	103.2	105.4	104.0
Cows milk	BYFA	21.7	99.6	100.0	104.6	109.6	117.8	119.3	134.0	134.6	119.0	104.2	98.6
Eggs	BYFB	3.6	87.7	100.0	87.5	86.2	98.8	99.4	90.0	107.6	92.3	85.0	80.3
Other animal products:													
Wool (clip)	BYFC	0.6	103.5	100.0	92.0	87.1	72.7	92.2	102.5	95.4	84.0	60.0	49.3

The price indices shown are all on the 1990 = 100 series.

Source: Stats (C & S) H, Ministry of Agriculture, Fisheries and Food: 01904 455253

16.8 Commodity price trends[1]
United Kingdom
Calendar years

			1989	1990	1991	1992	1993	1994	1995	1996	1997	1998	1999
Wheat £ per tonne	KVAA	Average ex-farm price[2]	104.9	109.8	116.5	120.5	124.2	106.4	115.6	112.5	88.7	..	..
Barley £ per tonne	KVAB	Average ex-farm price[2]	106.7	108.8	107.8	113.9	113.6	105.4	107.6	103.7	81.2	..	..
Oats £ per tonne	KVAC	Average ex-farm price[2]	98.5	106.4	105.9	115.1	128.8	108.4	101.4	107.4	83.5	..	..
Rye £ per tonne	KVAD	Average ex-farm price[2]	106.80	114.60	118.50	115.20	113.40	112.81	107.88	113.88	..	..	..
Hops £ per tonne	KVAE	Average farm-gate price	2 662	2 922	3 211	3 208	3 357	4 005	3 595	3 360	3 550	3 676	3 859
Potatoes £ per tonne	KVAF	Average farm-gate price[3]	89.47	98.66	93.02	75.19	64.14	125.77	187.66	100.54	65.96	121.57	120.49
Sugar beet £ per tonne	KVAG	Producer price[4]	27.87	31.47	31.42	38.02	36.47	34.74	38.34	37.72	32.86	31.85	..
Oilseed rape	KVAH	Average market price[5]	286.00	280.00	248.00	133.00	153.03	185.43	177.73	186.85	160.23	164.27	..
Apples £ per tonne	KPUE	Dessert average farm-gate price[6]	385.6	524.1	596.2	310.3	291.8	337.0	418.6	528.0	525.7	480.3	426.3
	KVAI	Dessert average market price	383.0	500.0	589.0	414.0	370.0	447.4	465.7	474.7	538.1	..	..
	KVAJ	Culinary average market price	286.0	408.0	420.0	312.0	327.0	446.4	405.9	462.8	558.4	..	..
	KPUJ	Culinary average farm-gate price	199.0	268.3	278.8	189.6	229.4	236.1	243.3	279.4	322.3	341.7	212.8
Pears £ per tonne	KPUG	Average farm-gate price	476.9	473.0	545.8	426.9	365.4	460.7	453.0	445.7	441.9	405.1	397.7
	KVAK	Average market price	402.0	485.0	468.0	461.0	380.0	408.3	447.5	441.7	433.1	394.2	..
Tomatoes £ per tonne	LQMH	Average farm-gate price[6]	551.1	669.8	584.9	481.2	535.5	617.8	582.4	756.2	554.0	603.9	572.4
	KVAL	Average market price[6]	559.0	694.0	604.0	494.0	552.8	675.2	624.0	700.1	655.6	..	..
Cauliflowers £ per tonne	KPUI	Average farm-gate price[6]	196.5	236.2	243.1	198.1	213.4	225.7	247.8	270.9	237.7	219.3	201.6
	KVAM	Average market price[6]	257.0	296.0	292.0	253.0	296.9	323.5	394.9	442.6	372.0	..	..
Cattle (rearing) £ per head	KVAN	1st quality Hereford/cross bull calves[7,13]	188.43	128.00	119.92	145.44	185.95	182.06	166.32	131.81	146.95	107.86	87.79
	KVAO	1st quality beef/cross yearling steers[13]	430.73	397.00	397.30	419.49	478.00	471.00	475.00	445.00	427.00	369.00	382.00
Cattle (fat) p per kg liveweight	KVAP	Clean cattle[8]	114.03	106.30	106.92	109.58	128.04	121.71	123.15	105.52	96.89	86.10	92.12

See footnotes on the second part of this table.

Source: Ministry of Agriculture, Fisheries and Food: 01904 455332

16.8
continued

Commodity price trends[1]
United Kingdom
Calendar years

			1989	1990	1991	1992	1993	1994	1995	1996	1997	1998	1999
Sheep (store) £ per head	KVAQ	1st quality lambs, hoggets and tegs[7]	36.10	33.80	35.50	37.90	35.56	40.02	44.46	46.83	53.42	31.28	28.66
Sheep (fat) p per kg estimated dressed carcase weight	KVAR KVAS	Great Britain[11] Northern Ireland[12]	184.47 202.50	174.47 170.94	148.16 179.41	182.12 172.37	218.96 199.50	236.88 221.95	236.40 214.41	283.13 260.46	239.02 228.23	192.46 179.06	180.27 165.71
Pigs £ per kg deadweight	KVAT	Average price clean pigs	112.92	111.74	102.42	115.12	103.02	99.57	118.84	137.73	110.83	80.65	78.53
Broilers p per kg carcass weight	KVAU	Average producer price	82.1	86.8	81.0	82.7	86.8	86.5	83.8	90.7	85.9	76.6	71.8
Milk p per litre	KVAV	Average net return to producers[9]	19.10	19.19	19.81	20.94	22.68	22.96	24.96	25.01	22.31	19.44	18.55
Eggs p per dozen	KVAW	Average producer price[10]	37.30	42.60	36.30	36.60	41.90	42.40	38.20	45.70	39.80	36.20	34.00
Wool p per kg	KHWQ	Average producer price for clip paid to producers by the British Wool Marketing Board	95.30	91.04	81.98	79.82	61.00	97.97	94.08	86.90	74.90	47.80	45.20

1 This table gives indications of the movement in commodity prices at the first point of sale. The series do not always show total receipts by farmers; for some commodities additional premiums or deficiency payments are made to achieve support price levels.

2 Weighted average ex-farm prices of United Kingdom cereals.

3 Weighted average price paid to growers for early and main crop potatoes in the United Kingdom. (includes all potatoes and a value for sacks)

4 Returns to growers figures since 1986 prices per 'adjusted' tonne at 16% sugar content.

5 Typical contract price adjusted to delivered basis and 40 per cent oil content.

6 Weighted average wholesale prices for England and Wales. From 1982, for England only. Average farm-gate price for England and Wales, crop year (June-May).

7 Average prices at representative markets in England and Wales.

8 Based on Meat and Livestock Commission all clean cattle prices.

9 Derived by dividing total value of output by the total quantity of output available for human consumption.

10 Average price of all Class A eggs weighted according to quantity in each grade.

11 Average of Great Britain weekly market prices as used to determine the level of ewe premium.

12 Average of Northern Ireland weekly market prices used to determine the level of ewe premium.

13 Category change 1988: formerly 1st quality yearling steers beef/dairy cross, now consists of Hereford/cross, Charolais/cross, Limousin/cross, Simmental/cross, Belgian/cross, other continental cross, other beef/dairy cross, other beef/beef cross.

Source: Ministry of Agriculture, Fisheries and Food: 01904 455332

17 Government finance

Government finance

Public sector *(Tables 17.1 to 17.3 and 17.5)*

In Table 17.1 the term public sector describes the consolidation of central government, local government and public corporations. General government is the consolidated total of central government and local government. The table shows details of the key public sector finances' indicators, consistent with the European System of Accounts 1995 (ESA95).

The concepts in Table 17.1 are consistent with the new format for public finances in the *Economic and Fiscal Strategy Report (EFSR),* (published by HM Treasury 11 June 1998). The public sector surplus on current budget in the *EFSR* is equivalent to net saving in national accounts plus capital tax receipts. Net investment is gross capital formation, plus payments less receipts of investment grants, less depreciation. Net borrowing is net investment less surplus on current budget. Net borrowing differs from the net cash requirement (see below) in that it is measured on an accruals basis whereas the net cash requirement is mainly a cash measure which includes some financial transactions.

Details of the public sector net cash requirement and the contributions to the net cash requirement are given in Table 17.2. The net cash requirement indicates the extent to which the public sector borrows from other sectors of the economy and non-residents to finance the balance of expenditure and receipts arising from its various activities. Part of the central government net cash requirement is needed to finance central government on lending to local government and public corporations. Their additional 'contributions' to the public sector are therefore equal to their net cash requirements *less* their direct borrowing from central government.

General government net cash requirement is the sum of the borrowing requirements of central government and local government *less* direct borrowing by local government from central government. The public sector net cash requirement is general government *plus* public corporations' net cash requirement *less* their direct borrowing from central government.

The net cash requirements for local government and public corporations are measured from the financing items rather than as the difference between receipts and payments because this information comes to hand more quickly.

Table 17.3 shows public sector net debt. Public sector net debt consists of the public sector's financial liabilities at face value minus its liquid assets - mainly foreign currency exchange reserves and bank deposits. General government gross debt (consolidated) in table 17.3 is consistent with the definition of general government

gross debt reported to the European Commission under the requirements of the Maastricht Treaty. More information on the concepts in table 17.1, 17.2 and 17.3 can be found in a guide to monthly public sector finance statistics, *GSS Methodology Series No 12,* the ONS First Releases *Public Sector Finances* and *Public Sector Accounts* and *Financial Statistics Explanatory Handbook* .

Table 17.5 (Part 1) shows the central government net cash requirement on own account, which is the net measure of all receipts and expenditure on central government funds and accounts, after excluding transactions which do not cross the central government boundary with the rest of the economy. Part 2 shows central government net cash requirement. The table shows the main financial instruments through which central government borrows to finance the net cash requirement. The details of the changes in the financial liabilities and assets of central government in aggregate match the net cash requirement.

Rateable values *(Table 17.12)*

Major changes to local government finance in England and Wales took effect from 1 April 1990. These included the abolition of domestic rating - replaced by the community charge (replaced in 1993 by the council tax), the revaluation of all non-domestic properties, and the introduction of the Uniform Business Rate. Also in 1990, a new classification scheme was introduced which has resulted in differences in coverage. Further differences are caused by legislative changes which have changed the treatment of certain types of property.

As a result, the analysis presented here for 1990 differs substantially from that of previous years and comparisons between 1990 and earlier years should be made with caution. With effect from 1 April 1995 all non-domestic properties were revalued. Although overall there was little change in rateable values, those for offices fell and there was a rise for all other main property types.

With effect from 1 April 2000 all non-domestic properties were revalued. Overall there was an increase in rateable values, the largest proportionate increase being for offices with all main property types showing rises.

Central government

The central government embraces all bodies for whose activities a Minister of the Crown, or other responsible person, is accountable to Parliament. It includes, in addition to the ordinary government departments, a number of bodies administering public policy but without the substantial degree of financial independence which characterises the public corporations; it also includes certain extra-budgetary funds and accounts controlled by departments.

The government's financial transactions are handled through a number of statutory funds, or accounts. The most important of these is the Consolidated Fund which is the government's main account with the Bank of England. Up to 31 March 1968 the Consolidated Fund was virtually synonymous with the term 'Exchequer' which was then the government's central cash account. From 1 April 1968 the National Loans Fund, with a separate account at the Bank of England, was set up by the National Loans Act, 1968. The general effect of this Act was to remove from the Consolidated Fund most of the government's domestic lending and the whole of the government's borrowing transactions and to provide for them to be brought to account in the National Loans Fund.

Revenue from taxation and miscellaneous receipts, including interest and dividends on loans made from Votes, continue to be paid into the Consolidated Fund. After meeting the ordinary expenditure on Supply Services and the Consolidated Fund Standing Services, the surplus or deficit of the Consolidated Fund (Table 17.4), is payable into or met by the National Loans Fund.

Table 17.4 also provides a summary of the transactions of the National Loans Fund. The service of the National Debt, previously borne by the Consolidated Fund, is now met from the National Loans Fund which receives (a) interest payable on loans to the nationalised industries, local authorities and other bodies, whether the loans were made before or after 1 April 1968 and (b) the profits of the Issue Department of the Bank of England, mainly derived from interest on government securities, which were formerly paid into the Exchange Equalisation Account. The net cost of servicing the National Debt after applying these interest receipts and similar items is a charge on the Consolidated Fund as part of the standing services. Details of National Loans Fund loans outstanding are shown in Table 17.7.

Details of borrowing and repayments of debt, other than loans from the National Loans Fund, are shown in Table 17.6.

Government finance

17.1 Public sector finances[1]
United Kingdom
Not seasonally adjusted

£ millions

		1989 /90	1990 /91	1991 /92	1992 /93	1993 /94	1994 /95	1995 /96	1996 /97	1997 /98	1998 /99	1999 /00
Surplus on current budget[2]												
General Government	ANLW	9 894	6 809	−8 268	−32 710	−38 709	−31 506	−25 779	−22 374	−1 336	9 878	20 255
Public sector	ANMU	7 661	3 177	−11 184	−35 697	−40 970	−33 952	−26 195	−23 057	−1 701	8 910	18 830
Net investment[3]												
General Government	−ANNV	10 823	13 840	12 549	13 835	11 980	13 499	10 704	6 795	4 687	4 081	3 595
Public sector	−ANNW	5 738	7 199	10 124	11 833	9 851	9 325	8 910	4 674	3 799	3 995	3 221
Net borrowing[4]												
General Government	−NNBK	929	7 031	20 817	46 545	50 689	45 005	36 483	29 169	6 023	−5 797	−16 660
Public sector	−ANNX	−1 923	4 022	21 308	47 530	50 821	43 277	35 105	27 731	5 500	−4 915	−15 609
Net cash requirement[5]												
General Government	RUUS	−2 982	239	13 420	36 577	46 070	38 096	34 489	24 152	1 830	−6 574	−9 699
Public sector	RURQ	−6 905	−776	13 856	36 180	46 162	36 688	31 485	22 728	1 112	−6 960	−8 687

1 National accounts entities as defined under the European System of Accounts 1995 (ESA95) consistent with the latest national accounts.
2 Net saving, plus capital taxes.

3 Gross capital formation, plus payments less receipts, of investment grants less depreciation.
4 Net borrowing = net investment minus surplus on current budget.
5 Previously called Public Sector Borrowing Requirement (PSBR).

Source: Office for National Statistics: 020 7533 5984

17.2 Contributions to the public sector net cash requirement
United Kingdom

£ millions

		1989 /90	1990 /91	1991 /92	1992 /93	1993 /94	1994 /95	1995 /96	1996 /97	1997 /98	1998 /99	1999 /00
Central government net cash requirement	RUUW	−4 575	−2 635	13 020	36 230	49 699	39 123	35 315	25 156	3 542	−4 535	−9 143
of which: own account	RUUX	−4 314	−3 092	11 830	42 312	48 850	39 057	35 628	24 995	2 650	−6 170	−10 556
Local government												
Direct borrowing from central government[1]	ABEC	2 262	1 472	639	−7 267	−654	−392	473	1 517	955	1 869	1 400
Net borrowing from other sources	ABEF	−967	1 817	973	1 506	−2 025	−610	−1 611	−2 357	−1 761	−2 166	−562
less Transactions in other public sector dept:												
Central government	ABEE	32	−32	19	−12	43	25	4	2	15	103	−19
Public corporations	AAEJ	−69	−10	3	−14	58	−66	−3	1	−1	4	−3
Net cash requirement	ABEG	1 332	3 331	1 590	−5 735	−2 780	−961	−1 139	−843	−820	−404	860
General government net cash requirement	RUUI	−5 505	−776	13 971	37 762	47 573	38 554	33 703	22 796	1 767	−6 808	−9 683
Public corporations:												
Direct borrowing from central government	ABEI	−2 523	−1 015	551	1 185	1 503	458	−786	−1 356	−63	−234	13
Net borrowing from other sources	ABES	−1 778	−216	−357	−599	−845	−633	−419	1 187	−295	−843	728
less Transactions in other public sector debt:												
Central government	ABEK	−236	−230	−225	865	531	1 267	2 495	1 340	356	−660	−298
Local authorities	ABEL	−142	14	−17	118	35	−34	−696	−85	4	−31	30
Net cash requirement	ABEM	−3 923	−1 015	436	−397	92	−1 408	−3 004	−1 424	−718	−386	1 009
Public sector net cash requirement	RURQ	−6 905	−776	13 856	36 180	46 162	36 688	31 485	22 728	1 112	−6 960	−8 687
Public sector net cash requirement excluding privatisation proceeds	RURS	−2 686	4 569	21 779	44 364	51 592	43 121	33 920	27 162	2 882	−6 890	−8 152

1 Excluding market transactions of central government in public sector debt; these transactions are included in 'Net borrowing from other sources.'

Source: Office for National Statistics: 020 7533 5984

17.3 Public sector net debt
United Kingdom

£ millions

		1992 /93	1993 /94	1994 /95	1995 /96	1996 /97	1997 /98	1998 /99	1999 /00
Cental government sterling gross debt:									
British goverment stock									
Conventional gilts	BKPK	130 642	168 414	186 666	208 943	231 869	232 292	223 105	218 687
Index linked gilts	BKPL	27 861	34 854	39 207	46 133	51 535	58 729	62 289	65 740
Total	BKPM	158 503	203 268	225 872	255 075	283 404	291 021	285 394	284 427
Sterling Treasury bills	BKPJ	5 307	3 483	8 051	10 781	4 996	2 106	4 721	4 453
National savings	ACUA	44 147	48 330	51 843	56 965	61 754	63 271	63 620	62 544
Tax instruments	ACRV	2 385	2 133	1 612	1 222	853	706	574	535
Other sterling debt[2]	BKSK	10 716	15 045	25 773	26 758	26 571	25 312	26 152	25 293
Central government sterling gross debt total	BKSL	221 058	272 259	313 151	350 801	377 578	382 416	380 461	377 252
Central government foreign currency gross debt:									
US$ bonds	BKPG	4 585	4 651	4 241	4 524	4 294	4 180	4 338	4 388
DM bonds[1]	EYST	2 062	2 018	2 245	2 219	1 828	–	–	–
ECU bonds	EYSJ	1 998	1 945	2 045	2 059	1 777	1 606	1 672	1 500
ECU/euro Treasury notes	EYSV	1 998	3 890	4 499	4 118	3 199	2 891	3 010	2 701
ECU/euro Treasury bills	EYSN	2 878	2 723	2 863	2 883	2 488	2 249	2 341	–
Other foreign currency debt	BKPH	5 371	1 632	1 018	982	752	537	456	365
Central government foreign currency gross debt total	BKPI	18 892	16 860	16 912	16 785	14 338	11 463	11 816	8 954
Central government gross debt total	BKPW	239 950	289 119	330 063	367 586	391 916	393 879	392 277	386 206
Local government gross debt total	EYKP	49 897	50 239	50 229	50 552	51 599	51 933	52 742	53 437
less									
Central government holdings of local government debt	–EYKZ	–41 527	–40 977	–40 707	–41 266	–42 555	–43 397	–45 273	–46 656
Local government holdings of central government debt	–EYLA	–81	–124	–149	–153	–155	–170	–273	–254
General government gross debt (consolidated)	BKPX	248 239	298 257	339 436	376 719	400 805	402 245	399 473	392 733
Public corporations gross debt	EYYD	16 194	23 867	26 916	26 595	26 158	26 044	26 775	26 812
less:									
Central government holdings of public corporations debt	–EYXY	–15 227	–22 951	–26 279	–25 980	–25 664	–25 668	–26 440	–26 453
Local government holdings of public corporations debt	–EYXZ	–11	–69	–3	–	–1	–	–4	–1
Public corporations holdings of central government debt	–BKPZ	–2 617	–2 854	–3 503	–5 723	–7 125	–7 485	–6 529	–6 169
Public corporations holdings of local government debt	–EYXV	–1 585	–1 620	–1 586	–890	–805	–810	–779	–812
Public sector gross debt (consolidated)	BKQA	244 993	294 630	334 981	370 721	393 368	394 326	392 496	386 110
Public sector liquid assets:									
Official reserves	AIPD	27 153	28 908	28 330	30 463	25 547	21 293	22 147	21 498
Central government deposits[3]	BKSM	1 631	1 775	1 816	1 808	2 067	2 292	1 762	1 879
Other central government	BKSN	3 386	1 250	–	–	–	–	–	4 756
Local government deposits[3]	BKSO	6 341	8 762	9 335	10 229	11 276	11 790	12 275	11 758
Other local government short term assets	BKQG	1 932	2 424	2 621	2 826	3 256	3 693	4 334	4 754
Public corporations deposits[3]	BKSP	1 166	1 353	2 622	3 089	1 778	1 469	2 029	1 455
Other public corporations short term assets	BKSQ	1 077	790	943	1 054	964	937	1 300	1 114
Public sector liquid assets total	BKQJ	42 686	45 262	45 667	49 469	44 888	41 474	43 847	47 214
Public sector net debt	BKQK	202 307	249 368	289 314	321 252	348 480	352 852	348 649	338 896
as percentage of GDP[4]	RUTO	32.2	37.5	41.1	43.1	44.0	41.9	39.6	36.7

1 Matured on 28 October 1997.
2 Including overdraft with Bank of England.
3 Bank and building society deposits.
4 Gross domestic product at market prices fro 12 months centred on the end
  of the month.

Source: Office for National Statistics: 020 7533 5984

17.4 Consolidated Fund and National Loans Fund: revenue and expenditure; receipts and payments

United Kingdom   Years ended 31 March

£ millions

		1989/90	1990/91	1991/92	1992/93	1993/94	1994/95	1995/96	1996/97	1997/98	1998/99	1999/00
Consolidated Fund												
Revenue												
Inland Revenue	KCWZ	76 674.3	82 320.7	79 509.6	76 345.9	77 270.6	87 230.4	97 100.9	103 892.4	117 632.8	128 249.8	139 384.0
Customs and Excise	KCXA	52 190.2	55 336.9	61 826.9	63 398.0	66 885.5	72 485.6	76 668.6	82 351.6	89 839.6	94 018.3	97 291.5
Motor vehicle duties	KCXB	2 920.0	2 971.4	2 945.3	3 196.0	3 752.3	3 805.9	4 043.6	4 217.5	4 543.0	4 666.3	4 893.0
National Non-Domestic Rates	KPOI	..	..	..	..	..	16 280.3	13 373.4	14 269.3	14 036.9	15 878.3	13 403.8
Miscellaneous receipts	KCXE	13 136.5	21 736.6	27 193.0	30 101.2	22 150.2	16 280.3	10 289.3	12 634.6	14 176.6	10 737.1	8 799.0
Total revenue	KCXF	144 921.6	162 366.1	171 474.8	173 041.2	170 058.6	191 272.0	201 475.8	217 365.4	240 228.9	253 549.8	263 771.3
Expenditure												
Supply services	KCXG	122 548.8	145 763.1	168 702.6	189 961.6	204 376.1	207 465.8	211 403.3	214 226.0	209 440.8	213 439.2	226 989.6
Debt interest[1]	KCXH	11 343.3	10 229.2	8 943.0	10 675.1	13 459.6	16 039.8	18 423.1	20 702.3	21 605.7	21 320.8	18 535.3
Payments to Northern Ireland	KCXI	2 683.1	2 927.7	2 944.9	2 632.1	3 090.3	4 052.6	3 903.5	3 685.2	4 581.5	4 709.3	3 104.4
Payments to the European Communities, etc	KCXJ	4 537.7	4 806.1	3 323.3	4 867.1	6 079.5	5 258.2	7 650.7	6 875.3	7 039.9	8 060.7	7 001.8
Other expenditure[2]	KCXL	380.7	503.7	276.3	117.7	−453.3	271.6	−14.0	876.2	−53.8	−62.1	223.7
Total expenditure	KCXM	141 493.6	164 229.8	184 189.7	208 253.6	226 552.2	233 088.0	241 366.5	246 365.0	242 614.1	247 467.9	255 854.8
Deficit met from the National Loans Fund	KCXN	−3 428.0	1 863.7	12 715.5	35 212.4	56 493.6	41 816.0	39 890.7	28 999.6	2 385.2	−6 081.9	−7 916.5
National Loans Fund												
Receipts												
Profits of the Issue Department of the Bank of England - income[5]	KZAW	1 237.1	2 247.3	1 816.5	1 350.8	996.6	955.2	1 275.5	1 200.9	1 604.8	1 600.9	1 327.3
Other miscellaneous receipts	KZAX	3.9	−	6.2	66.7	106.6	4.8	4.4	3.6	5.0	5.0	4.4
Interest on loans	KCXO	6 282.4	5 429.0	5 925.1	5 100.7	4 695.2	4 564.5	4 598.7	4 393.5	5 103.6	4 409.7	4 533.3
Service of the National Debt - balance met from the Consolidated Fund	KCXP	11 335.5	10 229.3	8 943.1	10 675.1	13 459.6	16 039.8	18 423.2	20 702.3	21 605.7	21 320.8	18 535.3
Gilt Edged Official Operations Account Net Income	KJDO	..	..	..	..	2.0	−	−	−	−	−	127.5
Total	KCXQ	18 858.9	17 905.6	16 690.9	17 193.3	19 260.0	21 564.3	24 301.8	26 300.3	28 319.1	27 336.4	24 527.8
Exchange Equalisation Account-sterling capital	KCXR	6 175.0	−1 050.0	300.0	3 574.5	400.0	1 250.0	2 750.0	2 150.0	3 650.0	1 880.0	975.0
Net borrowing[4]	KCXS	−	3 684.7	12 112.0	25 907.6	58 939.5	39 848.1	37 688.8	27 547.9	−	−	4 997.3
International Monetary Fund-maintenance of sterling holdings	KCXT	−	−	59.8	47.6	−	−	−	82.1	707.0	181.2	−
Profits of the Issue Department of the Bank of England: capital appreciation	KZAY	..	..	..	..	..	..	..	18.8	21.2	19.3	1.7
Reduction of National Debt Commissioners' Liability in respect of the National Savings Bank Investment Account	KCXU	−	−	−	−	−	−	−	−	−	−	−
Change in balances and other items	KCXV	−	−	−	−	−	−	−	−	−	−	−
NILO Gilt-Edged operations A/C	KJDL	−	−	−	−	2 500.0	2 500.0	2 500.0	2 000.0	2 500.0	2 500.0	5 000.0
Total	KCXW	25 033.9	20 540.3	29 162.7	46 723.0	81 099.5	65 162.4	42 938.8	58 099.1	35 197.3	31 916.9	35 501.8
Payments												
Service of the National Debt:												
Interest	KJDM	18 679.9	17 730.6	16 516.3	17 009.5	19 107.0	21 334.7	24 004.0	25 942.5	27 877.8	26 792.1	24 073.7
Management and expenses	KCXY	179.0	175.0	174.6	183.8	153.0	229.6	297.8	357.8	441.3	544.3	454.1
Total	KCXZ	18 858.9	17 905.6	16 690.9	17 193.3	19 260.0	21 564.3	24 301.8	26 300.3	28 319.1	27 336.4	24 527.8
Consolidated Fund deficit met from the National Loans Fund	KCYA	−3 435.7	1 863.7	12 714.9	35 212.4	56 493.6	41 816.0	39 890.7	28 999.6	2 385.2	−6 081.9	−7 916.5
Net repayment[4]	KCYB	7 923.3	−	−	−	−	−	−	−	2 482.1	3 558.2	−
Net lending[3]	KCYC	1 538.3	623.9	−243.1	−6 787.0	−286.6	−974.8	334.1	280.6	−4.2	1 766.3	1 255.9
International Monetary Fund-maintenance of value of sterling holding	KCYD	149.1	147.1	−	1 104.3	632.5	226.2	202.1	−	−	−	126.1
International Monetary Fund-additional subscription	KCYE	−	−	−	−	−	−	−	−	−	2 826.5	−
NILO Gilt-Edged Operations A/C	KJDN	−	−	−	−	−	2 500.0	2 500.0	2 500.0	2 000.0	2 500.0	2 500.0
Discharge of Treasury Liability to the Bank of England Issue Department	KPUK	..	−	−	−	−	30.7	11.9	18.6	15.1	11.4	8.5
Debt Management Account	ZAFB	..	..	..	..	..	..	..	..	..	..	15 000.0
Total	KCYF	25 033.9	20 540.3	29 162.7	46 723.0	81 099.5	65 162.4	42 938.8	58 099.1	35 197.3	31 916.9	35 501.8

1 Payment to National Loans Fund representing its payments for the service of the National Debt *less* its receipts of interest on loans outstanding, etc.
2 Includes net issues to Contingencies Fund.
3 Minus sign indicates a net issue repayment.

4 See Table 17.6.
5 Prior to 1996-97, receipts from the Bank of England for appreciation of the assets of the Issue Department were included in the total amount for the profits of the Issue Department.

Source: HM Treasury: 020 7270 1586

17.5 Central government net cash requirement
United Kingdom
Years ended 31 March

£ millions

		1989/90	1990/91	1991/92	1992/93	1993/94	1994/95	1995/96	1996/97	1997/98	1998/99	1999/00
Inland revenue	ACAB	76 673	82 322	79 353	76 292	77 289	87 255	97 120	103 957	117 632	128 249	139 384
Customs and excise	ACAC	52 190	55 336	61 827	63 398	66 885	72 486	76 670	82 351	89 840	94 019	97 290
Social security contributions[1]	ABIA	31 020	33 013	34 391	35 420	36 985	40 659	42 882	45 121	49 255	53 227	54 606
Interest and dividends	RUUL	11 362	10 997	10 924	9 828	9 595	8 380	9 607	9 082	9 557	9 455	8 637
Other receipts[2]	RUUM	3 107	14 798	16 052	16 529	17 870	17 082	19 289	20 906	20 848	19 618	20 202
Total cash receipts	RUUN	174 352	196 466	202 547	201 467	208 624	225 862	245 568	261 417	287 132	304 568	320 119
Interest payments	RUUO	18 090	17 465	16 538	17 528	19 160	21 998	24 452	27 554	27 807	27 031	24 278
Privatisation proceeds	ABIF	−4 219	−5 345	−7 923	−8 184	−5 430	−6 433	−2 435	−4 434	−1 770	−70	−535
Net departmental outlays[3]	RUUP	156 167	181 254	205 762	234 435	243 744	249 354	259 179	263 292	263 745	271 437	285 820
Total cash outlays	RUUQ	170 038	193 374	214 377	243 779	257 474	264 919	281 196	286 412	289 782	298 398	309 563
Own account net cash requirement	RUUX	−4 314	−3 092	11 830	42 312	48 850	39 057	35 628	24 995	2 650	−6 170	−10 556
On lending to local government	ABEC	2 262	1 472	639	−7 267	−654	−392	473	1 517	955	1 869	1 400
On lending to public corporations	ABEI	−2 523	−1 015	551	1 185	1 503	458	−786	−1 356	−63	−234	13
Central government net cash requirement	RUUW	−4 575	−2 635	13 020	36 230	49 699	39 123	35 315	25 156	3 542	−4 535	−9 143

1 Excluding Northern Ireland contributions
2 Including some elements of expenditure not separately identified.
3 Net of certain receipts.

		1992/93	1993/94	1994/95	1995/96	1996/97	1997/98	1998/99	1999/00
Central government funds and accounts									
National Loans Fund:									
Total payments	ACAU	10 407	18 973	20 648	24 631	26 581	28 309	29 100	25 786
Total receipts	ACAQ	17 193	19 260	21 593	24 286	26 282	28 318	27 335	24 527
Less surplus from consolidated fund	ACAP	−35 213	−56 494	−41 817	−39 889	−28 983	−2 386	6 083	7 859
Borrowing required	ACAX	28 426	56 205	40 871	40 235	29 279	2 376	−4 318	−6 602
Surplus of National Insurance Funds[2]	ACAY	−6 033	903	2 304	674	326	1 798	3 053	2 262
Departmental balances and miscellaneous	ACAZ	−1 615	5 585	−539	4 192	3 857	−3 046	−2 947	109
Northern Ireland central government debt	ACBA	156	−20	15	−52	59	−82	−111	−170
Financing of the central government net cash requirement analysed by type of instrument									
Net cash requirement	RUUW	36 230	49 699	39 123	35 315	25 156	3 542	−4 535	−9 143
Liabilities									
Coin	−EYMW	33	97	121	74	136	145	219	192
Sterling Treasury bills	NAVG	−4 321	−1 821	4 566	2 733	−5 787	−2 890	2 614	−274
British government securities	ANTA	30 468	46 411	21 206	26 607	26 492	6 285	−8 910	−1 203
National savings	−AACE	4 352	4 111	3 570	5 109	4 821	1 554	365	−1 055
Tax instruments	−AACF	−329	−252	−521	−390	−369	−147	−135	−39
Loans from MFIs	ANTB	−4 113	3 400	9 028	−292	−1 342	−1 468	2 576	1 332
Northern Ireland cg debt	−AACH	7	−27	−3	−7	−4	−21	−18	−12
ECS liabilities	−AACI	−50	−43	−24	−35	−9	4	−4	–
Deposits with cg from other sectors	ANTC	693	1 242	1 406	1 393	990	156	−1 637	−947
Government foreign currency debt	−AACL	6 966	−1 639	−25	−401	−248	−1 803	−45	−2 221
Other government overseas financing	−AACM	−100	−94	−93	−94	−88	−91	−98	−98
Assets									
NILO lending (except PWLB)	ANTD	388	−124	−122	−97	253	140	−2	−118
Net change in official reserves	AIPA	2 184	−1 442	62	705	635	1 902	3	167
Deposits with MFIs	ANSZ	52	−117	−48	13	−325	−224	537	−4 866

1 This is equal to National Loans Fund borrowing and special transactions (net) *less* receipts from other central government funds, etc.
2 A negative item represents a surplus, a positive item a deficit.

Sources: HM Treasury;
Office for National Statistics: 020 7533 5984

17.6 Borrowing and repayment of debt
United Kingdom
Years ended 31 March

£ millions

		1989/90	1990/91	1991/92	1992/93	1993/94	1994/95	1995/96	1996/97	1997/98	1998/99	1999/00
Borrowing												
Government securities: new issues	KQGA	–	3 269.3	15 920.7	33 601.1	55 959.2	32 137.5	34 150.3	40 800.8	28 484.4	12 048.0	26 426.5
National savings securities:												
National savings certificates	KQGB	1 256.2	2 658.1	3 549.1	3 453.4	3 381.5	2 187.9	3 425.9	3 695.5	4 435.2	3 028.7	1 962.7
Capital bonds	KQGC	288.0	188.7	282.1	524.8	556.2	521.5	504.8	450.8	619.0	469.6	35.4
Income bonds	KQGD	1 482.9	1 629.1	1 329.1	1 251.2	1 940.8	1 255.7	780.7	1 272.7	1 043.4	1 371.7	653.4
Deposit bonds	KQGE	2.4	–	–	–	–	–	–	–	–	–	–
British savings bonds	KQGF	–	–	–	–	–	–	–	–	–	–	–
Premium savings bonds	KQGG	256.5	185.9	246.5	378.6	931.5	1 837.2	2 040.6	2 552.5	3 158.8	3 652.8	3 449.4
Save As You Earn	KQGH	76.4	88.2	94.3	85.3	76.4	66.5	50.8	34.1	20.7	11.4	5.0
Yearly plan	KQGI	88.8	71.0	87.0	109.9	112.4	116.5	94.1	–	–	5.2	–
National savings stamps and gift tokens	KQGJ	0.5	11.4	–	–	–	–	–	–	–	–	–
National Savings Bank Investments	KQGK	1 434.7	1 491.2	1 215.1	1 227.9	1 370.5	1 368.1	1 312.1	1 478.7	1 282.3	1 085.0	901.6
Children's Bonus Bonds	KGVO	–	–	127.0	95.5	91.2	118.9	144.9	352.4	255.3	205.0	58.5
First Option Bonds	KIAR	–	–	–	859.4	1 026.0	812.0	826.4	1 139.8	1 152.9	1 001.8	34.3
Pensioners Guaranteed Income Bond	KJDW					786.1	1 190.3	2 104.2	2 863.8	1 126.9	201.0	590.7
Treasurer's account	KWNF	..	..	..	..	..	..	..	21.1	39.9	17.1	13.6
Individual Savings Account	ZAFC	..	..	..	..	..	..	..	..	..	–	257.8
Fixed Rate Savings Bonds	ZAFD	..	..	..	..	..	..	..	..	..	–	175.9
Certificate of tax deposit	KQGL	1 065.9	1 343.1	1 137.7	607.2	470.6	91.2	76.2	109.4	84.1	66.4	121.4
Nationalised industries', etc temporary deposits	KQGM	29 728.0	25 855.0	20 709.0	19 350.0	28 700.9	29 294.0	36 870.6	53 198.2	46 375.9	39 962.4	40 343.3
British Gas corporation deposits	KQGN	–	–	–	–	–	–	–	–	–	–	–
Sterling Treasury bills (net receipt)	KQGO	7 282.5	–	–	–	–	5 196.1	2 606.1	–	–	3 546.2	–
ECU Treasury bills (net receipt)	KQGP	625.3	429.2	–	–	–	–	–	–	–	–	–
ECU Treasury notes (net receipt)	KDZZ	–	–	1 066.4	1 396.0	2 073.2	429.8	–	–	–	–	721.1
Ways and means (net receipt)	KQGQ	1 753.9	4 107.5	2 530.5	–	9 007.0	8 891.7	1 162.3	511.1	–	183.6	5 599.0
Other debt : payable in sterling :												
Interest free notes	KQGR	323.6	319.1	161.2	1 045.6	796.6	382.6	247.4	99.2	32.4	2 130.9	373.5
Other debt : payable in external currencies	KHCY	588.1	1 939.8	40.0	33 147.7	9 243.9	–	–	2 565.2	–	–	–
Total receipts	KHCZ	46 253.7	43 586.6	48 495.7	97 133.6	116 524.0	85 897.5	86 397.4	111 145.3	88 111.2	68 986.8	81 723.1
Repayment of debt												
Government securities : redemptions	KQGS	17 068.4	6 806.0	7 841.5	8 351.8	7 390.5	9 333.3	4 652.7	14 488.4	20 678.9	18 575.5	19 815.8
Statutory sinking funds	KQGT	2.8	2.7	2.5	2.5	2.4	2.3	2.2	2.2	2.1	2.0	2.0
Terminable annuities:												
National Debt Commissioners	KQGU											
National savings securities:												
National savings certificates	KQGV	2 879.1	2 187.4	1 653.6	1 092.5	2 208.0	1 612.6	2 258.4	3 263.7	4 058.5	3 449.0	2 405.2
Capital bonds	KQGW	5.9	23.5	14.6	21.1	398.0	647.7	509.0	698.3	1 160.5	888.3	324.2
Income bonds	KQGX	1 094.9	831.3	729.0	955.2	1 000.7	1 181.8	1 256.9	1 394.0	1 148.9	880.8	1 686.3
Deposit bonds	KQGY	202.5	138.4	86.8	80.9	71.8	72.3	72.5	64.8	72.6	84.2	70.2
Yearly Plan	KQGZ	81.0	127.5	107.1	99.8	88.9	77.0	101.9	96.3	113.2	120.0	141.8
British savings bonds	KQHA	–	–	–	–	–	–	–	–	–	–	–
Premium savings bonds	KQHB	185.7	194.0	154.3	153.4	181.0	333.0	590.1	869.3	1 203.1	1 398.4	1 923.8
Save As You Earn	KQHC	87.9	89.6	103.6	116.9	96.3	92.3	98.7	70.1	68.2	37.1	34.5
National savings stamps and gift tokens	KQHD	0.1	11.1	–	–	0.7	–	–	–	–	–	–
National Savings Bank Investments (repayments)	KQHE	2 056.6	1 775.3	1 796.1	2 039.0	1 646.3	1 745.3	1 755.8	1 837.0	2 175.7	2 027.0	1 886.3
Children's Bonus Bonds	KGVQ	–	–	0.1	1.0	1.2	4.3	0.1	257.8	187.9	183.2	69.3
First Option Bonds	KIAS	–	–	–	4.6	1 085.1	969.9	732.7	833.9	1 283.0	1 055.5	298.1
Pensioners Guaranteed Income Bond	KPOB	–	–	–	–	57.0	104.5	185.0	318.8	897.8	935.3
Treasurer's account	KWNG	..	..	..	..	..	..	..	1.2	11.8	13.7	16.4
Individual Savings Account	ZAFE	..	..	..	..	..	..	..	..	..	..	12.3
Fixed Rate Savings Bonds	ZAFF	..	..	..	..	..	..	..	..	..	..	2.8
Certificates of tax deposit	KQHF	797.1	1 192.3	1 116.5	936.9	722.6	612.1	466.0	478.9	229.0	199.9	159.9
Tax reserve certificates	KQHG	–	0.1	0.1	–	–	–	–	–	–	–	–
Nationalised industries', etc temporary deposits	KQHH	29 314.0	25 833.0	21 186.0	18 477.0	28 098.5	28 557.8	35 263.1	51 979.3	46 835.7	41 776.9	41 089.4
Debt to the Bank of England	KPOC	–	–	–	–	–	11.0	–	–	–	–	–
British Gas Corporation (Repayment of Deposits)	KQHI	–	–	–	–	–	–	–	–	–	–	–
Sterling Treasury bills (net repayment)	KQHJ	–	140.3	1 191.0	4 882.1	1 547.5	–	–	4 009.6	1 928.5	–	3 014.8
ECU Treasury bills (net repayment)	KJEG	..	..	..	..	73.3	–	–	–	–	–	2 492.9
ECU Treasury notes (net repayment)	KSPA	..	..	..	..	..	..	439.1	318.3	3.3	13.2	–
Ways and means (net repayment)	KQHK	..	..	–	6 786.3	–	–	–	–	5 815.4	–	–
Other debt: payable in sterling :												
Interest free notes	KQHL	170.8	169.6	268.3	155.8	101.3	225.2	301.3	87.6	1 215.5	850.5	246.4
Other	KQHM	0.1	0.1	0.1	–	–	–	–	–	–	–	–
Other debt : payable in external currencies	KQHN	229.3	379.7	132.5	27 068.7	12 870.4	514.5	103.6	2 661.7	2 082.7	92.0	98.1
Total payments	KQHO	54 177.0	39 901.9	36 383.7	71 226.0	57 584.5	46 049.4	48 708.6	83 597.4	90 593.3	72 545.0	76 725.8
Net borrowing	KQHP	–	3 684.7	12 112.0	25 907.6	58 939.5	39 848.1	37 688.8	27 547.9	–	–	4 997.3
Net repayment	KHDD	7 923.3	–	–	–	–	–	–	–	2 482.1	3 558.2	–

Source: HM Treasury: 020 7270 1586

17.7 Consolidated Fund and National Loans Fund: assets and liabilities
United Kingdom
At 31 March in each year

£ millions

		1990	1991	1992	1993	1994	1995	1996	1997	1998	1999
Consolidated Fund											
Total estimated assets	KQIA	6 820.0	14 951.0	19 852.9	18 872.0	26 914.5	33 992.4	33 809.0	36 177.4	36 061.0	36 148.0
Subscriptions and contributions to international financial organisations	KQIB	2 866.1	4 329.6	4 315.2	5 009.2	5 438.2	5 898.1	6 470.8	6 528.9	6 660.8	7 059.7
International Bank for Reconstruction and Development	KQIC	215.7	224.8	236.3	259.8	274.5	265.2	271.6	265.0	262.5	266.0
International Finance Corporation	KQID	41.6	39.3	39.4	53.1	60.9	62.0	73.1	74.9	72.9	75.6
International Development Association	KQIE	1 979.5	2 127.3	2 343.3	2 576.0	2 785.4	3 005.5	3 205.8	3 372.7	3 562.2	3 733.3
African Development Bank	KQIF	65.9	80.8	91.2	108.1	127.9	141.2	148.3	162.9	180.0	199.1
Asian Development Bank	KQIG	142.3	155.8	173.0	180.9	188.9	201.5	214.6	240.4	272.5	304.6
Caribbean Development Bank	KQIH	20.9	24.6	27.5	29.4	31.2	32.6	34.2	34.1	34.6	36.8
European Investment Bank	KQII	277.7	1 550.3	1 252.8	1 588.9	1 713.7	1 876.4	2 166.6	2 036.5	1 840.7	2 083.1
European Bank for Reconstruction and Development	KPOD	..	..	22.3	61.3	99.4	146.3	189.4	175.6	164.2	179.2
Inter-American Development Bank	KQIJ	87.5	89.9	89.4	109.8	112.5	107.2	119.6	117.5	219.3	127.8
International Fund for Agricultural Development	KQIK	31.8	34.7	36.9	38.5	40.2	42.7	44.2	46.1	48.8	51.0
Multilateral Investment Guarantee Agency	KQIL	3.2	3.0	3.0	3.5	3.5	3.2	3.4	3.2	3.1	3.2
Amounts due from overseas governments	KQIM	1.3	–	–	–	–	–	–	–	–	–
War of 1939-45	KQIN	–	–	–	–	–	–	–	–	–	–
Other	KQIO	1.3	–	–	–	–	–	–	–	–	–
Loans from Votes	KQIP	2 257.1	2 420.3	4 047.3	6 709.2	11 057.4	13 599.7	12 967.0	13 684.7	14 050.0	11 546.3
Issues of public dividend capital:	KQIQ	1 629.0	1 617.9	1 642.7	4 920.0	7 979.2	11 467.0	12 161.1	12 424.8	13 157.1	16 238.5
British Airways Board	KQIR	–	–	–	–	–	–	–	–	–	–
British Steel Corporation	KQIS	–	–	–	–	–	–	–	–	–	–
Royal Ordnance Factories	KQIT	–	–	–	–	–	–	–	–	–	–
National Enterprise Board	KQIU	–	–	–	–	–	–	–	–	–	–
Royal Mint	KQIV	7.0	7.0	7.0	7.0	7.0	7.0	7.0	7.0	7.0	7.0
Post Office	KQIW	22.0	–	–	–	–	–	–	–	–	–
Scottish Development Agency	KQIX	7.9	–	–	–	–	–	–	–	–	–
Welsh Development Agency	KQIY	15.5	15.5	13.5	12.6	11.6	10.9	9.8	8.9	8.8	8.6
British Aerospace	KQIZ	–	–	–	–	–	–	–	–	–	–
British Shipbuilders	KQJA	1 576.6	1 595.4	1 597.4	1 598.3	1 598.3	1 598.3	1 598.3	1 598.5	1 598.3	1 598.3
Patent Office	KIAT	–	–	6.3	6.3	6.3	6.3	6.3	6.3	6.3	6.3
NHS Trusts	KIAU	–	–	1 325.8	3 279.6	6 336.2	9 603.1	10 173.8	10 349.7	11 078.0	14 158.7
Companies House	KIAV	–	–	16.9	15.9	15.9	15.9	15.9	15.9	15.9	15.9
Central Office of Information	KIAW	–	–	0.3	0.3	0.3	0.3	0.3	0.3	0.3	0.3
Chessington Computer Centre	KPOE	–	–	–	–	3.5	3.5	3.5	–	–	–
Buying Agency	KWNH	..	..	..	..	..	0.1	0.4	0.4	0.4	0.4
Defence Evaluation and Research Agency	KWNI	..	..	..	..	..	128.8	253.0	274.5	274.5	275.4
Fire Service College	KWNJ	..	..	..	..	..	16.7	16.7	16.7	16.7	16.7
Land Registry	KWNK	..	..	..	..	..	55.4	55.4	61.5	61.5	61.5
Medicines Control Agency	KWNL	..	..	..	..	..	1.6	1.6	1.6	1.6	1.6
Meteorological Office	KZAZ	..	..	..	..	..	..	..	58.9	58.9	58.9
Registers of Scotland	KZBA	..	..	..	..	..	..	..	4.3	4.3	4.3
Vehicle Inspectorate	KWNM	..	..	..	..	..	19.1	19.1	20.3	20.3	20.3
Driving Standards Agency	LQMI	..	..	..	..	..	..	..	..	3.5	3.5
Queen Elizabeth II Conference Centre	LQMJ	..	..	..	..	..	..	..	..	0.8	0.8
Contingencies Fund - capital	KQJB	0.6	942.0	1 097.0	947.0	347.0	447.0	297.0	977.0	577.0	277.0
Balance on revenue accounts	KQJC	66.3	237.2	725.2	477.6	358.7	1 433.6	1 096.1	954.9	1 546.0	1 026.5
Privatisation receipts	KIAX	–	5 403.9	6 701.0	809.0	1 734.0	1 147.0	817.0	1 607.1	70.1	–
Total liabilities	KQJD	123 397.0	128 386.2	–	–	–	–	333 927.9	364 803.0	364 950.8	363 625.5
Liability to balance National Loans Fund	KQJE	121 170.9	125 807.1	142 306.7	182 102.2	240 351.0	286 055.9	331 164.9	362 506.5	362 582.5	361 065.3
Payment from Votes:	KQJF	68.3	67.6	66.9	66.1	65.2	64.3	63.4	62.4	61.3	60.2
Married quarters for Armed Forces	KQJG	68.3	67.6	66.9	66.1	65.2	64.3	63.4	62.4	61.3	60.2
Liability to Post Office Superannuation Fund	KQJH	–	–	–	–	–	–	–	–	–	–
Post-war credits outstanding and interest due - estimated	KQJI	46.2	46.1	46.1	46.0	46.0	46.0	45.9	45.9	45.9	45.9
Revenue paid over in advance of collection	KQJJ	0.5	–	8.3	–	83.7	37.0	–	28.2	13.8	177.9
Inland Revenue	KQJK	–	–	–	–	–	–	–	–	–	177.9
Customs and Excise	KQJL	0.5	–	–	–	–	–	–	28.2	–	–
Broadcast receiving licences	KQJM	–	–	–	–	–	–	–	–	–	–
Vehicle Excise Duty	KQJN	–	–	8.3	–	83.7	37.0	–	–	13.8	–
National insurance surcharge - Great Britain	KQJO	–	–	–	–	–	–	–	–	–	–
National insurance surcharge - Northern Ireland	KQJP	–	–	–	–	–	–	–	–	–	–

Source: HM Treasury: 020 7270 1586

17.7
continued

Consolidated Fund and National Loans Fund: assets and liabilities
United Kingdom
At 31 March in each year

£ millions

		1990	1991	1992	1993	1994	1995	1996	1997	1998	1999
Consolidated Fund (continued)											
Promissory notes issued by											
Minister of Overseas Development	KQJQ	2 111.1	2 465.1	770.3	979.5	1 002.6	996.7	1 005.8	1 021.9	822.1	963.1
International Development Association	KQJR	650.0	705.3	489.4	673.1	670.5	656.5	663.2	673.6	484.0	612.3
African Development Fund	KQJS	71.2	77.1	92.1	100.7	106.6	93.2	86.2	95.3	95.2	105.6
Asian Development Bank	KQJT	2.1	1.4	0.1	–	–	–	–	–	–	–
Asian Development Fund	KQJU	119.9	108.7	92.1	108.7	131.8	140.5	127.6	136.0	120.5	105.4
Caribbean Development Bank	KQJV	–	–	0.1	0.1	1.2	1.3	1.4	1.3	1.3	1.3
Special Development Fund	KQKC	9.5	8.1	8.3	6.9	8.0	9.5	10.6	13.2	15.8	16.4
European Community/International Development Association Special Action Account	KQJW	–	–	–	–	–	–	–	–	–	–
European Investment Bank	KQJX	86.6	61.2	–	–	–	–	–	–	–	–
Inter-American Development Bank	KQJY	1.6	1.7	1.7	2.6	2.2	1.3	2.0	1.8	1.9	1.0
Fund for special operations	KQJZ	23.4	22.5	22.5	15.4	16.4	13.1	11.3	8.8	6.3	2.6
International Fund for Agricultural Development	KQKA	15.3	16.2	17.8	16.1	18.2	15.8	14.2	12.3	14.2	16.5
International Bank for Reconstruction and Development	KQKB	48.2	34.2	31.9	30.2	24.2	39.2	60.7	71.7	81.9	94.3
European Bank for Reconstruction and Development	KIAY	–	–	14.3	20.4	19.9	20.9	21.0	6.1	–	7.7
United Nations Environment Programme	KJEH	–	–	–	5.3	3.6	5.4	7.6	1.8	1.0	–
Other contributions and instalments due in respect of international subscriptions, etc	KQYX	1 083.3	1 429.0	2 125.1	1 520.7	2 165.8	1 499.6	1 647.9	1 138.1	1 425.2	1 313.1
National Loans Fund											
Total assets	KQKD	192 981.4	198 703.4	214 527.6	248 643.5	306 872.6	349 159.5	390 681.8	419 548.9	418 444.7	421 635.7
Total National Loans Fund loans outstanding	KQKE	56 154.1	56 777.9	55 492.8	48 705.9	48 470.8	47 496.1	46 600.9	46 746.8	46 742.6	48 513.6
Loans to nationalised industries:											
Post Office	KQKF	–	–	–	–	–	–	–	–	–	–
British Coal	KQKG	1 145.9	387.4	257.7	180.0	–	–	–	–	–	–
Electricity Council	KQKH	–	–	–	–	–	–	–	–	–	–
North of Scotland Hydro-Electric Board	KQKI	–	–	–	–	–	–	–	–	–	–
Scottish Hydro-Electric	KQKJ	527.8	534.9	–	–	–	–	–	–	–	–
South of Scotland Electricity Board	KQKK	–	–	–	–	–	–	–	–	–	–
Scottish Power	KQKL	548.8	508.6	–	–	–	–	–	–	–	–
Scottish Nuclear Ltd	KQKM	205.0	203.2	201.3	199.2	196.8	194.1	96.1	–	–	–
British Gas Corporation	KQKN	–	–	–	–	–	–	–	–	–	–
British Steel Corporation	KQKO	–	–	–	–	–	–	–	–	–	–
British Airways Board	KQKP	–	–	–	–	–	–	–	–	–	–
Railtrack	KTCR	..	..	..	..	..	1 287.7	–	–	–	–
European Passenger Services	KTCS	..	..	..	..	..	99.0	761.2	–	–	–
Civil Aviation Authority	KQKQ	146.9	216.3	271.2	311.9	403.7	453.3	476.1	447.5	420.9	365.7
British Airports Authority	KQKR	–	–	–	–	–	–	–	–	–	–
British Railways Board	KQKS	202.8	938.5	1 040.8	1 923.9	2 445.6	749.2	718.3	601.2	573.7	546.2
British Transport Docks Board	KQKT	–	–	–	–	–	–	–	–	–	–
British Waterways Board	KQKU	22.8	21.6	20.0	19.2	18.6	18.3	18.2	18.2	18.2	18.2
National Freight Corporation	KQKV	–	–	–	–	–	–	–	–	–	–
National Bus Company	KQKW	–	–	–	–	–	–	–	–	–	–
Scottish Transport Group	KQKX	–	–	–	–	–	–	–	–	–	–
British National Oil Corporation	KQKY	–	–	–	–	–	–	–	–	–	–
British Aerospace	KQKZ	–	–	–	–	–	–	–	–	–	–
British Shipbuilders	KQLA	–	–	–	–	–	–	–	–	–	–
British Telecommunications	KQLB	–	–	–	–	–	–	–	–	–	–
Regional Water Authorities	KQLC	–	–	–	–	–	–	–	–	–	–
Loans to other public corporations:											
New Towns - Development Corporations and Commission	KQLD	2 481.0	1 714.6	1 441.5	1 303.9	1 130.1	1 008.8	314.3	122.2	36.2	8.0
Scottish Special Housing Association	KQLE	–	–	–	–	–	–	–	–	–	–
Scottish Homes	KQLF	796.1	786.4	654.5	401.2	399.4	397.3	395.0	392.5	259.8	190.9
Housing Corporation (Scotland)	KQLG	–	–	–	–	–	–	–	–	–	–
Housing Corporation (England)	KQLH	1 744.1	1 611.3	1 021.4	986.0	899.0	869.9	926.3	848.7	4.0	4.0
Housing for Wales	KQLI	139.9	125.8	96.6	86.7	86.4	69.2	59.0	–	–	–
Covent Garden Market Authority	KQLJ	0.4	–	–	–	–	–	–	–	–	–
National Enterprise Board	KQLK	–	–	–	–	–	–	–	–	–	–
Land Authority for Wales	KQLL	7.6	6.8	8.8	10.3	6.2	3.2	3.2	1.3	1.3	–
Scottish Enterprise	KQLM	5.7	5.4	4.6	2.7	1.9	1.3	0.6	0.5	0.1	–
Welsh Development Agency	KQLN	2.8	2.4	1.8	1.5	1.2	0.9	1.1	1.2	1.2	0.9
Land Registry Trading Fund	KPOF	–	–	–	–	54.9	–	–	–	–	–
Development Board for Rural Wales	KQLO	8.8	8.8	8.8	8.8	8.8	8.8	7.9	4.1	4.0	4.0
Royal Mint	KQLP	0.1	–	–	–	–	–	–	–	–	–
Royal Ordnance Factories	KQLQ	–	–	–	–	–	–	–	–	–	–
The Crown Suppliers	KQLR	23.7	–	–	–	–	–	–	–	–	–
Crown Agents	KQLS	2.8	2.5	2.5	2.3	2.1	2.0	1.9	–	–	–
Her Majesty's Stationery Office	KQLT	22.6	16.8	10.6	6.7	3.3	–	7.0	–	–	–
Urban Development Corporations	KQLU	0.8	0.4	0.8	0.7	1.0	–	–	–	–	–
Harbour Authorities	KQLV	42.3	36.3	33.4	7.1	1.5	0.8	0.7	0.6	0.5	0.4
Commonwealth Development Corporation	KQLW	–	–	–	–	–	–	–	–	–	–
UK Atomic Energy Authority	KQLX	64.0	106.7	111.0	149.8	125.0	147.3	141.0	–	–	–

Source: HM Treasury: 020 7270 1586

17.7

Consolidated Fund and National Loans Fund: assets and liabilities
United Kingdom

continued At 31 March in each year

£ millions

		1990	1991	1992	1993	1994	1995	1996	1997	1998	1999
National Loans Fund (*continued*)											
Loans to other public corporations: (continued)											
Central Office of Information	KJEI	–	–	1.3	1.0	0.8	0.5	0.3	–	–	–
Registers of Scotland	KZBB	..	..	..	..	..	..	..	6.4	5.6	5.1
East of Scotland Water Authority	KZBC	..	..	..	..	..	..	..	163.0	229.0	288.0
North of Scotland Water Authority	KZBD	..	..	..	..	..	..	..	155.0	189.2	242.0
West of Scotland Water Authority	KZBE	..	..	..	..	..	..	..	185.0	304.9	425.6
Loans to local authorities	KQLY	46 567.0	48 087.1	48 742.3	41 464.6	40 979.2	40 440.7	40 969.2	42 134.0	42 951.1	44 742.7
Loans to private sector:											
Shipbuilding Industry Board	KQLZ	–	–	–	–	–	–	–	–	–	–
Shipowners (Ship credit scheme)	KGVR	–	–	–	–	–	–	–	–	–	–
Housing associations	KGVS	15.8	14.9	14.6	14.1	13.8	13.2	12.7	0.5	0.5	0.5
Building societies	KGVT	–	–	–	–	–	–	–	–	–	–
British Nuclear Fuels Ltd	KGVU	1.3	–	–	–	–	–	–	–	–	–
British Aerospace plc	KGVV	1.1	–	–	–	–	–	–	–	–	–
Loans within central government:											
Northern Ireland Exchequer	KGVW	1 357.6	1 373.1	1 480.3	1 558.3	1 626.2	1 666.3	1 627.4	1 602.5	1 681.1	1 611.2
Married quarters for Armed Forces	KGVX	68.3	67.6	66.9	66.1	65.2	64.3	63.4	62.4	61.3	60.2
Redundancy Fund	KGVY	–	–	–	–	–	–	–	–	–	–
Other assets:											
Exchange Equalisation Account - capital	KGVZ	10 025.0	11 075.0	10 774.5	7 200.0	6 800.0	5 550.0	2 800.0	650.0	–	–
Subscriptions and contributions to international financial organisations:											
International Monetary Fund	KGXE	4 904.6	4 785.5	4 885.3	6 893.0	7 066.4	7 172.2	7 102.6	6 241.2	5 895.6	9 048.1
Gilt-Edged Official Operations Account -advances outstanding	KPUF		–	–	–	2 500.0	2 500.0	2 500.0	3 000.0	2 500.0	2 500.0
-surplus not paid to the National Loans Fund	KPUH	–	–	–	–	2.0	–	–	–	141.6	190.8
Borrowing included in national debt but not brought to account by 31 March	KGXF	726.7	257.8	1 068.2	3 742.5	1 682.4	385.2	513.4	404.7	568.6	317.9
National Debt Commissioners' liability in respect of the National Savings Bank's Investment Fund	KCYG	–	–	–	–	–	–	–	–	–	–
Other	KCYH	–	–	–	–	–	–	–	–	–	–
Consolidated Fund liability	KCYI	121 170.9	125 807.1	142 306.7	182 102.2	240 351.0	286 055.9	331 164.9	362 506.2	362 596.4	361 065.3
Total liabilities											
National Loans Fund - national debt outstanding	KCYJ	192 981.4	198 703.4	214 527.6	248 643.5	306 872.6	349 159.5	390 681.8	419 548.9	418 444.7	421 635.7

Source: HM Treasury: 020 7270 1586

17.8

British government and government guaranteed marketable securities[1]
Nominal values of official and other holdings by maturity[2,3,4]

At 31 March in each year

£ millions

		1990	1991	1992	1993	1994	1995	1996	1997	1998	1999	2000
Total holdings	KQMO	125 018	122 437	133 121	162 642	209 507	232 486	262 262	290 259	297 366	291 788	290 630
Up to 5 years	KQMP	36 523	34 933	40 363	46 019	58 437	69 011	81 122	90 357	86 094	95 112	95 131
Over 5 and up to 15 years	KQMQ	53 395	56 309	61 239	72 612	94 308	101 960	111 510	125 401	131 758	124 603	116 910
Over 15 years (including undated)	KQMR	35 100	31 194	31 520	44 010	56 762	61 515	69 630	74 501	79 515	72 074	78 589
Official holdings:[4]												
Total	THAA	10 308	10 892	8 799	4 138	6 239	6 614	7 186	6 858	6 345	6 394	7 560
Up to 5 years	THAB	4 992	4 406	3 478	1 434	1 685	2 007	2 345	2 850	2 499	2 600	2 649
Over 5 and up to 15 years	THAC	4 145	5 415	4 323	1 826	3 194	3 700	3 774	3 041	2 726	2 989	2 791
Over 15 years (including undated)	THAD	1 170	1 071	998	879	1 359	907	1 068	967	1 120	805	2 120
Market holdings:												
Total	THAE	114 710	111 544	124 323	158 503	203 268	225 872	255 075	283 402	291 021	285 394	283 070
Up to 5 years	THAF	31 531	30 527	36 885	44 585	56 751	67 004	78 777	87 508	83 595	92 512	92 482
Over 5 and up tp 15 years	THAG	49 250	50 894	56 916	70 786	91 115	98 260	107 736	122 360	129 032	121 614	114 119
Over 15 years (including undated)	THAH	33 930	30 123	30 522	43 131	55 403	60 608	68 562	73 536	78 395	71 269	76 469

1 The government guaranteed securities of nationalised industries only. A relatively small amount of other government guaranteed securities is excluded.

2 Securities with optional redemption dates are classified according to the final redemption date.

3 The nominal value of index-linked BGS has been raised by the amount of accrued capital uplift.

4 Official holdings have changed following the introduction of the central bank sector into the UK national accounts. These holdings now principally include those of the National Investment and Loans Office and other government departments. The Issue and Banking Departments of the Bank of England are classified within the central bank sector, and so as part of the market.

Source: Bank of England: 020 7601 4068

17.9 National savings
Year ended 31 March

£ millions

		1989 /90	1990 /91	1991 /92	1992 /93	1993 /94	1994 /95	1995 /96	1996 /97	1997 /98	1998 /99	1999 /00
Department for National Savings												
Receipts												
Total	KQNA	5 562.9	6 408.9	7 704.7	8 485.5	10 336.2	9 246.9	11 596.9	13 353.5	12 565.6	10 212.9	8 966.4
Capital bonds	KQNB	284.0	185.6	338.3	476.6	566.4	511.2	500.5	482.7	583.6	238.1	29.2
National Savings Certificates:												
5yr Fixed Interest	KQNC	632.6	696.7	2 119.6	1 894.7	1 929.1	1 083.6	1 519.8	1 805.9	1 753.4	1 174.4	704.1
5yr Index-linked	KQND	634.6	1 503.2	1 500.8	1 600.0	1 434.9	1 083.2	1 949.8	1 871.8	2 640.4	1 734.1	551.9
2yr Fixed Interest	YZZZ	..	..	..	..	..	..	..	..	..	..	437.9
2yr Index Linked	ZCEZ	..	..	..	..	..	..	..	..	..	..	285.6
Yearly Plan	KQNE	90.1	74.2	89.3	115.7	118.2	117.5	97.0	0.7	–	–	–
Save As You Earn:												
Fixed Interest (1st, 2nd and												
4th issues)	KQNF	76.2	83.2	94.1	85.5	76.9	66.7	49.9	33.4	20.3	11.2	6.3
Index-linked (3rd issue)	KQNG	0.2	–	–	–	–	–	–	–	–	–	–
Income bonds	KQNH	1 512.1	1 605.6	1 355.9	1 241.2	1 948.9	1 228.9	802.4	1 263.6	1 044.1	1 365.4	642.2
First Option bonds	KHYZ	–	–	–	885.0	247.0	95.6	194.3	398.3	149.2	110.1	25.1
Investment Account	KQNI	1 491.5	1 515.7	1 247.7	1 107.4	1 392.9	1 393.1	1 299.2	1 478.3	1 270.1	1 045.4	918.6
Premium Savings bonds	KQNJ	249.4	185.7	257.5	384.5	998.2	1 826.2	2 075.7	2 578.1	3 199.6	3 622.9	3 618.4
Ordinary Account	KQNK	592.2	559.0	566.0	604.4	636.1	635.6	627.3	643.1	653.0	622.3	641.7
Children's Bonus bonds	KHCU	–	–	135.5	90.5	92.6	116.8	144.9	124.3	109.7	73.4	57.3
5yr Pensioners' bonds	KJRB	..	..	..	..	895.0	1 088.5	2 336.1	2 651.4	1 104.2	199.1	234.4
2yr Pensioners' bonds	ZCFA	..	..	..	..	..	..	..	..	..	..	373.6
Deposit bonds	KQNL	–	–	–	–	–	–	–	–	–	–	–
Indexed-income bonds	KQNM	–	–	–	–	–	–	–	–	–	–	–
British Savings bonds	KQNN	–	–	–	–	–	–	–	–	–	–	–
Treasurer's Account	KXCY	–	–	–	–	–	–	–	21.9	38.0	16.5	13.2
ISA's	ZCFB	..	..	..	..	..	..	..	..	..	..	257.0
Fixed Rate Savings Bond	ZCFC	..	..	..	..	..	..	..	..	..	..	169.9
Repayments												
Total	KQNO	9 432.0	7 339.8	6 495.7	5 853.8	8 051.0	7 759.8	8 756.9	11 048.5	13 201.7	11 665.7	10 960.9
Capital bonds	KQNP	5.0	23.6	14.9	21.8	345.3	678.3	453.1	776.6	1 143.5	649.7	325.1
National Savings Certificates:												
5yr Fixed Interest - Principal	KQNQ	2 498.2	1 455.3	1 193.4	647.9	1 292.6	843.0	840.1	1 838.8	2 256.2	1 934.3	1 182.2
- Accrued Interest	KQNR	1 642.6	991.0	738.7	417.4	670.9	437.2	474.8	937.0	1 021.4	645.6	391.6
5yr Index-linked - Principal	KQNS	394.4	412.9	418.8	448.2	913.5	761.7	1 419.7	1 432.7	1 803.5	1 520.1	1 200.5
- Accrued Interest/												
Index-linking, etc.	KQNT	370.6	403.3	396.6	378.5	598.1	425.8	672.0	613.6	703.1	527.5	373.7
2yr Fixed Interest - Principal	ZCFD	..	..	..	..	..	..	..	..	..	..	3.0
- Accrued Interest	ZCFE	..	..	..	..	..	..	..	..	..	..	–
2yr Index-linked - Principal	ZCFF	..	..	..	..	..	..	..	..	..	..	1.5
- Accrued Interest/												
Index-linking, etc.	ZCFG	..	..	..	..	..	..	..	..	..	..	–
Yearly Plan:												
Principal	KQNU	82.4	124.2	106.5	98.4	89.5	77.0	102.0	96.3	119.5	111.8	99.3
Interest	KQNV	23.6	43.2	40.9	35.7	30.3	26.2	42.1	39.2	43.6	30.6	27.0
Save As You Earn:												
Fixed Interest - Principal	KQNW	40.9	59.3	74.4	88.7	86.1	85.0	96.7	69.1	67.4	35.9	35.2
- Accrued Interest	KQNX	9.7	13.3	16.0	18.2	18.1	19.2	21.9	17.9	18.5	9.1	7.9
Index-linked - Principal	KQNY	45.0	24.2	29.4	26.5	9.3	7.4	1.8	0.9	0.8	0.6	0.5
- Accrued Interest/												
Index-linking	KQNZ	33.7	27.1	38.5	38.9	14.3	12.2	3.3	1.6	1.5	1.2	1.0
Income bonds	KQOA	1 091.2	824.2	719.9	956.0	1 000.3	1 180.1	1 256.2	1 392.0	1 141.9	880.7	1 685.1
First Option bonds	KHYY	–	–	–	4.8	375.8	288.4	126.5	139.1	335.2	205.5	283.8
Investment Account	KQOB	2 074.3	1 904.0	1 803.9	1 780.0	1 677.1	1 777.2	1 797.2	1 856.0	2 177.1	1 981.6	1 888.2
Premium Savings bonds	KQOC	186.4	193.4	153.7	153.4	181.0	333.0	590.4	869.0	1 203.1	1 398.4	1 683.0
Ordinary Account	KQOD	733.2	700.9	663.7	658.1	674.7	676.8	676.5	692.3	703.4	684.6	676.4
Children's Bonus bonds	KHCV	–	–	0.1	0.9	1.2	1.8	2.6	30.8	39.8	52.4	69.5
5yr Pensioners' bonds	KJRE	..	..	..	..	..	56.7	104.8	172.5	331.4	903.1	922.1
2yr Pensioners' bonds	ZCFH	..	..	..	..	..	..	..	..	..	..	8.4
Deposit bonds	KQOE	197.6	137.7	85.3	79.8	72.4	72.2	73.5	65.5	76.6	79.0	67.1
Indexed-income bonds	KQOF	3.2	2.2	1.0	0.6	0.5	0.6	1.7	6.5	2.6	–	–
British Savings bonds:												
Before maturity	KQOG	–	–	–	–	–	–	–	–	–	–	–
On maturity	KQOH	–	–	–	–	–	–	–	–	–	–	–
Treasurer's Account	KXCZ	–	–	–	–	–	–	–	1.1	11.6	14.0	15.8
ISA's	ZCFI	..	..	..	..	..	..	..	..	..	..	12.4
Fixed Rate Savings Bond	ZCFJ	..	..	..	..	..	..	..	..	..	..	0.6

Source: Department for National Savings: 020 7605 9314

17.9 National savings
Year ended 31 March
continued

£ millions

		1989/90	1990/91	1991/92	1992/93	1993/94	1994/95	1995/96	1996/97	1997/98	1998/99	1999/00
Department for National Savings												
Interest accruing												
Capital bonds	KQOO	12.2	42.0	76.8	130.8	223.1	218.8	214.6	249.9	172.0	146.9	126.6
National Savings Certificates:												
5yr Fixed Interest	KQOP	675.0	525.7	443.3	521.2	604.2	622.2	703.7	787.6	557.8	485.3	432.5
5yr Index-linked	KQOQ	422.0	477.0	351.7	267.8	303.9	458.5	655.2	671.9	690.3	502.7	344.1
2yr Fixed Interest	ZCFK	–	–	–	–	–	–	–	–	–	–	1.0
2yr Index-linked	ZCFL	..	..	..	..	..	..	..	..	..	..	1.0
Yearly Plan	KQOR	42.8	40.9	36.7	32.5	30.5	34.1	37.5	38.0	28.3	17.2	14.0
Save As You Earn:												
Fixed Interest (1st, 2nd and 4th issues)	KQOS	13.6	14.4	18.3	18.8	18.3	18.0	18.3	14.6	11.7	5.7	4.9
Index-linked (3rd issue)	KQOT	26.3	21.1	8.8	1.1	0.3	0.9	0.4	0.5	0.5	0.5	0.1
First Option bonds	KIAJ	–	–	–	–	70.7	40.4	31.8	40.4	54.8	48.4	40.1
Investment Account	KQOU	831.2	1 007.8	864.4	657.7	541.8	529.1	518.5	509.0	497.8	464.5	335.7
Ordinary Account	KQOV	64.0	60.9	58.2	57.3	44.6	42.8	35.5	36.2	29.4	30.6	15.7
Childrens Bonus bonds	KHCW	–	–	–	9.3	14.4	19.2	27.0	98.9	73.7	66.6	66.9
Deposit Bonds	KQOW	97.4	95.4	77.9	59.8	46.4	41.4	39.4	38.3	37.2	31.5	22.9
Treasurer's Account	KXDA	–	–	–	–	–	–	–	–	–	–	6.2
ISA's	ZCFM	..	..	..	..	..	..	..	..	..	..	6.0
Fixed Rate Savings Bond	ZCFN	..	..	..	..	..	..	..	..	..	..	1.2
Total	KQOX	2 184.5	2 285.2	1 936.1	1 756.3	1 898.2	2 025.4	2 281.9	2 485.3	2 153.5	1 799.9	1 418.9
Amounts remaining invested												
Capital bonds	KQOY	490.7	694.7	1 094.9	1 680.5	2 124.7	2 176.4	2 438.4	2 394.4	2 006.5	1 741.8	1 572.5
National Savings Certificates												
5yr Fixed Interest - Principal	KQOZ	5 879.2	5 120.6	6 046.8	7 293.6	7 930.1	8 170.7	8 850.4	8 817.5	8 314.7	7 554.8	7 076.7
- Accrued Interest	KQPA	2 658.7	2 193.4	1 898.0	2 001.8	1 935.1	2 120.1	2 349.0	2 199.6	1 736.0	1 575.7	1 616.6
5yr Index-linked - Principal	KQPB	2 923.2	4 013.5	5 095.5	6 247.3	6 768.7	7 090.2	7 620.3	8 059.4	8 896.3	9 110.3	8 461.7
- Accrued Interest, Index-linking, etc.	KQPC	1 426.4	1 500.1	1 455.2	1 344.5	1 050.3	1 083.0	1 066.2	1 124.5	1 111.7	1 086.9	1 057.3
2yr Fixed interest - Principal	ZCFO	..	..	..	..	..	..	..	..	..	..	434.9
- Accrued Interest	ZCFP	..	..	..	..	..	..	..	..	..	..	1.0
2yr Index-linked - Principal	ZCFQ	..	..	..	..	..	..	..	..	..	..	284.1
- Accrued Interest/ Index-linking, etc.	ZCFR	..	..	..	..	..	..	..	..	..	..	1.0
Yearly Plan:												
Principal	KQPD	491.1	441.1	423.9	441.2	469.9	510.4	505.4	409.8	290.3	178.5	105.0
Interest	KQPE	75.4	73.1	68.9	65.7	65.9	73.8	69.2	68.0	52.7	39.3	29.8
Save As You Earn:												
Fixed Interest - Principal	KQPF	184.9	208.8	228.5	225.3	216.1	197.8	151.0	115.3	68.2	43.5	18.4
- Accrued Interest	KQPG	21.4	22.5	24.8	25.4	25.6	24.4	20.8	17.5	10.7	7.3	4.4
Index-linked - Principal	KQPH	116.2	92.0	62.6	36.1	26.8	19.4	17.6	16.7	15.9	15.3	15.2
- Accrued Interest/ Index-linking, etc.	KQPI	114.0	108.0	78.3	40.5	26.5	15.2	12.3	11.2	10.2	9.5	9.2
Stock on the National Savings Register (DNS only)	KQPJ	868.4	963.1	1 026.2	1 180.3	1 198.6	1 392.7	1 530.7	1 541.1	1 468.5	–	–
Income bonds	KQPK	8 181.8	8 963.2	9 599.2	9 884.4	10 833.0	10 881.8	10 428.0	10 299.6	10 205.2	10 689.9	9 647.0
First Option bonds	KIAK	–	–	–	880.2	822.1	669.7	769.3	1 068.9	937.7	890.7	672.1
Investment Account	KQPL	8 007.0	8 626.5	8 934.7	8 919.8	9 177.4	9 322.4	9 342.9	9 474.2	9 065.0	8 593.3	7 959.4
Premium Savings bonds	KQPM	2 334.0	2 326.3	2 430.1	2 661.2	3 478.4	4 971.6	6 456.9	8 166.0	10 162.5	12 387.0	13 717.7
Ordinary Account	KQPN	1 555.3	1 474.3	1 434.8	1 438.4	1 444.4	1 446.0	1 432.3	1 419.3	1 398.3	1 366.6	1 347.6
Children's Bonus bonds	KHCX	–	–	135.4	234.3	340.1	474.3	643.6	836.0	979.6	1 067.2	1 121.9
5yr Pensioners' bonds	KJRG	–	–	–	–	895.0	1 926.8	4 158.1	6 637.0	7 409.8	6 705.8	6 018.1
2yr Pensioners' bonds	ZCFS	..	..	..	..	..	..	..	..	..	..	365.2
Deposit bonds	KQPO	779.7	737.4	730.0	710.0	684.0	653.2	619.1	591.9	552.5	505.0	460.8
Indexed-income bonds	KQPP	19.1	16.9	15.9	15.3	14.8	14.2	12.5	6.0	–	–	–
British Saving bonds	KQPQ	–	–	–	–	–	–	–	–	–	–	–
National Savings stamps and gift tokens	KQPR	2.1	1.9	1.8	1.8	1.7	1.7	1.6	1.6	1.6	1.6	1.6
Treasurer's Account	KXDB	–	–	–	–	–	–	–	20.8	47.2	49.7	53.3
ISA's	ZCFT	..	..	..	..	..	..	..	..	..	..	250.6
Fixed Rate Savings Bond	ZCFU	..	..	..	..	..	..	..	..	..	..	170.5
Total administered by DNS	KQPS	36 128.6	37 577.4	40 785.5	45 327.6	49 529.2	53 235.8	58 495.6	63 296.3	64 741.1	63 619.7	62 473.5

Source: Department for National Savings: 020 7605 9314

17.10

Income tax: allowances and reliefs
United Kingdom

£

		1990 /91	1991 /92	1992 /93	1993 /94	1994 /95	1995 /96	1996 /97	1997 /98	1998 /99	1999 /00	2000 /01
Personal allowances												
Personal allowance	KDZP	3 005	3 295	3 445	3 445	3 445	3 525	3 765	4 045	4 195	4 335	4 385
Married couples allowance[1]	KDZR	1 720	1 720	1 720	1 720	1 720	1 720	1 790	1 830	1 900	1 970	..
Age allowance:[2]												
Personal (aged 65-74)	KSOH	3 670	4 020	4 200	4 200	4 200	4 630	4 910	5 220	5 410	5 720	5 790
Personal (aged 75 or over)	KSOI	3 820	4 180	4 370	4 370	4 370	4 800	5 090	5 400	5 600	5 980	6 050
Married couple's (either partner between 65-74 but neither partner 75 or over)	KEDI	2 145	2 355	2 465	2 465	2 665	2 995	3 115	3 185	3 305	5 125	5 185[7]
Married couples (either partner 75 or over)	KEIY	2 185	2 395	2 505	2 505	2 705	3 035	3 155	3 225	3 345	5 195	5 255
Income limit	KEOO	12 300	13 500	14 200	14 200	14 200	14 600	15 200	15 600	16 200	16 800	17 100
Marginal fraction		1/2	1/2	1/2	1/2	1/2	1/2	1/2	1/2	1/2	1/2	1/2
Additional personal allowance[3]	KEPG	1 720	1 720	1 720	1 720	1 720	1 720	1 790	1 830	1 900	1 970	..
Widow's bereavement allowance[4]	KEPH	1 720	1 720	1 720	1 720	1 720	1 720	1 790	1 830	1 900	1 970	..
Blind person's allowance[5]												
Single or married (one spouse blind)	KSOJ	1 080	1 080	1 080	1 080	1 200	1 200	1 250	1 280	1 330	1 380	1 400
Married (both spouses blind)	KSOK	2 160	2 160	2 160	2 160	2 400	2 400	2 500	2 560	2 660	2 760	2 800
Life Assurance Relief[6]												
(Percentage of gross premium)	KFDR	12.5 or Nil	12.5 or Nil	12.5 or Nil	12.5 or Nil	12.5 or Nil	12.5 or Nil	12.5 or Nil	12.5 or Nil	12.5 or Nil	12.5 or Nil	12.5 or Nil

1 Following the introduction of Independent Taxation from 1990-91 the married couple's allowance was introduced. It is payable in addition to the personal allowance and between 1990-91 and 1992-93 went to the husband unless the transfer condition was met. The condition was that the husband was unable to make full use of the allowance himself and in that case he could transfer only part or all of the married couple's allowance to his wife. In 1993-94 all or half of the allowance could be transferred to the wife if the couple had agreed beforehand. The wife has the right to claim half the allowance. The married couple's allowance and allowances linked to it, were restricted to 20 per cent in 1994-95 and to 15 per cent from 1995-96.

2 The age allowance replaces the single allowance, provided the taxpayer's income is below the limit shown. From 1989-90, for incomes in excess of the limit, the allowance is reduced by £1 for each additional £2 of income until the ordinary limit is reached (before it was £2 for each £3 of additional income). The relief is due where the taxpayer is aged 65 or over in the year of assessment.

3 The additional personal allowance may be claimed by a single parent (or by a married man if his wife is totally incapacitated) who maintains a resident child at his or her own expense. This allowance has been abolished from April 2000.

4 Widow's bereavement allowance is due to a widow in the year of her husband's death and in the following year provided the widow has not remarried before the beginning of that year. This allowance has also been abolished from April 2000.

5 The blind person's allowance may be claimed by blind persons (in England and Wales, registered as blind by a local authority) and surplus blind person's allowance may be transferred to a husband or wife.

6 Relief on life assurance premiums is given by deduction from the premium payable. From 1984-85, it is confined to policies made before 14 March 1984.

7 At least one of the partners must be aged 65 before April 2000 to be entitled to the MCA. This means that only people born before 6 April 1935 are entitled to MCA.

Source: Board of Inland Revenue: 020 7438 4335

17.11 Rates of Income tax
United Kingdom

	1991/92		1992/93		1993/94		1994/95		1995/96	
	Bands of taxable income (£)[1]	Rate of tax (%)	Bands of taxable income (£)[1]	Rate of tax (%)	Bands of taxable income (£)[1]	Rate of tax (%)	Bands of taxable income (£)[1]	Rate of tax (%)	Bands of taxable income (£)[1]	Rate of tax (%)
Lower rate	-	-	1 - 2000	20	1 - 2 500	20	1 - 3 00	20	1 - 3 200	20
Basic rate	1 - 23 700	25	2 001 - 23 700	25	2 501 - 23 700	25[2]	3 001 - 23 700	25[2]	3 201 - 24 300	25[2]
Higher rate	over 23 700	40	over 23 700	40	over 23 700	40	over 23 700	40	over 24 300	40

	1996/97		1997/98		1998/99		1999/00		2000/01	
	Bands of taxable income (£)[1]	Rate of tax (%)	Bands of taxable income (£)[1]	Rate of tax (%)	Bands of taxable income (£)[1]	Rate of tax (%)	Bands of taxable income (£)[1]	Rate of tax (%)	Bands of taxable income (£)[1]	Rate of tax (%)
Lower rate	1 - 3 900	20	1 - 4 100	20	1 - 4 300	20	1 - 1 500	10[4]	1 - 1 520	10[4]
Basic rate	3 901 - 25 500	24[3]	4 101 - 26 100	23[3]	4 301 - 27 100	23[3]	1 501 - 28 000	23[5]	1 520 - 28 400	22[5]
Higher rate	over 25 500	40	over 26 100	40	over 27 100	40	over 28 000	40[6]	over 28 400	40[6]

1 Taxable income is defined as gross income for income tax purposes less any allowances and reliefs available at the taxpayer's marginal rate.
2 The basic rate of tax on dividend income is 20%.
3 The basic rate of tax on dividends and savings income is 20%.
4 The starting rate also applies to savings.
5 The basic rate of tax on dividends is 10% and savings income is 20%
6 The higher rate of tax on dividends is 32.5%.

Source: Board of Inland Revenue: 020 7438 4335

17.12 Rateable values
England and Wales
At 1 April in each year

	Unit	1990[2]	1991[2]	1992[2]	1993[2]	1994[2]	1995[2]	1996[2]	1997[2]	1998[2]	1999[2]	2000
Number of properties	Thousands											
Total-all classes	KMIH	"	1 685	1 709	1 734	1 737	1 734	1 723	1 726	1 725	1 719	1 720	1 711
Domestic: total	KMII	"	..	..	..	..	..	..	..	..	..	..	..
Commercial: total	KMIN	"	1 190	1 211	1 227	1 230	1 227	1 223	1 228	1 225	1 223	1 279	1 272
Shops and cafes	KMIO	"	576	572	570	567	565	562	497	491	488	484	478
Offices	KMIP	"	223	234	243	248	251	252	255	255	257	258	261
Other	KMIQ	"	392	405	413	415	411	409	476	479	478	537	533
On-licensed premises: total	KMIR	"	55	55	55	55	55	60	59	59	59	60	61
Entertainment and recreational: total	KMIS	"	95	95	94	93	92	87	87	87	81	80	79
Cinemas	KMIT	"	1	1	1	1	1	1	1	1	1	1	1
Theatres and music-halls	KMIU	"	1	1	1	1	1	1	1	1	1	1	1
Other	KMIV	"	94	94	93	92	91	86	85	86	80	79	76
Public utility: total	KMIW	"	15	15	15	15	15	9	8	8	9	9	8
Educational and cultural: total	KMIX	"	42	42	42	42	41	41	41	41	41	41	41
Miscellaneous: total	KMIY	"	53	53	59	58	58	56	55	55	56	61	65
Industrial: total	KMIZ	"	234	237	241	244	247	248	249	249	250	250	246
Value of assessments	£ million											
Total-all classes	KMHA	"	32 916	34 214	35 608	35 263	34 129	33 912	34 245	34 299	33 909	33 649	41 309
Domestic: total	KMHB	"	..	..	..	..	..	..	..	..	..	..	..
Commercial: total	KMHG	"	19 566	20 659	21 440	21 336	20 662	19 626	19 822	19 859	19 733	20 649	27 088
Shops and cafes	KMHH	"	7 229	7 382	7 472	7 335	7 068	7 780	6 094	5 959	5 860	5 840	6 801
Offices	KMHI	"	6 787	7 545	8 093	8 239	8 027	5 587	5 630	5 641	5 624	5 575	8 625
Other	KMHJ	"	5 550	5 732	5 876	5 762	5 568	6 260	8 098	8 259	8 249	9 234	11 663
On-licensed premises: total	KMHK	"	679	691	698	679	642	968	969	970	980	997	1 311
Entertainment and recreational: total	KMHL	"	951	994	1 025	1 022	988	1 009	1 018	1 033	1 040	1 045	1 309
Cinemas	KMHM	"	18	21	24	25	24	32	32	36	39	45	61
Theatres and music-halls	KMHN	"	21	21	22	21	19	21	21	21	21	20	28
Other	KMHO	"	912	951	979	975	946	956	965	975	979	980	1 220
Public utility: total	KMHP	"	3 485	3 493	3 518	3 505	3 424	3 455	3 469	3 488	3 380	3 361	3 349
Educational and cultural: total	KMHQ	"	1 981	1 994	1 970	1 883	1 813	1 873	1 883	1 894	1 773	1 672	1 826
Miscellaneous: total	KMHR	"	806	823	1 375	1 367	1 319	1 429	1 500	1 494	1 464	1 439	1 769
Industrial: total	KMHS	"	5 448	5 559	5 583	5 470	5 280	5 550	5 584	5 561	5 540	5 463	5 968

1 The detailed breakdown of the various rateable value bands for houses and flats is not available after 1985.
2 See chapter text.

Source: Board of Inland Revenue: 020 7438 6314

17.13 Local authorities: gross loan debt outstanding[1]
At 31 March in each year

£ millions

		1990	1991	1992	1993	1994	1995	1996	1997	1998	1999	2000
United Kingdom												
Total debt[2]	**KQBR**	59 982	57 985	56 331	55 943	55 869	..	..	..	..	..	..
Public Works Loan Board	**KQBS**	46 499	48 001	48 717	41 447	40 803	40 388	40 445	41 683	42 901	44 701	46 044
Northern Ireland Consolidated Fund[2]	**KQBT**	208	239	93	109	126	138	157	175	220	..	..
Other debt	**KQBU**	13 275	9 745	..	..	..	..	..	..	..	..	..
England and Wales												
Total debt	**KQBV**	51 689	49 914	48 187	47 357	46 695	..	..	..	..	..	..
of which Public Works Loan Board	**KQBW**	*39 969*	*41 025*	*41 501*	*34 082*	*33 132*	*32 448*	*32 617*	*33 660*	*34 606*	*36 049*	*37 172*
Scotland												
Total debt[3]	**KQBX**	8 192	7 948	8 005	8 429	8 999	9 984	10 850	..	..	..	..
of which Public Works Loan Board	**KQBY**	*6 530*	*6 976*	*7 216*	*.7 365*	*7 671*	*7 940*	*7 828*	*8 023*	*8 295*	*8 652*	*8 872*
Northern Ireland												
Total debt[2]	**KQBZ**	101	123	139	157	175	186	183	211	225	250	..

1 The sums shown exclude inter-authority loans and debt transfers, and temporary loans and overdrafts obtained for the purpose of providing for current expenses. No deduction has been made in respect of sums held in sinking funds for the repayment of debt.

2 The Northern Ireland Loans Fund was abolished on 1 April 1983 and its functions transferred to the Northern Ireland Consolidated Fund.

3 The data for 1991 is taken from information supplied by the Chartered Institute of Public Finance and Accountancy. Data for 1996 is before transfer of responsibility for Water & Sewerage and the Scottish Childrens Reporters Administration.

Sources: Department of the Environment (1981 to 1990);
Public Works Loan Board: 020 7270 3874;
Department of the Environment for Northern Ireland: 028 9054 0707;
Welsh Office (1981 to 1990);
Chartered Institute of Public Finance and Accountancy (England and Wales, 1991)

17.14 Revenue expenditure of local authorities

	1997/98 outturn £m	1998/99 outturn £m	1999/2000 budget[7] £m	1999/2000 adjusted budget[5,6] £m	2000/2001 budget[8] £m	Difference 2000/2001 over 1999/2000 adjusted budget[9]	
						£m	%
England							
Education	18 908	19 946	22 591	21 802	23 529	1 727	7.9
Personal social services	8 454	9 059	9 693	9 713	10 288	575	5.9
Police	6 498	6 693	7 083	7 095	7 304	209	2.9
Fire	1 338	1 402	1 496	1 496	1 543	47	3.1
Highway maintenance	1 628	1 621	1 736	1 806	1 879	73	4.0
EPC services	14 297	14 751	15 469	15 507	16 295	788	5.1
Comprising:							
Civil defence and other Home office	556	558	578	578	612	34	5.9
Magistrates courts	308	309	317	317	323	6	1.9
Parking and public transport	659	695	680	680	786	106	15.6
Housing benefit and council tax administration[1]	5 531	5 520	5 817	5 817	5 989	172	3.0
Non HRA housing	367	400	430	430	434	4	0.9
Libraries and art galleries	745	881	937	937	1 021	84	9.0
Sports and recreation centres	537	562	533	533	542	9	1.7
Local environmental services	3 474	3 675	4 848	4 848	5 071	223	4.6
Other[5]	2 121	2 150	1 330	1 368	1 517	149	10.9
Net current expenditure	51 123	53 471	58 067	57 419	60 838	3 419	6.0
Capital charges	1 970	1 968	2 117	2 123	2 038	-85	-4.0
CERA[2]	712	717	744	744	658	-86	-11.6
Interest receipts	-1 053	-1 143	-758	-758	-788	-30	4.0
Other non-current[3]	3 897	3 992	2 291	2 291	2 349	58	2.5
Gross revenue expenditure[4]	56 650	59 005	62 461	61 818	65 094	3 276	5.3
Specific grants outside AEF	-9 395	-8 816	-8 694	-7 944	-8 205	-261	3.3
Revenue expenditure	47 256	50 189	53 767	53 874	56 888	3 014	5.6
Specific & special grants inside AEF	-1 825	-2 334	-2 368	-2 458	-3 484	-1 026	41.7
Net revenue expenditure	45 431	47 855	51 399	51 416	53 403	1 987	3.9
Other adjustments	-1	-67	-50	-50	-31	19	-38.0
Use of reserves	54	243	-810	-810	-550	260	-32.1
Budget requirement	45 483	48 030	50 539	50 556	52 823	2 267	4.5
SSA reduction grant	-123	-102	-68	-68	-18	50	-73.5
Police grant	-3 243	-3 375	-3 505	-3 511	-3 627	-116	3.3
Revenue support grant	-18 649	-19 480	-19 875	-19 886	-19 437	449	-2.3
Central Support Protection Grant	-	-	-52	-52	-34	18	-34.6
Council Tax Benefit Subsid Limitation Scheme	-	-	32	32	54	22	68.8
Non-domestic rates	-12 027	-12 531	-13 612	-13 612	-15 407	-1 795	13.2
Other items	-201	-211	-181	-181	-46	135	-74.6
Precepts/demand on collection fund	11 241	12 332	13 278	13 278	14 200	922	6.9
Scotland							
Net revenue expenditure on general fund	6 508	6 732	7 041	..	7 174	133	2

1 Administration and payment of housing benefit and administration of Council Tax.
2 Capital Expenditure charged to the Revenue Account.
3 Includes:
 (i) Gross expenditure on council tax benefit.
 (ii) Expenditure on council tax reduction scheme.
 (iii) Discretionary (non-domestic) rate relief.
 (iv) Flood defence payments to the National Rivers authority (now Environment Agency)
 (v) Payments in respect of grant maintained schools.
 (vi) Bad debt provision.
4 This measure of expenditure is referred to as "Gross Revenue Expenditure" on local authority returns, but is actually net of expenditure met by sales, fees, charges and interest receipts, and excludes most expenditure on the housing revenue account and on trading services.

5 Includes Other income for licence fees etc.
6 Adjustments made for changes to the mandatory student awards system, further education discretionary awards, costs of audit and on inspection associated with Best Value, Carers Grant, Highways maintenance and work previously carried out by the Highways Agency, and other minor changes.
7 For Scotland figure for 1999/2000 is a provisional outturn figure, not a budget figure.
8 Scotland figure for 2000/20001 is a budget estimate not actual budget.
9 For Scotland only, the difference is between the 2000/2001 budget over 1999/2000 provisional outturn.

Sources: Department of the Environment, Transport and the Regions: 020 7890 4163;

Scottish Executive, Economic Advice & Statistics: 0131 244 7033

17.14 Revenue expenditure of local authorities
continued

	1993/94 outturn	1994/95 outturn	1995/96 outturn	1996/97 outturn	1997/98 outturn	1998/99 outturn	1999/2000 budget	2000/2001 budget
Wales[1]								
Education	1 265	1 253	1 276	1 307	1 328	1 385	1 427	1 476
Personal social services	352	426	482	528	560	595	619	668
Police	273	282	298	321	344	353	372	395
Fire & civil defence[2]	70	69	74	80	83	90	96	100
Highways maintenance	146	150	157	147	143	142	145	146
Other services	777	840	909	901	914	942	963	1 023
Comprising:								
Other Home office[2]	28	31	32	35	35	37	34	35
Magistrates courts	17	19	19	21	21	22	19	20
Parking and public transport	15	14	15	16	15	17	18	20
Housing benefit and council tax administration	244	279	307	335	340	347	360	377
Non HRA housing	15	15	17	17	18	17	17	19
Libraries and art galleries	35	35	37	37	38	47	50	52
Sports and recreation centres	50	49	53	50	51	55	55	54
Local environmental services	229	240	255	231	238	244	265	273
Other	144	159	174	158	160	156	146	172
Capital charges	188	187	202	219	243	248	265	263
CERA	37	43	63	15	19	19	19	19
Interest receipts	-39	-43	-55	-30	-39	-42	-18	-24
Gross revenue expenditure	3 068	3 207	3 407	3 489	3 595	3 732	3 887	4 066
Specific grants outside AEF	-444	-451	-475	-499	-474	-486	-458	-434
Revenue expenditure	2 624	2 755	2 932	2 990	3 121	3 246	3 429	3 633
Specific grants inside AEF	-70	-73	-70	-73	-75	-84	-68	-81
Net revenue expenditure	2 554	2 682	2 862	2 918	3 046	3 163	3 361	3551
Use of reserves	46	16	-76	-10	-24	-1	-17	-11
Budget requirement	2 599	2 699	2 786	2 908	3 022	3 162	3 343	3 540
Council tax reduction scheme grant	-	-	-	-45	-17	-31	-22	-17
Police grant	-139	-142	-156	-166	-171	-180	-181	-186
Revenue support grant	-1 668	-1 739	-1 717	-1 790	-1 731	-1 798	-1 890	-2031
Non-domestic rates	-470	-464	-520	-459	-584	-612	-656	-638
Other items	-	-	-	-	-	-	-	-
Precepts/demand on collection fund	322	354	393	448	519	541	594	668
Northern Ireland								
Total expenditure[3]								
Capital	56.4	65.3	47.4	73.7	65.2	77.2		
Other	214.1	227.8	251.7	294.6	304.3	324.6		
Total income	235.0	251.3	243.5	301.1	370.4	407.3		

1 For definitions of the above please e-mail: LGFS.Transfer@Wales.gsi.gov.uk.
2 For 1996/97 and previous years, civil defence was included in "Other Home Office" and not "Fire".
3 "Capital" and "Other" figures cannot be added to give "Total" figure because of double counting of loan charges, which are recorded as both "Capital" and "Other" expenditure.

Sources: National Assembly for Wales: 029 2082 5355; Department of the Environment for Northern Ireland: 028 9054 0707

17.15 Funding of revenue expenditure
Years ended 31 March

£ millions

		Domestic rating system		Community charge system			Council tax system							
		1988 /89	1989 /90	1990 /91	1991[13] /92	1992 /93	1993 /94	1994 /95	1995 /96	1996 /97	1997 /98	1998 /99	1999[12,6] /00	2000[12,6] /01
England														
Revenue expenditure[1]														
1999/00 prices £m[5]	KRTM	48 729	48 447	48 396	50 173	51 701	49 748	51 524	51 484	51 774	51 155	52 601	54 977	56 888
Cash £m	KRTN	31 240	33 282	35 851	39 472	42 020	41 506	43 602	44 827	46 532	47 256	50 189	53 767	56 888
Government grants[2]														
Cash £m	KRTO	13 201	13 481	12 927	18 620	20 968	21 685	23 679	23 335	23 003	23 840	25 291	25 867	26 566
Per cent	KRTP	42	41	36	47	50	52	54	52	49	50	49	48	47
Non- domestic rates[3]														
Cash £m	KRTQ	8 819	9 595	10 429	12 408	12 306	11 584	10 692	11 361	12 743	12 034	12 531	13 619	15 407
Per cent	KRTR	28	29	29	32	29	28	25	25	27	25	25	25	27
Domestic rates, community charges & council taxes[4]														
Cash £m	KRTS	8 957	9 713	12 251	8 533	9 521	8 912	9 239	9 777	10 461	11 241	12 332	13 278	14 200
Per cent	KRTT	29	29	34	22	23	21	21	22	22	24	24	25	25
Wales[7]														
Revenue expenditure	ZBXH	1 956	2 122	2 217	2 473	2 644	2 624	2 755	2 932	2 990	3 121	3 246	3 429	3 633
General government grants[8,13]	ZBXI	1 249	1 327	1 250	1 660	1 753	1 807	1 881	1 873	2 001	1 957	2 009	2 093	2 234
Specific government grants[9,13]	ZBXG	..	..	59	64	69	70	73	70	73	75	84	68	81
Share of redistributed non- domestic rates	ZBXJ	..	..	443	525	536	470	464	520	459	584	612	656	638
Community charge/council tax income[10]	ZBXK	..	..	477	231	299	323	354	394	449	483	542	596	670
Other[11]	ZBXL	..	..	−12	−7	−12	−46	−17	75	9	22	−	15	9

1 1981/82 to 1989/90: net expenditure financed from relevant grants rates and balance. 1990/91 onwards: "Revenue expenditure to compare with TSS" ie expenditure financed from revenue support grant, specific grants within Aggregate External Finance, special grants, non domestic rates, community charges/council taxes and balances. Also includes spending met by community charge grant (1991/92), and additional grant for teacher pay (1992/93), SSA reduction grant (1994/95 to 1999/00), police grant (1995/96 to 2000/01), Central Support Reduction Grant (1999/00 to 2000/01) and Greater London Authority Grant (2000/01). This line is not the total of the others. The difference is due to funding by balances and other adjustments.

2 1981/82 to 1989/90: Aggregate Exchequer Grant 1990/91 onwards: revenue support grants, specific and special grants within AEF, community charge grant (1991/92), teachers' pay award additional grant (1992/93), SSA reduction grant (1994/95 to 1999/00), police grant (1995/96 to 1999/00) and Central Support Reduction Grant (1990/00 to 2000/01) and Greater London Authority Grant (2000/01).

3 1981/82 to 1989/90 net of rate relief. 1990/91 onwards: distributable amount from non-domestic rate pool. 1993/94 onwards: includes City Offset.

4 1981/82 to 1989/90: gross of domestic rate rebates. 1990/91 to 1992/93: gross of community charge benefit and community charge transitional relief/community charge reduction scheme grant. 1993/94 onwards: gross of council tax benefit and council tax transitional reduction scheme.

5 Revenue expenditure at 1999/00 prices have been calculated using the GDP deflator. Major function changes include:
(i) Responsibilities for municipal bus service transferred to public transport companies in 1986;
(ii) Funding of Polytechnic and higher education colleges transferred to Polytechnics and colleges Funding Council (PCFC) on 1 April 1989;
(iii) Increasing responsibilities as a result of care in the community since 1 April 1993;
(iv) Funding of colleges of further education and sixth form colleges transferred to the Further Education Funding Council (FEFC) on 1 April 1993.

6 Budget Estimate for England.

7 This table provides a general indication of the trend in the financing of revenue expenditure. Comparisons between the rates (prior to 1990/91), community charge (1990/91 to 1992/93) and council tax systems must be made with caution since expenditure definitions and categories differ. For example, specific and supplementary grants within aggregate exchequer grant (included under government grants prior to 1990/91) are not comparable in coverage to those within aggregate external finance (included 1990/91 onwards). Also the split between domestic and non-domestic rates, and rebates relating to each, prior to 1990/91 has been estimated. The components do not add to the totals for technical reasons; these include rounding and authorities' use of balances.

8 Includes all unhypothecated grants, namely revenue support grant, police grant, council tax reduction scheme grant and the adjustment to reverse the transfer out of nursery voucher monies in 1997/98. Also see footnote 13.

9 Comprises specific and supplementary grants within aggregate external finance, excluding police grant. Also see footnote 13.

10 This includes community council precepts, and income covered by community charge/council tax benefit grant, but excludes council tax reduction scheme grant.

11 This includes use of, or contribution to, local authority reserves and other minor adjustments.

12 Budget for Wales.

13 In 1991/92, a grant of £140 per taxpayer was given to local authorities in Wales to reduce community charge bills. Although identified separately from revenue support grant in 1991/92, it has been included under that heading as it was added into revenue support grant in subsequent years.

Sources: Department of the Environment, Transport and the Regions: 020 7890 4163;

National Assembly for Wales: 029 2082 5355

17.16 Local authority capital expenditure and receipts
Years ended 31 March

£ millions

England		1994	1995	1996	1997	1998	1999
		1994/95 final outturn	1995/96 final outturn	1996/97 final outturn	1997/98 final outturn	1998/99 final outturn	1999/00 provisional outturn
Expenditure							
Housing[1]	KRUB	2 039	1 999	1 746	1 665	1 921	1 837
Transport	KRUC	1 436	1 374	1 176	1 086	994	1 028
Education[2]	KRUD	1 061	1 011	1 047	1 114	1 236	1 344
Personal Social Services	KRUE	195	198	191	148	135	127
Fire services	KRUF	72	63	49	50	48	47
Agriculture, fisheries and food	KRUG	33	53	55	51	52	30
Sport and recreation	KRUH	175	192	201	194	217	242
Protective services[3]	KRUI	314	341	290	272	288	318
Urban and regeneration programmes[4]	KRUJ	653	564	725	649	628	588
Single regeneration budget - environment[5]	KRUK	609	530	683	604	545	526
Single regeneration budget - other departments[5]	KRUL	44	34	42	45	83	62
Other environment	KRUM	9	1	..	..	..	..
Other services							
Environment	KRUN	880	898	730	847	885	1 065
Other departments	KRUO	69	61	65	127	142	176
Social Housing Grant	KRUP	331	364	338	330	328	330
Total	KRUR	7 257	7 119	6 612	6 533	6 874	7 132
Receipts							
Housing	KRUS	1 391	1 203	1 049	1 289	1 514	2 104
Transport	KRUU	47	14	49	13	49	104
Education	KRUT	128	75	120	133	82	95
Personal Social Services	KRUV	45	40	57	43	52	46
Fire services	KRUW	3	3	5	9	3	5
Agriculture, fisheries and food	KTDH	16	9	12	12	12	15
Sport and recreation	KRUX	13	15	9	13	10	19
Protective services	KRUY	56	58	82	71	76	146
Other services							
Environment	KRUZ	463	359	545	544	687	955
Other departments	KRVA	69	44	52	54	45	38
Total	KRVB	2 230	1 821	1 980	2 181	2 530	3 527

1 Excludes expenditure on Estate Action and Housing Association Grant.
2 Includes grant maintained and voluntary aided schools.
3 Includes police, probabtion and aftercare, civil defence and magistrates' courts.
4 Includes expenditure on Estate Action schemes.
5 Includes environmental services, consumer protection, careers and sheltered employment and museums, galleries and libraries.

Source: Department of the Environment, Transport and the Regions: 020 7890 4076

17.17 Capital expenditure and income

£ millions

	Expenditure			Income				
	Expenditure on land works, etc	Capital assigned to repayment of debt	All expenditure	Loans	Government grants	Miscellaneous	All income	Gross debt at end of year
Financial year								
	KRVC	KRVD	KRVE	KRVF	KRVG	KRVH	KRVI	KRVJ
1970/71	1 792	150	1 942	1 516	106	349	1 970	13 384
1971/72	1 938	170	2 109	1 605	116	421	2 143	14 450
1972/73	2 418	213	2 631	2 030	122	531	2 682	16 105
1973/74	3 286	225	3 511	2 781	143	619	3 544	18 300
1974/75[1]	3 712	127	3 839	3 209	128	498	3 835	18 884
1975/76	3 917	198	4 115	3 285	177	647	4 109	21 930
1976/77	3 783	312	4 095	3 097	249	803	4 149	24 534
1977/78	3 487	352	3 839	2 677	255	981	3 913	26 282
1978/79	3 621	390	4 011	2 627	351	1 139	4 117	27 103
1979/80	4 249	331	4 580	2 992	385	1 367	4 745	30 187
1980/81	4 476	413	4 889	2 900	492	1 864	5 256	32 076
1981/82	4 061	563	4 623	2 527	470	2 177	5 174	34 069
1982/83	5 090	634	5 724	3 358	416	3 100	6 874	36 231
1983/84	5 890	562	6 452	3 538	379	3 294	7 211	38 698
1984/85	6 352	515	6 867	3 381	327	3 283	6 991	40 554
1985/86	5 748	348	6 096	3 008	360	3 239	6 607	40 138
1986/87	5 899	328	6 227	2 814	388	3 878	7 081	43 033
1987/88	6 091	486	6 577	2 953	297	4 286	7 536	44 904
1988/89	7 166	658	7 824	2 985	270	6 122	9 376	47 295
1989/90	9 590	474	10 064	2 919	440	6 110	9 469	48 695

			Income				Capital receipts set aside[2,4]	Credit ceiling[3]	Provision for credit liabilities[3]
	Gross capital expenditure	Credit approvals used	Government grants	Capital receipts	Other income	Total income			
Financial year									
At 1 April 1990	-	-	-	-	-	-	4 241	42 167	4 241
	KRVK	KRVL	KRVM	KRVN	KRVO	KRVP	KRVQ	KRVR	KRVS
1990/91	6 869	2 786	907	3 165	542	7 400	2 022	41 125	5 677
1991/92	6 572	3 140	1 041	2 251	674	7 106	1 353	41 234	6 502
1992/93	6 567	3 229	1 210	2 110	619	7 168	908	37 051	6 282
1993/94	7 124	2 948	1 279	3 310	651	8 188	356	37 941	6 041
1994/95	6 950	2 722	1 176	2 458	724	7 080	1 409	37 673	6 921
1995/96	6 910	2 264	1 484	1 966	1 278	6 992	1 160	37 103	7 677
1996/97	6 420	2 120	1 388	2 183	1 132	6 823	1 039	37 261	8 520
1997/98	6 298	2 099	1 262	2 349	1 129	6 839	1 186	36 711	8 594
1998/99	6 630	2 334	1 160	2 662	1 413	7 659	1 130	36 791	7 274

1 Reorganisation of local government in April 1974 transferred responsibility for various services to regional health and water authorities.
2 Excluding Social Housing Grant and European Regional Development Fund (ERDF) grants.
3 At end of year.
4 Gross receipts received in year.

Source: Department of the Environment, Transport and the Regions: 020 7890 4076

17.18 Expenditure of local authorities
Scotland

Year ended 31 March

£ thousands

Out of revenue [1]

		1988/89	1989[8]/90	1990/91	1991/92	1992/93	1993/94	1994/95	1995/96	1996/97	1997[11]/98	1998/99
Total	KQTA	6 198 024	6 794 154	7 429 771	7 985 137	8 560 071	8 713 471	9 111 751	9 690 424	9 196 125	9 566 936	10 033 985
General Fund Services:	KQTB	4 771 959	5 212 273	5 650 719	6 093 642	6 542 916	6 589 420	6 904 228	7 324 381	7 151 759	6 679 396	7 021 038
Education[2]	KQTC	1 977 117	2 174 652	2 390 134	2 564 363	2 757 058	2 537 582	2 563 049	2 654 158	2 629 961	2 512 725	2 649 170
Libraries, museums and galleries	KQTD	74 991	83 712	103 489	109 181	117 243	125 791	132 055	149 427	138 483	121 387	124 648
Social work[2]	KQTE	483 888	559 013	668 792	733 067	806 613	914 436	1 045 638	1 222 693	1 289 928	1 315 387	1 394 142
Law, order and protective services[2]	KQTF	514 793	580 977	653 197	704 943	763 917	804 616	828 480	866 567	816 315	931 795	952 940
Roads[3]	KQTG	467 912	506 562	561 522	589 564	633 874	650 555	684 452	676 116	716 570	440 712	546 945
Environmental services[4]	KQTH	336 953	221 857	264 507	283 968	305 645	322 534	330 039	351 689	329 674	343 565	349 413
Planning	KQTI	127 816	125 298	162 566	174 380	188 753	202 027	211 346	226 073	210 827	163 380	179 078
Leisure and recreation	KQTJ	237 221	276 331	338 532	362 560	383 081	396 874	405 083	451 952	426 422	364 853	368 023
Central administration[9]	KQTK	226 432	305 743	–	–	–	–	–	–	–	–	–
Other services[2,4]	KQTL	219 355	258 196	383 221	445 968	456 198	516 842	580 561	591 766	562 462	456 219	430 790
Other general fund expenditure[5]	KQTM	105 481	119 932	124 759	125 648	130 534	118 163	123 525	133 940	31 117	29 373	25 889
Housing	KQTN	1 325 226	1 330 796	1 473 950	1 573 590	1 672 566	1 738 427	1 806 022	1 924 930	2 000 684	1 658 935	1 754 686
Trading services:	KQTO	206 320	371 017	429 861	443 553	475 123	503 787	525 026	575 053	74 799	75 976	79 644
Water supply	KQTP	151 002	168 347	188 478	203 847	218 864	239 291	255 081	274 773	–	–	–
Sewerage[6]	KQTQ	–	154 436	176 449	185 216	194 576	200 036	209 323	233 525	–	–	–
Passenger transport	KQTR	188	263	560	603	859	681	685	794	2 849	1 524	121
Ferries	KQTS	4 158	5 358	6 596	4 508	8 336	7 203	7 574	7 744	6 831	7 512	8 930
Harbours, docks and piers	KQTT	36 967	25 757	23 428	28 008	27 811	16 215	16 804	15 301	13 482	12 884	15 697
Airports	KQTU	1 142	–	–	–	–	–	–	–	–	–	–
Road bridges	KQTV	8 459	7 942	9 277	9 629	9 508	10 948	7 579	11 755	12 759	16 064	16 408
Slaughterhouses	KQTW	3 121	3 366	2 737	1 427	1 282	985	976	1 000	794	850	228
Markets	KQTX	2 184	..	..	6 086	8 145	8 462	8 615	10 336	14 278	13 479	13 161
Other trading services	KQTY	–901	5 548	22 336	4 229	5 742	19 966	18 389	19 825	23 806	23 663	25 099
Loan charges:[11] Total	KQTZ	1 215 398	1 199 706	1 267 466	1 327 639	1 343 768	1 346 433	1 383 167	1 451 179	1 121 448	1 126 637	1 152 728
Allocated to :												
General Fund services	KMHV	538 518	538 693	567 143	607 867	631 479	649 212	677 377	710 801	639 380	651 982	710 371
Housing	KMHW	602 914	504 201	530 566	542 248	528 488	505 407	499 904	504 162	475 507	471 274	438 556
Trading services	KMHX	73 966	156 812	169 757	177 524	183 801	191 814	205 886	236 216	6 561	3 381	3 801

On capital works [7]

		1988/89	1989[8]/90	1990/91	1991/92	1992/93	1993/94	1994/95	1995/96	1996/97	1997/98	1998/99
Total	KQUA	1 142 074	1 262 076	1 249 744	1 276 006	1 344 250	1 428 545	1 518 362	1 528 167	889 572	813 900	815 981
General Fund Services:	KQUB	450 701	617 013	589 921	620 287	650 779	699 250	760 564	767 795	540 127	540 096	541 769
Education[2]	KQUC	72 144	81 643	75 166	81 007	92 584	85 619	113 121	114 128	101 898	112 753	125 341
Libraries, museums & galleries	KQUD	6 031	5 389	7 223	9 225	15 319	11 077	12 822	16 757	11 602	9 974	13 231
Social work[2]	KQUE	23 448	24 801	25 797	26 017	32 940	29 040	29 067	30 298	20 658	19 660	22 554
Law, order and protective services[2]	KQUF	27 257	29 789	23 378	19 903	28 230	32 951	33 635	35 847	41 326	37 701	37 727
Roads	KQUG	125 870	167 797	159 467	164 333	179 275	189 525	198 178	187 988	116 881	108 227	113 954
Environmental services[4]	KQUH	70 541	15 708	12 738	12 798	13 239	18 905	16 595	14 580	10 226	21 193	18 397
Planning	KQUI	30 076	30 897	55 899	84 900	69 065	76 477	102 152	103 221	51 182	69 648	50 854
Leisure and recreation	KQUJ	33 714	55 885	43 872	51 490	44 774	74 563	65 411	57 243	36 232	29 692	40 926
Administrative buildings & equipment[10]	KQUK	42 919	22 857	32 251	29 996	24 980	17 888	23 994	14 693	40 014	45 374	35 107
Other services[2,4]	KQUL	18 701	182 247	154 130	140 618	150 373	163 205	165 589	193 040	110 108	85 814	83 678
Housing	KQUM	629 816	501 082	504 378	485 131	460 140	467 811	497 997	517 593	345 713	270 005	268 135
Trading Services:	KQUN	61 557	143 981	155 445	170 588	233 331	261 484	259 801	242 779	3 732	3 799	6 077
Water supply	KQUO	51 470	61 991	63 872	77 000	109 655	128 081	123 564	107 064	–	–	–
Sewerage[6]	KQUP	–	65 417	77 096	88 035	113 998	127 047	130 634	131 684	–	–	–
Passenger transport	KQUQ	24	–	–	–	–	–	–	–	–	–	–
Ferries	KQUR	1 573	3 422	846	773	18	–	376	355	521	770	268
Harbours, docks and piers	KQUS	5 703	3 222	8 444	336	5 020	2 300	1 982	1 218	934	1 175	1 626
Airports	KQUT	262	59	14	2	2	184	173	763	1 149	439	–
Road bridges	KQUU	1 440	2 276	237	380	694	799	830	805	277	973	2 791
Slaughterhouses	KQUV	67	170	73	56	87	1 068	139	63	112	69	54
Markets	KQUW	313	–	–	–	–	–	–	–	–	–	–
Other trading services	KMHY	705	7 424	4 863	4 006	3 857	2 005	2 103	827	739	373	1 338

1 Gross expenditure less inter-authority and inter-account transfers.
2 From 1989/90 Education includes careers service (previously Other Services); Social work includes sheltered employment (previously Other Services); Other services includes district courts (previously Law, order and protective services), public analyst (previously Environmental services) and Housing loans and grants (previously Housing).
3 Including general fund support for transport (LA and NON-LA).
4 From 1989/90 onwards burial grounds and crematoria are included within Environmental services. From 1981/82 to 1988/89 (inclusive) they were included within Other services.
5 General fund contributions to Housing and Trading services (excluding transport), are also included in the expenditure figures for these services. From 1996/97 water and sewerage are excluded from other general fund expenditure.

6 From 1989/90 onwards Sewerage is shown as a trading service (previously included in Environmental services).
7 Expenditure out of loans, government grants and other capital receipts.
8 From 1980/81 to 1988/89 inclusive, revenue contributions to capital are recorded as expenditure in **both** the revenue and capital summaries. Table 17.19 details the amount of these contributions. From 1989/90 revenue contributions to capital are excluded from the capital summary and shown **only** in the revenue summary.
9 From 1990/91 Central Administration expenditure is included in the relevant service expenditure.
10 Prior to 1990-91 was called Central Administration.
11 From 1997/98 loan charges are not included within individual service totals.

Source: Scottish Executive, Economic Advice & Statistics: 0131 244 7033

Government finance

17.19 Income of local authorities: classified according to source
Scotland
Year ended 31 March

£ thousands

		1988/89	1989/90	1990/91	1991/92	1992/93	1993/94	1994/95	1995/96	1996/97	1997/98	1998/99
Revenue account												
Rates[1,2,3]	KQXA	2 050 666	1 265 922	1 351 627	1 414 346	1 336 395	1 258 863	1 198 575	1 310 721	1 313 531	1 326 129	1 437 646
Community charges	KQXB	–	867 519	890 645	802 005	932 994	–	–	–	–	–	–
Council tax	KPUC	–	–	–	–	–	822 830	918 502	976 465	968 153	1 070 405	1 146 366
Government grants												
RSG[4]:	KQXC	–	2 346 281	2 495 840	2 706 629	3 546 958	3 582 127	3 741 567	3 716 567	3 649 694	3 520 461	3 483 815
Needs element	KQXD	1 690 000	–	–	–	–	–	–	–	–	–	–
Resources element	KQXE	215 800	–	–	–	–	–	–	–	–	–	–
Domestic element	KQXF	91 900	–	–	–	–	–	–	–	–	–	–
Rate rebate grant[2]	KQXG	189 632	24 164	30 941	37 304	33 741	41 772	39 860	4 456	496	–	–
Community charge grant[5]	KIMJ	..	..	..	437 105	15 512	–	–	–	–	–	–
Community charge rebate grants	KQXH	–	187 182	192 378	112 904	153 231	–	–	–	–	–	–
Council tax rebate grants	KPUD	–	–	–	–	–	166 015	186 219	193 937	226 132	260 424	274 940
Other grants and subsidies[6]	KQXI	796 789	808 535	882 296	951 871	1 049 899	1 118 978	1 179 327	1 236 160	1 347 706	1 480 890	1 642 045
Sales	KQXJ	55 881	49 439	50 001	45 134	54 399	61 970	59 182	64 284	59 059	46 874	39 595
Fees and charges[7]	KQXK	1 070 254	1 185 303	1 288 728	1 410 355	1 435 951	1 421 565	1 471 320	1 528 270	1 539 611	1 625 952	1 668 223
Other income[6,7]	KQXL	126 990	123 212	132 009	161 791	184 581	194 151	209 819	207 005	162 825	189 496	190 934
Capital account												
Sale of fixed assets	KQXM	295 736	446 097	416 838	415 475	413 083	441 600	529 528	500 838	499 143	327 569	335 037
Loans	KQXN	774 490	682 767	..	..	..	..	..	..	..	..	..
Government grants	KQXO	25 134	..	..	..	..	..	..	..	..	..	..
Revenue contributions to capital	KQXP	14 391	11 812	48 997	73 896	111 710	163 228	134 156	197 606	119 641	149 423	204 982
Transfer from special funds	KMHZ	1 904	1 513	2 196	1 218	1 751	7 902	10 679	9 035	2 652	36 929	26 959
Other receipts	KMGV	38 715	23 156	24 649	23 110	42 631	32 554	38 736	29 571	45 067	32 118	45 028
Total income	KMGW	7 438 282	..	..	..	..	..	..	..	..	..	..

1 Excluding government grants towards rate rebates and domestic element of rate support grant (RSG). Including domestic water rate receipts.

2 Until 1982/83, certificated rate rebates paid in respect of supplementary benefit recipients were included with rate income. From 1983/84 onwards, they are included as part of rate rebate grant.

3 From 1989/90 rates refer to non-domestic rates only.

4 From 1989/90 onwards, RSG is not broken down into the three elements.

5 Payment to local authorities in respect of the £140 reduction in community charge awarded.

6 Until 1986/87, government grants not specific to service, eg grants towards job creation, were included under other income. From 1987/88, these are included under other grants and subsidies.

7 Prior to 1984/85 rents are treated as other income. From 1984/85 onwards rents are included with fees and charges.

Source: Scottish Executive, Economic Advice & Statistics: 0131 244 7033

17.20 Income of local authorities from government grants[1]
Scotland

Year ended 31 March

£ thousands

		1988/89	1989/90	1990/91	1991/92	1992/93	1993/94	1994/95	1995/96	1996/97	1997/98	1998/99
General fund services[2]	KQYA	274 707	295 169	339 619	368 717	403 437	428 927	450 056	468 660	487 734	557 536	690 569
Education	KQYB	15 801	11 510	17 809	17 699	20 439	21 791	17 452	17 186	18 324	61 960	92 368
Libraries, museums and galleries	KQYC	664	57	80	106	154	108	247	123	137	326	627
Social work	KQYD	4 434	8 311	10 561	24 817	32 626	36 734	48 091	50 230	57 576	59 892	62 167
Law, order and protective services	KQYE	185 772	211 304	235 477	253 548	274 149	288 835	295 600	312 812	330 767	359 811	366 961
Transport[7]	KQYF	12 641	4 127	4 580	3 325	3 540	1 993	4 315	4 788	403	237	97 649
Environmental services	KQYG	4 491	150	50	56	50	84	82	42	119	159	89
Planning	KQYH	770	4 144	971	947	785	1 310	867	3 030	3 337	4 885	2 695
Leisure and recreation	KQYI	2 606	1 522	1 739	1 503	1 396	1 476	1 609	1 830	1 509	1 856	1 509
Central administration[3]	KQYJ	1 344	867	–	–	–	–	–	–	–	–	–
Other services	KQYK	46 184	53 177	68 352	66 716	70 298	76 596	81 793	78 619	75 562	68 410	66 504
Housing	KQYL	537 496	510 201	538 042	577 321	640 127	684 519	723 604	762 172	856 435	920 700	948 232
Trading services	KQYM	9 720	3 165	4 024	4 739	5 405	4 954	4 009	4 557	–	–	–
Water supply	KQYN	7 363	3 132	3 998	4 139	4 255	4 823	4 009	4 459	–	–	–
Ferries	KQYO	213	–	–	1	46	47	–	–	–	–	–
Other trading services	KQYP	2 144	33	26	599	1 104	84	–	98	–	–	–
Capital grants[4,5]	KQYQ	–	..	..	..	..	..	..	..	..	..	..
General fund services	KQYR	–	..	..	..	..	..	..	..	..	..	..
Other services	KMGX	–	..	..	..	..	..	..	..	..	..	..
Grants not allocated to specific services[6]	KMGY	2 187 332	2 557 627	2 719 159	3 293 942	3 749 442	3 789 914	3 781 426	3 721 023	3 650 190	3 520 461	3 483 815
Total	KMGZ	3 009 255	..	3 600 844	4 244 719	4 798 411	4 908 314	4 959 095	4 956 412	4 994 362	4 998 697	5 122 616

1 Including grants for capital works.
2 Until 1986/87, excludes government grants not specific to services, eg grants towards job creation. From 1987/88 includes such grants.
3 From 1990/91 Central Administration income is included in the relevant service income.
4 From 1989/90 service breakdown no longer includes capital grants.

5 From 1990-91, the total income from government grants does not include capital grants.
6 Revenue support grant, community charge grant and rate and community charge rebate grants.
7 The significant increase in 1998/99 is due to the different reporting of a grant in aid of expenditure on rail passenger services in the Strathclyde Passenger Transport area.

Source: Scottish Executive, Economic Advice & Statistics: 0131 244 7033

17.21 Expenditure of local authorities
Northern Ireland
Years ended 31 March

£ thousand

		Out of revenue and special funds										
		1988 /89	1989 /90	1990 /91	1991 /92	1992 /93	1993 /94	1994 /95	1995 /96	1996 /97	1997 /98	1998 /99
Total	KQVA	167 303	179 404	193 450	203 650	214 107	230 666	251 737	252 794	294 563	304 305	413 698
Libraries, museums and art galleries	KQVB	683	3 606	3 881	4 030	4 644	5 647	7 214	8 481	10 956	13 928	14 571
Environmental health services:												
Refuse collection and disposal	KQVC	26 418	26 366	29 363	32 131	33 582	39 952	42 109	41 284	52 267	56 246	56 360
Public baths	KQVD	3 105	1 457	1 571	1 808	1 505	1 562	1 648	1 703	1 838	2 585	2 634
Parks, recreation grounds, etc	KQVE	59 871	63 284	68 593	74 439	80 601	91 258	101 319	100 418	111 884	115 302	118 396
Other sanitary services	KQVF	21 543	24 990	24 237	26 251	27 593	32 074	34 582	35 706	39 545	39 682	42 923
Housing (grants and small dwellings acquisition)[1]	KQVG	1 092	1 008	1 130	860	792	873	553	472	489	545	358
Trading services:												
Gas supply	KQVH	6 631	7 997	3 472	–	–	–	–	–	..	..	..
Cemeteries	KQVI	3 846	4 335	4 492	4 908	5 044	5 352	5 984	5 489	5 120	5 626	5 887
Other trading services (including markets, fairs and harbours)	KQVJ	5 348	6 491	7 340	7 778	7 335	7 123	6 587	4 254	8 672	7 016	10 779
Miscellaneous	KQVK	38 768	39 870	49 371	51 445	53 011	46 825	51 741	54 987	63 792	63 375	161 790
Total loan charges	KQVL	13 588	18 154	19 430	20 226	21 693	19 194	20 797	21 122	24 363	34 823	26 413
Loan charges included in terms of expenditure above:												
Allocated to rate fund services	KQVM	11 221	13 216	15 155	16 777	18 785	..	..	..	..	..	..
Allocated to trading services	KQVN	1 969	4 513	3 904	3 102	2 689	..	..	..	..	..	..
Not allocated	KQVO	398	425	371	347	219	..	..	..	..	..	..

		On capital works[1]										
		1988 /89	1989 /90	1990 /91	1991 /92	1992 /93	1993 /94	1994 /95	1995 /96	1996 /97	1997 /98	1998 /99
Total	KQVP	33 943	34 955	37 800	42 005	52 908	63 870	56 031	60 629	72 910	69 159	81 869
Libraries, museums and art galleries	KQVQ	343	683	997	919	2 008	3 833	1 225	1 466	890	1 158	4 019
Environmental health services:												
Refuse collection and disposal	KQVR	5 107	3 917	7 254	6 363	4 629	7 013	8 907	8 772	10 401	9 136	8 831
Public baths	KQVS	271	73	189	225	156	35	143	213	1 000	2 669	8 107
Parks, recreation grounds, etc	KQVT	8 951	14 343	18 654	19 239	29 205	26 736	20 914	23 732	26 749	28 884	32 033
Other sanitary services	KQVU	1 333	1 666	1 844	2 053	2 094	1 657	1 883	2 233	1 894	2 739	1 716
Housing (including small dwellings acquisition)[1]	KQVV	104	84	254	441	164	–	18	–	–	192	224
Trading services:												
Gas supply	KQVW	86	22	–	–	–	–	–	–	–	–	–
Cemeteries	KQVX	1 161	597	795	690	673	267	198	714	322	167	689
Other trading services (including markets, fairs and harbours)	KQVY	4 125	4 493	2 762	4 738	3 043	4 231	2 954	357	5 456	6 145	4 438
Miscellaneous	KQVZ	12 462	9 077	5 051	7 337	10 936	20 098	19 789	23 142	26 198	18 069	21 812

1 Expenditure met out of loans, government grants for capital works, sales of property and other capital receipts.

Source: Department of the Environment for Northern Ireland: 028 9054 0707

17.22 Income of local authorities
Northern Ireland
Classified according to source   Years ended 31 March

£ thousand

		1988 /89	1989 /90	1990 /91	1991 /92	1992 /93	1993 /94	1994 /95	1995 /96	1996 /97	1997 /98	1998 /99
Total income	KQWA	201 189	216 779	234 037	224 082	284 923	..	..	..	..	..	..
Capital receipts: total	KQWB	26 421	30 127	33 860	36 022	53 523	63 151	44 567	61 502	67 724	63 242	64 585
Loans	KQWC	11 012	15 557	20 417	19 166	25 736	..	..	..	..	..	..
Government grants	KQWD	4 366	5 638	5 607	8 945	16 140	..	..	..	..	..	..
Other sources	KQWE	11 043	8 932	7 836	7 911	11 647	..	..	..	..	..	..
Other income: total	KQWF	130 646	135 587	145 168	163 500	178 834	..	..	..	..	..	..
Rates	KQWG	97 564	101 883	108 829	124 106	136 460	145 306	150 991	163 405	178 897	191 141	202 843
Government grants Housing[1]	KQWH	32 541	33 311	36 005	39 095	42 002	..	..	..	..	..	..
Grants and small dwellings acquisition	KQWI	541	393	334	299	372	..	..	..	..	..	..
Miscellaneous income	KQWJ	26 454	30 515	36 903	37 619	40 360	..	..	..	..	..	..
Trading services												
Total (capital and revenue)	KQWK	17 668	20 550	18 106	16 967	12 206	..	..	..	..	..	..
Gas: total	KQWL	7 954	7 599	6 362	–	–	..	..	..	..	..	..
Loans	KQWM	–	–	–	–	–	..	..	..	..	..	..
Government grants	KQWN	2 216	5 742	4 883	–	–	..	..	..	..	..	..
Miscellaneous	KQWO	5 738	1 857	1 479	–	–	..	..	..	..	..	..
Cemeteries: total	KQWP	1 833	2 122	2 427	2 507	2 796	..	..	..	..	..	..
Loans	KQWQ	904	866	1 216	1 063	1 241	..	..	..	..	..	..
Government grants	KQWR	11	99	116	123	243	..	..	..	..	..	..
Miscellaneous	KQWS	918	1 157	1 095	1 321	1 312	..	..	..	..	..	..
Other trading: total	KQWT	7 881	10 829	9 317	14 460	9 410	..	..	..	..	..	..
Loans	KQWU	2 739	4 662	4 670	6 365	2 751	..	..	..	..	..	..
Government grants	KQWV	1 330	1 857	23	1 288	1 420	..	..	..	..	..	..
Miscellaneous	KQWW	3 812	4 310	4 624	6 807	5 239	..	..	..	..	..	..

1 Including annuity repayments made by borrowers under the Small Dwellings Acquisition scheme.

Source: Department of the Environment for Northern Ireland: 028 9054 0707

17.23 Income of local authorities from government grants[1]
Northern Ireland
Classified according to services,   Years ended 31 March

£ thousand

		1988 /89	1989 /90	1990 /91	1991 /92	1992 /93	1993 /94	1994 /95	1995 /96	1996 /97	1997 /98	1998 /99
Total	KQXV	40 464	46 648	46 634	49 450	59 807	..	..	..	..	..	..
Allocated to specific services:												
Environmental health services	KQXW	6 500	7 596	8 355	11 179	18 945	..	..	..	..	..	..
Housing	KQXX	–	–	–	–	–	–	..	..	..	..	..
Other services	KQXY	4 958	9 017	6 012	4 300	4 960	..	..	..	..	..	..
Not allocated to specific services[2]	KQXZ	29 006	30 035	32 267	33 974	35 902	36 139	40 203	41 295	41 267	36 485	41 369

1 Including grants for capital works.
2 Assistance to local authorities under various Local Government Acts.

Source: Department of the Environment for Northern Ireland: 01232 540707

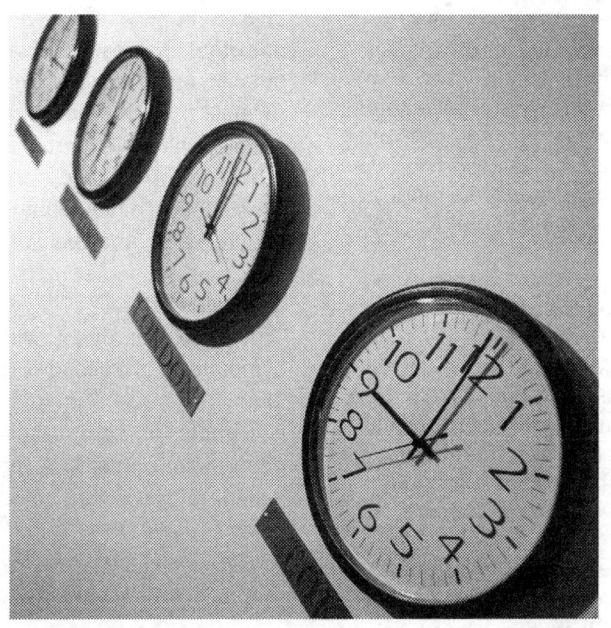

18 External trade and investment

External trade and investment

External trade *(Table 18.1 and 18.3 to 18.6)*
The statistics in Table 18.1 are on a Balance of Payments (BoP) basis; all other statistics in this section are on an Overseas Trade Statistics (OTS) basis, compiled from information provided to H M Customs and Excise by importers and exporters, which values exports 'f.o.b.' (free on board) and imports 'c.i.f.' (including insurance and freight). In addition to deducting these freight costs and insurance premiums from the OTS figures, coverage adjustments are made to convert the OTS data to a BoP basis. Adjustments are also made to the level of all exports and EU imports to take account of estimated under-recording. The adjustments are set out and described in the annual ONS *'Pink Book' (United Kingdom Balance of Payments)*. These adjustments are made to conform to the definitions in the 5th edition of the IMF Balance of Payments Manual.

Aggregate estimates of trade in goods, seasonally adjusted and on a BoP basis are published monthly in the ONS First Release UK Trade. More detailed figures are available from the ONS Databank and are also published in the Monthly Review of External Trade Statistics (Business Monitor MM24). Detailed figures for EU and non-EU trade on an OTS basis are published by The Stationery Office in Overseas Trade Statistics of the United Kingdom.

A fuller description of how trade statistics are compiled can be found in Statistics on Trade in Goods (Government Statistical Service Methodological Series).

Import penetration and export sales ratios *(Table 18.2)*
The ratios were first introduced in the August 1977 edition of *Economic Trends* in an article 'The Home and Export Performance of United Kingdom Industries'. The article described the conceptual and methodological problems involved in measuring such variables as import penetration.

The industries are grouped according to the 1992 Standard Industrial Classification. The four different ratios are defined as follows:

Ratio 1: percentage ratio of imports to home demand
Ratio 2: percentage ratio of imports to (home demand plus exports)
Ratio 3: percentage ratio of exports to total manufacturers sales
Ratio 4: percentage ratio of exports to (total manufacturers sales plus imports)

Home demand is defined as total manufacturers sales plus imports minus exports.

Ratio 1 is commonly used to describe the import penetration of the home market. Allowance is made for the extent of a domestic industry's involvement in export markets by using Ratio 2; this reduces as exports increase.

Similarly Ratio 3 is the measure normally used to relate exports to total sales by UK producers and Ratio 4 makes an allowance for the extent that imports of the same product are coming into the UK.

Overseas trade in services *(Tables 18.7 and 18.8)*
These data relate to overseas trade in services and cover both production and non-production industries (excluding the Public Sector). In terms of types of services traded this equates to trade in royalties, various forms of consultancy, computing and telecommunications services, advertising and market research and other business services. A separate inquiry covers the Film and Television industries. The surveys cover receipts from the provision of services to residents of other countries (exports) and payments to residents of other countries for services rendered (imports). "Residents of other countries" is defined as companies, governments and individuals.

Sources of data
The OTIS surveys (which consist of a quarterly component addressed to the largest businesses and an annual component for the remainder) are based on a sample of companies derived from the Inter-departmental Business register. The companies are asked to show the amounts for their imports and exports against the geographical area to which they were paid or from which they were received - irrespective of where they were first earned.

The purpose of the OTIS survey is to record international transactions which impact on the UK's Balance of Payments, hence companies are asked to exclude from their earnings trade expenses such as the cost of services purchased abroad. Trade in service exports or imports which are included in invoices for the export or import of goods are excluded as they are already counted in the estimates for trade in goods. However, earnings from third country trade i.e. from arranging the sale of goods between two countries other than the UK and where the goods never physically enter the UK (known as merchanting), are included. Earnings from commodity trading are also included. Together these two comprise "Trade Related Services".

"Royalties" are the largest part of the total trade in services collected in the OTIS survey: these cover transactions for items such as printed matter, sound recordings, performing rights, patents, licences, trade marks, designs, copyrights, manufacturing rights, the use of technical "know-how" and technical assistance.

Balance of payments *(Tables 18.9 to 18.12)*
Tables 18.9 to 18.12 in this section are derived from *United Kingdom Balance of Payments 2000 edition - the ONS Pink Book*. The following general notes to the tables provide brief definitions and explanations of the figures and terms used. Further notes are included in the *Pink Book*.

Summary of Balance of Payments

The Balance of Payments consists of the current account, the capital account, the financial account and the International Investment Position. The **current account** consists of trade in goods and services, income and current transfers. **Income** consists of investment income and a new category compensation of employees. The **capital account** mainly consists of capital transfers and the **financial account** covers financial transactions. The **International Investment Position** covers balance sheet levels of UK external assets and liabilities. Every credit entry in the balance of payments accounts should, in theory, be matched by a corresponding debit entry so that total current, capital and financial account credits should be equal to, and therefore offset by, total debits. In practice there is a discrepancy termed **net errors and omissions**.

The Current Account

Trade in goods

The goods account covers exports and imports of goods. Imports of motor cars from Japan, for example, are recorded as debits in the trade in goods account whereas exports of vehicles manufactured in the UK are recorded as credits. Trade in goods forms a component of the expenditure measure of Gross Domestic Product (GDP).

Trade in services

The services account covers exports and imports of services (eg, civil aviation). Passenger tickets for travel on UK aircraft sold abroad, for example, are recorded as credits in the services account whereas the purchases of airline tickets from foreign airlines by UK passengers are recorded as debits. Trade in services, along with trade in goods, forms a component of the expenditure measure of Gross Domestic Product (GDP).

Income

The income account consists of compensation of employees and investment income and is dominated by the latter. Compensation of employees covers employment income from cross-border and seasonal workers which is less significant in the UK than in other countries. Investment income covers earnings (eg, profits, dividends and interest payments and receipts) arising from foreign investment and financial assets and liabilities. For example, earnings on foreign bonds and shares held by financial institutions based in the UK are recorded as credits in the investment income account, whereas earnings on UK company securities held abroad are recorded as investment income debits. Investment income forms a component of Gross National Income (GNI) but not Gross Domestic Product (GDP).

Current transfers

Current transfers are composed of central government transfers (eg, taxes and payments to and receipts from the European Union) and other transfers (eg, gifts in cash or kind received by private individuals from abroad or receipts from the EU where the UK government acts as an agent for the ultimate beneficiary of the transfer). Current transfers do not form a component either of Gross Domestic Product (GDP) or of Gross National Income

(GNI). For example payments to the UK farming industry under the EU Agricultural Guarantee Fund are recorded as credits in the current transfers account while payments of EU agricultural levies by the UK farming industry are recorded as debits in the current transfers account.

Capital Account

Capital account transactions involve transfers of ownership of fixed assets, transfers of funds associated with acquisition or disposal of fixed assets, and cancellation of liabilities by creditors without any counterparts being received in return. The main components are migrants transfers, EU transfers relating to fixed capital formation (regional development fund and agricultural guidance fund) and debt forgiveness. Funds brought into the UK by new immigrants would, for example, be recorded as credits in the capital account, while funds sent abroad by UK residents emigrating to other countries would be recorded as debits in the capital account. The magnitude of capital account transactions are quite minor compared with the current and financial accounts.

Financial Account

While investment income covers earnings arising from overseas investments and financial assets and liabilities, the financial account of the balance of payments covers the flows of such investments. While earnings on foreign bonds and shares held by financial institutions based in the UK are, for example, recorded as credits in the investment income account, the acquisition of such foreign securities by UK based financial institutions are recorded as net debits in the financial account as portfolio investment abroad. Similarly the acquisitions of UK company securities held by foreign residents are recorded in the financial account as net credits as portfolio investment in the UK.

International Investment Position

While the financial account covers the flows of foreign investments and financial assets and liabilities, the International Investment Position records the levels of external assets and liabilities. While the acquisition of foreign securities by UK based financial institutions are recorded in the financial account, as net debits, the total holdings of foreign securities by UK based financial institutions are recorded as levels of UK external assets. Similarly the holdings of UK company securities held by foreign residents are recorded as levels of UK liabilities.

Overseas direct investment
(Tables 18.13 to 18.18)

Direct investment refers to investment that adds to, deducts from or acquires a lasting interest in an enterprise operating in an economy other than that of the investor, the investor's purpose being to have an effective voice in the management of the enterprise. (For the purposes of the statistical inquiry, an effective voice is taken as equivalent to a holding of 10 per cent or more in the foreign enterprise.) Other investments in which the investor does not have an effective voice in the management of the enterprise are mainly portfolio investments and these are not covered here. Cross-border investment by public corporations or in property (which is regarded as direct investment in the national

External trade and investment

accounts) is not covered here, but is shown in the balance of payments. Similarly direct investment earnings data are shown net of tax in Tables 18.15 and 18.18 but are gross of tax in the balance of payments.

Direct investment is a financial concept and is not the same as capital expenditure on fixed assets. It covers only the money invested in a related concern by the parent company and the concern will then decide how to use the money. A related concern may also raise money locally without reference to the parent company.

The investment figures are published on a net basis, that is, they consist of investments net of disinvestments by a company into its foreign subsidiaries, associate companies and branches.

Definitional changes from 1997

The new European System of Accounts (ESA(95)) definitions were introduced from the 1997 estimates. The changes were as follows:

i)   Previously for the measurement of direct investment, an effective voice in the management of an enterprise was taken as the equivalent of a 20 per cent shareholding. This is now 10 per cent.

ii)   The Channels Islands (Jersey, Guernsey etc.) and the Isle of Man have been excluded from the definition of the economic territory of the UK. Prior to 1987 these islands were considered to be part of the United Kingdom.

iii)   Interest received or paid was replaced by interest accrued in the figures on earnings from direct investment. There is deemed to be little or no impact arising from this definitional change on the estimates.

The definitional changes have been introduced from 1997 only. The data prior to 1997 have not been reworked in Tables 18.13 to 18.18. For clarity, the Offshore Islands are identified separately on the tables. The breaks in the series for the other definitional changes are not quantified but are relatively small. More detailed information on the effect of these changes was published in the business monitor, MA4 – Overseas Direct Investment in February 2000.

Sources of data

The figures in Tables 18.13 to 18.18 are based on annual inquiries into overseas direct investment for 1998. These were sample surveys which involved sending around 900 forms to UK businesses investing abroad and 1700 forms to UK businesses in which foreign parents and associates had invested. The tables also contain some revisions to 1997 as a result of new information coming to light in the course of conducting the 1998 annual inquiries. Further details from the 1998 annual inquiries, including analyses by industry and by components of direct investment, were published in 2000 in MA4, Overseas Direct Investment, one of the ONS Business Monitor series of publications. Updated figures for 1998 and 1999 were published in a First Release in December 2000.

Country allocation

The analysis of inward investment is based on the country of ownership of the immediate parent company. Thus, inward investment in a UK company may be attributed to the country of the intervening overseas subsidiary, rather than the country of the ultimate parent. Similarly, the country analysis of outward investment is based on the country of ownership of the immediate subsidiary. As an example, to the extent that overseas investment in the UK is channelled through holding companies in the Netherlands, the underlying flow of investment from this country is overstated and the inflow from originating countries is understated.

Further information

More detailed statistics on overseas direct investment are available on request from Simon Harrington, National Statistics, Overseas Financial & Coordination Division, Room 1.075, Government Buildings, Cardiff Road, Newport, Gwent NP10 8XG. (Telephone: 01633 812406, fax: 01633813306,e-mail simon.harrington@ons.gov.uk).

18.1 Trade in goods United Kingdom On a balance of payments basis[1]

		1989	1990	1991	1992	1993	1994	1995	1996	1997	1998	1999
Value(£ millions)												
Exports of goods	BOKG	92 611	102 313	103 939	107 863	122 039	135 260	153 725	167 403	171 783	164 092	165 667
Imports of goods	BOKH	117 335	121 020	114 162	120 913	135 358	146 351	165 449	180 489	183 693	184 629	192 434
Balance on trade in goods	BOKI	−24 724	−18 707	−10 223	−13 050	−13 319	−11 091	−11 724	−13 086	−11 910	−20 537	−26 767
Price index numbers 1995 = 100												
Exports of goods	BQKR	78.9	81.7	82.8	84.5	95.0	96.9	100.0	100.8	95.2	90.3	89.8
Imports of goods	BQKS	79.3	81.2	82.2	82.9	91.2	94.3	100.0	100.1	93.8	88.0	86.8
Terms of trade[2]	BQKT	99.5	100.6	100.7	101.9	104.2	102.8	100.0	100.7	101.5	102.6	103.5
Volume index numbers 1995 = 100												
Exports of goods	BQKU	72.6	77.2	78.0	79.9	82.8	91.3	100.0	107.7	116.5	117.9	121.6
Imports of goods	BQKV	86.5	86.5	81.9	87.3	90.6	94.6	100.0	109.1	119.0	129.1	138.7

1 Statistics of trade in goods on a balance of payments basis are obtained by making certain adjustments in respect of valuation and coverage to the statistics recorded in the *Overseas Trade Statistics*. These adjustments are described in detail in *The Pink Book 1999*.

2 Export price index as a percentage of the import price index.

Source: Office for National Statistics: 020 7533 6064

18.2 Import penetration and export sales ratios for products of manufacturing industry [1,2,3]
United Kingdom: SIC 92

			1994	1995	1996
Ratio 1:Imports/Home Demand					
Description		SIC Division			
Total of divisions below	BAZI			50	52	56
Textiles[2]	BAZJ	17	46	47	47
Wearing Apparel: Dressing and dyeing of fur	BAZK	18	61	60	65
Chemicals and Chemical products	BAZL	24	48	52	57
Ratio 2:Imports/Home Demand plus Exports					
Description					
Total of divisions below	BAZM		34	36	37
Textiles[2]	BAZN	17	36	36	36
Wearing Apparel: Dressing and dyeing of fur	BAZO	18	47	45	49
Chemicals and Chemical products	BAZP	24	31	34	35
Ratio 3:Exports/Sales					
Description					
Total of divisions below	BAZQ		47	49	53
Textiles[2]	BAZR	17	34	37	36
Wearing Apparel: Dressing and dyeing of fur	BAZS	18	45	46	49
Chemicals and Chemical products	BAZT	24	51	53	59
Ratio 4:Exports/Sales plus Imports					
Description					
Total of division below	BAZU		31	32	34
Textiles[2]	BAZV	17	22	23	23
Wearing Apparel:Dressing and dyeing of fur	BAZW	18	24	25	25
Chemicals and Chemical products	BAZX	24	35	35	39

1 The ratios were re-instated in the July 1995 edition of *Monthly Digest of Statistics* after a gap of seven years. They contained figures collected under the PRODCOM Inquiry which was introduced in 1993 and the data was regarded as provisional. Please note that the current tables have been calculated using revised data for 1994.

2 Previously included duplicate trade data for certain headings.

3 Division 23 (Coke, refined petroleum products and nuclear fuel) and SIC 24610 (manufacture of explosives, are excluded from the analysis), SIC 27100 (Basic Iron and Steel and of ferro-alloys) is not incorporated in PRODCOM and therefore also does not form part of the analysis.

4 Division 13 (Mining of Metal Ores) not published in 1995.

5 Division 16 data has a large revision as Excise Duty is now excluded from PRODCOM data.

Source: Office for National Statistics: 01633 813065

18.2
Import penetration and export sales ratios for products of manufacturing industry [1,2,3]

continued

United Kingdom: SIC 92

			1994	1995	1996
Ratio 1 Imports/Home Demand					
Description		*SIC Division*			
Total of divisions below	BAZY		44	45	46
Mining of Metal Ores[4]	BAZZ	13	101	..	..
Other Mining and Quarrying	BBAM	14	106	135	169
Food products and beverages	BBAN	15	21	22	23
Tobacco products	BBAO	16	9	14	14
Textiles	BAZJ	17	46	47	47
Wearing Apparel: Dressing and dyeing of fur	BAZK	18	61	60	65
Tanning and dressing of leather:luggage,		19			
handbags, saddlery, harness and footwear	BBAP		69	73	74
Wood products of wood and cork (except furniture)		20			
articles of straw and plaiting materials	BBAQ		42	37	34
Pulp, paper and paper products	BBAR	21	37	39	36
Publishing, printing and reproduction of recorded media[2]	BBAS	22	7	7	7
Chemicals and chemical products	BAZL	24	48	52	57
Rubber and plastic products[2]	BBAT	25	29	29	27
Other non metallic mineral products	BBAU	26	20	20	20
Basic metals [2]	BBAV	27	61	64	66
Fabricated metal products (except machinery and equipment)[2]	BBAW	28	19	20	19
Machinery and equipment not elsewhere classified	BBAX	29	60	61	60
Office machinery and computers	BBAY	30	113	128	102
Electrical machinery not elsewhere classified	BBAZ	31	53	56	58
Radio, television and communication equipment and apparatus	BBBA	32	94	92	98
Medical, precision and optical instruments, watches and clocks	BBBB	33	72	76	79
Motor vehicles, trailers and semi-trailers	BBBC	34	55	53	59
Other transport equipment	BBBD	35	56	54	47
Furniture and manufacturing not elsewhere classified	BBBE	36	48	48	48
Ratio 2 Imports/Home Demand plus Exports					
Description		*SIC Division*			
Total of divisions below	BBBF		32	32	33
Mining of Metal Ores[4]	BBBG	13	98	..	..
Other Mining and Quarrying	BBBH	14	48	54	59
Food products and beverages	BBBI	15	18	19	20
Tobacco products	BBBJ	16	6	8	8
Textiles	BAZN	17	36	36	36
Wearing Apparel: Dressing and dyeing of fur	BAZO	18	47	45	49
Tanning and dressing of leather:luggage,		19			
handbags, saddlery, harness and footwear	BBBK		54	55	56
Wood products of wood and cork (except furniture)		20			
articles of straw and plaiting materials	BBBL		40	36	33
Pulp, paper and paper products	BBBM	21	32	35	31
Publishing, printing and reproduction of recorded media[2]	BBBN	22	6	7	6
Chemicals and chemical products	BAZP	24	31	34	35
Rubber and plastic products[2]	BBBO	25	24	24	22
Other non metallic mineral products	BBBP	26	17	16	16
Basic metals[2]	BBBQ	27	44	44	46
Fabricated metal products (except machinery and equipment)[2]	BBBR	28	16	16	16
Machinery and equipment not elsewhere classified	BBBS	29	36	36	35
Office machinery and computers	BBBT	30	56	58	53
Electrical machinery not elsewhere classified	BBBU	31	36	38	38
Radio, television and communication equipment and apparatus	BBBV	32	48	47	52
Medical, precision and optical instruments, watches and clocks	BBBW	33	41	42	44
Motor vehicles, trailers and semi-trailers	BBBX	34	41	39	41
Other transport equipment	BBBY	35	33	31	29
Furniture and manufacturing not elsewhere classified	BBBZ	36	36	35	36

See footnotes on the first part of this table.

Source: Office for National Statistics: 01633 813065

18.2
continued

Import penetration and export sales ratios for products of manufacturing industry [1,2,3]

United Kingdom: SIC 92

			1994	1995	1996
Ratio 3 Exports/Sales					
Description		*SIC Division*			
Total of divisions below	BBCK		40	42	43
Mining of Metal Ores[4]	BBCL	13	151	..	..
Other Mining and Quarrying	BBCM	14	105	131	158
Food products and beverages	BBCN	15	16	17	16
Tobacco products	BBCO	16	32	46	46
Textiles	BAZR	17	34	37	36
Wearing Apparel:Dressing and dyeing of fur	BAZS	18	45	46	49
Tanning and dressing of leather:luggage,		19			
handbags, saddlery, harness and footwear	BBCP		50	55	55
Wood products of wood and cork (except furniture)		20			
articles of straw and plaiting materials	BBCQ		6	6	6
Pulp, paper and paper products	BBCR	21	18	19	19
Publishing, printing and reproduction of recorded media[2]	BBCS	22	10	11	9
Chemicals and chemical products	BAZT	24	51	53	59
Rubber and plastic products[2]	BBCT	25	26	26	25
Other non metallic mineral products	BBCU	26	20	21	22
Basic metals[2]	BBCV	27	50	55	56
Fabricated metal products (except machinery and equipment)[2]	BBCW	28	18	19	18
Machinery and equipment not elsewhere classified	BBCX	29	63	64	64
Office machinery and computers	BBCY	30	115	130	102
Electrical machinery not elsewhere classified	BBDK	31	50	53	56
Radio, television and communication equipment and apparatus	BBDL	32	94	93	98
Medical, precision and optical instruments, watches and clocks	BBDM	33	73	77	80
Motor vehicles, trailers and semi-trailers	BBDN	34	44	44	51
Other transport equipment	BBDO	35	61	62	55
Furniture and manufacturing not elsewhere classified	BBDP	36	39	40	39
Ratio 4 Exports/Sales **plus Imports**					
Description		*SIC Division*			
Total of divisions below	BBDQ		27	29	29
Mining of Metal Ores[4]	BBDR	13	2	..	..
Other Mining and Quarrying	BBDS	14	55	60	65
Food products and beverages	BBDT	15	13	14	13
Tobacco products	BBDU	16	30	43	43
Textiles	BAZV	17	22	23	23
Wearing Apparel: Dressing and dyeing of fur	BAZW	18	24	25	25
Tanning and dressing of leather: luggage,		19			
handbags, saddlery, harness and footwear	BBDV		23	25	24
Wood products of wood and cork (except furniture)		20			
articles and straw and plaiting materials	BBDW		4	4	4
Pulp, paper and paper products	BBDX	21	13	12	13
Publishing, printing and reproduction of recorded media[2]	BBDY	22	10	10	9
Chemicals and chemical products	BAZX	24	35	35	39
Rubber and plastic products[2]	BBDZ	25	20	20	19
Other non-metallic mineral products	BBEA	26	17	18	19
Basic metals	BBEB	27	28	30	30
Fabricated metal products (except machinery and equipment)[2]	BBEC	28	15	16	15
Machinery and equipment not elsewhere classified	BBED	29	40	41	42
Office machinery and computers	BBEE	30	50	55	48
Electrical machinery not elsewhere classified	BBEF	31	32	33	35
Radio, television and communication equipment and apparatus	BBEG	32	49	49	47
Medical, precision and optical instruments, watches and clocks	BBEH	33	43	45	45
Motor vehicles, trailers and semi-trailers	BBEI	34	26	27	30
Other transport equipment	BBEJ	35	40	43	39
Furniture and manufacturing not elsewhere classified	BBEK	36	25	26	25

See footnotes on the first part of this table.

Source: Office for National Statistics: 01633 813065

18.3 United Kingdom exports, by commodity[1]

£ million BOP-consistent basis seasonally adjusted

		1990	1991	1992	1993	1994	1995	1996	1997	1998	1999
0. Food and live animals	BOGG	4 265	4 657	5 276	5 864	6 312	7 089	7 006	6 575	6 280	5 903
Of which:											
01. Meat and meat preparations	BOGS	603	666	829	997	1 229	1 470	1 081	925	745	660
02. Dairy products and eggs	BQMS	456	445	534	658	695	821	735	744	745	683
04 & 08. Cereals and animal feeding stuffs	BQMT	1 283	1 393	1 545	1 600	1 523	1 705	2 012	1 799	1 711	1 560
05. Vegetables and fruit	BQMU	263	294	332	315	398	456	474	455	408	434
1. Beverages and tobacco	BQMZ	2 730	2 997	3 401	3 302	3 734	4 115	4 337	4 519	3 939	4 026
11. Beverages	BQNB	2 084	2 225	2 435	2 654	2 865	2 988	3 141	3 302	2 880	3 006
12. Tobacco	BQOW	646	772	966	648	869	1 127	1 196	1 217	1 059	1 020
2. Crude materials	BQOX	2 154	1 914	1 865	2 152	2 400	2 728	2 585	2 486	2 269	2 082
Of which:											
24. Wood, lumber and cork	BQOY	27	25	25	22	45	46	52	52	57	69
25. Pulp and waste paper	BQOZ	52	38	39	22	50	66	56	64	48	54
26. Textile fibres	BQPA	494	466	486	505	572	637	611	567	493	446
28. Metal ores	BQPB	630	530	458	627	664	772	658	641	555	516
3. Fuels	BOPN	8 398	7 637	7 479	9 053	9 498	9 951	11 594	11 004	7 515	9 853
33. Petroleum and petroleum products	ELBL	8 074	7 284	7 172	8 605	9 085	9 393	10 943	10 229	7 020	9 050
32, 34 and 35. Coal, gas and electricity	BOQI	324	353	307	448	413	558	651	775	495	803
4. Animal and vegetable oils and fats	BQPI	88	94	85	118	171	221	208	264	243	198
5. Chemicals	ENDG	13 079	13 700	14 931	17 708	18 819	21 019	22 194	21 883	22 107	22 999
Of which:											
51. Organic chemicals	BQPJ	3 326	3 450	3 692	4 476	4 733	4 928	5 159	4 970	4 913	5 483
52. Inorganic chemicals	BQPK	944	991	1 179	1 247	1 120	1 237	1 191	1 181	1 161	1 124
53. Colouring materials	CSCE	1 185	1 212	1 277	1 452	1 480	1 618	1 642	1 577	1 543	1 536
54. Medicinal products	BQPL	2 240	2 542	2 983	3 777	4 013	4 929	5 338	5 413	5 858	6 261
55. Toilet preparations	CSCF	1 155	1 292	1 466	1 699	2 013	2 127	2 410	2 567	2 450	2 457
57 & 58. Plastics	BQQA	2 106	2 110	2 129	2 525	2 802	3 280	3 296	3 161	3 194	3 145
6. Manufactures classified chiefly by material	BQQB	15 717	15 495	15 427	17 743	19 594	22 482	23 172	22 655	21 248	20 235
Of which:											
63. Wood and cork manufactures	BQQC	116	117	129	133	171	190	228	250	254	275
64. Paper and paperboard manufactures	BQQD	1 530	1 613	1 726	1 878	2 052	2 352	2 346	2 309	2 200	2 021
65. Textile manufactures	BQQE	2 428	2 337	2 444	2 657	2 958	3 285	3 475	3 418	3 261	3 004
67. Iron and steel	BQQF	3 012	2 994	2 996	3 216	3 665	4 349	4 067	3 635	3 318	2 571
68. Non-ferrous metals	BQQG	2 181	1 966	1 748	1 954	2 234	2 868	2 682	2 771	2 437	2 123
69. Metal manufactures	BQQH	2 084	2 155	2 192	2 313	2 640	3 090	3 355	3 364	3 588	3 527
7. Machinery and transport equipment[2]	BQQI	40 756	42 860	43 768	49 362	55 913	65 412	73 453	78 937	78 038	78 711
71 - 716, 72, 73 & 74. Mechanical machinery	BQQK	13 966	13 425	13 921	15 158	16 287	18 350	20 503	22 313	22 702	21 857
716, 75, 76 & 77. Electrical machinery	BQQL	14 727	15 391	16 042	21 063	24 930	30 682	32 984	34 218	34 472	35 838
78. Road vehicles	BQQM	7 072	8 341	8 679	8 510	9 666	11 657	14 295	14 799	14 560	15 040
79. Other transport equipment	BQQN	4 991	5 703	5 126	4 631	5 030	4 723	5 671	7 607	6 304	5 976
8. Miscellaneous manufactures[2]	BQQO	12 862	12 749	13 580	15 080	17 322	18 880	20 900	21 517	20 556	20 165
Of which:											
84. Clothing	CSCN	1 645	1 874	2 035	2 370	2 722	3 060	3 358	3 257	2 983	2 768
85. Footwear	CSCP	269	309	332	417	479	519	597	605	539	529
87 & 88. Scientific and photographic	BQQQ	3 988	4 155	4 351	4 816	5 360	5 904	6 598	6 972	6 713	6 726
9. Other commodities and transactions	BOQL	2 264	1 836	2 051	1 657	1 497	1 828	1 954	1 943	1 897	1 495
TOTAL UK EXPORTS	BOKG	102 313	103 939	107 863	122 039	135 260	153 725	167 403	171 783	164 092	165 667

1 The numbers on the left hand side of the table refer to the code numbers of the *Standard International Trade Classification*, Revision 3, which was introduced in January 1988.

2 Sections 7 and 8 are shown by broad economic category in table E2 of the *Monthly Review of External Trade Statistics*.

Source: Office for National Statistics: 020 7533 6064

18.4 United Kingdom imports, by commodity[1]

£ million BOP-consistent basis seasonally adjusted

		1990	1991	1992	1993	1994	1995	1996	1997	1998	1999
0. Food and live animals	BQQR	9 796	9 779	10 701	11 260	11 678	12 931	14 049	13 329	13 203	13 343
Of which:											
01. Meat and meat preparations	BQQS	1 796	1 752	1 920	1 918	1 885	2 239	2 544	2 236	2 008	2 152
02. Dairy products and eggs	BQQT	874	827	1 060	1 011	1 095	1 078	1 194	1 101	1 111	1 176
04 & 08. Cereals and animal feeding stuffs	BQQU	1 344	1 364	1 628	1 775	1 684	1 782	1 917	1 994	1 806	1 722
05. Vegetables and fruit	BQQV	2 790	2 826	2 919	3 041	3 288	3 821	4 178	3 902	4 014	4 030
1. Beverages and tobacco	BQQW	1 815	1 830	1 912	2 086	2 154	2 416	2 791	2 885	3 001	3 184
11. Beverages	EGAT	1 465	1 398	1 488	1 672	1 797	1 966	2 208	2 344	2 549	2 786
12. Tobacco	EMAI	350	432	424	414	357	450	583	541	452	398
2. Crude materials	ENVB	5 175	4 230	4 228	4 603	5 045	5 895	5 864	5 674	5 073	4 942
Of which:											
24. Wood, lumber and cork	ENVC	1 273	943	930	1 048	1 302	1 143	1 203	1 239	1 098	1 089
25. Pulp and waste paper	EQAH	713	556	569	503	578	979	656	572	480	511
26. Textile fibres	EQAP	499	411	435	451	577	636	639	590	448	420
28. Metal ores	EHAA	1 306	1 084	1 030	1 051	1 031	1 358	1 476	1 461	1 316	1 319
3. Fuels	BQAT	7 914	7 623	7 123	7 476	6 345	6 162	7 287	6 826	4 890	5 625
33. Petroleum and petroleum products	ENXO	6 443	6 010	5 562	6 011	5 144	5 062	6 120	5 680	3 975	4 842
32, 34 and 35. Coal, gas and electricity	BPBI	1 471	1 613	1 561	1 465	1 201	1 100	1 167	1 146	915	783
4. Animal and vegetable oils and fats	EHAB	350	358	388	454	499	561	686	603	553	574
5. Chemicals	ENGA	10 454	10 599	11 205	13 012	14 177	17 491	18 117	17 423	17 352	18 622
Of which:											
51. Organic chemicals	EHAC	2 537	2 528	2 695	3 113	3 429	4 673	4 722	4 467	4 507	4 803
52. Inorganic chemicals	EHAE	927	995	914	985	1 064	1 087	1 233	1 107	1 016	1 056
53. Colouring materials	CSCR	625	599	661	872	790	930	1 001	976	1 004	958
54. Medicinal products	EHAF	1 120	1 328	1 603	2 027	2 260	2 787	3 062	3 104	3 303	4 124
55. Toilet preparations	CSCS	732	773	913	1 015	1 195	1 365	1 478	1 507	1 620	1 756
57 & 58. Plastics	EHAG	3 126	2 932	2 936	3 321	3 678	4 601	4 345	4 171	3 899	3 819
6. Manufactures classified chiefly by material	EHAH	21 102	19 792	19 905	21 659	23 869	27 773	28 731	28 030	27 661	26 815
Of which:											
63. Wood and cork manufactures	EHAI	904	780	801	871	999	1 037	1 080	1 083	1 085	1 145
64. Paper and paperboard manufactures	EHAJ	3 884	3 742	3 674	3 756	4 183	5 205	4 971	4 555	4 496	4 323
65. Textile manufactures	EHAK	3 774	3 586	3 778	3 969	4 403	4 808	5 080	5 007	4 855	4 385
67. Iron and steel	EHAL	2 597	2 538	2 433	2 568	2 909	3 622	3 612	3 340	3 199	2 466
68. Non-ferrous metals	EHAM	2 861	2 439	2 473	2 844	2 918	3 756	3 722	3 628	3 707	2 942
69. Metal manufactures	EHAN	2 476	2 412	2 460	2 540	2 818	3 237	3 488	3 563	3 735	3 763
7. Machinery and transport equipment[2]	EHAO	45 277	41 417	45 577	53 417	60 063	68 073	76 189	80 581	83 212	88 550
71 - 716, 72, 73 & 74. Mechanical machinery	EHAQ	11 490	10 568	11 142	11 811	13 109	15 152	16 554	17 051	17 139	17 289
716, 75, 76 & 77. Electrical machinery	EHAR	17 508	17 467	19 154	23 568	26 171	31 501	35 326	35 816	36 865	40 843
78. Road vehicles	EHAS	12 031	9 786	11 616	14 509	15 921	17 842	20 264	21 728	22 440	24 080
79. Other transport equipment	EHAT	4 248	3 596	3 665	3 529	4 862	3 578	4 045	5 986	6 768	6 338
8. Miscellaneous manufactures[2]	EHAU	17 223	16 618	18 103	19 983	21 339	22 530	25 010	26 582	27 881	28 990
Of which:											
84. Clothing	CSDR	3 702	3 927	4 256	4 698	4 781	5 179	6 063	6 632	7 021	7 475
85. Footwear	CSDS	1 113	1 115	1 102	1 231	1 430	1 514	1 772	1 913	1 861	2 036
87 & 88. Scientific and photographic	EHAW	3 862	3 889	4 051	4 621	4 842	5 387	6 007	6 070	6 099	6 177
9. Other commodities and transactions	BQAW	1 914	1 916	1 771	1 408	1 182	1 617	1 765	1 760	1 803	1 789
TOTAL UK IMPORTS	BOKH	121 020	114 162	120 913	135 358	146 351	165 449	180 489	183 693	184 629	192 434

1 The numbers on the left hand side of the table refer to the code numbers of the *Standard International Trade Classification*, Revision 3, which was introduced in January 1988.

2 Sections 7 and 8 are shown by broad economic category in table E2 of the *Monthly Review of External Trade Statistics*.

Source: Office for National Statistics: 020 7533 6064

18.5 United Kingdom exports, by area

£ million BOP-consistent basis seasonally adjusted

		1990	1991	1992	1993	1994	1995	1996	1997	1998	1999
European Union:	**ENOF**	58 878	63 118	64 976	69 212	76 993	89 684	95 965	95 908	95 726	97 283
EMU members:	**QAKW**	54 128	58 619	60 208	63 787	70 812	82 364	88 179	88 329	88 228	90 082
Germany	**ENYO**	13 039	14 513	15 185	16 055	17 363	20 274	20 761	20 650	20 598	20 350
France	**ENYL**	10 792	11 739	11 493	12 184	13 678	15 290	17 132	16 581	16 453	16 809
Italy	**CHNO**	5 536	6 111	6 137	6 078	6 848	7 895	8 043	8 200	8 611	7 781
Netherlands	**CHNP**	7 411	8 166	8 491	8 099	9 610	12 362	13 516	13 901	12 987	13 544
Belgium & Luxembourg	**CHNQ**	5 573	5 819	5 706	7 131	7 376	8 312	8 538	8 444	8 449	9 188
Irish Republic	**CHNS**	5 235	5 234	5 733	6 352	7 172	7 806	8 683	9 347	9 610	10 716
Portugal	**CHNU**	1 020	1 075	1 164	1 372	1 260	1 471	1 683	1 750	1 723	1 701
Spain	**CHNV**	3 791	4 354	4 509	4 484	5 137	6 110	6 738	6 730	7 174	7 484
Finland	**CHMZ**	1 035	845	995	1 118	1 317	1 718	1 818	1 569	1 434	1 347
Austria	**CHMY**	696	763	795	914	1 051	1 126	1 267	1 157	1 189	1 162
Non-EMU members	**QAKZ**	4 750	4 499	4 768	5 425	6 181	7 320	7 786	7 579	7 498	7 201
Sweden	**CHNA**	2 675	2 444	2 435	2 893	3 417	4 160	4 429	4 444	4 394	4 012
Denmark	**CHNR**	1 393	1 394	1 557	1 613	1 825	2 113	2 216	2 089	2 057	2 044
Greece	**CHNT**	682	661	776	919	939	1 047	1 141	1 046	1 047	1 145
Other Western Europe:	**HCJD**	4 664	4 559	4 298	5 317	5 772	6 417	7 332	7 850	7 673	6 514
Of which:											
Norway	**EPLX**	1 315	1 329	1 409	1 505	2 047	2 002	2 051	2 607	2 689	2 064
Switzerland	**EPLV**	2 404	2 124	1 839	2 282	2 480	2 729	3 185	2 958	2 902	2 751
Turkey	**EOBA**	615	742	690	1 047	821	1 149	1 554	1 734	1 614	1 215
Iceland	**EPLW**	89	97	92	148	110	138	152	153	161	160
North America:	**HBZQ**	15 473	13 645	14 741	17 779	19 722	20 450	22 357	23 871	24 793	27 872
Of which:											
USA	**EOBB**	13 197	11 550	12 640	15 403	17 081	17 901	19 761	20 900	21 721	24 297
Canada	**EOBC**	1 936	1 729	1 637	1 848	1 935	1 804	1 970	2 147	2 178	2 552
Mexico	**EPJX**	266	280	302	336	393	277	317	428	545	583
Other OECD countries:	**HCII**	5 711	5 229	5 348	6 666	7 795	9 390	11 015	10 784	8 770	9 159
Of which:											
Japan	**EOBD**	2 580	2 246	2 172	2 673	3 047	3 814	4 295	4 177	3 151	3 303
Australia	**EPMA**	1 621	1 341	1 340	1 611	1 957	2 140	2 488	2 457	2 218	2 164
South Korea	**ERDM**	612	780	644	805	987	1 162	1 313	1 228	675	950
Poland	**ERDR**	219	351	589	732	716	953	1 364	1 355	1 188	1 182
New Zealand	**EPMB**	431	259	258	335	422	440	475	409	340	326
Czech Rep	**FKML**	..	..	..	290	383	571	722	712	699	741
Hungary	**QALC**	120	133	157	209	263	296	349	438	487	491
Oil exporting countries:	**HDII**	5 427	5 758	6 051	6 589	5 811	6 296	7 933	9 404	7 313	5 552
Of which:											
Dubai	**QALI**	437	486	548	681	624	701	750	866	833	791
Saudi Arabia	**ERDI**	1 927	2 213	1 969	1 844	1 534	1 621	2 436	3 656	2 614	1 489
Indonesia	**FKMR**	190	202	315	333	371	518	813	674	368	389
Brunei	**QALF**	217	210	211	328	422	251	545	536	249	125
Rest of the World	**HCHW**	12 163	11 633	12 450	16 472	19 170	21 490	22 801	23 962	19 818	19 286
Of which:											
Brazil	**FKMO**	319	331	270	422	539	679	851	1 030	927	748
China	**ERDN**	457	316	425	755	868	832	744	924	861	1 220
Egypt	**QALL**	290	275	251	347	378	385	432	501	505	544
Hong Kong	**ERDG**	1 202	1 357	1 597	2 177	2 356	2 664	2 942	3 223	2 680	2 329
India	**ERDJ**	1 216	988	937	1 155	1 340	1 689	1 717	1 575	1 247	1 461
Israel	**ERDL**	550	518	583	895	1 060	1 113	1 274	1 180	1 082	1 306
Malaysia	**ERDK**	580	577	633	985	1 346	1 192	1 169	1 210	679	949
Pakistan	**FKMU**	245	266	308	336	362	342	347	270	235	226
Philippines	**FKMX**	155	143	202	313	364	436	397	601	303	240
Russia	**ERDQ**	..	..	..	561	728	871	1 016	1 234	932	547
Singapore	**ERDH**	1 015	997	1 137	1 459	1 811	2 072	2 159	2 049	1 604	1 611
South Africa	**EPME**	1 084	1 001	1 071	1 149	1 452	1 837	1 892	1 637	1 534	1 290
Taiwan	**ERDP**	419	511	552	681	752	965	949	1 035	875	872
Thailand	**ERDO**	404	456	473	677	769	838	981	866	390	468

Source: Office for National Statistics: 020 7533 6064

18.6 United Kingdom imports, by area

£ million BOP-consistent basis seasonally adjusted

		1990	1991	1992	1993	1994	1995	1996	1997	1998	1999
European Union:	ENOS	70 548	65 463	69 910	74 497	82 530	93 908	100 199	99 944	101 021	103 719
EMU members	QAKX	64 433	59 832	64 013	68 465	75 798	86 736	92 665	92 529	94 156	96 497
Germany	ENYS	19 503	17 312	18 588	19 910	21 904	26 254	27 206	25 641	25 039	26 468
France	ENYP	11 472	10 771	11 945	13 437	15 027	16 371	17 846	17 756	17 587	17 851
Italy	CHNW	6 565	6 237	6 609	6 663	7 510	8 269	8 819	9 549	9 724	9 311
Netherlands	CHNX	10 219	9 802	9 676	8 977	10 081	11 525	12 421	12 332	13 381	13 401
Belgium & Luxembourg	CHNY	5 585	5 350	5 601	6 683	7 092	8 013	8 618	9 059	9 395	9 471
Irish Republic	CHOA	4 382	4 310	4 945	5 453	5 908	7 053	7 247	7 393	7 785	8 478
Portugal	CHOC	1 145	1 017	1 141	1 236	1 286	1 466	1 661	1 764	1 790	1 812
Spain	CHOD	2 896	2 646	2 952	3 268	3 686	4 360	5 048	5 099	5 725	5 894
Finland	CHNC	1 731	1 490	1 636	1 880	2 277	2 501	2 646	2 544	2 323	2 362
Austria	CHNB	935	897	920	958	1 027	924	1 153	1 392	1 407	1 449
Non-EMU members:	QALA	6 115	5 631	5 897	6 032	6 732	7 172	7 534	7 415	6 865	7 222
Sweden	CHND	3 502	3 073	3 201	3 570	4 204	4 543	4 776	4 696	4 351	4 601
Denmark	CHNZ	2 218	2 177	2 326	2 136	2 174	2 201	2 359	2 319	2 151	2 222
Greece	CHOB	395	381	370	326	354	428	399	400	363	399
Other Western Europe:	HBTS	9 153	8 481	8 407	9 489	9 374	10 341	11 387	10 801	9 759	10 629
Of which:											
Norway	EPMX	4 115	4 138	3 798	4 027	3 711	4 175	4 790	4 687	3 431	3 561
Switzerland	EPMV	4 157	3 641	3 830	4 590	4 677	4 981	5 210	4 668	4 770	5 329
Turkey	EOBU	539	391	446	515	610	768	898	993	1 105	1 214
Iceland	EPMW	255	233	233	242	233	244	257	229	250	283
North America:	HCRB	16 592	15 457	15 298	17 960	19 379	22 293	24 910	27 311	27 919	28 116
Of which:											
USA	EOBV	14 063	13 336	13 221	15 886	17 233	19 615	22 069	24 355	24 892	24 431
Canada	EOBW	2 225	1 869	1 824	1 805	1 827	2 300	2 407	2 483	2 518	3 033
Mexico	EPJY	170	143	149	160	233	288	322	371	366	397
Other OECD countries:	HDJQ	9 123	8 795	9 890	11 418	12 257	13 699	13 717	14 587	14 951	15 934
Of which:											
Japan	EOBX	6 247	6 269	7 051	8 140	8 584	9 276	8 584	9 040	9 121	9 251
Australia	EPNA	960	808	953	954	1 035	1 068	1 239	1 319	1 366	1 359
South Korea	ERDY	893	857	890	1 029	1 068	1 505	1 949	2 155	2 201	2 825
Poland	ERED	330	293	338	429	533	616	573	596	654	671
New Zealand	EPNB	450	362	405	474	527	555	604	554	518	574
Czech Rep	FKMM	..	..	..	234	271	312	356	449	551	580
Hungary	QALD	96	97	112	145	232	358	404	467	533	666
Oil exporting countries:	HCPC	2 538	2 565	2 857	3 600	3 049	2 930	3 263	3 328	3 183	3 269
Of which:											
Dubai	QALJ	84	90	175	123	123	169	207	284	337	437
Saudi Arabia	ERDU	673	879	900	1 208	757	649	656	838	789	794
Indonesia	FKMS	286	387	501	665	728	814	855	860	868	941
Brunei	QALG	134	137	109	288	275	111	252	283	161	67
Rest of the World	HCIF	13 071	13 403	14 555	18 394	19 759	22 278	27 011	27 723	27 798	30 765
Of which:											
Brazil	FKMP	672	714	830	872	891	936	941	911	884	972
China	ERDZ	545	657	891	1 279	1 592	1 843	2 112	2 383	2 820	3 405
Egypt	QALM	134	122	130	180	245	235	269	258	278	257
Hong Kong	ERDS	1 841	1 995	2 242	2 894	2 988	3 364	3 900	4 153	4 370	4 940
India	ERDV	746	725	808	1 050	1 249	1 363	1 542	1 550	1 384	1 431
Israel	ERDX	475	424	454	530	555	659	797	842	875	1 003
Malaysia	ERDW	723	849	1 032	1 350	1 166	1 414	2 277	1 933	1 896	1 965
Pakistan	FKMV	221	297	256	312	348	344	372	362	338	321
Philippines	FKMY	208	214	225	266	237	335	857	728	855	987
Russia	EREC	..	..	..	792	781	916	1 218	1 418	1 393	1 316
Singapore	ERDT	947	1 050	1 113	1 558	1 836	2 101	2 463	2 590	2 342	2 365
South Africa	EPNE	1 008	897	811	964	941	1 058	1 165	1 323	1 352	1 645
Taiwan	EREB	1 134	1 184	1 305	1 561	1 535	1 640	2 000	2 237	2 219	2 641
Thailand	EREA	453	591	600	746	884	987	1 137	1 167	1 263	1 300

Source: Office for National Statistics: 020 7533 6064

18.7 Services supplied (exports) and purchased (imports)[1,2]: 1998

£ millions

	Exports	Imports	Net
Business services			
Legal	240	155	86
Accounting	413	82	331
Management consulting	913	299	614
Advertising	775	405	370
Market research	272	107	165
Research and development	1 784	620	1 164
Insurance: premiums	-	52	-52
claims	3	1	2
Financial Services	241	101	140
Property	11	6	5
Other business services	2 540	1 010	1 530
Telecommunications services			
Communications	1 122	1 240	-118
Computer	1 333	419	914
Information	177	17	160
Technical services			
Architectural	59	11	48
Engineering (consulting, process etc.)	2 679	992	1 688
Surveying	30	31	-1
Construction	285	108	177
Agriculture	26	14	12
Mining	25	16	9
Other technical	919	366	553
Miscellaneous services			
Operational leasing	33	68	-35
Cultural services			
TV and radio services	102	16	86
Music services (excluding royalties)	14	5	9
Other cultural	120	38	83
Royalties	3 419	2 954	466
Trade related services			
Own account earning	290	46	244
Commission	446	322	124
Commodity trading	65	55	10
Management services to affiliated companies	916	619	297
All other services	1 187	353	835
WORLD TOTAL	20 441	10 526	9 915

1 Due to rounding, the sum of constituent items may not always equal the total shown.
2 Data excludes the following industries: Financial, Film and TV, Travel and Transport, Public Sector (including Education) and Law Society members.

Source: Office for National Statistics

18.8 Overseas trade in services[1,2] by country: 1998

£ millions

	Exports	Imports	Net
European Union	7 227	3 636	3 591
Austria	63	43	21
Belgium/Luxembourg	758	317	441
Denmark	237	129	108
Finland	178	48	129
France	961	750	211
Germany	1 568	867	702
Greece	58	26	32
Irish Republic	1 006	315	691
Italy	380	219	161
Netherlands	1 212	625	587
Portugal	76	52	24
Spain	408	126	283
Sweden	319	117	202
EU Institutions	2	4	-2
EFTA	1 222	596	626
Iceland	2	3	-
Norway	518	178	340
Switzerland	701	415	286
Other European countries	9 472	4 776	4 696
Czech Republic	48	17	31
Poland	49	14	35
Russia	59	30	29
Channel Islands	115	23	92
Isle of Man	4	10	-6
Turkey	67	28	40
Liechtenstein	4	23	-19
Rest of Europe	676	400	277
Africa	607	147	460
South Africa	181	44	137
Rest of Africa	426	104	323
America	6 084	4 045	2 039
Brazil	73	16	57
Canada	348	120	228
Mexico	38	3	35
USA	4 920	3 664	1 255
Rest of America	705	242	463
Asia	3 885	1 358	2 528
China	83	20	63
Hong Kong	234	118	116
India	83	69	14
Indonesia	53	12	41
Israel	33	53	-20
Japan	738	351	387
Malaysia	135	40	95
Pakistan	87	22	65
Phillippines	23	8	15
Saudi Arabia	1 226	314	912
Singapore	192	45	147
South Korea	181	23	158
Taiwan	22	10	12
Thailand	65	18	47
Rest of Asia	731	255	476
Australia and Oceania	369	193	176
Australia	271	129	142
New Zealand	44	20	24
Rest of Australia and Oceania	54	44	10
Rest of World Unallocated	24	7	17
International Orgainisations	-	-	-
WORLD TOTAL	20 441	10 526	9 915
Economic Zones			
OCED	14 921	8 560	6 362
NAFTA	5 306	3 788	1 518
Central and Eastern Europe	174	57	117
OPEC	1 657	427	1 230
ASEAN	480	127	353
CIS	197	47	150
NICs1	629	196	433
Offshore Financial centres	757	253	504
ACP	314	73	242

1 Due to rounding, the sum of constituent items may not always equal the total shown.

2 Data excludes the following industries: Financial, Film and TV, Travel and Transport, Public Sector (including Education) and Law Society members.

Source: Office for National Statistics

18.9 Summary of balance of payments in 1999
United Kingdom

£ millions

	Credits	Debits
1. Current account		
A. Goods and services	229 649	244 878
1. Goods	165 667	192 434
2. Services	63 982	52 444
2.1. Transportation	11 538	13 930
2.2. Travel	14 293	22 634
2.3. Communications	1 484	1 694
2.4. Construction	267	85
2.5. Insurance	4 111	569
2.6. Financial	6 992	205
2.7. Computer and information	1 928	500
2.8. Royalties and licence fees	4 387	3 840
2.9. Other business	17 083	6 130
2.10. Personal, cultural and recreational	782	490
2.11. Government	1 117	2 367
B. Income	109 099	100 767
1. Compensation of employees	960	759
2. Investment income	108 139	100 008
2.1 Direct investment	33 820	22 302
2.2 Portfolio investment	27 928	27 819
2.3 Other investment (including earnings on reserve assets)	46 391	49 887
C. Current transfers	18 278	22 362
1. Central government	9 464	7 278
2. Other sectors	8 814	15 084
Total current account	**357 026**	**368 007**
2. Capital and financial accounts		
A. Capital account	1 562	786
1. Capital transfers	1 476	680
2. Acquisition/disposal of non-produced, non-financial assets	86	106
B. Financial account	185 997	180 144
1. Direct investment	52 326	125 288
Abroad		125 288
1.1. Equity capital		95 024
1.2. Reinvested earnings		19 845
1.3. Other capital[1]		10 419
In United Kingdom	52 326	
1.1. Equity capital	21 402	
1.2. Reinvested earnings	6 875	
1.3. Other capital[2]	24 049	
2. Portfolio investment	115 602	5 432
Assets		5 432
2.1. Equity securities		17 915
2.2. Debt securities		−12 483
Liabilities	115 602	
2.1. Equity securities	74 341	
2.2. Debt securities	41 261	
3. Other investment	18 069	50 063
Assets		50 063
3.1 Trade credits		−435
3.2 Loans		16 815
3.3 Currency and deposits		33 357
3.4 Other assets		326
Liabilities	18 069	
3.1. Trade credits	−	
3.2. Loans	6 616	
3.3. Currency and deposits	12 128	
3.4. Other liabilities	−675	
4. Reserve assets		−639
4.1. Monetary gold		−412
4.2. Special drawing rights		38
4.3. Reserve position in the IMF		626
4.4. Foreign exchange		−891
Total capital and financial accounts	**187 559**	**180 930**
Total current, capital and financial accounts	**544 585**	**548 937**
Net errors and omissions	4 352	

1 Other capital transaction on direct investment abroad represents claims on affiliated enterprises less liabilities to affiliated enterprises

2 Other capital transactions on direct investment in the United Kingdom represents liabilities to direct investors less claims on direct investors

Source: Office for National Statistics

18.10 Summary of balance of payments
Balances (credits less debits)
United Kingdom

£ millions

	Current account										
	Trade in goods	Trade in services	**Total goods and services**	Compensation of employees	Investment income	**Total income**	**Current transfers**	**Current balance**	Capital account	Financial account	Net errors & omissions
	LQCT	KTMS	KTMY	KTMP	HMBM	HMBP	KTNF	HBOG	FKMJ	HBNT	HHDH
1946	−101	−274	−375	−20	88	68	166	−141	−21	181	−19
1947	−358	−197	−555	−19	159	140	123	−292	−21	552	−239
1948	−152	−64	−216	−20	252	232	96	112	−17	−58	−37
1949	−137	−43	−180	−20	234	214	29	63	−12	−103	52
1950	−54	−4	−58	−21	426	405	39	386	−10	−447	71
1951	−692	32	−660	−21	365	344	29	−287	−15	426	−124
1952	−272	123	−149	−22	265	243	169	263	−15	−229	−19
1953	−244	123	−121	−25	238	213	143	235	−13	−177	−45
1954	−210	115	−95	−27	261	234	55	194	−13	−174	−7
1955	−315	42	−273	−27	175	148	43	−82	−15	34	63
1956	50	26	76	−30	237	207	2	285	−13	−250	−22
1957	−29	121	92	−32	257	225	−5	312	−13	−313	14
1958	34	119	153	−34	303	269	4	426	−10	−411	−5
1959	−116	118	2	−37	269	232	−	234	−5	−68	−161
1960	−404	39	−365	−35	235	200	−6	−171	−6	−7	184
1961	−144	51	−93	−35	259	224	−9	122	−12	23	−133
1962	−104	50	−54	−37	346	309	−14	241	−12	−195	−34
1963	−123	4	−119	−38	416	378	−37	222	−16	−30	−176
1964	−551	−34	−585	−33	420	387	−62	−260	−17	392	−115
1965	−263	−66	−329	−34	467	433	−66	38	−18	49	−69
1966	−111	44	−67	−39	413	374	−89	218	−19	16	−215
1967	−601	157	−444	−39	411	372	−117	−189	−25	172	42
1968	−708	341	−367	−48	357	309	−89	−147	−26	672	−499
1969	−214	392	178	−47	543	496	−120	554	−23	−838	307
1970	−18	455	437	−56	612	556	−82	911	−22	−864	−25
1971	205	590	795	−63	560	497	−51	1 241	−23	−1 441	223
1972	−736	665	−71	−52	518	466	−51	344	−35	462	−771
1973	−2 573	760	−1 813	−68	1 283	1 215	−316	−914	−39	971	−18
1974	−5 241	1 065	−4 176	−92	1 429	1 337	−340	−3 179	−34	3 162	51
1975	−3 245	1 393	−1 852	−102	706	604	−317	−1 565	−36	1 554	47
1976	−3 930	2 465	−1 465	−140	1 385	1 245	−507	−727	−12	420	319
1977	−2 271	3 219	948	−152	−120	−272	−469	207	11	−3 665	3 447
1978	−1 534	3 679	2 145	−140	386	246	−958	1 433	−79	−2 798	1 444
1979	−3 326	3 965	639	−130	540	410	−961	88	−103	−97	112
1980	1 329	3 717	5 046	−82	−1 346	−1 428	−452	3 166	−4	−3 238	76
1981	3 238	3 834	7 072	−66	−369	−435	−88	6 549	−79	−6 612	142
1982	1 879	3 069	4 948	−95	−461	−556	−285	4 107	6	−2 010	−2 103
1983	−1 618	3 941	2 323	−89	1 205	1 116	−140	3 299	75	−4 068	694
1984	−5 409	4 341	−1 068	−94	2 497	2 403	−126	1 209	107	−8 009	6 693
1985	−3 416	6 619	3 203	−120	132	12	−988	2 227	185	−2 902	490
1986	−9 617	6 505	−3 112	−156	3 028	2 872	−2 045	−2 285	135	−2 341	4 491
1987	−11 698	6 686	−5 012	−174	1 677	1 503	−2 074	−5 583	333	5 065	185
1988	−21 553	4 330	−17 223	−64	1 355	1 291	−1 605	−17 537	235	15 135	2 167
1989	−24 724	3 917	−20 807	−138	74	−64	−2 620	−23 491	270	19 024	4 197
1990	−18 707	4 010	−14 697	−110	−448	−558	−4 258	−19 513	497	17 529	1 487
1991	−10 223	4 471	−5 752	−63	−1 890	−1 953	−669	−8 374	290	9 990	−1 906
1992	−13 050	5 674	−7 376	−49	2 164	2 115	−4 821	−10 082	421	5 716	3 945
1993	−13 319	6 623	−6 696	35	650	685	−4 607	−10 618	309	9 447	862
1994	−11 091	6 528	−4 563	−170	7 940	7 770	−4 665	−1 458	33	−6 082	7 507
1995	−11 724	8 915	−2 809	−296	6 272	5 976	−6 912	−3 745	534	937	2 274
1996	−13 086	8 897	−4 189	93	8 018	8 111	−4 522	−600	736	1 781	−1 917
1997	−11 910	12 414	504	83	11 087	11 170	−5 051	6 623	804	−13 186	5 759
1998	−20 537	12 582	−7 955	−10	14 255	14 245	−6 370	−80	473	−4 677	4 284
1999	−26 767	11 538	−15 229	201	8 131	8 332	−4 084	−10 981	776	5 853	4 352

Source: Office for National Statistics

18.11 Balance of Payments: current account
United Kingdom

£ millions

		1989	1990	1991	1992	1993	1994	1995	1996	1997	1998	1999
Credits												
Exports of goods and services												
Exports of goods	LQAD	92 611	102 313	103 939	107 863	122 039	135 260	153 725	167 403	171 783	164 092	165 667
Exports of services	KTMQ	29 272	31 188	31 426	35 428	40 039	43 507	48 687	52 900	57 543	61 382	63 982
Total exports of goods and services	KTMW	121 883	133 501	135 365	143 291	162 078	178 767	202 412	220 303	229 326	225 474	229 649
Income												
Compensation of employees	KTMN	476	543	551	551	595	681	887	911	1 007	840	960
Investment income	HMBN	81 799	88 186	84 419	74 549	78 825	82 639	97 086	101 669	106 898	108 392	108 139
Total income	HMBQ	82 275	88 729	84 970	75 100	79 420	83 320	97 973	102 580	107 905	109 232	109 099
Current transfers												
Central government	FJUM	4 924	4 294	6 746	4 254	5 306	5 008	4 845	6 754	5 979	6 381	9 464
Other sectors	FJUN	5 161	5 956	7 493	7 386	7 958	7 801	8 518	14 632	9 326	9 043	8 814
Total current transfers	KTND	10 085	10 250	14 239	11 640	13 264	12 809	13 363	21 386	15 305	15 424	18 278
Total	HBOE	**214 243**	**232 480**	**234 574**	**230 031**	**254 762**	**274 896**	**313 748**	**344 269**	**352 536**	**350 130**	**357 026**
Debits												
Imports of goods and services												
Imports of goods	LQBL	117 335	121 020	114 162	120 913	135 358	146 351	165 449	180 489	183 693	184 629	192 434
Imports of services	KTMR	25 355	27 178	26 955	29 754	33 416	36 979	39 772	44 003	45 129	48 800	52 444
Total imports of goods and services	KTMX	142 690	148 198	141 117	150 667	168 774	183 330	205 221	224 492	228 822	233 429	244 878
Income												
Compensation of employees	KTMO	614	653	614	600	560	851	1 183	818	924	850	759
Investment income	HMBO	81 725	88 634	86 309	72 385	78 175	74 699	90 814	93 651	95 811	94 137	100 008
Total income	HMBR	82 339	89 287	86 923	72 985	78 735	75 550	91 997	94 469	96 735	94 987	100 767
Current transfers												
Central government	FJUO	2 055	1 995	3 218	3 506	4 156	4 795	4 795	5 056	5 087	6 585	7 278
Other sectors	FJUP	10 650	12 513	11 690	12 955	13 715	12 679	15 480	20 852	15 269	15 209	15 084
Total current transfers	KTNE	12 705	14 508	14 908	16 461	17 871	17 474	20 275	25 908	20 356	21 794	22 362
Total	HBOF	**237 734**	**251 993**	**242 948**	**240 113**	**265 380**	**276 354**	**317 493**	**344 869**	**345 913**	**350 210**	**368 007**
Balances												
Trade in goods and services												
Trade in goods	LQCT	−24 724	−18 707	−10 223	−13 050	−13 319	−11 091	−11 724	−13 086	−11 910	−20 537	−26 767
Trade in services	KTMS	3 917	4 010	4 471	5 674	6 623	6 528	8 915	8 897	12 414	12 582	11 538
Total trade in goods and services	KTMY	−20 807	−14 697	−5 752	−7 376	−6 696	−4 563	−2 809	−4 189	504	−7 955	−15 229
Income												
Compensation of employees	KTMP	−138	−110	−63	−49	35	−170	−296	93	83	−10	201
Investment income	HMBM	74	−448	−1 890	2 164	650	7 940	6 272	8 018	11 087	14 255	8 131
Total income	HMBP	−64	−558	−1 953	2 115	685	7 770	5 976	8 111	11 170	14 245	8 332
Current transfers												
Central government	FJUQ	2 869	2 299	3 528	748	1 150	213	50	1 698	892	−204	2 186
Other sectors	FJUR	−5 489	−6 557	−4 197	−5 569	−5 757	−4 878	−6 962	−6 220	−5 943	−6 166	−6 270
Total current transfers	KTNF	−2 620	−4 258	−669	−4 821	−4 607	−4 665	−6 912	−4 522	−5 051	−6 370	−4 084
Total (Current balance)	HBOG	**−23 491**	**−19 513**	**−8 374**	**−10 082**	**−10 618**	**−1 458**	**−3 745**	**−600**	**6 623**	**−80**	**−10 981**

Source: Office for National Statistics

18.12 Balance of payments: summary of international investment position, financial account and investment income

United Kingdom

£ billions

		1989	1990	1991	1992	1993	1994	1995	1996	1997	1998	1999
Investment abroad												
International investment position												
Direct investment	HBWD	123.2	120.7	126.2	149.7	170.3	173.9	200.9	207.8	226.5	301.1	418.5
Portfolio investment	HHZZ	227.3	197.3	253.0	316.9	456.4	414.4	487.2	535.1	626.7	685.5	771.6
Other investment	HLXV	566.0	555.9	533.6	650.0	694.7	719.0	819.5	864.2	1 066.2	1 102.6	1 130.9
Reserve assets	APDD	26.3	22.5	26.0	28.3	29.7	30.7	31.8	27.3	22.8	23.3	22.2
Total	HBQA	**942.8**	**896.4**	**938.8**	**1 144.9**	**1 351.2**	**1 337.9**	**1 539.4**	**1 634.4**	**1 942.2**	**2 112.5**	**2 343.2**
Financial account transactions												
Direct investment	-HJYP	21.5	10.6	9.1	11.1	17.9	22.2	28.2	22.5	38.9	71.9	125.3
Portfolio investment	-HHZC	38.9	15.9	32.4	28.7	89.6	-21.8	39.3	59.8	51.9	36.7	5.4
Other investment	-XBMM	35.5	52.5	-20.5	30.7	45.7	28.9	48.1	137.3	168.4	15.9	50.1
Reserve assets	-AIPA	-5.4	0.1	2.7	-1.4	0.7	1.0	-0.2	-0.5	-2.4	-0.2	-0.6
Total	-HBNR	**90.4**	**79.0**	**23.6**	**69.0**	**153.8**	**30.4**	**115.3**	**219.2**	**256.8**	**124.4**	**180.1**
Investment income												
Direct investment	HJYW	18.7	17.5	14.5	15.2	19.1	23.8	26.9	30.9	32.3	32.0	33.8
Portfolio investment	HLYX	12.8	13.9	15.1	17.5	20.4	21.9	25.3	25.3	28.8	25.9	27.9
Other investment	AIOP	48.4	55.1	53.2	40.4	37.8	35.3	43.2	43.9	44.4	49.3	45.2
Reserve assets	HHCB	1.9	1.7	1.7	1.5	1.5	1.6	1.7	1.6	1.4	1.1	1.2
Total	HMBN	**81.8**	**88.2**	**84.4**	**74.5**	**78.8**	**82.6**	**97.1**	**101.7**	**106.9**	**108.4**	**108.1**
Investment in the UK												
International investment position												
Direct investment	HBWI	100.1	113.5	121.0	123.1	128.2	122.6	137.9	147.6	167.1	192.8	243.1
Portfolio investment	HLXW	194.1	189.2	208.8	247.0	306.9	320.0	386.4	429.6	588.4	686.7	882.9
Other investment	HLYD	597.5	602.0	605.9	752.2	879.7	873.1	1 007.5	1 059.1	1 269.3	1 351.2	1 365.4
Total	HBQB	**891.8**	**904.6**	**935.7**	**1 122.3**	**1 314.8**	**1 315.6**	**1 531.8**	**1 636.3**	**2 024.8**	**2 230.7**	**2 491.4**
Financial account transactions												
Direct investment	HJYU	18.6	18.6	9.1	9.2	10.3	6.1	12.9	16.6	22.6	38.4	52.3
Portfolio investment	HHZF	18.2	13.4	11.0	9.4	28.4	33.2	37.2	44.2	27.2	17.9	115.6
Other investment	XBMN	72.6	64.6	13.5	56.1	124.6	-15.0	66.1	160.2	193.9	63.4	18.1
Total	HBNS	**109.4**	**96.6**	**33.6**	**74.7**	**163.3**	**24.3**	**116.2**	**220.9**	**243.7**	**119.7**	**186.0**
Investment income												
Direct investment	HJYX	12.7	9.3	6.4	7.3	12.9	12.3	15.6	18.7	17.3	11.7	22.3
Portfolio investment	HLZC	14.9	15.1	14.3	13.2	14.0	16.5	20.3	20.7	24.9	28.0	27.8
Other investment	HLZN	54.2	64.3	65.6	51.9	51.3	46.0	54.8	54.2	53.6	54.4	49.9
Total	HMBO	**81.7**	**88.6**	**86.3**	**72.4**	**78.2**	**74.7**	**90.8**	**93.7**	**95.8**	**94.1**	**100.0**
Net investment												
International investment position												
Direct investment	HBWQ	23.1	7.2	5.2	26.6	42.1	51.3	63.0	60.2	59.4	108.3	175.4
Portfolio investment	CGNH	33.2	8.1	44.2	69.9	149.5	94.4	100.8	105.5	38.3	-1.2	-111.3
Other investment	CGNG	-31.5	-46.0	-72.3	-102.2	-184.9	-154.1	-188.0	-194.9	-203.1	-248.5	-234.5
Reserve assets	APDD	26.3	22.5	26.0	28.3	29.7	30.7	31.8	27.3	22.8	23.3	22.2
Net investment position	HBQC	**51.0**	**-8.2**	**3.1**	**22.5**	**36.4**	**22.2**	**7.6**	**-1.9**	**-82.6**	**-118.1**	**-148.3**
Financial account transactions												
Direct investment	HJYV	-2.9	8.0	–	-1.8	-7.6	-16.1	-15.2	-6.0	-16.3	-33.5	-73.0
Portfolio investment	HHZD	-20.7	-2.5	-21.4	-19.3	-61.2	55.0	-2.1	-15.6	-24.8	-18.8	110.2
Other investment	HHYR	37.1	12.1	34.0	25.5	78.9	-44.0	18.1	22.9	25.5	47.5	-32.0
Reserve assets	AIPA	5.4	-0.1	-2.7	1.4	-0.7	-1.0	0.2	0.5	2.4	0.2	0.6
Net transactions	HBNT	**19.0**	**17.5**	**10.0**	**5.7**	**9.4**	**-6.1**	**0.9**	**1.8**	**-13.2**	**-4.7**	**5.9**
Investment income												
Direct investment	HJYE	6.0	8.2	8.1	7.9	6.1	11.5	11.2	12.2	15.0	20.3	11.5
Portfolio investment	HLZX	-2.1	-1.2	0.7	4.3	6.4	5.5	5.0	4.5	3.9	-2.1	0.1
Other investment	CGNA	-5.7	-9.2	-12.3	-11.5	-13.5	-10.6	-11.7	-10.2	-9.3	-5.1	-4.7
Reserve assets	HHCB	1.9	1.7	1.7	1.5	1.5	1.6	1.7	1.6	1.4	1.1	1.2
Net earnings	HMBM	**0.1**	**-0.4**	**-1.9**	**2.2**	**0.6**	**7.9**	**6.3**	**8.0**	**11.1**	**14.3**	**8.1**

Source: Office for National Statistics

18.13 Net outward direct investment by UK companies analysed by area and main country [1,2]

£ millions

		1988	1989	1990	1991	1992	1993	1994	1995	1996	1997	1998
Europe	GQBX	5 773	5 620	5 844	3 978	4 911	6 171	9 241	9 184	13 321	19 964	22 804
EU	CAUU	5 360	5 941	5 103	3 919	4 613	6 146	8 278	9 457	13 432	17 368	11 444
Austria	CBJD	41	32	58	45	16	13	102	90	102	16	26
Belgium & Luxembourg	CAUV	17	301	−211	316	−191	160	132	438	991	1 536	−703
Denmark	CAUW	50	105	43	66	47	237	64	416	−176	47	−92
Finland	CBJE	6	13	4	−1	7	10	26	112	28	−5	105
France	CAUX	1 821	1 484	1 158	486	628	471	423	1 515	2 375	2 380	908
Germany	CAUY	505	797	187	155	536	1 333	1 261	1 478	1 184	1 078	1 409
Greece	CAUZ	4	52	42	37	167	44	84	163	106	302	303
Irish Republic	CAVA	56	299	144	388	895	1 082	100	776	755	450	1 135
Italy	CAVB	298	358	548	258	222	282	298	406	421	447	496
Netherlands .	CAVC	2 011	1 644	2 258	985	1 585	2 436	4 615	2 953	6 577	9 804	7 492
Portugal	CAVD	109	202	159	61	237	25	169	159	56	112	−15
Spain	CAVE	471	573	699	982	217	−31	460	431	735	864	−169
Sweden	CBJG	−29	82	15	141	249	84	546	522	277	335	555
EFTA of which	CAVG	−5	−163	497	−42	163	−84	645	−594	−12	2 195	8 652
Norway	CBJF	−235	170	32	35	156	92	662	−255	96	1 997	627
Switzerland	CBJH	232	−333	465	−74	−1	−177	−16	−338	−110	197	8 016
Other European Countries of which	GQBY	417	−159	244	100	135	110	317	322	−97	402	2 708
Russia[3]	GLAA	..	..	2	−2	..	11	115	39	132	448	−170
UK offshore islands	GLAC	−	−	−	−	−	−	−	−	−	−933	2 447
America of which	GQBZ	12 129	13 000	2 181	2 628	2 657	8 673	8 464	13 460	3 277	13 953	49 360
Bermuda	CBKZ	621	25	276	−438	506	586	349	291	142	−43	460
Brazil	CBLA	260	269	211	89	121	38	291	473	692	337	322
Canada	CAVK	535	542	894	318	−106	5	−4	244	−159	823	582
Chile	GQCA	62	49	19	80	−22	101	76	220	89	168	171
Colombia	GQCB	−	48	20	−264	..	−245	204	123	100	241	..
Mexico	GLAD	57	−136	27	39	114	44	42	79	110	760	145
Panama	GLAE	198	−14	−13	100	211	−100	94	75	103	..	319
USA	CAVJ	10 472	11 676	47	2 235	1 321	7 975	6 549	11 840	1 837	10 509	45 709
Asia	GQCI	578	798	888	853	959	1 596	2 049	1 657	2 823	2 251	−742
Near and Middle East Countries of which	CBKF	−81	−7	244	489	44	−239	253	154	28	350	1 646
Gulf Arabian countries[4]	GQCC	−71	−47	239	476	27	−236	250	116	30	260	1 534
Other Asian Countries of which	GQCD	660	806	644	364	915	1 834	1 796	1 503	2 794	1 901	−2 388
Hong Kong	CAVN	119	−161	−250	−245	−18	456	128	734	730	−359	1 525
India	GLAF	14	38	42	2	−27	139	87	61	110	171	208
Indonesia	GLAG	24	32	−46	74	−59	69	92	−28	155	170	32
Japan	CAVM	102	230	235	−4	13	−49	245	169	378	383	21
Malaysia	CBKN	94	−32	159	140	272	363	286	28	184	731	612
Singapore	CBKQ	191	509	344	232	569	528	590	−48	535	352	−5 581
South Korea	GLAH	3	27	4	20	37	44	27	47	32	−26	231
Thailand	GLAI	25	67	40	24	51	103	177	245	194	103	187
Australasia & Oceania of which	GQCE	2 362	783	999	1 239	1 280	658	959	2 596	1 843	827	211
Australia	CBJO	1 789	654	913	1 089	989	655	625	2 258	1 472	737	215
New Zealand	CBJP	488	76	−24	66	110	71	264	67	244	255	−116
Africa of which	GQCF	74	1 290	196	606	300	262	327	707	561	623	46
Kenya	GLAJ	19	30	47	22	23	33	9	67	24	73	40
Nigeria	CBJY	−12	..	−12	227	138	347	−197	−271	−94	234	−87
South Africa	CAVO	−8	414	22	151	72	314	170	466	−25	401	−210
Zimbabwe	CBKD	59	51	52	72	59	36	28	16	25	1	42
World Total	CDQD	20 916	21 491	10 108	9 304	10 107	17 358	21 040	27 604	21 823	37 619	71 678
OECD	GQCG	19 194	18 868	7 731	7 673	7 343	14 864	16 880	23 686	17 545	33 212	67 449
Central and Eastern Europe[5]	GQCH	−	5	2	18	37	41	168	194	201	214	460

1 Net investment includes unremitted profits.
2 Minus sign indicates net disinvestment overseas.
3 Prior to 1995 Russia covers other former USSR countries, the Baltic States and Albania.
4 Includes Abu Dhabi, Bahrain, Dubai, Iraq, Kuwait, Oman, Other Gulf States, Qatar, Saudi Arabia and Yemen.
5 Includes Albania, Belarus, Bulgaria, Croatia, Czech Republic, Estonia, Hungary, Latvia, Lithuania, Poland, Romania, Serbia and Montenegro, Slovakia and Slovenia.

Sources: ONS Overseas Direct Investment Inquiries: 01633 813314;
Bank of England

18.14 Level of UK outward direct investment - book value of net assets analysed by area and main country at year end

£ millions

		1988	1989	1990	1991	1992	1993	1994	1995	1996	1997	1998
Europe	GQCJ	26 175	30 626	34 450	37 272	44 213	57 853	66 705	76 434	87 582	99 263	119 547
EU	CDLN	23 163	27 826	31 610	34 312	40 620	53 914	61 674	72 808	83 902	92 072	98 564
Austria	CDLZ	169	244	336	384	371	379	454	734	578	461	515
Belgium & Luxembourg	CDLO	1 675	1 814	1 590	2 505	3 804	2 687	3 189	3 172	5 326	5 701	4 384
Denmark	CDLP	564	778	757	739	863	1 301	1 538	2 803	2 273	2 123	2 345
Finland	CDMA	83	101	102	80	122	104	117	271	215	217	251
France	CDLQ	4 698	6 173	6 898	7 290	8 043	8 619	10 357	12 913	13 128	11 368	10 943
Germany	CDLR	3 963	4 303	4 217	3 998	3 804	5 974	8 442	9 215	8 943	8 328	9 367
Greece	CDLS	81	189	159	156	288	294	203	500	465	366	653
Irish Republic	CDLT	1 297	1 659	2 048	2 743	3 333	4 169	4 436	4 587	6 282	6 182	7 555
Italy	CDLU	1 462	1 941	2 093	2 400	2 427	2 287	2 475	2 698	3 196	3 064	3 148
Netherlands	CDLV	6 265	6 442	8 287	8 369	11 980	23 190	25 228	29 906	37 676	48 240	53 277
Portugal	CDLW	516	739	865	1 032	1 171	1 195	932	1 210	1 190	1 023	992
Spain	CDLX	1 828	2 737	3 498	3 796	3 471	2 820	3 157	3 399	3 477	3 748	3 400
Sweden	CDMD	565	707	761	821	942	894	1 146	1 401	1 154	1 250	1 714
EFTA of which	CDLY	2 130	2 495	2 511	2 545	2 968	3 303	4 113	2 522	2 161	1 533	10 494
Norway	CDMC	385	549	522	542	736	803	1 513	1 244	1 171	1 116	393
Switzerland	CDME	1 745	1 943	1 989	2 003	2 232	2 500	2 594	1 279	988	415	10 097
Other European Countries of which	GQCK	882	306	329	415	626	636	918	1 103	1 520	5 658	10 489
Russia[1]	GQAA	..	10	9	10	20	7	26	120	238	401	251
UK offshore islands	GQAB	–	–	–	–	–	–	–	–	–	2 690	7 130
America of which	GQCU	55 898	66 515	62 381	62 939	74 868	77 003	75 390	83 275	67 592	80 324	140 271
Bermuda	CDOA	2 252	2 589	4 630	4 628	5 382	4 869	5 403	5 504	5 295	4 942	4 615
Brazil	CDOB	1 289	1 452	1 250	1 345	1 880	1 963	2 059	2 323	2 421	2 214	1 592
Canada	CDML	5 877	6 516	6 219	6 253	6 766	7 162	4 919	5 395	4 563	5 748	5 127
Chile	GQCT	190	252	207	363	416	481	439	666	670	970	1 137
Colombia	GQCS	..	..	..	594	1 109	839	1 071	1 207	1 274	1 197	1 593
Mexico	GQAC	324	314	405	428	504	419	334	350	553	1 327	795
Panama	GQAD	204	169	100	232	630	435	507	467	744	..	..
USA	CDMM	42 613	50 933	45 532	45 367	54 688	57 380	55 174	62 159	49 170	59 083	121 782
Asia	GQCL	6 927	7 996	8 285	9 633	12 230	14 118	16 095	18 038	19 916	19 389	18 863
Near & Middle East Countries of which	CDNH	345	373	314	749	748	698	754	788	676	917	2 938
Gulf Arabian countries[2]	GQCM	315	294	229	657	592	617	660	704	586	658	2 583
Other Asian Countries of which	GQCR	6 582	7 623	7 970	8 884	11 482	13 419	15 341	17 250	19 239	18 472	15 925
Hong Kong	CDNN	2 142	2 059	1 654	1 895	2 753	3 569	3 373	4 033	4 636	4 406	5 294
India	GQAE	301	312	341	302	245	490	601	498	532	703	707
Indonesia	GQAF	213	281	264	316	222	272	295	418	391	801	622
Japan	CDMP	1 205	1 398	1 591	1 674	1 998	1 936	2 613	2 397	2 437	1 605	1 716
Malaysia	CDNQ	709	690	706	845	1 285	1 750	2 119	1 813	2 164	2 411	2 049
Singapore	CDNT	1 469	2 134	2 449	2 691	3 516	3 706	4 445	5 287	5 822	5 186	2 508
South Korea	GQAG	26	45	57	69	114	155	183	250	238	154	165
Thailand	GQAH	92	138	205	253	359	404	511	920	1 053	1 009	748
Australasia & Oceania of which	GQCN	9 777	11 284	9 951	10 210	11 222	12 287	13 517	13 985	14 636	13 312	12 538
Australia	CDMO	8 544	9 979	8 924	9 057	9 605	10 299	11 153	11 365	12 213	10 598	9 585
New Zealand	CDMQ	889	1 069	696	700	930	1 443	1 689	1 670	1 640	1 663	1 648
Africa of which	GQCQ	3 438	4 526	3 868	4 039	4 080	4 570	5 409	4 955	4 876	5 873	4 496
Kenya	GQAI	216	246	267	233	249	165	673	276	237	361	415
Nigeria	CDNA	60	639	325	419	490	754	681	335	321	1 060	561
South Africa	CDMR	1 911	2 296	2 012	2 239	2 311	2 622	2 202	2 827	2 429	2 527	1 660
Zimbabwe	CDNF	424	435	402	324	411	248	331	262	200	192	124
World Total	CDOO	102 215	120 948	118 935	124 093	146 613	165 831	177 116	196 687	194 601	218 162	295 716
OECD	GQCO	85 419	100 632	97 637	100 517	118 430	136 247	142 332	159 476	157 652	175 434	251 999
Central & Eastern Europe[3]	GQCP	1	3	9	36	123	106	460	427	622	1 782	2 581

1 Prior to 1995 Russia covers other former USSR countries, the Baltic States and Albania.
2 Includes Abu Dhabi, Bahrain, Dubai, Iraq, Kuwait, Oman, Other Gulf States, Qatar, Saudi Arabia and Yemen.
3 Includes Albania, Belarus, Bulgaria, Croatia, Czech Republic, Estonia, Hungary, Latvia, Lithuania, Poland, Romania, Serbia and Montenegro, Slovakia and Slovenia.

Sources: ONS Overseas Direct Investment Inquiries: 01633 813314; Bank of England

18.15 Net earnings from direct investment overseas by UK companies analysed by area and main country [1] [2]

£ millions

		1988	1989	1990	1991	1992	1993	1994	1995	1996	1997	1998
Europe	GQCV	3 483	4 548	4 727	4 182	3 315	5 182	7 033	8 289	9 700	10 440	11 013
EU	CAWG	3 085	4 045	4 198	3 721	2 499	4 450	6 138	7 251	8 557	8 994	9 504
Austria	CBLQ	53	36	49	43	54	35	52	73	82	65	51
Belgium & Luxembourg	CAWH	263	299	165	259	404	412	387	308	358	297	601
Denmark	CAWI	64	86	91	71	115	207	115	286	208	191	197
Finland	CBLR	17	17	9	–	24	22	30	43	–	36	58
France	CAWJ	514	805	688	598	279	50	607	619	999	1 036	970
Germany	CAWK	546	595	623	617	260	381	834	1 032	951	844	727
Greece	CAWL	16	34	22	12	50	58	−202	−106	172	122	88
Irish Republic	CAWM	161	171	265	414	393	669	516	639	847	1 112	1 197
Italy	CAWN	182	173	220	175	75	113	219	272	327	268	337
Netherlands	CAWO	964	1 449	1 674	1 141	758	2 459	2 986	3 248	3 748	4 143	4 400
Portugal	CAWP	87	135	124	93	83	53	162	188	184	96	154
Spain	CAWQ	190	178	219	197	−5	39	234	338	493	561	437
Sweden	CBLT	27	68	50	103	12	−48	200	310	188	224	289
EFTA of which	CAWS	194	451	476	433	740	639	792	899	963	991	837
Norway	CBLS	−14	114	242	214	281	119	267	224	311	242	123
Switzerland	CBLU	208	337	233	219	459	520	524	675	652	747	705
Other European Countries of which	GQCW	204	52	53	28	75	95	103	139	180	454	672
Russia[3]	GQAJ	..	..	1	..	..	2	3	12	24	−30	−213
UK offshore islands	GQAK	–	–	–	–	–	–	–	–	–	225	692
America of which	GQCX	6 840	7 525	6 962	4 624	5 530	6 126	8 007	10 254	10 698	11 867	11 504
Bermuda	CBNK	251	376	269	449	562	428	446	509	506	70	441
Brazil	CBNL	365	366	227	87	182	193	348	432	650	380	332
Canada	CAWW	531	650	464	189	175	283	357	374	571	913	843
Chile	GQCY	38	44	35	88	118	139	195	263	265	236	146
Colombia	GQCZ	32	41	64	21	−40	16	−22	28	23	53	2
Mexico	GQAL	46	8	12	−2	41	43	48	52	74	145	89
Panama	GQAM	14	11	54	17	−27	69	51	45	67	..	180
USA	CAWV	4 964	5 499	5 402	3 255	4 065	4 621	5 894	7 803	8 034	9 339	9 358
Asia	GQDA	1 501	1 873	2 114	2 355	2 636	2 792	3 449	2 501	3 776	3 249	4 145
Near & Middle East Countries of which	CBMS	180	221	235	303	342	283	297	262	241	475	924
Gulf Arabian countries[4]	GQDB	179	234	249	300	317	273	293	260	212	424	874
Other Asian Countries of which	GQDC	1 321	1 652	1 879	2 053	2 293	2 509	3 152	2 239	3 536	2 774	3 221
Hong Kong	CAYB	632	485	439	440	846	972	1 427	1 362	1 463	623	925
India	GQAN	50	63	88	77	−2	−190	121	100	81	124	192
Indonesia	GQAO	1	29	25	71	18	60	48	71	87	143	108
Japan	CAWY	88	125	72	115	182	142	199	212	281	313	160
Malaysia	CBNA	139	152	182	197	229	248	221	248	332	360	250
Singapore	CBND	322	611	967	1 010	839	977	781	−144	883	795	1 329
South Korea	GQAP	16	14	7	10	5	8	29	40	34	17	35
Thailand	GQAQ	8	30	34	17	28	78	84	75	101	95	23
Australasia & Oceania of which	GQDD	1 215	1 627	854	541	960	1 233	2 131	2 044	2 269	1 950	1 540
Australia	CBMB	1 082	1 590	925	535	809	991	1 776	1 587	1 747	1 503	1 087
New Zealand	CBMC	116	15	−98	5	73	213	302	322	319	278	146
Africa of which	GQDE	769	1 035	869	986	844	1 465	737	807	1 055	965	671
Kenya	GQAR	33	47	47	36	41	34	41	46	35	94	81
Nigeria	CBML	116	197	159	273	280	498	−27	−35	61	46	49
South Africa	CAWZ	424	595	410	425	280	488	366	438	503	521	398
Zimbabwe	CBMQ	75	80	73	81	77	54	58	58	50	58	57
World Total	GLAB	13 808	16 608	15 526	12 688	13 285	16 796	21 355	23 894	27 498	28 470	28 872
OECD	GQDF	10 294	12 425	11 486	8 279	8 624	11 454	15 578	18 567	20 621	22 601	22 146
Central & Eastern Europe[5]	GQDG	–	1	2	1	7	11	−24	16	15	118	71

1 A minus sign indicates net losses.
2 Net earnings equal profits of overseas branches plus UK companies' receipts of interest and their share of profits of overseas subsidiaries and associates. Earnings are after deducting provisions for depreciation and overseas tax on profits, dividends and interest.
3 Prior to 1995 Russia covers other former USSR countries, the Baltic States and Albania.
4 Includes Abu Dhabi, Bahrain, Dubai, Iraq, Kuwait, Oman, Other Gulf States, Qatar, Saudi Arabia and Yemen.
5 Includes Albania, Belarus, Bulgaria, Croatia, Czech Republic, Estonia, Hungary, Latvia, Lithuania, Poland, Romania, Serbia & Montenegro, Slovakia and Slovenia.

Sources: ONS Overseas Direct Investment Inquiries: 01633 813314;
Bank of England

18.16 Net direct investment in the UK analysed by area and main country [1][2]

£ millions

		1988	1989	1990	1991	1992	1993	1994	1995	1996	1997	1998
Europe	GQDH	7 279	7 971	8 042	4 910	4 044	2 202	3 065	4 626	6 931	8 394	14 705
EU	CAYO	5 282	5 617	7 628	4 578	3 433	1 589	3 367	3 555	4 673	6 905	2 061
Austria	CBOB	8	1	62	11	−45	13	60	21	20	18	126
Belgium & Luxembourg	CAYP	307	853	296	201	65	−427	357	520	6	174	1 003
Denmark	CAYQ	121	198	154	122	91	97	76	68	151	228	197
Finland	CBOC	26	56	36	8	54	−42	32	−36	2	193	126
France	CAYR	868	1 870	1 551	1 333	802	−37	310	1 004	1 321	2 647	−470
Germany	CAYS	278	460	1 610	396	1 261	656	71	2 090	835	1 123	205
Greece	CAYT	..	..	..	..	..	..	..	..	..	..	2
Irish Republic	CAYU	121	230	229	137	−32	49	224	−35	221	1 127	688
Italy	CAYV	83	26	−42	45	−37	80	177	328	−184	−32	−1
Netherlands	CAYW	3 142	1 613	2 085	2 335	1 135	1 244	1 915	−633	2 610	1 180	343
Portugal	CAYX	..	..	..	..	..	..	..	..	..	..	−1
Spain	CAYY	49	130	3	−11	3	14	21	17	66	71	80
Sweden	CBOE	285	185	1 658	5	129	−56	119	184	−379	147	−233
EFTA of which	CAZB	2 021	2 310	431	327	674	550	−176	1 036	2 211	1 512	12 249
Norway	CBOD	218	−52	201	−71	−34	49	−131	124	1 060	182	−122
Switzerland	CBOF	1 803	2 363	229	399	710	501	−44	912	1 151	1 320	12 366
Other European Countries of which	GQDI	−24	44	−17	5	−62	64	−125	36	47	−21	395
Russia[3]	GQAS	−24	28	−26	−11	..	49	–	19	61	19	..
UK offshore islands	GQAT	–	–	–	–	–	–	–	–	–	−74	421
America of which	GQDJ	1 669	7 019	6 266	1 898	3 720	5 993	2 344	8 750	7 210	10 615	21 757
Canada	CAZF	168	610	−264	265	−45	33	−246	−438	444	374	−123
USA	CAZE	1 288	6 415	5 095	1 879	3 748	5 142	2 138	9 293	6 742	10 045	21 533
Asia	GQDK	1 092	1 378	1 931	255	630	570	186	−189	412	402	493
Near & Middle East Countries	GQAU	−27	114	−54	137	251	115	78	58	64	103	111
Other Asian Countries of which	GQAV	1 120	1 264	1 986	118	380	456	110	−248	348	299	382
Hong Kong	GQAW	109	10	10	53	280	106	45	−124	10	15	42
Japan	CAZH	1 130	1 238	2 091	48	−21	277	4	−379	209	288	56
Singapore	GQAX	8	4	9	7	9	14	2	40	1	41	16
South Korea	GQAY	..	..	..	..	..	43	2	85	−8	−78	178
Australasia & Oceania of which	GQDL	1 530	990	852	1 328	323	995	387	−647	992	714	826
Australia	CBOJ	1 575	846	957	937	340	995	260	−708	1 096	721	940
New Zealand	CBOK	−45	..	−105	391	−17	–	127	60	−104	−6	−113
Africa of which	GQAZ	−8	47	64	27	99	111	63	117	118	170	853
South Africa	CAZJ	−30	..	38	30	85	58	50	125	109	149	603
World Total	CBDH	11 562	17 405	17 155	8 418	8 816	9 871	6 046	12 654	15 662	20 296	38 633
OECD	GQBA	11 432	17 188	15 727	8 428	8 221	8 636	5 346	12 511	15 235	19 758	36 782
Central & Eastern Europe[4]	GQBB	–	4	–	–	−7	–	−141	15	−19	14	−1

1 Net investment includes unremitted profits.
2 A minus sign indicates net disinvestment in the UK.
3 Prior to 1995 Russia covers other former USSR countries, the Baltic States and Albania.
4 Includes Albania, Belarus, Bulgaria, Croatia, Czech Republic, Estonia, Hungary, Latvia, Lithuania, Poland, Romania, Serbia & Montenegro, Slovakia and Slovenia.

Sources: ONS Overseas Direct Investment Inquiries: 01633 813314;
Bank of England

18.17 Level of UK inward direct investment - book value of net liabilities analysed by area and main country at year end

£ millions

		1988	1989	1990	1991	1992	1993	1994	1995	1996	1997	1998
Europe	GQDM	28 990	37 610	40 606	45 205	46 928	47 770	47 281	52 144	55 856	58 037	67 241
EU	CDOT	23 593	28 711	33 707	38 036	39 547	40 266	39 998	43 493	43 774	44 927	48 789
Austria	CDPF	37	40	104	103	−30	93	428	412	280	79	175
Belgium & Luxembourg	CDOU	1 679	1 357	1 634	1 812	1 817	1 801	2 221	2 170	1 233	1 856	2 424
Denmark	CDOV	561	696	685	701	877	1 339	1 072	1 127	850	927	1 278
Finland	CDPG	192	291	423	364	437	300	356	352	334	444	557
France	CDOW	3 923	6 148	7 427	9 000	8 749	7 880	7 728	8 289	9 147	13 880	13 440
Germany	CDOX	1 973	2 543	4 239	4 597	5 627	5 921	5 589	8 854	9 508	10 078	10 218
Greece	CDOY	..	..	..	..	..	..	..	..	..	..	..
Irish Republic	CDOZ	276	491	1 069	840	865	681	956	686	703	1 837	2 392
Italy	CDPA	444	623	597	649	845	875	839	1 223	988	824	982
Netherlands	CDPB	12 871	14 571	14 182	16 547	16 715	18 477	18 511	17 173	18 692	12 131	14 208
Portugal	CDPC	..	..	..	..	..	..	..	..	..	..	..
Spain	CDPD	143	194	318	329	356	346	178	164	78	247	338
Sweden	CDPI	1 482	1 732	3 025	3 058	3 274	2 542	2 105	2 908	1 871	2 521	2 655
EFTA of which	CDPE	4 882	8 248	6 794	7 040	7 308	7 225	7 111	8 188	11 735	12 379	16 733
Norway	CDPH	705	725	748	661	647	701	506	665	1 571	1 866	1 520
Switzerland	CDPJ	4 176	7 521	6 044	6 375	6 657	6 519	6 605	7 523	10 164	10 422	15 137
Other European Countries of which	GQDN	515	651	105	129	73	280	172	463	..	..	..
Russia[1]	GQBC	306	374	18	18	−51	43	24	80	212	..	..
UK offshore islands	GQBD	–	–	–	–	–	–	–	–	–	341	1 241
America of which	GQDU	33 333	43 591	49 721	49 682	50 910	55 209	55 918	59 420	62 253	77 408	97 518
Canada	CDPM	3 762	4 935	4 104	4 427	4 065	4 101	4 593	2 652	3 517	4 129	3 629
USA	CDPN	28 257	37 093	43 784	44 434	46 001	49 537	49 829	55 129	55 956	70 270	90 341
Asia	GQDO	3 941	5 729	7 184	7 378	6 935	7 655	7 782	7 934	8 072	9 166	9 289
Near & Middle East Countries	GQBE	573	1 119	1 110	1 372	1 099	1 427	2 027	1 324	1 274	1 450	1 406
Other Asian Countries of which	GQBF	3 368	4 609	6 073	6 006	5 836	6 228	5 755	6 609	6 797	7 715	7 883
Hong Kong	GQBG	93	402	406	200	422	262	233	19	31	56	216
Japan	CDPQ	3 082	3 965	5 648	5 346	4 929	5 427	5 105	5 542	5 888	6 562	6 624
Singapore	GQBH	26	29	47	..	..	415	421	500	503	757	412
South Korea	GQBI	..	..	..	−43	−28	−3	−203	12	−206	−305	−99
Australasia & Oceania of which	GQDP	5 104	6 297	7 937	8 715	9 135	9 560	9 644	8 527	7 707	7 354	7 713
Australia	CDPP	5 052	6 081	6 799	7 655	8 083	8 598	7 968	7 021	6 169	6 003	5 877
New Zealand	CDPR	52	..	912	832	824	844	1 676	1 506	1 538	1 351	1 492
Africa of which	GQBJ	284	357	313	393	501	811	712	861	766	991	1 782
South Africa	CDPS	241	..	263	342	438	618	549	665	578	743	1 220
World Total	CDPZ	71 652	93 554	105 760	111 373	114 409	121 005	121 336	128 885	134 654	152 956	183 544
OECD	GQBK	68 716	89 287	101 702	107 814	110 816	116 082	116 171	123 761	128 475	145 336	173 424
Central & Eastern Europe[2]	GQBL	..	238	29	29	24	21	10	258	14	24	53

1 Prior to 1995 Russia covers other former USSR countries, the Baltic States and Albania.
2 Includes Albania, Belarus, Bulgaria, Croatia, Czech Rebuplic, Estonia, Hungary, Latvia, Lithuania, Poland, Romania, Serbia & Montenegro, Slovakia and Slovenia.

Sources: ONS Overseas Direct Investment Inquiries: 01633 813314; Bank of England

18.18 Net earnings from direct investment in the UK analysed by area and main country [1][2]

£ millions

		1988	1989	1990	1991	1992	1993	1994	1995	1996	1997	1998
Europe	GQDQ	2 305	2 734	2 007	1 243	2 482	4 833	3 661	5 432	6 401	5 746	−432
EU	CBDJ	2 052	2 256	1 689	1 025	1 932	3 556	3 659	4 657	5 631	5 231	1 835
Austria	CBOR	1	−3	−8	..	..	−5	94	30	55	13	8
Belgium & Luxembourg	CBDK	151	72	−3	−53	−1	224	272	249	209	139	336
Denmark	CBDL	72	117	88	42	−17	92	18	152	137	171	228
Finland	CBOS	−13	−10	−43	−71	−36	−52	2	88	74	80	62
France	CBDM	287	297	420	377	340	633	227	836	705	1 239	269
Germany	CBDN	182	117	169	22	221	576	507	700	706	563	−447
Greece	CBDO	..	..	..	..	..	..	..	..	..	..	20
Irish Republic	CBDP	165	78	−4	−27	−12	74	92	155	141	222	336
Italy	CBDQ	54	30	−73	−55	−24	97	246	196	318	430	203
Netherlands	CBDR	1 010	1 443	1 148	927	1 731	1 820	2 076	2 070	3 053	2 034	493
Portugal	CBDS	..	..	..	..	..	..	..	..	..	..	−8
Spain	CBDT	25	28	−	−29	−5	55	17	42	69	106	65
Sweden	CBOU	120	112	13	−56	−177	46	107	127	146	219	270
EFTA	CBDW	233	464	316	146	846	1 188	−33	685	709	408	−2 252
of which												
Norway	CBOT	51	42	17	−14	−35	27	12	11	−58	121	−180
Switzerland	CBOV	183	423	301	338	885	1 161	−45	675	768	277	−2 077
Other European Countries	GQDR	20	13	2	−104	−296	88	36	89	60	108	−14
of which												
Russia[3]	GQBM	..	9	2	..	..	55	1	15	31	..	..
UK offshore islands	GQBN	−	−	−	−	−	−	−	−	−	33	17
America	GQDV	5 210	6 072	5 131	2 948	2 391	4 917	4 992	5 824	7 589	6 775	7 074
of which												
Canada	CBEA	235	448	273	199	47	234	506	228	281	65	153
USA	CBDZ	4 727	5 492	4 602	2 951	2 284	4 441	4 372	5 606	6 986	6 512	6 690
Asia	GQDS	513	481	102	193	107	106	172	459	300	−332	−778
Near & Middle East Countries	GQBO	10	29	−119	−89	−31	16	−8	112	89	96	43
Other Asian Countries	GQBP	504	453	222	283	139	90	181	347	211	−428	−822
of which												
Hong Kong	GQBQ	85	−27	−23	47	207	52	4	−2	28	21	−185
Japan	CBEC	405	456	261	246	−41	45	171	334	151	−502	−557
Singapore	GQBS	2	2	−12	3	−2	4	1	5	−	41	−77
South Korea	GQBT	..	..	..	..	..	7	15	−6	−6	−11	−25
Australasia & Oceania	GQDT	540	−185	−302	74	211	418	327	472	594	860	594
of which												
Australia	CBOZ	522	−194	−168	92	222	410	330	479	566	830	519
New Zealand	CBPA	18	9	−134	−18	..	8	−1	−6	28	..	79
Africa	GQBU	44	56	−6	3	..	19	25	49	44	55	29
of which												
South Africa	CBED	35	65	−6	−1	6	9	21	38	35	46	..
World Total	CBEV	8 612	9 158	6 932	4 461	5 197	10 293	9 176	12 235	14 928	13 103	6 484
OECD	GQBV	8 204	8 844	6 831	4 878	5 371	9 998	9 118	12 081	14 388	12 583	6 455
Central & Eastern Europe[4]	GQBW	..	−	−	−	2	1	24	60	13	18	−11

1 A minus sign indicates net losses.
2 Net earnings equal profits of UK branches plus overseas investors' receipts of interest and their share of the profits of UK subsidiaries and associates. Earnings are after deducting provisions for depreciation and UK tax on profits and interest.
3 Prior to 1995 Russia covers other former USSR countries, the Baltic States and Albania.
4 Includes Albania, Belarus, Bulgaria, Croatia, Czech Republic, Estonia, Hungary, Latvia, Lithuania, Poland, Romania, Serbia & Montenegro, Slovakia and Slovenia.

Sources: ONS Overseas Direct Investment Inquiries: 01633 813314;
Bank of England

19 Research and development

Research and development

Research and development
(Tables 19.1 to 19.5)

Research and experimental development (R&D) is defined for statistical purposes as 'creative work undertaken on a systematic basis in order to increase the stock of knowledge, including knowledge of man, culture and society, and the use of this stock of knowledge to devise new applications'.

R&D is financed and carried out mainly by businesses, the Government, and institutions of higher education. A small amount is performed by non-profit-making bodies. Gross Expenditure on R&D (GERD) is an indicator of the total amount of R&D performed within the UK: it has been approximately 2 per cent of GDP in recent years. Detailed figures are reported each year in a First Release published in March ONS (2000) 119 and the August edition of the ONS's *Economic Trends*. Table 19.1 shows the main components of GERD.

The ONS conducts an annual survey of expenditure and employment on R&D performed by Government, and of Government funding of R&D. The survey collects data on outturn and planning years. Until 1993 the detailed results were reported in the *Annual Review of Government Funded R&D* produced by the Office of Science and Technology (OST). From 1997 the results have appeared in OST's *Science, Engineering and Technology Statistics* publication. Table 19.2 gives some broad totals for gross expenditure by Government (expenditure before deducting funds received by Government for R&D). Table 19.3 gives a breakdown of net expenditure (receipts are deducted).

The ONS conducts an annual survey of R&D in business. Tables 19.4 and 19.5 give a summary of the main trends up to 1998. The latest set of results from the survey will be available in a First Release dated 17 November 2000 and a Business Monitor (MA14) to be published in January 2001.

Statistics on expenditure and employment on R&D in Higher Education Institutions (HEIs) are based on information collected by Higher Education Funding Councils and HESA (Higher Education Statistics Agency). In 1994 a new methodology was introduced to estimate expenditure on R&D in HEIs. This is based on the allocation of various Funding Council Grants. Full details of the new methodology are contained in SET 2000 available on the Office of Science and Technology Web Site at http://www.dti.gov.uk/ost/

The most comprehensive international comparisons of resources devoted to R&D appear in Main Science and Technology Indicators published by the Organisation for Economic Co-operation and Development (OECD). The Statistical Office of the European Union and the United Nations, also compile R&D statistics based on figures supplied by member states.

To make international comparisons more reliable the OECD have published a series of manuals giving guidance on how to measure various components of R&D inputs and outputs. The most important of these is the Frascati Manual which defines R&D and recommends how resources for R&D should be measured. The UK follows the Frascati Manual as far as possible.

For information on available aggregated data on Research and Development please contact Jane Morgan on 01633 813109, (e-mail jane.morgan@ons.gov.uk).

19.1 Cost of research and development: analysis by sector

	Work performed within each sector													
	1992		1993		1994		1995		1996		1997		1998	
	£m	%	£m	%	£m	%	£m	%	£m	%	£m	%	£m	%
Sector carrying out the work (£m cash terms)														
Government	1 846	15	1 928	14	2 051	15	1 462	10	1 495	10	1 427	10	1 487	10
Research Councils	-	-	-	-	-	-	581	4	575	4	590	4	591	4
Business enterprise	8 489	67	9 069	67	9 204	66	9 254	65	9 431	65	9 657	65	10 231	66
Higher education	2 129	17	2 312	17	2 623	19	2 696	19	2 792	19	2 893	20	3 040	20
Private non-profit	224	2	232	2	168	1	177	1	177	1	190	1	203	1
Total	12 689	100	13 541	100	14 046	100	14 172	100	14 470	100	14 758	100	15 553	100

	Finance provided by each sector													
	1992		1993		1994		1995		1996		1997		1998	
	£m	%	£m	%	£m	%	£m	%	£m	%	£m	%	£m	%
Sector providing the funds (£m cash terms)														
Government	4 239	33	4 400	32	4 657	33	2 611	18	2 494	17	2 421	16	2 619	17
Research Councils	-	-	-	-	-	-	1 078	8	1 092	8	1 135	8	1 128	7
Higher Education Funding Councils	-	-	-	-	-	-	1 018	7	1 027	7	1 033	7	1 085	7
Higher education	99	1	103	1	116	1	119	1	120	1	123	1	130	1
Business enterprise[1]	6 461	51	6 974	52	7 025	50	6 796	48	6 846	47	7 321	50	7 351	47
Private non-profit	435	3	451	3	495	4	511	4	546	4	579	4	621	4
Abroad	1 455	11	1 613	12	1 753	12	2 039	14	2 345	16	2 146	15	2 618	17
Total	12 689	100	13 541	100	14 046	100	14 172	100	14 470	100	14 758	100	15 553	100

1 Including research associations and public corporations.

Source: Office for National Statistics: 01633 813109

19.2 Gross Central Government expenditure on research and development

£ millions

	1993/94		1994/95		1995/96		1996/97		1997/98		1998/99	
	Intra-mural	Extra-mural[1]	Intra-mural	Extra-mural[1]	Intra-mural	Extra-mural[1]	Intra-mural	Extra-mural[1]	Intra-mural	Extra-mural[1]	Intra-mural	Extra-mural[1]
Defence	731	1 680	707	1451	692	1562	804	1429	774	1 639	818	1 436
Research councils	584	700	589	783	599	823	592	851	608	852	608	865
Higher Education Institutes	-	968	-	1 017	-	1 018	-	1 027	-	1 033	-	1 085
Other programmes	425	626	414	552	374	572	290	628	253	681	266	714
Total (ex NHS)	1 739	3 974	1 710	3 803	1 665	3 975	1 686	3 935	1 635	4 205	1 692	4 100

1 Including work performed overseas and excluding monies spent with other government departments.

Source: Office for National Statistics: 01633 813109

319

Research and development

19.3 Net central government expenditure on research and development, using European Union objectives for R&D expenditure

£ millions

		1988/89	1989/90	1990/91	1991/92	1992/93	1993/94	1994/95	1995/96	1996/97	1997/98	1998/99
Exploration and exploitation of the earth	KDVP	99.5	123.7	145.2	143.9	120.5	98.8	106.8	105.2	95.4	81.3	78.5
Infrastructure and general planning of land-use	KDVQ	66.8	71.7	74.1	64.2	85.6	96.7	98.1	94.1	98.8	98.9	103.5
Control of environmental pollution	KDVR	58.4	53.0	70.3	71.9	69.5	108.7	117.2	131.8	128.7	136.2	142.8
Protection and promotion of human health (ex NHS)	KDVS	221.7	264.1	292.0	298.4	341.5	383.1	397.2	416.0	427.4	445.1	450.1
Production, distribution and rational utilization of energy	KDVT	177.3	157.7	141.7	133.0	120.0	96.8	55.5	52.3	43.2	41.0	28.0
Agricultural production and technology	KDVU	209.4	197.7	198.6	216.2	261.1	284.6	263.4	281.9	257.0	268.9	255.5
Industrial production and technology	KDVV	399.2	455.2	478.8	399.0	394.1	458.7	184.4	165.8	144.6	102.8	61.6
Social structures and relationships	KDVW	95.7	101.6	110.8	115.5	141.9	149.1	141.9	137.1	120.7	114.7	154.7
Exploration and exploitation of space	KDVX	148.0	146.3	155.2	134.2	149.1	187.4	161.5	153.0	164.1	164.4	142.5
Research financed from General University Funds	KDVY	800.0	799.0	835.0	919.1	963.3	968.4	1 017.9	1 018.6	1 027.5	1 033.3	1 085.1
Non-oriented research	KDVZ	249.5	257.3	287.6	287.6	337.1	267.3	612.5	653.5	680.5	671.0	677.0
Other civil research	KDWA	13.8	11.9	11.0	35.5	23.8	34.0	22.2	24.7	20.5	21.6	25.8
Defence	KDWB	1 957.2	2 132.7	2 154.7	2 208.8	2 071.1	2 268.6	2 021.9	2 098.9	2 143.5	2 312.1	2 099.5
Total (ex NHS)	KDWC	4 496.5	4 771.8	4 955.1	5 027.4	5 078.6	5 402.3	5 200.4	5 332.9	5 351.8	5 491.2	5 304.5

Source: Office for National Statistics: 01633 813109

19.4 Intramural expenditure on Business Enterprise R&D At Current Prices and Constant Prices

£ millions

(i) Current Prices

		Total				Civil				Defence		
		1996	1997	1998		1996	1997	1998		1996	1997	1998
Total	KDWD	9 431	9 657	10 231	KDWN	8 071	8 214	8 698	KDWX	1 360	1 443	1 533
Manufacturing Total	KDWE	7 035	7 360	7 872	KDWO	5 767	6 055	6 455	KDWY	1 268	1 304	1 417
Chemicals	KDWF	2 479	2 831	2 926	KDWP	2 477	2 829	2 926	KDWZ	2	2	–
Mechanical engineering	KDWG	668	709	730	KDWQ	395	407	455	KDXA	273	302	276
Electrical machinery	KJRT	1 313	1 181	1 320	KJTC	896	803	916	KJUL	417	377	404
Aerospace	KDWJ	812	893	1 039	KDWT	359	412	485	KDXD	453	481	554
Transport equipment	KDWK	977	966	983	KDWU	967	955	947	KDXE	10	11	36
Other manufacturing	KDWL	787	779	874	KDWV	673	648	727	KDXF	113	131	147
Services	KDWM	2 396	2 297	2 359	KDWW	2 304	2 158	2 243	KDXG	92	139	116

(ii) 1995 Prices

		Total				Civil				Defence		
		1996	1997	1998		1996	1997	1998		1996	1997	1998
Total	KDXH	9 137	9 102	9 405	KDXR	7 819	7 742	7 996	KDYB	1 318	1 360	1 409
Manufacturing Total	KDXI	6 815	6 937	7 236	KDXS	5 587	5 707	5 934	KDYC	1 228	1 229	1 303
Chemicals	KDXJ	2 402	2 668	2 690	KDXT	2 400	2 667	2 690	KDYD	2	2	–
Mechanical engineering	KDXK	647	668	671	KDXU	383	384	418	KDYE	264	285	254
Electrical machinery	KKKJ	1 272	1 113	1 213	KKKK	868	757	842	KKKX	404	355	371
Aerospace	KDXN	787	842	955	KDXX	348	388	446	KDYH	439	453	509
Transport equipment	KDXO	947	911	904	KDXY	937	900	871	KDYI	10	10	33
Other manufacturing	KDXP	762	734	803	KDXZ	653	611	668	KDYJ	109	123	135
Services	KDXQ	2 321	2 165	2 169	KDYA	2 232	2 034	2 062	KDYK	89	131	107

Source: Office for National Statistics: 01633 813109

19.5 Sources of funds for R&D within Business Enterprises in the United Kingdom

		Total				Civil				Defence		
		1996	1997	1998		1996	1997	1998		1996	1997	1998
Funds for Business Enterprise R&D												
£m cash terms												
Total	KDYL	9 431	9 657	10 231	KDYT	8 071	8 214	8 698	KDZB	1 360	1 443	1 533
Government funds	KDYM	934	1 005	1 190	KDYU	242	288	403	KDZC	693	717	787
Overseas funds	KDYN	2 031	1 811	2 246	KDYV	1 728	1 486	1 865	KDZD	303	325	381
Mainly own funds	KDYO	6 465	6 840	6 796	KDYW	6 102	6 439	6 431	KDZE	364	401	365
Funds for Business Enterprise R&D												
Percentage												
Total	KDYP	100	100	100	KDYX	100	100	100	KDZF	100	100	100
Government funds	KDYQ	10	10	12	KDYY	3	4	5	KDZG	51	50	51
Overseas funds	KDYR	22	19	22	KDYZ	21	18	21	KDZH	22	22	25
Mainly own funds	KDYS	69	71	66	KDZA	76	78	74	KDZI	27	28	24

Source: Office for National Statistics: 01633 813109

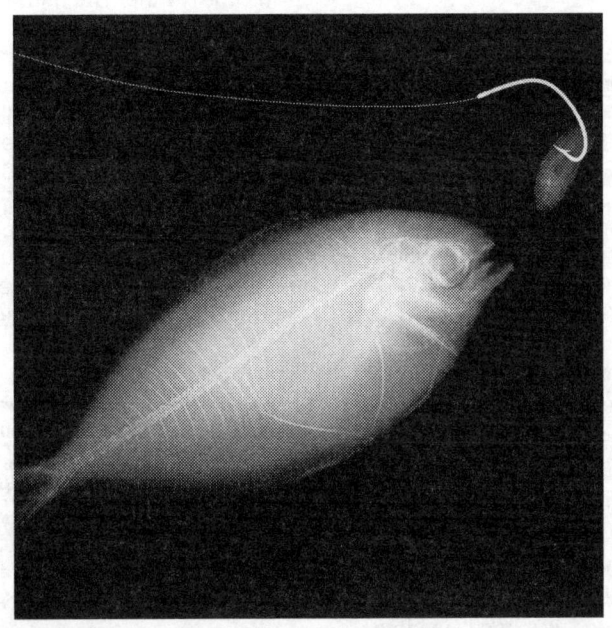

20 Agriculture, fisheries and food

Agriculture, fisheries and food

Agricultural censuses and surveys
(Tables 20.3, 20.5 and 20.13)
The coverage for holdings detailed in Tables 20.3, 20.5 and 20.13 includes all main and minor holdings for each country. Scotland now includes minor holdings and Northern Ireland data is now based on all active farm business, therefore data here will differ from previous editions.

Estimated quantity of crops and grass harvested
(Table 20.4)
The estimated yields of sugar beet and hops (Table 20.4) are obtained from production figures supplied by British Sugar plc, and the main hop producers in England and Wales. In Great Britain potato yields are estimated in consultation with the British Potato Council.

Forestry *(Table 20.6)*
Statistics for state forestry are from the Annual Reports and Accounts of Forest Enterprise in Great Britain and the Forest Service in Northern Ireland.

For private forestry in Great Britain, statistics on new planting and restocking are based on records of the Woodland Grant Scheme, and timber removals are estimated from a survey of the largest timber harvesting companies. Productive woodland is based on data obtained from censuses of woodlands and adjusted to reflect subsequent changes. Figures are based on results from the 1995 National Inventory of Woodlands.

Average weekly earnings and hours of agricultural and horticultural workers
(Tables 20.7 and 20.8)
Since 1998, data on the Earnings and Hours of Agricultural and Horticultural workers has been collected via an annual telephone survey. This annual survey collects information for a snapshot in time, relating to the month of September. The survey covers seven main categories of workers and in 1999 data was collected on about 1 200 workers. Prior to 1998, data was collected from a monthly postal survey, which mainly covered male full time workers.

The survey provides data which is used by the Agricultural Wages Board when considering wage claims and by the Ministry of Agriculture, Fisheries and Food in considering the cost of labour in agriculture and horticulture.

Fisheries *(Tables 20.14 and 20.15)*
Data relating to the weight and value of landings of fish in the United Kingdom (Table 20.14) is generally obtained from sales notes completed at fish market auctions.

Fishing fleet information (Table 20.15) is obtained from vessel registers maintained by the Ministry of Agriculture, Fisheries and Food in England and Wales and the Scottish Office Agriculture and Fisheries Department.

Estimated average household food consumption in Great Britain - national food survey *(Table 20.16)*

The sample
The National Food Survey results are derived from the responses of a random sample of private households throughout Great Britain. Although the survey was extended to include Northern Ireland in 1996, the results given are for Great Britain in order to preserve continuity. The person most responsible for the catering arrangements of the household is designated as the main diary keeper; he or she records details of all items of food for human consumption brought into the home during the course of a week. Until 1997 about 8 000 households in Great Britain participated in the Survey. From 1997 a more efficient sample design was introduced and the sample for Great Britain was reduced to around 6 000 households. A description of the sampling methods is given in the annual reports; the latest is *National Food Survey* 1998.

Household
A group of persons living in the same dwelling and sharing common catering arrangements. The size of the household is defined in terms of the number of persons who spend at least four nights in the household during the week of the survey and also have at least one meal a day from the household food supply on at least four days. The head of the household and the main diary keeper are regarded as 'persons' in all cases.

Food obtained for consumption
Purchases of selected foods for home consumption during the Survey week (including purchases in bulk and, exceptionally, school milk) plus any garden or allotment produce, etc, consumed during the week. For a few minor miscellaneous items, expenditure is recorded but not the quantity (eg artificial sweeteners). The survey also includes information on confectionery and soft and alcoholic drinks brought home and, published from 1994, on food and drink consumed outside the home.

Although the quantity of food purchased or obtained free during the survey week will differ from the actual consumption of an individual household, the average quantity of food for a large number of households will equal the average consumption if there is no general change in the level of larder stocks.

20.1 Outputs, inputs and income at current prices
United Kingdom
Calendar years

£ millions

		1989	1990	1991	1992	1993	1994	1995	1996	1997	1998	1999[14]
Outputs[1]												
Cereals:												
wheat	KFKA	1 363	1 426	1 689	1 682	1 783	1 723	2 079	2 315	1 851	1 652	1 545
barley	KFKB	847	776	714	855	845	846	1 110	1 184	977	781	739
oats	KFKC	44	53	52	58	72	81	89	86	71	60	57
rye, mixed corn & triticale	KFKD	3	4	3	4	6	7	9	9	9	8	8
1. Total production of cereals	KFKF	2 257	2 259	2 458	2 599	2 704	2 657	3 287	3 594	2 907	2 502	2 349
Other crops:												
oilseed rape	KFKG	270	283	349	268	411	373	379	421	406	407	356
linseed	KIBT	11	15	39	84	184	39	41	40	51	67	129
sugar beet	KFKH	254	276	310	386	353	343	355	358	329	295	291
hops	KFKI	16	16	22	19	23	22	18	21	21	15	14
peas and beans for stockfeed	KFKJ	116	117	107	123	186	147	135	129	129	112	115
hay and dried grass	KFKK	14	22	21	16	17	19	21	21	19	14	14
grass and clover seed	KFKL	17	18	15	15	14	16	15	21	23	20	19
straw	LUJX	159	213	164	116	219	249	321	222	169	184	185
unspecified crops[2]	LUJY	37	40	44	33	46	55	56	61	52	51	49
2. Total production of other crops	KFKN	895	999	1 072	1 061	1 454	1 262	1 340	1 293	1 199	1 166	1 173
3. Total production of potatoes	KFKO	495	571	521	533	385	707	1 088	634	387	624	755
Horticulture:												
vegtables	KFKP	929	1 021	980	936	915	999	1 065	1 082	962	984	963
fruit	KFKQ	262	260	284	269	257	235	241	268	202	242	246
ornamentals	KFKR	467	508	522	529	567	595	615	658	680	659	682
fruit, vegtables and tomato seeds	KFKS	7	6	6	9	8	8	8	8	7	8	8
4. Total production of horticulture	KFKT	1 665	1 795	1 792	1 742	1 746	1 837	1 928	2 016	1 851	1 893	1 899
Livestock												
finished cattle and calves	KFKU	2 162	1 975	2 072	2 022	2 392	2 486	2 583	2 550	2 278	1 990	1 996
finished sheep and lambs	KFKV	1 008	1 017	1 141	1 164	1 250	1 242	1 345	1 300	1 200	1 133	1 007
finished pigs	KFKW	1 061	1 065	1 016	1 141	1 036	1 032	1 169	1 366	1 195	881	782
poultry	KFKX	1 002	1 079	1 079	1 124	1 271	1 336	1 333	1 501	1 482	1 347	1 247
other livestock	KFKY	117	122	127	135	136	135	143	149	156	153	153
5. Total production of livestock	KFLA	5 350	5 257	5 435	5 586	6 086	6 231	6 572	6 866	6 311	5 503	5 184
Livestock products:												
milk	KFLB	2 727	2 793	2 789	2 925	3 187	3 278	3 508	3 504	3 161	2 718	2 673
eggs[3]	KFLC	383	439	410	397	427	432	399	467	428	400	359
clip wool	KFLD	52	49	42	41	30	46	46	40	35	24	21
unspecified livestock products	KFLE	24	26	21	23	24	22	24	23	25	21	25
6. Total production of livestock products	KFLF	3 186	3 306	3 262	3 386	3 667	3 778	3 977	4 034	3 649	3 162	3 078
Capital formation in livestock												
cattle	KUJZ	381	321	236	442	651	580	359	229	394	302	198
sheep	LUKA	188	171	125	144	128	154	142	134	213	149	120
pigs	LUKB	13	17	16	20	15	13	11	23	18	1	5
poultry	LUKC	88	106	110	114	120	112	122	130	131	135	126
7. Total capital formation in livestock	KFLI	670	616	487	719	914	858	634	515	756	586	449

1 Output is a net of VAT collected on the sale of non-edible products. Figures for total output include subsidies on products, but not other subsidies.

2 Includes turf, other minor crops and arable area payments for fodder maize.

3 Includes the value of duck eggs and exports of eggs for hatching.

4 For years prior to 1992 the split between compounds and straights has been estimated based on the split present in later years.

5 Landlords' expenses are included within farm maintenance, miscellaneous expenditure and depreciation of buildings and works.

6 Includes livestock and crop costs, water costs, insurance premia, bank charges, professional fees, rates, and other farming costs.

7 Includes Environmentally and Nitrate Sensitive Areas, Countryside Steward-ship, Countryside Premium, Tir Cymen, Tir Gofal, Moorland, Habitat, Farm Woodland and Organic Farming Schemes.

8 Includes guidance premium for beef and sheepmeat production, Pilot Beef and Sheep Extensification Scheme, non-agricultural horse grazing and farm accounts grant as well as historic data for fertiliser and lime grant and payments to small scale cereal producers.

9 Excludes the value of work done by farm labour on own account capital formation in buildings and works.

10 Interest charges on loans for current farming purposes and buildings and less interest on money held on short term deposit.

11 Rent paid (after deductions) is the rent paid on all tenanted land includ- ing 'conacre' land in Northern Ireland, less landlords' expenses and the benefit value of dwellings on that land.

12 Rent received (after deductions) is the rent received by farming landowners from renting of land to other farmers less landlords' expenses and the benefit value of dwellings on that land. (This series starts in 1996 following a revision to the methodology of calculating net rent.)

13 Total net rent is the net rent flowing out of the agricultural sector paid to non farming landowners, including that part of tenanted land in Northern Ireland. (Although there has been some updating of the technical pro- cedures for calculating this figure, it corresponds with the previous net rent variable.)

14 Provisional

Source: Ministry of Agriculture, Fisheries and Food: 01904 455089

20.1

Outputs, inputs and income at current prices
United Kingdom

Calendar years

£ millions

		1989	1990	1991	1992	1993	1994	1995	1996	1997	1998	1999[14]
Other agricultural activities												
contract work	LUKD	350	375	401	430	463	495	544	596	569	565	590
leasing out milk quota	LUKE	30	44	32	42	104	127	136	169	120	99	70
leasing out ewe premium	LUKF	–	–	–	–	5	6	7	5	4	4	5
leasing out suckler cow premium	LUKG	–	–	–	–	1	1	1	1	1	6	6
8. Total other agricultural activities	LUOS	380	419	433	472	573	629	688	770	694	674	671
9. Total inseparable non-agricultural activities	LUOT	207	243	265	286	313	340	344	382	399	461	494
10. Gross output at basic prices	KFLT	15 104	15 465	15 725	16 385	17 841	18 298	19 857	20 105	18 154	16 571	16 053
11. Total subsidies (less taxes) on product	LUOU	401	448	660	804	1 763	1 686	2 107	2 782	2 588	2 438	2 362
12. Output at market prices (10-11)[5]	LUOV	14 704	15 017	15 065	15 580	16 078	16 612	17 750	17 323	15 566	14 133	13 691
of which												
transactions within the agricultural idustry	LUNP	..	..	..	..	..	..	..	..	..	..	..
feed wheat	LUNQ	62	62	95	114	81	75	55	67	79	80	68
feed barley	LUNR	209	228	255	265	233	201	199	206	193	164	154
feed oats	LUNS	18	19	22	19	21	22	16	16	12	10	12
seed potatoes	LUNT	14	25	17	23	13	14	41	34	10	15	32
straw	LUNU	150	203	156	109	207	236	308	212	160	173	173
contract work	LUNV	350	375	401	430	463	495	544	596	569	565	590
leasing of quota	LUNW	30	44	32	42	110	133	144	175	125	109	81
total capital formation in livestock	LUNX	670	616	487	719	914	858	634	515	756	586	449
Intermediate consumption (expenditure net of reclaimed VAT)												
(Expenditure net of reclaimed VAT)												
Feedingstuffs												
compounds[4]	LUNY	1 833	1 761	1 734	1 671	1 764	1 689	1 806	1 960	1 772	1 524	1 422
straights[4]	LUNZ	815	783	771	742	761	812	885	873	734	635	661
feed purchased from other farms	LUOA	288	308	371	399	336	297	271	289	284	254	233
other costs	LUOB	–	–	–	69	72	76	84	80	71	68	69
13. Total feedingstuffs	KFMB	2 936	2 852	2 876	2 881	2 932	2 874	3 046	3 201	2 860	2 480	2 385
Seeds												
cereals	KFMC	126	121	123	114	114	112	121	124	103	88	87
other	KFMD	178	205	189	207	180	209	264	255	225	234	246
14. Total seeds	KFME	304	326	312	321	293	321	385	379	328	322	333
15. Total fertilisers and lime	KFMM	897	934	903	839	758	847	931	1 022	990	822	775
16. Pesticides	KFMN	525	516	545	531	547	558	589	648	672	652	628
Farm maintenance[5]												
occupier	KCOZ	202	201	202	226	247	282	308	295	301	263	249
landlord	KCPA	64	63	64	64	64	64	64	69	72	71	70
17. Total farm maintenance	KCPB	265	264	265	291	311	346	373	364	373	334	319
Miscellaneous expenditure												
machinery repairs	KFMO	556	578	612	601	637	629	722	746	724	702	686
machinery fuel and oil	KFMP	291	324	335	328	349	343	355	400	398	367	391
veterinary expenses and medicines	KCPC	195	211	222	231	253	274	289	297	308	286	271
power and fuel(mainly electricity)	KCPD	194	215	254	247	249	247	242	250	234	224	229
imported livestock	LUOC	40	40	31	37	35	33	25	19	23	14	18
straw for bedding	LUOD	150	203	156	109	207	236	308	212	160	173	173
contract work	LUOE	350	375	401	430	463	495	544	596	569	565	590
leasing of quota	LUOF	30	44	32	42	110	133	144	175	125	109	81
other farming costs[5,6]	KCPG	1 188	1 249	1 401	1 563	1 605	1 665	1 684	1 856	1 920	1 903	1 858
18. Total miscellaneous expenses	KCPH	2 995	3 239	3 443	3 587	3 908	4 056	4 312	4 550	4 460	4 342	4 297

See footnotes on the first part of this table.

Source: Ministry of Agriculture, Fisheries and Food: 01904 455080

20.1 continued

Outputs, inputs and income at current prices
United Kingdom
Calendar years

£ millions

		1989	1990	1991	1992	1993	1994	1995	1996	1997	1998	1999[14]
19. Total intermediate consumption	KCPM	7 922	8 132	8 344	8 450	8 749	9 002	9 636	10 164	9 684	8 952	8 737
20. Gross value added at basic prices (10-19)	LUOG	7 182	7 333	7 381	7 935	9 092	9 295	10 221	9 941	8 469	7 619	7 316
Consumption of Fixed Capital												
buildings and works	LUOH	649	691	636	568	568	582	640	681	671	683	698
landlord[5]	KCPP	116	123	115	105	105	110	120	128	139	113	115
other	KCPQ	533	568	520	463	463	472	520	553	532	570	583
plant, machinery and vehicles	KCPR	1 021	1 061	1 097	1 109	1 141	1 179	1 230	1 295	1 327	1 332	1 321
cattle	LUOI	314	283	318	330	577	529	416	315	395	321	216
sheep	LUOJ	132	150	148	120	137	141	174	189	155	106	132
pigs	LUOK	14	14	16	18	14	15	17	18	15	9	9
poultry	LUOL	101	102	109	118	108	108	121	130	123	147	137
21. Total Consumption of Fixed Capital	KCPS	2 230	2 301	2 324	2 263	2 546	2 554	2 598	2 629	2 687	2 598	2 513
22. Net value added (at basic prices)(20-21)	KCPT	4 952	5 032	5 057	5 673	6 546	6 741	7 624	7 313	5 782	5 021	4 803
Other subsidies												
animal disease compensation	LUOM	8	6	7	6	11	7	7	6	16	10	19
set-aside	LUON	9	18	25	33	168	222	206	163	90	87	171
Agri-Environment schemes[7]	ZBXC	9	10	13	24	37	57	80	86	103	140	165
other[8]	LUOO	10	8	9	10	8	8	8	9	9	9	10
vehicle licenses	ZBXD	27	27	32	34	40	42	46	54	56	59	59
23. Total other subsidies less taxes	LUOP	8	16	22	39	183	252	256	210	162	187	307
24. Net value added at factor cost(22+23)	LUOQ	4 960	5 048	5 079	5 711	6 729	6 993	7 879	7 523	5 945	5 208	5 110
25. Total compensation of employees[9]	LUOR	1 581	1 713	1 780	1 786	1 789	1 831	1 839	1 877	1 929	1 975	1 963
26. Interest[10]	KCPU	922	1 007	835	713	523	536	586	552	621	685	598
Rent												
net rent paid[11]	ZBXE	159	151	161	175	179	182	176	271	281	297	286
net rent received[12]	ZBXF	..	..	..	..	..	..	..	74	79	79	76
27. Net rent expenditure[13]	KCPV	159	151	161	175	179	182	176	197	202	218	210
28. Total income from farming (24-25-26-27)	KCQB	2 298	2 178	2 303	3 037	4 239	4 445	5 279	4 897	3 193	2 330	2 339

See footnotes on the first part of this table.

Source: Ministry of Agriculture, Fisheries and Food: 01904 455080

20.2 Output and input volume indices
United Kingdom
Calendar years

1995=100

		1988	1989	1990	1991	1992	1993	1994	1995	1996	1997	1998
Outputs[1]												
Cereals:												
wheat	LUKH	80.4	96.0	95.5	103.0	98.8	90.4	93.4	100.0	111.4	105.4	109.1
barley	LUKI	120.8	121.0	105.1	96.1	108.8	89.1	88.6	100.0	115.5	112.8	102.6
oats	LUKJ	80.0	67.8	75.1	75.0	71.0	73.1	86.0	100.0	89.5	90.8	91.6
rye, mixed corn & triticale	LUKK	65.6	78.8	95.3	79.4	90.8	86.0	91.1	100.0	96.9	95.7	103.2
1. Total production of cereals	LUKL	93.1	103.0	97.9	99.9	100.8	89.4	91.6	100.0	112.2	107.4	106.6
Other crops:												
oilseed rape	LUKM	84.7	77.6	79.2	105.2	99.4	89.5	100.3	100.0	112.7	122.0	126.5
linseed	LUKN	32.6	42.7	77.3	201.6	279.4	239.0	116.0	100.0	107.3	131.7	177.6
sugar beet	LUKO	96.7	96.2	93.7	103.2	120.4	114.6	103.4	100.0	123.6	131.5	116.3
hops	LUKP	115.5	112.3	110.7	144.0	114.6	126.2	107.0	100.0	127.3	118.1	80.9
peas and beans for stockfeed	LUKQ	164.8	125.0	133.9	115.1	119.0	160.0	127.7	100.0	101.8	123.0	125.8
hay and dried grass	LUKR	118.8	112.7	129.0	129.0	106.9	108.6	104.3	100.0	102.4	97.1	83.6
grass and clover seed	LUKS	146.2	170.4	176.0	135.9	126.1	116.0	132.7	100.0	98.0	107.1	154.9
straw	LUKT	69.6	71.7	86.8	75.5	65.0	74.0	78.5	100.0	85.2	74.4	70.7
unspecified crops[2]	LUKU	102.0	86.0	87.2	85.2	82.0	95.5	122.2	100.0	120.3	105.6	90.4
2. Total production of other crops	LUKV	95.3	89.2	94.5	104.2	105.5	106.4	99.6	100.0	107.5	112.4	110.8
3. Total production of potatoes	LUKW	104.0	97.3	99.8	97.5	121.8	104.6	98.4	100.0	107.5	101.8	92.7
Horticulture:												
vegtables	LUKX	111.0	109.6	104.4	107.0	110.6	107.0	107.5	100.0	105.0	102.5	99.0
fruit	LUKY	103.1	122.4	107.1	112.9	128.4	107.4	104.7	100.0	104.8	73.4	86.7
ornamentals	LUKZ	81.3	84.0	87.7	89.6	88.8	89.9	91.0	100.0	104.0	105.4	106.3
fruit, vegtable and tomato seeds	LULA	117.1	117.7	104.6	105.9	113.9	97.3	97.9	100.0	98.2	100.6	102.2
4. Total production of horticulture	LULB	99.0	102.0	98.4	101.2	105.0	100.9	101.2	100.0	104.6	99.9	100.1
Livestock												
finished cattle and calves	LULC	93.4	100.2	100.5	104.4	96.7	93.0	99.3	100.0	76.2	76.9	77.3
finished sheep and lambs	LULD	87.8	97.6	100.5	103.4	100.0	98.9	99.9	100.0	95.3	92.4	97.9
finished pigs	LULE	102.4	94.7	96.4	100.6	100.2	102.4	105.6	100.0	100.4	108.9	110.3
poultry	LULF	80.7	77.8	81.0	85.7	87.5	92.5	98.1	100.0	103.6	107.1	107.6
other livestock	LULG	94.5	95.9	95.8	94.8	102.4	99.4	97.7	100.0	100.6	103.0	104.4
5. Total production of livestock	LULH	90.4	93.2	94.8	98.7	95.7	95.7	100.1	100.0	90.5	92.5	94.1
Livestock products:												
milk	LULI	102.6	101.3	103.4	100.2	99.1	99.8	101.3	100.0	99.6	100.6	99.1
eggs[3]	LULJ	110.7	97.5	100.9	104.6	102.3	101.3	100.7	100.0	100.3	103.0	104.8
clip wool	LULK	101.3	110.4	110.4	105.5	105.4	99.7	96.7	100.0	95.1	96.9	100.8
unspecified	LULL	83.0	119.4	131.2	101.9	111.2	110.8	91.9	100.0	84.1	96.0	94.9
6. Total production of livestock products	LULM	103.2	100.9	103.2	100.7	99.6	100.0	101.1	100.0	99.5	100.8	99.7
Capital formation in livestock:												
cattle	LULN	88.2	111.4	101.9	78.4	126.2	121.1	119.3	100.0	94.2	105.2	96.0
sheep	LULO	123.5	134.7	115.3	77.6	119.2	99.0	135.4	100.0	83.4	131.2	121.7
pigs	LULP	74.3	132.2	173.2	168.9	183.6	167.6	143.5	100.0	182.1	191.4	31.1
poultry	LULQ	103.3	86.1	95.5	92.9	89.4	101.9	101.0	100.0	101.5	108.5	100.2
7. Total capital formation in livestock	LULR	101.6	114.9	107.1	83.9	119.6	115.0	119.3	100.0	94.7	115.6	104.2
Other agricultural activities												
contract work	LULS	96.2	93.7	92.4	89.9	89.9	91.6	94.4	100.0	104.6	107.3	111.0
leasing out milk quota	LULT	33.1	44.6	56.6	65.4	68.4	79.1	90.9	100.0	102.8	111.7	119.8
leasing out ewe premium	LULU	91.2	91.2	91.2	91.2	91.2	91.2	88.9	100.0	65.0	48.9	43.2
leasing out suckler cow premium	LULV	54.8	54.8	54.8	54.8	54.8	54.8	42.8	100.0	68.8	52.5	52.7
8. Total other non-agricultural activities	LULW	86.5	86.1	86.8	86.1	86.4	89.0	93.5	100.0	104.0	107.9	112.3
9. Total inseparable non-agricultural activities	LULX	79.8	81.3	83.7	85.4	89.1	95.3	101.4	100.0	106.6	106.3	102.8

1 Output is net of VAT collected on the sale of non-edible products. Figures for total output include subsidies on products, but not other subsidies.
2 Includes turf, other minor crops and arable area payments for fodder maize.
3 Includes the value of duck eggs and exports of eggs for hatching.
4 Gross Output at basic prices includes subsidies (less taxes) on products.
5 Descriptions of terms used in this table are provided in the Annex.

6 Landlords' expenses are included within farm maintenance, miscellaneous expenditure and depreciation of buildings and works.
7 Includes livestock and crop costs, water costs, insurance premia, bank charges, professional fees, rates, vehicle licence costs and other farming costs.

Source: Ministry of Agriculture, Fisheries and Food: 01904 455080

20.2

Output and input volume indices
United Kingdom
Calendar years

1995=100

		1988	1989	1990	1991	1992	1993	1994	1995	1996	1997	1998
10. **Gross output** (at basic prices)[4,5]	LULY	94.8	97.1	97.3	98.5	100.1	97.5	99.5	100.0	100.2	100.8	100.5
of which												
transactions within the agricultural industry												
feed wheat	LULZ	108.2	110.2	112.2	161.0	190.4	141.2	145.7	100.0	119.8	139.3	130.4
feed barley	LUMA	100.6	103.4	108.8	120.9	124.3	107.3	105.0	100.0	105.2	113.1	100.0
feed oats	LUMB	101.9	100.2	99.6	114.1	92.4	97.7	124.6	100.0	92.8	88.6	98.3
seed potatoes	LUMC	131.8	138.5	139.9	125.0	175.1	134.7	100.2	100.0	112.2	123.2	101.9
straw	LUMD	100.0	100.0	100.0	100.0	100.0	100.0	100.0	100.0	100.0	100.0	100.0
contract work	LUME	68.4	70.5	86.3	74.4	63.5	72.9	77.6	100.0	84.5	73.3	69.5
leasing of quota	LUMF	96.2	93.7	92.4	89.9	89.9	91.6	94.4	100.0	104.6	107.3	111.0
total capital formation in livestock	LUMG	30.6	41.2	52.3	60.4	63.2	79.3	90.5	100.0	101.5	109.6	117.1
Intermediate Consumption (formerly known as inputs)[5] (Expenditure net of reclaimed VAT)												
Feedingstuffs:												
compounds	LUMH	153.8	150.6	150.3	148.3	95.0	97.8	100.0	100.0	101.1	96.9	102.0
straights	LUMI	88.1	88.1	88.1	88.1	88.1	93.0	99.1	100.0	90.3	88.3	83.1
feed purchased from other farms	LUMJ	102.2	104.4	108.8	128.2	135.2	113.2	114.3	100.0	107.5	117.0	106.2
other costs	LUMK	94.0	94.0	94.0	94.0	94.0	97.4	100.4	100.0	99.0	98.3	100.4
13. Total feedingstuffs	LUML	100.8	99.1	99.4	100.1	96.9	97.9	101.1	100.0	99.2	96.1	97.0
Seeds:												
cereals	LUMM	125.3	119.3	111.4	107.0	92.8	95.9	95.1	100.0	104.5	104.6	96.9
other	LUMN	91.9	94.2	106.9	102.0	107.7	103.4	100.4	100.0	100.3	99.6	99.1
14. Total seeds	LUMO	103.8	103.3	108.6	103.9	102.1	100.6	98.5	100.0	101.6	101.2	98.4
15. Total fertilisers and lime	LUMP	91.1	98.2	101.1	100.8	99.4	95.1	100.7	100.0	97.7	98.5	100.5
16. Pesticides	LUMQ	101.0	110.8	99.9	97.1	93.1	94.5	92.1	100.0	101.4	105.5	108.5
Farm maintenance:[6]												
occupier	LUMR	83.8	83.2	79.1	77.0	85.7	90.9	99.0	100.0	96.2	95.2	88.9
landlord	LUMS	110.8	108.4	106.5	106.5	105.6	104.7	102.7	100.0	98.0	96.2	95.4
17. Total farm maintenance	LUMT	88.4	87.4	83.7	82.1	89.0	93.2	99.6	100.0	96.5	95.4	90.0
Miscellaneous expenditure:												
machinery repairs	LUMU	111.7	107.0	102.9	102.4	93.8	94.8	91.1	100.0	97.5	94.0	92.4
machinery fuel and oil	LUMV	123.4	109.8	108.7	108.7	105.7	105.1	104.1	100.0	96.6	95.4	93.8
veterinary expenses and medicines	LUMW	70.3	74.9	78.4	79.1	81.1	87.7	95.0	100.0	99.9	102.2	97.6
power and fuel (mainly electricity)	LUMX	102.6	91.5	92.2	104.3	96.7	97.8	100.1	100.0	99.8	99.1	100.7
imported livestock	LUMY	370.7	260.9	240.1	181.4	209.3	125.3	124.2	100.0	85.3	108.4	76.4
straw for bedding	LUMZ	68.4	70.5	86.3	74.4	63.5	72.9	77.6	100.0	84.5	73.3	69.5
contract work	LUNA	96.2	93.7	92.4	89.9	89.9	91.6	94.4	100.0	104.6	107.3	111.0
leasing of quota	LUNB	30.6	41.2	52.3	60.4	63.2	79.3	90.5	100.0	101.5	109.6	117.1
other farming costs[6,7]	LUNC	87.9	92.4	89.6	92.4	95.4	98.5	101.5	100.0	99.3	101.7	102.4
18. Total miscellaneous expenses	LUND	93.7	93.0	92.4	93.2	92.0	94.5	96.7	100.0	98.5	99.1	99.0
19. Total intermediate consumption (formerly known as Gross input)[5]	LUNE	96.2	96.5	96.2	96.3	94.5	95.8	98.3	100.0	98.9	98.5	98.8
20. **Gross Value Added** (10-19)[5]	LUNF	93.2	97.8	98.5	100.9	106.5	99.3	100.8	100.0	101.5	103.3	102.1
Consumption of fixed capital:												
buildings and works	LUNG	98.2	98.7	99.2	99.6	99.7	99.8	100.0	100.0	99.5	98.8	97.8
landlord[6] other	LUNH	112.0	110.5	109.1	107.5	105.7	103.7	102.0	100.0	97.5	94.8	91.9
plant, machinery and vehicles	LUNI	106.9	105.7	103.9	102.0	100.1	99.1	99.3	100.0	101.5	101.9	100.3
cattle	LUNJ	79.9	83.4	82.4	95.6	79.4	87.7	87.4	100.0	104.7	93.7	93.2
sheep	LUNK	68.8	78.4	82.8	76.7	81.8	86.0	102.4	100.0	96.8	79.5	79.6
pigs	LUNL	105.1	91.9	91.5	103.2	104.0	101.0	109.8	100.0	92.1	101.1	111.1
poultry	LUNM	99.2	101.6	94.6	93.9	95.6	92.1	98.3	100.0	102.7	102.9	109.8
21. Total consumption of Fixed Capital	LUNN	96.0	97.0	96.3	97.1	94.5	95.5	96.9	100.0	101.2	98.7	98.0
22. **Net value added** (at basic prices)[5]	LUNO	91.8	97.9	99.2	102.4	111.9	100.8	102.4	100.0	101.6	105.0	103.6

See footnotes on the first part of this table.

Source: Ministry of Agriculture, Fisheries and Food: 01904 455080

20.3 Agriculture-land use
United Kingdom
Area at the June census[1]

Thousand hectares

		1989	1990	1991	1992	1993	1994	1995	1996	1997	1998	1999
Total Agricultural area	KFEU	18 929	18 884	18 854	18 849	18 890	18 850	18 746	18 753	18 653	18 593	18 579
Crops	KSJA	5 139	5 015	4 957	4 982	4 520	4 470	4 544	4 722	4 990	4 972	4 709
Bare fallow	KIJQ	69	68	67	53	50	46	43	37	29	34	33
Total tillage	KIJR	5 208	5 082	5 025	5 035	4 569	4 516	4 586	4 759	5 020	5 005	4 742
All grass under 5 years old	KFEM	1 561	1 606	1 608	1 584	1 582	1 456	1 407	1 395	1 405	1 303	1 226
Total arable land	KFEN	6 770	6 689	6 633	6 618	6 152	5 972	5 993	6 154	6 425	6 308	5 968
All grasses 5 years old and over	KFEO	5 303	5 316	5 327	5 279	5 274	5 388	5 375	5 354	5 282	5 350	5 449
Total tillage and grass	KFEP	12 073	12 005	11 960	11 897	11 426	11 360	11 368	11 507	11 706	11 658	11 417
Sole right rough grazing	KFEQ	4 997	4 965	4 950	4 943	4 879	4 825	4 785	4 760	4 657	4 624	4 575
Set aside[2]	KSJB	..	72	97	160	677	728	633	509	306	314	572
All other land on agricultural holdings including woodland	KSJC	623	607	614	618	680	712	734	751	763	777	789
Total land on agricultural holdings	KSJD	17 693	17 648	17 620	17 619	17 661	17 626	17 520	17 527	17 432	17 372	17 352
Common rough grazing (estimated)	KFER	1 236	1 236	1 233	1 230	1 229	1 224	1 226	1 226	1 221	1 221	1 227
Crops	KSJE	5 139	5 015	4 957	4 982	4 520	4 470	4 544	4 722	4 990	4 972	4 709
Cereals	KSJF	3 876	3 660	3 502	3 489	3 033	3 043	3 182	3 359	3 514	3 420	3 141
Wheat	KFDA	2 083	2 014	1 981	2 067	1 759	1 811	1 859	1 976	2 036	2 045	1 847
Barley	KFDB	1 654	1 518	1 395	1 299	1 166	1 108	1 193	1 269	1 359	1 255	1 179
Oats	KFDC	119	107	104	100	92	109	112	96	100	98	92
Mixed corn	KFDD	5	4	4	4	3	3	3	3	2	2	2
Rye[3]	KFDE	7	8	9	8	6	7	8	8	9	10	8
Triticale[4]	KIHX	8	9	11	11	7	6	7	7	8	10	13
Other arable crops (excluding potatoes)	KSJG	881	970	1 074	1 115	1 128	1 073	1 003	996	1 126	1 193	1 211
Oilseed rape	KFEH	321	390	440	421	377	404	354	356	445	506	417
Sugar beet not for stock feeding[5]	KFEG	197	194	196	197	197	195	196	199	196	189	183
Hops[6]	KIHZ	4	4	4	4	3	3	3	3	3	3	3
Peas for harvesting dry and field beans	KSJH	215	216	203	208	244	228	195	178	197	213	202
Linseed[7]	KSJI	17	34	92	144	150	58	54	49	73	99	209
Other crops	KSJJ	127	132	141	141	157	185	201	211	211	211	197
Potatoes	KGRS	175	177	177	181	171	164	172	178	166	164	178
Horticultural	KSJK	208	208	204	198	188	189	187	189	185	177	179
Vegetables grown in the open	KSJL	141	142	139	135	126	127	130	132	126	123	126
Orchard fruit	KSJM	36	34	34	33	32	32	28	28	30	28	28
Soft fruit	KSJN	15	15	15	14	13	13	12	12	11	10	9
Ornamentals[8]	KSJO	14	14	14	14	14	14	15	14	14	13	12
Glasshouse crops	KFEF	2	2	2	2	2	2	2	2	2	2	2

1 Includes estimates for minor holdings for all countries. In previous editions minor holdings were excluded for Scotland and therefore data here will differ from previous editions. Also, Northern Ireland data are now based on all active farm business.

2 Figures are for England only in 1990 and 1991 and Great Britain only in 1992.

3 Figures are for England and Wales only.

4 Figures are for Great Britain only.

5 Figures are for England and Wales only.

6 Figures are for England and Wales only for 1989 and England only from 1990.

7 Figures are for England and Wales only from 1989 to 1991 and 1992 Great Britain only.

8 Includes non-commercial orchards.

Source: Agricultural Departments: 01904 455332

20.4 Estimated quantity of crops and grass harvested[1,2]
United Kingdom

Thousand tonnes

		1989	1990	1991	1992	1993	1994	1995	1996	1997	1998	1999
Cereals												
Wheat	KFQA	14 033	14 035	14 362	14 095	12 890	13 320	14 310	16 100	15 020	15 470	14 870
Barley	KFQB	8 073	7 911	7 632	7 368	6 050	5 950	6 840	7 790	7 830	6 630	6 580
Oats	KFQC	529	520	522	503	480	600	615	590	575	585	540
Mixed corn for threshing	KFQD	18	17	15	16	14	13	16	12	11	6	10
Rye for threshing	KFQE	36	40	49	37	30	43	43	51	53	42	45
Maize for threshing[3]	KFQF	940	1 035	1 695	1 975	2 730	..	..	..	..	..	..
Potatoes												
Early crop[4]	KFQG	366	437	359	411	426	337	373	325	386	336	341
Main crop[4]	KFQH	5 956	6 106	6 000	7 402	6 647	6 203	6 033	6 900	6 739	6 081	6 759
Fodder crops												
Beans for stockfeeding	KFQI	450	474	423	445	612	454	319	318	377	378	397
Turnips, swedes[5]	KFQJ	905	920	835	760	620	..	..	..	..	..	..
Fodder beet and mangolds[5]	KFQK	600	640	715	710	655	..	..	..	..	..	..
Maize for threshing or stock-feeding[3]	KFQL	940	..	..	..	..	..	..	..	..	..	..
Kale, cabbage, savoys and kohl rabi	KFQN	565	535	610	515	485	..	..	..	..	..	..
Peas harvested dry for stock-feeding	KFQP	277	320	224	209	266	246	229	239	297	259	284
Other crops												
Sugar beet[6]	KFQQ	8 115	7 902	8 701	10 148	9 666	8 720	8 431	10 420	11 084	10 002	10 328
Rape grown for oilseed	KFQR	950	1 258	1 278	1 166	1 100	1 243	1 224	1 412	1 527	1 569	..
Hops	KFQS	5	5	6	5	6	5	4	6	5	4	..
Horticultural crops												
Vegetables grown in the open												
Brussels sprouts	KFQW	124	100	97	115	98	105	78	80	78	73	79
Cabbage (including savoys and spring greens)	KFQX	460	393	388	402	381	401	342	360	310	284	272
Cauliflowers	KFQY	308	306	312	341	310	289	243	238	195	192	173
Carrots	KFQZ	503	486	544	608	591	633	512	624	623	618	675
Parsnips	KFRA	47	47	49	60	64	70	63	75	96	91	91
Turnips and swedes	KFRB	140	128	156	158	141	139	125	139	116	118	125
Beetroot	KFRC	93	89	87	74	93	87	73	72	74	70	63
Onions, Dry bulb	KFRD	256	217	213	235	274	274	225	285	336	342	391
Onions, Salad	KFRE	30	20	23	28	24	25	24	28	26	25	26
Leeks	KFRF	66	64	68	72	60	61	62	54	46	52	52
Broad beans	KFRG	12	13	20	17	11	12	11	10	10	13	12
Runner beans including French	KFRH	44	28	37	39	46	36	30	35	35	30	24
Peas, Green for market	KFRI	8	8	8	6	6	6	8	7	8	7	7
Peas, Green for processing	KFRJ	206	238	223	211	209	181	198	216	168	152	143
Celery	KFRK	56	46	49	44	41	42	39	38	39	35	40
Lettuce	KFRL	206	197	194	206	145	178	192	188	158	152	155
Rhubarb	KFRM	30	27	28	21	20	21	20	20	20	21	23
Protected crops												
Tomatoes	KFRN	130	134	133	122	110	108	113	117	115	109	117
Cucumbers	KFRO	96	101	104	90	104	83	88	86	82	84	84
Lettuce	KFRP	48	50	47	44	37	34	31	28	25	21	20
Fruit crops												
Total Dessert Apples	KFRQ	202.4	179.0	148.3	164.7	167.1	175.9	138.5	105.4	96.0	97.8	133.9
Total Culinary Apples	KFRR	197.7	125.7	157.2	161.8	158.7	130.2	134.9	118.5	91.1	85.9	114.1
Pears	KFRS	36.9	34.1	36.0	30.8	30.7	32.5	29.7	35.8	33.0	26.3	22.7
Plums	KFRT	10.7	7.2	21.5	21.1	11.8	11.0	14.4	19.6	12.1	6.4	9.3
Cherries	KFRU	3.2	1.5	1.0	3.8	2.4	1.3	3.5	3.6	0.6	0.9	1.3
Soft fruit	KFRV	101.5	102.3	102.0	95.0	92.5	76.2	75.6	80.8	58.0	59.6	67.9

1 For vegetables; output marketed for the calendar year; for horticultural crops output marketed for the crop year.

2 Except for sugar beet and hops, the production area for England and Wales is the area returned at the June census together with estimates for very small holdings (known as minor holdings). In Scotland and Northern Ireland the area returned at June is also the production area except that estimates for minor holdings are included in Scotland for potatoes and in Nothern Ireland for barley, oats and potatoes.

3 From 1979 maize for threshing is included with maize for stockfeeding.

4 Revised basis of calculation adopted which prevents direct comparison with post - 1980 figures and earlier years.

5 Before 1977 fodder beet was included with turnips and swedes for stockfeeding. In 1977, as a result of changes in the census categories, fodder beet was included with mangolds in England and Wales but continued to be included with turnips and swedes for stockfeeding in Scotland and Northern Ireland. Scotland collected fodder beet separately for the first time in 1986.

6 From 1991 figures are adjusted to constant 16% sugar content.

Source: Agricultural Departments: 01904 455332

20.5 Cattle, sheep, pigs and poultry on agricultural holdings[1]
United Kingdom
At June each year

Thousands

		1989	1990	1991	1992	1993	1994	1995	1996	1997	1998	1999
Total cattle and calves	KFSB	12 101	12 192	12 003	11 924	11 851	11 954	11 857	12 040	116 637	11 519	11 423
of which:												
dairy cows	KFCT	2 866	2 848	2 771	2 683	2 668	2 716	2 603	2 587	2 478	2 439	2 440
beef cows	KFCU	1 525	1 632	1 700	1 731	1 784	1 809	1 840	1 864	1 862	1 947	1 924
heifers in calf	KFCV	799	763	738	768	803	775	775	818	848	787	763
Total sheep and lambs	KFSG	43 588	44 469	44 166	44 540	44 436	43 813	43 304	42 086	42 823	44 471	44 656
of which:												
ewes and shearlings	KSJP	20 368	20 787	20 665	20 732	20 881	20 861	20 830	20 550	20 696	21 260	21 458
lambs under one year old	KFSF	21 897	22 380	22 213	22 607	22 394	21 758	21 350	20 443	21 032	22 138	22 092
Total pigs[2]	KFSQ	7 606	7 548	7 695	7 707	7 853	7 892	7 627	7 590	8 072	8 146	7 284
of which:												
sows in pig and other sows for breeding	KSJQ	671	671	690	683	698	691	654	649	683	675	603
gilts in pig	KSJR	98	110	109	110	117	106	101	107	116	103	85
Total fowls	KFSV	121 029	125 357	128 025	124 842	131 093	126 653	127 035	..	..	..	149 867
of which:												
table fowls including broilers	KFSU	70 509	73 944	76 111	73 748	79 940	75 696	77 177	..	106 937	98 244	101 625
laying fowls[3]	KFSS	34 101	33 624	33 416	33 348	32 965	32 682	31 837	..	34 286	29 483	29 258
growing pullets	KFSR	9 487	10 530	11 102	10 849	10 750	10 388	10 210	..	11 510	9 860	9 583

1 Includes estimates for minor holdings for all countries. In previous editions minor holdings were excluded for Scotland and therefore data here will differ from previous editions. Also Northern Ireland data are now based on all active farm business.
2 Figures for Scotland and Northern Ireland have been revised and therefore data here will differ from previous editions.
3 Excludes fowls laying eggs for hatching.

Source: Agricultural Departments: 01904 455332

20.6 Forestry
Years ending 31 March

Area - thousand hectares, Volume - million cubic metres

		1989/90	1990/91	1991/92	1992/93	1993/94	1994/95	1995/96	1996/97	1997/98	1998/99	1999/00
Forest area[1]												
United Kingdom	KUAA	2 400	2 411	2 427	2 438	2 455	2 469	2 485	2 504	2 521	2 659	2 795
Great Britain	KUAB	2 326	2 336	2 350	2 361	2 377	2 390	2 405	2 423	2 440	2 577	2 713
Northern Ireland	KUAC	74	75	77	77	78	79	80	81	81	82	82
Forestry Commission (Great Britain)												
Productive woodland	KUAD	864[5]	859	855	845	827	815	804	795	785	780	774
Net disposals of forestry land[2]	KUAE	5.1	2.2	4.7	6.5	14.1	9.6	8.2	9.6	10.3	4.1	4.3
New planting[3]	KUAF	4.1	3.5	3.0	2.4	1.4	0.9	0.4	0.5	0.1	0.1	–
Restocking[3]	KUAG	7.9	7.6	8.3	8.5	7.9	7.9	7.5	7.9	7.8	7.9	8.2
Volume of timber removed[4]	KUAH	3.5	3.4	3.9	4.1	4.3	4.3	4.2	4.7	4.7	5.3	5.6
Total estates	KUAI	1 140	1 133	1 128	1 115	1 100	1 089	1 080	1 073	1 062	1 057	1 053
Private forestry (Great Britain)												
Productive woodland	KUAJ	1 266	1 281	1 298	1 317	1 344	1 367	1 392	1 417	1 444	1 542	1 673
New planting[3]	KUAK	15.6	15.6	14.3	15.5	16.1	18.5	15.3	16.4	16.2	16.2	17.0
Restocking[3]	KUAL	6.3	7.2	7.9	8.1	8.5	6.2	5.8	6.6	5.6	5.5	6.4
Volume of timber removed[4]	KUAM	3.6	3.3	3.1	2.9	3.0	3.8	4.2	4.0	4.4	3.9	3.8
State afforestation in Northern Ireland												
Land under plantation	KUAN	58.5	58.8	60.6	60.8	60.8	61.0	61.0	60.9	61.0	61.0	60.8
Plantable land acquired during year	KUAO	0.6	0.4	0.3	0.4	0.4	0.1	0.1	0.1	0.1	0.3	0.1
Total area planted during year	KUAP	1.0	1.0	0.9	0.9	0.8	0.8	0.8	0.6	0.7	0.7	0.7
Total estates	KUAQ	74.6	74.8	75.1	75.2	75.5	75.5	75.3	75.5	75.5	75.7	75.7

1 Includes unproductive woodland.
2 Disposals less acquisitions, for plantations and plantable land.
3 New planting is planting on ground not previously carrying forest; Restocking is replacing trees after felling.

4 Standing volume overbark; private forestry figures are for calendar years ending previous December.
5 The apparent decrease in 1989/90 is mainly the result of re-classification of certain woodland types within the Forestry Commission.

Sources: Forest Service Agency, DARDNI;
Forestry Commission: 0131 334 0303

Agriculture, fisheries and food

20.7 Average weekly earnings and hours of male agricultural workers[1,2,3]
England and Wales
For the month of September 1995 to 1999

		1995	1996	1997	1998	1999
Average weekly earnings (£) 95% confidence interval	LQML	272.27 (+/-£10.02)	288.33 (+/-£13.59)	286.01 (+/-£11.57)	301.24 (+/-£12.69)	301.22 (+/-£11.88
Average weekly hours worked 95% confidence interval	LQMM	50.5 (+/-1.4)	52.4 (+/-1.8)	50.9 (+/-1.3)	50.7 (+/-1.5)	50.9 (+/-1.4)
Average earnings/hours (£) 95% confidence interval	LQMN	5.39 (+/-£0.10)	5.50 (+/-£0.12)	5.62 (+/-£0.12)	5.94 (+/-£0.18)	5.92 (+/-£0.15)
Number of workers in the sample		239	172	244	274	292

1 Total earnings of regular full time male workers, including all payments-in-kind, valued where applicable in accordance with the Agricultural Wages Order.
2 Aged 20 and over in September 1994 and 19 and over from September 1995.
3 Results exclude earnings and hours of hire farm managers.

Source: Agricultural Departments: 01904 455332

20.8 Average weekly earnings and hours of different types of agricultural workers[1,2]
England and Wales
For the month of September 1999

	Full time		Part time[3]		Casual[4]		
	Male	Female	Male	Female	Male	Female	Managers
Average weekly earnings (£) 95% confidence interval	301.22 (+/-£11.88)	225.58 (+/-£11.58)	113.87 (+/-£14.64)	99.60 (+/-£9.99)	167.50 (+/-£18.67)	109.57 (+/-£12.20)	437.26 (+/-£29.71)
Average weekly hours worked 95% confidence interval	50.9 (+/-£1.4)	42.5 (+/-£1.1)	22.1 (+/-£2.3)	21.5 (+/-£1.7)	34.3 (+/-£3.2)	25.6 (+/-£2.8)	..
Average earnings/hour (£) 95% confidence interval	5.92 (+/-£0.15)	5.31 (+/-£0.22)	5.15 (+/-£0.39)	4.63 (+/-£0.23)	4.89 (+/-£0.20)	4.29 (+/-£0.15)	..
Number of workers in the sample	292	103	114	124	183	124	129

1 Total earnings of workers, including all payments-in-kind, valued where applicable in accordance with the Agricultural Wages Order.
2 Aged 19 and over.
3 Part time workers are defined as working less than 39 basic hours per week.
4 Casual workers are employed on a temporary basis.

Source: Agricultural Departments: 01904 455332

20.9 Sales for food of agricultural produce and livestock
United Kingdom

		Unit	1989	1990	1991	1992	1993	1994	1995	1996	1997	1998	1999
Cereals:		Thousand											
Wheat[1,2]	KCQK	tonnes	4 228	4 347	4 269	4 212	3 865	4 234	4 674	4 845	4 749	4 662	4 818
Barley	KCQL	"	5 026	3 791	3 849	3 599	2 762	3 190	3 776	3 692	3 411	3 483	3 410
Oats[3]	KCQM	"	239	222	215	222	208	215	216	235	259	273	270
Potatoes[4]	KCQN	"	6 085	5 911	5 799	5 994	6 357	6 491	5 923	6 123	6 261	5 986	5 863
Milk[5]:													
Milk utilised for liquid consumption	KCQO	Million litres	6 859	6 892	6 893	6 966	7 026	6 926	6 922	6 838	6 748	6 739	6 853
Milk utilised for manufacture	KCQP	Million litres	7 258	7 489	7 022	6 876	6 880	7 134	6 918	6 934	7 059	6 875	7 041
Total milk available for domestic use[6]	KCQQ	Million litres	14 485	14 751	14 282	14 189	14 228	14 420	14 255	14 194	14 258	13 973	14 238
Hen eggs in shell	KCQR	Million dozens	763	804	818	806	791	787	774	775	794	792	743
Animals slaughtered:													
Cattle and calves:													
Cattle	KCQS	Thousands	3 414	3 478	3 568	3 355	2 944	3 089	3 266	2 291	2 264	2 297	2 217
Calves	KCQT	"	28	46	49	33	19	22	26	24	20	32	75
Total	KCQU	"	3 442	3 524	3 617	3 387	2 963	3 112	3 292	2 315	2 284	2 329	2 292
Sheep and lambs	KCQV	"	19 618	20 012	20 918	19 428	18 864	18 962	19 311	18 049	16 660	18 688	19 116
Pigs:													
For bacon:													
Used wholly[7]	KCQW	"	1 966	1 903	14 091	14 143	14 265	14 681	14 021	13 897	15 132	15 872	14 350
Used in part	KCQX	"	3 449	3 281	..	..	..	..	..	..	..	..	..
Other uses	KCQY	"	8 767	8 694	..	..	..	..	..	..	..	..	..
Sows and boars	KCQZ	"	331	325	366	373	356	389	355	324	363	415	379
Total	KCRA	"	14 514	14 203	14 457	14 515	14 620	15 069	14 376	14 221	15 496	16 286	14 728
Poultry:[8] slaughtered	KCRB	Millions	644	670	693	689	715	807	774	814	842	844	833

TIME SERIES. The figures for cereals and for animals slaughtered relate to periods of 52 weeks (53 weeks in 1987, 1992 and 1998).

1 Flour millers' receipts of home-grown wheat.
2 Following the receipt of additional data, figures have been revised back to 1992 and are not strictly compatible with those for earlier years.
3 Oatmeal millers' receipts of home-grown oats.
4 Total sales for human consumption in the UK.

5 Data to 1994 sourced from the Milk Marketing Boards. Data from 1995 sourced from surveys run by the agricultural departments. 1994 includes two months of data sourced from the surveys run by the agricultural departments.
6 The totals of liquid consumption and milk used for manufacture may not add up to the total available for domestic use because of adjustments for dairy wastage, stock changes and other uses, such as farmhouse consumption, milk fed to stock and on farm waste.
7 From 1991, data series quotes the number of clean pigs slaughtered for all pig meat.
8 Total fowls, ducks, geese and turkeys.

Source: Ministry of Agriculture, Fisheries and Food: 01904 455332

20.10 Stocks of food and feedingstuffs[1]
United Kingdom

At end-December in each year

Thousand tonnes

		1989	1990	1991	1992	1993	1994	1995	1996	1997	1998	1999
Wheat and flour (as wheat)	KCRC	918	860	1 461	1 839	1 255	1 236	1 036	1 012	984	1 047	848
Barley (GB only)	KCRD	1 043	1 120	1 489	2 028	1 401	1 375	1 542	1 502	1 441	1 224	1 373
Maize	KCRE	70	41	36	109	23	32	33	25	45	67	43
Oilcake and meal[2]	KCRF	148	153	93	107	92	108	103	89	79	69	72
Oilseeds and nuts (crude oil equivalent)	KCRG	24	25	18	11	17	28	34	25	18	12	18
Vegetable oil (as crude oil)	KCRI	85	109	89	94	90	109	96	100	99	98	97
Marine oil (as crude oil)	KCRJ	11	9	9	8	8	18	17	10	4	–	–
Butter[3]	KCRK	55	74	65	63	34	19	11	14	7	11	22
Meat and offal[4]	KCRL	85.0	150.8	212.0	218.2	198.7	102.5	76.9	129.5	161.9	156.8	84.2
Raw coffee[5]	KCRM	7	11	10	10	12	13	11	8	7	8	7
Tea[6]	KCRN	51	48	43	40	44	43	38	39	37	38	38
Sugar	KCRO	860	824	824	888	1 069	1 016	766	807	1 003	928	..
Chocolate and sugar confectionery[7]	KCRP	..	..	..	..	..	..	..	..	..	..	..

1 Recorded stocks, including stocks in bond or held by the main processors.
2 Excluding castor meal, cocoa cake and meal.
3 In addition to stocks in public cold stores surveyed by MAFF, closing stocks include all intervention stocks in private cold stores.

4 Stocks of imported and home-produced meat and offal held in public cold stores, excluding poultrymeat, bacon and ham.
5 Including manufacturers' stocks and additional public warehouses.
6 Covering stocks held by primary wholesalers and held in public/private warehouses.
7 Manufacturers' stocks only.

Source: Ministry of Agriculture, Fisheries and Food: 01904 455332

20.11 Processed food and animal feedingstuffs: production
United Kingdom

Thousand tonnes

		1989	1990	1991	1992	1993	1994	1995	1996	1997	1998	1999
Flour milling:												
Wheat milling: total[8]	KFTA	5 032	4 875	4 796	5 022	5 236	5 290	5 338	5 501	5 535	5 707	5 668
Home produced[8]	KFTB	4 161	4 273	4 185	4 192	3 781	4 106	4 598	4 772	4 667	4 582	4 701
Imported	KFTC	871	605	611	830	1 455	1 184	740	729	868	1 125	966
Flour produced[8]	KFTD	3 928	3 879	3 851	3 975	4 120	4 232	4 292	4 454	4 439	4 526	4 497
Offals produced[8]	KFTE	1 076	999	968	1 045	1 123	1 078	1 079	1 111	1 112	1 221	1 181
Oat milling:												
Oats milled by oatmeal millers	KFTF	221	231	216	225	207	209	217	250	259	272	266
Products of oat milling	KFTG	129	132	124	124	105	102	110	123	129	154	157
Seed crushing:												
Oilseeds and nuts processed	KFTH	1 725	1 877	1 710	1 807	1 903	2 035	2 122	2 466	2 587	2 683	2 398
Crude oil produced, including production of maize oil	KFTI	589	630	583	636	658	739	779	862	909	915	832
Oilcake and meal produced, excluding castor meal, cocoa cake and meal	KFTJ	1 077	1 193	1 081	1 125	1 187	1 242	1 305	1 541	1 614	1 687	1 484
Production of home-killed meat: total including meat subsequently canned	KFTK	2 330	2 376	2 455	2 392	2 262	2 358	2 376	2 080	2 150	2 265	2 130
Beef	KFTL	976	1 000	1 018	970	858	915	973	701	695	704	675
Veal	KFTM	1	2	2	1	1	1	1	1	1	1	2
Mutton and lamb	KFTN	366	370	385	362	349	352	364	345	321	356	361
Pork	KFTO	718	735	772	786	783	807	761	778	875	937	829
Offal[1]	KFTP	268	270	278	274	270	284	277	255	258	267	261
Production of poultry meat[2]	KFTQ	1 116	1 148	1 211	1 226	1 289	1 344	1 397	1 461	1 502	..	..
Production of bacon and ham, including meat subsequently canned	KFTR	204	191	193	189	216	233	245	241	239	236	233
Production of milk products:												
Butter[3]	KFTS	140	151	132	127	141	148	133	130	139	137	141
Cheese (including farmhouse)	KFTT	288	320	309	332	338	341	362	377	377	366	368
Condensed milk: includes skim concentrate and condensed milk used in manufacture of chocolate crumb	KFTU	207	204	198	206	191	196	181	206	214	192	177
Milk powder: excluding buttermilk and whey powder												
Full cream	KFTV	95	70	79	84	71	83	90	83	96	97	102
Skimmed	KFTW	133	166	143	106	132	142	117	108	109	107	102
Cream, fresh and sterilised; including farm cream[3]	KFTX	208	230	254	240	255	274	281	281	268	266	275
Sugar: production from home-grown sugar-beet (as refined sugar)	KFTY	1 267	1 241	1 220	1 472	1 433	1 263	1 469	1 324	1 524	1 557	..
Production of compound fats:												
Margarine and other table spreads[4]	KFTZ	489	486	481	477	493	487	490	491	461	448	421
Solid cooking fats	KFUA	121	122	117	116	129	109	110	123	109	131	125
Production of other processed foods:												
Jam and marmalade	KFUB	181	–	..	..	..	..	..	..	..	..	..
Syrup and treacle[6]	KFUC	52	51	51	49	52	50	48	–	–	..	..
Canned vegetables[5]	KFUD	732[3]	–	–	..	..	..	..	..	..	..	..
Canned and bottled fruit[5]	KFUE	37	..	..	..	..	..	..	..	..	..	..
Chocolate confectionery	KSJS	498	539	534	532	563	573	592	608	569	568	553
Sugar confectionery	KSJT	309	320	303	300	302	322	322	351	345	337	317
Cocoa beans excluding re-exports	KFVX	115	125	148	159	171	163	160	189	174	172	168
Soups, canned and powdered	KFUF	–	..	..	..	..	..	..	..	..	..	..
Canned meat	KFUG	118	91	147	..	..	..	..	..	..	..	..
Canned fish	KFUH	9	..	..	..	..	..	..	..	..	..	..
Biscuits, total disposals of home produced	KFUI	–	–	..	..	..	..	..	..	..	..	..
Breakfast cereals, other than oatmeal and oatmeal flakes	KFUJ	278	286	290	303	302	325	335	343	359	349	354
Glucose	KFUM	542	546	557	568	580	593	607	642	637	644	630
Production of soft drinks (million litres):												
Concentrated	KFUN	555	557	..	..	..	..	..	..	..	..	..
Unconcentrated	KFUO	4 112	4 316	..	..	..	..	..	..	..	..	..
Compound feedingstuffs: total[7]	KFUP	10 713	10 564	10 374	10 514	11 141	11 402	11 609	11 801	11 304	11 206	11 404
Cattle food[7]	KFUQ	3 947	3 909	3 798	4 098	4 271	4 347	4 476	4 430	3 926	3 844	4 264
Calf food[7]	KFUR	347	324	280	242	261	286	307	277	227	198	187
Pig food[7]	KFUS	2 158	2 276	2 361	2 489	2 561	2 547	2 453	2 566	2 759	2 740	2 435
Poultry food[9]	KFUT	3 216	3 212	3 062	2 737	3 123	3 179	3 243	3 286	3 324	3 213	3 139
Other compounds[7]	KFUU	1 045	843	873	948	925	1 043	1 130	1 249	1 168	1 210	1 378

TIME SERIES. The figures relate to periods of 52 weeks (53 weeks in 1987, 1992 and 1998) with the following exceptions which are on a calendar year basis: butter, cheese, cream, canned meat, soft drinks, condensed milk and milk powder, canned vegetables, canned and bottled fruit, jam and marmalade, and soups.

Please note production of Poultry Feed by Integrated Poultry Units has been;

1992 = 2 555 ('000) tonnes
1993 = 2 679 ('000) tonnes
1994 = 2 767 ('000) tonnes
1995 = 2 892 ('000) tonnes
1996 = 3 012 ('000) tonnes
1997 = 3 072 ('000) tonnes
1998= 3 105 ('000) tonnes
1999= 2 943 ('000) tonnes

These figures have been revised following the receipt of more up-to-date information.

1 Including poultry offal.
2 Total of fowl, ducks, geese and turkeys (carcass weight).
3 Includes cream from the residual elements of low fat milk production.
4 Table spreads are only included from 1986 onwards.

5 From 1981 the method of collecting these figures has changed. They are therefore not comparable with previous years.
6 This survey ceased at the end of 1995.
7 Figures from 1992 onwards have been revised to include data on blended cattle and sheep feeds and are therefore not strictly compatible with earlier years. In 1996, mainly as a result of the introduction of the Beef Assurance Scheme, the Ministry became aware of a number of feed mills that it had not been surveying. Data from these mills has now been included in these figures back to 1992. Total production from these mills has been in the range of 110 000 to 135 000 tonnes each year.
8 Following the receipt of additional data, figures have been revised back to 1992 and are not strictly compatible with those for earlier years.
9 It was found that data for Poultry food had previously contained some mills whose production or part of their production should have been recorded against the Integrated Poultyr Unit (IPU) series. Production for these sites has now been moved from the Poultry food series to the IPU series. This data was available from 1992 onwards. Earlier years have been estimated in order to make the Poultry food series comparable.

Source: Ministry of Agriculture, Fisheries and Food: 01904 455332

20.12 Food and animal feedingstuffs: disposals

Thousand tonnes

		1989	1990	1991	1992	1993	1994	1995	1996	1997	1998	1999
Flour[8]	KFPU	3 858	3 830	3 798	3 932	4 076	4 200	4 290	4 457	4 434	4 528	4 487
Sugar (as refined sugar): total disposals	KFPV	2 354	2 332	2 297	2 319	2 154	2 196	2 177	2 200	2 040	2 143	..
For food in the United Kingdom[1]	KFPW	2 336	2 320	2 280	2 292	2 123	2 165	2 157	2 180	2 007	2 106	..
Syrup and treacle[5]	KFPX	52	51	51	49	52	50	48	–	–	..	..
Meat and fish:												
Fresh and frozen meat and offal, including usage for canning:												
Beef and veal	KFPY	1 219	1 104	1 130	1 145	1 094	1 228	1 206	804	865	872	942
Mutton and lamb	KFPZ	506	517	511	497	470	474	504	501	468	496	497
Pork	KFVA	811	814	847	877	895	922	926	963	1 039	1 116	1 062
Offal[6]	KFVB	345	329	324	335	316	327	337	297	308	303	310
Poultry-meat[3,4]	KFVC	1 160	1 217	1 257	1 338	1 373	1 744	1 486	1 567	1 550	1 636	1 672
Bacon and ham, including usage for canning	KFVD	463	451	446	428	453	457	473	502	477	468	461
Dairy products:												
Butter	KFVI	283	245	245	258	279	284	255	240	256	238	244
Cheese	KFVJ	476	515	509	560	523	559	577	617	614	632	645
Condensed milk[2]	KFVK	212	218	211	218	202	208	195	217	229	205	190
Milk powder, excluding buttermilk and whey powder:												
Full cream	KFVM	99	76	81	91	75	91	97	94	105	107	112
Skimmed	KFVN	149	170	157	136	144	149	138	95	104	91	127
Hen eggs in shell	KFVO	780	864	853	831	821	837	818	833	838	819	790
Oils (as crude oil):												
Vegetable oil	KFVP	1 501	1 465	1 488	1 492	1 567	1 905	1 960	2 010	1 780	2 449	..
Marine oil for the manufacture of margarine and compound fat	KFVQ	141	..	115	103	105	115	114	58	37	12	..
Potatoes	KFVR	6 085	5 911	5 799	5 994	6 357	6 491	5 923	6 123	6 261	5 986	5 863
Other foods:												
Chocolate confectionery	KFVT	578	603	621	640	667	696	674	698	672	697	679
Sugar confectionery, excluding medicated	KFVU	359	366	362	367	366	382	380	410	420	415	402
Tea excluding re-exports	KFVV	162	145	152	147	157	149	141	148	152	145	133
Raw coffee	KFVW	98	104	101	108	116	119	105	116	118	122	115
Barley:[9]												
For brewing and distilling and for food	KFVY	5 095	3 858	3 917	3 436	2 682	3 092	3 574	3 579	3 439	3 502	3 322
Maize (including maize meal): total disposals	KFVZ	1 405	1 659	1 510	1 433	1 414	1 382	1 409	1 372	1 429	1 445	1 238
Animal feed	KCRT	176	292	145	148	152	173	154	156	174	194	198
Oilcake and meal	KCRQ	3 174	3 569	3 470	3 646	3 891	4 152	4 462	4 429	4 041	3 677	4 035
Wheat milling offals	KCRR	1 169	1 133	1 064	1 086	1 170	1 121	1 131	1 156	1 159	1 273	1 209
Fish and poultry meal for animal feed,[7] figures relate to sales	KCRS	439	394	383	430	382	385	378	257	233	216	194

TIME SERIES. The figures relate to periods of 52 weeks (53 weeks in 1987, 1992 and 1998) with the following exceptions which are on a calendar year basis: fish and potatoes; condensed milk; milk powder; butter and sugar.

1 Including sugar used in the manufacture of other foods subsequently exported. Excluding sugar in imported manufactured foods.

2 Includes skim concentrate and condensed milk used in the manufacture of chocolate crumb.

3 Provisional.

4 Total of fowls, ducks, geese and turkeys.

5 This survey ceased at the end of 1995.

6 Including poultry offal.

7 Before a ban on 29 March 1996 this included both mammalian meat and bone meal and poultry meat.

8 Following the receipt of additional data, figures have been revised back to 1992 and are not strictly compatible with those for previous years.

9 From 1992 figures exclude sales of barley and barley screenings and are not strictly compatible with those from earlier years.

Source: Ministry of Agriculture, Fisheries and Food: 01904 455332

20.13 Number of workers employed in agriculture [1,2]
United Kingdom
At June in each year

Thousands

	Regular workers					Seasonal or casual workers			All workers			Salaried managers[3]
	Total	Whole - time		Part - time		Total	Male	Female	Total	Male	Female	
		Male	Female	Male	Female							
	KAXV	KAXW	KAXX	KAXY	KAXZ	KAYA	KAYB	KAYC	KAYD	KAYE	KAYF	KAYG
1989	186.6	114.7	15.2	29.2	27.6	88.3	54.0	34.3	274.9	197.8	77.1	7.8
1990	183.3	109.7	15.7	29.9	28.0	90.5	55.6	35.0	273.8	195.2	78.6	8.1
1991	176.9	104.7	15.0	29.7	27.4	86.6	53.8	32.8	263.5	188.2	75.3	7.9
1992	169.9	99.9	14.8	29.1	26.1	86.2	54.4	31.9	256.2	183.3	72.8	7.8
1993	165.3	96.5	13.7	29.8	25.3	85.4	55.0	30.4	250.7	181.3	69.4	7.6
1994	161.0	93.6	13.2	30.0	24.2	82.2	53.9	28.4	243.2	177.5	65.7	7.8
1995	157.4	90.4	13.0	30.0	24.1	83.7	56.5	27.2	241.2	176.8	64.3	7.7
1996	156.4	89.2	12.6	31.2	23.4	81.5	55.6	25.8	237.9	176.0	61.9	7.8
1997	154.2	87.5	12.5	31.2	22.9	80.9	55.4	25.6	235.0	174.1	61.0	7.8
1998	155.6	88.0	13.1	29.7	24.7	79.5	55.0	24.4	235.0	172.8	62.2	12.3
1999	144.7	82.7	11.9	27.5	22.6	73.0	51.8	21.2	217.7	162.0	55.7	14.1

See chapter text.

1 Includes estimates for minor holdings for all countries. In previous editions minor holdings were excluded for Scotland and therefore data here will differ from previous editions. Also, Northern Ireland data are now based on all active business.

2 Figures exclude school children, farmers, partners and directors and their spouses and most trainees.

3 Great Britain only.

Source: Agricultural Departments: 01904 455332

20.14 Landings of fish by United Kingdom vessels: live weight and value into United Kingdom

		Quantity (thousand tonnes)							Value (£ thousand)					
		1994	1995	1996	1997	1998	1999		1993	1994	1995	1996	1997	1998
Total all species	KSJU	687.6	725.6	635.9	593.3	552.5	506.5	KSLN	425 593	454 466	478 209	491 045	467 694	448 005
Total wet fish	KSJV	576.5	601.0	504.3	467.2	428.3	389.8	KSLO	318 431	326 720	333 174	343 045	314 712	323 297
Brill	KSJX	0.5	0.5	0.5	0.5	0.4	0.3	KSLP	1 502	1 927	2 201	2 639	2 244	1 674
Catfish	KSJY	1.4	1.0	1.1	1.0	0.8	0.7	KSLQ	1 867	1 669	1 474	1 449	1 152	1 070
Cod	KSJZ	65.7	74.4	75.7	71.0	72.7	46.8	KSLR	64 915	65 090	65 772	69 752	67 641	79 450
Dogfish	KSKA	8.2	10.9	9.7	8.6	7.4	6.9	KSLS	7 327	6 291	7 684	7 002	5 586	5 535
Haddock	KSKB	92.9	85.3	89.1	82.6	82.8	71.3	KSLT	54 710	61 017	54 734	54 333	44 778	57 131
Hake	KSKC	3.2	3.1	2.8	2.7	2.5	3.9	KSLU	11 535	8 363	7 361	7 346	6 375	5 117
Lemon Soles	KSKD	4.8	4.6	5.1	5.2	4.7	4.5	KSLV	11 073	11 931	10 115	11 897	11 786	10 620
Ling	KSKE	8.1	9.8	9.2	9.4	10.0	8.8	KSLW	5 210	5 832	7 483	6 945	6 568	8 291
Megrims	KSKF	4.7	5.1	6.0	6.0	5.3	5.0	KSLX	8 543	9 210	9 227	10 430	9 467	8 573
Monks or Anglers	KSKG	17.7	22.2	29.7	25.6	18.5	15.5	KSLY	32 271	34 328	39 451	51 468	45 947	38 540
Plaice	KSKH	17.5	15.5	12.5	12.9	11.5	9.5	KSLZ	21 499	19 937	17 573	16 013	15 484	13 185
Pollack (Lythe)	KSKI	2.9	3.3	2.9	3.0	2.6	2.3	KSMA	3 074	2 564	2 935	2 563	2 491	2 423
Saithe	KSKJ	12.5	12.8	13.3	12.3	10.1	10.4	KSMB	4 671	4 875	5 625	5 674	4 894	4 971
Sand Eels	KSKK	8.7	7.3	9.3	14.5	11.6	6.8	KSMC	124	424	398	505	815	742
Skates and Rays	KSKL	7.3	7.6	8.3	7.2	6.8	5.6	KSMD	5 899	6 322	6 543	7 451	6 215	6 403
Soles	KSKM	2.8	2.8	2.5	2.3	2.0	2.0	KSME	12 795	13 454	14 200	14 068	14 800	13 960
Turbot	KSKN	1.0	0.8	0.8	0.7	0.6	0.5	KSMF	4 521	5 238	4 667	5 006	4 263	3 614
Whiting	KSKO	41.8	39.8	37.3	34.5	26.7	25.4	KSMG	20 748	20 135	18 918	18 962	15 939	13 380
Whiting, Blue	KSKP	1.9	3.4	3.5	12.4	27.8	38.4	KSMH	137	90	180	190	693	2 003
Whitches	KSKQ	2.1	2.3	2.3	2.3	1.9	2.2	KSMI	2 305	2 867	2 915	3 068	2 263	1 587
Other Demersal	KSKR	8.9	12.9	13.3	13.2	12.7	15.7	KSMJ	8 730	10 709	17 028	16 614	16 000	14 794
Total Demersal[1]	KSKS	314.7	325.4	334.8	327.9	319.3	282.6	KSMK	283 860	292 276	296 485	313 377	285 402	293 882
Herring[2]	KSKT	86.1	95.9	72.3	57.4	39.5	45.3	KSML	9 716	9 756	11 105	8 742	6 430	4 897
Horse Mackerel	KSKU	9.5	26.2	22.0	5.5	5.1	2.1	KSMM	378	835	2 636	2 966	878	783
Mackerel[2]	KSKV	155.9	140.4	60.8	63.2	54.4	41.3	KSMN	22 055	21 230	20 860	15 645	19 822	21 754
Pilchards	KSKW	2.1	6.8	6.8	4.7	4.7	3.5	KSMO	632	277	680	959	696	765
Sprats	KSKX	7.6	5.9	7.2	8.3	5.0	14.3	KSMP	954	1 535	1 080	1 175	1 386	1 112
Tuna	KSKY	0.4	0.1	..	..	..	0.1	KSMQ	652	707	246	66	46	44
Other Pelagic	KSKZ	0.1	0.2	0.3	0.1	0.2	0.6	KSMR	185	104	82	116	52	61
Total Pelagic	KSLA	261.7	275.6	169.5	139.3	108.9	107.2	KSMS	34 571	34 444	36 689	29 668	29 309	29 416
Cockles	KSLB	22.3	25.4	24.2	19.5	12.1	14.2	KSMT	3 440	3 070	3 544	3 266	3 632	4 162
Crabs	KSLC	19.2	21.7	20.3	22.5	27.2	23.0	KSMU	15 810	20 397	21 346	22 226	24 264	32 290
Lobsters	KSLD	1.1	1.3	1.3	1.5	1.6	1.8	KSMV	9 353	10 688	11 896	11 888	13 060	14 343
Mussels	KSLE	10.3	9.5	12.3	9.6	12.7	8.4	KSMW	1 431	1 986	2 976	4 574	3 102	3 502
Nephrops	KSLF	29.8	31.1	29.0	31.1	28.6	31.1	KSMX	48 883	56 366	60 704	57 164	63 480	56 810
Periwinkles	KSLG	2.3	2.4	2.4	2.9	2.0	1.2	KSMY	1 150	1 554	1 954	2 046	2 735	1 892
Queens	KSLH	3.0	2.9	2.3	5.6	8.1	5.9	KSMZ	2 879	1 789	1 929	1 225	1 954	2 887
Scallops	KSLI	14.0	15.7	17.1	18.5	20.1	19.1	KSNA	13 787	21 209	24 279	27 036	27 576	30 156
Shrimps/Prawns	KSLJ	1.4	2.7	2.7	1.0	2.2	2.0	KSNB	1 858	1 981	3 517	3 257	960	2 751
Squid	KSLK	1.3	1.6	1.4	1.6	2.2	2.1	KSNC	2 482	2 824	3 783	2 987	4 044	4 362
Other shellfish	KSLL	6.2	10.4	18.7	12.2	7.6	8.0	KSND	6 494	5 881	9 106	12 332	8 176	7 553
Total shellfish	KSLM	111.1	124.6	131.6	126.1	124.2	116.7	KSNE	107 567	127 746	145 035	148 000	152 983	160 708

1 Includes fish roes.
2 Includes transshipments ie caught by UK boats but not actually landing at UK ports. These quantities are transshipped to foreign vessels in coastal waters and are later recorded as exports.

Source: Agricultural Departments: 01904 455332

20.15 United Kingdom fishing fleet
At 31 December each year[1]

Number

		1992	1993	1994	1995	1996	1997	1998	1999
By size									
10m & under	**KSNF**	7 376	7 666	7 194	6 319	5 606	5 474	5 487	5 409
10.01 - 12.19m	**KSNG**	1 450	1 361	1 167	1 016	800	732	628	577
12.20 - 17.00m	**KSNH**	787	751	680	622	540	523	491	468
17.01 - 18.29m	**KSNI**	232	220	193	187	164	162	154	154
18.30 - 24.38m	**KSNJ**	697	657	610	574	509	471	443	414
24.39 - 30.48m	**KSNK**	200	210	211	212	223	227	226	224
30.49 - 36.58m	**KSNL**	120	124	126	127	114	104	89	80
over 36.58m	**KSNM**	117	119	116	117	117	119	121	122
Total over 10m	**KSNN**	3 603	3 442	3 103	2 855	2 467	2 338	2 152	2 039
Total UK fleet (excluding Islands)	**KSNO**	10 979	11 108	10 297	9 174	8 073	7 812	7 639	7 448
By segment									
Pelagic gears	**KSNP**	76	69	68	67	58	49	50	46
Beam trawl	**KSNQ**	227	240	212	220	215	153	123	114
Demersal trawls & seines	**KXET**	..	..	..	..	1 040	..	..	..
Demersal trawls	**KSIX**	1 039	988	854	856	..	..	..	..
Nephrop trawls	**KSIY**	566	560	593	528	411	..	..	..
Seines	**KSIZ**	255	203	197	165	..	..	..	..
Demersal, Seines & Nephrops	**JZCI**	..	..	..	..	..	1 428	1 318	1 235
Lines & Nets	**KSNR**	339	329	300	267	224	214	187	172
Shellfish: mobile	**KSNS**	214	181	206	194	265	227	241	243
Shellfish: fixed	**KSNT**	306	312	305	283	339	352	311	301
Distant water	**KSNU**	16	14	13	12	15	13	14	12
Under 10m	**KSNV**	7 831	8 128	7 607	6 757	6 091	6 022	6 027	5 920
Non-active/non-TAC	**KSNW**	692	668	472	371	–	–	–	–
Other: Mussel Dredgers	**JZCJ**	..	..	..	..	..	3	2	2
Total UK fleet[2]	**KSNX**	11 561	11 692	10 827	9 720	8 658	8 461	8 271	8 104

1 Prior to 1990 the figures referred to vessels that were active; after 1990 the
figures refer to vessels in the registered fleet for which the data are currently under review.
2 The UK figures here include Channel Islands and Isle of Man.

Source: Ministry of Agriculture, Fisheries and Food: 01904 455332

20.16 Estimated household food consumption by all households in Great Britain

Grammes per person per week

		1989	1990	1991	1992	1993	1994	1995	1996	1997	1998	1999
Liquid wholemilk[1] (ml)	KPQM	1 377	1 232	1 104	995	898	870	812	776	712	693	634
Fully skimmed (ml)	KZBH	190	193	198	213	217	207	204	137	158	164	167
Semi skimmed (ml)	KZBI	432	516	579	752	814	863	899	935	978	945	958
Other milk and cream (ml)	KZBJ	237	228	247	262	249	252	255	259	248	243	248
Cheese	KPQO	115	113	117	114	109	106	108	111	109	104	104
Butter	KPQP	50	46	44	41	40	39	36	39	38	39	37
Margarine	KPQQ	98	91	89	79	70	43	41	36	26	26	20
Low and reduced fat spreads	KZBK	46	45	47	51	52	74	72	79	77	69	71
All other oils and fats (ml for oils)	KPQR	66	67	60	74	69	70	69	71	62	62	58
Eggs (number)	KPQS	2.29	2.20	2.25	2.08	1.92	1.86	1.85	1.87	1.78	1.74	1.68
Preserves and honey	KPQT	50	48	51	45	42	43	39	41	41	38	33
Sugar	KPQU	183	171	167	156	151	144	136	144	128	119	107
Beef and veal	KPQV	171	149	152	141	133	131	121	101	110	109	110
Mutton and lamb	KPQW	85	83	86	71	66	54	54	66	56	59	57
Pork	KPQX	89	84	82	72	80	77	71	73	75	76	69
Bacon and ham, uncooked	KPQY	95	86	85	77	77	77	76	77	72	76	68
Bacon and ham, cooked (including canned)	KPQZ	35	32	33	33	35	38	39	33	41	40	39
Poultry uncooked	JZCH	207	211	202	216	222	209	215	233	221	218	201
Cooked poultry (not purchased in cans)	KYBP	13	15	14	15	16	20	22	23	33	33	35
Other cooked and canned meats	KPRB	70	62	60	68	60	63	63	62	52	49	48
Offals	KPRC	16	14	13	12	11	9	9	7	7	5	5
Sausages, uncooked	KPRD	72	68	62	61	60	61	63	63	63	60	58
Other meat products	KPRE	165	163	173	183	194	203	211	207	209	216	221
Fish, fresh and processed (including shellfish)	KPRF	74	69	65	67	71	71	68	72	70	70	70
Canned fish	KPRG	27	29	30	32	30	30	29	31	31	29	31
Fish and fish products, frozen	KPRH	47	47	43	43	44	44	46	50	46	46	42
Potatoes (excluding processed)	KPRI	1 009	996	959	901	875	812	803	805	745	715	673
Fresh green vegetables	KPRJ	290	277	259	250	240	245	225	233	251	246	245
Other fresh vegetables	KPRK	486	459	461	475	477	464	470	489	497	486	500
Frozen potato products	KYBQ	80	73	82	92	98	103	99	113	106	111	113
Other frozen vegetables	KPRL	110	112	117	106	105	107	101	94	94	88	87
Potato products not frozen	JZCF	62	62	59	75	80	82	89	92	90	89	86
Canned beans	KPRM	126	124	123	120	112	111	117	125	122	118	112
Other canned vegetables (excl. potatoes)	KPRN	122	117	120	124	114	103	110	113	104	99	92
Other processed vegetables (excl. potatoes)	LQZH	42	41	43	50	52	55	48	55	52	54	59
Apples	KPRO	206	201	190	187	179	180	183	175	179	181	169
Bananas	KPRP	113	125	129	144	151	162	176	185	195	198	202
Oranges	KPRQ	84	81	76	72	62	65	66	63	62	63	50
All other fresh fruit	KPRR	204	198	216	216	224	238	247	263	276	274	290
Canned fruit	KPRS	61	52	52	51	48	46	45	43	44	37	38
Dried fruit, nuts and fruit and nut products	KPRT	36	36	39	38	39	36	34	36	35	34	30
Fruit juices (ml)	KPRU	214	202	250	222	236	240	244	258	277	304	284
Flour	KPRV	93	91	81	81	82	62	57	70	54	55	56
Bread	KPRW	834	797	752	755	757	758	756	752	746	742	717
Buns, scones and teacakes	KPRX	33	34	39	40	39	38	36	47	43	41	40
Cakes and pastries	KPRY	69	70	79	76	79	85	85	87	93	88	87
Biscuits	KPRZ	149	149	147	148	142	138	135	150	138	137	132
Breakfast cereals	KPSA	126	127	134	132	129	134	135	140	135	136	134
Oatmeal and oat products	KPSB	16	15	19	15	14	11	11	13	16	11	13
Other cereals and cereal products	JZCG	192	187	204	217	218	218	251	304	293	270	284
Tea	KPSC	46	43	42	39	36	38	39	38	36	35	32
Instant coffee	KPSD	14	14	15	14	13	13	12	13	11	12	11
Canned soups	KPSE	77	68	69	70	66	68	64	72	70	71	67
Pickles and sauces	KPSF	66	67	69	72	77	77	80	84	92	96	91

Note: Chapter text contains a description of the National Food Survey.
1 Including also school and welfare milk.

Sources: Ministry of Agriculture, Fisheries and Food (National Food Survey);
020 7270 8563

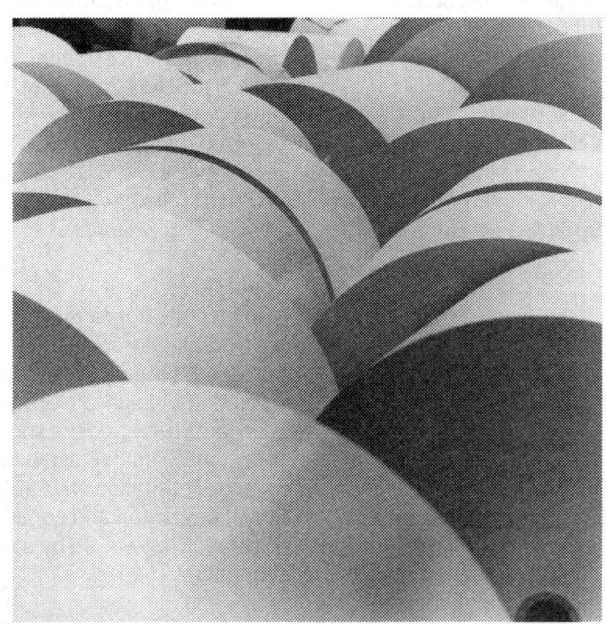

21 Production

Production

Production survey (Table 21.1)

The Annual Business Inquiry (ABI) provides information about the structure of industry in the United Kingdom. The results meet a wide range of needs for government, economic analysts and the business community at large. In official statistics the inquiry is an important source for the national accounts and input-output tables, but also provides weights for the indices of production and producer prices. Inquiry results also enable the United Kingdom to meet statistical requirements of the European Union.

Contributors for the Inquiry were selected under a stratified random sampling scheme. The strata used were industry and employment size group. The sampling fractions varied by industry but, in general, smaller enterprises had a lower chance of selection. All the largest enterprises in each industry were selected.

Data for 1998 comes directly from the new ABI and the previous years have been revised in line with these levels. Data for 1986 - 1992 on SIC(80) is unaffected.

Manufacturers sales by industry (Table 21.2)

This table shows the total manufacturers sales for products classified to the 1992 Standard Industrial Classification and collected under the PRODCOM (Products of the European Community) Inquiry since its introduction in 1993. Some data is not available for confidentiality reasons or where data has not been published for a given period. Detailed product sales data together with exports and imports data are available in the Product Sales and Trade quarterly and annual reports (PRQ and PRA series.

Number of local units in manufacturing industries in 2000 (Table 21.3)

This table shows the number of local units (sites) in manufacturing by employment sizebands. The class-ification breakdown is at division level (2 digit) as classified to the 1992 Standard Industrial Classification held on the Inter Departmental Business Register (IDBR). This register became fully operational in 1995 and combines information on VAT traders and PAYE employers in a statistical register comprising 2 million enterprises (businesses), representing nearly 99% of economic activity. Business Monitor PA1003 - Size Analysis of United Kingdom Businesses provides further details and contains detailed information on enterprises in the UK including size, classification and location. Additionally, this information is available for manufacturing local units.

Total inland energy consumption (Table 21.4)

This table shows energy consumption by fuel and final energy consumption by fuel and class of consumer. Primary energy consumption covers consumption of all primary fuels for energy purposes. Primary fuels are coal, gas, oil and primary electricity (i.e. electricity generated by hydro and nuclear stations and also electricity imported from France through the interconnector). This measure of energy consumption includes energy that is lost by converting primary fuels into secondary fuels, ie the energy lost burning coal to generate electricity or the energy used by refineries to separate crude oil into fractions, in addition to losses in distribution. The other common way of measuring energy consumption is to measure the energy content of the fuels supplied to consumers. This is called final energy consumption. It is net of fuel used by the energy industries, conversion, transmission and distribution losses. The figures are presented on a common basis, measured as energy supplied and expressed in million tonnes of oil equivalent. So far as practicable the user categories have been grouped on the basis of the SIC92 although the methods used by each of the supply industries to identify end users are slightly different. Chapter 1 of the *Digest of UK Energy Statistics* (published by The Stationery Office) gives more information on these figures.

Coal (Table 21.5)

Since 1995, aggregate data on coal production has been obtained from the Coal Authority. In addition main coal producers provide data in response to an annual DTI inquiry which covers production (deepmined and opencast), trade, stocks and disposals. HM Customs and Excise also provide trade data for solid fuels. The DTI collects information on the use of coal from Iron and Steel Statistics Bureau and consumption of coal for electricity generation is covered by data provided by the electricity generators.

Gas (Table 21.6)

Production figures, covering the production of gas from the UKCS offshore and onshore gas fields and gas obtained during the production of oil, are obtained from returns made under the DTI's Petroleum Production Reporting System. Additional information is used on imports and exports of gas and details from the operators of gas terminals in the UK to complete the picture.

DTI carry out an annual survey of gas suppliers to obtain details of gas sales to the various categories of consumer. Estimates are included for the suppliers with the smallest market share since the DTI inquiry covers only the largest suppliers (i.e. those more than about 0.5% per cent share of the UK market).

Electricity (Tables 21.7 - 21.9)

The electricity Tables 21.7 to 21.9 cover all generators and suppliers of electricity in the United Kingdom.

The relationship between generation, supply, availability and consumption is as follows:

Electricity generated
less electricity used on works
equals electricity supplied (gross)
less electricity used in pumping at pumped storage stations
equals electricity supplied (net)
plus imports (net of exports) of electricity
equals electricity available
less losses and statistical differences
equals electricity consumed.

In table 21.7 'major power producers' are those generating companies corresponding to the old public sector supply system, ie. AES Electric Ltd., Anglian Power Generation, Barking Power Ltd., British Nuclear Fuels plc., BNFL Magnox, British Energy plc., Coolkeeragh Power Ltd., Corby Power Ltd., Derwent Cogeneration Ltd., Eastern Merchant Generation Ltd., Elm Energy and Recycling (UK) Ltd., Edison Mission Energy Ltd., Fellside Heat and Power Ltd., Fibrogen Ltd., Fibropower Ltd., Fibrothetford Ltd., First Hydro Ltd., Fife Power Ltd., Humber Power Ltd., Hydro-Electric, Indian Queens Power Ltd., Keadby Generation Ltd., Lakeland Power Ltd., Magnox Electric plc., Medway Power Ltd., Midlands Power (UK) Ltd., National Power, NIGEN, Nuclear Electric, Peterborough Power Ltd., PowerGen plc., Premier Power Ltd., Regional Power Generators Ltd., Rocksavage Power Company Ltd., Sita Tyre Recycling Ltd., Scottish Nuclear, Scottish Power, Scottish and Southern Energy plc., Seabank Power Ltd., SELCHP Ltd. (South East London Combined Heat & Power Ltd.), South Western Electricity, Sutton Bridge Power Ltd., Teesside Power Ltd., TXU Europe Power Ltd

In Table 21.9 all fuels are converted to the common unit of million tonnes of oil equivalent, ie the amounts of oil which would be needed to produce the output of electricity generated from those fuels.

More detailed statistics on energy are given in the *Digest of United Kingdom Energy Statistics 2000*. Readers may wish to note that the production and consumption of fuels are presented using commodity balances. A commodity balance shows the flows of an individual fuel through from production to final consumption, showing its use in transformation and energy industry own use.

Oil and oil products *(Tables 21.10 - 21.12)*
The data on the production of crude oil, condensates and natural gases given in Table 21.10 are collected by the DTI direct from the operators of production facilities and terminals situated on UK territory, either on land or on the UK continental shelf. Data is also collected from the companies on their trade in oil and oil products. This data is used in preference to the foreign trade as recorded by HM Customs & Excise in the Overseas Trade Statistics.

Data on the internal UK oil industry (ie on the supply, refining and distribution of oil and oil products in the UK) is collected by the UK Petroleum Industry Association. This data, reported by individual refining companies and wholesalers and supplemented where necessary by data from other sources, provides the contents of Tables 21.11 and 21.12. The data is presented in terms of deliveries to the inland UK market. This is regarded as an acceptable proxy for actual consumption of products. The main shortcoming is that whilst changes in stocks held by companies in central storage areas are taken into account, changes in the levels of stocks further down the retail ladder (such as stocks held on petrol station forecourts) are not. This is not thought to result in a significant degree of difference in the data.

Iron and steel *(Tables 21.13 - 21.15)*

Iron and steel industry
The general definition of the UK iron and steel industry is based on groups 271 "ECSC iron and steel", 272 "Tubes", and 273 "Primary Transformation" of the UK Standard Industrial Classification (1992), except those parts of groups 272 and 273 which cover cast iron pipes, drawn wire, cold formed sections and Ferro alloys.

The definition excludes certain products which may be made by works within the industry such as refined iron, finished steel castings, steel tyres, wheels, axles and rolled rings, open and closed die forgings, colliery arches and springs. Iron foundries and steel stockholders are also considered to be outside of the industry.

Statistics
The statistics for the UK iron and steel industry are compiled by ISSB Ltd. from data collected from UK steel producing companies with the exception of trade data which is based on HM Customs data.

Crude steel is the total of usable ingots, usable continuously cast semi finished products and liquid steel for castings.

Production of finished products is the total production at the mill of that product after deduction of any material which is immediately scrapped.

Deliveries are based on invoiced tonnages and will include deliveries made to steel stockholders and service centres by the UK steel industry.

For more detailed information on definitions etc please contact ISSB Ltd. on 020 7343 3900.

Construction *(Tables 21.21 - 21.22)*
Table 21.21 shows the value of contractors' output in the construction industry in Great Britain. Contractors' output is defined as the amount chargeable to customers for building and civil engineering work done in the relevant period. The data comes from surveys run by the Department of the Environment, Transport and the Regions (DETR). As well as being an important input to the National Accounts, it is used by the government and the construction industry in their efforts to fully understand the industry, and also by Eurostat.

Table 21.22 shows the value of new orders in the construction industry; this is also collected by DETR. This information relates to contracts for new construction work awarded to main contractors by clients in both the public and private sectors; it also includes speculative work, undertaken on the initiative of the firm, where no contract is awarded. New orders are used as a good indicator of future output.

Motor vehicle production *(Table 21.25)*
The figures represent the output of United Kingdom based manufacturers classified to Class 34.10 (motor vehicles) of the Standard Industrial Classification 1992. They are derived from the Motor Vehicle Production

Production

Inquiry (MVPI).
These figures include vehicles produced in the form of kits for assembly. The value of the kit must be 50% or more of the value of a corresponding complete vehicle.

Drink and tobacco *(Tables 21.26 and 21.27)*
Data for these tables are derived by Customs and Excise from the systems for collecting excise duties. Alcoholic drinks and tobacco products become liable to duty when released for consumption in the UK. Figures for releases include both home-produced products and commercial imports. Production figures are also available for potable spirits distilled and beer brewed in the UK.

Alcoholic drink *(Table 21.26)*
The figures for Imported and other spirits released for home consumption include gin and other UK produced spirits, for which a breakdown is not available.

Since June 1993 beer duty has been charged when the beer leaves the brewery or other registered premises. Previously duty was chargeable at an earlier stage (the worts stage) in the brewing process, and an allowance was made for wastage. Figures for years prior to 1994 include adjustments to bring them into line with current data. The change in June 1993 also led to the availability of data on the strength; a series in hectolitres of pure alcohol is shown from 1994.

Made wine with alcoholic strength from 1.2% to 5.5% is termed 'coolers'. Included in coolers are alcoholic lemonade and similar products of appropriate strength. Prior to 1989 coolers were included under the heading of made wine other than coolers.

Tobacco Products *(Table 21.27)*
Releases of cigarettes and other tobacco products tend to be higher in the period before a Budget. Products may then be stocked, duty paid, before being sold.

21.1

Production survey: summary table
United Kingdom

	Estimates for all firms (£ million)					
			Stocks and work in progress			
	Gross output (Production)[1]	Gross value added	At end of year	Change during year	Capital expenditure *less* disposals	Wages and salaries
Standard Industrial Classification: Revised 1992						
Production and construction Sections C-F[3]						
	KSCC	KSCD	KSCE	KSCF	KSCG	KSCH
1993	543 365.8	172 245.6	..	..	22 360.0	86 856.8
1994	569 687.4	184 692.2	..	..	23 625.4	89 779.8
1995	509 908.9	194 984.3	77 441.9	..	26 335.4	..
1996	623 698.0	202 188.5	71 956.3	620.2	25 548.5	90 761.4
1997	636 620.7	215 385.4	71 978.0	−137.8	32 023.7	95 799.3
1998	637 766.1	214 618.7	70 797.6	472.9	34 008.9	98 838.4
Production industries (Revised definitions) Sections C-E[3]						
	KSCK	KSCL	KSCM	KSCN	KSCO	KSCP
1993	447 043.9	148 130.6	56 730.9	430.1	20 938.0	73 590.0
1994	482 313.6	159 800.4	57 971.3	3 472.0	22 078.5	75 990.5
1995	509 908.9	165 899.9	62 226.5	5 208.2	24 718.7	75 726.5
1996	526 474.7	170 962.6	58 035.1	124.8	24 093.4	75 837.2
1997	538 824.8	181 569.0	58 371.4	−1 150.0	30 148.9	79 000.0
1998	534 265.8	180 107.5	55 625.8	−622.8	32 225.7	82 244.2
Mining and quarrying Section C[3]						
	KSCS	KSCT	KSCU	KSCV	KSCW	KSCX
1993	7 445.4	2 622.4	1 206.1	−75.8	397.8	1 934.9
1994	5 951.4	2 079.0	629.1	−92.4	331.8	934.7
1995	6 312.4	2 522.6	617.3	−89.7	353.8	970.5
1996	6 797.3	3 021.5	665.9	13.9	550.7	1 079.9
1997	26 839.0	16 530.1	1 214.0	17.2	4 799.1	2 280.1
1998	25 784.7	14 188.5	1 143.8	52.7	6 326.8	2 273.6
Mining and quarrying of energy producing materials Subsection CA[3]						
	KSDA	KSDB	KSDC	KSDD	KSDE	KSDF
1993	3 881.6	1 323.6	..	..	235.8	1 384.0
1994	2 172.2	813.8	409.1	−86.0	78.6	364.0
1995	2 588.9	937.8	391.6	−108.5	97.3	420.7
1996	2 386.8	1 042.8	387.4	−12.9	161.7	453.7
1997	23 014.6	14 759.4	926.3	−9.1	4 537.4	1 710.9
1998	21 672.5	12 575.4	734.8	18.7	6 005.8	1 677.6
Mining and quarrying except energy producing materials Subsection CB						
	KSDI	KSDJ	KSDK	KSDL	KSDM	KSDN
1993	3 563.7	1 298.8	..	..	161.9	550.8
1994	3 779.3	1 265.2	220.1	−6.4	253.2	570.7
1995	3 723.6	1 584.7	225.7	18.8	256.5	549.8
1996	4 410.5	1 978.6	278.5	26.7	389.1	626.1
1997	3 824.4	1 770.7	287.7	26.3	261.7	569.1
1998	4 112.3	1 613.1	409.0	34.0	321.1	596.0
Manufacturing (Revised definition) Section D						
	KSDQ	KSDR	KSDS	KSDT	KSDU	KSDV
1993	392 893.6	127 841.4	52 842.5	802.0	14 541.2	67 029.4
1994	429 419.0	140 466.1	55 397.6	4 306.5	15 702.1	70 646.6
1995	454 324.7	147 282.5	59 760.4	5 406.6	19 028.5	70 687.1
1996	472 455.4	151 209.8	55 879.9	132.4	19 030.6	71 348.6
1997	468 011.2	148 690.8	55 701.4	−1 142.6	20 247.8	73 384.8
1998	463 418.0	150 097.4	52 912.7	−584.1	20 315.9	76 449.3

See footnotes on the last part of this table.

Source: Office for National Statistics: 01633 812929

21.1

Production survey: summary table
United Kingdom

	Gross output (Production)[1]	Gross value added	Stocks and work in progress		Capital expenditure *less* disposals	Wages and salaries
			At end of year	Change during year		
Standard Industrial Classification: Revised 1992			,			
Manufacture of food; beverages and tobacco Subsection DA						
	KSDY	KSDZ	KSEA	KSEB	KSEC	KSED
1993	72 816.2	18 336.8	6 844.9	−37.3	2 574.7	7 878.1
1994	75 552.4	19 373.3	6 881.4	296.9	2 552.9	8 174.9
1995	78 160.3	18 924.5	7 270.2	407.5	2 662.4	7 826.9
1996	81 784.3	20 346.5	7 335.1	529.6	2 489.6	7 807.9
1997	77 578.1	20 041.1	7 615.6	259.0	2 665.3	8 213.0
1998	73 412.2	19 336.6	8 021.9	−229.5	2 763.2	8 272.7
Manufacture of textile and textile products Subsection DB						
	KSEG	KSEH	KSEI	KSEJ	KSEK	KSEL
1993	17 066.2	6 715.8	2 441.5	130.0	429.4	3 877.7
1994	18 251.6	7 086.9	3 095.6	452.3	512.9	3 943.0
1995	19 032.6	7 155.9	2 978.1	206.3	497.0	3 938.9
1996	19 545.7	7 580.2	2 820.0	17.5	598.2	4 004.1
1997	18 966.5	7 663.7	3 045.6	28.8	506.3	4 146.1
1998	17 317.6	6 704.2	2 896.4	−145.1	553.4	4 009.5
Manufacture of leather and leather products Subsection DC						
	KSEO	KSEP	KSEQ	KSER	KSES	KSET
1993	2 778.0	1 061.3	420.3	19.9	61.3	677.7
1994	3 000.7	1 068.4	520.8	57.2	75.9	651.5
1995	2 452.5	844.5	384.6	26.4	67.7	609.7
1996	2 544.3	933.7	400.7	5.0	54.7	445.3
1997	2 201.3	786.8	408.8	45.1	49.0	428.6
1998	1 982.0	673.5	410.6	−9.5	41.7	410.2
Manufacture of wood and wood products Subsection DD						
	KSEW	KSEX	KSEY	KSEZ	KSFA	KSFB
1993	5 435.2	1 687.2	621.8	39.4	146.2	972.9
1994	6 592.0	1 885.5	746.0	92.2	136.8	1 145.6
1995	6 647.8	2 068.2	753.0	13.0	165.0	1 175.8
1996	6 442.7	2 085.8	644.8	−7.0	173.4	1 133.5
1997	6 153.9	2 217.9	667.2	14.8	237.5	1 135.9
1998	5 769.1	2 255.6	590.5	14.5	254.4	1 224.3
Manufacture of pulp, paper and paper products; publishing and printing Subsection DE						
	KSFE	KSFF	KSFG	KSFH	KSFI	KSFJ
1993	36 806.4	15 614.7	2 620.0	74.3	1 812.3	7 437.3
1994	40 965.0	17 109.0	3 087.1	374.2	1 956.0	8 335.6
1995	43 870.8	18 283.0	3 477.9	483.0	2 294.7	8 156.5
1996	45 970.0	19 029.7	3 046.6	−212.4	1 889.7	8 588.5
1997	42 152.0	17 716.9	3 034.9	−44.5	2 087.2	8 631.3
1998	42 813.6	18 452.9	2 850.8	−9.6	1 960.5	9 071.0
Manufacture of coke, refined petroleum products and nuclear fuel Subsection DF						
	KSFM	KSFN	KSFO	KSFP	KSFQ	KSFR
1993	22 700.1	2 436.0	1 490.1	−99.6	797.6	708.0
1994	22 507.8	2 360.6	1 171.5	26.9	646.1	716.3
1995	22 552.8	2 965.6	1 264.9	225.3	814.5	693.3
1996	25 602.3	2 485.1	1 169.4	−96.1	756.9	722.3
1997	25 617.1	2 023.6	1 171.1	−175.0	703.5	669.1
1998	25 628.4	2 321.0	918.4	−162.9	728.4	809.1

See footnotes on the last part of this table.

Source: Office for National Statistics: 01633 812929

21.1
continued

Production survey: summary table
United Kingdom

	Estimates for all firms (£ million)					
			Stocks and work in progress		Capital expenditure	Wages
	Gross output (Production)[1]	Gross value added	At end of year	Change during year	less disposals	and salaries

Standard Industrial Classification: Revised 1992

Manufacture of chemicals, chemical products and man-made fibres
Subsection DG

	KSFU	KSFV	KSFW	KSFX	KSFY	KSFZ
1993	40 066.3	13 424.4	5 344.7	154.6	2 057.1	5 590.9
1994	42 930.5	14 405.9	5 577.8	285.6	2 074.9	5 705.5
1995	46 033.4	15 931.5	6 188.6	475.4	2 451.7	5 986.2
1996	47 135.9	15 701.6	5 954.1	274.2	2 848.4	5 815.2
1997	46 817.8	14 581.8	5 595.1	−44.5	2 917.4	5 929.1
1998	44 970.8	14 278.8	5 709.8	114.3	3 302.5	6 078.9

Manufacture of rubber and plastic products
Subsection DH

	KSGC	KSGD	KSGE	KSGF	KSGG	KSGH
1993	16 352.2	6 408.7	1 663.7	57.3	829.6	3 502.5
1994	18 307.5	7 048.9	1 833.1	184.5	828.4	3 718.7
1995	19 312.6	7 069.5	1 950.4	183.4	1 007.2	3 809.3
1996	20 119.8	7 551.1	1 981.0	28.7	1 020.1	3 955.1
1997	20 368.3	7 834.2	1 908.3	33.7	1 071.5	4 096.1
1998	20 374.4	8 009.2	2 009.0	56.3	1 097.7	4 241.3

Manufacture of other non-metallic mineral products
Subsection DI

	KSGK	KSGL	KSGM	KSGN	KSGO	KSGP
1993	10 112.8	4 124.8	1 327.3	−89.2	461.3	2 302.0
1994	11 917.2	5 105.1	1 490.0	111.6	466.5	2 489.8
1995	12 857.1	5 472.1	1 583.3	131.7	649.4	2 605.0
1996	12 102.6	5 345.5	1 519.0	100.5	688.9	2 477.0
1997	11 888.8	5 092.2	1 526.8	16.6	571.4	2 484.0
1998	11 334.5	4 865.7	1 426.1	30.7	630.6	2 394.2

Manufacture of basic iron and of ferro-alloys
Subsection DJ

	KSGS	KSGT	KSGU	KSGV	KSGW	KSGX
1993	38 353.6	13 902.5	4 289.7	66.6	1 160.7	8 445.8
1994	43 151.3	15 471.5	4 560.1	281.6	1 369.9	8 816.0
1995	47 670.0	17 539.0	4 993.6	546.8	1 591.3	9 163.1
1996	47 273.7	16 788.1	4 637.8	14.8	1 792.4	9 167.8
1997	43 343.9	16 335.4	4 289.2	−23.1	1 744.1	8 888.0
1998	44 359.3	17 374.8	4 270.9	−124.7	2 040.4	9 517.8

Manufacture of machinery and equipment not elsewhere specified
Subsection DK

	KSHA	KSHB	KSHC	KSHD	KSHE	KSHF
1993	28 529.1	10 510.4	4 983.7	−72.8	790.1	6 508.2
1994	31 497.0	11 622.7	5 287.3	180.5	976.5	6 946.0
1995	35 977.4	12 922.8	5 933.3	391.9	1 171.7	7 217.6
1996	36 274.6	13 103.7	5 329.2	64.6	1 254.1	7 048.0
1997	36 174.2	13 372.9	5 483.3	96.0	1 108.6	7 354.6
1998	35 663.5	13 295.0	5 061.6	28.0	989.9	7 548.0

Manufacture of electrical and optical equipment
Subsection DL

	KSHI	KSHJ	KSHK	KSHL	KSHM	KSHN
1993	47 475.1	15 534.5	7 804.0	379.6	1 704.3	8 993.5
1994	51 419.3	18 058.0	7 849.3	637.7	2 051.5	9 266.3
1995	55 412.8	18 711.3	8 127.2	808.4	2 720.0	8 888.5
1996	59 062.8	19 151.1	7 501.1	−229.6	2 445.9	9 207.8
1997	61 089.5	18 963.6	7 337.1	16.1	2 792.3	9 536.3
1998	62 162.0	19 477.5	6 830.8	−38.2	2 682.3	10 205.7

See footnotes on the last part of this table.

Source: Office for National Statistics: 01633 812929

21.1
continued

Production survey: summary table
United Kingdom

			Estimates for all firms (£ million)			
	Gross output (Production)[1]	Gross value added	Stocks and work in progress		Capital expenditure *less* disposals	Wages and salaries
			At end of year	Change during year		

Standard Industrial Classification: Revised 1992

Manufacture of transport equipment
Subsection DM

	KSHQ	KSHR	KSHS	KSHT	KSHU	KSHV
1993	43 736.7	14 093.0	11 725.4	100.0	1 450.2	7 697.7
1994	49 484.3	14 991.9	11 688.5	1 177.9	1 683.5	7 755.5
1995	49 786.1	14 346.7	13 136.6	1 388.0	2 477.6	7 758.2
1996	53 829.3	15 547.5	11 960.6	−447.9	2 550.4	8 040.1
1997	60 159.3	16 204.4	11 728.6	−1 427.5	3 236.8	8 736.3
1998	62 215.3	16 968.4	10 349.0	−214.5	2 749.7	9 539.4

Manufacture not elsewhere classified
Subsection DN

	KSHY	KSHZ	KSIA	KSIB	KSIC	KSID
1993	10 665.9	3 991.3	1 265.4	79.2	266.4	2 437.0
1994	13 842.5	4 878.5	1 609.0	147.4	370.2	2 981.9
1995	14 558.4	5 047.9	1 718.7	119.4	458.5	2 858.2
1996	14 767.4	5 560.3	1 580.6	90.3	468.0	2 935.9
1997	15 500.5	5 856.4	1 889.8	61.7	556.9	3 136.5
1998	15 415.4	6 084.2	1 566.9	105.9	521.2	3 127.2

Electricity, gas and water supply
Section E

	KSIG	KSIH	KSII	KSIJ	KSIK	KSIL
1993	46 704.9	17 666.8	2 682.3	−296.1	5 999.0	4 625.8
1994	46 943.1	17 255.3	1 944.5	−742.0	6 044.5	4 409.2
1995	49 271.7	16 094.9	1 848.9	−108.7	5 336.5	4 068.9
1996	47 222.0	16 731.4	1 489.3	−21.4	4 512.0	3 408.8
1997	43 974.6	16 348.1	1 456.0	−24.5	5 102.1	3 335.1
1998	45 063.0	15 821.6	1 569.3	−91.3	5 582.9	3 521.3

Construction
Section F

	KSIO	KSIP	KSIQ	KSIR	KSIS	KSIT
1993	96 322.0	24 115.0	..	..	1 422.0	13 266.7
1994	87 373.8	24 891.8	..	..	1 547.0	13 789.3
1995	..	29 084.4	15 215.3	..	1 616.7	..
1996	97 223.3	31 225.8	13 921.2	495.4	1 455.1	14 924.2
1997	97 795.9	33 816.4	13 606.6	1 012.2	1 874.7	16 799.3
1998	103 500.3	34 511.2	15 171.8	1 095.7	1 783.2	16 594.2

See footnotes on the last part of this table.

Source: Office for National Statistics: 01633 812929

21.1 Production survey: summary table
United Kingdom

continued

	Estimates for all firms							
	(£ million)							
			Stocks and work in progress				Average number of persons employed[2] (000s)	Gross value added per person employed (£)
	Gross output (Production)[1]	Gross value added	At end of year	Change during year	Capital expenditure less disposals	Wages and salaries		
Standard Industrial Classification: Revised 1980								
Production and construction Divisions 1 - 5[3]								
	KABW	KABX	KAFE	KAFF	KAFG	KAFH	KAFI	KAFJ
1986	311 772	107 141	..	−224	13 669	59 705	6 468	16 565
1987	345 812	117 216	..	..	14 797	..	6 448	18 177
1988	386 112	131 584	..	..	18 026	..	6 487	20 283
1989	421 674	144 135	..	..	21 000	..	6 494	22 195
1990	454 031	149 788	..	..	21 666	..	6 364	21 530
1991	440 770	142 849	..	..	20 736	..	5 919	24 134
1992	447 431	145 012	..	..	20 248	..	5 698	25 448
Production industries (Revised definition) Divisions 1 - 4[3]								
	KAFK	KAFL	KAFM	KAFO	KAGP	KAIA	KAIB	KAIC
1986	268 313	93 958	47 028	225	13 032	48 854	5 346	17 576
1987	297 798	102 748	49 501	2 113	14 019	52 040	5 309	19 354
1988	326 814	114 523	52 676	..	16 789	56 202	5 341	21 443
1989	355 406	123 709	55 391	..	19 578	61 594	5 334	23 194
1990	380 790	129 106	55 699	..	20 591	65 782	5 202	24 821
1991	374 221	124 543	52 984	..	20 115	67 159	4 884	25 501
1992	385 042	127 369	54 423	..	19 616	67 934	4 683	27 199
Manufacturing (Revised definition) Divisions 2 - 4								
	KAID	KAIE	KAIF	KAIG	KAIH	KAII	KAJF	KAJG
1986	232 499	80 955	42 979	515	8 705	43 426	4 878	16 595
1987	254 683	89 745	44 797	2 111	9 754	46 429	4 874	18 412
1988	283 434	99 934	48 338	3 459	12 170	50 664	4 932	20 261
1989	309 020	108 291	51 510	3 530	14 499	55 492	4 953	21 863
1990	319 295	111 051	51 546	376	14 308	59 712	4 840	22 945
1991	308 909	105 606	48 722	−2 202	13 100	60 793	4 538	23 274
1992	319 515	108 144	50 167	819	12 094	61 727	4 369	24 752
Energy and water supply industries Division 1[3,4]								
	KAJH	KAJI	KAJJ	KAJK	KAJL	KAJM	KAJN	KAJO
1986	35 814	13 003	4 049	−740	4 327	5 428	468	27 799
1987	43 116	13 003	4 704	2	4 269	5 611	435	29 916
1988	43 380	14 589	4 338	281	4 620	5 539	409	35 704
1989	46 386	15 418	3 882	−132	5 080	6 102	380	40 508
1990	61 495	18 055	4 152	100	6 282	6 070	362	49 920
1991	65 312	18 937	4 262	−40	7 016	6 366	346	54 674
1992	65 526	19 226	4 256	−56	7 522	6 207	314	61 262
Coal extraction, coke ovens and manufacture of solid fuels Classes 11 and 12								
	KAJP	KAJQ	KAJR	KAJS	KAJT	KAJU	KAJV	KAJW
1986	4 007	2 513	546	8	507	1 828	160	15 691
1987	3 859	2 266	468	−72	507	1 878	132	17 166
1988	3 924	2 375	557	89	401	1 639	112	21 207
1989	3 700	2 030	533	−24	347	1 724	90	22 556
1990	3 466	1 853	566	29	297	1 406	76	24 382
1991	3 550	1 881	751	109	215	1 237	66	28 415
1992	3 029	1 401	602	−152	123	1 066	50	28 020
Extraction of mineral oil and natural gas Class 13[5]								
	KAMY	KANE	KAPF	KAQL	KARG	KARY	KATL	KAYU
1986	11 861	9 000	..	−89	2 579	..	23	391 322
1987	12 664	10 088	..	54	2 042	..	28	360 275
1988	10 062	7 625	..	−56	2 214	..	29	262 941
1989	10 411	7 457	..	28	2 706	..	31	240 532
1990	11 924	7 923	..	−90	3 568	..	37	214 143
1991	12 168	7 510	..	..	5 126	..	33	227 561
1992	12 132	7 866	..	..	5 420	..	30	262 193

See footnotes on the last part of this table.

Source: Office for National Statistics: 01633 812929

21.1
continued

Production survey: summary table
United Kingdom

	Estimates for all firms							
	(£ million)						Average number of persons employed[2] (000s)	Gross value added per person employed (£)
			Stocks and work in progress					
	Gross output (Production)[1]	Gross value added	At end of year	Change during year	Capital expenditure *less* disposals	Wages and salaries		

Standard Industrial Classification: Revised 1980

Mineral oil processing
Class 14

	KAYV	KAYW	KAYX	KAYY	KAYZ	KAZA	KAZB	KAZC
1986	9 080	1 337	994	−541	301	199	14	93 139
1987	16 328	1 349	996	−20	223	226	15	91 198
1988	15 173	1 609	738	−176	334	254	16	102 685
1989	16 528	1 960	791	222	303	268	15	131 910
1990	19 016	2 492	1 029	192	343	279	14	174 213
1991	19 010	1 484	728	−279	416	292	13	110 581
1992	18 606	1 434	788	53	420	310	13	107 281

Other energy and water supply
Classes 15 to 17[4]

	KAZD	KAZE	KAZF	KAZG	KAZH	KAZK	KAZN	KAZO
1986	22 727	9 153	2 509	−208	3 518	3 401	293	31 215
1987	22 929	9 388	3 240	94	3 535	3 508	287	32 711
1988	24 282	10 605	3 043	368	3 885	3 646	282	37 607
1989	26 157	11 428	2 558	−330	4 430	4 109	276	41 390
1990	39 013	13 710	2 556	−121	5 642	4 384	270	50 778
1991	42 752	15 572	2 783	..	6 384	4 836	267	58 366
1992	43 893	16 391	2 866	..	6 979	4 831	250	65 564

Extraction of minerals and ores other than fuels; manufacture of metals, mineral products and chemicals
Division 2

	KAZP	KAZQ	KAZR	KAZS	KAZT	KAZU	KBAB	KBAC
1986	46 618	15 700	7 068	−216	2 249	6 669	655	23 961
1987	51 645	18 427	7 505	470	2 680	7 226	653	28 223
1988	58 159	21 202	8 058	610	3 216	7 946	662	32 036
1989	63 288	22 068	8 679	563	3 907	8 789	676	32 641
1990	62 684	20 839	8 666	1	4 008	9 385	656	31 782
1991	59 157	19 453	8 263	−494	3 365	9 562	614	31 685
1992	59 953	19 796	8 159	−77	3 000	9 680	585	33 835

Extraction and preparation of metalliferous ores
Class 21

	KBAD	KBAG	KBAH	KBAI	KBAJ	KBAL	KBAM	KBAN
1986	25	4	6	−	6	12	1	4 486
1987	19	−1	12	6	11	11	1	1 925
1988	3	2	1	−	−	2	−	10 454
1989	3	1	−	−	−	2	−	4 447
1990	−	−	−	−	−	2	−	−6 773
1991	−	−	−	−	−	−	−	−
1992	−	−	−	−	−	−	−	−

Metal manufacturing
Class 22

	KBAO	KBAQ	KBAR	KBAS	KBAT	KBBB	KBBC	KBBD
1986	11 134	2 956	2 008	−25	417	1 593	153	19 278
1987	12 368	3 539	2 055	120	461	1 622	142	24 848
1988	14 549	4 247	2 298	219	580	1 766	141	30 124
1989	15 600	4 236	2 302	−13	688	1 878	141	30 002
1990	14 685	3 638	2 086	−183	692	1 980	136	26 578
1991	12 700	3 063	1 844	−246	504	1 913	124	24 745
1992	12 319	2 943	1 723	−121	402	1 810	112	26 262

Extraction of minerals nes
Class 23

	KBBE	KBBG	KBBH	KBBI	KBBJ	KBBL	KBBM	KBBN
1986	659	343	41	−3	30	98	10	34 578
1987	670	350	43	3	43	102	9	37 191
1988	743	370	41	−2	70	111	10	39 028
1989	717	371	41	5	63	116	9	39 648
1990	717	385	52	12	66	126	9	42 803
1991	698	368	48	−1	35	123	8	43 679
1992	637	309	42	−	34	120	7	40 772

See footnotes on the last part of this table.

Source: Office for National Statistics: 01633 812929

21.1
continued

Production survey: summary table
United Kingdom

			Estimates for all firms					
			(£ million)					
			Stocks and work in progress				Average number of persons employed[2] (000s)	Gross value added per person employed (£)
	Gross output (Production)[1]	Gross value added	At end of year	Change during year	Capital expenditure *less* disposals	Wages and salaries		

Standard Industrial Classification: Revised 1980

Manufacture of non-metallic mineral products
Class 24

	KBBO	KBBQ	KBBR	KBBS	KBBT	KBBV	KBBW	KBBX
1986	9 021	3 848	1 170	−13	431	1 780	200	19 274
1987	10 013	4 364	1 185	10	601	1 964	202	21 583
1988	11 786	5 308	1 257	54	822	2 251	214	24 816
1989	12 936	5 650	1 455	190	1 028	2 526	220	25 719
1990	12 631	5 256	1 567	114	891	2 616	210	25 063
1991	11 196	4 510	1 502	−25	480	2 517	190	23 732
1992	10 865	4 237	1 496	−26	407	2 473	180	23 599

Chemical industry
Class 25

	KBBY	KBDB	KBDC	KBDD	KBDE	KBDG	KBDH	KBDI
1986	24 889	8 221	3 738	−171	1 318	3 061	281	29 298
1987	27 620	9 814	4 099	324	1 504	3 392	287	34 166
1988	30 153	10 869	4 357	344	1 712	3 681	287	37 862
1989	33 014	11 394	4 776	380	2 048	4 124	296	38 449
1990	33 601	11 120	4 838	42	2 271	4 507	290	38 265
1991	33 553	11 100	4 755	−209	2 235	4 855	283	39 270
1992	35 050	11 894	4 779	84	2 113	5 143	278	42 725

Production of man-made fibres
Class 26

	KBDJ	KBDL	KBDM	KBDN	KBDO	KBDQ	KBDR	KBDS
1986	889	329	105	−4	47	125	11	30 454
1987	956	362	112	6	59	135	11	33 113
1988	925	405	104	−6	32	136	10	39 752
1989	1 018	418	106	2	81	143	10	42 824
1990	1 048	439	123	17	88	155	9	46 606
1991	1 010	411	114	−13	111	153	9	45 542
1992	1 081	414	118	−15	43	133	7	54 948

Metal goods, engineering and vehicle industries
Division 3

	KBDT	KBDV	KBDW	KBDX	KBDY	KBEB	KBEC	KBED
1986	87 583	34 104	23 855	879	3 183	20 242	2 156	15 821
1987	95 497	36 453	24 394	716	3 182	21 286	2 116	17 231
1988	108 319	41 058	26 144	1 775	4 092	23 199	2 131	19 269
1989	120 878	45 674	28 134	2 259	5 149	25 400	2 130	21 440
1990	126 974	47 571	27 960	−38	5 300	27 730	2 111	22 535
1991	120 192	43 669	26 121	−1 456	4 834	28 132	1 964	22 233
1992	124 847	43 259	27 552	568	4 259	28 078	1 863	23 222

Manufacture of metal goods nes
Class 31

	KBEE	KBEG	KBEH	KBEI	KBEJ	KBEL	KBEM	KBEN
1986	10 611	4 298	1 581	27	350	2 610	322	13 339
1987	11 331	4 560	1 653	100	407	2 750	316	14 428
1988	12 954	5 229	1 872	176	536	3 088	325	16 090
1989	14 340	5 776	1 962	139	644	3 450	335	17 265
1990	15 364	6 272	2 014	−45	629	3 816	338	18 524
1991	14 400	5 729	1 828	−180	490	3 700	308	18 596
1992	14 054	5 694	1 746	−55	454	3 705	293	19 423

Mechanical engineering
Class 32

	KBEO	KBEQ	KBER	KBES	KBET	KBEV	KBEW	KBEX
1986	23 541	9 651	5 886	−62	711	5 958	615	15 681
1987	24 351	9 966	5 710	51	696	5 973	586	16 995
1988	27 463	11 079	5 905	356	801	6 491	586	18 901
1989	31 186	12 622	6 277	456	1 029	7 170	590	21 401
1990	33 296	13 300	6 184	−100	1 136	7 902	588	22 596
1991	31 270	12 568	5 541	−467	930	8 001	547	22 963
1992	31 223	12 491	5 485	−386	819	8 069	521	23 965

See footnotes on the last part of this table.

Source: Office for National Statistics: 01633 812929

21.1 Production survey: summary table
United Kingdom
continued

	Estimates for all firms							
	(£ million)							
			Stocks and work in progress				Average number of persons employed[2] (000s)	Gross value added per person employed (£)
	Gross output (Production)[1]	Gross value added	At end of year	Change during year	Capital expenditure *less* disposals	Wages and salaries		
Standard Industrial Classification: Revised 1980								
Electrical and electronic engineering and manufacturing of office machinery and data processing equipment								
Classes 33 and 34								
	KBEY	KBFR	KBFV	KBFW	KBFX	KBGG	KBGN	KBHO
1986	24 729	9 914	5 676	135	950	5 389	590	16 795
1987	27 401	10 861	5 868	261	999	5 796	590	18 408
1988	31 379	12 434	6 411	369	1 288	6 372	599	20 758
1989	34 104	12 650	6 772	450	1 444	6 878	590	21 440
1990	35 254	12 750	6 810	51	1 300	7 236	566	22 526
1991	33 996	12 008	6 196	−412	1 162	7 578	534	22 504
1992	34 785	11 389	6 152	−332	1 115	7 520	504	22 597
Manufacture of motor vehicles and parts thereof								
Class 35								
	KBHP	KBHQ	KBHR	KBHS	KBHT	KBHU	KBHV	KBHW
1986	15 410	4 657	2 907	173	677	2 688	261	17 844
1987	17 629	5 112	2 925	82	612	2 804	258	19 814
1988	20 882	5 564	3 363	409	925	3 180	265	20 967
1989	23 399	6 686	3 637	301	1 339	3 519	267	25 067
1990	23 660	6 331	3 880	180	1 522	3 826	268	23 663
1991	21 053	4 768	3 061	−837	1 778	3 807	246	19 399
1992	23 526	5 956	3 183	88	1 385	3 842	234	25 463
Manufacture of other transport equipment								
Class 36								
	KBHX	KBHY	KBHZ	KBJU	KBJV	KBJW	KBJX	KBJY
1986	10 889	4 401	7 055	599	387	2 871	284	15 485
1987	11 854	4 695	7 461	366	354	3 183	282	16 640
1988	12 245	5 218	7 688	347	402	3 192	268	19 449
1989	14 163	6 417	8 540	883	526	3 414	262	24 497
1990	15 552	7 291	8 143	−69	570	3 911	265	27 487
1991	15 545	6 806	8 584	410	324	4 012	257	27 090
1992	17 040	5 876	9 988	1 100	334	3 881	234	25 148
Instrument engineering								
Class 37								
	KBJZ	KBLI	KBNN	KBNO	KBNP	KBNQ	KBNR	KBNS
1986	2 674	1 183	750	7	109	726	82	14 350
1987	2 932	1 259	776	20	114	779	83	15 128
1988	3 396	1 533	906	118	140	875	87	17 685
1989	3 685	1 522	947	30	167	968	88	17 393
1990	3 847	1 627	928	−56	144	1 039	85	19 056
1991	3 928	1 791	911	30	150	1 033	78	22 909
1992	4 217	1 852	998	27	153	1 061	77	24 053
Other manufacturing industries								
Division 4								
	KBNT	KBNU	KBNV	KBNW	KBNX	KBNY	KBNZ	KBRO
1986	98 298	31 151	12 056	−147	3 273	16 513	2 067	15 067
1987	107 540	34 865	12 897	926	3 892	17 917	2 106	16 556
1988	116 957	37 674	14 135	1 074	4 862	19 519	2 140	17 607
1989	124 854	40 548	14 696	708	5 442	21 305	2 147	18 889
1990	129 638	42 641	14 920	413	4 999	22 596	2 073	20 568
1991	129 560	42 485	14 338	−251	4 901	23 100	1 960	21 682
1992	134 715	45 088	14 456	327	4 835	23 970	1 921	23 469
Food, drink and tobacco manufacturing								
Class 41/42								
	KBRP	KBRQ	KBRR	KBRS	KBRT	KBRU	KBRV	KBRW
1986	47 023	10 801	4 808	−384	1 275	4 735	582	18 572
1987	49 272	11 696	4 844	66	1 453	5 082	594	19 692
1988	52 004	12 134	5 190	267	1 660	5 406	592	20 483
1989	55 029	13 268	5 482	314	1 909	5 882	598	22 191
1990	58 298	14 390	5 867	407	2 076	6 364	591	24 347
1991	60 237	14 875	5 914	139	2 132	6 774	577	25 796
1992	61 826	15 616	5 845	295	2 102	6 980	564	27 693

See footnotes on the last part of this table.

Source: Office for National Statistics: 01633 812929

21.1

Production survey: summary table
United Kingdom

continued

	Estimates for all firms							
	(£ million)							
			Stocks and work in progress				Average number of persons employed[2] (000s)	Gross value added per person employed (£)
	Gross output (Production)[1]	Gross value added	At end of year	Change during year	Capital expenditure less disposals	Wages and salaries		

Standard Industrial Classification: Revised 1980

Textile industry
Class 43

	KBRX	KBRY	KBUE	KBUF	KBUG	KBUH	KBUI	KBUJ
1986	6 788	2 503	1 207	−4	265	1 504	229	10 929
1987	7 571	2 873	1 338	125	271	1 623	228	12 596
1988	7 930	2 980	1 448	96	353	1 709	225	13 234
1989	7 942	2 962	1 484	10	296	1 791	216	13 745
1990	7 648	2 941	1 338	−82	251	1 785	196	15 035
1991	7 384	2 842	1 236	−101	234	1 795	182	15 625
1992	7 544	2 956	1 253	8	281	1 843	172	17 130

Footwear and clothing industries and manufacture of leather and leather goods
Classes 44 and 45

	KBUK	KBUL	KBUM	KBUN	KBUO	KBUP	KBUR	KBUS
1986	7 143	2 864	1 342	45	174	1 798	341	8 399
1987	7 800	3 104	1 509	198	194	1 904	341	9 103
1988	8 217	3 229	1 618	125	212	2 042	341	9 470
1989	8 321	3 288	1 565	−4	188	2 066	320	10 277
1990	8 499	3 448	1 620	82	192	2 104	298	11 570
1991	7 965	3 219	1 436	−56	156	2 060	270	11 944
1992	8 305	3 405	1 462	19	144	2 123	258	13 198

Timber and wooden furniture industries
Class 46

	KBUT	KBUV	KBUW	KBUX	KBUY	KBUZ	KBVA	KBVB
1986	7 112	2 393	1 119	51	197	1 513	193	12 428
1987	8 335	2 884	1 230	155	271	1 647	198	14 544
1988	9 783	3 339	1 405	137	351	1 925	213	15 705
1989	10 138	3 478	1 418	82	397	2 082	215	16 207
1990	10 295	3 459	1 383	1	260	2 186	207	16 715
1991	9 464	3 165	1 232	−120	225	2 110	189	16 755
1992	9 448	3 137	1 205	−41	259	2 130	186	16 883

Manufacture of paper and paper products; printing and publishing
Class 47

	KBVC	KBVE	KBVF	KBVG	KBVH	KBVI	KBVJ	KBVK
1986	19 396	8 364	1 982	91	870	4 653	439	19 065
1987	21 914	9 327	2 156	169	1 070	5 051	446	20 908
1988	24 824	10 464	2 451	213	1 521	5 517	456	22 956
1989	27 389	11 469	2 589	199	1 771	6 142	469	24 454
1990	28 304	12 004	2 534	−46	1 398	6 582	462	25 983
1991	28 357	12 102	2 489	−23	1 474	6 719	442	27 377
1992	30 168	13 023	2 559	39	1 300	7 006	438	29 759

Processing of rubber and plastics
Class 48

	KBVL	KBVM	KBVN	KBVO	KBVP	KBVR	KBVS	KBVT
1986	8 379	3 274	1 125	44	419	1 777	204	16 084
1987	9 869	3 876	1 280	135	549	2 011	214	18 075
1988	11 028	4 214	1 362	124	651	2 250	225	18 729
1989	12 542	4 704	1 494	64	763	2 578	237	19 867
1990	13 085	5 026	1 555	46	710	2 794	234	21 451
1991	12 886	4 976	1 465	−104	581	2 872	224	22 257
1992	13 923	5 510	1 525	9	644	3 067	224	24 579

Other manufacturing industries
Class 49

	KBVU	KBVV	KBVW	KBVX	KBVY	KBVZ	KBWA	KBWB
1986	2 458	952	475	11	73	534	81	11 747
1987	2 778	1 106	540	78	86	597	84	13 223
1988	3 171	1 314	662	112	115	670	88	14 914
1989	3 492	1 378	666	43	119	763	93	14 906
1990	3 507	1 372	622	6	111	786	85	16 128
1991	3 269	1 305	568	14	99	770	77	16 975
1992	3 501	1 441	607	−2	104	821	79	18 204

See footnotes on the last part of this table.

Source: Office for National Statistics: 01633 812929

21.1
continued

Production survey: summary table
United Kingdom

	Estimates for all firms							
	(£ million)						Average number of persons employed[2] (000s)	Gross value added per person employed (£)
			Stocks and work in progress					
	Gross output (production)[1]	Gross value added	At end of year	Change during year	Capital expenditure *less* disposals	Wages and salaries		
Standard Industrial Classification: Revised 1980								
Construction Division 5								
	KBWC	KBWE	KBWF	KBWG	KBWH	KBWI	KBWJ	KBWK
1986	43 459	13 183	..	..	637	10 851	1 122	11 751
1987	48 013	14 168	..	..	779	11 948	1 140	12 696
1988	59 298	17 061	..	..	1 237	13 261	1 146	14 880
1989	66 268	20 426	..	..	1 422	13 018	1 160	17 605
1990	73 240	20 681	..	..	1 076	16 311	1 163	17 782
1991	66 549	18 306	..	..	621	15 442	1 035	17 683
1992	62 390	17 642	..	..	631	16 000	1 016	17 373

1 Figures for gross output include a substantial amount of duplication represented by the total value of partly manufactured goods sold by one industrial establishment to another. The extent of duplication varies from one census industry to another.
2 The figures include working proprietors but exclude outworkers.

3 Figures for mineral oil and natural gas are not included for 1986-1996.
4 Figures for stocks and work in progress exclude water undertakings and work in progress in the gas industry.
5 Figures for stocks and work in progress exclude goods on hand for sale.

Source: Office for National Statistics: 01633 812929

21.2 Manufacturers sales by industry[1]

£ millions

Industry		SIC (92)	1996	1997	1998	1999
Other mining and quarrying						
Quarrying of stone for construction	KSPF	14110	..	..	..	..
Quarrying of limestone, gypsum and chalk	KSPG	14120	..	..	..	..
Quarrying of slate	KSPH	14130	..	..	..	..
Operation of gravel and sand pits	KSPJ	14210	..	..	..	..
Mining of clays and kaolin	KSPK	14220	..	..	..	..
Mining of chemical and fertilizer minerals	KSPL	14300	138	60	158	..
Production of salt	KSPM	14400	..	..	..	..
Other mining and quarrying n.e.c.	KSPN	14500	54	65	64	..
Manufacture of food products and beverages						
Production and preserving of meat	KSPO	15110	3 646	3 646	3 353	..
Production and preserving of poultry meat	KSPP	15120	1 679	1 650	1 587	..
Bacon and ham production	KSPQ	15131	1 264	1 159	1 014	..
Other meat and poultry meat processing	KSPR	15139[2]	3 361	3 470	3 514	..
Processing and preserving of fish and fish products	KSPS	15200	1 532	1 384	1 397	..
Processing and preserving of potatoes	KSPT	15310	..	1 148	1 151	..
Fruit and vegetable juice	KSPU	15320	488	..	405	..
Processing and preserving of fruit and vegetables n.e.c.	KSPV	15330	2 024	1 966	1 935	..
Crude oils and fats	KSPW	15410	525	587	635	476
Refined oils and fats	KSPX	15420	567	486	489	462
Margarine and similar edible fats	KSPY	15430	478	465	443	442
Operation of dairies	KTEH	15510	..	5 794	5 756	5 593
Ice cream	KSPZ	15520	..	..	..	..
Grain mill products	KSQA	15610	2 927	2 827	2 681	2 707
Starches and starch products	KSQB	15620	482	441	376	378
Prepared feeds for farm animals	KSPI	15710	2 558	2 987	3 488	3 489
Prepared pet foods	KSQC	15720	..	1 458	1 321	1 142
Bread; fresh pastry goods and cakes	KSQD	15810	3 824	3 908	4 299	..
Rusks and biscuits; preserved pastry goods and cakes	KSQE	15820	3 281	..	3 101	..
Sugar	KSQF	15830	1 383	1 308	1 205	..
Cocoa; chocolate and sugar confectionery	KSQG	15840	3 139	3 333	3 312	3 323
Macaroni, noodles, couscous and similar farinaceous products	KSQH	15850	..	..	..	..
Processing of tea and coffee	KSQI	15860	1 349	1 384	1 484	..
Condiments and seasonings	KSQJ	15870	..	..	..	..
Homogenised food preparations and dietetic foods	KSQK	15880	..	..	..	..
Manufacture of other food products n.e.c.	KSQL	15890	..	1 519	1 848	1 871
Distilled potable alcoholic beverages	KSQM	15910	2 263	2 030	2 087	..
Production of ethyl alcohol from fermented materials	KSQN	15920	..	..	..	..
Wines	KSQO	15930	62	83	161	..
Cider and other fruit wines	KSQP	15940	486	517	464	..
Other non-distilled fermented beverages	KSQQ	15950	–	–	–	..
Beer	KSQR	15960	5 458	5 455	4 719	..
Malt	KSQS	15970	..	..	296	..
Mineral waters and soft drinks	KSQT	15980	..	..	2 867	..
Manufacture of tobacco products						
Tobacco products	KSQU	16000	2 616	2 622	2 482	2 440
Manufacture of textiles						
Preparation and spinning of textile fibres	KSQV	17100	..	837	1 000	886
Textile weaving	KSQW	17200	..	518	1 073	972
Finishing of textiles	KSQX	17300	..	778	715	630
Soft furnishings	KSQY	17401	..	723	492	448
Canvas goods, sacks etc	KSQZ	17402	..	145	123	160
Household textiles	KSRA	17403	..	926	896	897
Carpets and rugs	KSRB	17510	..	1 103	1 083	1 031
Cordage, rope, twine and netting	KSRC	17520	..	100	82	80

1 The data are collected under the PRODCOM inquiry which was introduced in 1993. The inquiry replaced the previous QSI/ASI inquiries.
2 Previously 15132.

Source: Office for National Statistics: 01633 813065

357

Production

21.2 Manufacturers sales by industry[1]
continued

£ millions

Industry	SIC (92)	1996	1997	1998	1999
Manufacture of textiles continued					
Nonwovens and articles made from nonwovens, except apparel	KSRD	17530	..	141	145	158
Lace	KSRE	17541	..	88	62	46
Narrow fabrics	KSRF	17542	..	..	233	223
Other textiles n.e.c.	KSRG	17549[2]	..	598	519	502
Knitted and crocheted fabrics	KSRH	17600	..	608	..	460
Knitted and crocheted hosiery	KSRI	17710	..	495	452	368
Knitted and crocheted pullovers, cardigans and similar	KSRJ	17720	..	1 007	759	664
Manufacture of wearing apparel; dressing and dyeing of fur					
Leather clothes	KSRK	18100	..	16	17	15
Workwear	KSRL	18210	..	..	290	285
Men's outerwear	KSRM	18221	..	894	763	618
Other women's outerwear	KSRN	18222	..	1 460	1 297	1 002
Men's underwear	KSRO	18231	..	581	553	440
Women's underwear	KSRP	18232	..	902	911	785
Hats	KSRQ	18241	..	..	70	..
Other wearing apparel and accessories	KSRR	18249[3]	..	212	652	611
Dressing/dyeing of fur; articles of fur	KSRS	18300	..	19	7	6
Tanning and dressing of leather; manufacture of luggage, handbags, saddlery, harness and footwear					
Tanning and dressing of leather	KSRT	19100	444	365	363	323
Luggage, handbags and the like, saddlery and harness	KSRU	19200	239	248	238	262
Footwear	KSRV	19300	1 295	1 026	899	764
Manufacture of wood and of products of wood and cork, except furniture; manufacture of articles of straw and plaiting materials					
Sawmilling and planing of wood, impregnation of wood	KSRW	20100	710	663	619	678
Veneer sheets	KSRX	20200	815	783	709	705
Builders' carpentry and joinery	KSRY	20300	1 972	1 972	2 038	1 832
Wooden containers	KSRZ	20400	567	515	500	449
Other products of wood	KSSA	20510	428	319	383	362
Articles of cork, straw and plaiting materials	KSSB	20520	35	29	..	28
Manufacture of pulp, paper and paper products					
Paper and paperboard	KSSC	21120	..	..	..	..
Corrugated paper and paperboard, sacks and bags	KSSD	21211	..	..	..	..
Cartons, boxes, cases and other containers	KSSE	21219[4]	..	..	..	..
Household and sanitary goods and toilet requisites	KSSF	21220	1 699	1 431	..	..
Paper stationery	KSSG	21230	928	813	739	685
Wallpaper	KSSH	21240	..	..	301	..
Other articles of paper and paperboard n.e.c.	KSSI	21250	..	..	..	..
Publishing, printing and reproduction of recorded media					
Publishing of books	KSSJ	22110	3 001	2 815	2 973	3 294
Publishing of newspapers	KSSK	22120	3 131	3 453	3 573	3 574
Publishing of journals and periodicals	KSSL	22130	5 649	5 754	6 164	6 652
Publishing of sound recordings	KSSM	22140	132	..	..	..
Other publishinig	KSSN	22150	423	417	476	527
Printing of newspapers	KSSO	22210	238	207	..	..
Printing n.e.c.	KSSP	22220	9 372	10 409	9 968	..
Bookbinding and finishing	KSSQ	22230	416	378	359	..
Composition and plate-making	KSSR	22240	723	618	566	..
Other activities related to printing	KSSS	22250	410	519	671	..
Reproduction of sound recording	KSST	22310	372	..	336	..
Reproduction of video recording	KSSU	22320	..	..	194	..
Reproduction of computer media	KSSV	22330	119	92	122	..
Manufacture of chemicals and chemical products					
Industrial gases	KSSW	24110	..	535	625	530
Dyes and pigments	KSSX	24120	..	1 114	1 017	1 046
Other inorganic basic chemicals	KSSY	24130	..	1 538	1 369	1 251
Other organic basic chemicals	KSSZ	24140	..	4 810	4 013	4 094
Fertilizers and nitrogen compounds	KSTA	24150	..	764	617	734

1 The data are collected under the PRODCOM inquiry which was introduced in 1993. The inquiry replaced the previous QSI/ASI inquiries.
2 Previously 17543.
3 Previously 18242.
4 Previously 21212.

Source: Office for National Statistics: 01633 813065

358

21.2 Manufacturers sales by industry[1]
continued

£ millions

Industry	SIC (92)		1996	1997	1998	1999
Manufacture of chemicals and chemical products continued						
Plastics in primary forms	KSTB	24160	..	..	3 305	3 498
Synthetic rubber in primary forms	KSTC	24170	..	207	346	..
Pesticides and other agro-chemical products	KSTD	24200	..	1 159		732
Paints, varnishes and similar coatings, printing ink and mastic	KSTE	24300	..	2 229	2 468	2 607
Basic pharmaceutical products	KSTF	24410	..	624	508	519
Pharmaceutical preparations	KSTG	24420	..	5 969	6 030	7 321
Soap and detergents, cleaning and polishing preparations	KSTH	24510	..	1 889	1 827	1 912
Perfumes and toilet preparations	KSTI	24520	..	..	2 465	2 550
Explosives	KSTJ	24610	..	122	123	101
Glues and gelatines	KSTK	24620	..	397	380	353
Essential oils	KSTL	24630	..	432	461	497
Photographic chemical material	KSTM	24640	..	1 158	1 204	..
Prepared unrecorded media	KSTN	24650	..	..	134	137
Other chemical products n.e.c.	KSTO	24660	..	2 193	2 206	2 321
Man-made fibres	KSTP	24700	..	..	754	671
Manufacture of rubber and plastic products						
Rubber tyres and tubes	KSTQ	25110	1 118	1 006	1 014	972
Retreading and rebuilding of rubber tyres	KSTR	25120	180	..	..	124
Other rubber products	KSTS	25130	1 687	1 740	1 802	1 717
Plastic plates, sheets, tubes and profiles	KSTT	25210	3 351	3 312	3 196	3 158
Plastic packing goods	KSTU	25220	..	..	..	..
Builders' ware of plastic	KSTV	25230	3 084	3 074	3 251	3 155
Other plastic products	KSTW	25240	3 793	3 867	3 918	4 191
Manufacture of other non-metallic mineral products						
Flat glass	KSTX	26110	271	168	159	..
Shaping and processing of flat glass	KSTY	26120	646	738	812	790
Hollow glass	KSTZ	26130	730	744	721	..
Glass fibres	KSUA	26140	349	320	314	298
Manufacturing and processing of other glass incl technical glassware	KSUB	26150	208	..	328	..
Ceramic household and ornamental articles	KSUC	26210	774	740	655	587
Ceramic sanitary fixtures	KSUD	26220	172	..	..	..
Ceramic insulators and insulating fittings	KSUE	26230	..	..	23	..
Other technical ceramic products	KSUF	26240	26	..	..	..
Other ceramic products	KSUG	26250	17	15	22	..
Refractory ceramic products	KSUH	26260	..	303	..	..
Ceramic tiles and flags	KSUI	26300	93	118	103	..
Bricks, tiles and construction products in baked clay	KSUJ	26400	..	601	582	..
Cement	KSUK	26510	647	706	..	774
Lime	KSUL	26520	..	..	..	..
Plaster	KSUM	26530	..	..	..	104
Concrete products for construction purposes	KSUN	26610	1 442	1 647	1 587	..
Plaster products for construction purposes	KSUO	26620	..	258	281	..
Ready mixed concrete	KSUP	26630	981	..	1 047	..
Mortars	KSUQ	26640	111	..	..	69
Fibre cement	KSUR	26650	105	..	96	99
Other articles of concrete, plaster and cement	KSUS	26660	135	127	..	122
Cutting, shaping and finishing of stone	KSUT	26700	205	206	225	..
Abrasive products	KSUU	26810	239	245	239	220
Other non-metallic mineral products n.e.c.	KSUV	26820	775	772	746	675
Manufacture of basic metals						
Cast iron tubes	KSUW	27210	..	154	127	121
Steel tubes	KSUX	27220	1 471	1 398	1 486	1 321
Cold drawing	KSUY	27310	234	223	216	..

1 The data are collected under the PRODCOM inquiry which was introduced in 1993. The inquiry replaced the previous QSI/ASI inquiries.

Source: Office for National Statistics: 01633 813065

Production

21.2 Manufacturers sales by industry[1]
continued

£ millions

Industry		SIC (92)	1996	1997	1998	1999

Manufacture of basic metals continued

Industry		SIC (92)	1996	1997	1998	1999
Cold rolling of narrow strip	KSUZ	27320	93	..	..	..
Cold forming or folding	KSVA	27330	166	157	157	..
Wire drawing	KSVB	27340	353	333	291	..
Other first processing of iron and steel n.e.c.	KSVC	27350	85	98	91	..
Precious metals production	KSVD	27410	252	285	234	267
Aluminium production	KSVE	27420	2 270	2 314	2 160	..
Lead, zinc and tin production	KSVF	27430	492	435	389	363
Copper production	KSVG	27440	..	1 046	856	751
Other non-ferrous metal production	KSVH	27450	671	634	605	505
Casting of iron	KSVI	27510	853	815	757	647
Casting of steel	KSVJ	27520	228	226	185	151
Casting of light metals	KSVK	27530	257	302	318	279
Casting of other non-ferrous metals	KSVL	27540	498	478	464	..

Manufacture of fabricated metal products, except machinery and equipment

Industry		SIC (92)	1996	1997	1998	1999
Metal structures and parts of structures	KSVM	28110	4 058	4 483	4 500	..
Builders' carpentry and joinery of metal	KSVN	28120	778	813	814	..
Tanks, reservoirs and containers of metal	KSVO	28210	385	354	366	..
Central heating radiators and boilers	KSVP	28220	552	593	606	..
Steam generators, except central heating hot water boilers	KSVQ	28300	618	510	533	..
Forging, pressing, stamping and roll forming of metal	KSVR	28400	2 393	2 250	2 207	2 068
Treatment and coating of metals	KSVS	28510	1 052	1 072	1 156	1 123
General mechanical engineering	KSVT	28520	2 811	2 824	2 808	..
Cutlery	KSVU	28610	241	206	220	..
Tools	KSVV	28620	1 106	1 086	1 024	941
Locks and hinges	KSVW	28630	703	723	663	680
Steel drums and similar containers	KSVX	28710	210	209	149	..
Light metal packaging	KSVY	28720	1 417	1 298	1 250	..
Wire products	KSVZ	28730	659	631	607	..
Fasteners, screw machine products, chain and spring	KSWA	28740	866	797	782	684
Other fabricated metal products n.e.c.	KSWB	28750	1 651	1 661	1 726	1 678

Manufacture of machinery and equipment not elsewhere classified

Industry		SIC (92)	1996	1997	1998	1999
Engines and turbines, except aircraft, vehicles and cycle engines	KSWC	29110	1 356	1 444	..	1 566
Pumps	KSWD	29121	..	..	..	1 036
Compressors	KSWE	29122	..	..	..	1 227
Taps and valves	KSWF	29130	..	..	..	1 159
Bearings, gears, gearing and driving elements	KSWG	29140	1 282	1 249	1 080	..
Furnaces and furnace burners	KSWH	29210	374	..	411	310
Lifting and handling equipment	KSWI	29220	2 737	2 641	2 753	2 759
Non-domestic cooling and ventilation equipment	KSWJ	29230	2 296	2 403	2 651	2 516
Other general purpose machinery n.e.c.	KSWK	29240	2 245	2 128	2 292	..
Agricultural tractors	KSWL	29310	..	1 047	1 060	920
Other agricultural and forestry machinery	KSWM	29320	602	592	619	619
Machine tools	KSWN	29400	1 906	2 090	2 025	1 900
Machinery for metallurgy	KSWO	29510	141	105	92	79
Machinery for mining	KSWP	29521	416	465	496	..
Earth-moving equipment	KSWQ	29522	932	1 028	1 020	..
Equipment for concrete crushing and screening and roadworks	KSWR	29523	589	501	499	..
Machinery for food, beverage and tobacco processing	KSWS	29530	893	780	656	661
Machinery for textile, apparel and leather production	KSWT	29540	391	400	683	255
Machinery for paper and paperboard production	KSWU	29550	393	286	318	234
Other special purpose machinery n.e.c.	KSWV	29560	2 216	2 277	2 129	1 963
Weapons and ammunition	KSWW	29600	2 086	1 673	1 724	1 503

1 The data are collected under the PRODCOM inquiry which was introduced in 1993. The inquiry replaced the previous QSI/ASI inquiries.

Source: Office for National Statistics: 01633 813065

21.2
Manufacturers sales by industry[1]

£ millions

Industry	SIC (92)	1996	1997	1998	1999
Manufacture of machinery and equipment not elsewhere classified continued					
Electric domestic appliances	KSYR	29710	1 923	2 025	1 870	1 744
Non-electric domestic appliances	KSWX	29720	498	515	..	495
Manufacture of office machinery and computers					
Office machinery	KSWY	30010	1 005	1 040	1 165	..
Computers and other information processing equipment	KSWZ	30020	11 968	9 974	9 801	9 291
Manufacture of electrical machinery and apparatus not elsewhere classified					
Electric motors, generators and transformers	KSXA	31100	2 635	2 719	2 324	2 236
Electricity, distribution and control apparatus	KSXB	31200	2 510	2 657	2 522	2 552
Insulated wire and cable	KSXC	31300	1 610	1 453	1 415	..
Accumulators, primary cells and batteries	KSXD	31400	526	499	482	500
Lighting equipment and electric lamps	KSXE	31500	1 348	1 333	1 293	1 267
Electrical equipment for engines and vehicles n.e.c.	KSXF	31610	..	1 161	1 144	1 065
Other electrical equipment n.e.c.	KSXG	31620	2 162	1 917	1 745	1 608
Manufacture of radio, television and communication equipment and apparatus					
Electronic valves and tubes and other electronic components	KSXH	32100	3 830	4 099	4 489	3 948
Telegraph and telephone apparatus and equipment	KSXI	32201	..	3 174	3 465	4 518
Radio and electronic capital goods	KSXJ	32202	2 290	2 984	3 004	4 194
Television and radio receivers, sound or video recording etc	KSXK	32300	3 488	3 717	3 400	3 371
Manufacture of medical, precision and optical instruments, watches and clocks					
Medical and surgical equipment and orthopaedic appliances	KSXL	33100	1 811	1 719	1 696	1 748
Instruments and appliances for measuring, checking, testing etc	KSXM	33200	4 811	4 895	4 733	..
Industrial process control equipment	KSXN	33300	654	764	735	..
Optical instruments and photographic equipment	KSXO	33400	876	926	939	989
Watches and clocks	KSXP	33500	85	91	88	..
Manufacture of motor vehicles, trailers and semi-trailers					
Motor vehicles	KSXQ	34100	20 383	20 839	20 868	21 877
Bodies (coachwork) for motor vehicles (exc caravans)	KSXR	34201	801	777	895	..
Trailers and semi-trailers	KSXS	34202	1 049	951	..	..
Caravans	KSXT	34203	387	392	340	..
Parts and accessories for motor vehicles and their engines	KSXU	34300	8 198	7 906	8 580	..
Manufacture of other transport equipment					
Building and repairing of ships	KSXV	35110	..	..	1 585	..
Building and repairing of pleasure and sporting boats	KSXW	35120	..	..	423	..
Railway and tramway locomotives and rolling stock	KSXX	35200	978	976	996	..
Aircraft and spacecraft	KSXY	35300	10 191	11 827	..	13 911
Motorcycles	KSXZ	35410	106	100	104	..
Bicycles	KSYA	35420	148	159	115	112
Invalid carriages	KSYB	35430	97	96	119	..
Other transport equipment n.e.c.	KSYC	35500	65	68	77	..
Manufacture of furniture; manufacturing not elsewhere classified					
Chairs and seats	KSYD	36110	2 348	2 300	2 421	2 373
Other office and shop furniture	KSYE	36120	1 429	1 296	1 286	1 294
Other kitchen furniture	KSYF	36130	920	1 026	908	1 076
Other furniture	KSYG	36140	2 104	2 160	1 950	2 234
Mattresses	KSYH	36150	390	467	493	491
Striking of coins and medals	KSYI	36210	..	..	..	..
Jewellery and related articles n.e.c.	KSYJ	36220	601	554	521	..
Musical instruments	KSYK	36300	63	..	62	55
Sports goods	KSYL	36400	292	264	269	266
Games and toys	KSYM	36500	601	507	465	448
Imitation jewellery	KSYN	36610	..	32	29	..
Brooms and brushes	KSYO	36620	179	192	174	175
Miscellaneous stationers' goods	KSYP	36631	284	287	267	269
Other manufacturing n.e.c.	KSYQ	36639[2]	474	501	504	..

1 The data are collected under the PRODCOM inquiry which was introduced in 1993. The inquiry replaced the previous QSI/ASI inquiries.
2 Previously 36632.

Source: Office for National Statistics: 01633 813065

21.3 Number of local units in manufacturing industries in 2000
United Kingdom
Standard Industrial Classification 1992 Division by Employment Sizeband

				Employment size					
	1 - 9	10 - 19	20 - 49	50 - 99	100 - 199	200 - 499	500 - 999	1 000+	Total
Number of local units									
Division									
15/16 Food products; beverages & tobacco	6 025	1 715	1 150	565	485	450	135	40	10 565
17 Textiles & textile products	3 855	770	665	350	265	145	20	-	6 075
18 Wearing apparel; dressing & dyeing of fur	4 490	955	605	220	145	115	15	-	6540
19 Leather & leather products	670	145	140	75	30	25	-	-	1 085
20 Wood & wood products	6 830	920	530	140	65	25	-	-	8 510
21 Pulp, paper & paper products	1 625	355	450	215	190	115	10	-	2955
22 Publishing, printing & reproduction of recorded media	24 365	2 985	1 610	580	330	185	35	10	30 110
23 Coke, refined petroleum products & nuclear fuel	165	25	30	25	15	10	10	5	285
24 Chemicals, chemical products & man-made fibres	2 430	540	570	365	280	195	70	30	4 480
25 Rubber & plastic products	4 295	1 225	1 095	465	340	175	30	5	7 630
26 Other non-metallic mineral products	5 090	740	565	305	175	105	20	5	7 010
27 Basic metals	1 480	340	370	185	135	100	20	10	2 650
28 Fabricated metal products, except machinery & equipment	21 845	4 100	2 545	845	400	170	20	-	29 930
29 Machinery & equipment not elsewhere classified	9 200	2 060	1 680	670	420	270	60	20	14 380
30 Office machinery & computers	1 000	135	105	40	35	35	10	10	1 370
31 Electrical machinery & apparatus not elsewhere classified	3 870	710	635	285	230	160	35	10	5935
32 Radio, television & communication equipment & apparatus	1 855	300	265	125	110	80	35	20	2 795
33 Medical, precision & optical instruments, watches & clocks	3 310	650	535	275	165	85	20	5	5 050
34 Motor vehicles, trailers & semi-trailers	1 520	355	370	185	150	155	45	30	2 810
35 Other transport equipment	1 690	245	205	95	75	80	40	30	2 465
36/37 Manufacturing not elsewhere classified	16 710	1 755	940	370	200	125	20	-	20 125
Total manufacturing (15/37)	122 320	21 025	15 075	6 390	4 245	2 805	650	235	172 750

1 The analysis follows the Division in the UK Standard Industrial Classification of Economic Activities 1992 - revised edition.
2 The data in this table is taken from the ONS publication Business Monitor *PA1003 - Size Analysis of United Kingdom Businesses* 1999 edition. The count of units refers to local units i.e. individual sites, rather than whole businesses.
3 All counts have been rounded to avoid disclosure.

Source: Office for National Statistics: 01633 813269

21.4 Total inland energy consumption
Heat supplied basis

Million tonnes of oil equivalent[1]

		1989	1990	1991	1992	1993	1994	1995	1996	1997	1998	1999
Inland energy consumption of primary fuels and equivalents[2]	KLWA	212.7	214.9	220.1	217.7	221.0	218.4	218.7	230.5	226.0	229.4	227.8
Coal[3]	KLWB	67.0	67.0	67.1	63.1	54.9	51.3	48.9	46.2	41.1	41.4	36.7
Petroleum[4]	KLWC	76.3	78.3	77.8	78.3	78.5	77.6	75.7	77.9	75.4	74.9	73.4
Primary electricity[5]	KLWD	19.2	17.7	19.2	20.4	23.4	23.1	23.1	23.8	24.8	25.2	24.4
Natural gas[6]	KLWE	49.5	51.2	55.3	55.1	63.0	64.9	69.2	80.9	82.7	85.8	90.9
less Energy used by fuel producers and losses in conversion and distribution	KLWF	66.5	67.6	68.3	65.8	68.3	68.4	69.9	72.0	72.2	74.0	71.0
Total consumption by final users[2]	KLWG	146.2	147.3	151.8	151.9	152.7	150.0	148.8	158.5	153.8	155.4	156.8
Final energy consumption by type of fuel												
Coal (direct use)[7]	KLWH	8.9	8.1	8.6	8.1	7.6	6.9	5.5	4.9	4.4	3.8	4.2
Coke and breeze	KLWI	4.6	4.3	4.0	3.9	3.9	1.2	1.2	1.0	0.8	0.9	0.9
Other solid fuel[7]	KLWJ	0.8	0.8	0.8	0.7	0.8	0.8	0.7	0.8	0.7	0.7	0.6
Coke oven gas	KLWK	0.6	0.6	0.6	0.5	0.6	0.8	0.7	1.3	0.8	0.7	0.6
Natural gas (direct use)[6]	KLWL	44.8	46.1	49.7	48.4	49.3	49.9	51.8	57.4	54.2	55.5	56.9
Electricity	KLWM	23.3	23.6	24.2	24.2	24.6	24.4	25.2	26.2	26.6	27.1	27.5
Petroleum (direct use)[8]	KLWN	62.7	63.3	63.5	64.6	65.4	65.2	63.8	66.1	65.4	65.8	65.0
Final energy consumption by class of consumer												
Agriculture	KLWP	1.3	1.3	1.4	1.4	1.4	1.4	1.3	1.4	1.3	1.4	1.3
Iron and steel industry	KLWQ	8.0	6.9	6.6	6.5	7.0	7.7	7.7	4.7	4.6	4.1	4.1
Other industries	KLWR	30.2	30.9	30.2	29.1	29.9	30.7	30.7	31.2	30.1	29.9	31.3
Railways[9]	KLWS	1.0	1.1	1.1	1.2	1.3	1.3	1.3	1.3	1.2	1.2	1.2
Road transport	KLWT	37.8	38.8	38.5	39.4	39.5	39.7	39.3	40.7	41.2	41.0	40.8
Water transport	KLWU	1.4	1.4	1.4	1.4	1.3	1.2	1.2	1.3	1.3	1.2	1.1
Air transport	KLWV	7.3	7.3	6.9	7.4	7.9	8.1	8.5	8.9	9.3	10.2	10.7
Domestic	KLWW	40.2	40.8	44.8	44.0	45.5	44.0	42.7	48.1	44.9	46.1	46.1
Public administration	KLWX	7.7	7.7	8.5	9.1	8.1	8.3	8.5	8.9	8.6	8.2	7.9
Commercial and other services[10]	KLWY	10.1	10.3	11.0	10.5	11.2	11.0	11.5	12.0	12.1	13.0	13.2

1 Estimates of the gross calorific values used for converting the statistics for the various fuels to them are given in the *Digest of United Kingdom Energy Statistics 1997*.
2 Including, from 1988, small amounts of primary heat sources (solar, geothermal, etc). Up to 1988 includes natural gas used for non-energy purposes (eg petrochemicals).
3 Including net trade and stock change in other solid fuels. Including, from 1988, solid renewable sources (wood, waste, etc).
4 Refinery throughput of crude oil, *plus* net foreign trade and stock change in petroleum products. Petroleum products not used as fuels (chemical feedstock, industrial and white spirits, lubricants, bitumen and wax) are excluded.

5 Primary electricity comprises nuclear, natural flow hydro, net imports of electricity, and from 1988 generation of wind stations.
6 Natural gas includes colliery methane, non-energy use of natural gas up to 1988, and from 1988, landfill gas and sewage gas.
7 Includes from 1988 solid renewable sources.
8 Includes briquettes, ovoids, Phurnacite, Coalite, etc, and from 1988 wood, waste etc used for heat generation.
9 Including fuel used at transport premises from 1990.
10 Including fuel used at transport premises prior to 1990.

Source: Department of Trade and Industry: 020 7215 5187

Production

21.5 Coal: supply and demand

Million tonnes

			1989	1990	1991	1992	1993	1994	1995	1996	1997	1998	1999
Supply													
Production of deep-mined coal	KLXA		79.6	72.9	73.4	65.8	50.5	31.9	35.2	32.2	30.3	25.3	20.9
Production of opencast coal	KLXB		18.6	18.1	18.6	18.2	17.0	16.8	16.4	16.3	16.7	14.8	15.3
Total	KLXC		98.2	91.0	92.0	84.0	67.5	48.7	51.6	48.5	47.0	40.0	36.2
Recovered slurry, fines, etc	KLXD		1.5	1.7	· 2.2	0.5	0.7	0.1	1.5	1.7	1.5	1.1	0.9
Imports	KLXE		12.1	14.8	19.6	20.3	18.4	15.1	15.9	17.8	19.8	21.2	20.8
Total	KLXF		111.8	107.5	113.8	104.8	86.6	64.9	69.0	68.0	68.3	62.4	57.8
Change in colliery stocks	KLXG	KSOL	1.3	−0.9	2.8	2.2	1.8	−4.2	−4.2	−3.0	0.7	−0.3	0.4
Change in stocks at opencast sites	KLXH		1.5	−0.1	−0.8	0.6	0.5	−0.5					
Total supply	KLXI		109.0	108.5	111.8	102.0	84.5	69.6	73.1	71.0	67.6	62.7	57.4
Home consumption													
Electricity supply industry[1]	KLXJ		82.1	84.0	83.6	78.5	66.1	62.4	69.7	65.0	56.9	57.9	49.7
Coke ovens	KLXK		10.8	10.9	10.0	9.0	8.5	8.6	8.7	8.6	8.8	8.7	8.6
Low temperature carbonization plants	KLXL	KYAM	0.8	0.8	0.8	0.6	1.3	1.2	1.0	0.9	0.9	0.6	0.6
Manufactured fuel plants	KLXM		0.9	0.8	0.7	0.7							
Collieries	KLXO		0.1	0.1	0.1	0.1	–	–	–	–	–	–	–
Industry[2,3]	KLXQ		6.8	6.3	6.4	6.6	5.3	4.9	4.0	3.1	3.0	2.5	2.8
Domestic:													
House coal [3,4]	KLXR	LUQM	3.1	2.5	2.7	2.9	2.7	1.9	1.2	1.3	1.3	2.4	2.7
Anthracite and dry steam coal [4,5,6]	KLXS		1.3	1.2	1.6	1.3	1.9	2.0	1.5	1.4	1.3		
Miners' coal	KLXT		0.7	0.6	0.5	0.4	–	–	–	–	–	–	–
Public services	KLXU		0.9	0.9	0.8	0.7	0.6	0.5	0.3	0.4	0.5	0.3	0.3
Miscellaneous	KLXV		0.2	0.3	0.3	0.2	0.2	0.2	0.2	0.2	0.2	0.1	–
Total home consumption	KLXW		107.6	108.3	107.5	100.6	86.6	81.7	77.0	71.3	63.3	62.9	64.7
Overseas shipments and bunkers	KLXX		2.0	2.5	1.7	1.0	1.1	1.2	0.9	1.0	1.1	1.0	0.8
Total consumption and shipments	KLXY		109.6	110.8	109.2	101.6	87.7	82.9	77.9	72.3	64.1	63.8	65.4
Change in distributed stocks[7]	KLXZ		0.4	−0.4	3.6	1.2	−3.6	−13.9	−4.4	−0.8	3.3	−1.0	0.6
Balance[8]	KLYA		1.0	1.9	−1.0	−0.8	0.4	−0.6	−0.4	−0.5	0.3	0.1	−8.6
Stocks at end of year													
Distributed[7]	KLYB		29.2	28.7	32.3	33.5	29.9	16.0	11.6	10.8	14.1	13.1	13.7
At collieries	KLYC	KSOM	6.9	6.0	8.8	10.9	12.7	8.5	7.1	4.2	4.8	4.6	5.0
At opencast sites	KLYD		3.2	3.0	2.2	2.8	3.3	2.8					
Total stocks	KLYE		39.2	37.8	43.3	47.2	45.9	27.3	18.7	14.9	18.9	17.7	18.6

TIME SERIES. Figures relate to periods of 52 weeks.
For 1990, figures relate to 52 weeks estimate for period ended 29 December 1990.

1 Includes quantities used in the production of steam for sale.
2 Colliery and opencast disposals to industry.
3 Includes estimated proportions of steam coal imports.

4 Colliery and opencast disposals to merchants.
5 Including disposals of imported anthracite.
6 Anthracite is also consumed under other categories, including miners' coal and manufactured fuel plants.
7 Great Britain. Stock change excludes industrial and domestic stocks.
8 This is the balance between supply and consumption, shipments and changes in known distributed stocks.

Source: Department of Trade and Industry: 020 7215 2717

21.6 Fuel input and gas output: gas sales[5]
Public supply

		Units	1989	1990	1991	1992	1993	1994	1995	1996	1997	1998	1999
Fuel input to gas industry													
Petroleum	KLZA	Million tonnes	–	–	–	–	–	..	..	..	..	..	..
Petroleum gases[1]	KIJY	Giga-watt hours	88	29	41	51	50	52	..	..	..	..	..
Total to gas works	KIKB	"	88	29	41	51	50	..	..	..	..	..	..
Natural gas for direct supply	KIKC	"	549 450	568 037	616 194	619 921	699 050	724 832	777 483	908 072	..	..	..
Total fuel input	KIKD	"	549 538	568 066	616 235	619 972	702 041	729 426	..	..	..	..	..
Fuel input to gas industry		Million tonnes of coal or coal equivalent											
Petroleum	KLZH	"	–	–	–	–	–	..	..	..	..	..	..
Petroleum gases[1]	KLZI	"	–	–	–	–	–	..	..	..	..	..	..
Total to gas works	KLZL	"	–	–	–	–	–	..	..	..	..	..	..
Natural gas for direct supply	KLZM	"	75.0	77.5	84.1	84.6	95.8	99.5	..	..	..	..	..
Total fuel input	KLZN	"	75.0	77.5	84.1	84.6	95.8	99.5	..	..	..	..	..
Gas output and sales		Giga-watt hours											
Gas output:													
Town gas	KIKE	"	29	29	29	28	32	30	..	..	..	..	..
Natural gas supplied direct	KIKF	"	549 450	568 037	616 194	619 921	699 050	724 832	777 483	908 072	..	..	..
Gross total available	KIKG	"	549 479	568 066	616 223	619 949	699 082	724 862	..	..	..	..	..
Own use[2]	KIKH	"	–2 960	–2 383	–3 007	–2 651	–2 930	–3 090	–3 311	–4 576	..	..	..
Statistical difference[3]	KIKI	"	–8 763	2 638	362	–26 166	29 667	–15 842	..	..	..	..	..
Total sales	KIKJ	"	537 756	553 045	594 854	591 132	666 485	705 930	..	..	..	..	..
Analysis of gas sales													
Fuel producers													
Power stations[4]	KIKK	"	6 108	6 404	6 561	17 894	81 778	114 575	145 790	190 691	250 155	266 600	313 319
Coal extraction and manufacture of solid fuels	KIKL	"	451	338	630	1 042	415	266	368	344	193	67	160
Coke ovens	KIKM	"	59	91	62	108	191	1	1	–	–	–	–
Petroleum refineries	KIKN	"	293	272	279	1 940	2 449	1 933	2 922	3 118	3 122	3 772	3 509
Nuclear fuel production	KIKO	"	410	422	496	508	565	550	467	874	923	989	1 021
Production and distribution of other energy	KIKP	"	193	145	270	447	178	114	352	437	487	549	629
Total final producers	KIKQ	"	7 514	7 672	8 298	21 939	85 576	117 439	149 900	195 464	248 021	262 795	318 637
Final users:													
Iron and steel industry	KIKR	"	13 693	13 594	12 565	13 908	15 577	20 327	20 689	21 460	20 577	21 020	21 936
Other industries	KIKS	"	141 319	146 122	139 488	132 936	132 719	143 979	149 097	165 019	13 888	13 264	14 282
Domestic	KIKT	"	290 557	300 410	333 963	330 100	340 162	329 710	326 010	375 841	345 532	355 895	356 067
Public administration	KIKU	"	34 828	35 376	40 030	43 817	38 725	41 119	47 208	52 011	53 203	52 345	51 365
Agriculture	KIKV	"	938	1 001	1 087	1 286	1 277	1 227	1 210	1 420	1 443	1 344	1 486
Miscellaneous	KIKW	"	48 907	48 844	59 394	54 769	58 917	58 790	61 502	66 504	59 022	64 441	68 050
Total final users	KIKX	"	530 242	545 347	586 527	576 816	587 377	595 152	605 715	682 255	644 524	665 381	513 186
Total sales	KIKY	"	537 756	553 019	594 825	598 755	672 952	712 592	755 615	877 719	892 545	928 176	831 823

Note: The breakdown of consumption by industrial users is made according to the 1980 Standard Industrial Classification, though only data from 1984 are available on this basis.
1 Butane, propane, ethane and refinery tail gases.
2 Used in works, offices, showrooms, etc.
3 Supply greater than recorded demand (-).Includes losses in distribution.

4 Pre-1987 auto-production of electricity is included under the relevant industry, post 1987 it is included under power stations. However, 1987 and 1988 are calculated on a different basis to 1989-1995.
5 It is no longer possible to present information on fuels input into the gas industry and gas output and sales in the same format as in the previous versions of this table. As such, users are directed to chapter 4 of the 2000 edition of the *Digest of United Kingdom Energy Statistics* published by the DTI, where more detailed information on gas production and consumption in the UK is available.

Source: Department of Trade and Industry: 020 7215 2717

21.7 Electricity: generation, supply and consumption
United Kingdom

Gigawatt-hours[6]

		1989	1990	1991	1992	1993	1994	1995	1996	1997	1998	1999
Electricity generated												
Major power producers[1]: total	KLUA	292 896	298 495	301 490	300 177	305 434	306 726	313 958	326 287	323 973	335 145	337 142
Conventional steam stations	KLUB	219 712	230 376	229 190	217 228	187 786	174 943	169 866	160 565	133 132	134 317	118 453
Combined cycle gas turbine stations	KJCS	..	..	312	2 991	22 811	36 971	48 720	65 880	86 974	93 832	114 242
Nuclear stations[7]	KLUC	71 734	65 749	70 543	76 807	89 353	88 282	88 964	94 671	98 146	100 140	96 281
Gas turbines and oil engines	KLUD	529	432	356	358	359	244	190	226	459	229	196
Hydro-electric stations:												
Natural flow	KLUE	4 002	4 393	3 777	4 591	3 522	4 317	4 096	2 801	3 337	4 357	4 422
Pumped storage	KLUF	1 910	1 982	1 523	1 697	1 437	1 463	1 552	1 556	1 486	1 624	2 902
Renewables other than hydro[2]	KLUG	2	4	3	45	165	506	570	588	439	646	646
Other generators[3]: total	KLUH	21 690	21 244	21 385	20 864	17 669	18 252	20 084	21 096	24 478	26 870	29 656
Conventional steam stations[4]	KLUI	15 241	15 014	15 230	15 049	14 865	14 263	15 387	16 028	17 451	17 820	18 072
Combined cycle gas turbine stations	KJCT	..	292	310	409	607	1 505	2 126	2 404	3 375	4 701	6 415
Hydro-electric stations (natural flow)	KLUK	747	814	847	840	780	777	742	560	832	880	930
Renewables other than hydro[2]	KILA	708	683	784	1 028	1 417	1 707	1 829	2 104	2 820	3 469	4 239
All generating companies: total	KLUL	314 585	319 739	322 875	321 043	323 102	324 978	334 042	347 383	348 451	362 014	366 798
Conventional steam stations[4]	KLUM	234 953	245 390	244 420	232 277	202 651	189 207	185 253	176 553	150 583	152 137	136 525
Combined cycle gas turbine stations	KJCU	..	292	622	3 400	23 418	38 475	50 846	68 284	90 349	98 533	120 657
Nuclear stations	KLUN	71 734	65 749	70 543	76 807	89 353	88 282	88 964	94 671	98 146	100 140	96 281
Gas turbines and oil engines	KLUO	529	432	356	358	359	244	190	226	459	221	196
Hydro-electric stations:												
Natural flow	KLUP	4 749	5 207	4 624	5 431	4 302	5 094	4 838	3 361	4 169	5 237	5 352
Pumped storage	KLUQ	1 910	1 982	1 523	1 697	1 437	1 463	1 552	1 556	1 486	1 624	2 902
Renewables other than hydro[2]	KLUR	710	687	787	1 073	1 582	2 213	2 399	2 692	3 259	4 115	4 885
Electricity used on works: Total	KLUS	20 263	19 611	20 111	20 237	19 287	17 491	17 411	17 697	16 503	17 686	17 456
Major generating companies[1]	KLUT	18 610	17 891	18 424	18 485	17 391	16 696	16 510	16 674	15 404	16 471	16 182
Other generators[3]	KLUU	1 653	1 720	1 687	1 752	1 896	795	901	1 023	1 099	1 215	1 274
Electricity supplied (gross)												
Major power producers[1]: total	KLUV	274 286	280 604	283 066	281 692	287 264	290 780	299 000	311 169	308 569	318 674	320 960
Conventional steam stations[5]	KLUW	208 675	218 957	217 947	205 897	178 312	166 883	162 084	153 170	127 075	127 581	112 552
Combined cycle gas turbine stations	KJCV	..	..	309	2 964	22 611	36 815	48 525	65 604	86 682	93 005	112 763
Nuclear stations	KLUX	63 602	58 664	62 761	69 135	80 979	79 962	80 598	85 820	89 341	91 186	87 672
Gas turbines and oil engines[5]	KLUY	494	403	310	311	324	233	181	216	344	210	186
Hydro-electric stations:												
Natural flow	KLUZ	3 992	4 384	3 767	4 579	3 513	4 265	4 051	2 763	3 299	4 344	4 409
Pumped storage	KLVA	1 812	1 892	1 465	1 635	1 388	1 417	1 502	1 507	1 439	1 569	2 804
Renewables other than hydro[2]	KLVB	2	3	3	37	136	455	506	533	389	572	574
Other generators[3]: total	KLVC	20 037	19 524	19 698	19 112	16 522	18 207	20 909	21 674	23 379	25 655	28 382
Conventional steam stations[4]	KLVD	14 326	14 082	14 312	14 033	13 836	14 183	15 815	16 340	15 583	15 143	18 146
Combined cycle gas turbine stations	KJCW	..	280	298	394	584	1 466	2 100	2 374	3 263	4 547	6 207
Hydro-electric stations (natural flow)	KLVF	654	806	839	832	772	769	733	585	823	868	917
Renewables other than hydro[2]	KIKZ	681	656	753	987	1 360	1 639	1 738	1 999	2 667	3 278	3 112
All generating companies: total	KLVG	294 323	300 128	302 764	300 804	303 815	308 987	319 909	332 843	331 948	344 328	349 342
Conventional steam stations[4,5]	KLVH	223 001	233 039	232 259	219 930	192 148	180 446	176 696	168 285	143 701	144 543	130 698
Combined cycle gas turbine stations	KJCX	..	280	607	3 358	23 195	38 281	50 625	67 978	89 945	97 552	118 970
Nuclear stations	KLVI	63 602	58 664	62 761	69 135	80 979	79 962	80 598	85 820	89 341	91 186	87 672
Gas turbines and oil engines[5]	KLVJ	494	403	310	311	324	233	181	216	344	210	186
Hydro-electric stations:												
Natural flow	KLVK	4 730	5 190	4 666	5 411	4 285	5 034	4 784	3 348	4 122	5 212	5 326
Pumped storage	KLVL	1 812	1 892	1 465	1 635	1 388	1 417	1 502	1 507	1 439	1 569	2 804
Renewables other than hydro[2]	KLVM	684	659	756	1 024	1 496	2 094	2 244	2 532	3 049	3 845	3 686
Electricity used in pumping												
Major power producers[1]	KLVN	2 572	2 626	2 109	2 257	1 948	2 051	2 282	2 430	2 477	2 594	3 774
Electricity supplied (net): Total	KLVO	291 751	297 502	300 654	298 547	301 868	306 936	317 627	330 413	329 471	341 734	345 568
Major power producers[1]	KLVP	271 714	277 978	280 956	279 435	285 316	288 729	296 718	308 739	306 092	316 080	317 186
Other generators[3]	KLVQ	20 037	19 524	19 698	19 112	16 552	18 207	20 909	21 674	23 379	25 655	28 382
Net imports	KGEZ	12 631	11 990	16 408	16 694	16 716	16 887	16 313	16 755	16 574	12 468	14 244
Electricity available	KGIZ	304 382	309 408	317 062	315 241	318 584	323 830	333 940	347 168	346 045	354 202	359 812
Losses in transmission etc	KGKW	24 983	24 988	26 221	23 788	22 838	31 000	30 020	31 300	26 949	29 161	29 872
Electricity consumption: Total	KGKX	279 399	284 420	290 841	291 453	295 746	292 830	303 920	315 868	319 101	325 040	329 940
Fuel industries	KGKY	9 001	9 986	9 794	9 984	9 615	7 518	8 070	8 850	8 290	8 130	8 315
Final users: total	KGKZ	270 398	274 434	281 048	281 468	286 130	285 310	295 849	307 024	310 820	316 910	321 625
Industrial sector	KGLZ	99 417	100 643	99 570	95 277	96 842	96 120	101 780	104 320	106 160	106 810	109 790
Domestic sector	KGMZ	92 270	93 793	98 098	99 482	100 456	101 407	102 210	107 513	104 455	109 610	110 408
Other sectors	KGNZ	78 711	79 997	83 380	86 711	88 833	87 790	91 860	95 190	100 190	100 490	101 430

1 Generating companies corresponding to the old public sector supply system. See chapter introduction.
2 Including wind and biofuels.
3 Larger establishments in the industrial and transport sectors generating 1 Gigawatt-hour or more a year.
4 For other generators, conventional steam stations cover all types of station not separately listed

5 Prior to 1986 gas turbines and oil engines are included with conventional steam stations.
6 1 Gigawatt-hour equals 1 million kilowatt hours.
7 Nuclear generators are now included under "major power producers" only.

Source: Department of Trade and Industry: 020 7215 5190

21.8 Electricity: plant capacity and demand
United Kingdom

Megawatts

		1991 end-March	1992 end-March	1993 end-March	1994 end-March	1995 end-March	1996 end-March	*1996* end-December[8]	1997 end-December[8]	1998 end-December[8]	1999
Major power producers[1]:											
Total declared net capability	KGON	69 320	66 336	63 377	66 901	64 923	66 100	69 090	68 288	68 390	70 091
Conventional steam stations	KGOO	51 365	48 309	44 860	41 143	38 453	38 242	38 230	37 395	35 039	35 427
Combined cycle gas turbine stations	KJCZ	..	229	1 129	5 463	8 364	9 034	12 052	12 252	14 680	16 143
Nuclear stations[7,9]	KGOP	11 353	11 353	11 353	11 894	12 037	12 762	12 916	12 946	12 956	12 956
Gas turbines and oil engines	KGOQ	3 130	2 968	2 539	2 248	1 895	1 890	1 721	1 526	1 492	1 333
Hydro-electric stations:											
Natural flow	KGOR	1 302	1 308	1 314	1 314	1 314	1 314	1 313	1 311	1 327	1 327
Pumped storage	KGOS	2 787	2 787	2 787	2 787	2 788	2 788		2 788	2 788	2 788
Renewables other than hydro	KGOT	3	2	15	52	72	71	70	70	108	117
Other generators[2]:											
Total capacity of own generating plant[3]	KGOU	4 205	4 210	4 122	3 622	3 818	4 025	4 181	4 408	4 763	5 214
Conventional steam stations[4]	KGOV	3 279	3 211	3 037	3 096	3 257	3 234	3 192	3 223	3 246	3 334
Combined cycle gas turbine stations	KJDA	76	102	150	150	153	343	410	551	780	1 052
Hydro-electric stations (natural flow)	KGOX	108	122	110	111	111	118	142	145	148	150
Renewables other than hydro	KILB	122	155	205	265	297	330	437	489	589	678
All generating companies: Total capacity[3]	KGOY	73 525	70 546	67 499	68 523	68 741	70 126	73 271	72 696	73 153	75 305
Conventional steam stations[4]	KGOZ	54 644	51 520	47 897	44 239	41 710	41 476	41 422	40 618	38 327	38 761
Combined cycle gas turbine stations	KJDC	76	331	1 279	5 613	8 517	9 377	12 462	12 803	15 418	17 195
Nuclear stations[7]	KGPM	11 353	11 353	11 353	11 894	12 037	12 762	12 916	12 946	12 956	12 956
Gas turbines and oil engines	KGPN	3 130	2 968	2 539	2 248	1 895	1 890	1 721	1 526	1 492	1 333
Hydro-electric stations:											
Natural flow	KGPO	1 410	1 430	1 424	1 425	1 425	1 432	1 455	1 456	1 475	1 477
Pumped storage	KGPP	2 787	2 787	2 787	2 787	2 788	2 788		2 788	2 788	2 788
Renewables other than hydro	KGPQ	125	157	220	317	369	401	507	559	697	795
Major power producers[1]:											
Simultaneous maximum load met[5]	KGPR	54 068	54 472	51 663	54 848	52 362	55 611	56 815	56 965	56 312	57 849
Major power producers[1]:											
System load factor[6] (percentage)	KGQY	62.2	62.9	66.6	63.8	67.3	65.4	65.5	65.4	67.2	66.1

1 See footnote 1 to Table 21.7.
2 See footnote 3 to Table 21.7.
3 Capacity figures for other generators are as at end-December of the previous year.
4 For other generators, conventional steam stations cover all types of stations not separately listed.
5 Maximum load in year to end of March.

6 The average hourly quantity of electricity available during the year ended March expressed as a percentage of the maximum demand.
7 The 1995 figure includes 300 MW of the 1 188 MW capacity of Sizewell B which began to produce electricity in March 1995.
8 From 1996 data are on a calendar year basis.
9 Nuclear generators are now included under "major power producers" only.

Source: Department of Trade and Industry: 020 7215 5190

21.9 Electricity: fuel used in generation
United Kingdom

Million tonnes of oil equivalent

		1989	1990	1991	1992	1993	1994	1995	1996	1997	1998	1999
Major power producers[1]: total all fuels	KGPS	74.10	72.20	72.90	71.30	72.32	71.65	72.72	74.61	73.17	75.33	73.63
Coal	FTAJ	50.7	49.0	49.0	46.0	38.3	35.9	35.0	32.4	27.7	29.0	24.1
Oil[2]	FTAK	5.6	6.8	5.9	5.0	4.4	3.6	3.1	3.0	1.4	0.8	0.8
Gas[3]	KGPT	–	–	–	1.0	6.3	9.1	11.4	15.2	19.2	20.4	24.2
Nuclear	FTAL	17.7	16.3	17.4	18.5	21.6	21.2	21.3	22.2	23.0	23.6	22.7
Hydro (natural flow)	FTAM	0.3	0.4	0.3	0.4	0.3	0.4	0.4	0.3	0.3	0.4	0.4
Other fuels used by UK companies[3]	KGPU	–	–	–	–	0.1	0.1	0.1	0.2	0.2	0.1	0.2
Net imports	KGPV	1.1	1.0	1.4	1.4	1.4	1.5	1.4	1.4	1.4	1.1	1.2
Other generators[4]: total all fuels	KGPW	6.1	5.2	5.4	6.7	4.5	3.5	5.8	6.0	6.5	7.0	7.1
Transport undertakings												
Gas	KGPX	0.2	0.2	0.2	0.2	0.2	0.2	0.2	0.2	0.2	0.2	0.2
Undertakings in industrial sector												
Coal	KGPY	0.9	1.0	1.0	1.0	1.3	1.2	1.3	1.2	1.3	1.3	0.9
Oil	KGPZ	1.6	1.6	1.7	3.1	1.4	0.5	1.0	1.0	0.9	1.0	0.9
Gas	KGQM	0.3	0.3	0.3	0.3	0.8	0.6	1.6	1.8	2.1	2.3	2.5
Hydro (natural flow)	KGQO	0.1	0.1	0.1	0.1	0.1	0.1	0.1	0.1	0.1	0.1	0.1
Other fuels	KGQP	1.7	1.8	1.9	1.1	1.0	1.0	1.7	1.8	1.9	2.2	2.4
All generating companies[4]: total fuels	KGQQ	80.2	77.4	78.3	78.0	76.8	75.2	78.6	80.6	79.7	82.4	80.7
Coal	KGQR	51.6	50.0	50.0	46.9	39.6	37.1	36.3	33.6	29.0	30.2	25.1
Oil	KGQS	7.1	8.4	7.6	8.1	5.8	4.1	4.1	4.0	2.3	1.8	1.8
Gas[3]	KGQT	0.5	0.6	0.6	1.5	7.0	9.9	13.3	17.2	21.5	22.9	26.9
Nuclear	KGQU	17.7	16.3	17.4	18.5	21.6	21.2	21.3	22.2	23.0	23.6	22.7
Hydro (natural flow)	KGQV	0.4	0.4	0.4	0.5	0.4	0.4	0.4	0.3	0.4	0.5	0.5
Other fuels used by UK companies[3,5]	KGQW	1.7	1.8	0.9	1.1	1.0	1.1	1.8	1.9	2.1	2.3	2.6
Net imports	KGQX	1.1	1.0	1.4	1.4	1.4	1.5	1.4	1.4	1.4	1.1	1.2

1 See footnote 1 to Table 21.7.
2 Includes oil used in gas turbine and diesel plant for lighting up coal fired boilers and Orimulsion.
3 For 1990 and 1991 gas used by major power producers was included with other fuels for reasons of confidentiality.

4 See footnote 3 to Table 21.7. Prior to 1987 'other generators' covers only transport undertakings and industrial hydro and nuclear stations. For years 1987 to 1989 figures for fuel used by other generators are largely estimated.
5 Main fuels included are coke oven gas, blast furnace gas, waste products from chemical processes and sludge gas.
6 Nuclear generators are now included under "major power producers" only.

Source: Department of Trade and Industry: 020 7215 5190

Production

21.10 Indigenous production, refinery receipts, imports and exports of oil[1]

Thousand tonnes

		1989	1990	1991	1992	1993	1994	1995	1996	1997	1998	1999
Total indigenous petroleum production[2]	KMBA	91 710	91 064	91 260	94 251	100 188	126 812	129 894	129 742	128 234	132 633	137 099
Crude petroleum[3]:												
Refinery receipts total	KMBB	88 840	89 735	92 523	92 789	97 400	93 771	93 572	96 721	97 032	94 071	89 345
Indigenous[4]	KMBC	39 585	37 754	35 932	35 472	36 680	42 174	44 872	49 449	47 589	46 382	50 886
Other[5]	KMBD	904	916	772	832	852	427	1 110	997	794	1 255	2 113
Net foreign arrivals[6]	KMBE	48 351	51 065	55 819	56 485	59 868	51 170	47 590	48 275	48 649	46 434	36 346
Foreign trade												
Imports[6]	KMBF	49 500	52 710	57 084	57 683	61 701	53 096	48 749	50 099	49 994	47 957	44 891
Exports												
Indigenous	KMBG	49 130	54 022	52 396	54 441	60 165	77 466	77 926	76 937	74 708	77 765	82 176
Other[7]	KMBH	1 332	1 878	1 406	1 536	2 225	2 359	1 761	2 219	1 805	2 051	3 362
Petroleum products												
Foreign trade												
Imports[6]	KMBI	9 479	11 005	10 140	10 567	10 064	10 441	9 878	9 316	8 705	11 327	11 953
Exports[6]	KMBJ	17 873	18 002	20 677	21 899	24 890	24 644	24 418	26 018	29 118	26 895	24 826
Net imports[6]	KMBK	−8 394	−6 997	−10 537	−11 332	−14 826	−14 203	−14 540	−16 702	20 413	−15 568	−12 873
Bunkers[8]	KMBL	2 396	2 538	2 486	2 546	2 478	2 313	2 465	2 664	2 961	3 080	2 329

1 The term 'indigenous' is used in this table for convenience to include oil from the UK Continental Shelf as well as the small amounts produced on the mainland.
2 Crude oil *plus* condensates and petroleum gases derived at onshore treatment plants.
3 Includes process(partly refined) oils.
4 Includes condensate for distillation.

5 Mainly recycled products.
6 Foreign trade as recorded by the petroleum industry and may differ from figures published in *Overseas Trade Statistics*.
7 Re-exports of imported crude which may include some indigenous oil in blend.
8 International marine bunkers.

Source: Department of Trade and Industry: 020 7215 5184

21.11 Throughput of crude and process oils and output of refined products from refineries[1]

Thousand tonnes

		1989	1990	1991	1992	1993	1994	1995	1996	1997	1998	1999
Throughput of crude and process oils	KMAU	87 699	88 692	92 001	92 334	96 274	93 162	92 743	96 661	97 024	93 797	88 285
less: Refinery fuel[2]:	KMAA	5 816	5 838	6 058	6 080	6 383	6 256	6 481	6 623	6 572	6 468	5 976
Losses	KMAB	491	568	467	471	308	261	129	152	86	233	324
Total output of refined products	KMAC	81 392	82 286	85 476	85 783	89 583	86 645	86 133	89 885	90 366	87 096	81 985
Gases:												
Butane and propane	KMAE	1 568	1 514	1 664	1 583	1 575	1 605	1 815	1 828	1 950	1 978	2 002
Other petroleum	KMAF	90	106	134	172	162	132	133	144	139	200	209
Naphtha and other feedstock	KMAG	2 073	2 139	2 515	3 040	2 696	2 794	2 711	2 824	2 854	2 335	2 465
Aviation spirit	KMAH	–	–	–	–	–	–	–	–	–	–	16
Motor spirit	KMAJ	27 237	26 724	27 793	27 980	28 394	27 562	27 254	28 046	28 260	27 392	25 587
Industrial and white spirit	KMAK	105	121	136	150	159	143	143	136	128	136	130
Kerosene:												
Aviation turbine fuel	KMAL	7 092	7 541	7 037	7 681	8 341	7 697	7 837	8 305	8 342	7 942	7 352
Burning oil	KMAM	2 309	2 344	2 446	2 450	2 707	2 967	2 924	3 510	3 336	3 471	3 603
Gas/diesel oil	KMAN	23 292	23 402	26 057	25 650	27 361	27 137	27 169	28 903	28 778	27 859	26 226
Fuel oil	KMAO	13 020	13 805	13 205	12 388	13 183	11 378	10 969	11 479	11 747	11 066	10 289
Lubricating oil	KMAP	1 050	974	973	1 163	1 264	1 296	1 261	1 111	1 231	1 134	920
Bitumen	KMAQ	2 393	2 454	2 302	2 336	2 450	2 569	2 459	2 189	2 258	2 190	1 667
Petroleum wax	KMAR	54	40	37	62	59	64	46	41	65	59	264
Petroleum coke	KMAS	564	586	555	535	621	679	759	714	598	694	648
Other products	KMAT	545	536	620	593	613	623	653	655	680	640	607

1 Crude and process oils comprise all feedstocks, other than distillation benzines, for treatment at refinery plants. Refinery production does not cover further treatment of finished products for special grades such as in distillation plant for the preparation of industrial spirits.

2 Comprising 2 681 thousand tonnes gases, 2 079 thousand tonnes fuel oil and 1 216 thousand tonnes other products in 1999.

Source: Department of Trade and Industry: 020 7215 5184

21.12 Deliveries of petroleum products for inland consumption

Thousand tonnes

		1989	1990	1991	1992	1993	1994	1995	1996	1997	1998	1999
Total (including refinery fuel)	KMCA	78 844	79 781	80 564	81 550	82 173	81 213	80 175	82 013	79 073	78 437	76 949
Total (excluding refinery fuel)	KMCB	73 028	73 943	74 506	75 470	75 970	74 957	73 694	75 390	72 501	71 969	70 973
Gases:												
Butane and propane:												
For gas works	KMCC	33	37	42	40	41	47	43	48	45	46	46
Other uses	KMCD	1 045	1 009	1 172	1 049	1 094	1 153	1 158	1 272	1 148	1 108	1 021
Other gases:												
Other uses	KMCF	49	48	63	58	48	88	98	101	73	69	74
Feedstock:												
For petroleum chemical plants	KMCG	5 816	5 115	5 935	5 970	5 921	6 199	6 227	6 228	6 088	6 322	6 650
Aviation spirit	KMCI	29	26	24	27	27	29	29	32	37	36	44
Dealers:												
4 star	KMCK	18 325	15 586	13 793	12 481	11 046	9 503	7 973	7 043	6 138	4 595	2 702
3 star	KMCL	2	–	–	–	–	–	–	–	–	–	–
2 star	KMCM	321	–	–	–	–	–	–	–	–	–	–
Unleaded	KMCN	4 543	8 060	9 587	10 942	12 193	12 859	13 529	14 926	15 694	16 841	18 435
Commercial consumers:												
4 star	KMCO	582	472	360	294	217	178	149	135	112	91	59
3 star	KMCP	14	–	–	–	–	–	–	–	–	–	–
2 star	KMCQ	31	–	–	–	–	–	–	–	–	–	–
Unleaded	KMCR	105	197	282	326	311	303	302	305	307	321	316
Motor spirit: total	BHOD	23 923	24 315	24 022	24 043	23 767	22 843	21 953	22 409	22 251	17 703	21 512
Industrial and white spirits	KMCS	207	171	162	159	164	170	178	184	195	179	165
Kerosene:												
Aviation turbine fuel	BHOE	6 564	6 589	6 176	6 666	7 106	7 284	7 660	8 049	8 411	9 241	9 659
Burning oil	KMCT	1 937	2 058	2 383	2 472	2 625	2 655	2 774	3 336	3 343	3 575	3 557
Gas/diesel oil:												
Derv fuel	BHOI	10 118	10 652	10 694	11 132	11 806	12 914	13 457	14 365	14 976	15 143	15 188
Other	BHOJ	8 323	8 046	8 031	7 871	7 782	7 491	7 227	7 631	7 326	7 244	6 806
Fuel oil	BHOK	11 125	11 997	11 948	11 481	10 770	9 275	7 975	6 854	3 936	2 935	2 186
Lubricating oils	BHOL	839	822	759	786	806	795	895	864	872	813	790
Bitumen	BHOM	2 423	2 491	2 514	2 555	2 523	2 595	2 420	2 146	2 015	1 967	1 963
Petroleum wax	KMCU	77	55	49	47	48	47	44	44	44	18	19
Petroleum coke	KMCV	120	112	154	682	778	911	1 008	1 210	1 095	887	939
Miscellaneous products	KMCW	399	403	380	433	484	461	549	617	644	538	354

1 Including a small quantity supplied for use as fuel by other consumers.

Source: Department of Trade and Industry: 020 7215 5184

21.13 Iron and steel
Summary of steel supplies, deliveries and stocks
United Kingdom

		Finished product weight - thousand tonnes										
		1989	1990	1991	1992	1993	1994	1995	1996	1997	1998	1999
Supply, disposal and consumption												
UK producers' home deliveries	KLTA	10 907	9 711	7 951	7 315	7 567	7 827	8 257	8 383	8 626	8 260	7 652
Imports excl steelworks receipts	KLTB	4 424	4 446	4 509	4 418	4 132	5 012	5 384	5 147	5 894	6 466	6 014
Total deliveries to home market (a)	KLTC	15 331	14 157	12 460	11 733	11 698	12 839	13 641	13 530	14 520	14 726	13 667
Total exports (producers, consumers, merchants)	KLTD	6 180	6 550	7 444	7 718	7 621	8 120	8 228	8 917	9 060	8 008	7 538
Exports by UK producers	KLTE	5 973	6 370	7 082	7 587	7 536	7 873	7 828	8 305	8 534	7 876	7 416
Derived consumers' and merchants' exports (b)	KLTF	207	180	362	131	85	247	400	612	526	132	122
Net home disposals (a)-(b)	KLTG	15 124	13 977	12 098	11 602	11 614	12 592	13 241	12 918	13 994	14 594	13 545
Consumers' and merchants' stock change	KLTH	220	−290	−400	60	60	390	..	..	..	..	..
Estimated home consumption	KLTI	14 904	14 267	12 498	11 542	11 554	12 202	13 241	12 918	13 994	14 594	13 545
Stocks												
Producers												
- ingots & semis	KLTJ	1 182	1 245	1 035	933	1 005	946	1 068	767	946	717	747
- finished steel	KLTK	1 692	1 563	1 719	1 573	1 425	1 389	1 274	1 515	1 358	1 495	1 318
Consumers	KLTL	1 700	1 590	1 400	1 410	1 300	1 470	..	..	..	..	..
Merchants	KLTM	1 230	1 050	840	890	1 060	1 280	..	..	..	..	..

		Crude steel equivalent - million tonnes										
		1989	1990	1991	1992	1993	1994	1995	1996	1997	1998	1999
Estimated home consumption												
Crude steel production[1]	KLTN	18.74	17.84	16.47	16.21	16.62	17.28	17.60	17.99	18.50	17.32	16.28
Producers' stock change	KLTO	−0.09	−0.08	−0.07	−0.30	−0.09	−0.12	0.01	−0.07	0.03	−0.11	−0.19
Re-usable material	KLTP	0.10	0.10	0.07	0.06	0.08	0.09	0.08	0.07	0.06	0.02	..
Total supply from home sources	KLTQ	18.93	18.02	16.61	16.57	16.79	17.49	17.67	18.13	18.53	17.45	16.47
Total imports[2]	KLTR	6.25	5.96	6.21	5.99	5.44	6.58	7.05	7.01	7.49	8.38	7.81
Total exports[2]	KLTS	7.49	7.66	8.72	9.07	8.95	9.55	9.63	10.26	10.43	9.25	8.70
Net home disposals	KLTT	17.69	16.32	14.10	13.49	13.28	14.52	15.09	14.88	15.59	16.58	15.58
Consumers' and merchants' stock change	KLTU	0.29	−0.37	−0.50	0.07	0.07	0.48	..	..	..	..	..
Estimated home consumption	KLTV	17.40	16.69	14.60	13.42	13.21	14.04	15.09	14.88	15.59	16.58	15.58

TIME SERIES. The figures relate to periods of 52 weeks (53 weeks in 1992).

1 Includes liquid steel for castings.
2 Based on HM Customs Statistics, reflecting total trade rather than producers' trade.

Source: Iron and Steel Statistics Bureau: 020 8686 9050 ext 126

21.14 Iron and steel
Iron ore, manganese ore, pig iron and iron and steel scrap
United Kingdom

Thousand tonnes

		1989	1990	1991	1992	1993	1994	1995	1996	1997	1998	1999
Iron ore												
Jurassic	KLOA	32	53	57	29	–	–	–	–	–	–	–
Hematite	KLOB	–	–	–	–	–	–	–	–	–	–	–
Production: total	KLOC	32	53	57	29	–	–	–	–	–	–	–
Home produced	KLOD	37	53	57	29	–	–	–	–	–	–	–
Imported	KLOE	18 563	17 935	17 833	17 235	17 507	18 161	18 670	19 720	20 820	19 532	18 739
Consumption: total	KLOF	18 600	17 988	17 890	17 264	17 507	18 161	18 670	19 720	20 820	19 532	18 739
Manganese ore												
Consumption	KLOG	339	340	383	308	152	64	32	48	37	22	14
Pig iron (and blast furnace ferro-alloys)												
Average number of furnaces in blast during period	KLOH	*11*	*10*	*8*	*8*	*8*	*8*	*8*	*9*	*9*	*9*	*9*
Production												
Steelmaking iron	KLOI	12 551	12 218	11 834	11 469	11 534	11 943	12 236	12 830	13 054	12 746	12 139
Foundry iron	KLOJ	87	102	50	73	–	–	–	–	–	–	–
Speigeleisen and ferro-manganese	KLOK	143	143	178	137	45	–	–	–	–	–	–
In blast furnaces: total	KLOL	12 781	12 463	12 062	11 679	11 579	11 943	12 236	12 830	13 054	12 746	12 139
In steel works and steel foundries	KLOM	12 771	12 358	11 836	11 463	11 554	11 889	12 121	12 753	13 044	12 746	12 139
In iron foundries	KLON	146	195	181	214	..	..	..	..	..	..	..
Consumption of pig iron: total	KLOO	12 917	12 553	12 017	11 677	11 554	11 889	12 121	12 753	13 044	12 746	12 139
Pig iron stocks (end of period)	KLOP	85	..	..	..	..	..	..	..	..	..	..
Iron and steel scrap												
Steelworks and steel foundries												
Circulating scrap	KLOQ	2 817	2 489	2 332	2 449	2 303	2 326	2 390	2 639	2 459	2 380	2 488
Purchased receipts	KLOR	5 172	4 730	3 694	3 739	4 149	4 533	4 688	4 130	5 418	4 045	3 433
Consumption	KLOS	7 904	7 251	6 085	6 190	6 550	6 874	7 012	6 828	7 207	6 408	5 884
Stocks (end of period)	KLOT	467	430	365	365	267	253	319	260	236	253	290
Iron foundries												
Arisings	KLOU	453	693	582	587	..	..	..	..	..	..	..
Consumption	KLOV	1 137	1 609	1 457	1 556	..	..	..	..	..	..	..
Stocks (end of period)	KLOW	64	..	..	..	..	..	..	..	..	..	..

TIME SERIES. The figures relate to periods of 52 weeks (53 weeks in 1992).

Source: Iron and Steel Statistics Bureau: 020 8686 9050 ext 126

Production

21.15 Iron and steel
Number of furnaces and production of steel
United Kingdom

		1989	1990	1991	1992	1993	1994	1995	1996	1997	1998	1999
Steel furnaces												
(Number in existence at end of period)[1]												
Total	KLPA	229	214	209	206	202	202	192	192	192	190	181
Open hearth	KLPB	–	–	–	–	–	–	–	–	–	–	–
Oxygen converters	KLPC	14	14	14	11	11	11	11	11	11	11	11
Electric	KLPD	215	200	195	195	191	191	181	181	181	179	170
Stock and tropenas	KLPE	–	–	–	–	–	–	–	–	–	–	–
Production of crude steel												
(thousand tonnes)												
Total	KLPF	18 740	17 841	16 474	16 212	16 625	17 286	17 604	17 992	18 499	17 315	16 284
by process												
Open hearth	KLPG	–	–	–	–	–	–	–	–	–	–	–
Oxygen converters	KLPH	13 627	13 169	12 540	12 092	12 330	12 909	13 082	13 758	13 986	13 426	12 634
Electric	KLPI	5 113	4 672	3 934	4 120	4 295	4 377	4 522	4 234	4 513	3 889	3 650
Stock and tropenas	KLPJ	–	–	–	–	–	–	–	–	–	–	–
by cast method												
Cast to ingot	KLPK	3 469	2 692	2 201	2 083	2 140	2 033	2 174	1 892	1 660	784	534
Continuously cast	KLPL	15 031	14 909	14 085	13 958	14 319	15 079	15 250	15 912	16 653	16 346	15 622
Steel for castings	KLPM	240	240	189	171	166	174	180	188	186	185	128
by quality												
Non alloy steel	KLPN	17 371	16 641	15 496	15 195	15 558	16 062	16 243	16 708	17 193	16 145	15 253
Stainless and other alloy steel	KLPO	1 369	1 200	978	1 017	1 067	1 224	1 361	1 284	1 306	1 170	1 031
Production of finished steel products												
(all quantities)[2](thousand tonnes)												
Rods and bars for reinforcement (in coil and lengths)	KLPP	1 219	1 241	1 151	1 130	1 229	1 269	1 154	1 182	1 118	1 133	893
Wire rods and other rods and bars in coil	KLPQ	1 417	1 407	1 272	1 327	1 427	1 524	1 642	1 536	1 565	1 492	1 407
Hot rolled bars in lengths	KLPR	1 243	1 336	1 192	1 178	1 140	1 275	1 311	1 499	1 716	1 791	1 542
Bright steel bars[3]	KLPS	340	318	257	281	295	363	424	357	385	336	311
Light sections other than rails	KLPT	326	325	324	349	294	306	286	298	302	318	264
Heavy and light rails and accessories / Other heavy sections	KGQZ KLPU KLPV	2 540	2 583	2 297	2 361	2 408	2 412	2 549	2 557	2 397	2 346	2 303
Hot rolled plates, sheets and strip in coil and lengths	KLPW	8 076	8 089	7 270	7 145	7 230	7 715	8 077	8 512	8 956	8 454	7 893
Cold rolled plates and sheets in coil and lengths	KLPX	3 976	3 749	3 592	3 532	3 635	3 835	4 100	4 221	4 437	4 288	3 914
Cold rolled strip[3]	KLPZ	388	357	286	222	229	243	267	246	255	259	233
Tinplate	KLQW	960	855	742	805	829	767	791	739	754	772	736
Other coated sheet	KLQX	1 568	1 657	1 647	1 795	1 865	2 021	2 306	2 366	2 534	2 610	2 475
Tubes and pipes[3]	KLQY	1 519	1 465	1 260	1 187	1 155	1 136	1 183	1 317	1 310	1 276	1 100
Forged bars[3]	KLQZ	16	16	7	4	2	2	3	3	3	3	2

TIME SERIES. The figures relate to periods of 52 weeks (53 weeks in 1992).

1 Includes steel furnaces at steel foundries.
2 Includes material for conversion into other products listed in the table.
3 Based on producers' deliveries.

Source: Iron and Steel Statistics Bureau: 020 8686 9050 ext 126

21.16 Non-ferrous metals

Thousand tonnes

		1987	1988	1989	1990	1991	1992	1993	1994	1995	1996	1997
Copper												
Production of refined copper:												
Primary	KLAA	54.0	49.3	48.6	47.0	16.6	10.4	10.7	11.1	12.0	13.0	9.1
Secondary	KLAB	68.3	74.7	70.4	74.6	53.5	31.7	35.9	35.6	43.0	43.6	51.3
Home consumption:												
Refined	KLAC	327.7	327.7	324.7	317.2	269.4	308.3	325.0	377.3	397.9	396.0	408.5
Scrap (metal content)	KLAD	137.7	132.1	129.7	126.3	118.5	83.2	77.9	88.0	81.0	81.0	69.0
Stocks (end of period)[1,2]	KLAE	11.7	12.2	14.5	11.7	9.3	9.7	9.3	8.1	7.5	6.6	12.8
Analysis of home consumption												
(refined and scrap):[3] total	KLAF	465.4	459.8	454.4	443.5	387.9	391.5	403.0	468.0	493.2	477.3	488.0
Wire[4]	KLAG	220.3	217.8	221.7	220.2	191.9	247.0	253.9	306.2	321.4	309.4	312.5
Rods, bars and sections	KLAH	62.5	57.3	55.5	54.4	52.7	51.5	53.2	54.9	59.0	58.3	58.3
Sheet, strip and plate	KLAI	62.5	66.3	59.2	54.4	37.1	31.0	30.7	33.0	37.1	34.0	36.5
Tubes	KLAJ	79.1	77.5	77.7	73.0	65.5	62.0	65.2	73.9	75.7	75.6	70.1
Castings and miscellaneous	KLAK	41.0	40.9	40.4	41.5	40.7	..	..	..	..	..	..
Zinc												
Slab zinc:												
Production	KLAL	81.4	76.0	79.8	93.3	100.7	96.8	102.4	101.3	106.0	96.9	107.7
Home consumption	KLAM	188.1	192.8	194.5	193.0	183.7	190.1	195.9	196.5	198.4	195.7	194.8
Stocks (end of period)	KLAN	14.0	13.2	13.9	12.2	11.2	11.4	11.4	10.5	9.8	10.5	10.1
Other zinc (metal content):												
Consumption	KLAO	52.6	51.7	49.6	52.4	49.5	46.7	45.4	45.0	46.8	41.3	41.5
Analysis of home consumption												
(slab and scrap): total	KLAP	240.7	244.4	244.1	245.4	233.2	236.8	241.3	241.5	245.2	237.1	236.3
Brass	KLAQ	55.8	54.1	51.1	51.4	47.2	40.9	41.6	42.6	45.2	39.1	41.6
Galvanized products	KLAR	95.8	101.4	104.3	104.7	96.6	103.4	105.1	107.4	110.7	110.3	108.4
Zinc sheet and strip	KLAS	4.0	4.1	4.0	3.6	3.6	4.1	4.0	4.6	3.0	3.0	3.3
Zinc alloy die castings	KLAT	44.0	43.5	43.1	44.4	45.4	45.2	46.5	46.5	46.5	46.5	46.5
Zinc oxide	KLAU	22.8	23.2	21.7	21.1	20.3	22.5	20.7	21.6	21.6	20.7	20.6
Other products	KLAV	18.3	18.2	19.8	20.2	20.2	20.8	23.4	18.8	18.2	17.5	16.1
Refined lead												
Production[5,6]	KLAW	347.0	373.8	350.0	329.4	311.0	346.8	363.8	352.5	320.7	351.4	384.1
Home consumption[6,7]												
Refined lead	KLAX	287.5	302.5	301.3	301.6	263.8	263.6	263.6	267.6	285.4	272.8	270.4
Scrap and remelted lead[6]	KLAY	36.6	37.0	35.0	32.5	33.6	38.7	35.2	38.5	41.6	43.4	39.1
Stocks (end of period)[8]												
Lead bullion	KLAZ	26.1	18.6	17.0	18.0	22.8	36.3	20.7	10.2	9.5	32.9	15.5
Refined soft lead at consumers	KLBA	24.4	26.7	25.7	22.3	21.8	24.5	25.0	23.5	24.9	28.8	29.1
In LME Warehouses (UK)	KLBB	2.8	–	11.0	12.1	8.0	9.0	9.5	6.1	0.4	3.0	2.4
Analysis of home consumption												
(refined and scrap): total	KLBC	324.1	339.4	336.4	334.0	297.4	302.3	298.8	306.1	327.0	316.2	309.5
Cables	KLBD	10.0	11.0	12.6	10.4	8.6	9.3	8.9	9.3	9.8	9.8	9.7
Batteries (excluding oxides)	KLBE	48.0	49.2	50.5	51.0	51.9	53.4	48.7	52.5	52.7	52.3	54.7
Oxides and compounds:												
Batteries	KLBF	49.0	51.4	51.7	52.8	54.2	53.1	53.9	55.2	56.2	54.9	56.1
Other uses[9]	KLBG	82.7	76.8	72.6	73.7	55.0	55.6	56.3	53.9	53.8	56.1	54.5
Sheets and pipes	KLBH	86.1	102.4	98.1	96.8	79.8	82.8	82.7	84.6	101.2	94.1	91.1
White lead	KLBI	..	..	..	..	..	..	..	..	..	..	..
Solder	KLBJ	7.4	9.0	9.1	8.0	7.7	7.4	7.4	7.4	7.4	7.4	7.4
Alloys	KLBK	13.6	13.5	13.4	14.0	12.2	14.7	14.1	15.3	15.9	12.1	9.4
Other uses	KLBL	27.3	26.1	28.4	27.5	28.0	26.2	26.8	27.9	30.0	29.5	26.6

See footnotes on the second part of this table.

Source: World Bureau of Metal Statistics: 01920 461274

Production

21.16 Non-ferrous metals

continued

		1989	1990	1991	1992	1993	1994	1995	1996	1997	1998	1999
Tin												
Tin ore (metal content):												
Production	KLBM	4.0	3.4	2.3	2.0	2.2	1.9	2.1	2.3	0.4	..	..
Tin metal[11]:												
Production[12]	KLBO	10.8	12.0	5.2	–	–	–	–	–	–	..	..
Home consumption[12]	KLBT	10.2	10.4	10.3	10.4	10.4	10.4	10.5	10.5	10.1	..	..
Exports and re-exports[13]	KLBQ	5.4	5.7	2.9	0.2	0.3	1.2	2.7	0.6	0.3	..	..
Stocks (end of period):												
Consumers	KLBR	1.0	1.0	1.0	1.0	1.0	1.0	1.0	1.0	1.0	..	..
Merchants and others	KLBS	..	..	..	..	..	..	..	..	..	..	..
Analysis of home consumption												
(excluding scrap): total	KLBT	10.2	10.4	10.3	10.4	10.4	10.4	10.5	10.5	10.1	..	..
Tinplate	KLBU	3.6	3.6	3.6	3.6	3.6	3.6	3.6	3.6	3.6	..	..
Alloys	KLBV	3.4	3.4	3.3	3.4	3.4	3.3	3.4	3.5	3.6	..	..
Solder	KLBW	1.0	1.0	1.1	1.1	1.1	1.1	1.1	1.1	1.1	..	..
Other uses	KLBX	2.2	2.4	2.3	2.3	2.3	2.4	2.4	2.3	2.3	..	..
Primary aluminium[14]												
Production	KLBY	297.3	289.8	293.5[13]	244.2	239.1	231.2	237.9	240.0	247.7	258.4	269.7
Despatches to consumers	KLBZ	494.2	520.2	485.4	587.2	815.3	610.6	459.4	593.7	456.4	648.5	480.1
Secondary aluminium												
Production	KLCA	220.0	201.4	195.1	197.3	236.2	224.3	229.7	261.0	242.7	274.8	258.3
Exports	KLCC	61.2	59.7	64.8	83.5	98.3	124.8	145.8	152.2	153.3	156.6	143.1
Fabricated aluminium												
Total despatches[15]	KLCD	544.8	547.7	518.0	598.2	592.0	643.1	648.3	633.5	663.2	668.5	668.7
Rolled products[16]	KLCE	236.2	261.0	269.4	328.9	309.3	346.4	359.2	327.9	350.4	352.5	349.7
Extrusions and tubes[17]	KLCF	163.1	157.9	129.1	132.8	136.2	142.7	142.1	149.6	160.8	168.0	181.7
Castings	KLCH	121.0	111.3	97.3	116.3	133.0	143.4	147.0	156.0	152.0	148.0	137.3
Refined nickel												
Production (including ferro-nickel)	KLCM	26.1	26.5	28.6	28.0	28.0	28.4	35.1	42.0	36.6	..	..

1 Unwrought copper (electrolytic, fire refined and blister).
2 Reported stocks of refined copper held by consumers and those held in London Metal Exchange (LME) warehouses in the United Kingdom.
3 Copper content.
4 Consumption for high-conductivity copper and cadmium copper wire represented by consumption of wire rods, production of which for export is also included.
5 Lead reclaimed from secondary and scrap material and lead refined from bullion and domestic ores.
6 From 1975, figures for production and consumption of refined lead include antimonial lead, and for scrap and remelted lead, exclude secondary antimonial lead.
7 Including toll transactions involving fabrication.
8 Excluding goverment stocks.

9 Includes values for White Lead wef 1986.
10 Separate data no longer available, see footnote 9.
11 Including production from imported scrap and residues refined on toll.
12 Primary and secondary metal.
13 Including re-exports on toll transactions.
14 Including primary alloys. Despatches to consumers are calculated as the despatches by UK industry plus imports, minus exports but deliveries to LME warehouses are not included.
15 Includes wrought, cast products, and excludes foil products.
16 Includes foil stock and excludes foil products.
17 Excluding forging bars, wirebars, and almost two-thirds of despatches of hot rolled rod.

Sources: World Bureau of Metal Statistics: 01920 461274;
Aluminium Federation: 0121 456 1103

21.17 Cotton, man-made fibres and wool

		Unit	1988	1989	1990	1991	1992	1993	1994	1995	1996	1997	1998
Raw cotton[1]													
Imports[9]	KLKC	Thousand	48	43	32	23	24	24	..	..	..	..	..
Home consumption: total	BKCA	tonnes	42	37	30	20	14	6	..	..	..	..	..
Stocks (end of period)	BKCB	"	4	3	1	1	–	1	..	..	..	..	..
Cotton waste													
Imports	KLKD	"	28.4	29.2	36.1	31.3	35.2	25.3	..	..	..	..	..
Cotton linters													
Imports	KLKE	"	13.6	18.0	13.7	16.1	19.0	5.2	..	..	..	..	..
Man-made fibres[2]													
Production: total	KLKF	"	280.1	272.5	273.2	267.4	261.9	240.6	206.9	195.3	..	..	..
Continuous filament yarn	KLKG	"	105.3	108.5	101.7	92.6	93.8	86.7	67.1	68.1	68.2	..	..
Staple fibre	KLKH	"	174.9	164.0	171.5	174.8	168.1	153.9	139.8	127.2	115.5	..	..
Cotton and man-made fibre yarn (including waste spinning)													
Production of single yarn[3]:													
100% Cotton	KJEK	"	33.2	25.9	20.4	11.2	6.4	7.3	5.3	5.5	5.8	4.8	3.9
Predominantly Cotton	KJEL	"	2.2	2.4	2.2	1.4	2.3	7.3	8.0	7.1	7.0	5.2	4.9
100% man-made fibre	KJEM	"	17.1	13.1	11.0	8.1	7.6	10.2	10.4	9.1	7.8	6.8	5.1
Mixtures including 50/50 blends	KJEN	"	29.8	26.6	24.4	21.3	19.3	16.3	16.4	15.9	15.5	14.1	13.3
Spindle activity (includes waste spinning)	KJEO	Millions	1.00	0.83	0.52	0.42	0.33	0.28	0.27	0.26	0.23	0.19	0.15
Yarn consumption:													
Cotton and predominantly Cotton yarns	KJEP	Thousand	31.5	30.6	28.0	24.1	23.6	20.7	19.1	17.9	19.0	11.8	10.8
100% man-made fibre spun yarns	KJEQ	tonnes	2.9	2.7	2.8	2.5	2.1	2.6	2.6	2.5	2.3	..	..
Spun mixture yarns	KJER	"	26.2	24.2	25.5	24.7	23.9	21.7	20.0	34.1	35.8	..	..
Continuous filament													
Man-made fibre yarn	KJES	"	34.6	35.2	34.4	31.8	33.0	33.0	32.0	30.2	33.0	..	..
Other	KJET	"	3.2	3.2	3.0	1.5	0.4	0.2	0.2	0.2	–	..	..
Other	LQYW	"	..	..	..	..	..	..	..	..	..	22.0	18.5
Cotton and man-made fibre weaving		Million linear metres											
Production of woven cloth:													
Cotton	KLKV	"	219	206	169	154	142	109	86	80	83	78	74
Man-made fibres	KLKW	"	212.5	217.4	223.4	197.1	195.8	191.3	187.8	179.6	184.6	161.5	152.4
Cotton/man-made fibre mixtures	KLKX	"	44.6	35.7	36.5	35.1	34.3	30.7	29.6	28.9	26.9	22.7	19.4
Loom activity													
Average number of looms running on cotton and man-made fibres	KLKY	Thousands	11.6	10.6	8.9	7.9	7.6	6.8	5.9	5.9	5.6	5.0	4.6
Wool													
Virgin wool (clean weight):		Million kilogrammes											
Production[4]	KLKZ	grammes	44	47	48	47	47	44	..	..	..	..	..
Imports[9]	KLLA	"	89	77	88	93	102	67	..	..	..	..	..
Exports[5]	KLLB	"	34	33	23	40	32	19	..	..	..	..	..
Stocks at 31 August	KLLC	"	21	21	20	28	26	19	..	..	..	..	..
Consumption:													
Wool	KLLD	"	104.5	97.2	93.6	87.9	92.3	89.6	86.5	84.4	79.9	..	..
Hair	KLLE	"	7.0	6.5	5.9	5.6	5.0	3.5	2.3	0.9	1.1	..	..
Man-made fibres	KLLF	"	53.9	45.9	40.6	37.7	36.4	38.8	39.6	31.7	37.3	..	..
Other fibres[6]	KLLG	"	10.0	8.9	6.4	5.6	5.7	5.9	5.4	7.0	6.7	..	..
Tops													
Production: total	KLLH	"	80.0	69.1	60.5	61.9	64.3	61.5	63.4	52.8	52.3	..	..
Wool and hair	KLLI	"	42.8	38.7	34.2	36.0	38.6	36.4	38.2	32.9	29.2	..	..
Man-made fibres	KLLJ	"	37.2	30.4	26.3	25.9	25.7	25.1	25.2	19.9	23.1	..	..
Worsted yarns[9]:													
Production	KLLK	"	60.2	52.4	47.2	44.8	47.0	44.4	43.0	39.1	40.3	..	..
Semi-worsted yarns[7]:													
Production	KLLL	"	13.5	12.7	11.4	7.6	7.0	6.8	7.1	5.5	5.0	..	..
Woollen yarn:													
Production	KLLM	"	78.3	74.9	72.7	66.1	68.2	67.0	68.1	63.7	62.6	..	..
Woven woollen and worsted fabrics[8]:		Million square metres											
Deliveries	KLLN	"	89.0	85.4	79.0	72.1	71.8	70.4	75.9	68.3	68.6	..	..
Blankets:													
Deliveries	KLLO	"	7.2	7.0	7.3	6.2	5.4	5.7	4.7	5.4	6.0	..	..

TIME SERIES. Figures for consumption of raw cotton, and production and consumption of cotton and man-made fibre yarn are for periods of 52 weeks (53 weeks in 1986).

1 From 1978 figures for consumption of raw cotton are for calendar months.
2 Figures are based on returns from producers (excluding waste) and include all man-made fibres in commercial production.
3 Includes waste spinning.
4 Estimated.
5 Including imported wool and wool from imported skins, scoured, etc in the United Kingdom.

6 Including noils, broken tops, wastes, mungo and shoddy.
7 Including all yarn spun on the worsted system.
8 Includes mixture and man-made fibre fabrics classified as wool or worsted, but excludes blankets.
9 From 1993 trade data does not include UK trade with other EU Member States.

Sources: British Man-made Fibres Federation;
Textile Statistics Bureau: 0161 620 7272

Production

21.18 Fertilisers
Deliveries to UK agriculture by Members of the Fertiliser Manufacturers' Association
Years ending 30 June[1]

Thousand tonnes

		1989	1990	1991	1992	1993	1994	1995	1996	1997	1998	1999
Nutrient Content												
N (nitrogen):												
Straight	KGRM	676	707	628	587	537	553	602	685	615	664	618
Compounds	KGRN	487	483	462	378	377	413	449	444	420	406	430
P_2O_5 (phosphate)	KGRO	337	318	278	227	218	236	272	284	287	296	291
K_2O (potash)	KGRP	431	417	364	287	284	299	343	353	356	360	357
Compounds - total product	KGRQ	3 049	2 967	2 742	2 254	2 216	2 378	2 656	2 688	2 664	2 620	2 727

1 Pre 1990 the year ended is 31 May.

Source: Fertiliser Manufacturers' Association: 01780 720422

21.19 Minerals: production

Thousand tonnes

Great Britain

		1989	1990	1991	1992	1993	1994	1995	1996	1997	1998	1999
Limestone	KLEA	107 908	9 775	91 999	86 000	90 069	102 844	90 933	82 442	84 252	85 382	82 714
Sandstone	KLEB	16 748	14 952	12 928	11 586	12 100	13 494	15 017	12 581	12 457	13 545	11 870
Igneous rock	KLEC	46 809	49 542	46 008	48 630	49 209	50 014	49 641	43 731	42 370	39 838	45 294
Clay/shale	KLED	19 011	15 864	13 038	12 155	10 891	12 464	13 930	11 804	11 322	12 230	11 355
Industrial sand	KLEE	4 380	4 132	4 201	3 615	3 587	4 038	4 344	4 861	4 704	4 662	4 092
Chalk	KLEF	13 877	13 129	10 317	9 171	9 076	10 236	9 949	9 239	9 550	9 934	9 667
Fireclay	KLEG	1 052	892	867	572	479	679	708	536	338	577	545
Barium sulphate	KLEH	70.0	68.0	86.0	77.0	33.0	34.0	74.0	93.0	57.0	64.0	59.0
Calcium fluoride	KLEI	122.0	119.0	78.0	76.0	70.0	50.0	46.0	..	58.0	52.0	46.0
Copper	KLEJ	0.5	1.0	0.2	–	–	–	–	–	–	–	–
Lead	KLEK	2.0	1.0	–	..	..	2.0	..	..	..	1.0	1.0
Tin	KLEL	3.8	3.4	2.3	2.0	2.2	1.9	2.0	2.1	2.0	–	–
Zinc	KLEM	5.8	6.7	1.0	..	..	..	..	..	–	–	–
Iron ore: crude	KLEN	4	4	..	4	..	2	2	1	2	2	1
Iron ore: iron content	KLEO	2	2	..	2	1	1	1	1	1	1	1
Calcspar	KLEP	22	34	8	4	3	..	..	..	13	15	..
China clay	KLEQ / KILC	4 190	4 042	3 744	2 732	2 852	2 977	3 076	2 654	2 798	2 866	2 841
Ball clay	KIMS				..	..	913	..	..	..	..	..
Chert and flint	KLER	..	14	5	..	..	..	..	..	..	..	6
Fuller's earth	KLES	265	228	202	203	153	193	150	183	162	111	83
Lignite	KLET	4	5	3	3	3	2	–	–	–	–	–
Rock salt	KLEU	594	815	2 088	..	..	..	..	..	..	..	..
Salt from brine	KLEV	..	..	1 319	..	..	..	..	..	..	..	..
Salt in brine	KLEW	..	..	..	3 401	4 076	4 009	3 548	3 512	3 561	..	..
Anhydrite	KLEX	..	..	..	..	..	..	..	–	–	–	–
Dolomite	KLEY	21 271	20 674	19 454	18 539	17 985	17 616	17 966	16 555	17 282	15 632	13 698
Gypsum	KLEZ	..	..	..	..	..	..	..	..	..	..	..
Slate[1]	KLFA	590	359	360	326	462	402	275	408	347	425	361
Soapstone and talc	KLFB	15	15	11	5	5	5	4	5	5	5	6
Sand and gravel (land-won)	KLFC	110 504	98 993	85 479	78 341	79 380	86 341	78 031	70 489	74 362	73 016	74 785
Sand and gravel (marine dredged)	KLFD	20 728	17 179	12 439	10 557	10 090	11 331	11 625	11 508	12 004	12 952	13 424

Northern Ireland

		1989	1990	1991	1992	1993	1994	1995	1996	1997	1998	1999
Clay and shale	KLFF	..	..	..	..	..	..	..	–	–	–	–
Sand and gravel	KLFG	4 554	4 030	3 832	3 697	4 318	5 109	5 262	7 684	5 138	5 300	5 517
Basalt and igneous rock (other than granite)	KLFH	7 463	7 691	7 787	9 024	8 557	6 480	7 564	6 974	6 286	6 107	9 538
Limestone	KLFI	3 485	2 866	2 861	3 398	3 236	..	3 703	4 122	3 500	3 892	8 771
Sandstone[2]	KLFJ	2 845	3 090	3 679	3 304	3 959	5 480	4 779	4 941	6 042	6 584	3 615
Granite	KLFL	..	..	..	..	..	..	..	–	–	–	–
Others[3]	KLFN	..	..	..	..	647	896	812	1 392	625	473	1 579

1 Includes waste used for constructional fill, and powder and granules used in manufacturing.
2 Prior to 1993 the 'Sandstone' heading was called 'Grit and conglomerate'. The new heading is all encompassing and was confirmed as correct with the Geological Survey in Northern Ireland.
3 Rock salt, Chalk, Diatomite and Fireclay.

Source: Office for National Statistics: 01633 812082

21.20 Building materials and components: production
Great Britain

		Unit	1989	1990	1991	1992	1993	1994	1995	1996	1997	1998	1999
Building bricks (excluding refractory and glazed)	KLGA	Millions	4 654	3 802	3 212	3 000	2 639	3 114	3 256	3 046	2 997	3 000	2 939
Cement[1]	KLGB	Thousand tonnes	16 849	14 740	12 297	11 006	11 039	12 307	11 805	12 214	12 638	12 409	12 697
Building sand[2]	KLGC	"	23 290	20 948	18 079	16 769	17 406	18 534	17 389	14 655	15 337	13 810	13 941
Concreting sand	KLGD	"	41 223	37 213	31 239	28 573	28 021	30 977	29 390	28 659	30 130	30 244	31 730
Gravel[3]	KLGE	"	66 718	58 010	48 598	43 557	44 043	48 162	42 877	38 683	40 899	41 914	42 538
Crushed rock aggregates:													
used as roadstone (coated)	KLGF	"	23 733	26 430	26 387	26 647	27 238	28 512	28 972	26 270	23 906	23 131	22 260
roadstone (uncoated)	KLGG	"	66 015	61 742	60 748	53 471	54 412	51 121	49 307	40 893	40 186	36 816	38 114
fill and ballast	KLGH	"	59 689	54 640	45 669	48 919	52 141	65 779	56 140	50 982	51 396	51 623	52 144
concrete aggregate	KLGI	"	19 356	18 804	15 203	14 929	15 786	16 345	16 419	14 748	18 300	20 146	20 080
Ready mixed concrete[1]	KLGJ	Million m^3	29.6	26.8	22.5	20.8	20.8	22.9	21.7	20.9	22.3	23.0	23.6
Fibre cement products	KLGK	Thousand tonnes	220.7	234.7	133.7	121.1	128.7	154.1	160.5	146.2	163.5	160.9	156.2
Clay roofing tiles[1]	KLGL	Thousand m^2	3 756	2 912	2 191	1 495	..	..	..	..	..	..	..
Concrete roofing tiles	KLGM	"	35 787	31 510	26 359	21 490	24 574	28 149	26 118	24 651	24 958	24 981	25 972
Concrete building blocks:[1]													
dense aggregate	KLGN	"	45 564	39 297	32 456	29 732	30 116	36 997	36 933	34 996	37 250	39 439	41 951
lightweight aggregate	KLGO	"	31 041	23 768	18 581	17 479	19 235	22 048	18 147	16 316	17 783	19 110	21 486
aerated concrete	KLGP	"	31 394	28 089	23 594	20 984	24 936	28 503	23 207	24 554	27 505	26 113	27 607
Concrete pipes[1]	KLGQ	Thousand tonnes	717	737	723	564	..	..	..	..	..	..	..
Roofing & architectural slates	KLGR	"	46.6	44.1	41.0	41.6	37.3	44.9	42.0	48.5	44.6	46.2	47.0
Gypsum (excluding anhydrite)	KLGS	"	..	..	..	..	..	..	..	..	..	..	..
Plaster	KLGT	"	..	..	..	..	..	..	..	..	..	..	..
Plasterboard	KLGU	Thousand m^2	..	..	..	..	..	..	..	..	..	..	..
Unglazed floorquarries[1]	KLGV	"	1 180	1 070	889	889	..	..	..	..	..	..	..
Unglazed tiles[1]	KLGW	"	1 521	1 349	934	493	..	..	..	..	..	..	..

1 United Kingdom.
2 Including sand and gravel used for coating.
3 Figures include hoggin, concrete aggregate, other purposes (excluding fill) and fill.

Source: Department of the Environment, Transport and the Regions: 020 7890 5593

21.21 Construction: Value of output in Great Britain[1]

£ millions

		1989	1990	1991	1992	1993	1994	1995	1996	1997	1998[2]	1999
All work: total	FGAY	52 150	55 307	51 115	47 472	46 323	49 439	52 643	55 243	58 352	62 060	65 658
New work: total	BLAB	29 320	30 762	27 726	24 814	23 556	25 086	26 672	27 926	29 928	32 491	35 419
New housing: total	KLQA	8 083	6 680	5 796	6 084	6 628	7 417	7 135	7 013	7 983	8 430	8 378
For public sector	BLAC	966	934	793	1 243	1 415	1 671	1 660	1 421	1 232	1 069	1 007
For private sector	BLAD	7 117	5 746	5 003	4 841	5 213	5 746	5 475	5 592	6 751	7 361	7 370
Infrastructure: total	KIAM	4 017	4 965	6 062	5 716	5 544	5 149	5 660	6 338	6 311	6 182	6 170
Other new work: total (excluding infrastructure)	KLQB	17 220	19 118	15 867	13 015	11 384	12 521	13 877	14 575	15 635	17 878	20 871
For public sector	BLAE	3 903	4 414	4 142	4 181	4 045	4 384	4 661	4 441	3 756	4 151	4 895
For private sector	KLQC	13 317	14 704	11 725	8 834	7 339	8 137	9 217	10 134	11 879	13 727	15 976
Private Industrial	BLAF	3 425	3 394	2 622	2 234	2 208	2 489	3 008	3 119	3 491	3 810	3 954
Private Commercial	BLAG	9 892	11 310	9 103	6 600	5 131	5 648	6 209	7 015	8 388	9 917	12 021
Repair and maintenance: total	BLAH	22 830	24 544	23 389	22 658	22 767	24 353	25 971	27 317	28 423	29 569	30 238
Housing: total[2]	KLQD	13 092	13 839	13 001	12 586	12 809	13 767	14 595	15 035	15 755	16 202	16 482
For public sector	BLBK	4 943	5 384	4 938	4 991	5 439	5 963	6 465	6 637	6 629	6 506	6 523
For private sector	BLBL	8 149	8 455	8 063	7 595	7 370	7 804	8 130	8 398	9 126	9 696	9 959
Public other work	BLAJ	4 982	5 488	5 291	5 087	4 916	5 211	5 398	5 252	5 079	5 220	5 383
Private other work	BLAK	4 755	5 218	5 098	4 985	5 042	5 375	5 978	7 030	7 590	8 147	8 374

1 Output by contractors, including unrecorded estimates by small firms and self-employed workers, and output by public sector direct labour departments - classified to construction in the *1980 Standard Industrial Classification*.
2 Provisional.

Source: Department of the Environment, Transport and the Regions: 020 7890 5583

21.22 Construction: Value of new orders obtained by contractors[1]
Great Britain

£ millions

		1989	1990	1991	1992	1993	1994	1995	1996	1997	1998	1999
New work: total	FHAA	27 142	22 491	19 455	17 493	19 965	21 285	22 065	22 834	24 806	27 477	26 079
Public housing	BLBC	872	683	875	1 246	1 668	1 386	1 182	1 073	995	933	969
Private housing[2]	BLBD	6 497	4 855	4 552	4 016	4 874	5 721	4 905	5 416	6 253	5 997	5 901
New housing: total	FGAU	7 370	5 538	5 427	5 263	6 542	7 106	6 087	6 487	7 248	6 930	6 869
Infrastructure:												
Water	KIBV	251	321	509	669	421	412	500	640	733	957	760
Sewerage	KIBW	332	491	429	469	447	389	394	481	656	737	789
Electricity	KIBX	271	187	301	281	211	170	218	294	382	359	254
Roads	KIBY	1 226	1 425	1 415	1 322	1 435	1 356	1 531	1 710	928	821	957
Gas, communications, air	KIBZ	339	391	441	554	642	494	904	745	693	745	713
Railways	KIDP	362	160	125	200	623	412	351	524	416	573	459
Harbours	KIDQ	180	216	203	252	220	218	273	270	182	287	246
Total	KIDR	2 690	3 190	3 423	3 746	3 998	3 451	4 170	4 664	3 991	4 479	4 030
of which												
- Public	KIDS	2 369	2 029	2 090	1 690	2 472	2 211	2 327	1 671	1 352	1 505	1 495
- Private	KIDT	592	1 161	1 333	2 056	1 525	1 240	1 843	2 993	2 639	2 974	2 700
Other public non-housing:												
Factories	KIDU	188	149	89	128	111	111	94	91	72	84	72
Warehouses	KIDV	48	14	14	54	23	38	29	14	27	20	24
Oil, steel, coal	KIDW	115	81	13	47	30	12	13	4	4	2	5
Schools and colleges	KIDX	471	527	584	584	655	658	710	708	749	770	791
Universities	KIDY	139	146	150	203	353	376	373	355	273	405	345
Health	KIDZ	824	663	578	644	697	752	717	674	491	769	635
Offices	KIFP	519	570	492	499	684	469	393	381	391	292	390
Entertainment	KIFQ	382	283	250	189	281	308	285	253	342	432	435
Garages	KIFR	75	56	44	28	42	49	51	28	34	19	32
Shops	KIFS	26	24	25	23	26	14	21	11	35	35	29
Agriculture	KIFT	6	5	17	14	44	22	12	8	33	17	9
Miscellaneous	KIFU	1 043	601	421	351	450	844	508	419	441	660	526
Total	KIFV	3 836	3 117	2 677	2 763	3 397	3 654	3 206	2 945	2 894	3 504	3 273
Private industrial:[2]												
Factories	KIFW	2 269	2 094	1 830	1 006	1 221	1 451	2 055	1 603	2 184	1 878	1 698
Warehouses	KIFX	706	648	438	426	429	498	594	663	901	1 014	821
Oil, steel, coal	KIFY	73	108	79	72	27	51	76	71	64	79	38
Total	KIFZ	3 049	2 850	2 347	1 503	1 677	1 999	2 725	2 337	3 149	2 971	2 558
Private commercial:[2]												
Schools, universities	KIHP	179	169	175	121	134	115	105	156	189	351	393
Health	KIHQ	295	271	369	193	179	255	288	277	356	651	411
Offices	KIHR	5 271	4 215	2 215	1 691	1 471	1 777	2 123	2 169	2 506	3 472	3 566
Entertainment	KIHS	1 418	1 195	1 111	747	751	928	940	1 407	1 847	2 244	2 224
Garages	KIHT	405	364	261	234	308	300	301	265	344	315	266
Shops	KIHU	2 086	1 345	1 222	1 034	1 278	1 453	1 871	1 795	1 937	2 154	1 901
Agriculture	KIBN	127	127	105	94	108	120	124	123	148	146	110
Miscellaneous	KIBO	149	109	123	103	122	127	126	198	198	259	335
Total	KIBP	9 927	7 796	5 581	4 218	4 351	5 075	5 877	6 390	7 525	9 593	9 184

1 Classified to construction in the *1980 Standard Industrial Classification*. Total figures only are available in this series prior to 1985.

2 Figures for private sector include work to be carried out by contractors on their own initiative for sale.

Source: Department of the Environment, Transport and the Regions: 020 7890 5583

21.23 Total engineering
Total turnover of UK based manufacturers[1,2,3]
Standard Industrial Classification 1992

£ millions

Activity heading Product group		1993	1994	1995	1996	1997	1998	1999
Class 29: Manufacture of machinery and equipment not elsewhere classified								
2911 Manufacture of engines and turbines except aircraft, vehicle & cycle engines	BBEM	1 653	1 649	1 764	1 616	1 417	1 492	..
2912 Manufacture of pumps and compressors	BBEN	2 368	2 466	2 780	2 739	2 698	2 897	..
2913 Manufacture of taps and valves	BBEO	1 441	1 504	1 589	1 569	1 536	1 648	..
2914 Manufacture of bearings, gears, gearing and driving elements	BBEP	1 381	1 505	1 616	1 720	1 574	1 562	..
2922 Manufacture of lifting and handling equipment	BBEQ	2 775	3 286	3 453	3 265	2 937	2 990	..
2923 Manufacture of non-domestic cooling and ventilation equipment	BBER	2 888	2 812	2 925	3 058	3 268	3 350	..
2924 Manufacture of other general purpose machinery not elsewhere classified	BBES	2 473	2 571	2 474	2 669	2 877	2 820	..
2940 Manufacture of machine tools	BBET	1 881	2 097	2 301	2 413	2 508	2 420	..
2952 Manufacture of machinery for mining, quarrying and construction	BBEU	1 864	2 230	2 231	2 203	2 496	2 575	..
2953 Manufacture of machinery for food, beverage and tobacco processing	BBEV	1 107	1 133	1 343	1 247	1 209	1 117	..
2954 Manufacture of machinery for textile, apparel and leather production	BBEW	504	443	495	460	419	379	..
2956 Manufacture of other special purpose machinery not elsewhere classified	BBEX	2 155	2 444	2 163	2 298	2 097	2 004	..
2971 Manufacture of electric domestic appliances	BBEY	2 122	2 314	2 233	2 230	2 266	2 247	..
Total	BBEZ	24 612	26 454	27 367	27 487	27 302	27 501	..
Class 30 : Manufacture of electrical and optical equipment								
3001 Manufacture of office machinery	BBFA	1 065	1 189	1 232	1 449	1 279	1 354	..
3002 Manufacture of computers and other information processing equipment	BBFB	9 218	10 769	12 105	12 166	13 518	14 068	..
Total	BBFC	11 958	11 958	13 337	13 615	14 797	15 422	..
Class 31 : Manufacture of electrical machinery and apparatus not elsewhere classified								
3110 Manufacture of electric motors, generators and transformers	BBFD	1 888	2 020	2 057	2 280	2 305	2 275	..
3120 Manufacture of electricity distribution and control apparatus	BBFE	2 999	3 155	3 428	3 784	3 582	3 488	..
3130 Manufacture of insulated wire and cable	BBFF	1 625	2 156	2 384	2 581	2 152	1 873	..
3140 Manufacture of accumulators, primary cells and primary batteries	BBFG	689	721	613	664	655	606	..
3150 Manufacture of lighting equipment and electric lamps	BBFH	1 365	1 496	1 589	1 732	1 670	1 575	..
3161 Manufacture of other electrical equipment for engines and vehicles not otherwise classified	BBFI	1 270	1 339	1 247	1 226	1 148	1 065	..
3162 Manufacture of other electrical equipment not elsewhere classified	BBFJ	2 532	2 677	2 808	2 764	2 705	2 924	..
Total	BBFK	12 368	13 564	14 126	15 031	14 217	13 806	..
Class 32 : Manufacture of radio, television and communication equipment and apparatus								
3210 Manufacture of electronic valves and tubes and other electronic components	BBFL	4 734	5 923	6 362	6 270	6 102	6 108	..
3220 Manufacture of television and radio transmitters and apparatus for line telephony and line telegraphy	BBFM	4 684	5 902	6 616	6 815	7 029	7 786	..
3230 Manufacture of television and radio receivers, sound or video recording or reproducing apparatus and associated goods	BBFN	3 241	3 858	4 257	4 978	4 707	4 425	..
Total	BBFO	12 659	15 683	17 235	18 063	17 838	18 319	..
Class 33 : Manufacture of medical, precision and optical instruments, watches and clocks								
3310 Manufacture of medical and surgical equipment and orthopaedic appliances	BBFP	1 986	1 883	2 015	1 967	1 772	1 716	..
3320 Manufacture of instruments and appliances for measuring, checking, testing, navigating and other purposes, except industrial process control equipment	BBFQ	6 307	6 030	6 066	6 693	6 440	6 147	..
3340 Manufacture of optical instruments and photographic equipment	BBFR	1 089	1 205	1 233	1 249	1 283	1 356	..
Total	BBFS	9 382	9 118	9 314	9 909	9 495	9 219	..

1 The figures shown represent the output of UK based manufacturers classified to Subsections DK and DL of the Standard Industrial Classification 1992. The figures shown are derived from the monthly production inquiry (MPI) and include estimates for non-responders and for establishments which are not sampled.

2 Orders on hand figures are given for the end of the period to which they relate.
3 The data on this table are not seasonally adjusted.

Source: Office for National Statistics: 01633 812786

21.24 Volume index numbers of turnover and orders for the engineering industries
United Kingdom

	Total			Home			Export		
	Orders on hand end of period (1995 average = 100)	1995 average monthly sales = 100		Orders on hand end of period (1995 average = 100)	1995 average monthly sales = 100		Orders on hand end of period (1995 average = 100)	1995 average monthly sales = 100	
		New orders[1]	Turnover		New orders[1]	Turnover		New orders[1]	Turnover

Total Engineering industries
SIC 1992 Class 29, 30, 31,32 and 33

	FGWA	FGWB	FGVT	FGVU	FGVV	FGVW	FGVX	FGVY	FGVZ
1991	99.4	85.3	86.8	96.9	85.7	88.4	103.4	84.7	84.7
1992	94.9	84.6	86.0	90.3	85.7	87.7	102.0	83.1	83.5
1993	95.6	87.5	87.3	92.0	92.6	92.1	101.3	80.4	80.7
1994	105.0	98.1	95.4	105.6	103.1	99.0	104.2	91.2	90.4
1995	98.4	98.0	100.0	100.0	98.3	100.0	95.9	97.7	100.0
1996	94.2	102.5	103.7	94.0	98.0	99.8	94.4	108.7	109.2
1997	97.1	107.3	106.4	97.5	102.0	100.9	96.5	114.7	114.1
1998	94.4	110.7	111.5	89.6	100.9	103.3	102.0	124.5	122.9
1999	106.1	119.3	115.8	104.8	113.7	109.1	108.5	127.1	125.3

Manufacture of Machinery and Equipment
SIC 1992 Class 29

	FGVB	FGVD	FGVF	FGVH	FGVJ	FGVL	FGVN	FGVP	FGVR
1991	103.2	99.6	101.0	95.3	98.8	102.0	115.6	101.1	99.2
1992	94.4	94.2	97.4	82.9	95.1	99.4	112.7	92.8	93.9
1993	95.0	96.4	96.2	84.9	100.9	100.2	111.0	88.9	89.5
1994	107.1	104.3	99.9	107.9	111.1	103.1	105.8	92.6	94.6
1995	97.9	96.7	100.0	97.9	96.5	100.0	97.8	97.0	100.0
1996	96.0	98.7	99.4	99.0	96.9	96.5	91.2	101.9	104.4
1997	100.6	99.6	98.0	105.7	97.6	95.3	92.6	103.1	102.6
1998	86.0	92.7	98.0	86.2	86.6	93.3	85.8	103.3	105.9
1999	88.4	93.4	92.6	91.8	92.2	90.2	82.9	95.6	96.6

Manufacture of Electrical and Optical Equipment
SIC 1992 Class 30, 31,32 and 33

	FGVC	FGVE	FGVG	FGVI	FGVK	FGVM	FGVO	FGVQ	FGVS
1991	96.4	77.0	78.6	98.1	77.1	79.3	93.9	76.8	77.7
1992	95.4	79.1	79.3	96.6	79.5	80.0	93.7	78.5	78.6
1993	96.2	82.4	82.2	98.0	87.1	86.8	93.7	76.4	76.4
1994	103.3	94.6	92.8	103.6	97.8	96.3	102.9	90.5	88.4
1995	98.8	98.8	100.0	101.8	99.5	100.0	94.4	98.0	100.0
1996	92.6	104.7	106.2	89.8	98.8	102.1	96.8	112.0	111.5
1997	94.3	111.7	111.3	90.7	104.9	104.6	99.5	120.3	119.6
1998	101.5	121.2	119.4	92.5	110.4	109.9	114.6	134.6	131.1
1999	120.9	134.3	129.3	115.7	127.9	121.6	128.4	142.3	139.1

1 Net of cancellations.
2 The percentage changes have been calculated on unrounded values and then rounded to the nearest half percentage point.

Source: Office for National Statistics: 01633 812786

21.25 Motor vehicle production
United Kingdom

		1989	1990	1991	1992	1993	1994	1995	1996	1997	1998	1999
Motor vehicles												
SIC 1992, Class 34-10 Passenger cars: total	**GKAJ**	1 299 082	1 295 610	1 236 900	1 291 880	1 375 524	1 466 823	1 532 084	1 686 134	1 698 001	1 748 258	1 786 623
1 000 c.c. and under	**GKAB**	133 135	93 039	15 918	22 037	98 034	98 178	95 198	108 645	119 894	112 044	113 204
Over 1 000 c.c. but not over 1 600c.c.	**GKAD**	716 784	809 219	496 822	793 307	709 615	729 397	814 873	845 084	829 079	814 595	776 111
Over 1 600 c.c. but not over 2 800 c.c.	**GKAF**	375 309	325 116	193 972	437 951	515 487	573 357	528 444	635 861	653 147	720 556	758 478
Over 2 800 c.c.	**GKAH**	73 854	68 236	26 001	38 585	52 388	65 891	93 569	96 544	95 881	101 063	138 830
Commercial vehicles: total	**GKDF**	326 590	270 346	217 141	248 453	193 467	227 815	233 011	238 314	237 706	227 379	185 905
Of which: Light commercial vehicles	**GKDH**	267 135	230 510	105 633	216 477	171 141	197 285	199 346	205 372	210 942	203 629	162 176
Trucks: Under 7.5 tonnes	**GKDJ**	17 687	10 515	5 379	9 558	4 755	8 154	9 523	8 913	6 254	5 006	4 107
Over 7.5 tonnes	**GKDL**	21 083	13 674	7 673	11 113	8 269	10 016	11 717	10 128	7 932	7 002	6 443
Motive units for articulated vehicles	**GKCV**	5 827	3 327	1 444	2 788	2 283	2 794	3 476	2 631	2 574	2 492	2 739
Buses, coaches and mini buses	**GKDN**	14 858	12 320	5 593	8 517	7 019	9 566	8 939	11 270	10 004	9 250	10 440

TIME SERIES. Figures for motor vehicles relate to periods of 52 weeks (53 weeks in 1983, 1988 and 1993).

Source: Office for National Statistics: 01633 812963

Production

21.26 Alcoholic drink
United Kingdom

			1989	1990	1991	1992	1993	1994	1995	1996	1997	1998	1999
Spirits[1]		Thousand hectolitres of alcohol											
Production	KMEA	"	4 211	4 676	4 476	4 219	3 974	4 114	4 507	4 868	5 297	5 145	4 705
Released for home consumption													
Home produced whisky	KMEE	"	430	413	383	356	374	383	310	321	312	289	323
Imported and other	KMEG	"	570	567	529	505	504	531	481	495	533	505	596
Total	KMEH	"	1 000	980	912	861	878	914	791	815	845	794	919
Beer[2]		Thousand hectolitres											
Production	KMEI	"	62 132	61 783	59 552	57 616	56 746	58 333	56 800	58 072	59 139	56 652	57 854
Released for home consumption	KMEL	"	65 303	65 184	63 038	60 973	59 177	60 575	59 129	59 894	61 114	58 835	58 917
		Thousand hectolitres of pure											
Production	JYXJ	alcohol	..	..	..	..	..	2 345	2 298	2 360	2 406	2 333	2 364
Released for home consumption	JYXK		..	..	..	..	..	2 453	2 410	2 448	2 504	2 439	2 428
Wine of fresh grapes													
Released for home consumption		Thousand											
Fortified	KMEM	hectolitres	327	378	357	345	335	329	358	359	323	370	316
Still table	KMEN	"	5 871	5 893	5 910	6 166	6 471	6 759	6 577	6 995	7 653	7 979	8 391
Sparkling	KMEO	"	392	365	316	292	296	297	315	358	382	416	576
Total	KMEP	"	6 669	6 636	6 583	6 803	7 102	7 385	7 250	7 712	8 358	8 765	9 283
Made-wine													
Released for home consumption													
Other than coolers	KMEQ	"	512	521	436	439	505	470	516	513	485	406	416
Coolers[3]	KJDD	"	79	185	263	433	485	549	903	1 781	1 151	1 243	1 846
Cider and perry													
Released for home consumption	KMER	"	3 263	3 666	3 713	4 398	4 496	4 811	5 575	5 656	5 513	5 548	6 022

1 Potable spirits distilled.
2 A new system was introduced for beer duty in June 1993. The figures in this table include adjustments to data prior to this date to bring them into line with current data.

3 Made wine with alcoholic strength 1.2% to 5.5%. Includes alcoholic lemonade of appropriate strength and similar product. Coolers were included with other made wine prior to 1989.

Source: HM Customs and Excise: 020 7865 5249

21.27 Tobacco products: released for home consumption
United Kingdom

			1989	1990	1991	1992	1993[1]	1994	1995	1996	1997	1998	1999
Cigarettes:		Thousand million											
Home produced	KMFA	"	87.5	87.4	85.3	76.4	86.4	79.4	70.8	73.8	71.1	67.8	28.2
Imported	KMFB	"	10.3	10.3	10.3	9.3	8.8	13.2	29.5	9.5	9.9	7.5	6.0
Total	KMFC	"	95.9	97.8	95.6	85.7	95.2	92.6	80.3	83.3	81.0	75.3	34.2
Cigars:		Million kg.											
Home produced	KMFD	"	2.3	2.1	1.9	1.8	1.7	1.6	1.5	1.4	1.3	1.2	0.9
Imported	KMFE	"	0.2	0.2	0.1	0.1	0.1	0.1	0.1	0.1	0.1	0.1	0.1
Total	KMFF	"	2.4	2.3	2.0	1.9	1.8	1.7	1.6	1.5	1.4	1.3	1.0
Hand-rolling tobacco:													
Home produced	KMFG	"	4.3	4.1	4.1	3.7	3.5	3.0	2.4	2.1	1.8	1.7	2.0
Imported	KMFH	"	–	–	0.1	0.1	0.1	0.1	0.1	0.1	0.1	0.1	0.1
Total	KMFI	"	4.3	4.1	4.1	3.7	3.6	3.2	2.6	2.3	1.9	1.8	2.0
Other smoking and chewing tobacco:													
Home produced	KMFJ	"	2.2	2.1	2.0	1.8	1.8	1.5	1.3	1.2	1.1	1.0	0.6
Imported	KMFK	"	0.1	0.1	0.1	0.2	0.1	0.1	0.1	0.1	0.1	0.1	0.1
Total	KMFL	"	2.3	2.2	2.1	2.0	1.9	1.6	1.4	1.3	1.2	1.1	0.7

1 1993 contained two Budgets, in March and November.

Source: HM Customs and Excise: 020 7865 5249

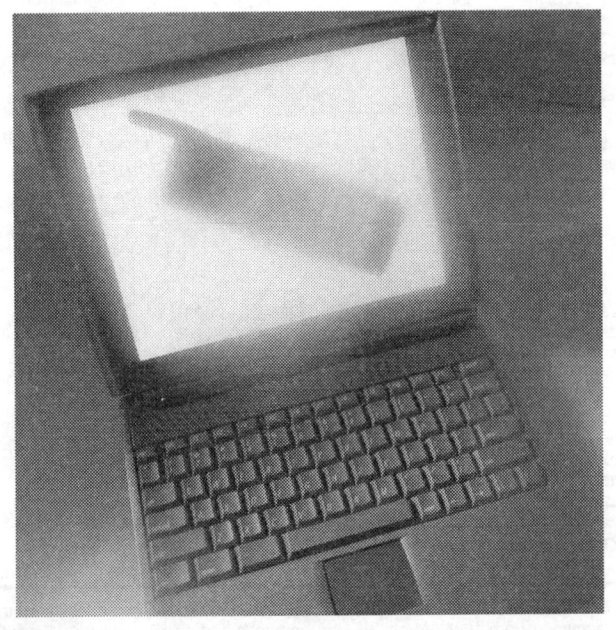

22 Banking, insurance etc

Banking, insurance etc

22.1 Bank of England

£ millions

		December										
		1989	1990	1991	1992	1993	1994	1995	1996	1997	1998	1999
Issue Department												
Liabilities:												
Notes in circulation	AEFA	16 849	17 283	17 466	17 542	18 218	20 055	21 262	22 407	23 715	24 573	27 232
Notes in Banking Department	AEFB	11	7	4	8	12	5	7	12	5	7	8
Assets:												
Government securities[1]	AEFC	13 946	14 672	11 791	7 808	6 816	11 468	14 552	16 524	16 416	15 826	17 264
Other securities[2]	AEFD	2 914	2 618	5 679	9 742	11 414	8 592	6 717	5 896	7 304	8 754	9 976
Banking Department												
Liabilities:												
Total[3]	AEFE	5 398	8 613	5 825	5 623	11 095	6 192	7 114	6 229	7 221	6 802	52 072
Public deposits[4]	AEFF	69	44	104	97	6 205	938	1 159	1 001	1 192	237	195
Bankers' deposits[5]	AEFH	1 750	1 842	1 813	1 553	1 700	1 855	2 001	2 021	2 800	1 388	1 357
Reserves and other accounts[6]	AEFI	3 565	6 713	3 894	3 959	3 175	3 385	3 941	3 193	3 214	5 163	50 506
Assets:												
Total	KCYT	5 398	8 615	5 825	5 623	11 095	6 192	7 114	6 229	7 221	6 802	..
Government securities	AEFJ	1 354	1 432	1 346	1 237	1 174	1 050	1 090	1 232	1 373	1 352	1 444
Advances and other accounts	AEFK	726	2 146	2 443	3 935	9 411	4 696	5 499	2 339	5 388	3 302	46 895
Premises, equipment and other securities[6]	AEFL	3 307	5 030	2 031	443	498	441	518	2 646	455	2 141	3 724
Notes and coin	AEFM	11	7	5	8	12	5	7	12	5	7	8

1 Including the historic liability of the Treasury of £11 million until 1993.
2 Including gilt and Treasury bill repurchase agreements (from 1994 - previously in "Government securities")
3 The only liability not shown separately is the Bank's capital (held by the Treasury) which has been constant at £14.6 million.
4 Excluding local government and public corporations' deposits which are included under Reserves and other accounts.

5 Up to 19 August 1981 these constituted the current accounts held at the Bank by the banks and discount houses. From the introduction of new arrangements for monetary control on 20 August, they consist of operational deposits held mainly by the clearing banks and non-operational cash ratio deposits for which institutions authorised under the Banking Act, deposit - taking UK branches of "European Authorised Institutions" and (from 1998) building societies are liable.
6 Large increases from 1999 arise from the Bank of England.

Source: Bank of England: 020 7601 3236

22.2 Value of inter-bank clearings[1]

£ billions

		1989	1990	1991	1992	1993	1994	1995	1996	1997	1998	1999
Bulk paper clearings												
Cheque (formerly general)	KCYY	1 030	1 089	1 084	1 052	1 065	1 075	1 097	1 161	1 196	1 214	1 225
Credit (formerly credit clearing)	KCYZ	107	109	104	101	97	93	92	94	94	92	88
High-value clearings												
Town	KCZA	6 754	4 776	2 228	1 387	1 069	681	59	–	–	–	–
CHAPS	KCZB	14 733	18 880	19 050	20 929	23 545	25 052	26 719	28 881	36 032	41 501	44 704
Electronic clearing	KCZC	526	668	772	803	836	941	1 055	1 251	1 432	1 602	1 761

1 Excludes inter-branch clearings and clearings in Scotland and Northern Ireland.

Source: Association of Payment Clearing Services (APACS): 020 7601 4340

22.3 Other banks' balance sheet[1]

£ millions

		1990	1991	1992	1993	1994	1995	1996	1997	1998[2]	1999[3]
Sterling liabilities											
Notes outstanding & cash loaded cards	TBFA	1 678	1 840	2 084	2 186	2 456	2 576	2 717	2 832	2 929	3 311
Sight deposits											
UK banks	TBFB	12 893	10 229	14 243	14 768	16 222	16 983	20 138	44 573	37 839	33 463
UK building societies	TBFC	..	..	..	..	..	..	..	950	1 277	841
UK public sector	TBFD	3 697	2 953	2 952	3 335	3 301	3 824	3 641	3 781	3 003	3 449
Other UK residents	TBFE	138 310	144 516	148 011	161 907	164 451	192 297	211 179	271 232	295 069	325 392
Non-residents	TBFF	14 760	14 466	15 094	15 075	16 425	18 690	17 707	37 730	43 528	44 581
Time deposits											
UK banks	TBFG	84 736	72 344	78 640	68 531	75 629	90 044	95 798	99 783	111 970	112 530
UK building sicieties	TBFH	–	–	–	–	–	–	–	5 682	4 362	4 254
UK public sector	TBFI	4 699	2 885	3 193	4 223	4 908	7 896	6 087	9 060	9 749	8 064
Other UK residents	TBFJ	148 934	154 223	157 979	162 053	166 505	190 707	210 045	284 630	295 925	282 789
of which TESSAs	TBFK	–	2 453	4 331	5 896	7 517	10 314	9 389	20 393	21 568	22 868
of which SAYE	TBFL	–	–	–	–	–	–	–	2 255	2 604	2 840
Non-residents	TBFM	67 349	57 718	58 550	58 583	62 905	68 274	63 995	91 040	97 954	116 967
Acceptances granted	TBFN	–	–	–	–	–	–	–	19 952	16 659	12 854
Liabilities under sale and repurchase agreements											
of which British govt. securities	TBFU	–	–	–	–	–	–	22 668	47 297	55 561	56 145
UK banks	TBFP	–	–	–	–	–	–	13 718	29 089	43 314	48 213
UK building societies	TBFQ	..	..	..	..	..	..	..	20	32	200
UK public sector	TBFR	–	–	–	–	–	–	2 279	6 044	–	–
Other UK residents	TBFS	–	–	–	–	–	–	7 703	18 114	20 918	17 165
Non-residents	TBFT	–	–	–	–	–	–	683	5 664	5 469	5 542
CDs and other short-term paper issued	TBFV	53 225	52 307	50 912	52 783	63 880	70 277	96 390	119 266	138 248	158 826
Total sterling deposits	TBFW	528 604	511 641	529 575	541 260	574 224	658 993	749 364	1 046 610	1 125 314	1 175 131
Sterling items in suspense and transmission	TBFX	11 920	11 349	10 317	11 011	8 412	10 423	12 120	16 055	15 714	17 307
Net derivatives	TBFY	..	..	..	..	..	..	..	8 186	8 342	8 324
Accrued amounts payable	TBFZ	..	..	..	..	..	..	..	20 713	24 632	22 122
Sterling capital and other internal funds	TBGA	62 020	65 908	68 640	71 833	78 775	82 160	90 464	103 463	103 867	100 576
Total sterling liabilities	TBGB	604 222	590 738	610 616	626 290	663 868	754 152	854 666	1 197 858	1 280 799	1 326 770
Foreign currency liabilities											
Sight and time deposits											
UK banks	TBGC	75 833	76 901	89 532	95 921	105 813	104 769	91 314	90 858	77 128	77 685
UK building societies	TBGD	..	..	..	..	..	..	..	1 027	639	681
UK public sector	TBGE	..	..	..	..	..	..	..	226	149	127
Other UK residents	TBGF	..	..	..	..	..	..	..	64 188	60 513	65 202
Non-residents	TBGG	440 307	432 000	543 883	580 951	618 769	696 380	605 439	716 573	766 934	736 792
Acceptances granted	TBGH	..	..	..	..	..	..	..	743	730	619
Sale and repurchase agreements											
UK banks	TBGJ	–	–	–	–	–	–	17 114	21 311	30 669	25 169
UK building societies	TBGK	..	..	..	..	..	..	..	–	–	–
UK public sector	TBGL	..	..	..	..	..	..	..	22	–	–
Other UK residents	TBGM	..	..	..	..	..	..	..	25 716	26 742	21 997
Non-residents	TBGN	–	–	–	–	–	–	61 307	100 935	118 909	115 357
CDs and other short-term paper issued	TBGO	70 973	65 648	73 814	61 017	67 869	89 032	101 005	131 620	124 151	151 009
Total foreign currency deposits	TBGP	637 509	608 685	754 851	790 361	851 856	972 832	975 619	1 153 220	1 206 562	1 194 637
Items in suspense and transmission	TBGQ	4 979	5 637	11 261	20 714	14 779	13 881	21 272	35 713	25 027	30 547
Net derivatives	TBGR	..	..	..	..	..	..	..	8 653	2 657	3 704
Accrued amounts payable	TBGS	..	..	..	..	..	..	..	21 996	25 184	18 081
Capital and other internal funds	TBGT	19 721	18 697	20 833	21 581	21 081	26 430	25 535	31 676	46 952	69 797
Total foreign currency liabilities	TBGU	662 209	633 019	786 945	832 656	887 716	1 013 143	1 022 426	1 251 258	1 306 381	1 316 766
Total liabilities	TBGV	1 266 430	1 223 757	1 397 561	1 458 946	1 551 584	1 767 295	1 877 092	2 449 116	2 587 180	2 643 536

1 The implementation of the review of banking statistics at end-September 1997 has resulted in several changes to this table:

a) The table now includes the business of all monthly and quarterly reporting banks in the UK; it formerly covered only the business of monthly reporting institutions.

b) The Channel Islands and Isle of Man are no longer treated as part of the UK for statistical purposes. Banking institutions in the Channel Islands and Isle of Man no longer have the option of being within the UK banking sector and their business, along with the business of offshore island branches of UK mainland banks, is now excluded from the figures within this table. Additionally, the business of the UK banking sector with offshore island residents and entities has been reclassified from UK residents to non-residents.

c) The table now contains more comprehensive detail of business with building societies. This business was previously included indistinguishably within the UK private sector elements of the table.

d) The aggregate balance sheet of the banking sector has been inflated because it is now reported on an accruals basis rather than a cash basis (accrued amounts payable/receivable are shown under liabilities and assets respectively). Additionally, acceptances have been brought onto the balance sheet and are shown under both Liabilities and assets.

2 With effect from 1998, the balance sheet of the Banking Department of the Bank of England is excluded from this table, and other banks' business with the Issue Department is reclassified from "UK public sector" to "UK banks".

3 Data for 1999 reflect the acquisition of Birmingham Midshires Building Society by Halifax plc during that year.

Source: Bank of England: 020 7601 3236

22.3 Other banks' balance sheet[1]
continued

£ millions

		1990	1991	1992	1993	1994	1995	1996	1997	1998[2]	1999[3]
Sterling assets											
Notes and coins	TBGW	3 956	3 920	4 454	4 711	4 983	5 357	4 812	5 225	6 698	9 047
With UK central bank											
Cash ratio deposits	TBGX	1 690	1 576	1 402	1 415	1 490	1 682	1 888	2 566	1 068	1 141
Other	TBGY	3	27	−42	183	103	113	533	217	383	676
Market loans											
UK banks	TBGZ	91 047	77 568	87 691	79 281	88 582	103 006	109 500	139 996	148 139	144 537
UK bank CDs	TBHB	20 271	19 661	20 620	19 028	23 632	26 767	36 922	62 584	65 510	75 070
UK bank commercial paper	TBHC	..	..	..	..	..	..	..	29	130	208
UK building societies CDs etc and deposits	TBHD	3 357	3 673	4 433	5 360	5 358	4 387	4 891	4 241	4 505	5 093
Non-residents	TBHE	28 707	23 978	33 734	43 571	44 582	47 470	50 585	79 367	84 162	74 403
Acceptances granted											
UK building societies	TBHF	..	..	..	..	..	..	..	–	–	–
UK public sector	TBHG	..	..	..	..	..	..	..	–	–	–
Other UK residents	TBHH	..	..	..	..	..	..	..	18 573	15 395	11 934
Non-residents	TBHI	..	..	..	..	..	..	..	1 379	1 264	920
Bills											
Treasury bills	TBHJ	3 242	4 045	1 952	1 561	4 166	10 404	1 652	554	779	2 750
UK bank bills	TBHA	..	..	..	..	..	..	..	18 221	14 110	11 426
UK building societies	TBHK	..	..	..	..	..	..	..	–	–	–
Other UK	TBHL	..	..	..	..	..	..	..	1 117	1 220	818
Non-residents	TBHM	..	..	..	..	..	..	..	309	207	206
Claims under sale and repurchase agreements											
of which British govt. securities	TBHT	–	–	–	–	–	–	26 030	47 158	56 639	64 943
UK banks	TBHO	–	–	–	–	–	–	16 853	27 611	41 969	39 667
UK building societies	TBHP	..	..	..	..	..	..	..	345	134	91
UK public sector	TBHQ	..	..	..	..	..	..	..	..	..	..
Other UK residents	TBHR	..	..	..	..	..	..	..	21 283	23 803	30 338
Non-residents	TBHS	..	..	..	..	..	..	..	6 873	5 907	6 310
Advances											
UK public sector	TBHU	1 701	1 788	2 397	3 309	3 526	3 549	2 912	3 872	3 402	2 566
Other UK residents	TBHV	359 586	366 459	366 096	371 086	380 615	426 936	460 107	636 162	672 812	732 649
Non-residents	TBHW	14 863	13 825	12 336	12 268	12 163	13 403	16 759	21 102	21 040	23 364
Banking dept. lending to central govt. (net)	TBNU	1 671	1 526	1 277	−5 407	−947	−1 801	948	−2 741	–	–
Investments											
British government stocks	TBHX	4 201	3 873	4 848	13 753	14 366	17 135	19 910	23 078	14 714	9 242
Other public sector	TBHY	306	334	236	204	303	409	303	282	215	124
UK banks	TBHZ	..	..	..	..	..	..	..	11 922	13 415	13 584
UK building societies	TBIA	3 105	3 966	4 767	5 492	4 769	4 639	4 898	2 875	2 222	2 506
Other UK residents	TBIB	..	..	..	..	..	..	..	45 133	48 780	57 391
Non-residents	TBIC	..	..	..	..	..	..	..	9 342	11 833	13 775
Items in suspense and collection	TBID	18 070	17 356	16 426	17 135	16 477	17 613	19 830	23 526	23 888	23 441
Accrued amounts receivable	TBIE	..	..	..	..	..	..	..	15 003	17 351	15 172
Other assets	TBIF	12 045	12 346	11 724	11 146	10 242	10 525	10 267	12 218	12 593	13 036
Total sterling assets	TBIG	609 785	597 389	617 158	630 527	668 960	755 937	852 075	1 192 263	1 257 650	1 321 485
Foreign currency assets											
Market loans and advances											
UK banks	TBIH	72 229	72 961	87 596	96 129	99 885	98 305	83 920	90 367	72 262	74 250
UK banks' CDs etc.	TBII	10 161	11 081	11 239	8 642	7 226	9 345	7 793	13 634	11 064	14 363
UK building societies CDs etc. and deposits	TBIJ	..	..	..	..	..	..	..	83	259	451
UK public sector	TBIK	39	29	4 061	3 421	28	38	36	25	45	21
Other UK residents	TBIL	70 419	59 592	65 836	71 326	76 538	102 061	72 213	76 356	83 968	88 848
Non-residents	TBIM	446 041	412 552	504 567	489 439	534 589	604 783	505 953	598 541	616 832	599 145
Claims under sale and repurchase agreement											
UK banks	TBIO	–	–	–	–	–	–	21 189	24 184	31 900	28 008
UK building societies	TBIP	..	..	..	..	..	..	..	–	–	–
UK public sector	TBIQ	..	..	..	..	..	..	..	22	–	–
Other UK residents	TBIR	..	..	..	..	..	..	..	55 945	39 764	33 027
Non-residents	TBIS	–	..	..	..	..	–	75 376	121 101	147 562	146 756
Acceptances granted	TBIT	..	..	..	..	..	..	..	743	729	618
Bills	TBIU	5 562	7 835	11 784	15 398	10 490	14 429	9 660	12 728	15 240	19 508
Investments											
British government stocks	TBIV	..	..	..	..	..	..	..	3 453	4 755	4 473
Other public sector	TBIW	..	..	..	..	..	..	..	–	–	–
UK banks	TBIX	..	..	..	..	..	..	..	2 850	4 310	8 607
UK building societies	TBIY	141	335	701	889	997	728	701	414	526	631
Other UK residents	TBIZ	..	..	..	..	..	..	..	4 055	4 584	5 679
Non-residents	TBJA	44 562	53 940	79 547	114 904	128 507	154 398	161 045	186 289	234 564	243 147
Items in suspense and collection	TBJB	3 753	4 557	9 981	19 371	15 572	17 598	21 664	40 175	30 228	29 705
Accrued amounts receivable	TBJC	..	..	..	..	..	..	..	23 672	27 820	20 163
Other assets	TBJD	1 510	1 370	1 586	2 791	1 868	1 817	1 809	2 214	3 111	4 647
Total foreign currency assets	TBJE	656 645	626 368	780 403	828 419	882 624	1 011 358	1 025 017	1 256 850	1 329 525	1 322 045
Total assets	TBJF	1 266 430	1 223 757	1 397 561	1 458 946	1 551 584	1 767 295	1 877 092	2 449 113	2 587 175	2 643 530
Holdings of own sterling acceptances	TBJG	20 286	19 081	21 988	21 814	18 274	18 721	21 521	1 823	2 137	1 724
Holdings of own FC acceptances	TBJH	4 824	5 474	1 439	914	640	1 153	1 031	291	170	146
Eligible banks' total sterling acceptances	TBJI	19 929	18 870	21 812	21 726	18 168	18 476	21 220	21 411	18 753	14 458
Eligible liabilities	TBJJ	400 584	401 451	406 885	425 353	440 032	507 279	564 648	768 082	807 803	849 290

See footnote on first part of this table.

Source: Bank of England: 020 7601 3236

22.4 Industrial analysis of bank lending to UK residents[1,2]

£ millions

	UK residents		Agriculture, hunting and forestry	Fishing	Mining & quarrying	Manufacturing			
	Total to	of which sterling				Total	Food, beverages & tobacco	Textiles & leather	Pulp, paper, publishing & printing
Amounts outstanding (sterling & other currencies)									
Loans & advances (including under repo & sterling commercial paper)									
	TBOA	TBOB	TBOC	TBOD	TBOE	TBOF	TBOG	TBOH	TBOI
1998	824 053	700 275	7 013	336	5 299	52 531	9 819	2 155	7 346
1999	887 815	765 839	7 479	360	4 672	57 904	10 598	2 027	7 321
Acceptances									
	TBQA	TBQB	TBQC	TBQD	TBQE	TBQF	TBQG	TBQH	TBQI
1998	15 734	15 395	3	–	354	5 948	3 023	89	278
1999	12 253	11 934	20	–	456	3 541	1 568	111	212
Total									
	TBSA		TBSC	TBSD	TBSE	TBSF	TBSG	TBSH	TBSI
1998	839 787		7 015	336	5 653	58 479	12 842	2 244	7 624
1999	900 067		7 499	361	5 128	61 444	12 166	2 138	7 532
of which in sterling									
	TBUA		TBUC	TBUD	TBUE	TBUF	TBUG	TBUH	TBUI
1998	715 670		6 942	329	3 402	41 566	10 116	1 822	5 051
1999	777 772		7 425	354	2 634	41 372	9 563	1 685	5 121
Facilities granted									
	TCAA		TCAC	TCAD	TCAE	TCAF	TCAG	TCAH	TCAI
1998	1 034 268		9 189	416	9 663	109 229	25 135	3 762	14 360
1999	1 134 378		9 627	441	10 452	115 494	26 172	3 416	12 919
of which in sterling									
	TCCA		TCCC	TCCD	TCCE	TCCF	TCCG	TCCH	TCCI
1998	852 055		9 073	409	4 661	68 074	15 088	3 109	7 951
1999	932 208		9 498	430	3 782	71 189	15 772	2 805	7 953

	Manufacturing					Electricity, gas and water supply		Construction
	Chemicals, man-made fibres, rubber & plastics	Non-metallic mineral products & metals	Machinery, equipment & transport equipment	Electrical, medical & optical equipment	Other manufacturing	Electricity, gas & heated water	Cold water purification & supply	
Amounts outstanding (sterling & other currencies)								
Loans & advances (including under repo & sterling commercial paper)								
	TBOJ	TBOK	TBOL	TBOM	TBON	TBOO	TBOP	TBOQ
1998	7 794	6 130	8 036	6 062	5 190	6 046	990	8 667
1999	7 261	6 673	9 320	8 644	6 061	7 041	794	9 177
Acceptances								
	TBQJ	TBQK	TBQL	TBQM	TBQN	TBQO	TBQP	TBQQ
1998	702	258	772	449	376	546	1	102
1999	317	427	468	195	242	525	10	85
Total								
	TBSJ	TBSK	TBSL	TBSM	TBSN	TBSO	TBSP	TBSQ
1998	8 496	6 388	8 808	6 511	5 566	6 592	991	8 769
1999	7 577	7 100	9 788	8 839	6 303	7 566	804	9 261
of which in sterling								
	TBUJ	TBUK	TBUL	TBUM	TBUN	TBUO	TBUP	TBUQ
1998	5 517	4 411	6 374	4 157	4 117	6 219	956	7 581
1999	4 767	4 892	6 637	4 052	4 656	7 014	602	8 078
Facilities granted								
	TCAJ	TCAK	TCAL	TCAM	TCAN	TCAO	TCAP	TCAQ
1998	16 348	11 477	15 487	13 864	8 796	17 273	4 049	14 310
1999	16 173	13 270	17 780	15 770	9 995	17 625	3 369	15 575
of which in sterling								
	TCCJ	TCCK	TCCL	TCCM	TCCN	TCCO	TCCP	TCCQ
1998	9 491	7 988	10 712	7 250	6 485	13 370	3 236	12 411
1999	9 515	8 842	11 713	7 272	7 316	12 881	2 262	13 672

1 This is a series of statistics based on the Standard Industrial Classification 1992 and comprises loans, advances (including under reverse repos), finance leasing, acceptances, facilities and holdings of sterling and euro commercial paper. It includes lending under the Department of Trade and Industry special scheme for domestic shipbuilding. Holdings of investments and bills and adjustments for transit items are not included. Figures are supplied by monthly reporting banks and grossed to cover quarterly reporters. They exclude lending to building societies and to residents of the Channel Islands and Isle of Man.

2 Data for 1999 reflect the acquisition of the Birmingham Midshires Building Society by Halifax plc during that year.

Source: Bank of England: 020 7601 3236

Banking, insurance etc

22.4 Industrial analysis of bank lending to UK residents[1,2]
continued

£ millions

		Wholesale and retail trade					Real estate, renting, computer and other business activities		
	Total	Sale & repair of motor vehicles & fuel	Other wholesale trade	Other retail trade & repair	Hotels and restaurants	Transport, storage & communication	Total	Development, buying, selling, renting of real estate	Renting of machinery & equipment
Amounts outstanding (sterling & other currencies)									
Loans & advances (including under repo & sterling commercial paper)									
	TBOR	TBOS	TBOT	TBOU	TBOV	TBOW	TBOX	TBOY	TBPA
1998	34 697	8 665	12 714	13 318	11 826	15 810	56 670	39 289	3 881
1999	34 307	9 216	12 810	12 281	12 690	18 853	64 159	45 005	4 302
Acceptances									
	TBQR	TBQS	TBQT	TBQU	TBQV	TBQW	TBQX	TBQY	TBRA
1998	2 185	309	1 161	715	212	177	348	19	83
1999	2 012	378	953	681	94	119	300	64	66
Total									
	TBSR	TBSS	TBST	TBSU	TBSV	TBSW	TBSX	TBSY	TBTA
1998	36 882	8 974	13 875	14 033	12 038	15 987	57 018	39 308	3 964
1999	36 319	9 593	13 763	12 963	12 784	18 972	64 459	45 069	4 368
of which in sterling									
	TBUR	TBUS	TBUT	TBUU	TBUV	TBUW	TBUX	TBUY	TBXA
1998	29 946	8 492	8 902	12 552	10 780	13 557	53 715	38 120	419
1999	29 339	9 161	8 537	11 641	11 500	15 345	60 623	43 964	320
Facilities granted									
	TCAR	TCAS	TCAT	TCAU	TCAV	TCAW	TCAX	TCAY	TCBA
1998	56 202	12 605	20 349	23 248	15 264	27 801	77 517	50 432	4 894
1999	58 944	13 664	21 687	23 593	16 490	50 783	87 620	58 154	5 241
of which in sterling									
	TCCR	TCCS	TCCT	TCCU	TCCV	TCCW	TCCX	TCCY	TCDA
1998	44 730	11 400	13 872	19 458	13 297	21 206	71 574	48 289	4 343
1999	46 095	12 229	14 178	19 688	14 172	26 555	81 026	56 183	4 557

	Real estate, renting, computer and other business activities					Recreational, personal & community service activities		Financial intermediation (excl. insurance & pension funds)	
	Computer & related activities	Legal, accountancy, consultancy & other business activities	Public administration & defence	Education	Health & social work	Recreational, cultural & sporting activities	Personal & community services activities	Total	Financial leasing corporations
Amounts outstanding (sterling & other currencies)									
Loans & advances (including under repo & sterling commercial paper)									
	TBPB	TBPC	TBPD	TBPE	TBPF	TBPH	TBPG	TBPI	TBPJ
1998	1 574	11 927	2 985	2 434	6 498	4 937	3 386	197 647	37 721
1999	1 939	12 913	2 301	2 894	6 868	5 764	3 636	203 764	39 633
Acceptances									
	TBRB	TBRC	TBRD	TBRE	TBRF	TBRH	TBRG	TBRI	TBRJ
1998	30	216	–	–	1	36	12	5 420	1 530
1999	22	148	–	–	1	78	4	4 593	1 547
Total									
	TBTB	TBTC	TBTD	TBTE	TBTF	TBTH	TBTG	TBTI	TBTJ
1998	1 604	12 142	2 985	2 434	6 499	4 973	3 398	203 066	39 251
1999	1 961	13 060	2 302	2 894	6 869	5 842	3 640	208 359	41 180
of which in sterling									
	TBVB	TBVC	TBVD	TBVE	TBVF	TBVH	TBVG	TBVI	TBVJ
1998	1 221	10 815	2 974	2 411	6 406	4 413	3 043	117 364	38 391
1999	1 439	11 340	2 285	2 870	6 743	5 049	3 349	132 870	39 998
Facilities granted									
	TCBB	TCBC	TCBD	TCBE	TCBF	TCBH	TCBG	TCBI	TCBJ
1998	3 042	19 148	4 700	3 216	7 872	7 903	4 646	227 134	43 374
1999	3 730	20 494	3 975	3 519	8 394	9 418	4 969	231 213	44 509
of which in sterling									
	TCDB	TCDC	TCDD	TCDE	TCDF	TCDH	TCDG	TCDI	TCDJ
1998	2 274	16 669	4 653	3 183	7 666	6 228	4 168	131 213	42 203
1999	2 812	17 474	3 858	3 491	8 159	7 597	4 551	145 828	43 087

See footnote on first part of this table.

Source: Bank of England: 020 7601 3236

22.4 Industrial analysis of bank lending to UK residents[1,2]

continued

£ millions

Financial intermediation (excl. insurance & pension funds)

	Non-bank credit grantors, excl. credit unions	Credit unions	Factoring corporations	Mortgage & housing credit corporations	Investment & unit trusts excl. money market mutual funds	Money market mutual funds	Bank holding companies	Securities dealers (f)	Other financial intermediaries
Amounts outstanding (sterling & other currencies)									
Loans & advances (including under repo & sterling commercial paper)									
	TBPK	TBPL	TBPM	TBPN	TBPO	TBPP	TBPQ	TBPR	TBPS
1998	13 665	29	2 746	10 217	4 187	15	10 985	81 761	36 322
1999	12 350	1	2 031	16 138	5 070	14	7 631	87 695	33 202
Acceptances									
	TBRK	TBRL	TBRM	TBRN	TBRO	TBRP	TBRQ	TBRR	TBRS
1998	1 651	–	67	22	59	–	46	152	1 893
1999	1 199	–	92	44	43	–	1	187	1 480
Total									
	TBTK	TBTL	TBTM	TBTN	TBTO	TBTP	TBTQ	TBTR	TBTS
1998	15 316	29	2 812	10 239	4 246	15	11 031	81 914	38 215
1999	13 549	1	2 123	16 182	5 113	14	7 632	87 882	34 682
of which in sterling									
	TBVK	TBVL	TBVM	TBVN	TBVO	TBVP	TBVQ	TBVR	TBVS
1998	13 787	6	2 671	10 239	2 670	12	8 761	21 449	19 377
1999	12 393	1	2 012	16 182	3 302	14	7 404	29 717	21 847
Facilities granted									
	TCBK	TCBL	TCBM	TCBN	TCBO	TCBP	TCBQ	TCBR	TCBS
1998	17 641	30	3 078	11 039	6 939	15	11 081	87 715	46 223
1999	15 322	23	2 193	17 024	8 123	54	7 724	92 051	44 190
of which in sterling									
	TCDK	TCDL	TCDM	TCDN	TCDO	TCDP	TCDQ	TCDR	TCDS
1998	15 013	6	2 877	11 033	4 900	12	8 797	22 722	23 648
1999	13 614	23	2 058	16 910	5 514	14	7 440	31 166	26 002

	Activities auxiliary to financial intermediation			Individuals & individual trusts		
	Insurance companies & pension funds	Fund management activities	Other	Total	Lending secured on dwellings inc. bridging finance	Other loans & advances
Amounts outstanding (sterling & other currencies)						
Loans & advances (including under repo & sterling commercial paper)						
	TBPT	TBPU	TBPV	TBPW	TBPX	TBPY
1998	15 621	1 031	2 412	387 217	314 592	72 625
1999	16 408	3 547	4 805	420 393	337 867	82 494
Acceptances						
	TBRT		TBRU	TBRV		
1998	322		7	59		
1999	336		31	47		
Total						
	TBTT	TBTU	TBTV	TBTW	TBTX	TBTY
1998	15 944	1 038	2 471	387 217	314 592	72 625
1999	16 744	3 578	4 852	420 393	337 899	82 494
of which in sterling						
	TBVT	TBVU	TBVV	TBVW	TBVX	TBVY
1998	14 953	410	1 680	387 022	314 558	72 464
1999	15 883	2 236	2 043	420 160	337 867	82 293
Facilities granted						
	TCBT	TCBU	TCBV	TCBW	TCBX	TCBY
1998	22 982	1 679	3 432	409 791	321 565	88 226
1999	24 387	5 765	5 995	450 323	349 535	100 789
of which in sterling						
	TCDT	TCDU	TCDV	TCDW	TCDX	TCDY
1998	19 961	911	2 468	409 565	321 531	88 034
1999	21 255	2 935	2 923	450 054	349 495	100 559

See footnote on first part of this table.

Source: Bank of England: 020 7601 3236

22.5 Industrial analysis of bank deposits from UK residents[1,2]

£ millions

	Total from UK residents	Agriculture, hunting and forestry	Fishing	Mining & quarrying	Manufacturing			
					Total	Food, beverages & tobacco	Textiles & leather	Pulp, paper, publishing & printing
Amounts outstanding (sterling & other currencies)								
Deposit liabilities (including under repos)								
	TDAA	TDAB	TDAC	TDAD	TDAE	TDAF	TDAG	TDAH
1998	712 068	3 065	111	3 669	34 681	3 618	1 350	3 119
1999	724 185	2 940	114	3 504	32 203	3 343	1 335	3 490
of which in sterling								
	TDCA	TDCB	TDCC	TDCD	TDCE	TDCF	TDCG	TDCH
1998	624 664	3 016	101	2 677	28 163	2 871	1 107	2 675
1999	636 859	2 900	104	2 236	25 062	2 598	1 103	2 948

	Manufacturing					Electricity, gas and water supply		Construction
	Chemicals, man-made fibres, rubber & plastics	Non-metallic mineral products & metals	Machinery, equipment & transport equipment	Electrical, medical & optical equipment	Other manufacturing	Electricity, gas & heated water	Cold water purification & supply	
Amounts outstanding (sterling & other currencies)								
Deposit liabilities (including under repos)								
	TDAI	TDAJ	TDAK	TDAL	TDAM	TDAN	TDAO	TDAP
1998	4 945	4 789	6 781	5 869	4 211	4 102	756	7 382
1999	4 816	3 570	6 123	5 776	3 749	3 737	1 074	8 369
of which in sterling								
	TDCI	TDCJ	TDCK	TDCL	TDCM	TDCN	TDCO	TDCP
1998	3 710	4 377	5 393	4 440	3 590	3 842	730	7 132
1999	2 907	3 129	4 696	4 513	3 169	3 580	1 041	8 122

	Wholesale and retail trade				Hotels and restaurants	Transport, storage & communication	Real estate, renting, computer and other business activities		
	Total	Sale & repair of motor vehicles & fuel	Other wholesale trade	Other retail trade & repair			Total	Development, buying, selling, renting of real estate	Renting of machinery & equipment
Amounts outstanding (sterling & other currencies)									
Deposit liabilities (including under repos)									
	TDAQ	TDAR	TDAS	TDAT	TDAU	TDAV	TDAW	TDAX	TDAY
1998	20 874	2 321	9 896	8 658	2 407	10 678	46 229	13 435	872
1999	21 912	2 406	9 550	9 955	2 830	14 475	52 711	14 236	1 150
of which in sterling									
	TDCQ	TDCR	TDCS	TDCT	TDCU	TDCV	TDCW	TDCX	TDCY
1998	17 785	2 217	7 314	8 254	2 370	8 692	43 214	13 077	770
1999	18 738	2 316	7 124	9 298	2 788	12 277	48 560	13 859	1 080

1 This is a series of statistics based on the Standard Industrial Classification 1992 and includes borrowing under sale and repurchase agreements (repo). Adjustments for transit items are not included. Figures are supplied by monthly reporting banks and grossed to cover quarterly reporters. They exclude deposits from building societies and residents of the Channel Islands and Isle of Man.

2 Data for 1999 reflect the acquisition of Birmingham Midshires Building Society by Halifax plc during that year.

Source: Bank of England: 020 7601 3236

22.5 Industrial analysis of bank deposits from UK residents[1,2]

continued

£ millions

Real estate, renting, computer and other business activities / Recreational, personal & community service activities / Financial intermediation (excl. insurance & pension funds)

	Computer & related activities	Legal, accountancy, consultancy & other business activities	Public administration & defence	Education	Health & social work	Recreational, cultural & sporting activities	Personal & community services activities	Total	Financial leasing corporations
Amounts outstanding (sterling & other currencies)									
Deposit liabilities (including under repos)									
	TDAZ	TDBA	TDBB	TDBC	TDBD	TDBF	TDBE	TDBG	TDBH
1998	4 007	27 914	10 270	3 854	6 664	4 551	9 173	123 382	3 871
1999	5 366	31 960	9 483	4 109	6 382	5 579	9 560	113 150	4 263
of which in sterling									
	TDCZ	TDDA	TDDB	TDDC	TDDD	TDDF	TDDE	TDDG	TCDJ
1998	3 329	26 038	10 145	3 758	6 579	4 058	8 803	69 681	42 203
1999	4 450	29 170	9 373	4 018	6 236	5 022	9 226	64 235	43 087

Financial intermediation (excl. insurance & pension funds)

	Non-bank credit grantors, excl. credit unions	Credit unions	Factoring corporations	Mortgage & housing credit corporations	Investment & unit trusts excl. money market mutual funds	Money market mutual funds	Bank holding companies	Securities dealers	Other financial intermediaries
Amounts outstanding (sterling & other currencies)									
Deposit liabilities (including under repos)									
	TDBI	TDBJ	TDBK	TDBL	TDBM	TDBN	TDBO	TDBP	TDBQ
1998	2 937	103	301	567	15 268	563	2 872	55 440	41 462
1999	2 556	108	156	901	13 155	408	3 841	53 857	33 904
of which in sterling									
	TDDI	TDDJ	TDDK	TDDL	TDDM	TDDN	TDDO	TDDP	TDDQ
1998	2 455	103	285	562	11 981	530	2 451	22 927	24 926
1999	1 913	93	134	901	10 719	395	3 450	19 975	23 071

Activities auxiliary to financial intermediation

	Insurance companies & pension funds	Placed by fund managers	Other	Individuals & individual trusts
Amounts outstanding (sterling & other currencies)				
Deposit liabilities (including under repos)				
	TDBR	TDBS	TDBT	TDBU
1998	56 183	27 781	9 122	327 134
1999	49 502	22 341	11 785	348 431
of which in sterling				
	TDDR	TDDS	TDDT	TDDU
1998	49 191	22 425	6 732	325 568
1999	43 394	16 109	6 793	347 046

See footnote on first part of this table.

Source: Bank of England: 020 7601 3236

22.6 Public sector net cash requirement and other counterparts to changes in money stock during the year

Not seasonally adjusted

£ millions

		1989	1990	1991	1992	1993	1994	1995	1996	1997	1998	1999
Public sector net cash requirement (surplus-)	ABEN	−9 274	−1 687	6 959	28 436	43 358	39 344	35 446	24 688	11 856	−6 400	−1 726
Sales(-) of public sector debt to M4 private sector	KHGZ	12 736	−767	−5 685	−20 268	−30 799	−23 426	−21 688	−19 241	−16 121	−1 517	−2 402
M4 lending[1]	AVBS	89 050	70 556	37 092	25 605	22 685	31 567	57 736	59 129	68 311	63 929	78 045
External and foreign currency finance of the public sector	KHJP	−3 385	2 947	−3 058	−12 647	−10 768	654	−3 640	−10 885	−2 493	−4 711	7 186
Other external and foreign currency flows[2]	AVBW	−13 625	−12 248	1 199	8 842	14 305	−7 692	−3 521	17 917	24 922	13 289	−47 052
Net non-deposit liabilities (increase-)	AVBX	−10 754	−8 443	−8 564	−12 013	−14 850	−15 064	−8 377	−12 213	−6 201	−7 900	−2 240
Money stock (M4)	AUZI	64 746	50 356	27 941	17 955	23 931	25 386	55 957	59 395	80 273	59 723	31 800

1 Bank and building society lending, plus holdings of commercial bills by the Issue Department of the Bank of England.
2 Including sterling lending to non-residents sector.

Source: Bank of England: 020 7601 5468

22.7 Money stock and liquidity

£ millions

		1989	1990	1991	1992	1993	1994	1995	1996	1997	1998	1999
Amounts outstanding at end-year												
Notes and coin in circulation with the M4 private sector[1]	VQKT	15 355	15 253	15 690	16 770	17 795	18 749	20 007	20 843	22 477	23 318	25 580
UK private sector sterling non-interest bearing sight deposits[2,3,4,5]	AUYA	31 240	29 282	29 388	28 659	34 515	33 487	35 435	38 433	38 936	37 261	43 012
Money stock (M2)[4,5,6]	VQXV	279 953	309 810	335 928	373 243	394 510	410 469	437 102	460 294	484 828	514 618	558 526
Money stock M4[4,5,7]	AUYM	426 322	477 128	504 113	517 919	544 097	567 195	623 542	682 999	722 199	782 850	813 868
Changes during the year[8]												
Notes and coin in circulation with the M4 private sector[1]	VQLU	898	−102	437	1 087	1 025	954	1 256	836	1 646	1 134	2 276
UK private sector sterling non-interest bearing sight deposits[2,3,4,5]	AUZA	−3 928	−2 056	−781	−322	4 203	1 084	1 783	3 527	5 366	−632	5 769
Money stock (M2)[4,5,6]	AUZE	21 064	18 339	22 987	9 807	18 853	17 613	26 570	24 358	36 013	30 299	42 100
Money stock M4[4,5,7]	AUZI	64 746	50 356	27 941	17 955	23 931	25 386	55 957	59 395	80 273	59 723	31 800

1 The estimates of levels of coin in circulation include allowance for wastage, hoarding, etc.

2 Non-interest bearing deposits are confined to those with institutions included in the United Kingdom banks sector (See Table 22.3).

3 Banks' data from 1986 onwards are adjusted by a proportion of sterling items in transit and suspense.

4 Revised rules on netting of customers' credit balances against their borrowing increased the UK private sector's outstanding balances of deposits and borrowing by £2.5bn at end-December 1993. Within retail deposit, £1.7bn of the increase was in NIB bank deposits. Re-netting during 1994 amounted to £1.7bn. Changes data have been adjusted to exclude these effects.

5 Building societies' data from 1992 onwards are affected by the revised treatment of building society transit items within M4.

6 With effect from the flow for December 1992, M2 comprises the UK non-monetary financial institutions and non-public sector, i.e. M4 private sector's holdings of notes and coin together with its sterling denominated retail deposits with UK monetary financial institutions.

7 From end-1986, the discrepancy in banks' reporting of their domestic sterling interbank business has been allocated mainly to the wholesale component of M4, rather than to net non-deposit sterling liabilities.

8 As far as possible the changes exclude the effect of changes in the number of contributors to the series, and also of the introduction of new statistical returns. Changes are not seasonally adjusted.

Source: Bank of England: 020 7601 5468

22.8 Selected retail banks' base rate[1]
Percentage rates operative between dates shown

Rate

Date of change	New rate	Date of change	New rate	Date of change	New rate
1986 Jan 9	12.50	Jun 29	9.50	Sep 12	5.75
Mar 19	11.50	Jul 4	9.50-10.00	Dec 7	6.25
Apr 8	11.00-11.50	Jul 5	10.00		
Apr 9	11.00	Jul 18	10.00-10.50	1995 Feb 2[1]	6.25-6.75
Apr 21	10.50	Jul 19	10.50	Feb 3	6.75
May 23	10.00-10.50	Aug 8	10.50-11.00	Dec 13	6.50
May 27	10.00	Aug 9	11.00		
Oct 14	10.00-11.00	Aug 25	11.00-12.00	1996 Jan 18	6.25
Oct 15	11.00	Aug 26	12.00	Mar 8	6.00
		Nov 25	13.00	Jun 6	5.75
1987 Mar 10	10.50			Oct 30	5.75-6.00
Mar 18	10.00-10.50	1989 May 24	14.00	Oct 31	6.00
Mar 19	10.00	Oct 5	15.00		
Apr 28	9.50-10.00			1997 May 6	6.25
Apr 29	9.50	1990 Oct 8	14.00	Jun 6	6.25-6.50
May 11	9.00			Jun 9	6.50
Aug 6	9.00-9.50	1991 Feb 13	13.50	Jul 10	6.75
Aug 7	10.00	Feb 27	13.00	Aug 7	7.00
Oct 23	9.50-10.00	Mar 22	12.50	Nov 6	7.25
Oct 29	9.50	Apr 12	12.00		
Nov 4	9.00-9.50	May 24	11.50	1998 Jun 4	7.50
Nov 5	9.00	Jul 12	11.00	Oct 8	7.25
Dec 4	8.50	Sep 4	10.50	Nov 5	6.75
				Dec 10	6.25
1988 Feb 2	9.00	1992 May 5	10.00		
Mar 17	8.50-9.00	Sep 16[1]	12.00	1999 Jan 7	6.00
Mar 18	8.50	Sep 17[1]	10.00-12.00	Feb 4	5.50
Apr 11	8.00	Sep 18	10.00	Apr 8	5.25
May 17	7.50-8.00	Sep 22	9.00	Jun 10	5.00
May 18	7.50	Oct 16	8.00-9.00	Sep 8	5.00-5.25
Jun 2	7.50-8.00	Oct 19	8.00	Sep 10	5.25
Jun 3	8.00	Nov 13	7.00	Nov 4	5.50
Jun 6	8.00-8.50				
Jun 7	8.50	1993 Jan 26	6.00	2000 Jan 13	5.75
Jun 22	8.50-9.00	Nov 23	5.50	Feb 10	6.00
Jun 23	9.00				
Jun 28	9.00-9.50	1994 Feb 8	5.25		

1 Data obtained from Barclays Bank, Lloyds TSB Bank, HSBC, National Westminster Bank whose rates are used to compile this series. Where all the rates did not change on the same day a spread is shown.

Source: Bank of England: 020 7601 4342

22.9 Average three month sterling money market rates[4]

Rate per cent

	1990	1991	1992	1993	1994	1995	1996	1997	1998	1999	2000
Treasury bills:[1] KDMM											
January	14.50	13.00	9.97	6.05	4.88	5.93	6.08	6.01	6.84	5.28	5.72
February	14.45	12.39	9.80	5.37	4.76	6.16	5.96	5.81	6.88	5.04	5.83
March	14.57	11.64	10.10	5.38	4.83	6.09	5.81	5.92	6.95	4.92	5.86
April	14.59	11.25	9.97	5.33	4.88	6.30	5.80	6.09	7.02	4.90	5.90
May	14.50	10.84	9.42	5.30	4.81	6.20	5.82	6.15	6.99	4.93	5.95
June	14.38	10.72	9.42	5.19	4.88	6.37	5.58	6.37	7.29	4.76	5.85
July	14.32	10.52	9.43	5.13	5.09	6.62	5.49	6.60	7.22	4.76	5.83
August	14.31	10.20	9.65	5.06	5.34	6.59	5.54	6.81	7.19	4.85	5.80
September	14.26	9.66	9.16	5.16	5.39	6.52	5.54	6.88	6.94	5.08	..
October	13.37	9.86	7.47	5.15	5.44	6.57	5.55	6.94	6.54	5.25	..
November	12.92	9.98	6.49	4.95	5.63	6.44	6.02	7.09	6.31	5.20	..
December	12.96	10.10	6.39	4.87	5.87	6.21	6.08	7.04	5.72	5.49	..
Eligible bill:[2] KDMY											
January	14.55	13.34	10.08	6.43	5.07	6.41	6.18	6.15	7.28	5.63	5.90
February	14.53	12.55	9.87	5.59	4.95	6.54	6.00	5.99	7.24	5.28	6.01
March	14.67	11.75	10.14	5.62	4.90	6.40	5.87	6.01	7.25	5.11	5.98
April	14.63	11.44	10.18	5.66	4.93	6.44	5.83	6.26	7.24	5.02	6.05
May	14.54	11.05	9.56	5.67	4.92	6.54	5.85	6.31	7.20	5.08	6.09
June	14.40	10.78	9.52	5.62	4.94	6.44	5.66	6.50	7.41	4.94	6.03
July	14.33	10.61	9.59	5.63	5.01	6.66	5.57	6.80	7.49	4.89	5.97
August	14.34	10.39	9.80	5.59	5.44	6.64	5.60	6.95	7.40	4.94	5.97
September	14.31	9.85	9.43	5.58	5.54	6.55	5.63	7.02	7.20	5.16	..
October	13.40	10.02	7.78	5.50	5.74	6.58	5.76	7.10	6.91	5.42	..
November	13.10	10.09	6.70	5.31	5.89	6.49	6.10	7.27	6.52	5.43	..
December	13.14	10.21	6.69	5.04	6.12	6.29	6.18	7.31	6.05	5.59	..
Interbank rate:[3] AMIJ											
January	15.16	13.97	10.65	6.94	5.39	6.56	6.36	6.32	7.48	5.80	6.06
February	15.11	13.25	10.37	6.16	5.22	6.75	6.16	6.19	7.46	5.43	6.15
March	15.29	12.40	10.62	5.98	5.16	6.66	6.05	6.20	7.48	5.30	6.15
April	15.21	11.95	10.62	5.98	5.21	6.67	6.00	6.38	7.44	5.23	6.21
May	15.15	11.53	10.06	5.97	5.17	6.72	6.02	6.45	7.41	5.25	6.23
June	14.97	11.24	9.98	5.89	5.13	6.64	5.85	6.66	7.63	5.12	6.14
July	14.95	11.09	10.15	5.95	5.20	6.80	5.73	6.96	7.71	5.07	6.11
August	15.00	10.89	10.35	5.84	5.53	6.79	5.75	7.15	7.66	5.18	6.14
September	14.91	10.29	9.99	5.91	5.67	6.72	5.77	7.21	7.38	5.32	..
October	14.03	10.40	8.32	5.76	5.91	6.73	5.94	7.26	7.14	5.94	..
November	13.64	10.48	7.21	5.57	6.06	6.64	6.30	7.54	6.89	5.78	..
December	13.81	10.78	7.15	5.33	6.37	6.49	6.35	7.62	6.38	5.97	..
Certificate of deposits:[3] KOSA											
January	15.10	13.86	10.53	6.82	5.29	6.48	6.31	6.27	7.44	5.74	6.02
February	15.05	13.18	10.27	6.00	5.14	6.67	6.11	6.14	7.42	5.38	6.10
March	15.20	12.33	10.51	5.87	5.09	6.59	6.01	6.15	7.43	5.26	6.09
April	15.15	11.86	10.50	5.84	5.12	6.62	5.96	6.33	7.40	5.19	6.17
May	15.09	11.44	9.95	5.86	5.10	6.66	5.98	6.39	7.37	5.22	6.19
June	14.90	11.13	9.89	5.77	5.06	6.56	5.79	6.62	7.59	5.09	6.10
July	14.90	10.99	10.04	5.81	5.11	6.72	5.69	6.92	7.66	5.03	6.08
August	14.94	10.79	10.21	5.71	5.45	6.73	5.71	7.12	7.61	5.14	6.09
September	14.87	10.21	9.83	5.79	5.58	6.66	5.74	7.17	7.34	5.28	..
October	13.97	10.30	8.17	5.65	5.81	6.68	5.89	7.22	7.09	5.86	..
November	13.53	10.37	7.04	5.46	5.97	6.58	6.25	7.50	6.82	5.72	..
December	13.68	10.67	7.02	5.23	6.25	6.44	6.29	7.57	6.32	5.89	..
Local authority deposits:[3] KDPX											
January	15.02	13.94	10.61	6.84	5.30	6.52	6.31	6.27	7.43	5.76	6.03
February	15.02	13.24	10.34	6.09	5.12	6.69	6.13	6.15	7.40	5.38	6.09
March	15.20	12.45	10.57	5.93	5.08	6.59	6.02	6.14	7.40	5.27	6.08
April	15.19	11.89	10.59	5.95	5.14	6.60	5.98	6.33	7.38	5.17	6.12
May	15.12	11.50	10.02	5.94	5.12	6.68	6.00	6.38	7.34	5.19	6.14
June	14.94	11.23	9.94	5.86	5.08	6.58	5.80	6.57	7.56	5.07	6.09
July	14.91	11.05	10.10	5.90	5.18	6.76	5.69	6.90	7.64	5.01	6.04
August	14.96	10.88	10.24	5.80	5.44	6.74	5.71	7.11	7.55	5.11	6.06
September	14.92	10.32	9.82	5.85	5.62	6.65	5.72	7.19	7.35	5.19	..
October	14.03	10.45	8.28	5.70	5.84	6.68	5.86	7.21	7.08	5.83	..
November	13.60	10.44	7.17	5.51	5.99	6.60	6.24	7.49	6.85	5.64	..
December	13.78	10.75	7.08	5.26	6.32	6.43	6.30	7.56	6.35	5.88	..

1 A full definition of these series is given in Section 7 of the ONS Financial Statistics Explanatory Handbook.
2 Average rate of discount at weekly (Friday) tender.
3 Working day average of the mean of the bid and offer discount rate.
4 Working day average of the mean bid and offer yield.

Source: Bank of England: 020 7601 4342

22.10 Average foreign exchange rates[1,2]

	1990	1991	1992	1993	1994	1995	1996	1997	1998	1999	2000
Sterling exchange rate index (1990 = 100) AJHX											
January	96.5	103.0	99.6	88.8	92.0	88.5	83.2	95.9	104.7	99.6	108.5
February	98.3	103.0	99.7	84.7	90.4	87.4	83.8	97.4	104.7	100.8	108.4
March	95.5	101.9	98.9	86.4	89.8	85.6	83.5	97.4	106.8	102.8	108.4
April	95.5	101.6	100.2	88.9	89.2	84.5	83.8	99.5	107.1	103.4	110.1
May	96.5	100.9	101.7	89.0	88.9	84.3	84.6	99.0	103.4	104.2	108.5
June	99.1	99.5	101.7	88.3	89.1	84.1	86.0	100.4	105.4	104.7	104.6
July	102.4	99.6	101.2	90.5	87.9	83.6	85.7	104.5	105.3	103.5	105.6
August	104.2	99.9	100.5	90.3	87.8	84.4	84.7	102.5	104.6	103.3	107.4
September	102.8	100.1	96.5	89.8	88.1	84.8	86.1	100.4	103.3	104.7	..
October	103.7	99.6	88.7	89.4	89.1	84.3	88.4	101.1	100.7	105.4	..
November	103.0	99.9	86.2	90.2	89.1	83.3	92.0	103.8	100.6	105.7	..
December	102.0	100.0	88.2	91.0	89.1	82.9	93.8	104.4	100.4	106.7	..
Sterling/US Dollar AJFA											
January	1.6523	1.9348	1.8127	1.5325	1.4940	1.5747	1.5306	1.6587	1.6353	1.6509	1.6402
February	1.6962	1.9655	1.7781	1.4386	1.4799	1.5720	1.5364	1.6246	1.6407	1.6276	1.5998
March	1.6246	1.8265	1.7238	1.4625	1.4917	1.6005	1.5271	1.6063	1.6620	1.6220	1.5802
April	1.6374	1.7502	1.7576	1.5472	1.4837	1.6074	1.5145	1.6295	1.6733	1.6105	1.5837
May	1.6778	1.7252	1.8109	1.5481	1.5029	1.5868	1.5152	1.6334	1.6366	1.6154	1.5075
June	1.7094	1.6499	1.8556	1.5099	1.5252	1.5949	1.5418	1.6446	1.6507	1.5950	1.5089
July	1.8081	1.6503	1.9186	1.4963	1.5463	1.5953	1.5539	1.6702	1.6437	1.5748	1.5088
August	1.8998	1.6841	1.9412	1.4911	1.5427	1.5681	1.5502	1.6034	1.6320	1.6073	1.4910
September	1.8786	1.7249	1.8559	1.5261	1.5651	1.5584	1.5597	1.6015	1.6822	1.6243	..
October	1.9454	1.7226	1.6577	1.5037	1.6057	1.5779	1.5862	1.6329	1.6952	1.6571	..
November	1.9647	1.7787	1.5275	1.4806	1.5886	1.5623	1.6626	1.6890	1.6620	1.6214	..
December	1.9257	1.8258	1.5536	1.4904	1.5595	1.5398	1.6647	1.6597	1.6705	1.6132	..
Sterling/Deutsche Mark AJFH											
January	2.793	2.920	2.856	2.475	2.604	2.409	2.236	2.660	2.971	2.784	3.169
February	2.843	2.908	2.877	2.362	2.567	2.360	2.252	2.722	2.974	2.843	3.179
March	2.769	2.931	2.865	2.407	2.523	2.249	2.256	2.725	3.036	2.915	3.203
April	2.761	2.979	2.895	2.468	2.520	2.218	2.282	2.788	3.032	2.944	3.272
May	2.790	2.963	2.936	2.488	2.491	2.239	2.323	2.782	2.904	2.970	3.257
June	2.879	2.940	2.917	2.496	2.484	2.232	2.356	2.840	2.958	3.007	3.106
July	2.962	2.947	2.860	2.566	2.426	2.214	2.336	2.992	2.954	2.974	3.139
August	2.983	2.936	2.816	2.529	2.413	2.264	2.298	2.950	2.919	2.962	3.223
September	2.950	2.925	2.683	2.472	2.424	2.276	2.349	2.863	2.860	3.023	..
October	2.965	2.911	2.455	2.463	2.441	2.232	2.424	2.868	2.778	3.030	..
November	2.917	2.884	2.424	2.517	2.446	2.215	2.513	2.926	2.795	3.072	..
December	2.879	2.856	2.455	2.549	2.451	2.218	2.583	2.952	2.788	3.120	..

1 Working day average
2 A full definition of these series is given in Section 7 of the ONS Explanatory Handbook.

Source: Bank of England: 020 7601 4342

22.11 Average FTSE Actuaries share indices[1,2]

	1990	1991	1992	1993	1994	1995	1996	1997	1998	1999	2000
FTSE 100 AJNO											
January	2 367.84	2 106.64	2 520.19	2 790.29	3 431.29	3 028.27	3 715.78	4 166.48	5 242.10	5 975.84	6 471.60
February	2 296.99	2 278.36	2 543.31	2 840.17	3 396.40	3 051.68	3 738.08	4 316.57	5 657.73	6 010.79	6 178.51
March	2 248.53	2 449.81	2 495.24	2 897.07	3 206.10	3 078.24	3 697.50	4 349.78	5 861.80	6 168.55	6 541.46
April	2 191.33	2 514.14	2 549.44	2 837.45	3 130.94	3 198.38	3 792.32	4 312.51	5 974.51	6 459.86	6 312.71
May	2 230.57	2 493.32	2 702.34	2 830.13	3 089.23	3 288.31	3 758.41	4 622.62	5 936.72	6 322.04	6 210.24
June	2 376.98	2 495.14	2 604.44	2 874.70	2 980.32	3 351.55	3 734.02	4 649.40	5 847.04	6 425.82	6 450.25
July	2 361.90	2 530.10	2 443.25	2 850.73	3 036.57	3 426.50	3 707.21	4 843.16	5 987.19	6 422.83	6 433.31
August	2 195.05	2 600.50	2 344.11	3 019.28	3 178.50	3 486.95	3 841.75	4 945.56	5 555.77	6 210.91	6 480.01
September	2 081.02	2 622.16	2 452.41	3 028.12	3 098.35	3 534.27	3 927.10	5 010.35	5 171.92	6 116.94	..
October	2 091.89	2 580.86	2 587.09	3 125.15	3 046.77	3 531.80	4 020.99	5 145.13	5 063.84	6 071.20	..
November	2 089.68	2 505.09	2 712.92	3 111.59	3 086.85	3 580.31	3 969.54	4 846.24	5 595.58	6 487.49	..
December	2 164.10	2 410.50	2 777.08	3 313.68	3 026.62	3 650.05	4 038.89	5 087.53	5 695.61	6 718.34	..
FT Non-Financials AJMG											
January	1 291.51	1 115.00	1 353.77	1 496.94	1 818.98	1 631.29	1 919.36	2 104.75	2 455.76	2 778.42	3 245.63
February	1 249.22	1 204.72	1 374.45	1 522.74	1 818.96	1 631.03	1 941.86	2 150.64	2 586.40	2 815.82	3 148.44
March	1 219.10	1 308.69	1 354.06	1 552.97	1 745.46	1 631.47	1 953.49	2 178.24	2 708.91	2 877.41	3 351.94
April	1 186.16	1 342.30	1 387.84	1 522.32	1 708.89	1 690.67	2 021.61	2 149.68	2 776.91	2 988.44	3 156.97
May	1 204.65	1 331.16	1 476.08	1 522.69	1 690.44	1 738.74	2 013.00	2 219.45	2 847.14	2 970.83	3 093.98
June	1 285.06	1 330.25	1 419.66	1 539.22	1 618.42	1 767.52	1 999.60	2 231.81	2 833.04	3 020.57	3 216.08
July	1 275.24	1 342.46	1 319.06	1 521.63	1 642.28	1 806.86	1 958.89	2 284.21	2 859.68	3 064.76	3 220.07
August	1 184.05	1 379.55	1 258.02	1 614.52	1 726.77	1 846.24	2 002.27	2 326.86	2 658.60	2 983.93	3 192.66
September	1 116.53	1 404.22	1 301.02	1 623.43	1 680.38	1 868.17	2 043.06	2 369.90	2 480.53	2 944.00	..
October	1 119.39	1 387.17	1 364.42	1 653.67	1 639.72	1 851.30	2 069.12	2 439.08	2 413.68	2 901.63	..
November	1 113.82	1 353.28	1 425.57	1 643.34	1 654.73	1 854.75	2 040.44	2 332.02	2 630.55	3 090.84	..
December	1 145.07	1 299.58	1 473.45	1 733.10	1 622.39	1 879.54	2 056.24	2 401.00	2 651.00	3 269.95	..
Financials AMAA											
January	1 621.71	1 333.92	1 385.89	1 718.78	2 619.71	2 084.15	2 916.24	3 674.44	4 968.04	5 145.56	5 280.33
February	1 583.14	1 464.83	1 384.60	1 822.76	2 607.79	2 125.71	2 942.72	3 919.61	5 542.60	5 263.96	4 884.58
March	1 520.56	1 591.19	1 346.68	1 888.45	2 324.02	2 170.51	2 837.38	3 876.31	5 732.81	5 566.39	5 109.08
April	1 500.51	1 594.89	1 353.29	1 901.37	2 240.03	2 264.66	2 866.93	3 825.30	5 801.80	5 992.44	5 267.23
May	1 476.32	1 548.06	1 505.57	1 926.91	2 164.18	2 350.00	2 898.78	4 331.40	5 497.77	5 762.16	5 319.47
June	1 556.43	1 507.79	1 452.21	2 011.94	2 111.15	2 411.52	2 867.16	4 281.17	5 274.89	5 837.41	5 530.31
July	1 543.97	1 513.55	1 352.32	2 065.80	2 129.92	2 466.78	2 886.69	4 468.02	5 352.53	5 734.03	5 585.71
August	1 406.57	1 584.38	1 267.47	2 175.74	2 197.58	2 526.20	3 078.43	4 647.61	4 914.36	5 575.43	5 997.42
September	1 284.25	1 605.07	1 348.16	2 174.42	2 181.71	2 599.72	3 149.04	4 634.33	4 410.37	5 489.99	..
October	1 312.97	1 531.22	1 483.95	2 310.58	2 137.44	2 691.46	3 292.82	4 787.52	4 319.56	5 388.54	..
November	1 337.08	1 455.47	1 622.84	2 289.99	2 188.27	2 805.33	3 300.68	4 407.61	4 877.76	5 765.55	..
December	1 386.04	1 348.81	1 645.58	2 502.99	2 134.40	2 879.80	3 418.82	4 756.91	4 955.84	5 706.70	..
Investments Trusts DEPG											
January	1 949.83	1 497.25	1 822.17	2 064.63	3 058.15	2 609.12	3 079.31	3 198.05	3 436.17	3 649.01	4 966.17
February	1 850.43	1 642.43	1 825.74	2 217.35	3 056.69	2 604.17	3 142.90	3 328.88	3 635.46	3 712.94	5 029.95
March	1 783.47	1 835.51	1 808.41	2 244.24	2 901.35	2 583.43	3 106.91	3 340.35	3 855.17	3 812.75	5 403.93
April	1 757.29	1 863.97	1 826.01	2 225.74	2 844.45	2 648.57	3 216.41	3 234.90	3 935.37	3 991.63	5 044.26
May	1 800.58	1 864.72	1 945.40	2 256.79	2 812.57	2 762.00	3 237.58	3 377.50	4 036.89	4 059.74	5 035.94
June	1 882.72	1 859.45	1 837.53	2 330.08	2 709.20	2 791.09	3 170.26	3 422.71	3 976.40	4 112.19	5 327.88
July	1 878.07	1 854.11	1 726.09	2 372.09	2 725.64	2 874.20	3 075.76	3 453.98	3 960.55	4 319.87	5 474.11
August	1 688.83	1 885.60	1 626.22	2 563.16	2 882.04	2 938.91	3 147.91	3 512.81	3 606.48	4 258.92	5 596.02
September	1 581.00	1 926.31	1 688.05	2 549.64	2 831.12	2 969.59	3 182.58	3 493.30	3 166.36	4 251.66	..
October	1 537.79	1 905.34	1 801.19	2 663.51	2 732.79	2 924.52	3 204.46	3 534.96	3 118.92	4 122.35	..
November	1 540.42	1 834.04	1 933.38	2 669.09	2 732.45	2 932.60	3 137.47	3 275.77	3 478.60	4 510.47	..
December	1 561.66	1 747.99	2 000.31	2 880.07	2 686.29	2 998.07	3 129.25	3 370.41	3 480.98	4 910.85	..
FTSE All Share AJMA											
January	1 184.51	1 010.79	1 203.08	1 351.60	1 710.35	1 501.87	1 818.72	2 041.99	2 455.05	2 715.41	3 072.11
February	1 146.53	1 095.30	1 218.70	1 384.99	1 709.09	1 506.17	1 839.78	2 105.82	2 624.19	2 757.57	2 947.10
March	1 115.82	1 190.90	1 199.04	1 415.40	1 619.80	1 511.04	1 836.04	2 121.89	2 740.51	2 841.78	3 126.10
April	1 087.87	1 217.27	1 225.16	1 393.70	1 582.06	1 566.98	1 892.47	2 092.74	2 799.69	2 976.58	3 000.08
May	1 100.35	1 203.75	1 310.73	1 397.10	1 559.27	1 614.69	1 889.96	2 203.40	2 814.73	2 935.82	2 959.31
June	1 170.76	1 198.76	1 260.28	1 419.94	1 497.44	1 643.59	1 875.05	2 207.24	2 775.66	2 982.44	3 076.22
July	1 162.07	1 208.52	1 171.62	1 413.38	1 517.70	1 680.80	1 844.67	2 269.94	2 804.19	3 000.90	3 085.70
August	1 075.21	1 244.49	1 114.82	1 498.55	1 591.47	1 718.13	1 899.46	2 324.27	2 597.71	2 920.81	3 114.63
September	1 008.65	1 265.42	1 156.91	1 505.06	1 554.01	1 743.26	1 938.37	2 357.80	2 397.79	2 880.46	..
October	1 009.41	1 245.25	1 221.44	1 544.80	1 516.65	1 739.84	1 973.94	2 422.75	2 338.00	2 835.95	..
November	1 007.00	1 210.28	1 284.96	1 535.11	1 533.46	1 755.17	1 951.91	2 293.45	2 571.19	3 024.26	..
December	1 040.25	1 156.90	1 324.08	1 628.88	1 502.42	1 783.30	1 976.41	2 388.17	2 595.88	3 146.68	..

1 Working day average
2 A full definition of these series is given in Section 7 of the ONS Explanatory Handbook.

Source: Bank of England: 020 7601 4342

22.12 Average Zero Coupon Yields[1,2]

	1990	1991	1992	1993	1994	1995	1996	1997	1998	1999	2000
Nominal Five Year Yield ZBRG											
January	11.07	10.47	9.54	7.46	5.89	8.63	6.85	7.15	6.18	4.30	6.28
February	11.44	9.97	9.34	7.06	6.23	8.53	7.12	6.82	6.10	4.46	6.13
March	12.30	10.04	9.71	6.94	6.96	8.45	7.45	7.07	6.09	4.69	5.89
April	12.51	10.06	9.53	7.23	7.58	8.25	7.52	7.28	5.93	4.66	5.80
May	12.21	10.15	9.08	7.47	7.97	7.95	7.53	6.94	5.95	4.95	5.82
June	11.57	10.33	9.10	7.34	8.45	7.77	7.46	6.96	6.04	5.28	5.61
July	11.60	10.15	9.08	7.02	8.27	7.89	7.30	7.01	6.12	5.49	5.58
August	11.72	9.93	9.45	6.62	8.47	7.70	7.19	6.97	5.80	5.75	5.65
September	11.68	9.57	9.18	6.59	8.71	7.47	7.18	6.72	5.32	6.00	..
October	11.25	9.65	8.06	6.43	8.64	7.56	6.97	6.51	4.94	6.25	..
November	10.92	9.70	7.46	6.35	8.49	7.21	7.18	6.69	4.92	5.86	..
December	10.66	9.72	7.65	5.89	8.49	6.88	7.20	6.46	4.51	5.90	..
Nominal Ten Year Yield ZBRH											
January	10.35	10.19	9.21	8.51	6.39	8.57	7.46	7.52	5.96	4.24	5.62
February	10.76	9.84	9.08	8.25	6.78	8.50	7.80	7.15	5.91	4.39	5.44
March	11.59	10.05	9.40	7.95	7.43	8.45	8.08	7.41	5.85	4.60	5.18
April	11.89	9.95	9.15	8.06	7.79	8.31	8.06	7.58	5.69	4.53	5.14
May	11.67	10.13	8.82	8.32	8.24	8.07	8.10	7.08	5.73	4.83	5.23
June	11.15	10.31	8.90	8.11	8.65	8.04	8.09	7.04	5.60	5.07	5.05
July	11.20	10.00	8.79	7.74	8.47	8.20	7.96	6.92	5.65	5.24	5.09
August	11.60	9.77	9.04	7.23	8.54	8.07	7.86	6.97	5.41	5.25	5.18
September	11.56	9.43	8.99	7.09	8.77	7.93	7.86	6.70	5.03	5.51	..
October	11.28	9.50	8.78	7.00	8.64	8.09	7.56	6.37	4.93	5.68	..
November	11.00	9.53	8.42	6.97	8.51	7.78	7.56	6.46	4.83	5.11	..
December	10.43	9.41	8.46	6.45	8.43	7.52	7.52	6.22	4.44	5.19	..
Nominal Twenty Year Yield ZBRI											
January	8.94	9.28	..	9.19	6.57	8.23	7.89	7.74	5.94	4.36	4.45
February	9.26	9.10	8.67	8.97	6.88	8.16	8.19	7.39	5.88	4.44	4.38
March	9.89	9.22	8.94	8.67	7.45	8.15	8.37	7.59	5.78	4.60	4.25
April	10.16	9.15	8.81	8.63	7.69	8.09	8.30	7.73	5.61	4.53	4.35
May	9.93	9.30	8.57	8.74	7.98	7.92	8.38	7.16	5.67	4.75	4.40
June	9.69	9.47	8.61	8.51	8.18	7.98	8.41	7.08	5.42	4.77	4.37
July	9.70	9.35	8.43	8.12	8.08	8.24	8.34	6.80	5.45	4.67	4.38
August	10.04	..	8.55	7.56	8.15	8.14	8.26	6.86	5.30	4.53	4.49
September	9.90	..	8.72	7.37	8.29	8.05	8.27	6.64	4.91	4.62	..
October	9.92	..	9.37	7.27	8.23	8.30	7.98	6.36	4.87	4.56	..
November	9.94	..	9.09	7.20	8.18	7.98	7.81	6.37	4.73	4.07	..
December	9.43	..	9.00	6.63	8.08	7.80	7.67	6.17	4.47	4.20	..
Real Ten Year Yield ZBRJ											
January	3.63	4.10	4.29	3.56	2.73	3.87	3.42	3.45	3.10	2.00	2.10
February	3.86	4.12	4.22	3.19	2.86	3.86	3.54	3.27	3.06	1.91	2.17
March	4.10	4.11	4.33	3.01	3.09	3.87	3.67	3.43	3.00	1.85	2.05
April	4.16	4.04	4.51	3.07	3.25	3.79	3.63	3.56	2.91	1.70	2.08
May	4.16	4.05	4.43	3.23	3.48	3.57	3.72	3.57	2.92	1.91	2.14
June	4.17	4.17	4.38	3.25	3.76	3.56	3.77	3.66	2.85	1.89	2.12
July	4.35	4.27	4.50	3.19	3.84	3.58	3.70	3.62	2.77	1.90	2.14
August	4.26	4.32	4.77	3.15	3.78	3.48	3.58	3.60	2.65	2.19	2.25
September	4.31	4.16	4.67	3.09	3.81	3.45	3.57	3.52	2.59	2.31	..
October	4.30	4.14	3.77	3.02	3.82	3.63	3.41	3.23	2.67	2.26	..
November	4.05	4.17	3.42	2.95	3.81	3.52	3.43	3.25	2.40	2.05	..
December	4.05	4.33	3.67	2.79	3.83	3.43	3.42	3.11	2.11	1.98	..
Real Twenty Year Yield ZBRK											
January	..	..	..	3.84	3.07	3.89	..	3.67	3.06	2.07	2.01
February	..	..	..	3.68	3.23	3.89	3.79	3.49	3.05	1.99	1.95
March	..	..	..	3.53	3.45	3.88	3.81	3.59	2.98	1.93	1.78
April	..	..	4.52	3.54	3.51	3.80	3.75	3.68	2.85	1.81	1.84
May	..	..	4.40	3.63	3.68	3.64	3.82	3.66	2.83	1.99	1.91
June	..	..	4.32	3.59	3.91	3.69	3.86	3.69	2.63	1.97	1.87
July	..	..	4.40	3.52	3.93	3.71	3.81	3.57	2.58	2.00	1.90
August	..	..	4.55	3.35	3.84	3.62	3.75	3.57	2.53	2.14	1.96
September	..	..	4.48	3.25	3.88	3.61	3.76	3.48	2.49	2.26	..
October	..	..	3.98	3.19	3.87	3.73	3.61	3.22	2.59	2.22	..
November	..	..	3.82	3.21	3.85	3.61	3.62	3.18	2.36	1.92	..
December	..	..	3.96	3.08	3.87	3.56	3.62	3.06	2.14	1.87	..

1 Working day average.
2 Calculated using the Variable Roughness Penalty (VRP) model.

Source: Bank of England: 020 7601 4342

22.13 Average Rates on Representative British Government Stocks[1]

	1990	1991	1992	1993	1994	1995	1996	1997	1998	1999	2000
5 Year Conventional Rate KORP											
January	11.51	10.66	9.57	6.88	5.76	8.61	6.78	7.19	6.33	4.25	6.36
February	11.90	10.16	9.34	6.72	6.05	8.52	7.02	6.86	6.24	4.41	6.23
March	12.78	10.22	9.75	6.62	6.72	8.44	7.56	7.08	6.26	4.65	6.01
April	13.01	10.23	9.54	6.91	7.33	8.26	7.43	7.30	6.11	4.66	5.95
May	12.67	10.27	9.09	7.10	7.74	7.96	7.61	6.98	6.14	4.93	5.97
June	12.01	10.41	9.12	7.01	8.22	7.79	7.52	7.01	6.31	5.27	5.78
July	12.03	10.25	9.13	6.70	8.06	7.90	7.35	7.09	6.14	5.49	5.75
August	12.06	10.04	9.50	6.35	8.31	7.69	7.21	7.02	5.84	5.80	5.81
September	12.01	9.67	9.13	6.34	8.61	7.45	7.20	6.78	5.34	6.04	..
October	11.48	9.74	7.80	6.17	8.57	7.54	.7.01	6.59	4.88	6.24	..
November	11.12	9.79	7.15	6.09	8.44	7.16	7.22	6.79	4.86	5.89	..
December	10.99	9.83	7.38	5.66	8.49	6.83	7.26	6.60	4.45	5.91	..
10 year Conventional Rate KORQ											
January	10.73	10.42	9.47	8.22	6.23	8.66	7.42	7.53	6.07	4.16	5.75
February	11.16	10.11	9.32	7.91	6.61	8.59	7.75	7.17	6.02	4.32	5.56
March	12.06	10.25	9.67	7.66	7.29	8.53	8.05	7.41	5.97	4.54	5.29
April	12.33	10.17	9.43	7.82	7.68	8.39	8.05	7.60	5.81	4.48	5.25
May	12.06	10.32	9.06	8.06	8.13	8.12	8.08	7.13	5.85	4.77	5.35
June	11.46	10.53	9.14	7.87	8.54	8.08	8.04	7.10	5.77	5.02	5.15
July	11.53	10.24	9.08	7.49	8.37	8.23	7.91	7.01	5.67	5.20	5.18
August	11.84	10.00	9.35	6.98	8.52	8.10	7.81	7.05	5.56	5.24	5.27
September	11.80	9.65	9.17	6.90	8.80	7.92	7.80	6.77	5.10	5.52	..
October	11.46	9.72	8.68	6.81	8.70	8.08	7.51	6.47	4.93	5.70	..
November	11.13	9.76	8.26	6.77	8.57	7.75	7.56	6.59	4.87	5.16	..
December	10.66	9.69	8.38	6.29	8.53	7.45	7.54	6.34	4.49	5.24	..
20 Year Conventional Rate KORR											
January	10.08	10.06	9.23	8.74	6.53	8.45	7.73	7.71	6.04	4.36	4.91
February	10.49	9.75	9.12	8.44	6.88	8.43	8.04	7.35	5.98	4.47	4.80
March	11.30	9.89	9.44	8.19	7.49	8.40	8.28	7.58	5.90	4.64	4.64
April	11.60	9.81	9.25	8.42	7.81	8.30	8.26	7.74	5.73	4.58	4.71
May	11.33	10.00	8.93	8.58	8.18	8.09	8.31	7.21	5.79	4.83	4.77
June	10.90	10.20	8.99	8.36	8.48	8.08	8.31	7.15	5.59	4.92	4.68
July	10.92	9.98	8.85	7.98	8.35	8.30	8.21	6.93	5.63	4.88	4.70
August	11.27	9.78	9.06	7.46	8.46	8.19	8.12	6.98	5.43	4.82	4.79
September	11.16	9.44	9.08	7.31	8.65	8.06	8.11	6.74	5.02	4.97	..
October	10.97	9.50	9.15	7.18	8.56	8.26	7.84	6.45	4.92	4.97	..
November	10.80	9.57	8.78	7.12	8.46	7.93	7.77	6.50	4.79	4.46	..
December	10.25	9.46	8.78	6.57	8.39	7.70	7.67	6.32	4.49	4.56	..
10 Year Index-Linked Rate KORS											
January	3.78	4.19	4.29	3.60	2.70	3.89	3.42	3.44	3.01	2.00	2.11
February	4.01	4.19	4.18	3.23	2.81	3.87	3.57	3.23	2.94	1.94	2.16
March	4.27	4.19	4.29	3.07	3.07	3.86	3.70	3.41	2.89	1.90	2.06
April	4.38	4.09	4.47	3.11	3.25	3.79	3.66	3.55	2.80	1.74	2.08
May	4.41	4.14	4.41	3.30	3.51	3.58	3.74	3.52	2.83	1.96	2.15
June	4.38	4.28	4.40	3.31	3.78	3.58	3.80	3.62	2.81	1.93	2.13
July	4.56	4.34	4.51	3.22	3.85	3.61	3.82	3.68	2.67	1.93	2.14
August	4.47	4.34	4.76	3.16	3.82	3.52	3.59	3.59	2.55	2.20	2.25
September	4.50	4.18	4.68	3.09	3.85	3.46	3.57	3.47	2.59	2.32	..
October	4.49	4.16	3.82	3.03	3.84	3.65	3.41	3.17	2.66	2.26	..
November	4.23	4.19	3.40	2.96	3.84	3.54	3.42	3.23	2.39	2.03	..
December	4.14	4.34	3.61	2.75	3.85	3.45	3.41	3.01	2.11	1.99	..
20 Year Index-Linked rate KORT											
January	3.76	4.23	4.34	3.84	2.96	3.91	3.58	3.62	3.01	2.06	2.01
February	3.94	4.23	4.32	3.64	3.11	3.89	3.70	3.43	3.01	1.97	1.98
March	4.14	4.25	4.49	3.50	3.35	3.89	3.82	3.55	2.92	1.93	1.83
April	4.23	4.17	4.59	3.51	3.45	3.81	3.77	3.65	2.80	1.81	1.90
May	4.24	4.23	4.42	3.62	3.64	3.64	3.84	3.61	2.79	1.99	1.97
June	4.20	4.35	4.35	3.57	3.88	3.67	3.88	3.65	2.61	1.97	1.94
July	4.34	4.40	4.42	3.48	3.90	3.71	3.72	3.68	2.56	1.97	1.96
August	4.32	4.40	4.61	3.32	3.83	3.62	3.75	3.54	2.51	2.12	2.03
September	4.40	4.25	4.55	3.22	3.87	3.60	3.74	3.43	2.51	2.23	..
October	4.43	4.25	4.00	3.15	3.86	3.74	3.60	3.17	2.58	2.18	..
November	4.29	4.27	3.77	3.14	3.85	3.62	3.59	3.16	2.35	1.91	..
December	4.20	4.39	3.94	2.98	3.86	3.55	3.58	3.02	2.12	1.88	..

1 Working day average.

Source: Bank of England: 020 7601 4342

22.14 Securities quoted on the Stock Exchange[1]
At last working day in March

£ millions

		1986	1987	1988	1989	1990	1991	1992	1993	1994	1995	1996
Total of all securities at market values	KDRV	1 247 580	1 547 845	1 427 397	1 861 091	2 106 147	2 195 213	2 054 927	2 605 093	3 225 921	3 342 381	4 077 109
British government and government guaranteed stocks[2]												
Nominal values	KDRW	128 850	138 777	142 857	133 780	117 857	118 702	130 143	150 803	200 282	217 283	262 246
Market values	KDRX	138 417	147 550	151 207	137 195	109 431	121 183	132 806	172 114	221 960	228 242	292 057
Other securities at market values:												
Irish government stocks	KDRY	8 398	9 727	11 026	10 730	11 834	11 878	13 359	14 003	15 366	14 445	17 320
Corporation stocks, public boards, etc	KDRZ	1 149	912	644	763	309	276	246	213	423	434	671
Dominion and foreign government and corporation stocks	KDSA	83 656	104 460	102 703	142 501	123 575	138 957	138 977	205 555	282 018	335 613	355 169
Company securities												
Total	KDSB	1 015 960	1 285 196	1 161 817	1 569 902	1 860 998	1 922 919	1 769 539	2 213 208	2 706 154	2 763 647	3 429 210
Loan capital	KDSC	9 004	12 013	11 820	13 621	16 788	14 129	15 164	16 407	22 216	21 758	24 872
Preference and preferred capital	KDSD	8 259	22 438	26 887	35 459	39 859	32 918	26 822	15 226	13 124	11 390	14 673
Ordinary and deferred capital[3]	KDSE	998 697	1 250 745	1 123 110	1 520 822	1 804 351	1 875 872	1 727 553	2 181 575	2 670 814	2 730 499	3 389 664

1 The stock exchanges of the United Kingdom and the Republic of Ireland form one exchange (The Stock Exchange).
2 Excluding marketable unlisted securities; including all outstanding amounts of 4 per cent Victory Bonds and 4 per cent Funding Loan, 1960-90 (that is, amounts for death duties and held by the National Debt Commissioners are included).

3 From 1978 shares of no par value are no longer distinguished separately.

Source: Council of The Stock Exchange

22.15 Capital issues and redemptions[1,2]

£ millions

			1989	1990	1991	1992	1993	1994	1995	1996	1997	1998	1999
Total issues and redemptions													
Gross issues	KDSF		24 382	18 821	26 735	20 649	40 615	39 110	25 929	38 354	38 217	33 000	54 989
Gross redemptions	KDSG		5 762	5 359	3 765	7 011	11 400	11 866	10 467	14 123	14 579	11 607	12 661
Issues *less* redemptions: total	KDSH		11 513	8 383	16 284	5 701	18 161	16 812	12 682	14 092	11 887	10 727	23 156
Loan capital	KDSI		13 344	13 001	11 498	12 744	22 561	24 640	20 888	29 493	29 960	28 624	37 639
Preference shares	DEDO		858	781	1 245	589	1 700	603	2 875	710	−881	−330	−438
Ordinary shares	DEDF		3 457	3 449	10 849	6 224	16 671	14 620	9 777	10 273	8 614	4 637	10 127
UK borrowers: total	DEDX		18 620	13 462	22 970	13 638	29 216	25 244	15 562	24 231	23 638	21 393	42 328
Local government	DEEA		–	–	1	1	−1	–	–	–	–	–	–
Listed public companies	KDSN		18 620	13 462	22 969	13 637	29 217	25 241	15 462	24 231	23 638	21 393	42 328
Non-resident borrowers: total	KDSO		5 274	2 878	5 132	1 829	9 289	3 285	2 153	9 452	10 790	3 935	3 356
Central government[3]	KIMI	KDSP	2 636	1 142	2 956	2 001	5 525	749	652	1 929	2 724	2 889	2 080
State, local government[3]		KDSQ											
Companies[4]	KHDR		2 638	1 736	2 176	−172	3 764	2 536	1 501	7 523	8 066	1 046	1 276

1 See footnotes on the second part of this table.

Source: Bank of England: 020 7601 3149

22.15 Capital issues and redemptions[1,2]
continued

£ millions

		1989	1990	1991	1992	1993	1994	1995	1996	1997	1998	1999
UK listed public companies												
All companies: total	KDSN	18 620	13 462	22 969	13 637	29 217	25 241	15 462	24 231	23 638	21 393	42 328
Loan capital	KDSS	14 305	9 232	10 875	6 824	10 845	10 021	2 810	13 248	15 905	17 086	32 639
Preference shares	KDST	858	781	1 245	589	1 700	603	2 875	710	−881	−330	−438
Ordinary shares	KDSU	3 457	3 449	10 849	6 224	16 672	14 617	9 777	10 273	8 614	4 637	10 127
Financial corporations: total	DEEC	10 384	6 737	7 815	5 427	12 523	11 774	−341	11 030	6 711	6 830	16 104
Loan capital	KDSW	8 448	5 868	6 027	3 898	7 488	6 972	−4 005	7 508	4 142	6 190	13 191
Preference shares	KDSX	264	214	660	459	1 221	138	1 538	868	−536	175	−438
Ordinary shares	DELC	1 672	655	1 128	1 070	3 847	4 664	2 126	2 654	3 105	465	3 351
Other companies: total	DEEB	8 236	6 725	15 154	8 210	16 694	13 470	15 903	13 201	16 927	14 563	26 224
Loan capital	KDTA	5 857	3 364	4 848	2 926	3 357	3 049	6 915	5 740	11 763	10 896	19 448
Preference shares	KDTB	594	567	585	130	479	465	1 337	−158	−345	−505	–
Ordinary shares	DEEY	1 785	2 794	9 721	5 154	12 824	9 956	7 651	7 619	5 509	4 172	6 776
UK listed public companies												
Financial companies: total	KDTD	10 383	6 735	7 817	5 426	12 553	11 774	−342	11 032	8 172	6 828	16 106
Monetary financial institutions	KDTE	6 789	4 614	2 856	1 972	4 764	3 763	−648	9 618	22	2 161	2 312
Insurance corporations	DELR	183	−157	63	394	1 694	501	578	1 007	1 805	617	1 843
Investment trust companies	DELS	938	439	841	709	3 027	4 118	1 415	1 537	927	427	231
Other[5]	KDTH	2 473	1 839	4 057	2 351	3 068	3 392	−1 687	−1 130	5 418	3 623	11 720
Other companies: total	DEEB	8 236	6 725	15 154	8 210	16 694	13 470	15 903	13 201	16 927	14 563	26 224
Manufacturing industries: total	KDTJ	3 782	2 522	5 611	4 460	7 100	4 811	9 536	1 888	1 849	−413	3 637
Minerals and metal manufacture	DEKN	610	209	1 170	1 116	447	76	534	−947	−549	−325	637
Chemicals and allied industries	DEKO	−59	628	338	51	2 043	283	1 759	1 124	854	−295	393
Metal goods, engineering and vehicles	DEKP	597	612	1 165	1 197	1 441	1 535	1 097	365	676	94	987
Electrical and electronic engines	DEKQ	196	104	219	339	119	376	868	447	451	145	167
Food, drink and tobacco	DEKR	1 589	40	1 289	561	1 136	1 242	3 730	−112	−279	−474	876
Other manufacturing	DEKS	849	929	1 430	1 196	1 947	1 302	1 548	1 011	696	442	577
Energy	DEKT	−1 414	704	817	539	1 413	1 173	948	1 821	1 781	1 829	3 255
Water	DEKU	−6	87	724	168	212	251	648	354	509	1 025	1 642
Construction	DEKV	131	533	852	238	662	1 284	53	623	703	54	258
Distribution, hotels and repairs	DEKW	1 544	1 048	3 121	1 064	2 191	1 137	901	854	1 481	1 242	1 291
Transport and communications	DEKX	691	499	843	418	872	912	1 134	3 744	4 769	6 946	10 220
Property companies	DEKY	1 774	338	1 402	212	2 007	1 873	1 370	1 907	2 798	1 196	1 605
Services	DEKZ	1 741	993	1 782	1 118	2 207	2 025	1 310	2 011	3 039	2 689	4 322

1 The estimates relate to new money raised on the main stock market by issues of ordinary, preference and loan capital (public issues, offers for sale, issues by tender, placings and issues to shareholders and employees) by listed public companies and local government in the United Kingdom; and by non-resident borrowers split between central governent, state and local governments and companies. The estimates include UK local government negotiable bonds (of not less than one year) issued to or through the agency of banks, discount houses, issuing houses or brokers. Mortgages, bank advances and any other loans redeemable in less than twelve months are excluded; so also are loans from UK government funds (including the former Industrial Reorganisation Corporation and the National Enterprise Board) but not government subscriptions to company issues made *pari passu* with the market. Issues to shareholders are included only if the sole or principal share register is maintained in the United Kingdom. Estimates of issues are based on the prices at which securities are offered to the market. Subscriptions are recorded under the periods in which they are due to be paid. Redemptions exclude share buy-backs. They relate to fixed interest securities of the kinds included as issues; conversion issues in lieu of cash repayment are included in the gross figures of both issues and redemptions. These figures include issues of debentures and loan stock carrying the right of conversion into, or subscription to, equity capital. Estimates for these issues *less* redemptions are: 1977 -5; 1978 -21; 1979 23; 1980 178; 1981 194; 1982 8; 1983 47; 1984 101; 1985 320.

The division between United Kingdom and non-resident company borrowers is determined by the location of the registered office. The industrial classification of companies is according to the primary occupation of the borrowing company or group and is based up to 1982 on the former *Standard Industrial Classification 1968* and from 1983 on the *Revised Standard Industrial Classification 1980*.

2 The estimates exclude issues on the unlisted securities market which was launched by the Stock Exchange in Novembere 1980. These issues are mainly of ordinary shares by industrial and commercial companies. Estimates of new money raised are: 1980 88; 1981 54; 1982 87; 1983 164; 1984 159; 1985 181; 1986 320; 1987 967; 1988 632; 1989 767; 1990 364; 1991 261.

3 Series now combined.

4 Non-resident companies including public corporations.

5 'Other' includes special finance agencies (listed public companies engaged in the provision of medium and long-term finance to industry eg ICFC) and those finance houses and other consumer credit grantors not included under banks and building societies.

Source: Bank of England: 020 7601 3149

22.16 Building societies[1]
United Kingdom

		1990	1991	1992	1993	1994	1995[2]	1996[2]	1997[2]	1998[2]	1999[2]
Number and balance sheets											
Societies on register											
(number)	KRNA	117	110	105	101	96	94	88	82	78	72
Share investors (thousands)	KRNB	36 948	37 925	37 533	37 809	38 150	38 998	37 768	19 234	21 195	21 774
Depositors (thousands)	KRNC	4 299	4 698	3 879	3 686	5 369	6 143	6 718	882	820	642
Borrowers (thousands)	KRND	6 724	6 998	7 055	7 140	7 222	6 906	6 586	2 703	2 934	2 868
Assets and liabilities (£ million)											
Liabilities:											
Shares	KRNE	160 538.2	177 519.4	187 108.4	194 975.1	201 812.2	200 682.0	196 546.4	90 092.8	103 289.8	109 137.7
Deposits and loans	KRNF	40 695.5	49 516.6	57 067.5	62 301.2	69 925.2	67 513.8	73 919.1	31 033.7	33 311.2	34 746.6
Taxation and other	KRNG	3 768.8	3 093.9	2 559.5	2 565.7	2 939.2	3 306.2	3 727.4	1 338.8	1 586.4	1 665.4
General reserves	KRNH	10 206.1	11 430.4	12 634.4	14 269.5	16 312.3	17 218.3	17 940.3	7 331.2	7 926.4	8 301.5
Other Capital	KRNI	1 639.7	2 419.4	3 144.7	3 900.9	4 125.7	3 498.0	4 762.3	1 643.9	1 550.7	1 529.2
Assets: total	KRNJ	216 848.3	243 979.7	262 514.5	278 012.4	295 114.6	292 218.3	296 895.5	131 440.4	147 664.5	155 380.4
Mortgages	KRNK	175 745.4	196 945.6	210 994.5	221 237.6	240 297.2	236 841.0	241 472.9	107 531.5	118 288.4	123 183.4
Investments	KHVZ KRNL	35 050.9	39 513.6	42 909.1	47 174.2	50 786.7	50 894.1	51 016.7	21 869.8	27 102.0	29 917.8
Cash	KRNM										
Other	KRNN	6 052.0	7 520.5	8 610.1	9 600.6	4 030.7	4 483.2	4 405.9	2 039.1	2 274.1	2 279.2
Current transactions (£ million)											
Mortgage advances	KRNU	43 081.0	42 948.0	34 989.0	32 259.0	34 829.0	34 673.0	38 488.0	28 771.7	21 988.3	23 997.9
Management expenses	KRNX	2 363.0	2 591.0	2 723.7	2 952.5	3 136.7	3 352.6	3 555.3	2 270.5	1 501.7	1 573.8

1 The figures for each year relate to accounting years ending on dates between 1 February of that year and 31 January of the following year.
2 The societies which have converted to the banking sector, namely Cheltenham & Gloucester (August 1995), National & Provincial (August 1996), Alliance & Leicester (April 1997), Halifax (June 1997), Woolwich (July 1997), Bristol & West (July 1997), Northern Rock (October 1997), and Birmingham Midshires (April 1999) have been included in flow figures (using flows up to the date of conversion), but have been excluded from the end of year balances.

Source: Building Societies Commission: 020 7676 1000

22.17 Consumer credit

£ millions

		1989	1990	1991	1992	1993	1994	1995	1996	1997	1998	1999
Total amount outstanding	**AILA**	48 406	52 578	53 555	52 609	52 330	..	..	..	..	..	..
	VZRD	49 036[9]	53 471[9]	54 416[9]	53 486[9]	53 295[9]	58 051[9]	68 205[9]	77 494	88 100	102 222	115 385
Total net lending[1]	**-AIKL**	6 521	4 439	2 245	284	2 423	..	..	..	..	..	..
	VZQC	6 764	4 616	2 318	484	2 653	5 743	8 234	11 215	12 013	14 490	14 471
Retailers[2]	**AAPP**	−1	50	37	25	69	83	−133	75	208	7	100
Building societies' class 3 loans[3]	**ALPY**	303	223	−45	−65	46	89	238	383	120	−22	10
Banks	**AIKN**	5 704	3 765	2 523	792	843	3 704	5 606	7 682	9 027	11 711	10 998
of which												
Credit cards	**VTFY**	540	1 761	774	126	700	..	..	..	..	..	..
	VZQS	540	1 761	774	138	719	1 483	2 103	3 029	3 507	4 854	5 258
Loans on personal accounts[4]	**VTGA**	5 007	1 981	1 805	615	156	..	..	..	..	..	..
Other	**VZQT**	6 224	2 855	1 544	346	1 934	4 261	6 132	8 186	8 505	9 636	9 213
Insurance companies[5]	**-AIKQ**	59	156	68	29	165	..	..	..	..	..	..
	RSBK	59	157	69	29	170	−178	39	−81	4	−16	−77
Non-bank credit companies	**-AGSJ**	607	254	−417	−483	1 332	1 856	2 222	2 805	2 287	2 409	2 928
Other specialist lenders	**VZQQ**	699	421	−266	−297	1 525	2 045	2 485	3 156	2 654	2 810	3 439
Total gross lending	**VZQG**	12 376	13 299	12 530	11 913	54 094	75 079	89 115	103 217	116 136	133 886	146 873
Narrower coverage[6]												
Total amount outstanding	**RLWE**	27 057	30 255	30 624	30 120	32 204	37 027	..	..	..	..	..
Total net lending[7]	**RLWF**	3 165	3 683	1 060	367	3 042	5 515	..	..	..	..	..
Total new credit advanced[8]	**RLBY**	41 521	46 336	47 098	48 865	54 859	62 050	..	..	..	..	..

1 Figures for net lending refer to changes in amounts outstanding adjusted to remove distortions caused by revaluations of debt outstanding, such as write-offs.
2 Self-financed credit advanced by food retailers, clothing retailers, household goods retailers, mixed business retailers (other than co-operative societies) and general mail order houses.
3 Class 3 loans advanced under the terms of the Building Societies' Act 1986.
4 Excludes loans for house purchase and bridging finance.
5 Prior to 1985 includes only policy loans.

6 Data relating to the narrower coverage covers finance houses and other specialist credit grantors, bank credit cards (operated under the VISA and Mastercard systems), and unsecured loans by building societies (since the end of 1986). Data no longer available from 1995.
7 Before 1987, net lending equals changes in amounts outstanding.
8 A high proportion of credit advanced in certain types of agreement, notably on credit cards, is repaid within a month. This reflects use of such agreements as a method of payment rather than a way of obtaining credit.

Source: Office for National Statistics: 01633 812789

22.18 End-year assets and liabilities of investment trust companies, unit trusts[1] and property unit trusts[2]

£ millions

		1989	1990	1991	1992	1993	1994	1995	1996	1997	1998	1999
Investment trust companies												
Short-term assets and liabilities (net):	CBPL	864	1 070	730	390	623	273	627	1 076	1 426	2 263	105
Cash and UK bank deposits	AHAG	462	642	397	340	387	443	1 009	1 087	1 577	2 647	1 227
Other short-term assets	CBPN	742	657	711	645	1 030	772	738	794	1 714	1 734	1 111
Short-term liabilities	−CBPS	−340	−229	−378	−595	−794	−942	−1 120	−805	−1 865	−2 118	−2 202
Medium and long-term liabilities and capital:	−CBPO	−24 496	−20 382	−23 417	−28 895	−36 140	−40 180	−43 882	−50 911	−54 821	−49 985	−57 491
Issued share and loan capital	−CBPQ	−4 692	−5 193	−5 076	−4 827	−8 286	−10 978	−13 250	−8 330	−9 350	−8 837	−8 565
Foreign currency borrowing	−CBPR	−70	−119	−135	−407	−473	−354	−1 061	−638	−658	−607	−867
Other borrowing	−CBQA	−698	−596	−733	−802	−849	−1 354	−622	−823	−1 296	−1 723	−1 604
Reserves and provisions, etc	−AHBC	−19 036	−14 474	−17 473	−22 859	−26 532	−27 494	−28 949	−41 120	−43 517	−38 818	−46 455
Investments:	CBPM	23 251	19 108	22 392	28 586	35 300	39 586	43 410	50 034	51 618	46 313	56 075
British government securities	AHBF	177	326	415	996	1 013	2 490	1 194	1 422	1 255	815	1 209
UK company securities:												
Loan capital and preference shares	CBGZ	903	687	720	814	854	1 000	846	832	1 317	1 359	1 414
Ordinary and deferred shares	CBGY	11 121	9 878	10 637	12 825	14 892	15 926	19 384	25 046	27 913	24 729	27 803
Overseas company securities:												
Loan capital and preference shares	CBHA	454	257	355	514	533	896	740	279	1 165	773	972
Ordinary and deferred shares	AHCC	10 259	7 392	9 105	11 943	16 886	17 873	19 485	21 047	17 747	17 844	23 158
Other investments	CBPT	337	568	1 160	1 494	1 122	1 401	1 761	1 408	1 631	1 051	1 519
Unit trusts												
Short-term assets and liabilities:	CBPU	2 026	2 315	1 698	2 099	2 673	3 266	3 116	3 822	4 627	6 883	5 894
Cash and UK bank deposits	AGYE	1 683	1 864	1 318	1 793	2 579	3 102	3 326	3 895	4 731	6 020	4 797
Other short-term assets	CBPW	488	710	628	920	1 013	1 364	986	1 201	467	1 343	1 545
Short-term liabilities	−CBPX	−145	−259	−248	−614	−919	−1 200	−1 196	−1 274	−571	−480	−448
Foreign currency borrowing	−AGYK	−63	−31	−47	−8	−39	−21	−1	–	–	–	–
Investments:	CBPZ	52 994	41 608	50 459	58 785	88 479	83 495	104 069	125 841	143 108	162 929	205 484
British government securities	CBHT	374	411	523	664	959	1 414	1 774	2 716	3 087	3 771	3 627
UK company securities:												
Loan capital and preference shares	CBHU	1 690	1 337	1 337	1 664	2 906	2 970	3 298	5 029	6 494	9 290	13 322
Ordinary and deferred shares	RLIB	28 808	25 529	29 546	33 356	49 657	43 335	59 122	67 509	85 742	93 410	119 496
Overseas company securities:												
Loan capital and preference shares	CBHV	453	347	516	570	864	1 001	2 145	1 288	1 834	1 801	3 012
Ordinary and deferred shares	RLIC	21 401	13 791	18 124	21 862	32 904	33 473	36 062	47 346	42 931	51 119	62 182
Other assets	CBQE	268	193	413	669	1 189	1 302	1 668	1 953	2 593	3 657	3 825
Property unit trusts												
Short-term assets and liabilities (net)	AGVC	78	136	86	73	212	253	186	343	351	254	205
Property	CBQG	1 020	948	1 241	1 373	1 492	2 197	1 807	2 582	3 875	2 740	2 722
Other assets	AGVL	26	21	–	34	60	11	11	11	167	197	436
Long-term borrowing	−AGVM	−6	−6	−8	−42	−42	–	−131	−45	−246	−106	−75

Note: Assets are shown as positive: liabilities as negative.
1 Including open ended investment companies (OEICs).
2 Investments are at market value.

Source: Office for National Statistics: 01633 812789

22.19 Self-administered pension funds: market value of assets
United Kingdom

End year

£ millions

		1993	1994	1995	1996	1997	1998	1999	2000
Total pension funds[1]									
Total net assets	AHVA	480 547	443 467	508 600	543 883	656 873	699 191	..	..
Short-term assets	RYIQ	20 279	22 617	26 114	31 521	35 368	39 005	..	..
British government securities	AHVK	34 280	41 855	52 659	57 784	80 534	91 084	98 828	..
UK local authority long-term debt	AHVO	81	250	81	89	156	183	184	..
Overseas government securities	AHVT	11 044	11 092	11 721	11 800	13 079	15 493	16 258	..
UK company securities									
Ordinary shares	AHVP	251 099	219 189	256 625	276 001	339 687	334 648	398 280	..
Other	AHVQ	5 759	3 935	7 064	6 181	5 617	8 168	9 658	..
Overseas company securities									
Ordinary shares	AHVR	84 118	74 813	82 164	84 163	104 187	108 884	119 139	..
Other	AHVS	2 103	3 045	1 184	4 909	3 851	3 842	4 520	..
UK loans and mortgages	RLDQ	260	44	34	83	160	22	..	..
UK land, property and ground rent	AHWA	21 931	24 353	21 317	21 638	24 176	24 355	30 495	..
Authorised unit trust units	AHVU	13 188	13 345	15 212	21 767	21 979	30 596	39 045	..
Property unit trusts	AHVW	1 905	2 463	2 485	2 666	3 219	3 211	3 952	..
Other assets	RKPL	38 761	31 318	36 352	30 628	32 978	47 136	..	..
Total liabilities	GQFX	4 261	4 852	4 412	5 347	8 118	7 436	..	..

1 These figures cover funded schemes only and therefore exclude the main superannuation arrangements in the central government sector.

Source: Office for National Statistics: 01633 812729

22.20 Insurance companies: balance sheet
Market values

End year

£ millions

		1991	1992	1993	1994	1995	1996	1997	1998	1999
Long-term insurance companies										
Assets										
Total current assets (gross)	RYEW	15 303	18 101	16 925	16 690	24 171	31 699	42 795	46 165	50 122
Agents' and reinsurance balances (net)	AHNY	788	799	457	−209	−157	−232	155	1 383	..
Other debtors[1]	RKPN	4 070	4 198	4 368	4 562	7 565	12 982	15 708	18 210	..
British government securities	AHNJ	36 584	50 970	72 575	64 921	80 268	90 996	107 847	127 903	..
UK local authority securities etc	AHNN	577	667	772	815	1 322	1 088	914	1 722	..
UK company securities[2]	RKPO	145 590	172 204	237 020	217 034	272 554	304 587	386 734	438 666	..
Overseas company securities	RKPP	28 120	32 101	49 087	48 195	59 950	62 378	73 428	82 122	..
Overseas government securities	AHNS	5 996	8 793	8 874	6 871	8 793	7 554	8 471	17 515	..
Loans and mortgages	RKPQ	7 771	8 345	7 885	6 833	7 305	6 653	8 271	11 027	..
UK land, property and ground rent	AHNX	32 185	30 074	33 939	35 914	35 596	36 209	42 275	45 903	..
Overseas land, property and ground rent	RGCP	160	124	144	151	118	114	98	252	..
Other investments	RKPR	1 447	2 663	3 096	4 644	2 162	3 886	3 416	5 654	..
Total	RFXN	278 591	329 039	435 142	406 421	499 647	557 914	690 112	796 522	..
Net value of direct investment in:										
Non-insurance subsidiaries and associate companies in the United Kingdom	RYET	3 044	2 569	2 288	2 547	2 773	3 033	3 426	3 035	..
UK associate and subsidiary insurance companies and insurance holding companies	RYEU	345	639	1 186	504	701	575	−239	148	..
Overseas subsidiaries and associates	RYEV	471	773	1 016	1 034	987	986	1 104	1 087	..
Total assets	RKBI	282 451	333 020	439 632	410 506	504 108	562 508	694 403	800 792	..
Liabilities										
Borrowing:										
Borrowing from UK banks	RGDF	1 701	1 162	1 234	1 570	1 907	2 234	3 027	3 252	4 213
Other UK borrowing	RGDE	1 372	1 007	553	982	796	1 349	786	1 040	1 064
Borrowing from overseas	RGDD	292	603	381	176	79	90	104	148	208
Long-term business:										
Funds	RKDC	238 145	280 276	354 711	357 263	424 866	470 893	581 009	669 301	764 587
Claims admitted but not paid	RKBM	927	951	1 035	1 085	1 419	1 441	1 436	1 712	..
Provision for taxation net of amounts receivable:										
UK authorities	RYPI	−907	−1 119	−141	−470	502	2 568	4 207	5 443	..
Overseas authorities	RYPJ	−13	−14	−20	29	−11	9	25	67	..
Provision for recommended dividends	RYPK	145	46	83	76	195	276	368	359	..
Other creditors and liabilities	RYPL	3 642	3 763	4 020	4 399	5 979	6 303	8 083	12 509	..
Excess of assets over above liabilities:										
Excess of value of assets over liabilities in respect of long-term funds	RKBR	36 032	43 511	74 160	42 608	63 255	71 817	89 790	96 456	96 456
Minority interests in UK subsidiary companies	RKTI	−	30	30	−	3	−	2	−	..
Shareholders' capital and reserves in respect of general business	RKBS	414	1 952	890	1 143	2 050	2 576	3 862	6 299	..
Other reserves including profit and loss account balances	RKBT	701	852	2 696	1 645	3 068	2 952	1 704	4 206	4 206
Total liabilities	RKBI	282 451	333 020	439 632	410 506	504 108	562 508	694 403	800 792	..

See footnotes on the second part of this table.

Source: Office for National Statistics: 01633 812729

22.20
continued

Insurance companies: balance sheet
Market values
End year

£ millions

		1991	1992	1993	1994	1995	1996	1997	1998	1999
Other than long-term insurance companies										
Assets										
Total current assets (gross)	RYME	5 774	6 523	6 467	7 426	8 318	11 559	12 628	8 524	5 956
Agents' and reinsurance balances (net)	AHMX	5 796	6 380	5 887	6 123	7 494	11 569	9 405	10 528	..
Other debtors[1]	RKPS	2 833	1 765	1 847	2 118	3 403	6 097	5 998	6 277	..
British government securities	AHMJ	6 359	8 378	11 474	12 320	14 363	16 893	15 666	16 409	..
UK local authority securities etc	AHMN	33	49	59	50	56	42	16	14	..
UK company securities[2]	RKPT	9 877	10 480	14 533	14 312	17 425	17 825	18 845	18 440	..
Overseas company securities	RKPU	3 776	3 747	4 163	3 578	4 422	5 072	6 594	8 676	..
Overseas government securities	AHMS	3 534	4 660	5 324	5 064	6 511	9 546	8 215	10 459	..
Loans and mortgages	RKPV	1 166	1 147	1 234	1 321	1 337	1 593	1 385	1 335	..
UK land, property and ground rent	AHMW	3 034	2 398	2 375	2 121	2 100	2 077	2 842	1 146	..
Overseas land, property and ground rent	RYNK	91	185	80	89	128	120	149	107	..
Other investments	RKPW	673	633	418	536	665	716	2 465	2 366	..
Total	RKAL	42 946	46 345	53 861	55 058	66 222	83 106	84 208	84 281	..
Net value of direct investment in:										
Non-insurance subsidiaries and associate companies in the United Kingdom	RYNR	1 724	2 617	2 214	2 474	2 449	3 195	6 950	5 553	..
UK associate and subsidiary insurance companies and insurance holding companies	RYNS	682	1 087	1 835	1 738	1 642	7 170	4 204	6 424	..
Overseas subsidiaries and associates	RYNT	8 534	9 908	12 275	11 854	15 485	14 859	16 402	14 239	..
Total assets	RKBY	53 886	59 957	70 185	71 124	85 798	108 330	111 764	110 497	..
Liabilities										
Borrowing:										
Borrowing from UK banks	RYMB	910	434	721	1 382	1 584	1 524	3 029	1 825	5 305
Other UK borrowing	RYMC	1 208	1 677	1 989	2 354	2 370	2 536	2 996	1 551	658
Borrowing from overseas	RYMD	1 202	1 296	1 103	1 626	1 876	1 976	1 202	1 600	1 857
General business technical reserves	RKCT	33 832	38 005	39 746	42 374	47 493	58 618	59 527	60 775	58 929
Long-term business:										
Funds	RKTF	–	–	–	–	–	–	–	–	..
Claims admitted but not paid	RKTK	–	–	–	–	–	–	–	–	..
Provision for taxation net of amounts receivable:										
UK authorities	RYPO	–148	–295	235	397	841	807	1 253	1 197	..
Overseas authorities	RYPP	18	24	14	22	16	22	7	11	..
Provision for recommended dividends	RYPQ	635	650	794	874	1 098	1 407	2 048	1 318	..
Other creditors and liabilities	RYPR	2 180	1 921	1 987	2 551	2 955	3 886	3 873	3 793	..
Excess of assets over above liabilities:										
Excess of value of assets over liabilities in respect of long-term funds	RKCG	–	–	–	–	–	–	–	–	..
Minority interests in UK subsidiary companies	RKCH	17	33	80	52	22	24	60	68	..
Shareholders' capital and reserves in respect of general business	RKCI	13 035	14 552	21 355	17 628	25 545	35 069	35 172	34 144	..
Other reserves including profit and loss account balances	RKCJ	997	1 660	2 161	1 864	1 998	2 461	2 597	4 215	..
Total liabilities	RKBY	53 886	59 957	70 185	71 124	85 798	108 330	111 764	110 497	..

1 Including outstanding interest, dividends and rents (net).
2 Including authorised unit trust units.

Source: Office for National Statistics: 01633 812729

404

22.21 Individual insolvencies

Number

		1988	1989	1990	1991	1992	1993	1994	1995	1996	1997	1998	1999
England and Wales													
Bankruptcies[1,2]	AIHW	7 717	8 138	12 058	22 632	32 106	31 016	25 634	21 933	21 803	19 892	19 647	21 611
Individual voluntary arrangements[3]	AIHI	779	1 224	1 927	3 002	4 686	5 679	5 103	4 384	4 466	4 545	4 901	7 195
Deeds of arrangement	AIHO	11	3	2	6	2	8	2	2	2	4	1	–
Total	AIHK	8 507	9 365	13 987	25 640	36 794	36 703	30 739	26 319	26 271	24 441	24 549	28 806
Scotland													
Sequestrations[4]	KRHA	1 401	2 301	4 350	7 665	10 845	6 828	2 182	2 188	2 503	2 502	3 016	3 195
Northern Ireland													
Bankruptcies[5,6]	KRHB	164	238	286	367	406	474	438	399	415	393	394	401
Individual voluntary arrangements[7]	KJRK	..	..	..	2	42	67	84	64	101	84	121	172
Deeds of arrangement	KRHC	–	–	–	–	–	–	–	–	–	–	–	1
Total	KRHD	164	238	286	369	448	541	522	463	516	477	515	574

1 Comprises receiving and administration orders under the Bankruptcy Act 1914 and bankruptcy orders under the Insolvency Act 1986.
2 Orders later consolidated or rescinded are included in these figures.
3 Introduced under the Insolvency Act 1986.
4 Sequestrations awarded but not brought into operation are included in these figures.

5 Comprises bankruptcy adjudication orders, arrangement protection orders and orders for the administration of estates of deceased insolvents.
6 Orders later set aside or dismissed are included in these figures.
7 Introduced under the Insolvency Northern Ireland order 1989.

Source: Department of Trade and Industry: 020 7215 3291/3305

22.22 Company insolvencies

Number

		1988	1989	1990	1991	1992	1993	1994	1995	1996	1997	1998	1999
England and Wales													
Compulsory liquidations	AIHR	3 667	4 020	5 977	8 368	9 734	8 244	6 597	5 519	5 080	4 735	5 216	5 209
Creditors' voluntary liquidations	AIHS	5 760	6 436	9 074	13 459	14 691	12 464	10 131	9 017	8 381	7 875	7 987	9 071
Total	AIHQ	9 427	10 456	15 051	21 827	24 425	20 708	16 728	14 536	13 461	12 610	13 203	14 280
Scotland													
Compulsory liquidations	KRGA	228	229	251	304	310	286	242	252	266	254	338	364
Creditors' voluntary liquidations	KRGB	168	199	219	312	360	265	202	189	175	223	228	208
Total	KRGC	396	428	470	616	670	551	444	441	441	477	566	572
Northern Ireland													
Compulsory liquidations	KRGD	62	69	73	112	79	73	69	72	68	60	53	53
Creditors' voluntary liquidations	KRGE	54	75	55	71	77	85	52	37	54	53	46	45
Total	KRGF	116	144	128	183	156	158	121	109	122	113	99	98

Source: Department of Trade and Industry: 020 7215 3291/3305

22.23 Industry analysis: bankruptcies and deeds of arrangement[1]
England and Wales

Number

		1989	1990	1991	1992	1993	1994	1995	1996	1997	1998	1999
Industry												
Self-employed												
Agriculture and horticulture	KRFY	142	198	266	313	277	231	218	168	155	157	183
Manufacturing:												
Food, drink and tobacco	KRFZ	9	31	48	56	34	33	30	31	18	21	17
Chemicals	KRLA	3	4	12	9	7	23	8	5	5	7	4
Metals and engineering	KRLB	180	240	424	634	612	523	396	411	413	378	385
Textiles and clothing	KRLC	77	63	152	174	160	95	114	91	76	81	87
Timber and furniture	KRLD	62	116	233	317	207	176	158	118	98	96	94
Paper, printing and publishing	KRLE	39	80	143	205	161	142	142	117	104	101	112
Other	KRLF	38	67	120	125	169	133	146	117	116	110	111
Total	KRLG	408	601	1 132	1 520	1 350	1 125	994	890	830	794	810
Construction and transport:												
Construction	KRLH	1 652	2 348	3 812	4 692	4 361	3 362	2 783	2 713	2 182	1 919	1 911
Transport and communication	KRLI	601	953	1 620	2 038	1 754	1 402	1 138	1 227	1 162	1 060	1 187
Total	KHGP	2 253	3 301	5 432	6 730	6 115	4 764	3 921	3 940	3 344	2 979	3 098
Wholesaling:												
Food, drink and tobacco	KRLJ	41	57	68	114	114	94	103	77	62	53	45
Motor vehicles	KRLK	4	8	21	48	21	28	33	36	28	20	22
Other	KRLL	67	81	122	220	191	160	122	101	78	92	83
Total	KHGQ	112	146	211	382	326	282	258	214	168	165	150
Retailing:												
Food, drink and tobacco	KRLM	401	595	895	1 001	1 107	981	782	662	546	514	438
Motor vehicles and filling stations	KRLN	131	155	362	399	412	343	316	327	276	238	241
Other	KRLO	490	807	1 442	2 159	2 087	1 615	1 566	1 268	1 048	971	1 032
Total	KHGR	1 022	1 557	2 699	3 559	3 606	2 939	2 664	2 257	1 870	1 723	1 711
Services:												
Financial institutions	KRLP	95	143	247	266	292	241	185	125	105	79	54
Business services	KRLQ	386	662	1 284	1 859	1 843	1 537	1 354	1 176	1 117	1 057	1 162
Hotels and catering	KRLR	718	867	1 481	2 366	2 437	2 102	1 956	1 736	1 603	1 309	1 376
Total	KHGS	1 199	1 672	3 012	4 491	4 572	3 880	3 495	3 037	2 825	2 445	2 592
Other	KHGT	724	1 014	1 857	2 530	2 315	1 893	1 732	2 161	2 077	2 157	2 179
Total: self-employed	KRLT	5 860	8 489	14 609	19 525	18 561	15 114	13 282	12 667	11 269	10 420	10 723
Other individuals												
Employees	KRLU	856	1 172	1 639	2 588	2 507	2 279	1 981	2 471	2 625	3 141	4 357
No occupation and unemployed	KRLV	698	1 107	2 811	4 325	4 816	3 696	2 859	3 294	3 051	3 384	4 457
Directors and promoters of companies	KRLW	305	427	667	965	862	628	484	368	310	272	330
Occupation unknown	KRLX	419	865	2 906	4 703	4 270	3 917	3 327	3 003	2 637	2 430	1 744
Total: other individuals	KRLY	2 278	3 571	8 023	12 581	12 455	10 520	8 651	9 136	8 623	9 227	10 888
Total bankruptcies and deeds of arrangements[1]	KRLZ	8 138	12 060	22 632	32 106	31 016	25 634	21 933	21 803	19 892	19 647	21 611

1 From January 1991 Industrial Analysis excludes Deeds of Arrangement.

Source: Department of Trade and Industry: 020 7215 3291/3305

22.24 Industry analysis: company insolvencies[1]
England and Wales

Number

Industry		1989	1990	1991	1992	1993	1994	1995	1996	1997	1998	1999
Agriculture and horticulture	KRMA	78	111	135	191	157	166	99	89	51	65	75
Manufacturing:												
Food, drink and tobacco	KRMB	105	109	171	215	213	142	130	163	93	89	67
Chemicals	KRMC	85	97	134	141	91	108	69	65	31	57	35
Metals and engineering	KRMD	697	972	1 344	1 621	1 381	932	681	658	591	594	698
Textiles and clothing	KRME	959	921	1 052	1 120	917	736	567	568	596	526	419
Timber and furniture	KRMF	302	391	527	508	333	252	267	249	181	149	190
Paper, printing and publishing	KRMG	425	552	856	830	777	579	452	438	364	426	387
Other	KRMH	468	792	939	1 014	878	859	681	599	613	652	780
Total	KRMI	3 041	3 834	5 023	5 449	4 590	3 608	2 847	2 740	2 469	2 493	2 576
Construction and transport:												
Construction	KRMJ	1 638	2 445	3 373	3 830	3 189	2 401	1 844	1 610	1 419	1 325	1 529
Transport and communication	KRMK	589	932	1 246	1 261	1 082	774	706	682	540	504	443
Total	KHGU	2 227	3 377	4 619	5 091	4 271	3 175	2 550	2 292	1 959	1 829	1 972
Wholesaling:												
Food, drink and tobacco	KRML	162	235	287	388	231	244	205	183	158	139	187
Motor vehicles	KRMM	69	107	152	186	142	112	83	95	41	60	38
Other	KRMN	428	724	841	672	639	638	678	429	340	364	394
Total	KHGV	659	1 066	1 280	1 246	1 012	994	966	707	539	563	619
Retailing:												
Food, drink and tobacco	KRMO	165	244	291	406	388	299	246	236	219	186	193
Motor vehicles and filling stations	KRMP	136	174	245	339	229	226	195	227	132	120	142
Other	KRMQ	738	1 181	1 578	1 732	1 388	1 186	1 127	956	891	847	919
Total	KHGW	1 039	1 599	2 114	2 477	2 005	1 711	1 568	1 419	1 242	1 153	1 254
Services:												
Financial institutions	KRMR	167	303	394	563	421	259	198	222	111	101	118
Business services	KRMS	952	1 558	2 396	2 788	2 415	1 807	1 525	1 500	1 528	1 617	1 831
Hotels and catering	KRMT	371	489	748	1 010	912	777	692	708	609	626	562
Total	KJRS	1 490	2 350	3 538	4 361	3 748	2 843	2 415	2 430	2 248	2 344	2 511
Other	KHGX	1 922	2 714	5 118	5 610	4 925	4 231	4 091	3 784	4 102	4 756	5 723
Total company insolvencies	KHGY	10 456	15 051	21 827	24 425	20 708	16 728	14 536	13 461	12 610	13 203	14 280

1 Including partnerships.

Source: Department of Trade and Industry: 020 7215 3291/3305

23 Service industry

Service industry

Annual retailing inquiries *(Table 23.1)*

A 'Sector Review' was published by the Office for National Statistics (ONS) on 14th September 2000 giving a wide range of statistics on the United Kingdom (UK) annual retailing inquiries from 1995 to 1998. The retailing inquiry forms part of the Annual Business Inquiry (ABI) conducted by the ONS, which also includes the catering, wholesaling, property, motor trades, service trades, production and construction industries.

The retailing Sector Review now gives, for the first time, a 4 year run of data and provides a wide range of information, more precise details of which a described below. Copies of two of the main Tables which appeared in the published Sector Review (Tables 1 and 2) are now included in this publication.

The inquiry covers only businesses which operate in and are involved in retailing; it does not cover retail activity carried out by businesses classified to other industries. It is undertaken on a stratified random sample of about 10,000 businesses classified to the retail division of the Standard Industrial Classification (SIC (1992)). The inquiry is conducted primarily for national accounts purposes, including the provision of estimates of output, stock changes and capital expenditure. It also provides a benchmark for the various series of short-term statistics and analyses the structure of retail trade.

The type of information collected in the inquiry is very extensive and covers areas such as turnover, purchases, capital expenditure, detailed commodity sales data, stocks, employment costs, taxes, duties and levies. There have also been some major changes to the previous publication (*Sector Review: Retailing - Data for 1996*), with the earlier tables either having been dispensed with completely or replaced by new tables in the most recent Sector Review. These changes, particularly the publication of 4 years data, now bring the retailing Sector Review into line with others within the ABI.

The ABI covers in its estimates all UK businesses registered for Value Added Tax (VAT) and/or Pay As You Earn (PAYE), classified to the 1992 Standard Industrial Classification (SIC (92)). The ABI obtains details on these businesses from the ONS Inter-Departmental Business Register (IDBR), which consists of companies, partnerships, sole-proprietorships, public authorities, central government departments, local authorities and non-profit making bodies. The main administrative sources of the IDBR are HM Customs and Excise for VAT details and Inland Revenue for PAYE details.

Discontinuities: There have been changes to the methodology used for 1997. The major change has been the move from stratification by turnover to employment. Data for 1995 and 1996 were calculated on a different basis from those of 1997 and 1998. In order to provide a link between the two data series, 1995 and 1996 data have been reworked to provide estimates on a consistent basis to 1997 and 1998. Other changes are:

* the treatment of outliers and the level of expansion have been amended since the 1996 inquiry;

* from 1998, Scotland has been sampled separately from England and Wales.
Contact point for data enquiries: Steve Watts: 01633 812536.

Retail trade: index numbers of value and volume *(Table 23.2)*

The main purpose of the Retail Sales Inquiry (RSI) is to provide up to date information on short period movements in the level of retail sales. In principle, the RSI covers the retail activity of every business classified in the retail sector (Division 52 of the 1992 Standard Industrial Classification) in Great Britain. A business will be classified to the retail sector if its main activity is one of the individual 4 digit SIC categories within Division 52. The retail activity of a business is then defined by its retail turnover i.e. the sale of all retail goods (note that petrol, for example, is not a retail good).

The RSI is compiled from the information returned to the statutory monthly retail trades inquiry. The inquiry is addressed to a stratified sample of 5000 businesses classified to the retail sector, the stratification being by 'type of store' (the individual 4 digit SIC categories within Division 52) and by size. The sample structure is designed to ensure that the inquiry estimates are as accurate as possible. In terms of the selection, this means that:
- each of the individual 4 digit SIC categories are represented, their coverage depending upon the relative size of the category and the variability of the data.
- within each 4 digit SIC category, the larger retailers tend to be fully enumerated with decreasing proportions of medium and smaller retailers.

The structure of the inquiry is updated every two or three years at the time of rebasing, by reference to the more comprehensive results of the Annual Retail Inquiry (ARI). The inquiry estimates are benchmarked to the ARI results at the same time. The monthly inquiry also incorporates a rotation element for the smallest retailers. This helps to spread the burden more fairly, as well as improving the representativeness between successive benchmarks.

During 1998, the retail sales index was rebased using detailed information from the 1995 annual retailing inquiry. The reference year is now set at 1995=100. Details of the work, together with revised figures for January 1990 to December 1997, were published in *ONS News Release* (98) 349 on 21 October 1998.

The latest summary statistics are published each month by *First Release*. More disaggregated value indices (not seasonally adjusted) are published each month in *Business Monitor SDM28*, available from NS Direct Sales, price £110 a year.

Motor trades and catering inquiries *(Tables 23.3 and 23.4)*

The motor trades and catering inquiries are conducted on a sample basis from the ONS's Inter Departmental Business Register (IDBR). In general the inquiries are addressed solely to businesses classified to these trades, in that businesses who may be engaged in the catering or motor trades as a subsidiary activity are excluded. (An exception is that the catering inquiry includes   certain large groups of managed public houses owned by breweries.) The results generally relate to the total activity of all businesses registered for VAT, including those with a VAT turnover beneath the mandatory registration threshold, and or businesses obtained from PAYE source.

23.1 Retail businesses
United Kingdom
All currency values are £ million

		1995[1]	1996[1]	1997	1998
Number of businesses	ZABE	209 386	211 062	218 333	216 000
Total turnover[2]	ZABL	185 222	201 951	207 489	220 998
Value added tax in total turnover	ZABM	17 614	19 523	20 410	21 791
Retail turnover[2]	ZABN	173 617	189 726	193 928	202 335
Non-retail turnover[2]	ZABO	11 605	12 226	13 561	18 662
Other income					
Value of commercial insurance claims received	ZABP	..	..	..	250
Subsidies received from UK government sources and the EC	ZAEN	..	..	..	24
Employment costs[3]	ZABQ	17 773	19 103	21 178	23 136
Gross wages and salaries	ZABR	16 164	17 342	19 165	20 689
Redundancy and severance payments	ZABS	..	..	..	148
Employers' National Insurance contributions	ZABT	1 609	1 761	2 013	1 550
Contributions to pension funds[5]	ZABU	..	..	..	748
Stocks					
Increase during year	ZABV	1 037	1 154	1 387	1 211
Value at end of year	ZABW	16 978	18 129	19 593	19 817
Total turnover[3] divided by end-year stocks (Quotient)	ZABX	9.9	10.1	9.5	10.1
Purchases of goods, materials and services[3]	ZABY	139 047	145 472	148 254	157 149
Goods bought for resale without processing	ZABZ	117 136	124 937	126 833	133 676
Energy and water products for own consumption[4]	ZACA	..	2 483	2 568	1 811
Goods and materials[4]	ZACB	..	..	..	3 290
Hiring, leasing or renting of plant, machinery and vehicles	ZACC	..	436	677	672
Commercial insurance premiums	ZACD	..	598	617	543
Road transport services	ZACE	..	1 830	2 051	2 051
Telecommunication services	ZACF	..	416	468	465
Computer and related services	ZACG	..	361	484	539
Advertising and marketing services	ZACH	..	2 162	2 491	2 369
Other services	ZACI	21 911	12 250	12 066	11 735
Taxes, duties and levies	ZACJ	..	2 678	3 534	3 592
National non-domestic (business) rates	ZACK	..	2 405	2 965	3 097
Other amounts paid for taxes, duties and levies	ZACL	..	273	569	495
Capital expenditure					
Cost of acquisitions	ZACM	6 325	6 327	7 713	8 259
Proceeds from disposals	ZACN	595	704	1 438	1 137
Net capital expenditure	ZACO	5 731	5 623	6 275	7 121
Amount included in acquisitions for assets under finance leasing arrangements	ZACP	..	..	..	283
Work of a capital nature carried out by own staff (included in acquisitions)	ZACQ	..	58	77	82
Gross margin					
Amount	ZACR	51 509	58 645	61 633	66 742
As a percentage of adjusted turnover[6]	ZACS	30.7	32.1	32.9	33.5
Approximate gross value added at basic prices	ZACT	29 598	37 895	39 720	43 130

1 Data for 1995 and 1996 were calculated on a different basis from those for 1997 and 1998 (see chapter introduction).
2 Inclusive of VAT.
3 Exclusive of VAT.
4 Previously combined with purchases of energy, water and materials for 1995 to 1997.
5 Previously combined with employers' National Insurance contributions for 1995 to 1997.
6 Turnover is adjusted to take out VAT.

Source: Office for National Statistics: 01633 812921/2476

23.1

Retail businesses
United Kingdom

continued   All currency values are £ million

£ million

		1995[2]	1996[2]	1997[2]	1998[2]
Total turnover	ZABL	185 222	201 951	207 489	220 998
Retail turnover	ZABN	173 617	189 726	193 928	202 335
1 Fruit and vegetables	ZACU	7 049	6 562	6 752	7 374
2 Meat, poultry and game	ZACV	8 560	8 735	8 494	9 046
3 Fish, crustaceans and molluscs	ZACW	1 346	1 389	1 580	1 572
4 Bread, cakes, flour and sugar confectionary	ZACX	7 589	7 755	8 168	8 195
5 Alcoholic drink	ZACY	7 958	8 076	8 569	9 112
6 Soft drinks	ZACZ	3 580	3 490	3 434	3 427
7 Tobacco and smokers' requisites	ZADA	8 420	9 256	8 749	8 865
8 Dairy products and eggs	ZADB	7 532	7 422	7 196	7 476
9 Canned and packaged foods[3]	ZADC	..	..	7 800	8 554
10 Other food for human consumption[3]	ZADD	20 417	21 884	13 769	15 073
11 Pharmaceutical preparations	ZADE	1 625	1 985	1 666	1 795
12 National Health Service receipts	ZADF	4 372	5 221	5 262	5 422
13 Medical and orthopaedic goods	ZADG	758	817	831	963
14 Perfumes, cosmetics and toilet articles	ZADH	6 881	8 666	7 106	7 342
15 Clothing fabrics, haberdashery etc.	ZADI	424	499	526	543
16 Household textiles	ZADJ	1 564	1 611	1 518	1 618
17 Men's wear and accessories[4]	ZADK	6 039	6 388	6 802	6 892
18 Ladies' wear and accessories[4]	ZADL	13 247	14 839	13 261	14 102
19 Adult clothing of fur and leather accessories	ZADM	271	315	361	367
20 Boys', girls' and infants' wear[5]	ZADN	2 717	2 845	2 790	2 945
21 Footwear[6]	ZADO	4 433	4 332	4 172	3 975
22 Leather and travel goods	ZADP	473	493	530	610
23 Domestic gas appliances	ZADQ	509	429	516	446
24 Soft furnishings	ZADR	1 171	1 341	1 503	1 624
25 Other household articles	ZADS	3 562	3 945	4 495	4 692
26 Domestic furniture	ZADT	4 552	6 316	7 299	7 527
27 Domestic electrical appliances	ZADU	3 238	3 787	4 168	4 230
28 Audio and visual equipment[7]	ZADV	3 991	3 926	3 708	3 885
29 Audio and video tape, records, compact discs etc.	ZADW	2 726	3 008	3 488	3 330
30 Home computers and computer software[8]	ZADX	..	..	2 516	2 696
31 Decorators and DIY supplies	ZADY	4 129	5 432	5 165	5 389
32 Wallpaper	ZADZ	388	489	566	533
33 Lawnmowers	ZAEA	201	247	246	278
34 Books, newspapers and periodicals	ZAEB	4 782	5 302	5 737	5 612
35 Stationary	ZAEC	1 493	1 553	1 913	1 754
36 Floor coverings	ZAED	2 236	2 367	2 537	2 719
37 Photographic and optical goods; spectacles and contact lenses	ZAEE	2 319	2 664	2 736	2 243
38 Office and telecommunications equipment[7]	ZAEF	1 909	2 682	1 143	1 129
39 Jewellery, silverware and plate; watches and clocks	ZAEG	2 766	2 766	3 246	2 783
40 Souvenirs, gifts and novelties	ZAEH	2 718	2 864	2 830	2 798
41 Prints and picture frames; works of art[9]	ZAEI	613	580	784	522
42 Stamps and coins; toys and games; sports and camping; cycles[10]	ZAEJ	4 816	5 545	6 805	7 982
43 Antiques and other second-hand goods[11]	ZAEK	976	1 173	1 416	1 649
44 Other goods not elsewhere specified	ZAEL	8 608	10 042	10 878	12 373
45 Hire and repair of personal and household goods[12]	ZAEM	655	687	899	875

1 Inclusive of VAT.
2 Data for 1995 and 1996 were calculated on a different basis from those of 1997 and 1998 (see chapter introduction).
3 "Canned and packaged foods" were combined with "Other food for human consumption" in 1995 and 1996.
4 Includes sports clothing and second-hand clothes in 1995 but excludes them in 1996, 1997 and 1998.
5 Includes sports clothing in 1995 but excludes them in 1996, 1997 and 1998.
6 Includes sports shoes in 1995 but excludes them in 1996, 1997 and 1998.
7 Includes computers and computer software in 1995 and 1996 but excludes them in 1997 and 1998.
8 Included in commodities 28 and 38 in 1995 and 1996.
9 Includes prams in 1995 and 1996 but excludes them in 1997 and 1998.
10 Excludes prams in 1995 and 1996 but includes them in 1997 and 1998; excludes sports clothing and footwear in 1995 and 1996 but includes them in 1997 and 1998.
11 Excludes second-hand clothes in 1995 and 1996 but includes them in 1997 and 1998.
12 The commodity values for 1995 and 1996 cover hire and repair whilst those for 1997 and 1998 only cover repair.

Source: Office for National Statistics: 01633 812921/2476

23.2 Retail trade: Index numbers of value and volume of sales[1]
Great Britain

Weekly average 1995 = 100, not seasonally adjusted

Value		Sales in 1995 £m	1989	1990	1991	1992	1993	1994	1995	1996	1997	1998	1999
All retailing:total	EAFY	166 681	75.3	80.5	84.1	87.3	92.0	96.3	100.0	105.4	112.0	116.4	120.3
All retailing:large	EAFZ	119 937	69	74	78	83	89	94	100	107	115	121	126
All retailing:small	EAGA	46 743	92	99	100	100	101	102	100	102	103	104	104
Predominantly food stores:total	EAFS	74 914	67.9	74.1	80.2	85.7	90.1	94.4	100.0	105.3	110.7	116.3	120.3
Predominantly food stores:large	EAGK	57 713	62	68	75	82	87	93	100	107	113	120	125
Predominantly food stores:small	EAGL	17 201	93	100	102	102	102	100	100	100	102	103	105
Non specialised food stores:total	EAGB	60 602	62	68	75	81	87	93	100	107	113	119	124
Non specialised food stores:large	EAGC	54 878	60	66	73	80	86	92	100	107	114	121	125
Non specialised food stores:small	EAGD	5 724	84	91	95	96	97	98	100	102	104	104	108
Specialised food stores	EAPP	14 311	96	101	103	105	105	102	100	100	101	103	105
Retail sale of fruit and vegetables	EAOZ	1 283	110	117	115	108	102	98	100	100	102	112	104
Retail sale of meat and meat products	EAPA	2 515	132	132	129	122	116	107	100	97	92	89	91
Retail sale of fish, crustaceans & molluscs	EAPB	266	144	157	147	128	123	109	100	95	91	78	61
Retail sale of bread cakes and confectionery	EAPC	1 796	84	91	95	99	102	102	100	100	103	109	108
Retail sale of alcohol and other beverages	EAPD	3 208	83	89	90	95	95	96	100	101	104	105	110
Retail sale of tobacco products	EAPE	3 944	90	97	102	108	109	106	100	100	103	106	111
Other specialised food stores	EAPF	1 296	101	107	108	105	110	105	100	97	100	102	111
Predominantly non-food stores:total	EAFT	83 184	79.6	84.2	85.8	87.2	92.4	97.0	100.0	105.8	113.6	116.8	120.7
Predominantly non-food stores:large	EAGM	55 351	74	78	81	83	89	95	100	107	118	122	128
Predominantly non-food stores:small	EAGN	27 832	90	97	97	96	100	102	100	104	105	107	106
Non specialised predominantly non-food stores:total	EAGE	15 035	76.1	80.7	84.5	88.1	93.4	96.4	100.0	108.2	115.5	116.9	120.2
Non specialised predominantly non-food stores:large	EAGF	12 070	77	80	84	87	92	95	100	108	115	117	121
Non specialised predominantly non-food stores:small	EAGG	2 964	74	83	91	98	106	103	100	109	116	115	115
Pharmaceutical,medical,cosmetic and toilet goods	EAPQ	3 165	69	74	81	89	97	97	100	102	109	113	116
Textiles,clothing,footwear and leather:total	EAFU	26 100	79.6	84.7	85.8	87.2	91.2	96.8	100.0	104.2	111.8	112.4	114.9
Textiles clothing footwear and leather:large	EAGO	20 352	73	77	80	84	89	95	100	106	116	118	121
Textiles clothing footwear and leather:small	EAGP	5 746	108	118	111	101	102	103	100	97	96	93	92
Retail sale of textiles	EAPG	699	94	105	105	106	127	117	100	99	105	106	108
Retail sale of clothing:total	EAGH	21 535	78	83	85	87	90	96	100	106	113	115	118
Retail sale of clothing:large	EAGI	17 606	73	77	80	84	89	95	100	108	118	120	124
Retail sale of clothing:small	EAGJ	3 928	103	110	106	99	99	101	100	95	92	92	91
Retail sale of footwear and leather goods	EAPH	3 864	88	96	91	87	92	100	100	97	105	98	99
Household goods stores:total	EAFV	19 770	82.0	84.1	85.9	86.9	92.9	97.0	100.0	107.9	118.3	124.8	130.3
Household goods stores:large	EAGQ	13 273	69	70	75	81	87	94	100	109	122	130	138
Household goods stores:small	EAGR	6 496	109	115	108	101	106	104	100	106	112	114	115
Retail sale of furniture, lighting etc	EAPI	6 400	95	96	94	94	101	103	100	108	122	128	127

1 Please see notes in the chapter text.

Source: Office for National Statistics: 01633 812609

23.2

Retail trade: Index numbers of value and volume of sales[1]
Great Britain

continued

Weekly average 1995 = 100, not seasonally adjusted

		Sales in 1995 £m	1989	1990	1991	1992	1993	1994	1995	1996	1997	1998	1999
Retail sale of electrical household appliances	EAPJ	7 727	77	79	80	79	86	91	100	108	119	124	132
Retail sale of hardware paint and glass	EAPK	5 642	77	81	87	91	96	100	100	107	114	122	131
Other specialised non-food stores: total	EAFW	22 280	79.5	85.4	86.3	87.1	92.5	97.3	100.0	104.1	110.0	114.8	119.3
Other specialised non-food stores: large	EAGS	9 655	81	89	85	81	89	94	100	103	119	124	137
Other specialised non-food stores: small	EAGT	12 624	77	83	87	92	95	100	100	105	103	108	106
Retail sale of books newspapers and periodicals	EAPL	4 078	76	84	88	92	97	99	100	104	109	117	118
Retail sale of floor covering	EAPM	1 045	94	93	91	92	98	99	100	107	116	99	90
Photo, optical and precision equipment office supplies and equipment	EAWH	2 676	98	113	112	111	97	97	100	104	103	104	115
Other retail sale in specialised stores nes	EAWK	10 201	83	89	87	83	90	95	100	105	112	120	128
Second-hand goods stores	EAQA	1 112	68	68	67	68	74	105	100	94	104	102	97
Other retail sale (non-store) and repair: total	EAFX	8 583	94.2	97.4	99.0	99.3	102.1	104.3	100.0	102.8	107.7	113.9	115.9
Other retail sale (non-store) and repair: large	EAGU	6 872	87	89	90	91	97	102	100	104	112	122	126
Other retail sale (non-store) and repair: small	EAGV	1 710	109	116	119	118	114	110	100	96	90	82	75
Retail sale via mail order houses	EAPN	6 629	82	87	89	92	98	103	100	103	109	117	123
Non-store retail exc mail order	EAPO	1 544	111	113	113	110	107	106	100	100	102	101	87
Repair of personal and household goods	EAPR	408	80	84	99	106	115	106	100	104	110	110	106
Volume													
All retailing	EAHC	166 681	92.4	93.0	91.8	92.4	95.3	98.8	100.0	103.1	108.5	111.7	115.6
Predominantly food stores	EAGW	74 914	88.0	89.4	90.4	93.1	95.0	98.1	100.0	101.8	105.9	108.8	110.8
Predominantly non-food stores	EAGX	83 184	93.5	93.9	91.0	90.3	94.2	98.4	100.0	104.4	111.2	114.3	119.9
Non specialised predominantly non-food stores	EAHI	15 035	94.0	94.3	92.9	93.6	97.0	99.0	100.0	106.0	111.5	111.5	114.7
Textiles,clothing, footwear and leather	EAGY	26 100	88.5	89.9	88.0	89.1	92.3	97.5	100.0	104.3	111.2	112.0	117.1
Household goods stores	EAGZ	19 770	91.3	89.7	87.0	86.5	92.2	97.3	100.0	106.8	117.2	125.2	135.2
Other specialised non-food stores	EAHA	22 280	100.9	102.5	97.1	93.8	96.7	100.1	100.0	101.4	105.7	109.2	113.2
Other retail sale (non-store) and repair	EAHB	8 583	111.8	109.4	105.7	103.8	105.0	106.1	100.0	101.4	105.7	111.6	115.2

1 Please see notes in the chapter text.

Source: Office for National Statistics: 01633 812609

	Number of businesses	Total turnover	Motor trades turnover	Retail sales of		Sales to other dealers of		Gross sales of used motor vehicles and motorcycles	Turnover from sales of petrol, diesel, oil and other petroleum products	Other motor trades sales and receipts (including parts and accessories, workshop receipts)	Non-motor trades turnover
				New cars	Other new motor vehicles and motorcycles	New cars	Other new motor vehicles and motorcycles				
	Number	£ million	£ million	£ million	£ million	£ million	£ million	£ million	£ million	£ million	£ million

Sale, maintenance and repair of motor vehicles and motorcycles; retail sale of automotive fuel (SIC 92 50.00)

	MKEQ	CMRH	CMRI	CMRJ	CMRK	CMRL	CMRM	CMRN	CMRO	CMRP	CMRQ
1995[2]	70 278	100 742	97 579	18 169	3 177	14 123	2 444	23 101	11 847	24 718	3 163
1996[2]	71 119	108 805	105 489	19 888	3 246	16 085	2 328	25 558	11 698	26 686	3 316
1997	72 527	119 065	115 442	23 119	3 311	15 762	2 395	28 328	12 871	29 656	3 623
1998	72 105	123 130	119 816	24 492	3 626	16 922	2 547	27 327	13 445	31 457	3 314

Sale of motor vehicles (SIC 92 50.10)

	MKER	EWRI	FDFZ	FDGA	FDGB	FDGC	FDGD	FDGE	FDGF	FDGG	FDHJ
1995[2]	39 473	69 177	68 425	16 517	2 740	14 076	2 352	20 839	1 328	10 573	752
1996[2]	36 383	76 920	76 009	18 877	2 878	16 053	2 225	23 793	1 271	10 912	911
1997	34 664	84 395	83 548	22 554	2 890	15 737	2 255	26 910	1 182	12 020	847
1998	31 196	87 035	86 122	23 897	3 125	16 896	2 435	26 124	1 379	12 266	913

Maintenance and repair of motor vehicles (SIC 92 50.20)

	MKES	FDHK	FDHL	FDHM	FDHN	FDHO	FDHP	FDHQ	FDHR	FDHS	FDHT
1995[2]	17 363	8 930	8 698	1 238	169	31	1	1 467	741	5 051	232
1996[2]	19 709	8 263	8 147	796	129	19	1	1 021	550	5 631	116
1997	22 027	8 008	7 829	417	78	20	5	662	286	6 361	179
1998	24 680	8 976	8 862	297	54	17	–	312	343	7 839	114

Sale of motor vehicle parts and accessories (SIC 92 50.30)

	MKET	FDIW	FDIX	FDIY	FDIZ	FDJA	FDJB	FDJC	FDJD	FDJE	FDJF
1995[2]	4 801	9 437	9 101	223	99	10	–	259	130	8 380	336
1996[2]	5 829	10 066	9 806	70	24	9	–	118	78	9 507	260
1997	6 583	10 741	10 567	9	21	–	–	70	79	10 388	174
1998	7 187	10 962	10 808	8	5	–	–	89	111	10 595	154

Sale, maintenance and repair of motorcycles and related parts and accessories (SIC 92 50.40)

	MKEU	FDKI	FDKJ	FDKK	FDKL	FDKM	FDKN	FDKO	FDKP	FDKQ	FDKR
1995[2]	1 276	1 054	1 024	95	168	4	91	291	10	365	30
1996[2]	1 231	1 019	996	15	214	–	102	342	3	320	23
1997	1 522	1 248	1 225	–	322	–	135	344	2	422	23
1998	1 782	1 274	1 196	–	441	–	112	281	1	361	78

Retail sale of automotive fuel (SIC 92 50.50)

	MKEV	FDLV	FDLW	FDLX	FDLY	FDLZ	FDMA	FDMB	FDMC	FDMD	FDME
1995[2]	7 365	12 144	10 331	96	1	2	–	245	9 638	349	1 813
1996[2]	7 967	12 537	10 531	130	1	4	–	284	9 796	316	2 006
1997	7 701	14 673	12 273	139	–	5	–	342	11 322	465	2 400
1998	7 260	14 883	12 828	290	1	9	–	521	11 611	396	2 055

1 Figures are exclusive of VAT.
2 Data for 1995 and 1996 were collected on a different basis from those for 1997 onwards.

Source: Office for National Statistics: 01633 812264

23.3 Motor trades[1]
United Kingdom
continued

	Purchases of goods, materials and services											
	Total purchases	Energy, water and materials	Used motor vehicles and motorcycles	Parts used solely in repair and servicing activities	Other goods for resale	Hiring, leasing and renting of plant, machinery and vehicles	Commercial insurance premiums	Road transport services	Telecommunication services	Computer and related services	Advertising and marketing services	Other services
	£ million	£ million	£ million	£ million	£ million	£ million	£ million	£ million	£ million	£ million	£ million	£ million

Sale, maintenance and repair of motor vehicles and motorcycles; retail sale of automotive fuel (SIC 92 50.00)

	CMNR	CMRS	COBU	CMRT	CMRU	CMRV	CMRW	CMRX	CMRY	CMRZ	CMSA	CMSB
1995[2]	87 908	..	20 751	..	57 452	..	..	..	..	..	..	..
1996[2]	94 753	505	23 001	5 739	59 599	183	328	299	226	132	1 316	3 425
1997	102 471	643	25 327	5 614	64 809	245	361	327	245	130	1 190	3 580
1998	106 431	1 636	24 673	6 236	67 545	228	343	326	249	186	1 464	3 545

Sale of motor vehicles (SIC 92 50.10)

	FDGH	FDGI	FDGJ	FDGK	FDGL	FDGM	FDGN	FDGO	FDGP	FDGQ	FDGR	FDGS
1995[2]	61 540	..	18 733	..	37 447	..	..	..	..	..	..	..
1996[2]	68 655	248	21 483	3 048	39 869	86	163	202	123	88	1 110	2 235
1997	74 663	298	24 065	2 803	43 307	106	179	191	133	88	998	2 495
1998	77 395	975	23 604	2 592	46 218	90	156	205	126	99	1 233	2 097

Maintenance and repair of motor vehicles (SIC 92 50.20)

	FDHU	FDHV	FDHW	FDHX	FDHY	FDHZ	FDIA	FDIB	FDIC	FDID	FDIE	FDIF
1995[2]	6 623	..	1 324	..	2 576	..	..	..	..	..	..	..
1996[2]	5 703	115	900	2 266	1 583	59	89	21	45	17	89	519
1997	5 102	176	604	2 291	1 235	97	102	37	49	18	70	423
1998	5 667	292	300	3 171	846	86	112	23	54	21	74	688

Sale of motor vehicle parts and accessories (SIC 92 50.30)

	FDJG	FDJH	FDJI	FDJJ	FDJK	FDJL	FDJM	FDJN	FDJO	FDJP	FDJQ	FDJR
1995[2]	7 826	..	226	..	6 664	..	..	..	..	..	..	..
1996[2]	8 107	69	101	291	7 044	31	42	69	40	21	82	317
1997	8 336	74	68	328	7 186	31	46	89	46	21	92	355
1998	8 624	169	144	346	7 089	43	50	88	53	42	111	489

Sale, maintenance and repair of motorcycles and related parts and accessories (SIC 92 50.40)

	FDKT	FDKU	FDKV	FDKW	FDKX	FDKY	FDKZ	FDLA	FDLB	FDLC	FDLD	FDLE
1995[2]	884	..	247	..	543	..	..	..	..	..	..	..
1996[2]	856	3	271	29	489	1	5	4	2	2	14	36
1997	1 060	17	293	43	629	1	8	4	4	1	11	49
1998	1 088	46	226	29	731	1	4	3	2	1	21	24

Retail sale of automotive fuel (SIC 92 50.50)

	FDMF	FDMG	FDMH	FDMI	FDMJ	FDMK	FDML	COBV	COBW	COBX	COBY	COBZ
1995[2]	11 035	..	221	..	10 222	..	..	..	..	..	..	..
1996[2]	11 432	70	246	105	10 614	6	29	3	16	4	21	318
1997	13 310	78	297	149	12 452	10	26	6	13	2	19	258
1998	13 657	154	399	98	12 661	8	21	7	14	23	25	247

1 Figures are exclusive of VAT.
2 Data for 1995 and 1996 were collected on a different basis from those for 1997 onwards.

Source: Office for National Statistics: 01633 812264

23.3
continued

Motor trades[1]
United Kingdom

	Taxes, duties and levies			Capital Expenditure			
	Total taxes and levies	National (non-domestic business) rates	Other amounts paid for taxes, duties and levies	Cost of acquisitions	Cost of disposals	Net capital expenditure	Work of a capital nature carried out by own staff (included in acquisitions)
	£ million	£ million	£ million	£ million	£ million	£ million	£ million

Sale, maintenance and repair of motor vehicles and motorcycles; retail sale of automotive fuel (SIC 92 50.00)

	CMSC	CMSD	CMSE	CMSF	CMSG	CMSH	CMSI
1995[2]	..	..	..	825	338	487	..
1996[2]	598	467	131	827	354	473	7
1997	692	500	192	1 550	570	980	14
1998	951	496	455	2 026	836	1 190	39

Sale of motor vehicles (SIC 92 50.10)

	FDGT	FDGU	FDGV	FDGW	FDGX	FDGY	FDGZ
1995[2]	..	..	..	566	275	291	..
1996[2]	330	216	114	617	311	306	5
1997	373	277	96	934	398	536	7
1998	610	240	370	1 225	655	570	27

Maintenance and repair of motor vehicles (SIC 92 50.20)

	FDIG	FDIH	FDII	FDIJ	FDIK	FDIL	FDIM
1995[2]	..	..	..	70	14	56	..
1996[2]	106	103	3	72	14	58	1
1997	142	84	58	266	38	228	4
1998	142	114	28	437	97	340	2

Sale of motor vehicle parts and accessories (SIC 92 50.30)

	FDJS	FDJT	FDJU	FDJV	FDJW	FDJX	FDJY
1995[2]	..	..	..	96	17	79	..
1996[2]	111	104	7	92	15	77	1
1997	105	80	25	238	81	157	3
1998	100	73	27	180	43	137	6

Sale, maintenance and repair of motorcycles and related parts and accessories (SIC 92 50.40)

	FDLF	FDLG	FDLH	FDLI	FDLJ	FDLK	FDLL
1995[2]	..	..	..	11	2	9	..
1996[2]	8	6	2	11	2	9	–
1997	12	11	1	24	6	18	–
1998	16	10	6	26	10	16	4

Retail sale of automotive fuel (SIC 92 50.50)

	COCA	COCB	COCC	COCD	COCE	COCF	COCG
1995[2]	..	..	..	82	30	52	..
1996[2]	43	38	5	35	12	23	–
1997	60	48	12	88	47	41	–
1998	83	59	24	158	31	127	–

1 Figures are exclusive of VAT.
2 Data for 1995 and 1996 were collected on a different basis from those for 1997 onwards.

Source: Office for National Statistics: 01633 812264

23.3
continued

Motor trades[1]
United Kingdom

	Stocks			Employment costs			Gross margin		Approximate gross value added at basic prices
	Increase during year	Value at end of year	Total turnover divided by end-year stocks	Total employment costs	Gross wages and salaries paid	National insurance and pension contributions	Amount	As a percentage of adjusted turnover	
	£ million	£ million	Quotient	£ million	£ million	£ million	£ million	Percentage	£ million

Sale, maintenance and repair of motor vehicles and motorcycles; retail sale of automotive fuel (SIC 92 50.00)

	CMSJ	CMSK	CMSL	CMSM	COBP	COBQ	COBR	COBS	COBT
1995[2]	953	10 294	9.8	5 683	5 082	601	23 492	23.3	13 787
1996[2]	888	11 127	9.8	6 206	5 564	642	21 354	20.7	14 816
1997	1 388	12 079	9.9	6 981	6 229	752	24 703	21.8	17 804
1998	1 133	12 862	9.6	7 660	6 802	858	25 809	22.1	17 464

Sale of motor vehicles (SIC 92 50.10)

	FDHA	FDHB	FDHC	FDHD	FDHE	FDHF	FDHG	FDHH	FDHI
1995[2]	729	8 003	8.6	3 068	2 728	340	13 726	19.9	8 366
1996[2]	748	8 786	8.8	3 381	3 024	357	13 268	18.0	8 904
1997	1 213	9 494	8.9	3 766	3 349	417	15 433	18.9	10 856
1998	948	10 233	8.5	4 048	3 594	454	15 569	18.4	10 274

Maintenance and repair of motor vehicles (SIC 92 50.20)

	FDIN	FDIO	FDIP	FDIQ	FDIR	FDIS	FDIT	FDIU	FDIV
1995[2]	57	645	13.8	1 221	1 100	121	5 087	57.0	2 364
1996[2]	30	558	14.8	1 366	1 230	136	3 544	59.1	2 588
1997	46	544	14.7	1 435	1 273	162	3 924	68.6	2 898
1998	28	515	17.4	1 718	1 517	201	4 687	80.7	3 317

Sale of motor vehicle parts and accessories (SIC 92 50.30)

	FDJZ	FDKA	FDKB	FDKC	FDKD	FDKE	FDKF	FDKG	FDKH
1995[2]	129	1 136	8.3	939	842	97	2 676	28.4	1 740
1996[2]	81	1 231	8.2	1 018	911	107	2 711	27.7	2 034
1997	66	1 329	8.1	1 231	1 104	127	3 225	31.0	2 449
1998	53	1 332	8.2	1 292	1 142	150	3 436	32.4	2 373

Sale, maintenance and repair of motorcycles and related parts and accessories (SIC 92 50.40)

	FDLM	FDLN	FDLO	FDLP	FDLQ	FDLR	FDLS	FDLT	FDLU
1995[2]	15	187	5.6	85	76	9	279	26.5	185
1996[2]	16	216	4.7	69	61	8	246	24.8	177
1997	26	263	4.7	93	83	10	309	25.6	213
1998	77	333	3.8	101	90	11	365	29.3	262

Retail sale of automotive fuel (SIC 92 50.50)

	COCH	COCI	COCJ	COCK	COCL	COCM	COCN	CMQN	CMQO
1995[2]	23	323	37.6	370	336	34	1 724	14.2	1 132
1996[2]	13	336	37.3	372	338	34	1 585	12.7	1 113
1997	37	449	32.7	456	420	36	1 812	12.5	1 388
1998	27	449	33.1	501	459	42	1 752	12.0	1 238

1 Figures are exclusive of VAT.
2 Data for 1995 and 1996 were collected on a different basis from those for 1997 onwards.

Source: Office for National Statistics: 01633 812264

23.4 Catering and allied trades
United Kingdom

| | | | Taxes and levies[3] | | | Capital expenditure[3] | | | |
	Number of businesses	Total turnover[2]	Total taxes and levies	National (non-domestic business) rates	Other amounts paid for taxes duties and levies	Capital acquisitions	Capital disposals	Net capital expenditure	Work of a capital nature carried out by your own staff (included in acquisitions)
	Number	£ million	£ million	£ million	, £ million	£ million	£ million	£ million	£ million
Total catering and allied trades (SIC 92 55.00)									
	MKEK	CMKX	CMLM	CMLJ	CMLL	CMLP	CMLQ	CMLK	CMLR
1995[1]	112 398	39 057	..	..	..	2 822	551	2 271	..
1996[1]	110 583	41 666	979	787	192	2 991	445	2 546	14
1997	110 245	45 844	1 082	899	183	3 877	465	3 412	14
1998	111 815	47 946	1 206	1 045	161	4 391	533	3 858	30
Hotels and motels (SIC 92 55.11 and 55.12)									
	MKEL	CMLW	CMML	CMMI	CMMK	CMMO	CMMP	CMMJ	CMMQ
1995[1]	12 563	8 226	..	..	..	612	125	487	..
1996[1]	12 163	8 933	244	226	18	782	195	587	3
1997	11 555	9 589	256	228	28	1 085	99	986	8
1998	11 374	10 333	267	261	6	1 189	105	1 084	3
Camping sites and other provision of short-stay accommodation (SIC 92 55.21 to 55.23)									
	MKEM	CMMV	CMNK	CMNH	CMNJ	CMNN	CMNO	CMNI	CMNP
1995[1]	3 065	1 440	..	..	..	194	22	172	..
1996[1]	3 094	1 620	43	43	..	159	15	144	1
1997	3 289	1 945	59	50	9	253	36	217	2
1998	3 435	2 089	67	61	6	271	63	208	2
Restaurants or cafes, take-away food shops (SIC 92 55.30)									
	MKEN	CMNU	CMOJ	CMOG	CMOI	CMOM	CMON	CMOH	CMOO
1995[1]	46 575	11 071	..	..	..	651	83	568	..
1996[1]	46 379	11 643	246	225	21	625	66	559	1
1997	46 984	12 660	272	250	22	719	62	657	2
1998	48 362	12 956	289	275	14	931	109	822	1
Licensed clubs with entertainment, independent, tenanted, managed public houses or wine bars (SIC 92 55.40)[5]									
	MKEO	CMOT	CMPI	CMPF	CMPH	CMPL	CMPM	CMPG	CMPN
1995[1]	46 395	14 868	..	..	..	1 300	310	990	..
1996[1]	45 134	15 484	423	270	153	1 364	164	1 200	8
1997	44 198	16 792	451	336	115	1 734	265	1 469	2
1998	44 283	17 820	559	429	130	1 909	251	1 658	..
Canteen operator, catering contractor (SIC 92 55.51 and 55.52)									
	MKEP	CMPS	CMQH	CMQE	CMQG	CMQK	CMQL	CMQF	CMQM
1995[1]	3 800	3 452	..	..	..	65	11	54	..
1996[1]	3 813	3 986	23	23	..	61	5	56	1
1997	4 219	4 858	44	35	9	86	3	83	–
1998	4 361	4 748	24	19	5	91	5	86	..

1 Data for 1995 and 1996 were collected on a different basis from those for 1997 onwards.
2 Inclusive of VAT.
3 Exclusive of VAT.

4 The 1995, 1996 and 1997 total turnover figure used to calculate these data excludes VAT.
5 Includes figures for managed public houses owned by breweries.

Source: Office for National Statistics: 01633 812264

23.4

Catering and allied trades
United Kingdom

continued

	Stocks[3]		Purchases of goods and services[3]									
	Increase during year	Value at end of year	Total purchases	Energy, water and materials	Goods for resale	Hiring, leasing of plant, machinery etc.	Commercial insurance premiums	Road transport services	Telecommun- ication services	Computer and related services	Advertising and marketing services	Other services
	£ million	£ million	£ million	£ million	£ million	£ million	£ million	£ million	£ million	£ million	£ million	£ million
Total catering and allied trades (SIC 92 55.00)												
	CMLN	CMLO	CMLI	CMKZ	CMLA	CMLB	CMLC	CMLD	CMLE	CMLF	CMLG	CMLH
1995[1]	37	767	19 951	..	8 476	..	..	..	..	..	..	..
1996[1]	38	787	19 966	6 108	7 971	208	281	62	154	36	477	4 669
1997	48	841	21 368	8 054	7 338	233	284	89	186	51	545	4 588
1998	54	981	22 460	9 227	7 035	269	271	51	190	61	577	4 779
Hotels and motels (SIC 92 55.11 and 55.12)												
	CMMM	CMMN	CMMH	CMLY	CMLZ	CMMA	CMMB	CMMC	CMMD	CMME	CMMF	CMMG
1995[1]	3	115	3 467	..	706	..	..	..	..	..	..	..
1996[1]	−10	130	3 413	1 211	548	66	83	14	64	15	173	1 239
1997	−1	137	3 532	1 487	506	68	73	27	60	17	162	1 132
1998	3	159	3 824	1 665	555	54	76	12	60	18	172	1 212
Camping sites and other provision of short-stay accommodation (SIC 92 55.21 to 55.23)												
	CMNL	CMNM	CMNG	CMMX	CMMY	CMMZ	CMNA	CMNB	CMNC	CMND	CMNE	CMNF
1995[1]	3	56	705	..	265	..	..	..	..	..	..	..
1996[1]	4	65	761	165	252	8	27	6	10	3	47	243
1997	8	87	886	172	278	11	23	5	10	5	55	327
1998	10	116	939	215	264	11	23	3	16	6	76	325
Restaurants or cafes, take-away food shops (SIC 92 55.30)												
	CMOK	CMOL	CMOF	CMNW	CMNX	CMNY	CMNZ	CMOA	CMOB	CMOC	CMOD	CMOE
1995[1]	10	179	5 669	..	1 783	..	..	..	..	..	..	..
1996[1]	6	185	5 725	2 212	1 679	21	66	15	30	5	119	1 578
1997	14	206	6 174	2 926	1 538	27	78	22	41	7	159	1 376
1998	14	217	6 312	2 973	1 575	45	61	10	41	11	151	1 445
Licensed clubs with entertainment, independent, tenanted, managed public houses or wine bars (SIC 92 55.40)[5]												
	CMPJ	CMPK	CMPE	CMOV	CMOW	CMOX	CMOY	CMOZ	CMPA	CMPB	CMPC	CMPD
1995[1]	18	359	8 440	..	5 367	..	..	..	..	..	..	..
1996[1]	29	338	8 203	1 298	5 143	86	93	17	41	4	125	1 396
1997	15	340	8 664	2 042	4 800	95	96	17	64	13	158	1 379
1998	20	407	9 148	2 796	4 389	96	96	15	62	17	160	1 517
Canteen operator, catering contractor (SIC 92 55.51 and 55.52)												
	CMQI	CMQJ	CMQD	CMPU	CMPV	CMPW	CMPX	CMPY	CMPZ	CMQA	CMQB	CMQC
1995[1]	3	58	1 670	..	355	..	..	..	..	..	..	..
1996[1]	9	69	1 864	1 222	349	27	12	10	9	9	13	213
1997	12	71	2 112	1 427	216	32	14	18	11	9	11	374
1998	7	82	2 237	1 578	252	63	15	11	11	9	18	280

See footnotes on the first page of this table.

Source: Office for National Statistics: 01633 812264

23.4 Catering and allied trades
United Kingdom
continued

	Employment costs[3]			Gross margin[4]			Accommodation	
	Total employment costs	Gross wages and salaries paid	National insurance and pension contributions	Amount	As a percentage of turnover	Value added at basic prices[4]	Number of establishments	Letting bedplaces
	£ million	£ million	£ million	£ million	Percentage	£ million	Number	Number

Total catering and allied trades (SIC 92 55.00)

	CMKY	CMKV	CMKW	CMQP	CMQQ	CMQR	CMLS	CMLT
1995[1]	7 742	7 133	609	24 950	74.7	13 475	..	..
1996[1]	8 214	7 570	644	27 812	77.8	15 639	..	..
1997	9 199	8 493	706	32 258	81.6	18 059	23 207	1 591 979
1998	10 146	9 351	795	34 427	83.1	18 950	23 962	1 672 755

Hotels and motels (SIC 92 55.11 and 55.12)

	CMLX	CMLU	CMLV	CMQS	CMQT	CMQU	CMMR	CMMS
1995[1]	2 059	1 887	172	6 354	90.0	3 593	–	–
1996[1]	2 179	1 998	181	7 062	92.7	4 182	–	–
1997	2 257	2 071	186	7 683	93.8	4 637	13 505	727 016
1998	2 453	2 239	214	8 242	93.7	4 981	12 995	694 150

Camping sites and other provision of short-stay accommodation (SIC 92 55.21 to 55.23)

	CMMW	CMMT	CMMU	CMQV	CMQW	CMQX	CMNQ	CMRR
1995[1]	237	217	20	1 000	79.2	560	–	–
1996[1]	255	235	20	1 180	82.6	672	–	–
1997	312	293	19	1 463	84.4	848	4 598	770 397
1998	351	327	24	1 606	86.3	933	5 074	868 867

Restaurants or cafes, take-away food shops (SIC 92 55.30)

	CMNV	CMNS	CMNT	CMQY	CMQZ	CMRA	CMOP	CMOQ
1995[1]	2 000	1 850	150	7 710	81.3	3 824	..	..
1996[1]	2 095	1 946	149	8 336	83.3	4 270	..	..
1997	2 405	2 231	174	9 373	86.0	4 717	655	29 815
1998	2 786	2 590	196	9 650	86.1	4 939	654	31 124

Licensed clubs with entertainment, independent, tenanted, managed public houses or wine bars (SIC 92 55.40)[5]

	CMOU	CMOR	CMOS	CMRB	CMRC	CMRD	CMPO	CMPP
1995[1]	2 305	2 131	174	7 310	57.7	4 237	–	–
1996[1]	2 418	2 227	191	8 082	61.2	4 877	..	–
1997	2 656	2 451	205	9 607	66.8	5 630	4 449	64 751
1998	2 982	2 752	230	10 912	71.4	6 052	5 239	78 614

Canteen operator, catering contractor (SIC 92 55.51 and 55.52)

	CMPT	CMPQ	CMPR	CMRE	CMRF	CMRG		
1995[1]	1 141	1 048	93	2 576	88.0	1 261		
1996[1]	1 267	1 164	103	3 152	90.3	1 638		
1997	1 569	1 447	122	4 132	95.3	2 227		
1998	1 574	1 443	131	4 017	94.3	2 045		

See footnotes on the first page of this table.

Source: Office for National Statistics: 01633 812264

SOURCES

This index of sources gives the titles of official publications or other sources containing statistics allied to those in the tables of this *Annual Abstract*. These publications provide more detailed analyses than are shown in the *Annual Abstract*. This index includes publications to which reference should be made for short-term (monthly or quarterly) series. No entry is made in this index for items where the data have been obtained from departmental records. Further advice on published statistical sources is available from the National Statistics Public Enquiry Service on the numbers provided on page ii.

Subject	Table number in *Abstract*	Government department or other organisation	Official publication or other source
1. Area			
	1.1	Ordnance Survey Ordnance Survey of Northern Ireland Office for National Statistics	Regional Trends (annual, The Stationery Office (TSO))
2. Parliamentary elections			
Elections	2.1	Home Office	Electoral statistics (series EL) Return of election expenses Vachers Parliamentary Companion
By-elections	2.2	Home Office	Social Trends (annual, TSO)
3. International development			
	3.1, 3.2	Department for International Development	Statistics on International Development (annual)
4. Defence			
	4.1 - 4.13	Ministry of Defence/ DASA	UK Defence Statistics 2000 (TSO)
5. Population and vital statistics			
Population	5.1 - 5.3, 5.5, 5.6	Office for National Statistics	*England and Wales*: Census reports 1911, 1921, 1931, 1951, 1961, 1971, 1981 and 1991 Census 1991, Key Population and Vital Statistics; Great Britain Digest of Welsh Statistics (annual, National Assembly for Wales)
		General Register Office (Scotland)	*Scotland*: Census reports 1951, 1961, 1971, 1981 and 1991 Census 1991, Key statistics for urban areas: Scotland
		General Register Office (Northern Ireland)	*Northern Ireland*: Census of population 1951, 1961, 1966 and 1971, 1981 and 1991
		Office for National Statistics	*England and Wales*: Series FM (Family statistics), DH (Deaths), MB (Morbidity), PP (Population estimates and projections), MN (Migration) and VS (Key population and vital statistics) Series PP1, Population estimates: The Registrar General's estimates of the population of regions and local government areas of England and
Wales			Population Trends (quarterly TSO) Health Statistics Quarterly (TSO)
		General Register Office (Scotland)	*Scotland*: Annual report of the Registrar General for Scotland Annual estimate of the population of Scotland
		General Register Office (Northern Ireland)	*Northern Ireland*: Annual report of the Registrar General
Projections	5.1 - 5.3	Government Actuary's Department Office for National Statistics	Series PP2, Population projections - national figures
Migration	5.7, 5.8	Office for National Statistics	Series MN (International migration) Population Trends (quarterly, TSO)
	5.9, 5.10	Home Office	Control of immigration statistics United Kingdom (annual)
Vital statistics	5.4, 5.11 - 5.21	Office for National Statistics	*England and Wales*: Series FM (Births, marriages and divorce statistics), DH (Deaths), MB (Morbidity), PP (Population estimates and projections), MN (International migration) and VS (Key population and vital statistics) Population Trends (quarterly, TSO)

SOURCES

Subject	Table number in *Abstract*	Government department or other organisation	Official publication or other source
	5.4, 5.11 - 5.20	General Register Office (Scotland)	*Scotland*: Annual report of the Registrar General for Scotland Quarterly return of births, deaths and marriages
		General Register Office (Northern Ireland)	*Northern Ireland*: Annual report of the Registrar General Quarterly return of births, deaths and marriages
	5.13	Northern Ireland Court Service	Northern Ireland Judicial Statistics (annual)
	5.17	Scottish Executive	
	5.22	Government Actuary's Department	*England and Wales*: Interim Life Table *Scotland*: Interim Life Table *Northern Ireland*: Annual Report of the Registrar General

6. Education

Subject	Table number in *Abstract*	Government department or other organisation	Official publication or other source
	6.1 - 6.11	Department for Education and Employment National Assembly for Wales Scottish Executive Northern Ireland Department of Education	Scottish Educational Statistics (annual, TSO) Northern Ireland Education Statistics (annual) Compendium of Education Statistics for the United Kingdom (annual) Northern Ireland Annual Abstract of Statistics Statistics of Education and Training in Wales (annual, Welsh Office)

7. Labour market

Subject	Table number in *Abstract*	Government department or other organisation	Official publication or other source
Labour Force Survey	7.1 - 7.3, 7.6, 7.9, 7.10, 7.12, 7.15 - 7.17	Office for National Statistics	Labour Market Trends (monthly, TSO)
	7.4, 7.5	Office for National Statistics	
	7.7	Cabinet Office	Civil Service Statistics (annual) Monthly Digest of Statistics (TSO)
	7.8	Department of the Environment Transport and the Regions (DETR) Scottish Executive National Assembly for Wales	Labour Market Trends (monthly, TSO) Annual Review of the Engineering Industry Training Board
Claimant count	7.11, 7.13 7.14, 7.27	Office for National Statistics	Labour Market Trends (monthly, TSO)
	7.18	Office for National Statistics	Labour Market Trends (monthly TSO) Monthly Digest of Statistics (TSO)
New Earnings Survey	7.19, 7.20, 7.23, 7.25	Office for National Statistics	New Earnings Survey (annual, ONS)
Average Earnings Index	7.21, 7.22	Office for National Statistics	Labour Market Trends (monthly, TSO) Monthly Digest of Statistics (TSO)
	7.24	Department of Enterprise, Trade and Investment (Northern Ireland)	New Earnings Survey Northern Ireland (annual) (some details in Northern Ireland Annual Abstract of Statistics)
	7.26	Department of Trade and Industry	Labour Market Trends (monthly, TSO)

8. Personal income, expenditure and wealth

Subject	Table number in *Abstract*	Government department or other organisation	Official publication or other source
	8.1 8.2	Office for National Statistics Board of Inland Revenue	Economic Trends, March 1997 (monthly, TSO) Inland Revenue Statistics (annual, TSO) Economic Trends (monthly, TSO)
	8.3 - 8.5	Office for National Statistics	Family Expenditure Survey, (annual) (1990 onwards edition-Family Spending) (annual, TSO)

9. Health

Subject	Table number in *Abstract*	Government department or other organisation	Official publication or other source
National health service	9.1	Department of Health National Assembly for Wales	Appropriation Accounts (annual) Health and Personal Social Services Statistics for England (annual) Health and Personal Social Services Statistics for Wales (annual)
	9.2	Scottish Health Service, Common Services Agency	

Subject	Table number in *Abstract*	Government department or other organisation	Official publication or other source
	9.3	Central Services Agency (Northern Ireland) Department of Health and Social Services (Northern Ireland)	Summary of Health and Personal Social Services Accounts (annual) Hospital Statistics (annual)
	9.4	Department of Health Scottish Health Service, Common Services Agency National Assembly for Wales	Health and Personal Social Services Statistics for England (annual)
Public health	9.5	Communicable Disease Surveillance Centre	Communicable Disease Statistics Series MB2 (annual) Annual Review of Communicable Diseases
		Scottish Health Service, Common Services Agency	Scottish Health Statistics (annual)
		Department of Health and Social Services (Northern Ireland)	Annual report of the Registrar General Northern Ireland Quarterly return of births, deaths and marriages
	9.6 - 9.8	Health and Safety Executive Department of Social Security	Health and Safety Statistics

10. Social protection

Subject	Table number in *Abstract*	Government department or other organisation	Official publication or other source
Social security pensions, benefits and allowances	10.1, 10.2,	Department of Social Security	National Insurance Fund Account (annual)
	10.4	Board of Inland Revenue	
	10.3, 10.5, 10.6 - 10.16	Department of Social Security Department of Health and Social Services (Northern Ireland)	Social Security Statistics (annual, TSO) Health and Personal Social Services Statistics for England (annual) Welsh Office: Health and Personal Social Services Statistics for Wales (annual)
Social services	10.17 - 10.21	Office for National Statistics Department for Education and Employment	Appropriation Accounts (annual) Northern Ireland Annual Abstract of Statistics
Housing	10.22	Office for National Statistics	

11. Crime and justice

Subject	Table number in *Abstract*	Government department or other organisation	Official publication or other source
	11.1	Home Office	Monthly Digest of Statistics (TSO)
	11.2	Home Office	*England and Wales*: Report of Her Majesty's Chief Inspector of Constabulary (annual)
	11.20 - 11.23	Scottish Executive Justice Department Royal Ulster Constabulary	*Scotland*: Report of Her Majesty's Chief Inspector of Constabulary for Scotland (annual) The Chief Constable's Annual Report
	11.3 - 11.11	Home Office	Criminal Statistics, England and Wales (annual) Prison statistics, England and Wales (annual) Digest of Welsh Statistics (annual, Welsh Office) Offences relating to motor vehicles, England and Wales (annual bulletin)
	11.12 - 11.17	Home Office	HM Prison Service Annual Report and Accounts April 1999 - March 2000
		Scottish Executive Justice Department	Recorded Crime in Scotland, 1999
	11.18, 11.19	Scottish Executive Justice Department	Prison Statistics Scotland, 1999 Scottish Prison Service Annual Report and Accounts 1999-00

12. Lifestyles

Subject	Table number in *Abstract*	Government department or other organisation	Official publication or other source
	12.1	Department for Culture, Media and Sport	DCMS Annual Report
	12.2	Office for National Statistics	Labour Market Trends (monthly, TSO)

SOURCES

Subject	Table number in *Abstract*	Government department or other organisation	Official publication or other source
	12.3	Office for National Statistics	GB Cinema exhibitor statistic First Release Monthly Digest of Statistics (TSO)
	12.4	Department for Culture, Media and Sport	British Film Institute Film and Television Handbook
	12.5	Department for Culture, Media and Sport	Digest of Tourist Statistics (annual) Sightseeing in the UK (annual)
		Office for National Statistics	Travel Trends (annual, TSO) Overseas Travel and Tourism First Release Monthly Digest of Statistics (TSO)
	12.6	Office for National Statistics	General Household Survey Report
	12.7	Gaming Board for Great Britain Office for National Statistics	Social Trends (annual, TSO)
Households	12.8	Office for National Statistics General Register Office (Scotland)	Census 1991 National Report Great Britain Part II 1991 Census. Household & Family Composition (10%) G.B.

13. Environment, water and housing

Subject	Table number in *Abstract*	Government department or other organisation	Official publication or other source
Environment	13.1 - 13.17	DETR	Digest of Environmental Statistics (annual, TSO)
	13.8, 13.9	Scottish Executive	
Housing	13.18 - 13.21	Office for National Statistics DETR	Housing and Construction Statistics (quarterly) Housing return for Scotland (quarterly) Housing in England (annual, TSO)
		National Assembly for Wales	Welsh Housing Statistics (annual, National Assembly for Wales)
		Scottish Executive	Housing return for Scotland (quarterly)
	13.22	Office of Water Services (OFWAT)	Digest of environmental protection and water statistics (annual)

14. Transport and communications

Subject	Table number in *Abstract*	Government department or other organisation	Official publication or other source
General	14.1, 14.2, 14.4	DETR	
	14.3	Office for National Statistics	
Road transport	14.5 - 14.11	DETR	Transport Statistics Great Britain (annual, TSO) Vehicle Licensing Statistics (annual, TSO) Monthly Digest of Statistics (TSO) Road accidents in Great Britain (annual, TSO) Monthly Digest of Statistics (TSO) Road accidents Wales (annual, National Assembly for Wales)
	14.12, 14.13	Department of the Environment for Northern Ireland	Transport Statistics NI
Rail transport	14.19, 14.20	DETR	Transport Statistics Great Britain (annual, TSO) Health and Safety Executive: Industry and Services (annual) Bulletin of Rail Statistics (quarterly)
	14.21, 14.22	Department of the Environment for Northern Ireland	Northern Ireland Annual Abstract of Statistics
Air transport	14.23 - 14.27	Civil Aviation Authority	Monthly Digest of Statistics (TSO) Civil Aviation Authority; Annual Statements of Movements, Passengers and Cargo Civil Aviation Authority; Monthly Statements of Movements, Passengers and Cargo Accidents to aircraft on the British Register (annual)
Sea transport	14.28, 14.29	DETR	Maritime Statistics (annual, TSO) Monthly Digest of Statistics (TSO)
Passenger movement	14.30	DETR Civil Aviation Authority	Monthly Digest of Statistics (TSO)

Subject	Table number in *Abstract*	Government department or other organisation	Official publication or other source
Communications	14.31	Royal Mail Parcel Force Subscription Services Ltd Post Office Counters Ltd	Monthly Digest of Statistics (TSO) Post Office report and accounts (annual)

15. National accounts

	15.1 - 15.22	Office for National Statistics	United Kingdom National Accounts (annual, TSO) Monthly Digest of Statistics (TSO) Economic Trends (monthly, TSO) UK Economic Accounts (quarterly, TSO) Consumer Trends (quarterly, TSO)

16. Prices

Producer prices	16.1, 16.2	Office for National Statistics	Producer Price Index Press Notice (monthly) Business Monitor MM22, Producer Price Indices (monthly, TSO) Monthly Digest of Statistics (TSO)
Consumer prices	16.3 - 16.5	Office for National Statistics	Monthly Digest of Statistics (TSO) Labour Market Trends (monthly, TSO) Business Monitor MM23, Consumer Price Indices (monthly, TSO)
	16.6, 16.7	Ministry of Agriculture, Fisheries and Food	Agricultural Statistics, United Kingdom (annual) MAFF Statistical Notice Agricultural Price Indices (Monthly) Monthly Digest of Statistics (TSO)
	16.8	Ministry of Agriculture, Fisheries and Food	Annual Review of Agriculture (annual)

17. Government finance

Central government	17.1 - 17.3	Office for National Statistics	Financial Statistics (monthly, TSO)
	17.4 - 17.7	HM Treasury Office for National Statistics	Consolidated Fund and National Loans Fund Accounts Financial Statistics (monthly, TSO)
	17.8	Bank of England	
Saving	17.9	Department for National Savings	Accounts of National Savings Bank Investment Deposit Accounts (annual) Ordinary Deposit Accounts (annual)
Central government	17.10, 17.11	Board of Inland Revenue	Inland Revenue Statistics (annual, TSO)
Rateable values	17.12	Board of Inland Revenue	Rates and Rateable values in England and Wales (annual) (Up to 1989)
Local authorities	17.13, 17.14	Department of the Environment, Transport and the Regions National Assembly for Wales	Local government financial statistics (England)(annual) Welsh local government financial statistics (annual)
		Public Works Loan Board	Annual report of the Public Works Loan Board
		Scottish Executive, Economic Advice and Statistics	Local financial returns (Scotland) (annual)
		Department of the Environment for Northern Ireland	
		Chartered Institute of Public Finance and Accountancy	
	17.15, 17.16	Department of the Environment, Transport and the Regions National Assembly for Wales	Local government financial statistics (England) (annual) Welsh local government financial statistics (annual)
	17.17	Department of the Environment, Transport and the Regions	Local government financial statistics (England) (annual)
	17.18 - 17.20	Scottish Executive, Economic Advice and Statistics	Local financial returns (Scotland) (annual)
	17.21 - 17.23	Department of the Environment, Transport and the Regions Northern Ireland	District Council - Summary of Statement of Accounts (annual)

SOURCES

Subject	Table number in *Abstract*	Government department or other organisation	Official publication or other source
18. External trade and investment			
	18.1 - 18.8	Office for National Statistics	Business Monitor MM24, Monthly Review of External Trade Statistics (monthly, TSO) Overseas Trade Analysed in Terms of Industries MQ10 (quarterly, TSO) Monthly Digest of Statistics (monthly, TSO) HM Customs & Excise: Overseas Trade Statistics of the UK (monthly, quarterly and annual)
	18.9 - 18.18	Office for National Statistics Bank of England	United Kingdom Balance of Payments (annual, TSO) Quarterly figures: UK Economic Accounts Financial Statistics (monthly, TSO)
19. Research and development			
	19.1 - 19.5	Office for National Statistics	Business Monitor MA14, Research and Development in UK Business (annual, ONS)
20. Agriculture, fisheries and food			
Agriculture	20.1, 20.2	Agricultural Departments	Agriculture in the United Kingdom 1999 (annual)
	20.3 - 20.5	Agricultural Departments	Agricultural Statistics; United Kingdom (annual) Scottish Agricultural Economics (annual) Welsh Agricultural Statistics (annual, National Assembly for Wales)
	20.6	Forestry Commission	Great Britain: Annual Report and Accounts of the Forestry Commission
		Department of Agriculture and Rural Development (Northern Ireland)	Northern Ireland Annual Abstract of Statistics
	20.7, 20.8	Agricultural Departments	
Food	20.9 - 20.12	Ministry of Agriculture, Fisheries and Food	Monthly Digest of Statistics (TSO)
	20.13	Agriculture Departments	Agricultural Statistics, United Kingdom (annual) As for notes 20.3 - 20.5
Fisheries	20.14, 20.15	Ministry of Agriculture, Fisheries and Food; Scottish Executive Agricultural Departments	*England and Wales*: Sea fisheries statistical tables (annual) *Scotland*: Fisheries of Scotland report (annual) Scottish Sea fisheries statistics (annual, TSO)
Food consumption	20.16	Ministry of Agriculture, Fisheries and Food	National Food Survey
21. Production			
Production survey	21.1	Office for National Statistics	Manufacturing Summary Volume (Business Monitor PA 1002) (annual, ONS) PACSTAT (CD-ROM) (annual, ONS)
Manufacturers sales	21.2	Office for National Statistics	Product Sales and Trade PRA1 to 92 and PRQ1 to 33 (ONS)
	21.3	Office for National Statistics	Size analysis of United Kingdom Businesses (Business Monitor PA1003) (annual, ONS)
Energy	21.4 - 21.12	Department of Trade and Industry (Energy Policy, Technology Analysis and Coal Unit)	Digest of United Kingdom Energy Statistics (annual) Energy Trends (monthly) PACSTAT (CD-ROM) (annual, ONS)
Iron and steel	21.13 - 21.15	Iron and Steel Statistics Bureau	Iron and steel industry: annual statistics published by the Iron and Steel Statistics Bureau Corporation Regional Trends (annual, TSO)
Industrial materials	21.16	World Bureau of Metal Statistics Aluminium Federation	World Metal Statistics (monthly) PACSTAT (CD-ROM) (annual, ONS)
	21.17, 21.18	British man-made fibres Federation Textile Statistics Bureau Fertiliser Manufacturers' Association	Monthly Digest of Statistics (TSO) PACSTAT (CD-ROM) (Annual, ONS)

Subject	Table number in *Abstract*	Government department or other organisation	Official publication or other source
	21.19	Office for National Statistics	Minerals (Business Monitor PA 1007) (annual, ONS) Natural Environment Research Council: United Kingdom Minerals Yearbook
		Department of Economic Development (Northern Ireland)	Northern Ireland Annual Abstract of Statistics
Building and construction	21.20	Office for National Statistics DETR	Minerals (Business Monitor PA 1007) (annual, ONS) Monthly Digest of Statistics (TSO) Housing and Construction Statistics (quarterly and annual)
	21.21, 21.22	DETR	Housing and Construction Statistics (quarterly and annual)
Engineering	21.23, 21.24	Office for National Statistics	PACSTAT (CD-ROM) (annual, ONS)
Motor vehicle production	21.25	Office for National Statistics	Business Monitor PM 34.10, (monthly, ONS) PACSTAT (CD-ROM) (annual, ONS) Sector Review- Motor Trades (formerly Business Monitor SDA27) (annual, TSO)
Drink and tobacco	21.26, 21.27	HM Customs and Excise	Annual report of the Commissioners of HM Customs and Excise
		Office for National Statistics	Monthly Digest of Statistics (TSO)

22. Banking, insurance, etc

Subject	Table number in *Abstract*	Government department or other organisation	Official publication or other source
Banking	22.1 22.3 - 22.5	Bank of England	Bank of England Annual Report and Accounts Bank of England Quarterly Bulletin
	22.2	Association of Payment Clearing Services	Annual report of the Bankers' Clearing House
	22.6	Bank of England	Financial Statistics (monthly, TSO)
	22.7 22.8 22.9 - 22.13	Bank of England Bank of England Bank of England	Bank of England Quarterly Bulletin Bank of England Quarterly Bulletin Monthly Digest of Statistics (TSO) Financial Statistics (monthly, TSO)
	22.14	Council of The Stock Exchange	Stock Exchange Fact Book (quarterly)
	22.15	Bank of England	Financial Statistics (monthly, TSO) Registry of Friendly Societies
Other financial institutions	22.16	Building Societies Commission	Report of the Chief Registrar incorporating the Report of the Industrial Assurance Commissioner (annual)
	22.17	Office for National Statistics	Business Monitor SDQ7, Assets and Liabilities of Finance Houses and Other Credit Companies (quarterly, ONS)
	22.18	Office for National Statistics	Financial Statistics (monthly, TSO) Monthly Digest of Statistics (TSO) Business Monitor MQ5, Insurance Companies; Pension Funds and Trusts Investments (quarterly, ONS) First Release
	22.19, 22.20	Office for National Statistics	Financial Statistics (monthly, TSO) Business Monitor MQ5, Insurance Companies; Pension Funds and Trusts Investments (quarterly, ONS)
Insolvency	22.21 - 22.24	Department of Trade and Industry	Insolvency Annual Report (DTI) Companies (DTI) Financial Statistics (monthly, TSO)

SOURCES

Subject	Table number in *Abstract*	Government department or other organisation	Official publication or other source
23. Service industry			
Retail trades	23.1	Office for National Statistics	Sector Review - Retailing (formerly Business Monitor SDA25) (TSO)
	23.2	Office for National Statistics	Business Monitor SDM 28, Retail Sales (monthly, ONS) Monthly Digest of Statistics (TSO)
Motor trades	23.3	Office for National Statistics	Sector Review- Motor Trades (formerly Business Monitor SDA 27) (TSO)
Catering	23.4	Office for National Statistics	Sector Review- Catering and Allied Trades (formerly Business Monitor SDA 28 (TSO)

INDEX

INDEX

INDEX

Figures indicate table numbers

INDEX

Figures indicate table numbers

INDEX

Printed in the United Kingdom for The Stationery Office
TJ003278   C45   578013   1/01   19585